The Emergence of Organizations and Markets

The Emergence of Organizations and Markets

John F. Padgett and Walter W. Powell

PRINCETON UNIVERSITY PRESS

Princeton & Oxford

Published by Princeton University Press,
41 William Street, Princeton, New Jersey 08540
In the United Kingdom: Princeton University Press,
6 Oxford Street, Woodstock, Oxfordshire OX20 1TW

press.princeton.edu

The cover displays a cross-section of fossilized stromatolites. These were bacterial colonies formed not long after the earth cooled. Stromatolites are arguably the earliest physical record we have of the origins of life. Composite of photos by Paul Carrara/National Park Service and Walter W. Powell.

Library of Congress Cataloging-in-Publication Data

The emergence of organizations and markets / edited by
John F. Padgett and Walter W. Powell.
p. cm.
Includes index.
ISBN 978-0-691-14867-0 (hbk.) —
ISBN 978-0-691-14887-8 (pbk.)
1. Organizational sociology. 2. Organization.
3. Industrial organization (Economic theory)
I. Padgett, John Frederick. II. Powell, Walter W.

HM786.E44 2012
302.3'5—dc23 2012004342

British Library Cataloging-in-Publication Data is available

This book has been composed in Sabon and Din

Printed on acid-free paper. ∞

Printed in the United States of America

10 9 8 7 6 5 4 3 2

This volume is dedicated to

HARRISON C. WHITE,
il maestro della bottega

Nihil ideo quoniam natumst in corpore, ut uti possemus, sed quod natumst id procreat usum.

(Nothing is born in the body for us to use it, but rather, having been born, it begets a use.)

—Lucretius, *De Rerum Natura* iv: 834–35 (first century B.C.)

Contents

Contributors

John F. Padgett is a social scientist at the University of Chicago, with a primary appointment in the Department of Political Science and courtesy appointments in the Departments of Sociology and History. He is also a visiting professor in the Faculty of Economics and Management at the Universitá di Trento in Italy. He was an external faculty member at the Santa Fe Institute from 1996 to 1999 and from 2005 to 2009 and a research professor there from 2000 to 2004.

Walter W. Powell is a sociologist at Stanford University, with a primary appointment in the School of Education and courtesy appointments in the Schools of Business and Engineering, and in Sociology, Communication, and Public Policy. He is co-director of Stanford's Center on Philanthropy and Civil Society. He has been an external faculty member at the Santa Fe Institute since 2001.

Peter McMahan is a Ph.D. student in the sociology department at the University of Chicago. His research interests center on microsociological foundations of group processes, with a focus on mathematical and statistical modeling.

Xing Zhong is a research fellow at Duke University, having received her Ph.D. from the sociology department at the University of Chicago in 2009. Her research interests include the emergence and evolution of networks, the social contexts and processes of technological innovation, and the development of organizational capabilities in emerging markets.

Jonathan Obert is a Ph.D. student in the political science department at the University of Chicago. His research interests include American political development and the creation of police and internal security forces, as well as processes of state formation more generally.

Andrew Spicer is an associate professor of international business at the Moore School of Business at the University of South Carolina. His research has examined privatization policies and outcomes in post-communist countries; the role of Western ideas and international organizations in shaping market reform policies; and the effects of national context and national identity on managers' ethical evaluations in international business settings.

Valery Yakubovich is an associate professor of management at the ESSEC Business School in France. He received his Ph.D. in sociology from Stanford University and, prior to joining ESSEC, taught at Chicago Booth and the Wharton School. His current projects explore organizational innovations in virtual firms and regional high-tech clusters, the interplay between formal hierarchies and social networks in large Russian firms, and the co-production of knowledge and social relations in organizations.

Stanislav Shekshnia is an affiliate professor of entrepreneurship at INSEAD and a senior partner at Ward Howell/Zest Leadership talent equity. His research concentrates on leadership, leadership development, and effective governance in emerging markets and organizations.

David Stark is the Arthur Lehman Professor of Sociology and International Affairs at Columbia University where he directs the Center on Organizational Innovation. His recent book, *The Sense of Dissonance: Accounts of Worth in Economic Life* (Princeton University Press, 2009), uses ethnographic methods to study the organizational structures that contribute to reflexivity. With Balázs Vedres, he coauthored "Structural Folds: Generative Disruption in Overlapping Groups" (*American Journal of Sociology*, 2010). Their current research on the historical network properties of creative teams is supported by the National Science Foundation.

Balázs Vedres is an associate professor of sociology at the Central European University in Budapest. His research furthers the agenda of understanding historical dynamics in network systems, combining insights from historical sociology, social network analysis, and studies of complex systems in physics and biology. His work combines historical sensitivities to temporal processes with a network analytic sensitivity to patterns of connectedness cross-sectionally. His article with David Stark (*American Journal* *of Sociology*, 2010) analyzes generative tensions in the historical evolution of business groups. The article won the 2011 Viviana Zelizer Award for best article in economic sociology, as well as the 2011 Roger V. Gould Prize.

Kurt Sandholtz is a doctoral candidate at Stanford's Center for Work, Technology, and Organization, and a visiting instructor at BYU Marriott School of Management. His work has appeared in *Organization Studies* and *Strategic Entrepreneurship Journal*.

Kelley Packalen is an associate professor of entrepreneurship in the School of Business at Queen's University in Kingston, Ontario. Her research is at the intersection of entrepreneurship and organization theory. She is broadly interested in the connection between the career biographies of founders and the networks they develop for their nascent firms. Kelley received her Ph.D. in industrial engineering from Stanford University.

Kjersten Whittington is an assistant professor of sociology at Reed College. In addition to regional dynamics, her research addresses how the structural and network organization of firms influences scientists' career trajectories and innovative output. Her work on this topic focuses on sex disparities in productivity in light of inventor collaborations across academic and industrial science contexts. She is also studying gender and motherhood dynamics among science professionals and, with collaborators, gendered decision making in venture capital contexts.

Jason Owen-Smith is an associate professor of sociology and organizational studies at the University of Michigan. He examines how science, commerce, and the law cohere and conflict in contemporary societies and economies. Together with collaborators, Jason works on projects that examine the dynamics of high-technology industries, the commercialization of academic research, and the science and politics of human embryonic stem cell research.

Jeannette A. Colyvas is an assistant professor in the School of Education and Social Policy and (by courtesy) Sociology and the Institute for Policy Research at Northwestern University. She holds a Ph.D. from Stanford University. Her published work has appeared in *Management Science*, *Research Policy*, *Minerva*, *Sociological Theory*, and *Research in Organizational Behavior*. Jeannette's current research examines university-industry interfaces, focusing on the translation of basic science into commercial application and its ramifications for careers, identities, and public science.

Spiro Maroulis is an assistant professor in the School of Public Affairs at Arizona State University, and Associate Director for Policy Informatics at the ASU Decision Theater. His research addresses problems involved with understanding the relationship between individual and collective behavior, particularly why strategic initiatives and change efforts so often provoke resistance and unanticipated responses inside organizations. Spiro received his B.S.E. from Duke University, M.P.P. from Harvard University, and Ph.D. from Northwestern University.

Lee Fleming is the director of the Coleman Fung Institute of Engineering Leadership in the UC–Berkeley College of Engineering. Previously he was the Albert Whitehead III Professor of Business Administration at the Harvard Business School. Working with large databases, he has empirically modeled invention as a process of recombinant search, the social networks of inventors, and the emergence of leadership in open innovation communities. He is currently investigating how non-compete contracts influence inventor mobility, firm strategy, and regional dynamics.

Lyra Colfer holds a Ph.D. in information, technology, and management from Harvard University. Her research examines the relationship between organizational structure and product architecture. She has applied multiple methods to evaluate the mirroring hypothesis, which posits that the structure of a development organization "mirrors" the design of the product it develops. She is currently working in the commercial software industry as a strategic consultant.

Alexandra Marin is an assistant professor of sociology at the University of Toronto. Her research examines how social networks operate in the labor market, focusing on how information holders make choices to share or withhold information. She is currently examining occupation closure and its effects on status attainment and network-based job search in the Canadian labor market.

Jonathan McPhie is currently a product manager at Google, Inc. While there, he has worked on a variety of projects covering online communications, web search, location services, and social networking. Jonathan previously worked as a research associate at Harvard Business School, where he conducted analyses of collaboration patterns in the U.S. patent database. Jonathan holds bachelor's and master's degrees in computer science from Harvard University.

Fabrizio Ferraro is an associate professor of strategic management at IESE Business School. He holds a Ph.D. in management from Stanford University. He has studied the emergence of novel organizational forms and institutions, including open-source software communities and sustainability reporting. He is now studying the emergence of the socially responsible investing field in finance and, more broadly, the relationship between social values and financial investing. He has published in the *Academy of Management Journal*, *Academy of Management Review*, and *Organization Science*. His article "Economics Language and Assumptions: How Theories Can Become Self-fulfilling" won the 2006 Best Paper Award from the *Academy of Management Review*.

Siobhán O'Mahony is an associate professor at the Boston University School of Management. Her research explores how technical and creative projects organize. She has examined high-technology contractors, open source programmers, artists, music producers, Internet start-ups, and corporate consortiums. She is interested in how people create organizations that promote innovation, creativity, and growth without replicating the bureaucratic structures they strive to avoid. Her work has appeared in *Administrative Science Quarterly*, *Organization Science*, *Academy of Management Journal*, *Research in Organizational Behavior*, *Research Policy*, *Research in the Sociology of Organizations*, *Industry and Innovation*, and the *Journal of Management and Governance*.

Illustrations

Tables

Acknowledgments

This book grew out of sustained conversations about evolution, novelty, and history at the Santa Fe Institute (SFI). John Padgett was a research professor at SFI from 2000 to 2004 and an external faculty member from 1996 to 2000 and from 2004 to 2009. Woody Powell has been an SFI external faculty member since 2001. From 1999 to 2009, Padgett and Powell co-directed an SFI program, the Co-evolution of States and Markets, originally supported financially by SFI and eventually by the Hewlett Foundation. The project was also supported financially by an NSF grant to Padgett through its Human and Social Dynamics initiative. This book is a product of that SFI program and of the many people who have contributed to it over the years.

Because of this institutional lineage, thanks go first to the SFI leaders who had the faith and the commitment to invest in the long-term vision of this book with its multiyear time horizon—especially Ellen Goldberg, president of SFI from 1996 to 2003, and Erica Jen, former vice president and current science board member at SFI. The Santa Fe Institute was and is a very special place where natural scientists from a variety of disciplines interact with social scientists from a variety of disciplines. Intellectual reaches of this magnitude are very unlikely to succeed, but SFI over the years has somehow managed to foster a series of innovative and out-of-the-box contributions by remaining committed to this mind-contorting stretch. Of course, interdisciplinarity is not enough for coherent conversation. One also needs topics or themes where joint conversation makes independent sense to both sides, and enough time and patience to carry it through. Evolution and the generation of novelty were the animating themes of our SFI program. These topics are at the frontier of sectors of the natural sciences ranging from biochemistry to systems biology. They are also at the frontier of historically oriented social science, as long as past abuses of evolutionary thinking in the social sciences and in politics are kept squarely in view. A mechanical transposition of biological mechanisms to "cultural evolution" in human systems dooms the project to intellectual failure in social science and in history. But SFI's glory has always been that it encourages deep rethinking of basic theories from new perspectives—to the benefit of the natural sciences as well as the social sciences. That SFI does so is due to the taste of its leaders. Ellen Goldberg and Erica Jen were those types of leaders. Ginger Richardson and Susan Ballati also deserve special thanks among the SFI staff (here, here for science being led by women!).

The structure of the SFI program Co-evolution of States and Markets was an annual, month-long research working group, with rotating membership, assembled each summer by Padgett and Powell at Santa Fe. Recurrent participants were Walter Fontana, Sanjay Jain, David Stark, and Douglas White. The chemist Fontana was an informal co-leader and inspiration of our group. He is the one who introduced Padgett and the rest of us to the core concept of autocatalysis as well as much else in systems biology and evolutionary chemistry.[1] The physicist Jain is a formal modeler of autocatalysis with wide and deep interests in biology and economics. The sociologist Stark brought a theoretical commitment to cognitive reflexivity and hybridity, as well as a substantive knowledge of Eastern Europe. The mathematical anthropologist White brought modeling and data-analysis skills in the field of social networks. Because of post-project changes in direction, not all of these core participants appear in this final volume, but they were within the conversational heart and soul of this venture. Besides the authors whose work appears in this book, the mostly historically oriented other participants in the SFI co-evolution program over the years have included Julia Adams, Christopher Ansell, Dan Carpenter, Bruce Carruthers,

[1] Fontana and Buss used the different label of "self-maintaining organization" for this concept (see chapter 2). For an amusing, not altogether serious profile of Padgett and Fontana at the beginning of this program, see *SFI Bulletin* 13 (Summer 1998): 14–17.

Elizabeth Clemens, Sam Cohn, Bruce Kogut, Paul McLean, Elena Obukhova, Pip Pattison, Charles Sabel, and Brian Uzzi.

For Padgett, end-game thanks go to the University of Trento, especially to Paolo Collini, dean of the faculty of economics and management, and to Enrico Zaninotto, director of the social science Ph.D. school. Padgett recently was given a part-time faculty position there, in large part because of their intellectual support of this project and its write-up. They and the Hewlett Foundation jointly sponsored a final conference that brought together chapter authors with University of Trento critics and discussants in the spectacular mountain village of Schenna in the high Tyrolean Alps. Special thanks go to Johanna Mair and her family for hosting us in their lovely resort hotel in Schenna. The University of Trento added an evolutionary-economics sensibility to this volume and may even deserve co-parentage with SFI as institutional lineage. Massimo Warglien at the University of Venice, Alessandro Lomi at the University of Bologna,[2] Anna Grandori at Bocconi University, Massimo Egidi at Luiss University, Fabio Pammolli and Massimo Riccaboni at IMT-Lucca, Andrea Ginsburg and David Lane at the University of Modena, and Richard Goldthwaite in Florence also deserve shout-outs on the Italian front. Padgett has guest taught at most of these places.

All of the thanks just mentioned involve the recent past. The deepest intellectual tap root of this book, however, is Harrison White. Two books have emerged out of the four-year seminar that White and Padgett co-taught at Harvard in the early 1980s—this one and the first edition of White's *Identity and Control*.[3] Knowledgeable readers will appreciate how differently our theoretical answers have evolved, but the foundational questions in these two books overlap strongly. "Structural" for Harrison meant not social determinism but the iteration of often clashing relational logics. He was obsessed with how social interaction, at fairly macrohistorical scales, constructed persons, and he infected Padgett with his obsession. Together we pored through obscure history book after history book, looking to uncover insightful gems and to construct always tentative "theories of the week." Apart from any particular theory or statistical technology, Harrison imparted to his graduate students and assistant professors (including Ron Breiger) the capacity to hold multiple perspectives in our minds simultaneously and the desire to ask big questions. That is why this volume is dedicated to him.

At the University of Chicago, Padgett continued to teach a historically oriented graduate course on organizations, perhaps with a little more structure than the wildly exuberant Harvard course. Hundreds of pages of written lectures have been produced for this Chicago course over the years, some of which have developed into chapters for this book. At Chicago, Padgett also had the distinct pleasure of running a weekly workshop for twenty years, Organizations and State Formation, with frequent co-leadership by the late Roger Gould and then by Gary Herrigel. I give thanks to them and to all my students, in particular Chris Ansell, Dan Carpenter, Bruce Carruthers, Jungwoon Choi, Zhiyuan Cui, Lauren Duquette, Wendy Espeland, Kevin Esterling, Dan Levinthal, Santi Furnari, Blair Gifford, Elizabeth McGhee Hassrick, Michael Heaney, Carla Hess, John Kenny, Steve Laymon, Doowan Lee, Dan McFarland, Paul McLean, Peter McMahan, Martina Morris, Jonathan Obert, Elena Obukhova, Sarah Parkinson, Roger Peterson, Katalin Prajda, Michael Reinhard, Ethel Santacroce, Andrew Schrank, Bat Sparrow, Guy Stuart, Xing Zhong, and Kuba Zielinski.

And finally to the deepest tap root of them all, and not just in matters intellectual. Wendy Griswold knows more about the ebbs and flows of this project, these people, and these ideas than anyone else. She is the love of my life. To her, I owe not just thanks but everything. Ray and Olivia, our kids, have felt this lengthy work effort loom large in background of their lives, causing extended absences from home by dad but also fun family trips. Both kids have grown up to be independent, active, and loving young adults, precious gifts to their parents. Distinct as we are, we make a good foursome. Had she lived, my mother also would have been pleased; her love continues to flow through all of us.

For Powell, annual visits to SFI were also highly generative. Conversations with Jennifer Dunne, Doyne Farmer, Doug Irwin, José Lobo, John Miller, Mark Newman, and Geoff West were especially rewarding. Doug White and Ken Koput were crucial to my understanding of modeling and visualizing network dynamics;

[2] Lomi is now at the University of Lugano.

[3] Harrison C. White, *Identity and Control: A Structural Theory of Social Action* (Princeton: Princeton University Press, 1992).

conversations with Dan McFarland and Jim Moody were critical as well.

At Stanford, early drafts of Powell's work were regularly presented at the Stanford Institute for Economic Policy Research (SIEPR) workshop. Thanks to Tim Bresnahan, Paul David, and Jenny Kuan for comments and sustaining the workshop. A Berkeley-Stanford work-in-progress conference with Dave Mowery and Bronwyn Hall and their students and Powell's students was very fruitful. Research support from the Columbia-Stanford project on Biomedical Innovation was much appreciated, as were the associated feedback and interactions with Annetine Gelijns, Dick Nelson, Nate Rosenberg, and Bhaven Sampat. Throughout this work, conversations with economist colleagues have been priceless, and Alfonso Gambardella, Franco Malerba, Doug North, and Fabio Pammolli deserve thanks for sharing ideas.

Financial support from several NSF grants and SFI sponsored the Powell "lab" and its weekly meetings from 2000 to 2007. The earliest members—Jason Owen-Smith, Kjersten Whittington, James Evans, Stine Grodal, Caroline Simard, Brandy Aven, Andrew Nelson, Kelley Porter Packalen, Jeannette Colyvas, Andrew Parker, Jarrett Spiro, and Kaisa Snellman—were indispensable in forging a robust intellectual community. I owe them all my thanks and love. The lab subsequently morphed into the Networks and Organizations workshop, with too many participants in recent years to even try to list here. But Dan Wang deserves a shout-out for being an anchor for that workshop. Current and former faculty colleagues Steve Barley, Kathy Eisenhardt, Henning Hillman, and Dan McFarland have provided ample commentary on work in progress, as have long-term friends Neil Fligstein and Marc Schneiberg. I had the great fortune to be assigned Tanya Chamberlain as an assistant when I arrived at Stanford, and she has been with me through the entire time on this book. All of my text, tables, and figures were fashioned into shape by Tanya. Without her work, care, acute sense of organization, and professionalism, this volume would not have been completed. I owe her immense thanks and appreciation for all we have been through together.

Earlier versions of Powell's chapters were tried out in many places, but several deserve special mention. Initial drafts of chapters 13–15 were presented at the University of Oxford as the Clarendon Lectures in Management. The late Anthony Hopwood, the Dean of the Saïd School, and David Musson of Oxford University Press were most genial hosts, and Victor Seidel arranged a lovely stay at Trinity College. A term at the Judge Institute at Sidney Sussex College at the University of Cambridge provided a subsequent opportunity to present the work. Dame Sandra Dawson, then Dean of the Judge, was a gracious host. A fellowship year at the Center for Advanced Study in the Behavioral Sciences provided a conducive environment to make further progress on the manuscript. Conversations about the book with Marion Fourcade, John Lucy, Andy Markovits, Martin Ruef, and Kate Stovel were highlights of the year. Finally, completing the book was made possible by spending much of spring 2011 at the University of Chicago Booth School of Business. Ron Burt had the good sense to know that John and I needed face time together to get the book finished.

As this project was launched, Powell moved from the University of Arizona to Stanford. I had the good luck that Ken Koput continued to work with me and that Jason Owen-Smith followed me to Stanford. The move to Palo Alto was further eased when my "adopted" father, Charles Perrow, continued his wonderful habit of following my moves, first to Yale, then Arizona, and for the past decade at Stanford. Every idea has been listened to, and every page read, by Chick. His friendship has been a constant for over three decades. When this project began, my son, Ian, was nine years old. His sharpest memories of Santa Fe are likely to be our whitewater rafting of the Taos Box stretch of the Rio Grande River or trips to Anasazi ruins in Bandelier National Park. But I also deserted Ian and my wife, Marianne Broome Powell, just as we were moving into a fixer-upper house on the Stanford campus. I got to go to "work" in Santa Fe as they rebuilt our new home. Their love and tolerance of many absences have made my scholarship possible. Marianne was always willing to educate me about the biomedical sciences, and as Ian grew into a college student, he read chapters and made critical comments. They lived all the details of this project, both its joys and challenges. Neither of them will ever really know how much they have helped and sustained me.

At Princeton University Press, Eric Schwartz, Karen Carter, and Peter Dougherty have been tolerant, professional, and encouraging, steadfast in their support. Jennifer Backer tackled the immense typescript manuscript and edited it with great care and good humor. J. Naomi Linzer composed an excellent index.

Finally, at the end of the day, John and Woody need to thank each other. We have been dogged in tracking down every intellectual lead, both for ourselves and for each other. Long-term collaboration and constructive feedback don't get any better than this.

The Emergence of Organizations and Markets

1

The Problem of Emergence

John F. Padgett ▪ Walter W. Powell

ORGANIZATIONAL NOVELTY

Darwin's question about the origin of species is worth posing and exploring as much in the social sciences as it was in biology. Human organizations, like living organisms, have evolved throughout history, with new organizational forms emerging and transforming in various settings: new types of banks and banking in the history of capitalism; new types of research organizations and research in the history of science; new types of political organizations and nations in the history of state formation. All of these examples are discussed in this book. The histories of economies and polities are littered with new organizational forms that never existed before. In biological language, this emergence of new organizational forms is the puzzle of speciation.

We economists, political scientists, and sociologists have many theories about how to choose alternatives, once these swim into our field of vision. But our theories have little to say about the invention of new alternatives in the first place. New ideas, new practices, new organizational forms, new people must enter from off the stage of our imaginary before our analyses can begin. Darwin asked the fundamental question, but our concepts are like those of Darwin before Mendel and Watson and Crick. We understand selection and equilibrium, but we do not understand the emergence of what we choose or of who we are. Our analytical shears are sharp, but the life forces pushing things up to be trimmed elude us.

Novelty almost by definition is hard to understand. Something is not genuinely new if it already exists in our current practice or imagination. The terms *innovation* and *invention*, as we use them in this book, mean the construction of something neither present nor anticipated by anyone in the population. We do not mean that planned incremental improvement on what already exists is not possible—quite the opposite. This type of learning occurs far more often than does the production of genuine novelty. The conundrum for both researchers and participants is that logical cognition, no matter how useful for refinement and improvement, is unlikely to be a fundamental process for generating novelty, because logic can only use axioms that are already there.

The literature on "organizational innovation" is voluminous, but that literature largely focuses on learning,[1] search,[2] and diffusion[3] and often uses patents as indicators.[4] The term *innovation* in organization theory refers to products and ideas, never to the emergence of organizational actors per se.[5] Social science studies processes of innovation, so defined, but mainly by abstracting

[1] See, for example, March 1991; Zander and Kogut 1995; Szulanski 1996; and Argote 1999.

[2] See, for example, Levinthal and March 1981; Hansen 1999; and Rivkin and Siggelkow 2003.

[3] See, for example, Strang and Meyer 1993; Guillén 1994; Davis and Greve 1997; and Simmons, Dobbin, and Garrett 2006.

[4] See, for example, Mansfield 1986; Griliches 1990; Jaffe, Trajtenberg, and Henderson 1993; Owen-Smith and Powell 2004; and Fleming and Sorenson 2004.

[5] Numerous scholars have lamented that the origins of institutions have been largely opaque to social scientists. Kreps (1990, 530) has remarked that whereas the economics literature emphasizes the effects of institutions, it "leaves open the question, where did institutions come from?" In an assessment of the sociological literature, Barley and Tolbert (1997) underscored the neglect of how institutional arrangements are created. More recently, in a comprehensive review of organizations research, Greenwood et al. (2008, 26) conclude that "institutional studies have not been overly concerned with how institutions arise."

from the content of innovation itself.[6] Lest this limitation be mistaken for criticism, it is important to remember that Darwin himself never truly answered his own question about the origin of species. He "only" analyzed the natural selection of populations of organisms within species, once species existed. Some parts of social science with an evolutionary sympathy have absorbed Darwin,[7] but natural (or artificial) selection alone does not solve his puzzle of speciation.

Besides this introductory chapter and a coda, this book contains fourteen historical case studies of the emergence of organizations and markets, plus three modeling chapters that apply concepts from biochemistry to social evolution. The case studies are divided into three clusters: four case studies on the European co-evolution of early capitalism and state formation, four case studies on Communist economic reform and transition, and six chapters about technologically advanced capitalism and science. These case studies, discussed below, were selected because all of them contain instances of the historical emergence of organizational novelty. Some chapters also discuss failed emergence as a control group. Not all of the chapters involve speciation in the radical sense of new to human history, but nearly half of them do. All involve speciation in the sense of organizational novelty in the context of the population under study.

The three modeling chapters in part 1 extract the foundational concept of autocatalysis from the existing chemistry literature on the origins of life and then apply this concept, through agent-based computer models, first to the self-organization of economic production and second to the evolution of primitive language and communication. These simple, biochemically inspired models are in no way rich enough to capture the phenomena or the array of emergence mechanisms observed in the historical case studies.[8] But they do provide an analytical framework for specifying with some precision the social science problem of emergence. In this volume, inductive histories and deductive models are viewed as complementary (not competitive) research strategies, both being dedicated to the discovery of social processes of organizational genesis and emergence.

Organizational genesis does not mean virgin birth. All new organizational forms, no matter how radically new, are combinations and permutations of what was there before. Transformations are what make them novel. Evolution, therefore, is not teleological progress toward some ahistorical (and often egocentric) ideal. It is a thick and tangled bush of branchings, recombinations, transformations, and sequential path-dependent trajectories, just as Darwin said it was. Invention "in the wild" cannot be understood through abstracting away from concrete social context, because inventions are permutations of that context.

Historical path dependency does not imply that there are no transformational principles at the base of endless open-ended generation. Scientific prediction in open-ended, creative systems such as life is not the specification of a fixed-point equilibrium. It is the description of processual mechanisms of genesis and selection in sufficient detail to be capable, in the rich interactive context of the study system, of specifying a limited number of possible histories. This is the biology, not the physics, view of science.

A barrier, however, inhibits social science investigation into processes of organizational emergence or speciation. Most social science proceeds according to the logic of methodological individualism. That is, the analyst takes as given some constitutive features of the hypothesized individual or actor (typically preferences, beliefs, and resources) and then derives aggregate or behavioral conclusions from them. "Actors" are objects imbued with boundaries, purposes, and choices whose teleological behavior is explained thereby. Useful as this approach is for many purposes, it creates in our understanding a black hole of genesis. To assume axiomatically that real people are *actors* makes them logically impenetrable to the theories built upon them. No theory can derive its own axioms. The problem is not that the social science concept of actor is not useful. The problem is that the atomic conception of actor precludes investigation into the construction and emergence of the real people and organizations that we refer to by that abstraction. The whole question of where novelty in actors comes from, so central to any theory of evolution, never arises in the first place.

In this book, we take the following as our mantra: *In the short run, actors create relations; in the long run, relations create actors.* The difference between methodological individualism and social constructivism is not for us a matter

[6] Fortunately there are some valuable exceptions: Hughes 1983; Bijker, Hughes, and Pinch 1987; Latour 1988; Hutchins 1995; Galison 1997; Sewell 2005.

[7] For example, Simon 1969; Nelson and Winter 1982; and Hannan and Freeman 1989.

[8] Colyvas and Maroulis in chapter 16, however, explicitly develop autocatalyic models for their biotechnology case.

of religion; it is a matter of time scale. In the short run, all objects—physical, biological, or social—appear fixed, atomic.[9] But in the long run, all objects evolve, that is, emerge, transform, and disappear. To understand the genesis of objects, we argue, requires a relational and historical turn of mind. On longer time frames, transformational relations come first, and actors congeal out of iterations of such constitutive relations. If actors—organizations, people, or states—are not to be assumed as given, then one must search for some deeper transformational dynamic out of which they emerge. In any application domain, without a theory of the dynamics of actor construction, the scientific problem of where novelty comes from remains unsolvable.

The example of the human body may help to fix the idea. Viewed from the perspective of ourselves, we seem solid enough: well bounded and autonomous. But viewed from the perspective of chemistry, we are just a complex set of chemical reactions. Chemicals come into us; chemicals go out of us; chemicals move around and are transformed within us. Solid as we may appear from the outside, no single atom in our body has been there for more than a few years. It is possible (and flattering) to see our physical selves as autonomous bodies exchanging food and other nutrients, but it is also possible to see ourselves as an ensemble of chemicals that flow, interpenetrate, and interact. Stability of the human body through time does not mean mechanical fixity of parts; it means organic reproduction of parts in flux. Viewed as chemical reactions, we are vortexes in the communicating material of life that wends through us all.

To explain the emergence of new organizational actors, we take as our starting inspiration—but not as our final model—biochemical insights about the emergence of life. At the theoretical level, our approach is a merger of social network analysis with autocatalysis models from biochemistry.[10] From social network analysis we appropriate an empirical commitment to fine-grained relational data on social and economic interactions through time. For us, emergence of organizations is grounded in transformations in social networks, which wend through organizations, bringing them to life. From autocatalysis we appropriate a commitment to discovering and formalizing processual mechanisms of genesis and catalysis, which generate self-organization in highly interactive systems. For us, nodes and ties in social networks are not reified dots and lines; they are the congealed residues of history—in particular, the history of iterated production rules and communication protocols in interaction. Learning at the human level is equivalent to co-evolution of rules and protocols at the "chemical" level. Actors thereby become vehicles through which autocatalytic life self-organizes.

We regard our infrastructural work of synthesizing social science with biochemistry as essential to defining rigorously the topic of organizational novelty (or more generally novelty of actors) in the first place. Through this, we hope to point the way toward a new path in new social science—namely, toward a theory of the co-evolution of social networks.[11] Actors fall out as derivations of that theory, but they are not the axiomatic starting points. In the rest of our introduction, after a brief overview of the book, we elaborate on this approach and show its empirical relevance.

In our empirical case studies, we find that novelty in new organizational form often emerges through spillover across multiple, intertwined social networks. Hence not autocatalysis within one network but interaction among autocatalytic networks is the key to generating novelty. The empirical chapters in this volume cover a wide sample of historical cases about the emergence of new forms of economic organizations and markets. Generally, throughout the volume, *actors* refers to organizations and *relations* to markets. With our emphasis on multiple networks, however, a central finding about the production of novelty in the economic realm will be that other types of social relations—for example, politics, kinship, and science—structure the "topology of

[9] We ourselves are methodological individualists when the study time frame is short.

[10] Autocatalytic theory, described below, is a branch (a chemistry branch) of so-called complexity theory. "Complexity theory" is an umbrella term that refers to a wide variety of mathematical models of self-organization dynamics in highly interactive and nonhomogeneous systems. As is explained in more detail in chapter 2, while the individual models within this family are very precise, the umbrella term itself is not. Hence, despite its current fashion, we do not use the term *complexity theory* again.

[11] This ambition parallels the objectives of systems biology. The caution, if not disdain, that many social scientists have toward evolutionary theory is based on their unfortunate experience with Social Darwinism. If evolutionary theory were still as atomistic and as functionalist (if not Panglossian) as that, we would share their aversion. Most social scientists, however, do not appreciate how far contemporary biologists have gone beyond the usefully simplifying yet dangerously simplistic assumptions of previous generations. The cutting-edge issue in systems biology no longer is the evolution of gene frequencies; it is the evolution of genetic regulatory networks.

the possible," that is, the specific ways and trajectories through which old economic organizational forms can evolve into new ones.

The empirical case studies of emergence in this volume illustrate and develop our central insight about constructive feedbacks across multiple networks. Part 2, comprising four chapters by Padgett, analyzes the emergence of four organizational inventions in the history of early financial capitalism and state formation—namely, the medieval corporation in thirteenth-century Tuscany, the partnership system in fourteenth-century Florence, the joint-stock company and federalism in seventeenth-century Netherlands, and the Reichstag and political parties in nineteenth-century Germany. Padgett, along with Jonathan Obert in the German case, demonstrates that these organizational inventions in early capitalism and state formation emerged from dynamic feedback among economic, political, religious, and kinship networks.

The four empirical chapters of part 3 analyze organizational emergence, sometimes perverse, in the postsocialist transitions in Russia, China, and Eastern Europe. Padgett compares the political logics of economic reform under Stalin, Khrushchev, and Gorbachev in the Soviet Union and under Mao and Deng Xiaoping in China, documenting in each of these five cases the path-dependent co-evolution between political mobilization and economic reform. Andrew Spicer carries the Russian reform story forward in his case study of the unexpected developments in the history of banking under Yeltsin. Valery Yakubovich and Stanislav Shekshnia examine a more successful case of market emergence in post-Soviet Russia: the telecom industry. David Stark and Balázs Vedres trace the development and reproduction over time of business groups in Hungary, with close attention to their interactions with domestic politics and foreign multinationals.

Part 4, made up of six chapters, focuses on contemporary science and technology sectors. Four chapters by Powell and colleagues apply our theoretical framework to the high-tech case of the emergence of the biotechnology industry within the life sciences. The first chapter, by Powell and Kurt Sandholtz, focuses on the genesis of the first generation of biotech firms in the late 1970s and early 1980s, analyzing how particular attributes and practices were assembled to produce new organizational models for science. The second chapter, by Powell, Kelley Packalen, and Kjersten Whittington, traces the rapid growth and catalysis of these first-generation firms, over the years 1988–2002, into an expansive multiple-network organizational field with distinctive regional locations. They compare the networks of three successful biotech industrial districts with eight failures to congeal. The third chapter, by Powell and Jason Owen-Smith, analyzes the open-elite recruitment dynamics of reproduction within this new industry. Jeannette A. Colyvas and Spiro Maroulis round out the biotech module with an agent-based model of the rapid spread of patenting in the life sciences in research universities. This chapter extends into new empirical ground the formal model of autocatalysis by Padgett, Peter McMahan, and Xing Zhong presented in chapter 3.

Focusing more on the information-technology industry, Lee Fleming and colleagues compare inventor networks in Boston and Silicon Valley, demonstrating the emergence of innovative cross-industry connectivity in Silicon Valley. This innovation stemmed from the career brokerage by IBM of postdoctoral scientists. Through detailed internal records, Fabrizio Ferraro and Siobhán O'Mahony trace the emergence and self-organization of an innovative open-source computing company called Debian, which is as much global community as company.

These empirically rich cases of organizational and market emergence are surveyed in short introductions to each part, which make explicit the links between theory and cases. The empirical chapters were selected on the basis of two criteria: (a) detailed multiple-network information, tracing not just actors but relations among actors; and (b) dynamic networks over time, spanning an observed organizational or market invention of interest. Readers interested in particular application domains may wish to focus on the section closest to their concerns. The rest of this introductory chapter elaborates the theoretical framework that has emerged from these detailed cases.

Our theoretical elaboration proceeds as follows. First, we describe the problem of organizational novelty in the context of multiple social networks. Second, we explain our core dynamic motor of autocatalysis both at the level of chemical and economic production and at the level of the biographical production of persons through interactive learning, communication, and teaching. Third, we describe eight network mechanisms of organizational genesis that we have discovered in our case studies. Finally, we point to the important outstanding issue of structural vulnerability to tipping. The question of multiple-network poisedness is, for us, the next research frontier.

INNOVATION VERSUS INVENTION

Sometimes defining the problem is half the work. To proffer a distinction we build on throughout this book: *Innovations* improve on existing ways (i.e., activities, conceptions, and purposes) of doing things, whereas *inventions* change the ways things are done. Under this definition, the key to classifying something as an invention is the degree to which it reverberates out to alter the interacting system of which it is a part.[12] To some extent we understand micrologics of combination and recombination. Yet the invention puzzle is that some innovative recombinations cascade out to reconfigure entire interlinked ecologies of "ways of doing things," whereas most innovations do not. The poisedness of a system to reconfiguration by an invention is as much a part of the phenomenon to be explained as is the system's generation of the invention itself. Invention in the wild cannot be understood through abstracting away from concrete social context because inventions are permutations of that context. But to make progress in understanding discontinuous change, we need to embed our analysis of transformation in the routine dynamics of actively self-reproducing social contexts, where constitutive elements and relations are generated and reinforced.

Figure 1.1 lays the groundwork for understanding this distinction between innovation and invention, viewed through the lens of multiple networks. In a cross-sectional view, all social systems look like this to a social-network analyst.[13] Each plane in the figure represents a different domain of activity. In the example of Renaissance Florence illustrated here, these are the economic domain, where goods are produced and exchanged among companies; the kinship domain, where babies are produced through marriage among families; and the political domain, where deals are made among factions within the state. Other domains not shown, such as religion and the military, could be added. Solid lines represent the "constitutive ties" of cooperation or partnership in production—firms, families, and factions, respectively.[14] Markets are sets of dotted lines within domains. The term *relational ties* is used when resource flows are recurrent and focused. The people participating in organizations and markets can be categorized in various ways, through either personal attributes or institutional memberships, as shown.

Our social science disciplines usually segregate their intellectual activities by analyzing only one domain at a time, as if the other domains and disciplines did not exist. At best, external domains are conceptually black-boxed as reified "environments" without examining their internal structures. In contrast, the whole point of a multiple-network perspective is to superimpose multiple domains, with their respective production and exchange networks, and to examine feedback dynamics. Vertical lines in figure 1.1, connecting superimposed dots, are people. Each dot in a plane is a role. In the economic domain, for example, the person may be a businessman; in the kinship domain, he may be a father; in the political domain, he may be a politician—all depending upon how he is attached to others in that domain. Properly speaking, individuals don't have goals; roles have goals.[15] Consistency of motivations across roles should in no way be presumed for complicated persons.[16]

It is well recognized by scholars in the social-network tradition that micropatterns of topological overlay among different types of social networks can induce cross-sectional behavioral effects.[17] At the social psychological level, different ways of nesting various roles in a single

[12] We understand that these definitions invert the way that Schumpeter used the terms. We believe that our definitions are more consistent with typical usage in English than were Schumpeter's. See, for example, http://www.oxforddictionary.com. Semantic matters are always slippery and debatable, however. The main thing is that readers understand what we mean.

[13] This figure is a cartoon of the relational database structure of Padgett's actual Florentine data set. See Padgett 2010 for details.

[14] These three types of lines correspond to the three types of autocatalysis discussed later in this chapter. Dotted lines correspond to production autocatalysis; solid lines correspond to cellular or biographical autocatalysis; and ovals correspond to public names, emerging out of linguistic autocatalysis.

[15] Profit maximization, for example, might be the goal of a businessman. But that is not the goal of a more complicated businessman-father-politician ensemble person. For this reason, "methodological individualism" is a misnomer. "Methodological role-ism" is a more accurate description of modeling practices in the segregated world of contemporary social science.

[16] This caveat makes the imputation of any meta- or cross-role utility function to individuals problematic because Von Neumann-Morgenstern axioms are likely to be violated. Without a well-defined utility function, the definition of maximization becomes unhinged. Cross-role consistency is of course possible, but that would be quite a social achievement. In this sense, rationality (narrowly conceived as individual maximization) is socially produced.

[17] Granovetter 1985.

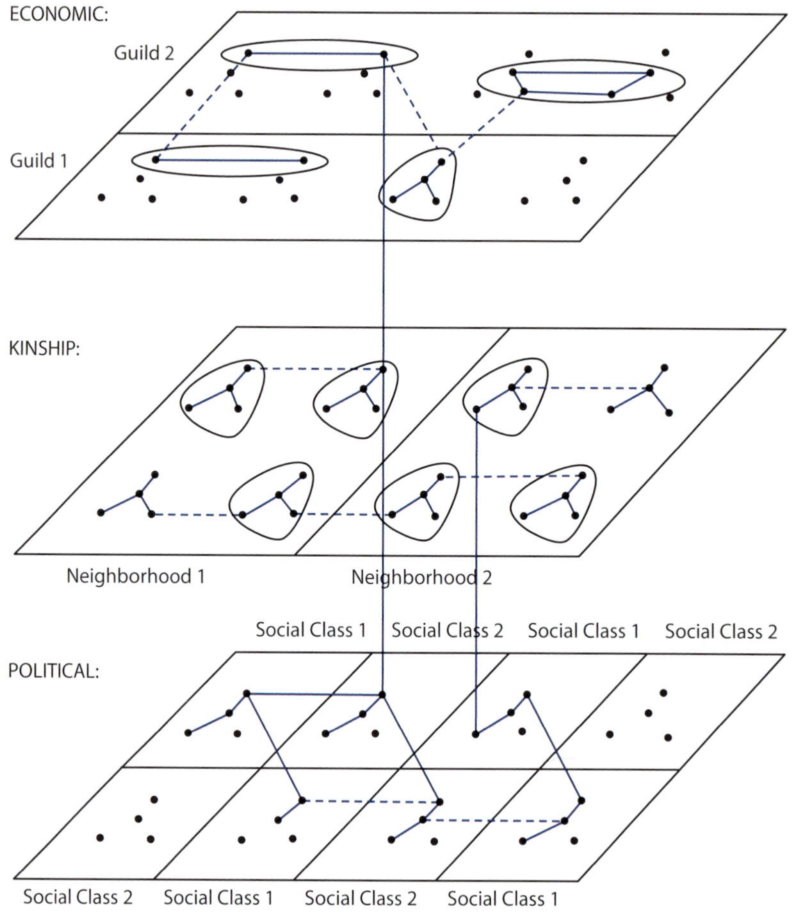

Figure 1.1 Multiple-network ensemble in Renaissance Florence. Solid lines are constitutive ties, dotted lines are relational social exchanges, and oblongs are formal organizations (families and firms). People in multiple roles are vertical lines connecting corresponding dots in domains of activity in which people are active. (Only two are shown for illustration.)

person can induce role strain, autonomy, informational access, or even freedom from social control. At the transactional level, the embeddedness or multiplexity of one type of tie in another can induce trust, normative reframing, or changes in time horizons.

Our interest is in how multiple-network topologies can shape the dynamics of emergence and evolution of organizational actors over time. Innovation in our usage is recombination through one of a variety of organizational genesis mechanisms of network folding.[18] Invention in our usage is the system tipping that might ensue as a cascade from the original innovation out through the multiple networks that originally induced it.

The network recombinant mechanisms of organizational genesis that we identify below involve transposing social relations from one domain into another. Sometimes this begins as a small-scale transposition, which then reverberates. Examples are marriage, university labs, or political patronage being used by local actors to

[18] We stick with the word *recombination* because that is so prevalent in the literature. But in our empirical cases the elements being recombined are not atomic entities, decoupled from their context, but rather nodes or ties in some network or other. For that reason, *network folding* more accurately describe the phenomena we observe than does the word *recombination*, which to our ears has atomistic overtones.

reorganize a business. Sometimes this involves larger population transpositions, where entire subsets of new networks are rewired into old ones. Rewiring then transforms both sides. Whatever the variant, topological overlay defines the routes through which relational practices flow. Relational flow occurs either via strategically located persons operating in multiple domains or via biographies that wend their way across domains. Where you sit in a multiple-network array affects both whom you can reach and who can reach you. In systems biology, the reachability constraint that underlying genetic networks impose on phenotypic evolution has been suggestively labeled "the topology of the possible."[19]

Organizational innovation, whatever its source, must reproduce in order to survive. To reproduce and to grow, organizations must succeed in attracting resource flows (dotted lines) and people flows (solid lines) into their primary fields of activity. Economic companies must succeed in product markets. But because companies' component persons and resources are embedded in other domains as well, organizations actually must survive in multiple selection environments. Politics, kinship, and maybe even religion, armies, or science must reproduce for particular types of economic firms to exist. Treating multifaceted people as reproducing flows through organizations makes the point about multiple selection environments more transparent than does focusing on products and financial flows alone.

In terms of figure 1.1, our empirical cases reveal that organizational innovation is vertical transposition of relational ties and practices across domains. Organizational invention, if it occurs, is horizontal spillover into relational and constitutive networks within domains. Organizational innovation becomes systemic invention (if it does) when local network transpositions spill over or cascade through reproductive feedback into the multiple global networks to which local relations are linked. People and skills are the usual channels through which these feedbacks are carried. If and when this chain reaction occurs, the selection environment itself for the organizational innovation is altered. This can lead to nonlinear rates of tipping—in other words, to the dynamics of punctuated equilibria. Sometimes (though rarely) invention spillover may even readjust the differentiation of domains themselves through restructuring vertical lines of multifunctional embeddedness.[20]

[19] Stadler et al. 2001; Fontana 2006.

Other labels for network cascade exist in the evolutionary literature. Co-evolution is distinguished from evolution in this literature like this: the selection environment remains fixed in evolution but it adjusts in co-evolution. When a selection environment is fixed, the performance criterion for any subunit is given, and the concept of optimum becomes well-defined in principle (even if it is impossible to reach or even perceive in practice). When selection environments are endogenously molded by the innovations they select, however, performance criteria migrate, and "optimum" loses the supporting scale upon which it is defined. Co-evolution retains notions of relative-reproduction "fitness" between systems, but it does not retain the notion of an objective optimum. Social Darwinist dreams of Panglossian progress thereby usefully vanish into an ethereal mist.

To make these general observations about innovation and invention more systematic requires precision in the motor behind multiple-network feedback. In this book, that engine primarily is autocatalysis. Figure 1.1 is a cross-sectional snapshot from what is actually a movie through time. Autocatalysis brings this otherwise static picture to reproductive life.

AUTOCATALYSIS

Production Autocatalysis

One place to look for inspiration about processes of social emergence is the origin of life. Human beings, as mentioned above, appear to us as solid and sturdy objects. But viewed as chemistry, our bodies are just a complex set of biochemical reactions, which reproduce themselves over time, given appropriate inputs from other organisms. Our self-image of temporal continuity notwithstanding, we are not the coherently bounded objects that we think we are but a chemical process

[20] As explained in the section on catalysis, if the analyst looks at figure 1.1 from the top down, viewing through superimposed domains, then he or she sees figure 1.1 as a Venn diagram. Patterns of overlaps among domains in the Venn diagram are defined by patterns of multifunctional memberships of people in figure 1.1. Change patterns of multifunctional embeddedness, therefore, and one changes patterns of domain differentiation. It is demonstrated in the ALL-chemistry models of chapter 3 that differentiation of domains (called "subsystems" in that chapter) is an automatic corollary of autocatalysis.

that renews itself for a while. From the chemical perspective, life itself can be defined as an interacting ensemble of chemicals that reproduces itself, in the face of turnover of its parts.[21]

Organizational actors are no different. The production and distribution of goods by firms are only half of what is accomplished in markets. Firms are also produced and transformed by the goods and people passing through them. Social structures should be viewed more as vortexes in the flow of social life than as buildings of stone. In organisms, social or biological, rules of action and patterns of interaction persist and reproduce in the face of continual turnover in component parts, be these cells, molecules, principals, or agents. In the flow of people through organizations, the collectivity is not renegotiated anew. Rather, within constraints, component parts are transformed and molded into ongoing streams of action.

To implement this processual view of social structure, in part 1 we build relational microfoundations, based on the biochemical literature on the origins of life. Autocatalysis is the core concept that we import. As reviewed in chapter 2, this concept was first developed and formalized by Manfred Eigen and Peter Schuster to explain the prebiotic chemical origin of life.[22] Abstracted from its chemical origins, autocatalysis can be defined as *a set of nodes and transformations in which all nodes are reconstructed through transformations among nodes in the set.* In the original biological context, nodes were chemicals, and transformations were chemical reactions.[23] Chemicals bump into other chemicals, triggering reactions that make new chemicals. If a chemical reaction network contains an autocatalytic set within it, then it reproduces itself through time, given appropriate energy inputs. Positive feedback loops or cycles of self-reinforcing transformations lie at the core of autocatalytic sets. Such cycles are at the foundation of chemical growth.[24]

Given autocatalysis, reproduction can be sustained even in the face of turnover in network components: destroy a segment of the network, and an autocatalytic network often (not always) can reconstruct its deleted segment. Self-repair is the crucial dynamic feature of autocatalytic sets that gives the set continuity through perilous times. Autocatalysis, in other words, is the network definition of life itself. In this context, the origin-of-life problem is finding prebiotic experimental conditions under which an initial random set of chemicals can self-organize and reproduce itself into an autocatalytic set. The maintenance-of-life problem is finding conditions that support self-repair and resilience.

In chapter 2, Padgett reviews the biological literature on autocatalysis for the benefit of social science readers. In chapter 3, Padgett, McMahan, and Zhong develop an agent-based model that extends this concept to the realm of economic production. There, products are like chemicals, and production rules are like chemical reactions. Actors are holding bins for production rules, through which products flow and are transformed. Economic "life" is the self-organization, through differential reproduction, of technological webs of production rules and product exchanges. These webs of production and exchange wend through multiple heterogeneous firms, constructing and reconstructing those firms, keeping them materially alive. In chapter 4, Padgett extends the production orientation of chapter 3 into communication. Not only do production rules reproduce, but communication protocols do as well. Social interaction networks thereby endogenously co-evolve with economic technology. At the level of communication, social "life" can be considered to be the self-organization of interaction protocols into language communities. Actors, either people or firms, thus become the vehicles through which life self-organizes, both in production (chapter 3) and in communication (chapter 4).

Actors—again, be they people or organizations—become who they are through learning and teaching. Autocatalysis does not challenge this fundamental insight. It just operationalizes

[21] From the physics and biological points of view, additional criteria are sometimes added to the definition of life. Physicists (e.g., Nicolis and Prigogine 1989) sometimes add the criterion of far-from-equilibrium throughput of energy. Biologists (e.g., Varela, Maturana, and Uribe 1974) may include the criterion of permeable encapsulation, like a cell. The various definitions of life are discussed in more detail in chapter 2.

[22] In 1967 Eigen received the Nobel Prize in chemistry.

[23] Autocatalysis or life, however, remains well defined even when entities other than chemicals are substituted into the "nodes" of the definition—for example, economic products, people, organizations, or words. When products are substituted, autocatalysis becomes "[a] set of economic products and production and exchange rules in which all economic products are re-created through transformations and exchanges among products in the set." This is like the Leontiev input-output (ecological) view of an economy. When people are substituted, autocatalysis becomes "[a] set of people and social interactions in which all types of people are re-created through social interactions among the people in the set."

[24] This is not to deny, of course, that negative feedback loops are also important to keep such growth bounded.

it and adds a more systemic emphasis on the network feedbacks induced in linked chains of learners. Actors learning through interaction is the same as production rules and communication protocols reproducing and diffusing among them. Through structured social interaction, endogenous or not, chains of rules and protocols assemble themselves via autocatalytic growth into technologies (chains of production rules), markets (chains of exchanged products), and language communities (chains of communication protocols).

Autocatalysis suggests a modification in how social-network analysts should conceptualize and measure network ties. Autocatalytic networks are networks of transformations, not networks of mere transmission. Neither information nor products are inert sacks of potatoes passing through passive networks-as-pipes. Information is transformed through communication protocols, and products are transformed through production rules. Either way, social networks don't just pass things; they do transformational work. Under this view, diffusion should be reconceptualized from mimicry to chain reactions. The autocatalytic self-organization of these chain-reaction transformations is emergence.

The connection between these microprocessual points and the macro-architecture of figure 1.1 is as follows. Findings from the autocatalytic production models of chapter 3 include these: Technological complexity increases as spatial constraints on exchange interaction are imposed. Altruism evolves because it supports repair of cycles better than selfishness, but selfishness can gain traction through stigmergy. Intelligence increases the speed of convergence to evolutionary equilibrium but does not alter that equilibrium. The agent-based finding most relevant to figure 1.1, however, is that multiple, overlapping production networks emerge spontaneously, without requiring any intervention by the experimenter. The emergence of multiple, differentiated yet partially overlapping domains of activity (the planes of figure 1.1), in other words, is a surprisingly automatic corollary of autocatalytic processes. "Domains" are sets of production rules and products that are autocatalytic. "Overlapping domains" means that some products, production rules, and/or communication protocols in these sets are shared. Multiple overlapping domains emerge in autocatalytic models because shared rules and products create synergistic feedbacks—both positive for stimulation and negative for regulation—between individual autocatalytic production networks. Because of such synergies, multiple networks that self-organize are reproductively more resilient than any one autocatalytic network alone.

Embedding of exchange of any sort (economic, political, kinship, or whatever) in multiple reinforcing networks means that innovations and inventions in any one domain are resisted. Resilient self-repair at the system level implies reproductive stickiness at the microlevel. The closer to the reproductive cyclic core of any autocatalytic system, the denser the networks of homeostatic feedback. This is why creative destruction is often an important prequel to innovation and invention.[25] This is also why invention, if and when it ever does break through, can appear as rapid "punctuated equilibria," with unintended spillover consequences for organizations in collateral domains. The problem of novelty would not be so difficult were not autocatalytic life in place to resist it. The further evolution proceeds, indeed, the harder it becomes to generate genuine novelty. Reshuffling and relabeling of superficially new things is breathlessly mistaken for innovation in advanced societies when actually that only reproduces the old.

Once the microdynamics of autocatalysis are folded into the network topology of figure 1.1, processes of network selection and organizational novelty become more well defined. Innovation or novelty in actors is a new partition of production rules or communication protocols into organizations or people. Organizational selection occurs whenever a new partition is reproducible through product and informational feedback with other interacting organizations of rules and protocols. Organizational novelty that survives without disturbing other partitions we label an organizational innovation. Organizational novelty that tips into disrupting other partitions, which collectively find their own modified autocatalysis, we label a systemic invention. The extent of spillover is obviously a matter of degree.

Autocatalysis is network self-organization and emergence, but that alone is not the same

[25] We modify Schumpeter's famous point about creative destruction, however, as follows: Unlike Schumpeter's famous characterization of "creative destruction" as the elimination of old businessmen and their replacement by new ones (Schumpeter 1947, 131–34; Schumpeter 1939, 87–101), we define "creative destruction" as the breakup of old networks and their replacement by new ones. Our version includes Schumpeter's version as a subset but is not limited to it. Many of our historical cases illustrate unintended innovation produced by conservative elites trying hard to resist it.

thing as novelty. Autocatalysis is our relational version of Darwinian selection—namely, successful reproduction that keeps networks alive, resilient, and maintaining themselves through perilous time. It operationalizes our point above that "to make progress in understanding discontinuous change, we need to embed our analysis of transformation in the routine dynamics of actively self-reproducing social contexts, where constitutive elements and relations are generated and reinforced." Network novelty, the Mendelian side, comes into focus when we discuss our eight network-folding mechanisms of organizational genesis. To fully understand organizational evolution, the network analogues of Darwin and Mendel have to be put together.

Biographical Autocatalysis

In our extension of autocatalytic theory to social applications, we distinguish three types of autocatalysis: (1) Production autocatalysis, just discussed (see also chapter 3), is the production and transformation of products through skills within cells and relational exchange ties among cells.[26] Here products flow through skills, and skills reproduce within cells. Exchange ties emerge to reinforce the flow of transformed products into self-reproducing life. (2) Cellular or biographical autocatalysis, to be discussed in this section and in chapter 4, is the production and flow of skills among cells through constitutive teaching between cells. Cells themselves learn new skills, die, and are replaced. Lineages of descent emerge to reinforce the flow of skills into inheritance across generations of cells. (3) Linguistic autocatalysis, adumbrated in chapter 4, means that words and symbols reproduce through conversational use in production. Linguistic autocatalysis does not play a central role in any of the organizational inventions we have observed empirically, but we fully recognize that the autocatalysis of language, and how this relates to organizational genesis, is an important topic for future research.[27]

The first type of autocatalysis, which produces products, is nested inside the second one, which produces biographies. More advanced autocatalytic systems are regulated through stochastically channeling biographies, whose intertwining directs the flows of skills and relational protocols.

The second level of biographical autocatalysis emerges because of cell death and turnover. One of the main findings of Eigen and Schuster, reconfirmed in the agent-based models in chapter 3, is that autocatalytic life beyond four chemicals/products cannot be sustained in a random (e.g., gaseous or liquid) topology. They called this the "complexity barrier" to the emergence of life. This is why complex life beyond four chemicals is always spatially embodied. In an economic context, this is why production organizations, such as firms, exist. Given embodiment of a far-from-equilibrium vortex, cell death sooner or later becomes inevitable.[28]

Faced with cell death and turnover, autocatalytic systems need cell replenishment and renewal to survive. In biological systems, genetic inheritance and phenotypic development are there to fill this gap. In social systems, teaching does the trick of overcoming death. Teaching of what? In our framework, "constitutive ties" mean that cells teach other cells production skills and relational protocols. Production skills have already been discussed: these are the rules or technologies that transform products into each other. Relational protocols are not literally the set of addresses or names of others with whom to have relational-exchange or constitutive-teaching network ties. They are the higher-order learning rules through which cells develop such lists of access from their own personal experience. Cell inheritance in the social context means passing production skills and relational protocols down from experienced cells to less experienced cells, including to blank cells. Teaching ties that percolate down induce biographies of descendants coming back up.

In this context of cell death and turnover, cellular autocatalysis can be visualized as a spiral through time of reproducing rules, analogous to the cycle in space of reproducing products in production autocatalysis. Even though particular cells come and go with finite lifetimes, collectively autocatalytic cells construct copies of their components through teaching. In the social examples in this book, this process of cells constituting each other happens gradually through

[26] "Cells" is our neutral synonym for actors, which can mean either people or organizations, depending upon the application.

[27] A recent book by Padgett's coauthor and former student Paul McLean (2007) points in a promising direction.

[28] Prigogine's famous phrase "far from equilibrium" (Nicolis and Prigogine 1989) refers to physical systems, such as life, but also other systems that spontaneously self-organize through a continuous influx of energy beyond some threshold. Interrupt the energy influx and such systems drop back to equilibrium—that is, they die.

interactional time, not all at once as in biological birth. Intertwined lineages of teaching are the social analogues of biological families.[29] Changes in lineages of teaching induce new types of biographies to emerge.

Cellular autocatalysis of cells and biographies usually crystallizes on a slower time frame than does production autocatalysis of products and skills. In our empirical cases, we often observe organizational innovation triggered by unanticipated transpositions of people from one domain to another, who carry with them production skills and relational protocols that mix with and transform skills and protocols already there. Organizational invention, following such innovation, is usually the slower process of the new innovation percolating around the networks in which it is embedded, tipping them into new topologies and interactional forms along the way. More radical episodes of this process lead to "innovation cascade." Restructured biographies are the medium through which network spillover is transmitted.

In this book we often speak of a two-stage process of organizational genesis and organizational catalysis. Organizational genesis is the transposition of skills and relational protocols that triggers innovation. Organizational catalysis is the slower process of absorbing innovation into transformed collateral networks through restructured biographies. If this happens (which is rare because preexisting autocatalyses resist it), this transmutes organizational innovation into systemic invention.

Multifunctionality—the participation of cells, skills, and relational protocols in more than one domain—lies at the center of how domains intersect. Hence multifunctionality lies at the center of the topology of how organizational innovations, wherever they come from, diffuse or do not diffuse into systemic invention. In terms of the Venn diagrams later in this chapter, multifunctionality is the pattern of shared overlap among distinct autocatalytic domains. Innovation spillover across domains, if it occurs, occurs through parts in common.

Biographical restructuring is particularly consequential, therefore, when it rewires how multifunctional cells or people are assembled across domains. Our more dramatic cases of systemic invention show transformations not just in particular domains—economics, politics, kinship, science—but in generic ways that people interact, across multiple domains. Renaissance Florence, to take one example, innovated not just in economics. It also developed a new generic way of interacting across social classes—namely, a patron-client relational protocol—that operated in politics, economics, kinship, and art, transforming all of these domains in the process. Early modern Netherlands, to take a second example, innovated not only in economics. It also developed a new generic way of interacting across geographical space—namely, a federalist relational protocol—that operated in politics, economics, and religion. Contemporary biotechnology, to take a final example, developed a new model for doing research and development—namely, privatized labs—that operated in markets, in universities, and even in government. These are transformations not just in individual domains but in how domains fit together.

Cellular autocatalysis, to sum up, is the self-sustaining feedback of cells teaching each other production skills and relational protocols within any one domain. Multiple-network cellular autocatalyses are the self-sustaining feedbacks of cells teaching each other production skills and relational protocols in multiple domains linked through parts in common. Altering the first changes careers. Altering the second changes biographies.

[29] See chapter 4 for a formal model of this.

MECHANISMS OF ORGANIZATIONAL GENESIS

Single autocatalytic networks generate life, but they do not generate novel forms of life. There is nothing outside of a single decontextualized network to bring in to recombine with what is already there. Self-organizing out of randomness into an equilibrium of reproducing transformations, the origin of life, was a nontrivial accomplishment, to be sure. But this is not quite speciation, which is the emergence of one form of life out of another.

Transpositions and feedbacks among multiple social networks are the source of organizational novelty. In the multiple-network framework, networks are the contexts of each other. Studying organizational novelty places a premium on measuring multiple social networks in interaction because that is the raw material for relational recombination. Of course in any real research project, one cannot measure everything, but that is a statement about research design, not a statement about reality.

In what follows, we extract and abstract the mechanisms of organizational genesis that we have discovered in our case studies. These genesis mechanisms involve network transpositions or linkages of one sort or another from one domain to another, which altered the flow of cross-domain biographies in reproducible ways. After describing the multiple-network genesis mechanisms that produced our observed organizational innovations, we then go on in each case to describe the catalysis mechanisms that elevated organizational innovation into organizational invention.

The word *recombination* is often used in the literature to refer to processes of generating novelty, but that word is too atomistic for our tastes. Here the people, practices, and relational protocols being recombined are attached to networks, with percolation consequences. *Network folding* more accurately describes the novelty-making processes that we see.

The eight network-folding (and also network-tearing) mechanisms of organizational genesis that we describe briefly in this section are these:

1) Transposition and refunctionality
2) Anchoring diversity
3) Incorporation and detachment
4) Migration and homology
5) Conflict displacement and dual inclusion
6) Purge and mass mobilization
7) Privatization and business groups
8) Robust action and multivocality

We regard this list of organizational genesis mechanisms as a start toward developing social-network analogues to Mendel's biological rules for recombining genes. The invention mechanisms are elaborated, and indeed were often discovered, in the empirical chapters in this volume.

Transposition and Refunctionality

Our first organizational genesis mechanism, transposition and refunctionality, is the movement of a relational practice from one domain to another and its reuse for a different function or purpose in the new domain. Transposition and refunctionality is not innovation in the usual sense of a new tool for an old purpose; this is innovation in the sense of a new purpose for an old tool.[30]

Relations and relational protocols originally developed in one autocatalytic network are inserted into another network and reproduce there, possibly tipping those networks in the process.

In chapter 6, Padgett documents the transposition, via the city council in Renaissance Florence, of the master-apprentice relationship in domestic guilds to the international world of merchant-finance, thereby making the partnership system. In chapter 13, Powell and Sandholtz document the transposition, via venture capital, of the scientific life-sciences lab from the university to the market, thereby making the dedicated biotechnology firm. To show the similarity in process of organizational genesis between these otherwise disparate cases, transposition and refunctionality is diagrammed in figure 1.2a for Florence and in figure 1.3a for biotech.

In the Florentine case, an employment relationship of master-apprentice was transposed, through the city council in response to the Ciompi revolt, from its original home in domestic guilds into the new more open world of international finance. Economic function altered thereby: a senior partner invested in a set of legally independent branch partners, who were traders and bankers. This transformed the master/senior partner from an entrepreneur into a financier. In outline, the partnership systems of Renaissance Florence resemble venture capitalists today.

Catalysis and reproduction of transposition and refunctionality in both the Florentine and the biotechnology cases were produced by the emergence of a new open elite of biographical flows, which broke down previous social boundaries. In the case of Florence, new-men bankers participating in partnership systems gradually intermarried with politically victorious segments of the old patricians. This class synthesis through social mobility made a new type of "Renaissance man," the merchant-republican. This restructured elite was based not on inherited blood and state service alone but also on patronage and aesthetic taste. Through intense social mimicry, the contemporary conception of

[30] Gould and Vrba (1982, 6) explain their term *exaptation* in the following way: "We suggest that characters evolved for other usages (or for no function at all), and later coopted for their current role, be called *exaptations*." This is essentially the same as our term *refunctionality*. Hence our research program for social science parallels that of Gould (2002) for biology. Gould and Vrba offer examples but no list of genesis mechanisms for how their exaptations are achieved. Like Gould, we emphasize the consistency of our search for historical mechanisms of speciation/genesis with Darwin's emphasis on natural selection. Also like Gould, we insist that natural selection operates at the network level of interacting systems, not only at the level of atomistic and individualistic genes.

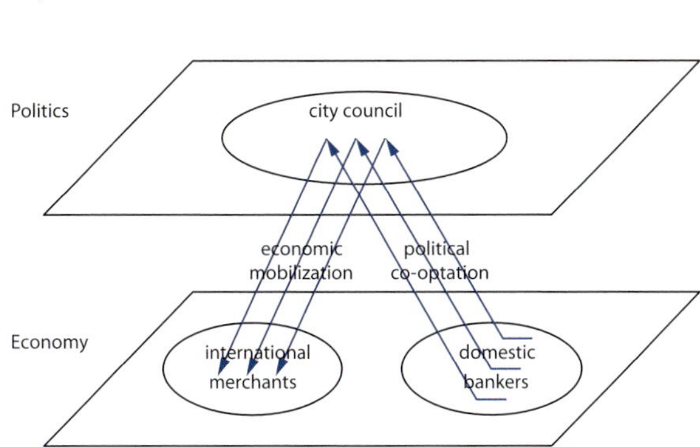

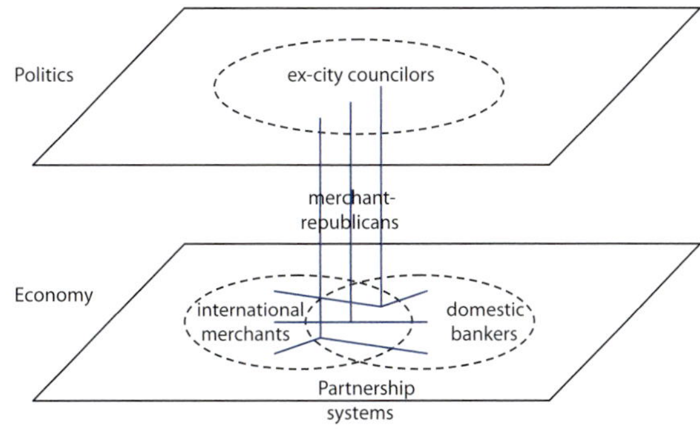

Figure 1.2a Partnership systems in Renaissance Florence: genesis.

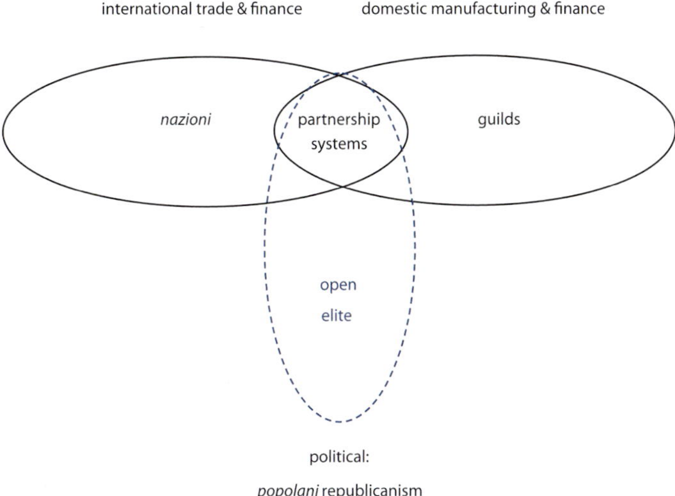

Figure 1.2b Partnership systems in Renaissance Florence: catalysis. Venn diagram oblongs are the domains of figure 1.1 viewed vertically from the top down, looking through the planes superimposed. Overlapping oblongs contain people active in multiple domains. In all the b figures in chapter 1, solid ovals refer to production autocatalysis, and dotted ovals refer to cellular autocatalysis.

Transposition:

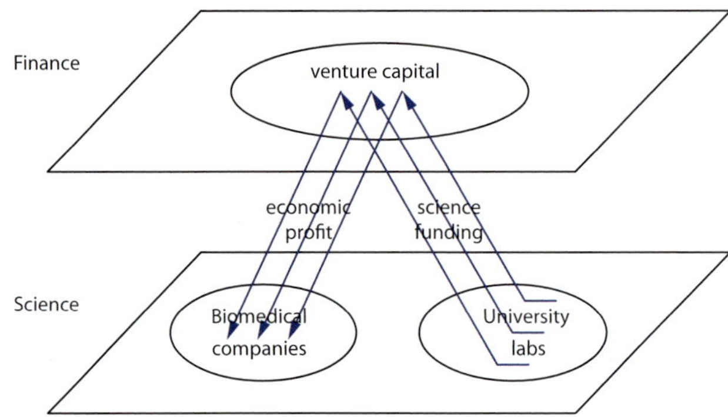

Refunctionality:

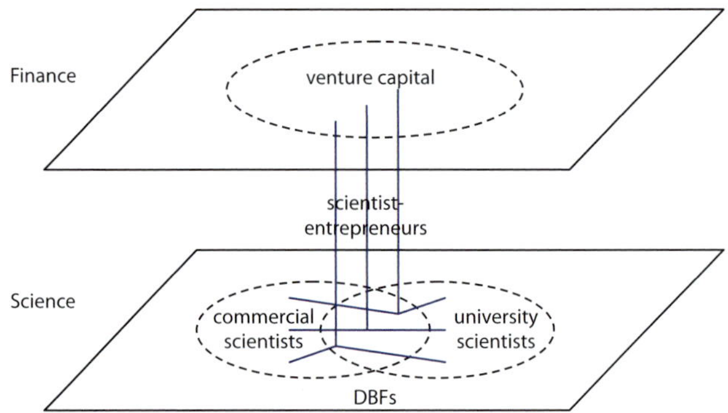

Figure 1.3a Dedicated Biotechnology Firms (DBF): genesis.

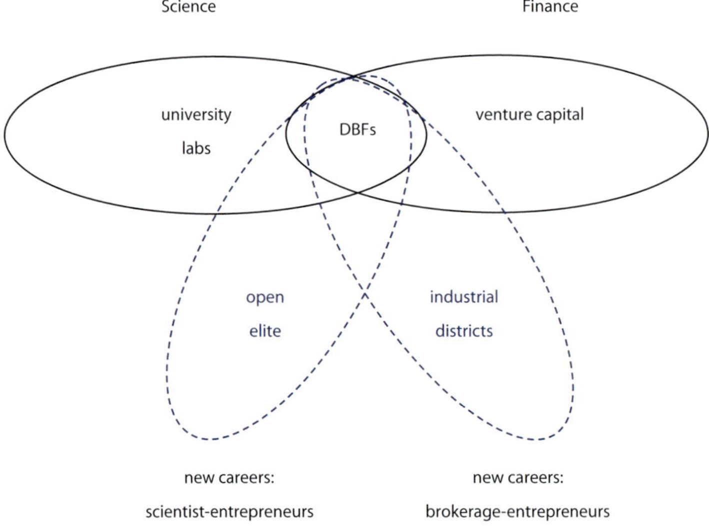

Figure 1.3b Dedicated Biotechnology Firms (DBF): catalysis.

"elite" became more a widely diffused ideal than a stable demographic reality.[31]

All b figures in this section illustrate the autocatalyses that locked in the organizational geneses shown in the corresponding a figures. The two figures are complimentary: innovation was produced by the organizational genesis mechanisms of figure a. Invention was generated by the organizational catalysis mechanism of figure b. In all the b figures of catalysis, black solid ovals represent production autocatalyses and blue dotted ovals represent cellular autocatalyses.

As documented in chapter 6, restructured channels of political and social co-optation transformed Florentine social mobility and biographies, thereby elevating partnership systems from an influential organizational innovation in the history of business to a new constitutive network in Florence's social and political elite. This new merchant-republican open elite, in turn, stimulated and bankrolled the famous sequence of artistic and political inventions that we label the Renaissance. The organizational invention of partnership systems in Florence triggered not only new banking but also new elite network structures.

In the case of contemporary biotechnology, the academic science laboratory was transposed, through venture capitalists in response to new gene manipulation technologies, from its cozy home in universities into the new more profit-oriented world of the market. Chapter 13 by Powell and Sandholtz analyzes the origins of the first generation of biotechnology companies, founded by amphibious scientists who carried scientific practices into the world of commerce. The result was the creation of a science-based firm, which was the product of overlapping networks of science, finance, and commerce. The setting is the 1970s, a time when landmark scientific discoveries in molecular biology triggered perturbations in university science, pharmaceutical research, and venture finance. The novel collection of organizational practices that coalesced into a new science-based commercial entity, the dedicated biotech firm, proved disruptive, as patenting was added to publishing as measures of scientific output. Amphibious scientist-entrepreneurs introduced academic norms into the start-up world while unwittingly conducting commercial values and metrics into the academy.

The case of biotechnology also illustrates the concept of open elite as a biographical catalysis mechanism, further emphasizing the parallelism across centuries of these two seemingly disparate cases. In chapter 15, Powell and Owen-Smith analyze the emergence of a core group of diverse, highly interconnected organizations, which they also dub an open elite. The animating question is why this group of organizations, which constitutes a structural backbone of the field, has not become an ossified gatekeeper but remains engaged in expansive exploration. The answer is found in their multiconnectivity, the multiple, independent pathways that link diverse types of research-focused organizations in a wide array of different activities. The analysis sheds light on how a select group of incumbent elites can absorb novel challenges from upstart organizations.

Anchoring Diversity

In addition to open elite, the case of biotechnology also exhibits a second catalysis mechanism, that of regional agglomeration or industrial districts, as illustrated in figure 1.3b. Eleven regional agglomerations of biomedical research, drug, development, and finance in the United States are analyzed by Powell, Packalen, and Whittington in chapter 14: three successful cases and eight unsuccessful ones. From the perspective of dedicated biotech firms (DBFs), industrial districts catalyze DBFs, but from the perspective of the districts themselves, life-science regional clusters can be considered higher-order emergent organizations themselves.

The three successful regional biotech agglomerations in the San Francisco Bay Area, Boston, and San Diego all profited from intense contractual collaborations among a diverse array of organizational forms, most notably public research organizations (such as universities and research institutes), venture capital, and dedicated biotechnology firms, but also others. In contrast, contractual collaboration in the eight unsuccessful regional agglomerations was led by a single organizational form: pharmaceuticals in New Jersey and Philadelphia, financial institutions in New York and Houston, the National Institutes of Health in Washington, D.C., supply companies in Los Angeles, and a DBF in Seattle. "Anchoring diversity" refers to the mediating role of

[31] See Padgett 2010 for elaboration on and statistical proof of these conclusions, based on two centuries of population and network data on changing social mobility and kinship in Florence. Padgett demonstrates that the driver behind social mobility between 1300 and 1500, particularly pronounced after the Ciompi revolt, was contradiction between three orthogonal and contending dimensions of social status: age of lineage, average household wealth, and membership in political factions during three intense crises.

community-oriented organizations—sometimes public research organizations, sometimes venture capitalists, sometimes DBFs themselves—in the cores of each of the three successful clusters. The activities of these so-called anchor tenants generated new organizations and fostered ties among others. Open norms of science, company spin-offs, and labor mobility are three of the network mechanisms that underlie the community-building orientation of these anchor tenants.

In chapter 17, Fleming, Colfer, Marin, and McPhie also analyze comparatively the emergence of industrial districts in Silicon Valley and Boston, exploring not only biotechnology but all of their high-tech industries together. Using a data set of inventors that patented in the United States from 1975 through 2002, they observe dramatic aggregation of regional inventor networks, first in Silicon Valley and three years later in Boston. Despite considerable similarity in the number of patents, inventors, technologies, and firms and in the overall density of ties, the inventors in Boston were more fragmented and specialized by industry than were the inventors in Silicon Valley. Drawing on interviews with inventors who did—and did not—create ties across each region's network components, they demonstrate the importance of "academic" institutions, both educational like Stanford and proprietary like IBM's Almaden Labs, for biographical linkage, information flow, and commercial science. Such training institutions enabled the earlier aggregation of Silicon Valley by encouraging the movement of young inventors into innovative bridging positions. This blending of local organizations and industries through the biographies of scientists enabled the formation of rich and generative ecologies between academic and corporate organizations and technologies.

Incorporation and Detachment

Our third organizational genesis mechanism involves the insertion of a connected chunk of one network into another, at first without detaching it from its original network. A hybrid organization forms in the (perhaps tension-laden) incorporation overlap. The hybrid eventually detaches to find its own new exchange relations. In chapter 5, Padgett illustrates this incorporation-and-detachment mechanism through the creation of the medieval merchant-banking corporation. This was the first ongoing organizational form of international finance in Europe that involved sedentary merchants in offices. The pope triggered this emergence by mobilizing Tuscan merchants from his hometown Champagne fairs into papal administration for the Italian crusades. The concept of "corporation" in economics thus originally had religious overtones, as in an organ in the body of Christ militant.[32] Later merchant-banks detached from the Church to find their own way in new patterns of international trade, which they pioneered. The incorporation and detachment process is diagrammed in figure 1.4a.

Catalyzed reproduction of this new organizational form proceeded through a cascade of induced innovations that percolated around the exchange networks in which the Tuscan medieval corporations were embedded. First, Tuscan bankers transferred their new state-finance methods to England, creating a new customs method of taxation there. Second, Tuscan bankers to the King of England used their new-found leverage over English wool to construct a textile industry back home to compete with Flanders and to give themselves a more stable commercial foundation than the profitable but very risky state finance. Finally, successful merchant-bankers slowly transformed themselves into noble patrilineages, using a *consorteria* relational protocol common to many noble social organizations in medieval times. Instead of "company out of family," this was "family out of company." Figure 1.4b shows this catalysis of merchant-banks through kinship. This organizational invention of a mercantile nobility set Italy onto a very different co-evolutionary trajectory than France or England.

Migration and Homology

The fourth organizational genesis mechanism that we document in this book is migration and homology, discussed in chapter 7 on early modern Netherlands by Padgett. The profoundly consequential modern organizational inventions of joint-stock company, stock market, and governmental federalism all were produced as by-products of this. The Dutch Revolt in the late seventeenth century triggered a massive migration of Protestant merchants and artisans from what is now Belgium into what is now Netherlands, within what was then the politically unitary Spanish Netherlands. Precocious southern merchants brought advanced commercial and

[32] The word *corpus* in Latin means body.

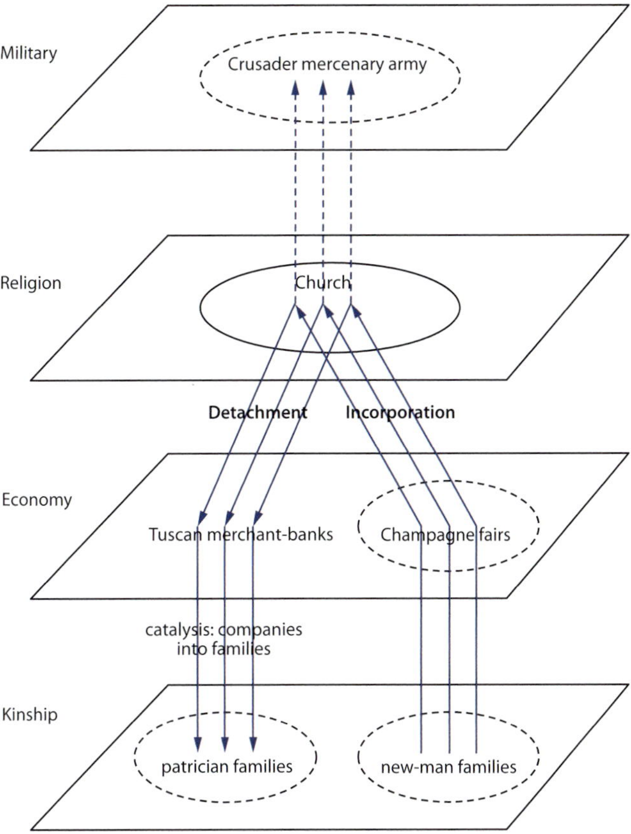

Figure 1.4a Medieval corporations in Dugento Tuscany: genesis.

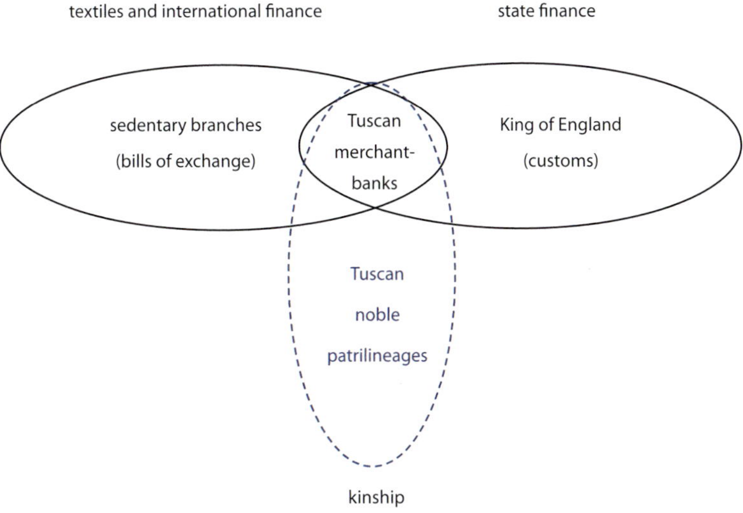

Figure 1.4b Medieval corporations in Dugento Tuscany: catalysis.

financial techniques, as well as economic connections throughout Europe, with them from Antwerp to Amsterdam to mix with the predominantly shipping skills already there. Southerners, no matter how wealthy, were not admitted to native political structures of regencies, which were inherited from the decapitated Spanish. But they were blended with native elites in the two collateral pillars of the Dutch Reformed Church and the Dutch East and West India Companies, which were homologous to and modeled on the federalism of the Dutch Revolt itself. The first joint-stock company and the first stock market, in the Amsterdam Bourse, were nautical extensions into overseas colonialism of the nascent Dutch federalist state. Padgett labels the three homologous pillars that reinforced each other to make the new country of the Netherlands "tripartite federalism." The genesis mechanism is illustrated and the story is told in figure 1.5a.

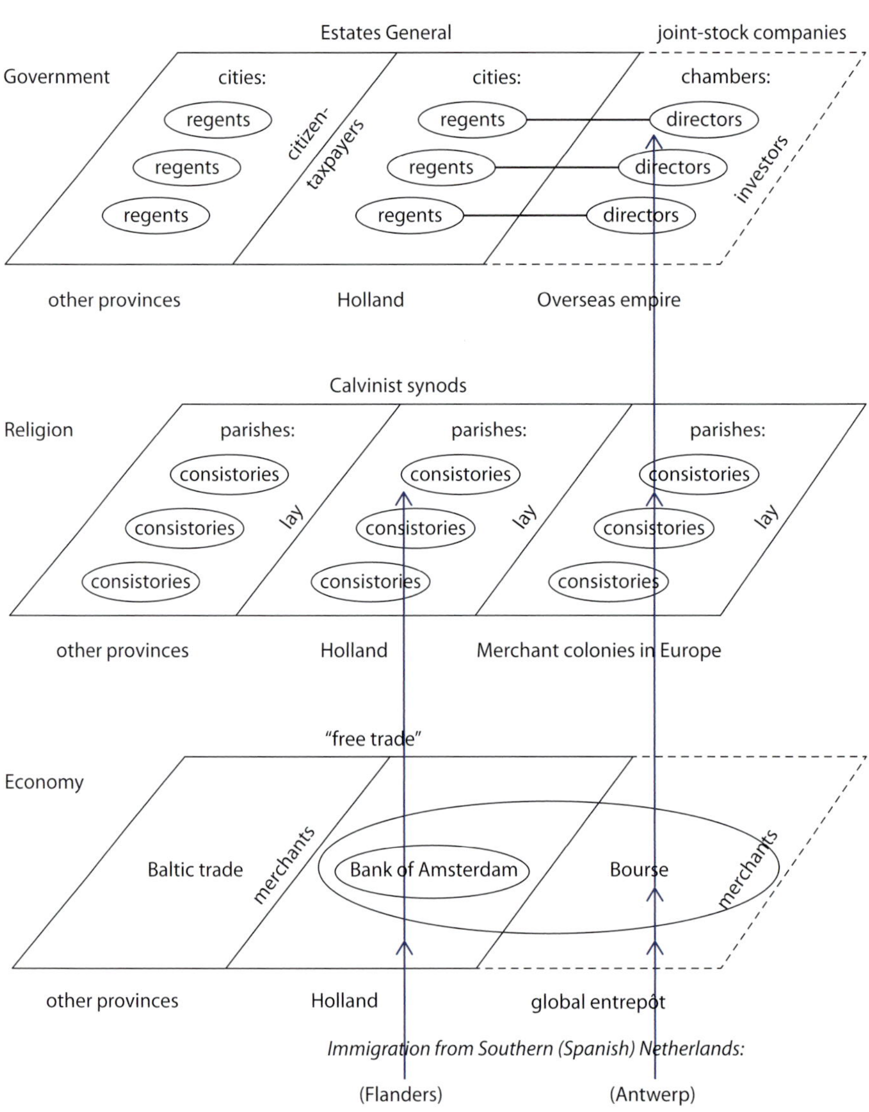

Figure 1.5a Joint-stock companies in early modern Netherlands: genesis.

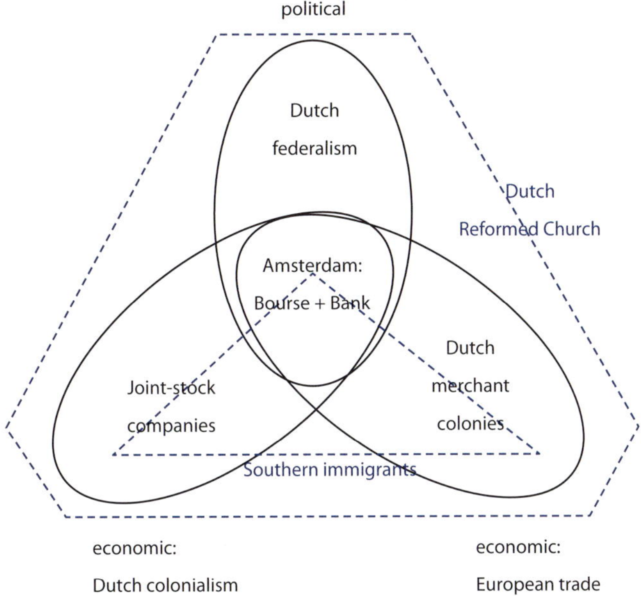

Figure 1.5b Joint-stock companies in early modern Netherlands: catalysis.

Biographical reconstruction to catalyze these organizational innovations into reproductive invention, Padgett argues, was accomplished through Calvinism. The Calvinist organizational system of consistories (boards of observant elders) was the midwife to bringing southerners and northerners into uneasy but ultimately successful communication and synthesis. "Lateral control," Padgett's label for public peer pressure, became a new generalized relational protocol through which the heterogeneous Dutch constructed their outward-looking mosaic. The final organizational invention of the Dutch central state bank, so influential for later British economic development, was essentially the consistory of the Amsterdam Bourse. The catalysis of Dutch economics and politics through the Dutch Reformed Church is summarized in figure 1.5b.

Conflict Displacement and Dual Inclusion

The organizational innovation in chapter 8 by Obert and Padgett is nothing less than the formation of Germany. More particularly, organizational genesis here means the assembly by Prussia in the nineteenth century of geographically disparate German principalities under a new constitutional umbrella of Reichstag, Bundesrat, and chancellery. Organizational catalysis in this context means the emergence of political parties and mass interest groups to manage this constitutional core in the name of German nationalism. Dual inclusion is the stapling together by Bismarck of the deeply contradictory principles of democracy and autocracy through his mutual-control balancing of "Prussia is in Germany, and Germany is in Prussia." This deep contradiction, built into the heart of the German state, drove forward the production of a succession of new political actors in German history.

Repeatedly in international wars with Austria and France and in domestic wars with Catholics and socialists, Bismarck used his characteristic style of conflict displacement to push forward institutional development. In a triad of mutually hostile relations, conflict displacement is the attack by an aggressor on a demonized other with the consequence of splitting a bystander, one segment of which joins into fragile alliance with the aggressor. Conflict displacement is a violent method of forming new ties by breaking old ones. Bismarck assumed the role of broker between the aggressor and the allied segment, but more deeply he assumed the role of charismatic hieratic authority that embodied the newfound unity of opposites.

Figure 1.6a diagrams how conflict displacement worked in the first episode of its use: Prussian war on Austria. Simultaneously with war,

Bismarck offered universal suffrage to conquered northern German subjects in a new German Reichstag legislature, thereby splitting them in sentiment from their princes, who had been allied with Austria. Instead of Prussian conqueror, Bismarck received the attribution of German liberator. Defeated and isolated German princes were co-opted into a new legislative upper house, the Bundesrat, and prostrate Austrian status superiors were treated leniently in peace.

To stabilize the reproduction of this dual-inclusion ensemble of Prussian autocracy and German democracy required not just clever tactics in war but the reconstruction of particularistic subjects biographically into German nationalists. Figure 1.6b illustrates this. An economic foundation for this reconstruction preceded Bismarck: the Zollverein or free-trade customs union that connected agricultural east with industrializing west into a budding domestic mass market.

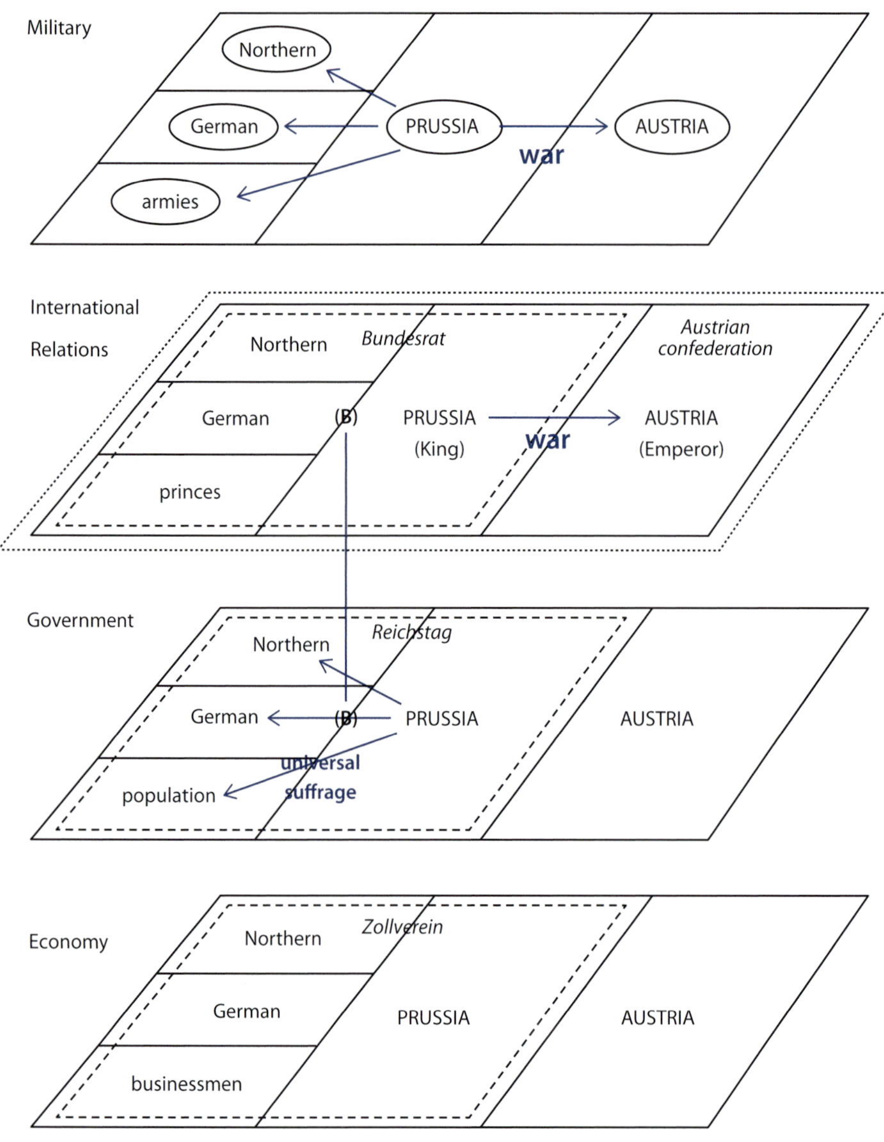

Figure 1.6a Nineteenth-century Germany: genesis through conflict displacement.

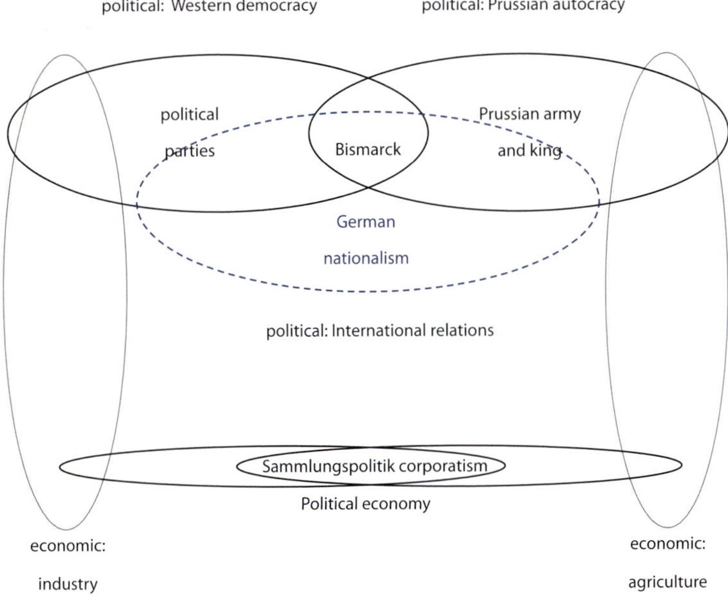

Figure 1.6b Nineteenth-century Germany: catalysis.

Economic potential was turned into political reality through two steps: elitist political parties of nationalism, of which Bismarck approved, and mass interest groups of nationalism, of which Bismarck did not. Early German political parties were parties of notables, suitable to Bismarck's elitist mentality. His otherwise successful conflict-displacement tactics, however, backfired seriously with Catholics and socialists, who responded to the conflict-displacement assaults on them by forming solidary mass political parties, an organizational portent of the future.

Conflict displacement was a powerful mechanism for constructing the German state, but that does not mean that it always worked as intended or that the resulting state functioned smoothly. Contra the mythology of Bismarck as genius, internal contradictions and pressures led to the explosive sequential production of new mass political organizations and movements, and ultimately down the road to World War I and beyond. They also changed Bismarck himself and what he was trying to achieve.

Purge and Mass Mobilization

In communism, dual hierarchy was the two hierarchies of Communist Party and central command economy arrayed parallel to each other with cross-cutting levels of overlapping inspection and control, like a ladder. In chapter 9, Padgett derives the political consequences of this multiple-network structure for the dynamics of economic reform under communism: under Stalin, under Mao, under Khrushchev, under Brezhnev/Kosygin, under Andropov, under Gorbachev, and under Deng Xiaoping. He shows that this structure imposed four and only four families of reform trajectory on leaders: mobilization of the top of the party, mobilization of the bottom of the party, mobilization of the economic ministries, and mobilization of economic factories. Reading history forward, not backward, Padgett interprets economic reform even under Gorbachev and Deng as a political dynamic within communism, not as a teleological imitation of Westerners.

The second, most radical of these reform trajectories is "purge and mass mobilization." In this, upper ranks of hierarchies are purged (and sometimes worse), and bottom tiers, often youthful, are raised up to take their place. Stalin did this first with collectivization and then with the Great Terror. Mao did this with collectivization and with the Cultural Revolution. Gorbachev tried unsuccessfully to do this with democratization. Even post-Communist Yeltsin, analyzed in a complementary chapter 10 by Spicer, did this in an inverted way with privatization. The organizational invention of the central command economy itself was produced by the first two waves of these purges and mass mobilizations under Stalin. Figure 1.7a illustrates Stalin's organizational intervention during the Great Terror.

Catalysis of the central command economy was accomplished by two types of biographical reconstruction. First, the "circular flow of power" through the *nomenklatura* system was the appointment and promotion by leaders of their supporters to selectorates, which then ratified them as leaders. Originally implemented at the top in the Central Committee, this method of central control reproduced downward throughout the Soviet system into localized "family circles." Little Stalins often defensively resisted the center they were imitating, thus requiring more purge and mass mobilization by the center to counter the resistance that the previous round had engendered. Figure 1.7b is a simple visualization. Second, by his mass murder of his own Communist Party in 1937–38, Stalin created so many job openings that an entire "generation of '38" of politically educated young red engineers rose rapidly through the ministries and the party to drive the Soviet economy toward massive industrial concentration. They used the huge

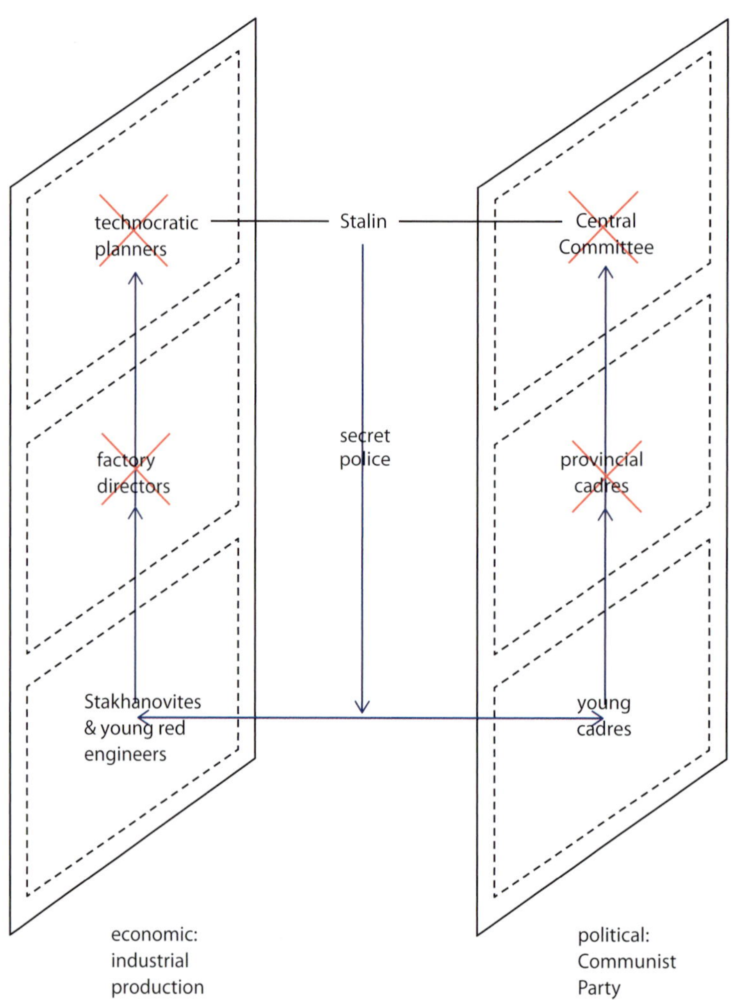

Figure 1.7a Soviet Central Command economy: genesis.

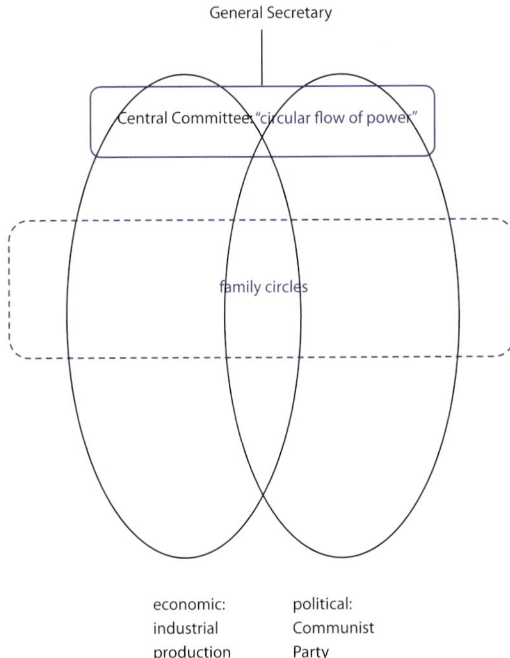

Figure 1.7b Soviet Central Command economy: catalysis.

factories and cities they built to defeat Hitler and thereby to lock in their own economic system by stigmergy.[33] This generation of '38 contained the entire leadership of the Soviet Union until Gorbachev.

Gorbachev was trying to reform and to revive communism, but he was driven quickly through the four reform trajectories that dual hierarchy presented to him until eventually he, too, was left with purge and mass mobilization. Democracy was Gorbachev's final mass mobilization tool, but it backfired for him disastrously, even as it induced the greatest political and economic transformation of our time.

Privatization and Business Groups

In chapter 10 Spicer analyzes Yeltsin's economic privatization program and its effect on the emergent stock market and banking system in post-Communist Russia. He demonstrates how little connection there was between utopian Western designs and Russian facts on the ground. Yeltsin's preeminent political objective, which trumped all else, was to destroy the Communist Party before it destroyed him. Viewed as politics, privatization was an inverted version of purge and mass mobilization: using economics to smash politics rather than the usual politics to smash economics.

Rather than an efficient means for capital-market investment, the first Russian stock market for privatization vouchers was an efficient means for swindle, theft, and a concentration of economic wealth. Through multiple-network chain reactions that Spicer describes, the first organizational innovation of the stock market cascaded into a sequence of collateral organizational innovations: the emergence of wealthy "new men" oligarchs; the emergence of a Yeltsin electoral political machine built upon these oligarchs; and finally the development of tight business groups, first through banks spun off from the state and then through Yeltsin's newly elected presidency. The case shows that organizational innovation and invention do not have to be confined to organizational forms that we approve of.

Two follow-on chapters examine the further evolution of business alliances and groups in postsocialist states, even though these chapters do not trace the evolutions of business groups back to their origins in privatization. Chapter 11 by Yakubovich and Shekshnia trace the emergence of the cell-phone industry in Moscow and St. Petersburg in the 1990s, Yeltsin's time. The organizational focus is on explaining successful versus unsuccessful business alliances between fragments of the Communist state—both in telecom and in military research—and various foreign telecom partners. Compared to the economic disasters in most parts of the Russian economy at this time, the emergence of the Russian cell-phone industry is a success story—what Gorbachev promised but delivered too rarely.

Chapter 12 by Stark and Vedres traces the development of business groups in Hungary through the first decade after the fall of communism, again the 1990s. They reveal the emergence of a dense population of different forms of Hungarian business alliances and groups—some rooted in domestic remnants of the Communist state, some connected to foreign partners, and many hybrids that combine the two. Instead of a sharp divide between an inefficient postsocialist segment of the Hungarian economy and an

[33] As discussed in chapter 3, stigmergy is the construction of a physical environment by a social-insect community; this construction then guides the future social evolution of that community. In the case of the Soviet Union, stigmergy was massive economic concentration in gigantic factories and cities.

efficient foreign-dominated sector, Stark and Vedres document blending of sectors through business partnerships and groups, a fact that they argue is conducive to fertile organizational innovation. For this book, the central point is that "market formation" in postsocialist states is a process of network evolution, in particular the evolution of business alliances. Stark and Vedres also document the penetration of Hungarian political parties onto the boards of large Hungarian firms; this adds a multiple-network component to their business-group analyses.

Robust Action and Multivocality

Our final organizational-genesis mechanism is robust action and multivocality. Robust actions are noncommittal actions that keep future lines of action open in strategic contexts where opponents are trying to narrow them. Robust action may ensue when a central broker bridges two segregated blocs of supporters through distinct networks. The broker's identities are ambiguous, not in the sense of being vague or uncertain but in the sense that multiple audiences attribute

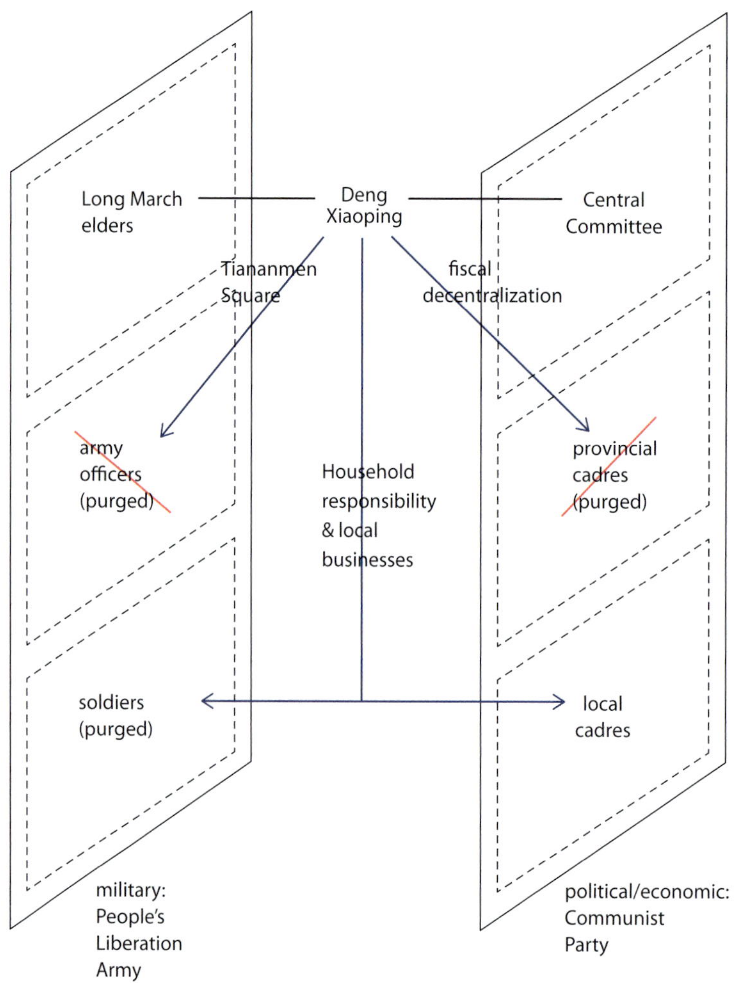

Figure 1.8a Chinese market economy: genesis.

different interests to the broker. Multivocality is the tactical capacity of robust-action brokers to sustain multiple attributions of identity through uttering sphinx-like statements that plausibly can be interpreted in multiple ways. Political polarization often drives both the structural process of segregation and the communicative process of inconsistent attributions. The archetypal example is Cosimo de' Medici, who used this tactic within his multiple networks to construct a centralized state in fifteenth-century Florence out of the pulverized social residues of class revolt and wars.[34]

In chapter 9 Padgett argues that robust action was also the successful network-bridging strategy employed by Deng Xiaoping in the 1980s to guide post-Mao China to economic development. Deng, like Cosimo, led from a backstage of informal power, not from formal office, and he issued only cryptic remarks about his reform intentions and policies, preferring to respond selectively to others' initiatives. The organizational invention produced by robust action in the early Chinese reform was local-government-as-entrepreneur, a combination of political patronage and profit orientation. As illustrated in figure 1.8a, market liberalization emerged from Deng's brokering among the residues of the Cultural Revolution.

At the end of the tumultuous and debilitating Cultural Revolution, the People's Liberation Army (PLA) was running the Chinese economy and government. Headed by elders from the Long March like himself, the post-Mao PLA was the original inherited power base for Deng. Viewed politically, decentralizing economic reform was a way for Deng to build a second patronage leg under his system of Communist control. The early household responsibility system in agriculture and local state businesses in light industry were popular reforms among wide segments of the party and PLA base. Selective fiscal decentralization to party provincial secretaries who supported Deng politically built a patronage machine at the province level, just as Stalin had done in his first Five-Year Plan and Khrushchev had done in his short-lived regional decentralization. Because of this conflation of markets within patronage and the Chinese decentralized state, what was good for politics was good for business, and what was profitable for business was good for political promotion. Ironically, Western economic advisers are everywhere to be seen in the failed Russian transition to a market economy, and they are nowhere to be seen in the successful Chinese transition to a market economy.

[34] Padgett and Ansell 1993.

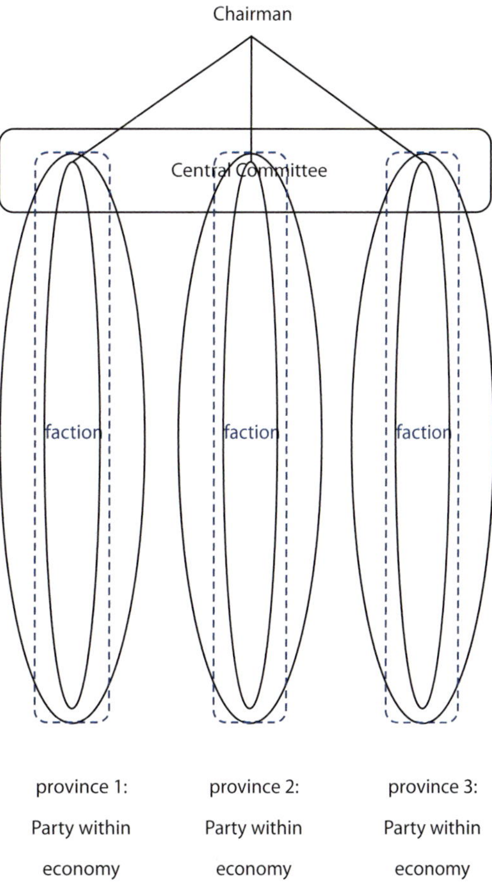

Figure 1.8b Mao's communist economy and party: catalysis.

Chapter 9 also demonstrates that this robust-action approach of Deng Xiaoping to economic-cum-political reform was possible only because of the radical administrative decentralization that Mao had engineered during the Great Leap Forward and the Cultural Revolution. Even though Mao opposed markets with every bone in his body, his administrative reforms made accessible what Deng achieved. Gorbachev's fundamental problem, in contrast, was that he was following Stalin rather than Mao. Figure 1.8b illustrates the comparative network point that Chinese informal political networks were organized vertically into factions, whereas Soviet informal political networks were organized horizontally into family circles. These networks channeled and indeed stimulated what the respective Communist leaders did, so much so that it is as reasonable to say that the systems constructed their leaders as it is to say that the leaders constructed their systems. In the short run, actors make relations; in the long run, relations make actors.

STRUCTURAL VULNERABILITY

In this volume we usually do not examine prior structural vulnerability to innovation and invention, although this is a crucial part of our theoretical framework.[35] This is the next research frontier. Certain network configurations of interacting rules, protocols, persons, and organizations are more poised to tip, in response to perturbation, than are others. Studying this empirically requires going back in time well before the original innovation ever occurred. Sometimes time-series data like that are available but sometimes they are hard to assemble, in part because organizational innovations often document themselves but not their old-fashioned predecessors. With formal modeling, the topic is easier to investigate, though those results are only suggestive.

One finding in the autocatalytic simulation models of chapters 3 and 4 is that reproductive stability of multiple-network systems is associated with redundancy, a dense spaghetti of overlaid and intertwined production networks with feedback cycles at their cores. Sometimes redundancy means the simple replication of networks of production rules, each copy distributed over different people. Sometimes redundancy means replication of multifunctional rules or people that bridge between networks in similar ways. Either way, redundancy is associated with reproductive stability because even if one of these autocatalytic networks is destroyed, there are other similar networks around to keep the ensemble going until a replacement is grown. Conversely, lack of redundancy is associated with reproductive fragility. This finding about redundancy suggests that sensitivity to system tipping—dramatic network cascades that we associate with organizational inventions—increases as redundancy is thinned out. Too much thinning and the system will collapse, but some threshold level of network thinning may move a highly redundant system toward being poised to tip.[36]

There are a number of possible ways that thinning can occur, setting the structural stage for invention. Political crises are one. The invention of the partnership system in Renaissance Florence logically had nothing to do with the Ciompi revolt. Nor did Deng's economic reforms logically follow from the Cultural Revolution. But both of these crises weakened the reproductive power of the previous multiple-network system. Crises alone do not predict what will happen next. That depends upon what the residues are, and how those are rewired into new autocatalysis.

Two metaphors may help fix our idea about the causal connection between political crises and organizational innovation. A meteor killed off the dinosaurs. Does that mean that an exogenous contingency caused the demise of that species? Yes and no. Over the millennia, many meteors struck the earth, but only that one caused the extinction. The structure of an ecology that receives a shock is just as important to system response as is the shock itself. Likewise, many political scientists argue that wars cause state formation. But some wars produce state formation, some cause collapse, some trigger revolution, and many do nothing. More than the perturbation itself is needed to explain emergence, even though perturbations are often involved. A second metaphor is the diamond cutter. Hit in one direction, a diamond cannot be broken with a sledgehammer. But tap the diamond along the lines of its natural cleavage, and it splits easily. Multiple-network social systems are like that. Perturbations often appear in the background of our organizational invention cases. But in differently interconnected systems, the same shock does not produce the same effect. Searching for simple input-cause and output-effect is a fantasy in densely connected feedback systems. Analyzing the percolation of perturbations through existing networks, no matter how

[35] Of the many empirical analyses in this book, the linked Communist cases in chapter 9 and the sequence of German episodes in chapter 8 come closest to qualifying as *longue durée* trajectories, where innovation episodes shape subsequent innovation episodes over decades and generations. Padgett's numerous empirical network studies of Renaissance Florence will also qualify once these are plugged into each other to make a sequence and a book.

[36] See footnote 25 for a comparison of our network version of "creative destruction" to Schumpeter's famous person-centered version.

data intensive, is essential for understanding system response to that perturbation.

Crisis, however, is not the only way in which redundancy can be thinned. The open-elite mechanism of organizational catalysis points to personnel turnover as another method for keeping organizational and production networks flexible and adaptive. This insight, however, needs to be treated with caution. Simply increasing the rate of hiring and firing is hardly an intelligent prescription for organizational learning. If the rate of turnover exceeds the rate of teaching, then degradation, not learning, ensues. Also there must be enough redundancy in the core of the organizational field that others can quickly take the place of nodes that exit. Because of this stable core, the open-elite method of fluidity is likely to generate more incremental innovations than is the crisis method of creative destruction.

One subtlety in managing fluidity that chemical engineers have brought to our attention is annealing. The more explosive the mix of elements being combined into hybrids, the more important it is to blend them in an oscillatory manner. Increase fluidity, decrease fluidity, increase fluidity, decrease fluidity. There is a time for exploration, and there is a time for consolidation. Done right, with sensitivity to the details of what is happening, this can lead to dampened oscillation and to successful hybridization. Done wrong, with insufficient sensitivity to context, this can lead to amplified oscillation, which is explosion.

A third way of thinning redundancy is counterintuitive in the sense that it involves making new ties rather than clipping old ones. The autocatalytic models in chapter 3 highlight the evolutionary role of parasites. These are chains of production rules that function as "free riders"—namely, others support their reproduction, but they do not support the reproduction of the rules that support them. Healthy autocatalytic systems can tolerate plenty of this with no threat to their cyclic core. The reason that parasites can lead to tipping and invention is that they might grow to form a new bridge of symbiosis between two autocatalytic networks previously interactionally distinct. Since they are parasites, they are more free to wander than are the rule chains upon which others depend. Thinning can happen as a second-order consequence of parasites because a new bridge formed by them can tip local competitive balances on either side of that bridge, leading to growth of one local network at the cost of another. Parasites may grow into becoming multifunctional.

A fourth mode of thinning redundancy that lies outside the autocatalytic models in this book is neutral drift. In models of neutral drift,[37] there is a sharp distinction drawn between genotype and phenotype. This distinction is equivalent in our terminology to relational networks of production rules versus constitutive networks of social persons. The phenomenon of neutral drift emphasizes that there are a number of functionally equivalent ways of genetically making the same phenotypic product. If selection operates on phenotype, not on genotype, as Darwin insisted, then all of these functionally equivalent ways are neutral from the point of view of selection. The micro rules are thereby free to wander randomly in evolution within selection constraints on their final products. Neutral drift is the network analogue to atomistic random mutation.

The relevance of this to the topic of organizational invention is that, just by chance, production-rule ensembles might reconfigure themselves within fixed phenotypes (or social networks) to become poised to tip into a nearby autocatalytic set. In the language of dynamic systems analysis, this is moving to the boundaries of basins of attraction. This creates a new phenotype. A new phenotype, so to speak, randomly bursts out of the chrysalis of the old. Of course there is no guarantee that this new phenotype can reproductively survive in the network of other phenotypes in which it finds itself. But to the macroscopic observer, this will appear to be almost spontaneous generation. In our chapters we have no examples of this, but we admit neutral drift as a logical possibility.

Much work on structural vulnerability remains to be done, especially on the empirical side. Studies of innovation and invention, including our own, are biased toward looking at successes more than at failures. We are proud to have included cases of failure as well as success in our case studies, but the ratio of studied failures to actual failures certainly is skewed. We do not apologize for this sample bias because much can be discovered this way about mechanisms of organizational genesis and catalysis. But we fully appreciate the need for complementary research designs that focus as much on the contextual

[37] See Ansel and Fontana 2000 and the literature cited therein.

detail of multiple-network systems before their innovation and invention as on the contextual detail of systems during and after their tips.

CONCLUSION

History is littered with the emergence of new organizational forms that altered the trajectory of the societies in which they appeared. Yet the emergence of novelty, especially novelty in human actors like people and organizations, is undertheorized in the social sciences. Novelty is fundamental to any analysis of evolution, yet that usually enters in from off the stage of our own imagination before our existing analytical tools can go to work. This book develops theories, models, mechanisms, and empirical cases in an effort to fill this gap in our collective understanding, especially in the domain of the emergence of new forms of organizations and markets. Each of the parts in this volume contains an introduction to clarify the connections between the overall framework in this introductory chapter and our detailed examples of organizational emergence. Both theory and cases benefit from a multidisciplinary perspective because organizational novelty comes from feedback among multiple social networks and domains. Chemistry, especially regarding the origins of life, does not provide all of the answers, but it at least asks the right questions—for social science as well as for biology.

REFERENCES

Ansel, Lauren W., and Walter Fontana. 2000. "Plasticity, Evolvability and Modularity in RNA." *Journal of Experimental Zoology (Mol. Dev. Evol.)* 288: 242–83.

Argote, Linda. 1999. *Organizational Learning: Creating, Retaining & Transferring Knowledge.* Norwell, MA: Kluwer Academic Publishers.

Barley, Stephen R., and Pamela S. Tolbert. 1997. "Institutionalization and Structuration: Studying the Links between Action and Institution." *Organization Studies* 18:93–117.

Bijker, Wiebe E., Thomas P. Hughes, and Trevor Pinch, eds. 1987. *The Social Construction of Technological Systems.* Cambridge, MA: MIT Press.

Davis, Gerald F., and H. R. Greve. 1997. "Corporate Elite Networks and Governance Changes in the 1980s." *American Journal of Sociology* 103:1–37.

Eigen, Manfred and Peter Schuster. 1979. *Hypercycle: A Principle of Natural Self-Organization.* Berlin: Springer-Verlag.

Fleming, Lee, and Olav Sorenson. 2004. "Science as a Map in Technological Search." *Strategic Management Journal 25(8–9):909–28.*

Fontana, Walter. 2006. "The Topology of the Possible." In *Understanding Change: Models, Methodologies and Metaphors*, ed. Andreas Wimmer and Reinhart Kossler. New York: Palgrave Macmillan.

Galison, Peter. 1997. *Image and Logic: A Material Culture of Microphysics.* Chicago: University of Chicago Press.

Gould, Stephen Jay. 2002. *The Structure of Evolutionary Theory.* Cambridge, MA: Harvard University Press.

Gould, Stephen Jay, and Elisabeth S. Vrba. 1982. "Exaptation—A Missing Term in the Science of Form." *Paleobiology* 8:4–15.

Granovetter, Mark. 1985. "Economic Action and Social Structure: The Problem of Embeddedness." *American Journal of Sociology* 91:481–510.

Greenwood, Royston, Christine Oliver, Kersten Sahlin, and Roy Suddaby. 2008. Introduction to *The Sage Handbook of Organizational Institutionalism*, ed. R. Greenwood et al., 1–47. London: Sage.

Griliches, Zvi. 1990. "Patent Statistics as Economic Indicators: A Survey." *Journal of Economic Literature* 28(4):1661–1707.

Guillén, Mauro. 1994. *Models of Management: Work, Authority, and Organization in a Comparative Perspective.* Chicago: University of Chicago Press.

Hannan, Michael, and John Freeman. 1989. *Organizational Ecology.* Cambridge, MA: Harvard University Press.

Hansen, Morten T. 1999. "The Search-Transfer Problem: The Role of Weak Ties in Sharing Knowledge across Organization Subunits."*Administrative Science Quarterly* 44:82–111.

Hughes, Thomas P. 1983. *Networks of Power: Electrification in Western Society, 1880–1930.* Baltimore: Johns Hopkins University Press.

Hutchins, Edwin. 1995. *Cognition in the Wild.* Cambridge, MA: MIT Press.

Jaffe, Adam B., Manuel Trajtenberg, and Rebecca Henderson. 1993. "Geographic Localization of Knowledge Spillovers as Evidenced by Patent Citations." *Quarterly Journal of Economics* 108(3):577–98.

Kreps, David. 1990. *A Course in Microeconomic Theory.* Princeton: Princeton University Press.

Latour, Bruno. 1988. *The Pasteurization of France.* Cambridge, MA: Harvard University Press.

Levinthal, Daniel, and J. G. March. 1981. "A Model of Adaptive Organizational Search." *Journal of Economic Behavior and Organization* 2:307–33.

Mansfield, Edwin. 1986. "Patents and Innovation: An Empirical Study." *Management Science* 32(2): 173–81.

March, James G. 1991. "Exploration and Exploitation in Organizational Learning." *Organization Science* 2:71–87.

McLean, Paul D. 2007. *The Art of the Network: Strategic Interaction and Patronage in Renaissance Florence.* Chapel Hill: Duke University Press.

Nelson, Richard R., and Sidney Winter. 1982. *An Evolutionary Theory of Economic Change*. Cambridge, MA: Harvard University Press.

Nicolis, Grégoire, and Ilya Prigogine. 1989. *Exploring Complexity*. New York: Freeman.

Owen-Smith, Jason, and Walter W. Powell. 2004. "Knowledge Networks as Channels and Conduits: The Effects of Spillovers in the Boston Biotechnology Community." *Organization Science* 15(1):5–21.

Padgett, John F. 2010. "Open Elite? Social Mobility, Marriage and Family in Florence, 1282–1494." *Renaissance Quarterly* 63:357–411.

Padgett, John F., and Christopher K. Ansell. 1993. "Robust Action and the Rise of the Medici, 1400–1434." *American Journal of Sociology* 98: 1259–1319.

Rivkin, Jan W., and Nicolaj Siggelkow. 2003. "Balancing Search and Stability: Interdependencies among Elements Organizational Design." *Management Science* 49:290–311.

Schumpeter, Joseph A. 1939. *Business Cycles: A Theoretical, Historical and Statistical Analysis of the Capitalist Process*. New York: McGraw-Hill.

———. 1947. *Capitalism, Socialism and Democracy*. New York: Harper.

Sewell, William H., Jr. 2005. *Logics of History: Social Theory and Social Transformation*. Chicago: University of Chicago Press.

Simmons, Beth, Frank Dobbin, and Geoffrey Garrett. 2006. "Introduction: The International Diffusion of Liberalism." *International Organization* 60:781–810.

Simon, Herbert A. 1969. "Architecture of Complexity." In *The Sciences of the Artificial*, 84–118. Cambridge, MA: MIT Press.

Stadler, Bärbel, Peter F. Stadler, Günter P. Wagner, and Walter Fontana. 2001. "The Topology of the Possible: Formal Spaces Underlying Patterns of Evolutionary Change." *Journal of Theoretical Biology* 213:241–74.

Strang, David, and John W. Meyer. 1993. "Institutional Conditions for Diffusion." *Theory and Society* 22:487–511.

Szulanski, G. 1996. "Exploring Internal Stickiness: Impediments to the Transfer of Best Practice within the Firm." *Strategic Management Journal* 17:27–43.

Varela, F. G., H. R. Maturana, and R. Uribe. 1974. "Autopoiesis: The Organization of Living Systems, Its Characterization and a Model." *BioSystems* 5:187–96.

Zander, Udo, and Bruce Kogut. 1995. "Knowledge and the Speed of the Transfer and Imitation of Organizational Capabilities: An Empirical Test." *Organizational Science* 6:76–92.

PART I

Autocatalysis

The three chapters on autocatalysis are foundational for the rest of the volume. This does not mean that the principles and mechanisms of organizational genesis and evolution discovered in the empirical case studies can be derived from these chapters on autocatalysis. Our empirical case studies of evolutionary dynamics in multiple networks contain their own discoveries, which can stand on their own. But "foundational" does mean that these three chapters on autocatalysis explain why there are organizations in the first place, capable of evolving as described in the case studies. Our answer is that organizations are one form of life. Human social organization has particular features—in particular, language—that set it apart from other forms of life. But it is still one form of life. As such, it shares with other forms the overarching principles and dynamics of life in general. It is these that explain the existence of organization, human and otherwise. We claim that the overarching self-organizational principles of life are largely (though perhaps not entirely) captured in the chemical concept of autocatalysis. We further claim—consistent with but extending Darwin in a relational way—that evolution, biological and social, emerges out of concatenations and selections of multiple reproductive autocatalyses in co-evolutionary feedback with each other.

The following three chapters stand in relation to each other as past, present, and future. Chapter 2 provides an extensive review, for the benefit of social scientists, of the biochemistry literature on the origins of life where the concept of autocatalysis figures most prominently. The chemical and empirical side (i.e., the actual scientific side) of that literature is reviewed first. There is a lively debate in that literature between scientists who subscribe to an RNA-first hypothesis and scientists who subscribe to a metabolism-first hypothesis about the origin of life. Both are different versions of autocatalysis, and a sensible conclusion could be that biological life really took off when a symbiosis developed between the two. After that, the chapter reviews past formal modeling in this area, which is spotty but highly suggestive. The chapter identifies Eigen's and Schuster's model of hypercycles[1] as the pathbreaking work that first placed empirical chemistry and formal models into fruitful dialogue with each other. Finally, the chapter reviews a less successful, more philosophical descendant of autocatalysis called autopoiesis, which is the guise under which autocatalysis first was presented to social scientists. Its flaws are identified. This volume seeks to do better by connecting social scientists back to the original science in biochemistry, not back to philosophy.

Chapter 3 represents the present. Padgett, Peter McMahan, and Xing Zhong develop further an agent-based model of economic production by Padgett, which itself was based on the chemical hypercycle model of Eigen and Schuster. Padgett and his colleagues show that certain limitations intrinsic to the original hypercycle model—in particular, complexity barriers and vulnerability to parasites—are overcome once autocatalysis takes place in a spatial context, rather than in random-topology liquids. Localized heterogeneity in spatial interaction induces the inscription of path dependencies into cells. This explains why life becomes enhanced once it

[1] Manfred Eigen and Peter Schuster, *The Hypercycle: A Principle of Natural Self-Organization* (Berlin: Springer-Verlag, 1979).

is embodied. The model also demonstrates why altruism and stigmergy[2] produce more complex rule-chemistries. Altruistic reproduction and stigmergy are superior to selfish reproduction and fixed environments, respectively, because of their superior capacities for self-repair. Beyond suggestive specifics, the hypercycle model and its extensions show how chemistry and economic production and trading in markets can be mapped onto each other, sparking insights for both sides.

Chapter 4 is the next frontier in autocatalytic modeling. Building on the model of production in chapter 3, communication in two forms is added in the formal models in chapter 4: symbolic communication through primitive language and genealogical communication through biographies. Because the topic of this book is emergence, only the most minimal representations of these human-like features are investigated. Language here emerges out of token feedbacks and social-interactional learning.[3] Genealogical descent and family organizations emerge out of reciprocity and teaching.[4] In the terminology of figure 1.1, the first cross-sectional type of communication is equivalent to the emergence of relational social-network ties, and the second longitudinal type of communication is equivalent to the emergence of constitutive social-network ties. With these human-like extensions beyond biochemistry, three types of autocatalysis emerge: production autocatalysis, where material objects are produced and exchanged; cellular or biographical autocatalysis, where actors are constructed through intercalated biographies; and linguistic autocatalysis, where symbols are passed and reproduced in conversations. The point of these extensions is not to leave biochemistry behind. These higher-order forms of autocatalysis remain biochemistry, with memory added. Much of what we humans egotistically admire about our specialness is emergent behavior out of that.

These chapters on autocatalysis are not meant to be the last word. They are invitations to social science to pursue an agenda. It is fair to say that these three chapters together sketch a vision of evolution that takes us up to primates. The rest of the volume pushes beyond that, into human history as we know it.

[2] Stigmergy is a concept from the social-insect literature that refers to the mutual feedback between social organizations and the physical environment that social organizations build for themselves.

[3] Padgett's guide to the emergence of language is Michael Tomasello, *Origins of Human Communication* (Cambridge, MA: MIT Press, 2008).

[4] Padgett's guide to the emergence of kinship is Bernard Chapais, *Primeval Kinship* (Cambridge, MA: Harvard University Press, 2008).

2

Autocatalysis in Chemistry and the Origin of Life

John F. Padgett

The purpose of this chapter is to provide background to social scientists on the concept of autocatalysis, drawn from chemistry and the literature on the origins of life. More comprehensive, though less focused, reviews of the early history of life from different theoretical perspectives are provided in Eigen, in Maynard Smith and Szathmáry, and in Margulis and Sagan.[1] The literature on the origin of life is tumultuous, much like the history of biological life itself. The placid and comforting image of Darwin's warm tidal pool as the physical locus for the first emergence of chemical life has been partly replaced (or at least challenged) in the current literature by violent volcanoes and thermal vents. The even more violent crashing of Venus- and Mars-sized proto-planets to create our Earth and its moon lies in the background of these early crescive volcanoes, which may have helped power early evolution. Obviously academic disputes do not compare in degree of violence to this, but much heat and constructive energy has been generated by an ongoing theoretical struggle between the RNA-first position, which places all its explanatory emphasis on the self-organization of nucleic acids, and the metabolism-first position, which focuses on the self-organization of simpler energy-processing chemistries that RNA and DNA later regulated and reproduced. A minority position insists that lipid cell vesicles came first, which both types of chemistry came to inhabit.

This literature review chapter cannot adjudicate these highly technical disputes, even though its assumption will be that all three contending positions have something valuable to contribute. Its purpose is more modest: to point out that the concept of autocatalysis lies at the foundation of all of these positions. The three schools of thought do not dispute the foundational importance of the concept of autocatalysis to the definition and emergence of life. They just dispute exactly which were the primary chemicals and chemical reactions involved in early autocatalysis. If the concept of autocatalysis ever succeeds in its transposition to the social sciences, we likewise can anticipate fruitful contention about exactly which types and combinations of autocatalysis are applicable to which historical episodes of organizational transformation.

This chapter proceeds in four sections: first, a definitional overview of the problem; second, a selective review of the current chemical literature on the origin of life; third, a brief review of formal modeling in this area; and finally a section on autopoiesis, the first not entirely successful attempt to transpose the concept of autocatalysis to the social sciences. I conclude with some remarks about Harrison White and William Sewell Jr., on whose work we build.

DEFINITIONS OF CHEMICAL AUTOCATALYSIS AND LIFE

The motivating puzzle for everyone who studies the origin of life on earth is that life arose very

[1] Eigen 1992; Maynard Smith and Szathmáry 1995; Margulis and Sagan 1995. Perhaps the best popular treatment is Capra 1996.

quickly, in geological time. The core facts, as described by Martin and Russell,[2] are these:

> The Earth is 4.5 billion years (Gyr) old, and the first ocean had condensed by ca. 4.4 Gyr. There are good reasons to believe that life arose here by ca. 3.8 Gyr, because carbon isotope data provide evidence for biological CO_2 fixation in sedimentary rocks of that age. By 3.5 Gyr, stromatolites were present, preserved microbial mats indicative of deposition by photosynthetic prokaryotes.[3] By ca. 1.5 Gyr, so-called acritarchs became reasonably abundant, microfossils of unicellular organisms that are almost certainly eukaryotes and are probably algae because of an easily preserved cell wall. By 1.2 Gyr, spectacularly preserved multicellular organisms appear that were very probably red algae.

In other words, as measured directly by fossils, life emerged about 20 percent of the way into the history of the earth. As measured indirectly by chemical traces, life emerged 15 percent of the way into the history of the earth. In such an early epoch, the originally molten earth was still quivering with volcanoes, left over from the giant collision of its birth and subsequent meteor bombardments. Life emerged so early in the history of the earth that the history of the earth itself is shaped by the history of life upon it—for example, the earth's atmosphere of oxygen, not to mention soil and oil.

The definition of life is contested but only in the sense that authors differ as to how many of the following list of items to include in the definition:

1. Thermodynamic throughput of energy
2. Autocatalysis or self-reproduction
3. Cellular enclosure
4. Evolution

This list is almost hierarchical, in the natural-science sense of that term:[4] namely, items lower in the list are included within and presuppose items higher in the list.

Throughput of energy is required not just as fuel for chemical reactions but also for self-organization of any kind, defined thermodynamically as a decrease in entropy. Maximal entropy is defined as randomness in an ensemble; hence decrease in entropy means increase in nonrandomness or order.[5] The Second Law of Thermodynamics states that any ensemble that is energetically isolated will gradually decay into complete randomness and that any ensemble that is energetically coupled to only one reservoir will gradually increase in entropy, going to equilibrium with its environmental reservoir. Material ensembles, in other words, gradually disintegrate and "die." The reason that living systems, which increase in order over developmental and evolutionary time, appear to violate the Second Law of Thermodynamics is throughput of energy. Here ensembles are attached to two reservoirs—an energy source from which order is drawn and an energy sink into which disorder is deposited.[6] Throughput of energy in physical and chemical ensembles induces alignment, patterning, or order into the elements of those ensembles. The earth itself is an ensemble experiencing a throughput of energy, since light from the sun during the day is radiated away as heat into outer space during the night.

Prigogine has done mathematically the most to analyze these "far-from-equilibrium" throughput systems, which he has labeled "dissipative systems."[7] Morowitz added the important addendum that cycling is part of the "pattern" produced by steady-state energy throughput.[8] All authors treat the throughput of energy as

[2] Martin and Russell 2003, 59–60 include citations for each of their numbers. To place these numbers in comparative perspective, the universe is 13.7 billion years old (Weintraub 2011); the sun is 4.6 Gyr; the Cambrian explosion, from which all animal phyla descend, is 0.53 Gyr (Gould 1989; Morris 1998); and humans (i.e., homo sapiens) arose .0002 billion years ago.

[3] Prokaryotes are simple single-celled bacteria, with no internal compartmentalization. Eukaryotes are complex and larger single-celled bacteria with extensive internal differentiation, including mitochrondria and a nucleus. Once aggregated, eukaryotes became cells in higher-level multicellular organisms.

[4] Simon 1969.

[5] The formula for entropy—namely, $S = -k\Sigma_i p_i \ln_e p_i$—is almost identical to that for information in Shannon-type information theory—namely, $I = -\Sigma_s p_s \ln_2 p_s$. Hence many authors equate entropy with information, even though Morowitz (1992, 74, 126) warns against such switching between interpretative contexts.

[6] No system violates the Second Law if both source and sink are included in the definition of "ensemble." Intermediate ensembles "defeat" the Law only through degrading the order in source into the disorder in sink.

[7] Prigogine [1955] 1967; Nicolis and Prigogine 1977, 1989. Prigogine won the Nobel Prize in 1977. The phrase *far from equilibrium* is potentially confusing for social scientists. In this context, it refers to thermodynamic equilibrium or disordered "death." *Steady state* is the term physicists use instead of equilibrium when referring to stable and reproducible patterns generated by throughput.

[8] Morowitz 1966; Morowitz 1968, 29–33.

A. Catalytic cycle in container
(Fenchel 2002, 32)

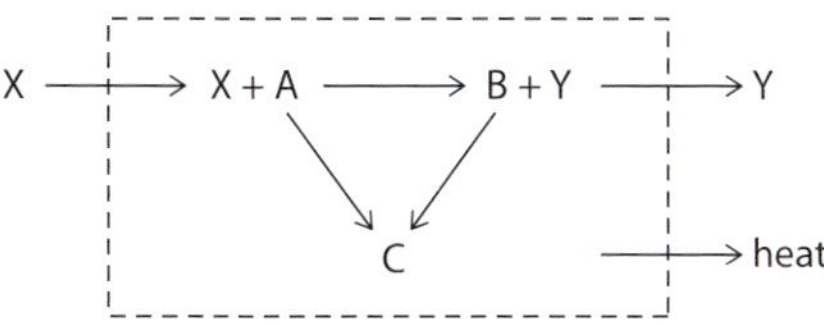

B. Example of autocatalytic reaction
(Morowitz 1992, 98)

A ⟶ C ⟶ D ⟵ B, meaning A + C→D
C
D + B→E
E→2 C

C. Example of autocatalytic reaction
(Fenchel 2002, 35)

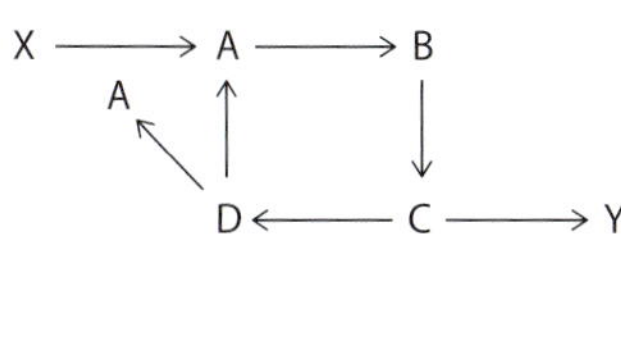

D. A general scheme of the self-reproducing cycle
(Gánti 2003a, 48)

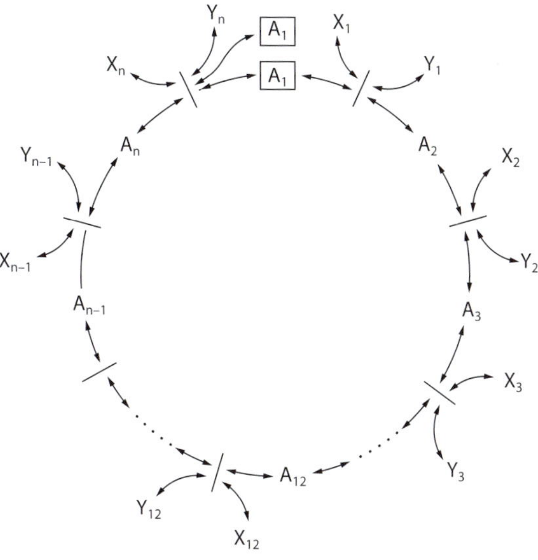

Figure 2.1 Examples of catalytic and autocatalytic chemical cycles.

a necessary precondition to life, but only a few of them treat this criterion as sufficient.[9] As Prigogine made clear, physical thermal convection systems are ordered dissipative systems, without being alive.

Autocatalytic systems are chemical dissipative systems with the criterion of self-reproduction added. The word *chemical*, unlike the word *physical*, implies transformation: elements interact not only by aligning with each other but also by changing each other. The most general definition of self-reproduction is that which was discussed in the introductory chapter to this book: "A set of nodes (in this case chemicals) whose transformational interaction reproduces the nodes in the set." In the face of inevitable dissipation and random decay in constituent chemical elements, chemical systems with the topology of autocatalysis have the potential (realized under favorable kinetic circumstances) to reconstruct their own lost components. In the steady-state case where energetic input equals energetic output, autocatalysis implies self-maintenance of the chemical network as a whole. At the micro level of individual chemicals, however, system self-maintenance is only achieved by the continual regeneration of the constituent chemicals to replace those that have been lost. Simple examples are given in figure 2.1. Self-repair of the system against perturbations that are not too severe is one corollary. If energy input exceeds energy

[9] See Schrödinger [1944] 1967 for a prescient analysis, before DNA was discovered, based on thermodynamics.

output, the autocatalytic system as a whole grows in chemical volume, perhaps physically to split. If energy input is less than energy output, the system as a whole declines in chemical volume, leading eventually to system collapse. I take autocatalysis, plus its necessary precondition of energy throughput, to be the minimal chemistry definition of life, even though other authors sometimes add other, more biological criteria to their definitions.

Because of the presence of DNA and RNA in all known forms of life on earth, it is important to stress that autocatalytic systems, so defined, include two subtypes of autocatalysis: (a) self-replication, where chemicals (given energy stimulation) "selfishly" reproduce themselves;[10] and (b) network replication, where chemicals "altruistically" reproduce each other. The RNA-first school of thought analyzes and emphasizes self-replication, whereas the metabolism-first school of thought emphasizes network replication, but all known living organisms have both versions of autocatalysis, in synergy. RNA and DNA cannot exist alone without being chemical components in a larger metabolic network that delivers energy to them to reproduce.[11] Conversely, network replication does exist in many metabolic cycles within cells (as emphasized by the metabolism-first school), but no empirical organism has yet been found where such metabolic cycles do not coexist with RNA/DNA.[12] The hypercycle model of Eigen and Schuster, reviewed below, is the simplest formal model representation of this symbiosis between these two subtypes of autocatalysis. It is for that reason that I take it as the basis for my own modeling in chapter 3.

In addition to energy throughput and autocatalysis, some authors insist on biological encapsulation as part of their definition of life, mostly because they subscribe to a third vesicle-first theory of the origin of life.[13] The argument in favor of the vesicle-first position is that chemical concentrations, of either RNA or metabolites, otherwise can never build up to requisite densities in an aqueous solution. In open water, promising chemistry is immediately diffused away. The argument against the vesicle-first position is the lack of a clear mechanism for these chemistries to jump inside their protective proto-cell walls, constructed out of porous hydrophobic lipids. This is the kind of chicken and egg problem that is common in the literature on the origins of life. Spatial embodiment and constraint also emerge as a strong theme in my autocatalytic models in chapter 3. Even so, I prefer to let that aspect emerge from reproduction dynamics rather than insert it by hand into the definition of life. Promising current lines of research, reviewed below, focus on studying other methods[14] of solving the concentration problem than lipid vesicles. These should not be excluded from the study of the origins of "life" by definitional fiat.

The early chemoton model of the Hungarian engineer Tibor Gánti,[15] working outside the mainstream but rightly admired by Maynard Smith and Szathmáry,[16] is an elegantly simple way to put all three who's-first schools of thought about the origin of life onto the same playing field. Gánti's core argument is the diagram reproduced in figure 2.2. All three chemical cycles are represented in this composite model: the self-reproducing metabolic cycle is represented by the circle of A's; self-reproducing nucleic acids are represented by the circle of pViVj's (p stands for polymer); and self-reproducing lipid cell walls are represented by the circle of Tm's. Production flows of X's and Y's into and out of the cell power the ensemble. Symbiosis is represented by couplings among the three cycles. Gánti shows through differential-equation analysis that the component behaviors of production and reproduction in his model change radically with subtle changes in symbiotic coupling. The chemoton

[10] Eigen (1971b, 172–78) draws the subtle but important distinction that DNA and RNA are not examples of true self-replication but of complementary instruction or template replication. This distinction has important implications for the reproducible diversity of nucleic acids sustained in steady state. In pure or true self-replication, simple monads (like worthless RNA strings composed of all As) take over through "cancerous" reproduction, leading to system collapse. See also Fontana and Buss 1994a, 20–21. This distinction between self-replication and template replication is ignored by Dawkins (1976) and his "selfish gene" followers.

[11] Viruses are exceptions only in the sense that they parasitically highjack other cells' metabolic machinery to do this job for them. As such, they are terribly useful for RNA experiments, but they cannot reproduce themselves. Bacteria, not viruses, are the first known autocatalytic forms of life.

[12] Catalysis of metabolic cycles using simpler and cruder methods, like pyrite surfaces containing iron and sulfur metals, however, is under active theoretical discussion and experimental development. Wächtershäuser 1990, 1992; Huber and Wächtershäuser 1997, 1998.

[13] Fox 1965; Varela, Maturana, and Uribe 1974; Morowitz 1992; Luisi 2006.

[14] Such as surface catalysis on pyrites or clay, and tiny compartments in porous rocks within thermal vents.

[15] Gánti 1975, 1979, 2003a, 2003b.

[16] Maynard Smith and Szathmáry (1995, 23) assert, "[W]e think that the abstract system of [Gánti, reproduced here as figure 2.2] is an excellent mental jumping-board for understanding the origin of life."

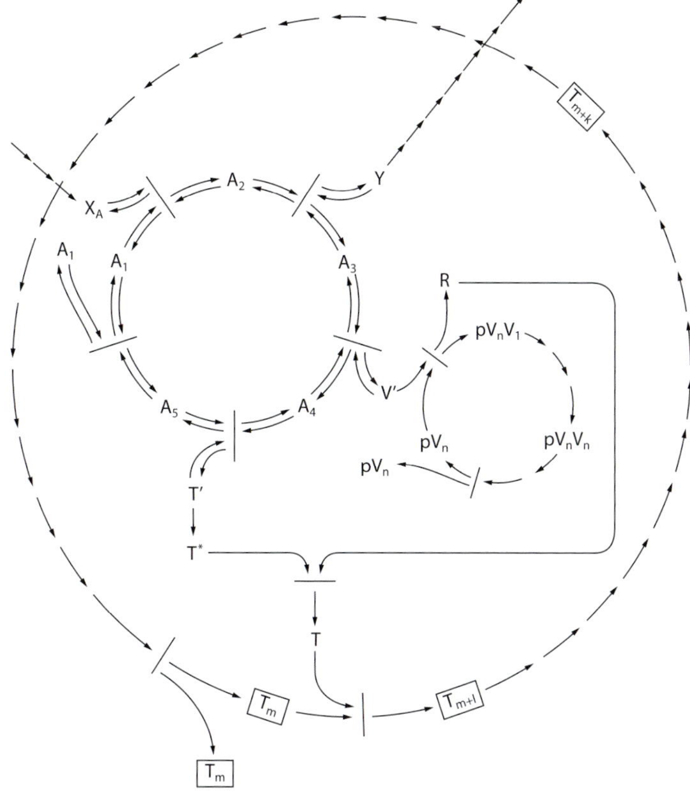

Figure 2.2 The chemoton (Gánti 2003a, 147).

model is very reminiscent of this book's overall theme of reproductive feedback between multiple social networks. Gánti does not address how this beautiful cellular symbiosis might have arisen historically.

Evolution is a commonly espoused fourth definition of life.[17] Evolution of course is at the heart of many of our theoretical agendas. But perhaps the most elegant argument against defining life as evolution is the reductio ad absurdum of Lynn Margulis:[18] if life is the capacity for evolution, then the mule is not alive. In ordinary English, the phrase *the evolution of life* presumes that there is a difference between these two terms. Defining life in terms of evolution has the practical effect of focusing analysis almost exclusively on the replication dynamics of RNA and DNA. Defining life in terms of autocatalysis has the practical effect of focusing analysis on the reproduction dynamics of entire chemical networks of metabolism and RNA/DNA, in symbiosis. The second gestalt is more potentially fruitful (and less dangerous) to transpose to the social sciences. The contrasting worldviews of reproducing networks versus replicating atomistic units are pregnant with consequences, both intellectual and political. That said, the whole point of mobilizing autocatalysis as a conceptual tool both in chemistry and in the social sciences is to derive consequences for the study of historical transformation and organizational evolution. Adopting the definition of life as autocatalysis does not mean arguing against Darwin; it just means emphasizing the relational side of Darwin.[19]

[17] A prominent example is Maynard Smith and Szathmáry 1995, 1999. The reissue of their academic book, *The Major Transitions in Evolution*, in a popular version as *The Origins of Life* is a give-away of their definitional equation of the two concepts. Autocatalysis remains an important component in their analysis of evolution, but they add many other features more specific to DNA and RNA (as is appropriate if the focus is on biological evolution, not life per se).

[18] Margulis and Sagan 1995, 18.

[19] Lest one think that the atomistic competition of Social Darwinism was the sum total of Darwin's own worldview, let me remind the reader of the closing paragraph of *Origin*

Chemical autocatalysis when coupled with a powering energy source and cellular enclosure leads naturally to cells that physically grow and eventually divide. Add a finite resource constraint to growing and dividing cells, and Darwin's natural selection is induced. All then that is missing for evolution is variation, which could be random or could be structured. Evolution, while not part of my and others' definition of life, easily grows out of the lower items on the list, once a few auxiliary features are added.

Speed of evolution, however, is another matter. It took about 70 percent of the earth's history before the early single-celled bacteria ever assembled into multicelled algae. And it took about 88 percent of the earth's history before anything as recognizable as organized critters with body plans emerged. If we were reasoning halfway into the history of the earth, I'm not sure that the concept of evolution would have entered our minds. The inventions of sex and cell death[20] were late arrivals in the history of evolution, which sped up biological evolution enormously, perhaps analogous to the invention of language in human evolution. None of these later steps is explained by autocatalysis alone, but autocatalysis remains a critical processual building block in higher-order explanations of evolutionary and historical transformations.

A. Outline of biochemical functions (Morowitz 1992, 135)

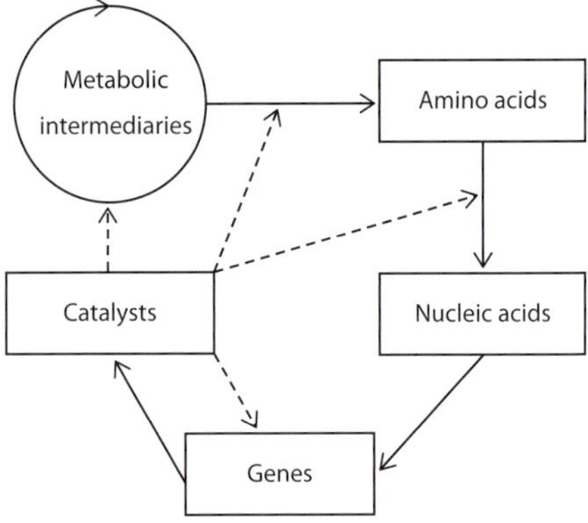

B. Outline of primitive biochemical functions (Morowitz 1992, 136)

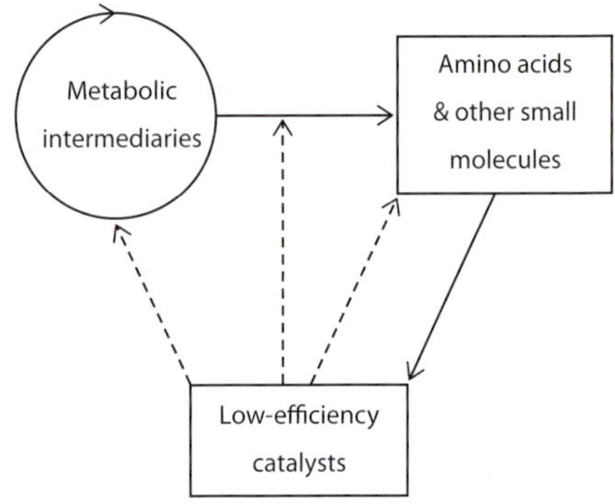

Figure 2.3 Simplified chemistry of life.

THE CHEMICAL ORIGIN OF LIFE

The details of biochemistry are incredibly complicated, even at the level of bacteria. Fortunately social scientists (who deal with enough complexity already) do not need to know those details in order to appreciate the structure and topology of the issues involved in the study of biological genesis. The questions asked in origins-of-life research are more useful to social scientists than are the specific answers generated in that subfield because social scientists have their own versions of these issues. The intellectual objective is to engage in interdisciplinary dialogue about challenging topics of interest to multiple disciplines, not to copy or mimic in either direction.[21]

Again Morowitz is useful to cut to the chase. Figure 2.3 reproduces two of his diagrams, which lay out in schematic overview the chemical structures both of currently living biochemistries and of posited primitive biochemistries. The generality is such that contending RNA-first and metabolism-first positions both can be accommodated. In currently living biochemical systems, metabolism generates amino acids and nucleobases (among other things), which are

of Species: "It is interesting to contemplate a tangled bank, clothed with many plants of many kinds, with birds singing on the bushes, with various insects flitting about, and with worms crawling through the damp earth, and to reflect that these elaborately constructed forms, so different from each other, and dependent upon each other in so complex a manner, have all been produced by laws acting around us" (Darwin [1859] 1993, 648). Competitive natural selection lies at the heart of Darwin's laws, to be sure, but intraspecies competition is structured within a tangled web of interspecies ecological and chemical flows that in ensemble more accurately warrant the label of (interdependent) co-evolution than of (autonomous) evolution.

[20] Bacteria can be killed, but they do not die if fed. Left to their own, they are immortal. Programmed death was an historical invention that imposed cell turnover and thus speeded evolution.

[21] Thanks again are due to the Santa Fe Institute, in particular Ellen Goldberg, Erica Jen, and Walter Fontana, for encouraging interdisciplinary dialogue across unusually distant disciplines.

assembled into nucleic acids, which are assembled into genes, which produce protein enzymes that control metabolism, as well as regulate other production links in the grand cycle.[22] The origin problem for this or any other autocatalytic cycle in equilibrium is that each step presupposes previous steps. How can anything be jump-started without the products produced by it? In particular protein enzymes are very complicated macromolecules that control virtually all chemistries in living organisms, and these are created by even more complex strings of genes in DNA. Did Deus ex machina do all this?

The second diagram in figure 2.3, representing primitive biochemistry, simplifies the autocatalysis problem without resolving it. Instead of complicated macromolecules like DNA and protein enzymes, researchers currently imagine "low-efficiency catalysts" to get the earliest autocatalytic chemical system moving. A variety of candidates for the very first iterations of this primitive cycle have been proposed, but nearly everyone now agrees that sooner or later those low-efficiency catalysts were primitive, short-stringed RNA. This is called the "RNA world" hypothesis.[23]

This hypothesis has become hegemonic in the field not because it solves everything but because it allows the simplification of the intractable top diagram in figure 2.3 into the "easier" bottom one. Prior to this simplification, DNA and protein enzymes both were considered enormously complicated macromolecules with various versions of RNA (tRNA, rRNA, mRNA, etc.)[24] serving only the intermediating function of translating between these complex worlds.[25] That is because this is what they do today. But focusing on complicated DNA and proteins directly makes their emergence seem virtually impossible. In the simplified RNA world of the alleged past, however, plastic and multifunctional RNA molecules did double duty: both as DNA inheritance machines and as protein catalysts of chemical reactions in cells. That doesn't mean that they did this very well, but over evolutionary time the "Darwin-Eigen Cycle" kicked in to induce greater specialization and genome precision.[26] This positive feedback loop, which generates genome complexity, is the following: "selection increases [RNA reproduction] fidelity → larger genome size → new functionality evolving → selection increases fidelity." As my first item of business in the formal-modeling section of this chapter, I will review Eigen's hypercycle and quasi-species models, which are referenced here. Molecular-Darwinian conceptual frameworks like these tell us not much in detail about how evolution did it, but they give contemporary biochemists confidence (justified or not) that the transition from the bottom diagram in figure 2.3 to the top one is "just" a matter of Darwinian engineering. Most evolutionary biochemists think they understand that, in principle at least.[27]

The hegemonic RNA-world hypothesis leaves open the question of how the bottom chemical structure in figure 2.3 evolved. To their credit, both of the contending RNA-first and metabolism-first positions have been motivated by exciting empirical findings. Simultaneous with the discovery of DNA,[28] the famous experiments by Stanley Miller,[29] way back in the 1950s, set the origin-of-life agenda for the next thirty years. Those experiments surprisingly generated amino acids just by sending electric sparks, which simulated lightning, through a gaseous mixture of methane, ammonia, hydrogen, and vaporized water. These gases simulated the ideas of Oparin and of Urey (Miller's teacher) about the presumed reductive atmosphere of early earth. Those experiments, together with laboratory syntheses of nucleobases,[30] gave

[22] Food energy inputs and outputs are implicit but not shown.

[23] The phrase is from Gilbert (1986), who suggestively drew attention to and labeled path-breaking experiments by Altman and Cech, which demonstrated catalytic production capacity for transfer RNA (tRNA) and ribosomal RNA (rRNA), respectively. Thereby ribosomes became "ribozymes." Two decades of experimental research on the RNA world since then are reviewed in Orgel 2004 and Penny 2005. I agree with Martin and Russell (2003, 64) that the label "RNA era" would have been more felicitous than "RNA world," in order to eliminate the connotation of a world being self-contained. But it is too late for linguistic corrections like this.

[24] http://en.wikipedia.org/wiki/List_of_RNAs.

[25] Woese (2002, 8745) suggestively emphasizes this "symbolic" or "linguistic" translation function of RNA between the DNA and protein worlds. He provocatively interprets the move from the bottom to the top diagrams in figure 2.3 as "The evolution of modern cells, then, had to begin with the onset of translation."

[26] Poole, Jeffares, and Penny 1998; Poole, Jeffares, and Penny 1999, 881; Penny 2005, 641.

[27] Margulis 1967, 1970, Marulis and Sagan 1995, and Margulis and Dolan 2002; Woese 1998, 2002; and Shapiro 2011 inject informed and healthy doses of skepticism into this consensus. I discuss their views at the end of this section.

[28] Watson and Crick 1953. One of the more famous conclusions in science is their comment, "It has not escaped our notice that the specific pairing we have postulated immediately suggests a possible copying mechanism for the genetic material."

[29] Miller 1953, 1955, 1957.

[30] Two decades of experiments are reviewed in Miller and Orgel 1974, 83–117. Oró and Kimball (1960) were the

empirical support to early pre-DNA hypotheses by Oparin and Haldane,[31] and by Darwin himself,[32] about life emerging from a "prebiotic soup." Another glance at the bottom diagram in figure 2.3 illustrates why all of this experimental ferment consolidated the RNA-first theoretical position:[33] primitive biochemical catalysts might have polymerized spontaneously out of amino-acid (→ protein) and/or nucleobase (→ RNA) components, which then could have triggered metabolism in nearby energy-rich chemicals.[34]

Alas, the exciting RNA-first position has confronted so far insuperable empirical difficulties, one of which is that no geochemist believes anymore the original assumption of Oparin-Urey-Miller about the highly reductive atmosphere of early earth, which made the amino-acid experiments work so well. The consensus now is that the atmosphere on early earth was composed mostly of nitrogen, carbon dioxide, and water vapor with a little bit of chemically more active carbon monoxide and methane possibly thrown in as non-steady-state transients from the moon-forming impact.[35] For a couple of decades, this stubborn fact about the early atmosphere threw into question the optimistic assumption of the RNA-first school that synthesizing amino-acid and nucleobase components of proteins and RNA, respectively, was easy.[36]

This empirical barrier to the RNA-first school of thought no longer seems as daunting as it once did. For one thing, Miller and his colleagues, right before he died, added a little iron to their previous neutral-atmosphere experiments, which seemed to solve the problem.[37] More significant, numerous amino acids and even nucleobases have been discovered on meteors from outer space, dating to the beginning of the solar system.[38] Whatever the chemical synthesis details, in other words, it once again seems a safe assumption that amino acids and nucleobases were there virtually from the beginning, not just on earth but all over the solar system. The emergence of life might not be just an earthly phenomenon.[39]

A second empirical problem has proved to be more recalcitrant. It has so far proven impossible to synthesize RNA in the lab from its nucleobase, ribosome (sugar), and phosphate components. This is the lower-right arrow in the bottom diagram of figure 2.3. Rather than review all the experimental difficulties, which I frankly do not understand, the conclusion of the most prominent RNA-first advocates in the field will be cited:

> A robust, prebiotically plausible synthesis of RNA, if achieved, will dramatically strengthen the case for the RNA world hypothesis. Despite nearly a half a century of effort, however, the prospects for such a synthesis have appeared somewhat remote.[40]

---

first to synthesize nucleobases. The Miller and Orgel book reported with considerable optimism on the state of the field and hopes of researchers in 1974. Even in 1974, however, everything was not rosy: "Nucleoside synthesis under plausibly prebiotic conditions has proved to be unexpectedly difficult, so much so that no really satisfactory method has been reported" (ibid., 112). See Oró, Miller, and Lazcano 1990 for an updated review.

[31] Oparin [1924] 1938; Haldane 1929.

[32] "It is often said that all the conditions for the first production of a living organism are now present, which could ever have been present. But if (and oh what a big if) we could conceive in some warm little pond with all sorts of ammonia and phosphoric salts,—light, heat, electricity &c. present, that a protein compound was chemically formed, ready to undergo still more complex changes, at the present day such matter wd be instantly devoured, or absorbed, which would not have been the case before living creatures were formed." Darwin to Joseph Hooker, February 1, 1871, http://bevets.com/equotesd.htm.

[33] The first to articulate this position was Muller (1926, 1966). See Lazcano 2010 for history.

[34] Indeed the hope was that ATP itself might also have been so catalyzed.

[35] Zahnle, Shaefer, and Fegley 2010; Zahnle et al. 2007; Sleep 2010.

[36] "A number of experiments were later carried out using CO and CO_2 model atmospheres. However, the synthesis of organic compounds by the action of electric discharges on neutral gas mixtures is much less efficient than when reduced model atmospheres are used. As the gas mixture becomes less reducing (less H_2, CH_4 or NH_3), the yields of organic compounds decrease drastically, with glycine being the only major amino acid synthesized. The presence of methane and ammonia appears to be especially important for the formation of diverse mixtures of amino acids. The main problem in the synthesis of amino acids and other biologically relevant organic compounds with non-reducing atmospheres appears to be the limited amount of hydrogen cyanide that is formed, which is a central intermediate in the Strecker amino acid synthesis and an important precursor for the synthesis of nucleobases" (Cleaves et al. 2008, 106). I have deleted numerous citations, present in the original, from this quote.

[37] Cleaves et al. 2008.

[38] Chyba et al. 1990; Chyba and Sagan 1992; Cronin and Chang 1993; Ehrenfreund et al. 2002; Martins et al. 2008.

[39] All along it has been recognized in the origin-of-life literature that so-called *Panspermia*—the importation into earth of spores of extraterrestrial organisms—cannot definitively be ruled out by our current evidence, especially in light of the enormous shower of meteors carrying organic compounds that descended upon the earth in its early years. However, no complicated macromolecules like nucleic acids and proteins have been found in meteors. An interesting new "aromatic world" hypothesis about the origin of life (Ehrenfreund et al. 2006; Ehrenfreund and Cami 2010) seeks to integrate the extraterrestrial influx of organic materials from early meteors into the existing theories. Moving out even beyond the solar system, Kuan et al. (2003) document the presence of glycine, the most common amino acid, in the Orion galaxy.

[40] Anastasi et al. 2008, 273.

> From our discussion of prebiotic chemistry we will conclude that the abiotic synthesis of RNA is so difficult that it is unclear that the RNA World could have evolved *de novo* on the primitive Earth. . . . The polymerization of nucleotides in aqueous solution is an uphill reaction and does not occur spontaneously to a significant extent. . . . Consequently, attempts to polymerize nucleotides from aqueous solution must necessarily make use of external activating agents. . . . It is possible that all of these, and many other difficulties will one day be overcome and that a convincing prebiotic synthesis of RNA will become available. However, many researchers in the field, myself included, think that this is unlikely and that there must be a different kind of solution to the problem of the origin of the RNA World.[41]

An uncharitable way of describing decades of hard experimental work is this:

> The notion of Hadean oceans chock-full of Oparin's prebiotic soup still enjoys some popularity, but the question remains of how a solution at equilibrium can start doing chemistry. Put another way, once autoclaved, a bowl of chicken soup left at any temperature will never bring forth life.[42]

In the language of autocatalysis, all the pieces of RNA seem to be there in the chicken soup. But there is something missing that turns those pieces into a cyclical chemistry that reproduces. For a while, porous clay seemed to be a promising spatial array within which nucleobases could self-organize.[43] But "there is as yet no experimental support for the idea of a self-replicating, informational clay mineral."[44] This is the unfortunate dead-end in which the RNA-first school of thought currently finds itself. The evolutionary road leading out from RNA seems clear, but the evolutionary road leading up to RNA is enshrouded in fog.[45]

The metabolism-first school of thought is a second crack at the origin-of-life problem. This theoretical position goes back to Oparin, but it received a large boost in popularity from the dramatic discovery of life in the late 1970s at the very bottom of the ocean around thermal vents oozing from deep inside the earth.[46] It was not so much the waving tube worms or giant clams that fascinated origin-of-life researchers but the thermal bacteria emerging from within the volcanic vents that provided the worms and the clams their food. This was not a warm tidal pond fueled by photosynthesis; this was life based on sulfur and iron.[47] Thermal vents reminded geochemists of early conditions on earth when volcanoes interacted chemically with oceans with much greater frequency than they do today.[48] This discovery, moreover, dovetailed nicely with the earliest application of genome sequencing to evolutionary questions, which placed thermal archaebacteria at or near the root of the evolutionary tree.[49] Far-from-equilibrium energy throughput obviously is not a problem with thermal vents.

On a basic level, the metabolism-first position and the RNA-first position both agree that autocatalysis in the form of Morowitz's second diagram in figure 2.3 must kick in for chemical life as we know it to emerge. The difference between these positions lies on the emphasis of the metabolism-first school on metallic surface catalysts, which are regarded as having jump-started cyclical metabolism before RNA evolved to do that job more efficiently.[50] Thermal vents are perfect for that job because they are porous rock funnels consisting largely of iron, sulfur, and nickel, arranged in tiny 3D compartments.[51] Thermal vent theory has been criticized because RNA is not stable at the high temperatures (~300° C) of "black smoker" cones.[52] But laterally away from the central rift, the temperature of thermal vents is not too high (~50–60° C), and mixture of magma material with convective seawater is more thorough.[53] In addition, many

[41] Orgel 2004, 100, 109, 114.

[42] Martin and Russell 2003, 62.

[43] Cairns-Smith 1982; Ferris 2002; Huang and Ferris 2003.

[44] Orgel 2004, 114. Orgel (1998) and Shapiro (2006, 107–17) provide more details on this negative assessment.

[45] Not everyone has given up. Anastasi et al. (2008) outline an experimental search procedure to exhaustively explore all the synthesis options involving compounds similar to RNA that have not been tried over the last fifty years.

[46] Corliss et al. 1979.

[47] Wächtershäuser 1992.

[48] Baross and Hoffman 1985, 329; Sleep 2010.

[49] Woese and Fox 1977; Woese, Magrum, and Fox 1978; Woese 1981, 1982, 1987; Achenbach-Richter et al. 1987; Iwabe et al. 1989; Woese, Kandler, and Wheelis 1990; Stetter 1996, 151; Woese 2000.

[50] Wächtershäuser 1988.

[51] Vivid pictures of what thermal-vent precipitates look like up close today, in laboratories, and 3.6 billion years ago (two fossils from Ireland) are shown in Martin and Russell 2003, 63 and Martin and Russell 2007, 1914. Thermal vents structurally have not changed over time.

[52] Miller and Bada 1988; Bada and Lazcano 2002.

[53] Russell et al. 1988; Corliss 1990; Martin and Russell 2007, 1914.

contemporary archaebacteria live in high temperatures (~80–110° C).[54]

Morowitz reminds us that "the chart of metabolic pathways is an expression of the universality of intermediary metabolism. The reaction networks of all extant species of organisms map onto a single chart, the great unity within diversity of the living world."[55] The metabolic network is far too complicated to reproduce in this chapter, but a wall-sized version of it, simplified, has been produced by the Roche pharmaceutical corporation.[56] At the core of this vast chemical network are a set of autocatalytic cycles: the Krebs or citric-acid cycle, which creates numerous biochemical components (like precursors to amino acids) out of food inputs (like carbohydrates, fats, and proteins); the Calvin or pentose-phosphate cycle, which fixes carbon in photosynthesis; the formose cycle, which processes sugars; the fatty-acid cycle, which makes lipids for cell walls; and the uric-acid cycle, which eliminates nitrogen waste. These core autocatalytic cycles are interlinked through metabolic pathways that lead from one to another through chemical-reaction chains. This whole multiple-network metabolic apparatus is regulated by protein enzymes, created by DNA and RNA in response to chemical feedbacks from the operation of the metabolic networks. In this sense, DNA and RNA function not only as inheritance machines for Darwinian evolution but also as chemical components within metabolism, which regulate it.

The metabolism-first school's approach to the origin of life is to shrink this vast metabolic system down to its minimal core and then to imagine chemical ways to construct that. A number of "minimal cores" have been proposed,[57] but the most popular has been the reductive or reverse citric-acid cycle (and components thereof). The reductive citric-acid cycle is the oxidative or regular citric-acid cycle run in reverse: "Where the Krebs cycle takes complex carbon molecules in the form of sugars and oxidizes them to CO2 and water, the reverse cycle takes CO2 and water to make carbon molecules."[58] The reductive citric-acid cycle is described in terms of both chemical outputs and chemical mechanics in figure 2.4. The reason for the metabolism-first school's substitution of reverse citric-acid cycle for normal (oxidative) citric-acid cycle is that the normal cycle requires biochemical input from the Calvin cycle, whereas the reductive citric-acid cycle can process primitive chemicals directly.[59]

A. Functional representation (Smith and Morowitz 2004,13169)

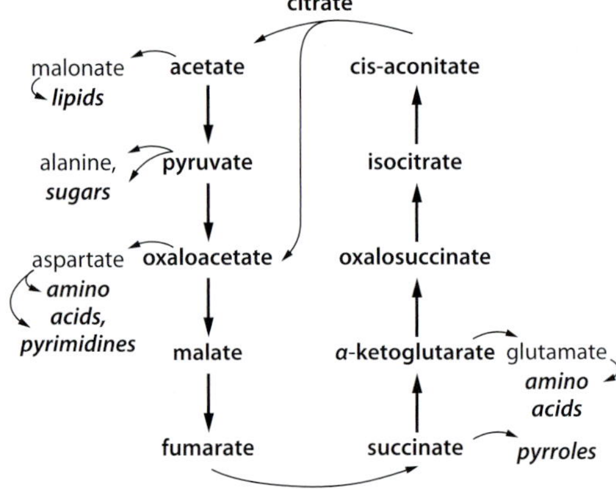

B. Chemical-mechanics representation (Cady et al. 2001, 3558)

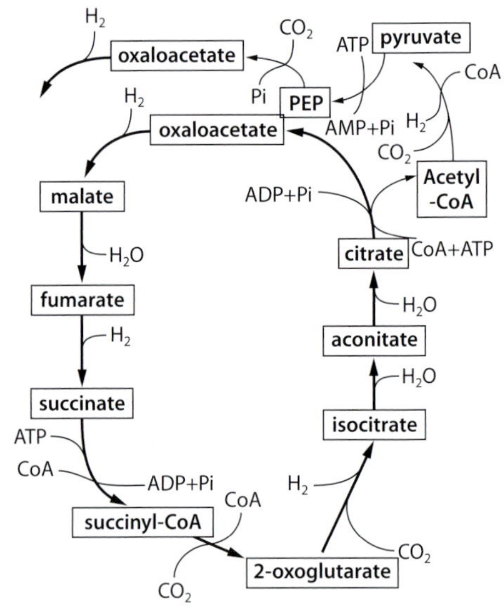

Figure 2.4 Reductive citric-acid cycle.

[54] Stetter 1996. Recently subterranean archaebacteria also have been discovered deep inside thermal hot springs in Idaho (Chappelle et al. 2002), far removed from any organic food other than primitive CO_2 and H_2. The authors speculate that if life exists on Mars, it will be of this form.

[55] Morowitz et al. 2000, 7704.

[56] See Dagley and Nicholson 1970, which breaks this into manageable pieces.

[57] A creatively "out of the box" suggestion by Jalbout (2008) is that the formose cycle, which makes sugars, formed in the gases of outer space. Formaldehyde and glycoaldehyde, key chemicals in that cycle, have been detected there by radio telescope. The formose cycle is the one metabolic cycle that is known to be possible without enzymes.

[58] http://en.wikipedia.org/wiki/Reverse_Krebs_cycle.

[59] Morowitz 1999; Smith and Morowitz 2004.

In addition, primitive bacteria without photosynthesis use the reductive citric-acid cycle.[60]

Given that only the primitive atoms of carbon, hydrogen, and oxygen are involved in the reductive citric-acid cycle itself,[61] the trick for the metabolism-first school is to find mineral or other catalysts that might process and assemble such prebiotic inputs into autocatalytic cycles. Going back to the useful simplicity of the lower diagram in figure 2.3, this is a focus on the lower-left catalytic arrow, as well as on the cyclic transformational arrow of metabolism itself.

Wächtershäuser[62] and Russell, Hall, and Martin[63] are the current theoretical leaders of the metabolism-first school. Russell, Hall, and Martin emphasize thermal vents more explicitly than does Wächtershäuser,[64] but both propose similar prebiotic chemistries: namely, the catalysis of various components of the reductive citric-acid cycle, along with molecular pathways leading into that, through surface metals, mainly iron- and nickel-sulfur compounds. Cody summarizes the decade's worth of experimental research[65] that has been devoted to these hypotheses, some of which has been carried out by his team. He reports mixed success: about half of the chemical reactions in the reductive citric-acid cycle have been synthesized without enzymes by metal-catalysis means but not the whole cycle. One of the core pathways leading into the cycle—the acetyl-CoA (Wood-Ljungdahl) pathway—seems to be the most promising chemical origin of the cycle itself, in part because that is easily synthesized.[66] This line of research is ongoing, much of it funded by NASA, without having yet reached definitive conclusion.

As always, the bottom diagram in figure 2.3 helps clarify the big picture. Considerable but not complete progress has been made on the lower-left catalytic arrow and on the cyclic constructive arrow of metabolism by the metabolism-first school of thought, using prebiotic metallic catalysts. Nobody worries about the horizontal constructive arrow going from metabolism to amino acids and the like because that is already well-known. The RNA-first school has made considerable progress synthesizing amino acids and nucleobases without requiring them to have been made by preexisting metabolism. The constructive arrow on the lower right, going from amino acids and so forth to primitive RNA, has been a major stumbling block. Fifty years of hard experimental labor by the best minds in biochemistry have not cracked that very tough nut. Once RNA falls into place, however, much sophisticated theoretical and experimental work exists to move from the bottom diagram to the top diagram of figure 2.3 through Darwinian means. Both autocatalytic diagrams together represent the emergence of life, as contemporary chemistry understands that.

A very recent review by Fry is judicious in its conclusion:

> This paper examines the RNA-first, the RNA-later, metabolism-first and preparatory-metabolism scenarios, assessing the weaknesses and strengths of each. I conclude that despite the recent theoretical advances in all these lines of research, and despite experimental breakthroughs, especially in overcoming several RNA-first hurdles, none of the examined paradigms has yet attained decisive experimental support. Demonstrating the evolvability of a potentially probiotic infrastructure, whether genetic or metabolic, is a most serious challenge. So is the experimental demonstration of the emergence of such an infrastructure under prebiotic conditions. The current agenda before origin-of-life researchers of all stripes and colors is the search for the experimental means to tackle all these difficulties.[67]

In the end it will be both sides (and their hybrids) working together to find a synthesis between

[60] Danson and Hough 1992.

[61] Morowitz et al. 2000.

[62] Wächtershäuser 1988, 1990, 1992, 1994, 1998, 2000, 2006, 2007.

[63] Russell and Hall 1997; Russell et al. 1988; Russell, Hall, and Turner 1989; Russell and Hall 1997; Russell, Daia, and Hall 1998; Martin and Russell 2003, 2007.

[64] The leaders differ in how they envision cell walls being constructed. Wächtershäuser (1994) has hypothesized that peptide ligands grow out from pyrite surfaces to contain and hold metabolic primitive reactions. Russell and Hall (1997) envision FeS bubbles forming within tiny thermal rock compartments, eventually to be supplanted by organic sulphide polymers, which shrink the membranes to increase chemical densities, and finally to be ejected into the open sea to meet their Darwinian fates. To my knowledge, neither of these cell-wall-origin suggestions has been evaluated experimentally.

[65] Cody 2004. For prominent examples of the research itself, see Huber and Wächtershäuser 1997, 1998; Cody et al. 2000, 2001, 2004; and Zhang and Martin 2006.

[66] Peretó et al. (1999) argue that the Wood-Ljungdahl pathway is more ancient than the reductive citric-acid cycle itself. Martin and Russell (2007, 1897) have recently integrated this suggestion by Cody into their updated protometabolism proposal for thermal vents. This now combines the Wood-Ljungdahl acetyl-CoA pathway with an incomplete reductive citric-acid cycle with the phosphorolysis suggestion of de Duve (1991).

[67] Fry 2011, 3.

their positions and their chemistries that carries the day. Chemical life as we know it, after all, is not genetics or metabolism but a symbiosis between the two.

Because of their resonance with themes in other chapters in this book, a couple of influential suggestions from cell evolution regarding symbiosis will also be mentioned here, applicable after cells are assumed to exist. Woese is the pioneer in tracing genealogies of the earliest bacteria, based on RNA sequencing.[68] Recent work of his,[69] the culmination of a career, draws the hegemonic image of the Darwinian genealogical tree into question, at least for bacterial origins, because horizontal gene transfer was prevalent among primitive bacteria with porous and poorly demarcated cell walls:

> The universal phylogenic tree is not an organismal tree at its base but gradually becomes one as its peripheral branchings emerge. The universal ancestor is not a discrete entity. It is, rather, a diverse community of cells that survives and evolves as a biological unit. This communal ancestor has a physical history but not a genealogical one.[70]

> Aboriginal cell designs are taken to be simply and loosely organized enough that all cellular componentry can be altered and/or displaced through horizontal gene transfer (HGT), making HGT the principal driving force in early cellular evolution. . . . The high level of novelty required to evolve cell designs is a product of communal invention, of the universal HGT field, not intralineage variation. It is the community as a whole, the ecosystem, which evolves. . . . As a cell design becomes more complex and interconnected a critical point is reached where a more integrated cellular organization emerges, and vertically generated novelty can and does assume greater importance. This critical point is called the "Darwinian Threshold."[71]

Only once this critical point in cellular integrity is reached do organismal species with Darwinian inheritance become well defined. As is illustrated in figure 2.5, followers of Woese have provocatively relabeled "the tree of life" in its origins as "the coral of life."[72] Needless to say, this Woese proposal of horizontal gene transfer is resisted by the narrowest of Darwinians, but it reflects the most up-to-date RNA-sequence analyses.[73] Margulis shows pictures of prokaryote bacteria today horizontally transferring their genes, in a kind of primitive sex.[74]

Margulis became widely known for a similar horizontal-transfer argument at the higher level of eukaryote cells.[75] Resisted at first, this argument is now considered standard wisdom. It was invented and labeled by earlier Russian authors as "endosymbiosis" or "symbiogenesis,"[76] but Margulis forcefully revived the hypothesis that complicated eukaryote cells (like those that comprise us) with nuclei and other internal parts arose historically by the ingestion, or perhaps infection, of one type of simpler bacteria cell by another. "The notion that eukaryote cells originated by endosymbiosis has been firmly established by molecular analysis of two organelles that contain their own DNA and ribosomes: the mitochondrion and the chloroplast.[77] DNA and ribosomal RNA sequencing demonstrate that the mitochondrion is a descendant of an alphaproteobacterium and that the chloroplast descended from a photosynthetic cyanobacterium.[78] Thus, the capacity of eukaryote cells to carry out oxidative metabolism and photosynthesis is clearly the result of symbiogenesis."[79] The details of how this ingestion or infection occurred in the first place, without either bacterium killing the other, are not entirely clear, but somehow or another both bacteria worked it out and benefited evolutionarily.[80] Symbiosis

[68] Obviously RNA sequencing cannot be used to penetrate into the origin of life deeper than RNA itself.

[69] Woese 1998, 2000, 2002. See also Fournier, Huang, and Gogarten 2009; Huang and Gogarten 2009; and Gaucher, Kratzer, and Randall 2010.

[70] Woese 1998, 6854.

[71] Woese 2002, 8742.

[72] Fournier, Huang, and Gorgarten 2009; Huang and Gorgarten 2009; Gaucher, Kratzer, and Randall 2010.

[73] Aravind et al. 1998; Kyrpides and Olsen 1999.

[74] Margulis and Sagan 1995, 95; Margulis and Dolan 2002, 52.

[75] Margulis 1967; Margulis 1970, 1981.

[76] Merezhkovsky 1909; Kozo-Polyansky [1924] 2010. The early twentieth-century history of botany in Russia is reviewed in Khakina 1992.

[77] Goodenough and Levine 1970.

[78] Bonen and Doolittle 1975; Zablen et al. 1975; Woese 1977; Gray, Burger, and Lang 1999.

[79] Shapiro 2011, 102.

[80] "The usual way of looking at mitochondria is as enslaved creatures captured to supply ATP for cells unable to respire on their own or to provide carbohydrate and oxygen for cells unequipped for photosynthesis. This master-slave arrangement is the common view of full-grown biologists, eukaryotes all. But there is another side. From their own standpoint the organelles might be viewed as having learned early how to have the best of possible worlds, with least effort and risk to themselves and their property" (Thomas 1974, 71).

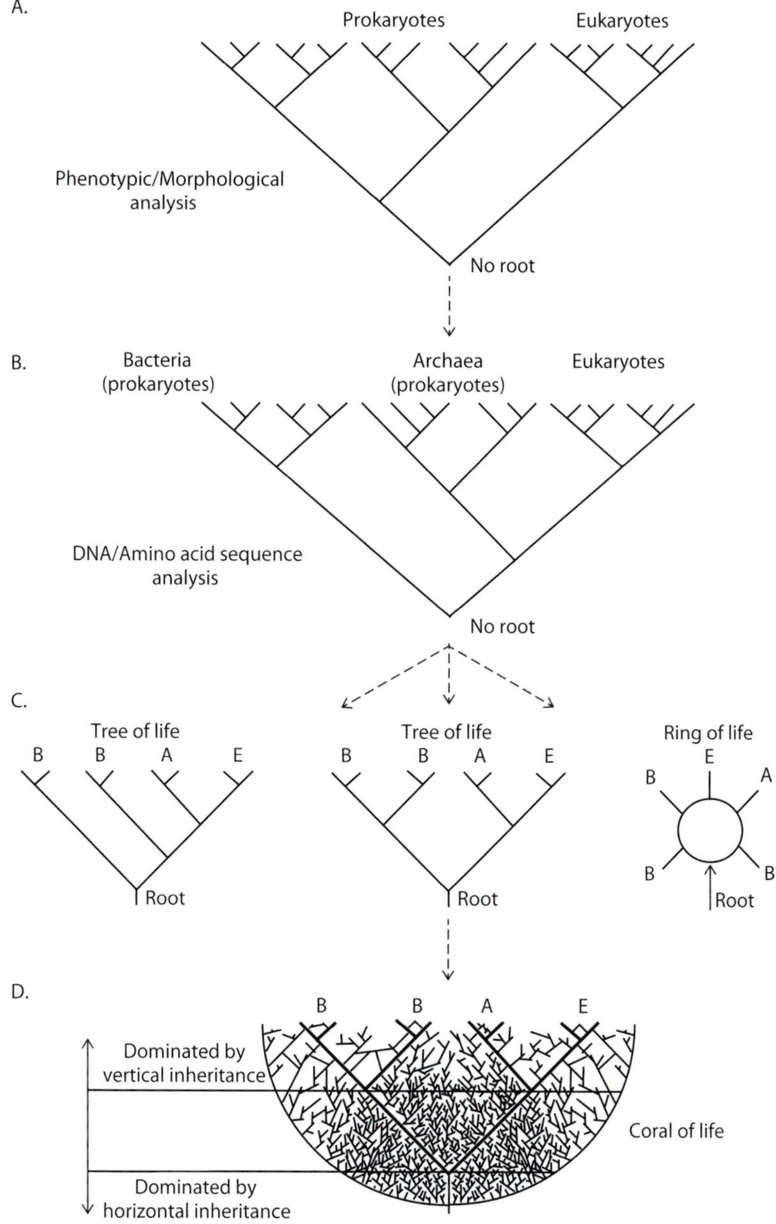

Figure 2.5 Changes in understanding of the tree of early life (Gaucher, Kratzer, and Randall 2010, 281).

operates not just at the level of the chemistry of genetics and metabolism within a simple cell but also at the phenotype level of how components of complicated cells fit together, coexist, and evolve.

Stephen Jay Gould has not written on autocatalysis and the origin of life and hence does not logically belong in this review. However, many social scientists know of his work because he undertook the intellectually daunting task of writing for a broad and diverse audience. "Punctuated equilibrium" and "exaptation" are the two scientific concepts most associated with his name, both of which are relevant for us. Punctuated equilibrium describes a phenomenon in the paleontological record not of instantaneous speciation but of rapid speciation.[81] Exaptation—similar to our own "transposition and refunctionality"—is the generation of novelty through the use of an old trait for a new purpose other than that for which it originally evolved.[82] In our empirical chapters, we show examples of both of these phenomena in human history. In this sense, we are building directly upon Gould's impressive powers of observation and insight. Our criticism is that we do not see Gould as having a theory to explain the phenomena that he astutely pointed to. Almost everything for him seems to be historical contingency.[83] A paleontologist, Gould was more concerned with documenting these understudied (and indeed resisted) evolutionary matters than he was with explaining them. Our proposition is that understanding the dynamics of multiple-network feedback and tipping is the next step in building upon the powerful insights that Gould has left us.

FORMAL MODELING OF AUTOCATALYSIS

Mathematical models have the same benefits and costs as other types of metaphors. Whereas reality has many things going on at once, models zero in on one aspect of reality at a time and, if they are good ones, impose the mental discipline of tracing through consequences not known beforehand. Through abstraction, models like other metaphors can function as translation devices across widely disparate domains and disciplines by identifying similarities not apparent in the details of particular fields. But the limitations of models should also be appreciated. Mathematical models should never be so glorified as to elide the distinction between them and reality. They are useful tools with which to think, not representations of the "essence" of reality, which is too rich and multitudinous to be reducible to anything as Platonic as "essence." At least nonindividualist models like autocatalysis focus attention on transformational interaction and feedback, important phenomena in any domain of emergence.

Formal models of chemical autocatalysis in the literature do not follow point by point the chemical research on the origin of life reviewed in the previous section. Indeed they are a bit splotchy in their coverage compared to the systematic, step-by-step approach of the empirical work. In this section I will discuss in most depth the first and most influential model of autocatalysis in chemistry: the hypercycle model of Eigen and Schuster. This model has been the most influential one in part because of its close connection with experimental work. After that, I will review other important models of autocatalysis by Kauffman, Fontana, and Jain.

The first model of autocatalysis in chemistry was the hypercycle model of Eigen and Schuster, proposed by Eigen in 1971 and developed by them in the 1970s.[84] As originally formulated, the hypercycle is a model of what is now called the RNA world. For orientation, this is the genetic component within the three-cycle simplification of the chemoton of figure 2.2. No autocatalytic model, other than the chemoton, deals with symbiosis among all three interacting autocatalytic systems—the metabolic, the genetic, and the cell wall.

Figure 2.6 presents the basic idea of the hypercycle model about autocatalysis in the RNA world. Figure 2.7 presents real genetic autocatalysis, which allegedly evolved out of the primitive RNA world. In the hypercycle model, but also in contemporary cellular reality, different types of self-replicating RNA and different types of protein enzymes make each other[85] in a self-constructing loop, which can be influenced by many environmental conditions and extracellular feedbacks. RNA reproduce themselves, once stimulated by a protein catalysis to do so. Assuming food, RNA make a second protein catalyst as well. Proteins act as catalysts for RNA, but once finished they (or their descendants) go out of the cell to regulate metabolism.[86] The full Eigen-and-Schuster model is complicated by

[81] Eldredge and Gould 1972; Gould 1989; Gould 2002, 745–1024; Fontana and Schuster 1998; Erwin 2000.

[82] Gould and Vrba 1982; Gould 2002, 1179–1295.

[83] Not that we are opposed to that; we just don't give it overwhelming status like he did. Our idea of a historically aware causal prediction is a constrained fan of trajectories through which history could evolve, not a single predetermined outcome. Gould probably would have agreed with this formulation, despite his occasionally very strong rhetoric about contingency (see, e.g., Gould 1989, 280–91).

[84] Eigen 1971a, 1971b; Eigen and Schuster 1979. By the time of this influential hypercycle work, Eigen had already received his 1967 Nobel Prize in Chemistry at the age of forty.

[85] RNAs construct proteins directly, out of raw-material amino acids in their local environment, whereas protein enzymes catalyze RNAs. The DNA in figure 2.7 did not exist in the earlier stage (figure 2.6) of the RNA world.

[86] Gilbert (1986) originally was excited by the experimental finding that some types of RNAs—so-called ribozymes—can also function as catalysts for RNA, like proteins do. This doesn't affect the hypercycle model itself much; it just implies

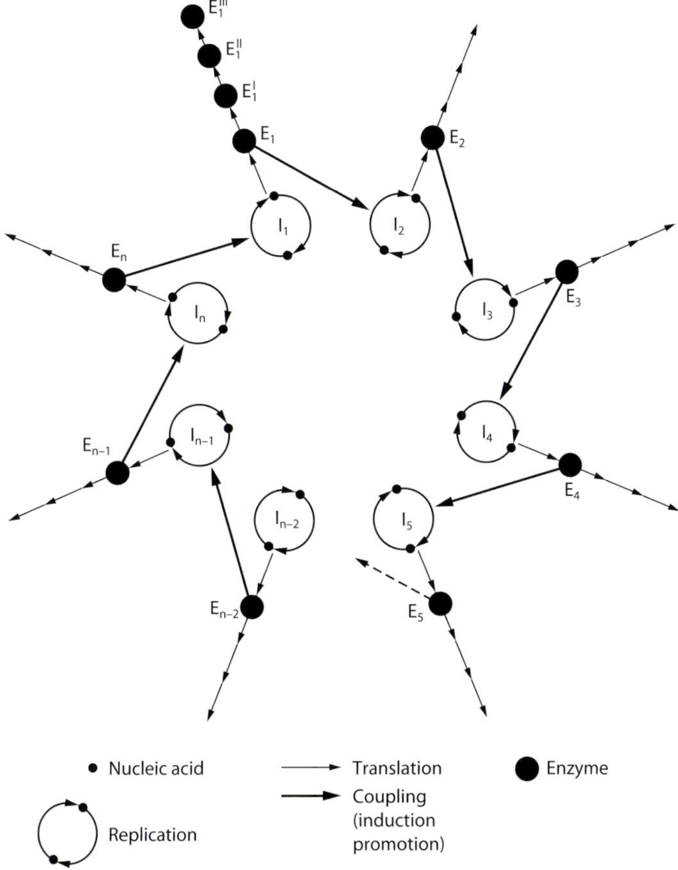

Figure 2.6 The hypercycle model of Eigen and Schuster (Eigen 1992, 110).

the fact that each "type of RNA" node in their chemical graph is actually a population distribution of genetically similar RNAs in an ensemble called by them a "quasi-species." Quasi-species are lineal descendants of RNA that emerge by mutation—namely, errors in self-replication—around a dominant and most reproductively efficient "wild type" of RNA. Hofbauer and Sigmund[87] simplify, as I do,[88] the full hypercycle of interacting quasi-species down into interacting "types of molecules" as nodes.

The hypercycle model is theoretically stimulating even for nonchemists because it places into a symbiotic relationship the two modalities of autocatalysis often regarded as contradictory: namely, "selfish" replication (RNA) and "cooperative" catalysis (enzymes). The theoretical contribution of Eigen and Schuster was to show how "cooperative" production networks are consistent with Darwinian natural selection in a primordial chemistry context. Because this Eigen-and-Schuster model is central to my extension of it in the next chapter, I spend more time reviewing it than I will spend reviewing subsequent models of chemical autocatalysis that appeared after this one.

Darwinian natural selection is modeled in hypercycles through "selfish" RNA self-replication. This induces competition in reproduction among quasi-species. Although obvious to biologists and chemists, it is worth a digression to spell out exactly what Darwin meant by natural selection in order to avoid misunderstanding

a direct catalytic link between some RNAs rather than one mediated by proteins.

[87] Hofbauer and Sigmund 1988, 87–107.

[88] In my transposition of this model to economic production, enzymes become products, and RNA becomes production rules. Padgett, Lee, and Collier 2003; Padgett, McMahan, and Zhong, this volume.

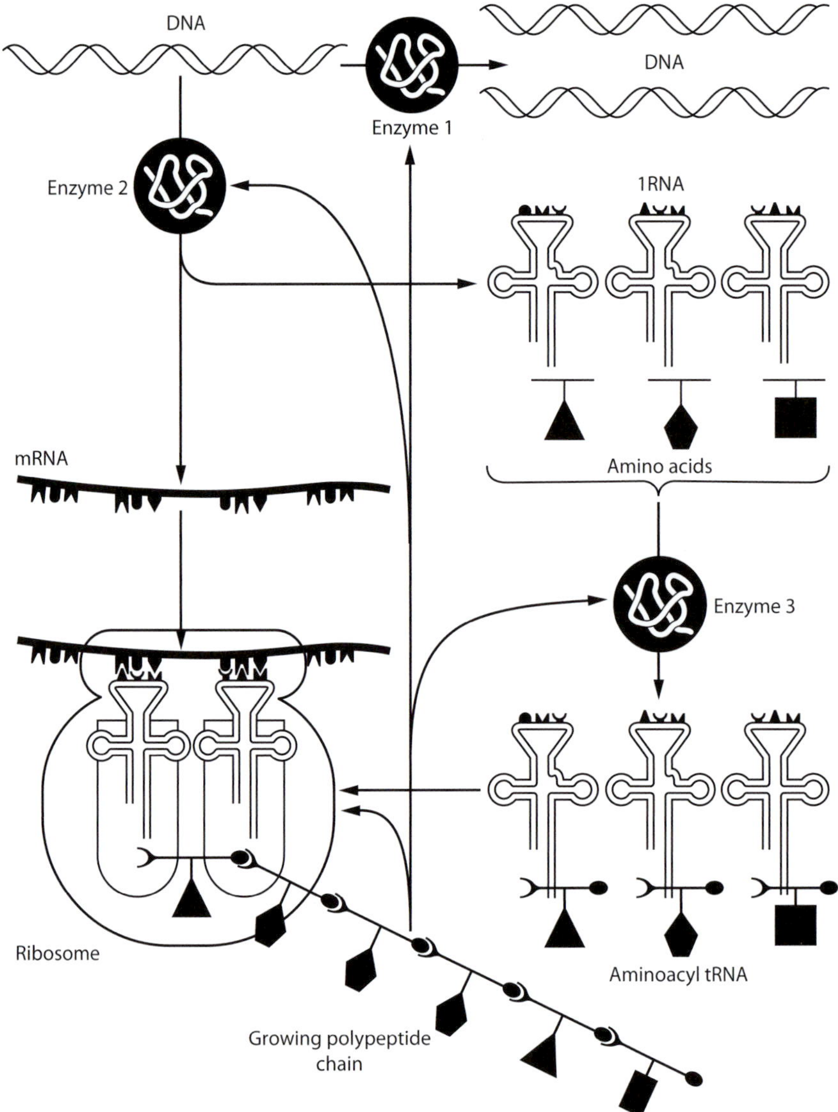

Figure 2.7 Full-blown genetic autocatalytic machinery (Eigen 1992, 76).

by social scientists, who frequently confuse that with Social Darwinism. Darwin's natural selection did not mean Spencer's "survival of (only) the fittest," much less the egotistical aggression presumed by most neoclassical economists. For Darwin, natural selection was almost a mathematical tautology. If population birthrates are proportional to population sizes (Malthus's idea), then exponential growth in population size is the consequence, assuming that birthrate is greater than death rate. With more than one population and a resource-budget limit on the total biomass possible for all populations put together, it is an accounting inevitability that higher growth-rate populations will crowd out lower growth-rate populations, perhaps driving some of them to extinction. This "natural selection" competition over resources is a demographic tautology, not a dog-eat-dog struggle among egotistical fighters. Indeed, change the birthrate assumption and "natural selection" changes:[89] a constant birthrate produces live-and-let-live mixed populations with linear growths and nobody selected out of existence. A greater than proportional quadratic birthrate produces winner-take-all competition with hyperbolic-growth populations, in which initial conditions determine victory as much as do underlying fundamentals, like birthrates.[90] Natural selection is not an inevitable fact of nature; long-term survival of fitter (i.e., higher birthrate) populations over less fit populations is a corollary of exactly how things reproduce.

"Selfish" self-replication of RNA or of anything else satisfies the proportional-growth Darwinian axiom and hence produces the Darwinian effect of "survival of the fittest." For Eigen and Schuster, as for all biologists, this type of selection is the sine qua non for demographic competition to lead to fitter populations, on average. Their distinctive contribution, however, was to demonstrate the negative consequences of self-replication alone for a second sine qua non of Darwinian evolution—namely, the production and maintenance of variation. This is the evolutionary reason why autocatalysis of the second network or "cooperative" variety comes into their RNA-world analysis.

There are two ways that unadulterated self-replication undermines variation, one intrinsic to their model in general and one having to do with the quasi-species component of their model. If there are no catalytic linkages between types of RNA in figure 2.6, then there is nothing but self-replication in the model, and demographic competition among populations with different net birthrates leads inexorably to selection of only one type: "survival of the fittest" in its starkest version. In ecology, this is called "competitive exclusion." Ecological coexistence and variety of multiple types of molecular species disappears.[91] Homogeneity in genotype and phenotype doesn't mean that life can't exist. It just means that life can't evolve.[92] Eigen and Schuster's original hypercycle model and the simpler versions by Hofbauer and Sigmund and by Padgett et al. all demonstrate that diversity in coexisting species is sustained only through catalytic interaction among chemical species.

Eigen's quasi-species extension to the baseline hypercycle model addresses variation within RNA species of genomes, in addition to "ecological" variation in numbers of types of RNA species. The core idea is the "error threshold." Mutation in RNA is conceived by Eigen as random errors that occur in copying during self-replication.[93] In "true self-instruction" where strings of nucleobases (A, C, G, U) reproduce in demographic competition, with no interactive feedback at all, RNA cannot exist because competitive exclusion produces mostly homogeneous nucleic strings (all A's or some other letter) that contain no instructional capacity.[94] Only when RNA develops the capacity to fold in on itself and to make complementary copies[95] of itself are populations of polymers with heterogeneous nucleobases sustainable. This complementarity between mirror images is the most primitive genetic hypercycle of all.

Above this 2-hypercycle level of complementary strands, Eigen shows that there is an "error threshold" limit to how long in length an RNA strand can grow to be, within isolated self-replicating (actually complementary-replicating) quasi-species, without catalytic support.[96] This is because there is a trade-off between RNA length and mutational copy-error rate: the higher the copy-error rate, the less capable long sequences are of maintaining their stochastic integrity, as stable probability distributions, over generations of self-replication. High copy-error rates lead to populations of RNA sequences drifting off into noise rather than remaining tightly clustered around maximally fit wild types. This means that even with complementary strands there is a limit to how complex RNA genomes can become with self-replication alone. Empirically, this limit is about the size of viruses. Eigen's error-threshold predictions about lengths of genomes and other aspects of hypercycle theory have been

[89] Eigen and Schuster 1979, 37.

[90] In economics, hyperbolic growth goes under the name "increasing returns." Crowd consumer behavior where buyers buy because others are buying—like computer interfaces or buzz in movies—is the archetype. Increasing returns is often discussed as one mechanism leading to path-dependence and to lock-in on inefficient equilibria. David 1985; Arthur 1994.

[91] Perhaps this is why there was so little evolution for most of earth's history: there were nothing but prokaryote bacteria around. Various theories of the Cambrian explosion exist, including ecological ones that new interspecies interactions like predation placed selection pressure on species to differentiate for defensive and offensive reasons. Erwin 1999; http://en.wikipedia.org/wiki/Cambrian_explosion#Ecological_explanations.

[92] Kirschner and Gerhart 1998.

[93] Shapiro (2011) challenges this traditional random conception of genetic mutation.

[94] Eigen 1971a, 490–96; Eigen 1971b, 172–75.

[95] The two mirror-image sides are called positive and negative copies.

[96] Eigen, McCaskill, and Schuster 1988.

confirmed in studies of viruses.[97] With catalytic or "symbiotic" hypercycle support from protein enzymes, however, copy-error rate goes down, and the various interdependent RNA quasi-species can all evolve beyond the complexity of viruses.[98]

For social scientists to appreciate the import of these findings, it might be helpful to translate them into the language of our world. It is as if in evolution the complexity of individuals can be increased through the social control of their reproduction by other types of individuals with whom they are in interaction. "Social control" has the connotation, and the reality, of decreasing variability at the micro level of the individual. Eigen's profound and counterintuitive observation, however, is that social-interactional control actually increases complexity and variability at the higher population level of the system itself when that control involves catalysis.[99]

If this Eigen-Schuster work is so good, and obviously I think it is, then what are the problems? For one thing, it doesn't address all of the outstanding issues. In particular, the hypercycle model is a model of the RNA world. As such, it says nothing about where RNA itself came from, a problem we have seen to be vexing indeed. Nor does it say anything about how RNA autocatalysis and metabolic autocatalysis (and cell-wall autocatalysis, for that matter) interrelate in the multiple-network symbiosis of a cell. Sins of omission like this, however, are hardly damning. No model does everything. Sins of omissions are just challenging agenda items for future research.

More significant theoretically are internal anomalies within the model itself. Hofbauer and Sigmund have derived that hypercycles are not dynamically stable for more than four types of chemical species, a finding confirmed in my own simulations.[100] This means that hypercycle catalysis alone cannot support five or more species in long-term-equilibrium existence without something else being added. The population of one or another of the species in such complicated ecologies soon or later is driven to zero, causing the entire interdependent cycle to unravel.

One solution to this "complexity barrier," as is shown in chapter 3 of this volume, is to embed hypercycles in two-dimensional interaction space. Eigen and Schuster's models presume a random topology of chemical interaction, as one would find in an aqueous solution. They have the primitive biotic pond of Darwin, Oparin, and Miller in the backs of their minds. Restrictive constraints on interaction possibilities, either through physical space (chapter 3) or through social networks (chapter 4), allow hypercycles to achieve a complexity of greater than five chemical species. In my spatial versions of the hypercycle model,[101] I have catalytic surfaces (like thermal vents) in the back of my mind. More important, social interactions are not random in social-network topology.

A second internal problem with the hypercycle model is the issue of parasites.[102] These are new chemical species introduced into well-functioning hypercycles either by mutation from an existing quasi-species or by migration from the outside. Parasites may (but do not necessarily) pose a number of problems for hypercycles: (a) they can reproduce so fast as to bleed existing species to death; (b) they can be more attractive to existing enzymes than to the old target, thereby breaking the chain; or (c) they can short-circuit existing hypercycles, not destroying them but making them simpler.[103] Critics propose that compartments—that is, cell walls—are required for solving these parasite problems. The only thing wrong with

[97] Spiegelman 1971; Domingo, Flavell, and Weissman 1976; Domingo et al. 1978; Domingo, Dávila, and Ortín 1980; Eigen and Winkler-Oswatitsch 1981a, 1981b; Biebricher, Eigen, and Luce 1981a, 1981b; Reanney 1982; Biebricher, Eigen, and Gardiner 1983, 1984, 1985; Eigen et al. 1991; Lee et al. 1997. On the evolutionary flip side for viruses, short RNA lengths mean high copy-error rates and hence the adaptive capacity of viruses to reconstruct themselves much more rapidly than can their hosts. Viruses are parasitic self-replicators that highjack hosts to survive.

[98] DNA polymers have developed error-correction mechanisms even beyond the enzyme-catalysis features of RNA and hence have become longer still, but that is another story.

[99] In chapter 4 I pursue this theme through the topic of teaching.

[100] Hofbauer and Sigmund 1988, 96; Padgett, Lee, and Collier 2003, 852–54; Padgett, McMahan, and Zhong, this volume. Eigen knew this (1971a, 506), but in his greater-than-four-species models, he permitted dead chemical species to come back to existence. As noted by Maynard Smith and Szathmáry (1995, 53), "this objection echoes the argument (Pimm and Lawton 1977) that ecological food chains are short because long chains are dynamically unstable."

[101] The idea of embedding hypercycles in spatial interaction structure was first pursued by Boerlijst and Hogeweg (1991, 1992). Their model produced interesting spiral-wave behavior, which emerged through making rule replication happen on adjacent bins rather than within the same bin, as in my model. While the Boerlijst-Hogeweg and my spatial-hypercycle models are cousins, they did not choose to explore the Hofbauer-Sigmund issue of dynamic instability. The Boerlijst-Hogeweg simulation model has been transposed into the analytical framework of partial differential equations by Cronhjort and Blomberg (1994) and Cronhjort (1995).

[102] Maynard Smith 1979; Bresch, Niesert, and Harnasch 1980; Niesert, Harnasch, and Bresch 1981.

[103] Bresch, Niesert, and Harnasch 1980, 402.

this parasite criticism is the implication that Eigen and Schuster didn't know this already.[104]

Both weaknesses in the original hypercycle model point to similar fixes. The physical embodiment of genetic autocatalysis or life—in space and/or in cellular compartments—helps the hypercyclic RNA world to power up into more complex evolution. This extended hypercycle model is the "Eigen-Darwin cycle" of molecular evolution that was mentioned above.[105] It is completely consistent with Darwin, but it emphasizes the relational side of Darwin.

Were one to have complete parallelism between formal modeling and the chemical literature on the origin of life, one would expect to find abstractions of autocatalysis on the metabolism-first side of the debate, analogous to Eigen and Schuster on the RNA side. With the autocatalysis model of Stuart Kauffman,[106] one finds something like this, but the fit between this model and the current metabolism-first chemical literature is far from seamless. "Metabolism-first" in the chemical literature focuses on the prebiotic catalysis of the reductive citric-acid cycle or some other chemical cycle in existing metabolisms. "Metabolism-first" in the model of Kauffman et al. focuses on the autocatalysis of polypeptides,[107] which in long versions are called proteins. The Kauffman model of autocatalysis, in other words, is a protein-first view of the origin of life. This model has both ancestors[108] and descendants.[109]

[104] Eigen (1971a, 508), for example, says clearly: "Neither 'individualization' nor 'compartmentalization' are inherent properties of the hypercycle—as are, for instance, the other properties mentioned above. However, where they occur after nucleation, they may offer a selective advantage and therefore are inevitable evolutionary consequences of the hypercycle. The advantages lie in the utilization of mutations. If a mutation—especially in the auxiliary [i.e., enzyme] function—turns out to be of advantage, it will be utilized by the whole 'disperse' system and therefore does not favor specifically the reproduction of the mutant—unless it occurs within a compartment. [For a virus example, see Eigen 1992, 102–4.] If it does so, it will favor that particular system which after individualization will also select against its precursors. The same is true for unfavorable mutations which—if they occur in a compartment—will affect (or even destroy) only their particular compartment and thus disappear, whereas otherwise they would pollute the whole system."

[105] Penny 2005.

[106] Kauffman 1986; Farmer, Kauffman, and Packard 1986; Bagley and Farmer 1992; Kauffman 1993, chap. 7. This model is foreshadowed but not developed in Kauffman (1971, appendix 6). Kauffman's second famous model of chemistry—the "rugged landscape" NK model of Boolean networks—is not reviewed here because that does not involve autocatalysis. See Kauffman 1969, 1971; Kauffman 1993, chaps. 2 and 5; and Levinthal 1997 for development and application of that.

[107] Polypeptides are polymer strings of amino acids.

[108] Calvin 1956, 1961; Rössler 1971; Dyson 1982, 1999.

[109] Segré and Lancet 1999; Hordijk and Steel 2004; Mossel and Steel 2005; Fishkis 2010.

In terms of our globally orienting figure 2.3B, the protein-first view is a focus on the catalytic dotted arrow in the lower right, going back up from "low-efficiency catalysts" to amino acids. The protein-first position is the hypothesis that polypeptide versions of low-efficiency catalysts can be self-organizing and autocatalytic.

The basic idea is presented in figure 2.8. Chemical reactions here involve the formation of polypeptides, that is, the connection and cleavage of simple components (like amino acids) and short strings into longer strings. The solid lines in figure 2.8 show the possible reaction pathways for smaller strings to be concatenated into longer strings but also for longer strings to disintegrate into their simpler components. Dotted lines represent indirect ("third party") catalysis effects, namely, the hypothesized effects that strings have on the production rates of connection and cleavage of other strings. "Spontaneous" concatenation options other than the catalyzed ones are logically possible, but since we know that catalyzed reactions will dominate a chemical system, the model zeroes in on them, randomly creating[110] chemical-reaction graphs like figure 2.8.

Autocatalysis in a system like this means that reaction graphs develop cycles, in which every polypeptide string (other than the basal food set) in the autocatalytic network is constructed out of interactions among the other strings. The model's question then becomes: when will self-sustaining production cycles emerge among random chemical networks? The two network-topology parameters of the random network in the model are these: (a) P, which is the probability that a randomly chosen reaction will be catalyzed (by someone), and (b) M, which is the maximum length of the polymer allowed in the system. The basic finding is that no matter what the P, autocatalysis is inevitable if M gets large enough. As Kauffman shows,[111] this result is the consequence of random-graph theory, in particular, the Erdös-Rényi proof that a large component will emerge in any random graph once the number of ties in the graph exceeds its number of nodes. As M goes up, the number of chemical nodes in the graph goes up, but for fixed P, the number of reaction ties goes up even faster than that. Sooner or later the growing

[110] "Randomly creating" means this: (a) randomly select strings to couple into concatenation/cleavage chains eligible for catalysis, and then (b) randomly select a third-party string to do the catalysis job.

[111] Kauffman 1993, 308–9.

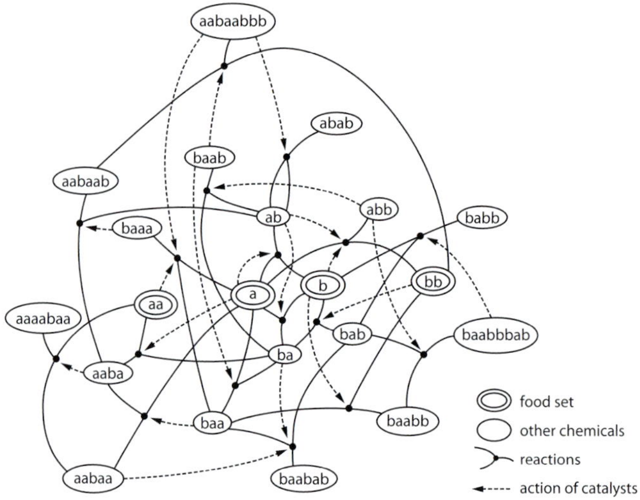

Figure 2.8 Autocatalysis of polymers (Farmer, Kauffman, and Packard 1986, 53). A typical example of a graph that might describe an autocatalytic set. The reactions are represented by nodes connecting cleavage products with the corresponding condensate. Dotted lines indicate catalytic pathways and point from the catalyst to the reaction being catalyzed.

number of ties will exceed the growing number of nodes, thereby triggering autocatalysis. Translated back into chemistry proper, the implication of the model is that networks of proteins alone can self-organize into and trigger life if polymer lengths can grow long enough.

This Kauffman et al. protein-first model has not been as influential as the Eigen-Schuster hypercycle model, in part because it has not been embedded in an ongoing line of experimental work,[112] as the Eigen-Schuster model has been. The simplifying assumptions of the polypeptide model have been criticized for being at variance with the behavior of real polypeptides.[113]

A second nonscientific reason for the relative lack of influence of the Kauffman model is the overreaching rhetoric with which he describes his findings in his books[114] as opposed to in his articles. In some of his more grandiloquent passages, Kauffman argues that autocatalysis is an alternative to Darwin. Kauffman is the only prominent advocate of autocatalysis who sees genesis and selection as being antithetical[115] rather than complementary. Perhaps he will be proven right and the rest of us wrong in the end. But most biologists and chemists believe Darwin needs to be supplemented not replaced. The quasi-religious reaction against Kauffman's inflated rhetoric is unfortunate, in my opinion, because his ideas and models deserve more thorough empirical investigation than they have received to date.

Only two more formal models of autocatalysis will be reviewed here, those of Sanjay Jain and Walter Fontana. Jain and Krishna[116] take an ecological approach to autocatalysis. They set up a community matrix of catalytic growth relations among species of either chemicals or animals, as is done in ecology.[117] Entries in such a community matrix of biological network interaction describe "who eats whom" and how fast one species contributes to the growth of another. An ecological network structure like this produces an equilibrium of relative population sizes, which may include oscillations, extinctions, and community

[112] But see Ashkenasy et al. 2004, which belatedly starts to address this empirical weakness.

[113] Orgel 2008. Orgel's serious criticisms are these: (a) No chemical reaction network is random, a fact that Kauffman never denied. (b) Polypeptides are hydrophobic, meaning that they naturally break up in water. This means that concatenation is only possible with an external coupling agent, which Kauffman never discusses. Once this coupling agent is admitted, the label "prebiotic" becomes dubious. (c) The assumption of fixed P is wrong. The discrimination capacity of short polypeptides is weak; only long proteins have the capacity to catalyze specific, targeted reactions. Weak discrimination at short lengths means that is difficult for polypeptide networks to get over the hump of low complexity to reach the nirvana of autocatalysis that is attainable only with long polypeptides.

[114] Kauffman 1993, 1995, 2000.

[115] Goodwin (1994), I should say, also believes this.

[116] Jain and Krishna 1998, 1999, 2001a, 2001b, 2002, 2003.

[117] See Case 2000, chap. 15.

collapses, as well as the stable coexistence of species.[118] The evolutionary aspect is that Jain and Krishna, at the end of each round's dynamic equilibrium, delete the row and column of the species with the lowest population in the community to simulate selection and then add a new substitute row and column with random coefficients to simulate "innovation" in the form of a new species entering the system. The interesting finding is that random community matrices, as they undergo evolution so defined, gradually constitute themselves as autocatalytic sets where species are linked into catalytic or feeding cycles.[119] Not only that, but autocatalytic sets have a particular dynamic, namely, autocatalytic sets that start small with only two species at the beginning grow in coverage to span the entire community, then collapse back either part of the way or all of the way to community disintegration. After partial or complete collapse, autocatalysis builds back up again, "replaying life's tape."[120] Figure 2.9 is a history of one of their simulation runs.

Jain and Krishna's model illustrates that forming autocatalytic sets of interacting populations in an ecological community is not particularly difficult. But getting them to hold onto what they have achieved is another matter. The ecological model of Jain and Krishna has variation and selection of evolving community networks, no mean achievement in modeling, but it has no retention mechanism to keep the system from collapsing back toward repeating history.

Finally, the λ-calculus model of autocatalysis by Fontana[121] (and its Kappa descendant)[122] is theoretically the most ambitious of them all, having no less of an objective than to construct a general-purpose computational language for chemistry. In this computer-science approach, nodes are primitive logic functions.[123] "Chemical reactions" are computations where one logic function operates on a second to produce a third. "Autocatalytic chemistry" is a self-organizing computational program, which can compute all the functions that comprise it—something like a set of functions that makes up a group or semigroup in algebra.[124] Instead of the word *autocatalysis*, Fontana and Buss call such a self-computing set of functions a *self-maintaining organization*, but the meaning is the same.[125]

What takes this programming out of the realm of logic and computer science and into the realm of chemistry and the origin of life is that fact that Fontana puts his λ-calculus primitive functions into an *in silico* "evolutionary vat" with functions flowing in and functions flowing out, and functions creating other functions in the meantime. His experiment is to observe what sorts of "autocatalytic chemistries" or self-maintaining organizations of computable functions emerge under various conditions. Figure 2.10 is a very simple representation, which (fortunately) does not require an understanding of λ-calculus itself.

The primary finding from this approach is that there are three classes of self-maintaining organizations that emerge in the computer experiments.[126] So-called L0 organizations are Eigen and Schuster hypercycles, where self-replication coexists with network autocatalysis. So-called L1 organizations are vastly more complicated and robust network-autocatalytic systems, which emerge when simple self-replication is prohibited.[127] So-called L2 organizations are symbiotic systems, formed by putting into the same vat two fully formed L1 organizations. L2 symbiosis becomes possible when a so-called glue set of tertiary functions emerges, not itself autocatalytic, which connects the two component autocatalytic sets into mutual support.

λ-calculus has features that make it not a perfect match with chemistry—in particular the feature that functions can have only one product upon application, unlike chemical reactions, which can have two or more. This is the reason that Fontana has moved on to Kappa, a new concurrent computer language specifically designed with chemistry in mind.[128] Perhaps λ-calculus fits a semantic network of concepts—where concepts

[118] May 1973; Pimm 1982, 1991; Newman and Palmer 2003; Solé and Bascompte 2006.

[119] Real ecologies are cycles, as long as you don't forget the bacteria in the community.

[120] This expression comes from Gould 1989, 45.

[121] Fontana 1992; Fontana and Buss 1994a, 1994b, 1996.

[122] Danos et al. 2007, 2009; Feret et al. 2009; Harmer et al. 2010.

[123] λ-calculus is a highly abstract, formal logic system invented by Alonso Church (1932, 1933; Revesz 1988) in the 1930s, which turned out to be foundational to the invention of computing in the 1950s.

[124] http://en.wikipedia.org/wiki/Group_(mathematics).

[125] "The constituent entities of a self-maintaining system characteristically engage in interactions whose direct outcome is the construction of other entities in the same class. Self-maintenance, then, is the consequence of a constructive feed-back loop: it occurs when the construction processes induced by the entities of the system permit the continuous regeneration of these same entities. The specific functional relationships between entities which collectively insure their continuous regeneration, we define as an organization. A theory of organization, so defined, is a theory of self-maintaining systems" (Fontana and Buss 1996, 56).

[126] Fontana and Buss 1994a, 1994b.

[127] This prohibition on self-replication makes L1 more a model of metabolism than of RNA.

[128] Danos and Laneve 2004.

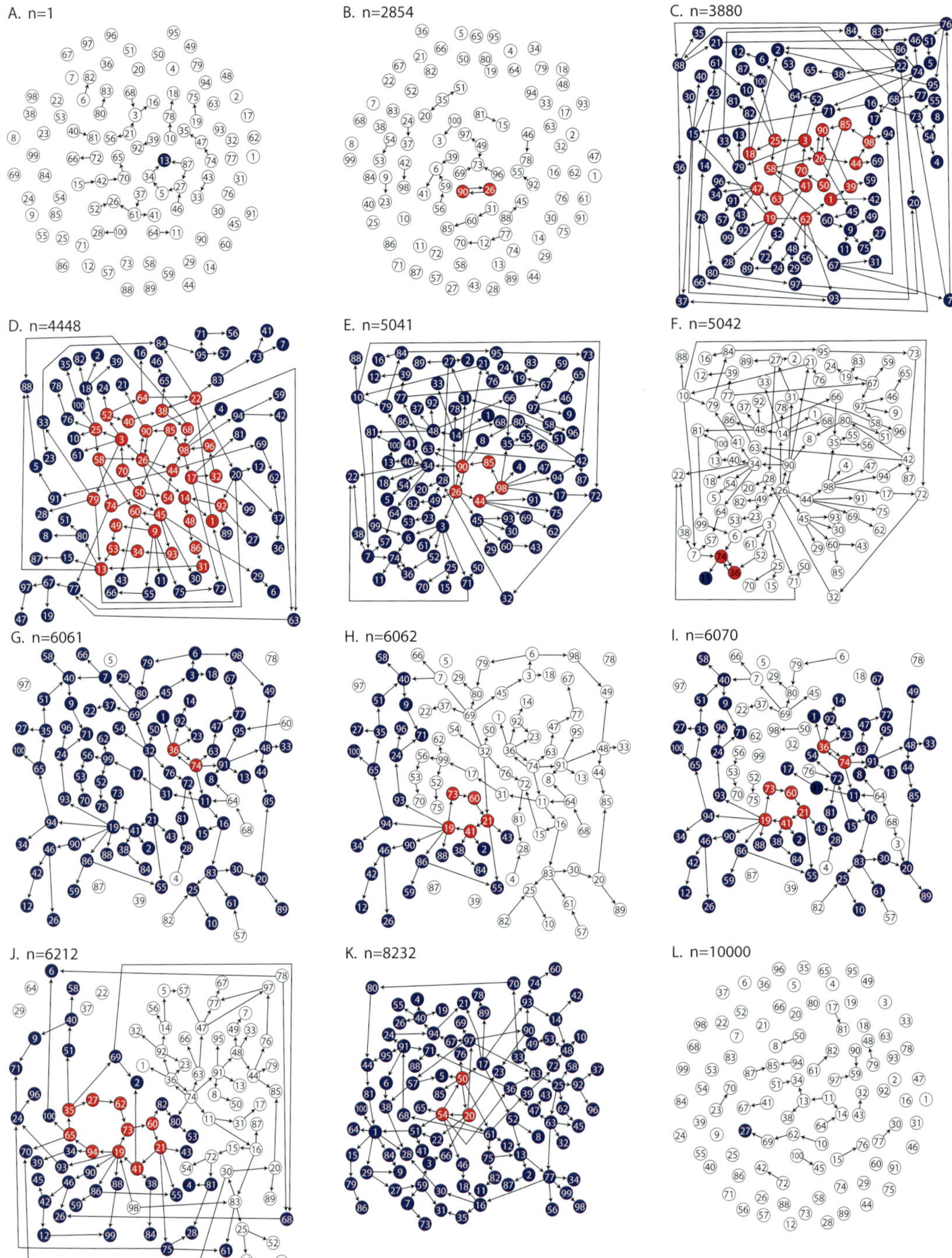

Figure 2.9 Jain and Krishna's ecological model of autocatalysis (Jain and Krishna 2003, 380).

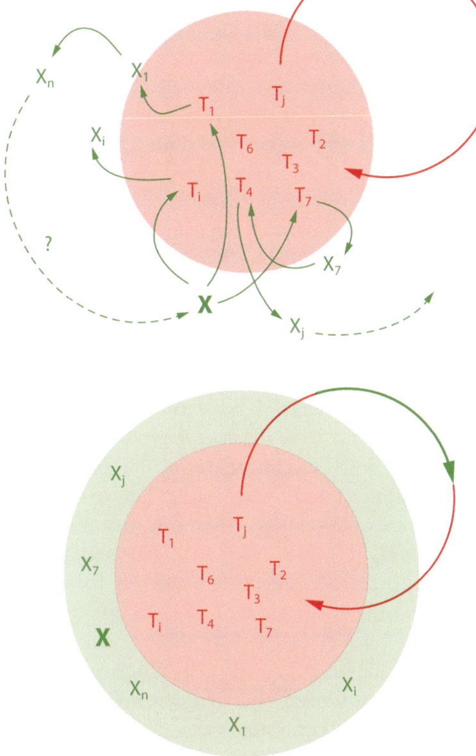

Figure 2.10 Fontana's λ-calculus model of autocatalysis (Fontana 2003, 26). The extension of a self-maintaining organization: A self-maintaining organization is schematically represented by a red set containing "red" components. The autocatalytic "red" organization is perturbed by a "green" component X, spawning a trail of consequences X_i. If that trail gives rise to a pathway that loops back to reproduce the original perturbing agent X, the "red" organization is extended in a self-maintaining fashion by a "green" layer (bottom).

transform concepts into other concepts—even better than it does chemistry. λ-calculus, after all, is symbolic logic at its base. If this proves to be the case, then this computer-science modeling framework might prove to be just as suggestive for the autocatalytic emergence of language as it is for the autocatalytic emergence of life.

All the formal models of autocatalysis reviewed in this section are by definition toy models. Whether their findings carry over into the real world of chemistry requires experimental and paleontological verification. Apart from the details of their individual fates, however, in ensemble they offer the promise that there are general principles about the emergence of life, which are there to be found underneath the enormous variety of particular histories of life forms. The models themselves are the "glue" that might be able to connect the biochemical sciences and the social sciences into symbiosis—or if not they themselves, then others like them. It is at least worth a try. Biochemists and social scientists both study "life" in its different manifestations. That doesn't mean that the word means exactly the same thing in its different realms. But it does mean that the two realms overlap, with evolutionary consequences for both sides.

AUTOPOIESIS

Social scientists are likely to have encountered the chemical concept of autocatalysis through the almost identical philosophical concept of "autopoiesis," invented by the Chilean biologists Maturana and Valera[129] and imported into sociology by the German social theorist Niklas Luhmann.[130] This pre-history and connotation are, from my perspective, most unfortunate. The concept of autopoiesis, unlike the concept of autocatalysis, was invented with no reference whatsoever to the extensive literature on the origin of life.[131] Its intellectual roots lay instead in cybernetic systems theory.[132] Because of this intellectual heritage, autopoiesis emphasizes autonomy and self-control, not interdependence; systems and subsystems, not self-organizing flux; and static equilibrium, not evolutionary dynamics. The concept of autopoiesis itself is fine, but what it is used for is not—at least not if the topic of interest is emergence and the production of novelty. In my opinion, Maturana-Varela and

[129] Varela, Maturana, and Uribe 1974; Maturana 1975, 1981; Maturana and Varela 1980; Varela 1979. Their label "autopoiesis," invented by them, derives from αὑτόσ = self, and ποιειυ = to make.

[130] Luhmann 1982, 1986a, 1989, 1990, [1984 in German] 1995.

[131] The papers by Maturana and Valera, just cited, contain remarkably few non-self citations: 4, 0, z, 23 citations, respectively. Only Varela (1979) makes a serious effort to engage with the field. That book is the only writing to cite Eigen and Schuster, who first published on hypercycles in 1971, but even its references to them are perfunctory.

[132] The first English translation of their 1973 Spanish book—eventually to become Maturana and Varela 1980—was published as a preprint (Maturana and Varela 1975) in the research center on cybernetics at the University of Illinois established by Heinz von Foerster.

Luhmann have taken a good idea and have run off with it in the wrong direction.[133]

The original definition of autopoiesis reveals its cybernetic roots:

> Autopoietic machines are homeostatic machines. Their peculiarity, however, does not lie in this but in the fundamental variable which they maintain constant. An autopoietic machine is a machine organized (defined as a unity) as a network of processes of production (transformation and destruction) of components that produces the components which: (i) through their interactions and transformations continuously regenerate and realize the network of processes (relations) that produced them; and (ii) constitute it (the machine) as a concrete unity in the space in which they (the components) exist by specifying the topological domain of its realization as such a network.[134]

Besides the convoluted English in which this is expressed,[135] there is nothing wrong with this autopoietic definition of biological life. It essentially combines items #2 and #3 in my four-element list in the section on the definition of life: their (i) is my (2) autocatalysis; their (ii) is my (3) cell wall; but (1) thermodynamic throughput and (4) evolution on my list are absent here.

The problems arise not in the definition, but in the implications they seek to draw:

> The consequences of this autopoietic organization are paramount: (i) Autopoietic machines are autonomous. . . . (ii) Autopoietic machines have individuality . . . (iii) . . . Their operations specify their own boundaries in the process of self-production. . . . (iv) Autopoietic machines do not have inputs or outputs.[136]

The motivation here is to use autopoiesis to specify "principles of biological autonomy," namely, principles of organizational self-development and self-control. Living systems, they want to claim, are self-directed systems, organizationally autonomous from the environments outside themselves. Nothing is said about the dynamics of how such a system could ever come to be. Given this motivation, it is not surprising that the only formal model Maturana and Varela ever developed was about cell-wall enclosure.[137] Consistent with this, the only biochemist whom I have discovered who has advocated their writings does research on cell compartmentalization.[138]

The main criticism I have of the autopoiesis approach is that it never goes beyond definition. Left there, "self-directed systems" become reified with no generative processes at all. Not really methodological individualism but essentialist individualism, if I can coin an awkward phrase. Talking about construction without investigating mechanisms of construction is not a theory of life.

Once the black box of construction is truly opened up, however, the dynamics of flux rush back in. "Autopoietic machines have no input or outputs" violates the first criterion of life that all dissipative systems require far-from-equilibrium throughputs of energy.[139] Autocatalysis does indeed imply that cyclic cores of self-reproducing chemical reactions exist. But it does not imply "organizational closure," where nothing but a cyclic core exists. "Parasites," which contribute nothing to self-maintenance, abound in autocatalytic systems, as is illustrated in chapter 3. Most of chemical metabolism topologically hangs off of cyclic cores rather being contained within them. Such "parasites" or metabolic pathways figure in channeling evolutionary tipping to new cores. Autopoiesis without paying attention to mutating or migrating rules is abolishing evolvability altogether. Perhaps the deepest problem is that the concept of autopoiesis, unlike the concept of autocatalysis, is crippled by being tied to a hierarchical-nesting vision of system boundaries and subsystems within systems. The notion of multiple networks and flows that intersect,

[133] Harrison White, an admirer of Luhmann, is trying to rescue the fruitful insights of Luhmann about communication from Luhmann's own systems-theory packaging. I will return to White's provocative reconstruction at the end of this section.

[134] Maturana and Varela 1980, 78–79.

[135] Maybe this version is better (or maybe not): "Autopoietic systems are systems that are defined as unities as networks of productions of components that recursively, through their interactions, generate and realize that network that produces them and constitute, in the space in which they exist, the boundaries of the network as components that participate in the realization of the network" (Maturana 1981, 21).

[136] Maturana and Varela 1980, 80–81; Varela 1979, 58: "This basic theoretical assumption, I now make explicit in the following. Closure thesis: Every autonomous system is organizationally closed."

[137] Varela, Maturana, and Uribe 1974.

[138] Luisi 2006; Damiano and Luisi 2010.

[139] Varela 1979 partially rectifies this error by distinguishing between organizational closure (in rules) and structural openness (in food). But even then, autocatalytic systems are not closed once mutation, migration, and evolution in rules are introduced.

interpenetrate, and collide through each other is nowhere to be found.

Perhaps Fontana has summarized best the biological version of this critique:

> In the past decades, molecular biology and the genome projects have opened many doors and worn out some hinge concepts in the process. We don't quite know anymore what a gene is. It used to be a stretch of DNA coding for one protein. But it turns out that most genes code for many variants of a protein. We used to think that a protein has a particular function. But a protein may be involved in so many processes and combine with so many other proteins into complexes with new interaction properties that the notion of a function has become elusive. We used to think that cells have types defined by genomic states, but there is too much consequential diversity within cells of the same type. We used to think of pathways that process information like pathways that transform metabolites. But now we know that few, if any, molecular signaling pathways are stand-alone entities. The cell resembles a combinatorially excitable medium more than a hard wired chip.[140]

It is flux, reproduction, and multifunctionality that make life different from cybernetic machines.

Multiple networks and how they intersect are at the heart of contemporary biochemistry in a way that old-fashioned cybernetic systems and subsystems, rooted in engineering, cannot begin to comprehend.

In this respect, Niklas Luhmann is more of the same. He emphasizes the closure and separation of the human social world from the rest of life rather than their interdependency.[141] "Self-referentiality"[142] is the core idea that Luhmann extracts from Maturana and Varela's concept of autopoiesis. He uses this idea to justify first defining human social autocatalysis in terms of communication and then to wall off symbolic communication into its own self-enclosed and self-referential world, like law,[143] decoupled from physical production and social interaction.

I am sympathetic to Luhmann's instinct to search for a distinctively human type of autocatalysis in the realm of communication and language (see chapter 4). But I am not sympathetic to his autopoiesis-derived assumption of autonomy and self-enclosure. Language studies from Wittgenstein to Tomasello[144] have emphasized—contra Chomsky[145]—the embeddedness of human communication practice and language in the physical and social contexts of their use. It thus seems a step backward, not a step forward, in our understanding of human communication to wall that off from the other forms of life in which language participates. For this backward step, the concept of autopoiesis is unfortunately to blame.[146]

Harrison White and Jan Fuhse[147] have excavated Luhmann for the parts worth saving. Luhmann, a German philosopher in lifelong adversarial conversation with his teacher Talcott Parsons, writes about as clearly as Parsons did and makes even fewer empirical references. Hence it is not always clear what Luhmann is talking about, nor does he make falsifiable statements.[148] White and Fuhse, however, usefully extract a Luhmann vision of social systems as communication that seems worthy of attention:

> A social system is constituted as an action system on the basis of communicative happenings, and using their operative means. The system generates a description of itself to steer the continuation of the process, the reproduction of the system. . . . Actions are constituted by processes of attribution. They come about only if, for whatever reasons, in whatever contexts, and with the help of whatever semantics ("intention", "motive", "interest"), selections can be attributed to systems."[149]

The detailed content of these "systems" is underspecified, but presumably what Luhmann

[140] Fontana 2008, 1.

[141] Luhmann 1986, 173: "The concept of autopoietic closure itself requires this theoretical decision [to separate social systems from living systems], and leads to a sharp distinction between meaning and life as different kinds of autopoietic organization. Meaning-using systems, moreover, have to be distinguished according to whether they use consciousness [for psychic systems] or communication [for social systems] as modes of meaning-based reproduction."

[142] Luhmann 1990.

[143] Luhmann 1987a, 1987b, 1989, 1992.

[144] Wittgenstein 1953; Kripke 1982; Lakoff 1987; Hanks 1996; Tomasello 2008.

[145] Kasher 1991.

[146] Mingers (2002), otherwise also an admirer of Luhmann, comes to a similar conclusion.

[147] White et al. 2007; Fuhse 2011.

[148] For a brief statement of my own epistemological criteria for good research, see the last section in Fowler et al. 2011. This involves systematic triangulation across heterogeneous data.

[149] Luhmann [1984 in German] 1995, 165–66. Attributional primacy was also the perspective of Mills (1940).

must mean is that communication regulates production activity. Behavioral action itself for Luhmann occurs off-stage, unexplained by communicative theory. Persons emerge through collective communications about them. Linguistic autocatalysis, on this view, would be the emergence of a set of classificatory attributions for actions, which attributions themselves reproduce through communication.

More specifically, Luhmann breaks down communication (and his vaguer "meaning") into three parts: information, utterance, and understanding. "Information" is the manifest content of the communication, pointing outward to elements in the world. "Utterance" is the part of the communication that refers to the relationship of the communicators. "Understanding" is the acknowledgment that proposed references both to the external object and to the relationship were accepted. Thus instead of the two-step action-reaction of production systems (though of course there is also learning), there is the three-step proposal-context-acknowledgment of communication. Luhmann, either himself or in White's and Fuhse's construction of him, says nothing about emergence (or about dynamics of any sort). But at least here is one specification of what a distinctively human linguistic autocatalysis might look like—a specification that takes language seriously without denying other forms of autocatalysis that intersect with it, namely, a set of three-step communication utterances that collectively reproduces itself through mutual acknowledgments.

Pointing is probably the best context, because so minimalist, for moving on from such definitions to study language emergence. Someone points to an object in the context of another. Communication occurs if the other responds by also pointing ("message received"), by taking an action, or by pointing to something else, thereby making a sequence of gestures. The object becomes a sign, and two observers become two cooperators. Not only that, but if sequences of gestures are strung together, then links across time—call this "narrative" if you want—are enabled. Tomasello reviews the experimental evidence on pointing by children and by primates.[150] Gärdenfors and Warglien provide a formal model.[151] Pointing to the addresses,[152] or if symbolized to the names, of bins of production rules is the approach taken in chapter 4. This adapts pointing to the attributional construction of people. Linguistic autocatalysis and production autocatalysis can co-evolve in attributional pointing because objects have transformational relations through production rules as much as do communications through addresses.[153]

CONCLUSION

In deference to my social-science audience, I end this literature review with a tribute to Harrison White. Throughout the stages in his career, White has been the pioneer in asking social constructivist questions from a multiple-social-network (or more generally a relational) perspective. This volume carries on his tradition of deriving social actors from concatenated social relations but pushes that tradition in the direction of large-scale historical transformations, evolution, and the genesis of organizational novelty.

Kinship is where the White approach came from.[154] Following an agenda derived from Lévi-Strauss,[155] the original focus was on deriving the concrete clan groups and alliances that would result from the iteration of "constitutional" rules of marriage and descent, applied over and over again to a closed tribal population. This empirical focus on kinship faded, and Lévi-Strauss's totalizing assumption of rule homogeneity fortunately was abandoned, but the basic idea of groups being generated out of the concatenated iteration of social networks was generalized, through the concept of structural equivalence, into a very influential algebraic and statistical-clustering way of analyzing social networks called blockmodeling.[156] This procedure knitted together multiple networks; it did not just analyze networks like kinship or economics one at a time in isolation from each other. Indeed "concatenation and iteration" usually meant multiplying the matrices of

[150] Tomasello 2008.

[151] Gärdenfors and Warglien forthcoming.

[152] Addressing is fundamental to parallel-processing or concurrent computation. See Milner 1993.

[153] Chapter 4 only begins to lays the groundwork for demonstrating this co-evolution. The objective there is to point to exciting challenges for future research more than to prove anything.

[154] White 1963.

[155] Lévi-Strauss [1949] 1969.

[156] Lorrain and White 1971; White, Boorman, and Breiger 1976; Boorman and White 1976. Prominent empirical applications of this approach are Breiger 1976, 1981a, and Padgett and Ansell 1993. Formal modeling through semigroup algebra was developed in Boorman and White 1976; Boyd 1991; and Pattison 1993.

multiple networks[157] and looking for algebraic equivalences. This approach to "emergence" was static and equilibrial, not evolutionary and dynamic, but it introduced new algebraic methods to the social sciences, which have resonance with the λ-calculus chemistry approach of Fontana and Buss.[158]

Individual (but not collective) dynamics were added by White to this stochastically stable macroblock structure through mobility.[159] Individuals biographically molded themselves into collective multiple-network structures through their own social mobility, reshaping themselves only to reproduce the patterns through which they flowed.

Recently White has backed away from this structuralist version of social constructivism, on which he built his career, in order to introduce more fluidity and even chaos. He did this by becoming more micro and by injecting linguistics, narrative, and conversation into the constitution of networks.[160] Both editions of *Identity and Control* include White's usual social constructivist questions but in the context of communication and instability, not in the context of structural order and reproduction.

This late career move by White has influenced a significant subset of the social-network community to become more "cultural."[161] There is irony in this influence. In sociology, "be more cultural" usually means little more than "take ideas and/or language seriously"[162] in the causal explanation of something. This formulation turns culture into independent and dependent variables, not process.[163] In debates with structuralists, incantations of "agency" are evoked, which often mean nothing more precise than free will or structural indeterminacy.[164] This is not what White is talking about at all. He rarely uses the word *culture* in fact, preferring to talk about communication and meaning-making as interactional processes that generate identities, not about culture as a set of hypostasized ideas in people's heads.[165]

The part of White's recent turn that resonates most strongly with this volume—and in particular with our mechanisms of organizational genesis—is his emphasis on switching across domains. Individual "identities" emerge out of such switching, of a variety of types,[166] because mismatch or turbulence from movement across domains needs restabilizing work.[167] Emergence of novelty is not discussed in White because his identities (of whatever form) are looking for stable footing,[168] not for change. But presumably this is where novelty would come from, according to White: the random bubbling up, in response to switching-based turbulence, of new types of identity that just happened to work. This is a quantum-mechanical view of social networks.

Introducing more fluidity into his earlier crystalline architectures was certainly a good move for White's long-term social constructivist agenda. But going all the way to the quantum mechanics of linguistic switching was not altogether helpful for maintaining empirical contact with large-scale historical change. Quantum mechanics explains why atoms bond into molecules and why they rearrange themselves in chemical reactions. But life is the autocatalytic iteration of sequences of such chemical reactions, folding and

[157] Multiplying matrices is the way to generate paths through multiple networks.

[158] For their discussion of functional equivalence and algebraic descriptions of λ-calculus microdynamics, see Fontana and Buss 1994a, 9–10, 22, and Fontana and Buss 1996.

[159] White 1970; Breiger 1981b; Padgett 1990, 2010.

[160] White 1992, 1995, 2008; Mische and White 1998; White and Godart 2007; White et al. 2007.

[161] Leading exemplars are Emirbayer and Goodwin 1994; Somers 1994; Emirbayer 1997; McLean 1998, 2007; and Mische 2003, 2007. Pachucki and Breiger 2010 provides a comprehensive review.

[162] Sometimes "take practices seriously" is also added to this list of independent variables, but then culture becomes hard to distinguish from production rules or skills.

[163] Abbott 2001.

[164] Fuchs 2001. If that is all agency means, then it is just a label for the (admittedly large) error term. Our own view, as stated in the introduction, is that the distinction between agency and structure is just a matter of time scales. Time scales, however, overlap and interpenetrate. Cf. Padgett 2010, 390–91.

[165] McLean (1998, 2007) is interactional in his treatment of "culture," in the way that White advocates. McLean astutely notes, for example, that identities were constructed in Florentine letter-writing, not by the linguistic conventions the Florentines used but by their ways of violating those conventions, creating images of selves that lurked behind.

[166] These different types of switching produce different types of "identities" constructed to deal with them, according to White: (1) Behavioral rules imported into a new setting may not fit or reproduce very well. Identity as local network position needs to be stabilized. (2) Alters in the new local context may not recognize the immigrant. Identity as attribution needs to be constructed. (3) Migration paths across multiple domains may be jagged and stochastic. Identities as career tracks need to be stabilized. (4) Alters in transient domains may not recognize the migrant's career path. Biographical narratives or stories about trajectories need to be spun. It does not help the precision of White's exposition that he uses the word *identity* to mean so many different things. Ambiguities notwithstanding, this quest for the social construction of persons through mismatches was profound.

[167] White does not refer to Heidegger, but this is like Heidegger's idea that consciousness is when things break down. Communication and linguistic work is required not when things go smoothly but when they do not.

[168] This is "control" in White's usage of the term. This usage derives from cybernetic control theory (e.g., Kalman filters).

feeding back on themselves, at a higher level of topology than the microbonds themselves. The macro world is not as bubbly as the micro world because of feedback. Creative efforts to communicate, trying to stabilize against turbulence, still need to be acknowledged and understood. The old Harrison of concatenation and iteration needs to be brought back in to give the new Harrison predictive purchase on the collective consequences of all of this identity bubbling.[169]

In his book *Logics of History*, the distinguished French historian and social scientist William Sewell Jr. provides a better level of optical resolution for the purposes of this volume. What are "Logics of History" for Sewell? Eventful transformations in social structures.[170] Okay, but what are "social structures" for Sewell? Recursive relationships between rules (or schemas) and resources, with rules transforming resources and resources reproducing rules.[171] This of course is the same thing as autocatalysis, although Sewell is not familiar with this term for life from chemistry.

There are fruitful complications, of course, in both Sewell's and our versions of autocatalysis. There are not just one but many forms of life, which interact, overlay, or more interestingly interpenetrate each other in chemical and human worlds alike. While random incremental change is not ruled out by either of us, revolutionary events are triggered by transpositions—of one variety or another—from one domain or form of life to another, which then reverberate through preexisting tensions or contradictions.[172] Transposition and reverberation together make up the invention of novel organizational species. The raw material out of which such variation comes is the array of domains and their channels of intersection. These channels define the "topology of the possible."[173] Because of this, multifunctional points of interpenetration are particularly fecund loci for plasticity and change, which is why such ambiguity is often surrounded by redundant controls.[174]

A key issue for Sewell, going back to the juxtaposition of his first two books,[175] is how the linguistic and the material worlds fit together. This also is an important issue for the transposition of the concept of autocatalysis from chemistry to the social sciences.[176] We do not solve this challenging issue in our book any more than Sewell does in his, although we, like Sewell, offer pointers toward resolution. Both Sewell and I agree, however, that the solution is not to wall off language and behavior from each other, pretending that they are autonomous media of transformation and exchange. The co-evolution of communication and production, in feedback with each other, is what makes this issue a hard intellectual problem—not only in the human realm but also in the chemical one.[177]

Powell and I feel justified in going ahead with our project, in spite of not yet having resolved how language fits in exactly with other forms of autocatalysis, because of our repeated empirical observations, in the case studies in this volume, that innovation in language usually lags, not leads, major organizational inventions.[178] All of the humans we observe in our cases have intentions and interpretations of one sort or another, expressed in language. The evolutionary problem is that rarely do these intentions and interpretations have much to do with how things actually turned out. "Great men" like Bismarck, Stalin, Mao, Deng, and Gorbachev[179] make dramatic appearances in this volume. They were part of but did not control the explosive events that they stimulated. Whirlwinds of time intersected though them. If "agency" means induced intent and learning, then fine. But if "agency" means the capacity to foresee and control complex chains of consequences, then no. Autocatalysis does not deny individual agency; it just endogenizes that as one time scale of life, interpenetrating with others.

[169] Pragmatists, who have an overly optimistic view of what is possible, have this same problem. See, e.g., Sabel and Zeitlin 1997.

[170] Sewell 2005, chaps. 3, 7, 8.

[171] Sewell 2005, chap. 4.

[172] For the "reverberate through preexisting tensions or contradictions" part, see Sewell 1994. For different operationalizations of the same generic point, see Skocpol 1979 and Markoff 1996.

[173] Ancel and Fontana 2000; Stadler et al. 2001; and Fontana 2003.

[174] The biological version of this is West-Eberhard 2003. The social version is Douglas 1966.

[175] Sewell 1980, 1985.

[176] See Padgett and McLean 2011 for one sustained attempt to blend statistical and textual evidence in syncopation. Padgett and McLean methodologically are both committed, jointly and separately, to such blendings, as is Powell. See the last chapter of this book for didactic elaboration.

[177] Biochemical systems communicate with each other through signaling pathways, like hormones, blood, the immune system, and the brain.

[178] Sewell 1980 does not challenge this temporal ordering, but Sewell 1994 does.

[179] I realize that with Gorbachev I am stretching the term *great men*. This, however, is only because, as I argue in chapter 9, his outcome was a disaster, not because his behavior was much different than the others.

I stand with White in concluding that, our Enlightenment pretensions notwithstanding, mostly we all play interpretive catch-up with events, trying to respond to the jaggedness of the unpredicted twists of a vibrant and vast social world far beyond our comprehension.[180] Most of the inventors I observe in history innovated opportunistically with relational tools that lay near at hand, often from conservative motivations such as fearing to lose what they already had.

This does not mean that language is unimportant in evolution. People respond in ways that are accessible to them—behaviorally in their repertoires of skills and production rules, interactionally through their communication networks, and cognitively in the linguistic categories that shape their perceptions of events. In their diverse intercalated responses, they build the vortexes they live in. Organizational novelty ultimately is the reconfiguration of these interacting streams into revised, interconnected autocatalyses.[181] Invention never eliminates the past; it rewires it. New life forms are a by-product of that.

REFERENCES

Abbott, Andrew. 2001. *Time Matters: On Theory and Method*. Chicago: University of Chicago Press.

Achenbach-Richter, L., R. Gupta, K. O. Stetter, and C. R. Woese. 1987. "Were the Original Eubacteria Thermophiles?" *Systematic and Applied Microbiology* 9:34–39.

Anastasi, Carole, Fabien F. Buchet, Michael A. Crowe, Alastair L. Parkes, Matthew W. Powner, James M. Smith, and John D. Sutherland. 2008. "RNA: Prebiotic Product, or Biotic Invention?" In Piet Herdewijn and M. Volkan Kisakürek, eds., *Origin of Life: A Chemical Approach*, 273–91. Zurich: Wiley-VCH.

Ancel, Lauren W., and Walter Fontana. 2000. "Plasticity, Evolvability, and Modularity in RNA." *Journal of Experimental Zoology (Molecular, Development, Evolution)* 288:242–83.

Aravind, L., R. L. Tatusov, Y. I. Wolf, D. R. Walker, and E. V. Koonin. 1998. "Evidence for Massive Gene Exchange between Archaeal and Bacterial Hyperthermophiles." *Trends in Genetics* 14:442–44.

Arthur, W. Brian. 1994. *Increasing Returns and Path Dependence in the Economy*. Ann Arbor: University of Michigan Press.

Ashkenasy, Gonen, Reshma Jagasia, Maneesh Yadiv, and M. Reza Ghadiri. 2004. "Design of a Directed Molecular Network." *Proceedings of the National Academy of the U.S.A.* 101:10872–77.

Bada, Jeffrey L., and Antonio Lazcano. 2002. "Some Like It Hot, But Not the First Biomolecules." *Science* 296:1982–83.

Bagley, Richard J., and J. Doyne Farmer. 1992. "Spontaneous Emergence of a Metabolism." In Christopher G. Langton, Charles Taylor, J. Doyne Farmer, and Steen Rasmussen, eds., *Artificial Life II: Santa Fe Institute Studies in Complexity*, 93–140. Reading: Addison-Wesley.

Baross, John A., and Sarah E. Hoffman. 1985. "Submarine Hydrothermal Vents and Associated Gradient Environments as Sites for the Origin and Evolution of Life." *Origin of Life* 15:327–45.

Biebricher, Christof K., Manfred Eigen, and Rüdiger Luce. 1981a. "Product Analysis of RNA Generated *de novo* by Q_β Replicase." *Journal of Molecular Biology* 148:369–90.

———. 1981b. "Kinetic Analysis of Template-Instructed a *de novo* RNA Synthesis by Q_βReplicase." *Journal of Molecular Biology* 148: 391–410.

Biebricher, Christof K., Manfred Eigen, and William C. Gardiner Jr. 1983. "Kinetics of RNA Replication." *Biochemistry* 22:2544–59.

———. 1984. "Kinetics of RNA Replication: Plus-Minus Asymmetry and Double-Strand Formation." *Biochemistry* 23:3186–94.

———. 1985. "Kinetics of RNA Replication: Competition and Selection among Self-Replicating RNA Species." *Biochemistry* 24: 6550–60.

Boerlijst, M. C., and P. Hogeweg. 1991. "Spiral Wave Structures in Pre-biotic Evolution: Hypercycles Stable against Parasites." *Physica D* 48:17–28.

———. 1992. "Self-Structuring and Selection: Spiral Waves as a Substrate for Prebiotic Evolution." In Christopher G. Langton, Charles Taylor, J. Doyne Farmer, and Steen Rasmussen, eds., *Artificial Life II: Santa Fe Institute Studies in Complexity*, 255–76. Reading: Addison-Wesley.

Bonen, L., and W. F. Doolittle. 1975. "On the Prokaryotic Nature of Red Algal Chloroplasts." *Proceedings of the National Academy of Sciences of the U.S.A.* 72:2310–14.

Boorman, Scott A., and Harrison C. White. 1976. "Social Structure from Multiple Networks. II. Role Structures." *American Journal of Sociology* 81: 1384–1446.

Boyd, John Paul. 1991. *Social Semigroups: A Unified Theory of Scaling and Blockmodeling as Applied to*

[180] Skocpol (1979, 14–18) and Tolstoy ([1869] 2010) are particularly emphatic on this point about mismatch between perception and reality, especially in times of turmoil. Also see Padgett and Ansell 1993, 1272–74. Herbert Simon's bounded rationality makes this mismatch between perception and reality into an existential condition of the brains of humanity without implying any despair. March and Simon 1958; Simon 1982.

[181] If production autocatalysis is reproducing transformations of products ($product_x$→$product_y$→ . . .), and cellular autocatalysis is reproducing transformations in social networks ($address_i$→$address_j$→ . . .), and linguistic autocatalysis is reproducing transformations in symbols ($symbol_\alpha$→$symbol_\beta$→ . . .), then the ultimate aspiration for evolutionary theories of change should be excavating and deriving accessible transitions among reproducing interpenetrations: ($product_x$→$symbol_\alpha$→$address_i$→ . . .).

Social Networks. Fairfax, VA: George Mason University Press.

Breiger, Ronald L. 1976. "Career Attributes and Network Structure: A Blockmodel Study of a Biomedical Research Specialty." *American Sociological Review* 41:117–35.

———. 1981a. "Structures of Economic Interdependence among Nations." In Peter Blau and Robert Merton, eds., *Continuities in Structural Inquiry*, 353–80. Beverly Hills, CA: Sage.

———. 1981b. "The Social Class Structure of Occupational Mobility." *American Journal of Sociology* 87:578–611.

Bresch, C., U. Niesert, and D. Harnasch. 1980. "Hypercycles, Parasites and Packages." *Journal of Theoretical Biology* 85:399–405.

Cairns-Smith, A. G. 1982. *Genetic Takeover and the Mineral Origins of Life*. Cambridge: Cambridge University Press.

Calvin, Melvin. 1956. "Chemical Evolution and the Origin of Life." *American Scientist* 44:248–63.

———. 1961. *Chemical Evolution*. Eugene: University of Oregon Books.

Capra, Fritjof. 1996. *The Web of Life: A New Scientific Understanding of Living Systems*. New York: Anchor Books.

Case, Ted J. 2000. *An Illustrated Guide to Theoretical Ecology*. New York: Oxford University Press.

Chappelle, Francis H., Kathleen O'Neill, Paul M. Bradley, Barbara A. Methé, Stacy A. Ciufo, LeRoy L. Knoble, and Derek R. Lovley. 2002. "A Hydrogen-Based Subsurface Microbial Community Dominated by Methanogens." *Nature* 415:312–15.

Church, Alonso. 1932. "A Set of Postulates for the Foundation of Logic." *Annals of Mathematics* 33:346–66.

———. 1933. "A Set of Postulates for the Foundation of Logic." *Annals of Mathematics* 34:839–64.

Chyba, Christopher, and Carl Sagan. 1992. "Endogenous Production, Exogenous Delivery and Impact-Shock Synthesis of Organic Molecules: An Inventory for the Origins of Life." *Nature* 355:125–32.

Chyba, Christopher F., Paul J. Thomas, Leigh Brookshaw, and Carl Sagan. 1990. "Cometary Delivery of Organic Molecules to the Early Earth." *Science* 249:366–73.

Cleaves, H. James, John H. Chalmers, Antonio Lazcano, Stanley L. Miller, and Jeffrey L. Bada. 2008. "A Reassessment of Prebiotic Organic Synthesis in Neutral Planetary Atmospheres." *Origins of Life and Evolution of the Biosphere* 38:105–15.

Cody, George D. 2004. "Transition Metal Sulfites and the Origins of Metabolism." *Annual Review of Earth and Planetary Science* 32:569–99.

Cody, G. D., N. Z. Boctor, J. A. Brandes, T. R. Filley, R. M. Hazen, and H. S. Yoder Jr. 2004. "Assaying the Catalytic Potential of Transition Metal Sulides for Abiotic Carbon Fixation." *Geochimica et Cosmochimica Acta* 68: 2185-2196.

Cody, George D., Nabil Z. Boctor, Timothy R. Filley, Robert M. Hazen, James H. Scott, Anurag Sharma, and Hatten S. Yoder Jr. 2000. "Primordial Carbonylated Iron-Sulfur Compounds and the Synthesis of Pyruvate." *Science* 289:1337–40.

Cody, G. D., N. Z. Boctor, R. M. Hazen, J. A. Brandes, Harold J. Morowitz, and H. S. Yoder Jr. 2001. "Geochemical Roots of Autotrophic Carbon Fixation: Hydrothermal Experiments in the System Citric Acid, H_2O-(±FeS)-(±NiS)." *Geochimica et Cosmochimica Acta* 65:3557–76.

Corliss, John B. 1990. "Hot Springs and the Origin of Life." *Nature* 347:624.

Corliss, John B., Jack Dymond, Louis I. Gordon, John M. Edmond, Richard P. von Herzen, Robert D. Ballard, Kenneth Green, David Williams, Arnold Bainbridge, Kathy Crane, and Tjeerd H. van Andel. 1979. "Submarine Thermal Springs on the Galápagos Rift." *Science* 203:1073–83.

Cronhjort, Mikael B. 1995. "Hypercycles versus Parasites in the Origin of Life: Model Dependence in Spatial Hypercycle Systems." *Origin of Life and Evolution of the Biosphere* 25:227–33.

Cronhjort, Mikael B., and Clas Blomberg. 1994. "Hypercycles versus Parasites in a Two Dimensional Partial Differential Equations Model." *Journal of Theoretical Biology* 169:31–49.

Cronin, J. R., and S. Chang. 1993. "Organic Matter in Meteorites: Molecular and Isotopic Analyses of the Murchison Meteorite." In J. M. Greenberg et al., eds., *The Chemistry of Life's Origins*, 209–58. Dordrecht: Kluwer Academic Publishers.

Dagley, S., and Donald E. Nicholson. 1970. *An Introduction to Metabolic Pathways*. New York: Wiley.

Damiano, Luisa, and Pier Luigi Luisi. 2010. "Towards an Autopoietic Redefinition of Life." *Origins of Life and Evolution of the Biosphere* 40:145–49.

Danos, Vincent, and Cosimo Laneve. 2004. "Formal Molecular Biology." *Theoretical Computer Science* 325:60–110.

Danos, Vincent, Jérôme Feret, Walter Fontana, Russell Harmer, and Jean Krivine. 2007. "Rule-Based Modelling of Cellular Signalling." *CONCUR 2007—Concurrency Theory. Lecture Notes in Computer Science* 4703:17–41.

———. 2009. "Rule-Based Modelling and Model Perturbation." *Transactions on Computational Systems Biology* 11:116–37.

Danson, Michael J., and David W. Hough. 1992. "The Enzymology of Archaebacterial Pathways of Central Metabolism." In M. J. Danson, D. W. Hough, and G. G. Lunt, eds., *The Archaebacteria: Biochemistry and Biotechnology*, 7–23. London: Portland Press.

Darwin, Charles. [1859] 1993. *The Origin of Species*. New York: The Modern Library.

David, Paul. 1985. "Clio and the Economics of QWERTY." *American Economic Review* 75:332–37.

Dawkins, Richard. 1976. *The Selfish Gene*. Oxford: Oxford University Press.

De Duve, C. 1991. *Blueprint for a Cell: The Nature and Origin of Life*. Burlington, NC: Neil Patterson.

Domingo. E., M. Dávila, and J. Ortín. 1980. "Nucleotide Sequence Heterogeneity of the RNA from a

Natural Population of Foot-and-Mouth-Disease Virus." *Gene* 11:333–46.

Domingo, E., A. Flavell, and C. Weissman. 1976. "In-vitro Site-Directed Mutagenesis: Generation and Properties of an Infectious Extra-Cistronic Mutant of Bacteriophage Q_{β}." *Gene* 1:3–25.

Domingo, E., D. Sabo, T. Tanaguchi, and C. Weissman 1978. "Nucleotide Sequence Heterogeneity of an RNA Phage Population." *Cell* 13:735–44.

Douglas, Mary. 1966. *Purity and Danger: An Analysis of the Concepts of Pollution and Taboo*. London: Routledge and Kegan Paul.

Dyson, Freeman J. 1982. "A Model for the Origin of Life." *Journal of Molecular Evolution* 18:344–50.

———. 1999. *Origins of Life*. Rev. ed. Cambridge: Cambridge University Press.

Ehrenfreund, Pascale, and Jan Cami. 2010. "Cosmic Carbon Chemistry: From the Interstellar Medium to the Early Earth." In David Deamer and Jack W. Szostak, eds., *The Origins of Life*, 21–34. Cold Spring Harbor, NY: Cold Spring Harbor Laboratory Press.

Ehrenfreund, Pascale, Steen Rasmussen, James Cleaves, and Liaohai Chen. 2006. "Experimentally Tracing the Key Steps in the Origin of Life: The Aromatic World." *Astrobiology* 6:490–520.

Ehrenfreund, P., W. Irvine, L. Becker, J. Blank, J. R. Brucato, L. Colangeli, S. Derenne, D. Despois, A. Dutrey, H. Fraaije, A. Lazcano, T. Owen, F. Robert, an International Space Science Institute ISSI-Team. 2002. "Astrophysical and Astrochemical Insights into the Origin of Life." *Reports on Progress in Physics* 65:1427–87.

Eigen, Manfred. 1971a. "Self-Organization of Matter and the Evolution of Biological Macromolecules." *Die Naturwissenschaften* 58:465–523.

———. 1971b. "Molecular Self-Organization and the Early Stages of Evolution." *Quarterly Reviews of Biophysics* 4:149–212.

———. 1992. *Steps toward Life: A Perspective on Evolution*. Oxford: Oxford University Press.

Eigen, Manfred, and Peter Schuster. 1979. *The Hypercycle: A Principle of Natural Self-Organization*. Berlin: Springer-Verlag. This book is a reprint of three original articles: "A. Emergence of Hypercycle," *Die Naturwissenschaften* 64 (1977): 541–65; "B. The Abstract Hypercycle," *Die Naturwissenschaften* 65 (1978): 7–41; and "C. The Realistic Hypercycle," *Die Naturwissenschaften* 65 (1978): 341–69.

Eigen, Manfred, and Ruthild Winkler-Oswatitsch. 1981a. "Transfer-RNA: The Early Adopter."*Die Naturwissenschaften* 68:217–28.

———. 1981a. "Transfer-RNA, an Early Gene?"*Die Naturwissenschaften* 68:282–92.

Eigen, Manfred, John McCaskell, and Peter Schuster. 1988. "Molecular Quasi-Species." *Journal of Physical Chemistry* 92:6881–91.

Eigen, Manfred, Christof K. Biebricher, Michael Gebinoga, and William C. Gardiner. 1991. "The Hypercycle: Coupling of RNA and Protein Biosynthesis in the Infection Cycle of an RNA Bacteriophage." *Biochemistry* 30:11005–18.

Eldredge, N., and S. J. Gould. 1972. "Punctuated Equilibria: An Alternative to Phyletic Gradualism." In T.J.M. Schopf, ed., *Models in Paleobiology*, 82–115. San Francisco: Freeman, Cooper.

Emirbayer, Mustafa. 1997. "Manifesto for a Relational Sociology." *American Journal of Sociology* 103:281–317.

Emirbayer, Mustafa, and Jeff Goodwin. 1994. "Network Analysis, Culture, and the Problem of Agency." *American Journal of Sociology* 99:1411–54.

Erwin, Douglas H. 1999. "The Origin of Bodyplans." *American Zoologist* 39:617–29.

———. 2000. "Macroevolution Is More than Repeated Rounds of Microevolution." *Evolution and Development* 2:78–84.

Farmer, J. Doyne, Stuart A. Kauffman, and Norman H. Packard. 1986. "Autocatalytic Replication of Polymers." *Physica D* 22:5–67.

Fenchel, Tom. 2002. *Origin and Early Evolution of Life*. Oxford: Oxford University Press.

Feret, Jérôme, Vincent Danos, Jean Krivine, Russ Harmer, and Walter Fontana. 2009. "Internal Coarse-Graining of Molecular Systems." *Proceedings of the National Academy of Sciences of the U.S.A.* 106:6453–58.

Ferris, J. P. 2002. "Montmorillonite Catalysis of 30-50 Mer Oligonucleotides: Laboratory Demonstration of Potential Steps in the Origins of the RNA World." *Origins of Life and Evolution of the Biosphere* 32:311–32.

Fishkis, Maya. 2010. "Emergence of Self-Reproduction in Cooperative Chemical Evolution of Prebiological Molecules." *Origin of Life and Evolution of the Biosphere* 41:261–75.

Fontana, Walter. 1992. "Algorithmic Chemistry." In Christopher G. Langton, Charles Taylor, J. Doyne Farmer, and Steen Rasmussen, eds., *Artificial Life II: Santa Fe Institute Studies in Complexity*, 159–209. Reading: Addison-Wesley.

———. 2003. "The Topology of the Possible." Unpublished paper originally written for this volume.

———. 2006. "The Topology of the Possible." In Andreas Wimmer and Reinhart Kössler, eds., *Understanding Change: Models, Methodologies, and Metaphors*, 67–84. New York: Palgrave Macmillan.

———. 2008. "Systems Biology, Models, and Concurrency." Paper presented to Symposium on Principles of Programming Languages. San Francisco.

Fontana, Walter, and Leo W. Buss. 1994a. "The Arrival of the Fittest: Toward a Theory of Biological Organization." *Bulletin of Mathematical Biology* 56:1–64.

———. 1994b. "What Would Be Conserved if 'The Tape Were Played Twice?'" *Proceedings of the National Academy of Sciences of the U.S.A.* 91:757–61.

———. 1996. "The Barrier of Objects: From Dynamical Systems to Bounded Organizations." In J. Casti and A. Karlqvist, eds., *Boundaries and Barriers*, 56–116. Reading, MA: Addison-Wesley.

Fontana, Walter, and Peter Schuster. 1998. "Continuity in Evolution: On the Nature of Transitions." *Science* 280:1451–55.

Fournier, Gregory P., Jinling Huang, and J. Peter Gorgarten. 2009. *Philosophical Transactions of the Royal Society. B.* 364:2229–39.

Fowler, James H., Michael T. Heaney, David W. Nickerson, John F. Padgett, and Betsy Sinclair. 2011. "Causality in Political Networks." *American Politics Research* 39:437–80.

Fox, Sidney W. 1965. "A Theory of Macromolecular and Cellular Origins." *Nature* 205:328–40.

Fry, Iris. 2011. "The Role of Natural Selection in the Origin of Life." *Origin of Life and Evolution of the Biosphere* 41:3–16.

Fuchs, Stephan. 2001. "Beyond Agency." *Sociological Theory* 19:24–40.

Fuhse, Jan A. 2011. "Networks from Communication." Unpublished manuscript.

Gánti, Tibor. 1975. "Organization of Chemical Reactions into Dividing and Metabolizing Units: The Chemotons." *BioSystems* 7:15–21.

———. 1979. *A Theory of Biochemical Supersystems and Its Application to Problems of Natural and Artificial Biogenesis.* Baltimore: University Park Press.

———. 2003a. *Chemoton Theory*. Vol. 1, *Theoretical Foundations of Fluid Machineries.* New York: Kluwer Academic.

———. 2003b. *Chemoton Theory*. Vol. 2, *Theory of Living Systems.* New York: Kluwer Academic.

Gärdenfors, Peter, and Massimo Warglien. Forthcoming. "The Development of Semantic Space for Pointing and Verbal Communication." In J. Hudson, U. Magnusson, and C. Paradis, eds., *Conceptual Spaces and the Construal of Spatial Meaning: Empirical Evidence from Human Communication.* Cambridge: Cambridge University Press.

Gaucher, Eric A., James T. Kratzer, and Ryan N. Randall. 2010. "Deep Phylogeny—How a Tree Can Help Characterize Early Life on Earth." In David Deamer and Jack W. Szostak, eds., *The Origins of Life*, 279–94. Cold Spring Harbor, NY: Cold Spring Harbor Laboratory Press.

Gilbert, Walter. 1986. "The RNA World." *Nature* 319: 618.

Goodenough, U. W., and R. P. Levine. 1970. "The Genetic Activity of Mitochondria and Chloroplasts." *Scientific American* 223:22–29.

Goodwin, Brian. 1994. *How the Leopard Changed His Spots.* New York: Simon and Schuster.

Gould, Stephen Jay. 1989. *Wonderful Life: The Burgess Shale and the Nature of History.* New York: Norton.

———. 2002. *The Structure of Evolutionary Theory.* Cambridge, MA: Harvard University Press.

Gould, Stephen Jay, and Elisabeth S. Vrba. 1982. "Exaption—A Missing Term in the Science of Form." *Paleobiology* 8:4–15.

Gray, M. W., G. Burger, and B. F. Lang. 1999. "Mitochondrial Evolution." *Science* 283:1476–81.

Haldane, J.B.S. 1929. "The Origin of Life." *The Rationalist Annual* 1929:148–69.

Hanks, William F. 1996. *Language and Communicative Practices.* Boulder, CO: Westview Press.

Harmer, Russ, Vincent Danos, Jérôme Feret, Jean Krivine, and Walter Fontana. 2010. "Intrinsic Information Carriers in Combinatorial Dynamical Systems." *Chaos* 20:037108.

Hofbauer, Josef, and Karl Sigmund. 1988. *The Theory of Evolution and Dynamical Systems.* Cambridge: Cambridge University Press.

Hordijk, Wim, and Mike Steel. 2004. "Detecting Autocatalytic, Self-Sustaining Sets in Chemical Reaction Systems." *Journal of Theoretical Biology* 227: 451–61.

Huang, J., and J. P. Gorgarten. 2009. "Ancient Gene Transfer as a Tool in Phylogenetic Reconstruction." *Methods in Molecular Biology* 532:127–39.

Huang, W., and J. P. Ferris. 2003. "Synthesis of 35-50 Mers of RNA Oligomers from Unblocked Monomers: A Simple Approach to the RNA World." *Chemical Communications* 2003:1458–59.

Huber, Claudia, and Günter Wächtershäuser. 1997. "Activated Acetic acid by Carbon Fixation on (Fe,Ni)S under Primordial Conditions." *Science* 276:245–47.

———. 1998. "Peptides by Activation of Amino Acids with CO on (Ni,Fe)S Surfaces: Implications for the Origin of Life." *Science* 281:670–72.

Iwabe, Naoyuki, Kei-ichi Kuma, Masami Hasegawa, Syozo Osawa, and Takashi Miyata. 1989. "Evolutionary Relationship of Archaebacteria, Eubacteria, and Eukaryotes Inferred from Phylogenetic Trees of Duplicated Genes." *Proceedings of the National Academy of Sciences of the U.S.A.* 86: 9355–59.

Jain, Sanjay, and Sandeep Krishna. 1998. "Autocatalytic Sets and the Growth of Complexity in an Evolutionary Model." *Physical Review Letters* 81: 5684–87.

———. 1999. "Emergence and Growth of Complex Networks in Adaptive Systems." *Computer Physics Communications* 121–22:116–21.

———. 2001a. "A Model for the Emergence of Cooperation, Interdependence and Structure in Evolving Networks." *Proceedings of the National Academy of Sciences of the U.S.A.* 98:543–47.

———. 2001b. "Large Extinctions in an Evolutionary Model: The Role of Innovation and Keystone Species." *Proceedings of the National Academy of Sciences of the U.S.A.* 99:2055–60.

———. 2002. "Crashes, Recoveries and 'Core-Shifts' in a Model of Evolving Networks." *Physical Review E* 65:026103.

———. 2003. "Graph Theory and the Evolution of Autocatalytic Networks." In Stefan Bornholdt and Heinz Georg Schuster, eds., *Handbook of Graphs and Networks: From the Genome to the Internet*, 355–95. Weinheim: Wiley-VCH.

Jalbout, Abraham F. 2008. "Prebiotic Synthesis of Simple Sugars by an Interstellar Formose Reaction." *Origins of Life and Evolution of the Biosphere* 38:489–97.

Kasher, Asa. 1991. *The Chomskyan Turn.* Oxford: Blackwell.

Kauffman, S. A. 1969. "Metabolic Stability and Epigenesis in Randomly Constructed Genetic Nets." *Journal of Theoretical Biology* 22:437–67.

———. 1971. "Cellular Homeostasis, Epigenesis and Replication in Randomly Aggregated Macromolecular Systems." *Journal of Cybernetics* 1:71–96.

———. 1986. "Autocatalytic Sets of Proteins." *Journal of Theoretical Biology* 119:1–24.

———. 1993. *The Origins of Order: Self-Organization and Selection in Evolution*. New York: Oxford University Press.

———. 1995. *At Home in the Universe: The Search for Laws of Self-Organization and Complexity*. New York: Oxford University Press.

———. 2000. *Investigations*. New York: Oxford University Press.

Khakhina, Liya Nikolaevna. 1992. *Concepts of Symbiogenesis: A Historical and Critical Study of the Research of Russian Botanists*. New Haven: Yale University Press.

Kirschner, Marc W., and John C. Gerhart. 1998. "Evolvability." *Proceedings of the National Academy of Sciences of the U.S.A.* 88:5969–73.

Kozo-Polyansky, B. M. [1924] 2010. *Symbiogenesis: A New Principle of Evolution*. Cambridge, MA: Harvard University Press.

Kripke, Saul A. 1982. *Wittgenstein on Rules and Private Language*. Cambridge, MA: Harvard University Press.

Kuan, Yi-Jehng, Steven B. Charnley, Hui-Chun Huang, Wei-Ling Tseng, and Zbigniew Kisiel. 2003. "Interstellar Glycine." *Astrophysical Journal* 593: 848–67.

Kyrpides, N. C., and G. J. Olsen. 1999. "Archaeal and Bacterial Hyperthermophiles: Horizontalgene Exchange or Common Ancestry?" *Trends in Genetics* 15:298–99.

Lakoff, George. 1987. *Women, Fire, and Other Dangerous Thing: What Categories Reveal about the Mind*. Chicago: University of Chicago Press.

Lazcano, Antonio. 2010. "Historical Development of Origins Research." In David Deamer and Jack W. Szostak, eds., *The Origins of Life*, 5–20. Cold Spring Harbor, NY: Cold Spring Harbor Laboratory Press.

Lee, David H., Kay Severin, Yohei Yokobayashi, and M. Reza Ghadiri. 1997. "Emergence of Symbiosis in Peptide Self-Replication through a Hypercyclic Network." *Nature* 390:591–94.

Lévi-Strauss, Claude. [1949] 1969. *The Elementary Structures of Kinship*. Boston: Beacon Press.

Levinthal, Daniel A. 1997. "Adaptation on Rugged Landscapes." *Management Science* 43:934–50.

Lorrain, François P., and Harrison C. White. 1971. "Structural Equivalence of Individuals in Social Networks." *Journal of Mathematical Sociology* 1:49–80.

Luhmann, Niklas. 1982. *The Differentiation of Society*. New York: Columbia University Press.

———. 1986. "The Autopoiesis of Social Systems." In Felix Geyer and Johnannes van der Zouwen, eds., *Sociocybernetic Paradoxes: Observation, Control and Evolution of Self-Steering Systems*, 172–92. Beverly Hills, CA: Sage.

———. 1987a. "The Unity of the Legal System." In G. Teubner, ed., *Autopoiesis and the Law*, 12–35. Berlin: de Gruyter.

———. 1987b. "Closure and Openness: On Reality in the World of Law." In G. Teubner, ed., *Autopoiesis and the Law*, 335–48. Berlin: de Gruyter.

———. 1989. "Law as a Social System." *Northwestern University Law Review* 83:136–50.

———. [1986 in German] 1989. *Ecological Communication*. Chicago: University of Chicago Press.

———. 1990. *Essays on Self-Reference*. New York: Columbia University Press.

———. 1992. "Operational Closure and Structural Coupling: The Differentiation of the Legal System." *Cardozo Law Review* 13:1419–41.

———. [1984 in German] 1995. *Social Systems*. Stanford: Stanford University Press.

Luisi, Pier Luigi. 2006. *The Emergence of Life: From Chemical Origins to Synthetic Biology*. Cambridge: Cambridge University Press.

March, James G., and Herbert A. Simon. 1958. *Organizations*. New York: Wiley.

Margulis, Lynn. 1967. "On the Origin of Mitosing Cells." *Journal of Theoretical Biology* 14:225–74.

———. 1970. *Origin of Eukaryote Cells: Evidence and Research Implications for a Theory of the Origin and Evolution of Microbial, Plant, and Animal Cells on the Precambian Earth*. New Haven: Yale University Press.

———. 1981. *Symbiosis in Cell Evolution*. San Francisco: W. H. Freeman.

Margulis, Lynn, and Michael F. Dolan. 2002. *Early Life: Evolution on the Precambrian Earth*. Boston: Jones and Bartlett.

Margulis, Lynn, and Dorion Sagan. 1995. *What Is Life?* Berkeley: University of California Press.

Markoff, John. 1996. *The Abolition of Feudalism: Peasants, Lords, and Legislators in the French Revolution*. University Park: Pennsylvania State University Press.

Martin, William, and Michael J. Russell. 2003. "On the Origin of Cells: A Hypothesis for the Evolutionary Transitions from Abiotic Geochemistry to Chemoautotrophic Prokaryotes, and from Prokaryotes to Nucleated Cell." *Philosophical Transactions of the Royal Society of London: Series B* 358:59–85.

———. 2007. "On the Origin of Biochemistry at an Alkalinehydrothermal Vent." *Philosophical Transactions of the Royal Society of London: Series B* 362:1887–1925.

Martins, Zita, Oliver Botta, Marilyn L. Fogel, Mark A. Sephton, Daniel P. Glavin, Jonathan S. Watson, Jason P. Dworkin, Alan W. Schwartz, and Pascale Ehrenfreund. 2008. "Extraterrestrial Nucleobases in the Murchinson Meteorite." *Earth and Planetary Science Letters* 270:130–36.

Maturana, Humberto R. 1975. "The Organization of the Living: A Theory of the Living Organization."

International Journal of Man-Machine Studies 7: 313–32.

———. 1981. "Autopoiesis." In Milan Zeleny, ed., *Autopoiesis: A Theory of Living Organization*, 21–30. New York: North Holland.

Maturana, Humberto R., and Francisco J. Varela. 1973. *De Máquinas y Seres Vivos*. Santiago, Chile: Editorial Universitaria.

———. 1975. *Autopoietic Systems: A Characterization of the Living Organism*. Biological Computer Laboratory. Reprint 9.4. University of Illinois.

———. 1980. *Autopoiesis and Cognition: The Realization of the Living*. Dordrecht, Netherlands: D. Reidel.

May, Robert M. 1973. *Stability and Complexity in Model Ecosystems*. Princeton: Princeton University Press.

Maynard Smith, John. 1979. "Hypercycles and the Origin of Life." *Nature* 280:445–46.

Maynard Smith, John, and Eörs Szathmáry. 1995. *The Major Transitions in Evolution*. Oxford: Oxford University Press.

———. 1999. *The Origins of Life: From the Birth of Life to the Origin of Language*. Oxford: Oxford University Press.

McLean, Paul D. 1998. "A Frame Analysis of Favor Seeking in the Renaissance: Agency, Networks, and Political Culture." *American Journal of Sociology* 104:51–91.

———. 2007. *The Art of the Network: Strategic Interaction and Patronage in Renaissance Florence*. Durham: Duke University Press.

Merezhkovsky, K. S. 1909. *The Theory of Two Plasms as the Basis of Symbiogenesis: A New Study on the Origins of Organisms*. Proceedings of Studies of the Imperial Kazan University. Publishing Office of the Imperial University (in Russian).

Miller, S. L. 1953. "A Production of Amino Acids under Possible Primitive Earth Conditions." *Science* 117:528–29.

———. 1955. "Production of Some Organic Compounds under Possible Primitive Earth Conditions." *Journal of American Chemical Society* 77: 2351–61.

———. 1957. "The Mechanism of Synthesis of Amino Acids by Electric Discharges." *Biochimica et Biophysica Acta* 23:480–89.

Miller, Stanley L., and Jeffrey L. Bada. 1988. "Submarine Hot Springs and the Origin of Life." *Nature* 334:609–11.

Miller, Stanley L., and Leslie E. Orgel. 1974. *The Origins of Life on the Earth*. Englewood Cliffs, NJ: Prentice-Hall.

Mills, C. Wright. 1940. "Situated Actions and Vocabularies of Motive." *American Sociological Review* 5:904–13.

Milner, Robin. 1993. "Elements of Interaction: Turing Award Lecture." *Communications of the ACM (Association for Computing Machinery)* 36: 78–89.

Mingers, John. 2002. "Can Social Systems Be Autopoietic? Assessing Luhmann's Social Theory." *Sociological Review* 50:278–99.

Mische, Ann. 2003. "Cross-Talk in Movements: Rethinking the Culture-Network Link." In Mario Diani and Doug McAdam, eds., *Social Movements and Networks*, 258–80. Oxford: Oxford University Press.

———. 2007. *Partisan Politics: Communication and Contention across Brazilian Youth Activist Networks*. Princeton: Princeton University Press.

Mische, Ann, and Harrison White. 1998. "Between Conversation and Situation: Public Switching Dynamics across Network Domains." *Social Research* 65:695–724.

Morowitz, Harold J. 1966. "Physical Background of Cycles in Biological Systems." *Journal of Theoretical Biology* 13:60–62.

———. 1968. *Energy Flow in Biology: Biological Organization as a Problem in Thermal Physics*. New York: Academic Press.

———. 1992. *Beginnings of Cellular Life: Metabolism Recapitulates Biogenesis*. New Haven: Yale University Press.

———. 1999. "A Theory of Biochemical Organization, Metabolic Pathways, and Evolution." *Complexity* 4:39–53.

Morowitz, Harold J., Jennifer D. Kostelnik, Jeremy Yang, and George D. Cody. 2000. "The Origin of Intermediary Metabolism." *Proceedings of the National Academy of Sciences of the U.S.A.* 97: 7704–8.

Morris, Simon Conway. 1998. *The Crucible of Creation: The Burgess Shale and the Rise of Animals*. Oxford: Oxford University Press.

Mossel, Elchanan, and Mike Steel. 2005. "Random Biochemical Networks: The Probability of Self-Sustaining Autocatalysis." *Journal of Theoretical Biology* 233:327–36.

Muller, H. J. 1926. "The Gene as the Basis of Life." *Proceedings of the International Congress of Plant Sciences* 1:897–921.

———. 1966. "The Gene Material as the Initiator and the Organizing Basis of Life." *American Naturalist* 100:493–502.

Newman, M.E.J., and R. G. Palmer. 2003. *Modeling Extinction*. New York: Oxford University Press.

Nicolis, Grégoire, and Ilya Prigogine. 1977. *Self-Organization in Nonequilibrium Systems: From Dissipative Structures to Order through Fluctuations*. New York: Wiley.

———. 1989. *Exploring Complexity*. New York: Freeman.

Niesert, U., D. Harnasch, and C. Bresch. 1981. "Origin of Life between Scylla and Charybdis." *Journal of Molecular Evolution* 17:348–53.

Oparin, A. I. 1924. *Proiskhozdenie Zhizny*. Moscow: Moskovskiy Rabochiy. Translated by Sergius Morgulis as *The Origin of Life*. New York: Macmillan, 1938.

Orgel, L. E. 1973. *The Origins of Life: Molecules and Natural Selection*. New York: Wiley.

———. 1998. "Polymerization on the Rocks: Theoretical Introduction." *Origin of Life and Evolution of the Biosphere* 28:227–34.

———. 2004. "Prebiotic Chemistry and the Origin of the RNA World." *Critical Reviews in Biochemistry and Molecular Biology* 39:99–123.

———. 2008. "The Implausibility of Metabolic Cycles on the Prebiotic Earth." *PLoS Biology* 6(1): e18.

Oró, J., and A. Kimball. 1960. "Synthesis of Adenine from Ammonia Cyanide." *Biochemical and Biophysical Research Communications* 2:407–12.

Oró, J., S. L. Miller, and A. Lazcano. 1990. "The Origin and Early Evolution of Life on Earth." *Annual Review of Earth and Planetary Sciences* 18: 317–56.

Pachucki, Mark A., and Ronald L. Breiger. 2010. "Cultural Holes: Beyond Relationality in Social Networks and Culture." *Annual Review of Sociology* 36:10.1–10.20.

Padgett, John F. 1990. "Mobility as Control: Congressmen through Committees." In Ronald L. Breiger, ed., *Social Mobility and Social Structure*, 27–58. Cambridge: Cambridge University Press.

———. 2010. "Open Elite? Social Mobility, Marriage, and Family in Florence, 1282–1494." *Renaissance Quarterly* 63:357–411.

Padgett, John F., and Christopher K. Ansell. 1993. "Robust Action and the Rise of the Medici, 1400–1434." *American Journal of Sociology* 98:1259–1319.

Padgett, John F., and Paul D. McLean. 2011. "Economic Credit in Renaissance Florence." *Journal of Modern History* 83:1–47.

Padgett, John F., Doowan Lee, and Nick Collier. 2003. "Economic Production as Chemistry." *Industrial and Corporate Change* 12:843–77.

Pattison, Philippa. 1993. *Algebraic Models for Social Networks*. Cambridge: Cambridge University Press.

Penny, David. 2005. "An Interpretive Review of the Origin of Life Research." *Biology and Philosophy* 20:633–71.

Peretó, J. G., A. M. Velasco, A. Becerra, and A. Lazcano. 1999. "Comparative Biochemistry of CO_2 Fixation and the Evolution of Autotrophy." *International Microbiology* 2:3–10.

Pimm, Stuart L. 1982. *Food Webs*. London: Chapman and Hall.

———. 1991. *The Balance of Nature? Ecological Issues in the Conservation of Species and Communities*. Chicago: University of Chicago Press.

Pimm, S. L., and J. H. Lawton. 1977. "Number of Trophic Levels in Ecological Communities." *Nature* 268:329–31.

Poole, Anthony M., Daniel C. Jeffares, and David Penny. 1998. "The Path from the RNA World." *Journal of Molecular Evolution* 46:1–17.

———. 1999. "Early Evolution: Prokaryotes, the New Kids on the Block." *BioEssays* 21:880–89.

Prigogine, Ilya. [1955] 1967. *Introduction to Thermodynamics of Irreversible Processes*. New York: Interscience Publishers.

Reanney, D. C. 1982. "The Evolution of RNA Viruses." *Annual Review of Microbiology* 36:47–73.

Revesz, G. E. 1988. *Lambda-Calculus, Combinators, and Functional Programming*. Cambridge: Cambridge University Press.

Rössler, Otto E. 1971. "Einsystemtheoretisches Modell zurBiogenese." *Zeitschriftfür Naturforschung B* 26:741–46.

Russell, M. J., and A. J. Hall. 1997. "The Emergence of Life from Iron Monosulphide Bubbles at a Submarine Hydrothermal Redox and pH Front." *Journal of the Geological Society, London* 154:377–402.

Russell, M. J., D. E. Daia, and A. J. Hall. 1998. "The Emergence of Life from FeS Bubbles at Alkaline Hot Springs in an Acid Ocean." In J. Weigel and M.W.W. Adams, eds., *Thermophiles*, 77–116. Philadelphia: Taylor and Francis.

Russell, M. J., A. J. Hall, and D. Turner. 1989. "In Vitro Growth of Iron Sulfide Chimneys: Possible Culture Chambers for Origin-of-Life Experiments." *Terra Nova* 1:238–41.

Russell, M. J., A. J. Hall, A. G. Cairns-Smith, and P. S. Braterman. 1988. "Submarine Hot Springs and the Origin of Life." *Nature* 336:117.

Sabel, Charles, and Jonathan Zeitlin. 1997. *World of Possibilities*. Cambridge: Cambridge University Press.

Sagan [née Margulis], Lynn. 1967. "On the Origin of Mitosing Cells." *Journal of Theoretical Biology* 14:225–74.

Schrödinger, Erwin. [1944] 1967. *What Is Life?* Cambridge: Cambridge University Press.

Segré, Daniel, and Doron Lancet. 1999. "A Statistical Chemistry Approach to the Origin of Life." *Chemtracts—Biochemistry and Molecular Biology* 12: 382–97.

Sewell, William H., Jr. 1980. *Work and Revolution in France: The Language of Labor from the Old Regime to 1848*. Cambridge: Cambridge University Press.

———. 1985. *Structure and Mobility: The Men and Women of Marseille, 1820–1870*. Cambridge: Cambridge University Press.

———. 1994. *A Rhetoric of Bourgeois Revolution: The Abbé Sieyes and "What Is the Third Estate?"* Durham: Duke University Press.

———. 2005. *Logics of History: Social Theory and Social Transformation*. Chicago: University of Chicago Press.

Shapiro, James A. 2011. *Evolution: A View from the 21st Century*. Upper Saddle River, NJ: FT Press Science.

Shapiro, Robert. 2006. "Small Molecular Interactions Were Central to the Origin of Life." *Quarterly Review of Biology* 81:105–25.

Simon, Herbert A. 1969. "The Architecture of Complexity." In *Sciences of the Artificial*, 84–118. Cambridge, MA: MIT Press.

———. 1982. *Models of Bounded Rationality: Behavioral Economics and Business Organization*. Cambridge, MA: MIT Press.

Skocpol, Theda. 1979. *States and Social Revolutions: A Comparative Analysis of France, Russia and China*. Cambridge: Cambridge University Press.

Sleep, Norman H. 2010. "The Haldean-Archaean Environment." In David Deamer and Jack W. Szostak, eds., *The Origins of Life*, 35–48. Cold Spring Harbor, NY: Cold Spring Harbor Laboratory Press.

Smith, Eric, and Harold J. Morowitz. 2004. "Universality in Intermediary Metabolism." *Proceedings of the National Academy of Sciences of the U.S.A.* 101:13168–73.

Solé, Richard V., and Jordi Bascompte. 2006. *Self-Organization in Complex Ecosystems*. Princeton: Princeton University Press.

Somers, Margaret R. 1994. "The Narrative Construction of Identity: A Relational and Network Approach." *Theory and Society* 23:605–49.

Spiegelman, Sol. 1971. "An Approach to the Experimental Analysis of Pre-Cellular Evolution." *Quarterly Reviews of Biophysics* 4:213–53.

Stadler, Bärbel M. R., Peter F. Stadler, Günter P. Wagner, and Walter Fontana. 2001. "The Topology of the Possible: Formal Spaces Underlying Patterns of Evolutionary Change." *Journal of Theoretical Biology* 213:241–74.

Stetter, Karl O. 1996. "Hyperthermophilicprocaryotes." *FEMS Microbiology Reviews* 18:149–58.

Thomas, Lewis. 1974. *The Lives of a Cell: Notes of a Biology Watcher*. New York: Bantam Books.

Tolstoy, Leo. [1869] 2010. *War and Peace*. Oxford: Oxford University Press.

Tomasello, Michael. 2008. *Origins of Human Communication*. Cambridge, MA: MIT Press.

Varela, Francisco J. 1979. *Principles of Biological Autonomy*. New York: North Holland.

Varela, F. G., H. R. Maturana, and R. Uribe. 1974. "Autopoiesis: The Organization of Living Systems, Its Characterization, and a Model." *BioSystems* 5:187–96.

Wächtershäuser, Günter. 1988. "Before Enzymes and Templates: Theory of Surface Metabolism." *Microbiological Reviews* 52:452–84.

———. 1990. "Evolution of the First Metabolic Cycles." *Proceedings of the National Academy of the U.S.A.* 87:200–204.

———. 1992. "Groundworks for an Evolutionary Biochemistry: The Iron-Sulfur World." *Progress in Biophysics and Molecular Biology* 58:85–201.

———. 1994. "Life in a Ligand Sphere." *Proceedings of the National Academy of the U.S.A.* 91:4283–87.

———. 1998. "The Case for a Hyper-thermophilic Chemolithoautrophic Origin of Life in an Iron-Sulfur World." In J. Weigel and M.W.W. Adams, eds., *Thermophiles*, 47–56. Philadelphia: Taylor and Francis.

———. 2000. "Life as We Don't Know It." *Science* 289:1307–8.

———. 2006. "From Volcanic Origins of Chemoautotrophic Life to Bacteria, Archae and Eukarya." *Philosophical Transactions of the Royal Academy: B* 361:1787–1808.

———. 2007. "On the Chemistry and Evolution of the Pioneer Organism." *Chemistry and Biodiversity* 4:584–602.

Watson, J. D., and F. H. Crick. 1953. "A Structure for Deoxyribose Nucleic Acid." *Nature* 171:737–38.

Weintraub, David A. 2011. *How Old Is the Universe?* Princeton: Princeton University Press.

West-Eberhard, Mary Jane. 2003. *Developmental Plasticity and Evolution*. Oxford: Oxford University Press.

White, Harrison C. 1963. *An Anatomy of Kinship: Mathematical Models for Structures of Cumulated Roles*. Englewood-Cliffs, NJ: Prentice-Hall.

———. 1970. *Chains of Opportunity: Systems Models of Mobility in Organizations*. Cambridge, MA: Harvard University Press.

———. 1981. "Where Do Markets Come from?" *American Journal of Sociology* 87:517–47.

———. 1992. *Identity and Control: A Structural Theory of Social Action*. Princeton: Princeton University Press.

———. 1995. "Network Switchings and Bayesian Forks: Reconstructing the Social and Behavioral." *Social Research* 62:1035–62.

———. 2002. *Markets from Networks: Socioeconomic Models of Production*. Princeton: Princeton University Press.

———. 2008. *Identity and Control: How Social Formations Emerge*. 2nd ed. Princeton: Princeton University Press.

White, Harrison C., and Frédéric C. Godart. 2007. "Stories from Identity and Control." *Sociologica* 3.

White, Harrison C., Scott A. Boorman, and Ronald L. Breiger. 1976. "Social Structure from Multiple Networks. I: Blockmodels of Roles and Positions." *American Journal of Sociology* 81:730–80.

White, Harrison C., Jan Fuhse, Matthias Thiemann, and Larissa Buchholz. 2007. "Networks and Meanings: Styles and Switchings." *Soziale Systeme* 13:543–55.

Wittgenstein, Ludwig. 1953. *Philosophical Investigations*. New York: Macmillan.

Woese, Carl R. 1977. "Endosymbionts and Mitochondrial Origins." *Journal of Molecular Evolution* 10:93–96.

———. 1981. "Archaebacteria." *Scientific American* 244:98–122.

———. 1982. "Archaebacteria and Cellular Origins: An Overview." *Zentralbl. Bakteriol. Parasitenkd. Infectionskr. Hyg. Abt. 1 Orig. Reihe C* 3:1–17.

———. 1987. "Bacterial Evolution." *Microbiological Reviews* 51:221–71.

———. 1998. "The Universal Ancestor." *Proceedings of the National Academy of the U.S.A.* 95:6854–59.

———. 2000. "Interpreting the Universal Phylogenic Tree." *Proceedings of the National Academy of Sciences of the U.S.A.* 97:8392–96.

———. 2002. "On the Evolution of Cells." *Proceedings of the National Academy of Sciences of the U.S.A.* 99:8742–47.

Woese, Carl R., and George E. Fox. 1977. "Phylogenic Structure of the Prokaryotic Domain: The Primary Kingdoms." *Proceedings of the National Academy of Sciences of the U.S.A.* 74:5088–90.

Woese, Carl R., Otto Kandler, and Mark L. Wheelis. 1990. "Towards a Natural System of Organisms: Proposal for the Domains Archaea, Bacteria, and Eucarya." *Proceedings of the National Academy of Sciences of the U.S.A.* 87:4576–79.

Woese, C. R., L. J. Magrum, and G. E. Fox. 1978. "Archaebacteria." *Journal of Molecular Evolution* 11: 245–52.

Zablen, L. B., M. S. Kissil, C. R. Woese, and D. E. Buetow. 1975. "Phylogenetic Origin of the Chloroplast and Prokaryotic Nature of Its Ribosomal RNA." *Proceedings of the National Academy of Sciences of the U.S.A.* 72:2418–22.

Zahnle, Kevin, Laura Schaefer, and Bruce Fegley. 2010. "Earth's Earliest Atmosphere." In David Deamer and Jack W. Szostak, eds., *The Origins of Life*, 49–66. Cold Spring Harbor, NY: Cold Spring Harbor Laboratory Press.

Zahnle, Kevin, Nick Arndt, Charles Cockell, Alex Halliday, Euan Nisbet, Franck Selsis, and Norman H. Sleep. 2007. "Emergence of a Habitable Planet." *Space Science Review* 129:35–78.

Zhang, Xiang V., and Scot T. Martin. 2006. "Driving Parts of Krebs Cycle in Reverse through Mineral Photochemistry." *Journal of the American Chemical Society* 128:16032–33.

3

Economic Production as Chemistry II

John F. Padgett ▪ Peter McMahan ▪ Xing Zhong

The production and distribution of goods by firms are only half of what is accomplished in markets. Firms also are produced and transformed through goods passing through them. This transformation is not just a matter of profits. Skills and the core competencies that define firms are developed and maintained through "learning by doing" and other learning processes that are triggered by exchange among firms. In periods of decentralization and outsourcing, like today, it is more evident than ever that linked chains of skills are distributed across firms. In this context especially, evolution in and learning of distributed skill sets reverberates directly into the reconstitution of firms. Evolving links among firms, in turn, guide and shape the recombinant new-product possibilities latent in distributed skill sets.

The duality of this co-evolution between product and organization is often ignored, as analysts assume away one side of the dynamics in order to focus attention on the other. A number of economists and social scientists are aware of the issue of co-evolution.[1] However, more tools are needed to help analyze the nonlinear and path-dependent dynamics of feedback among evolving networks that such processes entail.

One place to turn for analytic inspiration is chemistry. From the chemical perspective, life is an interacting ensemble of chemicals that reproduces itself through time, in the face of turnover of its parts.[2] Biological organisms are not fixed entities; they are autocatalytic networks of chemical transformations, which continually reconstruct both themselves and their physical containers. The origin-of-life problem, in this view, is how such an ensemble can self-organize and sustain itself from a soup of random chemicals in interaction and flux.

This chemical perspective can be applied to the analysis of co-evolution of products and firms through the following analogy. Skills, like chemical reactions, are rules that transform products into other products. Products, like chemicals, are transformed by skills. Firms, like organisms, are containers of skills that transform

The "II" in the title refers to fact that this chapter is a major extension of "Economic Production as Chemistry" by Padgett, Lee, and Collier, published in *Industrial and Corporate Change* 12, no. 4 (2003): 843–77. The extension in question is from the SOLO H to the ALL chemistry. We gratefully acknowledge the financial support of the National Science Foundation (program on Human and Social Dynamics) and the Hewlett Foundation, which funded the development of both the first and this second round of these agent-based models.

[1] See, e.g., March and Simon 1958; Nelson and Winter 1982; Hughes 1983, 1987; Dosi, Giannetti, and Toninelli 1992; Dosi, Nelson, and Winter 2000; Malerba and Orsinigo 1993; Nelson 1994, 1995; Warglien 1995; Powell 1996; McKelvey 1997; Coriat and Dosi 1998; Rosenkopf and Tushman 1998; Murman 2003; and Padgett and McLean 2006.

[2] From the physics and biological points of view, additional criteria to the definition of life are sometimes added. Physicists (e.g., Prigogine and Glansdorff 1971) sometimes add the criterion of far-from-equilibrium throughput of energy. Biologists (e.g., Maturana and Varela 1980) sometimes add the criterion of permeable encapsulation. We agree that from a thermodynamic point of view throughput of energy is fundamental, but this criterion is necessary not sufficient. There are many dissipative systems that are not living. Energy throughput is modeled here through environmental urns. Permeable encapsulation is very helpful to sustain chemical metabolism over time, but primitive life can exist without it. Our models explicitly show the importance of spatial embodiment for breaking the complexity barrier.

products. Trade, like food, passes transformed products around through exchange networks, renewing skills and thereby firms in the process. In the macroeconomic aggregate, product inputs flow into and outputs flow out of this trading network of firms and skills. Economic "life" exists if an autocatalytic network of interlinked skills and products can emerge and renew itself in the face of continual turnover and "death" in its component skills and products.

Firms in this view are sites through which distributed and living "chemical reaction" production processes flow. At a minimum, firms can be considered to be mere collection bins for diverse skills. Trading among firms regulates both the activation and the evolution of skill sets distributed across firms. Composition of skills within firms evolves, among other methods, through learning by doing: the more a skill is used, the more the skill is reinforced. Skills not used are forgotten. These two processes of learning and forgetting impose selection pressure on an evolving network-of-skills-through-firms production system. The origin-of-life problem for markets is to discover how a randomly distributed set of skills across firms can self-organize, through exchange and learning, into a coherent product-transformation network,[3] which then reproduces itself through time and "grows" a set of firms to sustain itself.

Inspired by a specific literature in chemistry on hypercycles, Padgett, Lee, and Collier (2003) developed one family of economic production models that operationalized this co-evolutionary perspective on markets. This chapter extends that modeling platform to cover a wider range of technological chemistries.

The "hypercycle" is a specific model of the chemical origin of life pioneered by Eigen and Schuster (1971, 1979) and extended by others.[4] From random distributions of chemicals, the hypercycle model seeks to find and to grow sets of chemical transformations that include self-reinforcing loops: {(1→2), (2→3), (3→4), . . . , (n→1)}. Chemical cycles are crucial to the emergence and maintenance of life because these are the motors that sustain the self-reproduction of metabolic networks in the face of continuous turnover in component chemicals. Without cycles, there is no positive feedback for growth. Without them, any chemical reaction left to itself will stop or "die." Eigen and Schuster, Hofbauer and Sigmund, and others have explored how variation in reaction rates, in chemical density, and in number of components affects the dynamic stability or "survivability" of various classes of hypercyclic chemical reactions within a well-stirred liquid reaction tank. Boerlijst and Hogeweg (1991), Padgett (1997), and Padgett, Lee, and Collier (2003) extended the investigation beyond the original liquid context to a spatial topology of interaction.

The hypercycle-modeling literature started with random distributions of interacting rules within linear or sequential rule sets, such as the one described above, and then searched for experimental conditions that would dynamically reproduce that rule set in the face of death. Here we relabel such linear-rule-set chemistries as SOLO H, which stands for "single hypercycle." In this chapter, we reproduce previous hypercycle (a.k.a. SOLO H) findings as benchmarks, but we also investigate a more general class of chemistries—namely, complete sets of interacting transformation rules {(i→j)} within experimentally varied maxima or n. Such complete families of chemistries we label ALL, standing for "all permutations."[5] For example, the ALL chemistry within a maximum of two products is {(1→2), (2→1)}. The ALL chemistry within a maximum of three products is {(1→2), (1→3), (2→1), (2→3), (3→1), (3→2)}; the ALL chemistry within a maximum of four products is {(1→2), (1→ 3), (1→4), (2→1), (2→3), (2→4), (3→1), (3→2), (3→4), (4→1), (4→2), (4→3)}; and so forth, up to experimentally controlled maxima of n products. The rule-set size of the ALL chemistry grows rapidly as $(n^2 - n)$, whereas the rule-set size of SOLO H grows only as n.

The discovery and nurturance of cycles within randomized rule sets are as important to the creation of life within the ALL chemistry as they are in the more restricted SOLO H chemistry. In either chemistry, without emergent cycles of rule reproduction there are no positive feedbacks for growth to combat endemic turnover or death. The difference is that in the ALL chemistry a great many distinct rule cycles are available to be discovered and reinforced, whereas in the SOLO H chemistry, there is only a single target type of cycle to try to grow and reinforce. This much larger space for exploration in ALL

[3] Such a network could be called a "metabolism" or a "technology," depending upon the application context.

[4] See, e.g., Hofbauer and Sigmund 1988; Kauffman 1986, 1993; and Fontana and Buss 1994. The full literature is reviewed in Stadler and Stadler 2002.

[5] Only redundant and dynamically degenerate rules of the form {(i→i)} are excluded.

opens the door for the possible emergence of multiple technological networks of linked rules, which functionally intertwine with each other, and of multiple trading networks of linked cells, which spatially overlap each other. This endogenous emergence of multiple networks is the main discovery that comes out of this extension from SOLO H to ALL. Multiple networks are not inserted "by hand" but rather self-organize out of the production and reproduction of constituent rules. Given the emergence of multiple production networks or "technologies" (called subsystems below), the structure of how such multiple networks overlay and dynamically feed back into each other becomes a topological topic from which to derive the consequences for system robustness and evolvability.[6]

Viewing economics as chemistry entails extraordinarily minimalist assumptions about economic production: Firms become nothing more than bins of transformation rules. Products randomly flow in and through these bins, without purpose. Rules reproduce or die only as functions of use. There is no guiding intelligence either at the level of the market or at the level of the firm.[7] In such a minimalist setup, the analytic question is: Can any coherent and self-reproducing systems of production (i.e., co-evolved sets of skills, products, and firms) emerge? And if they can, what mechanisms affect the likelihood of such emergence? A priori one might not expect much complex economic organization to be possible from randomly iterated rules. Yet the history of chemical and biological life on earth suggests that minimalist systems can generate astounding complexity under the right circumstances. Intelligence, we speculate, may not have been necessary for markets or organizations to emerge. We are not arguing thereby that humans are no more complicated than chemicals. We are arguing that a surprising amount of social and economic organization does not depend on humans being complicated.

CHEMISTRY MODELS OF ECONOMIC PRODUCTION: SOLO H AND ALL

We shall describe both variants of our chemical model of economic production in pseudo-algorithmic fashion because we have implemented it in the form of an agent-based simulation.[8] First we shall describe our core models of production and learning. These will give the logic of our core "dependent variable": autocatalytic-network emergence. Then we shall describe experimental variations of our core model—type of chemistry, number of products, interaction topology, mode of learning, input environment, and input search method. These are the "independent variables" that may affect the likelihood of autocatalytic-network emergence and of the structures of any production networks and firms that do emerge.

The simplest version of our spatial hypercycle model has been solved analytically, with closed-form solutions already published.[9] We do not reproduce those mathematical results here.[10]

Core Model of Production

1. There are three components in the model: rules ("skills"), balls ("products"), and bins ("firms").
2. Rules/skills transform balls/products into other balls/products, according to one of two families of chemistries: SOLO H and ALL.
3. Balls/products are indexed by i = 1, 2, 3, . . . , n. The parameter n serves two functions: it indexes each member of the two chemistry families, and it characterizes the relative

[6] Cf. Wagner and Altenberg 1996; Wagner 2005; Fontana 2005.

[7] This is not only bounded rationality, this is the absence of consciousness altogether.

[8] The original SOLO H agent-based model, publicly available for both demonstration and open-source modification, can be found at http://repast.sourceforge.net under the application module HYPERCYCLE. Repast is a comprehensive software framework and library for creating agent-based simulations, built in the Java language. It was developed at the Social Science Research Computing Center at the University of Chicago. Peter McMahan has reprogrammed this Java-based Repast model into the R computing language and has developed the extension to the ALL chemistry. This R version of the model, used to generate the results reported in this chapter, is available for both demonstration and open-source modification on Padgett's webpage: http://home.uchicago.edu/~jpadgett. Extensive docking tests were performed to verify that SOLO H performs identically in both the Java and the R implementations.

[9] Padgett, Lee, and Collier 2003, 861–62, 871–77.

[10] In economics, though not in physics, there is a fruitless methodological debate about agent-based modeling versus analytic modeling. Our position is that one can and should do both—namely, solve simple settings analytically and then scale up through computer modeling. Analytic solutions are more transparent than computer simulations but frequently require the imposition of highly restrictive and unrealistic homogeneity assumptions. In particular the move from nonspatial homogeneity to spatial heterogeneity causes problems for analytic tractability. Computers can numerically solve highly nonlinear models with heterogeneous agents in nonhomogeneous topologies, and there is no reason not to let them do so as long as one can understand the results.

"complexity" of the particular rule set under investigation.

4. Rules/skills are contained in bins/firms. At the beginning of each simulation, skills are just randomly distributed across available firms, without any logic. The number of firms initially is large.
5. Bins/firms are arrayed on a spatial grid with wrap-around boundaries. Each firm has eight possible nearest-neighbor trading partners—the so-called Moore neighborhood structure of physical space.
6. At each asynchronous iteration of the model, a random rule is chosen "looking for action." The firm containing that rule/skill reaches into the input environment (modeled as an urn) and draws an input ball/product. If the input ball/product selected is compatible with that rule, then the ball/product is transformed according to that rule. (For example, if a firm possessed an activated (1→2) skill, and it drew a 1 as input from the urn environment, then it would transform the input 1 into the output 2.) If the ball/product selected could not be processed by the activated rule, then input ball/product passes through the firm into the output environment (also modeled as an urn) unchanged.
7. Products successfully transformed within the firm are passed randomly to one of the firm's eight possible trading partners. If that trading partner possesses a compatible skill, then it transforms the product further and passes that along in a random direction. (For example, if the second firm possessed a (2→3), then after receiving the output 2 from the first firm, it would transform the 2 into a 3 and then pass that on to a third firm or possibly back to the first.) In this way, transformed products pass through sequences or chains of skills.
8. Bins/firms continue passing around transformed products among themselves until the product lands on a firm that does not possess a compatible skill to transform it further. At that point the product is ejected into the output environment, and a new input ball is selected to begin the iterative process all over again.

Overall, the production process looks like this: Input balls/products come in from an input environment then pass in random directions through randomly distributed production chains of skills, being transformed en route, until they pass back out into an output environment. For this random production process to self-organize into coherence, there must be some sort of feedback mechanism. For us, this is learning by doing.

Core Model of Learning

1. "Learning by doing" is modeled in chemical fashion as follows: If one skill transforms a product and passes it on to a second skill that transforms it further ("can use it"), then a skill is reproduced. We call such a sequence a "successful transaction," since both sides of the exchange transform products.[11] Which of the two skills is reproduced in a successful transaction—sender or receiver—is an experimental variation within the model, which will be discussed below.
2. "Forgetting" is modeled in chemical fashion as follows: Whenever one skill reproduces anywhere in the system, another skill, randomly chosen from the overall population of skills, is killed off. The total population volume of skills in the population thereby is held constant.[12]
3. Once a firm loses all its skills, it "goes bankrupt" or "dies," never to recover any skills.

Learning by firms is equivalent here to reproduction of their skills. Learning by firms and reproduction of skills, we argue, are the same process, just described at different levels of analysis. This is like a germ's eye view of disease: instead of focusing on the organism getting sick, we focus instead on the reproduction and spread of germs. If bins are analogized to firms and skills to people, then the reproduction of a skill is analogous to the hiring of a new employee. The numerical distribution of skills/rules across bins is then analogous to the size distribution of firms. Firms learn and adapt in our model, but the underlying mechanism is not conscious reasoning; it is the reproduction of their inherited skills through use.[13] Firms are kept alive or are killed off solely through the

[11] Final consumption is the output urn.

[12] This conservation-of-skills assumption mimics the conservation-of-mass assumption in real chemistry. While perhaps too harsh an assumption for many human populations, this constraint is a minimalist, chemistry-style way to model competition among firms.

[13] In future extensions of this model, we intend to add diffusion of skills among trading firms in order to mimic "teaching." That extension is outlined in the next chapter.

"chemical" reactions of technological skills that operate through them.

This combination of learning, forgetting, and dying imposes selection pressure on the production system of skills. In the face of inexorable forgetting, skills must reproduce in order to survive. In the harsh conservation-of-skills setup employed here, indeed, the very success of rules in one place in the system imposes sharply competitive selection pressure on rules elsewhere in the system. Heavily used subsets of the distributed skill set reproduce, and rarely used subsets of the distributed skill set disappear. The death of a firm is an absorbing state that permanently eliminates its unsuccessful skills.[14] As the skill composition of rules within firms thereby evolves, surviving firms congeal spatially into mutually reinforcing trading clusters, reminiscent of cities. And production chains of compatibly sequenced rules self-organize their way through these spatially contiguous clusters of firms.

A conscious desire to cooperate, indeed consciousness at all, is not necessary for mutually reinforcing trading firms to emerge and to survive. In this model, the minimal requirement for long-term survival, both of firms and of clusters, is to participate in at least one spatially distributed production chain that closes in on itself to form a loop. Not all production chains within a trading cluster need be closed into loops. And more than one loop within a cluster is certainly possible—more than one loop of the same sequence in the case of SOLO H or more than one loop of multiple sequences in the case of ALL. In either case, loops within distributed chains of skill are crucial, not for production itself but for the competitive reproduction of skills. Loops set up positive feedbacks of growth in skills that give firms that participate in them the reproductive ability to outproduce firms that do not. Put another way, clusters of firms can produce products with or without cycles, but firms whose skill sets participate in production chains that include loops have the further capacity to keep renewing each other endogenously through time. This is the chemical definition of life.

Technological loops do not imply that individual production runs move endlessly (and pointlessly) in cycles. Particular products are transformed only through segments of these global technological chains, distributed across firms. But in ensemble production rules must help each other reproduce through overlapping production runs forming cycles in order for self-sustaining metabolism or "life" to persist through time. Topologically autocatalysis is the set of nodes (here rules) with transformation or reproduction arrows coming into them from other nodes in the set. This set is not all cycles, but there are always at least some cycles at the core.

From our chemical perspective, therefore, the secret to understanding competitive success, both of firms and of spatial clusters, is to find the conditions that foster the spontaneous self-organization of skills into self-reinforcing cyclic production chains, which wend their way through firms, knitting them together in trade and helping them reproduce each other through continuous learning.

Experimental Variations

There are six "independent variables"—that is, experimental treatments in the simulation model—whose effect on the likelihood of finding and sustaining self-organized autocatalytic networks of skills will be explored in this chapter.

1. Type of Chemistry

The SOLO H and the ALL sets of initial production rules have already been described.[15]

2. Complexity

A parametrically fixed volume of rules or skills is scattered randomly around the space of firms at the beginning of each run. In this chapter there are always 200 specific instantiations of rules being scattered, chosen uniformly from the relevant chemistry's rule set. We vary the composition or "complexity" of the rule set so scattered, "complexity" being indexed by n. We shall vary n from 2 to 9: that is, within each of our chemistries, we shall explore 2-ball/product rule sets, 3-ball/product rule sets, and so forth, up to a maximum of 9-ball/product rule sets. Presumably the more complex and thin the resulting rule sets, the more difficult it will be to find and to sustain living production chains.[16]

[14] Allowing the entry of new firms is another obvious extension to our model that we do not explore here, but that is explored in the next chapter.

[15] We also explored a variant of ALL, called ALL (no reciprocity), explained in footnote 36.

[16] In the extreme case of ALL 9-ball chemistry, for example, there are only $200/(9^2-9)=2.778$ initial instances of each specific rule being randomly scattered over the 100 firms. Rounding of numbers of specific rule instantiations (to 3 or to 2 in this example), necessary to maintain a total of 200, was done randomly.

3. Interaction Topology

The basic spatial topology for trading to be explored in this chapter is the 10 × 10 wrap-around grid. That is, at the beginning of each run, there are 100 firms, one firm per cell in the grid, each of which can trade products with their eight nearest neighbors. This is the so-called Moore neighborhood topology.[17]

As experimental baseline, we shall compare the hypercycle behavior of this spatial topology to that of the nonspatial "well-stirred liquid reactor" topology, more traditional in chemistry. In nonspatial or random topology every rule is equally likely to pass a product to any other surviving rule, irrespective of spatial or firm location.

A major finding in the existing hypercycle literature[18] is that nonspatial hypercycles are dynamically stable up to 4-elements, but not beyond that. In other words, in nonspatial interaction when hypercyclic or SOLO H rule sets are 5-elements and up, one or more of the component chemicals is always driven to zero during the reaction process, thereby breaking the reproductive loop and causing the hypercycle to "crash." This is a "complexity barrier" that self-organizing hypercycles, and hence "life," cannot penetrate when chemical interaction is nonspatial or random. Padgett (1997) and Padgett, Lee, and Collier. (2003) have shown that in spatial interaction topologies, dynamically stable hypercycles of complexity 5-elements and above can be grown, albeit at increasingly lower frequencies at higher levels of complexity. Spatial interaction, in other words, can break the complexity barrier. Presumably this is one reason why complex chemical life is embodied. We shall reconfirm here both the Hofbauer and Sigmund (1988) nonspatial findings and the Padgett (1997; Padgett, Lee, and Collier 2003) spatial findings in a new context.

4. Learning/Reproduction

In the spatial topology setting, there are two variants of "learning by doing" that can and will be explored.[19]

[17] Padgett (1997) investigated 4-neighbor (von Neumann) neighborhoods. In future work, described in the next chapter, we shall investigate endogenous topologies. That extension will allow investigation of the emergence and impact of social, not just spatial, protocols.

[18] Hofbauer and Sigmund 1988, 96.

[19] In nonspatial interaction, these two reproduction modes behave identically (see appendix in Padgett, Lee, and Collier 2003). Space is what separates target from source. In Padgett 1997, a third mode was also explored: "joint reproduction," where both rules in a successful transaction reproduce. Because two rules are reproduced in joint reproduction, two offsetting skills need to be killed off.

(a) "Source reproduction" is where the originating rule in a successful transaction is reproduced.
(b) "Target reproduction" is where the receiving rule in a successful transaction is reproduced.

For example, if (1→2) receives a 1 from the input environment, transforms it into a 2, and then successfully passes that 2 onto a neighboring (2→3), which transforms it again, then source reproduction is where the initiating (1→2) reproduces, and target reproduction is where the recipient (2→3) reproduces.[20] Variation in mode of reproduction thus defines who benefits from the transaction.

We think of source reproduction as akin to "selfish learning" because the active initiator of the successful transaction reaps the reward. And we think of target reproduction as akin to "altruistic learning" because the passive recipient of the successful transaction reaps the reward. "Selfish" and "altruistic" are verbal labels that accurately characterize who benefits. In using these suggestive labels, however, one should avoid importing motivational connotations. In the minimalist models developed here, there are no motivations—just actions and reactions, like in chemistry.

Padgett (1997) and Padgett, Lee, and Collier (2003) have demonstrated that, in comparison with source reproduction, target reproduction dramatically increases the likelihood of growing stable hypercycles. And it also increases the spatial extensiveness and complexity of the firm cluster that hypercycles produce. Both of these findings will be reconfirmed here but extended with quantitative variation to more general chemistries.

In addition to these model variations, two more experimental manipulations will be performed here that vary the input or resource environment in which autocatalytic networks grow. Such experiments were not possible in Padgett's earlier work (1997) because in the original framework there was no explicit modeling of products or of product environments.

5. Input Environment

Input environments of resources or products can be conceived as fixed or variable, and they can be conceived as rich or poor.

[20] Of course the recipient (2→3) could easily turn into an initiator in the next tick if a neighboring (3→4) is subsequently found.

Among fixed resource environments,

(a) "rich" input environments will be modeled by letting the input urn of resources contain all n possible inputs, never to be depleted even as products/resources are withdrawn; and
(b) "poor" input environments will be modeled by letting the input urn of resources contain only one possible input (by convention, we call that "1"), not depleted even as products/resources are withdrawn.

Among variable resource environments,

(c) "endogenous" input environments will be modeled by letting the input urn be reconstructed over time by the outputs of the production system. Under the endogenous-environment variant, in other words, our model will withdraw one input product, transform it into other products through distributed production chains, and then place the final output back into the original input urn; and
(d) endogenous environments can be rich or poor, depending upon initialization of the input urn, which endogenous gradually modifies.

Presumably rich input environments are more congenial to autocatalytic-network emergence than are poor environments. What is less clear a priori is the relative ranking of endogenous environments. Given that we have defined "rich" virtually as nirvana (namely, as "all possible inputs available all the time, never to be depleted"), our expectation is that nothing can outperform that. However, modelers of social-insect behavior[21] have discovered that "stigmergy"—the ability of social insects to transform their physical environments into nests, mounds, paths, and the like—can sometimes exert surprisingly powerful feedback onto the development of social organization. Consistent with arguments in this social-insect tradition, Padgett et al. (2003) discovered in SOLO H that stigmergy performed almost as well as fixed-rich in target reproduction and that stigmergy even outperformed fixed-rich in source reproduction. Target reproduction remained superior, but source-reproduction-plus-stigmergy performed second best in survival rates, spatial extensiveness, and technological complexity.

[21] See, for example, Camazine et al. 2001.

6. Input Search

The final experimental manipulation possible within our model varies the precision of search through the input environment.

(a) "Random search" is when an activated rule reaches into the input environmental urn and chooses inputs randomly in proportion to what is there.
(b) "Selective search" is when an activated rule reaches into the input environmental urn and selects the exact input it needs to transform, if it is there.

Random search is like literal chemistry.[22] Selective search is more like animal behavior.[23] This is the only place in the model where we vary degree of intelligence. We originally expected the more intelligent selective-search procedure to outperform the stupid random-search procedure in finding and nurturing production hypercycles. Padgett et al. (2003) discovered to their surprise that selective search affected speed to equilibrium but not any properties of the equilibrium itself. Search intelligence, in other words, sped up evolution, but it did not alter the outcome of evolution. Because of this earlier finding, we do not focus on this independent variable in this chapter. Instead we fix the search method at random in order to direct our attention elsewhere.

To sum up the logic of our modeling enterprise: Chemistry teaches us that life is an ensemble of products and transformation rules that reproduces itself through time. Distributed economic production activity qualifies under this minimal definition, especially if the fragility and malleability of both firms and their skills are recognized. We take the analogy between economic and chemical exchange to its extreme by assuming away all human rationality and even consciousness, holding on to only the features of blind adaptive learning and selection. We will demonstrate that firms, production chains, and even "cities" can emerge and reproduce under these minimalist assumptions. We hope thereby to discover structural and interactive imperatives that help foster economic self-organization.

[22] Metaphorically we think of this as "the intelligence of an atom, bouncing around."

[23] Metaphorically we think of this as "the intelligence of a cow, looking for grass."

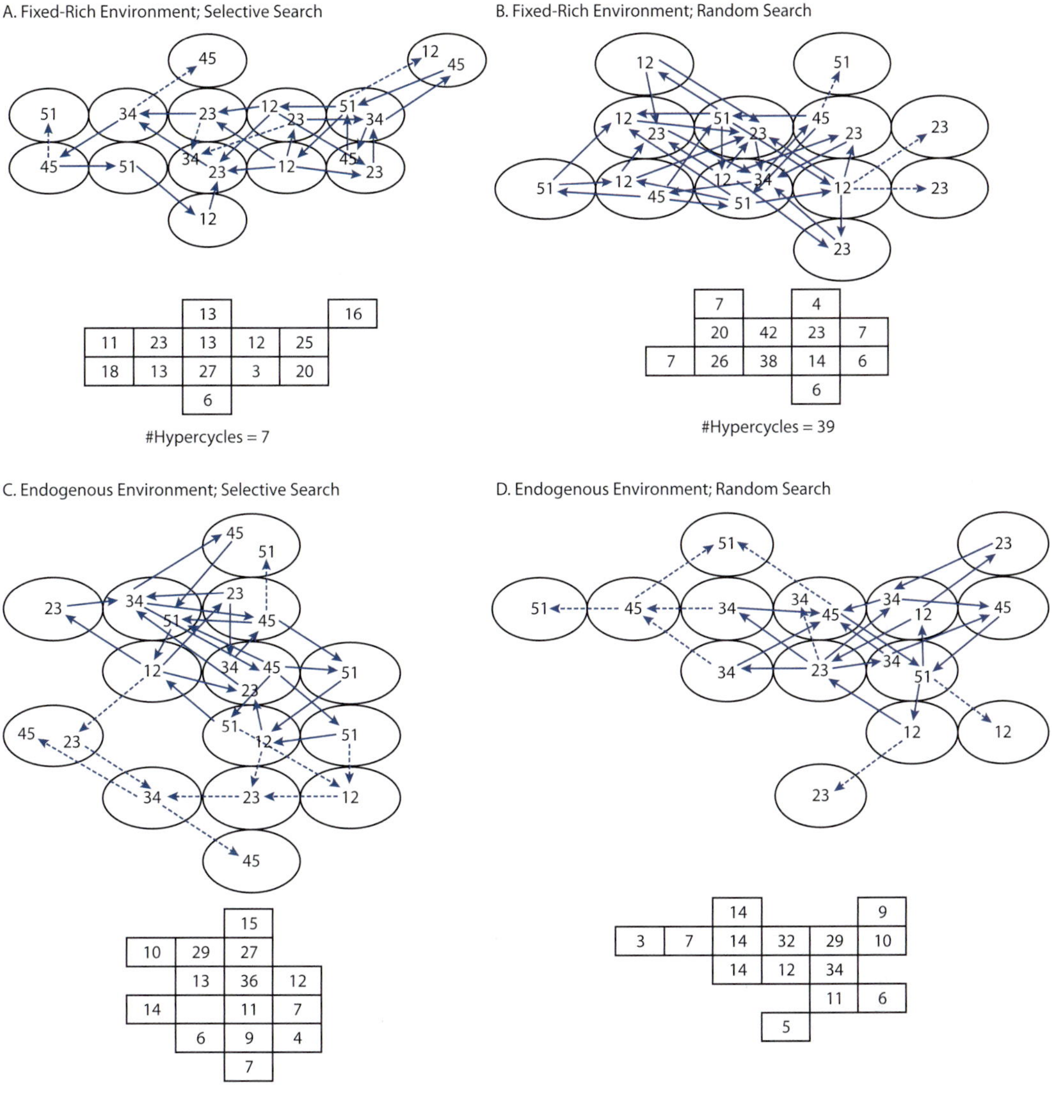

Figure 3.1 Representative 5-skill hypercycles at equilibrium under target reproduction. Ellipses are firms; within ellipses, number pairs are skills; products flow along arrows. Solid arrows participate in hypercycles. Dotted arrows link to parasite rules. Boxes give the total volume of rules (~employees) contained within corresponding ellipses.

RESULTS: EMERGENCE OF AUTOCATALYTIC NETWORKS IN SOLO H

Figure 3.1 presents a small sample of successful equilibria of our agent-based hypercycle model as they would appear on the computer screen.[24] "Success" means that at least one autocatalytic network was found and survived the selection process to reliably reproduce itself.[25] To interpret

[24] To download and observe the models themselves, see footnote 8.

[25] "Survived the selection process" operationally means this: Through experience, we learned how long it took on average for rule networks no longer to change topologically. Adding 50 percent to these experiential estimates yielded the following stopping parameters: 270,000 ticks for 2-ball runs; 410,000 for 3-ball runs; 580,000 for 4-ball runs; 770,000 for 5-ball runs; 980,000 for 6-ball runs; 1,210,000 for 7-ball runs; 1,460,000 for 8-ball runs; and 1,720,000 for 9-ball runs.

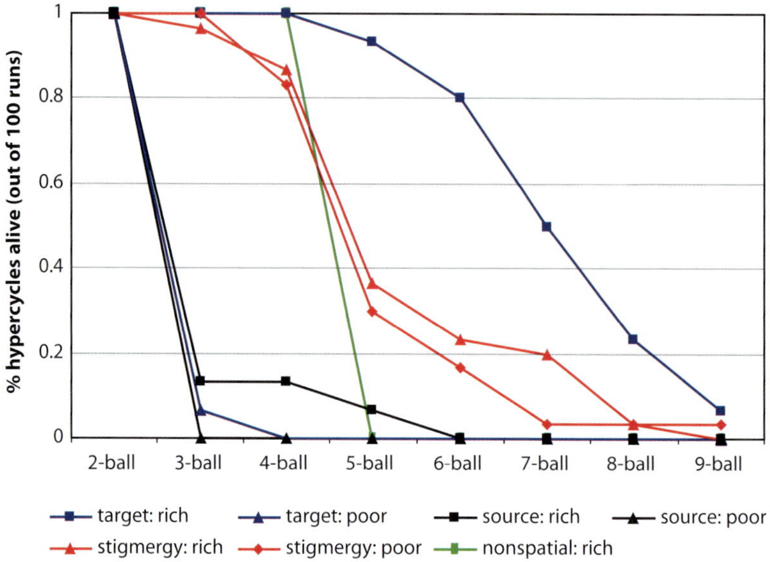

Figure 3.2 Survival of autocatalytic networks: hypercycle (i.e., SOLO H) chemistry.

the figure: (a) ellipses are surviving bins or firms; (b) numbers within the ellipses are surviving rules (a 51 in this figure stands for (5→1)); (c) lines are products being passed between firms and their rules; (d) solid lines are trades that participate in cycles; and (e) dotted lines are trades that do not participate in cycles (so-called parasites or free riders). The entire ensemble resembles a city of spatially contiguous firms, trading among each other through distributed production rules.[26]

Were one to observe on the computer screen the dynamics leading up to such equilibria, they would look like this: At first random rules pass around random products in all directions, like popcorn in a vat. Soon, however, where production-rule cycles randomly exist underneath the apparent chaos, clusters of more fervent production-cum-trading activity tend to congeal, with firms outside these clusters starting to die off. Gradually, a period of intercluster competition ensues, with the final outcome being either no surviving cluster or only a single surviving cluster. If any cluster survives, it is usually the largest cluster. The outcome of no survivor is due to dynamic instability in the underlying distributed technology network—such a system just did not reliably reproduce its component rules in the face of inevitable rule-component death. The outcome of no more than one surviving "cooperative" cluster is due to competitive exclusion—if production-network clusters do not reproduce better than their neighbors, those neighboring networks extract more input resources, gradually starving them out of existence. Competitive exclusion in this model ultimately is the selection consequence of all rules facing the same input environment/urn.

This dynamic is observed in both SOLO H and ALL variants of the model, with varying probabilities. The experimental questions to explore thus become: What conditions affect the likelihood of any autocatalytic network of production rules growing and surviving? And given survival, how are production network structures shaped by experimental conditions? We shall answer these questions first for the old SOLO H chemistry and then for the new chemistry ALL.

Figure 3.2 presents our results for SOLO H. These results reproduce, for longer run times,[27] the findings of Padgett, Lee and Collier (2003).

[26] Padgett (1997) interpreted pictures like these to be people in a workgroup or children in a playground. The principles of self-organization in our chemistry model are quite general, potentially applicable to many evolutionary scales from chemistry to ecology. We do not mean to imply that no important differences exist across scales, but in this line of modeling we choose to emphasize instead potentially universal principles common to life at any scale.

[27] Compare footnote 18 in Padgett, Lee, and Collier 2003 to footnote 25 in this chapter. We had faster server-style computers at our disposal this time, compared to the laptops in 2003.

Figure 3.2 presents on its y-axis our first-order dependent variable: long-term probability[28] of hypercycle survival. Figures 3.3 and 3.4, which we will discuss shortly, present comparable information for the ALL chemistry. All these present on their x-axes varying degrees of complexity in the simulated economies: simple 2-ball/product technologies, somewhat more complicated 3-product technologies, and so forth, up to our most complex 9-product rule set. Different lines within these graphs present the results of our various experimental manipulations: interaction topology, learning mode of reproduction, and input environment. As explained above, all these runs used the mindless random-search method of choosing inputs.

We shall unpack the findings in figure 3.2 one independent variable at a time.

The Effect of Spatial Topology

As Hofbauer and Sigmund (1988) have shown analytically, and as we have already mentioned, nonspatial hypercycles face a dynamic "complexity barrier" at the level of 5-elements and above. In the nonspatial or "liquid" topology of random interaction, where there are no firms, the volumes of the various reproducing skills undergo accelerating oscillations under a hypercycle regime with complex rule sets until eventually one skill is driven to zero, thereby breaking the reproductive loop and causing the overall hypercycle to "crash." This finding is reconfirmed in our simulations; hypercycle survival rates abruptly plummet from 100 to 0 percent in the nonspatial portion of all of our figures, as complexity passes the threshold from 4-skills to 5-skills.

In sharp contrast to this dynamic instability among 5+ skills, once spatial constraints on interaction are introduced—that is, once firms with delimited trading patterns are permitted—then higher complexity in skill sets becomes dynamically possible (albeit not 100 percent of the time). This finding is illustrated in figure 3.2: for complexity 5-skills and above, survival rates of spatial hypercycles can become superior to survival rates of nonspatial hypercycles. This statement is especially true for target reproduction operating under rich environments. But it is also true for "stigmergy"—that is, for source reproduction operating under endogenous environments (of either rich or poor initial configuration).[29] This statement is not true for either mode of reproduction operating under fixed poor environments; those provide too few nutrients for any but the simplest 2-product hypercycles to survive.

Another way of expressing these findings is this: Nonspatial "freedom of trade" of every skill with every other, with no firms to restrict and channel that trade, generates so much volatility in skill reproduction that high complexity becomes dynamically unsustainable. The opposite extreme—complete internalization of all skills within a single firm—eliminates entirely the trade that renews learning. Skills spatially dispersed through clusters of firms are necessary (but not sufficient) in our model for complex economic production networks to be sustainable. Simple economies (with four or fewer products) do not need firms or spatial clusters of firms to reproduce. But complicated economies (with five or more products) do. This is the chemistry reason for why spatially embodied firms exist in the first place—to break the complexity barrier.[30]

The mechanistic reason for this result is that physical space "breaks the symmetry" of homogeneous interaction and thereby allows heterogeneous "memory" of past interaction history to accrue within bins/firms. Through learning by doing, accretions of successes and failures in their past interaction become inscribed into the rule competencies of the two trading firms. The way this works is as follows: Successful transactions reproduce compatible skills that are located in neighboring firms. This sets up positive feedback between compatible-skilled neighbors: the more skills are activated, the more they reproduce; the more they reproduce, the more they are activated. The volume of skills in a firm at any given point in time thereby becomes the cumulative history of past interaction with its neighbors. Conversely, nonreproducing rules are "forgotten" because all skills are killed off randomly in the population. Rules not participating

[28] Each of the points in these graphs represents the average of 100 simulation runs.

[29] Stigmergy, as modeled by endogenous input urn, can be defined for either source or target reproduction. But in the case of target reproduction, an endogenous environment produces the same results as fixed-rich environments (see Padgett, Lee, and Collier 2003). In this chapter, therefore, "stigmergy" is confined to "stigmergy under source reproduction," where it makes a big difference.

[30] A colorful way of rephrasing this result is to ask: Can life exist in the gases of Jupiter? The hypercycle answer is yes, but only up to the complexity of four chemicals. For life more complex than this, cells or bodies are required.

in positive feedbacks with spatial neighbors thereby go extinct. The long-term success or failure of any given firm is the path-dependent consequence not only of that firm's own history but also of that firm's neighbors' histories.

None of this heterogeneous path-dependence would have occurred without physical space or without some social-network functional equivalent to space.[31] Spatial or social constraint on interaction breaks the symmetry of firms potentially trading with all other firms and allows localized skill in homogeneities to form. Positive feedback through continued trading then inscribes the memory of past interactive success into the structure of each co-adapting firm, thereby permitting the nonspatial complexity barrier to be breached.

A secondary mechanism behind the effectiveness of spatial clustering is chaining. The physical act of passing products around orchestrates sequences of learning. Not only do compatible neighbors generate positive feedbacks in their own growths but they also trigger other compatible neighbors. Once hypercyclic clusters begin to emerge, microfeedback loops are evoked and orchestrated more efficiently. Perhaps this is one evolutionary reason for why artifacts, either physical or symbolic, are helpful for humans learning in groups.[32] The mere act of passing around transformed products, even when purposeless, coordinates learning sequences of humans through chaining.

The Effect of Reproduction/Learning Mode

Embedding production and trading in physical (or social) space has a second non-obvious consequence: it induces an asymmetry between target and source reproduction.[33] Without bins/firms, there is no difference between "selfish" and "altruistic" because without bins/firms there are no phenotypic actors to begin with to be selfish or not.

In the production and nurture of spatial hypercycles, target reproduction is superior to source reproduction. This is shown in figure 3.2 by the fact that the survival plots of target reproduction are displaced to the right of the corresponding survival plots of source reproduction. In fixed poor environments, this difference is trivial because there almost everything dies. But in fixed rich environments, the difference is very dramatic. Rephrasing this finding at a different level of analysis, spatial hypercycles of whatever complexity are easier to grow when learning by firms is altruistic than when it is selfish.

As explained in Padgett 1997, the basic mechanism that produces this superiority is repair. Target reproduction combats dynamic instability in a way that source reproduction does not. The process of dynamic instability, which causes hypercycles to crash, is this: if one skill reproduces too rapidly, competition drives other skills to zero, thereby breaking the reproductive loop of skills upon which all depend. Spatial topology distributes this dynamic into overlapping series of neighborhoods, thereby inducing local heterogeneity, which may provide a partial buffer. But source reproduction, or selfish learning, does not really attack the basic dynamic instability itself. In source reproduction, an initial activated rule passes on its transformed product to a neighboring compatible rule, which causes the original activated rule to reproduce. Frequently activated rules thereby reproduce more frequently, like a cancer, often driving out of existence even compatible neighbors on whom they depend for their own survival. As we shall see in the next subsection, endogenous environments sometimes can ameliorate the negative effects of this uncontrolled growth, but that does not eliminate the underlying instability problem.

In sharp contrast, an initial activated rule in target reproduction passes on its transformed product to a neighboring compatible rule, thereby causing the recipient (not the sender) rule to reproduce. Here the more frequently the initial sender rule is activated, the more frequently the second recipient rule reproduces. This difference induces soothing homeostatic feedback: increased activation in the sender rule leads to increased reproduction in the recipient rule, which leads to increased probability of death (and hence activation next time) in the sender rule. In this way, high volumes of skills in firms reach in to low-volumes of skills in their compatible neighbors to build them back up. Threatening peaks and valleys of rule concentrations along loops in the hypercycle are smoothed, and hypercycles thereby repair themselves.

This simulates altruistic behavior, even though no skill or firm is trying to aid the public good. Target reproduction does not guarantee that a hypercycle will survive, but it does alleviate

[31] Cf. Cohen, Riolo, and Axelrod 2001.

[32] Cf. Hutchins 1995.

[33] Padgett, Lee, and Collier (2003, 871) have demonstrated that in nonspatial topology, target and source reproduction mathematically become identical processes.

directly through repair the dynamic instability problem that afflicts both the nonspatial and the spatial source-reproduction settings.

Padgett, Lee, and Collier (2003, 858) demonstrate analytically how this repair mechanism works in a special simplified case of the model.

The Effect of Input Environment

Figure 3.2 also points to the existence of a second repair mechanism, more relevant to source reproduction than to target reproduction. The label "stigmergy" in figure 3.2 and in all subsequent figures refers to the combination of endogenous input environment with source reproduction. Figure 3.2 demonstrates for SOLO H that while stigmergy never reaches the nirvana of target reproduction operating in a rich environment, the addition of endogenous environment to source is capable of regulating source reproduction out of its otherwise self-destructive behavior.

The mechanism behind this surprising result is not the direct repair of neighbor by neighbor, as in target reproduction, but is indirect repair via the intermediary of the input environment. As explained above, the basic problem is that source reproduction generates self-destructive ("cancerous") growth. The more skills are activated, the more they reproduce, the more they are activated, et cetera, until the neighbor upon whom that skill depends is destroyed. Endogenous environments do not eliminate this cancerous growth, but they help control it in the following way: The more a skill is activated, the more it consumes its own input from the environment and transforms it into something possibly useful for its compatible neighbor. If this product is not given directly to a compatible neighbor, then it is tossed back into the endogenous urn. The environment of compatible resources for low-volume skills thereby is enriched, while the environment of compatible resources for high-volume skills is starved.[34] This does not eliminate peaks and valleys around the hypercycle, as the more direct skills-to-skills intervention of target reproduction almost does—thus target reproduction remains superior to stigmergy. But the indirect skills-to-environment-to-skills method of regulation, induced by environmental endogeneity, can function to keep skill-volume peaks within bounds.

[34] This limiting of growth through nutrient starvation resembles the anti-angiogenesis type of cancer treatment.

This is like what social insects do.[35] Bees communicate directly, but ants coordinate their behavior with one another indirectly through modifying their environment (e.g., through pheromones) in ways that feed back into their own behaviors. This leads not to static equilibrium behavior but to flexible physical structures (like trails) that have the capacity to adapt, both to exogenous shocks and to what the ant colony itself does.

Further supporting this analogy is our observation that product outputs in our model do not converge to a fixed composition under endogenous environments. Peaks of modal product production stochastically change through time, like waves, even in hypercycle equilibrium. Such moving peaks are observed to be very sharp under selective search, whereas they are more gentle under random search.

No particular production output is favored over any other in the self-organizing model of this chapter. But were purposeful production to be introduced, the varying waves of production that hypercyclic production chains produce naturally in endogenous environments reveal that output could be adapted easily to changing circumstances in the short run. Hypercycles of production, in other words, generate flexible arrays of products, not just a single product. Conversely, monocultures of overspecialization are ruled out: In the long run, output *has* to shift around or else the natural repair mechanism of endogenous environment will be disabled.

The Effect of Search Intelligence

The main finding about degree of search intelligence by Padgett, Lee, and Collier (2003) was a negative one. Contrary to our expectations, selective search did not improve the chances of hypercycle emergence over random search. Equilibria were reached more speedily under selective than random search, but both the probabilities of survival and the structures of the final networks were the same. For this reason, we have chosen not to focus on this independent variable in this chapter.

Instead we just repeat our earlier conclusion about intelligence in search: "Search efficiency is not all it is sometimes cracked up to be. Search efficiency may be beneficial for a particular agent. But search efficiency through a given structure does not itself alter the evolution of

[35] See the models in Camazine et al. 2001.

that structure. More generally, intelligence is not necessary for complexity to emerge—a point we knew already from observing evolution. Rather the evolutionary sequence might have been the opposite: complexity is necessary for intelligence to emerge" (Padgett, Lee, and Collier 2003, 863).

RESULTS: EMERGENCE OF AUTOCATALYTIC NETWORKS IN ALL

Figures 3.3 and 3.4 present the survival probabilities for the ALL chemistry, comparable to those just presented in figure 3.2 for SOLO H. In general, the relative effects of our independent variables in ALL are reassuringly similar to the rank ordering observed in SOLO H, but the absolute probabilities are changed dramatically. It is much easier for *something* to survive in ALL than it is for specifically targeted hypercycles to emerge in SOLO H. While initially surprising to us, in hindsight there is not much of a puzzle in the higher absolute values. Even in high-n ALL chemistries, where the potential for complexity is great, what actually survives is often very simple. To take an extreme example

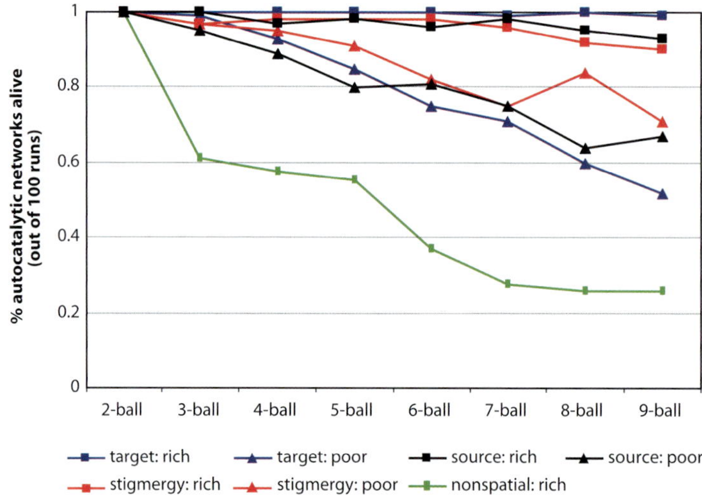

Figure 3.3 Survival of autocatalytic networks: ALL chemistry.

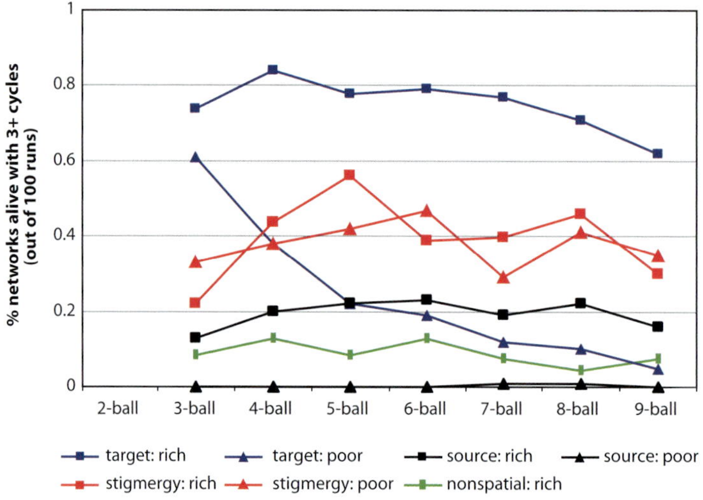

Figure 3.4 Survival of autocatalytic networks: ALL chemistry, 3+ cycles.

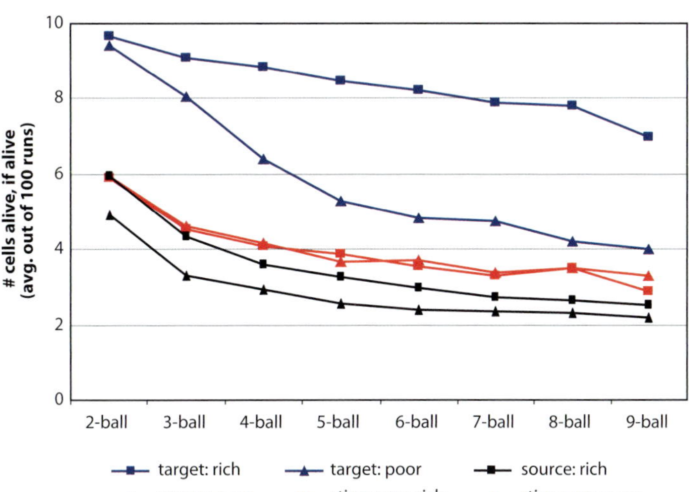

Figure 3.5 Population of cells: ALL chemistry.

for illustration, in a 9-product ALL chemistry, the equilibrium could turn out to be only the simpleton 2-product hypercycle: {(5→8), (8→5)}. Fortunately autocatalytic networks within ALL are not usually this boring, but if possible equilibria are unconstrained then the likelihood of finding *something* is high. The real question for the ALL chemistry, therefore, is not the likelihood of producing something but the likelihood of producing something complex and interesting.

In figure 3.4 we therefore re-present the same set of ALL-chemistry runs but this time measuring only the probability of finding and nurturing to equilibrium "complex" autocatalytic networks, where "complex" for this purpose means "cycles involving three or more distinct rules." Using this measure of survival, target reproduction in a fixed rich environment produces complex networks about 80 percent of the time, regardless of the number of balls/products. In contrast, source reproduction operating in a fixed rich environment produces complex networks about 20 percent of the time. Stigmergy, operating in either rich or poor initial environments, produces complex networks about 40 percent of the time. Source reproduction in poor environments never produces complex networks. Target reproduction in poor environments can do so, at declining rates (from 60 to 5 percent) as complexity increases. The symmetry-breaking and repair mechanisms lying beneath these comparative results have already been explained.[36]

What are the autocatalytic networks that emerge in the ALL chemistry like? Figures 3.5 through 3.8 present structural properties of the autocatalytic networks that survive in ALL, given that they survived in the first place.

Figure 3.5 plots the average number of surviving firms that comprise emergent autocatalytic networks in ALL. Target reproduction generates, on average, quite robust spatial clusters of eight or nine firms, regardless of chemistry complexity level, if the resource environment is rich. Even in poor resource environments, where the constraints on life are very severe, target reproduction can foster the emergence of small clusters of nine, declining to four firms. Source reproduction, in contrast, produces mainly boring two-firm dyads, although at low levels of

[36] We also ran a different procedure for evaluating survival rates above and beyond the lowest level of 2-product cycles. Namely, we implemented a modification of the ALL chemistry, which we label ALL (no reciprocity). This procedure kept the ALL rule set intact but did not reward with reproduction any reciprocal dyad in which firms just passed the same two products back and forth. Turning rubber into tires, and then tires back into rubber, happens all the time in real chemistry but seems rather pointless in human analogues. Somewhat surprising to us was the result that disabling low-level reciprocity did not much affect the ability of the ALL chemistry to generate more complicated trading patterns one way or the other. The presence or absence of "pointless" production behavior does not seem to matter for the emergence of more complex production behavior. Graphs proving these statements are available upon request.

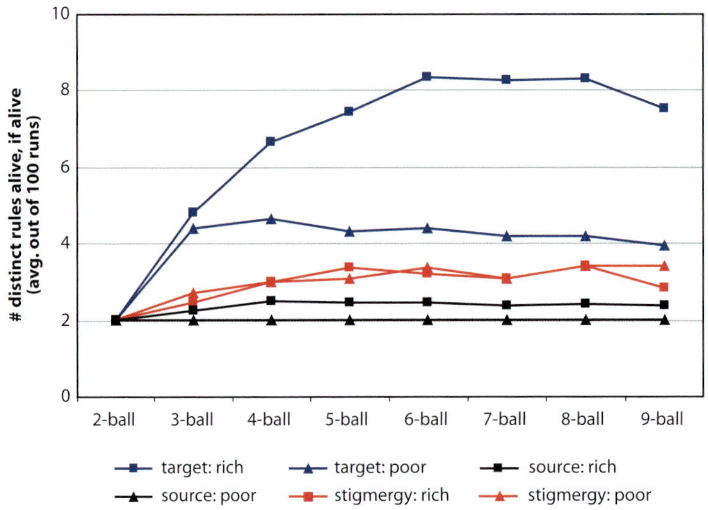

Figure 3.6 Rule complexity: ALL chemistry.

chemical complexity the number of surviving simple firms is higher. Stigmergy—which combines source reproduction with endogenous environment—helps raw source reproduction, as expected, but not as dramatically as it did in SOLO H. In the ALL rule set there are many more rules than in the SOLO H rule set; therefore, the benefits from the indirect repair in stigmergy are spread more thinly.

Figure 3.6 plots the number of distinct rules in ALL's surviving autocatalytic networks, which we call the "rule complexity" of the distributed production network. "Distinct" means unique types of rules in the entire population. These rules/skills are typically duplicated in different firms; hence the total volume of individual rules in the production networks (i.e., 200) is much larger than the number of distinct rules in the networks.

The rank ordering of experimental effects is similar for rule complexity as it was for population of firms, with target reproduction dominating this measure of complexity success, stigmergy second, and raw source reproduction last. Even more so than in SOLO H, target reproduction in ALL is the main route for generating complex autocatalytic networks. One interesting wrinkle emerges from examining the ratio of rule complexity to population. For target reproduction in both rich and poor environments, this ratio rises as the number of products increases. This means that more distinct rules on average become packed into surviving firms as the chemistry diversifies. That is, firms themselves become more complex: firms with more than one skill sit at the center of autocatalytic networks. This was also true in SOLO H chemistry.[37] Evolution therefore requires embodiment in two senses: physical space is necessary to break interaction symmetries, and phenotypic bins become more complex as the production networks that evolve through them advance. This second feature of complex phenotypes is true only for target, not source, reproduction.[38]

So far, our findings in the ALL chemistry differ quantitatively but not qualitatively from our earlier findings in the SOLO H chemistry. Scientific replications contribute to our confidence in the robustness of the findings, but they do not make for new news. The primary way in which the networks in ALL qualitatively extrapolate beyond the networks in SOLO H is presented in figure 3.7. ALL chemistry differs from SOLO H chemistry in being capable, through its richness, of generating multiple types of coexisting production networks or technologies, not just a single one. It does so to the extent measured in

[37] Padgett, Lee, and Collier 2003, 864–65.

[38] The advances in communication discussed in the next chapter will remove this restriction. For primitive Moore space communication, like we have here, however, this restriction stands. In this chapter, it is very hard for "selfish" production systems to get off the ground. More generally in this family of autocatalytic models, it is evolution in communication—in particular, the capacity to distinguish among alters—that will prove to be the key advance that permits "selfishness" to evolve.

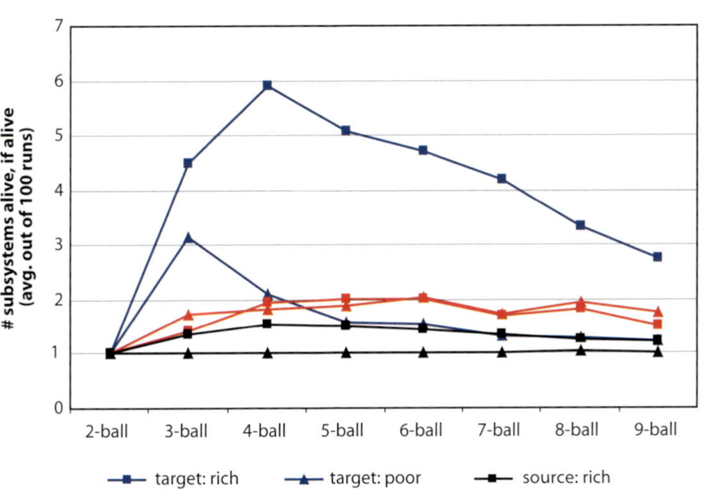

Figure 3.7 Subsystem complexity: ALL chemistry.

figure 3.7. SOLO H chemistry generated many overlapping cycles, as was apparent in figure 3.1, but these were always the same type of cycle, redundantly piled on top of each other like spaghetti. In ALL, by contrast, multiple *types* of networks are symbiotically intertwined with each other, dynamically supporting and regulating each other's reproduction. This is not only emergence but also differentiation into multiple subsystems.[39]

"Subsystems" are defined in figure 3.7 by distinct cycles. A distinct cycle is a cyclic chain of production rules in which no rule is repeated. Distinct cycles can and do share rule or even rule-sequence components, this being the meaning of "intertwined." Figure 3.7 reports the average number of subsystems or technologies, so defined, that existed in the surviving autocatalytic networks generated by the experiment indicated. Ours is the only experimental platform of which we are aware that spontaneously generates multiple types of networks.

The specific findings in figure 3.7 are these: Source reproduction rarely rises above its single type of network of minimal complexity. Stigmergy increases subsystem complexity on average to the coexistence of two types of production networks. Target reproduction in a poor environment also generates on average two subsystems. But target reproduction, when it operates in a rich resource environment, proliferates networks into subsystem-complexity levels of up to six distinct cycles! Obviously we are still far removed from the complexity of real organic chemistry, but at least our minimalist model offers some insight into how the rich combinatorics and diversity of living chemistries assemble themselves spontaneously for subsequent evolution to work on.

Why does the maximal subsystem complexity of six distinct production networks arise in the ALL chemistry of four products (twelve rules)? Not proof, but a clue, comes from the findings of Eigen (1971, 506) in the liquid context. He has shown that the rule-concentration dynamics for four products (four rules in SOLO H chemistry) are the most volatile possible without crashing. The specific numbers don't transpose because of the differences in both chemistry and space, but the suggestion is that there is an intermediate range of rule complexity whose concentration dynamics sweep out a wide range of rule-permutation exploration before crashing. Up to a point, volatility is good: many combinations can be tried and tested to see if they can fit. The point beyond which this is true is when volatility kills off the component rules themselves. In this specific model, an ALL chemistry of twelve rules, seven of which on average survive, seems to be capable of finding and sustaining the largest number of distinct technological networks. Richer chemistries allow an even larger number of rules on average to survive, but those do not self-organize into as high a topological complexity.

[39] In chapter 1, these subsystems were called "domains."

Table 3.1.
Distribution of Cycle Lengths (ALL chemistry)

Network Complexity: cycle success rates (out of 30 runs)

Target	any-cycle	2-cycle	3-cycle	4-cycle	5-cycle	6-cycle	7-cycle	8-cycle	9-cycle
2-ball	30	30							
3-ball	30	30	18	15		8			
4-ball	30	30	20	20	11	9	4		
5-ball	30	30	13	20	6	3	1		
6-ball	30	27	17	18	8	5	2		
7-ball	30	26	20	13	8	3		1	
8-ball	30	28	14	20	4	9	3	2	1
9-ball	30	28	10	15	2	1	1		

Network Complexity: cycle success rates (out of 30 runs

Source	any-cycle	2-cycle	3-cycle	4-cycle	5-cycle	6-cycle	7-cycle	8-cycle	9-cycle
2-ball	30	30							
3-ball	30	30	1	4					
4-ball	30	30		3					
5-ball	28	28		4					
6-ball	30	29	1	5					
7-ball	29	29		5					
8-ball	28	26	2	5					
9-ball	28	28		2					

Network Complexity: cycle success rates (out of 30 runs

Stigmergy	any-cycle	2-cycle	3-cycle	4-cycle	5-cycle	6-cycle	7-cycle	8-cycle	9-cycle
2-ball	30	30							
3-ball	30	30	2	8		1			
4-ball	26	26	1	10		1			
5-ball	29	29	7	10	1	1			
6-ball	23	23	6	7	1	2			
7-ball	26	22	11	5	1	2			
8-ball	24	23	7	5	1	3			
9-ball	19	18	4	3		1		1	

Note: All runs are based on Rich Environment and Random Search settings.

More fine-grained detail on the distinct cycles reported in figure 3.7 is provided in table 3.1. There "distinct cycles" are broken down by the length of the production-rule cycles. One can see that target reproduction generates not only more distinct cycles but also longer and more elaborate distinct cycles. Long and complex cycles build on top of and wend themselves through simpler cycles at their base.

Why is target reproduction the primary route to complex autocatalytic production networks in ALL? We have already provided one answer: repair. "Altruistic" neighbors in target reproduction, unlike "selfish" neighbors in source reproduction, directly reach in to reproduce low-volume rules threatened with extinction. But this repair answer applies equally to SOLO H and to ALL chemistries. The relative superiority of target reproduction, however, is even more pronounced in ALL than it was in the spatial hypercycle chemistry. Something about the more complex multiple-network context of ALL appears to boost the generic advantage of target's direct-repair mechanism and to dampen (without eliminating) the generic advantage of stigmergy's indirect-repair mechanism.

The reason for this extra boost is revealed in figure 3.8, which plots the volumes of "parasite rules" produced by our various experiments. Recall from our discussion of figure 3.1

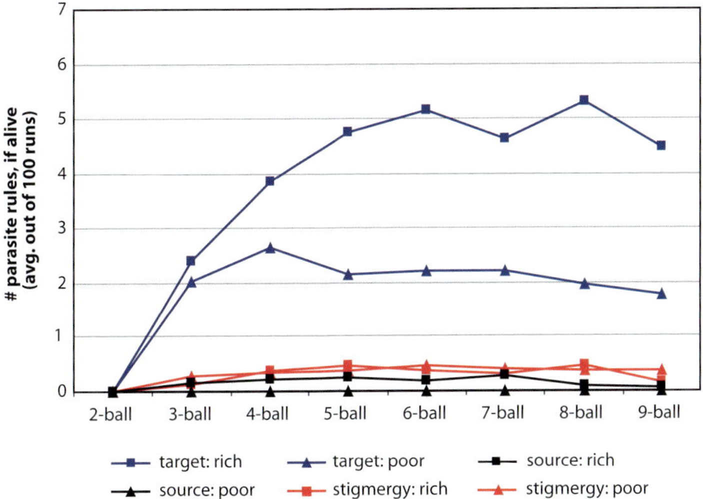

Figure 3.8 Free riding: ALL chemistry.

that "parasites" were defined as surviving rules in an autocatalytic network that do not themselves participate in reproductive cycles. These are free riders, in social science terminology, that live only by feeding on the (re)productive work of others. Figure 3.8 reveals parasites to be rampant in target reproduction and absent in all versions of source reproduction, including stigmergy. Source reproduction effectively eliminates parasitic free riders. In economics this is usually considered a good thing because efficiency is thereby improved. But in living chemistries, unlike in neoclassical markets or prisoners' dilemmas, aggressive weeding of free riders stops the emergence of all but the simplest forms of life.

An examination of visualizations of equilibrial ALL production networks, similar to the ones in figure 3.1, uncovered the reason why. While sometimes parasites in ALL shoot out into unproductive space, as they do in figure 3.1, other times parasites in ALL become the bridges for linking and symbiotically "coordinating" multiple networks. This is not the only mechanism for multiple-network coordination—shared components or multifunctionality is a second device for interlinking distinct cycles. With parasites as bridges, however, entire cycles reach in to neighboring cycles to support them in the face of weakness. One cycle's relative growth through competition bleeds into propping up its competitor, thereby enriching the multiple-cycle ensemble as a whole. The basic repair principle in target reproduction scales up, in other words, from neighbors reaching in to help each other to entire neighborhoods reaching in to help each other, sort of like international trade. There is no collective-good intentionality in this, of course. Self-repairs, both dyadic and intercyclic, are unintentional by-products of target reproduction.

When viewed dynamically, the coordination of multiple networks and the tolerance of parasites thus are causally connected. Today's parasite, from the perspective of production, might evolve into tomorrow's regulatory superstructure, not through intent and certainly not through foresight but because competitive subsystems tolerate each other better through them. In hindsight, one might have preferred to hold on to the parasites that later turned out to be regulators and to eliminate those that never did anything useful. But evolution has no hindsight, there being no end point to be privileged. Like it or not, the road to living complexity is littered with free riders. Certainly too many free riders can kill you, especially in harsh competition. But one polices parasites at the cost of restricting evolvability.[40]

Multifunctionality is when "parasites" (this time so-to-speak) themselves link up into higher-order cycles of greater length than the subsystems they span (see table 3.1). Overlapping distinct cycles have a "conflict of interest." On the one hand, they are competing for the same input

[40] Cf. March 1982, 1991.

resources, just like disjoint cycles. On the other hand, they share components whose growth or decline affects the survivability of both. Target versus source reproduction affects the relative balance of these two cross-pressures, with target tipping the balance toward multifunctional sharing of components, as well as toward parasite bridges. Symbiotic solutions for competitive multiple-network coexistence are not inevitably found, but more time is granted for groping toward solutions. Long cycles essentially are the epiphenomena of this chaining of shorter cycles via shared components. But the fact that these epiphenomena are themselves cycles gives a little boost to the shared components and hence to the sustainability of multiple networks in the autocatalytic system as a whole.

SUMMARY AND DISCUSSION

Even within our chemical perspective, this chapter has not fully addressed the issue of the coevolution of technology and industry because the evolution of products has not been modeled explicitly. That is the next step. What this chapter has done, however, is establish four principles of social organization that provide sufficient foundations for the unconscious evolution of technological complexity: structured topology, altruistic learning, stigmergy, and multiple networks.

1. Unstructured interaction topologies are not conducive to the emergence of complex technologies. Without help through embodiment, long sequences of skills cannot dynamically regulate their own stable reproduction. "Structured topology" does not have to mean spatial, as it does here.[41] But constraints on interaction are necessary, first, in order to break the symmetry of full mixing and induce localized heterogeneity, and second, in order to allow positive reproductive feedback to turn that raw heterogeneity into path-dependent memory of past successes. This is the chemistry answer to why firms exist:[42] dynamic barriers of technological complexity can be transcended once global is transformed into the concatenation of locals.

   Classic spatial clusters receive the benefits of physical space naturally. In an era of globalization, interconnected firms may not be so fortunate. What our model implies is that perfect (i.e., random) fluidity or liquidity induces instability in the reproduction of rules that destroys complex emergence beyond a simple technology. If physical space no longer provides enough stabilizing constraint on interaction, some social substitute needs to be found for technological progress to remain possible.
2. The potential benefits of localized embodiment are more easily reaped through altruistic learning than through selfish learning. When recipients, not initiators, of transactions reap the reproductive rewards, complex technologies are more readily nurtured because they repair themselves. Free riding happens, but that does not threaten system stability. More important than policing free riders is enriching learning feedbacks among core actors, on whom parasites can feed if life is strong enough.

   This conclusion is consistent with anthropological emphases on gift giving in primitive economies.[43] It is also consistent with sociological observations about the persistence of generous behavior in modern economies.[44] Ours may not be the only explanation of generosity. But repair—both between dyads and between cycles—is one evolutionary reason for the natural selection of altruism in competitive economies of all sorts. Altruistic learning stabilizes the reproduction of distributed technological skills, on which all depend.[45]
3. When altruistic learning is not present for whatever reason, then stigmergy—the endogenous construction of resource environments—is second best.

[41] Cf. Cohen, Riolo, and Axelrod 2001.

[42] Padgett discusses why the traditional explanations for the firm given in neoclassical economics—namely, transaction-cost economics and principal-agent theory—are inadequate from a biological perspective: "Such a transposition of 'the firm' down into a series of dyadic negotiations overlooks the institutionalized autonomy of all stable organizations. In organisms, social or biological, rules of action and patterns of interaction persist and reproduce even in the face of constant turnover in component parts, be these cells, molecules, principals, or agents. In the constant flow of people through organizations, the collectivity typically is not renegotiated anew. Rather, within constraints, component parts are transformed and molded into the ongoing flow of action" (1997, 199–200).

[43] Mauss [1899] 1967; Sahlins 1972.

[44] Macauley 1963; Granovetter 1985; Uzzi 1996; Herrigel 1996; Padgett and McLean 2011.

[45] This may come as news to some rational choice theorists, but it will not come as a surprise to parents and teachers.

Entomologists[46] have shown that stigmergy flexibly can coordinate sophisticated collective behavior among myopic social insects. We have shown that stigmergy also can regulate the cancerous growth of selfish learners, keeping chains of distributed skills alive. When rule chemistries are restricted, as in SOLO H, stigmergy may be enough to permit the evolution of complexity. As rule chemistries become richer, as in ALL, stigmergy still helps but may be insufficient by itself because the benefits of indirect repair become distributed too widely.[47]

Adams (1966, 1996) has long argued that cities are crucial to the history of technology. His exemplar case is Mesopotamia, where spatial feedbacks between settlements and rivers guided the joint emergence of urban concentration, irrigation technology, and the shapes of the rivers themselves. Of course our model is far too minimalist for real history, but it may illustrate one reason why the spatial reorganization of land into cities and the development of complex technologies proceeded hand in hand. Technology creates cities, as we all know; less obviously, the spatial products of technology channel and orchestrate the social forces that produce it.

4. In the ALL chemistry, where many simultaneous production networks become possible, parasites help the emergence and self-regulation of multiple networks through constructing synergistic bridges among these subsystems or "domains." Parasites construct "hypercycles on top of hypercycles" that can stabilize both the lower-order and higher-order production networks through inducing the multifunctional sharing of components. In disarticulated networks, production networks in this model are harshly competitive; they cannot coexist. But in functionally interconnected and spatially overlapping networks, parasites and multifunctionality become bridging mechanisms through which emergent economies dynamically grope their way through controlled volatility toward higher-order symbiosis among differentiated technologies.

[46] See, for example, Bonabeau, Dorigo, and Theraulaz 1999; Camazine et al. 2001.

[47] Spatial stigmergy in the next chapter, where resources are distributed heterogeneously over space, rather than homogeneously in urns, will overcome this problem.

In this chapter we have developed a few simple tools, imported from chemistry, that enable us to investigate systematically the co-evolution of distributed technology and social organization. Extreme assumptions about the absence of consciousness are imposed by our specification. The payoff of such extreme simplification is the discovery of four social-organizational principles enabling technological evolution. How robust such principles are to alternate specifications remains an important issue to explore in the future. Steps in this direction are taken in the next chapter. Regardless of the answer to that question, however, we hope at a minimum to have demonstrated that complex cognition is not necessary for the emergence and functioning of complex economies, just as March and Simon (1958) argued long ago.[48]

REFERENCES

Adams, Robert McCormick. 1966. *The Evolution of Urban Society: Early Mesopotamia and Prehispanic Mexico*. Chicago: Aldine.

———. 1996. *Paths of Fire: An Anthropologist's Inquiry into Western Technology*, Princeton: Princeton University Press.

Boerlijst, M. C., and P. Hogeweg. 1991. "Spiral Wave Structures in Pre-Biotic Evolution: Hypercycles Stable against Parasites." *Physica B* 48:17–28.

Bonabeau, Eric, Marco Dorigo, and Guy Theraulaz. 1999. *Swarm Intelligence: From Natural to Artificial Systems*. Oxford: Oxford University Press.

Camazine, Scott, Jean-Louis Deneubourg, Nigel R. Franks, James Sneyd, Guy Theraulaz, and Eric Bonabeau. 2001. *Self-Organization in Biological Systems*. Princeton: Princeton University Press.

Cohen, Michael D., Rick L. Riolo, and Robert Axelrod. 2001. "The Role of Social Structure in the Maintenance of Cooperative Regimes." *Rationality and Society* 13:5–32.

Coriat, Benjamin, and Giovanni Dosi. 1998. "Learning How to Govern and Learning How to Solve Problems: On the Co-evolution of Competencies, Conflicts and Organizational Routines." In A. Chandler, P. Hagstrom, and O. Solvell, eds., *The Dynamic Firm: The Role of Technology, Strategy, Organization and Regime*. Oxford: Oxford University Press.

Dosi, Giovanni, Renato Giannetti, and Pier Angelo Toninelli. 1992. *Technology and Enterprise in a Historical Perspective*. Oxford: Clarendon Press.

[48] March and Simon went beyond our point to also argue that social structures enable human cognition by mapping the world down to levels that we can comprehend.

Dosi, Giovanni, Richard Nelson, and Sidney Winter. 2000. *The Nature and Dynamics of Organizational Capabilities*. Oxford: Oxford University Press.

Eigen, Manfred. 1971. "Self-Organization of Matter and the Evolution of Biological Macromolecules." *Naturwissenschaften* 58:465–523.

Eigen, Manfred, and Peter Schuster. 1979. *The Hypercycle: A Principle of Natural Self-Organization*. New York: Springer-Verlag.

Elster, Jon. 1983. *Sour Grapes: Studies in the Subversion of Rationality*. Cambridge: Cambridge University Press.

Fontana, Walter F. 2005. "The Topology of the Possible." In A. Wimmer and R. Kossler, eds., *Understanding Change: Models, Methodologies and Metaphors*. New York: Palgrave Macmillan.

Fontana, Walter F., and Leo W. Buss. 1994. "The Arrival of the Fittest: Toward a Theory of Biological Organization." *Bulletin of Mathematical Biology* 56: 1–64.

Granovetter, Mark. 1985. "Economic Action and Social Structure: The Problem of Embeddedness." *American Journal of Sociology* 91:481–510.

Herrigel, Gary. 1996. *Industrial Constructions: The Sources of German Industrial Power*. Cambridge: Cambridge University Press.

Hofbauer, Josef, and Karl Sigmund. 1988. *Dynamical Systems and the Theory of Evolution*. Cambridge: Cambridge University Press.

Hughes, Thomas P. 1983. *Networks of Power: Electrification in Western Society, 1880–1930*. Baltimore: Johns Hopkins University Press.

———. 1987. "The Evolution of Large Technological Systems." In Wiebe Bijker, Thomas Hughes, and Trevor Pinch, eds., *The Social Construction of Technological Systems*. Cambridge, MA: MIT Press.

Hutchins, Edwin. 1995. *Cognition in the Wild*. Cambridge, MA: MIT Press.

Jain, Sanjay, and Sandeep Krishna. 1998. "Autocatalytic Sets and the Growth of Complexity in an Evolutionary Model." *Physical Review Letters* 81: 5684–87.

Kauffman, Stuart A. 1986. "Autocatalytic Sets of Proteins." *Journal of Theoretical Biology* 119:1–24.

———. 1993. *The Origins of Order: Self-Organization and Selection in Evolution*. New York: Oxford University Press.

Macauley, Stuart. 1963. "Non-Contractual Relations in Business: A Preliminary Study." *American Sociological Review* 28:55–67.

Malerba, Franco, and Luigi Orsinigo. 1993. "Technological Regimes and Firm Behavior." *Industrial and Corporate Change* 2:45–71.

March, James G. 1982. "The Technology of Foolishness." In J. G. March and J. P. Olsen, eds., *Ambiguity and Choice in Organizations*. Universitetsforlaget: Bergen, Norway.

———. 1991. "Exploration and Exploitation in Organizational Learning." *Organization Science* 2:71–87.

March, James G., and Herbert A. Simon. 1958. *Organizations*. Wiley: New York.

Maturana, Humberto, and Francisco Varela. 1980. "Autopoiesis: The Organization of the Living." In *Autopoiesis and Cognition*. Dordrecht, Holland: D. Reidel.

Mauss, Marcel [1899] 1967. *The Gift: Forms and Functions of Exchange in Archaic Societies*. New York: Norton.

May, Robert M. 1974. *Stability and Complexity in Model Ecosystems*. Princeton: Princeton University Press.

McKelvey, Maureen. 1997. "Co-evolution in Commercial Genetic Engineering." *Industrial and Corporate Change* 6:503–32.

Murman, J. Peter. 2003. *Knowledge and Competitive Advantage: The Co-evolution of Firms, Technology and National Institutions*. Cambridge: Cambridge University Press.

Nelson, Richard R. 1994. "The Co-evolution of Technology, Industrial Structure, and Supporting Institutions." *Industrial and Corporate Change* 3: 47–64.

———. 1995. "Recent Evolutionary Theorizing about Economic Change." *Journal of Economic Literature* 33:48–90.

Nelson, Richard R., and Sidney G. Winter. 1982. *An Evolutionary Theory of Economic Change*. Cambridge, MA: Belknap Press of Harvard University Press.

Padgett, John F. 1986. "Rationally Inaccessible Rationality." *Contemporary Sociology* 15:26–28.

———. 1992. "Learning from (and about) March." *Contemporary Sociology* 21:744–49.

———. 1997. "The Emergence of Simple Ecologies of Skill: A Hypercycle Approach to Economic Organization." In W. Brian Arthur, Steven N. Durlauf, and David A. Lane, eds., *The Economy as an Evolving Complex System II*. Reading, MA: Addison-Wesley.

Padgett, John F., and Paul D. McLean. 2006. "Organizational Invention and Elite Transformation: The Birth of the Partnership System in Renaissance Florence." *American Journal of Sociology* 111: 1463–1568.

———. 2011. "Economic Credit in Renaissance Florence." *Journal of Modern History* 83: 1-47.

Padgett, John F., Lee, Doowan, and Nick Collier. 2003. "Economic Production as Chemistry." *Industrial and Corporate Change* 12(4): 843–77.

Powell, Walter W. 1996. "Inter-organizational Collaboration in the Biotechnology Industry." *Journal of Institutional and Theoretical Economics* 152: 197–215.

Prigogine, Ilya, and Paul Glansdorff. 1971. *Thermodynamic Theory of Structure: Stability and Fluctuations*. New York: Wiley.

Rosenkopf, Lori, and Michael L. Tushman. 1998. "The Co-evolution of Community Networks and Technology: Lessons from the Flight Simulation Industry." *Industrial and Corporate Change* 7:311–46.

Sahlins, Marshall. 1972. *Stone Age Economics*. New York: Aldine.

Stadler, Barbel M. R., and Peter F. Stadler. 2002. "Molecular Replicator Dynamics." Santa Fe Institute working paper 02-09-049.

Uzzi, Brian. 1997. "The Sources and Consequences of Embeddedness for the Economic Performance of Organizations." *American Sociological Review* 42: 35–67.

Wagner, Andreas. 2005. *Robustness and Evolvability in Living Systems*. Princeton: Princeton University Press.

Wagner, Gunter, and Lee Altenberg. 1996. "Complex Adaptations and the Evolution of Evolvability." *Evolution* 50:967–76.

Warglien, Massimo. 1995. "Hierarchical Selection and Organizational Adaptation." *Industrial and Corporate Change* 4:161–86.

4

From Chemical to Social Networks

John F. Padgett

The goal of this chapter is to sketch the quasi-evolutionary stages necessary to move step-by-step from the chemical autocatalysis (a.k.a. "life") of the last chapter to a social autocatalysis that bears at least minimal resemblance to human interaction. I do not regard "complexity" or even "intelligence" as the crucial feature distinguishing chemical from social autocatalysis for the simple reason that the complexity and intelligence of biochemical systems are overwhelming to anyone who has looked into them. I am committed in this section of the book to understanding how the social builds out of and on top of, rather than displaces, the biochemical foundations of complexity and life. The key difference I see between chemical and social is language, with all that that implies. Biochemical systems also communicate, so extending my simple hypercyclic autocatalysis models of chemical production to include equally simple models of cellular communication is the central task of this chapter. "Chemical" and "social" throughout this chapter are labels used to distinguish "production autocatalysis" from "communication or linguistic autocatalysis," rather than to distinguish literal chemical systems from literal human systems, because it is not always the case that human systems are more complex than chemical ones, even on the dimension of communication.

As in the previous chapter, I continue to proceed self-consciously in the spirit of minimalism in order to keep the focus on simple mechanisms of learning, adaptation, and reproduction. I do not want to become overwhelmed by the complexity of the outcomes created through concatenating these simple mechanisms. This minimalist research strategy means that these are only toy models. The bulk of this book is devoted not to deductive models but to the inductive discovery of empirically real network mechanisms of organizational and market genesis. I feel, however, that neither induction nor deduction has a monopoly on the discovery of mechanisms.[1] Good ideas can be found in a variety of ways. Regardless of research style, the goal in this volume is the always same: to uncover network mechanisms of organizational and market genesis, in other words, to find out how network novelty emerges and self-organizes.

Two distinct extensions to the autocatalytic production model of the last chapter are outlined in this chapter. The first extension is to what might be called cross-sectional communication. This is the development of cell-to-cell communication capacity through tokens or symbols of products. Not only are products exchanged among cells, but tokens or symbols of those products are exchanged as well. Symbol passing, I show, enables endogenous learning—namely, the capacity for cells to identify and interact selectively with each other through addresses. These focused relations of exchange were labeled "relational ties" in chapter 1. Adding further the capacity of cells to transform symbols leads to emergent language: namely, to a network of symbols that are transformed into other symbols.[2]

The core evolutionary problem to which cross-sectional communication responds, I will

[1] If forced to choose, however, I would place more of my bet on the inductive approach.

[2] This definition of language as an autocatalytic network of transformed symbols parallels the last chapter's definition of technology as an autocatalytic network of transformed products.

argue, is adaptation to heterogeneous and fluctuating distributions of resources ("food") in the environment. Symbolic communication—and the selective interaction that follows from this—enables flexible reconfiguration of production networks to keep the autocatalytic system reproductively alive in the face of environmental perturbation. Species can adapt to environmental volatility in one of two ways: (a) organisms/cells can move to catch spatially fixed, even if temporally fluctuating, resources; or (b) organisms/cells can remain stationary, moving and passing fluctuating resources around among themselves. In terms of movement, these inverse approaches are equivalent, as in special relativity. But in terms of evolution, I argue that the second approach—characteristic of both human and biochemical cellular systems—induces the more refined communication system, which empowers further evolution.

The second extension is to what might be called longitudinal communication. This is the communication or transfer not of product symbols among cells but of action rules among cells. If the recipient cell involved in the diffusion already exists, this rule transfer is like teaching. If the recipient cell did not exist before this transfer brought it to life, this rule transfer is like cell birth or inheritance. Either way, teaching/inheritance transfers of rules among cells were labeled "constitutive ties" in chapter 1.

The evolutionary problem to which constitutive ties respond, I argue, is cell death. Constitutive ties can emerge without product symbols: this second extension does not require cross-sectional communication to operate. But it does require a communicative capacity to recognize and remember parentage—specifically the cellular addresses ("names" if symbolized) of parents. The simplest longitudinal communication requires identification and memory of only one generation deep; more sophisticated longitudinal communication is the identification and memory of multiple generations. Addressing parentage induces compounded kinship relations among cells, which are the traces in cell memories of transmissions of rules among living and dead cells. Biography and kinship emerge from the concatenated cell memories of parentage in the face of cell death.

I develop these two extensions—to cross-sectional communication ("relational ties") and to longitudinal communication ("constitutive ties")—one section at a time. The details of these extensions derive from internal autocatalytic logic, but their inspiration derives from Tomasello (2008) for the first type of communication and from Chapais (2008) for the second type of communication. Their impressive books—on the evolution of human language and on the evolution of human kinship, respectively—derive their persuasiveness from their strong empirical groundings in primate research. In a penultimate third section, I put these two modes of communication together, showing how categorization and collective self-consciousness through names emerge from their conjuncture.

Semantically, the toy models of communication autocatalysis in this chapter—like the models of production autocatalysis in the last chapter—can be interpreted on either of two levels of application. Cells can be interpreted either as people or as organizations. If cells are interpreted as people, then rules are skills and transferring rules between cells means teaching. At the end of this chapter, cells as people will be aggregated into families, my model representation of the first emergent formal organizations. If cells are interpreted already as organizations, then rules are people and transferring rules between cells means interfirm mobility and careers. Aggregating cells interpreted as organizations means emergent industries, which are families of rule or skill (i.e., technological) descent in my model representation. For the most part in this chapter, I adopt the semantic stance of interpreting cells as people and rules as skills. Occasionally I switch to interpreting cells as organizations and rules as people, just to remind the reader of the communication models' two potential levels of application.

I. CROSS-SECTIONAL COMMUNICATION THROUGH SYMBOLS

Simple language emerges in this model in three steps:

(a) Endogenous learning within the spatial context of the previous chapter

- This is enabled through adding distribution rules.

(b) Long-distance exchange, via passing tokens or symbols

- This is enabled through adding communication rules.

(c) Symbol transformation

- This is enabled through adding language rules.

The adaptation problem for these methods of communication to solve, as already mentioned, is heterogeneous and fluctuating resource environments. To model this, change the assumption in the previous chapter of a single input urn, homogeneously accessible to all cells, to a new assumption of multiple (10 × 10 = 100) heterogeneous input urns, one accessible for each spatially located cell. To be consistent, likewise change the assumption of a single homogenous output urn to a spatially distributed set of (10 × 10 = 100) heterogeneous output urns, one accessible for each cell. Cells "looking for action" at the beginning of production chains draw randomly from their own input urn and then do various things depending upon what they find. At the tail ends of production chains, cells always deposit products that they cannot transform into their own output urn. This model setup parallels that of connectionist neural nets: a vector of inputs is drawn in, processed iteratively through a transformation network, and then deposited into a vector of outputs. This analogy to neural nets suggests that social communication networks might be usefully perceived from afar as one type of computational brain.

With this spatial allocation of input urns to cells, any environmental pattern of spatial heterogeneity and temporal fluctuation of interest to the researcher can be modeled. The parallel to last chapter's homogeneous poor environment (only one input ball in the input urn) would be this chapter's heterogeneous poor environments (only one input ball in each input urn but different balls in different urns). The parallel to last chapter's homogeneous rich environment (all input balls present in the input urn) would be this chapter's heterogeneous rich environments (all input balls potentially present in all input urns but in different probabilities). The parallel to last chapter's stigmergy environment (draw input ball from homogeneous output urn) would be each cell drawing inputs from its own output urn.[3] Temporal fluctuations can be imposed on this input-urn spatial array by any method desired, including switching around the spatial assignments of input urns to cells. Through these means, all the models developed in this chapter can be subjected to various forms of environmental abuse. Of particular interest are mismatches between input-urn products and cellular production-rule capacities and whether the system can cope.

Ia. Spatial Endogenous Learning

The first, rather limited, flexibility that can be built into the previous chapter's spatial production model is not to change the topologies of those autocatalytic production networks but instead simply to modify and focus the product flows through those existing networks in response to changing experience. "Endogenous learning" is my term for modifying the cellular destinations of products, through address registries.

To model this idea, first let me re-represent last chapter's spatially bound cell by making explicit the Moore neighbor destinations to be found there. Before I represented a production rule, with the Moore neighbor destination hardwired, this way:

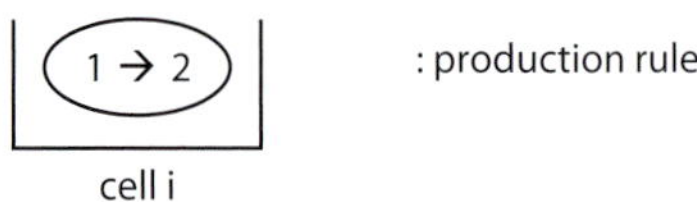

Now let me make explicit what was implicit (because hardwired) before.

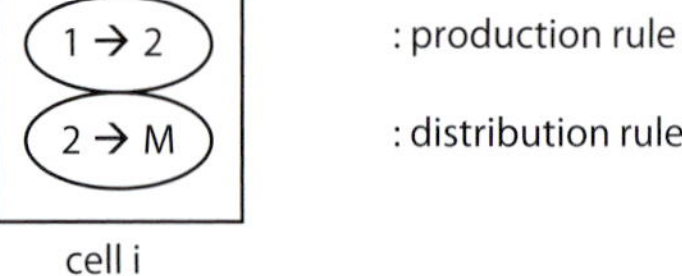

In words, the production rule means "transform input product 1 into output product 2." The distribution rule means "send product 2 to M," where M stands for "a Moore neighbor" (one-eighth probability to each of those neighbors). Together these mean "transform 1 into 2 and send it randomly to one of the eight Moore neighbors." There is nothing new here, other than making explicit that which was previously implicit.[4]

Making distribution rules explicit opens the door to learning about good versus bad

[3] Since by definition that draw is useless to the cell, there must be some method of passing that "worthless" draw on to someone else who can use it for this heterogeneous stigmergy option to go anywhere.

[4] Of course it was explicit in the programming code itself.

destinations—that is, destinations j that can use the output from cell i as inputs into their own production rules (thereby completing a "successful transaction") versus destinations k that possess no production rule that can transform cell i's delivered output. All that is necessary for endogenous learning of good destinations is to add memory into the distribution rule in order to register the addresses of "successful transaction" deliveries. I use the symbol □ to denote a blank space, waiting to be filled:

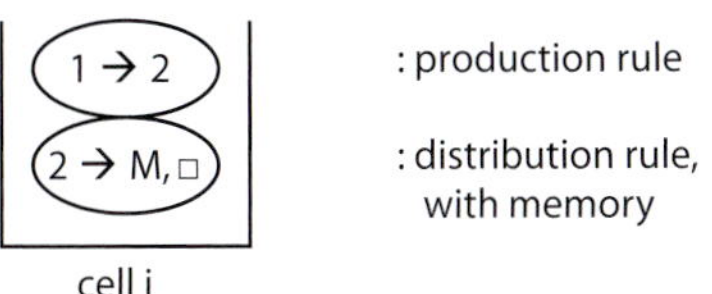

With this memory capability added, endogenous learning can work like this:

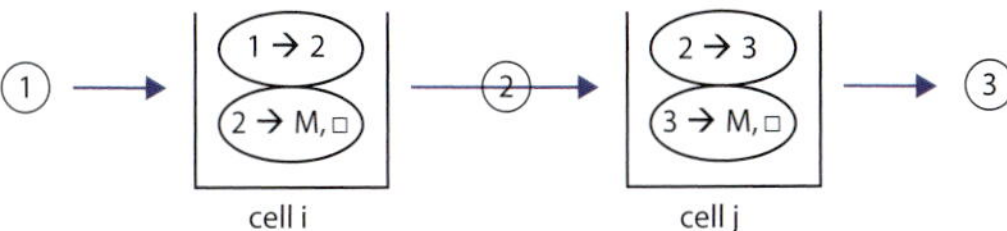

making a "successful transation" that is recorded as:

Of course one or the other of these production rules is also reproduced, depending on whether source reproduction (cell i's rule reproduces) or target reproduction (cell j's rule reproduces) is switched on.[5] The endogenous-learning point here, however, is that address j is inserted into cell i's distribution rule, registering the fact that cell i knows that cell j successfully transformed what was passed to him by i. I assume for Moore neighbors like i and j that cell i's observation of cell j's success is unproblematic because they are physically contiguous. Cell i can "see" or "feel" what neighbor cell j did. This observational transparency breaks down when cells i and j are not spatial neighbors.

Behaviorally the implication of having the address j in cell i's distribution-rule memory is that the next time that cell i produces a 2, it will send it with 50 percent probability to M and with 50 percent probability to j.[6] Transactional success, in other words, increases the chances of returning to successful destinations in the future. This is interactional learning—a "relational tie" in the terminology of chapter 1.[7] More successful experiences lead to ever greater probability of focusing on productive, not just random, destinations.

Positive experiences cannot be registered forever, for memory registers will explode. Therefore I impose an experimentally manipulable "maximum memory size" for distribution and communication rules. Think "ten" for illustrative discussion: in addition to the hardwired M, only nine additional addresses can be stored or remembered in distribution or other rules. If new addresses keep coming in, old ones eventually are thrown out or forgotten in order of their age. Because of this memory constraint, recent experiences of success are remembered and old ones are forgotten.[8]

The adaptive consequence of implementing endogenous learning within spatial interaction constraints will be to permit the focusing and refocusing of volumes of flow within existing

[5] "Reproduction of production rule" in this endogenous-learning context means "reproduction of the production rule, along with its attached distribution rule." The original distribution rule is reproduced, plus or minus any addresses learned by the parent. If the distribution rule is reproduced including learned addresses, that is Lamarckian reproduction. If it is reproduced without learned addresses, that is Darwinian reproduction. In the latter case, the new empty-register base rule of the offspring can later learn its own addresses, through its own experiences.

[6] "Sending to M," once again, means one-eighth probability sending to any of the eight Moore neighbors of cell i. If there were more than one address in memory, destinations would be chosen proportionately. For example, if the distribution registry contained M, j and k, then there would be a 33 percent chance of sending the next indicated output to M, 33 percent chance of sending to j, and 33 percent chance of sending to k. For another example, if distribution registry contained M, j, and a second j (due to two positive experiences), then there would be a 33 percent of sending to M and 67 percent chance of sending to j.

[7] Indeed, sending to spatial M in memory could be considered "transactional" or random exchange, while sending to cell j in memory could be considered "relational" or focused exchange.

[8] It occurred to me to model addresses like I do production-rule reproduction—namely, if one address is added, another random one is killed off elsewhere in the system. However, a common distinction drawn between physical reality and information is that the physical reality is constrained by laws of conservation of matter and energy, whereas information can expand without limit. Thus I chose the cell-level memory-capacity constraint in the text, which imposes weak selection pressure but not the harsher selection regime of fixed population size.

spatial autocatalytic networks. This can cope with modest and incremental environmental fluctuations, which do not extend spatially much beyond the site of the autocatalytic network itself. This degree of adaptive flexibility is limited at best.

Ib. Long-Distance Endogenous Learning through Symbols

Spatial contiguity was powerful in the elementary production context of the last chapter because it focused interaction and enabled "memory"—not in the explicit sense modeled here but in the implicit sense of building up compatible rules next to each other through successful interaction and reproduction. Conversely, nonspatial or random interactive topologies did not concentrate interaction and "memory" enough to produce living systems beyond a complexity level of four products.[9] With endogenous learning, however, it is possible to find a different method for focusing interaction and memory—namely, through explicit memory in address registers. This can substitute for the implicit memory that spatial contiguity had provided. Endogenous relational ties, in other words, can construct their own "social space," supplementing (and perhaps eventually transcending) physical Moore space.

For social space to emerge, the barrier of long distance in physical space needs to be overcome. Without physical contiguity, non-neighboring cells cannot discover whether their (perhaps unknown) partner successfully processed the output sent to them. For rule reproduction and address registry updating to occur, sending cells need some sort of a feedback signal from their partner to tell them the result of their shipment. Such feedback signals in my models are the origins of symbols. They emerge first to transcend physical space—think of tokens or written words that can carry far over physical space—but once emergent these signal tokens or "words" can be adapted to other purposes. Oral words carry over short physical spaces. In this model that is M, not R.[10]

Feedback signals to transcend physical space can be modeled through enabling communication rules in cells to pass tokens or symbols:

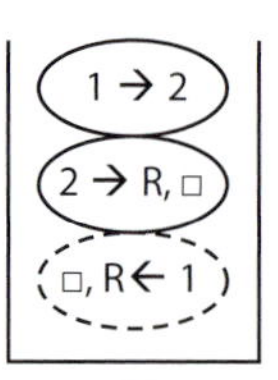

: production rule

: distribution rule

: communication rule

I use the notation of solid circles or ellipses to refer to physical products and dotted circles or ellipses to refer to tokens or symbols. The symbol "R" stands for Random destination, similar to the "M" in the previous section, which stood for Moore neighborhood destination. (Once symbols are enabled, a spatial M or a nonspatial R in the distribution rule becomes a viable design choice again. Endogenous learning through feedback signals enables R to work, whereas nonspatial random interaction did not work in physical space.)

This is how feedback signals through symbols work to traverse spatial distance:

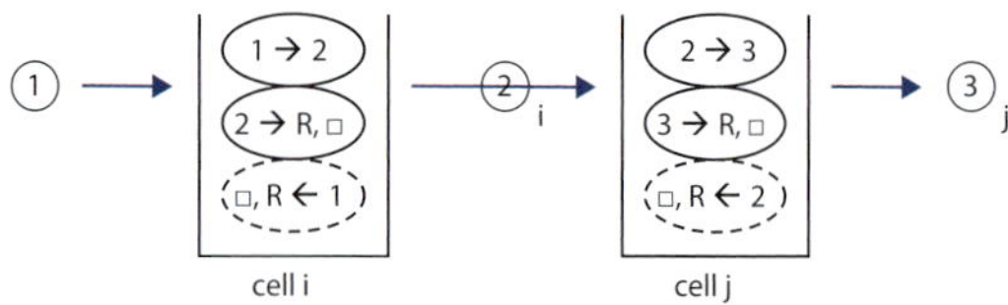

Making a "successful transaction" that triggers a feedback signal:

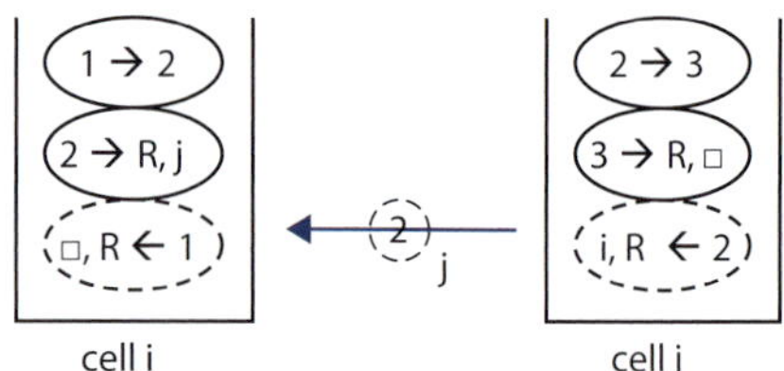

After this, one of the production-distribution-communication rule ensembles reproduces, either in cell i or in cell j depending upon source or target reproduction.

The two reverse flows, product and symbol, each modify the address registries of recipients through carrying subscripts that identify their cellular source. These subscripts of source inform long-distance recipients who each other is.[11]

[9] This was Eigen's and Schuster's "complexity barrier."

[10] If spatial contiguity does not imply immediate transparency of observation of a neighbor's reaction, then symbols are necessary even for endogenous learning in Moore space.

[11] Because of my metaphor of product as ball, I tend to think of these subscripts as like a little dab of paint on the

Recording subscripts in address registers enables endogenous learning over distance, as well as memory of past successes. Even after the transaction is over, recipient cell j knows through his own communication rule that a successful input 2 came from cell i, and source cell i knows through his own distribution rule that cell j experienced transactional success in the past when he sent him a 2. So he is more likely to send that to him again in the future if the occasion ever arises of another output product 2.

No complicated cognition is required to enable explicit memory. All that is necessary is to record the sources of products and symbols in address registries. Biological systems can do this; symbols and products being carried through blood.

Once symbolic tokens and communication rules exist for signaling successful transactions, another function can be layered onto the communication system with no modification of the system itself—namely, to request inputs. All that is necessary is to reverse the sequence of flows: instead of doing product flow first and then symbol flow, do symbol flow first and then product flow. This presents a simulacrum of intentionality, but it really is nothing more than a different sequence of stimulus and response. One striking implication of this is that human intentionality is a by-product of symbolization. "Future" is just a symbolic representation that we present to ourselves. Future cannot really drive our present actions; only learned symbolic representations of future can do that. Causality is always non-teleological, for humans as much as for atoms, functionalist (mis)reasoning notwithstanding.

Requests for inputs are initiated at the outset of production chains in this model by production rules "looking for action" from input balls drawn from their cell's input urn. In the failed case of drawing a useless ball, the rejected input draw is deposited immediately into the cell's output urn. In the models of last chapter, that was the end of the initiation story, and some other randomly chosen production rule "looking for action" would try again. Now, however, with symbols there is an additional response possible to input-urn failure: namely, to request from someone else the input product one is looking for. Once address registries have been primed by previous endogenous learning (a precondition for requests to function correctly), that scenario looks like the following.

The request is this:

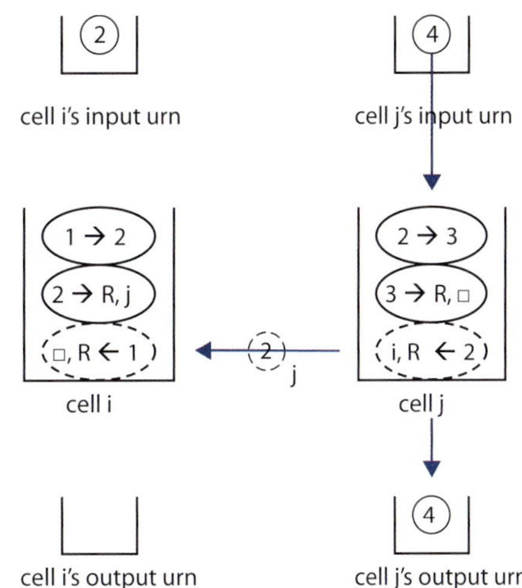

And the reply is this, assuming that the desired 2 is in fact in cell i's input urn:

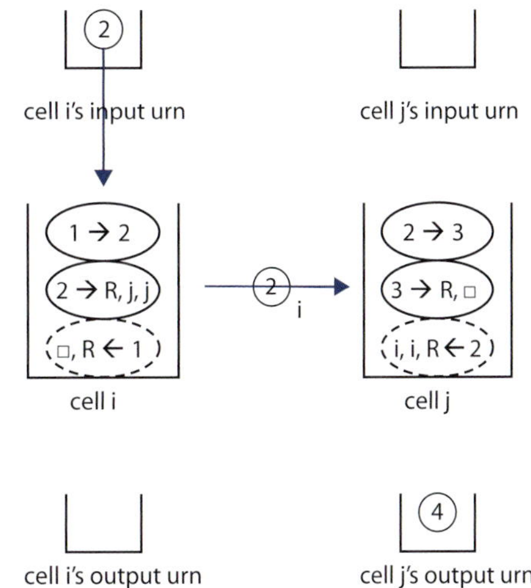

This request scenario is basically a temporal inversion of the previous feedback-signal scenario, reversing the sequence of symbol and product flows. At the end, endogenous learning recorded two addresses in each registry because the transaction was repeated, in reverse order. The signal-feedback sequence must be run first so as to initiate a relationship tie in the first place. After that, symbols and products can be passed back and forth in any order. Requests and signal feedbacks are thus mirror images of each other; requests just "highjack" signaling for a different purpose.

The adaptive significance of long-distance endogenous learning, using symbols, is that

ball, but obviously any sign perceptible to j will do. Signatures on letters are another metaphor.

autocatalytic production networks now can be spatially extended over wider territory, especially if target reproduction is implemented. This is adaptive to environmental heterogeneity and volatility because a wide catchment area allows many "useless" input products to be gathered and transferred through requests to cells that can use them. Cellular exploration of virgin territory—hence spatial mobility of the production network itself—will not be implemented until there are constitutive ties. But within the setting of relational ties, both wider spatial search of input urns and more efficient usage and transfer of input balls from those urns increase the adaptive capacity of the network as a whole.

Ic. Symbol Transformation

Now consider language as a network of transformations of symbols, one that is autocatalytic in the usual sense: transformations within the network reproduce nodes of the network. This is not a Chomsky conception of language as static and primordial grammar. It is a dynamic conception of language as symbols and as symbol-transformation rules, constructed and reproduced by conversation. Consider product symbols, introduced in the last section, as nouns if you will. And consider symbol-transformation rules, which will be introduced in this section, as verbs if you will. Production chains of words through symbol-transforming cells are like conversations. Conversation chains of nouns and verbs abstracted from their speakers are like sentences. Language as combinatorial grammar (universal or not) is not modeled here, but language as conversational syntax is, in my minimalist manner.

Consider the following extension of a (now call it full-fledged) production-rule ensemble:

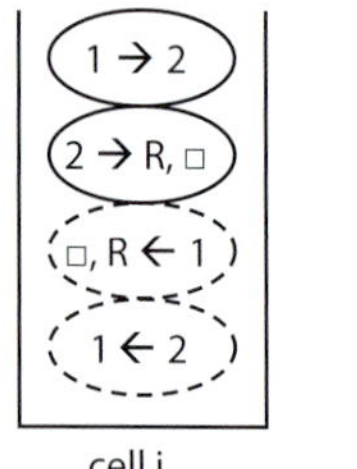

: production rule

: distribution rule

: communication rule

: language rule

All of the capabilities described so far—autocatalytic production and distribution of material products, endogenous learning in memory, and signaling and requests of symbolic products—are included in this simple setup; language rules are just layered on top, to mimic evolution. The language rule transforms an incoming symbol of product 2 into an outgoing symbol of product 1. The communication rule then sends that symbolic output to a destination in its address registry. The language-transformation setup within the cell mirrors the production-transformation setup in the cell, except in reverse direction. After endogenous learning, address registers in the two memory banks of material distribution and symbolic communication usually will not be the same.

To see how language works in this model, let's take it one step at a time. Endogenous learning through signaling feedback of transactional success works the same way as before, to prime address registries:

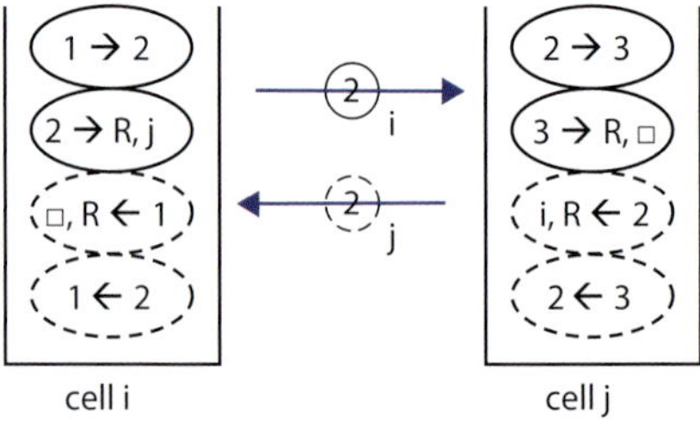

With language rules, however, requests can turn into a chain, not just a dyadic exchange of symbol for product. This occurs when recipient cell i does not successfully draw from its input urn the product requested by cell j. With symbol-transformation capacity, this failure of cell i's draw can turn into a subsequent request by cell i, repeating the request process but this time for itself:

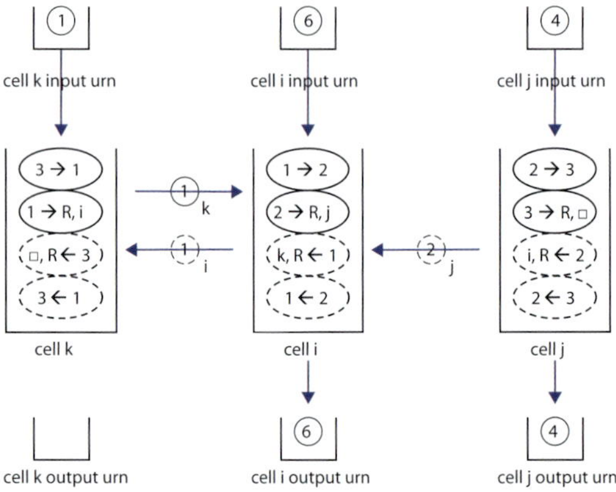

Cell j was the one who made the initial request, but cell i is the one who benefited directly by transforming j's request into its own after being unable to satisfy j's request. Notice in this arrangement of relational ties, however, that the production rules of (3→1), (1→ 2), and (2→3) themselves form a hypercycle. In this situation, signal feedback will fill in the indicated blanks in the address registries with the addresses necessary to complete the relational cycle.[12] This relational cycle among cells focuses the distributional flows of products into the autocatalytic cycle of production among their respective production rules. Not only that, but this relational cycle among cells also focuses the communicative flow of symbols into a chain of requests that searches over multiple input urns for resources, thereby transcending the limits of cells' own local environments. Cell j did not benefit directly from its original request. But it benefited mightily indirectly through keeping the hypercycle that sustains it alive. This communicative cooperation among members of a hypercycle, through passing symbols, vastly increases the adaptability of hypercycles to changes in environmental input urns by moving inputs to where they can be useful, thereby triggering production chains that wend through everyone.

It remains to translate this model into computer code in order to explore the robustness of these adaptive capacities under different environmental and design variations. From the results in the last chapter, I take it as a given that everything will work better, leading to more complex hypercycles, if target ("altruistic") is selected as the reproduction mode of production rules rather than source ("selfish"). The above analysis of request chains implies similarly that everyone will be better-off if no one gets too upset by others transforming their requests into something else. Once distributional and communicative cycles are recognized, self-interest in the long run (i.e., maximizing reproduction) does not equal self-interest in the short run (i.e., maximizing production).

If target reproduction and language are implemented, I speculate that small hypercycles—call these modules—are more likely to reach out to each other through symbolic and product exchange to link up into vaster hypercycles of collectively much greater complexity. Bridges to other hypercycles are "parasites" from the point of view of the local module hypercycle, draining it of valuable resources. Hence bridges of cross-hypercycle product and symbol flow are fragile at their outset. But if they can hang in there long enough to discover a compensating reverse flow, then a sort of "international trade" can develop that is mutually beneficial to both modules.

Using as my example only one good exchanged in international trade, figure 4.1 illustrates what I have in mind about growth in complexity. In that diagram I have used a visual mnemonic to fit everything in: namely, hiding the distribution, communication, and language rules underneath the production-rule cover of the ensembles. Similarly, symbol flows (both requests and signal feedbacks) are not shown, but these go in reverse directions to the indicated material-product flows. Implicitly all address registers are primed through past endogenous-learning experiences.

It is worth emphasizing that the "R" components in address registries were crucial in the discovery of cross-module bridges like these in the first place. This is the initial random exploration or outreach that signal feedback sometimes reinforces into relational ties of reproductively useful focused exchange.[13]

The point of figure 4.1 is to show how long-distance "international trade" of products and symbols between hypercyclic modules builds complex higher-order hypercycles out of module components. Just following the outer border, for example, a 9-element hypercycle has been constructed on top of the three 3-element hypercycles. Computer simulation will be necessary to discover the parametric circumstances of this higher-order construction, but I hypothesize that both target reproduction and language contribute to building higher-order complexity in reproductive hypercycles. Target reproduction alone can do this as long as everything is spatially clustered. But language in conversation is necessary to extend this higher-order complexity over longer distances, perhaps to include more diverse modules than are encountered locally, thereby enriching the aggregate complexity that wends across modules.[14]

[12] Namely j in cell k's communication rule and k in cell j's distribution rule.

[13] The mechanics of endogenous learning imply that the probability of random "exploration" goes down as that of successful "exploitation" of found partners goes up. But the existence of a fixed limit on address memory implies that exploration never goes to zero. For example, if the memory limit is ten, the probability of random search with an output product or a request cannot go below 10 percent. Conversely, a higher emphasis on random search when one's past success rate has been low makes intuitive sense. Such unsuccessful cells are getting desperate: either they find an exchange partner soon or they will go extinct.

[14] Note that local modules are not necessarily destroyed by linkage. But they might be in some circumstances of overwhelming international-trade volume. Simulation is required to weigh the balancing forces to see when component systems collapse and if so how that ramifies.

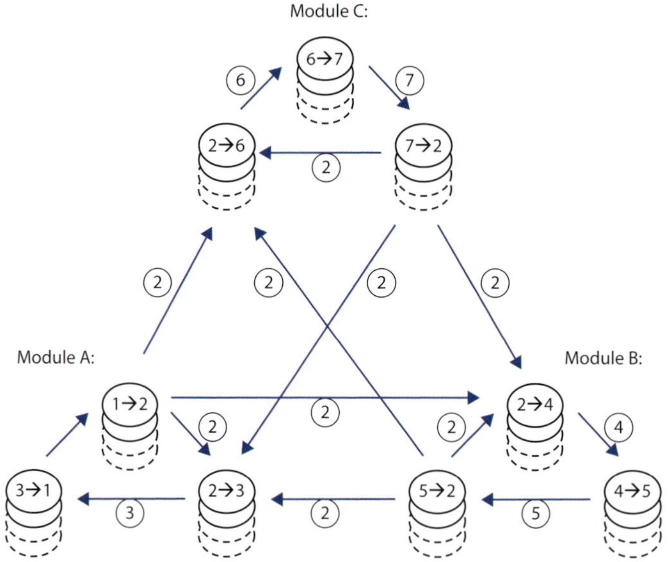

Figure 4.1 Hypercycles linked through "International Trade."

II. LONGITUDINAL COMMUNICATION THROUGH TEACHING

IIa. The Problem of Cell Death

Besides adaptation to environmental heterogeneity and fluctuation, there is a second threat to hypercyclic life, lying in the heart of itself: namely, cell death. A glance back at figure 3.1 in the previous chapter should be enough to convince the reader that sudden termination of cells—especially cells located at the core of the system—presents an enormous risk for system collapse. Target reproduction and spatial contiguity are excellent mechanisms for endowing autocatalytic production systems with capacities to repair their component production rules in the face of stochastic internal noise. Symbolic communication, as shown in the last section, extends this repair capacity of production autocatalysis to cope with environmental fluctuation and to transcend spatial contiguity, up to a point. These reproduction and communication mechanisms repair the distributions of production rules in and among cells when cells are assumed to be given. If an entire cell containing rules is obliterated at one stroke, however, there is no production-rule seed left in that location to grow back. Death of cells propagates downstream to kill other rules (and eventually cells) in the autocatalytic system that were dependent upon the production of the dead cell for their own survival. The extent and speed of propagation of fatality depend upon how central the dead cell was.

The autocatalytic model of Jain and Krishna (1998), discussed in chapter 2, demonstrates that system collapse like this is not necessarily the end of the world for autocatalytic life. Given incoming flux from the chemical environment, new autocatalytic cycles can eventually self-organize again from scratch—until the next system collapse. The problem that catastrophic cell death poses for evolution, therefore, is not the emergence of life itself but rather the preservation of enough of previous life to permit its next iteration to be a progressive step in complexity and not just a repeat of origin history.[15]

A process of cell death can be overcome through a compensating process of cell birth. No cell-birth process has yet been introduced into my autocatalytic models, apart from random initialization. The task of the present section is to rectify this omission, thereby exploring the evolutionary significance of cell death. Periodically purging autocatalytic systems through cell death and birth, I will show, accomplishes three things according to the logic of my models:

[15] Compare this to the Soviet experience under Gorbachev, analyzed in chapter 9.

1) It permits not only rule distributions to move within cellular topologies but also cellular topologies themselves to migrate across physical space through changing populations of nodes.
2) Depending upon the details of the birth process, production rules themselves can evolve, within whatever chemistry is enabled at the outset.
3) Lineages of production-rule descent emerge to keep social systems of communication and teaching together as they physically migrate and as technologies evolve within them. Constitutive family networks of "longitudinal" teaching and inheritance of production rules are central in understanding how distributed communication and production networks respond to cell death.

In ensemble, these three consequences add up to the conclusion that cell death, serious short-run threat to system life notwithstanding, is fundamental to an autocatalytic life that has the capacity to evolve as well as to reproduce and survive. Constitutive networks of teaching and inheritance need to emerge in this model to make this true.

IIb. Definitions: Cell Birth, Cell Death, Cellular Autocatalysis

The main step up the evolutionary ladder in this section is to enable cells to pass their production rules (if model base is the last chapter) or production-rule ensembles (if model base is the first half of this chapter) to other cells. If the recipient cell already possesses production rules, I call this passing of rules "teaching." If the recipient is merely an empty bin, I call it "cell birth." "Inheritance" is the production rule passed. From the perspective of the giver, teaching and cell birth are identical in my model; the only difference is the capacity of the receiver. Without the giving of rules, cell death cannot be overcome.

Giving away rules is altruistic in this model in the sense that depleting a cell's stock of production rules increases the chance that the stock will fall to zero, thereby killing the cell. We have seen repeatedly in autocatalytic models, however, how short-term survival costs to the cell can be overcome by long-term survival gains if autocatalytic cycles are triggered downstream, which then feed back. Target reproduction was an example of that in the previous chapter.

Cell death means that 100 percent of the production rule or production-rule ensemble contents of a cell are destroyed. This of course already existed in the model, in the sense that all production rules in a cell could gradually die out. This section adds the possibility that the contents of cells will be destroyed catastrophically all at once, at some small but fixed probability. Fixed *cell-death rate* means that such catastrophic cell deaths are not related to performance (in the sense of reproduction rates of rules, due to successful transactions), even though gradual noncatastrophic cell deaths were so related. This fixed-probability feature of catastrophic death simulates real organisms: plants and animals, including humans, don't live forever, no matter how successful they are.

All versions of the model fix the aggregate population size of production rules. This induces competitive selection, even without catastrophic cell death. Every time one rule successfully reproduces, another rule somewhere randomly is killed off. Catastrophic cell death under fixed rule-population size implies that deceased rules have to be replaced. Two different options for rule replacement after cell death will be explored:

(a) Random scatter of cell contents: take existing production-rule contents of the dead cell and randomly scatter them on the 10×10 grid. This preserves the existing aggregate distribution of rules, but it disrupts their previous useful locations. The chance that these replacement rules will successfully reintegrate into the autocatalytic system will be higher than in method (b), if the autocatalytic system survives long enough to allow this gradually to happen.
(b) Random draws from start-up chemistry: go back to original chemistry, from which rules first were drawn at initialization, and randomly draw a new set of replacement rules, equal in number to the ones just killed off. This random influx of new rules opens the door not just to survival but to progressive evolution in rules and in rule-chain technologies, with new rules possibly being successfully added to or supplanting old ones, in modified hypercycles. Perturbation of this magnitude subjects existing autocatalytic systems to more abuse than does the milder scattering method (a). Autocatalytic repair must be correspondingly stronger to induce

> enough resilience into the system to permit new rules to be explored without system collapse. The kinship and biography features in this section give autocatalytic repair this boost at the cellular (not just the rule) level.

The gift of rules, either by teaching or by cell birth, will enable the possibility of catastrophic cell death to be overcome, without system collapse, if the following definition of *cellular autocatalysis* is satisfied. Cellular autocatalysis is when the rule contents of dead cells in hypercycle cores can always be replaced by production-rule gifts from other cells in such a way as to repair the hypercycle core. In cellular autocatalysis, cycles of constitutive ties among cells are fundamental for the cell-birth replacement of catastrophic cell deaths. This is analogous to production autocatalysis, where cycles of relational trading among rules were fundamental for the rule-reproduction repair of random rule deaths.

IIc. Mitosis

The most primitive and conservative method of cell birth is mitosis—namely, the splitting of an existing cell into two. In this model, mitosis is easily implemented. At a fixed, experimentally manipulable, and presumably small *cell birthrate*, choose the cell in which a production rule has most recently reproduced and split its rule contents randomly into two subsets. No spatial movement is required; hence two cells now sit on top of each other in the same bin location i, the sum contents of which are identical to what had been contained in the previously unified cell i. No adjustments in trading partners' address registries are required: they still reference location i and choose the desired production rule therein (out of either resident cell) to interact with.

The only conservative point of mitosis is to buffer against cell death. At a fixed, experimentally manipulable, and presumably small *cell death rate*, choose one live cell to kill off, irrespective of any performance features of that cell other than that it is alive. Then using replacement method (a) or (b), scatter replacement rules randomly into all 10×10 bins, as in the original initialization. Making the mitosis of a particular cell proportionate to the reproduction of rules contained therein makes the splitting of large cells more likely than that of small cells. Since cells with a large number of rule copies are located topologically in hypercycle cores, this means that core locations, with two mitosis cells resident, are more likely to have replacements built in if one of them is randomly selected for destruction. Mitosis, in other words, buffers autocatalytic cores from system collapse.[16] Autocatalytic trading itself will then rebuild the surviving offspring cell back up to its parent's equilibrium rule-number size.

Mitosis combined with replacement method (b) comes close to embodying pure Darwinian evolution within an autocatalytic network context. No cross-location diffusion or learning of rules is enabled. Mitosis is conservative in that it accomplishes nothing directly other than buffering. No spatial mobility or constitutive networks are enabled. If replacement method (b) is used, the likelihood of successful rule evolution is not zero, but it is very small, more like bacteria than like animals. Given cell death, however, mitosis is a nontrivial step toward preserving existing life for subsequent random evolutionary exploration.

IId. Teaching in Moore Space

Cell birth not as stationary mitosis but as spatial diffusion is the first step in this model toward plant- and eventually animal-like evolution in cell-network topology itself. The most primitive method of teaching other cells—that is, of passing rules from one cell to another—is to send randomly to some spatially adjacent Moore neighbor a production rule (or production-rule ensemble) that has just been reproduced. No address-registry guidance of destination is implied in simple spatial diffusion. A small, experimentally manipulable *gift rate* parameter can be set to control the likelihood of sending such a rule, conditional on rule reproduction.[17] Sending recently reproduced rules implies that only "surplus rules" are sent, and the pre-gift stock of rules in the giver is not depleted.[18] Sending reproduced rules also implies that fecund rules,

[16] Buffering is not perfect, however, since the random division of rules into two cells does not guarantee that all rule types in the parent will be represented in each of the two offspring cells.

[17] To compare results, this *gift rate* parameter for spatial diffusion can be calibrated to be equivalent to the *cell birthrate* parameter of the previous section on mitosis.

[18] Survival probability of the giver, therefore, is not directly reduced, compared to before the gift. It is, however, indirectly reduced, compared to what it would have been had it kept the rule. In the latter sense, this is altruistic behavior. Whether long-run stimulation of hypercycles downstream is sufficient to overcome this opportunity cost to self remains to be seen.

which successfully reproduce a lot, send out more offspring rule gifts than do barely activated rules.[19] If spatial diffusion of the rule is to a neighbor cell that already has rules, I call this teaching. If spatial diffusion of the rule is to a neighboring location without preexisting rules, I call this cell birth.

Since there is no guidance to rule giving in simple spatial diffusion, there is no guarantee of anything useful coming out of this random spatial giving, but one example of a successful new cell birth that increases the resilience of the system is as follows:

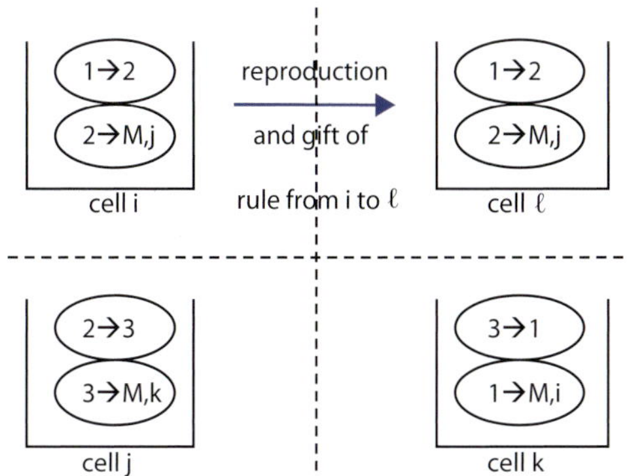

In this example, cells i, j, and k already had established a 3-product hypercycle among themselves, with endogenous learning in their distribution-rule address registries to reinforce and focus their own product flows into relational ties.[20] With spatial diffusion implemented, however, now cell i's rule has reproduced and has been given randomly, with probability *gift rate*, to i's neighboring bin ℓ. Since, by construction, bin location ℓ had been empty before the gift, a new offspring cell ℓ was thus born through parent cell i's gift. The reason that location ℓ was a perspicacious target in this example is that cell k, which produces the required input product 1, happened to be spatially contiguous with compatible new cell ℓ, as well as with compatible parent cell i. Thus cell k eventually will give its output of product 1 to cell ℓ, through M in its distribution rule, and thus will learn to add address ℓ to its distribution rule once it observes a successful transaction with the neighbor.[21] The existing 3-product hypercycle thereby expanded topologically from three to four cells.

Spatial diffusion/teaching is a more topologically labile way to buffer against cell death than is mitosis. Its buffering function is similar: if cell i dies, cell ℓ carries on without the (1→2→3→1) hypercycle being disrupted. And if cell ℓ dies, cell i does the same. If it gets lucky in its destination, spatial diffusion of rules can create cell redundancy in hypercycles through cell-network topological extension, just as mitosis did in its more spatially restricted way. Given the requirement of destination luck, however, spatial diffusion alone is less efficient in buffering than is mitosis.

Possibly offsetting this inferiority in buffering against cell death of spatial diffusion to mitosis is the superiority of spatial diffusion in cell-network mobility. The simple spatial-diffusion method of cell birth can lead a spatially contiguous hypercycle colony to adjust its cell composition and topology to migrate incrementally as a whole to heterogeneous resource environments that are more congenial to the colony's reproduction and growth. This migration is slow, to be sure, because the colony must remain spatially contiguous. But slow incremental movement is a whole lot better than mitosis, which does not move at all. Ecologically this is more like plants than it is like bacteria (mitosis) or animals (next section). Mitosis stretches out the time to hypercycle collapse, but it does not avert the inevitability of eventual collapse and rebound. Spatial diffusion, on the other hand, takes a more aggressive stance against cell death—namely, to build new hypercycles on the spatial borders of colonies, which slowly search for more fruitful resource environments. This collective spatial search has no intent; it is an unintended byproduct of rule giving.

IIe. Reciprocity

The next evolutionary advance to be modeled in this chapter is the recognition of parentage. Recognition of parentage enables mutual gift giving or reciprocity. And reciprocity, in turn, enables both parent and offspring automatically to reconstruct the other if either of them dies.[22]

[19] This is fitness in the biological sense: more babies.

[20] Endogenous learning through address registries is not necessary to make this example work. Nothing but spatial Ms, as in the previous chapter, would suffice. But endogenous learning makes spatial diffusion more efficient.

[21] As in the last section, overt symbols are not required for this feedback in spatially contiguous settings because direct observability is presumed. In long-distance transactions, in contrast, symbols are required.

[22] I don't mean literally to reconstruct the other (bring them back from the dead) but to construct a new cell that contains copies of the dead cell's rules in its previous location.

Reciprocity is the constitutive-tie analogue to endogenous learning for the relational ties of the last section. Just as endogenous learning was enabled through address subscripts on products that flow, so reciprocity in this section will be enabled through address subscripts on rules that flow. Address subscripts, both on product flows ("cross-sectional communication") and on rule flows ("longitudinal communication"), are the proto-linguistic tricks that turn Brownian motion into focused communication.

The following diagram illustrates rule addressing and its practical consequences for recording parentage and enabling reciprocity:

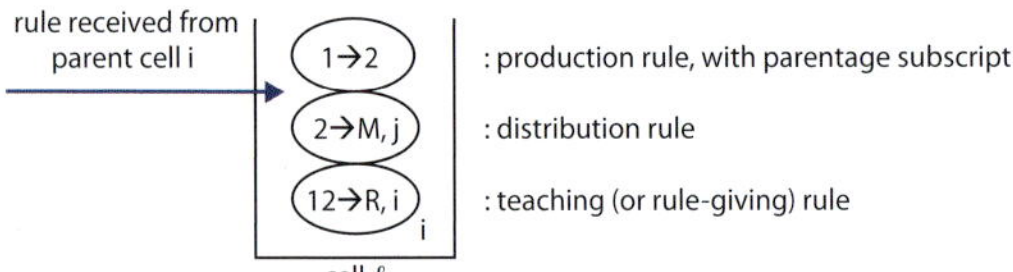

In this illustration, an off-screen parent cell i has given its reproduced rule ensemble to bin location ℓ, thereby creating a new offspring cell ℓ. Address j in cell i's (now also cell ℓ's) distribution rule came from the endogenous learning of cell i through its previous trading experience. Including distribution address j in rule diffusion is equivalent to assuming Lamarckian inheritance. This strikes me as plausible for social systems, even if not for biological systems. Social scientists might call this privileged access: a father giving his son access to his business contacts, for example. If the reader disagrees, he or she can register their complaint by substituting M,□ for M,j at this point. The communication and language rules of the last section, which process product symbols, are not included in this illustration in order to make the point that it is possible for kinship to evolve without preexisting language.[23] But if language has been enabled, then those two supplements are transferred as well in the complete rule ensemble that cell i transfers.

The new feature here, in addition to the rule-address subscript that records parentage, is the teaching rule. This tells cell ℓ where to give its own reproduced rule at the small conditional probability of *gift rate* ("12" is simply my shorthand that stands in for the current 1→2 rule ensemble). "R" in the teaching-rule address registry says to send the rule ensemble to some random location in the 10 × 10 grid. The address i in the teaching-rule address registry says to send the rule ensemble back to parent i. If those are the only two elements present in the registry, then each option occurs at a .5 probability. Inserting the rule-address subscript i, which indicates parentage, into the teaching-rule address registry of the offspring is the way my autocatalytic model represents reciprocity. Cells give back, when and if they can, to cells that have made them.

Let us walk through how reciprocity works. First with the probability of *gift rate*, a reproduced rule ensemble from cell i is sent to some randomly selected cell ℓ after a successful transaction by i (via either target or source reproduction, as the case may be):

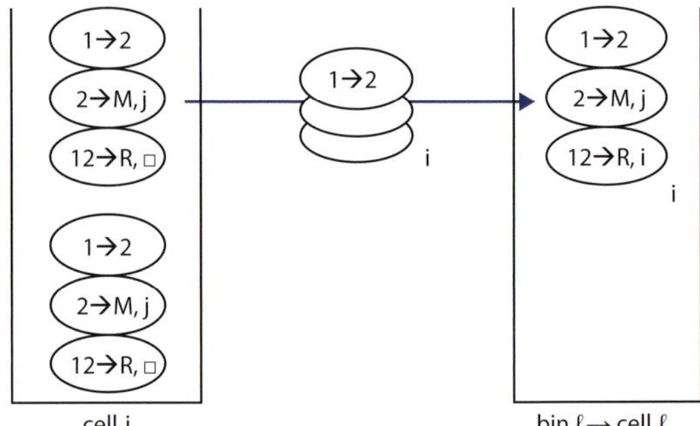

This gift of a rule from cell i to empty bin ℓ makes a new cell ℓ:

Now if this reproduced rule from parent cell i was sent to a location where it cannot transact successfully with its new Moore neighbors and thus reproduce, then the whole exercise was a waste of a good rule, and it will die off. On the other hand, if ℓ got lucky enough to be Moore adjacent to a production rule that produced product 1 as that rule's output, then the new rule in ℓ will get its required input-product "food" and thus may reproduce itself. This could occur through trading with an M spatial neighbor, if a compatible rule is adjacent, or it could occur through its long-distance parent's trading partner j, if Lamarckian inheritance is implemented (as it was here).

[23] This controversial point follows the argument of Chapais (2008, 48–59). However once the distribution rule substitutes R for M (a.k.a. long-distance "international trade"), then symbols become not optional but required, as has already been shown.

In the event of successful rule reproduction in offspring ℓ, there is a .5 times *gift rate* chance that it will be sent back to the rule's parent, if reciprocity is implemented:

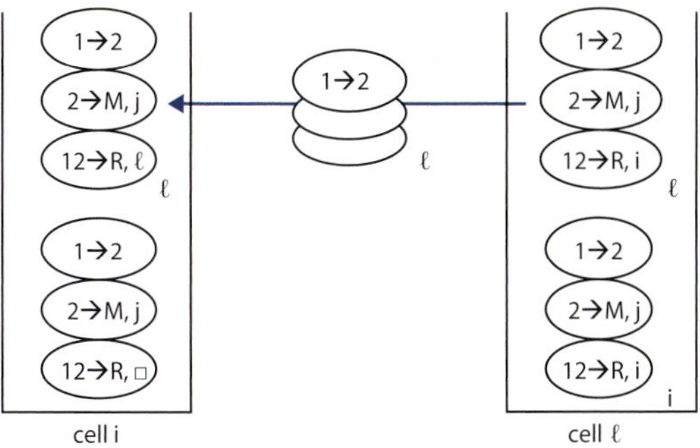

After these two reciprocal exchanges, this leaves:

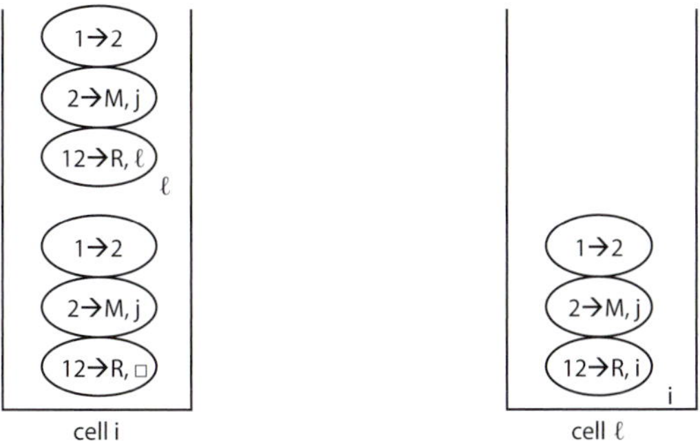

Any distribution-rule addresses of useful neighbors picked up by ℓ will also be passed back to i (given Lamarckian inheritance), although that is not shown in the figures. Plus of course any of these rules in i and in ℓ could also have been killed off at any time by the selection pressure of successful reproduction elsewhere in the system. When all is said and done, reciprocity enables cells not only to make each other (that is true even without reciprocity) but also to know who made them, simply by consulting the address indices on their own rules. That is the germ, but not the full flowering, of kinship.

The key for enabling reciprocity is the subscript pasted on the transferred rule. Under reciprocity (and under full kinship in the next section), rules have affixed upon them the cell identity of their maker when they reproduce. As in the previous section on language, cell memory requires no complex mental cognition. It requires only a registry in which to record address tokens. Only starting rules, randomly installed at the initialization of the simulation, have no subscripts of parentage.

Once dyadic reciprocity flows between parent and offspring become enabled, entire hypercycle colonies can be interlinked to keep each other alive, as illustrated in figure 4.2.

None of this is inevitable. Addressing, *gift rate*, and other parameters must be efficient enough to allow the coupled autocatalytic systems to repair each other quickly through reciprocal rule flows before the inexorable catastrophic cell deaths percolate into system collapse. The higher the rates of reciprocal rule flows going back and forth between all pairs of parents and offspring the more resilient both autocatalytic systems become. This is yet another illustration of the introductory chapter's general point that organisms and actors exist only as vortexes of flows that reconstruct them.

An anthropological reader will recognize figure 4.2 as "restricted exchange" in Lévi-Strauss's alliance theory of kinship.[24] This chapter shares with Chapais the desire to resituate Lévi-Strauss's powerful structuralist insights onto evolutionary foundations.

IIf. Generalized Exchange

It is surprisingly easy and natural in this autocatalytic model to move from Lévi-Strauss's reciprocal exchange between parental dyads to his generalized exchange within kin groups. All that is necessary is to increase address indexing of parentage from one generation to multiple generations. Generalized exchange is reciprocity in groups, not just in pairs.

By "multiple generations" I mean enabling subscripts that inscribe sequences of parentage, like $(1\rightarrow 2)_{ijk}$, instead of subscripts that inscribe only the immediate parent, as in the $(1\rightarrow 2)_i$ of direct reciprocity. Each time a production rule is passed from one cell to the next, the most recent giver appends its cell ID onto the existing subscript of the rule rather than replacing it. Multiple subscripts identify the sequence or biography of gift giving, from original creator to most recent giver, rather than identifying only the most recent giver. As sequences of rule gifts wend their way across multiple donors

[24] Levi-Strauss [1949] 1969. See also White 1963. In Lévi-Strauss's version of the diagram, women are exchanged as constitutive ties among male groups, who reproduce through them.

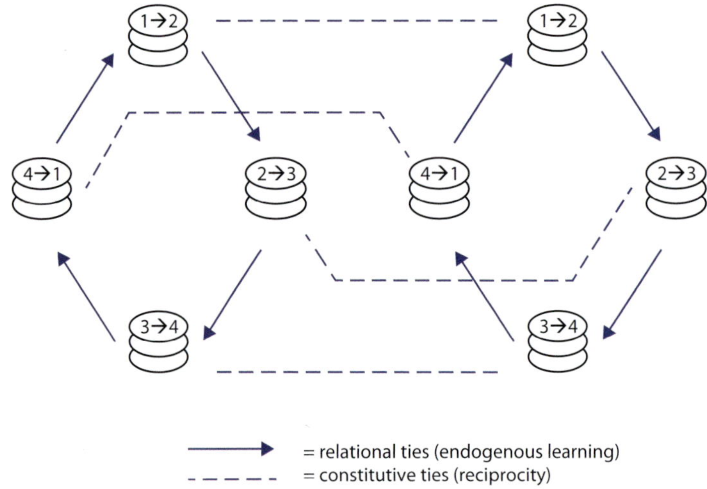

Figure 4.2 Hypercycles linked through "Reciprocity."

and recipients, kinship inheritance relations of descent are induced. Eventually nonproductive rules are killed off by successful reproduction elsewhere. But to the extent that rules survive, family relations of descent are selected and become known to cellular participants through the subscript labels on the living rules that constitute who they are.

Let us see how this chaining works, assuming that the passed rules successfully reproduce in their new locations:

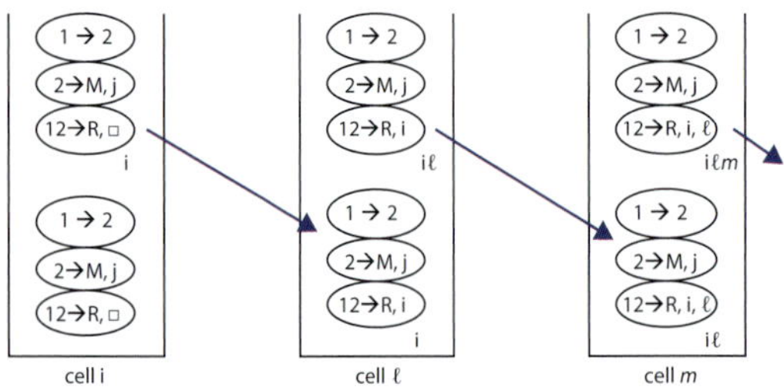

Rules at first move outward to new locations just through R, but reciprocity still links them probabilistically back to their ancestors—albeit now to grandparents and others as well as to parents—up to whatever maximum genealogical depth is permitted in the simulation. I continue to illustrate Lamarckian inheritance of distribution-rule addresses, though once again this is a design option, contingent upon researcher taste.

The logic of giving rules under dyadic reciprocity, previously discussed, is now extended to cover more recipients. (a) Cell i's reproduced rule has only its own subscript i on it,[25] and so with *gift rate* probability it is passed on to a random destination, which in this example happens to be cell ℓ. (b) The gift-rule ensemble in cell ℓ now has parent i as well as R in its teaching-rule address registry. Hence if that gift rule reproduces, then with .5 times *gift rate* probability, cell ℓ selects i from its (R,i) option set and sends its reproduction back to its parent, as in direct reciprocity. (This is not shown in the diagram.) But with .5 times *gift rate* probability it selects R and hence passes the newly reproduced rule to a random destination, which in this example happens to be the third location *m*. (c) Cell *m* now has R, i, and ℓ in its teaching-rule registry. That means that if its received rule in turn reproduces, then with .33 times *gift rate* probability, that newly reproduced rule will be sent to its parent ℓ (not shown). And with the same probability, it will be sent to its grandparent i (not shown). With the same probability, it will be sent to yet a fourth new location through R.

Once cellular autocatalysis kicks in, through chains like this looping back into itself to make cycles that reproduce, parentage subscripts sort themselves into "families," meaning a set of cell addresses whose parentage subscripts heavily overlap. In its closed-form limit, a set of cells, for example, {cell i, cell ℓ, cell *m*, cell *n*}, all would contain cycling production rules like $(1{\rightarrow}2)_{i\ell mn}$.

[25] A rule present from initialization has no subscript, as shown. But random-gift behavior would have been same if rule in cell i had contained only the subscript i.

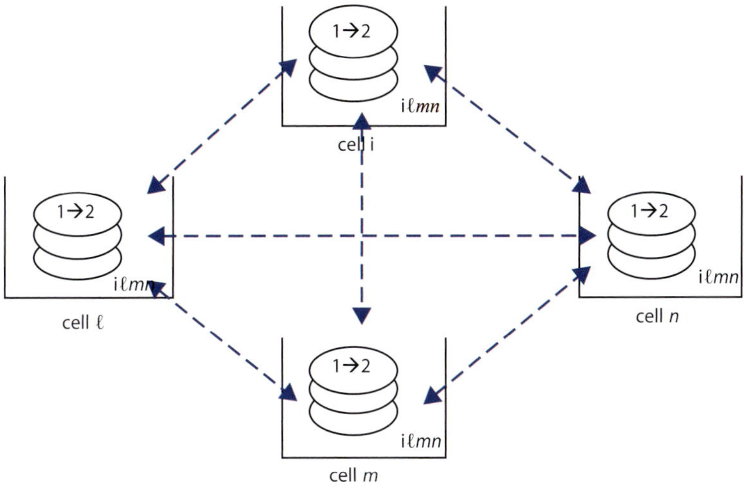

Figure 4.3 Cellular autocatalysis or "Families."

Behaviorally families generate self-consistent subscripts like this, and thereby themselves as a collectivity, through generalized exchange. Family members pass around constitutive rules among themselves, reconstructing themselves through replacement of rules, even in the face of cell death. Figure 4.3 is a portrait of a fully developed family, which emerges in cyclic closed form only after member cells' parentage indices have converged through repeated generalized exchange.

A family in these models is thus really the same thing as cellular autocatalysis, except that parentage indices make cells aware of each other. Through inherited indices on the rules that comprise them, cells know who other family members are and treat them accordingly. (The developmental sequence here is actually the reverse: through reciprocity in teaching, they construct who their family is.) In anthropological terms, this is more like kinship than it is like lineage because there is no constraint here that everyone descends from a single apical ancestor. Nor do families necessarily have to converge completely to self-consistent closed forms, as in figure 4.3. If only partial convergence occurs, then rule indices in family members will overlap without being identical, and "family" is more a cluster in constitutive-tie kinship space than it is a fully bounded group.

For expositional simplicity, I have drawn the figures in this chapter with only one type of production rule in each cell. We know from the simulations of the previous chapter, however, that it is common in autocatalytic systems for cells to have multiple rules or skills contained within them. This multifunctionality of cells was constructed by multiple hypercycles of trading redundantly lying on top of each other. If these multiple hypercycles all comprised the same set of rules, as they were in the SOLO H chemistry, then this is mere redundancy, good for collective resilience. If these multiple hypercycles comprised different (but intersecting) sets of rules, as they were in the ALL chemistry, then this was the emergence of multiple domains. In the current context of constitutive ties and families, multifunctionality of cells means that such cells can be in multiple families at once, once families emerge through generalized exchange. Families here are not mutually exclusive; they overlap (like bilateral kinship) through multifunctional cells that contain more than one type of production rule.

While there are more subtleties than can be captured in any toy model, as an approximation dyadic reciprocity is characteristic of primate kinship, according to the synthetic survey of Chapais (2008). Chimps and other apes can easily recognize and reciprocate with direct kin but not so easily with indirect kin. And generalized exchange is characteristic of primeval hominoid kinship, before (perhaps shortly before) language evolved. Of course there are no real data on hominoids at the very origin of the human race that can tell us whether language or family structure preceded the other in evolutionary sequence. But the modeling in this chapter is consistent with Chapais's claim that kinship could have evolved before language. Tomasello (2008), from the language end, also argues on the basis of primate evidence that human language emerged out of (and was driven by) processes of social interaction and cooperation rather than the reverse. All of this points to the conclusion that selfishness seems the wrong place to start in understanding human evolution.

III. COGNITION AND CATEGORIZATION

In this last section before the conclusion, I put together the previous two sections. First I add the symbol passing of the section on cross-sectional communication, through relational trading ties, to the rule passing of the section on longitudinal communication, through constitutive-kin ties. This combination of symbols with kin illustrates how "cultural evolution" through symbol passing can substitute for Lamarckian inheritance without evoking silly cultural-evolution concepts like memes.[26] Next I show how simple "cognitive" arithmetic operators on parentage address strings induce different kinship structures—for example, clan versus lineage. Primitive processing of address strings implies different logics of attributed founding within kin groups. Finally I introduce categorical names for kin groups, which reify alleged founders into collective labels or names for the kin groups they helped bring into existence. These symbolic labels or tags[27] for collectivities are most useful for nonkin, who can learn through these categories to generalize their successful personal experience with some traders to those traders' kin, with whom they have had no direct experience. The otherwise vague concept of collective "identity" thus has two distinct meanings in the modeling framework of autocatalysis. Internally, collective identity of a kin group is the set of parentage records of who made whom. Externally, collective identity of a kin group is the name or label attached to that group by outsiders who are trading with them. There can be interesting and historically consequential slippage between these two distinct (internal and external) processes of the social construction of group.[28]

[26] These sociobiology ideas are silly because they force a parallelism between ideas and genes that is not there. If cultural evolution exists (as I believe it does), it exists because of the distinctive recombinant logics of language, not because culture mimics biological genetics.

[27] Holland 1995.

[28] Cf. Padgett and Ansell 1993, 1273.

IIIa. Communication among Kin

Once generalized-exchange kin know who each other are, it is costless to kin members to pass along to their parentage their own feedback tokens or symbols of trading success—to "talk" to them in essence. This is how pheromone communication works among ants, except that ants do not have kin specificity in their communication. Passing product symbols of trading success among kin leads to convergence in the address registries of distribution rules among kin: "My friend is your friend," in essence. This is precisely what Lamarckian inheritance did in the previous section of this model. Hence with communication among kin, Lamarckian inheritance becomes dispensable. Symbolic communication among kin is the functional equivalent of biological inheritance of learning. With it, experiences are pooled and the pace of collective learning speeds up drastically compared to the socially isolated situation of every cell having to discover and learn useful trading partners on its own. Language and kinship, while perhaps having evolved separately, are synergistic in their reinforcement of each other, leading ultimately to increased rates of reproduction of rules within kin.

This is how communication about trading success between kin works:

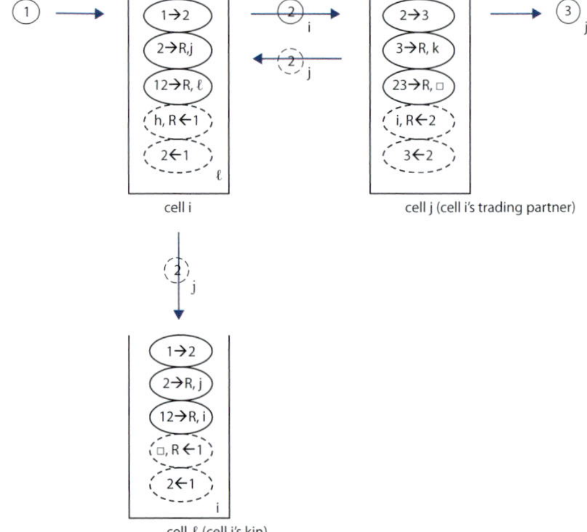

That is, instead of cell i discarding its feedback symbol of transactional success from cell j after registering j in its own distribution-rule address registry, cell i just passes that symbol along to its offspring cell ℓ, thereby allowing cell ℓ also to insert j in its distribution-rule address registry. There is no reproductive cost to cell i in doing so, so why not, once the kinship motivation is there. After such a communication between kin, whenever either cell i or cell ℓ next receives the product 1 as input, both are more likely to send their output of product 2 to relational-tie partner cell j, who can use it. This leads to future transactional success for both kin, not just for the original parent who directly experienced it. As mentioned above, this is a kinship-specific version of pheromones among ants.[29]

IIIa. Founders and Group Names

Throughout the autocatalytic modeling section of this book, the focus insistently has remained fixed on social interaction processes that are nonconscious and noncognitive—nonhuman, many would also say, though I disagree with this last appellation. Cells in the autocatalytic modeling approach are merely spatially arrayed holding tanks, with addresses, that do no internal processing other than transforming products and registering addresses. (This is not to say that the social processes modeled thereby cannot function as sophisticated distributed intelligence, like neural nets.) There were two reasons for this insistent focus on noncognition within cells. First, the goal of this modeling section on autocatalysis is evolutionary: tracing the continuities, not the discontinuities, among all forms of life, from chemical to human. And second, the goal of the book as a whole is the discovery of social processes of generating organizational novelty. New organizational forms that are already understood by participants do not really count as evolutionary novelty to us. Almost by definition, novelty (at least at the level of analysis of the species or the invention) means the production of something genuinely not known before. Our empirical chapters identify numerous cases of the historical production of organizational novelty. These almost always involve unanticipated spillover across multiple networks.

All this notwithstanding, we obviously do not deny that humans have cognition. By this we mean that they are able to process and transform symbols mentally. It's just that it violates the evolutionary purpose of this section of the book to jump immediately to full-blown human cognition and act as if the rest of the evolution of life does not matter for human capacity and behavior. In this subsection, I take my first baby step toward introducing human cognition.

The simplest "mental" calculation I can think of for cells to process the symbolic information contained within them is to sum the address registries of their compatible rule ensembles. What does this mean?

For the constitutive-tie address register of subscript indexes on rule ensembles, this means two calculations: counting the number of appearances of addresses within single rule ensembles and summing those counts across similar rule ensembles. As an illustration:

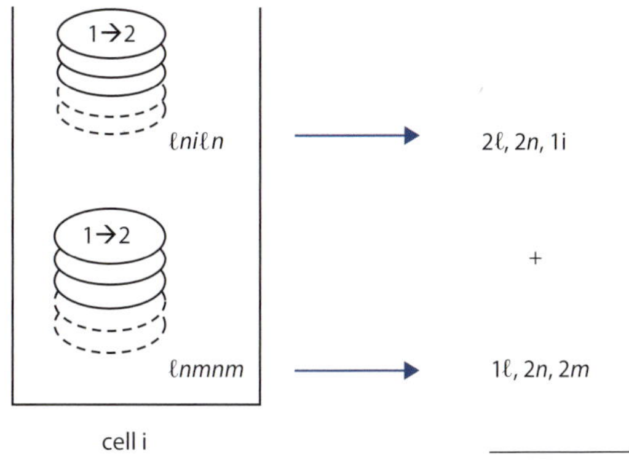

In this example, cell i's first production rule had the parentage, made through generalized-exchange gifts from its fellow kin {i,ℓ,m,n}, of ℓ→*n*→i→ℓ→*n*→i. Cell i's second production rule, of the same type, had the teaching history of ℓ→*n*→*m*→*n*→*m*→i.

Without the "mental" addition operators on the right-hand side of the diagram, cell i's own generalized-exchange behavior would be this: If the input product 1 arrived into i, one of these two eligible rules would be selected randomly and its output product 2 would be distributed according to the information contained in its distribution-rule registry. If that production led to reproductive success of the rule, through a successful transaction, then with *gift-rate* probability, one of the addresses in that rule's subscript would be chosen as a target for passing that reproduced rule gift to its kin (with or without Lamarckian inheritance involved).

With the "mental" addition operators on the right-hand side of the diagram, cell i's generalized-exchange behavior would be this: If the input product 1 arrived into i, one of these two eligible rules would be selected randomly and its output product 2 would be distributed

[29] Dancing among bees, to signal where food is, is functionally similar to pheromones among ants.

according to the information contained in its distribution-rule registry. If that production led to reproductive success of the rule, through a successful transaction, then with *gift-rate* probability, target addresses for receiving the reproduced rule would be chosen according to the aggregated probabilities of the summation. Namely, 3/10 probability that ℓ receives the rule gift, 4/10 probability that m receives the rule gift, and so forth.

What is the difference in behavior between cognition and no cognition in this simple gift-giving example? Virtually nothing. The behavioral giving probabilities are identical, except for possibly different likelihoods of reproductive success because of differing distribution-rule registries. To the extent that either Lamarckian inheritance or symbolic communication among kin is implemented, however, even that heterogeneity will go away. There is no selection pressure at the cellular level, in other words, for simple additive cognition to emerge.

There could be serious selection benefits for simple cognition, however, not at the individual level of the cell but at the collective level of the kin group if these simple mental calculations of internal "kinship identity" are made public by the cell into a kinship name for itself. I propose that the simplest naming nomenclature is just to make the address of the founding ancestor of your kin group into your own last name.[30] In this chapter, I self-consciously use kinship as my semantics because the evolutionary and anthropological literature on this topic is rich and deep. But I hope that it is clear to the reader that I believe that the interactional processes underlying the emergence of primitive kin groups, including their naming, carry over to the social foundations of the other forms of organization covered in this book.

How can kin names emerge out of simple cognition, applied to generalized exchange? Easy: all that is necessary is for cells to advertise the results of their parentage calculations on the outside of themselves in an augmented addressing scheme. Instead of the original spatial address "cell i," now make the kin name "cell i(*n*)," where i is now the cell's first name, and cell i's kin group founder *n* is now cell i's last name or surname.

[30] Not coincidentally, given my empirical research, this is exactly how family names emerge in Renaissance Florence, as in many other places. For example *di Piero*, meaning "son of Piero," turns after a while into the *Pieri* family, if Piero gave rise to numerous successful progeny. See Padgett 2010.

Different kinship structures derive from different cognitive definitions of ancestral "founder." If the ancestor mentioned most frequently in cell i's parentage summation is chosen to be declared cell i's ancestral "founder," then the kinship system is a clan. Clans are big-men kin systems where kinship groups fluidly form and re-form, depending upon who distributes the most gifts.[31] If the progenitor mentioned first in cell i's aggregated parentage list is chosen to be declared ancestral "founder," then the kinship system is a lineage. Lineages are more stable kinship structures than clans, where records of descent are maintained.[32] Since rule gifts cycle in generalized exchange, it is more cognitively demanding to figure out temporal sequence across multiple rules than it is to figure out simple frequency. For this reason, I speculate that fluid clans preceded stable lineages in kinship evolution.

To illustrate this simple kinship-based self-labeling process, I re-present the previous simple-cognition diagram, with the last step of ancestral naming added:

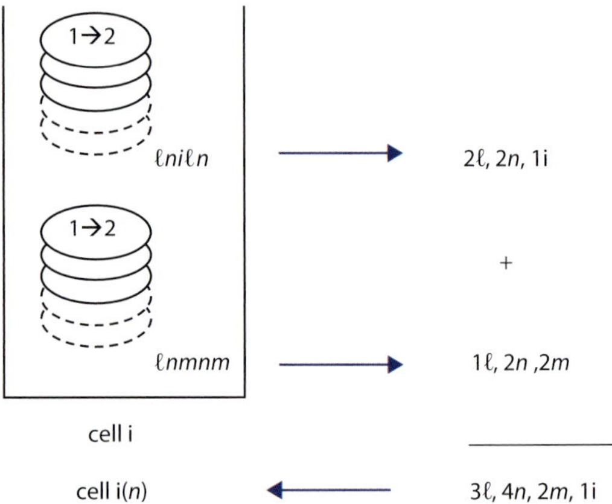

In this example, the clan, not the lineage, naming procedure was employed. (Last name would have been ℓ in the case of lineage.)

A dynamic advantage of placing group names in an autocatalytic context is that group names—and hence the attributed collective identities they embody—evolve along with the parentage registries upon which they are based. Rule ensembles reproduce and are killed off according to the learning-by-doing mechanisms in product autocatalysis. Cell collections of rules are catastrophically killed off and reconstructed according to the teaching and reciprocity mechanisms

[31] A classic analysis is Strathern 1971.
[32] A classic analysis is Evans-Pritchard 1940.

in cellular autocatalysis. Parentage registries are flushed and remade as by-products of rule reproduction and repair. Evolving kin names in this autocatalytic model is a formalization of Douglas's central point (1986) that group formation is a process of members writing and rewriting their own history. For both Douglas and me, rewriting history does not mean that objective facts are made up, only that they are selectively remembered and forgotten.

In particular, as cellular autocatalysis settles into closed-form families and drives members' parentage registers to become similar, members' attribution of their founders' names will also converge, and family names will spread and become agreed upon.[33] Conversely, breakage in cellular autocatalysis through cell death will cause underlying parentage registries to diverge. But this breakage in teaching cycles percolates up into fissure among family members' last names only with a time lag, as the weight of learned history must be slowly overcome. Perhaps this time lag is sufficient to enable the broken cellular autocatalysis to reconstruct itself as a family. But perhaps not, which then leads to splintering and redefinition of kin groups.

IIIc. Categorization

That is what group names are, but what do they do? Why is there selective advantage to kin members in adopting a public collective name based on the names of their founders? My answer is the same as for any advertisement: they let your customers find you.

The behavioral implication of public last names is that products and product symbols now become indexed by i(*n*) instead of by i alone. Just to be clear, this can be illustrated in my earlier endogenous-learning diagram:

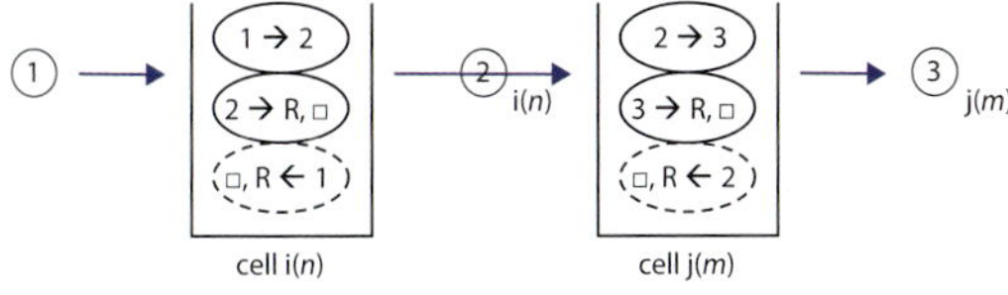

making a "successful transation" that triggers a feedback signal:

[33] Padgett (2010) presents an empirical analysis of two centuries of such family evolution in Renaissance Florence. Changing last names is part of this.

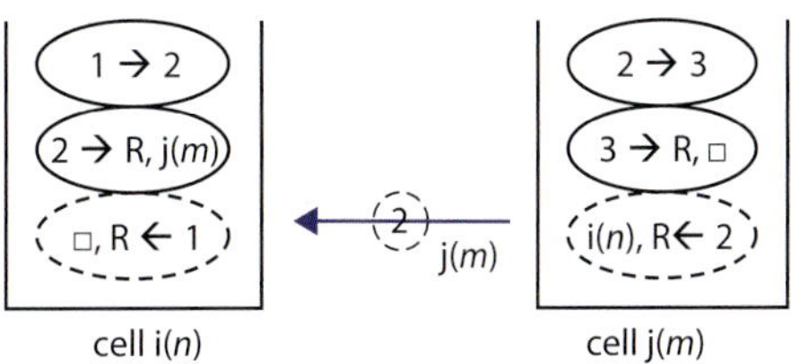

Hence over time, given endogenous relational learning, both distribution-rule and communication-rule address registries will fill up with addresses containing both first (spatial) and last (kinship) names.

The question is: how can recipient cells use this extra naming information about their trading partner's family membership? The next evolutionary step I propose is that of generalization. If recipient cells can abstract from the string of last names of their successful trading partners the abstract category N, which is the collective name of trading partners' kin group, then more refined search procedures become enabled.

In the mechanics of address registries, this means adding the kin-group label N to a cell's registry in addition to what is already there: namely, its random-search R and the various individual addresses that comprise its learned relational ties. One simple generalization mechanism that achieves this is that an N gets added to a cell's address registry once the number of last names in its relational-tie list exceeds some threshold.

To illustrate this with a threshold of three, applied to the registry of a distribution rule:

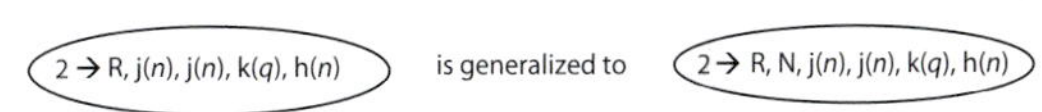

Exploratory search for trading partners by the cell now becomes more focused and targeted. In addition to the already existing search options of "go back to your friends" and "try a random destination," a third search option appears: "try the kin of your (especially good) friends." This third option of N is random search within the addresses that share the last name of *n*, but this is vastly more focused and fruitful than searching randomly through R all possible destinations, many of which will contain no rules at all. The cellular autocatalysis process that undergirded the emergence of families in the first place makes it highly likely that cells with the last name of N will contain similar rules to those with whom one has already experienced success. And the stronger the autocatalysis, the more that *n*'s will diffuse, increasing the odds of their frequency in registries exceeding the threshold of generalization into N.

Family names, therefore, give selective advantage to kin members who adopt them not because of any coordination advantages they give to members themselves—who after all have far more precise information about their parentage than what is contained in crude last-name labels. Rather, family names give selective advantage to kin members because they increase the efficiency with which compatible trading partners can find them.

Cellular cognition had no evolutionary reason to emerge from the individualistic perspective of the cell by itself. The autocatalytic combination of communicative kin names with primitive cellular cognition, however, suggests that it was the emergence of kin groups that built the platform for simple cognition and categorical generalization to gain evolutionary advantage. I do not claim that this evolutionary leap from kinship to individual cognition and categorical generalization was simple to achieve. But I do claim, along with Tomasello and Chapais, that the step-by-step emergence of human language was a deeply social process with dynamic consequences for the individual human mind.

CONCLUSION

In this conclusion, I make three points. First, I draw together the various processual strands discussed in this chapter into a macro-architectural portrait of how the pieces fit together. The connection between this chapter and figure 1.1 is thereby clarified. Second, I note the intimate connection between processes of cellular autocatalysis and repair, analyzed in this chapter, and the capacity of product autocatalysis, which they regulate, to tolerate evolutionary turnover in its constitutive product rules. Finally, I stress the fundamental difference between the relational approach of autocatalysis to theorizing about evolution and the individualist approach of Social Darwinism to theorizing about evolution. This distinction is crucial to the reception and reworking of evolutionary thinking by social scientists and historians.

Consider the highly aggregated functional representation of an autocatalytic system in figure 4.4. The word *functional* in this context means that the spatial and hence the individual cellular level of description is suppressed and that only macroeconomic interrelations of reproducing rules are portrayed. Within each macro box

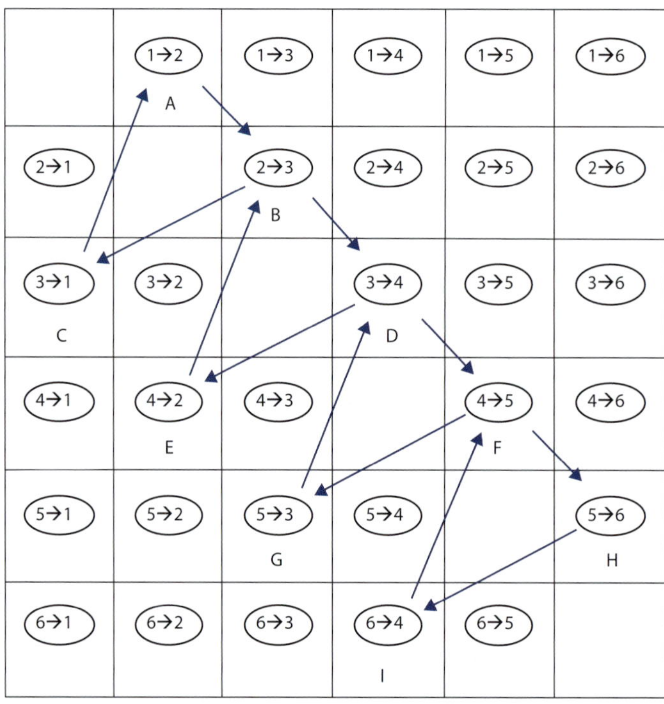

Figure 4.4 Functional aggregation of linked hypercycles.

of type of production rule are contained the numerous individual cells that contain that rule. Indeed, since cells may contain multiple types of rules, multifunctional cells are members of more than one rule category, making a thicket of cross-box connections underneath this aggregated functional representation.[34] Rule types not linked by autocatalytic feedback flows of products between them will eventually die out, killing cells that do that job. Only linked boxes, therefore, contain life.

Domains are classes of rule cycles: four triadic ones in this example. There could be—and most likely are for redundancy reasons—tens or hundreds of specific hypercycles linking particular cells in the various domain classes shown here. Multifunctional rules participate in more than one domain, thereby linking them in dynamic reproductive support. Rules and cells participating in more than one domain are the hinges through which invention spillover (or system collapse) may occur.

Functional categories contain within them all cells that contain the designated production rule. Cells within functional categories thus are eligible for cellular-autocatalytic reconstruction through constitutive ties of teaching and reciprocity among themselves. If generalized exchange exists, these constitutive ties may fold themselves into families and clans of parentage descent. More than one family can emerge within each functional category, but if selection pressures of competitive exclusion are strong, one clan may come to outcompete (outreproduce) the others. Capital letters in figure 4.4 are my way of representing the collective names of the clans so formed, under the assumption that there is only one surviving clan per niche. If more than one clan coexists in each niche, then more than one clan name (each designated by a capital letter) would have been shown. Spatial separation increases the chances of clan coexistence.

This macrofunctional diagram of autocatalysis is like the blockmodels in social network analysis.[35] Relational ties of trading induce structurally equivalent sets of cells, containing similar production rules. Two advances on that foundational work are introduced here: Blockmodels dynamically emerge, and structural-equivalence blocs become aware of themselves through communication. This parallels Marx's famous distinction between class-in-itself and class-for-itself without his radical politics or teleological history.

In the autocatalytic models of communication in this chapter, new product-transformation rules enter the system following catastrophic cell death through rule-replacement method (b)—namely, random new replacement draws from the original chemistry. Even if they previously had been killed off, all possible rules in the original chemistry reenter the system in this method, like flux or gentle rain dropping randomly down onto all spatial locations. The empirical chapters in the rest of this book uncover far more interesting and realistic genesis mechanisms than this—more recombinatoric (with spillover) than random. This simple-minded method of random flux will have served its analytical function, however, if it highlights and parameterizes the causal relationships between technological evolvability, social communication, and hypercycle repair, once computer implementation has been completed.

Even without demonstration through computer simulation, it is clear that the stronger the autocatalytic forces of product and cellular repair, the higher the rate of rule flux that can be tolerated and hence the higher the rate of technological search and evolvability that can be achieved without reproductive collapse. It is no accident that higher forms of life evolve faster than lower forms of life. First impression notwithstanding, rule evolvability and system stabilization are in fact correlated. New product-transformation rules may disrupt existing hypercycles, as well as extend them. The capacity of hypercycles flexibly to reconstruct and to repair themselves sets limits on the rates of new rules they can safely absorb. Evolutionary progress to more complex hypercycles will never be smooth, no matter what the buffers. System collapses of some magnitude are both inevitable and useful for clearing the way to subsequent advances. But ragged and stochastic drifts upward in technological complexity are increasingly likely as more sophistication in communication is enabled. Even though bacteria and humans both evolve, humans evolve faster because of their communication and cooperation through product and identity symbols.

In this chapter, I have developed and modeled the following three arguments. Through

[34] Multifunctional cells, containing more than one type of product rule, have as many last names as they do types of product cells, for example, i(*n*,*m*). Although inconsistent with human patrilineage, this is perfectly consistent with human bilateral kinship systems. More generally, multiple cross-cutting group memberships hardly seem odd in human contexts.

[35] White, Boorman, and Breiger 1976.

endogenous learning and product symbols in relational-trading ties, communication and language enable autocatalytic production networks to adapt to heterogeneous and fluctuating resource environments. Through reciprocity and generalized exchange in constitutive-teaching ties, the gift giving of rules overcomes cell death through kinship, better allowing product rules to evolve. Symbols and address registries are the minimalist mechanisms that induce these two types of networks to self-organize and to repair themselves through both cross-sectional and longitudinal communication. Putting language and kinship together enables the emergence of group categorization and simple individual cognition.

The autocatalytic approach suggests a different understanding of cultural evolution than is present in Social Darwinism and in its intellectual progeny like sociobiology, evolutionary psychology, and neoclassical economics. Instead of slavishly imitating traditional population genetics models through derivative concepts like "cultural memes" and "survival of the fittest," researchers interested in understanding evolutionary processes at higher levels of phyla are advised instead to study the development of communication and how that articulates with material foundations. Darwinist selection processes—understood in their biological sense of relative rates of reproduction—are fundamental, I argue, to such evolutionary development. But Darwinian selection can and does operate in networks of symbiotic exchange, not just in individualist competition, as Social Darwinism presumes. Indeed it operates more efficiently and resiliently when such networks are characterized by cooperation, communication, and altruism.

Cells, my minimalist model of people, make each other through gift exchange.[36] This way of talking grates on methodological-individualist ears, but it correctly conveys the relational construction of nodes inherent in autocatalytic systems. Inheritance of the reproductive success of individual cells in such a constructive system is inscribed in the population of rules within that cell, but it is also inscribed in the address registers and rule populations of other cells. Altruistic costs to individual cells in the short run are often outweighed in autocatalysis by reproductive benefits to them in the long run, when and if production feedback cycles are triggered downstream.

The problem with evolutionary theory as currently misused in the social sciences, therefore, is not Darwin per se. It is the individualist gestalt into which Darwinist selection has too often been inserted. The emergence of organization in autocatalysis means not the domination and defeat of others but rather the teaching and repair of others. Language, kinship, and cognition are facilitative of that.

[36] An empirical illustration of this idea is Padgett and McLean's study (2011) of economic credit in Renaissance Florence. Through both statistical analysis of commercial loans and textual examination of merchant letters, this study demonstrates that anthropological gift exchange lay at the foundation of early commercial capitalism and banking.

REFERENCES

Chapais, Bernard. 2008. *Primeval Kinship*. Cambridge, MA: Harvard University Press.

Douglas, Mary. 1986. *How Institutions Think*. Syracuse: Syracuse University Press.

Eigen, Manfred, and Peter Schuster. 1979. *The Hypercycle: A Principle of Natural Self-Organization*. New York: Springer-Verlag.

Evans-Pritchard, E. E. 1940. *The Nuer*. Oxford: Clarendon Press.

Holland, John H. 1995. *Hidden Order: How Adaptation Builds Complexity*. Reading, MA: Addison-Wesley.

Jain, Sanjay, and Sandeep Krishna. 1998. "Autocatalytic Sets and the Growth of Complexity in an Evolutionary Model." *Physical Review Letters* 81:5684–87.

Lévi-Strauss, Claude. [1949] 1969. *The Elementary Structures of Kinship*. Boston: Beacon Press.

Padgett, John F. 2010. "Open Elite? Social Mobility, Marriage, and Family in Florence, 1282–1494." *Renaissance Quarterly* 63:357–412.

Padgett, John F., and Christopher K. Ansell. 1993. "Robust Action and the Rise of the Medici, 1400–1434." *American Journal of Sociology* 98: 1259–1319.

Padgett, John F., and Paul D. McLean. 2011. "Economic Credit in Renaissance Florence." *Journal of Modern History* 83:1–47.

Strathern, Andrew. 1971. *The Rope of Moka: Big-Men and Ceremonial Exchange in Mount Hagen, New Guinea*. Cambridge: Cambridge University Press.

Tomasello, Michael. 2008. *Origins of Human Communication*. Cambridge, MA: MIT Press.

White, Harrison C. 1963. *The Anatomy of Kinship*. Englewood Cliffs, NJ: Prentice-Hall.

White, Harrison C., Scott A. Boorman, and Ronald L. Breiger. 1976. "Social Structure from Multiple Networks. I: Blockmodels of Roles and Positions." *American Journal of Sociology* 81:730–80.

PART II

Early Capitalism and State Formation

This introduction provides a cursory overview of the four chapters contained in the historically oriented segment of the book—just enough to enable the reader to compare the global structures of the emergence analyses. Historical details of course differ dramatically across the four cases because the time periods analyzed are so distinct: medieval, Renaissance, early modern, and industrial age. Taken in ensemble, these four chapters are snapshots of the historical coevolution of state and market in Europe. In each chapter I argue that foundational organizational inventions in early capitalism and in European state formation were intimately related. Such inventions often cascaded or spilled across domains, reorchestrating production networks in the process. Sometimes the empirical focus of attention in these chapters is more on the economic side, sometimes it is more on the political side, but ultimately the causal engine for emergence always is feedback between politics and economics. Repeatedly I show that organizational invention in the history of Europe, both in economics and in politics, was a systemic tipping in how multiple autocatalytic networks fit together, either in support or in disruption of each other. In all of the cases, indeed, I observe that war (civil or international) was a necessary but not sufficient prerequisite for reproductive networks to restructure each other. Something had to loosen up the previous system enough for it to become poised to tip.[1]

In the empirical cases in this part, I further find that synergistic feedback between economic and political production networks is not enough for organizational innovation to stabilize itself into systemic invention. The reproduction of people—not just the reproduction of activities and skills—has to change for innovation to become invention. Organizations in the autocatalytic framework are comprised of people, who in turn are comprised of skills. Skills are linked through technologies of production, and people are linked by communication through relational protocols. Relational protocols have to adapt to restructured technologies for those to become other than transitory. To return to the metaphor of chemistry: relational protocols catalyze production networks.

In the four chapters that follow, the nature of the regulatory system that reconstructs people through reshaping their intertwined biographies of interaction differs from case to case. In chapter 5, on medieval corporations, we see that noble patrilineages served this catalyzing function. The operation of corporate merchant-banks was reinforced by the fact that bankers came

[1] I disagree with Schumpeter's famous characterization of "creative destruction" as the elimination of old businessmen and their replacement by new ones. In lieu of this, I would define "creative destruction" as the breakup of old networks and their replacement by new ones. This includes Schumpeter's version but is not limited to it. In my historical cases, old elites frequently are observed to adapt and innovate for conservative (even reactionary) reasons. They intended to keep everything, especially their own positions of power and influence, the same but unintentionally changed themselves in the process. More consistent with my historical observations is Arthur L. Stinchcombe ("Social Structure and Organization," in *Handbook of Organizations*, ed. J. G. March [Chicago: Rand-McNally, 1965]), who hypothesized a causal connection between political upheaval and rate of economic organizational innovation without specifying anything about the content of innovation. My argument is not that war always leads to organizational invention. Repressive reversion to previous equilibria and complete system collapse are perfectly plausible alternative outcomes. In order to understand which historical trajectories are most likely, one needs to carefully investigate multiple networks and their feedbacks.

to reshape themselves into nobles. In chapter 6, on Florentine partnership systems, open-elite republicanism played this catalyzing role. New-men financiers were absorbed into elite marriage networks, thereby transforming the new elite through a patron-client relational protocol. In chapter 7, on early modern Netherlands, jointly emergent Dutch federalism on the state side and the joint-stock company and stock market on the economic side were catalyzed and reinforced by the "lateral-control" relational protocol of Calvinism in the Dutch Reformed Church. In chapter 8, on nineteenth-century Germany, state and market were connected through a new and fragile German nationalism manipulated through war by Bismarck. German nationalism was reinforced on the ground by the emergence of a domestic mass market, but the intensity of internal contradictions and the fragility of the catalytic framework of nationalism made nineteenth-century German history more volatile than most.

In figures 1.2b, 1.4b, 1.5b, and 1.6b in chapter 1, I denote for visual clarity the core production networks of economy and polity in each of this part's historical cases by solid ovals. Goods are produced in economy ovals, and militaries and war are produced in polity ovals. There are rich organizational and network structures within each of these production domains, which are discussed in the chapters themselves. In contrast, I denote the regulatory networks that construct people and their relational protocols by dotted ovals: kinship, religion, nationalism, and open-elite republicanism, as the case may be. There also are rich organizational and network structures within each of these regulatory ovals, which are discussed in the chapters. To understand the connection between the Venn diagram representations that are referred to in this section and the layer-cake representation used in figure 1.1, just imagine that you the analyst are looking at the layer-cake representation from the top down. Three-dimensional stacked layers visually become flattened into two-dimensional Venn diagram overlays. The vertical lines that represent multifunctional people in figure 1.1 turn into overlapping segments in the Venn diagrams. Multifunctionality or domain overlap is the key to feedback dynamics in both representations. In both representations, feedback across domains comes from parts in common.

The following sections give a précis or abstract of each of the four historical chapters, using the Venn diagrams as templates for comparison.

THE EMERGENCE OF CORPORATE MERCHANT-BANKS IN DUGENTO TUSCANY

Corporate merchant-banks, the largest private enterprises in medieval Europe, effectively invented international finance, with sedentary branch offices, bills of exchange, complex single-entry accounting, and ongoing loans for state leaders. The mechanism of organizational genesis for these large merchant-banks was "incorporation and detachment." The French pope in the 1260s mobilized traveling Tuscan merchants from his hometown Champagne fairs into the papal administration as the fiscal wing of his Italian crusade against the Holy Roman Emperor. Transient mercantile credit arrangements from the fairs thereby were combined with administrative letter-writing techniques and stationary physical locations from the Church. The permanence of church office was imprinted onto the fluidity of merchant partnerships.

A chain reaction of subsequent adjustments in state finance and in international trade ensued, as papal merchant-bankers slowly wound down their church loans and moved on to other business. First, some of these merchant-bankers transported to the king of England their new state-finance methods of extracting money from the fairs. They helped invent and then administered as repayment the customs method of taxing wool bound for Flanders. Second, control over high-quality English wool gave them leverage to build a textile industry in Florence, which then competed with Flanders. This provided a stable trading base to complement their lucrative but highly volatile and risky returns from state finance. Third, Tuscan sedentary offices created an alternative to the distribution channel of the Champagne fairs for luxury goods to circulate from manufacturers to wealthy customers all over western Europe. The Champagne fairs slowly declined as luxury goods moved instead through the "visible hands" of the Tuscan merchant-bankers.

The human, biographical construction side of this was noble patrilineage. Corporate merchant-banks were not built socially on the backs of preexisting noble families. Rather banks evolved into noble patrilineages through their financial success, using the social device of the *consorteria*. I call this not "company out of family," as the previous literature has it, but "family out of company." *Consorteria* was a plastic, multifunctional relational protocol for pooling assets that medieval men used to assemble military militia, defensive tower societies, blocs of land, and noble families. While originally triggered by the Church, merchant-banks lasted over generational time, even as they left the orbit of the Church, because of their progressively intensified social grounding in patrilineage. As Tuscan (and Venetian and Genoese) merchants rose to attain patrician status, the Italian nobility acquired mercantile overtones quite absent in their French and English counterparts.

A simple picture of all this is provided in figure 1.4b. Seen in macroscopic aggregate, Tuscan merchant-banks organizationally sat at the intersection of the otherwise distinct relational-flow domains of international trade, state finance, and noble kinship. Their multifunctional network position is why organizational innovations cascaded from one domain to another.

TRANSPOSITION AND REFUNCTIONALITY: THE BIRTH OF PARTNERSHIP SYSTEMS IN RENAISSANCE FLORENCE

The Florentine partnership system was a legally decentralized "network star" organizational form for doing diversified business in international trade and finance and in domestic textile manufacturing. A single dominant financier (or a small group of them) was tied by distinct founding contracts and account books to multiple businesses and entrepreneurs in different industries—all in all, not radically different from the venture capitalist of today. Chapter 6 argues that this economic innovation in business organization was the unintended consequence of political suppression of the Ciompi revolt, which was a quasi-Marxist rebellion by wool and other workers.

The organizational genesis mechanism behind the emergence of the Renaissance Florentine partnership systems was "transposition and refunctionality." Transposition in this case means that master-apprentice relational protocols from the world of guilds were imported into the previously patrilineage world of Florentine international finance. This occurred because of political co-optation: for political reasons, domestic or *cambio* bankers were recruited into the inner circles of the new post-Ciompi ruling elite. For macroeconomic reasons, these co-opted *cambio* bankers were then ordered to go out and reconstruct Florentine economic connections with the rest of Europe, which had been destroyed by civil and international war. Employment relations between senior partners and branch managers in international finance were thereby remade from lifelong corporate kin into short-term dyadic contracts. Refunctionality in this case means that short-term senior-junior partnership relations spilled over into commercial credit. Highly liquid current accounts and double-entry bookkeeping quickly spread from credit relations among businesses within partnership systems, to credit relations among businesses across partnership systems, to credit relations among import-export Florentine businesses at large. The liquidity advantages of these credit techniques, built on top of the dense social networks that undergirded them, were the basis for the market dominance of Florentine companies in European international finance.

Reproduction of this organizational spillover from economics to politics back to economics was catalyzed by social mobility. Successful financiers-cum-republicans were blended through marriage into the older patriciate. On the one hand, this "open elite" infusion of previous guildsmen into the ruling classes led to the diffusion downward of elitist political and kinship values as grateful new men mimicked their social superiors. On the other hand, this open-elite social mobility of financiers transformed the Florentine patriciate as a whole from aristocrats into republicans. Status became transformed from blood and state service into refined aesthetic taste. Cross-class patronage became the new relational protocol through which status, profit, and power were all pursued.

Partnership systems, which were an important innovation in the history of commercial capitalism, thus ultimately became one constitutive network in a new multinetwork republican-cum-merchant open elite. The dominant relational language within this new Renaissance elite, in politics, in marriage, in business, and in art, was patronage. Figure 1.2b illustrates this in succinct terms that emphasize the multifunctionality of Florentine partnership systems.

COUNTRY AS GLOBAL MARKET: NETHERLANDS, CALVINISM, AND THE JOINT-STOCK COMPANY

The amazingly creative Dutch Revolt, stretching from 1560 to 1610, triggered not just a single organizational invention but a whole raft of them in different domains: in economics, the joint-stock company, the stock market, and the central bank; in politics, state federalism; and in religion, the Calvinist Dutch Reformed Church. Chapter 7 argues that these organizational innovations were all interlinked through their common genesis mechanism of "migration and homology." Migration refers to two tidal waves of persecuted Calvinist merchants and artisans out of what is now Belgium into what is now the Netherlands, but within what was then the unitary region of the Spanish Netherlands. Homology refers to parallel organizational structures of nested councils in three institutional pillars: regents in federalist governments, consistories and synods in the Dutch Reformed Church, and boards of directors and shareholders in joint-stock companies and stock markets. Organizational innovations, shaped through civil, religious, and colonial wars, cascaded from domain to domain because they came to operate through the shared relational protocol of "lateral control" or public peer pressure.

Figure 1.5b simplifies the following multiple-network feedback story. Tax struggles lay at the base of the Dutch Revolt, but these "normal" struggles between local aristocrats and their monarch escalated into antihierarchical revolution because the Spanish reacted to growing Protestantism with the Inquisition. Formally, Dutch federalism was the decapitation of the previous Spanish imperial administration of indirect rule. Ultimately Dutch federalism cohered instead of fragmented, however, because of the financial dominance of the province of Holland within the United Provinces of the Netherland and the financial dominance of Amsterdam within Holland. Radical federalist decentralization through corporate voting was managed by tightly networked oligarchies of mercantile regents. One new and innovative mechanism for elite control was "ownership" of Dutch provincial states through purchasing government bonds. These originally were floated by the Spanish to fight their own wars but then revived by the rebels who had administered them.

Calvinism of course was antihierarchical in its essence. This led to an underground church organization of local consistories (boards of elders) and regional synods (migrant ministers with representatives of consistories). When Calvinist merchants and artisans from the south were persecuted and fled not only to northern Netherland but to other cities in Protestant Europe, they carried with them this church organization of public peer pressure and punishment of misbehavior through shame. Upon the success of the partly religious Dutch Revolt, this underground Calvinist movement became elevated into a state-sponsored Dutch Reformed Church. At this point interconnections and frictions between rigorist ministers and libertine regents surfaced and dominated intra-Dutch politics. Tensions were resolved, when they were resolved, through overlapping memberships on regency and consistory councils. This intercalation increased both the span of control and the legitimacy of moderately devout merchant regents.

The political success of the Dutch Revolt also turned southern merchant migrants to non-Dutch cities into sedentary colonies of Dutch merchants, who channeled their goods back into the Amsterdam Bourse. Family partnerships bridged these migrant merchants back to their natal homes, and churches were the social centers of these ex-pat communities. Within the central Amsterdam Bourse or trading entrepôt itself, highly experienced southerners from Antwerp poured in to mix with native northern Dutch merchants in markets (but not in politics or in intermarriage). The micro consequence was a blending and diffusion between the nautical business skills of the northerners and the financial and luxury-goods skills of the southerners. The macro consequence was the reconsolidation of intra-European trade from Antwerp to Amsterdam, with the major demographic difference being that traders were no longer cosmopolitans from all over Europe but instead were more monopolistically Dutch. Bilateral trading between nations at Antwerp shifted to integrated multilateral trade at Amsterdam, brokered almost exclusively through the Dutch. A new Amsterdam central bank operated like the consistory of this Amsterdam Bourse, regulating not through impersonal law but through public, transparent, and highly personal observation and peer pressure. All this was the economic foundation of the fabulously wealthy "Golden Age" of Holland.

Finally, co-evolution spilled over into colonialism and the birth of the joint-stock company. Trading impetus outward into the Far East was a dramatic continuation of the European migration by Dutch Calvinist merchants, reinforced by clear strategic and economic imperatives to decrease dependency on the Portuguese. The joint-stock company organizational form of the new Dutch East India Company (VOC) was a projection of the Dutch federalist state. Company stocks were like government bonds. The wealthy public owned both. Boards of directors of VOC chambers were like city and provincial regencies. Rich regents sat on both councils. The VOC was an ensemble of city chambers with voting rights, just like a Dutch province. The "private" Dutch East India Company indeed essentially was the new province of Indonesia, expanding the modular Netherlands through colonialism. The public-private distinction that we are so used to today makes little sense in the historical origins of the "private" joint-stock company, just as it makes little sense in the origins of "public" governmental federalism.

Padgett labels this whole ensemble of three intercalated federalisms—in politics, in religion, and in economics—tripartite federalism. Multiple organizational inventions in all of these domains were different facets of a single punctuated tipping in the system as a whole.

CONFLICT DISPLACEMENT AND DUAL INCLUSION IN THE CONSTRUCTION OF GERMANY

Chapter 8, by Jonathan Obert and Padgett, focuses on the nineteenth-century formation of Germany. Organizational innovation was the assembly by Prussia of geographically disparate German principalities under the new constitutional umbrella of Reichstag, Bundesrat, and chancellery. Organizational catalysis was the emergence of political parties and interest groups—and underneath those, of German nationalism—to manage the constitutional core. The multiple-network invention was dual inclusion: namely, the stapling together of the deeply contradictory principles of democracy and autocracy through "Prussia is in Germany, and Germany is in Prussia." This deep contradiction built into the heart of the German state generated a sequence of new political actors in German history.

Repeatedly in international wars with Austria and France and in domestic wars with Catholics and socialists, Bismarck used his characteristic style of conflict displacement to drive forward institutional development. In a triad of mutually hostile relations, conflict displacement is the attack by an aggressor on a demonized other with the intent (or at least the consequence) of splitting a bystander, one segment of which then joins the aggressor in a fragile alliance. Conflict displacement forms new ties by breaking old ones. Bismarck assumed the charismatic mantle of hieratic authority thereby—the broker between the aggressor and the allied segment, indeed the embodiment of their newfound unity.

To stabilize the reproduction of this dual-inclusion ensemble required not just clever tactics in war but the reconstruction of particularistic subjects into German nationalists. An economic foundation for this preceded Bismarck: the Zollverein or free-trade customs union that linked agricultural east with industrializing west into a budding domestic mass market. Potential was turned partly into reality through two steps: elitist political parties of nationalism, of which Bismarck approved, and mass interest groups of nationalism, of which Bismarck did not. Early German political parties were parties of notables, suitable to Bismarck's elitist mentality. His otherwise quite successful conflict-displacement tactics, however, backfired seriously with the Catholics because of their local parish network roots. The unintended result was the consolidation of the first disciplined mass-based political party in Germany, a portent of the future. Bismarck's brokerage control over the Reichstag seriously decreased.

Bismarck's war on the socialists triggered a second, even larger disciplined mass political party, the Socialist Democratic Party (SDP). Bismarck's conflict displacement intent, and partial achievement, was to segue out of Reichstag party politics and to set up an alternative corporatist state that could manage the economy through elite interest groups (the famous "marriage of iron and rye") and could appeal to public (especially worker) support through administrative social welfare. In some circles, Bismarck is celebrated for this as the founder of the European welfare state. But democratic legitimacy was undercut, as the whole point was to try to reassert elite control in the face of rapidly growing mass parties.

The huge populist mass movements of the Agrarian League and the Navy League, which led directly to World War I, developed after Bismarck's watch. But Obert and Padgett argue that these were logical extensions of the dual-inclusion state that Bismarck had assembled. They were set up in the name of their sainted hero, even against policy preferences Bismarck had expressed when he was still alive. The hieratic authority of Bismarck influenced German history beyond his death.

It is easy to portray Bismarck as a great man because of the historical importance of his conflict displacement style. Without denying him his due, Obert's and Padgett's central organizational point is to embed the leadership of Bismarck into his fulcrum position within dual inclusion, whipsawed by the deeply contradictory forces of democracy and autocracy that he had coupled. Brokerage for Bismarck was not the quiet equipoise of a Cosimo de' Medici or a Deng Xiaoping. It was the wild oscillations of an athletic surfer. This required considerable skill to remain upright, but the oscillations were due to forces beyond his control. Conflict displacement, while perhaps a genetic disposition for Bismarck, was also forced upon him by the monsters that he had catalyzed. Bismarck made dual inclusion, but it also made him.

The Venn diagrams in chapter 1 highlight what is in common in these four historical narratives of organizational, market, and state emergence. Historical details differ greatly of course, but the basic logics of autocatalysis are present in all cases: organizational genesis into innovation through coupling domains of production autocatalysis, and organizational catalysis into invention through layering in the constitutive autocatalysis of people. For organizational innovation to become organizational invention, new products, new skills, new relational protocols, and new people must flow through new organizations, bringing them to life.

5

The Emergence of Corporate Merchant-Banks in Dugento Tuscany

John F. Padgett

The idea of the corporation in its modern sense of a joint-stock company with limited liability did not exist in the Middle Ages. Then there was no limited liability, no stock market, no Industrial Revolution with factory production. Still, economic historians do speak of a Commercial Revolution in the "long 1200s" of the late 1100s into the early 1300s.[1] Along with the formation of the internationally oriented Champagne fairs in France, the rise of the large unitary merchant-bank in Tuscany ranks among the most important features of this Commercial Revolution.[2] Instead of mobile merchants from many nations traveling with their wares to and from central markets in France, a network of Italian (mostly Tuscan) merchant-banks developed in the mid-1200s effecting international movements of both goods and currency through themselves. Such banks were constructed out of sedentary merchants arranged in geographically distributed *filiali* or branches, sending letters to each other. Despite its geographical dispersion, this medieval Tuscan company was unitary in two legal senses: (a) a single multiple-year partnership contract, with different partners often heading different branches, and (b) a single master account book, located in the head office back home, in which all activities were tabulated and held accountable. An impressive list of early innovations in basic business technique followed this "rise of the sedentary merchant": regularized business correspondence, bills of exchange,[3]

I thank William Caferro, Fabrizio Ferraro, and Enrico Zaninotto for their helpful comments and questions.

[1] Gras 1939; Lopez 1976; Sapori 1970; De Roover 1963; Spufford 1988; Goldthwaite 2009.

[2] I will not analyze in this chapter the opening of trading routes to the Levant, which involved Genoa, Venice, and Pisa, even though these eastern trade routes provided part of the flow of trade underneath the Commercial Revolution. This flow from the east involved spices and other luxury goods. Florence, Siena, and Lucca were more centrally involved in the countervailing flow from the west, involving woolen textiles produced in Flanders, and later in Florence, and silk textiles produced in Lucca. During the height of the Champagne fairs, Genoese merchants participated in both sides of these trade flows. Geographically distributed Tuscan merchant-banks, however, gradually displaced the Champagne fairs in the late 1200s.

[3] In the absence of much surviving internal business records from the 1200s, it is impossible to prove the causal relationship that led from corporate organizational form to innovations in business technique. Nonetheless, what little data there are point in this direction. Bills of exchange between cooperating banks are first mentioned explicitly in 1291 in two business letters by the Cerchi company, one of the Florentine merchant-banks of this study, operating in England. The language suggests that this technique was routine by this date. Usher (1943, 80) draws the causal connection between bills of exchange and organizational form: "These new types of financial transactions are closely related to developments in the form of business enterprise. They rest upon the establishment of more or less permanent branch houses and agencies." Before the bill of exchange between sedentary bankers was the *instrumentum ex causa cambia* (De Roover 1963, 67). This notarized contract, used heavily by the Genoese, also transferred money between places and currencies but on a legal contractual basis through notaries rather than as a private relational understanding among bankers

complex account books,[4] and the making of deposits into investments.[5]

Beneath these fundamental innovations in business technique achieved by the sedentary merchant-bankers of the 1200s (the so-called Dugento), I maintain, lay the organizational invention of the corporation—not in the modern sense of joint-stock ownership but in the medieval sense of corporate body. This medieval-style corporation grew up within the Roman-law framework of the partnership, but it developed a temporal permanence and a continuity transcending its partners. The English word *corporation* is descended from the Latin *corpus* or body. In the context of the Italian medieval company,[6] the *corpo* was the starting capital contributed by its founding partners (*compagnie* or *soci*). Operationally, *corpo* was used to initiate a joint financial account (*ragione sociale*) in which the economic transactions and financial obligations of all the partners were effected and registered. The *ragione sociale* implemented in a practical way two organizational ideas: (a) unlimited liability of all the partners, and (b) corporate economic and legal existence, above and beyond that of its constitutive members. In medieval terms, the rise of the "corporation" meant a move from a temporary alliance of companions or *compagnie*, with fluid partners, to the corporate body of a *società*, with stationary branches or *filiali*. The Roman-law form of the founding partnership contract did not change,[7] but there was a new reality and a new sense of continuity through time—continuity through generational time—that had not existed before in business.

In medieval times, the words *company* (*compagnia*) and *corporation* (*societas*) did not refer exclusively to an economic enterprise. Guilds of educators could be corporations,[8] as could militia companies of soldiers,[9] as could protection alliances of noble families,[10] as could protection alliances of anti-noble families.[11] Whatever the activity, from the perspective of the Church what was required to transform a voluntary contract among men into an organizational body that transcended those men was incorporation into the body of Christ (later to be called the body politic). Legally speaking, this amounted to a charter or a commission, either from the pope or from the king.[12] Medieval merchants were business partners (companions or *compagnie*) in principal-agent alliances before their transformation into corporations. But upon incorporation, the larger *compagnie* became something more—namely, collective enterprises with geographical spread, temporal depth, and corporate liability.

My thesis in this chapter will be that religious incorporation was more than a metaphor in the origins of the Dugento merchant-banks. Tuscan merchant companies or *compagnie* became merchant-banking corporations or *società* when they were mobilized by the pope into crusade—to become the state-finance arm of the "body of Christ militant," if you will. Reproduction of this new organizational form beyond its origins in the crusades came through the refunctionality of these economic corporations first into English customs and wool and then into the patrilineage kinship system of Tuscan city-state elites. As social context changed, Tuscan merchant-banks were released from their crusader origins in the Church and developed new social interactions and economic functions. But the organizational inflection point of economic development in international banking, I shall argue, was catalyzed

[4] Similarly, advances in accounting are linked to the emergence of this new unitary and corporate form of banking. Fragments of a cash book from the large Salimbene company of Siena in 1277–82 document through references to missing books the existence of a complex accounting system of at least a half-dozen interrelated account books (De Roover 1974, 127). Such an accounting system was very sophisticated, but it does not imply the existence of double-entry bookkeeping.

[5] Sapori [1939] 1955b.

[6] The word *company*, in turn, descends from *compagnie* or companions. As I will explain later in this chapter, the organizational terms *compagnia* and *società* had elastic meanings in the Middle Ages, going well beyond the domains of economic production and exchange.

[7] "In general, the conceptions of a corporation held by civil and canon lawyers of the thirteenth century were lacking in precision. A corporation might be called a *corpus*, *universitas*, *communitas*, *collegium*, *societas*, or even . . . a *consortium* or *schola*" (Post 1934, 422). Maitland (1900, xxii–xxiii), however, insists on the sharp distinction between *societas* and *universitas*. I am no Roman-law scholar, but I see a slippage between rigid legal language, which did not change much, and social realities, which were fluid.

[8] Post 1934. The language used in this Parisian case was *universitas*. Organizationally, I do not think that the Tuscan merchant-banks and the Parisian university were the same, but there was a similar *corpo* sensibility behind both.

[9] Waley (1969, 165–66) discusses these *societas militum*. Cf. the Tolomei company below, which appears in the papal registers both as an economic company and as a soldier company. This is not the mystery it appears to modern eyes: In the 1200s, Italian merchants could turn themselves into Guelf cavalry just by getting onto horses, especially if they were noble. Sapori (1970, 9–14) emphasizes the militarism of Italian merchants of this period.

[10] See Santini 1887 on *società della torre*.

[11] See Waley 1969, 183–86 on *societas populi*.

[12] The pope, kings, and Holy Roman Emperor contested political and legal supremacy in this period.

by the Church—a fact that is not discussed in the economic-history literature.

Simple quantitative indicators of the organizational invention being discussed are the numbers of partners and employees. In the Champagne fairs of the early 1200s, merchants were organized into small partnerships of *compagnie* (often brothers or friends) that went to the fairs together, either as cloth merchants or as money changers. These numerous small companies were fluid both geographically and in partner composition.[13] The corporate merchant-banks of the second half of the 1200s and the first half of the 1300s, in contrast, were both large and organizationally stable. Exact numbers are very hard to come by in this era of sparse surviving business records, but indicators are good enough. During the early 1300s, after the period of this chapter, the largest three Florentine merchant-banks were the Bardi, the Peruzzi, and the Acciaiuoli. In 1310 the Bardi bank had 16 partners; in 1330 it had 11.[14] Over the time period of 1310 to 1345, the Bardi bank employed 346 factors.[15] During the period from 1300 to 1335, the number of partners in the Peruzzi bank ranged from 14 to 21.[16] Over the time period of 1331 to 1343, the Peruzzi bank employed 133 factors.[17] The Acciaiuoli employed 53 factors in 1341.[18] More data on 22 early fourteenth-century Florentine companies are provided in a sixty-one-page memo on my website.[19]

Data as precise as this are difficult to obtain for the 1200s. But according to Kaeuper, the Ricciardi company of Lucca had 74 factors and partners active from 1256 to 1300.[20] According to data from the papal registers and the English Liberate rolls, recorded in the appendix to this chapter, the Bonsignori company of Siena had at least 66 factors and partners active from 1250 to 1267, and the Scali company of Florence had at least 35 factors and partners from 1229 to 1269. By the standards of the Middle Ages, these are all large numbers.

In contrast to these large merchant-banks of the mid-1200s to mid-1300s, the largest Florentine bank of the 1400s was the famous Medici bank. Organizationally this was a partnership system, not a unitary corporation.[21] In 1435 the Medici holding company (central office) had only four partners, with seven branch managers as collateral junior partners in their respective branches.[22] In 1469, the Medici bank had a total of sixty employees in all branches, including both clerks and factors.[23] The unitary corporate merchant-banks of the 1200s and early 1300s, in other words, were often larger than the largest bank of the 1400s. The Tuscan merchant-banks in late Dugento and early Trecento were the largest private economic enterprises in Europe in the late Middle Ages.

The organizational invention of the corporation in its medieval sense, I intend to show, was induced by mobilization of the market, in the form of the Champagne fairs, by the Catholic Church for purposes of state finance—namely, to fund its Italian crusades against the Holy Roman Emperor. War pulled the markets into the Church to create something new. Crucial business techniques were invented in the fluid-merchant world of the Champagne fairs.[24] But the organizational drive toward sedentary *filiali* was imprinted on the market by the visible hand of the Church. The Church was not just an organizational model to imitate; it actively mobilized Tuscan bankers into becoming papal administrators. The contemporary but separate organizational techniques of Church and business thereby merged. This fusion quickly and directly transformed banks as organizational forms; it slowly and indirectly transformed banking practice.

On a practical level, the financial problem the Church faced was this: landed church assets were spread all over Europe, transcending the national boundaries of kingdoms. Asset dispersion in the "universal church" required comparable geographical dispersion among the Church's financial agents to mobilize those resources. On an ideological level, the fundamental Augustinian "two body" conception of human community—living simultaneously on earth and on the way to heaven—tried to impose an impersonal office conception of organization onto the deeply personalistic world of European feudalism. The mechanism of ideological influence on economic

[13] The same can be said for the sea-voyage *commenda* of Venice and Genoa, although these lie beyond the land-oriented scope of this chapter. See Lopez and Raymond 1955.

[14] Sapori 1926, 243–49.

[15] Sapori 1955a, 730–54.

[16] Sapori 1955, 665–69.

[17] Sapori 1955a, 718–29.

[18] De Roover 1963, 86.

[19] Padgett 2005.

[20] Kaeuper 1973, 56–59.

[21] See Padgett and McLean 2006 and chapter 6 in this volume for more details.

[22] De Roover 1963, 81; De Roover 1966, 377–79.

[23] De Roover 1963, 86.

[24] In particular the idea and methods of procurator or agent. See Face 1958 and Berlow 1971.

organization was not prescriptive command. It was the dual functionality of private merchant and papal administrator—in other words, being embedded in two worlds at once.

I shall call this bridging mechanism of organizational invention "incorporation and detachment." From the perspective of the state, private merchants (*mercatores*), operating in the fairs and organized as partnerships of companions (*compagnie*), were administratively absorbed or incorporated into the pope's curia (*in nostra camera*) to run papal finance. After the pope's wars were over, these new corporations (*societas*) partially detached themselves and discovered new business for themselves—first with the king of England and then with wealthy aristocratic customers all over Italy, France, and England. From the perspective of the market, these new private unitary merchant-banks operated in and began to dominate international trade, so much so that the Champagne fairs that originally spawned them were eventually driven out of business in the late 1200s in wool-textile trade and in the early 1300s in money exchange.

In this chapter, I shall develop this thesis about the organizational invention of medieval banks in several stages. After this introduction, I present a brief literature review, just to place my thesis in historiographical context. Next I state my argument in "mechanisms of invention" terms compatible with the goals of this volume. Then I offer a macrohistorical survey of the primary political and economic events of this period, including both the rise of the Champagne fairs on the economic front and the Italian crusades or wars between the pope and the Holy Roman Emperor on the political front. My co-evolutionary narrative seeks to identify the intersection of these two streams of development, tracing consequences for both state and market. Next I offer an organizational analysis of the development of partnership structures among Italian merchant-bankers, as observed and coded from the papal registers of 1243 to 1268,[25] from the English Liberate rolls from 1228 to 1307, and from secondary sources.[26] In the penultimate section, I derive some consequences of this organizational form for the evolution of the patrician family. Ultimately the seed of corporate merchant-banks found fertile soil to reproduce in the *consorteria* social framework of Tuscan patrilineage. The mid-1200s social-network context of the Church was replaced by the late 1200s social-network context of noble patrilineage. The conclusion will offer a brief coda about the fourteenth-century extinction of this organizational form.

[25] These raw data—namely, eighty-seven pages of extracts from these registers, in Latin—are posted on my webpage: http://home.uchicago.edu/~jpadgett. For the English reader, Lunt (1934, 302–4, 306, 317–18, 330–31, 338–39) has translated a small sample of this material.

[26] This material—in the form of 123 pages of extracts from various secondary sources—is also posted on my webpage: http://home.uchicago.edu/~jpadgett.

PREVIOUS LITERATURE

There are quite a few specialist studies of particular companies and towns, mostly written in languages other than English. Curiously, much of the intensive work of this type was done early in the twentieth century, apparently now having gone out of favor, at least outside Italy. I shall utilize these valuable case studies in the section below on organizational evolution.

At the level of broad synthesis, there is not as much; there are only a few authors, who are heavily cited by everyone else. Being economic historians, these synthetic authors explain the rise of merchant-banks through economic factors alone. Robert Lopez (1976) coined the term *Commercial Revolution*. The sweep of his vision is vast, but he emphasizes the traditional themes of trade opening to the east and the consequent rise of the Champagne fairs, as well as the theme of improvement in agriculture. Genoa, Venice, and shipping loom large in his account. Raymond de Roover (1963), without exactly contradicting Lopez, emphasizes instead the "internal" development of superior business techniques. The Tuscan merchant-banks were the culmination of the Commercial Revolution according to de Roover, but the Church and war are not part of his discussion. Peter Spufford (1988) is a monetarist who emphasizes in his work the discovery, in the late 1100s, of large volumes of silver in Germany and to a lesser extent in Italy, outside Siena. Spufford's monetarist focus was fresh when his book was published, but it applies to an earlier period than that with which we are dealing in this chapter. Without denying in any way their importance to macroeconomic takeoff, agriculture, trade, and silver are simply assumed as background in this chapter. My focus instead is on organizational form.

More than anyone else, Armando Sapori (1926, 1955a, 1955b, 1970) studied the large, unitary merchant-banks that are the topic of this chapter. His work is the point of departure here.

Sapori proposed that Italian unitary merchant-banks emerged through three stages of development.[27] First, companies were built on the basis of families. Second, family companies reached out to recruit outside partners in order to extend their start-up capital (*corpo*). Finally, family-plus-outsiders mobilized depositors to extend their working capital (even though that *sopracorpo* did not technically count as *corpo*). This simple developmental scheme, driven by growth in capital, will provide a null hypothesis against which my own alternative, more political account can be evaluated.

In my own papal register data on merchant-banks of the mid-1200s, which will be presented later in the chapter, I shall find empirical problems with Sapori's developmental scheme. It is not that I shall find no relationship between family and company. But I shall find the causality reversed. Instead of Sapori's "company emerging out of family," I shall find "family emerging out of company." The family-alliance (*consorteria*) hypothesis of Blomquist[28] I believe more accurately describes the initial structure of the mid-Dugento Tuscan merchant-banks that I see in the papal registers. From that beginning, family reproduction of partners within the banks, through generational time, transformed merchant nuclear families into magnate patrilineages. The relative dominance of a single "noble" family within the bank thereby grew. Challenging someone with the authority and depth of knowledge of Sapori is not to be done lightly, but I shall report my findings and leave it to future research to sort through the apparent contradictions.

To the best of my knowledge, this papal explanation for the birth of the Italian unitary merchant-bank is original in the historiographical literature.[29] Researchers on the Bonsignori company have certainly understood the papal connection, but I try to generalize the insights of case-study specialists.

MECHANISM OF ORGANIZATIONAL INVENTION: "INCORPORATION AND DETACHMENT"

Stated at an abstract level suitable for this comparative volume, the mechanism of organizational invention I find illustrated by this Dugento Italian case is "incorporation and detachment." Namely, small and fluid organizational forms of partnership, originally adapted to the Champagne-fair world of the market, were absorbed or incorporated into the new domain of state finance, first by the pope in the 1260s and then by the English king in the 1270s. Organizational invention ensued: Fluid and temporary partnerships evolved into "corporations" (*società*), in the medieval sense of that word defined earlier in the chapter—to repeat the definition: (a) a unitary *corpo* and *ragione sociale* that outlived its contributing partners, with (b) sedentary and more or less permanent geographical branches or *filiali*. Legally, the partnership contract, with its implicit unlimited liability, was elastic enough[30] to absorb this fundamental change in organizational form without requiring any change in Roman law.[31]

In my previous research on Renaissance Florence, I discovered three other multiple-network mechanisms for inventing new forms of organization: namely, "transposition and refunctionality,"[32] "fusion and hybridity,"[33] and "multivocality and robust action."[34] All of these organizational-invention mechanisms involve recombining *different types* of preexisting networks in new ways. Multiple functionality—the participation of hybrid actors in more than one domain—is a common feature of these four mechanisms. "New ideas," coming out of nowhere, are not.[35]

Innovation does not by itself imply that "it worked." To survive beyond antiquarian curiosity, any organizational innovation must first fit into, and be reproduced by, the autocatalytic flows out of which it emerged. This is the

[27] Sapori 1970, 45–49.

[28] Blomquist 1980, 1982.

[29] For a later period, Renouard (1941) discusses the link between Florentine bankers and the pope.

[30] Indeed, as will be discussed below, "partnership" was an organizational concept that could be extended to other than economic purposes—for example, military militias (*societas militum*), family alliances (*consorterie*), and joint-ownership tower societies (*società delle torri*).

[31] For an analogous elastic expansion, in nineteenth-century America, of the legal template of "commercial contract" to cover the radically different meanings of merchant custom, "meeting of the wills," and standardized obligations, see Horwitz 1977.

[32] Padgett 2001; Padgett and McLean 2006 and this volume.

[33] Padgett 2006.

[34] Padgett and Ansell 1993.

[35] For this reason, I dismiss the concept of "genius" or "great man" as a scientific explanation, even if such a person exists. The use of such labels generally implies that the researcher has not understood social context deeply enough to uncover the exact sequence of moves that were made. Galison (2003) deconstructs even Einstein into the sequence of his intellectual moves, involving trains as well as physics.

meaning of "selection" in an autocatalytic network context.[36] If those flows themselves are altered, then the word (systemic) *invention* is warranted, above and beyond just the word (organizational) *innovation*. Innovation is a new form of organization or artifact. Invention is a system tip induced by that innovation—a change in the selection regime that reproduces that innovation.[37] When, as in this case, there are two flows being combined—for example, international trade flows, centered on the Champagne fairs, and state finance flows, centered on popes and kings—then the dual-functionality innovation must be reproduced by two (not necessarily consistent) flows at once. Innovation in banks would become invention in banking[38] if the emergence of the new organizational form of bank transformed both the international-trade flows and the state-finance flows in which it participated in some way that reproduced that organizational form.

Dugento Tuscan merchant-banks qualify as an invention because they altered, without interrupting, international trade flows. The geographical dispersion of sedentary merchants in their interconnected *filiali* delivered luxury goods and textiles to (high-end) consumers more directly than did the traditional market of the Champagne fairs. The fairs gradually declined in the late 1200s and early 1300s, inversely with the rise of the sedentary merchants. This alteration in international trade flows did not occur suddenly. Merchant trade at the Champagne fairs declined in the late 1200s, but currency exchange continued; only in the early 1300s did currency exchange itself at the Champagne fairs decline, leading to the extinction of the fairs.

Dugento Tuscan merchant-banks also qualify as an invention because they altered, without interrupting, state finance. Individual Italian bankers (*campsores*), sometimes in syndicate, gave short-term loans to popes even before the rise of the large, unitary merchant-banks. With the help of the newly emergent merchant-banks, however, popes and later the English king could assemble money for their armies more quickly, taking loans from their Italian bankers in anticipation of extraordinary tax assessments, which were collected slowly and painfully. Merchant-bankers were repaid, often directly, from the state collections of substantial tax revenues that came in later. Because of this administrative arrangement of sharing tax collection, Italian merchant-banks became insinuated into, and indeed became partial authors of, the budding state-finance administrative machineries of their sponsors.

In the 1270s the English king Edward I introduced a wrinkle into this loans-against-future-taxes financial system, originally invented by the popes, which would have enormous consequences for the developing economy of Florence. Mercantilist English law prohibited the export of precious metal from the kingdom, so loans to the English king had to be repaid in raw wool, coming largely from monasteries. The introduction of a new English customs system, with Italian merchant-bankers participating in its administration and design, was the innovative solution for achieving this repayment. Organizational innovation in papal banking redounded into organizational invention in English state fiscal administration, which supported the original banking innovation. The enormous consequence for the Florentine economy was the diversion of high-quality English wool exports from their original destination of Flanders to the newly developing textile industry of Florence. Florence thereby came to displace Flanders as the primary center for wool-textile production in Europe.

With this new macroeconomic link between wool textiles and state finance came high merchant profits to couple with enormous (but risky) banking profits. The large unitary merchant-banks entered a self-sustaining "takeoff" phase, with steady merchant business anchoring their highly volatile state-finance business.

A final autocatalytic flow involved people, not money or goods. Originally Italian bankers were smallish money changers, sometimes but not always Jewish, tainted with the odor of usury. Participation in international trade could improve their social prestige from mere domestic money changers to international merchant-bankers—a considerable climb in social status, though still below the rank of nobility. In the fluid stage of the early 1200s, traveling Italian merchants clustered abroad in expatriate communities and neighborhoods called *nazioni*, with the permission of local potentates. Social bonds within *nazioni* could become close—the social foundation for economic cooperation

[36] This definition of "selection" is essentially identical with biologists' conception of "fitness" as relative reproduction but not with economists' conception of "fitness" as relative performance.

[37] Padgett and McLean 2006, 1468–71.

[38] I thank Walter Fontana for suggesting the useful distinction between banks and banking, a distinction upon which Goldthwaite (2009) also insists.

among overseas nationals—but in the early period local potentates did not grant permission to stay in their territory for more than three or four months at a time.

With the rise of the large, unitary merchant-banks in the mid-1200s, however, international merchant-bankers became associated with popes and kings. Such legitimation and protection attracted substantial deposits from lay and clerical aristocracies all over Europe. A multiplier effect on the growth of capital thus kicked in, a point that Sapori in particular has emphasized. My compatible point, from a social mobility perspective, is that such customers gave to successful leaders of large, unitary merchant-banks a plausible claim for noble status for themselves. This is my finding of "family coming out of company." Successful bankers in unitary banks became noble-mimicking patrilineages through bringing sons and relatives into the bank and through purchasing property in their native city and in its countryside.[39] This social consolidation contributed to the longevity and corporate character of the bank: company *corpo* became family patrimony. It also integrated bankers into the ruling patriciate of their city.

Once these audacious claims by merchants to noble status were recognized by their feudal peers, a spillover occurred into Italian elite family structure. A subset of Italian feudal nobility became more mercantile than their French, English, and German counterparts. In the tumultuous politics of the 1200s, which will be described a bit later in the chapter, fragile Italian communal elites had every incentive to reach out for sympathetic allies, as long as the volume of such families was not too substantial. This process of gradual and highly restricted[40] social absorption reached a point in Florence such that merchant families like the Bardi and the Cerchi were declared magnates in 1293, along with other more truly feudal families.[41]

The sequence of organizational invention just described is presented visually in figure 5.1, which identifies by circled numbers the temporal sequences of cross-network spillover in this simplified diagram of European political economy.

[39] Blomquist is particularly good at demonstrating these patrilineage spillovers for the companies and families of Lucca.

[40] Restricted because there were not that many large unitary merchant-banks.

[41] This observation speaks to a longstanding debate in Florentine political historiography: see Ottokar 1962, among others.

To summarize, the Dugento mechanism of organizational invention was the pope reaching into the Champagne fairs to absorb the international merchant-bankers he found there. The unitary merchant-banks thereby created warrant the label "invention," not just "innovation," because of the systemic spillovers they induced, which reinforced the reproduction of these banks. These multiple-network systemic spillovers included the following: (a) the deflection of international trade from the Champagne fairs of the banks' origin into themselves; (b) the development of the capacity of state finance to anticipate slow revenues; (c) the creation of the English system of customs; (d) the growth of the Florentine textile manufacturing industry; and (e) the absorption of elite merchants into noble family systems of patrilineage. This autocatalytic ensemble of multiple-network flows made not just innovative banks but a Commercial Revolution.

MACROHISTORICAL OVERVIEW

Such at least is my causal interpretation, based on considerable reading of primary and secondary sources.[42] Now what about evidence and proof? In this section I provide a macrohistorical narrative of the wars and political context of the organizational development of the Tuscan unitary merchant-banks. I provide new evidence from the papal registers dating the main innovative incorporation intervention by Pope Urban IV to 1262. In the next section, using both papal registers and existing case studies, I trace the "dependent variable" that responded to this papal intervention, as best I can with imperfect data—namely, growth and transformation in the partnership and branch structures of Italian merchant-banks.

(a) Champagne Fairs

The economic seeds out of which the Tuscan unitary merchant-banks grew were the short-term partnerships and agency relations among the geographically fluid Italian merchants who participated in the Champagne fairs outside Paris and in *nazioni* expatriate communities in England, in Flanders, and in other parts of France. The first documented "caravan merchants" to

[42] Again, see the lengthy extracts of primary and secondary sources, in various languages, that appear on my webpage (Padgett 2009a, 2009b).

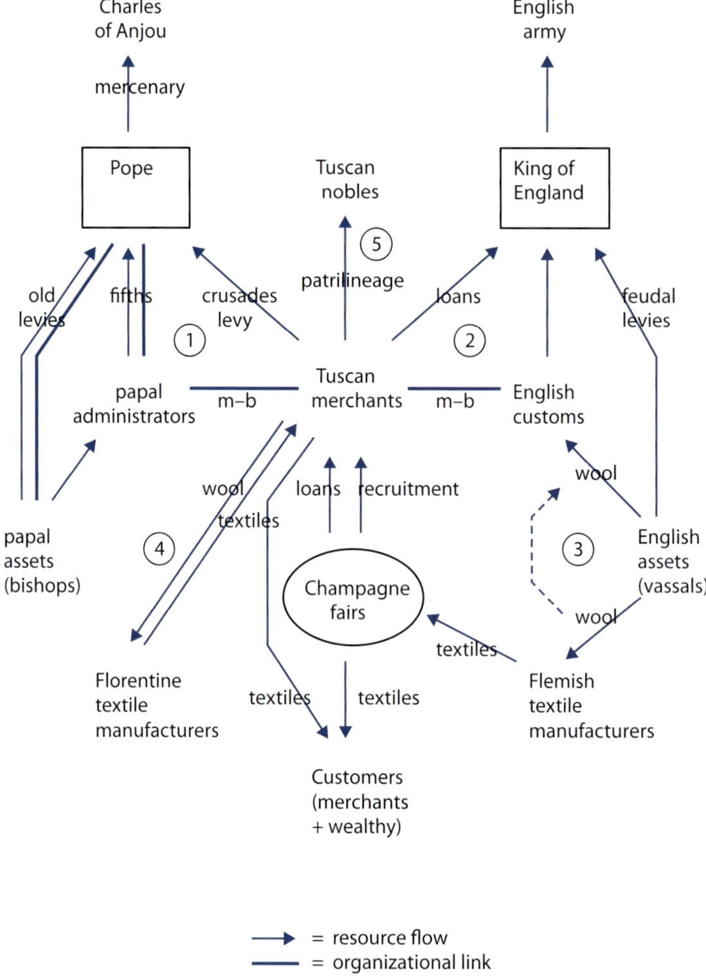

Figure 5.1 Sequence of emergence of Dugento Tuscan merchant-banks.

the Champagne fairs, in the 1190s, were from Arras in Flanders and from Asti in the Italian Alps.[43] By 1253 the Genoese had moved to a position of dominance in this merchant trading and exchange business.[44] Italian merchants moving within the orbits of their *nazioni* and hometowns developed short-term agency or "power of attorney" relations[45] with each other in order to take care of each other's business in cities while they were absent. These delegation contracts were primarily between merchants from the same hometown. Longer-term partnerships, to the extent they existed, were often between brothers. The Genoese in particular, because of their sea trade, had the capacity to extend these

[43] Reynolds 1952.

[44] According to Face (1969, 76): "Using as my criterion their appearance as principals in a contract drawn on a fair of Champagne in the fourth volume of the unpublished cartulary of the Genoese notary Bartholomeus de Fornarion for the year 1253, I have identified 278 individuals as belonging to that group of merchants who dominated the trade between Genoa and Champagne in the middle of the thirteenth century. . . . Of these 278 individuals, 146 or approximately 52% are Genoese; 50 or approximately 12% are Florentines; 21 are Sienese; 7 are from Lucca; 6 are from Parma; 4 are from Pistoia; and 3 are from Cremona. In contrast there remain only 6 Asti men. To my knowledge there are no longer any men from Arras in the group." Of course, the fact that the source for this information was a Genoese notary may inflate the estimated Genoese percentage somewhat.

[45] More specifically, delegation contracts of *procurator*, *nuncio*, or *misso*. See Face 1958.

agency or procurator relations east to the Levant, as well as north to Champagne.[46]

The Champagne fairs sprung into existence, probably in the mid-1100s, as a result of the macroeconomic conjuncture of the development of trading routes to the Levant, the discovery of silver in Germany, and the emergence of textile production in Flanders. In its origins, the Champagne fairs had nothing to do with papal finance.

(b) Crusades

Local feudal fighting was of course a constant during this period. But the really big military actions were the crusades. The incorporation intervention that mattered for the invention of corporate banks was not the usual crusades directed toward Jerusalem but the unusual crusades directed back inward toward Italy itself—the so-called Italian crusades of the popes against the Holy Roman Empire starting in 1254 and recurring intermittently until 1302.[47]

Financing of the First Crusade (1096–99) was a decentralized affair of the crusaders themselves, mostly feudal lords but also poor pilgrims, who mobilized their own troops and funds.[48] In the Second, Third, and Fourth Crusades (1147–49, 1187–92, 1202–4), kings started to exert more centralized control, starting in the Third Crusade through levying special taxes mostly on the towns and on the church properties in their reigns.[49] The Fourth Crusade demonstrated the weakness of secular control from the perspective of the Church: the crusaders and their Venetian shippers struck a private deal to capture Constantinople instead of continuing on to conquer the Holy Land.

In the Fifth Crusade (1217–21), Popes Innocent III and Honorius III started to develop the fiscal administrative machinery necessary to exercise centralized papal control. More or less standardized taxes on dispersed church properties were collected by appointed papal nuncios and bureaucrats rather than by local bishops alone.[50] The Knights Templar, as early papal "bankers,"[51] were used to move precious metals collected from local churches and monasteries all over Europe to the East, there to be distributed by papal legates, like Pelagius. Such centralized fiscal distribution blurred the line between crusaders and mercenaries.

Many strides in papal fiscal administration thus were made, including within the pope's central office or *camera* (literally "bedroom"). Without these, the later Italian merchant-banks would have had no one on the papal administration side to work with. But the dramatic failure[52] of the Seventh Crusade (1248–54), led by an alliance between Pope Innocent IV and King/Saint Louis IX of France, illustrated the weakness of even this improved system: neither slowly assembled monies (i.e., precious metals) nor troops could be delivered fast enough in emergency situations.

(c) Italian Crusades

Enter the Holy Roman Emperors—first the dashing Frederick II (1194–1250), then his tough sons, legitimate Conrad IV (1228–54) and illegitimate Manfred (1232–66), then his adolescent grandson Conradin (1252–68). From their inherited and wealthy base in Sicily, as well as from their disorderly homeland in Germany, all of these emperors aspired to making their grandiose but chimeral titles into reality. All that was necessary was to take over the popes' heartland of Italy using a military squeeze play.

This was not an unattainable goal because all of Italy was militarily fractious at the time—too busy fighting their neighbors to come together to defend "themselves," whatever that meant.[53] Upon Frederick II's revival of the pope-versus-emperor wars,[54] all these local feudal bands of Italian nobles clustered themselves into Guelf and Ghibelline factions. Technically the labels meant "pro-pope" and "pro-emperor," respectively, but these military bands were concerned primarily about their hostile neighbors. Hence their titular "leaders" could not always rely on

[46] Face (1969) provides a colorful example.

[47] The narrative in this subsection draws heavily from Grossman 1965 and Housley 1982.

[48] Or else scavenged them en route.

[49] The first general tax levy was called the Saladin Tithe, a precursor to national taxation. Nobles usually escaped these levies because they (a) directly participated in the military; (b) paid someone to take their place; or (c) simply refused, when the king did not have enough power to coerce them.

[50] Lunt 1934, 1939.

[51] Bankers is in quotes because this refers to physical transport only; no loans were involved.

[52] Including the Muslim capture and ransom of the French king for an amount equivalent to an entire year's tax revenue in France.

[53] Waley 1969 is an especially good survey account of the politics and domestic warfare of the Italian communes during this period. Jones 1997 is a learned but less readable version.

[54] The Investiture Controversy had been in 1075.

them.[55] What this meant for Frederick and for his opponent popes Gregory IX and Innocent IV was that whenever any of them blew a whistle, they could assemble a hodgepodge of unpredictable Italian noble militia to supplement whatever core troops they had. All this made for a very combustible military situation in Italy throughout the 1200s.

Wars in Italy broke out repeatedly: between Frederick and Pope Gregory in 1237–41, between Frederick and Pope Innocent in 1246–48, and between Manfred and Pope Innocent in 1254. With the Tuscan Ghibelline victory in 1260 in support of Manfred at Montaperti (outside of Siena), the emperors' dream of control over Italy seemed finally within reach. Since 1232 the popes no longer even had a stable home in Rome: they fled from one mountain top to another, in search of security and friends, all the while frantically issuing papal letters and missives that made it seem like their bureaucracy still functioned.[56] The popes were in very grave danger indeed, in spite of their administrative reforms.

Overall, then, the Dugento presents to modern eyes a contradiction: on the economic side, a budding "modernity" of trade, contracts, and markets; on the military side, a bewildering morass of feudal fighting at multiple scales, always with armies of questionable loyalty. These were the raw social-network materials out of which the new Tuscan merchant-banks were built.

(d) Pope Urban IV

Figure 5.2 presents data on the total number of papal missives or commands issued per year, from 1243 to 1268, as recorded in the papal registries of four consecutive mid-Dugento popes (see the bibliography). Figure 5.3 presents data on the subset of these papal letters that mentioned Italian bankers.[57] Figure 5.2 demonstrates a heavy papal workload, whose temporal rhythms were tied to their successive wars with the Holy Roman Emperor. Figure 5.3 shows that while the first connections between popes and Italian bankers certainly preceded Urban IV,[58] it was only under his reign that Italian bankers suddenly became actively organized into these strenuous war efforts. One effect of this mobilization appears to be that the efficiency of missive-issuing behavior by Urban IV skyrocketed: he issued nearly two thousand letters in 1264, in preparation for his upcoming war with Manfred.[59] Even this unprecedented effort underestimates that year's amazing letter-production rate, since Pope Urban died on September 11, 1264, thereby depriving the time series of over three months of otherwise observable behavior.[60]

What led Urban IV strenuously to mobilize Italian bankers into his war-making fiscal machinery? The problems that Italian merchant-bankers could solve, which the Knights Templar could not, have already been mentioned: (a) transfer of money using *cambium* contracts through their dispersed network of agents (rather than lugging precious metal around on horses) and, most important of all, (b) loans, using capital raised at the Champagne fairs. Italian bankers could solve the fiscal speed and hence the military coordination problems that plagued tax extraction at that time.

Obviously these economic-efficiency advantages were fundamental for lock-in and selection. They represented a major innovation in state finance. But this statement of fiscal consequences is not enough to explain Urban's act of innovation. Given the fairs of Champagne, other popes before Urban could have done the same thing. Both motive and opportunity were there. But only Urban did it. Functionalist explanations of consequence, however helpful for understanding selection, are not causal explanations of genesis.

Urban IV's predecessor, Pope Alexander IV, had the major strategic idea but not the organizational skills or knowledge to pull it off—namely, to preach "crusade" against the "Anti-Christ" in Italy. The Jerusalem experience of generalized tax levies on church properties (e.g., the *decima*) thereby came on line, and Italian Guelf militias were catalyzed. Some complained that this was

[55] Famous theater line: "enter stage right, Guelfs and Ghibellines fighting."

[56] Reading the bureaucratic formality of the papal registers while noticing the skittish movements of the popes who issued these "commands" makes for a somewhat poignant experience. These popes quite literally were running for their lives, barely escaping a number of military traps.

[57] The complete list of these missives, with verbatim extracts from each, is presented in Padgett 2009a.

[58] A fact to which I shall return later.

[59] "The character of the new pope [Urban IV] was well described by a Sienese merchant, who wrote of him that 'he does what he wishes and no one dares contradict him; he acts more like a temporal lord than a pope and he wants to make the land submit to him as much as he can; no pope since Alexander III has been so constant in his deeds and words'" (Waley 1961, 165).

[60] Did Pope Urban IV die of overwork?

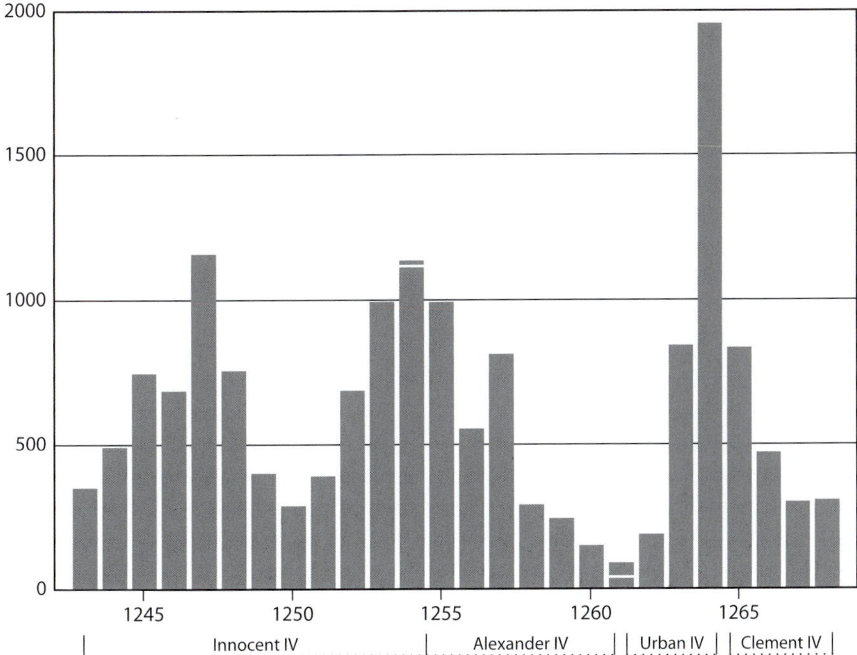

Figure 5.2 Total number of papal letters, 1243–68.

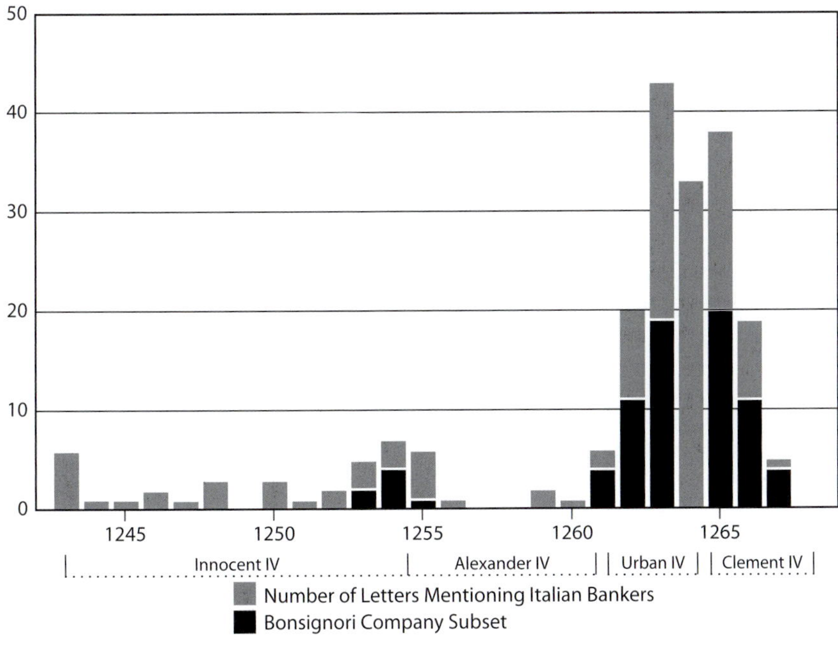

Figure 5.3 Number of letters mentioning Italian bankers.

a perversion of the crusader ideal.[61] But for the popes of the time, this was a life-or-death matter.

Alexander's specific and quite plausible idea was to preach this crusade in England, where King Henry III had previously expressed his interest to Innocent IV in commuting Henry's earlier "true" crusader pledge into a "Sicilian Venture" that allowed his second son, Edmund, to invade and to take over Sicily instead of going off himself to the Holy Land. In spite of Innocent's intense struggle with Frederick, this pious pope said to Henry, in effect: "No thanks, go off to the Holy Land." Which Henry never did.

Pope Alexander, on the other hand, decided to take up Henry on his offer after all. Taxes on English church properties were raised for the Sicilian venture, but tax collection was so slow and English resistance so high[62] that enough money never could be assembled quickly enough. The incomplete tax revenues ended up in who-knows-whose pockets. Eventually this "illegitimate" tax extraction led to the Barons' Revolt in 1258, to the military defeat of King Henry, and to the temporary loss of Henry's power.[63]

Pope Urban took this failed English idea of Alexander and made it French. Urban himself was French, from Troyes in Champagne, not Italian like his predecessors. His previous job had been Patriarch of Jerusalem, in which capacity he was intimately familiar with (normal) crusade finance. One result was that Charles of Anjou, brother of King/Saint Louis IX, was chosen to be the pope's champion instead of Edmund of England. "Crusade" against the Holy Roman Anti-Christ was launched using church properties in France as the tax base and the Champagne fairs as liquidity. Charles of Anjou himself was to contribute nothing except himself and his troops. A prince and future king in name but a mercenary in fact.

Presumably Urban became familiar with the merchant-banking techniques of the Genoese while in his previous job. So then why did he choose the Tuscans and not the Genoese to be his Italian merchant-bankers? Because his Tuscan merchant-bankers were politically Guelf, and the Genoese were not.[64]

As crusade finances were preached and Tuscans chosen to administer them, unsuccessful Alexander and successful Urban attached these cameral merchants,[65] as they were now called, to the existing papal collection system for its normal levies. First the Bonsignori company of Siena, and later others, were declared *campsores domini papae*, or official bankers to the pope.[66] On the one hand, this involved giving large loans to the pope. On the other hand, this involved transferring papal tax monies from papal nuncios, bishops, and abbots to the pope. By 1277 this also involved being the depositories for papal tax revenues collected overseas.

For such new papal tax-collection activities to be acceptable to local kings—the king of England under Alexander's failed Sicilian venture and the king of France under Urban's successful Angevin venture—there had to be authorizing commissions for the Tuscans from the pope, acceptable to the kings. Such commissions granted permanent residency to the Tuscan cameral merchants, quite an extension from the transient three-month authorizations previously granted to visiting Italian merchants, organized in their *nazioni* communities. Permanent residency of merchants, a prerequisite for permanent organizational branches, grew within this legal umbrella.

Transferring and holding papal tax revenues gave the Italian bankers an enormous float that they could invest for their own profits, through their own international trade. Private merchant activity and papal banking activity were therefore simpatico: merchants made huge money without popes paying much. With papal (and soon regal) business providing the stable and more or less legally secure foundation, wealthy prelates and barons started making large deposits in Tuscan merchant-banks, as Sapori has emphasized. The earliest such deposits indeed were for the purpose of paying taxes. Later more voluntary investments had ecclesiastical courts to back them up. As Lunt (1934, 56) puts it, "The prominent position held by the Italian bankers in European financial affairs must be attributed in no small degree to the business and protection of the papacy."

Such was the sequence of moves that led to Urban's administrative innovation. Urban himself

[61] Housley 1982, 37.

[62] Gasquet 1905, 347–74.

[63] This interlude of King Henry as only a figurehead led to the creation of Parliament. In 1265 his son Edward I defeated the barons and restored full monarchy, taming but not eliminating the Parliament. The Barons' Revolt of 1258, of course, built upon the more famous Magna Carta revolt of 1215.

[64] The intimate intertwining of Tuscan finance and Tuscan politics will be examined later in the chapter.

[65] Lunt 1934, 51–56; Lunt 1939, 599–603.

[66] Jordan 1909, 9–44. In his letters addressed to third parties, Urban IV himself referred to his chosen bankers not with this official language but with the more personal language of *nostri et ecclesie Romane devoti* (nos. 171–72, 426, 508, 518–21, 536, 542, 562, 2245).

had a foot in both worlds—the Champagne fairs and the Church, especially the "Church militant" of the crusades. His French biography made mobilization of the market for the church a natural, especially given his Italian predecessor's creative perversion of the idea of the crusade.

However created, Urban's innovation of using Tuscan merchant-bankers as papal fiscal agents locked in because it worked decisively on the military battleground. Urban never lived to see the culmination of his extraordinary efforts. But unlike the previous war failures of Innocent and Alexander, the subsequent (also French) pope, Clement IV, and his champion, Charles of Anjou, won a decisive battle in 1266 at Benevento over the fearsome Manfred, killing him directly on the battlefield and seizing his treasure. Another decisive battle over the grandson Conradin in 1268 at Tagliacozzo eliminated him as well. Major emergency loans by Tuscan merchant-bankers, against future tax collections, were essential in these mercenary victories. The Hohenstaufen dynasty of the Holy Roman Empire thereby came to a permanent end, though other papal wars of various sorts continued, eventually even against Charles of Anjou.

As a subplot in these Italian crusades, Florence temporarily swung Ghibelline in 1260 after Montaperti, with many Florentine Guelf noble families becoming exiles, but then swung back to Guelf in 1266 after Benevento, with many Florentine Ghibelline noble families exiled. Civil war raged, and much of the city and its tower houses were physically destroyed. Similar domestic upheaval occurred in Siena. Reverberations across levels of analysis are common in this period.

(e) The English Customs Service

The next chapter in this political-economic narrative of banking invention is the creation of the English customs service in 1275, which taxed the flow of English wool to Flanders. This new service enabled new English king Edward I, Henry's first son, to copy Pope Urban IV's fiscal innovation and to transplant it to England. Italian merchant-bankers were to be repaid in wool because precious metals legally could not be taken out of the country by private citizens. Figure 5.4 documents the simultaneity of this creation of the English wool customs and the intense involvement of the Ricciardi company of Lucca at the outset of the long reign of Edward I.

The diffusion of the basic idea to Edward also involved the crusades, a great mixer and shaker in this period. While still a prince, Edward led the failed Ninth "true" Crusade (1271–72) to the Holy Land, belatedly fulfilling his father's pledge. During his slow return, he dawdled for a year in Gascony, then under his own inheritance. Luke Natale of Lucca, acting in the traditional role of transient banker/money changer for the crusades, traveled with Edward during his perambulations and became close friends with him. Luke already had been part of the networked Luchese *nazione* in England, out of which the huge Ricciardi company of Lucca was soon to spring.[67] I have no "smoking gun" quote to prove this, but I presume that Luke educated Edward about the virtues of Urban IV's recent innovations. Siena and Florence, after all, were not distant from Lucca, and Tuscans mingled in their *nazioni*. For implementation in England, the only hitch was that there needed to be a way to repay loans by the Italian merchant-bankers (like Luke himself). Since Lucca as a city was economically founded on silk manufacturing and trading, the solution lay close at hand. The Luchese *nazione* in England already moved around textiles as a business and was quite prepared to diversify its mercantile trade from silk to wool, as were the Sienese and Florentine *nazioni*. Thus Urban IV's innovation diffused to England through the self-interested intermediation of the Tuscan merchant-bankers themselves. They then implemented their own advice by inserting their respective *nazioni* into the king's fiscal administration.

The English creation of the wool customs in 1275 was an enormous step toward centralized monarchy. A new and centralized flow of tax revenues was made available to the king, independent of Magna Carta–type fiscal constraints, upon which the Barons' Revolt had recently insisted. The serious financial-cum-political problems that Henry the father had experienced were solved by Edward the son—with help from Italians, who had implemented an originally French idea. Patent-law assumptions about private property notwithstanding, ownership of "inventions" becomes distributed when systems tip.

Overall, my contention is that organizational invention in the "visible hand" of the market was rooted in state finance—or more precisely, in the simpatico linkage between international trade and state finance.

[67] More details on this will follow.

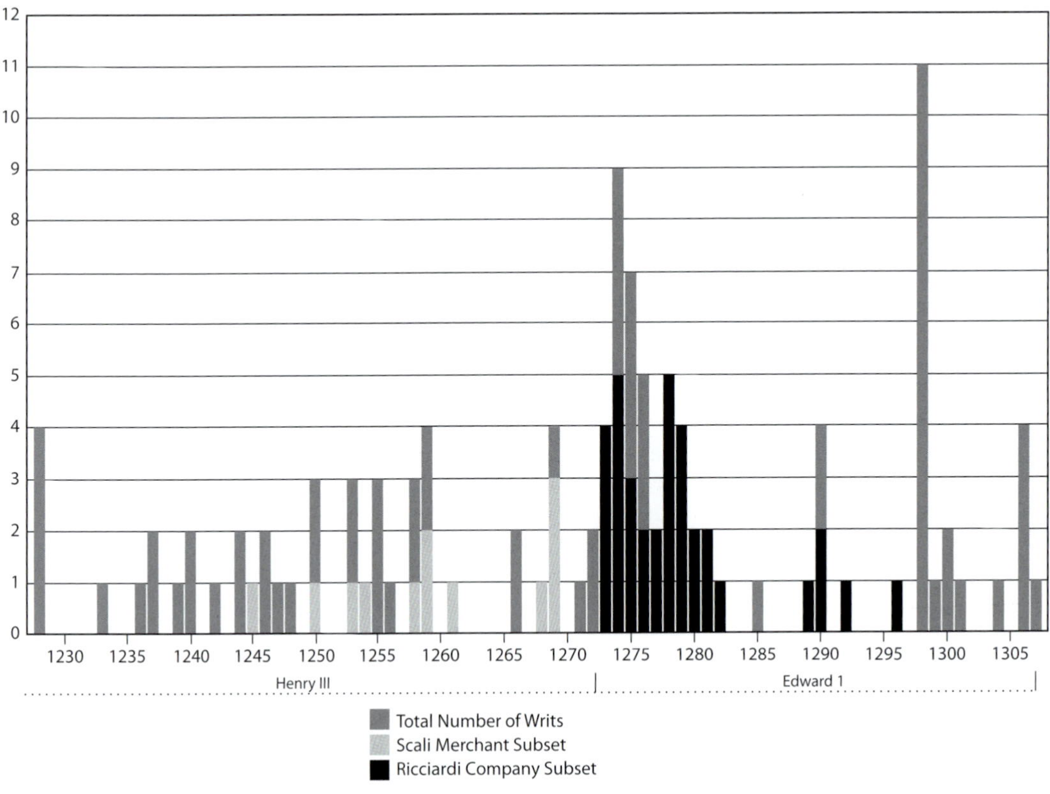

Figure 5.4 Italian bankers in extract from liberate rolls of king of England.

ORGANIZATIONAL EVOLUTION

In appendices A–D I present four case studies in tabular form of the organizational development and transactional activity of the largest banks from this period. The case studies are the Bonsignori company of Siena, the Scali company of Florence, the Tolomei company of Siena, and the Ricciardi company of Lucca. These tables array by year the transactional references that I have found to these companies in multiple secondary sources and in two primary sources: (a) the papal registers of Popes Innocent IV, Alexander IV, Urban IV, and Clement IV; and (b) extracts from the Liberate Rolls of the king of England, assembled by Bond (1839). The case-study tables document both the origins and the explosive growth in the 1260s of the Bonsignori, Scali, and Tolomei companies under the sponsorship of the popes (although in the Tolomei case this growth was aborted). They also document the origins and the rapid growth in the 1270s of the Ricciardi company under the sponsorship of King Edward I of England.

In appendix E, I provide a comprehensive snapshot of the twenty banks that were absolved from excommunication by Pope Urban IV in 1263 (plus four more in 1265) at the height of his most intensive mobilization of Tuscan merchant-bankers into supporting his Italian crusade against Manfred, both economically and politically.

(a) Origins of Case-Study Companies

As far as my sources enable us to see them, most of the early partners in these four large case-study banks were drawn from the transient Italian merchant communities or *nazioni* in Champagne and in England. They were then mobilized into cross-*nazioni* corporations by the popes or, in the Ricciardi case, by the English king.

The largest early Tuscan bank was the Bonsignori company of Siena. One is tempted to say that numerous famous later Florentine banks (e.g., Frescobaldi, Bardi, Peruzzi) were modeled on this early template, except for the fact that numerous such banks were born at almost the same time.[68] The Bonsignori were the largest, the most favored, and the most successful of the first-generation corporate banks.

The brothers Bonifacio di Bonsignore and Orlando di Bonsignore[69] were bankers (*campsores*) who operated in Genoa and Champagne.[70] In 1252 Bonifacio first appear[illegible]ve been appointed offici[illegible] (*campsor domini pa*[illegible]ans to the Church we[illegible]racter, by which I me[illegible] by temporary syndi[illegible]eshuffled across transac[illegible]

In 1255 o[illegible]di Bonsignore" partn[illegible]s reorganized—throw[illegible]o and incorporating o[illegible]most important of which w[illegible]onaventura di Bernardino. The apparent reason for this becomes clearer through the English Liberate Rolls. Bonaventura's father, Bernardino di Prosperino, had been active in loaning money to the king of England, for expenses and the like, along with other Sienese residents in England. These loans were also not really corporate in character but were offered by syndicates of *nazione* merchants, who reshuffled among themselves.[72] The new nonfamily partnership between Orlando di Bonsignore and Bonaventura di Bernardino (and others), in other words, was a partnership connection between Champagne and England. We shall see similar cross-geographical links develop at the same time in the Scali company.

Why the timing of this? This is the period of the failed English Sicilian venture. Pope Alexander IV gave to King Henry III of England permission to label as a "crusade" Henry's desire to send his second son, Edmund, to invade Sicily, thereby attacking the Holy Roman Emperor. Alexander authorized the collection of crusade tithes on English church property. As discussed above, ultimately this failed, leading to the Barons' Revolt in England. The point here is that this first triggering of the sedentary Bonsignori "corporation" was due to Alexander's early drive toward Italian-crusade papal finance.

In addition to internal English political constraints, a second reason for the failure of this particular war mobilization effort was Alexander's passivity in directing this tax-collection effort (as indicated in figure 5.2). Alexander delegated the collection of taxes on English church property to his hated[73] legates. In sharp contrast, Pope Urban IV directed his own frantic tax-collection drive himself, sending out orders all over France and Italy, but mainly France, in a much more centralized style.

While the details of the early formation of the Scali company are of course different, the broad contour is similar. Contra the general argument of Sapori, the core of the Scali company was not really the della Scala family at all. Rather it was a clique of four Florentine merchants resident in England—Amieri Cosa, Spigliato di Cambio, Rocco di Cambio, and Mainetto Spini. These merchants had been importing cloth into England since 1229, the beginning of Italian *nazioni* communities in England. These merchants also offered a variety of loans to the king from 1245 to 1254 in the reshuffling syndicate manner typical of the time, one deal of which involved Jacobo della Scala.[74]

The alliance between this clique and the della Scala family took place in 1255 through 1257. In 1255 a large loan was given in Gascony to King Henry III's first son, Prince Edward (later King Edward I), in order to raise some troops.[75] In 1256 a substantial partnership in England crystallized to service the Sicilian venture. In

[68] See appendix E for a quasi-census.

[69] In this context "di" means "son of." Such a name ("John son of Paul"), with no surname, connotes a nonpatrician status. Indeed the relative lack of wealth of the early Bonsignori was verified by Chiaudano (1935, 113–14) using early Sienese tax censuses.

[70] See Chiaudano 1935 on Genoa.

[71] English (1988, 12n8) thinks that Bonifacio's appointment by Innocent IV was due to his past link to the previous *campsor domini papae* of Pope Gregory IX, Angelerio Solaficu from Siena. This is quite plausible, but I could not verify that and hence do not record Angelerio in the Bonsignori table.

[72] Indeed the appendix shows that temporary syndicate partners in England of Bernardino di Prosperi later became regular partners in the Scali and Tolomei companies.

[73] The chronicle of Matthew Paris reflects contemporary English attitudes toward this tax collection and toward Italian bankers in general: "The usurers called Chorsins, who went under the name Christians, found a place of refuge and peace in England. First tolerated, and then afterwards openly protected by the pope, they unblushingly called themselves merchants or money-changers of the pope. Prelates were suspended from the collation to benefices until the pope's avarice on behalf of his unworthy barbarians [i.e., mercenaries], who never appeared in England" ([1247–50] 1986, 275; see also pp. 98, 103, 165).

[74] The family surname "della Scala" indicates a higher social status than the others.

[75] Borsari 1994, 19.

1257 Jacobo's son Cavalcante joined this new company on a permanent basis, thereby contributing the company's name.[76]

Syndicate loans directly to the English crown continued in 1258 and 1259, but in 1261 we see the massive entry of a greatly enlarged "Scali" company into the pope's own service. This was the year that the Scali company was appointed *campsores domini papae*, joining the Bonsignori company in this role.[77] The appointment of this second "favored banking company" was made by Pope Alexander IV at the very end of his life, probably in order to strengthen his (failed) financial connection to England. The Bonsignori had restructured themselves to strengthen their own English connection, but their economic roots remained primarily in France. The "Scali," however, had been in England from the Italian *nazioni* beginning.

The Tolomei company comes closest to fitting the Sapori model of "family plus outsiders" because of the extensive involvement of the patrician Tolomei family, mostly in small loans to the city government. But even these various Tolomei family members combined and recombined in their transactions in a fluid manner.

The Tolomei case is complicated by the fact that when the pope first mobilized them into papal finance, during the failed Sicilian venture, he actually mobilized two companies of them. The first was the earlier family-dominated business. This set of partners moved for a few years into papal finance but then dropped out and went back to wool trading. The second apparently new company, the Scotti-Tolomei company, was an alliance between three of the Tolomei with numerous other Sienese, including four of the Scotti. This second company was appointed official *campsores domini papae* by Alexander late in his life. This second company also did not stay long in papal finance. Urban launched an investigation into its unsatisfactory financial performance.[78] The first Tolomei company was called in to broker a compromise between Pope Urban and the Scotti-Tolomei. While the first Tolomei company escaped blame in the matter, neither company figured as major papal bankers again.

I do not have much partnership data over time on the Scotti-Tolomei, probably because they did not last long. But the fact that the regular Tolomei, when they dropped back to normal wool merchants, also dropped back to shifting partnership patterns is the exception that proves the rule.

My fourth and final case study of the Ricciardi company shows how the popes' financial innovation worked when it was transposed ten years later to England by the finally new[79] king Edward I. King Edward made an extension to this state-finance system of enormous consequence for the wool industry in Florence: the introduction of a wool customs to pay back Tuscan bankers' loans to the English king.

The first page of the Ricciardi table in the appendix, which takes us through 1266, demonstrates that originally there were two almost completely distinct sets of Lucchese merchants who later combined into the unified Ricciardi company: one set operating in Lucca, the other set operating in England. The Lucchese merchants in Lucca were manufacturing fine silk cloth. The Lucchese merchants in England were selling that silk cloth to wealthy clients, including to King Henry III himself. The Ricciardi name descended from the Lucca half of this cooperation—in particular, from one Ricciardo di Graziano di Ricciardo, a silk dyer or *tintor*. Each of these two geographically distinct subsets of merchants demonstrated considerable fluidity in their partnerships—namely, partnerships formed and re-formed among merchants within these two locations over time. The "almost" part of the first sentence in this paragraph refers to the one exception of Peregrino Sesmundi, who in 1241 apparently moved from Lucca to England, thereby creating the only partnership bridge in these early data between these two subsets of merchants.

Based on these data, historians have assumed that an integrated Ricciardi company existed in the 1240s and 1250s, with one branch making silk and the other branch selling silk. In my opinion, this reads history backward: inferring early structure from what followed. No doubt there were cooperative exchange relations between these two complementary halves of the supply

[76] I hypothesize that the Scali name was chosen for the firm, in spite of its leadership by others, because of the superior social status of that name. An alternative hypothesis is that the name was chosen because of the greater capital contribution of della Scala. But no partnership contracts, which would list capital contributions, of any of these companies survive. Later the less prestigious Cambii family spun out of the Scali company to form their own company. When they did so they took on a new, more noble family name for themselves: the de Mozzi.

[77] Jordan 1909, 11.

[78] Jordan 1909, 15; Lunt 1939, 602–3; Mucciarelli 1995, 105–6.

[79] King Henry III's reign lasted fifty-six years. King Edward I's own reign lasted thirty-five years.

chain. But I don't see the evidence, such as it is,[80] as demonstrating anything more than regularized cooperation.

The Ricciardi company exploded in partnership size, however, in the 1270s, with geographical branches appearing not only in England but also in Ireland and Paris. The original Lucca silk-manufacturing branch recedes from sight in the sources, but an extensive partnership list in 1286 leads to the presumption that the silk-manufacturing "home office" was still there, in the misty background. The Lucca branch itself was overshadowed by the transformation of the Ricciardi company into the primary bankers of the English king. As a consequence, the most important partner of the company was no longer one of the Ricciardi family but rather Lucasio Natale (Luke of Luka in English sources), the personal banker and friend of King Edward I.

Judging from timing, the triggering event in this transformation of the Ricciardi company appears to be loans[81] given to the still prince Edward in Genoa in 1272 during his leisurely return to England from his failed Ninth Crusade. Lucasio Natale had accompanied Edward throughout his crusade, such travels building upon the earlier social and business ties established between his compatriots and King Henry III in their previous roles as silk salesmen to the king.[82] It seems plausible to assume from their speed of implementation, immediately after Edward's November 1272 accession to the throne, that the financial innovations by Edward—namely, to appoint the Ricciardi company as favored state financiers and to make wool customs the mechanism of repayment—were rooted in these travel conversations and these loans between Lucasio and Prince Edward. Through *nazioni* linkages with other Tuscan bankers abroad, Lucasio would have been well informed about the contemporary financial innovations made by his Sienese and Florentine colleagues. If this is correct, then Tuscan bankers were not only the beneficiaries but also the (self-interested) authors of innovation in English state finance.

Tuscan bankers in general, and the Ricciardi company in particular, benefited greatly in trade from their increased control over the flow of English wool exports in repayment for their loans to the English king. In 1273, 24.4 percent of all licensed wool exports from England were in the hands of Tuscan companies. The distribution of wool export trade in that year is as follows:[83]

Scotti of Piacenza	2140 sacks
Riccardi of Lucca	1080 sacks
Frescobaldi of Florence	880 sacks
Bardi of Florence	700 sacks
Nicholas Testa of Lucca	700 sacks
Macci of Florence	640 sacks
Falconieri of Florence	620 sacks
Cerchi of Florence	400 sacks

The number of wool exports in the hands of Tuscan companies that were seized by the king twenty years later in 1294, a crisis year, were as follows:[84]

Riccardi of Lucca	412 sacks
Frescobaldi of Florence	360 sacks
Cerchi Neri of Florence	350 sacks
Cerchi Bianchi of Florence	301 sacks
Mozzi of Florence	261 sacks
Pulci of Florence	257.5 sacks
Frescobaldi Neri of Florence	154 sacks

These English wool-export lists give a hint of the growth in numbers of Tuscan unitary merchant-banks during the second half of the Dugento, after the initiating events analyzed here.[85]

(b) Pope Urban IV and the Corporate Organizational Form

Before he was elected pope in 1261, Urban IV was Jacques Pantaléon of Troyes. Troyes was the largest of the four towns that comprised the Champagne fairs. Urban IV, in other words, was from the Champagne fairs. Speaking a bit

[80] To repeat footnote 75, no founding contract of any partnership has survived from this period, so this disagreement in interpretation of the data is not capable of definitive resolution.

[81] Kaeuper 1973, 81; Del Punta 2004, 163. In 1255 Edward had received large loans in Gascony from the Scali, so he was directly familiar with Tuscan bankers. That previous event had triggering consequences for the Scali company as well.

[82] As is well-known, by Weber among others, state financial administration and the "king's wardrobe" blended in medieval government. Indeed the literal translation of the papal *camera* is the pope's "bedroom." Orlando Bonsignori, Pope Innocent IV's favorite banker, slept in the pope's bedroom, though I assume not in the pope's bed.

[83] Schaube 1908, 68, 183, reproduced in Kaeuper 1973, 43–44.

[84] Kaeuper 1973, 44.

[85] A longer list of sixteen Tuscan firms active in England, from 1283, is provided in Lunt 1939, appendix VI, pp. 641–65. Blomquist (1971, 173–78) provides a valuable comprehensive list of export-oriented companies in Lucca in 1284, which includes more than companies involved in English trade.

metaphorically, Urban IV was himself the incorporation of the fairs into the papacy. Speaking less metaphorically, he knew how they worked. This knowledge was used and polished through his appointment in 1255 as Patriarch of Jerusalem, shortly after the disaster of the failed Seventh Crusade.[86] Rather than being an insular man of Rome,[87] Urban IV was a man comfortable in the extended trading and military networks of medieval Europe.[88]

In figure 5.2 we have already seen evidence of Urban IV's capacity for hard work, most of which involved financing Charles of Anjou's army for war against Manfred. Urban IV did not delegate like Alexander IV; he took charge personally. Looking a bit more into the details of figure 5.3 reveals an interesting wrinkle in Urban's mobilization of Italian bankers. At first, Pope Urban IV relied heavily on the Bonsignori company, which he had inherited from his predecessors. The switch from projected English troops to projected French troops, after all, actually played to Bonsignori strengths. In 1264 at the very peak of Urban IV's frenzy, however, he dropped the Bonsignori company entirely, relying instead on a diversified range of other banks. One long-term consequence of this shift in centralized papal strategy was to propel the diffusion of the corporate organizational form beyond a few papal favorites out into the market at large.

What lay behind Urban's sudden shift toward diversification? I suggest that Urban IV's tactical approach in 1264 was not inconsistent with the Champagne fair experience of Jacques Pantaléon—except that the companies involved now emerged at a vastly larger scale and scope than before, with permanent branches instead of fluid partnerships. Urban IV from Champagne was using the market logic of Champagne to mobilize for war.[89]

Reasonable as this cognitively predisposing factor may be, Edward English has discovered that Urban had more on his mind than efficient market logic when he chose his bankers. The Guelfs and the Ghibellines of Siena and Florence had just had their battle of Montaperti in 1260, resulting in Ghibelline victory and in the installation of pro-emperor regimes in both Siena and Florence. This was the battle that led to the nadir of the popes' fortunes in Italy. Urban was basically surrounded by his enemies. His strategy for counterattack was to excommunicate both Ghibelline cities but then to target with absolution particular lists of Guelf allies and potential allies.[90] Foremost among these absolution lists were companies of merchants and companies of soldiers.[91] These lists are the source of the 1263 quasi-census of internationally oriented Florentine and Sienese companies presented in the appendix. It is worth noting that most of the new companies in this 1263 list are Florentine, not Sienese. Not all of the companies absolved in 1263 were ultimately used for papal finance in 1264 (at least in the data I coded), but many of them were. This may be the first intimation of a gradual takeover of papal business by the Florentines. If so, it places the politics of Guelf versus Ghibelline at the center of the explanation of the economic victory of Florence over Siena in the late Dugento.[92]

There was a political logic involved in the diversification of banks, in other words, as well as a market logic. Not only the original Bonsignori and Scali companies but also most of the Guelf-inclined international bankers in Siena and Florence were mobilized into Urban's crusade against Manfred—in opposition to the regimes of their own cities.[93] Papal oil was thrown on

[86] This was the crusade where the army of King/Saint Louis IX was defeated in Egypt. He was captured and ransomed for about one year's revenues of the entire kingdom of France.

[87] Indeed, as I mentioned above, he was too much on the run ever to reside in Rome.

[88] See footnote 58.

[89] Padgett and McLean (2006) call such examples of "old tool for new purpose" as the organizational- invention mechanism of "transposition and refunctionality."

[90] English 1988, 21. See Urban IV letters vol. 1, nos. 71, 161; vol. 2, nos. 175, 362–64, 410–11, 428–30, 447, 463, 465, 501, 532, 557, 570, 701; vol. 3., nos. 86, 124, 143.

[91] For companies of nobles, see Urban IV letters nos. 175, 274 (January 5, 1263; March 6, 1263). For companies of merchants, see Urban IV bulls nos. 161, 362–24, 410–11, 428–30, 447, 463, 465, 501, 511, 532, 557, 570, 701–3. (Dates range from July 5, 1263, to August 3, 1264.) The two missives absolving nobles contained long lists of companies of *nobiles viri*, whereas the missives absolving merchant companies were on a case-by-case basis. Note that nobles were absolved before merchants; this supports English's interpretation of a political motivation to Urban's technique of mobilizing Tuscany for crusade—namely to excommunicate en masse Siena and Florence but then to absolve Guelf factions within the cities that supported him. Nobles and merchants were just different wings of the church militant, in Urban's eyes.

[92] I do not deny the additional crucial importance of the new Florentine wool industry in this economic victory.

[93] This contested civil-war context led sometimes to strange contradictions. Orlando Bonsignori, for example, the "lead" partner of the Bonsignori banking company of the pope, actually aligned himself with the Ghibelline regime of Siena—so much so that he fought in the Sienese Ghibelline army at Montaperti against his papal employer's allies the Guelfs. This is someone who chose city over company, suffering exile as a consequence. Needless to say, Orlando laid low in the papal registers after this political choice, with Bonaventura emerging instead as the economic leader. But Orlando

the fires of Tuscan civil wars. When Charles of Anjou finally defeated Manfred in 1266, previously exiled Sienese and Florentine Guelfs triumphantly returned to their cities, exiled ruling Ghibellines in their turn, and destroyed their tower houses. Powerful noble Ghibelline families[94] fled to the hills and to friendlier cities, bitterly plotting their revenge and giving Dante much to write about.

The aspect of this story that interests us here is the organizational consequence of this successful mobilization, both political and economic, of Tuscan bankers for Italian crusade. Corporate organizational form, in the medieval sense of that term, is evident in the four case studies in the appendix in the following ways:

1. Home-office (director) partner roles and branch-office (nondirector) partner roles are distinguished linguistically in the papal-letter documents.[95] In the appendix, this linguistic differentiation of roles is indicated by underlining the letter number of the home-office partner, where such language appears.
2. Branches are indicated by the geographical clustering of different nondirector partners (*soci* in the documents) into specialized transaction locations.[96]
3. In contrast, director-partners are characterized by geographical diversity, as they write "home office" letters to all of their branches.
4. Under the reign of Urban IV, the highly corporate language of *societas*[97]—as in *Societas Ricciardorum*—first appears in the papal registers, although it is not yet common.[98] Language such as in footnote 94 was more commonly used instead. Lack of standardization in language is yet another indicator of how new this emergent organizational form was.

I have emphasized the temporal simultaneity of the emergence of the corporate organizational form in Tuscan banking and of financial mobilization by the popes for their Italian crusades. It seems clear that papal finance linked the Champagne fairs to war. For where, after all, did the Tuscan bankers get their original monies for loans to the pope, and later to the English king, in the first place? From the fairs.

I want to close this section by speculating about why the corporate organizational form in particular. Different aspects of this form were connected to different aspects of bankers' connection with the pope. "Large" seems induced by the magnitude of the extraordinary crusade taxes on Church properties, under the constraint that only a few favored banks were selected for the job. "Geographically dispersed" seems induced by the geographical dispersion of those Church assets. Loan money could be raised centrally in Champagne, but repayment was scattered all over Europe. Tuscan bankers had to be stably attached to papal administrators all over Europe for them to be repaid. The official church office of the *campsores domini papae* was the legal method to achieve this most securely. These practical aspects lead us toward but not quite all the way to the concept of "corporate."

Corporate in the medieval sense meant body, in particular collective body, as in "body of Christ."[99] This conception implied the continuity of the organization beyond the participatory contributions of its members—as in procession, it was hoped, all the way to heaven.[100] I see no evidence whatsoever of Tuscan merchant-bankers

still functioned officially as one of the four directors of the firm. Pope Urban IV's effort to splinter the politics of Tuscan cities, in other words, sometimes splintered the politics of his companies instead. Perhaps this was one triggering stimulus that led Urban to drop the Bonsignori in 1264 as primary bankers.

[94] Listed in Libro di Montaperti.

[95] An example would be "Andree Jacobi, Facio Juncte et Bonsignori Raynerii, sociis delectorum filiorum Rolandi Bonsignoris, Bonaventura Bernardini et Raynerii Jacobi, civium et mercatorum Senensium, campsorum camere nostre" (*Registres d'Urbain IV*, 2, n9). Here Andrea di Jacopo, Facio di Giunte, and Bonsignore di Raineri were carrying out in France a financial order issued by Urban IV in the name of their company directors Orlandino di Bonsignore, Bonaventura di Bernardino, and Raineri di Jacopo. Lunt (1934, 306) translates a similar example as "take care to assign that money in our name to the beloved sons Andrew Jacobi and James Gregorii, colleagues of the beloved sons, Bonaventura Bernardini and Rayner Jacobi, citizens and merchants of Siena" (*Registres d'Urbain IV*, 2, n. 154).

[96] This criterion alone is not decisive because it could also indicate only *nazioni*, as mentioned above. Indeed members of branch offices of unitary firms were still members of *nazioni* communities, just like their more fluid colleagues. But this criterion, even by itself, does rule out "caravan merchants" (Reynolds 1952).

[97] This contrasts with the previous language of *soci* or partners.

[98] Urban IV: letter number 159 (July 5, 1263). Under Clement IV, the language becomes somewhat more frequent: letter numbers 86, 124, 731, 803. But still not as common as it becomes later, when language is more standard.

[99] Cf. Kantorowicz 1957.

[100] Duby (1980) provides a rich discussion of "body of Christ," "procession," and "crusade" ideology in practical political use within the highly conflictual context of twelfth-century France.

thinking in terms of religious theology. But the pope certainly treated them as part of the "body of Christ militant," along with other more overtly military arms of that "procession" called crusade. They became absorbed—officially with titles, missives, and commissions—into the papal cameral administration of taxes. This was not just one aspect of their business (although it was that); this was the legal and economic foundation for most of their subsequent "private" business. The central organizational consequence of this absorption or incorporation, in my view, was continuity—residential continuity, regularized business-flow continuity, long-term loans, legal-liability continuity across partners, and finally social-attributional continuity, both by bankers of themselves and by others of them. The practical innovations in business technique discussed at the beginning of this chapter—namely, regularized business correspondence, bills of exchange, complex account books, and long-term investment—presuppose organization continuities of these sorts. In the next section, I evaluate how Tuscan bankers turned this organizational continuity into social reality through passing their business down through the generations of their newly constructed patrilineages.

One quotidian way in which corporate business technique was imparted to Tuscan merchants by their Church absorption should not escape mention just because it is obvious. Where might Tuscan merchants have gotten their revolutionary idea of a home office sending regular correspondence to sedentary *filiali*? To whose letters, after all, were they themselves responding? Long before merchants adapted missives to private business, volume upon volume of papal registers bear silent testimony to the sophistication of medieval church organization.[101] Even though I have never seen this suggestion in the literature, it does not seem so outlandish to suggest that Tuscan unitary bankers absorbed a secular version of church organization into themselves when they became agents of—indeed when they became part of—the papal *camera*.

The "origin of banking" framing of most economic historiography on unitary merchant-banks and otherwise is modernist in that it looks to explain economic consequences by economic causes.[102] I too am interested in explaining organizational genesis. But I insist that the multiple social-network contexts of inventions be taken seriously, for these are the raw materials being recombined into invention. Multifunctionality and spillover are rife in social invention processes, in part because of objective turmoil but also in part because other times and places may not parse "the economic," "the political," and "the social" as we do. Scientific explanation requires historical sensitivity to context, to mentalité, and to feedback.[103]

FAMILY OUT OF COMPANY

Church documents in the 1200s were in Latin. Hence second names ending in "i" usually implied the ablative "of"—for example, "Franciscus Guidi" meant "Francis son of Guido." Because of this medieval method of naming, kinship relations can be inferred from names. With two names strung together to make a person, one can infer the nuclear-family kinship relations of brother and father[104] but not that of cousin. With three names strung together in ablative form, first cousins can be identified. As ablatives evolved into surnames,[105] more distant "clan" relations can be inferred from a common surname. Patricians or nobles in the Dugento often added a "de" to their last names. Hence both kinship and social status can be inferred directly from names—a fact of course that was no accident to the people involved.

According to the documents that I examined, when Sapori referred to the first stage of unitary company development as "family," he must have been referring to nuclear family. Non-noble persons, with only ablative names, overwhelmingly predominated in the Dugento partnership lists,

[101] Chandler (1977) is not making so different an argument when he points to military antecedents of the revolutionary nineteenth-century industrial organization of the railroad.

[102] Recent efforts by economic historians to be multidisciplinary, such as Greif 2006, do so only by translating politics and kinship into their economic aspects rather than by taking alternative logics on their own historical terms.

[103] It would take me too far afield to develop this point, but I am arguing here for a processual or "mechanism" (Hedstrom 2005) view of science rather than an input-output "covering law" view of science. This processual view makes go away much of the usually assumed contradiction between history and science.

[104] Although not without some chance of error in cases where two unrelated persons had fathers with the same first name.

[105] Three names strung together implies self-consciousness of lineage, at least at the common grandfather level. As such self-consciousness of lineage develops, grandchildren and beyond can turn their ablative ancestor name "of Guido" into a new surname for themselves of "Guidi." See Padgett 2010.

even though noble family names do occasionally appear. Interestingly, however, the overall company name, once it developed, frequently referred to the noble member of the partnership, even though that member may not have been the true economic leader.[106] An example discussed above is the Scali company—named after Jacobus de Scala, even though that company was founded and led primarily by a clique of four nonpatrician merchants in the Florentine *nazione* in England. Using the family name of the company to infer the "family foundation" of the company, therefore, is a surprisingly precarious enterprise, at least for the mid-Dugento.

In this section I shall measure kinship connections among partners directly. I shall find that Blomquist's *consorteria* hypothesis fits the cross-sectional partnership data of the mid-Dugento better than does Sapori's more famous "core family plus outsiders" hypothesis. Viewed over time, Sapori's "company out of family" portrait is not wrong as long as the word *family* refers to alliances of mostly non-noble nuclear families. This caveat is not commonly observed in the literature, wherein the family name of the company is usually what is referenced. When the word *family* means patrilineage, I find that the image of "family out of company" fits the data much better, with merchant nuclear families growing into patrician patrilineages if the unitary company succeeded.

Summary statistics about kinship relations among the partners of the companies whose excommunication Pope Urban IV had absolved in 1263–64, and Pope Clement IV absolved in 1265, are as follows:[107]

proportion partners in largest-family (nuclear or otherwise) subset of partners

$= (\Sigma_i \text{ \# largest family subset}_i) / (\Sigma_i \text{ \# partners}_i)$
$= 71 / 197 = .360$

proportion partners in any-family (nuclear or otherwise) subset of partners

$= (\Sigma_i \text{ \# partners with any kin as partners}_i) / (\Sigma_i \text{ \# partners}_i)$
$= 124 / 197 = .629.$

Small companies with four or fewer partners do not really fit my unitary-bank definition. If these are excluded, then the kinship proportions shrink to .297 and .600,[108] respectively.

The connection between kinship and unitary merchant-banks therefore was high. But this connection was not just a single core family per company. Within these companies there were about as many partners in kinship relations outside the largest kin group as there were partners within the largest kinship group. If Dugento companies are to be described as "family plus outsiders," then it must be understood that "outsiders" had many family relations among themselves. Indeed, simple inspection of the lists shows that Dugento unitary companies were alliances of families—not alliances of noble patrilineal families, like the military tower societies,[109] but alliances of merchant nuclear families.

Blomquist (1980, 18) has noticed this already, with regard to the Ricciardi company:

> Despite its legal status as a simple partnership, the Ricciardi enterprise appears to have been similar functionally to the consortial organizations into which the families of the Lucchese urban elite commonly banded together. I am suggesting here that the large-scale international *societas* differed from a consortium (in Lucca called *consortatus*) only in that its purpose was to engage in commerce and finance rather than to provide political and [military] refuge for its members.

One further documentary example confirms directly Blomquist's hypothesis of a Dugento parallel between *societas* and *consorteria*. The absolution for the (regular) Tolomei company of Siena appeared in a long list[110] of other Sienese "companies," most of whom were composed of *socii nobilium*—a term that did not appear otherwise in my extract of papal letters about Italian merchant-banks. Comparison with another letter[111] to the exiled Guelf militia of Siena in 1263 confirms the impression that the first list was a list of soldier companies, not of merchant

[106] "Leader" in this sentence is defined in terms of the transactional behavior documented in the appendix. As I have said numerous times, no partnership contracts survive from this period; these would have listed the start-up capital investment of the various partners. It is possible, indeed likely, that noble families contributed more than their fair share of the *corpo*, even if they were passive investors.

[107] Readers are free of course to look in the appendix at the particular companies comprising these aggregate statistics. I included all absolved companies, including the Bonsignori, Scali, and Tolomei, in the statistics.

[108] The exact ratios are (52/175) and (105/175).

[109] Santini 1887; Waley 1969, 170–78.

[110] *Registre d'Urbain IV*, 2, n. 175 (5 January 1263).

[111] *Registre d'Urbain IV*, 2, n. 274 (6 March 1263).

companies. The Tolomei company was apparently both a merchant company and a soldier company at the same time,[112] probably because the family in question was noble.

Medieval Italian documents from the 1200s refer to *societas militum*,[113] which were noble families or alliances of noble families organized into cavalry bands. City militias were alliances of such bands.[114] The Tuscan civil wars of the 1260s between Guelfs and Ghibellines were carried out by *societates* of noble soldiers from Florence and Siena. The Tuscan financial mobilization of the 1260s by Urban IV, as we have seen, was carried out by *societates* of mostly non-noble merchants from Florence and Siena. Urban's purpose in absolving the merchant companies from his excommunication of their fellow citizens was to mobilize them[115] for war—specifically for his "religious" crusade against Manfred—which he successfully did. This intertwining of military with economic with religious organization, all in the name of crusade, can't get much more intimate than this. With crusade the pope spanned deep social-class divisions within Tuscan cities[116] and united pro-pope but fractious social segments in Florence, Siena, and Lucca into "Guelf."

Blomquist's observation about *societas* as *consorteria* adds an important subtlety to our point about papal absorption. Yes, incorporation imparted continuity ideologically through the "body of Christ militant" and practically through papal administration. But the modular units being so incorporated were medieval at their core: *societas militum* and the like. Odd as it may seem to us, unitary merchant-banking companies in Tuscany were in their origins the economic wing of a holy army that the pope built for his Italian crusade. The family-alliance or *consorteria* nature of the internal partnership structure of unitary banks reflected the way that Dugento Italy normally organized itself into militia. Diversification of one favored merchant company, the Bonsignori, into a state-finance "market" of economic companies paralleled the assembly of noble military companies into a feudal army.

Once released from their papal origins, international merchant-banking companies preserved their organizational imprinting as modular *consorterie*, reinforced in the late 1200s not by war but by kinship.

As discussed earlier, "corporate" in the medieval sense implied collective continuity through time. One hypothesized implication of continuity for economic organization is that partners of corporate companies should recruit their sons to replace them, to carry on their successful business after they died. To test this hypothesis, one needs lists of partners over generational time. In my 1260s case, this means lists of the partners into at least the 1280s. With only three case studies that do this, my conclusions about this hypothesis can only be suggestive. Nonetheless, for what they are worth: (1) five of the twenty-three partners in the Bonsignori company of 1289 were descendants of Bonsignori company partners in the previous generation;[117] (2) eight of the sixteen partners of the Scali company of 1282 and 1284 were descendants of Scali company partners in the previous generation;[118] and (3) five of the seventeen partners of the Ricciardi company of 1286 were descendants of Ricciardi partners in the previous generation.[119]Are these numbers high? I have no baseline model against which to evaluate statistically these numbers. But they at least are not inconsistent with the "sons replace fathers" continuity hypothesis. As telling as anything is the obvious fact that these three companies (and quite a few others)

[112] See the registration of *Registres d'Urbain IV*, 2, n. 175 in the 1263 column of appendix C. Orlando Bonsignori is another prominent Sienese example of a merchant who was also a soldier. The linguistic and social ambiguity of the Tolomei persisted in the deliberations of the Siena city council in 1293: "Cum societas et nobiles viri de societate filiorum ser Jacobi de Talomeis" (cited in Mucciarelli 1995, 19).

[113] Waley 1969, 166, 183.

[114] Waley (1969, 83): "Joint inheritance might cause the obligation to fall on a number of co-heirs, particularly at a time when there had been no recent review of cavalry service: those owing it would then have to provide a cavalryman between them. This must considerably have complicated the task of organizing the militia, for nearly two-thirds of the Florentine horses recorded in the *Libro di Montaperti* (1260) were owed jointly by *consortes*." Waley (1969, 135): "The approximate numbers of Florentine cavalrymen engaged in the four great battles of 1260 to 1325 are as follows: 1260 (Montaperti) 1,400."

[115] "Them" here means both noble soldiers and non-noble merchants.

[116] I have not the space to go deeply into these social-class cleavages, but they were deep. In 1250, for example, the Florentine non-noble Popolo rose up militarily, on their organizational foundation of guilds, to make a ten-year interlude of republican government. This lasted until the Ghibelline victory at the battle of Montaperti in 1260. The emergence of this non-noble (even anti-noble) *societas populi* roughly in the same period as the merchant-bank *societas* may not be causally connected, but together they imply a partial diffusion of noble forms of social organization, like *societas* and *consorteria*, downward.

[117] Four were the same people and hence do not count in the denominator.

[118] One was the same person and hence does not count in the denominator.

[119] Six were the same people and hence do not count in the denominator.

reproduced their organizational survival over decades in the first place. The fluid partnerships and syndicates of the Italian merchants in overseas *nazioni* before the 1260s did not do this. The "Scali" as a company, for example, survived over generations; the partners comprising it biologically reproduced as partners as well. In the future, I hope to continue my coding of the papal registers in order to increase the number of merchant-banks with which to evaluate further this hypothesis.

Blomquist provides evidence about a yet third kinship aspect of "corporate" on which I have no data. In my relational data set on Trecento and Quattrocento Florence, I have rich quantitative information on the marriage, economic, and political networks of Florentines.[120] I have no such network-contextual information on Dugento Florence. But in his archivally rich case study[121] of the Ricciardi and the Guidiccioni families of Lucca, who allied to make the Ricciardi company, Blomquist unearthed considerable information about the marriages, property purchases, and neighbors of members of these two families. Those data demonstrate something that I cannot—namely, that many of even the "non-kinship outsiders" partners in the company were linked to the dominant two families by marriage or by other means.

> The evidence at hand seems sufficient to warrant the conclusion that the Ricciardi Company was in fact a long term alliance for commercial ends between families descending from the early partners in the enterprise, an alliance that was augmented by recruiting new members from other families which were through blood, marriage, consortial or neighborhood ties already linked to the group. I would assume that admission to partnership status of an individual lacking these ties must have been rare. (1980, 18)

Much of the analysis in this section extends and confirms this superb but unfortunately obscure[122] case study by Blomquist.

All these pieces about kinship add up to my section conclusion: Successful leadership of unitary merchant-banks transformed merchant nuclear families into noble patrilineages—that is, "family out of company." This unitary-bank channel of social mobility was very restricted compared to the republican channels of the Renaissance.[123] But the consequence when it happened was the same: the diffusion of corporate versions of "the family" from the nobility down to mimicking merchants in the form of patrilineage. Again, Blomquist's rich case study of the Ricciardi and the Guidiccioni of Lucca provides details that my study cannot—namely, the purchase and construction of large blocks of real estate, both in the heart of the city (tower houses) and in the areas of the countryside or *contado* from which the family had emigrated. Profits from the bank provided the money for these real estate purchases. But other Florentine banking families apparently made the same social-mobility journey—namely, descendants of Spigliatus and Rustichellus Cambii turned into the Mozzi, descendants of Manetto Spine turned into the Spini, descendants of Bonaguide Bardi turned into the Bardi, descendants of Circulus Oliverii Circuli turned into the Cerchi, and descendants of Lambertus Fruscobaldi turned into the Frescobaldi. These family names are prominent as companies in the English wool-export lists reported above. But they are also prominent on the 1293 list of Florentine magnates declared to be legally excluded from ever holding public office in the future.[124] This magnate category was created by a "populist" revolt against patricians.[125] How quickly successful unitary-bank families of the 1260s took on a noble behavior that made them hated in populist eyes![126]

To close this section, I want to emphasize the common consortial logic of many forms of Dugento social organization—in the domain of economics, in the domain of military, in the domain of real estate, and in the domain of family. To try too hard to distinguish whether a family name referred to a patrilineage or to a unitary company ignores the consortial logic of both. Family was property, at least in the patrilineage sense of family. And property was family, at least in the patrimony sense of *corpo*. We are very far away from modern kinship concepts like romance.

[120] Padgett and Ansell 1993; Padgett and McLean 2006, 2011; Padgett 2010.

[121] Blomquist 1980, 1982.

[122] According to the Web of Science, in the thirty years since their publication, each of Blomquist's excellent *Actum Luce* articles has been cited exactly once.

[123] Cf. Padgett 2010.

[124] Lansing 1991.

[125] "Populist" is in quotes because many of the revolters were patricians themselves, in alliance with middle-class guilds.

[126] This point about nobility through unitary banks helps make sense of a puzzle in the political history of Florence: how merchants could have gotten onto a list of feudal magnates in the eyes of contemporary *popolani*. See Ottokar 1962.

Multifunctionality was everywhere in the organizations of the 1200s. This is a social science way of saying that the linked concepts of *societas* and *consorteria*[127] were plastic social-organizational tools of the Dugento, capable of mobilization for a variety of purposes. All sorts of micromotivations underlay the construction of particular such organizations—profit, war, social mobility. But both actively and passively, the Church stood behind them all, sending these motivations down particular organizational trajectories. Dugento organizational inventions were secular recombinations of social relations and concepts in a religious tool kit of practices.[128]

CONCLUSION

If the Tuscan corporate merchant-banks were born because of the pope, they survived because of the king of England. Repayment through the customs service turned wool into simultaneously a commodity in international trade and a commodity in state finance. Wool had to be manufactured into textiles both for merchants to make their profit and for the king to make his soldiers. As sedentary merchant-banks expanded, the Florence wool-textile industry grew and the Champagne fairs declined. Tuscan (now mostly Florentine) merchant-banking houses simultaneously funded international trade in wool textiles and funded kings in state finance. The textile business often depended on the state-finance business for its authorization.

This autocatalytic feedback lasted until the famous bankruptcies of the Bardi and Peruzzi companies in Florence in 1342. But in truth, this trading system had been in decline since the turn of the century: the Bonsignori company went bankrupt in 1298; the Ricciardi company went bankrupt in 1300; the Frescobaldi company went bankrupt in 1313; and the Scali company went bankrupt in 1326.

My own data from the Florentine banking guild's annual registration of banks[129] also trace a grim picture of steady decline in total numbers of registered bankers in the guild from 1299 onward: 355 partners in 1299, 313 partners in 1300, 277 partners in 1301, 238 partners in 1314, 146 partners in 1320, 116 partners in 1323, 100 partners in 1329. The bankers in these guild registration lists were extremely heterogeneous in nature, ranging from humble local money changers to grand international merchant-bankers. But even if we restrict our attention to the larger banks in these lists—those with more than five partners—the same story of early fourteenth-century decline appears:[130]

Bonciani company (7) last observed in 1300
Abbati company (8) last observed in 1300
Tedaldi company (7) last observed in 1300
Canigiani company (12) last observed in 1301
Marini company (9) last observed in 1301
Guadagni company (6) last observed in 1314
Macci company (14) last observed in 1314
[no family name] company (8) last observed in 1314
Pazzi company (17) last observed in 1314
Sassetti company (10) last observed in 1314
dell'Antella company (7) last observed in 1329
Peruzzi company (21) bankrupt in 1342

These declines were due to a series of wars between the king of England and the king of France. Secular wars between England and France were not as profitable for Tuscan merchant-banks as were the "holy" crusades in the peninsula of Italy. The reason for this difference is directly related to the flow of wool, which passed through France. The Italian crusades and the fiscal reforms of Edward I had fueled that flow, but subsequent wars with France by Edward II and Edward III had disrupted it. The king of France never adopted the innovative state-finance methods of Pope Urban IV. King Philip the Fair of France attacked England in part by jailing Italian merchants resident in France and confiscating their goods. In the name of usury. The kings of England in their turn, with their smooth state finance failing, shortsightedly also jailed their own bankers and confiscated their goods.[131] In spite of the English king's questionable credit rating, for a while one Tuscan banker replaced another in the king's service: the

[127] Here I am using the term *consorteria* both in its sense of family alliance and in its sense of patrilineage. Kent (1977) has emphasized that in the Renaissance the word *consorteria* came to be more restricted to mean "patrilineage" itself. The earlier Dugento meaning of "family alliance" had faded away, along with the reality of that form of social organization. Most likely one reason for this fade was the emergence of the republic, which undercut the military function of patrilineage.

[128] The tool-kit metaphor and idea is borrowed from Swidler 1986.

[129] Archivio di Stato di Firenze, *Arte del Cambio* 11.

[130] In parentheses, I list the largest number of registered partners of the named company during 1299–1329.

[131] This perhaps being one benefit of outsourcing state finance.

Ricciardi company was followed by the Frescobaldi company, which was followed by the Bardi company. Eventually profits in the wool trade were not sufficient to offset their shabby royal treatment. At the end, Edward III owed the Bardi company the equivalent of an entire year's English production in wool. Edward wouldn't pay it, and the organizational invention whose birth has been analyzed in this chapter became extinct. Busts following booms have been with us in history for a long time.

Ultimate extinction notwithstanding, the Tuscan unitary merchant-bank was an amazing organizational invention, especially for its time. Bills of exchange and account books changed banking forever, and the Commercial Revolution moved Europe out of its economic backwater. Dare I utter that historiographically out-of-fashion sentiment that the Middle Ages ended? If so, then this chapter has argued that the Middle Ages ended through the recombination of organizational elements that were, by themselves, deeply medieval. The "rise of capitalism" was real, but that does not mean that one coherent logic called "traditionalism" was displaced with another called "modernism." Traditionalism and modernity are two influential (and egocentric) concepts that I regard as without either historical or scientific precision.

For us as social scientists, the lessons of this venture into history are "incorporation and detachment" as one multiple-network folding mechanism for organizational genesis, with catalytic spillover into neighboring networks to reproduce and grow that genesis. Medieval invention in banking was not inevitable, but "historical contingency" does not have to mean something as intellectually flabby as a great idea, a great man, or even an accident. Multiple systems can feed back into each other occasionally to produce unpredictable tipping effects when such interacting systems are poised. Properly understood to exclude teleology and Social Darwinism, nonlinear path dependence is as characteristic of invention in social evolution as it is of speciation in biological evolution.

APPENDIXES: TRANSACTIONS FROM PAPAL REGISTERS AND ENGLISH LIBERATE ROLLS

Appendix A. Bonsignori Company (Siena): 1250–89

Table 5A.1.
Bonsignori Company Members and Their Transactions, 1250–56

Bonsignori company (Siena)	1250	1251	1252	1253	1254	1255	1256
Bonsignore di Bernardo (1203: salt)							
Bonifacius Bonsignoris	4815		5608, 6777a	L/6264,6386, 6381,6861, 6878	7342,7406, 7489,7980,	8034	XXVIII
Orlandius Bonsignoris	4815		5608	L/6264,6386, 6446,6861	7197,7406	Ch (dir.)	1148
Orlando Bartolomei Malavolti		L/5469		6381		Ch	
Aldebrandinus Bartholomei				6381			
Hugolinus Belmontis[b]		L/5469		L/6264,6386	7197,7489	165	1148
Capitino Buctin/ Capucino Buccic[c]						165	1148
Bartholomeo Guidii Ciabacte						165	1148
Andrea Iacobi						Ch	
Facius Juncte				L/6264			
Bartholomeo Christophori				6861,6878			
Theobaldum Thebalducii		L/5469					
Rainerium Tetii		L/5469					
Albizo Deuteaute					7342		
Bernardino Prosperini Cendonazi				XXIII,XXV,XXIV	8034		
Bonaventure Bernardini				6381, 6446	7980	Ch,165, XXVIII	1148
Aldebrando Aldebrandini				XXIII,XXV		XXVII, XXVIII	
Ruskitello Cambii[d]				XXIII			
Amanatto Spinetti5				XXIII			

Notes:

[a]First mention as campsor domini papae (actually campsoris nostri).

[b]This reorganization (initiation?) of company connected to Sicilian venture (see Chiaudano 1935, 114). Scali also mobilized as campsors papae at this time.

[c]In June 1255, part of Tolomei company (English 1988, 15).

[d]In June 1255, part of Tolomei company (English 1988, 15).

[e]Part of Scali company (though not really consolidated yet).

Table 5A.2.
Bonsignori Company Members and Their Transactions, 1261–63

Bonsignori company (Siena)	1261	1262	1263
Orlandi Bonsignoris	9,L/44,48,51,L186	53,209	157, 220,277,491
Raynerii Jacobi	9,L/44,48,L186	L/40,73,121,L/179, 180,182,209	491
Bonaventura Bernardini	9,L/44,48,51,L186	L/40,53,73,L/179, 182,209	157,159,161,166,172,173, 174,175,176,177,178,220, 277,370,480,491,426
Francisci Guidonis		73,121,L/179,180, 182	159,161,166,172,173,176, 177,277,370,480,426
Hugolinus Bellimontis			172,426
Facius (Bonifacius) Juncte	9	72,76	172,426
Jacobo Gregorii		L/40,73,180,182	163
Andree Jacobi	9	L/40,72,76,180,182, 209	157,159,163, 220,370,480, 491
Tholomeo Manenti			157,159,163,166,172, 220, 370,480,426
Bonsignori Raynerii	9	73,180,182,209	157,159,163,166,172,220, 370,480,491,426
Manno Ildebrandini		73,209	163,491
Jacobo Gilli		73	157,220
Raynerio Bonaccursi	48,51,L186	53,L147	159,163,166,173,220
Deutavivae Guidi	L/44,48,51,L186	53,L147	
Ildebrando Ildebrandini			173
Jacopo Ildebrandini			177
Castraleone Hugolini			177
Jacopo Romei			177,277
Gregorio dicto Gonnella			177
Martinello Rubei			177
Rostorius Juncte			163
Bonadota Capud Nigri			163
Corrado Jacobo	(87)		
Jacobus Curradi			161
Vivolo Salvanelli	(87)	121,L/179	161,176
Venturae Cambii	(87)	121	161,176
Ventura Benedicti		L/179	161
Lottus Ugolini			161

Table 5A.3.
Bonsignori Company Members and Their Transactions, 1265

Bonsignori company (Siena)	1265
Orlandi Bonsignoris	1427,731,1428
Bonaventura Bernardini	1427,726,728,729,730,731,735,738,739,746,747,753,754,755,756,1428,1464,1465,1480,1482
Raynerii Jacobi	1427,728,729,730,746,747,753,755,756,1428,1465
Francisci Guidonis	1427,726,728,729,730,731,735,738,739,746,747,748,753,755,756,1428,1464,1465,1469
Facius (Bonifacius) Juncte	1427,728,746,747,753,1428,1464
Restauro Juncte	1464,1480
Andree Jacobi	
Bonsignori Raynerii	1427
Raynerio Bonaccursi	
Tholomeo Manenti	1427
Manno Ildebrandini	1427
Blandum Aldebrandi	1427
Jacobo Gilii	1427,746,753,1480,1482
Hugoni Jacobi	1427,728,746,747,753,1428,1464,1480,1482
Jacobo Egidi	728,747,1464
Lotto Hugolini	1427,728,746,753,1428,1464
Gascum Trapillicini	1427,1464,1480,1482
Bindum Aldebrandini	1427
Aldebrandum Aldebrandini	1427,729,730,755,756
Paltonem Deutesalvi	1427,729,730,755,756
Facium Berignonis	1427,755,756
Gregorio Peruti	731
Jacobo Gregorii	738,739
Vivolum Salvanelli	1427
Gregorium Rigoli	1427
Deutaiuvam Guidi	1427
Bindum Falconis	1427
Bonfilium Contadini	1427
Incontratum Philippi	1427
Jacobum Skermi	1427
Conradum Jacobi	1427
Bettum Ferrantis	1427
Tholomeum Jacobi	1427
Thomam Viviani	1427
Leonardum Jannis	1427
Facium Ranerii	1427
Pacchinam Ranerii	1427
Meum Monaldetti	1427

Notes: red = France (anywhere else); blue = England; pink = Montpelier; orange = Champagne; green = Spain; purple = Charles of Anjou. Underlining indicates leadership language (i.e., not in transaction, but referenced). Parentheses = not Bonsignori company. Arabic numbers are papal missive #s; hence connected to papal curia. Latin numbers are Liberate Roll #s; hence connected to king of England. "Ch" refers to information from Chiaudano 1930, 1935; "L" refers to information from Lunt 1934, 1939; "E" refers to information from English 1988.

Table 5A.4.
Bonsignori Company Members and Their Transactions, 1266–67

Bonsignori company (Siena)	1266	1267
Orlandi Bonsignoris	761,789	798,
Bonaventura Bernardini	761,779,783,784,794,1483,1484	797,798,
Raynerii Jacobi	761,779, L173	
Francisci Guidonis	779,780,781,783,784,788,1483,1484	
Facius (Bonifacius) Juncte	779,784,1483,1484, L173	
Guidoni Juncte	1483,1484	803,804
Restauro Juncte	1483,1484	804
Hugoni Jacobi	783,1483,1484	803,804
Raynerio Jacobi	783,1483	
Andree Jacobi	761	
Bonsignori Raynerii	761	
Manno Ildebrandini	761	
Raynerio Bonaccursi		
Tholomeo Manenti		
Jacobo Gilii		
Jacobo Egidi	1483,1484	
Lotto Hugolini	779,784,1483,1484	798
Aldebrando Aldebrandini		
Jacobo Aldobrandini		797
Paltono Deutesalvi		
Gregorio Peruti		
Jacobo Gregorii	794	
Pultrono Frederici	794	
Facio Berignonis		
Gasconi Trapillicino	1483,1484	
Bartholomeo Henrici	1484	803
Gregorio Gonnelle		798

Table 5A.5.
Bonsignori Company Partners and Their Capital, 1289

Soci e capitani della Compagnia dei figli di Bonsignore (Societas filioum Bonsignoris) nel 1289:

Figli di Orlando Bonsignore	Soci estranei alla famiglia Bonsignori e loro capitali	
1. Fatius eques	6. Bonaventura Bernardini	6800 lib.
2. Ugo	7. Rainerius Iacobi	5200 lib.
3. Guilelmus	8. Pagnus Giliocti	3000 lib.
4. Bonsignore	9. Fatius Berignonis	3000 lib.
Figlio di Bonifazio Bonsignore	10. Conradus Berignonis	2500 lib.
5. Nicolaus eques	11. Manfredus Ranucii de Balzis	3000 lib.
	12. Gerius Montanini	3000 lib.
	13. Mevius domini Orlandi de Malavoltis	2500 lib.
	14. Bindus Aldobrandi	2500 lib.
	15. Tura Bartholomei	2500 lib.
	16. Claritus Iohannis	2500 lib.
	17. Thalomeus Manentis	2100 lib.
	18. Ventura o Tura Bonamici	1500 lib.
	19. Arbor Bernardini	1200 lib.
	20. Bartholomeus Henrici	–
	21. Vannes Henrici	–
	22. Mattheus Albizi	–
	23. Angelus Benvenuti	–
Total capital		40,800 lib.

Source: Chiaudono 1935, 134–35.

Appendix B. Scali Company (Florence): 1229–84

Table 5B.1.
Scali Company Members and Their Transactions, 1229–59

Scali company (Florence)	1229	1233	1235	1245	1249
Mainetto Robertin				XV	
Bonaccorso Inglesk		B:Eng.			
Amieri Cose	B:Engl.	B:Eng.	B:Eng.	XV	
Spigliato Cambii[a]	B:England		B:Eng.	XV	
Rocco (Rustichello) Cambii[c]			B:Eng.		
Manetto Spini (Spineti)			B:Eng.		B:Eng.
Pietro Benincase[d]					
Ranieri Abbati					
Hugoni (dicto Mazze) Simonetti					
Deuteayuto Guillelmi					
Jacopo della Scala					B:Eng.(+others)
Cavalcante (Cante) de Scala					
Jacobi Giberti[e]					
Hugoni Gilberti					
Benvenuto Will'i					
Gerardo Ricobaldi					
Bernardo Persperin[f]					
Aldebrando Aldebrandini[g]					
Jacobo Dananzaci					
Berardo Ricobaldi					
Petro de Sabaudia					
Luterio Bonycase					

Notes: red = France (anywhere else); blue = England; purple = Gascony. Underlining indicates leadership language (i.e., not in transaction, but referenced). Arabic numbers are papal missive #s; hence connected to papal curia. Latin numbers are Liberate Roll #s; hence connected to king of England. "B" indicates information from Borsari 1995.

[a]Due to strange English spellings, I assume Spigliato Cambi = Spinello Campano.

[b]These loans were part of Sicilian venture: a papal-English taxation joint venture. But some of them went straight to the king. Jordan (1909, 11) says Scali made *campsor papae*.

[c]Rocco Cambi = Rustichello Cambi, according to both Borsari (1995) and Kay (1970).

[d]Due to strange English spellings, I assume Pietro Benincase = Petro Bonacaso.

[e]As of 1262, he is in Bellindotti company.

[f]As of 1255, his son, Benvenuto Bernardini, is part of Bonsignori company of Siena.

Table 5B.1 (*continued*)

1250	1253	1254	1255	1256	1257	1258	1259
				B:Eng.	B:Eng.		
			B:Gasc.	B:Eng.[b]			
	XXIII	XXVI	B:Gasc.	B:Eng.	B:Eng.	XXXIII	XXXV,XXXVII
XXI	XXIII	XXVI	B:Gasc.	B:Eng.	B:Eng.		
			B:Gasc.	B:Eng.			
				B:Eng.			
XXI				B:Eng.			
				B:Eng.			
		7529	B:Gascony				
					B:Eng.		
	7069	7529,7227					
XXI							
XXI							
XXI							
	XXIII						
	XXIII					XXXIII	XXXV
						XXXIII	XXXV
						XXXIII	XXXV
							XXXVII
							XXXVII

Table 5B.2.
Scali Company Members and Their Transactions, 1261–69

Scali company (Florence)	1261	1262	1263	1264	1265	1268	1269
England							
Jacobum Cambii				1012			
Diritta (Dricta) Cambii			A,363	519			
Rucco (Rustichello) Cambii[a]	XXXVIII	B:p/E,L/125	A,363,479,327	519			
Manetto (Maynetto) Spine	XXXVIII	B:p/E,L/125	A,363,479	519	1469		
Lotherio Benincase		B:p/E	A,363,479	519,1012			
Ranieri Abbati		B:p/E,L/125	A,363,479,327	519		XLI	XLIII,XLIV,XLV
Hugonetto (Mace) Simonetti							XLIII,XLIV,XLV
Florence and elsewhere							
Amieri Cose	B:p		A,363	519,1012			
Jacobus (Lapus) Amierii Cose	B:p		A,363,212	519,1012			
Jacopo de Scala	B:p	B:p/E,L/125	A,363,327	519,1012	726		
Cavalcante (Cante) Jacobi de Scala	B:p,22		A,363,212	519,1012			
Spina Jacobi de Scala	B:p		A,363,212	519,1012			
Teghia Jacobi de Scala			A,363,212	519	1469		
Thomasio (Maso) Spiliati	B:p,22		A,363,212	519	1469		
Pietro Benincase	B:p	B:p/E,L/125	A,363	519,1012			
Dino Perini	B:p	B:p/E,L/125					
Jacobo Lecca	B:p		A,363,212	519	726		
Campana Francisci	B:p		A,363,212	519,1012			
Hugo (Ugo) Spine	B:p		A,363	519			
Teghia Amadoris	B:p		A,363,212	519			
Gerardinus Beliotti	B:p		212				
Rustichello Tedaldi	B:p						

Notes: Arabic numbers are papal missive #s; hence connected to papal curia; "p" means pope. Latin numbers are Liberate Roll #s; hence connected to king of England. "p/E" indicates pope/England relations; "B" indicates information from Borsari 1995; "L" indicates information from Lunt 1934, 1939; "A" indicates information from Arias 1902: "Sottomissione dei Banchieri Fiorentini alla Chiesa."

[a]Cambii family later becomes the magnate family of de Mozzi. Therefore, Mozzi (also Spini) bank spins out of Scali bank.

Table 5B.3.
Scali Company Members, 1282–84

Scali company (Florence) 1282 and 1284	
Cieffus Bonisegne	Martini IV die 13 septembris 1282 et die 13 augusti 1284 datis
Maynettus Hugonis	Martini IV die 13 septembris 1282 et die 13 augusti 1284 datis
Lapus de Scala	Martini IV die 13 septembris 1282 et die 13 augusti 1284 datis
Jacobus Aymerii Cosae	Martini IV die 13 septembris 1282 et die 13 augusti 1284 datis
Johannes Aymerii Cosae	Martini IV die 13 septembris 1282 et die 13 augusti 1284 datis
Albertus Aymerii Cosae	Martini IV die 13 septembris 1282 et die 13 augusti 1284 datis
Folia Aymerii Cosae	Martini IV die 13 septembris 1282 et die 13 augusti 1284 datis
Alamannus Aymerii Cosae	Martini IV die 13 septembris 1282 et die 13 augusti 1284 datis
Castellanus Lapi	Martini IV die 13 septembris 1282 et die 13 augusti 1284 datis
Lippus Petri Benincasae	Martini IV die 13 septembris 1282 et die 13 augusti 1284 datis
Riccasrdus Petri Benincasae	Martini IV die 13 septembris 1282 et die 13 augusti 1284 datis
Tegla Amadoris	Martini IV die 13 septembris 1282 et die 13 augusti 1284 datis
Bonacosa Cosa Fulchi	Martini IV die 13 septembris 1282 et die 13 augusti 1284 datis
Ugolinus de Vichio	Martini IV die 13 septembris 1282 et die 13 augusti 1284 datis
Lotherius Bonaguide	Martini IV die 13 septembris 1282 et die 13 augusti 1284 datis
Bonapresa Importuni	Martini IV die 13 septembris 1282 et die 13 augusti 1284 datis

Source: Jordan 1902, 1909.

Appendix C. Tolomei Company (Siena): 1223–79

Table 5C.1.
Tolomei Company Members and Their Transactions, 1223–60

Tolomei company (Siena)	1223	1226	1227	1230	1243
Ranierio Raulii			M:lc		
Catalano di Alfano		M:lc			
Bartolomeo di Guazzolino		M:lc			
Manente d'Uguccione	EM:cl.	M:lc			
Tolomeo di Tolomeo della Piazza	EM:cl.	M:lc	M:lc	M:lc	
Tavena di Tolomeo Tolomei				M:lc	
Lotterengo di Tolomeo Tolomei				M:lc	
Pelacane di Tolomeo Tolomei				M:lc	
Jacopo della Piazza					
Tolomeo di Jacobo Tolomei					
Cristoforo di Tolomeo Tolomei					
Jacobo di Tolomeo Tolomei					
Rinaldo di Jacobo Tolomei					
Cristoforo di Jacopo Tolomei					
Andrea di Cristoforo Tolomei					
Lotterengo d'UguccioneTolomei					
Bartolomeo di Pietro Tolomei					
Orlando Bonasera					347
Deutaviva di Guido					
Turchio di Ranieri					
Leo di Teodorico					
Ofriduccio di Rustibello					
Dietisalve di Benintende					
Accarigi di Ranuccio					
Petrus Montanarius					
Johannes Cesarii					
Raynaldus Renerii					
Jacobi Theci					
Luca Ricovarii					
Montanino Deutesalve					347
Bartholomeo Comitis					347
Henrico Deuteaiut					347
Jacobo Rustikino					347
Hugolino Gentili					347
Albizo Deuteaiut					347
Capitano di Bucce[c]					
Ugolino di Belimonte[d]					

Notes: "cl." = cloth; "lc" = loan to city; "p" = pope; "v" = vescovo; "Ch." = Champagne; "Eng." = England; "Fl." = Flanders.

[a]The loans below are from various combinations of these Tolomei, over this period of time. Not clearly integrated into unified block of *soci* yet.

[b]This, on the other hand, is a single loan to the pope Mucciarelli 1995, 99–100.

[c]Also a partner in Bonsignori company.

[d]Also a partner in Bonsignori company.

Table 5C.1 (*continued*)

1248	1251–53	1253	1254	1255	1255[xvi]	1255	1257	1260
	M:lc[a]			453				
	M:lc							
	M:lc							
	M:lc			453	M:p[b]	ME:p		
M:lc							E:Ch	
	M:lc						E:Ch.	
	M:lc			453	M:p	ME:p	E:Ch.	
M:lc								
		6468			M:p	ME:p,28,29		
	M:lc					E:p		E:Eng.
						ME:p,28,29		
	M:lc				M:p			
		6468			M:p	ME:p,28,29		
		6468			M:p			
					M:p			
					M:p			
					M:p			
					M:p			
						29		
						29		
		6468	7981					
		6468						
		6468						
		6468						
				ME:p				
				ME:p				

Table 5C.2.
Tolomei Company Members and Their Transactions, 1262–79

Tolomei company (Siena)	1262	1263	1264	1265	1269	1279
Orlando di Baldistricca Tolomei	E:Siena					
Tolomeo di Jacobo Tolomei	E:Siena				E:exile	
Pietro di Cristoforo Tolomei	E:Siena	175		745		
Andrea di Cristoforo Tolomei	E:Ch.	175	521?	745,E:Ch.	E:Ch.	
Minus di Cristoforo Tolomei		175				
Guillelmus et		175				
Meus Raynaldi, eorum nepotes		175				
Tholomei Reginaldi				745		
Christofori Tholomei				745		
Lotheringi Uguicionis				745		
Federigo Doni	E:Fl.	175		745,E:Eng.	E:Fl.	
Tebaldus Alteville		175				
Bartholomeus et Aringherius Jacobi			521?			
Tolomeo di Rinaldo Tolomei						
E:Siena						
Luca di Bonsignore						E:Ch.
Tofano di Bonsignore						E:Ch.
Cino di Pietro						E:Ch.

Table 5C.3.
Scotti and Tolomei Company Members and Their Transactions, 1255–62

Scotti and Tolomei company (Siena)	1255	1256	1258	1262[a]
Petrus Scotti Dominici	J	M:p	J	46
Rinaldus Tolomei	J		J	
Tholomeo Raynaldi				46
Reinaldum Rainerii		M:p		
Gregorius Bernardini			J	46
Lotteringus Corradi			J	46
Jacobus Raynaldi			J	46
Christoforus Tolomei		M:p	J	46
Raynucius (Raynerius) de Vallestricte			J	46
Aldebrandinus Tholomei			J	46
Petrus Christophori			J	46
Raynucius (Raynalducio) Johannis			J	46
Bonuncuntrus Scotti Dominici			J	46
Scotto Dominici				46
Jacobus Romei			J	46
Rubeus Consilii			J	46
Raynerius Citadini			J	46
Paulus Albertini			J	46
Jacobus Balioni			J	
Ventura Martini			J	
Bonrestorus Scotti			J	
Jacobus Ugolini			J	
Bonagratia Ardimanni			J	
Bencivenne Consilii			J	
Ventura Fornari		M:Eng.		
Raniero Barbotti		M:Eng.		
Ermino Erminii		M:Eng.		
Giacomo Teci		M:Eng.		

Notes:

[a]This is actually the "trial" of Scotti-Tolomei bank by Pope Urban IV. Alexander IV had appointed this company as *campsores papae*, but for some reason Urban IV became unhappy with them.

Appendix D. Ricciardi Company (Lucca): 122?–1286

Table 5D.1.
Ricciardi Company Members and Their Transactions, 122?–1266

Ricciardi company (Lucca)	122?	1227	1231	1234	1241
Paganino Guidiccioni				P:Luc.	
Aldibrandino Guidiccioni					
Bandino del Lucano Bugianensis					
Opizi (Opitone) Malisardi					
Ricciardo di Graziano di Ricciardo, tintor	P:Luc.	P:Luc.	BP:Luc.	P:Luc.	BP:Luc.
Perfetto di Graziano di Ricciardo			BP:Luc.		
Gottifredo di Conetto			BP:Luc.		
Orlandino del Antelmino Minusvetti					
Alamanno (monete contraffatte)	P:Lucca				
Rosselmo del Mainetto Minusvetti	P:Lucca				
Mainetto Minusvetti	P:Lucca				
maestro Giovanni	P:Genoa				
Orlandino Arnolfi					BP:Luc.
Guglielmo Rosciompelli					BP:Luc.
Peregrino Sesmundi					BP:Luc.
Reynerodetto Senaci Guidiccioni					
Henrico Saraceni					
Bartholomeo Bendini					
Luco (Luke) Natali					
Reiner Magiari					
Baroncinus di Gualterius de Vulturna					
Richardo Guidechonis					
Theobaldino Maniumac					
Guido Panichi: procurator only					

Note: ( ) = not yet part of comp.

Table 5D.1 *(continued)*

1245	1247	1251	1253	1254–55	1256	1263	1266
	BP:Luc.						
	BP:Luc.						
	BP:Luc.						
	BP:Luc.						
BP:Luc.							
K:England		RK:Eng.	K:Eng.	RKP:Eng.			
K:England		R:Eng.		RKP:Eng.			
		RK:Eng.	K:Eng.	RKP:Eng.			
				RKP:Eng.			
				RKP:Eng.	K:Eng.	K:Eng.	
						K:Eng.	
					(K:Eng.)	(K:Eng.)	
							(K:Cham)
							(K:Cham)
						(P:Genoa)	

Table 5D.2.
Ricciardi Company Members and Their Transactions, 1272–86

Ricciardi company (Lucca)	1272	1273	1276–83	1283	1284	1286
dominus Andree Parentii Ricciardi						A:Luc.
Philippi domini Raynerii Ricciardi						A:Luc.
Ricciardus domini Raynerii Ricciardi						A:Luc.
Pagani/uccio Guidi Guidiccionis					B:Luc.	A:Luc
Guidiccione Paganini Guidiccionis					B:Luc.	A:Luc.
Raynerii Bandini						A:Luc.
Philipucii Talgardi						A:Luc.
Saraceni Macchi	P:G[a]					A:Luc.
Iohannis Gambardi						A
Lucasio Natale[b] (Luke de Luka)	P:G	KP:Eng.	KP:Eng.	L:Eng.		(d.1279)
Bandino del Lucano		P:Eng.				
Uguccione Maghiari		P:Eng.				
Ranieri (Raynerius) Maghiarii[c]		K:Eng.	RKPL:Eng	L:Eng.		A
Orlandino di Pogio[d] (Podio)			RKP:Eng.	L:Eng.		
Henricus de Podio			K:Eng.	L:Eng.		K:Gascony
Bartolotto del Buggianese Bandini			P:Eng.,Paris	L:Eng.	B	
Matteo Rosciompelli			RKP:Eng.	L:Eng.		
Adiuti Rosciompili			K:Eng.			A
Vannes Rosciompeli					B	A
Abbate Talgardi			K:Eng.	L:Eng.		A
Giovanni Simonetti Sismondi	P:G		KP:Eng.	L:Eng.		A
Riccardo Paganini Guidiccionis[e]	P:G		KP:Eng.	L:Eng.	B:Luc.	
Tommasinus Paganini Guidi Guidiccionis		K:Eng.	KP:Eng.	L:Eng.	B:Luc.	A
Aldebrandino Guidiccioni			K:Eng.			
Federigi Venture			K:Eng.			A
Riccardo Bonifacii[f]						K:Eng.
Baroncino Gualteri[g] (in England 23 yrs. before)			RK:Eng.	L:Eng.		K:left comp
Brunetto Baroncini Gualteri						K:left comp
Riccardo Baroncini Gualteri						K:left comp
Opizzo (Opiso) Malisardi (in-law of Gualteri)	P:G		K:Eng.			K:left comp
Hugolino Rosciompelli		R:Ire.	K:Ireland			
Percival Gerarducci			K:Ireland			
Bendino Panichi (Peruchi)	P:G		KP:Ireland			A:Ireland
Ghirardo Chimbardi						K:Ireland
Francesco Malisardi						KP:Ireland

Riccardo Rosciompelli		K:Gascony		
Francesco Maneumach		K:Paris		
Lotto Aldebrandini		K:Paris		
Bindo di Giovanni Simonetti		P:Paris?		
Barchetta Barche		P:Paris?	B	
Ricciardinus domini Bonfatii Gottori			B	
Labro Volpelli	K:Eng.	KP:curia		KP:curia
Dino Tadolini		P:curia		
Frederigus Sarracini Incallocchiati				A:Ravenna
Nicolucius Bonacursii Mignosii				A:Ravenna
Guido Panichi, procurator only[h]	(P:Genoa)			
Bandino de Fondora, procurator only	(P:Genoa)			

Notes: R = Re; K = Kaeuper; B = Blomquist; P = Del Punto; L = Lunt; A = Arias.

[a]P:G refers to one-shot loan in 1272 at Genoa to Prince Edward (future Edward I), coming back from crusades. See Del Punta 2004, 163.

[b]Liberate Roll #s: In 1273: 48, 49, 49b, 50. In 1274: 52, 53, 56, 57, 58. In 1275: 61, 64, 65. In 1276: 68, 71.

[c]Liberate Roll #s: In 1278: 76, 78. In 1279: 79, 82. In 1280: 83.

[d]Liberate Roll #s: In 1277: 72, 73. In 1278: 74, 75, 76, 77. In 1280: 80, 80b, 84. In 1296: 95.

[e]Liberate Roll #s: In 1281: 86. In 1289: 89. In 1290: 90, 93. In 1292: 94.

[f]Liberate Roll #s: In 1290: 90, 93.

[g]Liberate Roll #s: In 1281: 85, 86. In 1282: 87. In 1285: 88.

[h]The exception that proves the rule? Genoa uses agents, not *filiali*.

Table 5D.3.
Ricciardi Company Members, Doing Business with Pope Martin IV

Ricciardi company (Lucca)	1286	Pope Martin IV
dominus Andree Parentii Ricciardi	A:Luc.	
Philippi domini Raynerii Ricciardi	A:Luc.	
Ricciardus domini Raynerii Ricciardi	A:Luc.	
Pagani/uccio Guidi Guidiccionis	A:Luc	J
Guidiccione Paganini Guidiccionis	A:Luc.	
Franciscus Guiditionis		J
Raynerii Bandini	A:Luc.	J
Philipucii Talgardi	A:Luc.	
Saraceni Macchi	A:Luc.	J
Iohannis Gambardi	A	
Ranieri (Raynerius) Maghiarii	A	J
Orlandino di Pogio[a] (Podio)		J
Henricus de Podio	K:Gascony	
Riccardus Pogii		J
Bartolotto del Buggianese Bandini		J
Adiuti (Adjustus) Rosciompili	A	J
Vannes Rosciompeli	A	
Abbate Talgardi	A	
Giovanni Simonetti Sismondi	A	J
Riccardo Paganini Guidiccionis[b]		J
Tommasinus Paganini Guidi Guidiccionis	A	J
Aldebrandino Guidiccioni		
Lotto Aldebrandini		J
Federigi Venture	A	
Riccardo Bonifacii[c]	K:Eng.	
Bendino Panichi (Peruchi)	A:Ireland	
Ghirardo Chimbardi	K:Ireland	
Francesco Malisardi	KP:Ireland	
Labro Volpelli	KP:curia	J
Dino Tadolini		J
Vantes Honestis		J
Ricciardinus domini Bonfatii Gottori		J
Paganellusseu Nellus Gualandi		J
Ghinus Christophori		J
Bonaventura Romanioli		J
Nicolutius Liene		J
Banus Pili Rictii		J

Notes: A = Arias; J = Jordan.

[a]Liberate Roll #s: In 1296: 95.

[b]Liberate Roll #s: In 1289: 89. In 1290: 90, 93. In 1292: 94.

[c]Liberate Roll #s: In 1290: 90, 93.

Appendix E. Companies Absolved from Excommunication, 1263–64

(Letter numbers from *Registres d'Urbain IV*, vol. 2)[132]

1 **de Burgo company** of Florence (n. 362: 5 August 1263)

Dulcis de Burgo
Boldus de Burgo
Hugo Monaldi
Moczius de Burgo
Gualterus de Burgo
Gerus de Burgo
Castra Gualfredi
Hugettus Symonetti
Spinellus Symonetti
Donatellus Octaviani
Dulcis Octaviani
Johannes Bonaviti
Rubeus Bacharelli
Lapus Stibaldi
Johannutius Bajamontis
Ranutius Ardingi

2 **Rimbertini company** of Florence (n. 364: 27 August 1263)

Philippus Radulphi
Frankettus Rembertini
Maynettus Rembertini
Jacobus Rembertini
Franciscus Rembertini
Frankettus Bencivenni
Raynaldus Uberti
Dosius Uberti
Ubertus Raynaldi
Pucius Raynaldi
Guelfus Raynaldi
Scolarius Radulphi
Rota Amannati
Michael Amannati
Bucca Amannati
Matheus Bonfilioli
Cantius Symonetti
Bonvicinus Nicolai

[132] This procedure makes these lists of partners complete, unlike the usual case with papal transactions. The Bonsignori, Scali, and Tolomei companies are not listed here because they were coded elsewhere in the appendix. Their Urban IV letter numbers and dates of absolution were the following, respectively: n. 161, 5 July 1263; n. 363: 27 August 1263; and n. 175, 5 January 1263. *Discipuli* or nonpartner employees were also included in the registers, but these are not reproduced here.

3 **Bardi company** of Florence (n. 410: 27 September 1263)

Gianni Bonaguide Bardi
Matheus Bonaguide Bardi
LapusBonaguide Bardi
Coltus Bonaguide Bardi
Riccus Beltrami
Guarnerius Mathei
Antoninus, filius Gerii

4 **Bellicozi company** of Florence (n. 411: 26 September 1263)

Cambius Manerii Bellicozi
Persus Manerii Bellicozi
Perus Manerii Bellicozi
GiannianusTebaldi
Zione Tebaldi

5 **Bellincioni company** of Florence (n. 428: 23 October 1263)

Ildebrandinus Bellincionis
Bellincione (Cione) Ildebrandinus Bellincionis
Cambiutius Ildebrandinus Bellincionis
Caccia (notarius) Bonciani
Cenni Bonciani

6 **Benvenuti del Bene company** of Florence (n. 429: 27 October 1263)

Ildebrandinus Benvenuti del Bene
Franciscum Benvenuti del Bene
Phylippus Benvenuti del Bene
Ugolinus Benvenuti del Bene

7 **Acquerelli "company"** of Florence (n. 430: 2 November 1263)

Ildebrandinus (judex) Gerardi de Acquerellis
Giacottus Gerardi de Acquerellis
Peroctus Gerardi de Acquerellis
Roggerus (patruus suus) quondam Ildebrandini de Acquerellis
Dinus Joseppi
Cervellinus (Cinus) Dini Joseppi
[but word *socii* not used in this "company"]

8 **de Bella company** of Florence (n. 447: 10 November 1263)

Comparinus Tedaldi de Bella
Janus Tedaldi de Bella
Hugo Melioris de Bella
Gabriel Donati Bucetunde
Dessus Donati Bucetunde

9 **Puccii et Dosii Albizi** of Florence (n. 463: 5 December 1263)

Dosius quondam Albizi
Pepus (Puccius) quondam Albizi

10 **Vinciguerre company** of Florence (n. 465: 23 December 1263)

Duccius Rogeri Vinciguerre
Nerus Rogeri Vinciguerre
Rusticus Rogeri Vinciguerre

11 **Phylippi company** of Florence (n. 501: 5 February 1264)

Cambius Phylippi
Raynerius Phylippi
Capiardinus Guillelmi Danielis
Lapus Bizochi Marci
Marcutius Bizochi Marci

12 **Rossi company** of Florence (n. 557: 29 April 1264)

Johannes Rossi
Catellus Rossi
Marus Rossi
Rossus Conradi (Cafagii)

13 **Abbati "company"** of Florence (n. 570: 14 May 1264)

Lambertus (Tuctius) Abbatis
Jacobus (clericus et procurator) Abbatis
[but word *socii* not used in this "company"]

14 **Cerchi** founder in Florence (not company) (n. 574: 28 May 1264)

Circulum Olivieri

15 **Frescobaldi company** of Florence (n. 701: 3 August 1264)

Bardus Lamberti Frascobaldi
Jacobus Lamberti Frascobaldi
Coppus Joseppi
Corbolinus Bencii

16 **Donosdei company** of Pistoia (n. 702: 3 August 1264)

Egidius Donosdei
Melior Pelegrini
Accursis Lesii
Bonadies Bonadiei
Henrigetti Bonadiei
Pecora Novanterii
Stancollus (Collus) Raynuzini
Meo (domini) Raynuzini
Matheus Thomasini
Bindus Armaleonis

17 **Ammannati company** of Pistoia (n. 703: 30 July 1264)

Bandinus Ammannati
Bartholomeus Ammannati
Framericus Baldeti
Fuccius Soffredi
Forese Jacobi
Corradutius Jacobi
Sarracenus Jacobi
Conte Montancolli

1265 companies absolved from excommunication

(Letter numbers from *Registres de Clement IV*)

18 **Cerchi "societate"** of Florence (again) (n. 86: 2 June 1265)

Circuli Oliverii Circuli
Bindus Galligaii de Mactis
Teglarius Tedaldi
Ubertus Cambii
Manfridus Oderici
Naddus Boniczi
Taldus Raynerii
Guiducius Oderici
Naddus Boniczi
Taldus Raynerii
Guiducius Cavalcanti
Bonsignore Bonaiuti

19 **Frescobaldi company** of Florence (again) (n. 87: 3 June 1265)

Jacobus Riccomandi
Albertinus Rote
Ghinus Fruscobaldi
Barduccius Lamberti Fruscobaldi
Jacobus Lamberti Fruscobaldi
Hugolinus Benivieni
Coppus Joseppi
Rainerius Joseppi
Corbolinus Benivi
Meliorellus Allioni
Puccinus Amatoris
Restorinus Spiliati

20 **Rubei et Arditionis company** of Florence (n. 143: 13 July 1265)

Fuctius Rubei
Cinus Jacobi Arditionis
Ricchus Jacobi
Julianus Ricchi
Clarus Oliverii
Riccus Bonaguide
Nerus Fornarii

Angelerius Bonelle
Petrus Corbizi
Ricchus Salvaterre

21 **Rimbottus Bonaiuti** of Siena (n. 158: 23 October 1265)

Rimbottus Bonaiuti
Tucius et Acherisius, filii ejus

REFERENCES

Primary Sources

Archivio di stato di Firenze. *Arte del Cambio* 11.

Bond, Edward Augustus, ed. 1840. *Extracts from the Liberate Rolls, relative to loans supplied by Italian merchants to the Kings of England in the thirteenth and fourteenth centuries*. London: J. B. Nichols and Son.

Les Registres d'Innocent IV. 1884. Vol. 1, par Élie Berger. Paris: Ernest Thorin éditeur.

Les Registres d'Innocent IV. 1887. Vol. 2, par Élie Berger. Paris: Ernest Thorin éditeur.

Les Registres d'Innocent IV. 1897. Vol. 3, par Élie Berger. Paris: Albert Fontemoing éditeur.

Les Registres d'Alexandre IV. 1902. Vol. 1, ed. C. Bourel de la Roncière. Paris: Albert Fontemoing, éditeur.

Les Registres d'Alexandre IV. 1917. Vol. 2, ed. Joseph de Loye, Pierre de Cenival. Paris: Fontemoing & cie., éditeurs.

Les Registres d'Alexandre IV. 1953. Vol. 3, ed. Auguste Coulon. Paris: Fontemoing & cie., éditeurs.

Les Registres d'Urbain IV. 1901. Vol. 1, ed. M. Jean Guiraud. Paris: Albert Fontemoing, éditeur.

Les Registres d'Urbain IV. 1901. Vol. 2, ed. M. Jean Guiraud. Paris: Albert Fontemoing, éditeur.

Les Registres d'Urbain IV. 1904. Vol. 3, ed. M. Jean Guiraud. Paris: Albert Fontemoing, éditeur.

Les Registres de Clément IV (1265–1268). 1893. Par M. Édouard Jordan. Paris: Albert Fontemoing, éditeur.

Vaughan, Richard, ed. [1247–50] 1986. *Chronicles of Matthew Paris: Monastic Life in the Thirteenth Century*. New York: St. Martin's Press.

Secondary Sources

Arias, Gino. 1902. *Studi e documenti di storia del diritto*. Firenze: Successori le Monnier.

Berlow, Rosalind Kent. 1971. "The Development of Business Techniques Used at the Fairs of Champagne from the End of the Twelfth Century to the Middle of the Thirteenth Century." *Studies in Medieval and Renaissance History* 8:3–32.

Blomquist, Thomas W. 1971. "Commercial Association in Thirteenth-Century Lucca." *Business History Review* 45:157–78. Reprinted posthumously in his *Merchant Families, Banking and Money in Medieval Lucca*.

———. 1980. "Lineage, Land and Business in the Thirteenth Century: The Guidiccioni Family of Lucca." *Actum Luce* 9:7–29. Reprinted in his *Merchant Families, Banking and Money in Medieval Lucca*.

———. 1982. "Lineage, Land and Business in the Thirteenth Century: The Guidiccioni Family of Lucca." *Actum Luce* 11:7–34. Reprinted in his *Merchant Families, Banking and Money in Medieval Lucca*.

———. 2005. *Merchant Families, Banking and Money in Medieval Lucca*. Burlington, VT: Ashgate Publishing.

Borsari, Silvano. 1994. *Una compagnia di Calimala: Gli Scali (secc. XIII–XIV)*. Macerata: Università degli studi di Mercerata.

Chandler, Alfred D. 1977. *The Visible Hand: The Managerial Revolution in American Business*. Cambridge, MA: Harvard University Press.

Chiaudano, Mario. 1935. "I Rothschild del Dugento: La Gran Tavola di Orlando Bonsignori." *Bullettino Senese di storia patria* Anno VI:103–42.

———. 1930. "Note e documenti sulla compagni dei Bonsignori." In *Studie documenti per la storia del diritto commerciale italiano nel sec. XIII*, 114–42. Torino: Istituto Giuridico della R Università.

De Roover, Raymond. 1963. "The Organization of Trade." In *The Cambridge Economic History of Europe*, vol. 3, *Economic Organization and Policies in the Middle Ages*, ed. M. M. Postan, E. E. Rich, and Edward Miller, 42–118. Cambridge: Cambridge University Press.

———. 1966. *The Rise and Decline of the Medici Bank, 1397–1494*. New York: Norton.

———. 1974. "The Development of Accounting prior to Luca Pacioli According to the Account Books of Medieval Merchants." Reprinted from his 1956 article as pp. 119–80 in *Business, Banking, and Economic Thought in Late Medieval and Early Modern Europe*. Chicago: University of Chicago Press.

Del Punta, Ignazio. 2004. *Mercanti e banchieri lucchesi nel Dugento*. Pisa: Pisa University Press.

Duby, George. 1980. *The Three Orders: Feudal Society Imagined*. Chicago: University of Chicago Press.

English, Edward D. 1988. *Enterprise and Liability in Sienese Banking, 1230–1350*. Cambridge, MA: The Medieval Academy of America.

Face, Richard D. 1958. "The Techniques of Business in the Trade between the Fairs of Champagne and the South of Europe in the Twelfth and Thirteenth Centuries." *Economic History Review* 10:427–38.

———. 1969. "Symon de Gualterio: A Brief Portrait of a Thirteenth-Century Man of Affairs." In *Economy, Society, and Government in Medieval Italy: Essays in Memory of Robert L. Reynolds*, ed. David Herlihy, Robert S. Lopez, and Vsevolod Slessarev, 75–94. Kent, OH: Kent State University Press.

Galison, Peter. 2003. *Einstein's Clocks, Poincaré's Maps: Empires of Time*. New York: Norton.

Gasquet, Abbot Francis A. 1905. *Henry the Third and the Church*. London: George Bell.

Goldthwaite, Richard A. 2009. *The Economy of Renaissance Florence*. Baltimore: Johns Hopkins University Press.

Gras, Norman S. B. 1939. *Business and Capitalism: An Introduction to Business History*. New York: F. S. Crofts.

Greif, Avner. 2006. *Institutions and the Path to the Modern Economy*. Cambridge: Cambridge University Press.

Grossman, Ronald P. 1965. "The Financing of the Crusades." Ph.D. diss., University of Chicago.

Hedstrom, Peter. 2005. *Dissecting the Social: On the Principles of Analytic Sociology*. Cambridge: Cambridge University Press.

Horwitz, Morton J. 1977. *The Transformation of American Law, 1780–1860*. Cambridge, MA: Harvard University Press.

Housley, Norman. 1982. *The Italian Crusades: The Papal-Angevin Alliance and the Crusades against Christian Lay Powers, 1254–1343*. Oxford: Clarendon Press.

Jones, Philip. 1997. *The Italian City-State: From Commune to Signoria*. Oxford: Clarendon Press.

Jordan, E. J. 1902. "La fallite des Buonsignori." In *Mélanges Paul Fabre: Études d'histoire du Moyen Age*, 116–35. Paris: Alphonse Picard et fils, 1902.

———. 1909. *De Mercatoribus Camerae Apostolocae, saeculo XIII*. Paris: Condate Rhedonum, Apud Oberthurtypographum.

Kaeuper, Richard W. 1973. *Bankers to the Crown: The Riccardi of Lucca and Edward I*. Princeton: Princeton University Press.

Kantorowicz, Ernst H. 1957. *The King's Two Bodies: A Study in Medieval Political Theology*. Princeton: Princeton University Press.

Kay, Richard. 1970. "Rucco di Cambio de' Mozzi in France and England." *Studi Danteschi* 47:49–53.

Kent, Francis William. 1977. *Household and Lineage in Renaissance Florence: The Family Life of the Capponi, Ginori, and Rucellai*. Princeton: Princeton University Press.

Lansing, Carol. 1991. *The Florentine Magnates: Lineage and Faction in a Medieval Commune*. Princeton: Princeton University Press.

Lopez, Robert S. 1976. *The Commercial Revolution of the Middle Ages, 950–1350*. Cambridge: Cambridge University Press.

Lopez, Robert S., and Irving W. Raymond. 1955. *Medieval Trade in the Mediterranean World*. New York: Columbia University Press.

Lunt, William E. 1934. *Papal Revenues in the Middle Ages*. New York: Columbia University Press.

———. 1939. *Financial Relations of the Papacy with England to 1327*. Cambridge, MA: The Medieval Academy of America.

Maitland, F. W. 1900. "Translator's Introduction." In Otto Gierke, *Political Theories of the Middle Age*, vii–xlv. Cambridge: Cambridge University Press.

McLean, Paul D. 2007. *The Art of the Network: Strategic Interaction and Patronage in Renaissance Florence*. Durham: Duke University Press.

Mucciarelli, Roberta. 1995. *I Tolomei banchieri di Siena: La parabola di un casato nel XIII e XIV secolo*. Siena: Protagon.

Olsen, Glenn. 1969. "Italian Merchants and the Performance of Papal Banking Functions in the Early Thirteenth Century." In *Economy, Society, and Government in Medieval Italy: Essays in Memory of Robert L. Reynolds*, ed. David Herlihy, Robert S. Lopez, and Vsevolod Slessarev, 43–63. Kent, OH: Kent State University Press.

Ottokar, Nicola. 1962. *Il Comune di Firenze alla fine del Dugento*. Torino: Giulio Einaudi.

Padgett, John F. 2001. "Organizational Genesis, Identity and Control: The Transformation of Banking in Renaissance Florence." In *Networks and Markets*, ed. James E. Rauch and Alessandra Casella, 211–57. New York: Russell Sage.

———. 2005. "Early Partnership Memo." Unpublished manuscript. http://home.uchicago.edu/~jpadgett.

———. 2006. "Organizational Genesis in Florentine History: Four Multiple-Network Mechanisms." Unpublished manuscript. http://home.uchicago.edu/~jpadgett.

——— 2009a. "Extracts from Papal Registers Involving Italian Bankers." Unpublished manuscript. http://home.uchicago.edu/~jpadgett.

———. 2009b. "Extracts from Secondary Literature about Dugento Italian Merchant-Bankers." Unpublished manuscript. http://home.uchicago.edu/~jpadgett.

———. 2010. "Open Elite? Social Mobility, Marriage and Family in Florence, 1282–1494." *Renaissance Quarterly* 63:357–411.

Padgett, John F., and Christopher K. Ansell. 1993. "Robust Action and the Rise of the Medici, 1400–1434." *American Journal of Sociology* 98:1259–1319.

Padgett, John F., and Paul D. McLean. 2006. "Organizational Invention and Elite Transformation: The Birth of the Partnership System in Renaissance Florence." *American Journal of Sociology* 111:1463–1568.

———. 2010. "Economic Credit in Renaissance Florence." *Journal of Modern History* 83:1–47.

Post, Gaines. 1934. "Parisian Masters as a Corporation, 1200–1246." *Speculum* 9:421–45.

Re, Emilo. 1914. "La compagnia dei Riccardi in Inghilterra." *Archivio della società Romana di storia patria* 37:87–138.

Renouard, Yves. 1941. *Les relations des papes d'Avignon et des compagnies commerciales et bancaires da 1316 à 1378*. Paris: E. de Boccard.

Reynolds, Robert L. 1952. "Origins of Modern Business Enterprise." *Journal of Economic History* 12:350–65.

Rhodes, Walter E. 1907. "The Italian Bankers in England and Their Loans to Edward I and Edward II." In *Historical Essays in Commemoration of the Jubilee of the Owens College, Manchester*, ed. T. F. Tout and James Tait, 137–68. Manchester: Manchester University Press.

Runciman, Steven. 1958. *The Sicilian Vespers*. Cambridge: Cambridge University Press.

Santini, P. 1887. "Società delle Torre in Firenze." *Archivio storico italiano* 20:25–58, 178–204.

Sapori, Armando. 1926. *La crisi delle compagnie mercantili dei Bardi a del Peruzzi*. Firenze: Leo S. Olschki.

———. 1947. *La compagnia dei Frescobaldi in Inghilterra*. Firenze: Leo S. Olschki.

———. [1939] 1955a. "Il personale delle compagnie mercantili del Medioevo." In *Studi di storica economica (secoli XIII–XIV–XV), volume secondo*, 695–763. Firenze: G. C. Sansoni.

———. [1939] 1955b. "Le compagnie mercantili Toscane del Dugento e dei primi del Trecento: La responsibilià dei compagni verso i terzi." In *Studi di storica economica (secoli XIII–XIV–XV), volume secondo*, 765–808. Firenze: G. C. Sansoni.

———. 1970. *The Italian Merchant in the Middle Ages*. New York: Norton.

Sayous, André-E. 1931. "Les mandats de Saint Louis sur son trésor et le movement international des capitaux pendent la septième croisade (1248–1254)." *Revue Historique* 56:254–304.

———. 1932. "Les opérations des banquiers Italiens en Italie et aux foires de Champagne pendent le XIIIe siècle." *Revue Historique* 57:1–31.

Spufford, Peter. 1988. *Money and Its Use in Medieval Europe*. Cambridge: Cambridge University Press.

Strayer, Joseph R. 1969. "Italian Bankers and Philip the Fair." In *Economy, Society, and Government in Medieval Italy: Essays in Memory of Robert L. Reynolds*, ed. David Herlihy, Robert S. Lopez, and Vsevolod Slessarev, 113–21. Kent, OH: Kent State University Press.

Swidler, Ann. 1986. "Culture in Action: Symbols and Strategies." *American Sociological Review* **51**: 273–86.

Usher, Abbott Payson. 1943. *The Early History of Deposit Banking in Mediterranean Europe*. Cambridge, MA: Harvard University Press.

Verlinden, O. 1963. "Markets and Fairs." In *The Cambridge Economic History of Europe*, vol. 3, *Economic Organization and Policies in the Middle Ages*, ed. M. M. Postan, E. E. Rich, and Edward Miller, 42–118. Cambridge: Cambridge University Press.

Waley, Daniel. 1961. *The Papal State in the Thirteenth Century*. London: MacMillan.

———. 1969. *The Italian City-Republics*. New York: McGraw-Hill.

Weber, Max. 2003. *The History of Commercial Partnerships in the Middle Ages*. Lanham, MD: Rowman and Littlefield.

Whitwell, Robert Jowitt. 1903. "Italian Bankers and the English Crown." *Transactions of the Royal Historical Society* 17:175–233.

———. 1904. "English Monasteries and the Wool Trade in the 13th Century." *Vierteljahrschrift fur Social-und Wirtschaftsgeschichte* 1–33.

6

Transposition and Refunctionality

The Birth of Partnership Systems in Renaissance Florence

John F. Padgett

Inventions of any sort are hard to understand. They seem to come out of the blue, a rupture with the past, yet close investigation always reveals historical roots. Individual geniuses sometimes create them, but is "genius" just our celebratory label for a process that worked, which we do not understand? To proffer a tentative distinction: innovations improve on existing ways (i.e, activities, conceptions, and purposes) of doing things, while inventions change the ways things are done. Under this definition, the key to classifying something as an invention is the degree to which it reverberates out to alter the interacting system of which it is a part. To some extent we understand micrologics of combination and recombination.[1] Yet the invention puzzle is that some of these innovative recombinations cascade out to reconfigure entire interlinked ecologies of "ways of doing things," whereas most innovations do not. The poisedness of a system to reconfiguration by an invention is as much a part of the phenomenon to be explained as is the system's production of the invention itself. Invention "in the wild" cannot be understood through abstracting away from concrete social context because inventions are permutations of that context.[2] But to make progress in understanding discontinuous change we need to embed our analysis of transformation in the routine dynamics of actively self-reproducing social contexts, where constitutive elements and relations are generated and reinforced.

Biological evolution stands as one exemplar that theoretical analysis (without prediction) is possible even in open-ended, endlessly generative systems of self-reproducing recombination and feedback. Imitation of biological science by the social sciences should never be slavish: social systems have no genes, and social systems have consciousness. But from biology comes the fundamental insight that organic entities, structures, and artifacts are not static "objects"; they are vortexes of cross-entity chemical flows that reproduce themselves.[3] Among other things, social systems are one form of "life."[4] As such, uncovering social analogues to cross-entity chemical flows, which transform and reproduce actors through interaction, is a prerequisite for systematically analyzing punctuated tippings or inventions in the reproductive dynamics of any human entity, be that a body, an organization, a market, or a city.

Renaissance Florence is the empirical site for this study of the historical process of socially embedded invention. While the uniqueness of the Italian Renaissance in world history may be debatable, the creativity of that particular place and time is not. Inventions in literature (Dante, Boccaccio), in art (Giotto, Masaccio, Donatello, Michelangelo), in letters (Petrarch), in architecture (Brunelleschi, Alberti), in science

This chapter is an abridged version (40 percent cut) of Padgett and McLean 2006.

[1] E.g., Barley 1990; March 1991; Powell, Koput, and Smith-Doerr 1996; Fleming 2002; Burt 2004.

[2] Hutchins 1995; Latour 1988; Galison 1997.

[3] Maturana and Varela 1980; Nicolis and Prigogine 1989; Fontana and Buss 1994; Padgett, Lee, and Collier 2003.

[4] Luhmann 1995; Padgett and Powell, this volume.

(Leonardo, Galileo), in constitutional design (Bruni, Savonarola), in political theory (Machiavelli, Guicciardini), and in business (Datini) were produced in breathtaking numbers and speeds. Indeed the most striking global feature about Renaissance Florence is the sheer multiplicity of domains in which inventions occurred: they seemed to cascade from one domain to another. These developments did not occur in isolation from the rest of northern Italy,[5] but Florence was a particularly catalytic site in the northern Italian Renaissance web of invention.

While there is no gainsaying these facts about inventiveness, recent historians have challenged the "renaissance" interpretation of late medieval Florence, preferring instead to emphasize the traditional and conservative character of the place.[6] The historiographical puzzle this revisionism poses is not which competing interpretation is correct. The puzzle is how both can be correct. How did such a traditional and conservative place, not at all motivated to innovate per se, nonetheless invent so prolifically? Large macrohistorical issues about the "rise of the West" are linked to the answer to this question.[7]

The particular Florentine economic invention whose emergence we will trace in this chapter is the discovery, in the late 1300s, of a new organizational form that Melis (1962) called the "business system" (*sistema di aziende*). We find his label imprecise, but what Melis (1962, 130) meant was not imprecise: a set of legally autonomous companies linked through one person or through a small set of controlling partners. In Melis's definition, "legally autonomous companies" meant either ownership by a single person (*individuale*) or ownership by a partnership of persons (*collettiva*). If at least one of the companies linked into the *sistema di aziende* is a partnership, then we will translate Melis's term as "partnership system." The partnership system was an innovation in company ownership in which a single controlling partner (or a small number of partners), if he did not manage the branch himself, made a set of legally separate partnership contracts with branch managers in different locations and/or industries. This new "network-star" ownership structure largely displaced earlier legally unitary companies, often built collectively by patrilineage families, which were common in the late 1200s and early 1300s.[8] Viewed formally, this splintering of a unitary company into overlapping parts was decentralization because it allowed various branches and business markets to be managed separately through legally independent account books. Viewed operationally, this devolution was centralization because it dissolved unitary committees of numerous owner-directors and substituted dominant ownership by just one or at most a few persons.[9] Melis (1962) himself studied the extraordinarily well-documented case of Francesco Datini, the famous "merchant of Prato" whose system lasted from 1382 to 1410.[10] The Datini system was among the first, if not the first, example of this new organizational form. De Roover (1966) studied the slightly later case of the Medici bank.

This new organizational form is important in the history of financial capitalism both because it protected owners (to some extent) against the unlimited-liability risk of complete financial ruin and because it easily allowed diversification into multiple product markets. The earlier unitary companies often had been generalist in character, doing whatever type of merchant or banking business made sense to it at the moment. The new partnership system was also generalist in ensemble, but each component company was more specialized than before. Component specialization required a more abstracted system of articulation among branches than before. This in our account was the organizational driver for the rapid diffusion of double-entry bookkeeping in Florence in the late 1300s.

A stock market did not yet exist in the Renaissance, but apart from this major difference in ownership structure, the invention of the partnership system in Renaissance Florentine banking is similar managerially to the shift in American manufacturing from the functional to the multidivisional form, discussed by Chandler (1962). In economic mentalité, Florentine partnership systems are early exemplars of the "financial conception of control" discussed by Fligstein (1990). Partnership systems are also members of the class of organizations that Powell (1990) called "network organizations"; indeed historically they may have been the first member of this class. Each of these modernist classifications is accurate, depending upon which aspect of the new organizational form one

[5] E.g., Witt 2003.
[6] Kent 1977; Kelly-Gadol 1977; Molho 1994.
[7] Lopez 1976; Abu-Lughod 1989.
[8] Sapori 1926; Renouard 1941.
[9] de Roover 1966, 78.
[10] See also Origo 1957.

chooses to emphasize. Viewed in the context of its time, however, partnership systems were sui generis, deeply embedded in the local Florentine and Tuscan context.

A companion article to this chapter, "Economic Credit in Renaissance Florence,"[11] examines this economic invention not at the level of organizational structure but at the level of organizational practice—namely, the operation and dramatic growth of economic credit in Renaissance Florence in the late 1300s and early 1400s. Ongoing relations of business credit were recorded primarily in the bookkeeping device of current accounts, tabulated in bilateral format. Extensive and deep credit relations among Florentine merchant-bankers were the primary reason for the century-long dominance of international finance in Europe by Florence. That companion article demonstrates the historical connection between the rise of intercompany credit and the invention and spread of partnership systems as new nodes of exchange in that credit.

THEORETICAL FRAMEWORK

Dynamic Multiple Networks

Inspired by biochemistry, our theoretical approach to the topic of organizational invention is to situate invention in the dynamics of reproduction of multiple networks—specifically, in the cross-network processes of transposition, refunctionality, and catalysis. Recombinant innovation in organizations is produced, this case study shows, when one or more social relations are transposed from one domain to another, mixing in use with relations already there. This transposition-induced hybridity is the raw material for invention, but that is only the first step. Refunctionality is when transposition leads not just to improvement in existing uses but, more radically, to new uses—that is, to new potential objects with which to interact and transform. Catalysis is when these new interactions feed back to alter the way existing relations reproduce. The entire multiple-network ensemble may tip into true invention when catalytic feedback loops are modified in the autocatalytic transformational process of network reproduction,[12] either by adding new positive feedback loops or by subtracting old negative feedback loops.

To draw out the operational meaning of this perspective for Florence, see figure 6.1 (reproduced in chapter 1 as figure 1.1). We represent "social context" by multiple-network architectures. Actors are clusters of relational ties. In the activity plane of economics, for example, collective actors called companies are composed of partnership ties. These companies trade with each other. In the domain of kinship, for another example, collective actors called patrilineages are composed of genealogy ties. These patrilineages marry each other. And in the domain of politics, collective actors called factions are composed of clientage ties. These factions do political deals with each other. We label the strong-tie relations that constitute collective actors "constitutive ties," and we label recurrent weak-tie relations through which actors deliver resources to each other "relational ties." Within each domain, relational ties "feed" constitutive ties. Reproduction is when constitutive ties, using input resources, make new constitutive ties.

All-important for a multiple-network setup, people are also conceived as constitutive ties: namely, they are cross-domain composites of roles. Purposes are domain-specific features of roles within individuals; they are not features of individuals per se. In figure 6.1, people are represented as vertical lines, linking roles across planes. Not all people participate in all networks at all levels, but many do, inducing patterns of multiple-network overlay or "social embeddedness."[13] Cross-domain connections, through people, regulate the reproductive formation of constitutive and relational ties. Conversely, network reproduction generates people as social actors by shaping and composing the roles that act though them. Patterns of social embeddedness are important for us not only because of "trust" but also because they regulate the dynamic reproduction of constitutive ties in each domain through the aligning and sequencing of multiple roles.

Multiple-network overlays frame and regulate the flows and processes that generate and reproduce the social relations that construct social actors, making them "alive." Uncovering generative flows is the prerequisite for empirically investigating qualitative tips in the dynamics of relational reproduction. Such system tips are how we conceptualize organizational invention.

[11] Padgett and McLean 2011.

[12] Maturana and Valera 1980; Kauffman 1993; Fontana and Buss 1994; Padgett, Lee, and Collier 2003.

[13] Granovetter 1985.

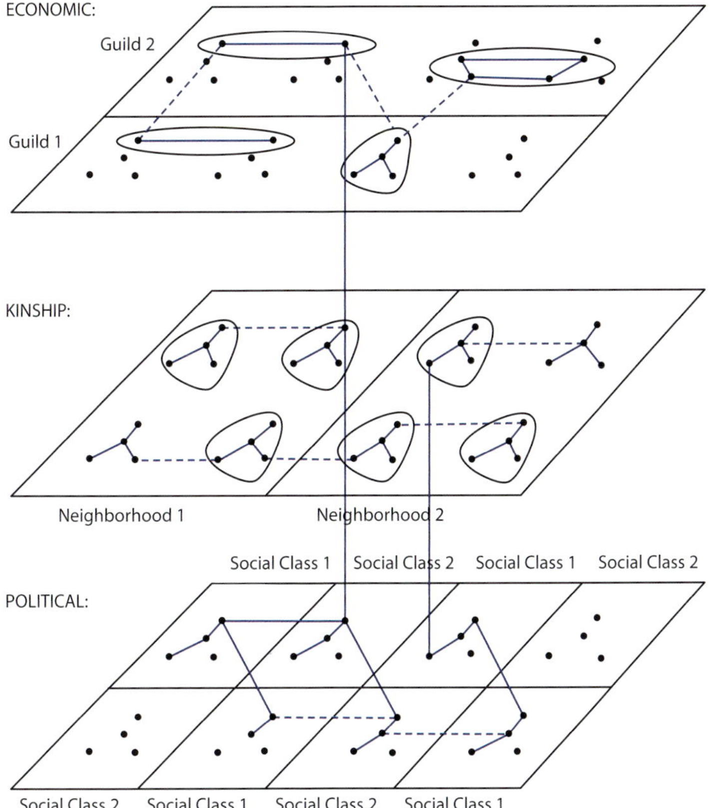

Figure 6.1 Multiple-network ensemble in Renaissance Florence. Solid lines are constitutive ties. Dotted lines are relational social exchanges. Oblongs are formal organizations (families and firms). People in multiple roles are vertical lines connecting corresponding dots in domains of activity in which people are active. (Only two are shown for illustration.)

If organizations are the units of analysis—firms, families, and factions—then one obvious flow through them, bringing them to life, is people: "In organizations, biological or social, rules of action and patterns of interaction persist and reproduce even in the face of constant turnover in component parts, be these molecules or people. In the constant flow of components through organizations, the collectivity typically is not renegotiated anew. Rather, within constraints, component parts are transformed and molded into the ongoing flow of action."[14] Attending to the flow of people, and to the action rules they bring with them, leads to an analytic focus on careers and biographies as these wend their way across organizations and domains. Organizations reproduce through people and other resources flowing through them. The structure of biographical flow among organizations, both within and across domains, channels constitutive-tie transpositions of previously acquired network ties and learned rules of action and interaction. Organizational structure is the blending, transformation, and reproduction, on-site, of networks and interaction rules transported by people into the site from numerous sources.[15] People, conversely, are the hybridized residues of past networks and rules acquired through interaction at their previous organizational sites.[16] In other words, both organizations and people are shaped, through network co-evolution, by the history of each flowing through the other.

[14] Padgett 1997, 200.

[15] Padgett 2001.

[16] Cf. Breiger 1974.

Florentine Transposition of Economic Networks into Politics (and Back Again)

In this chapter the general theoretical framework presented above will play out in Florentine history as follows: After the Ciompi revolt of 1378, as part of a political reconsolidation-repression to be discussed below, domestic or cambio bankers were mobilized into core political offices within the republican state. Before this political mobilization, cambio bankers operated for the most part domestically within the city, changing money and doing deposit banking for their Florentine customers. They participated in state offices through the medium of their guild. International trading (mostly of woolen cloth), on the other hand, was the province of socially high-status merchants often organized into large unitary family firms. This international versus domestic division of labor was reinforced administratively by the guild structure—Arte della Calimala for international traders of finished cloth and Arte del Cambio for domestic bankers. With aggressive political mobilization of them by elite moderates after the Ciompi revolt, however, cambio bankers systematically were pulled up into the "jet stream" of international trading, thereby injecting domestic banking organizational forms and accounting practices into international trading. In what follows I show that a majority of the new partnership systems were constructed by cambio bankers reaching overseas to construct new trading branches abroad. This engagement in international trade had been inhibited, though not prohibited, by the guild system before the Ciompi revolt. Making bankers into city councillors is our example of transposition of roles across domains through collectively restructuring political biographies.

As cambio bankers were transported into new settings, both economic and political, they brought with them their old master-apprentice logics of contracts and careers. They then adapted these to the new international-trading setting, blending with the patrilineage family logics already there. The result was a modularized hybrid—short-term contracts with both family and nonfamily branch managers—in other words, the partnership system. Refunctionality occurred when this new organizational form led Florentine businessmen to discover new ways for companies to relate to each other in the market—through current accounts, credit, and double-entry bookkeeping. Together transposition and refunctionality created the potential for revolutionizing international finance via modularity and liquidity, depending upon how the rest of the multiple-network system of Florence responded to these innovations.

The catalysis that catapulted this organizational innovation into systemic invention, which restructured both banking and elites, was the social embedding of this partnership system into marriage and clientage. In politics the Ciompi revolt triggered the formation of a "republican oligarchy" to succeed "guild corporatism"[17] in two stages. After 1393, a more conservative political regime succeeded the major-guild moderate innovators of 1382–92. Higher-status *popolani* and magnates demographically took over the partnership systems that had been developed (for the most part) by cambio bankers. This second stage of biographical transposition brought economic partnerships into tighter correlation with elite marriages. This in turn established sinews for the percolation of partnership-system economic techniques, like current accounts, out into the broader network structure of the ruling social elite at large, making that elite itself more mercantile in its thinking. For markets, this new correlation of partnership with marriage provided social foundations for *fiducia* (trust) within the merchant community to make the credit system function. The final product, on the one hand, was a vibrant financial system that dominated European international finance for a century. On the other hand, it was an intensely status-conscious but politically permeable merchant elite that created generalists ("Renaissance men") for whom economics, politics, family, art, and philosophy were all refractions of each other.

In sum, the economic invention in late medieval Florence of the partnership system was one corollary (not the only corollary) of elite transformation. As the social-network constituents of the Florentine elite shifted from patrilineage and guild into marriage and clientage, new business forms were invented, new political mobilization techniques were developed, and kinship was incrementally rewired to emphasize marriage. Each of these organizational changes spilled over to support the other to create a multiple-network ensemble that we might label the Renaissance oligarchic-republican regime.

The "rise of financial capitalism" here is not a grand teleological process of inevitable modernization. It was rooted instead in particular places and histories, which refashioned their

[17] Najemy 1982.

own multiple networks in crucial punctuated-equilibrium moments. Florence was unusually creative in part because of its tumultuous political history, which repeatedly transposed and refunctionalized its underlying social networks. Florentine elites invented not because they wanted to but because they had to, conservatively to preserve their threatened positions. Naturally there is more to explaining invention than political turmoil, but in the case of Renaissance Florence that was the core mechanism that recomposed its economic, political, and kinship networks into tipping.[18] Other case studies, like the ones in this book, no doubt will add to the list of annealing mechanisms that induce transposition, refunctionality, and catalysis in social networks in such ways that evolution, not collapse, is the result.[19]

This chapter will develop this argument in several stages. After reviewing prior historical research on Florentine partnership systems, I pinpoint the exact timing of this invention to be 1383. Most of the partnership system builders of this period will be identified to be cambio bankers, who politically were mobilized into government at increased rates after the Ciompi revolt. After identifying the innovators, I then describe the politics of the Ciompi revolt and its repression in some detail and show how political mobilization created a post-Ciompi republican oligarchy, absorbing cambio bankers and other businessmen into this newly augmented elite through marriage. This social embeddedness of banking in marriage catalyzed the reproduction of partnership systems in economics and helped transform the new oligarchy politically into mercantile republicans. *Tutti insieme*, post-revolt Renaissance Florence is a dramatic example of the punctuated co-evolution of economic markets and political elites.

DOCUMENTING THE EMERGENCE OF FLORENTINE PARTNERSHIP SYSTEMS

Existing Literature

The previous literature on the Florentine partnership system, both overviews and detailed case studies, was reviewed extensively in the article out of which this abridgment is drawn.[20] That review will not be repeated here, except to note that the two most important works that precede this study are the study of the Datini system by Melis (1962) and the study of the Medici system by de Roover (1966).

As documented in these and other studies, the complete set of organizational features that Datini and the Medici employed to construct and to manage their businesses were these:

1. legally distinct partnerships with branch managers (or the owner) in each location
2. separate sets of account books for each branch
3. diversification of companies into multiple industries
4. a "holding company" arrangement, in which Datini's Florentine partnership owned parts of other partnerships[21]
5. centralized oversight of branches through vast numbers of business letters between Datini and his branch partners and through regular meetings between Datini and his branch partners
6. double-entry bookkeeping in bilateral format
7. current accounts both among partnership-system companies and with major trading partners[22]

The first element in this list narrowly defines the partnership system, but the historical significance of the system comes from this whole package of organizational correlates working together.

Quantitative Documentation of Growth and Diffusion

The article out of which this abridgment was drawn also went to considerable length to document the precise timing of the invention and diffusion of this new organizational form. The reason for temporal precision was to narrow down causality. The previous literature had documented the form and operation of the partnership system but not the exacting timing of its invention and diffusion. Based on primary sources, this documentation was presented in a

[18] Cf. Stinchcombe 1965.

[19] See Powell and Sandholtz, this volume, for another example of transposition and refunctionality.

[20] Padgett and McLean 2006.

[21] Melis [1965] 1991, 169.

[22] de Roover [1956] 1974, 144–49.

thirteen-page appendix[23] and in an online sixty-one-page memo.[24]

Just to summarize, the primary findings about the timing of emergence were these:

1. Francesco di Marco Datini, the famous and well-documented "Merchant of Prato,"[25] was indeed one of the original founders of the partnership system, who first developed his new organizational form in 1383.[26]
2. But four other partnership systems, none documented like that of Datini with surviving internal business records, were also founded that same year: Vieri di Cambio de' Medici, Davanzato and Manetto di Giovanni Davanzati, Francesco di Neri Ardinghelli, and Ardingo di Corso Ricci and Gualtieri di Sandro Portinari. What had appeared to previous scholarship as the invention of a single business genius (Datini) was actually a simultaneous invention by a cluster of interrelated Florentine and Pratese businessmen.
3. All of the original inventors, except Datini, were Florentine cambio bankers who had been in business under more traditional organizational forms prior to their simultaneous adoption.
4. Given its first appearance in 1383, the new organizational form diffused rapidly through the upper reaches of the Florentine and then the Tuscan economies. The original article documents forty-eight such systems in Florence before 1400, and it discusses other examples in Lucca and in Pisa during the post-1390 period.
5. The size distribution of number of partners in cambio banks (information contained in annual guild registers) underwent a sudden shift exactly in 1382 as the organizational role of many of them shifted to being headquarters for partnership systems.

Composition of Post-Ciompi Partnership Systems

So much for timing, now what about agency? That is, other than Francesco Datini, Vieri di Cambio de' Medici, and the others already mentioned, who exactly were the Florentines who collectively invented the partnership system?

Table 6.1 shows the industrial composition and the centralization frequencies of the newly emergent partnership systems listed in the appendix of Padgett and McLean (2006). While some of the new partnership systems, like that of Datini himself, emerged out of international trading, the bulk of them, like that of Vieri de' Medici, emerged through a fusion of cambio banking with international trading. The role of wool-manufacturing companies in the emergence of partnership systems was minor. Among the twenty-four cambio-plus-international-fusion partnership systems, nineteen were formed sequentially by cambio bankers entering into international trading or merchant banking. Only five (including Datini) were formed in the reverse order, by international traders entering into cambio banking. In other words, Florentine partnership systems primarily emerged in the industry domains of domestic banking and international trading, fusing them together, with cambio bankers taking the lead in organizing this fusion.

Table 6.2 presents statistical information on who the post-Ciompi partnership-system innovators were in time periods both earlier and later than 1383. Poisson regressions were performed to discover the social and political features of the active Florentine businessmen who organized the most companies. The dependent variable in these regressions is the number of legally distinct companies in which a businessman is a partner. Businessmen involved in many companies were the organizers and central commanders of partnership systems. Archival sources for the data in these regressions are listed in the notes to the table.

Before the 1378 Ciompi revolt, the only businessmen who participated in multiple industries in statistically significant numbers, few in absolute numbers as these were, were guild consuls—that is, elected political leaders of the banking, the wool, and to a lesser extent the international trading guilds. The pre-Ciompi regressions in table 6.2 reflect the fact that business careers were specialized within guilds until guildsmen reached the pinnacle of success, at which point they might branch out into other economic activities, using their originally more specialized company as a base.

With the onset of partnership systems, the sociopolitical backgrounds of businessmen engaged in multiple companies changed. In 1385–99, immediately after the Ciompi revolt, businessmen

[23] Padgett and McLean 2006, 1548–60.
[24] Padgett 2005.
[25] Origo 1957.
[26] Melis 1962, 130.

Table 6.1.
Industrial Composition of 1385–99 Partnership Systems

# of partnership systems	Int'l trading + cambio bank	Int'l trading only	Int'l trading I+ wool manufacturing	Cambio bank + wool manufacturing
3+ partnerships	13 (11)	7 (4)	1 (0)	0 (0)
2+ partnerships	11 (10)	9 (3)	3 (0)	3 (2)
Total	24 (21)	16 (7)	4 (0)	3 (2)

Source: Padgett and McLean 2006, appendix A.

Note: Numbers in parentheses indicate the number of centralized partnership systems.

participating in two or more partnerships were distinguishable sociopolitically in two ways from businessmen involved in only one company: (a) politically they were mobilized into the 1384 *balìa* and the 1393 *reggimento*, and (b) socially they married upper-class popolani wives. Why did these particular political and social factors correlate with the economic activity of founding partnership systems?

Balìe were special ad hoc committees set up to reform the Florentine political constitution, sometimes in minor, sometimes in major ways.[27] The 1384 *balìa* was set up to reform the wool manufacturers' industry and guild,[28] a central locus of *ciompi* agitation. The *reggimento* was the set of Florentines successfully elected to be eligible for the Priorate, or city council[29] through an election procedure called the scrutiny.[30] As such it was Florence's political ruling class. To say that partnership-system businessmen were disproportionately members of these two groups is to say that, for those years at least, they were members of the political elite.

It is not surprising that the 1378 *balìa* coefficient, during the height of the Ciompi revolt itself, is not statistically significant. But it is interesting that in 1382, a year associated with repression of the Ciompi revolt, the political membership variables of 1382 *balìa* and 1382 *reggimento* were *not* statistically significant predictors of partnership-system builders. This temporal pattern of coefficients helps us interpret direction of causality: it was the new 1382 post-Ciompi political elite that subsequently recruited and co-opted businessmen (about to become partnership-system businessmen) into the political elite rather than these businessmen who created the new political elite in the first place.

The other statistically significant effect in table 6.2, for 1385–99, is for marriage to popolani wives. In the republican conception of status in Renaissance Florence, social class was defined as the political age of one's patrilineal family—namely, the year in which one's male ancestors first were elected to city council. The highest-prestige popolani were the politically founding generation of the Florentine families who first entered the Priorate during 1282–1342—namely, the era between the constitutional founding of the republic and its first major political convulsion in 1343. To say that partnership-system businessmen disproportionately married popolani wives is to say that they were being absorbed into the social elite, whether or not they were born into it.

The natal social-class coefficients reveal that the 1385–99 partnership-system businessmen (unlike their 1427 successors) were not themselves necessarily born into the social elite. Instead they were socially quite heterogeneous in class background—some high prestige like Vieri de' Medici and some low prestige like Francesco Datini. Either way, they wound up marrying popolani wives, indicating a systematic process of social as well as political co-optation. Even outsider Datini from Prato took a popolani Florentine wife.

The vector of 1427 coefficients shows how these partnership-system businessmen settled into the social structure of Florence over time. Businessmen's marriages to popolani wives (and now also to magnate wives) became an even more powerful predictor of their capacity to build partnership systems than it was the case in 1385–99. The big change from the late 1300s to 1427 was that partnership-system businessmen themselves became more homogeneously elitist

[27] Molho 1968a.
[28] A.S.F., *Arte della Lana* 46.
[29] Kent 1975.
[30] Najemy 1982.

Table 6.2.
Social and Political Embedding of Businessmen in Multiple Companies

Poisson regression coefficients over time:

	Number of Industries		Number of Partnerships	
	Alberti int'l. 1348–58	Pisa 1369	Datini 1385–99	Catasto 1427
	Cambio 1348–58 + Wool 1353	+ Cambio 1369 + Wool 1382	+ Cambio 1385–99 + Wool 1382	(all industries except "other")
Social Class				
Popolani	1.110	1.003	.342	**.688****
Magnate	[collinear]	[collinear]	.608	**1.030****
New Man	.718	1.465	.110	.007
Social Class of Wife				
Popolani	.736	.541	**.673****	**.766*****
Magnate	.559	.147	.365	**.713***
New Man	1.722	.815	.497	–.079
Political Office				
Priorate	–2.144	.054	–.288	.160
Calimala Consul	[–∞]	1.299	**.985***	–.307
Cambio Consul	**1.572***	**2.691*****	.198	–.341
Lana Consul	.907	**2.389*****	–.744˙	.322
Mercanzia	1.909	-.993	–.345	–.470
Balìa 1378			.408	
Balìa 1382			–.234	
Reggimento 1382			–.574	
Balìa 1384			**.746***	
Balìa 1393			–.200	
Reggimento 1393			**.995****	
Political Factions				
Albizzi	[–∞]	.523	.726	
Ricci	.602	**1.178***	–.333	
anti-Ciompi			.331	
pro-Ciompi			–.818	
Albizzeans				.095
Mediceans				**1.371*****
Quarter				
Santa Croce	1.187	.068	–.217	.057
Santa M. Novella	.126	.520	–.345	–.169
San Giovanni	–.022	–.183	.042	.260

Log likelihood	−54.4	−79.2	−311.0	-287.1
# obs. (persons)	850	502	829	533
L.R. chi^2	17.31	88.6	79.3	93.9
prob > chi^2	.185	.000	.000	.000
pseudo R^2	.137	.359	.113	.141

Sources:

1. **Numbers of industries and partnerships:** (a) 1348–99 annual censuses of cambio banking partnerships: ASF, *Arte del Cambio* 14. (b) 1348–58 companies with whom Alberti *nuovi* did business: Goldthwaite, Settesoldi, and Spallanzani 1995. (c) 1369 companies that shipped goods through the port of Pisa: Silva 1908; Peruzzi 1868, 219-22. (d) 1385–99 companies with whom Datini did business: Mellis 1962, tables 27, 28, 31, 32, 35, 36, 39, 40. (e) 1353 census of active wool manufacturers: ASF, *Arte del Lana* 20. (f) 1382 census of wool-manufacturing companies: ASF, *Arte del Lana* 46. (g) 1427 Catasto: ASF, *Catasto* 64-85.

2. **Social class:** (a) Magnates: Lansing (1991, 239–42) records original patrilineage membership in 1293 and 1295. See Klapisch-Zuber 1985 for important qualifications about changing membership in this group over time. (b) Popolani, new men and new-new men: defined by the date that an ancestor from patrilineage first entered Priorate, as recorded in A.S.F., *Manoscritti* 248–52. "Popolani" are defined by first date in Priorate between 1282 and 1342; "new men" are defined by first date in Priorate between 1343 and 1377; "new-new men" are defined by first date in Priorate between 1378 and 1433. See Padgett and Ansell 1993, 1261 for a time-series plot of rates of new entry of families into the Priorate, which makes obvious the discreteness of the political cohorts of families defined by these particular dates.

3. **Marriages:** recorded from multiple sources, but primarily A.S.F., *Manoscritti Carte dell'Ancisa* 348–61.

4. **Political offices:** (a) Priorate: Newberry library copy of A.S.F., *Manoscritti* 248–52. (b) Mercanzia: A.S.F., *Mercanzia* 129. (c) Merchant guild consuls: http://www.stg.brown.edu/projects/tratte. (d) Banking guild consuls: A.S.F., *Arte del Cambio* 12. (e) Wool guild consuls: http://www.stg.brown.edu/projects/tratte. (f) 1378 balìa: Gherardi [1389] 1876, 505. (g) 1382 balìa: Stefani [1385] 1903, 394–96; later additions or *arroti* in A.S.F., *Balìa* 17, 22. (h) 1384 balìa: A.S.F., *Arte della Lana* 46:154-66. (i) 1393 balìa: A.S.F., *Balìa* 17:80–86, 105–7. (j) Reggimento 1382: Ildefonso di San Luigi 1770, 125–260. (k) Reggimento 1393: A.S.F., *Tratte* 357, 7–20.

5. **Political factions:** (a) Albizzi and Ricci: Brucker 1968: no specific pages, narrative references throughout book. (b) Pro-Ciompi and anti-Ciompi: Stefani ([1385] 1903): (c) Albizzeans and Mediceans: Kent 1978, 1352–57.

6. **Neighborhood, both** *gonfalone* **and quarter:** (a) 1351: A.S.F., *Estimo* 306. (b) 1378: A.S.F., *Prestanze* 367–69, *Estimo* 268. (c) 1427: A.S.F., *Catasto* 64–85.

Notes:

(1) Given that businessmen participated as partners in at least one company or industry (see table 1 in Padgett and McLean 2006, 1481), the dependent variable is number (minus one, to fit Poisson format) of partnerships, or industries in the first two periods, that Florentine businessmen owned or participated in. "Number of Industries" is used as a proxy for number of companies in 1348–58 and 1369 periods because organizational systems, where companies were legally split into multiple partnerships, did not then exist. Nonetheless single unitary firms sometimes participated in multiple markets in these earlier times at the low rates shown in table 1, Padgett and McLean 2006, 1481.

(2) On the independent variable side, only marriages and political offices with dates prior to the last date of the logit regressions (i.e., 1358, 1369, 1399, 1427, respectively) are included in these estimations. Negative binomial regressions performed slightly better than Poisson regressions for the latter two periods, though the differences in estimated coefficients are quite minor. Nonetheless, Poisson regressions were used throughout table 6.2 to preserve comparability across all four regressions. The first two regressions would not converge using a negative binomial due to the absence of fat tails (see table 1 in Padgett and McLean 2006).

$^{***}p < .001$

$^{**}p < .01$

$^{*}p < .05$

$^{(*)}p < .06$

in social-class background. By 1427, natal birth into the popolani and magnate social classes had become strongly associated with leadership of partnership systems. Indeed by 1427, the social distinction between popolani and magnates had been largely effaced: these two upper social classes fused in the economic domain, as they gradually took over the partnership systems that others had created. It is facts like these that lend credence to the "oligarchic" interpretation of the Albizzean regime.[31]

The statistically significant 1427 coefficient for the Medici faction is consistent with existing historiography. The Medici bank was a crucial component in the new Medici political party.[32] To put this point more generally: ultimately, economic organizational invention, in the form of new partnership networks, became incorporated into the organizational structure of political parties, thereby changing the dynamic of state formation in Florence. After a number of intervening decades, economic invention eventually cascaded back into political invention.

I have not yet coded from the archives *balìa* and *reggimento* data for 1427, so my interpretation for that period needs to be provisional. But there is no evidence in table 6.2 to suggest that political mobilization, in the form of political officeholding, played an important role in the ongoing maintenance of the Florentine partnership system after its birth. Political mobilization was clearly related to economic partnership-system building in the 1383–99 phase of its genesis. But forty years later, during the phase of its ongoing reproduction, natal social class had taken over as the dominant social embedding for partnership systems. Marriage to popolani wives remained the network that dynamically bridged the transition between these two phases, guiding the partnership system from its political genesis to its social-class institutionalization.

EXPLAINING THE EMERGENCE OF FLORENTINE PARTNERSHIP SYSTEMS

Given these newly discovered facts about the Florentine invention of the partnership system in the 1380s, my causal explanation of these facts will be developed in the following stages. First, summarizing the extensive secondary literature on this topic, I briefly describe the Ciompi revolt and the stages of its repression. Second, I examine the roles of both cambio bankers and international merchants in the political reconstructions of the state and of the elite after the Ciompi revolt. Demobilization of guilds and politicization of marriage and clientage were central features in these reconstructions. Next I show how the social logics of cambio-banking and international-merchant partnerships, viewed separately as individual spokes of the partnership system, changed through this elite reconsolidation process, enabling those components to fit together organizationally and to be reproduced socially. In the final section of this chapter, I adumbrate the economic consequences of these organizational transformations for bookkeeping, liquidity, and credit in the Florentine banking system.

The Ciompi Revolt and Its Repression

The Ciompi revolt was the only (temporarily) successful workers revolution in European preindustrial history.[33] Some prominent Florentine historians do not accept this economic-class characterization,[34] even though the direct involvement of wool workers and other *popolo minuto* or "little people" (collectively called *ciompi* or "comrades" by contemporaries) in violently overthrowing the state and in evicting large numbers of popolani and magnates from Florence was indeed the most striking feature of this dramatic event in 1378. The major reason for their rejection is because the objectives of the *popolo minuto* emphasized guild-corporatist demands for inclusion and citizenship rather than overthrow of the means of production. Seen in the light of contemporaries, however, the political "reforms" proposed and forcibly implemented for a short time by the *ciompi* were radical indeed.[35] Here we shall narrate these searing events with an emphasis on the role of and the impact on international merchants and domestic bankers who collectively invented the partnership system.

The Ciompi revolt emerged out of the War of the Eight Saints (1375–78) with the papacy. Intense political struggle between two elite factions had been building up for two decades before this

[31] Schevill [1936] 1963; Martines 1979; Cohn 1980.
[32] Padgett and Ansell 1993.

[33] Rodolico [1899] 1968; Cohn 1980; Stella 1993; Trexler 1998.
[34] Brucker 1968, 1977; Najemy 1981, 1982.
[35] Cohn 2006.

climatic war, with a "conservative" side (the Albizzi faction in alliance with the Parte Guelfa) consistently pushing for restriction of the republican franchise to patrician families and with a "liberal" side (the Ricci faction in alliance with artisan guilds) consistently pushing to open the franchise to new men who had recently established themselves in the city economy.[36] Three traumatic events in the 1340s—namely, the 1342 bankruptcies of the large Bardi and Peruzzi banks, the 1343 political convulsion that economic crash triggered, and the 1348 Black Death, which killed about two-thirds of the Florentine population[37]—had opened up both the economy and the political regime to an infusion of new men (*gente nuova*). This post-1343 infusion generated deep resentment on the part of the older patricians who had founded the republic in 1282. Political struggle between patricians and new men had been a consistent trope in late medieval Florence—even more so than in other Italian city-states because of high rates of economic and social mobility. Contradictorily, each generation of elites between 1200 and 1500 sponsored mobility in the economic domain but resisted it in the political domain. The political expression of this underlying social-mobility contradiction, however, changed substantially through time.

In the 1343–78 generation, political struggle was manifest in an escalating series of McCarthyite purges (*ammonizione*) by both factions—the Albizzi-faction-cum-Parte Guelfa side purging selected liberals through denouncing them as Ghibellines and the Ricci-faction-cum-guild side purging targeted conservatives through denouncing them as magnates.[38] The 1375–78 war with the pope, then resident in Avignon, was perhaps inevitable given the two territorial consolidations by Florence in Tuscany and by the pope in central Italy, which collided. Internationally, the pope through his spiritual interdict of Florence organized a largely (though not completely) successful boycott of European trade with Florentine businessmen, temporarily crushing the Florentine economy.[39] Domestically, war with the pope desecrated deep and longstanding Guelf loyalties in many Florentines, especially among traditionalist patricians. Ultimately the rejection of city-state loyalty to the pope set the stage for the birth of civic-humanist republicanism.[40] But in the short run this intersection of domestic with international politics fueled Florentine factional struggle to the boiling point. Each side, but in particular the Guelf side, progressively denounced and purged the other to the point where eventually Salvestro d'Alamanno de' Medici led liberal guild forces in the burning of conservative houses and the forcible eviction from Florence of many Parte Guelfa leaders on June 18, 1378.

This violence within the citizenry opened the door to the potentially revolutionary entrance of previously disenfranchised *ciompi* onto the public stage. On July 21 and then again on August 31, waves of wool workers organized as a "mob" surged into the streets and public squares of Florence, forcibly dissolving with plunder and arson the existing government and demanding reorganization of the state in order to incorporate themselves as three new guilds. These new guilds provided the organizational core of the temporarily victorious *ciompi* state: an expanded guild-corporatist alliance between previously nonguild workers and minor-guild artisans, which lasted only six weeks. Throughout these tumultuous events, conservative popolani and magnates left Florence in droves in fear of their lives, and all export-oriented economic activity, already damaged by the pope's interdict, ceased.

It is not the purpose of this chapter to explain the Ciompi revolt itself, but historians have pointed to a (contested) combination of three factors as causes: (a) chronic dissatisfaction of wool workers with political disenfranchisement, due to their economic subordination within the guild system; (b) the self-immolation of elites in factional struggle, the liberal side of which had systematically raised enfranchisement expectations; and (c) a wool-industry economic slump, due both to short-run pressures from the papal war and to long-term pressures from the growth of a competitive English textile industry,[41] which constricted the import of high-quality English wool to Florentine putting-out *botteghe*, thereby generating unemployment.[42] In future research I hope to "endogenize" the Ciompi revolt by explaining it as the consequence of chronic contradiction in fourteenth-century Florence between the two organizing principles of patrilineage and

[36] Brucker 1962.
[37] Herlihy and Klapisch-Zuber 1985, 69.
[38] Brucker 1962.
[39] Trexler 1974.
[40] Baron 1966.
[41] Carus-Wilson 1967; Carus-Wilson and Coleman 1963.
[42] Hoshino 1980; Franceschi 1993a.

guild, which the short-term pressures mentioned above intensified.

More important in this chapter is the reaction of various exiled and nonexiled groups to this searing political event. Florentine reaction developed in three stages, each of which involved progressively more elitist actors. The first stage was not really an elite reaction at all; it was the countermobilization on September 1, 1378, of minor-guild artisans to take back "their" guild-corporatist state from six weeks of control by nonguild *ciompi*. Minor guildsmen, led by liberal popolani like Salvestro Medici, Tommaso Strozzi, Giorgio Scali, Benedetto Alberti, and Uguccione Ricci, confronted radical wool workers in the streets and defeated them in combat. The largest and most radical of the new *ciompi* guilds was disbanded, and a relatively democratic guild-corporatist state was established, which lasted from 1378 to 1382.

The second stage of reaction, in January 1382, was essentially a coup d'état by "cloth manufacturers and bands of aristocrats, who had armed their servants and retainers, and the peasants from their country estates."[43] The constitutional *balìa* produced by this coup abolished the remaining two minor guilds set up by the *ciompi*, burned the 1378 regime's scrutiny bags, and forcibly tilted officeholding away from artisans back toward the major guilds like international traders, cambio bankers, and wool cloth manufacturers (*lanaiuoli*), who had been in charge before the revolution. Rather than purely reactionary in character, this second-stage counterrevolution was led by factional "moderates"—that is, wealthy major guildsmen in the political center who opposed factional extremes on both the left and the right. Their guiding policy was elite "consensus,"[44] in the pursuit of which, ominously, deeply reactionary exiles and magnates were invited to return to Florence. This elitist but relatively moderate regime of 1382–93 was the "favorable business climate" that induced Francesco Datini to return to Tuscany in 1383, thereby initiating the construction of his partnership system.

The third and final stage of counterrevolution occurred in 1393 with the accession to power of Maso degli Albizzi and his "oligarchic" allies. Reinforced by an international context of dangerous wars with Milan, returning conservatives resumed their purging ways, first in 1387 and then in 1393, this time more selectively targeting the most powerful remaining leaders of the liberal popolani—namely, the Alberti family of international merchant bankers. With the Alberti and their close popolani allies sent into exile, the Albizzi-led regime destroyed remaining guild-consul scrutiny bags and held new elections to restructure the political *reggimento* by fusing elite moderates with elite conservatives.

There has been a lively debate in the historiographical literature about the character of this post-Ciompi Albizzean regime. The traditional interpretation shared by chroniclers and historians alike[45] is that the Albizzean regime was an oligarchy, politically dominated by a fairly well-defined set of conservative families, mostly popolani but also including new men and magnate sympathizers. But Hans Baron's (1966) famous book on civic humanism emphasized the forward-looking philosophical and patriotic vision of republicanism forged by this "oligarchy" in its wars with Milan. In support of this revisionist interpretation, careful empirical analyses by Molho (1968b), Witt (1976), and Najemy (1982) have shown the high rate of election of new individuals in the 1382 and 1393 scrutinies, well beyond any purported closed circle of elite families. Najemy (1982, 276–300) resolved this contradiction to some degree by showing that openness in election was offset by tight institutional controls (e.g., *accoppiatori* and *borsellini*) on the translation of election into real political power. But still this dual vision of oligarchy versus republicanism remains to confound clear understanding of the period.

Following Najemy (1982), our position on this puzzle will be that the entire 1282–1382 century in Florence can be understood as a long-term contradiction between the patrilineage and the guild modes of organizing social, economic, and political mobility. The original Popolo-regime pattern in the 1250s was older elites organized into patrilineages confronting rising groups organized into guilds. But the dynamic of political development came from organizational crossover in the late 1200s and early 1300s—namely, popolani dominating markets and the state through major guilds and new men mimicking patrilineages in their family structure.[46] Najemy focused on the formal institutional and electoral sides of this organizational contradiction. The complementary focus here is to trace this deep contradiction through the evolution of

[43] Brucker 1977, 60.
[44] Najemy 1982.

[45] E.g., Machiavelli [1524] 1988; Guicciardini [1512] 1994.
[46] Padgett 2006.

social networks. Padgett (2010) traces mobility patterns through marriage networks over two hundred years, demonstrating the contesting principles at work. Civic-humanist republicanism was the early fifteenth-century ideological face of this underlying social-network reorganization of mobility channels into the reconstituted Florentine elite.

Biographical Transposition: The Political Co-optation of Cambio Bankers

To repeat, for editorial clarity: "transposition" was the political co-optation of guild-based cambio bankers into high political office. "Refunctionality" was the conversion of these co-opted domestic bankers into international system builders. And "catalysis" was the absorption of partnership systems into socially elite marriage networks.

During the reaction to the Ciompi revolt, domestic cambio bankers, more so than international merchants, were mobilized strongly into the republican institutions of the state. Table 6.3 documents this point. In the post-Ciompi period of 1380–99, 26–36 percent of cambio bankers and 51–59 percent of cambio-banking companies were represented at some time in the city council or Priorate of the city, up from pre-Ciompi representation rates of 15–25 percent and 35–38 percent, respectively. In the more

Table 6.3.
Political Mobilization of Cambio Bankers and International Merchants

Cambio Banking

	% Bankers					% Partnerships				
	1348–62	1363–76	1380–89	1390–99	1427	1348–62	1363–76	1380–89	1390–99	1427
Governing offices of the state										
Priorate	.254	.147	**.262**	**.356**	.272	.353	.376	**.514**	**.587**	.405
Mercanzia	.063	.043	**.235**	**.244**	.087	.057	.113	**.436**	**.482**	.108
Balìe										
1378 Balìa			.027					.069		
1382 Balìa			.040					.073		
1384 Balìa			**.154**					**.362**		
1393 Balìa				**.106**					**.255**	
Reggimenti										
1382 Scrutiny			**.248**					**.512**		
1393 Scrutiny				**.313**					**.605**	

International Trading

	% Merchants				% Partnerships	
	1348–58	1369	1385–99	1427	1385–99	1427
Governing offices of the state						
Priorate	.297	**.479**	.167	.100	.263	.149
Mercanzia	.122	.028	.131	.100	.175	.108
Balìe						
1378 Balìa			.012		.035	
1382 Balìa			.024		.018	
1384 Balìa			.083		.088	
1393 Balìa			.048		.105	
Reggimenti						
1382 Scrutiny			.107		.105	
1393 Scrutiny			.167		.228	

Note: On the left, these are percentages of businessmen on the identified political bodies. On the right, these are percentages of partnerships with at least one partner on the identified political bodies. For Priorate and Mercanzia, time periods refer, for example, to "bankers active in 1348–62 who were ever on Priorate before 1362."

economically focused Mercanzia or commercial court, political mobilization of cambio bankers was even more dramatic: from 4–6 percent of cambio bankers and 6–11 percent of cambio-banking partnerships in the Mercanzia before the revolt, to 23–24 percent and 44–48 percent after the revolt, respectively. These high cambio-banker representation rates compare with the much lower representation rates of 13–17 percent for international merchants and 17–26 percent for international merchant-banking companies during 1380–99. Temporally refined *balìe* representation rates reveal the post-Ciompi mobilization inflection point exactly to be 1384, a date that makes perfect sense in light of the Ciompi-revolt narrative above: Cambio bankers did not initiate the 1382 second-stage major-guild regime that quickly mobilized them, but by 1393 they were fully integrated into the Albizzean "oligarchic" or "civic humanist" regime.

This differential political mobilization of cambio bankers, compared to that of international merchants, is surprising in light of the strictly economic history of the period. The pope emerged victorious in his 1375–78 war with Florence not because of the military power of his weak mercenary armies but because of the economic power of his spiritual interdict of Florentine merchants—namely, his ordering other cities' merchants not to trade with Florentines under the sanction of withholding sacraments. Florentine international merchants, not everywhere but in many places,[47] were decimated economically by this interdict, as foreign merchants seized their goods and exiled them back to Florence. From the perspective of rebuilding the damaged Florentine economy, it was the international merchant-bankers, not the domestic cambio bankers, that most needed political support.

To probe this and other aspects of the political mobilization of cambio bankers, I present tables 6.4 and 6.5. Within the context of a sampling universe of tax censuses of the entire male head-of-household population of Florence, these two tables present various social and political predictors of active participation in cambio banking (table 6.4) and in international trading (table 6.5), at various points in late medieval time. Numerous findings in these logit regressions are of interest, to which I shall return, but the answer to the current puzzle about the greater political mobilization of cambio bankers than international merchants is to be found in the political-faction section of those logit-regression tables. Both before and during the Ciompi revolt, cambio bankers and international merchants were politicized into the various factional struggles of the time, as was the entire city. But in the struggle between the Albizzi and Ricci factions, cambio bankers were neutral, and in the Ciompi struggle itself cambio bankers were politicized into both sides equally. In contrast, international merchants by 1369 had swung predominantly to the guild side.[48] The political redoubt of the leading Alberti family, later to be exiled by conservatives in 1387 and 1393, was the most internationally oriented guild of them all—the Arte della Calimala, home of international traders and import cloth finishers.

Leaders of the moderate regime of 1382–93 were *lanaiuoli* and other domestically based major guildsmen—socially and economically "elite" but politically opposed to both factional extremes. They had experienced decades of violent political and street warfare among fractious elite families, which had opened the door to revolution from below. These moderate major guildsmen desperately wanted to reestablish peace and control both for their own sanity and in order to rebuild the manufacturing and export economy upon which their livelihood depended, so damaged by war with the pope. Instead of crushing opposition, they sought to achieve the difficult objective of annealing conflicting forces back into economic and political synergy. Statistical support for this "leading reform role of the moderates" interpretation is given by the disappearance of all significant political-faction coefficients in tables 6.5–6.7 after 1382. Because of the sequentiality of annealing, the crushing of pro-Ciompi revolutionary forces in 1382 did not automatically imply that reactionary forces took over.

The political problem faced by the 1382 moderate-elite regime trying to restore order was the following: Repression of the radical *ciompi* obviously was the sine qua non, but that had already been accomplished by the 1378 regime of minor guilds and liberal popolani. The next step was to solve the structural problem of the guild-corporatist constitutional order, which had served major guildsmen so well in earlier generations but had badly malfunctioned. The *ciompi* had hijacked this institutional order to

[47] Trexler 1974.

[48] Brucker 1962, 124–27.

Table 6.4.
Political and Social Embedding of Cambio Bankers

Logit coefficients	1348–62	1363–76	1380–89	1390–99	1427
Patrilineage					
Cambio patrilineages	**1.624*** **	**3.229*** **	**2.199*** **	**2.534*** **	**2.196*** **
Social Class					
Popolani	.267	–.765**	–.008	–.388	.098
Magnate	.210	–.130	.347	–.138	**.732***
New man	**.815***	.106	.541	.483	-.003
Social Class of Wife					
Popolani	**.961*** **	**1.258*** **	**.689***	**.660** **	**1.836*** **
Magnate	.022	–.550	.180	.008	**1.113***
New man	**1.595** **	**1.799** **	**1.437** **	**.164**	**1.343***
Political Offices					
Priorate	**1.091*** **	–.060	.339	.319	**1.211*** **
Mercanzia	**1.021***	.835	**1.486*** **	**1.219*** **	.296
Balìa 1378		.198	.185	.524	
Balìa 1382		.081	–.394	.005	
Reggimento 1382		**.669***	.231	–.625	
Balìa 1384		**2.658*** **	**1.622*** **	**1.283** **	
Balìa 1393			–.756	–.354	
Reggimento 1393			**1.192*** **	**1.694*** **	
Political Factions					
Albizzi	.234	–.548	–.131	–.158	
Ricci	.997(*)	.122	–1.526	–1.230	
anti-Ciompi		**1.289***	.503	.721	
pro-Ciompi		**1.089***	–.474	-.517	
Albizzeans					.564
Mediceans					**1.405** **
Quarter					
Santa Croce	.074	–.198	.331	.070	.372
Santa Maria Novella	.467	**.796** **	**.712** **	**.606***	–.177
San Giovanni	.384	.313	**.771** **	**.597***	.477
Log likelihood	-576.7	-467.7	-574.2	-594.2	-416.1
# observations (persons)	5,005	7,129	7,129	7,129	8,376
L.R. chi^2	138.2	250.1	299.1	342.9	180.8
prob > chi^2	.000	.000	.000	.000	.000
pseudo R^2	.107	.211	.207	.224	.179

Sources: See citations in table 6.2.

Notes:

(1) In each logit regression, the universe of persons to whom these cambio bankers were compared was the time-appropriate tax census (i.e., 1351 *Estimo*, 1378 *Prestanze*, or 1427 *Catasto*) of household heads, plus those household heads' fathers.

(2) Only marriages and political offices with dates prior to the last date of the logit regressions (i.e., 1362, 1376, 1389, 1399, 1427, respectively) were included in estimations.

(3) "Cambio patrilineages" were patrilineages with three or more members in the cambio banking industry during the time period in question.

***$p < .001$

**$p < .01$

*$p < .05$

(*)$p < .06$

Table 6.5.
Political and Social Embedding of Merchant-Bankers

Logit coefficients	Alberti 1348–58 (Intl+Pisa+Florence)	Pisa 1369 (Int'l+Pisa+Florence)	Datini 1385–99 (Int'l+Pisa)	Catasto 1427 (Int'l+Pisa)
Patrilineage				
Int'l m-b patrilineages	**2.287*****	**2.964*****	**2.937*****	**2.098*****
Social Class				
Popolani	-.665	-.375	.048	-.089
Magnate	-1.367**	-1.413	-.352	-.060
New man	.392	-.113	.320	-1.492*
Social Class of Wife				
Popolani	**1.368*****	.781	**.821****	**2.333*****
Magnate	**1.492*****	**1.243***	-.431	**1.579****
New man	1.173	**1.755***	.550	1.364
Political Offices				
Priorate	**.977****	**2.385*****	-.985(*)	-.865
Mercanzia	**1.581****	-1.657	.730	**1.675****
Balìa 1378		**1.260*****	-.557	
Balìa 1382		.128	.436	
Reggimento 1382		**1.038****	-.010	
Balìa 1384		**1.598****	**1.510****	
Balìa 1393			-.649	
Reggimento 1393			**1.376****	
Political Factions				
Albizzi	**1.431***	.983	-1.150	
Ricci	**1.863****	**1.550***	.057	
anti-Ciompi		.529	.746	
pro-Ciompi		**1.907*****	.028	
Albizzeans				**1.425****
Mediceans				**2.202*****
Quarter				
Santa Croce	.396	.529	-.509	-.247
Santa Maria Novella	.487	.616	-.189	-.653
San Giovanni	**.771***	.081	-.519	-.174
Log likelihood	-313.9	-257.9	-389.0	-321.6
# observations (persons)	5,005	7,129	7,129	8,376
L.R. chi^2	142.8	279.9	135.1	166.0
prob > chi^2	.000	.000	.000	.000
pseudo R^2	.185	.352	.148	.205

Sources: See citations in table 6.2.

Notes:

(1) In each logit regression, the universe of persons to whom these international merchant-bankers were compared was the time-appropriate tax census (i.e., 1351 *Estimo*, 1378 *Prestanze*, or 1427 *Catasto*) of household heads, plus those household heads' fathers.

(2) Only those marriages and political offices with dates prior to the last date of the logit regressions (i.e., 1362, 1376, 1389, 1399, 1427, respectively) were included in estimations.

(3) "International merchant-banking patrilineages" were patrilineages with three or more members in the international merchant-banking industry during the time period in question.

(4) The first two of these regressions include merchant bankers whose companies were resident in Florence, as well as those whose companies were resident elsewhere (i.e., international + Pisa), because the primary data in these two periods did not differentiate residence well. Because of this, some of the overlap across industries, in these two periods only, is tautological.

***$p < .001$

**$p < .01$

*$p < .05$

(*)$p < .06$

mobilize revolution, and minor guildsmen with their liberal popolani allies had used it to seize control from major guilds, both immediately before and immediately after the Ciompi revolt. Najemy (1981) has shown how the economic-class tension associated with the Ciompi revolt shredded political cohesion within the guild of wool manufacturers, and presumably within other major guilds as well, thereby enabling these defeats.

Whatever the reasoning, the 1382–93 regime moved quickly to dismantle the autonomy of those very guilds, both major and minor, which had previously been the institutional foundation of their own economic and political power. In 1382, all elected guild consuls became subject to the approval of the Mercanzia; in 1383 and 1390 the Mercanzia exercised this review power to alter the results of the election of consuls in the cloth retail and silk guild; and finally in 1393 the *balìa* burned all guilds' scrutiny bags, which contained the results of previous consul elections, and requested that the Mercanzia appoint guild consuls directly "by hand."[49] In addition, in 1384 a special-purpose *balìa* of major guildsmen, including both cambio bankers and international merchants, was appointed to reform the wool-manufacturers' guild.[50] The previous constitutional system of federated economic and political self-governments by guilds was dismantled, in other words, in favor of more direct "oligarchic" oversight by those in control of the central institutions of the republican state (namely, the Priorate, the *balìe*, and the Mercanzia).

Previous histories have not always clearly differentiated between moderate and conservative elements in the post-Ciompi oligarchic-cum-republican regimes. Nor have they precisely identified the differing roles of various major guildsmen, such as wool manufacturers, cambio bankers, and international merchants, in this constitutional reconstruction. The data show clearly, however, that the 1382 reformers actively reached out to cambio bankers for allies in their institutional reforms. But they did not reach out similarly to international merchants, apparently because they were often not politically reliable. This mobilization collectively lifted cambio bankers to political heights not previously attainable.

This co-optation strategy by political moderates fits neatly with the findings of Molho (1968b), Witt (1976), and Najemy (1982), who demonstrated the high degree of openness by the post-1382 "oligarchic" regime to the (highly selective) election of newcomers. Cambio bankers were not the only ones being co-opted. In pursuit of their annealing objectives, elite-but-moderate reformers reached out for support in all sympathetic directions, as long as they, not the guilds, controlled the routes of access. But whereas many were mobilized as clients, cambio bankers were mobilized into the very core of the regime.

Without sharply distinguishing between moderates and conservatives, Najemy puts the same point eloquently, if somewhat cynically, like this:

> In short, as the number of participants reached new heights, real power in the system underwent an unprecedented process of centralization. The thousands of individual Florentine citizens who willingly entered the lists of the electoral lottery, each nourishing his private hope of elevation to the priorate, gave the republican regime a stability it had not previously known. They played the game as faithful creatures of the regime, hardly aware that their own acquiescence in the illusion of political equality, their very willingness to play by rules they no longer shared in defining, and their acceptance of participation without actual power were the bedrock of consensus on which the stable and elitist polity of fifteenth-century Florence was built. Even less were they aware of having created the conditions that shaped the new republican ideology of civic humanism. (1982, 299–300)

Organizational Refunctionality: Domestic Bankers into International System Builders

From the perspective of our theoretical framework for analyzing organizational invention, co-optation of bankers into politics was biographical transposition. This led to organizational refunctionality—namely, the perception of new purposes for old practices and tools. The old practices and tools were those of the domestic cambio bankers; the new perceptions and purposes were those of international trade.

Twenty-five to 30 percent of cambio bankers were elevated into the central institutions of the state—the Priorate, the *balìe*, and the Mercanzia—where government policy was made. This political promotion introduced these domestic deposit bankers to international contacts and

[49] Najemy 1972, 582–601; Franceschi 1993b, 886–89.
[50] A.S.F., *Arte della Lana* 46, 164–66.

to an internationalist perspective from which they had previously been, if not excluded, then inhibited by the specialized guild system. Before the Ciompi revolt, a few cambio bankers had sometimes engaged in international trading on the side, but that was hardly their primary activity. International trading instead had been dominated by merchants in the Calimala guild, not by bankers in the Cambio guild. Now, however, the state urgently needed to rebuild its war-damaged, export-oriented wool-manufacturing and international trading economies. Cambio bankers were recruited into this economy-rebuilding effort, and they became a core part of the very state that was recruiting them.

As shown in tables 6.4 and 6.5, the 1384 special-purpose *balìa* on the wool industry[51] was one prong in this rebuilding effort in which cambio bankers were centrally involved. This *balìa* reformed the terms of trade and the administration of disputes, fines, and fees among various members of the wool industry (manufacturers, dyers, laborers, etc.) in an apparent effort simultaneously to restructure this recently politically explosive guild and to revive this crucial but declining economic sector in Florence. Apart from this important industry-specific *balìa*, I am aware of no other special governmental commission that was set up to propose other economic reforms. Rather there was "just" the strong encouragement and backing of the state for those who wished to fill the international-trading vacuum. In future research into the records of these governmental bodies, I hope to elaborate the precise form this encouragement took.

Whatever the particular inducements, some experienced cambio bankers—men like Vieri di Cambio de' Medici and Manetto di Giovanni Davanzati, but also some international merchant-bankers like Francesco Datini and Tommaso di Guccio Soderini—responded to the new opportunities to expand their business by opening new branches in overseas cities. In addition, a new generation of cambio bankers—men like Giovanni di Bicci de' Medici, Francesco di Simone Tornabuoni, and Giovanni di Jacopo Orlandini, descended from the earlier generation of cambio bankers—broadened their domestic base into international merchant-banking. A few newcomers, like Niccolò da Uzzano, did the reverse and extended their international trading origins into cambio banking. The specific issue is, how did this flow of domestic banking into international trading trigger the invention of the partnership system, which organizationally fused these two industries?

My answer has two parts: careers and practices. Before the Ciompi revolt, the guild system had channeled economic careers into industrial specialization, which also became one important basis for political representation. After the Ciompi revolt, the guild system was effectively dismantled and a more centralized system of elite monitoring of the activities of businessmen was imposed, through the Mercanzia. This breakdown of effective intermediation through corporatist organizations "individualized" the biographical flows of businessmen through the state, inducing political and eventually social stratification. Selected businessmen from various industries were placed onto the same political career tracks through the Priorate, the *balìe*, the Mercanzia, and other republican offices of the state. Thereby it became easier, through dialogue and shared position within leading formal and informal (*consulte e pratiche*) councils of the state, and without the constraint of corporate representation, for each major guild's businessmen to see the world more easily from the perspective of the other major guilds. This is similar to the social-network concept of structural equivalence,[52] except here we have parallel career flows instead of highly correlated network profiles. The cognitive implication of career-flow equivalence, I hypothesize, was to replace the specialized perspective of industry and guild with the generalized perspectives of "Florence" and "business."

The precise micromechanism that translated this new career-flow equivalence into partnership systems was the transposition of cambio bankers' existing master-apprentice way of making domestic partnerships[53] onto the international stage. In their domestic companies, cambio bankers were used to short-term (often three-year) renewable partnership contracts between cambio masters and a series of ex-apprentice younger junior partners, who fully expected to split from their master's company upon financial success to form their own firms. For compensation, the junior partner received a share of the profit higher than his share of the capital contribution as reward and incentive for hard labor. These were exactly the typical terms of formal contracts between founders and

[51] A.S.F., *Arte della Lana* 46, 164–66.

[52] White, Boorman, and Breiger 1976.

[53] Padgett 2001, 227.

branch managers in partnership systems, except that in partnership systems there were simultaneously many such contracts with multiple branch managers, often spanning more than one industry. This cambio-banking guild partnering logic, previously constrained to be sequential because of its domestic and specialized-industry guild setting, was unleashed to become modular, cross-cutting multiple geographical settings and industries. Thereby it supplanted the older unitary patrilineage form of international merchant-banking, which after the 1340s was very much on the ropes in any event.

There were macroeconomic forces moving this industrially diversified partnering logic down the tracks of geographical diversification as well. The War of Eight Saints with the pope had altered the landscape of European trading outlets. Before this war, Florentine long-distance international trade, mostly in woolen cloth, traveled primarily along an almost straight line from London and England in the north, down through Flanders, Paris and Avignon in France, to Genoa, Milan, and Pisa in northern Italy, and continuing on to Rome and Naples in southern Italy.[54] Venice[55] and other smaller Italian cities also were in Florence's international trading network, off this primary geographical axis. The spiritual interdict of the pope, with its mixed success in host cities of organizing boycotts and exiles of resident Florentine businessmen, helped diversify this economic geography. To simplify a complex topography: after the war, England and Avignon went down and Spain and Venice went up, as relative Florentine trading partners, in immediate response to their respective national profiles of cooperating—or not—with the pope.[56]

To be sure, the various political responses of host countries to anti-Florentine pressure from the pope reflected their own economic interests. That is, they reflected ongoing economic trends. The fact remains that after the war, the king of England expelled Italians for decades in his successful import-substitution effort to develop domestic wool production. Exports of high-quality raw English wool to Florence plummeted,[57] which had deleterious consequences for the Florentine wool-manufacturing industry.[58] Trading connections with Catalonia and Mediterranean Spain, on the other hand, centered on silk and raw wool, blossomed.[59] And Venice, also in response to its War of Chioggia with Genoa, liberalized its free-trade policy, thereby currying the favor of Florentine merchants.[60]

Thus when Florentine international trading revived after the Ciompi revolt, Florentine companies, using their new organizational tool of partnership systems, faced a more dispersed economic geography than before, centered as much on the western Mediterranean as on the old French route to London. This was the "demand side" facing the "supply side" of new partnership systems. Modularity had a wide variety of geographical sockets to plug into.

To summarize, my contention about organizational refunctionality is that when cambio bankers flowed through newly centralized political institutions, these institutions transposed existing ways of doing economic business into new purposes. Politically moderate elite leaders of the new regime were just trying conservatively to reestablish control and to rebuild their decimated economy. But the unintended consequence of their co-opting cambio bankers and select international businessmen into their electoral system was to catalyze cambio bankers and their international partners into reshaping themselves. Sequential cambio partnerships became transformed into modularized simultaneous partnerships, which spanned industries. This new organizational form permitted the ready exploration of geographically dispersed markets, which had been produced through the war with the pope.

Multiple-Network Catalysis: Embedding Partnership Systems in Elite Marriage

Political co-optation in response to revolt explains the transposition and refunctionality mechanisms of organizational genesis. But for novel innovation to become transformative invention, there must be something more. Innovation must reverberate out into collateral ways of doing business, thereby reshaping the interactive system in which the invention is embedded. This is the difference between the incremental evolution of banks, which is variation within species, and the punctuated evolution of banking, which is emergence of new species. The same

[54] E.g., Goldthwaite, Settesoldi, and Spallanzani 1995, xlv–lxxx.
[55] Mueller 1997, 255–75.
[56] Trexler 1974, 44–108.
[57] Carus-Wilson and Coleman 1963.
[58] Franceschi 1993a.
[59] Lopez 1952, 347.
[60] Mueller 1997, 266.

post-Ciompi political process in Florence that induced organizational innovation, however, also rewired the social embedding of partnership into surrounding networks, thereby altering the contextual feedbacks that reproduced that invention. The Florentine partnership system was not just the incremental diffusion of a good organizational idea; it was part of a larger punctuated-equilibrium reconstitution of the Florentine elite, which resituated the Florentine business community within its surrounding social and political contexts. Some call this a shift from medieval to Renaissance.

To demonstrate this changing social embedding of economic partnership in late medieval Florence, I present tables 6.6 and 6.7, which disaggregate partnership systems into their constitutive parts—namely, cambio partnerships and international merchant-banking partnerships, viewed separately. Tables 6.6 and 6.7 present logit regressions on partnership dyads in these two industries over time. These logit-regression tables report the effects of many contextual social and political variables on economic partnership.

The strongest time-series message in these tables is marriage, but before I discuss those results I shall discuss three other statistically significant findings in tables 6.6 and 6.7, as interesting preliminaries. The first is essentially a reconfirmation of the discussion in the section about biographical transposition: Political mobilization of cambio bankers, through the 1380–99 Priorate, the 1384 *balìa*, the 1393 *balìa*, and the 1393 *reggimento*, had a significant effect on the formation of cambio banking partnerships. Table 6.5 showed that cambio bankers were mobilized politically after the suppression of the Ciompi revolt. Table 6.6 shows that this mobilization had an impact on cambio bankers' partnership behavior—namely, mobilized bankers were significantly more likely to form partnerships. Table 6.7 shows the same *not* to be true for international merchant-bankers. While international merchants were also mobilized into the 1384 *balìa* and the 1393 *reggimento*, this lesser mobilization had no detectable effect on their partnering behavior. Political mobilization not only affected cambio businessmen, it also affected their banks.

Second, examination of the coefficients for natal (not in-law) family in table 6.6 reveals the following trend: The causal importance of family—both at the level of the nuclear family and at the level of the patrilineage—for predicting the likelihood of forming cambio-banking partnerships declined smoothly in magnitude over the 1348 to 1427 period. But it remained statistically significant throughout. The same trends are revealed in table 6.7 for international merchant-banking partnerships over the shorter observable time period of 1385–99 to 1427. These results confirm the gradual decline of natal family as an organizing principle of economic partnership throughout the early Renaissance, just as Goldthwaite (1968) has argued. On the other hand, these results also confirm the historical continuity of patrilineage in early Renaissance Florence, as Kent (1977) has counterargued. Both historians were correct in their assessments; they just emphasized different sides of the late medieval kinship transition. "Family" did not go away in importance in Renaissance Florence; its economic role changed. The medieval dominance of the patrilineal father-son relation became supplemented, and to some degree supplanted, by early Renaissance economic relationships among in-laws. More specifically in the kinship history of Florentine elite families, the *consorteria* horizontal solidarity of medieval families, rooted primarily in factional feuds, land, and the military,[61] evolved into more internally differentiated Renaissance patrilineages, with sharp wealth distinctions between senior and cadet branches and with diffuse and negotiable membership boundaries.[62] Economic evolution and kinship evolution were linked.

Third, examination of the coefficients for neighborhood in table 6.6 reveals the following temporal pattern: Statistically significant effects of residence-in-same-*gonfalone* on cambio partnerships declined and then rose in magnitude over time. These results are consistent with those of Kent and Kent (1981; Kent 1987), who argued for the general importance of neighborhood in structuring sociality of all kinds in Renaissance Florence, at the level of the sixteen *gonfaloni* or administrative wards in the city. But they also are more specifically consistent with the overall thesis of the dissolution of guild, rooted in neighborhood, and then the consolidation of clientage, also rooted in neighborhood but in a different way. Like family, neighborhood never went away in its structuring impact in Renaissance Florence; rather its specific catalytic relationship with economic networks was reconfigured. Before the Ciompi revolt, guild brought cross-class neighbors together in

[61] Lansing 1991.
[62] Herlihy 1985; Fabbri 1991; Molho 1994.

Table 6.6.
Political and Social Embedding of Cambio Banking Partnerships

Logit coefficients	1348–62	1363–76	1380–89	1390–99	1427
Patrilineage					
Nuclear family	**8.273*****	**7.998*****	**6.296*****	**5.830*****	**4.006*****
Patrilineage (excl. nucl.)	**3.720*****	**2.435*****	**3.245*****	**2.966*****	**2.487*****
Marriage					
Nuclear in-law partners	.851	1.055	**2.888*****	**1.102****	**1.379****
Patrilineage intermarriage	**.684***	-.602	**1.566*****	**.382(*)**	**.915*****
to Popolani	**.182***	**.300****	**.455*****	.115	.014
to Magnates	-.215	-.184	-.331	-.626***	-.024
to New men	**.433****	**.680*****	.036	-.594***	-.579
Neighborhood					
Same *gonfalone*	**1.268*****	**.956*****	**.483*****	**.614*****	**1.129*****
Same quarter (excl. *gonfalone*)	**.384*****	-.034	**.270****	**.457*****	.327
Social Class					
Both popolani	-.168	.018	-.099	-.028	**.883****
Both magnates	-2.515***	.235	.315	-1.092***	**1.240***
Between popolani & magnates	-.317*	.113	-1.377***	**.703*****	**1.006****
Between popolani & new men	-1.409***	-.446**	-.545***	-.600***	.288
Both new men	-1.293***	-.176	-.695***	**.422****	**2.343*****
Both new-new men			-.256	.211	.577
Political Offices					
Priorate	-.100	**.388****	**.340*****	.124	-.138
Cambio Consuls	**.414*****	-.388***	-.348***	.008	.068
Mercanzia	-.528**	-.722***	-.146	-.068	.025
Balìa 1378		.004	.152	.014	
Balìa 1382		.353	-.198	.213	
Reggimento 1382		.181	.136	.016	
Balìa 1384		.128	**.181***	.087	
Balìa 1393			**.384*****	**.286****	
Reggimento 1393			**.369*****	**.200***	
Political Factions					
Albizzi	-.435*	**.762*****	-.116	-.964**	
Ricci	.145	**.874*****	-.841**	-.552*	
anti-Ciompi		.113	-.327*	.152	
pro-Ciompi		.074	-.049	-.181	
Albizzeans					-.037
Mediceans					-.161
Log likelihood	-3837.6	-2340.1	-3546.9	-4332.2	-628.3
# observations (dyad-year)	81,535	36,688	75,288	97,060	12,430
L.R. chi^2	3044.4	1306.1	1605.3	2173.6	349.0
prob > chi^2	.000	.000	.000	.000	.000
pseudo R^2	.284	.218	.185	.201	.217

Sources: See citations in table 6.2.

Notes:

(1) The (0/1) logit dependent variable equaled one if the dyadic partnership actually formed sometime in the time period in question, and it equaled zero if the dyadic partnership was possible but never formed in the time period in question. The universe of "possible partnerships" was constructed by dyadically crossing all cambio bankers who were observed to have been active as partners in the industry, solo or with somebody, during the time period in question.

(2) Only those marriages and political offices with dates prior to the last date of the logit regressions (i.e., 1362, 1376, 1399, 1427, respectively) were included in estimations.

(3) "Patrilineage intermarriage" was calculated on basis of existence of at least one intermarriage between patrilineages (excluding a direct nuclear in-law) in the thirty years prior to last date of regressions.

(4) Political offices, factions, and marriages with social class were coded as (0/1/2), depending on the number of partners in the category in question.

***$p < .001$

**$p < .01$

*$p < .05$

(*)$p < .06$

Table 6.7.
Political and Social Embedding of Merchant-Banker Partnerships

Logit coefficients	Alberti 1348–58	Pisa 1369	Datini 1385–99	Catasto 1427
Patrilineage				
Nuclear family			**5.138*** **	**3.865*** **
Patrilineage (excl. nuclear)			**3.591*** **	**2.058*** **
Marriage				
In-law partners			[-∞]	**2.395***
Patrilineage intermarriages			[-∞]	**.682** **
to Popolani			.056	-.152
to Magnate			-.229	-.327
to New Men			-.753	-.391
Neighborhood				
Same *gonfalone*			**.970(*)**	-.264
Same quarter (excl. *gonfalone*)			.193	**.619** **
Social Class				
Both popolani			.118	-.080
Both magnates			.226	-.670
Between popolani & magnates			-1.337	.319
Between popolani and new men			[-∞]	[-∞]
Both new men			.417	[no cases]
Both new-new men			[-∞]	1.485
Political Offices				
Priorate			.347	-.161
Calimala Consuls			-.699	**1.006***
Mercanzia			-.997	-.205
Balìa 1378			[collinear]	
Balìa 1382			.426	
Reggimento 1382			-.183	
Balìa 1384			.073	
Balìa 1393			-.595	
Reggimento 1393			.534	
Political Factions:				
Albizzi			.836	
Ricci			2.621	
anti-Ciompi			1.127	
pro-Ciompi			-1.478	
Albizzeans				.130
Medicieans				.268
Log likelihood			-275.1	-623.2
# observations (dyads)	[insufficient data]	[insufficient data]	13,366	7,260
L.R. chi^2			185.7	199.0
prob > chi^2			.000	.000
pseudo R^2			.252	.138

Sources: See citations in table 6.2.

Notes:

(1) The (0/1) logit dependent variable equaled one if the dyadic partnership actually formed sometime in the time period in question, and it equaled zero if the dyadic partnership was possible but never formed in the time period in question. The universe of "possible partnerships" was constructed by dyadically crossing all international merchant-bankers who were observed to have been active as partners in the industry, solo or with somebody, during the time period in question.

(2) Only marriages and political offices with dates prior to the last date of the logit regressions (i.e., 1362, 1376, 1399, 1427, respectively) were included in estimations.

(3) "Patrilineage intermarriage" was calculated on basis of existence of at least one intermarriage between patrilineages (excluding a direct nuclear in-law) in the thirty years prior to last date of regressions.

(4) Political offices, factions, and marriages with social class were coded as (0/1/2), depending on the number of partners in the category in question.

(5) [-∞] means "independent variable = 1 predicts partnership = 0 perfectly," so variable dropped from logit regression.

***$p < .001$

**$p < .01$

*$p < .05$

(*)$p < .06$

banking partnership through the social model of master and apprentice. After Ciompi, clientage brought cross-class neighbors together somewhat in banking partnership but even more so in credit,[63] through the social model of patron and client.

On the core issue of the increasing social embeddedness of economic partnership in marriage, there are two modalities of marriage embeddedness presented in tables 6.6 and 6.7: (a) the intermarriage of the partners themselves, either at the level of their nuclear families or at the level of their patrilineage families, and (b) the marriage of partners into various social classes, elite or otherwise. The logic of the first modality is multiplexity: namely, intermarriage with one's partner meant that economic and in-law kinship roles were mixed, with normative framing consequences for each of those roles. The logic of the second modality is access: namely, marriage to popolani meant that businessmen and their companies had kinship access into socially elite and usually politically powerful families, whether or not they themselves were elite.

The simplest message about marriage in both tables is that both forms of partnership embeddedness in marriage increased after the Ciompi revolt. But there was a difference in the fate of these two marriage influences after the 1380–89 period of partnership-system invention. Direct multiplexity mattered in all periods from 1380 onward. For this reason, the economic logic of partnership and the social logic of marriage became intertwined in how partners viewed each other.

The second dimension of marriage access into the popolani social elite was crucial during the 1380–89 period of invention, but it faded from statistical significance thereafter. During the invention period of 1380–89, cambio-banker founders were diverse in social-class backgrounds, consistent with their roots in the guilds. It did not matter whether cambio bankers were themselves popolani; what mattered was whether they had married into the popolani elite. After the founding generation had passed, however, bankers of more prestigious popolani social-class backgrounds took over these new central economic roles. New-men cambio bankers involved in innovative partnership systems were either absorbed through marriage into the newly reconfigured elite or were pushed aside.[64]

All of these marriage results are far more muted for international merchants. Only in 1427 do the two direct intermarriage coefficients in table 6.7 for international merchant partnerships achieve statistical significance. And never is *parentado* marriage into the popolani important for international merchants forming partnerships among themselves. Consistently the pattern here is of deeply socially embedded cambio bankers linking up with relatively unembedded international merchants to form partnership systems. Cambio bankers, being physically resident in Florence, were more connected into (and presumably more constrained by) their social and political contexts than were Florentine international merchants, who lived much of their active business lives abroad. To put this another way, in the period after the Ciompi revolt, residentially domestic bankers, newly connected to international merchants through partnership systems, helped broker those sometimes new merchants into the dense social-network structure of their own Florence back home.

This increased correlation between partnership and marriage has the testable corollary that the economic value of marriage should increase. Chabod (1995, 103) provides information on average Florentine dowry prices over time among families established enough to write surviving *ricordanzi* (private diaries). Consistent with the time series that we expect, the average price of the Florentine dowry reported by Chabod rose from 592 florins (n = 18) in 1314–49, to 845 florins (n = 24) in 1350–99, to 925 florins (n = 54) in 1400–1449, to 954 florins (n = 35) in 1450–99. The price of dowries rose so high, indeed, that money circulating among elite families through daughters came to be central in the maintenance of patrilineage economic position within the elite.[65]

The post-Ciompi fusion of cambio bankers into the popolani elite, therefore, changed the Renaissance meaning of banking partnership in two ways. In the first transposition-plus-refunctionality stage, political mobilization brought master-apprentice logic out of the guild world into the international domain to produce partnership systems, as has already been discussed. But in the second network-catalysis stage, social incorporation of cambio bankers into the popolani elite brought the logic of marriage, and hence dowry, out of the world of popolani kinship into banking, reinforcing and rewiring the social embedding of banking partnerships into

[63] Padgett and McLean 2011.
[64] Padgett 2010.
[65] Molho 1994.

the elite. Dowries came to be used as start-up capital.[66] And marriage logic applied to partnership reinforced industrial diversification: one's son-in-law was often in a different occupation from oneself. Once economic partnership became correlated with and symbolically framed as marriage, it took on the normative overtones and the catalytic reproductive support of the older popolani and magnate elites who embraced it.

This second causal stage of catalysis-through-embedding-in-marriage also fits neatly into the temporal history of the oligarchic reaction to the Ciompi revolt, just as did the first causal stage of transposition-and-refunctionality-through-co-optation. In 1382, consensus-oriented major-guildsmen moderates reached out to their "right" of patrician exiles by inviting everyone home, to their "left" of new men through relatively open electoral access, and to the "center" of cambio bankers through direct mobilization. It was primarily rapprochement with conservatives, culminating in the rise of Maso degli Albizzi in 1393, that led to the renewed "oligarchic" political dominance of the popolani. Consistent with what Baron (1966), Molho (1968b), Witt (1976), and Najemy (1982) have argued, however, this popolani oligarchic dominance was not achieved through methods of exclusion. It was achieved through methods of political, economic, and kinship co-optation. This turned non-popolani families mentally and behaviorally into popolani wannabes.

Whether the leaders of the 1382 regime were as foresighted and strategic as this narrative makes them appear is doubtful. Unlike Cosimo de' Medici in 1434 a couple of generations later,[67] the almost forgotten 1382 moderates are not among the most famous and celebrated names in Florentine history. Just because they achieved lasting success does not imply that they were unusually clever. More plausible than rational choice as microdecisional foundation is learning—in which intelligent but adaptive agents are channeled by events into adopting a new perspective that redefines their own rationality.[68] Cosimo de' Medici appears both to us and to contemporaries like a genius because the same historical forces that produced him also constructed a glorified political position or stage for him, far above that of other men.[69] The 1382 moderates in contrast are forgotten because they knit together a "consensual" republican regime in which many citizens had at least the illusion of access and influence. Both Cosimo de' Medici and the 1382 moderates were equally inventors—products of their time who changed their time. That they did so was not because they were superior in cognitive abilities, intelligent though no doubt they were. What they shared in common instead was the more profound perspicacity to observe the ways that others were moving tumultuously around them well enough to blend those others' biographies into reproducing sequences that can be called careers. New self-reproducing biographical sequences, in turn, induce new perspectives and goals in those shaped by them.

No greater testament to the achievement of the 1382 elite moderates can be made than to point to the speed of the ideological demise of deeply entrenched medieval loyalty to the pope and of the subsequent rise of civic-humanist republicanism to take its place.[70] The 1382 moderates did not themselves make the intellectual revolution of the Renaissance. But they altered the social-network feedbacks in Florentine history enough to make that intellectual cascade appear almost inevitable in hindsight.

ECONOMIC CONSEQUENCES: THE EVOLUTION OF BANKING

Most banks today are shining lobbies and offices, temples to modernism and the capitalist spirit. Renaissance banks did not look like this of course. They, too, had their *palazzi*,[71] from which modern bank lobbies are descended, but they were smaller and more intimate in physical and manpower size. In spite of this difference, however, Renaissance banks also epitomized—indeed they were central in inventing—financial capitalism, namely, partnership systems, limited liability, double-entry bookkeeping, and current accounts. The historiographical puzzle is the one that opened this chapter: How could such a traditionalist time and place, not motivated to innovate, nonetheless have invented so prolifically? In particular how did it invent financial capitalism? The political context of the Ciompi revolt and the post-Ciompi homology between partnership and marriage have taken us a considerable way

[66] Brucker 1967, 114, 121.
[67] Padgett and Ansell 1993.
[68] March 1999.
[69] Brown 1961.
[70] Baron 1966.
[71] Goldthwaite 1972.

toward understanding the changing Renaissance meaning of the partnership company. Now I show how this change in partnership logic transformed the banks internally.

Melis (1962) and de Roover (1966) have already documented at length these organizational changes. In this section I extend their strictly economic inquiry by analyzing this economic transformation more explicitly in its social context. I examine banks not as disaggregated sets of businessmen dyads, as in the logit regressions of the previous section, but holistically as coherent collective actors. In particular, I demonstrate transformation in the role of the lead banker from guild-based entrepreneur to partnership-system financier. Closely connected with the partnership system were important changes at the level of transactional practice—namely, widespread adoption of double-entry bookkeeping, current accounts, and economic credit. Together these organizational changes in partnership and credit transformed international banking and finance. But that subsequent diffusion is a story for another time.

Bookkeeping

At the level of bookkeeping, *conti correnti* (current accounts) registered repeat relational trading based on credit. These spread rapidly among Florentine bankers after 1380. *Conti di esercizio*, which emerged at about the same time,[72] were a similar bookkeeping device for registering credit between bankers and manufacturers. Double-entry bookkeeping as an algorithm, which for the first time permitted an integrated calculation of assets, debts, and profit, was invented decades earlier, perhaps in Genoa, perhaps in Tuscany. But in Florence this technique diffused widely only after 1380.[73] Bilateral or *contrapposto* format was a visualization of current accounts in Florentine bankers' account books: namely, a client's (person or company) debits (*dare*) were listed neatly on the left-side page (*verso*) of the company's account book, and the client's credits (*avere*) were listed on the right-side facing page (*recto*) of the same account book. With bilateral format, businessmen could see easily the state of each of their various economic relationships at a glance, laid out for them neatly on the pages. This is in contrast with earlier chronological listings of transactions with complex cross-referencing to how these were cleared. And it is in contrast with the earlier clustering of debits in the first half of an account book and credits in the second half, again with complex transactional cross-referencing to how these were cleared.[74] Bilateral format categorized transactions into economic relations, whereas earlier methods (including notarized contracts) coded transactions just as transactions. This conceptual transformation in business practice from transactional to relational accounting, I argue, was in Florence one corollary of the partnership system.

Piera Morlacchi and Ethel Santacroce have examined seventy-seven Florentine account books located in the Archivio di stato in Florence from the period 1259–1427 in order to trace the emergence of the bilateral format in Florence over time. This sample of account books was drawn from two exhaustive inventories of extant account books compiled by Richard Goldthwaite,[75] one covering the years 1211 to 1355 and another covering the years 1363 to 1427.[76] Fifty-one of these account books were *libri di debitori e creditori* (and equivalents like *libri del dare e dell'avere*) company account books from merchant banking, cambio banking, and the wool and silk industries. For comparability, they coded only these books. The full coded data set, with citations to all qualifying account books, is provided by Morlacchi (2005).

Without double-counting multiple account books in single companies, the results of this survey were as follows: (a) during 1259–99, 0/10 = 0 percent of the companies kept their books in bilateral format or *contrapposto*; (b) during 1300–1349, 0/7 = 0 percent of the companies were *contrapposto*; (c) during 1350–77, 0/3 = 0 percent were *contrapposto*; (d) during 1382–99, 5/5 = 100 percent were *contrapposto*; (e) during 1400–1427, 12½ /14 = 89 percent were *contrapposto*. There was a sharp and unambiguous transition to bilateral format in Florentine company account books exactly around 1382, the date that the partnership system was born.

To verify this apparently causal connection between the partnership system and bilateral format more closely, we examined carefully the first Florentine cases of bilateral format that survive: Paliano di Falco and Francesco Datini. Ethel

[72] Melis [1972] 1987; Dini 2001.
[73] de Roover [1956] 1974.
[74] de Roover [1956] 1974.
[75] Namely, Goldthwaite, Settesoldi, and Spallanzani 1995, cxxvii–cxxxii.
[76] Goldthwaite, private communication.

Santacroce transcribed the *ricordi* of Paliano di Falco, the first known Florentine to adopt bilateral format on October 12, 1382. Paliano di Falco was a cambio banker who enrolled in the Arte del Cambio in 1369 and soon afterward began running his own small bank as a solo *cambiatore* in 1370 and 1371. Paliano next appears in our records, through his *ricordi*, as a Perugia-resident partner within the Florentine partnership system of Giovanni Portinari and Ardingo Ricci, who themselves were Florentine cambio bankers; they started their company in Florence in 1372. The home-office account books of Portinari and Ricci have been lost, but the fact that Paliano initiated bilateral format on exactly the same day on which the partnership in Perugia between Paliano and Ardingo Ricci was formed[77] suggests a linkage between these two adoption events, even though Paliano's *ricordi* was actually a personal, not a company, account book. Paliano does not say so explicitly, but we presume that Paliano's bookkeeping practice conformed with that of his new senior partners. Very telling is the notation *scriverollo alla viniziana* at the outset of Paliano's account book, suggesting that he knew that he was adopting an accounting technique borrowed from the Venetians.

To confirm even further this connection between partnership systems and bilateral-format bookkeeping, Piera Morlacchi consulted many of the account books of Francesco Datini, preserved in the Archivio di Stato in Prato (and hence not part of the previous sample). As hypothesized, Datini's adoption of bilateral format in his bookkeeping procedures coincided perfectly in date with his adoption of the partnership system. Datini did not use bilateral format early in his career when he ran his unitary trading company in Avignon. Indeed, even after he left that city, his original company in Avignon lagged behind in adopting *contrapposto*, not switching to bilateral format until 1398. Rather, Datini's first adoption of bilateral format and double-entry bookkeeping was in his new Pisa branch in 1383, where he initiated his partnership system. Subsequent branches adopted bilateral format as they were founded: in Florence in 1386, in Genoa in 1391, and in Barcelona in 1393.

The final example of the microconnection between partnership system and bilateral double-entry bookkeeping is Averardo di Francesco de' Medici. A ninety-page fragment of Averardo's account book has survived from 1395, two years after Averardo in Florence formed a partnership system with his father, Francesco, in Genoa. This account book was in bilateral-format double-entry bookkeeping.[78]

Therefore, if the account-book survey and the first three known examples of usage are any guides, in Florence the adoption of the partnership system and the adoption of *contrapposto*-format bookkeeping were two sides of the same organizational invention. Florence did not itself invent bilateral-format bookkeeping, but it perceived this accounting technique as facilitating the management of its new partnership system.

My interpretation of the causal linkage is as follows: Bilateral format and double-entry bookkeeping were useful in managing centrally the heterogeneous companies that the partnership system created because bilateral format lumped dense and recurrent flows with clients into easily visible current accounts. Cross-branch, within-system transfers were the densest flows that required such inspection and central approval.

Heavily used current accounts among inside partners and employees, called *conti interni*, existed in older unitary companies. In older Florentine companies, *conti externi* with outside clients were transactionally specific, with little recurrent use.[79] Partnership systems almost tautologically took *conti interni* and turned them into *conti externi*. As such, the logics governing internal transfers became externalized into the domain of intercompany relations, especially as external business relations became more correlated with the enforceable "trust" inherent in Florentine elite structure. Intrasystem transfer of credits among branches was the transitional step toward intercompany transfer of credits across systems. As the partnership system diffused, credit protocols, such as current accounts and bilateral format, were standardized and rapidly spread.

Economic Credit

Bookkeeping evolution was not an expression of some impersonal and teleological "spirit of capitalism" that left traditionalism behind, à la Weber. Current accounts, bilateral formats, and double-entry bookkeeping were the formalization and measurement of deeply personalistic

[77] A.S.F., *Carte Strozziane*, serie II, 7, p. 4.

[78] Ceccherelli 1913.

[79] Goldthwaite, Settesoldi, and Spallanzani 1995, cxiii, cxvi.

and multivocal relationships, which transcended economics. It is within these relationships themselves, and not in the formal accounting of them, that the secrets of Florentine financial capitalism—namely, merchant trust or *fiducia*, organizational flexibility, and credit liquidity—are to be found.

In Padgett and McLean 2011, which analyzes commercial credits among 406 export-oriented companies in the 1427 *catasto* (tax register), these claims are documented. Among international merchant-banks, large domestic merchant-banks, and wool- and silk-manufacturing companies, extensive, deep, and recurrent commercial credit relations developed, all of which were managed through current accounts in bilateral accounting format. Total credit-to-asset leverage ratios rose to industry averages of 5:1 in the banking sectors. Export-oriented companies routinely extended each other commercial credit, in the course of their repeated business with each other, even without having paid off previous debts. Statistical analyses in that article revealed that repeat-business commercial credit relations between companies were highly correlated with personal and political relations between businessmen in different companies. Personal embedding of cross-company commercial ties included relations of kinship and neighborhood, which linked partners in different companies. Political embedding of cross-company commercial ties included the participation of businessmen in the elected political office of Priorate or city council. Election to city council, indeed, was like a public certification of one's honor. (The Italian word *onore* means political offices as well as personal honor.) This had implications for the creditworthiness of one's company as well as for the marriage-worthiness of one's daughter.

Sophisticated account books may look to insufficiently knowledgeable observers as the epitome of an impersonal mathematical measurement that abolishes personal favoritism. The Florentines knew better. Underneath their dry account-book entries was a rich social-network world full of dense knowledge about each other.[80] Clients were not strangers or automatons to whom businessmen were "objectively" loaning money and goods. Florentine businessmen knew tons about each other, beyond what was written in their books. This personalism behind the account books was not a marginal aspect, on the edges of impersonal markets. The densest and most high-volume flows of Florentine commercial credit and business coursed through personal and political ties, precisely measured and documented in bilateral current accounts.

From Entrepreneur to Financier

For the remainder of this chapter, I focus on data from the annual census of cambio-bank partnerships, administered by the Florentine banking guild,[81] as a regulatory check on usury. The full registration of such banks is heterogeneous in nature, ranging from individual money changers, to domestic deposit banks, to international merchant-banks, to headquarters of partnership systems. But this was the soil out of which partnership systems first emerged. With these data I can demonstrate, with a temporal precision not possible for other industries, changing organizational form at the level of individual component companies, not just of ensembles of companies. In particular in this section, I document organizational change in the role of senior partner from entrepreneur to financier, before and after the Ciompi revolt. In the next section, I show how guild and family principles fused into a mixed-kinship form of cambio banks after Ciompi.

Figure 6.2 sets the stage. Immediately after the suppression of the Ciompi revolt, there was a dramatic growth in the demographic representation in cambio banking of partners with popolani social-class backgrounds. Other social classes were not purged, but popolani families captured almost all of the successful post-Ciompi economic rebound in banking after the war with the pope. Partnership systems were how this economic rebound was achieved. The disproportionate social-class character of this rise is consistent with the political-mobilization and social-incorporation mechanisms already identified. These popolani bankers were men like Vieri di Cambio de' Medici—located physically in Florence, deeply involved in politics, simultaneously building internationally oriented partnership systems and transforming their cambio banks into the headquarters of those partnership systems. In the original transposition-and-refunctionality stage of organizational innovation, the inventors of partnership systems were not all popolani, but in the catalysis stage of organizational reproduction, cambio bankers with popolani social-class backgrounds took over.

[80] McLean 1998, 2007.

[81] A.S.F., *Arte del Cambio* 11, 14.

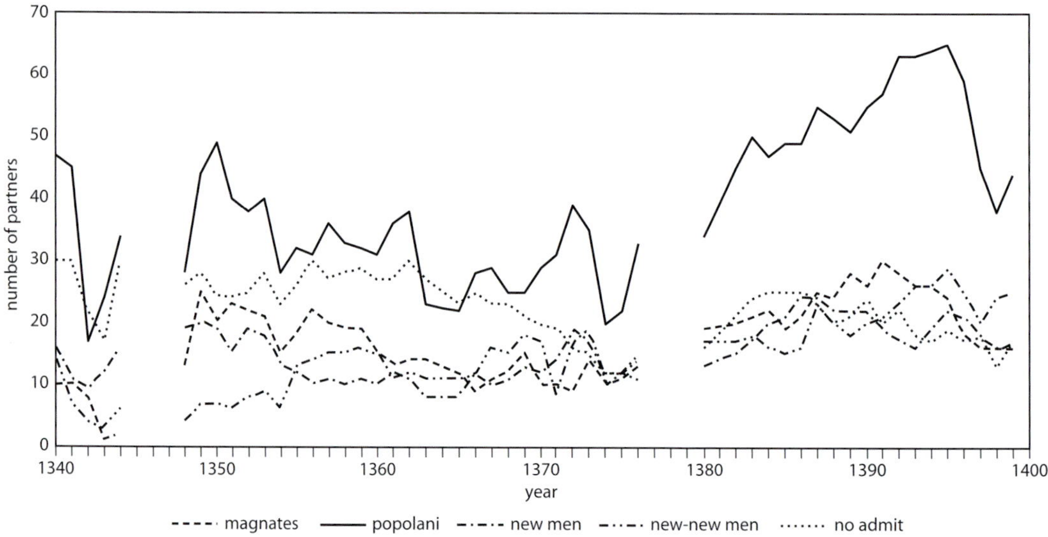

Figure 6.2 Number of cambio bankers, by social class, in the fourteenth century.

Table 6.8 presents a cross-tabulation of these 1348–99 cambio-bankers, arranged into partners and subdivided by social class, where the partnership dyad is ordered by relative experience in banking. That is, the rows contain the more senior partner, as defined by years of active experience in the industry, and the columns contain the more junior partner, defined the same way. Only nonfamily partnerships (including the nonfamily component of mixed-kinship companies) are cross-tabulated in this manner because partners within families are by definition within the same social class. The right-hand half of table 6.8 presents a simple tabular compression to help the reader see quickly the asymmetries in this table.

Before the Ciompi revolt nonfamily cambio banking partnerships were organized according to the guild logic of master and apprentice. In the context of this table, this means that relative experience and relative social prestige were, in the aggregate, highly correlated. A junior partner of lower social class would "apprentice" himself with no status difficulty to a senior partner of higher social class. But junior partners of higher social class never violated (in the aggregate) the Florentine status hierarchy by "apprenticing" themselves to senior partners of lower social status than themselves. Just because banking was based on guild did not mean that bankers were not deeply conscious of status and social class distinctions among themselves. The only exception to this pre-Ciompi "rule" of occupational authority mimicking social-class status was the peculiar position of magnates—high social status within feudal patrilineage logic but low social status in guild corporatist thinking. All in all, guilds were internally socially stratified, as was all of Florence, but these cross-class partnerships acted as a powerful engine of economic mobility for lower social classes.

After the Ciompi revolt, in sharp contrast to this guild-based equation of vertical occupational experience with vertical social class, two complementary horizontal layers of class-endogamous "alliances" developed: (a) popolani and magnates were more likely to form banking partnerships with each other than with the middle and the lower social classes, and (b) new men and new-new men were likewise more likely to form cambio banking partnerships with each other than with upper classes, presumably in response to fewer opportunities extended to them by the upper classes. A two-tiered segmentation of companies within the domestic-banking industry therefore developed—an upper-class tier of popolani and magnates, which integrated international-merchant and domestic-banking businesses into partnership systems, and a middle-class tier of new men and new-new men, carrying on the traditional domestic banking.

The most striking information contained in table 6.8 is the inversion of the occupational experience ordering of the popolani before and after

Table 6.8.
Relative Experience of Nonfamily Cambio Banking Partners (including nonfamily subset of mixed companies)

1348–76

	Less Experience in Cambio Banking						%MExp.> LExp.		Less Experience					
More experience:	P	NM	NNM	M	ND	Total		More experience:	P	NM	NNM	M	ND	Total
Popolani	191	49	56	78	157	531	+.424	Popolani	0	+	+	++	++	+++
New men	36	13	17	45	52	163	+.716	New men	-	0	+	+	+	++
New-new men	38	4	52	22	40	156	+.083	New-new men	-	-	0	+	+	+
Magnates	27	6	12	26	60	131	-.388	Magnates	--	-	-	0	+	--
No date	81	23	7	43	100	254	-.379	No date	--	-	-	-	0	---
Total	373	95	144	214	409	1235		Total	---	--	-	++	+++	

1380–99

	Less Experience in Cambio Banking						%MExp.> LExp.		Less Experience					
More Experience:	M	NM	ND	NNM	Pop.	Total		More experience:	M	NM	ND	NNM	Pop.	Total
Magnates	13	17	29	18	131	208	+.518	Magnates	0	0	0	0	++	++
New men	8	16	25	55	65	169	+.174	New men	0	0	0	+	0	+
No date	30	22	36	6	99	193	-.045	No date	0	0	0	0	0	0
New-new men	17	27	15	24	82	165	-.098	New-new men	0	-	0	0	0	-
Popolani	69	62	97	80	240	548	-.110	Popolani	--	0	0	0	0	--
Total	137	144	202	183	616	1283		Total	--	-	0	+	++	

Source: A.S.F. *Arte del Cambio* 14.

Notes:

"+" ≡ [(i,j) – (j,i)] ≥ 10; "++" ≡ [(i,j) – (j,i)] ≥ 50

"-" ≡ [(i,j) – (j,i)] ≤ -10; "--" ≡ [(i,j) – (j,i)] ≤ -50

the Ciompi revolt. In the pre-Ciompi guild logic, high-status popolani were also more occupationally experienced, on average. These were entrepreneurs: founding, owning, and running their own companies. In sharp contrast, after the Ciompi revolt, popolani surprisingly descended to the bottom of the occupational experience hierarchy. This did not necessarily mean that popolani had few years of experience in the industry. But it did mean that, whatever their own experience levels, popolani tended to partner with others of even more experience in the industry than themselves. No more reaching down to youngsters, except perhaps their own kin, in-laws, or clients. Instead they searched out and hired branch-manager partners who really knew the business and then turned over daily management of that business to them, with close supervision of course.

This is evidence not just for the evolution of organizational forms but also for the evolution of authority roles. Instead of senior partners doing the daily work themselves, they delegated that to branch partners, assuming for themselves the role of investor-supervisor—something roughly akin to the actively monitoring of venture capitalists today.[82] In addition to measuring clients, account books helped senior partners to keep tabs on their branch managers and to evaluate their relative performances from afar.

In the previous section I did not mention Padgett and McLean's negative finding (2011, 22) that social class was *not* a statistically significant determinant of commercial credit among companies in 1427. This is in contrast to the strong social-class basis of cambio-bank partnerships, just demonstrated. Putting these two findings together, economic relations across social classes were transposed from guild partnership before the Ciompi revolt to commercial credit after the Ciompi revolt. This bears an eerie resemblance to contemporary social-network developments in politics. Especially after the third conservative stage of 1393, victorious political elites closed in on themselves within oligarchic-republican institutions like *balìe*, Mercanzia, and *consulte e pratiche*, even as they absorbed lower-class supporters into the Priorate through clientage and marriage. In economics they did something similar—social closure through partnership but social openness through commercial credit. In both the economic and political domains, elite control was increasingly exercised not directly but from behind the stage of active daily decision making by others.

[82] Cf. Gompers and Lerner 1999.

Popolani Mixed-Kinship Banks

How did these mostly popolani cambio bankers reconstruct their Florentine domestic banks to link into and indeed to become central nodes within their partnership systems? Table 6.9 gives over-time data on the differential kinship character of cambio banks that participated in partnership systems with both international and domestic activities versus cambio banks that did not. "Not" means traditional domestic bankers who maintained their guild roles as deposit bankers and money changers, in the parlance of the day called *banchieri*, *cambiatori*, or *tavolieri*.[83] The first half of table 6.9 subdivides cambio banks (actually partner-years of cambio banks) into (a) whether the bank had only a single owner, (b) whether the partners all came from the same family (nuclear or patrilineage), (c) whether they came from a mixture of same family and nonfamily backgrounds, or (d) whether they all came from different families. The second half of the table records whether this kinship modality of cambio banks affected participation in international trading, above and beyond normal domestic deposit-bank business.

The message in table 6.9 is the growth in importance, after the Ciompi revolt, of the mixed-kinship or hybrid type of cambio bank. In raw numbers, the percentage of partner-years involved in the mixed type of cambio bank rose from 17 percent before Ciompi to 31 percent in 1427. More important to us, the likelihood of partners in such mixed-form banks engaging in international trading rose from 26 percent before Ciompi to 40 percent in 1427. Always the mixed form was more likely to engage in international trading than family or nonfamily cambio banks, but this differential grew after Ciompi. The key point is this: At the nodal center of the new partnership systems lay cambio banks that had been restructured through blending family (patrilineage) and nonfamily (guild) logics into hybridized economic headquarters.

These internal organizational developments can be illustrated perfectly with the Medici banks. As can be seen in more detail in Padgett and McLean 2006 (1549–50), the original

[83] LaSoursa 1904; Usher 1943; De la Roncière 1973; Goldthwaite 1985.

Table 6.9.
Family Types of Cambio Banking Partnerships

A. Aggregate percentage distribution

	Solo	Family	Mixed	Nonfamily	Total
1357–66	.265	.159	.177	.399	1.00
1367–76	.325	.171	.173	.332	1.00
1380–89	.275	.153	.190	.382	1.00
1390–99	.254	.173	.217	.357	1.00
1427	.152	.161	.312	.375	1.00

B. Percentage also in other merchant-banking activities or partnerships

	Solo	Family	Mixed	Nonfamily	Total
1357–66	.078	.239	.266	.107	.149
1367–76	.094	.130	.264	.134	.143
1380–89	.090	.095	.350	.123	.153
1390–99	.096	.125	.316	.268	.210
1427	.118	.333	.400	.190	.269

Source: Annual cambio bank censuses, plus 1427 *catasto*.

Notes:

(1) Unit of analysis is partner-year.

(2) "Solo" defined as company with only one owner. "Family" defined as company with all partners in the same nuclear or patrilineage (= "same last name") families. "Mixed" defined as company with some partners in same family but also with some other partners from different families. "Nonfamily" defined as company with all partners in different families.

(3) For overlaps of cambio banking with other industries/companies, 1357–66 and 1367–76 periods use "merchant banker" to be 1369 Pisa list, hence the word *activities* in the title; 1380–89 and 1390–99 periods use Melis's Datini list of partnerships; 1427 uses industry code = 1,2,3 in *catasto*. (See Padgett and McLean 2011.) Starting date of 1357 chosen to make 1357–76 period comparable (twenty years) to 1380–99 period.

Medici bank of Vieri di Cambio de' Medici started out as a domestic cambio bank, which had been founded in 1349. Before 1380, that successful cambio bank had been built entirely on the basis of nonfamily partnerships with many social classes, in classic guild manner. In 1382 or 1384 for the first time, however, Vieri di Cambio built his partnership system by using his distant nephew (and past apprentice) Francesco di Bicci de' Medici both to diversify internationally into Genoa and to make his domestic bank into a mixed-family form. Francesco's brother Giovanni di Bicci soon followed as partner-cum-branch-manager of Vieri's new Rome branch in 1385. After 1382, even the meaning of "nonfamily" partner changed: for example, one of Vieri's domestic banking partners, Niccolò di Riccardo Fagni, married Vieri's sister Cilia in 1399 after her first husband and Vieri had died.

The timing of these economic system-building moves was not accidental: Vieri was very active in Ciompi and post-Ciompi politics. Like the classic guildsman that he was, Vieri participated heavily in his own Arte del Cambio guild, serving as consul seven times before the Ciompi revolt. Despite his long years of guild service, however, Vieri never attained the exalted levels of the Mercanzia or the Priorate until after the Ciompi revolt—in 1383 and 1392, respectively. This institutional elevation was status recognition of Vieri's very active Ciompi and post-Ciompi involvement in the political reconstruction of the republic: Vieri was a member of every one of the reforming *balìe* in our data set (1378, 1382, 1384, and 1393). Leading up to the Ciompi revolt, Vieri di Cambio de' Medici had been a conservative leader of the Parte Guelfa, clearly aligned with the Albizzi faction and personally involved in anti-Ghibelline persecutions.[84] Despite his undoubted personal conservatism, Vieri served on the revolutionary 1378 *balìa* under the leadership of his firebrand cousin Salvestro

[84] Brucker 1962, 204, 340, 343n.

d'Alamanno de' Medici.[85] In reward for this service the Ciompi regime knighted him in 1378.[86] Even as late as 1393, artisans in street battles appealed futilely to Vieri, and to his cousin Michele de' Medici, for leadership.[87] This contradictory political behavior by Vieri can only be understood in the context of the cross-cutting social-network position of the Medici family itself.[88] To call Vieri a "political moderate" is too simple, but he clearly operated on both sides of the fence, whatever his own conservative views. His cross-cutting network position pushed him late in life into a position of inventive leadership within both the republican state and economic partnership systems.

These points could be illustrated at even greater length by the more famous Medici bank of Giovanni di Bicci and Cosimo di Giovanni, which descended from Vieri di Cambio, but de Roover (1966) has already done that job. The only aspect of that later famous Medici bank I would like to highlight here is their increased reliance on a higher social class of general and branch managers. In the early Medici bank of Vieri di Cambio, only 30 percent of the nonfamily partners had been either popolani or magnates. In the later Medici bank of Giovanni di Bicci and Cosimo di Giovanni, 64 percent of the nonfamily partners before 1427 were popolani or magnates.[89] In 1413 Cosimo himself married into the Bardi family of his bank's general managers. These changing personnel policies of the two Medici banks were quite consistent with overall trends in Florentine banking during the Albizzean republican era.

The popolani economic behavior of constructing mixed-kinship forms of cambio banks at the peak of one's career was consistent, I suggest, with the social behavior of any popolani patriarch—supporting through patronage and generosity one's own kin, in-laws, friends, and neighbors[90] in pursuit of the honor and glory of the patrilineage one leads. This generalized *padrone* role came to be gradually well-known within Florentine elite circles during the Renaissance.[91] What was new in this role, right after the Ciompi revolt, was the combination of this behavior from the kinship domain with behavior in the economic domain, thereby displacing the previously dominant role of guild master. First the cross-network relationship between banking and politics was rewired, and then the cross-network relationship between banking and kinship was rewired, locking in the first so tightly that it operated almost automatically. To be a calculating merchant and to be a generous patriarch-patron were no longer so distinct: a merchant was a patron, and a patron was a merchant.

Open Elite?

Throughout this study and throughout the historiography on the Florentine Renaissance, there has lurked the recurrent interpretative dilemma of oligarchy versus republicanism. On the one hand, there is plenty of evidence to support the oligarchic interpretation. After the Ciompi revolt, popolani elites took over backstage political institutions, even as they opened up election to city council. Clientage was the new method of elite control over the Priorate. And economically, socially elite popolani families moved into a position of dominance over newly created partnership systems, even though those systems distributed commercial credit widely. It is easy to see the force of Najemy's resolution of this interpretative dilemma: namely, that republican "consensus" was a sham to legitimate reconsolidated elite domination. My economic data on partnership, indeed, support Najemy's (and Molho's) view.

On the other hand, on balance I lean more toward the republican interpretation. How can that possibly be? Padgett (2010) presented extensive data to show not only that across two centuries popolani families married very widely across social classes but also that their social openness in marriage was at its peak in the supposedly oligarchic period under discussion. Therefore to say that economic and political elites were reorganizing themselves around high social-status popolani marriage (a true statement) is not to say that these elites were exclusionary in the core networks that constituted themselves. Political and social co-optation was not a sham. It reorganized the very elites doing the co-opting. The openness of Florentine elite families to organizational and social-network change was the secret to their resilience across tumultuous history. Out

[85] Gherardi [1389] 1876, 505.
[86] Stefani [1385] 1903, 324.
[87] Brucker 1977, 141n.
[88] Brucker 1957; Padgett and Ansell 1993.
[89] de Roover 1966, 377–78.
[90] Klapisch-Zuber 1985, 68–93.
[91] Alberti [1433] 1971.

of conservative motivations they adjusted their networks, thereby unintentionally reconstituting themselves.

Padgett (2010) also presented data on the consequences of political and economic co-optation for Florentine kinship. Over two centuries, generations of Florentine middle-class parvenu mimicked and absorbed the patrilineage kinship model of their social superiors, thereby extending the social reach of this patriarchal ideal. During the same time, however, the magnate citadel of this patrilineage model of kinship collapsed. The Florentine middle classes, in other words, increasingly imitated an upper-class kinship ideal (exemplified by magnates) that was in serious demographic decline. It was not as much upper-class families that emerged victorious as it was the upper-class family ideal, which diffused downward to parvenu. This ideal transformed middle-class families that aspired to it. Evolution of Florentine families during the Renaissance is yet another example of the mantra of our book: In the short run, actors create relations; in the long run, relations create actors.

"Republicanism" is open; "oligarchy" is closed. The Renaissance Florentine resolution to this contradiction, I suggest, was a politically and socially open elite that conceptualized itself as purer and higher than the rest of humanity. It was not only the older popolani elite that found this vision of merchant-plus-citizen-plus-patron (the cultured and generalist "Renaissance man") attractive to walk toward.

All of this system building and political reorganization added up to great wealth for Florentine bankers. Padgett and McLean (2006, 1536) document a progressive increase in the wealth of domestic bankers, relative to upper levels of the population as a whole, from 1351 to 1378 to 1403 to 1427, especially among the upper reaches of bankers, before its decline in 1460 after the period of our study. Coupled with the transformation in multiple social identities that produced this wealth, great wealth for Florentine bankers as individuals also translated into wealth for all the artists and clients they now sponsored. Perhaps we need not belabor the point that the artistic inventions traditionally associated with the onset of the Renaissance—for example, the new linear perspective of Brunelleschi, Masaccio, and Donatello—are dated around 1400, the terminus of the twenty-year banking and political consolidation that is analyzed here. The creation of great wealth and social-network patronage are the links between the well-known artistic story of the Renaissance and our own economic-political account.[92]

CONCLUSION

Despite the fact that Renaissance Florentines invented financial capitalism and much else that we associate with modernity, Paul McLean and I agree with contemporary historians who stress the traditionalist mentalité of the era. Florentines were too drenched in concerns with family, marriage, status, and clientage, not to mention the ever-looming threat of early mortality,[93] to appear cognitively to be very much like us, even though they frequently did things that were like what we do. Social science efforts to impose modernist models of ourselves on the past do violence to our comprehension of that past. More important, they lead us to miss the opportunity to learn what the ancients have to teach us, about social science among other things. Listening to—not testing preconceived ideas about—the past is how to learn.

Vasari ([1550] 1991) and Burckhardt ([1878] 1990) created the concepts of individual genius and Renaissance to explain the remarkable achievements of late medieval Florence. But if we try to listen to the Florentines of the past through systematic sifting of their voluminous records, then we can learn about those achievements' institutional and social-network dimensions, which do not speak straightforwardly to us in words. What those aggregated thousands of archival voices have told us, albeit in our own descriptive language, not in theirs, is transposition, refunctionality, and catalysis. Organizational inventions (as opposed to innovations) are transpositions of relational logics from one domain to another, which attain new purposes in the new domain, whose reproduction is positively reinforced to the point that it alters interactions among others in the new domain. Florentine inventions were more than good ideas. They were discontinuous system tippings, rooted in reproductive feedbacks among dynamic multiple social networks. This process explains how genesis and path-dependence historically go hand in hand.

[92] Cf. Kent 2000.
[93] Cohn 2002.

Transposition, refunctionality, and catalysis are "network folding" mechanisms that collectively produce organizational inventions. Important as Renaissance Florence is in its own right, the discovery of these mechanisms is a theoretical contribution beyond even this paradigmatic case because it opens the black boxes of "stochastic process" and "genius," the usual two nonexplanations of invention. In biology, life is the self-organization and reproduction of two forms of chemical flow: metabolic flow of food among species within generations and genetic flow of DNA within species across generations. Speciation is the reorganization and reproduction of these chemical transformations. This chapter has proposed an analogous perspective on the emergence of actors out of intersections of social-relational flows within a multiple-network architecture. "Metabolic flow" among organizations was operationalized as personal biographies. Biographies wend through organizations and transform the people flowing through them, usually into reproducing the roles and interests contained within those organizations. Not often but occasionally when catalyzed to do so, biographies and the people flowing along mobility paths tip their own self-regulation and transform themselves. "Genetic flow" was operationalized as organizational reproduction of relational logics. Selection in the multiple domains of markets, politics, and kinship lock in sets of relational logics that catalyze each other, not always optimally, through co-evolution. Interdependent "ways of doing things" usually require predictability in inputs and outputs collectively to function. But occasionally, the rewiring of old logics into new purposes opens a new trajectory for path-dependent system transition. We look to transformational feedback between interlinked biographies, on the one hand, and the reproduction of relational logics, on the other, to analyze the poisedness of a multiple-network system either to equilibrial lock-in or to organizational tipping and invention.

Specifically, the Florentine invention of the partnership system was a hybridization of the two relational logics of patrilineage and guild through the means of political republicanism. Rechanneling the political biographies of guildsmen, after the guild system had been politically defanged, broke down the previous segregation of patrilineal logic in international business and guild logic in domestic business. And it blended modular guild partnership methods from domestic cambio banking into the patrilineal world of international trade. A decisive system-tipping move into politics (not entirely by choice) dramatically increased the number of Florentines eligible for and nominated to political office at the same time as selection procedures for those offices were centralized. The more or less direct effect in politics was an explosion of patron-client relations. Organizational change in economics was an indirect effect as the *padrone* role emerged in Florence to influence the partnership and credit logics of the upper tier of business as well. In kinship continued pressure on the patrilineage internally to differentiate may have been a third consequence, although that was also a long-term trend. All of these interlinked organizational changes were aspects of the emergence of a new style of elite—part businessman, part politician, part patriarch, part intellectual esthete—that we have come to call the Renaissance man. In network terms, we interpret this emergence as an expression of an underlying transformation in the core relational logics of the society from patrilineage and guild to marriage and clientage.

This chapter has focused more on mechanism than on structural preconditions. More research into the earlier period[94] is required to uncover the exact topology of the patrilineage-guild ensemble that tipped into the Ciompi revolt. But even at our current level of understanding, it is clear why Florence had a different evolutionary trajectory than did Venice and Genoa, the two most obvious comparative cases. Namely, even though the relational logic of patrilineage was similar in all three cities, the relational logic of guild was strong only in Florence.

Venice and Genoa had their own forms of economic invention, to be sure, but not in international finance or partnership systems. Patrilineage was pervasive everywhere within the elites of northern Italy,[95] but guild corporatism was politically weak in the comparison cities, depriving those cities of the guild half of the Florentine fusion. Perhaps related to this historical fact, neither city experienced the degree of social mobility–driven political turmoil that Florence did. Venice exhibited great stability in its legally closed aristocracy; hence it was known as the *serenissima* (most serene) republic. The corollary in Venetian banking of this almost caste-like political stability was a strict segregation between domestic deposit banking,

[94] Cf. Brucker 1962; Najemy 1982; Padgett 2006.
[95] Waley 1969.

in which the small number of specialized Rialto bankers excelled, and international banking, which was delegated to the Florentines.[96] Rich Venetian merchants were shippers and traders,[97] not mixed-mode merchant-bankers like the Florentines. And Genoa, like Florence before the Black Death, had deep and persistent factional feuds and civil wars based on patrilineage.[98] The corollary in Genoese banking of this intra-elite turmoil and distrust was a strong transactionalist focus, with economic actors on both the domestic and international levels spreading around short-term economic partnerships, investments, and accounts among many alters to cushion risk.[99] In coarse-grained contrast to Venice on the one side and to Genoa on the other, post-Ciompi Florence appears to be relational and oligarchic with porous (because of co-optation) elite boundaries.

Besides the deep interconnection between organizations and elite networks, one final matter about which the Florentines can teach us is the perspectival construction of identity. As developed by Brunelleschi and Masaccio and explained by Alberti ([1435] 1991), visual perception of objects operates through linear perspective, in which the two-dimensional spatial arrangement of objects in a painting are artfully arranged to create the illusion of a third dimension—a line stretching from a focal-point location on the horizon in the painting back toward the viewer, which invites the viewer to movement into the painting. I believe that the partnership system, with its array of account books at its base, had a similar effect on the perceptions of Florentine businessmen. In a modularized partnership system, the senior owner is both inside (entrepreneur) and above (financier) his array of companies at the same time. The multiplicity of heterogeneous account books that he is forced to manage, keeping track of complex cross-flows of goods, finance, and credit, necessitated systematization and abstraction analogous to the arrangement of space in a linear-perspective painting.[100] Current accounts, which really were reified people and customers, were arrayed mathematically, with double-entry bookkeeping used to calculate the financial flows and the businessman's own line of movement, called profit. Businessmen always want to make money in some loose sense, as well as do other things. But the precision involved in "maximization of profits" over multiple streams of transactions is inconceivable without the array of cross-connected account books that lies at the base of the partnership system. In the sense of perception, the account books themselves induced the Florentine businessman to walk into this line of movement. More generally, I conclude that goals are our cognitive perspectives on the trajectories of flows, financial and biographical, to which organizational networks subject us in their processes of reproduction.

I end on this note of appreciation: innovation in the sense of getting someone to try something new is relatively easy. Invention in the sense of getting an entire system to tip into a new trajectory of evolution is extremely hard. Because of this, I salute both the *ciompi* and the forgotten 1382 moderates for helping make the Florentine Renaissance and, in the very long run, part of us.

[96] Mueller 1997, 3–32, 255–87.
[97] Lane 1967.
[98] Hughes 1975a, 1975b, 1977; Epstein 1996.
[99] Heers 1991, 77–80, 136–41.
[100] Cf. Baxandall [1972] 1988.

REFERENCES

Archival Primary Sources

Archivio di Stato di Firenze [A.S.F.]. *Arte del Cambio* 11, 14, 15, 16: Annual guild censuses of banks doing business in Florence, covering periods 1340–1399 and 1460–1520. (Books for intervening period 1400–1459 unfortunately are lost. After 1500, censuses appear to be unreliable.)

A.S.F. *Arte del Cambio* 12: Matriculants (1330–1500) and consuls (1280–1500) of the banking guild.

A.S.F. *Arte della Lana* 20: 1353 census of active wool manufacturers.

A.S.F. *Arte della Lana* 46: 1382 census of wool manufacturing firms by the wool guild (pp. 114–17); 1384 *balìa* membership and decisions (pp. 154–66).

A.S.F. *Balìe* 17: 1378 *balìa* membership (pp. xx); 1382 *balìa* membership (pp. 22, see also Stefani pp. 394–96); 1393 *balìa* membership (pp. 80–86, 105–7).

A.S.F. *Carte Strozziane*, serie II, 7: *ricordi* of Paliano di Falco, 1382–1404. A.S.F., *Catasto* 15–63 (*Portate dei Cittadini*): Original 1427 tax submissions of Florentine citizens.

A.S.F. *Catasto* 64–85 (*Campioni dei Cittadini*): Scribal summaries of citizens' 1427 tax submissions. [Thanks to the labors of David Herlihy and Christianne Klapisch-Zuber, a computerized subset of this information, not including the debitori and creditori analyzed here, is available online at http://www.stg.brown.edu/projects/catasto. These researchers also deposited a microfilm copy of the *campioni* documents themselves at the Center for Research Libraries at the University of Chicago.]

A.S.F. *Estimo* 306: 1351 tax assessments of Florentine residents. [Microfilm copy generously donated to Padgett by Samuel Cohn.]

A.S.F. *Estimo* 268: misfiled 1378 *prestanza* tax assessment for Santo Spirito residents.

A.S.F. *Manoscritto* 545: Arte della Calimala matriculation.

A.S.F. *Manoscritti Carte dell'Ancisa* 348–61: Fourteen volumes of hand-transcribed marriage information from Renaissance Florentine dowry contracts, originals mostly now lost, produced in the seventeenth-century by Pierantonio dell'Ancisa.

A.S.F. *Mercanzia* 129: List of members (1310–1500) of the commercial court.

A.S.F. *Prestanze* 367–69: 1378 tax assessments of Florentine residents, Santa Croce, Santa Maria Novella, and San Giovanni residents. [Microfilm copy generously given to Padgett by Samuel Cohn.]

A.S.F. *Prestanze* 1989–2020: 1403 tax assessments of Florentine residents.

A.S.F. *Prestanze* 834–37: 1458 tax assessments of Florentine residents.

A.S.F. *Tratte* 357: 7–20: 1393 electoral results, winners being *reggimento*.

Archivio di Stato di Lucca. *Corte dei Mercanti*, n. 82–86: *Libri dei mercanti, 1371, 1372, 1381, 1407 e 1488*. Along with Lazzareschi (1947), these are censuses of Lucca companies.

Archivio di Stato di Prato. *Datini* 1, 4–6, 16–22, 357–60, 365, 555, 723–25, 799: various account books of Francesco Datini, consulted in order to identify dates of adoption of bilateral or *contrapposto* bookkeeping format.

Newberry Library, Chicago. *Priorista descritto a Tratte riscontro con quello delle riformagioni e con alter scritture publiche*: An eighteenth-century hand copy of the official list of elected Priors, the *Priorista Mariani* original of which is A.S.F., *Manoscritti* 248–52. [Thanks to the labors of the late David Herlihy and Burr Litchfield, this information can now be obtained online at *www.stg.brown.edu/projects/tratte*.]

Published Primary Sources

Alberti, Leon Battista. [1433] 1971. *The Albertis of Florence: Leon Battista Alberti's* Della Famiglia, ed. Guido Guarino. Lewisburg, PA: Bucknell University Press.

———. [1435] 1991. *On Painting*. London: Penguin Books.

Brucker, Gene, ed. 1967. *Two Memoirs of Renaissance Florence: The Diaries of Buonaccorso Pitti and Gregorio Dati*. New York: Harper Torchbooks.

Frangioni, Luciana, ed. 1994. *Milano fine trecento: Il carteggio Milanese dell'Archivio Datini di Prato*. Firenze: Opus libri.

Gherardi, Alessandro, ed. [1389] 1876. *Diario d'Anonimo Fiorentino dall'anno 1358 al 1389*. Deputazione sugli studi di storia patria, eds., *Documenti di storia italiana*. Firenze: M. Cellini.

Goldthwaite, Richard A., Enzo Settesoldi, and Marco Spallanzani, eds. 1995. *Due libri mastri degli Alberti: Una grande compagnia di Calimala, 1348–1358*. Firenze: Cassa di Risparmio di Firenze.

Guicciardini, Francesco. [1512] 1994. *Dialogue on the Government of Florence*. Cambridge: Cambridge University Press.

Machiavelli, Niccolò. [1524] 1988. *Florentine Histories*. Princeton: Princeton University Press.

Silva, P. 1908. "L'ultimo trattato commerciale tra Pisa e Firenze." *Studi storici diretti da F. Crivellucci* 27: 679–83.

Stefani, Marchionne di Coppo. [1385] 1903. *Cronica Fiorentina di Marchionne di Coppo Stefani*, ed. Niccolò Rodolico. Città di Castello: S. Lapi editore.

Villain-Gandossi, Christiane, ed. 1969. *Comptes du sel (Libro di ragione e conto di sale) de Francesco di Marco Datini pours acompagnie d'Avignon, 1376–1379*. Paris: Bibliothèque nationale.

Secondary Sources

Abu-Lughod, Janet. 1989. *Before European Hegemony: The World System A.D. 1250–1350*. Oxford: Oxford University Press.

Barley, Stephen R. 1990. "The Alignment of Technology and Structure through Roles and Networks." *Administrative Science Quarterly* 35:61–103.

Baron, Hans. 1966. *The Crisis of the Early Italian Renaissance: Civic Humanism and Republican Liberty in an Age of Classicism and Tyranny*. Princeton: Princeton University Press.

Baxandall, Michael. [1972] 1988. *Painting and Experience in Fifteenth Century Italy*. Oxford: Oxford University Press.

Breiger, Ronald L. 1974. "The Duality of Persons and Groups." *Social Forces* 53:181–90.

Brown, Allison M. 1961. "The Humanist Portrait of Cosimo de' Medici, Pater Patriae." *Journal of the Warburg and Courtauld Institutes* 26:186–221.

Brucker, Gene A. 1957. "The Medici in the Fourteenth Century." *Speculum* 32:1–26.

———. 1962. *Florentine Politics and Society, 1343–1378*. Princeton: Princeton University Press.

———. 1968. "The Ciompi Revolution." In *Florentine Studies: Politics and Society in Renaissance Florence*, ed. Nicolai Rubinstein, 314–56. London: Faber.

———. 1977. *The Civic World of Early Renaissance Florence*. Princeton: Princeton University Press.

Burckhardt, Jacob. [1878] 1990. *The Civilization of the Renaissance in Italy*. New York: Penguin.

Burt, Ronald S. 2004. "Structural Holes and Good Ideas." *American Journal of Sociology* 110:349–99.

Carus-Wilson, E. M. 1967. "Trends in the Export of English Woolens in the Fourteenth Century." In

Medieval Merchant Venturers: Collected Studies, 239–64. London: Methuen.

Carus-Wilson, E. M., and Olive Coleman. 1963. *England's Export Trade, 1275–1547*. Oxford: Clarendon Press.

Ceccherelli, Alberto. 1913. *I libri di mercatura della Banca Medici, e l'applicazione della partita doppia a Firenze nel secolo XIV*. Firenze: R. Bemporad e figlio.

Chabod, Isabelle. 1995. "La dette des Familles: Femmes, lignages et patrimoinies a Florence aux XIV et XV siècles." Ph.D. diss., European University Institute.

Chandler, Alfred D. 1962. *Strategy and Structure: Chapters in the History of the American Industrial Enterprise*. Cambridge, MA: MIT Press.

Cohn, Samuel K. 1980. *The Laboring Classes in Renaissance Florence*. New York: Academic Press.

———. 2002. *The Black Death Transformed: Disease and Culture in Early Renaissance Europe*. New York: Oxford University Press.

———. 2006. *Lust for Liberty: The Politics of Social Revolt in Medieval Europe, 1200–1425*. Cambridge, MA: Harvard University Press.

De la Roncière, Charles M. 1973. *Un changeur florentin du Trecento: Lippo di Fede del Sega (1285 env.–1363 env.)*. Paris: Ècole pratique des hautes ètudes.

De Roover, Raymond. [1956] 1974. "The Development of Accounting prior to Luca Pacioli According to the Account Books of Medieval Merchants." In *Business, Banking, and Economic Thought in Late Medieval and Early Modern Europe by Raymond de Roover*, ed. Julius Kirshner, 119–79. Chicago: University of Chicago Press.

———. [1965] 1974. "The Antecedents of the Medici Bank: The Banking House of Messer Vieri di Cambio de' Medici." In *Business, Banking, and Economic Thought in Late Medieval and Early Modern Europe by Raymond de Roover*, ed. Julius Kirshner, 260–72. Chicago: University of Chicago Press.

———. 1966. *The Rise and Decline of the Medici Bank, 1397–1494*. New York: W. W. Norton.

Dini, Bruno. 2001. "Le forme e le tecniche del presititon el tardo Medioevo." In *Manifattura, commercio e banca nella Firenze medievale*. Firenze: Nardini editore.

Epstein, Steven. 1996. *Genoa and the Genoese, 958–1528*. Chapel Hill: University of North Carolina Press.

Fabbri, Lorenzo. 1991. *Alleanza matrimoniale e patriziato nella Firenze del' 400: Studio sulla famiglia Strozzi*. Firenze: Leo S. Olschki editore.

Fleming, Lee. 2002. "Finding the Sources of Technological Breakthroughs: The Story of Hewlett-Packard's Thermal Ink-Jet." *Industrial and Corporate Change* 11:1059–84.

Fligstein, Neil. 1990. *The Transformation of Corporate Control*. Cambridge, MA: Harvard University Press.

Fontana, Walter, and Leo Buss. 1994. "The Arrival of the Fittest: Toward a Theory of Biological Organization." *Bulletin of Mathematical Biology* 56:1–64.

Franceschi, Franco. 1993a. *Oltreil "Tumulto": I lavoratori fiorentini dell'Arte della Lana fra Tre e Quattrocento. Firenze*: Leo S. Olschki editore.

———. 1993b. "Intervento del potere centrale e ruolo delle Arti nel governo dell'economia fiorentina del Trecento e del primo Quattrocento: Linee generali." *Archivio Storico Italiano* 151:863–909.

Galison, Peter. 1997. *Image and Logic: A Material Culture of Microphysics*. Chicago: University of Chicago Press.

Goldthwaite, Richard A. 1968. *Private Wealth in Renaissance Florence*. Princeton: Princeton University Press.

———. 1972. "The Florence Palace as Domestic Architecture." *American Historical Review* 77:977–1012.

———. 1983. "Organizzazione economica e struttura famigliare." In Donatella Rugiadini (redactor), *I ceti dirigenti nella Toscana tardo comunale*, 1–14. Firenze: Francesco Papafava editore.

———. 1985. "Local Banking in Renaissance Florence." *Journal of European Economic History* 14: 5–55.

Gompers, Paul, and Josh Lerner. 1999. *The Venture Capital Cycle*. Cambridge, MA: MIT Press.

Granovetter, Mark. 1985. "Economic Action and Social Structure: The Problem of Embeddedness." *American Journal of Sociology* 91:481–510.

Heers, Jacques. 1991. *Genova nel '400: Civiltà mediterranea, grande capitalismo e capitalismo popolare*. Milano: Jaca book. [Italian translation of French original.]

Herlihy, David. 1985. *Medieval Households*. Cambridge, MA: Harvard University Press.

Herlihy, David, and Christiane Klapisch-Zuber. 1985. *Tuscans and Their Families: A Study of the Florentine Catasto of 1427*. New Haven: Yale University Press.

Hoshino, Hidetoshi. 1980. *L'Arte della Lana in Firenze nel basso medioevo*. Florence: Leo S. Olschki editore.

Hughes, Diane Owens. 1975a. "Urban Growth and Family Structure in Medieval Genoa." *Past and Present* 66:3–28.

———. 1975b. "Domestic Ideals and Social Behavior: Evidence from Medieval Genoa." In *The Family in History*, ed. Charles Rosenberg. Philadelphia: University of Pennsylvania Press.

———. 1977. "Kinsmen and Neighbors in Medieval Genoa." In *The Medieval City*, ed. Harry Miskimin and David Herlihy. New Haven: Yale University Press.

Hutchins, Edwin. 1995. *Cognition in the Wild*. Cambridge, MA: MIT Press.

Kauffman, Stuart A. 1993. *The Origins of Order: Self-Organization and Selection in Evolution*. New York: Oxford University Press.

Kelly-Gadol, Joan. 1977. "Did Women Have a Renaissance?" In *Becoming Visible: Women in European*

History, ed. Renate Bridenthal and Claudia Koonz. Boston: Houghton Mifflin.

Kent, Dale. 1975. "The Florentine Reggimento in the Fifteenth Century." *Renaissance Quarterly* 28: 575–638.

———. 1978. *The Rise of the Medici: Faction in Florence, 1426–1434*. Oxford: Oxford University Press.

———. 2000. *Cosimo de' Medici and the Florentine Renaissance*. New Haven: Yale University Press.

Kent, D. V., and F. W. Kent. 1981. *Neighbours and Neighbourhood in Renaissance Florence: The District of the Red Lion in the Fifteenth Century*. Locust Valley, NY: J. J. Augustin.

Kent, Francis William. 1977. *Household and Lineage in Renaissance Florence*. Princeton: Princeton University Press.

———. 1987. "Ties of Neighborhood and Patronage in Quattrocento Florence." In *Patronage, Art, and Society in Renaissance Italy*, ed. F. W. Kent and Patricia Simons, 79–98. Oxford: Clarendon Press.

Klapisch-Zuber, Christiane. 1985. *Women, Family, and Ritual in Renaissance Italy*. Chicago: University of Chicago Press.

Lane, Frederic C. 1967. *Andrea Barbarigo, Merchant of Venice 1418–1449*. New York: Octagon Books.

Lansing, Carol. 1991. *The Florentine Magnates: Lineage and Faction in a Medieval Commune*. Princeton: Princeton University Press.

LaSoursa, Saverio. 1904. *L'organizzazioni dei cambiatori fiorentini nel medioevo*. Cerignola: Tip. edit. dello "scienza e diletto."

Latour, Bruno. 1988. *The Pasteurization of France*. Cambridge, MA: Harvard University Press.

Lopez, Robert S. 1952. "The Trade of Medieval Europe: The South." In *Cambridge Economic History of Europe*, ed. M. Postan and E. E. Rich. Cambridge: Cambridge University Press.

———. 1976. *The Commercial Revolution of the Middle Ages, 950–1350*. Cambridge: Cambridge University Press.

Luhmann, Niklas 1995. *Social Systems*. Stanford: Stanford University Press.

March, James G. 1991. "Exploration and Exploitation in Organizational Learning." *Organization Science* 2:71–87.

———. 1999. *The Pursuit of Organizational Intelligence*. Malden, MA: Blackwell.

Martines, Lauro. 1979. *Power and Imagination: City-States in Renaissance Florence*. New York: Vintage Books.

Maturana, Humberto, and Francisco Valera. 1980. *Autopoiesis and Cognition: The Realization of the Living*. Boston: Reidel Publishing.

McLean, Paul D. 1998. "A Frame Analysis of Favor Seeking in the Renaissance: Agency, Networks and Political Culture." *American Journal of Sociology* 104:51–91.

———. 2007. *The Art of the Network: Strategic Interaction and Patronage in Renaissance Florence*. Durham: Duke University Press.

McLean, Paul D., and John F. Padgett. 1997. "Was Florence a Perfectly Competitive Market? Transactional Evidence from Renaissance." *Theory and Society* 26:209–44.

Melis, Federigo. 1962. *Aspetti della vita economica medievale: Studi nell'Archivio Datini di Prato*. Siena: Leo S. Olschki editore.

———. [1972] 1987. "La grande conquista trecen tesca del 'credito di esercizio'e la tipologia dei suo istrumentisino al XVI secolo." In *La Banca pisana e le origini della banca moderna*, ed. M. Spallanzi. Firenze: Le Monnier.

———. [1946–77] 1991. *L'azienda nel medioevo*. Firenze: Le Monnier.

Molho, Anthony. 1968a. "The Florentine Oligarchy and the Balìe of the Late Trecento." *Speculum* 43:23–51.

———. 1968b. "Politics and the Ruling Class in Early Renaissance Florence." *Nuova Rivista Storica* 52: 401–20.

———. 1994. *Marriage Alliance in Late Medieval Florence*. Cambridge, MA: Harvard University Press.

Morlacchi, Pierangela. 2005. "List of Florentine Account Books, Coded for Bilateral Format." http://home.uchicago.edu/~jpadgett.

Mueller, Reinhold C. 1997. *The Venetian Money Market: Banks, Panics, and the Public Debt, 1200–1500*. Baltimore: Johns Hopkins University Press.

Najemy, John M. 1972. "The Guilds in Florentine Politics, 1292–1394." Ph.D. diss., Harvard University.

———. 1981. "Audiant Omnes Artes: Corporate Origins of the Ciompi Revolution." In *Il Tumulto dei Ciompi: Un Momento si Storia Fiorentina ed Europea*, 59–93. Florence: Leo S. Olschki editore.

———. 1982. *Corporatism and Consensus in Florentine Electoral Politics, 1280–1400*. Chapel Hill: University of North Carolina Press.

Nicolis, Grégoire, and Ilya Prigogine. 1989. *Exploring Complexity*. New York: Freeman.

Origo, Iris. 1957. *The Merchant of Prato: Francesco di Marco Datini*. New York: Penguin Books.

Padgett, John F. 1994. "Marriage and Elite Structure in Renaissance Florence, 1282–1500." http://home.uchicago.edu/~jpadgett. Forthcoming in *Redes: Revista hispana para el análisi de redes sociales*.

———. 1997. "The Emergence of Simple Ecologies of Skill: A Hypercycle Approach to Economic Organization." In *The Economy as an Evolving Complex System II*, ed. Brian Arthur, Steven Durlauf, and David Lane, 199–222. Reading, MA: Addison-Wesley.

———. 2001. "Organizational Genesis, Identity, and Control: The Transformation of Banking in Renaissance Florence." In *Networks and Markets*, ed. James E. Rauch and Alessandra Casella, 211–57. New York: Russell Sage Foundation.

———. 2005. "Early Florentine Companies, 1300–1378." http://home.uchicago.edu/~jpadgett.

———. 2006. "Organizational Genesis in Florentine History: Four Multiple-Network Processes." http://home.uchicago.edu/~jpadgett.

———. 2010. "Open Elite? Social Mobility, Marriage and Family in Florence, 1282–1494." *Renaissance Quarterly* 63:357–411.

Padgett, John F., and Christopher K. Ansell. 1993. "Robust Action and the Rise of the Medici, 1400–1434." *American Journal of Sociology* 98:1259–1319.

Padgett, John F., and Paul D. McLean. 2006. "Organizational Invention and Elite Transformation: The Birth of Partnership Systems in Renaissance Florence." *American Journal of Sociology* 111: 1463–1568.

———. 2011. "Economic Credit in Renaissance Florence." *Journal of Modern History* 83:1–47.

Padgett, John F., Doowan Lee, and Nick Collier. 2003. "Economic Production as Chemistry." *Industrial and Corporate Change* 12:843–77.

Peruzzi, Simone Luigi. 1868. *Storia del commercio e dei banchieri di Firenze in tutto il mondo conosciuto dal 1200 al 1345*. Firenze: M. Cellini e comp.

Powell, Walter W. 1990. "Neither Market nor Hierarchy: Network Forms of Organization." In *Research in Organizational Behavior*, ed. B. Straw and L. L. Cummings, 295–336. Greenwich, CT: JAI Press.

Powell, Walter W., Kenneth W. Koput, and Laurel Smith-Doerr. 1996. "Inter-organizational Collaboration and the Locus of Innovation: Networks of Learning in Biotechnology." *Administrative Science Quarterly* 41:116–45.

Renouard, Yves. 1941. *Les relations des papes d'Avignon et des compagnies commerciales et bancaires de 1316 a 1378*. Paris: E. de Boccard.

Rodolico, Niccolò. [1899] 1968. *Il Popolo Minuto*. Firenze: Leo S. Olschki.

Rubinstein, Nicolai. 1966. *The Government of Florence under the Medici (1434 to 1494)*. Oxford: Oxford University Press.

Sapori, Armando. 1926. *La crisi delle compagnie mercantili dei Bardi e dei Peruzzi*. Firenze: Leo S. Olschki editore.

Schevill, Ferdinand. [1936] 1963. *Medieval and Renaissance Florence*. New York: Harper Torchbooks.

Stella, Alessandro. 1993. *La revolte des Ciompi: Les hommes, les lieux, le travail*. Paris:

Stinchcombe, Arthur L. 1965. "Social Structure and Organization." In *Handbook of Organizations*, ed. J. G. March. Chicago: Rand-McNally.

Trexler, Richard C. 1974. *The Spiritual Power: Republican Florence under Interdict*. Leiden: E. J. Brill.

———. 1980. *Public Life in Renaissance Florence*. Ithaca: Cornell University Press.

———. 1998. *The Workers of Renaissance Florence*. Asheville, NC: Pegasus Press.

Usher, Abbott. 1943. *The Early History of Deposit Banking in Mediterranean Europe*. Cambridge, MA: Harvard University Press.

Vasari, Georgio. [1550] 1991. *The Lives of the Artists*. New York: Oxford University Press.

Waley, Daniel. 1969. *The Italian City-Republics*. New York: World University Library.

White, Harrison C., Scott A. Boorman, and Ronald L. Breiger. 1976. "Social Structure from Multiple Networks. I: Blockmodels of Roles and Positions." *American Journal of Sociology* 81:730–50.

Witt, Ronald G. 1976. "Florentine Politics and the Ruling Class, 1382–1407." *Journal of Medieval and Renaissance Studies* 6:243–67.

———. 2003. *In the Footsteps of the Ancients: The Origins of Humanism from Lovato to Bruni*. Boston: Brill.

7

Country as Global Market

Netherlands, Calvinism, and the Joint-Stock Company

John F. Padgett

In this chapter I address the multifaceted organizational puzzle that is the Dutch Revolt. During these tumultuous events, which I bracket between 1560 and 1610, many transformative organizational inventions were produced in short order, almost like a cascade. In the domain of states, cities in the northern half of the Spanish Netherlands assembled themselves into the new organizational form of a federation, which called itself the United Provinces of the Netherlands. In the domain of religion, Calvinism emerged from Reformation rebellion into an official state church, the Dutch Reformed Church. In the domain of economics, the joint-stock company—so influential in later economic history—was invented, in conjunction with emergent Dutch colonialism. Overseas colonialism was one facet of a broader centralization of European commercial and trading networks, constructed by Dutch merchant middlemen and centered in their glorious global Amsterdam entrepôt and Bourse.[1] The first stock market emerged within the confines of this international goods-exchange market.

The thesis of this chapter is that these disparate organizational inventions[2] causally were linked in this period through the assembly of network coordination principles that I shall call "lateral (or horizontal) control." Manifest most obviously in councils but extended ultimately to markets, public peer pressure is not unique to the Dutch. But the degree to which the Dutch constructed parallel arrays of nested councils, in multiple domains, is to the best of my knowledge unprecedented in European history. Tripartite federalism is my label for the macro-architecture of this multiple-domain ensemble of councils in government, in religion, and in economics. Inner ruling oligarchies were constructed through overlapping memberships in these three parallel arrays of councils. Wide participation and literally buy-in was attained through investment in them by the Dutch citizenry.

In addition to profits, interpersonal and family ties were the lifeblood of this system; hence the phrase "impersonal markets" is deeply misleading. But the new lattice of tripartite federalism geographically extended interpersonal networks outward beyond Holland into European and global merchant colonies without losing lateral-control discipline. Centrally brokered "free trade" grew up around these colonial ligaments and autocatalyzed these new Dutch organizational inventions into reproduction and rapid growth. Indeed, the distinctively Dutch combination of state federalism, Calvinism,

[1] The word *Bourse* derived from an earlier international goods-exchange in Bruges, which had been situated in a small square dominated by an inn of the Van der Buerse family (Blondé, Gelderblom, and Sabel, 2007, 157). In both Amsterdam and Antwerp, the word *Bourse* came to refer to the large open-air building constructed to contain the voluminous trading negotiations taking place inside and around that building.

[2] Historians have discussed another organizational invention that some associate with the Dutch Revolt—namely, the "military revolution" of army structure and tactics based on precise troop and bullet movements, enabled through incessant drilling. See Richards 1967. Contra Richards, Parker (1988) has emphasized instead Italian roots, based on fort construction. Given the controversy about this topic, I leave it to one side. Rogers (1995) provides an overview of the debate.

and international trade grew so explosively in the seventeenth century that the period is still known by many as the "Golden Age" of Dutch economic hegemony.[3]

It is easy to trace historical continuities in the building blocks of Dutch federalism—both in public finance and in the regent ruling oligarchies of Dutch cities—to sixteenth-century Spanish administration. The Dutch Revolt was rooted in the same tax struggles between an aggrandizing king (in this case Spanish) and a defensive, particularist nobility (in this case Dutch) that one sees everywhere in medieval and early modern Europe. The Protestant Reformation, however, newly popular among urban artisans and merchants all over northern Europe, added a toxic element, which induced "normal" tax struggles to explode into Inquisition, iconoclasm, and persecution, with escalating violence on both sides. The waves of Calvinist merchant refugees produced by religious war were the dynamics, in my analysis, that triggered the cascade of Dutch organizational inventions from state federalism, to the Dutch Reformed Church, to the joint-stock company, to centrally brokered international trade. Naturally, the causal threads I assemble into this overall system-feedback "tipping" are not always simple and direct. For example, while the consistory organization of underground and refugee Calvinism is perhaps the purest exemplar of lateral control, frequently libertine regents used lateral control to manage harder-core Calvinists as much, if not more, than the reverse. And contra Max Weber, I will not argue that Calvinism caused the spirit of capitalism through changing interpretations of salvation. My argument instead will be organizational: namely, that religiously induced mass migration blended complementarities in business skills and networks through connecting financially advanced refugee merchants from southern Spanish Netherlands (today's Belgium) with shipping-oriented merchants in northern Spanish Netherlands (today's Netherlands). Together these constructed a global naval trade empire, which broke out of and then challenged the Spanish empire that had spawned it, in a way that neither could have done alone. The various newly born institutional lattices of state federalism, Dutch Reformed Church, and joint-stock company mixed these two populations, skill sets, and networks together in mutually reinforcing synergistic ways. In my historical account, country did not make international market, nor did international market make country. In early modern Netherlands, lateral-control emergent organizations and markets simultaneously created each other in co-evolutionary feedback through the catalyzing mediation of revolutionary Calvinist politics and migration.

This chapter is not based on primary archival research, as were the previous two chapters. It is a synthesis of a large secondary literature, mostly in English.[4] As such, my contribution is not to add to the stock of factual knowledge about the Dutch Revolt, which has impressive historiographies in each of the domains (government, religion, economy) to be discussed. The contribution instead is to propose an overarching interpretative framework of organizational genesis and system feedback, through which each of these domains, usually studied separately, interacted to create organizational novelty.

LATERAL CONTROL AND FEDERALIST TIERS

Figure 7.1 outlines the argument in this chapter visually. The lateral-control "councils" at the base of the Dutch federalist system were these: (a) the oligarchic regents of Dutch cities in the governmental domain; (b) the consistories of Calvinist church parishes in the religious domain; and (c) two distinct but complementary organizational subunits in the economic domain, namely, directors of joint-stock companies for overseas colonialism and geographically concentrated merchant colonies within Europe itself. City regents were self-recruiting oligarchies or *vroedschap* of elite ruling councilmen, who theoretically (absent overthrow) served their terms for life. Consistories were the councils of rotating elders and ministers, who governed and controlled Calvinist parishes. Directors were boards of large shareholders, who made major policy decisions for joint-stock companies. Merchant colonies were sedentary Dutch merchants living permanently abroad. These merchants organized themselves locally through parishes (not always

[3] Of course whether the age is "Golden" or not depends upon one's perspective.

[4] While I know the languages necessary to carry out primary research in the previous two chapters, I do not know Dutch. Because of this, this chapter will be unsatisfactory to historians, especially to Dutch historians, to whom I am deeply indebted. With apologies to them, I hope that the restricted linguistic foundation will prove sufficient to serve the chapter's social science objective, which is to discover new mechanisms of organizational genesis.

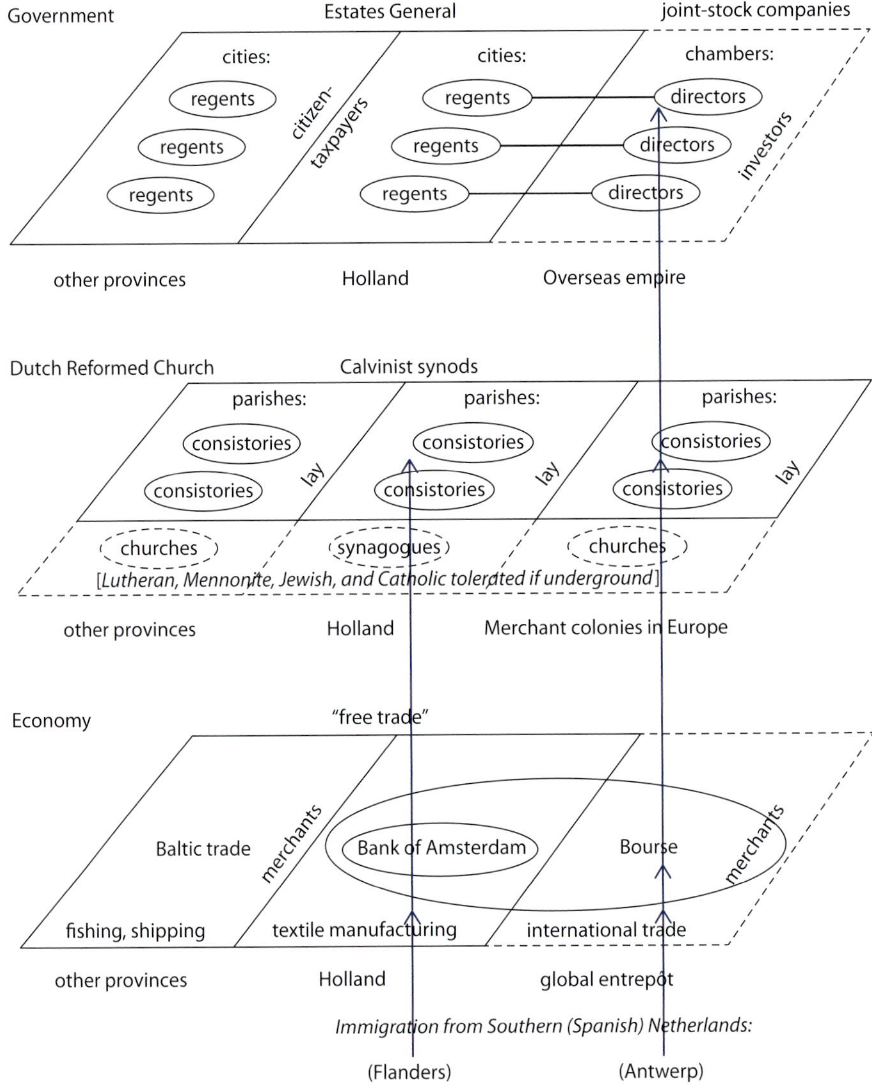

Figure 7.1 Migration and homology: the birth of Netherlands and the joint-stock company.

Calvinist), connecting back to the metropole via family partnerships.

These four sets of organizational building blocks each had their own evolutionary history, which will be discussed below. Hence none of them was a simple reflection of the others. Despite the only loose coupling among their distinct evolutions, all were homologous in the sense of being coordinated and disciplined through lateral/horizontal control. After the Dutch Revolt, no longer were political regents or religious parishes embedded in Spanish- or Catholic-style hierarchies of top-down command. Having lopped off their respective heads, Dutch state and Dutch religion were decentralized: their constitutive subunits had decisional autonomy. Schismatic tendencies are always inherent from the get-go in radical decentralizations like this. If fissures are not offset by countervailing mechanisms of coordination and control, then decentralized ensembles will not self-stabilize enough to persist through time, much less reproduce and grow. Before showing how this Dutch system evolved, I will itemize how lateral control worked in the mature seventeenth-century Dutch system.

Three complementary lateral-control mechanisms were present in the Dutch federalist ensemble diagrammed in figure 7.1: publicity within each councillor arena, segmentary opposition within each federalist tier of councils, and cross-cutting intersections (like chain mail) of multiple federalist arrays.

Councils take interpersonal interactions and make them public, observable to all in within eye- and ear sight. Transparency is achieved to the degree that important conversations among members take place within, not outside, the public observation of the council. Public visibility induces homogeneity in the information and perceptions that each participant has about the others. People are not standardized, but perceptions of them are. Visibility in and of itself strengthens peer pressure. Miscreants under investigation by Calvinist consistories feared the public announcement and confession of their own sins before their peers in their parish more than they did any private sanction.[5] The physicality of the bounded public square that was the Amsterdam Bourse in itself disciplined the international market of Dutch merchants who traded goods from all over the world there. When provincial estates and the national Estates General shifted from meeting rarely, at the behest of the king, to meeting regularly on a fixed and frequent schedule, the internal discipline of those legislatures changed markedly. Public visibility of course does not solve all problems. However, attributional and reputational perceptions of observers are aligned thereby, a nontrivial social accomplishment.

Segmentary opposition is an anthropological model of multilayered kinship politics in which high-frequency conflicts among lower subunits switch into alliance in response to low-frequency conflicts among higher aggregates that contain those subunits, only to dissolve back again into feud among subunits once peace at the upper level returns.[6] Applied to provincial Netherlands, this means rival neighboring towns aligning into provinces against rival provinces, which in turn coalesce into nation only in the face of an overwhelming enemy like Spain. Peace with Spain and the whole thing falls apart. This baseline model has much truth in it: early Netherlands was indeed very provincial, fractious, and fragile. Without institutional and network mechanisms to cross-cut these fissures, nascent Netherlands would have dissolved. Before the evolution of such mechanisms, however, the preservation and religious intensification of almost permanent war with Spain was the sine qua non. There would have been no Netherlands without the Inquisition and Protestantism. Tax revolts were chronic in this period, but they alone didn't cause abandonment of hierarchy itself.

Given a confederation externally propped up by segmentary opposition, internal stability (moving toward institutionalized federalism proper) began to emerge through negotiated pacts of balances of power. In the Netherlands, "contracts of correspondence" were negotiated contractual agreements among towns within provinces, and among provinces in the national federation, about their ratios of fiscal responsibility and about their relative corporate voting rights within nested legislatures. The first Dutch East India joint-stock company (the VOC) emerged from the bottom up in 1602 also like this. Long-distance trading companies (*voorcompagnieën*), sponsored by various Dutch port cities, were merged into six financially autonomous city-based chambers, each represented on an overall VOC coordinating board or council of directors (Heren Zeventien) according to negotiated voting ratios.[7] The result was a massive, militarized private trading company owned by stockholders. The result was also an overseas province within the United Provinces of the Netherlands—essentially the new colonial province of Indonesia. Both the Dutch overseas joint-stock companies and the Dutch domestic federalist state itself were hybrid public-private organizations.

Lateral control in the third federation tier of the Dutch Reformed Church worked like this: parish consistories were assembled into regional conferences, called colloquies or *classes*, which in turn were assembled into provincial conferences, called synods.[8] Theological and organizational disputes within consistories (of which there were many) were forwarded to *classis* or synod assemblies of peer consistories, the majority judgments of which were considered authoritative for member consistories. Disagreements among provincial synods or unusually salient disputes within prominent *classes* were settled in rare but highly consequential national synods

[5] Pettegree 1986, 192.
[6] Evans-Pritchard 1940.
[7] Bruijn, Gaastra, and Schöffer 1987, 6–15.
[8] Benedict 2002, 281–85.

comprised of representatives from all consistories in the Netherlands. Prestigious but nonvoting representatives from other national Calvinist synods were in attendance there. Federalism in Calvinism, federalism in the Dutch state, and federalism in joint-stock companies each had distinctive genealogies. These three federalist tiers hence were not reflections of each other, but there were clear homologies in organizational form in seventeenth-century Netherlands across multiple domains, based on similar nested-councils principles.

Homology, however, doesn't necessarily mean synergy. Homology can also lead to competition and cleavage. Internal politics within the early and still fragile Netherlands was rent by intense struggles for control over the new Dutch Reformed Church. Regents in the political tier, so-called libertines, frequently wanted an open version of the official Calvinist church, tolerant of all religions except Catholics, because that was useful for state control over the broad population. Calvinist ministers, in contrast, wanted a narrower and purer church only for the elect, with theocratic veto over state policy. Alliances of regent magistracies were mobilized on the first side of this dispute. Alliances of Calvinist consistories, sometimes aided by military Stadholders, were mobilized on the second side. Was the Dutch Revolt in essence a political struggle for liberty? Or was it a godly victory for Protestantism?

This bitter contestation was never resolved constitutionally. It was resolved instead, when it was resolved, through overlapping memberships in constituent councils. This is the third meaning of lateral control: intercalation of federalist tiers. Once enough regents and elite merchants became elders in Calvinist consistories, religious demagogues and their artisan allies were tethered. And once enough urban regents were devout, it became possible for the state to back Calvinism without theocracy being proclaimed. The compromise brokered by this intercalation was distinctly Dutch: Calvinism became monopolistic in public churches and sacred places, but Erasmus-style tolerance of other religions was accepted in private homes and hearts. The percentage of the Dutch population who were Calvinist never exceeded 30 percent in the period under study. Both regents and the general population were Dutch Reformed in name, but that did not necessarily imply that they were devout or even that they were Protestant. After the Dutch Revolt, with all of its religious terrors and counterterrors, there were more Catholics in the United Provinces of the Netherlands than there were Calvinists.

Intercalation also occurred between the Dutch state and the "private" joint-stock companies. In the 1590s the original exploratory *voorcompagnieën* were financially backed but not organizationally controlled by the cities that had sponsored them.[9] With their 1602 merger into the large and monopolistic Dutch East India Company, however, city regents gained the power of appointing "their" chamber's directors. The eligible pool of directors still had to be large shareholders, but shareholders lost their previous right to elect themselves as directors. This understandably was a contentious issue that could have disrupted the smooth management of Dutch colonialism, but when many regents were rich merchants and vice versa, there were plenty of "moderate" oligarchic brokers around to smooth organizational frictions.

Simultaneous memberships in governing councils, across multiple domains, of course created merchant-oriented urban oligarchies within each wealthy Dutch city. Ultimately Dutch tripartite federalism worked, despite its severe provincial and religious fissures, because there was this set of tight urban oligarchies at its core, each of which radiated out laterally through governments, churches, and businesses. In the next section I explain how this federalist system emerged and why the general public for the most part accepted oligarchic control of themselves.

MIGRATION AND HOMOLOGY: THE ORGANIZATIONAL GENESIS OF TRIPARTITE FEDERALISM

Migration did not create the northern governmental institutions of regents and provinces, nor did it create the economic foundation of Baltic trade, but Calvinist migration from southern Spanish Netherlands (Flanders, Brabant, and Walloons: today's Belgium), I argue, extended the leftovers of Spanish imperial administration into tripartite federalism and exploded the Dutch economy into global domination of international trade. Because of this analysis, I label the organizational genesis mechanism operating in this chapter as "migration and homology." That is, kernels of governmental federalism already present in the north were elaborated and

[9] Bruijn, Gaastra, and Schöffer 1987, 1–6.

extended to global scale by cosmopolitan economic and religious networks introduced into the north by a diaspora of Calvinist merchant immigrants, who fled Spanish persecution not only to northern Netherlands but also to other places in Protestant Europe. The coupling and merger of complementary northern and southern economic networks was supported by federalist homologies in the religious and governmental organizational forms of Dutch natives and Calvinist immigrants.

Before there was Amsterdam, there was Antwerp. We sometimes forget that the label "Spanish empire" in the 1500s is a bit of a misnomer. Habsburg dominions included within their enormous reach not only Spain (internally balkanized into Castile, Aragon, and other regions) but also the geographically noncontiguous regions of Austria, Burgundy, Netherlands (north and south), southern Italy (including Sicily), and North and South America. The Portuguese empire, including Brazil, the East Indies, and parts of Africa, was not Habsburg but was effectively allied. The first European global empire after ancient Rome, therefore, was not the Dutch; it was the loose dynastic ensemble of Habsburg-Spanish-Portuguese dominions, militarily centered in Castile. The Castilian core was militantly Catholic, at religious war not just with the Protestant Reformation in the north but also with Islam at home and in the east. The lengthy Spanish Reconquista against the Moors continued into the late fifteenth century, and wars with Ottoman Muslims in the Mediterranean and Austria raged throughout the sixteenth century. The Spanish Inquisition targeted not only Protestants. Muslims, Jews, heretic Catholics, and native Americans also were either converted or killed by an evangelizing, purifying, and crusading Castilian regime. This regime saw itself, not without reason, as religiously under siege at a global level.

In the 1500s numerous global economic trade flows in this sprawling ensemble converged in the Spanish Netherlands and were cleared mostly in the Antwerp entrepôt.[10] Portuguese spices were imported into Antwerp for distribution to Europe, prominently through wealthy southern German merchants like the Fuggers, who brought silver and other metals to exchange.[11] Fine Spanish wool was imported into Flanders to support a thriving local textile industry, which sold much of its product to Hanseatic League merchants resident in Bruges.[12] Unfinished English woolen cloth was imported by the monopolistic English Merchants Adventurers into Antwerp for dyeing and subsequent sale.[13] Italians brought high volumes of their silks to distribute to high-toned merchants of many nationalities, clustered there.[14] On the north-south axis, shipbuilders and ship captains from the northern Netherlands brought grain down in bulk from the Baltics (mostly from Danzig, the port outlet for Prussian agrarian Junkers) for local consumption but also for reexport to Spain and Portugal and later to Italy.[15] Return voyages carried Portuguese and French salt and French wines. Once the gold and especially silver treasures from the Americas started to pour into Seville in the mid-sixteenth century,[16] much of this treasure was reassigned to Antwerp both to repay huge Fugger state-finance loans and to cover Spanish trade deficits rooted in the backwardness of its own domestic industry. Because of this, the largest money market in Europe grew up in Antwerp, cheek to jowl with its trade entrepôt.[17] Merchants as well as states flocked there for financing and loans.[18]

In some pro-Holland historiography, sixteenth-century Antwerp is pejoratively labeled a "passive" market, in denigrating contrast to the "active" market that was seventeenth-century Amsterdam.[19] These labels mean that most of the merchants trading at Antwerp were not natives but cosmopolitan foreigners, coming from away to interact with each other on Antwerp soil, usually alternating their time between Antwerp and home.[20] In contrast, most of the merchants importing and trading in Amsterdam were Dutch,[21] buying goods overseas and shipping them into Amsterdam for sale to others or for reexport by themselves. Trade at Antwerp was thus bilateral, whereas in Amsterdam it was multilateral or triangular—that is, brokered.[22] While this characterization is accurate for the Antwerp of the early 1500s, pro-Belgian literature has stressed that native Antwerp businessmen, working as commission agents for foreigners,

[10] Brulez 1970; van der Wee 1993, 87–114; Heere 2009, 91.
[11] Ehrenberg 1928; Harreld 2004.

[12] Phillips 1983.
[13] Ramsay 1986; Dietz 1978.
[14] Subacchi 1995.
[15] Christensen 1941; Wieringa 1983; van Tielhof 2002.
[16] Hamilton 1970, 34.
[17] Van der Wee 1977.
[18] Stabel, Blondé, and Greve 2000.
[19] This literature, mostly in Dutch, is reviewed and criticized in Lesger 2006, 1–6.
[20] Goris 1925.
[21] Blondé, Gelderblom, and Sabel 2007, 170.
[22] Brenner 1993, 599.

gradually picked up cutting-edge business skills and networks, becoming full-fledged merchant companies themselves over the first half of the sixteenth century.[23] Antwerp, not Amsterdam, was the place where advanced Italian financial techniques, like bills of exchange and double-entry bookkeeping, first diffused into the native businesses of northern Europe.

When the Spanish Inquisition and the Dutch Revolt, which will be discussed below, produced a series of increasingly massive waves of Calvinist refugees out of parts of the Spanish Netherlands under Spanish control, textile artisans from Flanders moved northward to Holland[24] (mostly to Leiden and Haarlem), and merchants from Brabant (mostly Antwerp) moved to tolerant Protestant cities in Germany, France, England, and Scandinavia, especially to cities where refugees had previous business connections. After the revolt was over, many of these refugee Calvinist merchants immigrated back to northern Netherlands, especially to Amsterdam, where business was starting to pick up.[25] But many also settled down into a permanent diaspora of Dutch merchant colonies, spread all over Europe. Specifically, London,[26] Norwich, and Sandwich in England, Hamburg,[27] Emden,[28] Frankfurt,[29] and Danzig[30] in Germany, Bergen and Stockholm[31] in Scandinavia, Archangel[32] in Russia, La Rochelle, Nantes,[33] and Bordeaux[34] in Atlantic (and Huguenot) France,[35] and even Livorno[36] in Catholic Italy developed colonies of Dutch merchants permanently residing in these places who were partners with and agents of other Dutch merchants back home, often family members. In the Baltic region, most of these outpost Dutch merchants originated from Holland and northern Netherlands, but in the other European cities mentioned they originated largely from the south, albeit with mixing in all cases.[37]

Figure 7.1 illustrates the consequences of this Calvinist diaspora for economic development within the new federalist Netherlands. Calvinist artisans in textile manufacturing fled from Flanders to Leiden and Haarlem in Holland, largely transferring that distinguished Flemish industry. Calvinist merchants and financiers from Antwerp and Brabant moved to Amsterdam and other cities in Holland and Zeeland, bringing the business practices and network connections of the Antwerp Bourse with them. One important such financial practice was the Antwerp innovation of negotiability in bills of exchange and promissory notes. In spite of their previous dominance of and innovation within Antwerp, Catholic Italian, Spanish, and German merchants did not make the transition to Amsterdam.[38] Calvinist merchant refugees, mostly from the south, also established Dutch merchant colonies—outlets and feeders for Amsterdam trade—in the largely Protestant cities just mentioned.

As a result of all this movement, Amsterdam's population exploded from 30,000 in 1550, to 65,000 in 1600, to 175,000 in 1650.[39] The population growths of Leiden and Haarlem also were impressive: 12,000 to 25,000 to 67,000, and 14,000 to 30,000 to 38,000, respectively. Outside Holland, Middelburg in coastal Zeeland grew from 7,000 to 20,000 to 30,000. Rotterdam grew from 7,000 to 13,000 to 30,000. The far-north shipbuilding port of Enkhuizen grew from 8,000 to 17,000 to 22,000. In short, the population of most of northern Netherlands (though not the agrarian east) expanded spectacularly after the successful Dutch Revolt. On the other side of the line of Spanish troops, it was a different story. Antwerp's population plummeted from 90,000 in 1550 to 47,000 in 1600[40] but rebounded somewhat to 70,000 in 1650. Ghent in Flanders shrank drastically from

[23] Edler 1938; Brulez 1959; van der Wee 1963, 325–32.

[24] Van Zanden 1993.

[25] Gelderblom (2003, 263) reports the social composition of the Amsterdam merchant community in 1609 to be the following: out of 1,350 merchants in his data set, 40 percent of them were from Amsterdam, 35 percent were from southern Netherlands, 20 percent were from other locations in the Dutch Republic, less than 5 percent were from Germany, and less than 5 percent were from Portugal. Blondé, Gelderblom, and Sabel (2007, 169) round these figures off into the following statement: "Two out of every three merchants trading in Amsterdam in the early seventeenth century had only settled there recently."

[26] Pettegree 1986; Grell 1989; Mitchell 1995.

[27] Schilling 1983.

[28] Pettegree 1992; Ramsay 1986.

[29] Soliday 1974.

[30] Bogucka 1990.

[31] Lindblad 1995; Müeller 1998.

[32] Lubimenko 1924; Kellenbenz 1973; Israel 1989, 43–48; Wijnroks 1993; van der Meiden 1993.

[33] Collins 1984.

[34] Voss 1995.

[35] Veluwenkamp 1996.

[36] Engels 1997.

[37] Israel 1989, 43–60; Gelderblom 2003, 269–75.

[38] "From a geographical point of view, merchants from England, Portugal and Germany seem relatively rare, while Italians and Spaniards are virtually absent. The most important group consisted of newcomers born and raised elsewhere in the Low Countries, especially in Antwerp and its hinterland" (Blondé, Gelderblom, and Sabel 2007, 170).

[39] All population figures taken from De Vries 1984, appendix 1, 271–72.

[40] Marnef (1996, 5) reports that the Antwerp population dropped from 104,081 in 1568 to 46,123 in 1591.

50,000 to 31,000 but also rebounded to 46,000. Bruges stagnated more than declined: 35,000 to 27,000 to 34,000.

The previously glorious economy of southern Spanish Netherlands was not completely destroyed, but it was damaged beyond repair. The Antwerp money market was kept alive through the continued influx of Spanish silver, largely to service the resident Spanish army. The partial rebound of Antwerp and other southern cities also was fueled by stay-behind Catholic merchants' residual trade with Spain and Portugal.[41] Catholic merchants south of the Spanish line maintained interpersonal, family, and business links with their Protestant brethren and old friends north of the line, thereby partially bridging through trade the deep collective political and religious divide.[42] In the sudden transition caused by the Dutch Revolt, Antwerp became an economic appendage of Amsterdam, whereas previously it had been the reverse.

REGENTS AND PUBLIC FINANCE

As mentioned above, the Dutch Revolt was not a corollary of the Protestant Reformation. It was rooted in the usual medieval and early modern struggles over taxes and autonomy between an aggrandizing monarch and a defensive provincial nobility. Indeed it was Inquisition actions by the Spanish crown itself, more than Dutch initiative, that first linked tax resistance to Protestantism. These historical roots of administrative tensions within the Spanish empire are consequential for understanding how emergent Dutch federalism eventually reacted to and absorbed Calvinist refugees.

Together with northern Italy, the Low Countries regions of Flanders, Brabant, and Holland were among the most urbanized parts of Europe, going back to medieval times. Burgundy in the 1400s, even before Spain in the 1500s, was the first overlord to impose a central administration onto this thicket of proud, prosperous, and rivalrous towns and cities.[43] City regents, so important for later Dutch decentralization and revolt, were originally an imperial governing institution created by Burgundy overlords and then reinforced and supported by Spanish overlords. They were urban elites co-opted into administrative service as local magistrates, under the supervision and command of their imperial bosses. *Vroedschappen* (a term signifying "men of ease") were twenty to forty typically wealthy councilmen in each city who recruited each other into councillor membership for life (as long as they weren't overthrown). Mayors (burgomasters), aldermen (*schepenen*), and sheriffs were rotating magistrate officers drawn from this small pool of qualified *vroedschappen*.[44] Family lineage was commonly the main criterion for oligarchic self-recruitment into the *vroedschappen* regents, but there was some limited room for incorporating a few new men.[45] In the highly unusual circumstances of the Dutch Revolt, these conservative city regents became radicalized against their Spanish overlords, but even so they were not likely to relinquish their own tightly held political power to refugees from rival towns, no matter how wealthy or religious those were.

At the higher provincial level, Burgundy overlords were the first to aggregate cities into provinces through corporate councils or estates, like one sees almost everywhere in western Europe at this time. For example, the Raad van Holland (Council of Holland) included representatives of the elite of many towns in Holland, but by 1500 only seven votes in that council really mattered: one vote each for the six "great cities" in Holland (Dordrecht, Leiden, Haarlem, Delft, Amsterdam, and Gouda, which always voted in this sequence) and one collective vote for agrarian nobles.[46] Spain's main contribution to imperial administration was to take this Burgundy system, inherited through Habsburg dynastic marriage, and strengthen its overlord center with a sequence of three regents or female relatives of the Spanish king, who acted in the king's name in conjunction with appointed Spanish nobles as influential advisers. These Spanish bosses were linked to provincial councils, and thence to regents, through an Estates General of appointed provincial governors called *stadholders*. These provincial governors invariably were selected from native noble families like Orange and Nassau; hence Spanish imperial administration, like that in so many other empires, was an "indirect rule" blending of top-down Spanish overlords with bottom-up Netherlands nobility and regents.

[41] Smolar 1965.
[42] Van der Laan 1988.
[43] Blockmans and Prevenier 1999.
[44] Israel 1995, 125–28.
[45] Burke 1974, 23–32; Adams 2005, 75–105.
[46] Tracy 1990, 14–19; Israel 1995, 276–84.

James Tracy has done the most to describe the public-finance transformation in the mid-1500s of this Spanish hierarchical administrative structure into a chrysalis of increasingly autonomous Dutch provincial federalism. As was often the case in these systems, war and fiscal overload produced a devolution of power down to the council levels where financing was to be found. Spanish imperial finance was fairly advanced and efficient for its day, but the sheer magnitude and number of its wars broke the bank. In the 1550s the major war was with France. There is no need in this chapter to review all the public-finance intricacies discussed by Tracy. The bottom line is that in their desperation to repay and thus escape exorbitant short-term loans from Antwerp bankers like the Fuggers, Spanish kings Charles V and Philip II turned to longer-term, lower-interest-rate government bonds, called *renten*, floated by cities and especially provinces in the Netherlands.[47] Investors were only willing to buy such government bonds to the degree that they were assured of repayment. Dutch regents, acting collectively through their provincial councils, agreed to float these bonds on behalf of the king only if they themselves controlled the collection and distribution of the taxes levied to repay the interest due on those bonds. This tax-collection mechanism ensured that bondholders were the first, not the last, to be repaid from future flows of Spanish taxes. This mechanism also ensured that the Spanish king himself moved from the front to the back of the line in disbursement priority for his own taxes. Bond sales were very successful under this mechanism, ultimately leading to victory over France, but the Spanish king lost administrative control over his Netherlands financial machinery thereby. Obviously he never would have agreed to this serious devolution of power had his own international and financial need not been extreme.

An unintended consequence of this Spanish financial reform was that citizenship relations were altered between local Dutch governments and their subjects. The biggest purchasers of government bonds were the regents themselves and their extended families.[48] In this sense, regents not only politically controlled their cities and provinces but also began economically to own those cities and provinces, as an investment. Not only regents bought government bonds. Anyone voluntarily could and did buy them, to the extent of their financial capability and interest. Tracy stresses that the Dutch innovation was not the idea of government bonds per se but rather the idea of voluntary instead of mandatory purchase (although the truth is that we can find an occasional Italian precedent, like the Florentine Dowry Fund, if we look hard enough). Citizens and even noncitizens became transformed from subjects to owners of their states—not owners equally, of course, but owners in proportion to their bond holdings. States became investments—investments that were economically secure and profitable to the extent that investors actually controlled those states politically. Republicanism in Renaissance Italy arguably attained something similar in its public finance,[49] but Italy never transcended its city-state basis. To Machiavelli's resounding consternation and dismay, the city-states of Italy never could ratchet up into federated provinces and country, as did the almost equally urbane Netherlands. The legacy of Spanish imperial control is the reason for this difference.

DUTCH REVOLT

Tax struggle escalated into armed revolt first because of the Inquisition and then because Calvinism radicalized resistance.[50] The first Protestants persecuted and executed by Spanish overlords in the Netherlands were not Calvinists; they were Anabaptists or Mennonites.[51] Calvinism as an organized religion with public ministers did not exist in the Spanish Netherlands until 1566. The "excessive" persecution of poor and mostly artisanal Anabaptists is not explicable in the context of Netherlands: they hardly represented much of a threat to anyone, in spite of a couple of incidents. It is explicable only in the broader context of the rapid antihierarchical growth of Protestantism in Germany, Scandinavia, and France, as well as Muslim threat from the east, as mentioned above. The Spanish were trying to nip the

[47] Tracy 1985. "Here it will suffice to note that while revenues roughly quadrupled during the reign of Charles V, government indebtedness on the Antwerp exchange increased by a factor of about sixty to one. Thus fiscal officials like Holland's Receiver for the *beden* sent their receipts directly to the counting houses of one or more of the great firms in Antwerp, and the bankers themselves took an active interest in the revenues by which their loans were secured" (Tracy 1990, 51). For the medieval analogue, compare chapter 5 in this volume.

[48] Tracy 1985, 139–92.

[49] Spufford 1995.

[50] This summary of the Dutch Revolt draws upon the detailed accounts in Parker 1977 and Israel 1995, 129–230.

[51] Marnef 1966, 84–85.

problem in the bud before they had to face yet another religious front. The Spanish Netherlands were indeed vulnerable to Protestant infection, as everyone knew. They were urban, literate, and at the intersection of trading routes through which Protestant Bibles and other printed literature poured in, eagerly consumed surreptitiously by the pious. In addition, at the elite level, humanism, in the local form of Erasmus, appealed to educated Dutch urban oligarchs for the same status reasons as it had previously to Italian urban oligarchs. Erasmus humanism stood not for the rejection of Catholicism but for its internal adjustment in the direction of literacy and theological toleration.[52] For its primary audience of Dutch urban elites, both in the north and in the south, humanism asserted a status order different from hierarchical sublimation to Spain and the pope.

Spanish persecution of Protestant "heretics," therefore, did not receive enthusiastic support and implementation from local officials, to say the least. In the face of this dragging of feet, and perhaps also in reaction to the recent devolution of his tax power, Philip II in consultation with Spanish advisers on the scene upped the ante. In 1561 he announced his administrative plan to expand and strengthen the bishoprics of the Dutch Catholic Church with inquisitorial powers that did not require compliance from local magistrates. This strengthening of a royalist pillar tried to end-run the previous indirect-control system and hence was a direct threat to Dutch nobles and regents. Five years of increasing public tension and outcry, provoked by relentless Spanish executions, culminated in the Petition of (Religious) Compromise, forcibly presented to Regent Margaret of Parma by two hundred mostly middling nobles in April 1566. This petition demanded immediate suspension of the Inquisition, under a scarcely veiled threat of rebellion. The regent temporarily agreed, forwarding the petition on to Philip, her brother.

Before Philip responded negatively, Calvinism burst into the Netherlands. In five months, Calvinist ministers, mostly Huguenots from neighboring France, spread all over the Spanish Netherlands, dramatically preaching outside towns in their famous hedge-preaching. The popular response was electric, with thousands turning out for their fiery and emotional sermons against Catholicism. This powerful response of course didn't come from nowhere but drew upon deep currents of reformist Catholicism and crypto-Protestantism that had been percolating privately in people's homes for decades. Researchers have tried to identify the social composition of this powerful popular response. Calvinism (or perhaps more precisely anti-Catholicism) appealed all across the social spectrum, but it was particularly resonant among artisans and merchants.[53] Even the regents and nobles who had presented the Petition of Compromise that had opened the door were scared by the out-of-control populism of this response.

By late summer these sermons had escalated into iconoclasm—the organized destruction of sacred images, statues, and stained-glass windows in Catholic churches, convents, and monasteries. Calvin himself in Geneva did not support this sacrilegious destruction of Catholic icons, but he did not control his own extremists. Predictably enough, this direct assault on the sacred sent Philip and the Castilians into hyperspace. Neither iconoclasm nor Philip's repressive response was an isolated Dutch event. The Catholic Counter-Reformation had been officially launched at the conclusion of the Council of Trent in 1563. Despite the sentiments of humanists like Erasmus and of Dutch nobles like William of Orange, reconciliation or compromise between Protestants and Catholics was no longer possible.

Obviously much can be and has been written about the dynamics of the Dutch Revolt from 1566 to 1585, and beyond. For my specific purpose of understanding organizational genesis, the central theme is how elite Dutch regents and populist Calvinists came uneasily to fit together, with organizational consequences for capitalist evolution and colonialism.

The organizational form of the Calvinist consistory—parish-governing boards of elders and minister, linked horizontally with each other in

[52] Israel 1995, 41–54.

[53] Marnef (1996) provides the best quantitative data on the social background of converts, based on Spanish persecutions in Antwerp. For persecuted Anabaptists, Marnef (1996, 77) reports occupations as follows: (a) for the early period of 1550–66: 84.2 percent crafts and applied arts and 12.7 percent trade and transportation; (b) for the later period of 1584–85: 51.4 percent craft and applied arts and 38.6 percent trade and transport. For persecuted Calvinists, Marnef (1996, 173) reports occupations as follows: (a) for the early period of 1550–66: 64.6 percent craft and applied arts and 22.0 percent trade and transportation; (b) for the "Wonderyear" of 1566: 14.5 percent crafts and applied arts and 54.3 percent trade and transportation; (c) for the period of 1567–77, 59.2 percent crafts and applied arts and 23.2 percent trades and transportation; (d) for the later period of 1584–85: 54.1 percent crafts and applied arts and 38.0 percent trades and transportation.

synods—had been invented in Geneva and exported to Huguenots in France.[54] Its disciplined, cellular structure was well suited to its original formative environment of undergrounds and refugees: migrant ministers circulated secretly among private clusters of "chosen people." Although rotating in office, local Calvinist elders were moral, patriarchal, and stern, not democratic or tolerant. As Weber stressed, the Calvinist ideal was active monasticism in the world: not indolent prayer surrounded by luxury but disciplined service to others in need of guidance. A less kind way of putting it is "holier than thou." Unlike Mennonite pacifism or Lutheran dependence on princes, Calvinist consistories reinforced a subversive and resilient militancy, useful for both offensive and defensive religious war.

Even with war in the east with Islam looming, in 1567 Philip sent ten thousand crack Spanish troops to the Netherlands, under the command of the ruthless Duke of Alva, to crush Dutch political and religious dissent. The duke's orders were simple: smash the impertinent rebellion without mercy. As Spanish troops marched through, many nobles and regents waffled and fell back into line, to the lasting scorn of their populations. Thousands of prosecutions and hundreds of executions followed. The few towns brave enough to resist were leveled to the ground with all inhabitants slaughtered, as examples. An estimated sixty thousand people fled from the Netherlands, mostly to Germany and England.[55] This was the first wave of Calvinist refugees, but it also included William of Orange and other Dutch nobles who had rebelled more for political than religious reasons. Emden on the North Sea was a particularly famous site of Calvinist regrouping.[56] Many less visible Calvinists and anti-Catholics went underground ("church under cross") but kept up a lively correspondence with refugee consistories abroad.[57] Calvin scornfully called those of his followers not willing to stand up and be martyred "Nicodemites."

Adding insult to injury, Philip II, short of money as always, insisted that the Dutch pay for their own repression. The most infamous of these new direct taxes was the Ten Penny, or 10 percent excise tax on all goods. When even the browbeaten and intimidated Estates General refused to authorize this self-flagellation, Philip sent Spanish administrators into cities and provinces and ordered local magistrates to collect the taxes upon penalty of fine and jail. Despite the brutality of his methods, the Duke of Alva succeeded for a couple of years at coercing enough money to pay for his own troops.[58] Needless to say, the previous more sophisticated method of government bonds, used to pay for the war with France, was abandoned.

Despite the temporary success of Alva's repression, in 1572 a second Dutch rebellion broke out again, this time even more widespread than the first. No longer mainly a religious issue of Inquisition, this second rebellion was a unified revolt for "liberty," supported by many Catholics as well as by Protestants. A group of overseas nobles, who called themselves Sea Beggars, organized themselves into a naval flotilla of pirates and captured strategic islands off the coast in Zeeland and southern Holland. These islands were strategic because they enabled a blockade of international trade to Antwerp, the economic heart of the Spanish Netherlands. One might think that this would not be such a big deal for crack Spanish troops, but these island seizures triggered a forest fire of uprisings of town militia all over the Spanish Netherlands in support of the Beggars. There were too many fires for the Spanish army to deal with all at once. William of Orange also took this opportunity to invade from Germany, with Lutheran financial support. Heroic and mythological stories of founding Dutch nationalism date from this second rebellion: the sieges of Haarlem and Leiden, the bursting of dikes to flood the Spanish, rains from the Almighty to deliver William to save starving Leideners, and so forth.

Ultimately this second rebellion was successful not so much because of the defeat of Spanish troops as because of the loss of revenue to pay for them. Philip II had to declare "bankruptcy"—that is, inability to pay his Antwerp creditors—in 1575. The deciding Battle of Lepanto against the Ottomans, after all, had been in 1571. Simultaneous wars against both the Ottomans and the Dutch were more than even New World treasure could pay for. This bankruptcy led to the mutiny of his troops in 1576, who took out this loss of their pay on wealthy Antwerp creditors through looting, pillaging, and raping (the so-called Spanish Fury). Even Dutch Catholics were outraged. In ignominy, Philip withdrew his troops southward from the Netherlands in order

[54] Lewis 1985; Prestwich 1985; Oberman 2009.
[55] Parker 1977, 119.
[56] Pettegree 1992. Other famous sites were London (Pettegree 1987) and Wesel (Spohnholz 2011).
[57] Pettegree 1987.
[58] Parker [1972] 2004, 119.

to deal with another Calvinist threat: the Saint Bartholomew's Day massacre in France, which led to religious civil war there.

Organizationally, the significant aspect of these dramatic events was the overthrow of regents who had supported the crown and their replacement by patriots. Not all regents were overthrown because many of them had switched sides, and religions, during the revolt. Not all of the new regents were religiously hard core, but all of them were at least nominally Calvinist. Catholic priests and Dutch royalists all left town with the Spanish troops. Catholic nobles and others who had supported the revolt on political grounds were permitted to stay, but they were denuded of their churches. Catholic churches were all turned over to the Calvinists and stripped. Overnight, Calvinism went from being a persecuted "church under the cross" to the official state religion. Many exiles flooded home. Understandably, these tended to be religiously devout.

In terms of social composition, new patriotic regents were more likely to be merchants than were older deposed regents, who had served the Spanish as administrators. Especially in Amsterdam, the center of the Baltic trade, *alteratie* regents were strongly mercantile in occupation, essentially working two jobs at once.[59] The second Dutch Revolt, in other words, did not directly change the political institutions of the Spanish legacy. It more just changed the personnel. The organizational innovation produced by the Dutch Revolt instead was the Dutch Reformed Church.

CALVINIST HOMOLOGY

Despite the close association of Calvinism with Dutch patriotism, only about one-tenth of the Dutch population was Calvinist in 1587.[60] Thirty years later, that percentage had risen to only about 30 percent, even though the Dutch Reformed Church was sponsored by the state.[61] One reason for this restriction in diffusion was that religious Calvinists wanted it that way. Membership had two meanings in Calvinism: the inner sanctum of participation in communion—this was the restricted matter of being among "the elect"—and listening to Sunday sermons, which was open to all. Regulation of publically observed behavioral morality by consistories applied to the first category of membership but not to the second.

There was always a tension between these two definitions of membership. Indeed in the 1610s and 1620s, shortly after the period with which this chapter is concerned, this tension led to the overthrow of the libertine Oldenbarnevelt political regime; this verged on exploding into an intra-Protestant civil war. The rigorist position of hard-core Calvinists emphasized the restricted definition of the elect. The ultimate political implication of this rigorous position was an autonomous state Church, controlled by its elders and ministers, with theocratic veto over everything the state did. The alternative libertine position of Dutch patriots and most regents emphasized the looser definition of Sunday attendance. The political implication of this expansive interpretation of church membership was state appointment of ministers, and integration and social control of the non-Catholic population at large. The libertine approach would have made Calvinism essentially the same thing as Protestantism. That was resisted vigorously by devout refugees, who had laid down their lives.

Within the new Dutch Reformed Church, horizontally aggregative *classes* were centered in cities, and synods followed the provincial boundaries of the Netherlands (except that Holland was split in two). Hence the new Dutch Reformed Church and the new Dutch nation had homologous structures: both were geographical federations. Homology can lead to competition as well as to synergy, as mentioned above. Both tendencies are observable in Dutch history, in oscillatory tension with each other, depending upon how regents and consistories fit together.

Competition between political and religious councils, and hence instability in overall dual federalism, developed when almost all regents were libertine and almost all consistory elders were rigorists. Extreme examples were Leiden,[62] Gouda,[63] and Utrecht,[64] where constitutional struggles over religion continued for decades, but more successfully managed tensions like those were present everywhere. Unity in the shared war against Spain was imperiled by deep division about whether this battle was in the name of

[59] Burke 1974, 26; Israel 1995, 193, 342–43.
[60] Israel 1995, 365; Benedict 2002, 191.
[61] Duke 1985, 109–10; Kaplan 1995, 143; Kooi 2000, 194.
[62] Kooi 2000.
[63] Hibben 1983.
[64] Kaplan 1995.

liberty or of God, and about who controlled the cities if they won.

Synergy between political and religious councils, and hence stability in overall dual federalism, developed when there was considerable overlap in personnel between regents and consistories. Examples of very high overlap were Dordrecht and Amsterdam, where pro-Calvinist factions took over city governments after coups.[65] These cities vigorously supported Calvinist church construction, and their regents granted autonomy to church elders to appoint their own ministers. Because they were largely delegating to themselves, why shouldn't they? Haarlem, Delft, and Rotterdam were examples of moderate overlap.[66] Their regents supported the Reformed Church but in evenhanded ways less likely to stir up sectarian passions.

The organizational reason that director overlap or interlock generated system stability, in my judgment, was the following positive feedback. Political regents were self-recruiting oligarchies. Even after the shock of the Dutch Revolt produced some turnover, these native elites went back to their well-established, self-enclosed ways. For them, tapping into the Dutch Reformed Church offered a powerful channel to populist identification and support, at least among anti-Catholics. Artisans had no direct access to elite regencies. But they had plenty of access to the Dutch Reformed Church, even after it became more oligarchic through director interlock. Like later democratic elections, Calvinism was a framework for making elite control popular and patriotic.

The other half of the feedback was this: Regents pushed back against hard-core Calvinists' inherent tendencies to be religiously exclusive. In exchange for giving all previously Catholic churches to Calvinists, regents insisted that mere attendance at Sunday sermons was enough to qualify for public office. Even more significant, libertine regents pushed, with considerable success, to tolerate the worship of other religions, even the Roman Catholic one, as long as that was done privately in believers' homes. Religious toleration was not sanctioned in law; it was just that regents intentionally did not enforce religious intolerance and persecution. To do that would be to stir up serious public order problems for themselves.

Hence Calvinism gave populist legitimation to closed regent oligarchies, and regents gave (undesired?) extension and oversight of society to the Dutch Reformed Church. Together this horizontal synergy between regents and consistories, when it occurred, locked in the decentralized city foundations of Dutch federalism and thereby inhibited the reenergization of noble hierarchies into absolutism that one sees elsewhere in Europe at this time.

A revealing comparison, which confirms this feedback analysis, is between Dutch Calvinists and French Huguenots.[67] The organizational structures and the social compositions of these two Calvinisms were the same. The difference was that very quickly Calvinism in France articulated with cleavages in the high nobility. This gave a regional inflection to religious struggle and war, which took place between Catholic nobles who dominated in the north and Huguenot nobles who dominated in the south. Huguenot nobles mobilized administrative clientele; as a result, in addition to the usual artisan and merchant social bases, French "Calvinist towns" meant the conversion of hierarchical public officials and lawyers. Noble leadership of Calvinism in France led temporarily to stronger armies, but it also led to weaker federalism. Simultaneously with the Dutch Revolt, Huguenot nobles assembled themselves into a military alliance called the United Provinces of the Midi, based on estate principles. Unlike the United Provinces of the Netherlands, this Huguenot government never had strong foundations in autonomous cities and towns. As will be seen in the next section, military defeat strengthened the resilient inner core of the United Provinces of the Netherlands, whereas it shattered the fragile United Provinces of the Midi.

In the intra-Protestant political crisis in 1619, when Holland Advocate Oldenbarnevelt was overthrown and executed, a Huguenot-like alliance emerged in the Netherlands.[68] Stadholder Maurits reached down to hard-core Calvinists to attack Oldenbarnevelt's political bloc of urban regents. (Amsterdam went with Maurits, which explains this aberration.) After the shock of Oldenbarnevelt's execution, the system gradually returned to its urban-regents foundation, but the incident shows that one needs to be cautious about drawing too sharp a contrast between the

[65] Kooi 2000, 206.
[66] Kooi 2000, 207–8.

[67] This paragraph draws on Prestwich 1985. See also Benedict et al. 1999.
[68] Israel 1995, 421–49.

Netherlands and France. In truth, Calvinism had the Janis-faced capacity to fit in two ways into the politics of the Netherlands—reinforcing urban regents or reinforcing native nobility—depending upon the nature of council overlaps. The causality is not that Calvinism caused Dutch federalism; it is that the decentralized federalism of Calvinism's organizational structure reinforced a decentralized version of Dutch city-based governmental federalism. Without such reinforcement, the contradictory legacies of Spanish imperial administration and medieval parochialism could have tipped in different ways.

MERCHANT DIASPORA

Philip II did not take the loss of his wealthy Spanish Netherlands lying down. As soon as war in the east with the Ottomans calmed down, and as soon as new fleets arrived from the Americas loaded with silver, Philip went back on the attack—this time invading from the south, as an outsider. Except for a Twelve Year Truce between 1609 and 1621, war between the Netherlands and Spain would last continuously for eighty years, until belated recognition of the Netherlands by Spain in 1648. The consequences of this long, drawn-out reinvasion, lasting throughout the late 1570s and 1580s, have already been adumbrated. Southern Spanish Netherlands (today's Belgium) was recaptured, along with major chunks of rural eastern Netherlands. Unconquered "Netherlands" now shrunk essentially to Holland, Utrecht, Zeeland, and Friesland. A major event was the fall of Antwerp in 1585 after a bitter siege of that brief Calvinist government. Huge numbers of refugees fled the avenging Spanish army from the previously prosperous south, leading to the dramatic population swings cited above.[69] This was the second tidal wave of Calvinist refugees produced by the Dutch Revolt.

With mercenaries fighting on the Dutch side as well as the Spanish, and city fortifications to be built, how was the resistance to be paid for? A onetime expropriation of Catholic properties helped. But beyond that, while taxation procedures differed province by province, the Dutch taxed themselves to fight the war at volumes much higher than the Spanish levies. In Holland, for example, regents patriotically (but also regressively) levied heavy sales taxes on their populations—the same thing as Alva's Ten Penny, which had contributed so much to the ruckus in the first place!

But even heavy taxes were not enough, because normal tax revenues came in too slowly to build fortifications and to pay soldiers' wages, neither of which could wait. Hence the Dutch also reverted to their government-bond system of long-term provincial *renten*, which they had invented under the Habsburgs.[70] By buying bonds, citizens voluntarily gave their governments more money, on top of the tax burdens they already bore. Absolutist contemporaries looked on at amazement at the Dutch fiscal system. "What kind of tax system is this? Subjects voluntarily lining up to give us money?" they enviously might have said to themselves. Three prerequisites seem necessary for such a government-bond system to work: money in the pockets of citizens, legitimacy of the government, and investor confidence that interest on the bonds will be paid. Decentralized federalism, where tax collectors, investors, and interest disbursers are all the same, was the secret to the last prerequisite.[71] The system worked so well that the government eventually raised enough money to beat back the Spanish to approximately the current border of Belgium and Netherlands. Amazingly enough, despite the massive fiscal demand, medium- and long-term interest rates remained low: 8 percent on average in the 1590–1600 decade of Netherlands fiscal consolidation, declining to 4–6 percent during the subsequent Golden Age of the seventeenth century.[72]

Calvinism did not produce this fiscal miracle directly. But it lay in the background of each of the three prerequisites. Even the simple matter

[69] Israel (1995, 308) roughly estimates migrants from the south to the north in the range of 100,000 to 150,000. "This was one of the four great west European migrations of early modern times, along with the expulsion of the Jews from Spain (1492), the Protestant exodus from the Habsburg Netherlands in the 1560s, and the flight of the Huguenots from France culminating in the late 1680s" (1995, 308).

[70] Tracy 2009.

[71] For 1628–75 in Amsterdam, 't Hart (2009) has documented that (a) the official receiver of excises and seller of government bonds (the same person) were wealthy merchants and regents themselves, (b) these offices passed down through kinship, and (c) the largest investors in government bonds were also wealthy merchants, frequently even relatives of the receivers. Dutch state receivers, unlike French or English kings, were very unlikely to renege on fiscal obligations to state investors, who were their own elite peers and relatives. The Dutch investing public at large, who did not share close oligarchic connections, nonetheless benefited from the fiscal probity of the system induced by these oligarchic ties.

[72] Dehing and 't Hart 1997, 53; Gelderblom and Jonker 2004, 668.

of money in citizens' pockets was affected by the roughly doubling of population and wealth in Holland as a result of the massive refugee flow of wealthy merchants and hardworking textile artisans from the south. This is why defeat strengthened Dutch federalism.

Southern diaspora, however, was not only to northern Netherlands. Calvinist merchants from the south, who had business ties all over Europe, also fled to the mostly Protestant locations where they had established business connections. Indeed one interesting kinship pattern to this migration was that frequently southern merchant families geographically would split up, with various members of the same family (occasionally with different religions) heading out to different European destinations, to carry on the family business in a more dispersed way.[73] Instead of Antwerp merchants trading with foreign merchants, with either side working on commission, now southern Dutch diaspora families traded internationally within themselves. Northern Dutch diaspora families did likewise, around the Baltic.[74] To some extent, this is a return to the Italian sedentary-merchant organizational form discussed in chapter 5. The difference is that medieval Italian kinship was patrilineal, whereas Dutch kinship was bilateral, where marriage ties counted as much in business partnerships as did natal ties.[75] Hence Italian family businesses at their height were larger than Dutch family businesses.

Bilateral business partnerships also fit in (I won't say which caused which) with sedentary merchant colonies abroad, within which intermarriage was common. Catholic merchants abroad usually had been, and still were, organized into *nazioni* or "nations." These were like guilds, through which native potentates and foreign merchants negotiated rules of conduct, which were administered by merchants through elected consuls. While some core foreign merchants and factors lived abroad permanently, most *nazioni* served as hotels for transient merchants traveling back and forth from home. Spanish and Italian merchants in southern Netherlands had been organized like this.[76] By the simple failure to permit them to live any longer in the country, "fifth columnists" like these Spanish and Italian merchants were prohibited from trade in the new Calvinist Netherlands.

For overseas Dutch merchants, there were no *nazioni* except in Catholic territories. Instead, churches served equivalent community-building functions. Calvinist consistories in the colonies organized religious, sociality, and social-welfare support for their Dutch expatriates, and they also imposed discipline, including over internal business transactions and disputes.[77] The growth of these overseas churches was virtually automatic, once Dutch merchants settled down, because Calvinism had grown up as a refugee church. I hesitate here to ascribe causality uniquely to Calvinism, however, because Mennonite churches in the Baltics,[78] Portuguese Jewish synagogues in Amsterdam,[79] and even a Dutch Catholic church in Livorno[80] may well have operated in similar ways. It would be more accurate to say that religious churches, not Calvinism, provided the community infrastructure to allow Dutch merchant colonies to thrive and reproduce all over Europe. That said, Dutch Reformed churches were the most important factor in stabilizing Dutch merchant colonies abroad and in keeping Dutch expats oriented to their homeland.[81]

ORGANIZATIONAL CONSEQUENCES OF MERCHANT DIASPORA

The world-leading Amsterdam Bourse of the seventeenth century is often described as a transplantation of the previously world-leading Antwerp Bourse of the sixteenth century because of the obvious founding importance of the skills, of the trading networks, and of the financial market brought to Amsterdam by migrating merchants from Antwerp. This is true enough as far as it goes, but transposition was not quite as simple as that. Synthesis of south with north was required. In this section I describe changes in economic organization and international trade wrought within Europe by this transposition. In the next section I describe parallel changes for the organization of trade with the East Indies

[73] Brulez 1959; Schilling 1983, 22–23; van der Laan 1988; Wijnroks 1993; Voss 1995, 49–52.

[74] Van Tielhof 2002, 25–28.

[75] Florentine elite kinship moved in this direction during the Renaissance, as discussed in chapter 6, but never as far as the bilateral Dutch.

[76] Phillips 2000; Fagel 2000; Blondé, Gelderblom, and Sabel 2007.

[77] Pettegree 1986, 195–98.

[78] Sprunger 1995.

[79] Vlessing 1995.

[80] Engels 1997, 131.

[81] Compare the Portuguese tendency of their resident merchants to go native in India.

and the Americas. The joint-stock company and Dutch colonialism emerged out of the latter, but the latter and the former were two sides of the same process of centralizing international trade flows through the Amsterdam entrepôt.

The Dutch Revolt did damage to international trading routes. Spanish and Italian merchants were evicted permanently from the Netherlands. While of course there was always smuggling and indirection, Spain's embargo in the first decade of the seventeenth century cut off Spain from trading with the Netherlands, even through Dutch merchants.[82] Portugal was not at war with the Netherlands, but in 1580 Spain took over Portugal through coercive dynastic absorption. The import of Portuguese spices from the East Indies thereby became imperiled, though the Zeeland sea blockade had stopped that from coming into Antwerp in any event. Portuguese merchants were not verboten like the Spanish and the Italian because most of them were Jews or semiconverted "New Christians," not really Catholics. English woolens imported into Antwerp by English Merchants Adventurers were also blockaded. During the revolt, the English preserved a small outpost in Middleburg, on the Zeeland coast, but mostly they decided to divert their woolen exports around Netherlands into Germany through Hamburg.[83] That new routing stayed, even after the rise of Amsterdam.[84] The previously crucial south German bankers, like the Fuggers, stopped coming to the Netherlands, although that was mostly due to their bankruptcy because of Spanish military overextension. Spanish treasure no longer was shipped directly to the Netherlands, although it still poured into southern territories, through Genoese intermediaries,[85] to pay for Spanish mercenary troops. The Baltic "mother trade" of grain with the north was unaffected by the war. That kept Amsterdam going through tough times. But that trade alone was a far cry from Antwerp in its prime.

In other words, reconstructing the network of international trade within Europe, after the obliteration of its central node, was not straightforward. Amsterdam was not inevitable. Genoa largely did take over in banking. Northern trading routes almost reconsolidated around Hamburg instead of Amsterdam.

As if the magnitude of economic reconstruction was not enough, the problems of social integration in the north of a tidal wave of refugees from the south were not trivial, no matter how much wealth and skills those immigrants brought. The political elite in the north was completely closed to new entries, from their own lower classes, much less to outsiders. Social prejudice against immigrants is probably universal, but northern prejudice against southerners with "Spanish" ways[86] was strong in deeply provincial Netherlands. Netherlanders, both north and south, were used to antagonism with neighboring cities, much less to almost overwhelming migration waves like this. Northern merchants complained about the allegedly unfair trading advantage that southern merchants possessed because of their previous economic connections. Northern textile artisans in Holland complained about skilled southerners taking their jobs. The two communities avoided intermarrying, probably for over a century. Except for the massive Dutch East India Company (to be discussed in the next section), business partnerships (often based on family) were not made between northern natives and southern immigrants. For this mélange to turn collectively into a business juggernaut that could dominate the seventeenth-century world is little short of miraculous.

The institutions that annealed tensions between north and south into complementarity, instead of competition, I argue were three: the Dutch Reformed Church, the Amsterdam Bourse, and Dutch colonialism.

Unlike Weber, I do not argue that Calvinism had direct ideological effects on the development of capitalism. (Italy, after all, evolved capitalism well enough without it.) But I do believe that the Dutch Reformed Church had strong indirect effects on organizations and social networks in the Netherlands, which prepared a fertile soil for commercial capitalism to continue to evolve. The indirect effect of Calvinism on governmental federalism has already been discussed. In addition to that, the Dutch Reformed Church was a shared meeting ground for northerners and southerners to pray together, socialize together, and even govern together. Dutch regencies were closed to southerners, but Dutch consistories were not. Thus to the extent that membership in regencies and consistories overlapped, as it did in healthy lateral-control federalism, Calvinist

[82] Israel 1989, 57.
[83] Ramsay 1986.
[84] Baumann 1990.
[85] Pike 1966.

[86] See the biting contemporary Dutch play *Spanish Brabanter* (Bredero [1617] 1982).

consistories became arenas where native leaders from the north and immigrant leaders from the south converged and negotiated, without regency itself being threatened. Of course such convergence was not trouble free: immigrants from the south were more devout on average than northerners, for obvious selection reasons. But when northerners and southerners were united organizationally within the Dutch Reformed Church, social tolerance of each other, at both leadership and mass levels, could be achieved, even if intermarriage could not.

On the more directly economic front, it is notable that southern and northern merchants did not usually form European partnerships together but that they did converge nonetheless in their respective skill sets. Before the revolt, northern merchants centered in Amsterdam specialized in shipping and in the Baltic bulk trade. Southern merchants centered in Antwerp specialized in the trade of luxury items and in banking. After the revolt, Dutch merchants from the north developed "rich trades" in the Baltics to supplement their preexisting dominance over the bulk trade of grain, salt, and herring.[87] This extension in business almost drove the Hanseatic League out of existence. And Dutch merchants from the south purchased and leased northern-built ships to manage their European trade more directly. While still using overland routes, they became more nautical in their capabilities. An early example of this was the push by southern merchants to Russia northward via the Arctic Ocean, initiated in 1577 and carried to fruition in the 1590s.[88] Southern merchants (*kassiers*) still predominated in private banking, in major part because of their connections with the money market that remained in Antwerp. But Italian bills of exchange and accounting techniques diffused to northerners, supplementing the English-style promissory notes (*letters obligation*) upon which they had relied previously.

The budding Amsterdam Bourse was the main arena in which business skills as well as goods and trading information were exchanged among Dutch merchants of all types: Calvinist merchants as well as merchants from other tolerated religions (i.e., Jews, Mennonites, Lutherans, and even Catholics as long as they were Dutch). Sometimes economists and other social scientists are quick to ascribe the magic of markets as due to "impersonality." In contrast, all of the chapters in this book argue that markets (of various sorts) emerge through orchestrating social networks, not through denying them. Dutch merchants on the Amsterdam Bourse knew very well who each other were; or if they did not, they could easily find a third party to tell them. What was distinctive about the trading networks in the open air of the Amsterdam Bourse was not their impersonality but their publicity. "Self-regulating markets" in this Dutch case did indeed mean the absence of overt government regulation. But Dutch federalism and the Dutch Reformed Church regulated the Bourse not from outside the market but from the insides of the Dutch Calvinist "market makers" who stood at its center, not only as international merchants but also as religious elders and as patriotic regents. This is regulation not in the sense of external law but in the sense of internal discipline.[89] In my account, this discipline was not so much a matter of internalized religious values[90] as it was a matter of being observed in three lateral-control arenas at once. Cheating and opportunism, moreover, are not as devastating for the emergence of markets as prevailing economic theory claims they are. Emergence models like those in chapters 2 and 3 teach us that if autocatalytic networks reproduce powerfully enough in their hypercyclic cores, parasites and free riders on the periphery can merrily exist without disrupting those cores.

All forms of life, including the Amsterdam Bourse, require feeding to survive. The Bourse would not have existed without the merchant colonies, refugee and otherwise, discussed in the last section. Northern and southern merchants avoided other than polite competition with each other in part through geographical (but not activity) specialization. Geographical specialization was not 100 percent, but on average northern merchants remained focused on the profitable Baltics, in particular on Danzig, even as the range of their goods traded expanded to include wine from Atlantic France, spices from the VOC, and timber from Norway to build their ships. Southern merchants imported caviar, furs, and similar goods from Russia, as well as iron, copper, and cannons from Sweden. Southerners traded with the rest of France and dominated the trade to Italy and the Levant.[91] Frankfurt was a major trading outlet to Germany for southerners.[92]

To the extent that trade with Spain continued, that was channeled through southerners. Up until

[87] Israel 1989, 49–52.
[88] Kellenbenz 1973.
[89] Cf. Gorski 2003, especially chap. 2.
[90] After all, only 10–30 percent of the Dutch population was Calvinist, in the sense of consistory-disciplined communion.
[91] Israel 1986, 92; Gelderblom 2003, 271.
[92] Soliday 1974.

1598 and during the Twelve Year Truce (1609–21), this trade was unimpeded on the Spanish end because they needed the grain, ship-making timber, and other products that the Dutch provided. The main difference from pre-revolt days was that instead of Spanish merchants abroad in the Netherlands, this trade was now managed by very vulnerable Dutch merchants in Spain (keeping their religion under wraps). During the years when Spain imposed an embargo on the Netherlands, such trade as survived was funneled through southerners trading with their Catholic merchant friends and relatives on the other side of the Netherlands border.

Portugal's decision to relocate part of its spice trade to Amsterdam was crucial for jump-starting the city into subsequent autocatalysis. Jews, not Calvinists, were the most important intermediaries here. This reconnection of the flow of East Indian spices to northern Europe, while economically rational, was not so much a centralized policy decision by the Portuguese crown (although they had to approve) as it was the movement to Amsterdam of the same Jewish traders who had operated in Antwerp.[93] Prerequisite for this population movement was the religious toleration that Dutch regents had thrust upon their rigorous Calvinist colleagues. Jewish merchants also brokered the importation of sugar from Brazil.

As similar as the Amsterdam entrepôt was to the Antwerp entrepôt—and the similarities are considerable—one huge macroeconomic difference was that international trade in Antwerp was bilateral whereas international trade in Amsterdam became multilateral. That is, in Antwerp, no matter how many foreign countries were co-present, it was always the goods (including money) from merchants of country A being exchanged for the goods (including money) from merchants of country B. In Amsterdam, in contrast, goods coming in from country A were traded internally among Amsterdam merchants and warehouses for who knows what goods from any other country that could then be shipped to country B. Dutch merchants could centrally re-route diverse products thereby to whichever country needed them most at that moment.[94] Multilateral trading was enabled because intermediate supply-chain merchants were almost all Dutch (of both northern and southern varieties). Many economic efficiency consequences flowed from this increased flexibility, including resiliency of the international trading network as a whole to bypass blockages and respond to shocks. As by-products, these efficiency consequences greatly help explain international merchants' lock-in to this new Dutch trading system. But economic consequences, while undoubtedly real, do not explain the causes of their organizational genesis in the first place. These initial causes are rooted in historical recompositions of multiple social networks.

Economic competition between European Dutch colonies and native merchants usually worked out in favor of the Dutch for two reasons: low shipping charges and low interest rates. Freight charges were low because the Dutch developed large, slow, and thinly manned merchant ships (*flutes*), well adapted to the peaceful circumstances of the Baltic.[95] As the need for naval violence increased, such ships would no longer be enough, but their continued existence gave the Dutch a pricing edge. Even more significant was low interest rates. This is where the public-finance reforms, based on decentralized federalism, helped enormously. Public interest rates were low, and private interest rates equilibrated accordingly. Interest-rate charges to overseas Dutch merchants were so low in fact that they could offer to buy locals' products even before the locals had produced them—a forward contract.[96] The anticipation was that Dutch profits in the future, on the basis of sales prices negotiated today, would more than compensate for the precommitment. Permanent residency in locals' cities, so that both sides knew each other well, was a prerequisite for this very modern merchant behavior. The more common form of credit in the older putting-out system had been in reverse: namely commission sales, where producers did not get their money until after the sale of their goods.

Perhaps the most striking of all unanticipated economic consequences of merchant diaspora was balance of payments. Netherlanders ran substantial bullion deficits both in their mother trade with the Baltics and in their East and West Indian colonial trade.[97] In the absence of Antwerp's earlier silver flow from south Germany, where was Amsterdam going to get this bullion,

[93] Swetschinski 2000.

[94] Lesger (2006, 183–211) provides an extensive review of the extant geographical literature on the centralization of international trade in the Amsterdam entrepôt. He usefully critiques the prevailing view of extreme centralization, emphasizing instead the circulation of Amsterdam goods around numerous "gateways" within the Netherlands. This geographical extension does not affect the multilateral trading points made here.

[95] Unger 1978.

[96] Christensen 1941, 392–93.

[97] Attman 1983.

required to pay for these imports? The answer of course was the only place possible—from Spain, their most bitter enemy. In order to pay Spanish troops, American silver poured in to the Spanish Netherlands as fast as the galleys could be unloaded in Seville.[98] Directly this went to the Antwerp money market, of course, not to Amsterdam. But merchant ties between remaining Catholic merchants in Antwerp and their Calvinist brethren in Amsterdam were strong. To the extent that Spanish troops spent their silver in Spanish Netherlands, this silver made its way to the other side of the border. When trade between Spain and Netherlands flowed freely, silver flowed in gushers because of Spanish trade deficits. But even when Spain blockaded direct trade between itself and the Netherlands, the indirect bullion pipeline through Antwerp flowed strongly as needed Dutch goods still went to Spain through various roundabout means.

Spain, in other words, was paying not only for its own army but also, to some extent, for that of its archenemy as well. Military overexpansion, on top of a weak domestic industrial base, burned silver holes in Spain's fiscal pockets. However, Netherlanders never would have been fueled by this Spanish profligacy had it not been for the numerous, cascading organizational innovations triggered by the Dutch Revolt.

DUTCH COLONIALISM AND THE JOINT-STOCK COMPANY

In 1602 the Dutch federalist state created the monopolistic Dutch East India Company (VOC) out of a merger of private *voorcompagnieën* in order to build a trading empire in Indonesia and, not coincidentally, in order to fight the Portuguese, who were now part of Spain. The first stock exchange grew up in a corner of the Amsterdam Bourse around the speculative trading of VOC shares. In 1609 the Dutch state created the public Bank of Amsterdam, which financially cleared all large transactions negotiated in the Bourse. Later in the seventeenth century this central bank also provided financial security to the Dutch government, both domestic and colonial. All of these immensely influential organizational inventions are deeply entrenched in the historiographical lore about "the rise of capitalism." Too often, however, these economic-history accounts are developed teleologically (or even heroically), ripped out from the rich political and social contexts that generated them.

The thesis in this section is that the organizational forms of these path-breaking capitalist innovations were extensions of Dutch federalism into its third pillar. These economic innovations were neither exclusively "public" nor exclusively "private." They occurred in an overlapping zone that challenges our own mental dichotomy between public and private. Driven mostly by Calvinist merchant elites and operating through networks that spanned governments and markets, these organizational innovations came to encompass much of Dutch society.

The push to the Indies was a continuation, albeit a dramatic one, of the Dutch merchant outmigrations already discussed. The first merchant initiatives in this direction, by southerners, were actually through the Arctic Sea, looking for a shortcut. Successful trade with Russia was established, but ice blocked the rest of the way. A Dutch sailor in Portuguese service told his compatriots valuable information about Portuguese navigation routes around Africa, so in 1595 Dutch merchants—sometimes northerners, sometimes southerners—initiated a series of nine exploratory shipping ventures (thirty-eight ships in all) to the East Indies, called *voorcompagnieën*.[99] These were like traditional shipping partnerships on steroids. That is, a set of enterprising merchants pooled their money to buy shares in their joint venture of outfitting, stocking, and perhaps building ships.[100] The distance (hence time to profit) and risk involved in these particular ventures, however, were beyond any of their experiences. They therefore sought to expand capital and diversify their risk by subdividing some of their own shares and selling those to outsider investors whom they knew. Thus arose a two-level partnership structure: directors who were the original entrepreneurs and passive "participants" who were uninvolved in company policy or decision making. Although this was new to the Netherlands, Italian *accomandite* partnerships also had had "silent" investors. Upon conclusion of their convoy voyage and distribution of the profits, these two-level partnerships were to be liquidated.

Governments did not initiate these exploration ventures, but they were not exactly passive observers either. Knowing that the Portuguese were out there, city governments where

[98] Parker [1972] 2004, 118–32, 257–60.

[99] Bruijn, Gaastra, and Schöffer 1987, 1–6.

[100] Riemersma 1952.

merchants resided subsidized the outfitting of their merchants' ships with defensive cannon. Over the short period of 1595 to 1602, three ventures from Amsterdam formed (one composed of native merchants and two composed of merchants of southern origins), two ventures from Middleburg sailed forth (one of northerners and one of southerners), and two ventures from Rotterdam went out (one northern and one southern). Intracity mergers orchestrated by burgomasters consolidated the *voorcompagnieën* in Amsterdam and Middleburg. Not all of these "private" partnerships were commercially successful, but the ones that were triggered a sensation upon their long delayed but richly laden returns.

The Dutch East India Company was a contentiously negotiated merger of all these *voorcompagnieën* partnerships, painstakingly orchestrated by the Advocate of Holland, Johan Oldenbarnevelt (later to be executed for insufficient Calvinist rigorism).[101] Reflecting the rivalries of the cities in which they were born, the respective *voorcompagnieën* were extremely competitive with each other in a potentially massively profitable race for East Indies loot. How could private competitors like that be induced to cooperate? The economic benefit of stabilizing crippling price competition was an argument based on private interest that Oldenbarnevelt made to the partnership directors over and over again. But everyone also realized that the Portuguese were not going to roll over and play dead. And everyone knew that Portuguese Jews were a very weak reed upon which to lean for maintaining spice imports from the east. If Amsterdam were to go beyond merely blockading Antwerp to irrevocably supplanting Antwerp, then direct contact with the East Indies was vital. *Voorcompagnieën* merchants thought primarily in terms of domestic economic monopoly; government officials thought primarily in terms of military and economic war; but each side understood well the other's compatible point of view.

Through this merger deal, the organizational structure of the budding Dutch East India Company became a reflection of Dutch provincial federalism. The six cities of Amsterdam, Middleburg, Rotterdam, Delft, Hoorn, and Enkhuizen became chambers in the contractual Dutch East India trading company. The aggregated VOC in turn became essentially a new governmental province: the colonial province of Indonesia (called Batavia by the Dutch, in honor of their mythical past).[102] In the federated United Provinces of the Netherlands, this ambiguity between public and private was not as radical an idea as it might sound to modern ears, which are more accustomed to the unified sovereignty of the nation-state. Directors of *voorcompagnieën* became the first directors of their respective VOC chambers. Silent-partner "participants" became shareholders in their city's chambers, which maintained legal autonomy for profit-disbursement purposes. An overarching board of VOC directors, drawn from the chamber directors and called the Heren Zeventien, made operational policy and supervised the entire ensemble.[103] This board mimicked a Dutch provincial Estate in the sense that top directors were drawn from chamber directors according to strict and fixed corporate ratios and that they were accountable to direction from those chambers. Silent stockholders owned shares in the VOC similar to the way in which *renten* government-bond holders owned shares in their local governments. Over time even the oligarchic self-recruitment of regents insinuated itself into governing boards of the VOC because city regents, not silent shareholders, appointed replacements (including themselves, if they owned enough stock) to vacated director positions in "their" chambers. The same Dutch federalist system of overlapping memberships for coordinating regents and Calvinist consistories reproduced itself within the councils of the Dutch joint-stock company. The organizational structure of the first "private" joint-stock company, in other words, was a projection of "governmental" Dutch federalism.[104]

Company stocks were like government bonds in another respect: they were both transferrable and salable on a secondary market. Secondary markets in fixed-interest government bonds, but not in company shares, had a long history in Italy. Organizationally so similar, both VOC stocks and government bonds were traded in the

[101] Den Tex 1973, 301–13. "[Oldenbarnevelt] looked upon [his own personal investment of 5,000 guilders] more as a contribution to a good cause, that of harming Spain, with the added bonus of a possible profit. For that time it was a good forecast. In the first few years dividends did not by any means come up to expectations. Oldenbarnevelt's creation, later to be the basis of fabulous wealth, was for the time what he intended it to be: an act of war" (313).

[102] Gorski 2000.

[103] Bruijn, Gaastra, and Schöffer 1987, 6–21; de Vries and van der Woude 1997, 382–96.

[104] "Governmental" is in quotes because Dutch federalism itself had a large component of private ownership through bonds, as explained above.

physically open marketplace of the Amsterdam Bourse just like any other commodity. Transfers in ownership were registered in the accounts of the issuing institutions, located virtually next door. One big difference between stocks and bonds, though, was that VOC shares were highly uncertain in their rates of return, whereas Dutch government bonds were reliable and boring in their low interest rates. As a result, the speculative secondary market in VOC shares boomed in a way that it never did for bonds.[105] Especially as shares became subdivided into smaller and smaller fractions by previous owners, the general Dutch public became swept up in a speculative fever. "Tulip mania" was the famous and rather bizarre by-product of this first mass exposure to the speculative stock market.[106]

This was economic invention to be sure, but viewing the Dutch East India Company as the political organization that it also was generates a different perspective on its functioning within Dutch society. Like the Dutch Reformed Church, the Dutch East India Company included within itself—both at the elite level of controlling merchants and at the mass level of enthusiastic "participants"—both natives from Holland and immigrants from the south. Both contentious sides came together within this federalist ensemble to make Asian colonialism. The title of this chapter—"Country as Global Market"—is not just a metaphor. International trade, and in particular colonialism in both Europe and Asia, stapled together disparate and contentious peoples into a single nation, which attained not exactly unity but synergy among its mosaic parts. Tripartite federalism—that is, the interlinking of three homologous federalisms—was the real multiple-network, systems-level invention of the Dutch. The stock market, the joint-stock company, governmental federalism, and the Dutch Reformed Church were all brilliant refractions of that.

The Dutch domestic system had implications for the structure of Dutch colonialism in Asia. The Portuguese had organized their spice trade through private contractors answerable to state administrative viceroys—a naval version of the conquistador system in the Spanish Americas. The Portuguese government itself did not trade; it provided military coercion to impose forts for its own merchants and to extract customs and tolls from Asian merchants.[107] One problem with this system was that Portuguese private contractors often married locals and went native. Another problem was that all the economic emphasis was on bilateral trade with the homeland. Profits from Asian spices were plenty high this way, but the demand for bullion flowing back was insatiable.

The Dutch system of integrating trade and military into the same decentralized and modular organization, in contrast, placed pressure on overseas agents to fund their own coercion. The famous (or infamous, depending upon your politics) VOC Indonesia manager Jan Pieterszoon Coen responded to this by maneuvering the VOC into the same brokerage position within East Indian trade that the Dutch held within Europe.[108] The VOC entered already well-established intra-Asian trading routes,[109] for example, bringing cottons from India to pay for Indonesian spices instead of using Dutch bullion. Trade with China, to take another example, was used to get silver out of Japan for use in India and elsewhere. Coen also strongly urged the construction of Dutch merchant colonies in Batavia, just like in Europe, although in this case it took the socially conservative Heren Zeventien a while to come around to his idea of importing Dutch women. One unfortunate way that Coen's rigorous Calvinism manifested itself in East Asia was that if he decided that locals were not fellow merchants but cheats, he was inclined to slaughter them and take over their spice islands.[110] Good local merchants, on the other hand, he treated like good local merchants. In his mind, it was the Portuguese and later the English, not the locals, who were the really intractable enemies.

I close with the last big organizational invention of the Dutch Revolt: the establishment of the public Bank of Amsterdam in 1609. Merchants operating on the Antwerp Bourse had financially cleared their transactions through a system of private exchange bankers (*kassiers*), not dissimilar to Florentine domestic *cambio* bankers. These were guildsmen of deposit bankers who manually offset accounts of their customers in the account books of themselves—sort of that day's electronic transfer. These privatized

[105] Neal 1990; Dehing and 't Hart 1997, 53–56; Gelderblom and Jonker 2004. The original, contemporary description of the Amsterdam stock market was de la Vega [1688] 1957.

[106] Goldgar 2007. Compare Andrew Spicer's examination of the Russian stock markets under Yeltsin, in chapter 10 of this volume.

[107] Steensgaard 1973, 60–113; Newitt 2005.

[108] Masselman 1963, 401.

[109] Meilink-Roelofsz 1963; Prakash 1998.

[110] Masselman 1963, 415–23.

Antwerp exchange bankers were technically quite sophisticated, evolving even the innovation of negotiable ("payable to bearer") promissory notes, which was a credit instrument beyond what even the Florentines had attained.[111] Many Antwerp *kassiers* moved from Antwerp to Amsterdam during the diaspora, along with so many of their peers. Since they could handle the banking business of the Amsterdam Bourse, there was not an obvious economic reason for replacing them, apart from some unsubstantiated fear of system collapse.[112] The archival record is apparently not clear about exactly who pushed for their substitution by a single state bank.[113] Genoa and Venice had such large and centralized state banks, which "many merchants" admired. And being southerners without integration into Amsterdam centers of power, they were politically vulnerable. My hypothesis is that the Bank of Amsterdam was simply a logical continuation of what Dutch regents were doing on other organizational fronts. The Bank of Amsterdam was a board of important Bourse merchants, appointed by Amsterdam regents, who demanded that all Bourse-negotiated bills of exchange and transactions over a certain size be cleared through accounts centrally monitored and observable by them. To call this a consistory of the Amsterdam Bourse is maybe pushing it a little. But transparent, disciplinary councils, which observe and intermediate between what others are doing, seem deeply built into the recently evolved Dutch relational genes.

Alternative explanations are not that plausible. Bullion deposits had to be large enough to fully back large transactions. Hence credit through overdrafts, like the Florentines did credit, was not the founding reason. Public finance, the primary reason for founding the Bank of England eighty years later, was marginal to the operation of the Bank of Amsterdam. Dutch public finance was in amazingly good shape even without a central bank. Because of its extremely conservative reserve policy, bullion from the Spanish New World kept piling up in the vaults of the Bank of Amsterdam. Seventy years later, when the French invaded and almost won, there was a run on the bank, but it did not collapse. This financial stability was important in sustaining a war effort in hard times. But consequentialist foresight of this temporal depth strains cognitive credulity. It is more consistent with contemporaneous context to say simply that the central Bank of Amsterdam was a consistory of the Amsterdam Bourse, which observed and enforced how all good Dutch merchants related to each other.

This combination of colonialist joint-stock company, Amsterdam Bourse, and Bank of Amsterdam economically knitted together northern native merchants and southern immigrant merchants into making a new country. In the domain of politics, southerners were not admitted into the running of the federalist state. In the domain of kinship, southerners did not often marry into or form family business partnerships with northerners. But in the "weak-tie" domain of economics and markets, southerners and northerners invested together and traded with each other, and they did so intensively. In the initial 1602 stock offering of 3.67 million guilders in the Amsterdam chamber of the VOC, 26.3 percent of the investors and 38.1 percent of the investments were made by southerners. Conversely, 68.7 percent of the investors and 55.1 percent of the investments were made by northerners, the left over by foreigners.[114] And in the Amsterdam Exchange Bank in 1609, 36.1 percent of the accounts and 44.6 percent of the capital turnover was held by southerners; 3.0 percent of the accounts and 2.1 percent of the turnover was held by Portuguese Jews; and the rest (61 percent and 53.3 percent, respectively) was held essentially by northerners.[115] These banking accounts encompassed all of the large-scale international-goods trading on the Amsterdam Bourse. For the somewhat later West Indies Company of 1622, the relative weight of southerners is even higher.[116] If not a seamless web, this is at least a very complementary mosaic.

While cleaved in politics and kinship, the Dutch northern and southern populations thus were bridged through economic markets. Hot-button religion could flip-flop tensions, injecting creative instability into the system, but more often than not Calvinism served to blend, more

[111] Van der Wee 1963, 333–68; van der Wee 1977, 322–32.

[112] There had been a collapse of domestic banking in Bruges in the late 1400s, but that was a hundred years before. De Roover 1948, 339–41; van der Wee 1963, 105–12.

[113] Van Dillen 1934, 79.

[114] Van Dillen 1958, 55.

[115] Lesger 2006, 155. By 1611 the southern percentages had climbed to 36.6 percent of accounts and 49.9 percent of capital turnover.

[116] According to van Hoboken (1960, 51), out of "the first twenty directors in 1622, it appears that ten of them were South Netherlanders, six were Counter-Remonstrant [Amsterdam] regents, two Remonstrant regents and two of unknown affiliation. . . . Applying the same computation for the whole list [of 66 directors] from 1622 to 1636, the result is: 33 South Netherlanders, 10 Counter-Remonstrant regents, 3 Remonstrant regents and 20 of unknown affiliation."

than segregate, migrants with natives. The organizational inventions of joint-stock company, stock market, central bank, governmental federalism, and the Dutch Reformed Church all emerged out of the amazingly creative Dutch Revolt. But even more than that, Netherlands itself as a country emerged from the confluence of geographically fluid Calvinism with geographically fluid international trade: a vortex annealed into balanced coherence through lateral control.

CONCLUSION

The spillover of organizational inventions from one domain to another is dramatic in this Dutch Revolt case—the federalism of a new nation, the establishment of rigorist Protestant Church, and the invention of three new economic organizational forms: the joint-stock company, the stock market, and the central bank. This multidomain amalgam, which I have dubbed "tripartite federalism," was neither state nor market but a curiously dynamic hybrid institutional form that sustained its life not by sending armies out to conquer land but by sending businessmen out to conquer economic trade, both within Europe and overseas. Each of these organizational inventions—so influential for later Western economic and political development—subsequently had its own history. But the organizational-genesis question posed by this case is, what led to the cascading of inventions, with each invention triggering and reinforcing the others? In mini-Cambrian explosions like this, economic, political, and religious histories do not appear in neat little piles, conveniently laid out for our contemporary disciplines, but rather all twisted and tangled together.

The answer found in this case is "migration and homology." Inventions cascaded from one domain to another, feeding back to reinforce all of them, because there was a homology of federalist organizational forms to be found in politics and in religion, and eventually in economics, that shaped the networks through which mobilization flowed. There were other networks in the Netherlands, of course, but as the tumultuous wars of the Dutch Revolt unfolded, rising parallel federalisms reinforced each other in powerful multiple autocatalyses that washed out (or at least diminished) ragged organizational alternatives like theocracy and nobility. At the beginning, there was no logical connection between tax revolt and Calvinism, except that Phillip II saw them as linked due to the georeligious contexts that pressed in upon him. In this sense, Phillip II of Spain created the distinctive Dutch organizational fusion of politics and religion as much as did the Dutch themselves. But such an accurate but proximate explanation misses the deeper histories that molded Dutch response. The Dutch federalism that rose up in rebellion against Spain was the temporal overlay of a deep history of economically vibrant medieval towns, with a middle history of early modern Spanish administration, with a recent history of tax resistance and reform. Most of the oligarchic Dutch city regents, who had been created by Phillip, turned against him when he launched an Inquisition upon them. Calvinism stepped in as the populist side of a revolt, with conservative regents as the more moderate leaders. Dutch federalism was the organizational body of the Spanish king with its head and its soul expunged.

In this chapter I have emphasized that federalist homology between oligarchic regents and fire-breathing Calvinist consistories was not achieved smoothly. The two overlapping populations struggled for control, as much as cooperated, whenever the Spanish peril was not imminent. Homology can lead to competition as easily as to symbiosis. It took massive migration to anneal the two prickly sides together. In part, northerners and immigrant southerners negotiated their détentes parish by parish, in the bowels of the Dutch Reformed Church. More consequentially they negotiated that in markets, as southern traders and financiers cooperated, and eventually merged, with northern traders and shippers. Markets were useful for solving problems in politics and religion, as well as in economics.

As chain-mail overlap between political regencies and religious consistories developed, with merchants playing the most active roles as brokers, Dutch republicanism became mercantile republicanism in its elite sinews. Calvinist diaspora had placed religious but financially and commercially sophisticated Protestant merchants from southern Netherlands all over Europe. These would become the foundation for a new entrepôt for the distribution through Europe of colonial wealth. Once the Amsterdam Bourse developed to supplant the Antwerp Bourse, economic autocatalysis became added to an already potent political-religious mix. To put a complex causal sequence simply, in order to make a point, the Dutch state pushed out into colonialism because southern Calvinist merchants had been pushed out into diaspora. Markets are as much the restructuring of biographies as they are the restructuring of trade.

Given this underlying impetus or flow, moreover, the exact organizational content of the new economic inventions followed directly from the federalist structures that spawned them: The divisional structure of the Dutch East India Company followed the pattern of Dutch provincial estates. The VOC board of directors was like a city council, and the directors themselves were regents for Indonesia. Company stocks were like government bonds, owned by wealthy and the public alike; both traded on secondary markets within the Amsterdam Bourse. The central bank was the consistory of the Bourse. All of these are major inventions in the history of economics. But they also directly reflect the noneconomic circumstances and context of their emergence. In chapter 2, I ended by saying, "Invention never eliminates the past; it rewires it. New life forms are a by-product of that." While true in general, the point seems especially pertinent in the case of the birth of the joint-stock company and stock market in the Netherlands.

REFERENCES

Adams, Julia. 2005. *The Familial State: Ruling Families and Merchant Capitalism in Early Modern Europe*. Ithaca: Cornell University Press.

Attman, Artur. 1983. *Dutch Enterprise in the World Bullion Trade, 1550–1800*. Göteborg: Kungl. Vetenskaps- och Vitterhets-Samhället.

Baumann, Wolf-Rüdiger. 1990. *The Merchants Adventurers and the Continental Cloth-Trade (1560s–1620s)*. Berlin: de Gruyter.

Benedict, Philip. 2002. *Christ's Churches Purely Reformed: A Social History of Calvinism*. New Haven: Yale University Press.

Benedict, Philip, Guido Marnef, Henk van Nierop, and Marc Venard, eds. 1999. *Reformation, Revolt and Civil War in France and the Netherlands 1555–1585*. Amsterdam: Royal Netherlands Academy of Arts and Sciences.

Blockmans, Wim, and Walter Prevenier. 1999. *The Low Countries under Burgundy Rule, 1369–1530*. Philadelphia: University of Pennsylvania Press.

Blondé, Bruno, Oscar Gelderblom, and Peter Sabel. 2007. "Foreign Merchant Communities in Bruges, Antwerp and Amsterdam, c. 1350–1650." In *Cultural Exchange in Early Modern Europe*. Vol. 2, *Cities and Cultural Exchange in Europe, 1400–1700*, ed. Donatella Calabi and Stephen Turk Christensen, 154–74. Cambridge: Cambridge University Press.

Bogucka, Maria. 1990. "Dutch Merchants' Activities in Gdansk in the First Half of the 17th Century." In *Baltic Affairs: Relations between the Netherlands and North-Eastern Europe, 1500–1800*, ed. J.Ph.S. Lemmink and J.S.A.M. van Koningsbrugge, 19–32. Nijmegen: Institute for Northern and Eastern European Studies.

Bredero, Gerbrand A. [1617] 1982. *The Spanish Brabanter*. Binghamton, NY: Medieval and Renaissance Texts and Studies.

Brenner, Robert. 1993. *Merchants and Revolution: Commercial Change, Political Conflict, and London's Overseas Traders, 1550–1653*. Princeton: Princeton University Press.

Bruijn, J. R., F. S. Gaastra, and I. Schöffer. 1987. *Dutch-Asiatic Shipping in the 17th and 18th Centuries*. The Hague: Nijhoff.

Brulez, Wilfred. 1959. *De firma della Faille en de international handel van vlaamse firma's in de 16e eeuw*. Brussels: Paleis der Academiën.

———. 1970. "The Balance of Trade of the Netherlands in the Middle of the 16th Century." *Acta Historiae Neerlandica* 4:20–48.

Burke, Peter. 1974. *Venice and Amsterdam: A Study of Seventeenth-Century Elites*. London: Temple Smith.

Christensen, Aksel E. 1941. *Dutch Trade to the Baltic about 1600*. Copenhagen: Munksgaard.

Collins, J. B. 1984. "The Role of Atlantic France in Baltic Trade: Dutch Traders and Polish Grain at Nantes, 1625–1675." *Journal of European Economic History* 13:239–89.

Dehing, Pit, and Marjolein 't Hart. 1997. "Linking the Fortunes: Currency and Banking, 1550–1800." In *A Financial History of the Netherlands*, ed. Marjolein 't Hart, Joost Jonker, and Jan Luiten van Zanden, 37–63. Cambridge: Cambridge University Press.

de la Vega, Joseph. [1688] 1957.*Confusion de confusions*. Boston: Harvard Graduate School of Business.

den Tex, Jan. 1973. *Oldenbarnevelt*. Vol. 1, *1547–1606*. Cambridge: Cambridge University Press.

de Roover, Raymond. 1948. *Money, Banking and Credit in Medieval Bruges*. Cambridge, MA: Medieval Academy of America.

De Vries, Jan. 1984. *European Urbanization, 1500–1800*. Cambridge, MA: Harvard University Press.

De Vries, Jan, and Ad van der Woude. 1997. *The First Modern Economy: Success, Failure and Perseverance of the Dutch Economy, 1500–1815*. Cambridge: Cambridge University Press.

Dietz, Brian. 1978. "Antwerp and London: The Structure and Balance of Trade in the 1560s." In *Wealth and Power in Tudor England*, ed. E. E. Ives, R. J. Knecht, and J. J. Scarisbrick, 186–203. London: Athlone Press.

Duke, Alastair. 1985. "The Ambivalent Face of Calvinism in the Netherlands, 1561–1618." In *International Calvinism, 1541–1715*, ed. Menna Prestwich, 109–34. Oxford: Clarendon Press.

Edler, Florence. 1938. "The Van der Molen, Commission Merchants of Antwerp: Trade with Italy, 1538–44." In *Medieval and Historiographical*

Essays in Honor of James Westfall Thompson, ed. James Lea Cate and Eugene N. Anderson, 78–145. Chicago: University of Chicago Press.

Ehrenberg, Richard. 1928. *Capital and Finance in the Age of the Renaissance: A Study of the Fuggers and Their Connections*. New York: Harcourt, Brace and Company.

Engels, Marie-Christine. 1997. *Merchants, Interlopers, Seamen and Corsairs: The "Flemish" Community in Livorno and Genoa (1615–1635)*. Hilversum: Verloren.

Evans-Pritchard, E. E. 1940. *The Nuer*. Oxford: Clarendon Press.

Fagel, Raymond. 2000. "Spanish Merchants in the Low Countries: Stabilitas Loci or Peregrinato?" In *International Trade in the Low Countries (14th–16th Centuries)*, ed. Peter Sabel, Bruno Blonde, and Anke Greve, 87–104. Leuven-Apeldoorn: Garant.

Gelderblom, Oscar C. 2003. "From Antwerp to Amsterdam: The Contribution of Merchants from the Southern Netherlands to the Commercial Expansion of Amsterdam (c. 1540–1609)." *Review of the Fernand Braudel Center* 3:247–82.

Gelderblom, Oscar, and Joost Jonker. 2004. "Completing a Financial Revolution: The Finance of the Dutch East India Company and the Rise of the Amsterdam Capital Market, 1595–1612." *Journal of Economic History* 64:641–72.

Goldgar, Anne. 2007. *Tulipmania: Money, Honor and Knowledge in the Dutch Golden Age*. Chicago: University of Chicago Press.

Goris, J. A. 1925. *Étude sur les colonies marchandes méridionales (Portugais, Espagnols, Italiens) à Avers de 1488 à 1567*. Louvain: Librairie Universitaire.

Gorski, Philip S. 2000. "The Mosaic Moment: An Early Modernist Critique of Modernist Theories of Nationalism." *American Journal of Sociology* 105:1428–68.

———. 2003. *The Disciplinary Revolution: Calvinism and the Rise of the State in Early Modern Europe*. Chicago: University of Chicago Press.

Grell, Ole Peter. 1989. *Dutch Calvinists in Early Stuart London: The Dutch Church in Ausin Friars, 1603–1642*. Leiden: Brill.

Hamilton, Earl J. 1970. *American Treasure and the Price Revolution in Spain, 1501–1650*. New York: Octagon Books.

Harreld, Donald J. 2004. *High Germans in the Low Countries: German Merchants and Commerce in Golden Age Antwerp*. Leiden: Brill.

Hart, Marjolein 't. 2009. "Mutual Advantages: State Bankers as Brokers between the City of Amsterdam and the Dutch Republic." In *The Political Economy of the Dutch Republic*, ed. Oscar Gelderblom, 115–42. Surrey: Ashgate.

Heere, Franz. 2009. *The Life and Times of the Fuggers*. Augsburg, Germany: Wißner-Verlag.

Hibben, C. C. 1983. *Gouda in Revolt: Particularism and Pacifism in the Revolt of the Netherlands, 1572–1588*. Utrecht: HES Publishers.

Israel, Jonathan I. 1986. "The Dutch Merchant Colonies in the Mediterranean during the Seventeenth Century." *Renaissance and Modern Studies* 30:87–108.

———. 1989. *Dutch Primacy in World Trade, 1585–1740*. Oxford: Clarendon Press.

———. 1995. *The Dutch Republic: Its Rise, Greatness, and Fall, 1477–1806*. Oxford: Clarendon Press.

Kaplan, Benjamin J. 1995. *Calvinists and Libertines: Confession and Community in Utrecht 1578–1620*. Oxford: Clarendon Press.

Kellenbenz, Hermann. 1973. "The Economic Significance of the Archangel Route (from the Late 16th to the Late 18th Century)." *Journal of European Economic History* 2:541–81.

Kooi, Christine. 2000. *Liberty and Religion: Church and State in Leiden's Reformation, 1572–1620*. Leiden: Brill.

Lesger, Clé. 2006. *The Rise of the Amsterdam Market and Information Exchange: Merchants, Commercial Expansion and Change in the Spatial Economy of the Low Countries c. 1550–1630*. Aldershot, UK: Ashgate.

Lewis, Gillian. 1985. "Calvinism in Geneva in the Time of Calvin and Beza, 1541–1608." In *International Calvinism, 1541–1715*, ed. Menna Prestwich, 39–70. Oxford: Clarendon Press.

Lindblad, J. Thomas. 1995. "Louis de Geer (1587–1652): Dutch Entrepreneur and the Father of Swedish Industry." In *Entrepreneurs and Entrepreneurship in Early Modern Times: Merchants and Industrialists within the Orbit of the Dutch Staple Market*, ed. C. Lesger and L. Noordegraaf, 77–84. Den Haag: Stichting Hollandse Historische Reeks.

Lubimenko, Madame Inna. 1924. "The Struggle of the Dutch with the English for the Russian Market in the Seventeenth Century." *Transactions of the Royal Historical Society*, 4th ser., 7:27–51.

Marnef, Guido. 1996. *Antwerp in the Age of Reformation: Underground Protestantism in a Commercial Metropolis, 1550–1577*. Baltimore: Johns Hopkins University Press.

Masselman, George. 1963. *The Cradle of Colonialism*. New Haven: Yale University Press.

Meilink-Roelofsz, M.A.P. 1963. *Asian Trade and European Influence in the Indonesian Archipelago between 1500 and about 1630*. The Hague: Nijhoff.

Mitchell, David M. 1995. "'It will be easy to make money': Merchant Strangers in London, 1580–1680." In *Entrepreneurs and Entrepreneurship in Early Modern Times: Merchants and Industrialists within the Orbit of the Dutch Staple Market*, ed. C. Lesger and L. Noordegraaf, 119–46. Den Haag: Stichting Hollandse Historische Reeks.

Müeller, Leos. 1998. *The Merchant Houses of Stockholm, c. 1640–1800: A Comparative Study of Early-Modern Entrepreneurial Behavior*. Uppsala: Studia Historica Upsaliensia 188.

Neal, Larry. 1990. *The Rise of Financial Capitalism: International Capital Markets in the Age of Reason*. Cambridge: Cambridge University Press.

Newitt, Malyn. 2005. *A History of Portuguese Overseas Expansion, 1400–1668*. London: Routledge.

Oberman, Heiko A. 2009. *John Calvin and the Reformation of the Refugees*. Geneva: Librairie Droz.

Parker, Geoffrey. 1977. *The Dutch Revolt*. Ithaca: Cornell University Press.

———. 1988. *The Military Revolution: Military Innovation and the Rise of the West, 1500–1800*. Cambridge: Cambridge University Press.

———. [1972] 2004. *The Army of Flanders and the Spanish Road, 1567–1659*. Cambridge: Cambridge University Press.

Pettegree, Andrew. 1986. *Foreign Protestant Communities in Seventeenth-Century London*. Oxford: Clarendon Press.

———. 1987. "The Exile Churches and the Churches 'Under the Cross': Antwerp and Emden during the Dutch Revolt." *Journal of Ecclesiastical History* 38:187–209.

———. 1992. *Emden and the Dutch Revolt: Exile and the Development of Reformed Protestantism*. Oxford: Clarendon Press.

Phillips, Carla Rahn. 1983. "Spanish Merchants and the Wool Trade in the Sixteenth Century." *Seventeenth Century Journal* 14:259–82.

Phillips, William D. 2000. "Merchants of the Fleece: Castilians in Bruges and the Wool Trade." In *International Trade in the Low Countries (14th–16th Centuries)*, ed. Peter Sabel, Bruno Blonde, and Anke Greve, 75–85. Leuven-Apeldoorn: Garant.

Pike, Ruth. 1966. *Enterprise and Adventure: The Genoese in Seville and the Opening of the New World*. Ithaca: Cornell University Press.

Prakash, Om. 1998. *The New Cambridge History of India*. Vol. 2, *European Commercial Enterprise in Pre-colonial India*. Cambridge: Cambridge University Press.

Prestwich, Menna. 1985. "Calvinism in France, 1559–1629." In *International Calvinism, 1541–1715*, ed. Menna Prestwich, 71–108. Oxford: Clarendon Press.

Ramsay, G. D. 1986. *The Queen's Merchants and the Revolt of the Netherlands*. Manchester: Manchester University Press.

Richards, Michael. 1967. "The Military Revolution, 1560–1660." In *Essays in Swedish History*, 195–225. Minneapolis: University of Minnesota Press.

Riemersma, Jelle C. 1952. "Trading and Shipping Associations in 16th Century Holland." *Tijdschrift voor Geschiedenis* 65:330–38.

Rogers, Clifford J., ed. 1995. *The Military Revolution Debate*. Boulder, CO: Westview Press.

Schilling, Heinz. 1983. "Innovation through Migration: The Settlements of Calvinist Netherlanders in Sixteenth- and Seventeenth-Century Central and Western Europe." *Social History* 16:7–33.

Smolar, Frank J. 1965. "Resiliency of Enterprise: Economic Crises and Recovery in the Southern Netherlands in the Early Seventeenth Century." In *From the Renaissance to the Counter-Reformation: Essays in honor of Garrett Mattingly*, 247–68. New York: Random House.

Soliday, Gerald Lymam. 1974. *A Community in Conflict: Frankfurt Society in the Seventeenth and Early Eighteenth Centuries*. Hanover, NH: Brandeis University Press.

Spohnholz, Jesse. 2011. *The Tactics of Toleration: A Refugee Community in the Age of Religious Wars*. Newark: University of Delaware Press.

Sprunger, Mary. 1995. "Entrepreneurs and Ethics: Mennonite Merchants in Seventeenth-Century Amsterdam." In *Entrepreneurs and Entrepreneurship in Early Modern Times: Merchants and Industrialists within the Orbit of the Dutch Staple Market*, ed. C. Lesger and L. Noordegraaf, 213–21. Der Haag: Stichting Hollandse Historische Reeks.

Spufford, Peter. 1995. "Access to Credit and Capital in the Commercial Centers of Europe." In *A Miracle Mirrored: The Dutch Republic in European Perspective*, ed. Karel Davids and Jan Lucassen, 303–37. Cambridge: Cambridge University Press.

Stabel, Peter, Bruno Blondé, and Anke Greve, eds. 2000. *International Trade in the Low Countries (14th–16th Centuries): Merchants, Organisation, Infrastructure*. Louvain, Belgium: Garant.

Steensgaard, Niels. 1973. *The Asian Trade Revolution of the Seventeenth Century: The East India Companies and the Decline of the Caravan Trade*. Chicago: University of Chicago Press.

Subacchi, Paola. 1995. "Italians in Antwerp in the Second half of the Sixteenth Century." In *Minderheden in Westeuropese steden (16de—20ste eeuw)*, ed. Hugo Soly and Alfons K. L. Thijs, 73–90. Brussels: Institut Historique Belge de Rome.

Swetschinski, Daniel M. 2000. *Reluctant Cosmopolitans: The Portuguese Jews of Seventeenth-Century Amsterdam*. London: Littman Library of Jewish Civilization.

Tracy, James D. 1985. *A Financial Revolution in the Habsburg Netherlands: Renten and Renteniers in the County of Holland, 1515–1565*. Berkeley: University of California Press.

———. 1990. *Holland under Habsburg Rule, 1506–1566*. Berkeley: University of California Press.

———. 2009. "Holland's New Fiscal Regime, 1572–1576." In *The Political Economy of the Dutch Republic*, ed. Oscar Gelderblom, 41–54. Surrey: Ashgate.

Unger, R. W. 1978. *Dutch Shipbuilding before 1800*. Assen: Van Gorcum.

van der Laan, P.H.J. 1988. "The Poulle Brothers of Amsterdam and the North Sea and Baltic trade, 1590–1620." In *From Dunkirk to Danzig: Shipping and Trade in the North Sea and the Baltic, 1350–1850*, ed. W. G. Heeres, L.M.J.B. Hesp, L. Noordegraaf, and R.C.W. van der Voort, 317–30. Hilversum: Verloren.

van der Meiden, G. W. 1993. "Isaac Massa and the Beginnings of Dutch-Russian Relations." In *Russians and Dutchmen*, ed. J. Braat, A. H. Huussenjr,

B. Naarden, and C.A.L.M. Willemsen, 27–40. Groningen: Institute for Northern and Eastern European Studies.

van der Wee, Herman. 1963. *The Growth of the Antwerp Market and the European Economy*. Vol. 2, *Interpretation*. Louvain, Belgium: Bureaux de Recueil.

———. 1977. "Monetary, Credit and Banking Systems." In *The Cambridge Economic History of Europe*. Vol. 5, *The Economic Organization of Early Modern Europe*, ed. E. E. Rich and C. H. Wilson, 290–392. Cambridge: Cambridge University Press.

———. 1993. *The Low Countries in the Early Modern World*. Aldershot, U.K.: Valorium.

van Dillen, J. G. 1934. "The Bank of Amsterdam." In *History of the Principal Public Banks*, ed. J. G. van Dillen, 79–123. The Hague: Nijhoff.

———. 1958. *Het oudste aandeelhoudersregister van der Kamer Amsterdam der Oost-Indische Compagnie*. 's-Gravenhage: Nijhoff.

van Hoboken, W. J. 1960. "The Dutch West India Company: The Political Background of Its Rise and Fall." In *Britain and the Netherlands: Papers Delivered to the Oxford-Netherlands Historical Conference, 1959*, ed. J. S. Bromley and E. H. Kossman, 41–61. London: Chatto and Windus.

van Tielhof, Milja. 2002. *The "Mother of All Trades": The Baltic Grain Trade in Amsterdam from the Late 16th to the Early 19th Century*. Leiden: Brill.

van Zanden, J. L. 1993. *The Rise and Decline of Holland's Economy: Merchant Capitalism and the Labour Market*. Manchester: Manchester University Press.

Veluwenkamp, J. W. 1996. "Merchant Colonies in the Dutch Trade System (1550–1750)." In *Kapitaal, Ondernemerschap en Beleid*, C. A. Davids, W. Fritschy, and L.A. van ser Valk, 141–64. Amsterdam: NEHA.

Vlessing, Odette. 1995. "The Portuguese-Jewish Merchant Community in Seventeenth-Century Amsterdam." In *Entrepreneurs and Entrepreneurship in Early Modern Times: Merchants and Industrialists within the Orbit of the Dutch Staple Market*, ed. C. Lesger and L. Noordegraaf, 223–43. Der Haag: Stichting Hollandse Historische Reeks.

Voss, Peter. 1995. "A Community in Decline? The Dutch Merchants in Bordeaux, 1650–1715." In *Entrepreneurs and Entrepreneurship in Early Modern Times: Merchants and Industrialists within the Orbit of the Dutch Staple Market*, ed. C. Lesger and L. Noordegraaf, 43–62. Der Haag: Stichting Hollandse Historische Reeks.

Weber, Max. [1904–5] 1930. *The Protestant Ethic and the Spirit of Capitalism*. London: Unwin.

Wieringa, W. J., ed. 1983. *The Interactions of Amsterdam and Antwerp with the Baltic Region, 1400–1800*. Leiden: Nijhoff.

Wijnroks, E. H. 1993. "Jan van de Walle and the Dutch Silk-Trade with Russia, 1578–1635." In *Russians and Dutchmen*, ed. J. Braat, A. H. Huussenjr, B. Naarden, and C.A.L.M. Willemsen, 41–58. Groningen: Institute for Northern and Eastern European Studies.

8

Conflict Displacement and Dual Inclusion in the Construction of Germany

Jonathan Obert ▪ John F. Padgett

In classifying regimes, political scientists often think in terms of archetypes—democracy, autocracy, oligarchy, republic, empire, dictatorship, totalitarianism. Such ideal-typing of political states leads to primitive understandings of evolutionary dynamics, little more than "transition" from one purported archetype to another. Most real states, however, are amalgams of multiple organizational principles, sometimes in tension, sometimes in compromise, sometimes in outright contradiction. Historians and area specialists are well aware of this complexity, but theoretically oriented social scientists have not provided many conceptual tools for analyzing hybridity.[1]

On the topic of multiplicity of principles, Bismarck can teach us. As a person, Bismarck was anything but consistent. A reactionary Junker, he implemented universal male suffrage. While repressing socialists, he made the first welfare state in Europe. From persecuting Catholics, he turned on a dime to embracing them. A master of aggressive warfare in the first half of his career, he meticulously negotiated "balance of power" to preserve the peace in the second half of his career. Throughout these oscillating contradictions, Bismarck constructed the most powerful state in Europe, assembling a hodgepodge of disparate German principalities under the umbrella of a geographically disarticulated Prussia.

Some categorize the late nineteenth-century German state that Bismarck assembled as "federalism."[2] Some call it "military autocracy."[3] With an eye to its future, many accuse it of "imperialism."[4] With an eye to alternative possible futures, others insist that it was a "democracy," even if a struggling one.[5] Some, following Marx, have applied the moniker of "Bonapartism."[6] In our opinion, the only mistake in any of these labels would be to fixate on any one of them to the exclusion of the others. Each ideal type highlights one slice of reality. But the real intellectual challenge is not classification. It is to understand how all these

The listing of Obert as first author is not because of the alphabet. The conflict displacement idea is his, and he did most of the research work.

[1] This is not to say that fragmentary efforts to understand organizational hybridity are not under way. From the institutionalist tradition, see Orren and Skowronek 1993; Orren and Skowronek 2004, 108–18; and Thelen 2004. From the pragmatist tradition, see Herrigel 2010 and Ansell 2011. From the networks tradition, see Padgett and Ansell 1993; Padgett and McLean 2006; and Padgett and Powell, this volume.

[2] Nipperdey 1986, 60–109; Mommsen 1995; Langewiesche and Schmidt 2000; Green 2001; Ziblatt 2006.

[3] Rosenberg 1958; Craig 1978.

[4] "Imperial Germany" is a label used by most historians almost non-self-reflexively, although the Wehler branch of the "Kehrite school" of historians has taken "social imperialism" as the dominant motif in nineteenth-century German history. See Kehr 1977; Wehler 1969, 1985; Stegmann 1970; and Berghahn 1971.

[5] Anderson 2000; Rauh 1977; Kreuzer 2001.

[6] Wehler 1969, 454–64; Wehler 1985, 55–62; Stürmer 1974. In this view, the trappings of democracy were only a way of legitimating autocratic rule.

seemingly contradictory aspects fit together organizationally to generate the most powerful state in Europe. Predicting multiple trajectories in German political history might be one payoff, we shall argue in the conclusion, from understanding feedbacks among multiple organizational principles.

Dual inclusion is the architectural invention that we see Bismarck using to fit together contradictory organizational principles. Dual inclusion means "Prussia is in Germany, and Germany is in Prussia."[7] Bismarck used this architecture to play off two logics of control: Prussia was used to control Germany, and Germany was used to control Prussia. Bismarck did not have an ideal type of state that he was trying to design. He had a style of mixing that took organizational elements that were already there and combined them in novel ways. Such combinations then had a life of their own, so he mixed them again. Bismarck in our opinion had no goal, in the sense of a specific ideal future that he was trying to attain.[8] He simply wanted to preserve himself in the fulcrum position[9] to enable his capacity to do future mixings. As times and circumstances changed, Bismarck changed. He was a chameleon, albeit a rather high-testosterone chameleon. Clear and decisive at any one moment, Bismarck oscillated wildly across time in the directionality of that decisiveness.[10]

It may be useful to compare Bismarck to the robust action of Cosimo de' Medici in Renaissance Florence[11] and Deng Xiaoping in Communist China.[12] Both Cosimo and Deng late in his life were quiescent sphinxes whose reactive moves and ambiguous utterances bore multiple plausible interpretations about their motives. On the surface, Bismarck's leadership style was exactly the opposite of this: blustering, loud, direct, and insulting. Over time, however, repeated sharp changes in Bismarck's direction had the same effect. What Bismarck clearly stood for at one moment was the opposite of what he just as clearly stood for at the next. Multivocality—namely, different audiences of enemies and friends reading in different identities to speakers—was the attributional consequence shared by these polar opposite leadership styles.

Figure 8.1 presents the specifics of the dual-inclusion structure that Bismarck constructed over time, both directly himself in his long reign from 1862 to 1890 and posthumously in the hostile Caprivi government that succeeded him. We will not go into the details of this figure now; it can serve as a developmental table of contents for the narrative to follow. We draw attention here only to the column structure of the figure.

Dual inclusion combined contradictory organizational logics because Prussia from the age of the Grand Elector constitutionally was an autocracy and federalist Germany after the creation of the parliament in 1866 constitutionally was a democracy, but militarily victorious Prussia was not changed thereby. Combining Prussia and Germany meant combining autocracy with democracy without either trumping the other.[13] Through a number of deeply conflictual iterations, Bismarck took these two inherited constitutional principles and constructed a "dual-inclusion" series of institutional bridges and emergent actors to intermediate between

[7] The earliest reference to dual inclusion, to our knowledge, was made by Cyprian of North Africa in the third century, who said: "The bishop in the church, and the Church is in the bishop" (Clarke 1986, 121). The second part of Cyprian's sentence refers to *charism* or the gift of grace/illumination from the Spirit, symbolized in ordination by the laying on of hands by fellow bishops (Dix 1946). Augustine's doctrine of grace through sacraments extended Cyprian's treatment of the bishop to the church at large (Willis 1950). This conception of orders carried through Aquinas (Lovejoy 1936) to become secularized in the three estates in France (Duby 1980) and in Ständestaat in the Holy Roman Empire (Poggi 1978, 36–59).

[8] Padgett and Ansell 1993, 1263–64.

[9] Pflanze's epic biography (1990a, 1990b, 1990c) emphasizes how Bismarck exploited and occupied the fulcrum position consistently throughout his career. According to Bismarck, "in chess one should never base a move on the positive assumption that the other player will in turn make a certain move. One must always reckon with the possibility that the opponent will at the last moment make a move other than expected and act accordingly. In other words, one must always have two irons in the fire" (Pflanze 1990a, 83). "This trade (politics) teaches us that one can be as shrewd as the shrewdest in the world and still at any moment go like a child into the dark" (ibid., 242). A grander version of his aggressively reactive approach to strategy was Bismarck's famous retrospection: "By himself the individual can create nothing; he can only wait until he hears God's footsteps resounding through events and then springs forward to grasp the hem of his mantle—that is all" (ibid., 80). Yet another statement was this: "It is a principle of creation and of the whole of nature that life consists of strife. . . . Without struggle there can be no life and, if we wish to continue living, we must also be reconciled to further struggles" (ibid., 80).

[10] Because of preference reversal, Bismarck violates axioms of utility theory, as formalized for example by Von Neumann and Morgenstern. Maximization of utility cannot be defined for Bismarck because consistent utility cannot be defined. Was he pursuing the interests of Germany or of Prussia? Of Junkers or of industrialists? Of the Kaiser or of himself? Precisely the lack of unambiguous answers to these questions was one secret to his success.

[11] Padgett and Ansell 1993.

[12] Padgett chapter 9, this volume.

[13] This deliberate silence about trumping was the "constitutional gap" (or Lücketheorie) about which there was so much contemporary legal debate. See Pflanze 1990a, 200–17, 341–51.

Democracy pillar	**Dual inclusion**	**Autocracy pillar**
Germany		
		Prussia

A. Constitutional and bureaucratic levels of analysis:

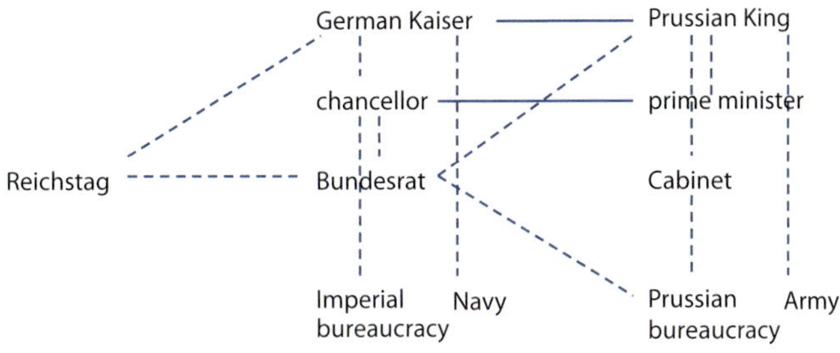

B. Political party level of analysis:

Center	Free Conservatives	Conservatives
Progressives	National Liberals	
Social Democrats		

C. Elite-networks and interest group level of analysis:

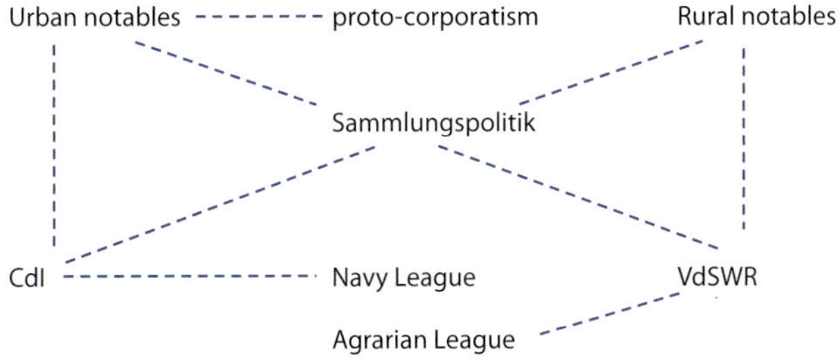

Figure 8.1 Late nineteenth-century Germany as dual inclusion.

them. Through these bridges each principle tried to control the other.

The dual-inclusion column in the middle of figure 8.1 was not itself an autonomous constitutional order. Rather, after Bismarck, democracy plus dual-inclusion brokerage together constituted "Germany." And autocracy plus dual-inclusion brokerage together constituted "Prussia." Prussia was in Germany and Germany was in Prussia because these new bridging institutions and political actors in the interface made them overlap and interpenetrate. This contradictory three-column ensemble could toggle between its two faces of "Germany" and "Prussia" depending upon which institutions and actors were activated in politics. Bismarck knew that and whipsawed the system accordingly.

How was dual inclusion constructed? Conflict displacement and hieratic authority were the political and social mechanisms, we argue, that Bismarck used to build dual inclusion. The term *conflict displacement* refers to Schattschneider's famous discussion of political party realignment.[14] Party realignment was one tool

[14] Schattschneider 1960, 60–75. Schattschneider is usually considered to be part of a broader literature in American politics on party realignment. Key (1955), Burnham (1970), and Sundquist (1983) are prominent advocates; Shafer (1991) and Mayhew (2002) are prominent critics. That literature has focused more on mass voting than on the elites, party factions

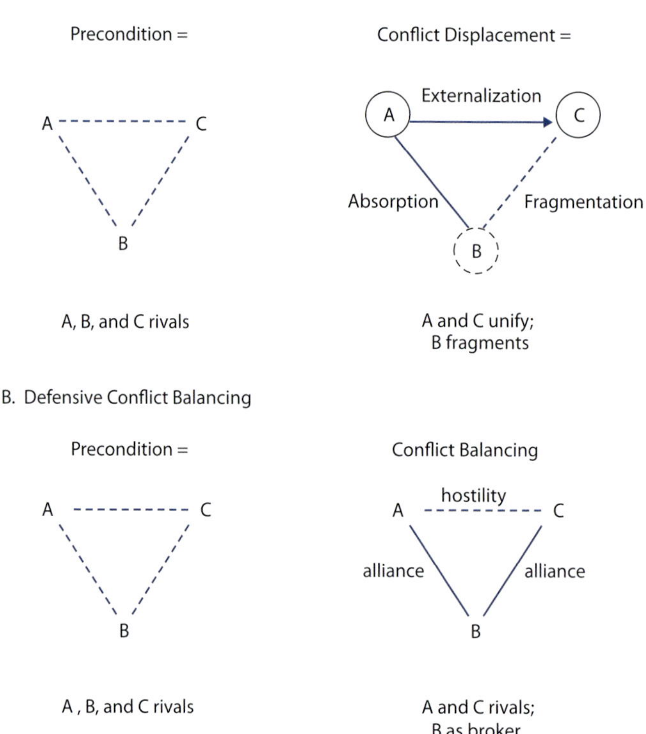

Figure 8.2 Conflict displacement.

in Bismarck's portfolio of state building. For Schattschneider, conflict displacement was a descriptive concept that highlighted the consequences of party structure for elite control in America. Schattschneider offered no detailed mechanism for achieving party realignment. We use the term *conflict displacement* more narrowly to refer to Bismarck's particular method of accomplishing party realignment, which distinctively relied on attacking and often demonizing outsiders. In addition to affecting political parties, Bismarck's tactic of conflict displacement allowed him to achieve constitutional design, bureaucratic control, and international order as well, depending upon who was attacked. We go so far as to suggest that conflict displacement was a built-in, almost genetic style for Bismarck, the action content of his so-called genius. He was remarkably subtle and creative in the timing and in the contextual application of this style, but in the end he was a one-trick pony. Plastic in identities and interests, Bismarck was rigidly constrained in his repertoire of action.[15] What was genius in one context could become suicidal in another, depending upon the conflicts and feedbacks in which he was embedded.

Our (Bismarck's) concept of conflict displacement is diagrammed in figure 8.2A. The initial precondition is (at least) three mutually hostile or rivalrous actors. An aggressor A is trying to influence antagonistic bystander B by attacking a third target C. We call the first attacking stage of conflict displacement "externalization" because the attack of A on C was generated in the first place by hostility between A and B. The intended impact of this attack on bystander B is to fragment B into two parts, one part supporting A and the other part supporting C. The more violent the attack of A on C, the deeper the

and "interests"that preoccupied Schattschneider. Like him, we focus more on the organization of political conflict into parties and factions than we do on mass voting. Claggett et al. (1982) provide an ecological analysis of mass voting in our period, which complements nicely our organizational focus.

[15] We perceive considerable consistency in Bismarck's style of action, though not in his goals, but Bismarck himself did not see it that way. He strongly believed that "there is no exact science of politics" and that "there are no rules and formulas" through which one might understand his political acts (quoted in Pflanze 1990a, 81).

fragmentation of B. If both the attack on C and the fragmentation of B are successful (they not always are), then A absorbs the sympathetic faction of B into alliance with itself, with A dominating the subordinate faction of B. The leader of A, for example, Bismarck, now becomes transformed into a broker between A and the allied subset of B. This alteration in leadership role gives the boss-turned-broker some degree of autonomy from his primary group affiliation of A. The two new allies remain rivalrous within the ruling coalition, even if they are no longer outright hostile. This internal rivalry preserves the fulcrum position of the broker.

We also diagram in figure 8.2B a close cousin of conflict displacement called conflict balancing. This was the famous "balance of power" international relations method to which Bismarck switched in the second half of his diplomatic career after the successful Franco-Prussian War.[16] Conflict displacement and conflict balancing appear to be opposites—the first is offensive, leading to war, the second is defensive, leading to peace. But figure 8.2 illustrates how these two strategies are actually the same logics, just seen from different role perspectives. Before 1870, Bismarck played the role of A, aggressively going to war. After 1870, once Germany had become "satiated," Bismarck switched to playing the role of B, trying to avoid having his new creation Germany itself becoming split by wars between powerful neighboring others. Conflict balancing in the latter case meant aggressive diplomacy to keep A (often Russia) from attacking C (often Austria).

We shall see that Bismarck used aggressive conflict displacement successfully in his war with Austria in 1866. He did this again successfully in his war with France in 1870. Bismarck transposed this originally international relations strategy down into domestic politics in his internal Kulturkampf "war" on the Catholic Church in 1871–75 but with only mixed success. He tried internal war again, this time more successfully in his sudden attack on the socialists in 1878, to produce a whole series of state-building innovations: first protectionism (the so-called Sammlungspolitik "marriage of iron and rye") in 1879–89, then proto-corporatist social welfare in 1881–87, and then the governing bloc of the Kartell in 1885–89. After Bismarck was deposed in 1890, his livid followers continued to practice the conflict displacement lessons of their master, albeit less subtly in a mass-mobilization manner of which the elitist Bismarck did not approve: namely, through the Agrarian League and the Navy League.

The demonized others of externalized assault (role C in figure 8.2), be they external or internal, were different in each of these conflict-displacement episodes. Bismarck sequentially attacked Austria, France, Catholics, and finally the socialists. After his deposition, mass supporters added the targets of Jews and England.[17] Crucial for understanding positive institution building are the changing bystander roles B. These are the institutions and the collective actors that emerged in the dual-inclusion column in figure 8.1. Bismarck himself launched initiating assaults alternately from the autocracy pillar of Prussia and from the democracy pillar of Germany. These were tactical preludes to segueing himself into the broker/fulcrum positions located in the dual-inclusion column that he had induced to emerge.

For conceptually understanding institutional and actor emergence, it is worth lingering a bit on the last stage of conflict displacement, absorption. "Fragmentation of B into alliance with A" actually is a more subtle, identity-changing process than the actor-centric representations in figure 8.2 imply. Louis Dumont long ago analyzed a status-based conception of hierarchy,[18] powerful in the history of humanity but no longer familiar to us. The word *hierarchy* to social scientists usually means an organizational tree of authority relations.[19] The word *hierarchy* to natural scientists means a nearly decomposable system,[20] that is, a nesting of sets of ever smaller modules within each other. In contrast to both of these, Dumont talked about Indian caste hierarchy as status incorporation, the archetypal example being pollution through gender (see figure 8.3).

The point of Dumont's diagram of patriarchy is that woman becomes MAN, that is, human, by virtue of fleeing her polluted side and instead finding her higher, purer self through submission to the exemplar of MAN, which is man. This is cultural domination. It is also an identity transformation of both man and woman through the incorporation relationship of MAN,

[16] Langer 1962; Joffe 1995.

[17] We need not belabor the point that Jews were only one of a list of demonized others in nineteenth-century Germany. Bismarck himself was not anti-Semitic; he used Jews heavily for financial support (see Stern 1977). Indeed one might argue that Bismarck was not deeply invested emotionally in any of his demonized enemies (Pflanze 1990a, 476). The Catholics come closest to being an exception (ibid., 368).

[18] Dumont 1970, 239–45. Padgett thanks Harrison White for educating him about hieratic authority in Dumont.

[19] Principal-agent is an economically oriented subset of this.

[20] Simon 1969, 84–118.

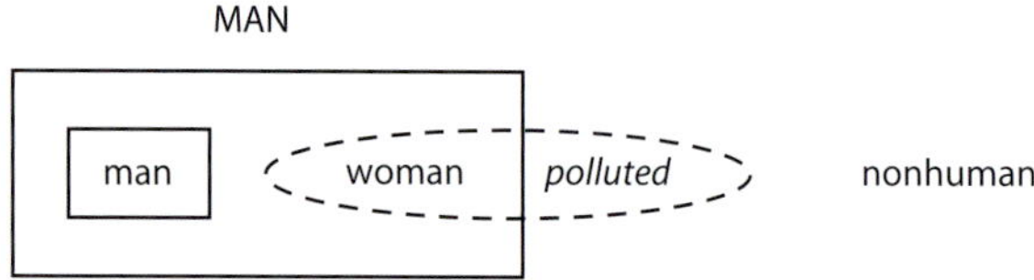

Figure 8.3 Hieratic authority.

accomplished through demonization of the nonhuman. Priestly authority of all stripes works like this, channeling people to God through denouncing their debased earthly selves. We give the label *hieratic* to this third form of hierarchy to avoid linguistic confusion with the other two definitions of hierarchy. Etymologically, the word *hieratic* has religious overtones, consistent with the concept's origins both in Hinduism and in Christianity.[21]

Dynamically, hieratic authority is achieved by man attacking nonhuman, splitting woman, and getting her to identify with MAN. Thus figures 8.2 and 8.3 are intimately related: Conflict displacement is a dynamic mechanism for inducing hieratic authority. As illustrated throughout this chapter, absorption in Bismarck's conflict displacement worked repeatedly like this. By attacking a demonized other, Bismarck hoped not only to fragment the targeted bystander but also to incorporate bystanders into identification with a higher form of themselves, epitomized by Bismarck himself. For smaller German principalities, Bismarck and his conquering Prussian army were not perceived as occupiers, as one might assume.[22] They were perceived as German nationalists. Conflict displacement drove hieratic authority and thereby the construction of dual inclusion. Nationalist collective actors repeatedly emerged out of bystanders, who then took it upon themselves to pursue Bismarck's oscillating agendas. Prussia was in Germany ultimately because of the Prussian army. But Germany was in Prussia because of hieratic sublimation.[23]

The rest of this chapter will illustrate and document these themes through synopses of the episodes adumbrated above: war with Austria in 1866, war with France in 1870, the Kulturkampf against the Catholic Church in 1871–75, continuous war against German socialists throughout the decade of 1878–89, and the rise of mass interest groups after Bismarck's fall from power. In all of these episodes we highlight the practical operation of conflict displacement and hieratic authority and show how iteration of these two processes kept adding layers to the gradual construction of dual-inclusion Germany. The underlying contradiction between democracy and autocracy never was resolved, with each pillar struggling mightily to control the other. This irreducible contradiction kept driving domestic political iterations forward through never-ending escalations among hostile actors who speciated and evolved. Bismarck could manage these contradictions (barely) through his fulcrum, but his successors could not. In the conclusion, we reflect on the macrohistorical dynamics generated by dual inclusion.

WARS WITH AUSTRIA AND FRANCE

Armed with an impeccable aristocratic Junker lineage and an early diplomatic career as Prussian ambassador first to the Frankfurt diet[24] and then to the Russian court, Otto von Bismarck was appointed by King Wilhelm I in 1862 to be his Prussian prime minister in order to battle the democratic[25] Prussian parliament or Landtag

[21] Christian versions of this are discussed in Dix 1946; Willis 1950; and Duby 1980. The archetypal example in medieval Christianity would substitute the corporate image of "Body of Christ" for the metaphor of MAN and replace the two genders with three occupational estates. This discussion of cultural ideology is intended to make it clear that German and especially Prussian concepts of estate-based authority and deference were important cognitive materials for Bismarck to work with. Subsequent discussion in this chapter makes it clear just how contested various cross-cutting hieratic authority conceptions became within Germany during the late nineteenth century.

[22] Annexation was not a smooth process, especially in Hanover (Schmitt 1985). Nevertheless, John (1987, 593–97) points out that Hanoverian liberals, while concerned about Prussianization, were also opportunists, using national integration as a chance for gaining national support for local political struggles.

[23] "Hieratic sublimation" means that Germany was in Prussia like MAN was in man.

[24] The Frankfurt diet was an assembly of representatives of German princes. This aristocratic confederation was set up by Metternich in 1817 in order to keep Austria in loose control of German-speaking Europe.

[25] "Democratic" in the sense of elected, but through an oligarchic three-class voting system that drastically favored wealthy property owners. The democratic Landtag was a

over the raging constitutional crisis of military funding. The aggressiveness of Bismarck's temperament dated back to his first substantial job as Prussian ambassador to the Frankfurt diet, where the brash youngster greeted his senior and distinguished Austrian counterpart, when first introduced, with cigar smoke in his face.[26] Bismarck bridled at the domination of Austria in the Frankfurt diet and peppered his superiors in Berlin with outlandish memos of unwanted foreign policy advice, many of which involved switching Prussian allegiance from Austria to France, that reviled homeland of the French Revolution and Napoleon. The autocratic king and his foreign policy advisers thought the young and brilliant Bismarck to be daft but humored him as an amusing devil's advocate. Plus he was a useful thorn in Austria's side, unswervingly faithful to the Prussian monarchy.[27]

Bismarck made no progress in striking a deal with the recalcitrant Landtag over military funding—the main reason he had been appointed to the position of prime minister. The Prussian king, like monarchs everywhere, wanted guaranteed military funding and complete discretion in running his army. In exchange for authorizing taxes, the Prussian Landtag, like parliaments everywhere, wanted annual budgets and parliamentary review. The king, with Bismarck's staunch support, refused utterly to grant this parliamentary trump card; hence there continued a constitutional standoff, with various extraparliamentary expedients carrying the army through. The parliamentary Liberal Party greatly outnumbered the royalist Conservative Party in the Landtag. The skewed voting system favored wealthy urban notables as well as wealthy rural notables. In such a rigid two-party-bloc parliament, Bismarck had nothing with which to maneuver. Civil war loomed again as an option, just as it did in 1848.

We need not be detained by the Danish Schleswig-Holstein incident in 1863,[28] except to note that Bismarck learned through this about military and diplomatic weakness in Austria. In 1866, with a brazen all-out military assault on Austria, Bismarck pulled the first and grandest conflict-displacement maneuver in his career. We can only speculate about the origins of this audacious plan in Bismarck's aggressively fertile mind.[29] But the overwhelming success of this war, on numerous levels, etched the formula for this glorious victory firmly in his learning for the rest of his life.

In terms of the conflict-displacement schema in figure 8.2, at the international relations level of analysis, Prussia under its leader Bismarck was the aggressor A, and Austria was the war target C. Bystanders B were the many other small German principalities in the Frankfurt diet. After the war with Austria in 1866, Protestant northern principalities were absorbed into Prussia to make the Northern German Confederation. After the subsequent war with France in 1870, largely Catholic southern principalities were also absorbed into the Northern Confederation to make the second Reich of Germany. With respect to state building, the Franco-Prussian War followed the same basic conflict-displacement script as did the Austro-Prussian War.[30]

Fragmentation of principality bystanders through these wars worked like this: With two big and rivalrous bullies in the Frankfurt diet, all of the smaller German states had an incentive to play off Prussia and Austria against one another in order to preserve their own autonomy. As in the conflict-balancing second panel of figure 8.2, bystanders before 1866 cultivated the friendship of each bully in order to stave off domination by the other bully. Sympathizers with Prussia were called Kleindeutsch (small Germany), and sympathizers with Austria were called Grossdeutsch

"gift" to the Prussian people by the Prussian king in 1848, that revolutionary year throughout much of Europe. The democratic Prussian Landtag had only been in existence for fourteen years before Bismarck's appointment. In 1848 Bismarck had bitterly opposed this extension of "democracy" to the Prussian people, favoring civil war instead.

[26] Taylor 1955, 33.

[27] Pflanze 1990a, 134–36, 142–60.

[28] On the Schleswig-Holstein crisis, see Koch 1984, 97–100.

[29] Pflanze (1990a, 74) argues that from the beginning of his political career, Bismarck was particularly attuned to the possibilities for breaking with Austria in the German Confederation to aggrandize Prussian power. Even though Bismarck supported the so-called Punctuation of Olmütz agreement with Austria in 1850, he actually "wavered between the seemingly opposite poles of the interest of state and the interest of conservative order." This balanced tension, in turn, allowed him to "resolve" the issue by recasting Prussia's interest as simultaneously both conservative *and* independently opposed to traditional subjugation to Austria in the Confederation. These mental gymnastics—reinforced by watching the old conservative alliance between Austria and Russia break up—probably had two effects. First, he started to view nationalism, in this early stage conceived only as Prussian independence tied to German strength, as a potentially "conservative" force. Second, he might have become aware, through the Crimean War, of how conflict among third parties might reconfigure alliances systematically (see Pflanze 1990a, 88–99, 136–39). Both became crucial elements of conflict displacement. Evidence that Bismarck thought in cross-level terms—seeing war as a diversionary solution to domestic conflicts—dates to 1860 (ibid., 183).

[30] Koch 1984, 105–21; Craig 1978.

(large Germany).[31] Without decisive action, there was no need for small principalities to choose between these two alternative Germanies. Decisive military defeat of Austria by Prussia in the battle of Königgrätz, however, severed protection links between Austria and the small German principalities.[32] The more Catholic dream of Grossdeutsch was destroyed. From the perspective of international relations, the battle of Königgrätz made small German principalities into low-hanging fruit for Prussia.

Conflict displacement, however, is not just military victory. The other crucial side is hieratic absorption. Simultaneously with his military assault on Austria, Bismarck the reactionary Junker offered universal suffrage[33] to all male voters in all German states through the creation of a new German legislature called the Reichstag. There had been a previous economic customs union called the Zollverein, which made this institutional extrapolation comprehensible. This move toward universal and unambiguously democratic suffrage reframed Prussian occupation into Kleindeutsch nationalism. Pflanze calls this move Bismarck's conservative hijacking of the previously liberal concept of nationalism, which had its origins in revolutionary France.[34]

Nationalist reframing worked not only because of rhetoric. Coupling military defeat with universal suffrage had two structural effects: cutting protection ties between German princes and their Austrian emperor at the top of each principality and strengthening bonds between autocratic Prussia and liberal urban notables at the base of each principality. Figure 8.4A visualizes this squeeze play. Vertical ties of "rally round the flag" between princes and their people, which one normally might expect to mobilize resistance to occupation, thereby were disabled.[35]

Figure 8.4B provides a visualization of how Bismarck took advantage of these induced cleavages to build an institutional state for Germany. Given internal fracture within each principality, Bismarck reached into the bases to co-opt the various federalized urban notables into his new Reichstag. Bismarck also reached into those fractured principalities' top halves to co-opt defanged princes into the upper branch of his new parliament, called the Bundesrat. The Bundesrat was established explicitly on federalist lines; each submissive prince was given the right to appoint delegates, in proportion to population size.[36] These new institutions of the Reichstag and the Bundesrat[37] mimicked

A. Conflict Displacement at International Relations level

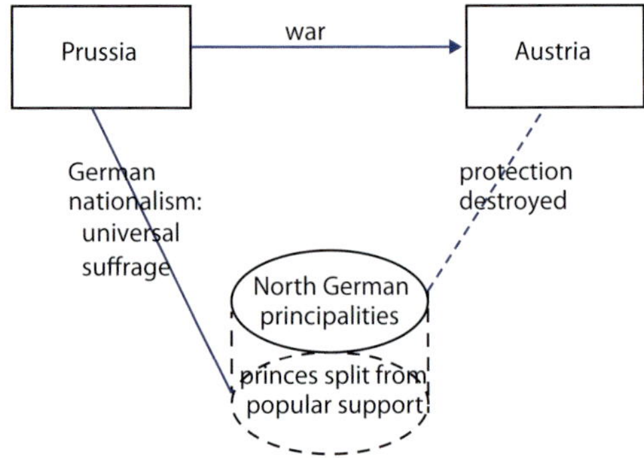

B. Conflict Displacement at Institutional level

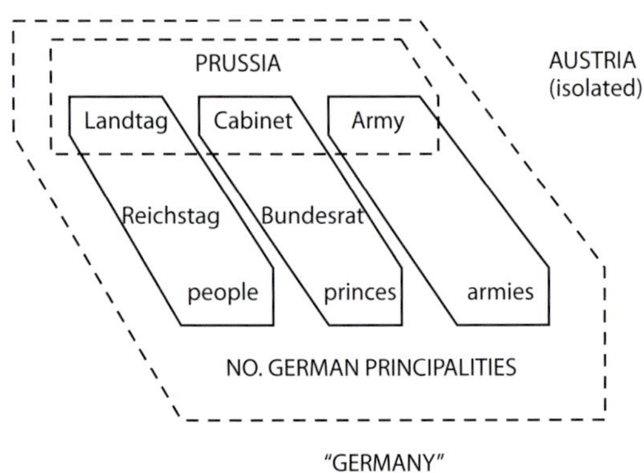

Figure 8.4A and B War with Austria (1866).

[31] Pflanze 1990a, 138–39. Green (2001, 193–94) notes that the *Kleindeutsch/Grossdeutsch* distinction was also rooted in different views of the state as unitary and federative, respectively. But Bismarck went across this cognitive grain by combining *Kleindeutsch* with the federative model.

[32] Koch 1984, 100.

[33] Not the skewed three-class version but full democratic one-man-one-vote.

[34] "If there is to be a revolution, we should rather make it than suffer it," Bismarck said in 1870 (Pflanze 1990a, 313). See also Pflanze 1990a, 308–9, and 1990b, 249–51.

[35] White (1976, 23–31) goes into this in some depth for Hesse. See also John 1987, 593–98.

[36] Actually Prussia took less than its fair share (17 out of 43 seats) to make submission easier to swallow.

[37] The Bundesrat combined two Prussian roles into one German institution. As the collective seat for the aristocracy, the Bundesrat legally was like the Prussia Upper House. But since princes usually appointed their own bureaucrats to do the real work of drafting government bills for the Reichstag, the Bundesrat functioned in practice more like the Prussian ministerial Cabinet. See Bonham 1985, 74–76.

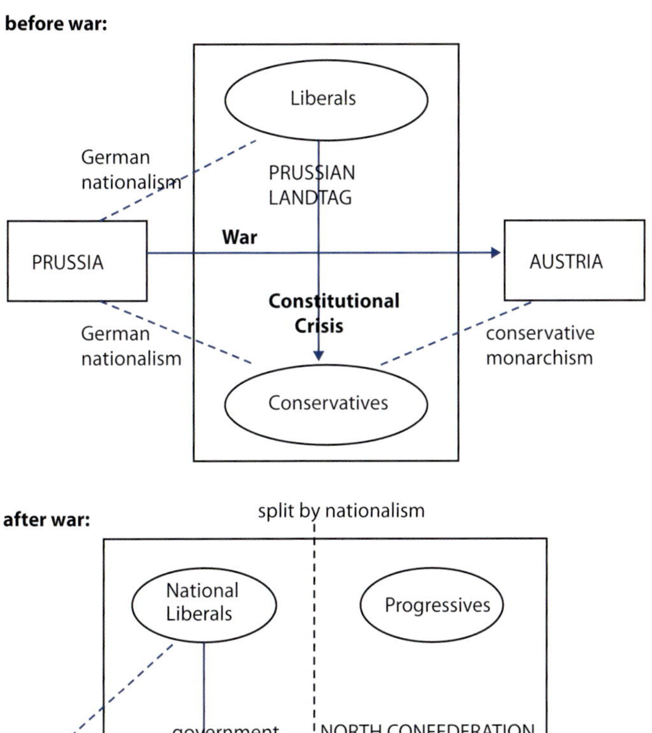

Figure 8.4C War with Austria: conflict displacement at political party level.

the Prussian Landtag and Upper House, except that they were more geographically extended and more democratic. Without going into detail, the Franco-Prussian War repeated this state-building strategy of conflict displacement for southern Germany, since France after 1866 had threatened to move in to play the counterbalancing role vacated by Austria.[38] After the Franco-Prussian War, the Reichstag and the Bundesrat became geographically coextensive with the Zollverein, the free-trade customs union. German parliamentary institutions thereby were made isomorphic with "natural" (even if heterogeneous) forces of industrial development and mass markets. "Germany" was now not only a manufactured legislature, it was also an autocatalytic economy.[39]

In his personal drafting of this German constitution, Bismarck did not neglect a role for himself. On the constitutional surface, the German

[38] Pflanze 1990b, 490–506; Koch 1984, 116–21; Bazillion 1990, 207–11.

[39] Herrigel (1996) points out that economic and transportation integration did not lead to sectoral uniformity but rather to complementary "autarkic" and "decentralized" economic regions.

chancellor was not a powerful position because it commanded no troops[40] and controlled little bureaucracy. The chancellor was instead a broker position, charged together with the Bundesrat with managing legislative relations between the German Reichstag and the Prussian government of king, bureaucracy, and army. To avoid putting all his eggs in this untried basket, Bismarck became German chancellor without giving up his old positions as Prussian prime minister and Prussian foreign minister. Officially, therefore, Bismarck was both German and Prussian at the same time. After talking his reluctant boss King Wilhelm I into adding the title of German Kaiser[41] to that of his cherished Prussian one, both Bismarck and his boss were German and Prussian simultaneously. The Kaiser, his chancellor, and the Bundesrat were the first three dual-inclusion institutions in Germany. These were neither pure democracy nor pure autocracy but betwixt and between.

In toto, what did the new constitutional ensemble look like? Formally the Reichstag was unambiguously democratic. But given that there were many rural notables in it with strong royalist sentiments, informally the Reichstag functioned to bridge liberal nationalist sentiments of parliamentary rights and free trade, rooted in urban areas, with imperial nationalist sentiments of conquest and autocracy, anchored in rural areas.[42] Bismarck at first was sanguine about the Reichstag because he assumed that the German public-at-large mostly was royalist.[43] The militarily glorious Prussia king, bureaucracy, and army anchored the pure autocracy column, under the influence but not really the legal control of the Reichstag. Symbolically the Kaiser loomed large, but at the beginning the only institutions holding together the contradictory pillars of democracy and autocracy were the small bridging offices of the chancellery and the Bundesrat. This was hardly a tightly integrated ensemble. The Reichstag was all that the broker Bismarck had to keep the Prussian autocracy, and especially its army, in check. It is no wonder that Bismarck was worried about foreign countries splitting him, just as he had split them.[44] The constitutional seeds of dual inclusion and fulcrum, however, had been planted.

POLITICAL PARTY REALIGNMENT

The first step toward strengthening this rickety edifice was political party realignment. A by-product of Bismarck's hijacking of nationalism for royalism was to split the previously stalemated Prussian Liberal and Conservative parties each into two segments. The old Liberal Party, which had stood for urban-oriented Landtag parliamentary rights and Zollverein free trade, split into the National Liberals and the Progressive parties, both in the German Reichstag and in the Prussian Landtag. The old Conservative Party, which had stood for rural-oriented monarchy and aristocracy, split into the Free Conservatives and the Conservatives.[45] The National Liberals and the Free Conservatives each were the centrist wing of their previous party. They both strongly supported national unification and Bismarck. The Progressives and the Conservatives each were the more polarized wing of their previous party. They both stood tough behind their earlier demands—namely, parliamentary and monarchic dominance, respectively.

This splintering of political parties was induced because of German nationalism, but it had policy consequences. The economically oriented National Liberals emphasized the free-trade side of liberalism, becoming more willing to compromise on parliamentary dominance.[46] The Free Conservatives emphasized the bureaucratic side of

[40] The army remained firmly Prussian, answerable only to the Prussian king. Other principalities' much smaller armies were either absorbed into the Prussian army or placed under its supervision (and command in times of war). Craig 1955, 219–20.

[41] This title signified the submission of other German kings to the "emperor." More practically, the Kaiser had the discretionary right of dissolving the Reichstag. It was as Prussian king, however, not as German Kaiser, that Wilhelm had the authority to make foreign policy and to go to war (Pflanze 1990a, 498–504).

[42] White 1976, 7–8; Sheehan 1978, 123–27; Langewiesche 2000, 95–97.

[43] Bismarck believed that universal male suffrage was, at its core, a "conservative principle . . . (providing) greater guarantees for the conservative conduct of parliament than any of the more artificial electoral laws that are calculated to achieve manufactured majorities" (quoted in Pflanze 1990a, 307).

[44] This is not really a chapter on Bismarck's famous "balance of power" international strategy. But it is notable that he shifted radically to that defensive posture immediately after his dramatic victory in the Franco-Prussian War. Not surprisingly, it took a while for other nations to accept his word that he had. See Pflanze 1990b, 247–58.

[45] Langewiesche 2000, 92–95; Berdahl 1965, 42–75; Pflanze 1990a, 335–38; Ritter 1913, 179. The proximate cause of this split was a vote over an "indemnity bill," which would have retroactively justified the Lückentheorie (Pflanze 1990a, 335–36).

[46] The organizational split between National Liberals and Progressives, in other words, drove a wedge between the economic and the parliamentary meanings of nineteenth-century liberalism, which had previously been linked. See, for instance, White 1976, 28–31, and Sheehan 1978, 124–37.

conservatism, no longer insisting on the interests of Junkers. These two new centrist parties found electoral support all over Germany, but National Liberals were especially strong in non-Prussian[47] geographical segments of the new Germany.

This political party realignment, which occurred immediately after the war with Austria, allowed Bismarck to break the logjam of the original constitutional crisis and to govern both the German and the Prussian parliaments through a nationalist and centrist alliance of the National Liberals and the Free Conservatives. Military funding bills now passed both legislatures with relative ease, subject only to parliamentary insistence on blanket (not detailed) reauthorization after five or seven years. At the level of political parties, externalization of the original domestic constitutional crisis into wars with Austria and France had solved the original crisis for which Bismarck had been hired.[48]

Figure 8.4C diagrams this political party realignment in a manner that Schattschneider would have liked. This representation highlights the continued possibility under Bismarck of toggling between two types of parliamentary politics. The more explosive cleavage was the primordial one between liberal and conservative, which had social roots in urban versus rural. This cleavage laid bare the basic contradiction between democracy and autocracy in all of its nakedness. Bismarck wanted to build across this chasm a nationalist politics of German state versus particularism. Not only did this obfuscate the danger of civil war, but also it formed a coalition out of his bellicose friends and polarized his opponents. There was no conceivable circumstance under which the Progressives and Conservatives, who despised each other, could have aligned against him.

What the hieratic schema adds to Schattschneider-style insights is an emphasis on struggle for collective identity—struggle for the German "soul" if you will. National Liberals and Free Conservatives both laid claim to a higher and more enlightened vision of liberalism and conservatism, respectively, than did their Prussia-embedded rivals—a nationalist German vision emphasized by Bismarck. Parties in late nineteenth-century Germany were not just disagreements over policy; they were also claims to cultural superiority and dominance.[49] As long as foreign war loomed on the horizon, the hieratic claim that Bismarck and his ruling coalition epitomized the greatness of Germany had cultural authority and electoral power. But when Bismarck shifted his international objectives to peace after 1870, this cultural authority and power started to wane. Under peacetime conditions, it is not surprising under the hieratic model to see alternative categorization schemas arise to challenge Bismarck's temporarily strong but in the long term fragile electoral hold on both Germany and Prussia.

To prepare our understanding of later, less successful applications of conflict displacement by Bismarck, it will prove useful to probe the micro social-network foundations of these political parties. The literature calls all of the parties mentioned so far Honoratioren parties, meaning parties of notables. Businessmen differed from landlords and professionals in many ways, but in one way these notables were all similar: they were leaders in their local communities, heavily involved in civic associations, and used to deference, respect, and votes from their social inferiors.[50] Social foundations of community-based deference long predated Bismarck, but it is worth noting that Bismarck's federalist constitution reinforced, rather than dampened, this elite politics of deference. We do not have the detailed social-network data that we had in previous projects,[51] but our impression from the secondary literature is that before unification these vertical deference ties, while diffuse, culminated loosely in the person of the local prince, although this traditional status system was far from tight. After Bismarck effectively (though not symbolically) decapitated the local princes, the no longer unified social-deference ties to notables split into parallel vertical trees, coordinated if at all only loosely through community civic associations.[52]

[47] The term *non-Prussia* in this context refers to the pre-1866 boundaries of Prussia.

[48] These domestic consequences of wars should not be confused, however, with the causes of those wars.

[49] Sheehan 1978, 15–17; Koch 1984, 135–37; Gross 1997, 545–48. Already in his famous 1858 "booklet" Bismarck had spoken of the relationship between Prussia and Germany in hieratic terms. He called Prussia a "pure German state [whose] needs and course of development [were] homogeneous with those of the rest of the German population" (Pflanze 1990a, 135). This claim by an agrarian Junker may have come as a surprise to the more urbanized and economically developed German principalities of the west.

[50] Nipperdey 1961, 9, 58–59; Sheehan 1978, 512–15; Retallack 1988a; Eley 1980, 22.

[51] Padgett and Ansell 1993; Padgett and McLean 2006, 2011; Padgett 2010.

[52] Sheehan 1978, 119–21, 123–26; White 1976, 27–31; John 1987; Retallack 1988a.

The implication of this social-network foundation for constitutional design is that federalism reinforced walls between communities of notables, thereby propping up the local deference ties to point toward the new center that had constructed those walls of segregation. Notables were poorly coordinated among themselves across communities, but federalism kept them minimally solidary within their communities.[53] This meant that Honoratioren parties had stable local foundations at the various Landtag and lower levels, but their parliamentary delegates in the Reichstag hardly existed as organizations. Indeed for the National Liberals and Free Conservatives, they were coordinated at their parliamentary cores pretty much only through Bismarck himself.[54] Federalism, while not ideal for Bismarck, served him well enough as long as he was faced only with the task of herding notable cats. He was the extraparliamentary leader upon whom their parliamentary cohesion came to depend. Federalism, while technically decentralization, operated practically in the hands of Bismarck as personalized centralization[55] because it reinforced him as broker and them as minimally cohesive parties. As long as nationalism could be used to beef up the electoral totals of those two ruling parties, Bismarck in his political-brokerage position could shift back and forth between using the National Liberals from "Germany" in order to pressure Prussia and using the Free Conservatives from "Prussia" in order to discipline the Reichstag. Whether this was enough depended upon electoral success, which in turn depended upon nationalist war.

KULTURKAMPF: THE PRIMARY FRONT

The Kulturkampf attack on the Catholic Church, launched one year after Bismarck's victory over France, is usually considered the greatest domestic political failure in Bismarck's career.[56] We will qualify this judgment with a mixed report card that distinguishes between primary and secondary targets. The only political party adjustment produced by the Franco-Prussian War, which folded heavily Catholic southern principalities into Germany, was the emergence of a new party of notables to defend Catholic interests, called the Center (Zentrum) Party.[57] This new party did not really fit into the dominant cross-cleavages of nationalism and liberalism. The military defeat of the Grossdeutsch empire had turned Catholics into a 30 percent minority within the new, predominantly Protestant Kleindeutsch Germany. Catholics had demonstrated no disloyalty, but Bismarck considered them a fifth-column, that is, potential targets for Austrian and French influence to try penetrate into his "pure" nationalist Germany.[58] For someone like Bismarck, sensitive to fracture, this was a potential vulnerability.

Kulturkampf was another conflict-displacement maneuver, this time directed at an internal enemy, not an external one. Pope Pius IX, viewed as directing Catholic disloyalty, was singled out for special demonization by Bismarck. In the middle of a nationalist uprising of his own (the Italian Risorgimento), the pope had recently issued a bull proclaiming papal infallibility in 1870 that had outraged both Italian nationalist and non-Catholic audiences. The majority of German bishops did not initially support this extreme assertion of papal centralization, though they eventually fell into line. In 1872, 1873, and 1875, Bismarck and his National Liberal Party responded to this pretext by passing three escalating bills that insisted on state supervision over Catholic schools and priestly appointments. Bismarck, through his deputy Falk, expelled the Jesuits and other religious orders.[59] The German Church responded by simply letting clergy and teaching vacancies go unfilled, essentially going out on strike.

Who were the bystander targets of this legislative assault on the Catholic Church? The primary target was the Center Party. Bismarck's

[53] Palmowski (1999, 680–89) argues that this process manifested itself in increased local polarization and political mobilization, particularly in municipal settings. In part this was the result of new political opportunities at the federal level, and in part it was the result of the need for local jurisdictional defense in a federal setting. At the same time, local notable politics did not lead to much formal party organization at the local level until later in the 1870s (Sheehan 1978).

[54] This is not to deny the importance of influential delegates (e.g., Lasker) capable of building coalitions within the caucus (see Sheehan 1968). These caucus coalitions, however, were always ad hoc, and the two government parties were deeply dependent on Bismarck's ability to forge majority alliances to maintain their own cohesion at the national level.

[55] This is not so unlike the organizational behavior of multidivisional firms (Chandler 1962) or partnership systems (Padgett and McLean 2006).

[56] Pflanze 1990b, 195–204, 310; Craig 1978; Ross 1998.

[57] Pflanze 1990b, 169–71, 183–87; Sperber 1984, 156–206; Anderson 1986.

[58] Pflanze (1990b, 189–93) traces the international context for Bismarck's thinking about the Kulturkampf. Bismarck was particularly worried about relations between the Vatican and France and believed he needed to stop the "continuing and open war of circles in the Catholic church against Prussia," one that included "an unnatural alliance" with "democrats and radicals" (quoted in Pflanze 1990b, 189–90).

[59] Gross (1997, 564–66) traces how the Liberals particularly singled out Jesuits, whom they suspected of collaborating with France, for attack.

hope was that "good German" Catholics could be separated from ultramontane infection, thereby isolating and purging a potentially cancerous fifth column not only from the outside influence of the pope but also from that of Catholic France and Austria. One weakness in Bismarck's conflict-displacement strategy was that there was nothing positive, analogous to universal suffrage, to offer to "good" Catholics. The Kulturkampf was all stick, no carrot.

Flush with success, Bismarck in the Kulturkampf transposed his international-relations strategy to the domestic arena.[60] There were numerous political consequences. On the primary front of battle, the Center Party was not fractured in any serious way.[61] Quite the contrary, regardless of what they thought of the pope, both the German clergy and the Catholic voters[62] rallied vigorously to the defense of the Center Party, transforming it indeed into the first mass-based political party in Germany. What had started as a party of notables, organizationally like the others, quickly became the political arm of a tightly defensive confessional community in reaction to Bismarck's religious attack.[63] Social clubs, schools, parishes, and welfare support provided a church-sponsored organizational foundation to mobilize Catholic voting masses, undergirding Catholic notables and disciplining them.[64] Bismarck's attempt to split the Center Party through conflict displacement backfired disastrously, producing the opposite of his intent.[65] The Reichstag for decades thereafter contained a solid, unsplittable bloc of about 100 Catholic delegates (out of 348 total) who sat there, like a pile of rocks in Bismarck's stomach, unable by themselves to overthrow him but always available to mix with others who might want to cause indigestion. Policy-wise, the Center stood first and foremost for decentralized federalism to protect themselves from central bureaucratic (read Prussian) control. Instead of strengthening dual inclusion, Bismarck with the Kulturkampf unintentionally strengthened the democratic pillar in Germany.

What does this failure tell us about the boundary conditions for successful conflict displacement? At the microlevel of organizational loyalties, conflict displacement is a battle between hieratic forces for fragmentation and absorption and "rally round the flag" forces for unified resistance. Whereas successful conflict displacement leads to cultural dominance, unsuccessful conflict displacement leads to strengthening the opposition. Conflict displacement is a risky all-or-nothing strategy, with potential consequences for escalation down the road.

Two organizational factors tipped the balance of forces toward the Catholic Church's successful rally-round-the-flag resistance during the Kulturkampf. German bishops were not monolithically behind the pope on papal infallibility, so simple "Catholic Church hierarchy" is not a sufficient answer. More powerful for resistance than priestly hierarchy was the organizational foundation of parishes. These were the schools and social clubs that contained Catholic voters, whose own children and parish priests were threatened by state supervision. The traditional politics of Honoratioren deference in the other parties had no equivalent cross-class organizations to bind notables to masses in such a personal and intimate way.

The second organizational feature of the Catholic Church that fostered its resistance was its cross-federal character. Protestant churches had intracommunity congregational governing structures, which more easily could be penetrated and controlled by community notables. If Bismarck controlled the local notables, he controlled their Protestant congregations. In contrast, organizational structures that cut across the federalist walls of local communities deeply threatened social layers of informal deference. We shall see again these two organizational features operate with the socialists, the Agrarian League, and the Navy League. Bismarck's persecution of the Catholic Church was the first step down the road of increasing tension between the notable and the mass ways of organizing politics.

KULTURKAMPF: THE SECONDARY FRONTS

While Catholics were the primary battlefront of the Kulturkampf, other fronts existed as well. Those produced more positive results for Bismarck. In the larger picture of dual-inclusion state building, Bismarck during the 1870s was

[60] Pflanze 1990b, 199.

[61] There was a tiny splinter of Catholic notables, for the most part with state jobs on the line, who fractured into the so-called Old Catholics. But their numbers were negligible. See Ross 1998, 35–52.

[62] Anderson 2000, 69–151; Anderson 1986, 84–91; Claggett et al. 1982, 657.

[63] Anderson 1986, 82–89; Sperber 1984, 187–91.

[64] Anderson 2000, 69–151; Blackbourn 1987, 187–91.

[65] For those who insist on interpreting Bismarck's "genius" as due to his superior intelligence, capable of calculating deep into the future, this is the decisive negative evidence. Our contrary view is that Bismarck was instead a one-trick pony, albeit someone extremely subtle in the flexible application of his trick.

swinging toward "Germany" to gain leverage over "Prussia." (In the 1880s he oscillated back.) We point to two related aspects of Kulturkampf success: Bismarck's improved holds over anti–Center Party alliances within the Reichstag and over the brand-new imperial and the well-established Prussian bureaucracies.

Just as the Catholic Center Party was consolidated by religious persecution, so too the polar-opposite National Liberal Party of notables was temporarily strengthened and unified by being selected as Bismarck's parliamentary instrument.[66] Proclaiming themselves the hieratic embodiment of German secular nationalism, the National Liberals temporarily achieved electoral dominance and staffed Bismarck's budding imperial bureaucracy.[67] This dual entrenchment made free trade the official economic policy of the 1870s Bismarck government. Because Bismarck himself had no strong opinions about economic matters, it was not an intellectual problem for him to delegate economic decision making to the National Liberals.

One significant down side for Bismarck of this useful alliance with National Liberals, however, was that it threatened the uniqueness of his fulcrum position. The Free Conservatives were never as large a party as the National Liberals.[68] Without a strong enough counterbalance to the National Liberals, Bismarck's discretion as broker between liberals and conservatives was impaired. There is evidence that the National Liberals carried the Catholic persecution further than Bismarck himself intended.[69] If so, then the liberal tail showed signs of starting to wag the Junker dog.

Another parliamentary front of the Kulturkampf was the ultraconservative faction within the Conservative Party. Almost simultaneously with the School Inspection Act of 1872, Bismarck proposed and pushed through the County Reorganization Act, which eliminated Junker hereditary ownership of local manorial government in the east.[70] In fact, Junkers numerically remained just as represented in the Landräte after the reform as before, but the legal basis for that control shifted from family to state appointment (after extensive consultation with local notables). Conservative resistance to this "traitorous" assault by Bismarck on the Junkers' homeland was understandably intense. He overcame that opposition only by convincing Wilhelm to pack the Prussian House of Lords with compliant new nobles.[71]

Why did Bismarck attack his Junker friends and relatives? Our answer, not surprisingly, is conflict displacement. So-called ultraconservatives (or ultras for short) dominated the Conservative Party both in the German Reichstag and in the Prussian Landtag.[72] Most important, they dominated the Prussian army officer corps. Edwin von Manteuffel was their reactionary leader. During the original constitutional crisis of the early 1860s, ultraconservatives had advocated and almost achieved open civil war and repression against parliamentary liberals.[73] Bismarck was hired as prime minister only after Wilhelm I had decided at the last minute against this. During the Franco-Prussian War, ultraconservatives in the army vigorously resisted Bismarck's "meddling" in military and diplomatic affairs. They were the core of the autocracy pillar of Prussia.

Bismarck throughout his whole career never touched this faction within the army. In 1883, indeed, he even supported it. As such Bismarck never got rid of pure autocracy. However, during the Kulturkampf period the influence of this dangerous group was curbed within the Conservative Party and within the Prussian civilian bureaucracy.

Parliamentary defeat suffered in the County Reorganization Act of 1872 fractured the losing Conservative Party into the ultras who previously had dominated and so-called New Conservatives who acquiesced to working within Bismarck's system.[74] The 1874 elections wiped

[66] Gross 1997, 564–65; Langewiesche 2000, 199–206.

[67] The most famous of Bismarck's National Liberal assistants was Rudolf Delbrück, who was appointed president of the chancellor's office. He was a strong proponent of economic and national liberalism and was instrumental in laying the administrative groundwork for the imperial bureaucracy. See Pflanze 1990b, 132–45, 207–45.

[68] The Free Conservatives had as their electoral foundation state bureaucrats and large industrialists. This made them into Bismarck's most reliable supporters. But the mass appeal of the Free Conservatives was always limited, especially when National Liberals stole their nationalist thunder. Bonham 1985, 65–67.

[69] In 1874 Bismarck perhaps disingenuously claimed that he "wanted to fight the Center as a political party, nothing more! If they [the ministers] had limited themselves to that, it would certainly have been successful. I am completely blameless for the fact that they went further and aroused the whole Catholic population" (quoted in Pflanze 1990b, 203–4).

[70] On the Kreisordnung, see Jacob 1963, 47–51; Muncy 1944; Berdahl 1965; and Pflanze 1990b, 207–13.

[71] Bismarck wanted to turn the House of Lords into a "circle of millionaires," including businessmen and professionals as well as landlords. This foreshadowed later proto-corporatist Prussian Economic Council.

[72] Berdahl 1965, 42–72.

[73] Craig 1955, 148–72.

[74] Berdahl 1965, vi, 242–47; Retallack 1988a; Pflanze 1990b, 206, 212–13, 340–44.

out ultras from both legislatures, leading to massive Conservative Party shrinkage.[75] In 1876 the Conservative Party reorganized itself with the New Conservative faction in the driver's seat. Ultras were not purged, but they assumed a subsidiary role within the party. This internal realignment was not enough to admit Conservatives into the government, but the road was paved for this in the future because they now had rejected Prussian particularism and had accepted German nationalism. It was not hard, after all, under hieratic authority to reinterpret Prussian military victory as German imperial glory.

All of the political-party effects of the Kulturkampf, both positive and negative from Bismarck's point of view, are diagrammed in figure 8.5A, which represents party realignment as Schattschneider would have done it. The nationalist ruling bloc of National Liberals and Free Conservatives was unified both by nationalism and by the demonization of Catholics. But secular Progressives, while outside the government, also supported the Kulturkampf.[76] The Conservative Party, especially Lutheran ultras within it, did not because of fear for their own church, but after their 1876 reorganization they were willing to cooperate with Bismarck on nationalist issues.[77] The result was a party system with a two-party ruling bloc at its center, with options of swinging either left (Progressive) or right (Conservative) as the opportunistic occasion required. An oppositional Center loomed as the mass-organized confessional other. This was how Bismarck organized democratic "Germany" to gain leverage over autocratic Prussia.

The internal realignment of the Conservative Party from ultraconservatives to collaborationist New Conservatives had its parallel within the bureaucracies.[78] The new imperial bureaucracy itself was built and staffed by National Liberals under the leadership of Rudolf Delbrück. It never was a control problem for Bismarck, even though the imperial bureaucracy drew upon coopted recruits from the Prussian bureaucracy.[79] On the more troublesome side of the powerful Prussian bureaucracy, Bismarck implemented two administrative changes, both involving dual hierarchy.[80] These two changes in bureaucratic control were made possible by the political marginalization of Prussian-particularist ultraconservatives.

First, the County Reorganization Act made local county-level Landräte governors answerable not only to the Prussian bureaucracy but also to the new imperial bureaucracy. Legally this was because local Landräte now were charged with enforcing German Reichstag laws as well as Prussian Landtag laws. This dual hierarchy made two career paths for Landräte officials: they could stay in their local posts for life, most likely coming to identify with their notable neighbors, or they could use the post as a stepping-stone to bureaucratic promotion, most likely coming to identify with the center. Even though they always had mixed loyalties, over time Landräte very slowly became more bureaucratic, less Junker in their background and orientation.[81] Interestingly enough, the imperial bureaucracy never developed field officials of its own. For this reason, there never was the structural option under dual inclusion for the democratic Reichstag ever to gain direct, unmediated control over any bureaucracy.[82] Bismarck, not the Reichstag, sat at the top of the newer branch of the Landräte's dual hierarchy, monopolizing brokerage.

Second, at the peak of the bureaucratic system, Bismarck used both the Kaiser/king and the German Bundesrat to undercut and control the Prussian ministerial cabinet. Prussian ministers (including Bismarck himself) were proud, prickly, and haughty because they were nobles by birth or appointment. To keep an eye on jealous colleagues, some of them ultraconservatives, Bismarck never resigned his Prussian posts of minister-president[83] and foreign minister, even after he became German chancellor. He insisted that other Prussian ministers, except the minister of war, report to the Prussian king through him only. Most important, Bismarck used his personal influence over the king to influence appointments.

Bismarck also used the trick of co-opting lower administrative levels in order to isolate his fellow Prussian ministers from controlling their

[75] Pflanze 1990b, 222. In the Prussian Landtag, the Old Conservative bloc was whittled down from 71 to 4 members in the 1873 elections.

[76] Gross 1997, 555–60.

[77] Berdahl 1965, 245–46.

[78] With reference to the bureaucracy, in 1877 Bismarck said: "Prussia is in greater need of Germanization than Germany of Prussianization" (quoted in Pflanze 1990b, 374).

[79] Morsey 1957, 1–18, 36–37, 251–52; Bonham 1985, 76–86; Pflanze 1990b, 129–53.

[80] Not to be confused with dual inclusion. Dual hierarchy simply means "employees answerable to two bosses." See Evans 1975.

[81] Muncy 1944, 188–90; Gillis 1971, 206.

[82] Jacob 1963, 29–34.

[83] Except for a few months in 1873. Pflanze 1990b, 143–44.

A. Political party cleavages

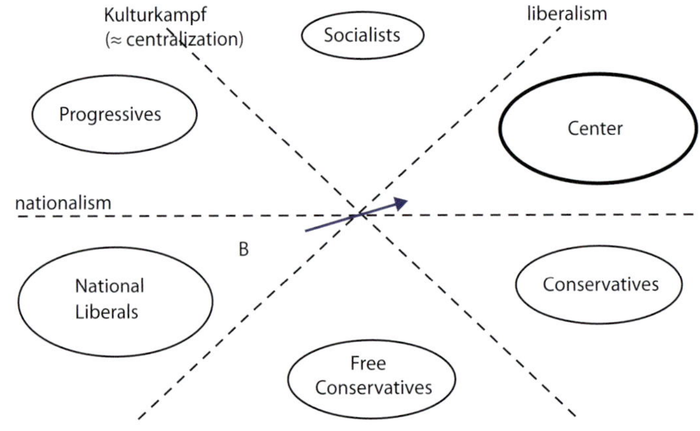

B. Hieratic authority

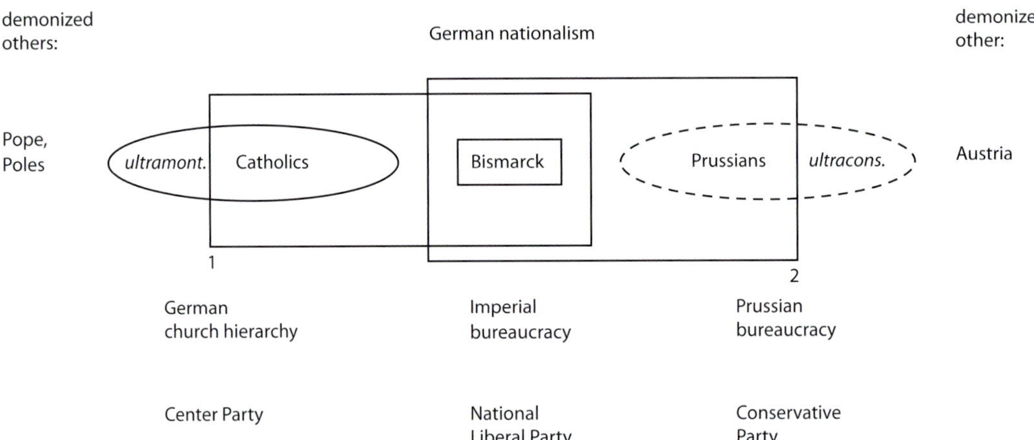

Figure 8.5 Kulturkampf (1871–75).

own ministries. Princely appointments to the Bundesrat were prohibited by Bismarck's constitution from being ministers; such appointments had to be high-level civil servants, the rank right below ministers. This Bundesrat appointment procedure effectively created two bosses for high-level state administrators—their own ministers in state cabinets and the new federalized German Bundesrat. To the extent that this absorption of Prussian high bureaucrats into German dual inclusion influenced their loyalties, pro-German sentiment built up in the bureaucratic layer right beneath the Prussian ministers.

To put political muscle behind both of these dual-hierarchy administrative tricks, Bismarck used the Kulturkampf to purge the Prussian bureaucracy of most of its Catholics.[84] A shock like this could have left no doubt in the minds of

[84] Anderson and Barkin (1982) have convincingly demolished the old myth, rooted in Kehr 1977, of a bureaucracy purge by Bismarck of liberals through his agent Robert von Puttkamer in 1881 and instead demonstrated an earlier purge by Bismarck of Catholics during Kulturkampf. See Gillis 1968, 123 and Gillis 1971, 206 for quantitative data on the Rhineland. The new imperial bureaucracy had no Catholics to begin with.

cautious Prussian bureaucrats that Bismarck was not someone to be taken lightly. This does not mean that the autocratic Prussian bureaucracy was transformed overnight into a bastion of Bismarck loyalists. Junker historical roots were too deep for that.[85] But lasting into the Wilhelmine period, the imperial bureaucracy was an obedient servant of the German chancellor, and the Prussian bureaucracy developed competing dual loyalties rather than being unambiguously Prussian particularist.[86] The Prussian bureaucracy was certainly never politically liberal, but it became predominantly New Conservative rather than ultraconservative. For Bismarck, this was an important distinction.

The Prussian army officer corps, however, remained ultraconservative.[87] If anything, their determination to resist control by Bismarck, and even discussion by the Reichstag, was deeper than ever. Kaiser/King Wilhelm I supported them in this.

Figure 8.5B assembles the various state-building consequences of Kulturkampf into the synoptic view of hieratic authority. Bismarck's demonizing assaults of conflict displacement on the pope (also the Poles) on one flank and on Austrian-sympathizing ultraconservatives on the other triggered new institutional and emergent-actor bridges of dual inclusion in the Reichstag and in the bureaucracies. The cultural cognition holding all this together was hieratic authority, with Bismarck himself at the charismatic center, personally epitomizing German nationalism. An unintentionally consolidated Center mass-party and a recalcitrant army officer corps on the two wings of dual inclusion were portents of the future.

The cultural grounding of the party cleavages in figure 8.5A in the hieratic authority of figure 8.5B implies that each cleavage was not just a policy disagreement. It was a claim by one side to cultural superiority and dominance over the other.[88] In liberal eyes, opponents were antimodern. In nationalist eyes, opponents were regional particularists. In Kulturkampf eyes, opponents were ultramontane subversives. The party most squarely on the opposing side of each cleavage epitomized the respective traitors, but adjacent parties could be seen as fellow travelers. Because of these hieratic interpretations of partisan conflicts, party cleavage was not polite policy disagreement. It was culture war for the soul of the new Germany. The slope from opposition to persecution was slippery.

ANTISOCIALISM AND PROTECTIONISM

In 1878 and 1879 Bismarck initiated a series of well-known actions that changed the course of German history: the negotiation of the so-called Sammlungspolitik.[89] Many commentators credit the lengthy depression that began in 1873 as triggering these events. But other countries experienced that worldwide depression, and only Germany started down the road of "social imperialism" to World War I. Can Bismarck's political realignment choices in 1878 and 1879, in delayed response to the depression, be explained by dual inclusion, conflict displacement, and hieratic authority?

Contemporary political science often reifies actors by assigning fixed goals. A typification of Bismarck as Germany would focus on electoral politics and on controlling the state bureaucracy as the motivational drivers of his state building. A typification of Bismarck as Prussia would focus on international relations and the military as his motivation for state building. In contrast to both of these assumptions about coherent goals, situating Bismarck within the contradiction between democracy and autocracy emphasizes his organizational brokerage role as a feedback channel through which contending political forces and levels of analysis reverberated. Even as he constructed dual inclusion through his favorite styles of conflict displacement and hieratic authority, Bismarck himself evolved in response. In the short run, actors create relations; in the long run, relations create actors.[90] Bismarck's policy inconsistencies and wild oscillations were not unrelated to the development of the contradictory system that he built.

Pflanze's biography makes it clear that even though the depression of 1873 was the economic crisis that ultimately led to the protectionist tariff

[85] Hintze 1975; Muncy 1944; Rosenberg 1958; Gillis 1968.

[86] According to lists of names in Bonham's dissertation (1985, 182, 217, 261, 327), in the 1890s imperial ministers and high bureaucrats supported the Caprivi and Bülow governments' economic "modernizing bills" 88 percent of the time, while Prussian ministers and high bureaucrats supported them 33 percent of the time.

[87] Craig 1955; Kitchen 1968.

[88] Gross (1997) traces how the Kulturkampf became tied to larger issues of German nationalism and national identity.

[89] The debate over Sammlungspolitik is enormous and includes contributions from the following sources: Gerschenkron 1943; Rosenberg 1967; Böhme 1966; Kehr 1977; Lambi 1963; Mommsen 1995; Barkin 1987; Stegmann 1970; Wehler 1985; and Eley 1974, 1976, 1980.

[90] Cf. Padgett and Ansell 1993; Padgett and McLean 2006; and Padgett and Powell, this volume.

legislation of 1879, it was the war-in-sight diplomatic crisis of May 1875 that was the more immediate stimulus to Bismarck's rethinking of his domestic political coalitions.[91] France and Austria were the two Catholic countries he had just defeated. France was the irreconcilable foe. A balancing coalition between France and Austria to counterattack Germany was the logical next step. To forestall this, Bismarck was generous to Austria in land and supported Austrian imperialist ambitions in the Balkans. Equally important, Bismarck cultivated close diplomatic ties with Russia in order to threaten Austria's flank in case it decided to reject German blandishments and to support France. The Three Emperors' League of 1873 was Bismarck's implementation of his new more defensive conflict-balancing approach to international relations.[92]

Bismarck's aggressively anti-Catholic posture during the Kulturkampf, however, undermined the credibility of his international-relations claim to have switched suddenly from bellicose conflict displacement to peaceful conflict balancing. Through a series of events that need not detain us, Russia and England diplomatically ganged up on Germany to insist that Bismarck be less aggressive toward France: "The rebuff that Bismarck experienced from other European powers in May 1875 was the greatest diplomatic defeat of his career."[93] From this moment forward, Bismarck looked to defuse the Kulturkampf and to find some alternative method of constructing a ruling coalition. Bismarck originally had mobilized mass support in 1866 by linking domestic parties to international politics, but international diplomacy eventually rebounded against his domestic political party realignments.

Meanwhile, the economic depression produced two political effects neither of Bismarck's making: a growth in electoral support among workers for the Social Democratic Party (SDP) and the emergence among heavy-industry businessen and large Junker landlords of elite interest groups to lobby for tariff protection from the government.[94]

Given the Marxism of their politicians and the radicalism of the recent Paris Commune, the currently small socialist party was not exactly a surprising new demon for Bismarck to select. But obtaining authorizing legislation to repress socialist printing presses and branch offices through police action was not easy in the left-leaning Kulturkampf coalition that Bismarck had assembled. Fortunately for Bismarck, two random assassination attempts on the Kaiser gave him the excuse to inflame public opinion against purported socialist assassins, to dissolve the Reichstag, and to launch a vigorous "wave the bloody shirt" electoral campaign against Progressive and National Liberal "defenders" of the socialists. This sudden attack of their leader on them took National Liberals by surprise. National Liberal opinion was split sharply about whether to defend legislative rights or to join Bismarck in demonizing the socialists.[95] Eventually in 1880, once protectionism was added to the two-pronged assault, the National Liberal Party officially fragmented between left-leaning "Secessionists," led by oppositional Edward Lasker, and pro-Bismarck remnants of the now shrunken and disoriented National Liberal Party.[96] Bismarck with his antisocialist aggression seemed to be cutting himself off at the knees, dramatically weakening his own ruling bloc.

Conservatives were thrilled by Bismarck's attack on the socialists and by the retreat from the Kulturkampf with which this new assault was correlated. A third political party realignment did not follow immediately from Bismarck's newest conflict-displacement maneuver. But the first stage of externalization had been laid for the second stage of absorption through protectionism to complete. Figure 8.6A diagrams the antisocialist attack;[97] figure 8.6B diagrams the protectionist realignment that ensued.

The abandoned Kulturkampf alliance of National Liberals and Free Conservatives had tilted to the left, in support of the democratic

[91] See Pflanze 1990b, 262–71, 322–25. "Most of his actions during the next four years stemmed from perceptions formed and initial decisions made during his Pomeranian recuperation [in summer] of 1875" (323). "In December 1875 Bismarck revealed his aims to Lucius: 'a division of the national liberals, strengthening of its right wing, and weakening of the Progressive party'" (324–25).

[92] Langer 1962, 25–26; Pflanze 1990b, 259–61. Bismarck articulated his famous "three out of five" rule, by which he practiced diplomacy in the 1870s and thereafter, in the Kissingen Dictation in 1877: "All [international] politics reduces itself to this formula: to try to be one of three, as long as the world is governed by an unstable equilibrium of five great powers" (ibid., 253). This statement of course violates his claim (see footnote 16) not to have any rules.

[93] Pflanze 1990b, 272.

[94] Pflanze 1990b, 282–93, 311–16; Rosenberg 1967; Lambi 1963; Böhme 1966; Wehler 1969.

[95] Pflanze 1990b, 392–408, 534–37; Sheehan 1978, 182–83, 191–95; Langewiesche 2000, 195–99, 209.

[96] Pflanze 1990b, 534–37; White 1976.

[97] Figure 8.6A shows that in sentiment antisocialism split Center as well as the National Liberals. That they did not fragment organizationally was due both to their more cohesive organization and to their subsequent support of protectionism.

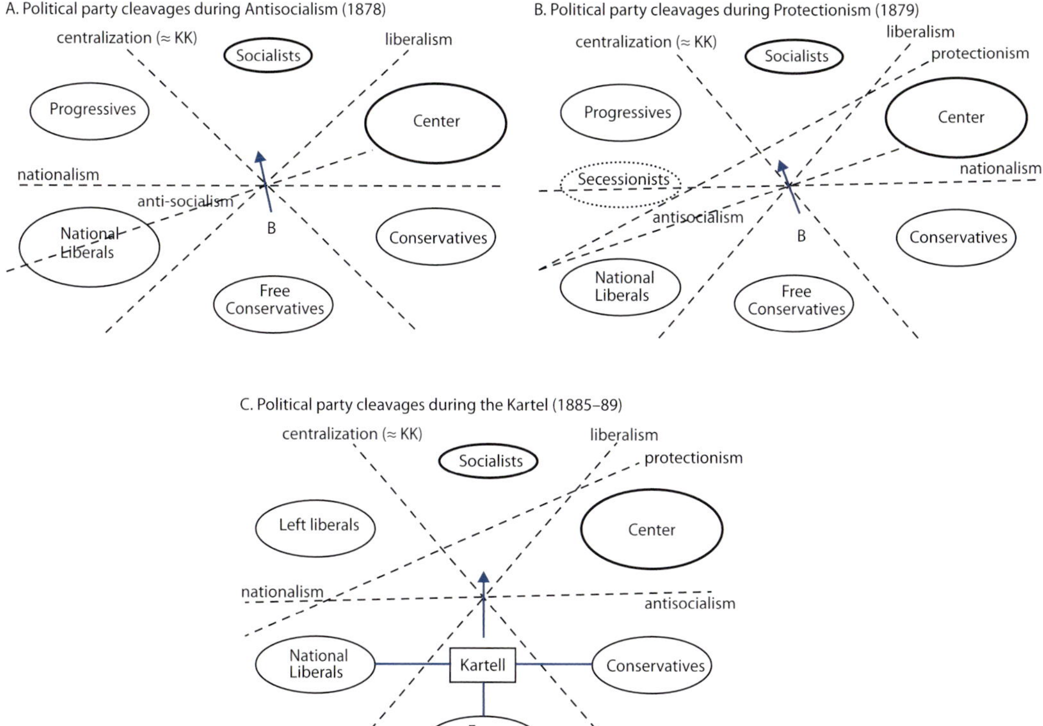

Figure 8.6A–C Antisocialism and protectionism (1878–1989).

pillar of "Germany." The new protectionist alliance of Free Conservatives, Conservatives, and a chastened rump of National Liberals tilted to the right. This was not a reversion to the autocratic pillar of "Prussia," because among other things the Conservatives had re-formed, but it was a shift back in that direction. The previously persecuted Center now turned into a very large swing vote that Bismarck could use opportunistically to oppose free-trade Progressives and Secessionists.

The second major political consequence of the depression, besides growth of socialists with subsequent realignment, was the formation of elite economic interest groups to lobby for tariff protection. The CdI for heavy industry and the VdSWR for large agriculturalists were the two most famous of these many new lobby groups.[98] Bismarck saw wide popular support for an active government initiative to respond to the depression, contrary to his own government's policies of free trade and laissez-faire. Bismarck responded by reaching outside his existing bureaucracies to consult extensively with elite members of these lobby groups and with businessmen whom he knew on his own. To industrialists' demands for tariffs, Bismarck added less popular agricultural tariffs.[99]

These were the conversations that led to the protectionist bill that realigned the parties again. Through extensive extragovernmental discussions with economic elites and interest groups at the peaks of both the industrial and the agrarian pillars of the economy, Bismarck negotiated personally his "marriage of iron and rye" tariff legislation, which was passed contentiously in 1879. The dramatic crescendo of this bill's passage was Bismarck's last-minute choice between parliamentary-rights concessions to National Liberals for the extra votes he needed and federalist concessions to Center for the extra votes

[98] Lambi 1963, 114–16, 140–44; Berdahl 1965, 233–35; Böhme 1966, 359–409; Pflanze 1990b, 311–16.

[99] Stern 1977, 184–204; Lambi 1963, 164–65, 180–90.

Stimulated positively by antisocialism and Sammlungspolitik but also perhaps threatened with proto-corporatism, leaders in each of the Honoratioren parties in Bismarck's protectionist coalition became very compliant over the course of the 1880s to Bismarck.[111] Our interpretation is that elite economic networks disciplined elite political networks. Bismarck orchestrated the tight electoral coordination of his three pro-government parties—namely, the Free Conservatives, the Conservatives, and the rump National Liberals—into an organized parliamentary bloc called the Kartell. These parties agreed not to run candidates against each other, effectively carving up the polity in a way parallel to the way that industrialists were beginning to divvy up markets.

This increased cohesion in Bismarck's own parliamentary bloc did not mean that he always had enough votes to dominate the Reichstag. The Center Party of one hundred delegates swamped any of the Kartell parties in size. The Progressives grew when the Secessionists joined them. Socialists would have ballooned if Bismarck had let them. It was only at the tail end of his career, in 1887–89, that the Kartell had enough votes by itself to be a majority. In the end, Bismarck's consolidation of an unsplittable Center Party constrained him severely.

But the Center's doctrinaire federalism, to protect Catholics against persecution, was compatible with Bismarck's shift back toward Prussia. Bismarck could wrangle Center votes as long as federalism was built into administrative implementation.[112] Political scientists usually think like the Center, namely, that federalism is a device for decentralization. For Bismarck, however, federalism was a device for Prussia to dominate Germany. Just as democracy was a device for Germany to dominate Prussia. In Bismarck's hands, federalism was the constitutional mechanism to protect and empower autocracy. Taken to its limits, federalism could be turned into the method for Staatsstreich, a coup d'état against the legislature in the name of Prussia.[113]

On the side of traditional bureaucracy, the most significant developments of the social-welfare era were two administrative reforms that pushed in different directions: Bismarck's increasing stranglehold over the Prussian civilian cabinet in 1880–82 and his authorization in 1883 of more administrative autonomy for the ultraconservative Prussian army. Both of these bureaucratic adjustments involved shifting back toward Prussia, but these two conservative Prussias were not exactly the same.

The stranglehold over the Prussian civilian cabinet was achieved through widespread turnover in ministerial appointments. Bismarck himself added the Prussian minister of commerce, in charge of social welfare, to his already crowded portfolio of jobs. Bismarck and Wilhelm left no doubt about the purpose of these high-level purges, demanding in 1882 that Prussian bureaucrats actively support the government's chosen parties at the electoral polls.[114]

Dismissing his war minister Kameke and his admiralty minister Stosch in 1883 was part of Bismarck's overall shake-up of the Prussian cabinet. But in these two cases, ministerial turnover was associated with less, not more, control over the military. The Prussian war minister was the only army official answerable to probing questions from Reichstag. The transition from Reichstag-friendly Kameke to the submissive Bronsart involved two crucial administrative changes: the right of the Chief of the General Staff to direct access to the Kaiser, without intermediation by his war minister, and the transfer of the army personnel office from the Prussian war ministry to the army's own internal Military Cabinet.[115] These two Bismarck-approved reforms, which had been pushed by the army for a long time, effectively made the autocratic pillar of the Prussian army uncontrollable by anyone other than the Kaiser/king. The war minister became the whipping boy of the Reichstag, constantly peppered with questions about the army, about which he knew almost nothing because the army wouldn't tell him. This was a major victory for the ultraconservatives, with whom previously Bismarck had struggled mightily but

[111] Retallack (1988a, 31–32), for instance, notes that "[party leader] Helldorf discussed [Conservative Party] propaganda in detail with Bismarck and his aides, sometimes changing only the odd word in the chancellor's drafts. . . . Helldorff's most immediate goal was to secure financial support from Bismarck. If the chancellor had any doubts about how the government might profit from such expenditure, Helldorff noted that these funds could help defray the costs of the Conservatives' brochure entitled 'Prince Bismarck and his Economic Policy.' . . . Given their reliance on Bismarck's good will, they had little choice but to accede to his desire of the Kartell."

[112] See the wrangling over the administration of the insurance bills of 1883 and 1884 (Pflanze 1990c, 161).

[113] In the name of "states' rights," Bismarck threatened both the Reichstag in 1882 and the Bundesrat in 1880. Pflanze 1990b, 525–26; 1990c, 77–78, 214.

[114] Pflanze 1990c, 23–38, 42.

[115] Craig 1955, 229; Pflanze 1990c, 39–40.

with whom now on this issue the Prussian Bismarck agreed.

MASS INTEREST GROUPS

Naturally enough, most narratives of nineteenth-century Germany either end with Bismarck or begin with Wilhelm II.[116] The organizational and emergent-actor reverberations of Bismarck's numerous conflict displacements, however, lasted until the end of the century. The main organizational innovation of the 1890s was the rise of mass interest groups, which arguably set the stage for some of what came later. The largest of these interest groups, reaching mass memberships of over three hundred thousand people each, were the Agrarian League and the Navy League.[117] The Agrarian League we interpret as Junkers reaching out from their native pillar of autocracy to ally with populists and to adopt the mass-mobilization organizational methods of democracy. The Navy League we interpret as industrialists reaching out from their native pillar of democracy to ally with nationalists and to adopt the militaristic methods of autocracy. Bismarck's "marriage of iron and rye" initiated the causal sequence that led to these transpositions of interest-group organization to the mass level, but Bismarck himself was an über-Honoratioren notable who preferred to operate through elite networks that he could discipline and bully. Mass nationalist appeal he wanted to leave concentrated in his person, not institutionalized into huge populist organizations beyond his control.

After the death of Wilhelm I, Bismarck's successor, Leo von Caprivi, with the support of his new boss, the brash young Wilhelm II, shocked Bismarck's support structures of Sammlungspolitik and Kartell in 1890 by retreating from protectionist tariffs. Caprivi sought instead to reconstruct a liberal and free-trade ruling coalition of Left-liberals and National Liberals, with possible swing support from the Center.[118] Caprivi even repealed the antisocialist repression of Bismarck, thereby allowing SDP to triple, then quadruple, then quintuple in size in the Reichstag over the 1890s. From his enforced retirement Bismarck railed and fumed; his nationalist and Junker supporters were livid at Caprivi's abandonment of Bismarck's policies and of Bismarck himself.

The inner circle of Sammlungspolitik—namely, the CdI interest group of heavy industrialists and the VdSWR interest group of Junker landlords—both bolted the government and moved into opposition. The Conservative Party also turned sharply into opposition. The Agrarian League, the first large mass interest group, grew out of intraparty dynamics within the Conservative Party, after these top-down stimuli.[119]

Bismarck's responsibility for these post-Bismarck developments was that the leaderships of the three Kartell parties had become so centralized that they lost touch with their regional offices and their Honoratioren notable bases. Intraparty vertical ties between center and periphery were not only weak but bred resentment about whose interests Kartell party leaders really served.[120] The Center and the SDP were cohesive mass-based parties, with deep organizational foundations. The National Liberals, Conservatives, and Free Conservatives, in contrast, were Honoratioren parties of notables whose horizontal cohesion had been created by Bismarck but whose vertical cohesion had been undermined by his intense co-optation of their leaderships.[121]

Party overcentralization mattered because yet another consequence of extended depression was that a wave of populist agrarian protest broke out all over Germany, just as it did in America. Banks, stock markets, and money were the focus of debt-related resentment in both countries. In Germany, Jews were well represented in financial institutions, so populism fueled anti-Semitism. The first manifestation of

[116] Bismarck lost his job at the ripe age of seventy-five basically because of Wilhelm II's succession to the throne. Egotistically, Wilhelm II wanted to make his own mark on history, which he did in an incompetent manner.

[117] For the Agrarian League, see Tirrell 1951; Puhle 1975; and Retallack 1988a. For the Navy League, see Kehr 1973 and Eley 1980.

[118] Barkin 1970; Bonham 1985, 101–82.

[119] Puhle 1975; Retallack 1988a; Hunt 1975, 513–14; Eley 1995.

[120] For Conservatives, see Retallack 1988a. For National Liberals, see White 1976, 84–158 and Eley 1980, 19–40.

[121] The proto-corporatism of trade associations in social welfare also undermined vertical cohesion by providing an alternate basis for notable aggregation. Following the lead of the Center and SDP to mass organization was impossible for the Kartell parties because that would have undermined their own local notable authority. The organizational analogues of parishes and unions for Conservatives were their landed estates and for National Liberals, their industrial factories. For notables to have organized these as voluntary political clubs, to give better organizational foundation to their parties, would have been to risk enabling resistance at the local level. Criticizing these parties for failing to respond "rationally" to universal-suffrage incentives, therefore, ignores the social-network foundations of these parties.

this populist and anti-Semitic wave was a small but loud Protestant group called the Christian Socialist Party. They allied with previously sidelined ultraconservatives at the Conservative Party's Tivoli conference in 1892 to overthrow the Bismarck-aligned leadership. This made the Conservative Party more Volk-ish and less controlled by traditional Junkers.[122]

Elite Junkers centered in the VdSWR reacted to this loss of control of "their" Conservative Party by reaching outside the party to form the nonpartisan Agrarian League. The Agrarian League was an antigovernment alliance between the VdSWR, the German Peasants' League, the Congress of German Farmers, and the Association for International Bimetallism.[123] This cross-class and also cross-regional[124] alliance of farmers was organizationally new: it was an interest group, like the VdSWR, but it was also mass based, like the Center and the SDP. The Agrarian League stood first and foremost against rolling back the agricultural tariff, but it also lobbied aggressively for all agrarian issues, including populist ones. It reactivated the dangerous urban-liberal versus rural-conservative cleavage that Bismarck had tried so hard to elide.

Riding on populism and money from Junkers, the Agrarian League built an organizational thicket of agricultural voluntary associations that did far more than just ask for votes. Cooperatives and other local economic organizations provided legal advice, mutual-aid welfare, crop distribution, and sometimes even fertilizer discounts. In this manner, the Agrarian League created an indebted mass base for Junkers in the East but also expanded to small independent farmers in the west and south who normally voted for National Liberals. National Liberal urban notables, counterintuitively, became beholden to the Junker-funded Agrarian League for rural votes to keep them in power.[125]

The Agrarian League thus became almost a confessional bloc, like the Center and the SDP mass parties. Unlike the Center's parishes and the SDP's unions, which organizationally had consolidated party elites with mass voters, however, agrarian mutual-aid societies crosscut and undercut notable parties, severing party elites from previously deferential voters. Junkers now were embedded in both the Agrarian League and the Conservative Party and could swing either way. But the Conservative Party found an organizational monster in its bowels, more populist and "unreasonable" than its notable self.

A similar story happened on the liberal side. Small interest groups, called the Colonial League and the Society for German Colonialism, grew up to support Bismarck's late colonial adventures. After Caprivi retreated from Bismarck's saber-rattling to emphasize peaceful free trade, aggressive nationalist sentiments concentrated in the Mittelstand (urban petit bourgeoisie) expanded these previously small interest groups into the Pan-German League. This league emphasized not only colonialism but also imperialist revanchism for German-speaking peoples everywhere, far more radical and militarily provocative than anything Bismarck had ever advocated. The National Liberal Party normally considered itself the exemplar of German nationalism, but it could not absorb radical Pan-Germans for three reasons: the inflammatory extremity of Pan-Germanist positions, the social and organizational gaps between notable party leaders and Mittelstand activists, and the fact that National Liberals traitorously supported Caprivi. Pan-Germanists felt that they were being loyal to their nationalist hero in a way that corrupt politicians were not. National Liberals were faced with the same deep alienation between co-opted elites and their mass electoral support as beset Conservatives.

In 1898 the Department of the Navy, under the leadership of Admiral Tirpitz, launched a well-organized propaganda and lobby campaign to build a modern German navy to challenge England on the seas. Tirpitz assembled twenty elite business interest groups, including the CdI, to back and fund his entrepreneurial efforts. The alliance between this set of elite businessmen and the Mittelstand Pan-Germans was not smooth, but eventually a symbiosis was organized, called the Navy League. Essentially the Pan-Germanists were absorbed into the more establishment Navy League, under the guidance of the Navy Department, with funding by business elites. Drawing heavily from a classic Mittelstand clientele, this new mass interest group was self-consciously nonpartisan and antiparty, like the Agrarian League that had preceded it.[126]

[122] Blackbourn 1986, 170–73; Retallack 1988b, 392–94; Eley 1995, 208–16.

[123] Retallack 1988a, 103.

[124] Junkers and the VdSWR were centered in their estates in Eastern Prussia, but the German Peasants' League was centered in small farms in mid- and western Germany, where National Liberals were strong.

[125] Hunt 1975, 517–18; Eley 1995, 216–23.

[126] Chickering 1984, 44–62; Eley 1980, 68–85.

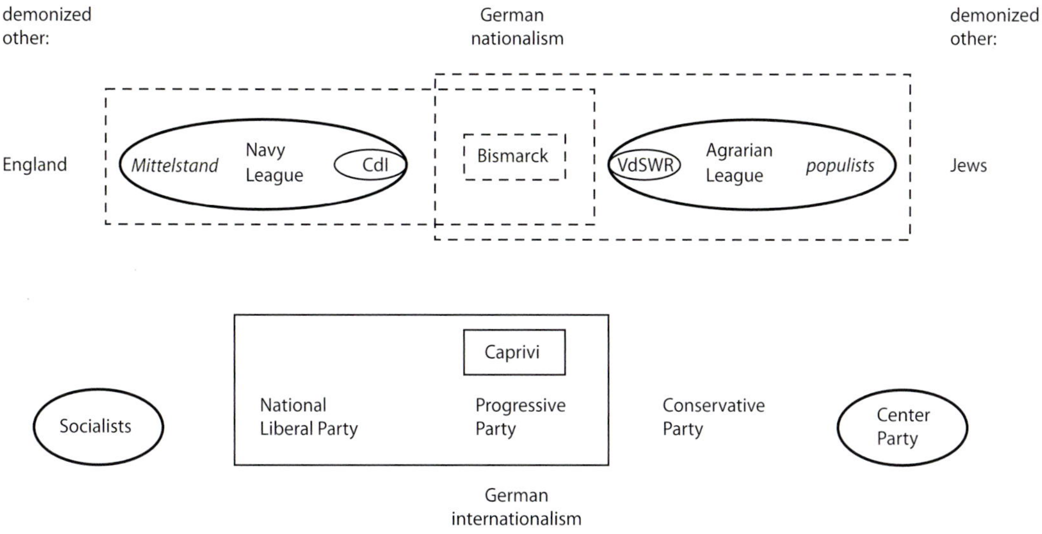

Figure 8.7 Hieratic authority during post-Bismarck rise of mass interest groups (1890s).

Organizationally, the Navy League functioned very differently than the Agrarian League. The Agrarian League was like a confessional bloc, replete with economic aid and voluntary associations that made a real difference in farmers' lives. The Navy League was like an ongoing patriotic festival, with parades, bands, bunting, dancing, and propagandistic plays and speeches. In the name of lobbying for military spending, the Navy League bombastically was preparing the nation for war with England. The Navy League built on the mass nationalism that Bismarck had fueled, through methods and against a target that Bismarck never approved of.

The central organizational point here is that militaristic organizational techniques taken from autocracy were used to mobilize voters who often voted liberal, just as the Agrarian League had used mass-party organizational forms taken from democracy to mobilize voters who often voted conservative. The two constitutional pillars of democracy and autocracy were interpenetrating each other through the emergent actors of mass interest groups, operating outside political parties. Bismarck mobilized nationalist masses through his own personal charisma. As Weber might have predicted,[127] the Navy League routinized Bismarck's absent charisma in ways that the original prophet more shrewdly would not have done. In this perverted way Bismarck's actions outlived him.

Figure 8.7 diagrams the emergence of Wilhelmine mass interest groups in terms of hieratic authority. Long after his death, the mythologized Bismarck epitomized German nationalism.[128] Competing groups clung to and indeed tore at his mantle. Early in the 1890s, while Bismarck was still alive, the Pan-German League, the anti-Polish Society for the Eastern Marches, the Agrarian League, and the Conservative and Free Conservative parties all loudly claimed to be acting in his name.[129] After Bismarck's death in 1898, the Navy League (founded 1989), Prime Minister Miquel's temporarily revived Sammlungspolitik (1897–1902), the Army reserve officer corps (1898–99), the Army League

[127] What the politician Weber (1978, 1392) actually said about Bismarck's legacy was this: "Above all, he left behind him a nation without any political will of its own, accustomed to the idea that the great statesman at the helm would make all the necessary political decisions."

[128] One measure of Bismarck's popularity in retirement was that on his eightieth birthday, in 1895, "Bismarck received several thousand packages, almost 10,000 telegrams, and 450,000 postcards, letters and publications" (Frankel 2005, 32). Another measure was his trip to Vienna to attend his son's wedding in 1892: "He enjoyed to the full the roaring applause of huge crowds that met him at every stop in Germany and even Austria" (Pflanze 1990c, 396). "Outside his room each night crowds filled the streets, including sixteen hundred torch-bearing students, while bands played, speeches were delivered, and patriotic songs sung" (Frankel 2005, 32).

[129] Frankel 2005, 33–79.

(founded 1912), and a Kartell of Productive Estates (1913) joined the chorus (or cacophony) of posthumous Bismarck worship.[130] Bismarck the archetypal state builder became a rallying cry for those on the right who found the current German government intolerable. In terms of Dumont's hieratic model of patriarchal authority, these groups were like polluted women reaching out to their man to construct a higher version of themselves as purified German MAN.[131] Bismarck's ghost was mobilized to fight new demonized others, like England and the Jews, whom the real Bismarck had never attacked.

As is also illustrated in figure 8.7, this mass mobilization of Bismarck mythology undercut the legitimacy of the German government and especially the Reichstag. Bismarck supposedly stood above the crass corruption and self-interest of political parties. Bismarck, as we have seen, in his last decade in power encouraged the proto-corporatism of economic interest groups to end run and to discipline parties. But these were elite machinations among Honoratioren notables. Once the interest-group organizational form was released into the mass public of populists and Mittelstand, proto-corporatism escaped central control. There was no more flywheel to fight against not just demons but the contradictory machine itself.

CONCLUSION

If Bismarck's innovative strategy of conflict displacement was brilliant, it was not because he foresaw and designed it all.[132] Conflict displacement built new forms of organizations and political actors not so much by adding new ties as by severing old ones. Through hieratic authority, the perturbed system then reconstructed itself under Bismarck's careful observation but not really under his control. At the beginning of his career, this chemist produced the organizational inventions that had made Germany: absorption of disparate principalities into Prussia, a national legislature of Reichstag and Bundesrat, party realignment from almost civil war to nationalism, and the harnessing of the autocratic Prussian army. At the middle and end of his career and after his death, he stimulated organizational monsters that drove German history down paths that he did not want: the Catholic and the socialist mass political parties during his lifetime, and the Agrarian League and Navy League mass populist movements after his fall from power and death.

Nineteenth-century German history, much less beyond, was so volatile because of the deep contradiction between democracy and autocracy built into the heart of the dual-inclusion political ensemble that Bismarck catalyzed. This contradiction was never resolved by anything Bismarck did; quite the opposite, he institutionalized it. The contradiction gave to Bismarck his fulcrum position on the seesaw, empowering him to tip one way or the other in response to whatever. But this fulcrum—so essential for holding together the ensemble—was a fragile and unstable balance point, requiring ever more conflict displacements to restore it. The forces underneath it were too strong for naive ideas like "control" to apply. Bismarck's leadership was wildly oscillatory, we argue, to some extent because of genetic disposition but more deeply because of the pulsating swings and conflicts between democracy and autocracy built into German dual inclusion. "Fulcrum" here does not mean the quiet and subtle equipoise of Cosimo de' Medici or Deng Xiaoping; athletic surfing is more like it. In the end, we don't accuse Bismarck of false modesty; we take him at his word when he famously said: "By himself the individual can create nothing; he can only wait until he hears God's footsteps resounding through events and then springs forward to grasp the hem of his mantle—that is all."[133] This self-description does not mean that Bismarck was not a genius. It just means that his conception of genius was less individualistic and egotistical, that is, more powerful, than is ours.

We hesitate to speculate about trajectories of German history in the face of so awesome a topic, about which many deeply informed scholars have thought. But it would be scientifically irresponsible of us not at least to point to logical consequences of our dual-inclusion model, for others to evaluate.

Bismarck did not create democracy and autocracy; he inherited these foundational pillars.

[130] Craig 1978, 274–78; Kehr 1977, 97–108; Kitchen 1968, 120–23; Coetzee 1990; Eley 1980, 316–21. The word *Sammlungspolitik*, literally meaning "bringing together politics," was coined by Miquel, not by Bismarck.

[131] An often reproduced poem read at Bismarck's funeral expressed this hieratic idea eloquently: "Bismarck was dead, is no longer dead,/ In your soul, which lifts itself,/ He rises before you, comes again and lives,/ Comes and is here,/ Omnipresent and near,/ Germany, your Bismarck, he lives" (Frankel 2005, 52).

[132] Contra Kissinger 1968.

[133] Quoted in Pflanze 1990a, 80.

What he did create, or at least catalyze, were three sequential versions of dual inclusion: centralized brokerage of federalism, operating through the chancellery and the Bundesrat; nationalistic political parties, operating through the Reichstag; and corporatist social welfare, operating through the "marriage of iron and rye" of private elite interest groups. Given that democracy and autocracy were stapled together in the first place, each of these three dual inclusions represents a possible trajectory of nineteenth-century German history. To understand the concept of "trajectory," it is useful to review how and why each of these evolved out of the others.

Constitutional federalism was a brilliant masterstroke that emerged from decapitation. Once the heads of German princes were separated from their body politics through the conflict displacement of international wars with Austria and France, the princely heads could be moved into the upper house of the new German Bundesrat and their populist bodies could be moved into the lower house of the new German Reichstag. Bismarck the chancellor managed communication between the two houses. Matters were not so simple with the Prussian king because he had won the wars. He instead was promoted upstairs to become German Kaiser. As long as Wilhelm I went along, the Prussian army followed. As Prussian king, Wilhelm's head was still firmly fixed to the autocratic body of his Prussian army and aristocracy. But as German Kaiser, William's relationship with his federalist German body was mediated through Bismarck.

Dual inclusion was organizational invention not just because it was institutionally new. The Kaiser, chancellery, Bundesrat, and Reichstag coupled together two domains of relational-tie autocatalysis, in the chemistry language of this book. Democracy was given geographical extension and aristocratic approval, enabling it to reproduce better. And militaristic autocracy was given money from a budding industrial economy, enabling it to reproduce better. So what's the problem? With positive feedbacks and a juggernaut like this, why didn't Bismarck proceed immediately to World War I, as some of his foreign neighbors feared and as some of his Prussian officers would have liked? Or to put it less anachronistically, why didn't Bismarck turn into another Napoleon?

The problem for Bismarck at this early stage of nation building was constitutive-tie or biographical autocatalysis,[134] in the terms of this book. For organizational innovations to reproduce over the long run they must reconstruct the people that populate them. At the cultural level, hieratic authority already had reconstructed Bismarck himself into the charismatic embodiment of the new Germany. "German nationalism" defined the people who worshiped this. But constitutive autocatalysis requires more than a warm glow after military victory. Warm glows must be translated into everyday lives for nationalism itself to reproduce. Without German nationalism built into the daily fabric of German federalism, the whole constitutional ensemble of Kaiser, chancellor, Bundesrat, and Reichstag became just another clever gimmick.

Bismarck's first approach to this problem was nationalist political parties. Hence the second type of dual inclusion grew organically out of the first. The first conflict displacement of war with Austria worked brilliantly to solve internal constitutional crisis of Prussia by splitting the Liberal (democratic) and Conservative (autocratic) political parties into a nationalist alliance of new centrist parties (National Liberals and Free Conservatives), opposing the polarized remnants of the two originals. All four of these parties were Honoratioren parties, that is, clubs of local notables. Bismarck's party realignment maneuvers, in other words, institutionalized German nationalism into centrist segments of the German upper classes. Nationalist sentiment in the lower classes remained mostly at the ephemeral level of warm glows after military victories.[135] Electoral success for Bismarck ebbed and flowed accordingly.

If history had stopped here, European wars still would have ensued, but they would have been of the polite diplomatic variety preferred by Bismarck and his Austrian predecessor Metternick rather than the brutal affairs desired by Napoleon or the Prussian army. Elite control by centrist notables, Bismarck foremost among them, would have been assured, mostly through the democratic pillar but with strong support from an imperialist Kaiser. Certainly Bismarck would have preferred for history to have stopped right here.

[134] Called "cellular autocatalysis" in the modeling language of chapter 4.

[135] There was, however, the additional issue of economic foundations. The Zolverein customs union had created the precedent of Germany as a mass domestic trading market. This was the appeal of "Germany" to industrialists and to a lesser (but not nonzero) extent to the consumers who benefited from the lower prices of free trade.

PART III

Communist Transitions

In world historical perspective, the collapse of the Soviet Union and the changes in China are the most significant organizational transformations of our time. Organizational developments in Europe and America are fascinating and revealing in their own right, but those events are incremental compared to what has happened in the former Communist bloc. If organizational innovations are recombinations of networks of skills and relational protocols into something new, and organizational inventions are the spillover of innovations into tipping the multiple domains in which they are embedded, then Communist transitions are an obvious contemporary place to look to study processes of organizational invention.

This conceptual framing of innovation/invention might seem odd to those who still believe in "transition" in the neoliberal sense of utter destruction of one system (communism) and its complete replacement by a new one (free-market capitalism). "Incomplete transition" is the only language available to those with such a totalizing vision, when confronted by uncomfortable pre- and post-transition facts that do not fit ideal types. Instead of studying Communist transition by measuring it against a normative standard, we propose instead to observe how historical networks responded to various types of "reform" perturbations. Seen in this manner, organizational innovation does not necessarily mean something that we approve of.

To be sure, the perspective of autocatalytic networks perceives "creative destruction" as integral to innovation and invention.[1] But without something more, destruction is nothing more than destruction. The autocatalytic perspective seeks to uncover endogenous dynamics of organizational innovation or genesis—that is, processes of preexisting multiple networks recombining and refolding themselves. And it also seeks to uncover endogenous dynamics of organizational catalysis—that is, processes of innovations fitting into preexisting autocatalytic networks of organizational reproduction, inducing those flows to tip or not. In addition to organizational innovation itself, systems have to be poised to tip for invention to ensue. This is far from easy, though this volume has oversampled on successful invention cases (though not exclusively so) in order to discover mechanisms. Failure to tip or reverberate means that the innovation ultimately fails, at least in its original form.

Chapters 9–12 observe processes of organizational innovation and invention in the communist bloc through the end of the 1990s. Chapter 9, by Padgett, compares the political, economic, and social-network dynamics of major economic reform campaigns within communism itself by Joseph Stalin, Nikita Khrushchev, Mao Zedong, Deng Xiaoping, and Mikhail Gorbachev. The transition to "capitalism" around 1990 in the Soviet Union and China appears unique in hindsight only from the perspective of its catastrophic result. Over their histories, Soviet, Chinese, and East European communisms frequently had tried to reform themselves economically in a

[1] Footnote 1 in part 2's introduction compares Schumpeter's person-centered notion of "creative destruction" with our own network-centered operationalization. Schumpeter's view was "out with old people and in with new ones." Ours is "break and recombine networks." Sometimes this involves personnel turnover, sometimes not, but always there are leftover, fractured residues that have to be folded back together, perhaps in new ways.

wide variety of ways. The dynamics of economic reform in the climactic 1980s were not as different, Padgett finds, from what had preceded it as is commonly assumed. It was the outcome more than the process that differed. Padgett analyzes the transition from communism to "capitalism" not from the outside perspective of capitalism but from the internal perspective of communism. Thereby he is trying to read history forward, as a finite set of alternative trajectories, not read history backward, as the teleological victory of superior efficiency (a synonym for us).

In particular, the emergence of the central command economy itself was at least as significant an organizational invention as any of the more capitalist organizations, markets, and states discussed in this volume. Dual hierarchy, constructed by Stalin, was the alignment and interpenetration of the two pillars of central command economy and Communist Party (CP), from their political tops in the Central Committee down to their organizational bases in factories. Dual hierarchy presented to reform-minded leaders (including Stalin himself) four basic constituency and network trajectories for political mobilization: (a) mobilization through the Communist Party hierarchy;[2] (b) mobilization around the CP hierarchy directly down to the party base;[3] (c) mobilization of economic ministries;[4] and (d) mobilization around the ministries directly down to the factory base.[5] Communist economic reform campaigns differed in important and consequential details across time and space, but in broad structural contour they were members of four and only four families.

The most powerful organizational genesis mechanisms that Padgett finds repeatedly in Soviet and Chinese communist reform histories are "purge and mass mobilization" and "robust action." Stalin was the master of the former; Deng Xiaoping was the master of the latter. Mao oscillated between these distinct leadership styles implicit in the system, with powerful results politically and ineffectual results economically. Gorbachev escalated rapidly from failed robust action in perestroika to purge and mass mobilization through democracy. The results were disastrous for him but revolutionary for the Soviet Union. Path dependence does not mean that history is foreordained. It means that Mao made accessible what Deng achieved, and that Stalin created the processual reform options for Gorbachev. Initiated by persons but beyond the control of any person, organizational genesis is shaped by living institutional and network structures inherited from the past, available to be folded, abused, and sometimes re-autocatalyzed.

Catalysis of the central command economy, created primarily by Stalin's purge and mobilization innovation technique,[6] was accomplished by two types of biographical reconstructions. First, the "circular flow of power" through the *nomenklatura* system was the appointment and promotion by leaders of their supporters to selectorates, which then ratified them as leaders in one-candidate elections. Originally implemented at the top in the Central Committee, this method of central control reproduced downward throughout the Soviet system into localized "family circles," which often passively resisted the center they were imitating. Second, by the Great Terror murder of his own Communist Party in 1937–39, Stalin induced so many job openings that an entire "generation of '38" of politically educated young red engineers rose rapidly through the party and the ministries to drive the Soviet economy toward massive concentration and to use the huge factories and cities they built to defeat Hitler. This generation of '38 contained the entire leadership of the Soviet Union until Gorbachev.

The next three chapters in the book—by Andrew Spicer, Valery Yakubovich and Stanislav Shekshnia, and David Stark and Balázs Vedres, respectively—cover different aspects of post-transition Russian and Hungarian reform during the 1990s, the first ten years after Communist transition. These are the Yeltsin years in Russia. Much of intense interest has occurred in the ten years since that first decade (e.g., Putin), but the primary focus of this book is on processes of organizational genesis. This places an empirical premium on studying transitional more than equilibrium moments.[7]

[2] Mao's Great Leap Forward and Stalin's first Five-Year Plan were examples of this, as were Khrushchev's regional economic councils and Deng's fiscal decentralization.

[3] Mao's Cultural Revolution and Stalin's Great Purges were examples of this, but so was Gorbachev's democratization.

[4] Stalin's post-purge mobilization for war with Hitler was the most prominent example of this, but the incremental reforms of Kosygin and Andropov are more modest examples.

[5] This was Hungarian-style reform, greatly desired by Gorbachev but never achieved by him.

[6] While the word *innovation* academically is justified in this context, morally this language is tongue-in-cheek, since what is being referred to are catastrophic events like collectivization and the Great Terror.

[7] Arguably of course, Russia was still very far from equilibrium at the turn of the century. We agree. Not carrying the

Chapter 10 by Spicer is an overview of Yeltsin's economic reforms, with a focus on the financial markets and banks associated with privatization. The architects of Russian reform hoped that private activity could be rapidly and irreversibly severed from the polity such that a "depoliticized" market would quickly fill the void left by the rapid destruction of the state planning system. In contrast, the emergence of a new market system actually evolved through a gradual process of economic experimentation and political settlement where the domains of states and markets were inextricably intertwined. Market reform policies helped dismantle the economic and political structures of the Soviet regime, but they did not dictate what emerged in its place.

Yeltsin's shock therapy of mass privatization was so sudden and so widespread not primarily because of an economic logic but for the political reason of needing to shatter the Communists before they could recover enough strength to overthrow him. Curiously enough, mass privatization (a.k.a. "capitalism") in the hands of Yeltsin was an inverted version of the traditional communist technique of purge and mass mobilization, where this time mass economics was mobilized to smash politics rather than the usual mass politics being mobilized to smash economics. The political objective of shattering communists beyond repair was achieved, but the economic consequence was not capital market efficiency (as overconfident economists had hoped) but swindle, fraud, and consolidation of property in the hands of a few: some old-time managers, some quick-witted newcomers. Spicer traces the rapid rise and rapid decline of the Russian stock market and its consequences for the emergence of Russian business groups, first centered on spun-off state banks and later centered on Yeltsin's own political machine. The stock market under Yeltsin was an organizational innovation that did not last. Oligarchic business groups, which wend across state and markets, were the organizational inventions under Yeltsin that did last, with continuing profound consequences for Russia today. Personnel have turned over dramatically under Putin, but the organizational form of nontransparent business groups has persisted and reproduced. These fabulously wealthy oligarchic business groups are neither "economics" nor "politics" but both.

Chapter 11 by Yakubovich and Shekshnia is a reminder that Russia is too large a country to be captured by a single narrative, no matter how insightful. The background turmoil of Yeltsin is hardly mentioned in this case study of the emergence of the cellular phone industry in Moscow and St. Petersburg. Rather, these are local stories about how fragments of the old Communist state—in particular traditional telecoms and a military research lab, both of which had highly qualified engineers—mostly successfully reached out to foreign partners to jointly found six new cellular companies. These are the types of stories that Gorbachev promised but too rarely delivered. This chapter confirms the basic message of chapter 10 that "market formation" in post-Communist Russia was not the spontaneous invisible hand of Adam Smith and Friedrich Hayek but instead was the visible-hand emergence of business alliances and groups. But the business alliances in question look quite different in the Yakubovich and Shekshnia chapter than they do in the Spicer chapter. Both versions were and are present in Russia.

Of particular interest in the Yakubovich and Shekshnia case study is the entrepreneurial military research lab, which successfully broke into the Moscow telecom market from the outside[8] in response to its otherwise catastrophic financial situation. This lab used its deep (but also nurtured) political connections with the federal regulatory state to construct a successful (and technologically compatible) partnership with a service-oriented foreign company. This explains the emergence of a "competitive" (i.e., two large providers) market in Moscow. In St. Petersburg, in contrast, a U.S. cell-phone manufacturer partnered directly with the St. Petersburg local state, with tons of clout but no technical expertise. This partnership failure explains the emergence of a "monopolistic" cellular market in St. Petersburg. Market structure in this Russian case study thus empirically comes down to the dynamics of business alliances. These business alliances wend in and out of the state in both chapters 10 and 11, but one case has pernicious overtones whereas the other case does not.

Chapter 12 by Stark and Vedres is a reprint of a 2006 article from the *American Journal of Sociology*, with new material on politics added.

story through to its conclusion, however, does not obviate an interest in organizational genesis processes that occurred during the years of Yeltsin.

[8] Outside the traditional telecom industry/ministry, that is, but certainly not from outside the ex-Soviet state.

The topic here again is business alliances and business groups. Stark and Vedres have collected data on the ownership of the 1,700 largest firms[9] in the Hungarian economy from 1987 to 2001. They have also collected data on memberships on the boards of directors of these same Hungarian firms. Consistent with findings in other post-socialist countries,[10] Stark and Vedres find massive patterns of domestic firms owning parts of each other, particularly early in the 1990s but also persisting throughout the decade. Many of these domestic firms were fragments of the previous, now fractured Communist state.[11] Especially given the timing, it is plausible to assume that many of these domestic business networks of cross-ownership had their roots in prior Communist economic relationships.

Stark and Vedres also find, however, the large-scale entry of foreign firms into the Hungarian economy in this decade, no doubt fueled by Hungary's entry into the European Union. Rather than keep themselves removed from native firms, many of these foreign firms sought to develop through joint ownership local partnerships and business alliances, reminiscent of the case study in chapter 11. This is not to say that the pattern of business cross-ownership networks is the same with and without foreign direct investment, but the distinction is certainly not as simple as "foreign firms stay removed from local networks" and "domestic firms are networked up to their eyeballs." Foreign and domestic firms interpenetrated through ownership in Hungary in interesting ways in the 1990s, the details of which no doubt will be further elaborated in future research.

Stark and Vedres also present evidence on Hungarian politicians sitting on the boards of Hungarian companies. This phenomenon is widespread, especially in the larger companies in Hungary. In subsequent work, Stark and Vedres have shown that this phenomenon has a partisan cast to it—namely, some large Hungarian companies have become connected through board membership with leftist parties, and others have become associated with rightist parties. This "politicization of the economy" is not a residue from communism but a result of post-socialist electoral politics. Party memberships on boards of directors are to Hungary as corporate campaign contributions are to America.

In terms of the overall theory in this volume—about production and cellular autocatalysis—the chapters in this volume stress the importance of reconfigured biographies to translating innovation into invention. Mass mobilization under communism—under Stalin, under Mao, and more pathetically under Gorbachev—was all about the massive reconstruction (intended and unintended) of biographical flows. We have argued that organizational innovations of all kinds ultimately have to be reinforced through the cellular autocatalysis of people via teaching for innovation to become absorbed into a multiple-network system as invention. In the case of Hungary, and even that of Russia, elite business biographies have moved as much onto the European stage as onto the national one. What implications this has for the evolution of European business networks and groups remains to be seen. Business networks at the national level that are open to foreign direct investment (FDI) could be consistent or inconsistent with closed cosmopolitan business networks at the European or even global levels. Whether or not this is a new European-level open elite remains to be seen. Tracing evolving business groups, alliances, and biographies both beyond national borders and more deeply into national states, therefore, may be a next research step in the study of post-Communist transitions.

[9] They defined "large firm" as being in the annual ranking of the top five hundred firms (based on revenue) in Hungary in any of the years from 1987 to 2001.

[10] But also consistent with findings in other parts of the world, notably East Asia.

[11] Privatization did not have nearly the magnitude of shock in Hungary as it did in Russia (which is not to belittle it) thanks to the previous reform experience of "market socialism" under Hungarian communism. This is Communist reform pattern (d) in Padgett's classification schema.

9

The Politics of Communist Economic Reform

Soviet Union and China

John F. Padgett

In 1983, two years before Mikhail Gorbachev came to power, Joseph Berliner, that doyen of Western research on Soviet industrial relations, wrote a remarkably prescient article that outlined the constrained options for reforming the Soviet economy and then evaluated the likelihood of political success for each strategy.[1] Berliner foresaw four realistic approaches to communist economic reform: the "conservative model," which tinkered "scientifically" with new techniques of central planning; the "reactionary model," which restored the alleged discipline and top-down control of the Stalinist period; the "radical model," which decentralized central planning to allow for Hungarian-style enterprise autonomy; and the "liberal model," which authorized a laissez-faire market for small private firms, surrounding an untouched central planned core of state-owned enterprises.[2] He ranked the likelihood of political success for each alternative in inverse proportion to their threat to entrenched ministerial power. Berliner's analysis was astute enough to predict the categories through which Gorbachev's reform program moved:[3] from Andropov-style discipline in 1985–86, to the Hungarian-like Law on State Enterprises in 1987, to the liberal Law on Cooperatives in 1988. He did not omnisciently foresee Gorbachev's final revolutionary choice of political democratization in 1989. And he mistakenly assumed that his alternatives were mutually exclusive. No one (including Gorbachev himself) foresaw the wild escalation that Gorbachev actually executed, much less the fall of the Soviet Union. But at least Berliner understood the structure of the economic-cum-political reform problems that Gorbachev faced.

In sharp contrast to Gorbachev's radical reforms, which led to the cataclysmic collapse of the Soviet Union, Deng Xiaoping famously introduced gradual economic reforms with no political change. This led to the most vibrant capitalist economy on earth today. Based on this sample of two and twenty-twenty hindsight, it is now conventional wisdom that gradual economic reform is superior to radical political change for inducing efficient economic markets. This lazy interpretation of communist-transition events in the 1980s is superficial in part because it is based on a shallow and teleological historical vision. Change one's temporal focus to the 1950s and 1960s, and the Soviet Union becomes

I thank Stanislav Markus, Andrew Spicer, Andrew Walder, Dali Yang, Valery Yakubovich, and especially Georgi Derluguian for their helpful comments.

[1] Berliner 1983.

[2] This last model had been the NEP (New Economic Policy) approach of Lenin and Bukharin in the mid-1920s before Stalin eliminated that in 1929 with his forced collectivization of agriculture and his wildly ambitious first Five-Year Plan.

[3] Brezhnev-style tinkering with central planning was the only one of Berliner's reform options that Gorbachev rejected out of hand, because of his commitment not to be Brezhnev.

enforcing fulfillment of the plan. At the very top, the Politburo and the Council of Ministers overlapped through shared members. The Central Committee formally was the governing body of the Communist Party, in charge of appointing the leader and Politburo (albeit usually in a rubber-stamp manner).[9] Meeting only occasionally, it was composed of high-level officials from both of the pillars: provincial secretaries, economic ministers, and the like. The secretariat or bureaucracy of the Central Committee was structured into departments that monitored the work of the Moscow-based economic ministries. Lower down at the provincial level,[10] provincial first secretaries were held responsible for the overall economic performance of enterprises in their region. They, jointly with the industrial ministers, appointed and fired enterprise managers in their region through the *nomenklatura* system. At the bottom of the dual-hierarchy system, communist workers and managers formed party cells within each plant to report the plant's performance up the party hierarchy as well as up the factory hierarchy. Party inspection and reporting, to check on laxity and corruption, was called *kontrol*.

Needless to say, things rarely worked as smoothly as this organization chart implies. In subsequent sections, I shall outline actual operations and compare across regimes. But the basic organizational ideas were not complicated. From the perspective of the economy, dual hierarchy operated to send management orders down the economic hierarchy and to monitor performance through information feedback up the political hierarchy. The two hierarchies were separated to inhibit lying. From the perspective of politics, dual hierarchy operated to instill communist values (e.g., "the Soviet man" or "the thought of Mao") into the productive personnel of the economy. Economics under communism was never just economics; it was also mass mobilization of the nation for the future.[11]

No matter how simplified this starting sketch of dual hierarchy, it is still useful enough to identify constrained trajectories for the politics of communist economic reform, were such a thing to become desired. First of all, it is obvious but worth saying that all reform must come top-down from the leader. The basic dual-hierarchy organizational system had too many cross-checking veto points for political initiative to have been possible from any other quarter. In addition, the "circular flow of power" (see footnote 9) gave any communist leader a secure base from which to launch initiatives. But leadership initiative alone was never enough to accomplish reform. For it to become more than just a decree, leadership initiative had to be taken up by others in the system and then achieve self-sustaining reproduction of those interests. The basic dual-hierarchy skeleton defined the alternative set of potential political allies that communist leaders looked to in order to carry their initiative, whatever that might happen to be. The options within the system were four: to reach down to provincial secretaries, to reach down to local party cadres, to reach down to economic ministries, and to reach down to state enterprises. A leadership initiative that appealed to none of these constituencies was greeted only by silence and obstruction. But if it appealed at least to one, then a sequence of events might ensue, tipping into reform or not.

As a first cut, the various reform drives in communist Soviet and Chinese history can be classified according to the primary constituency the leader reached out to. The most tumultuous of such reform drives—Mao's Cultural Revolution and Stalin's Great Purges—involved the leader reaching around provincial party leaders directly down to local party cadres. Such extraordinary mass-mobilization events were not outside "normal" communist history; they were simply the most dramatic of the inbuilt modalities of reform available to communist leaders. Indeed, seen from the internal perspective of communist reform history, not from our perspective of the West, Gorbachev's revolutionary call for political democracy in 1989 was similar in strategic style to the demagogues Stalin and Mao.[12] I demonstrate below that all three of these leaders

[9] Leadership control over the Central Committee was achieved through the "circular flow of power," discussed below: namely, leaders appointed provincial secretaries and ministers who joined the Central Committee, which voted on the succession and renewal of the leaders. See Daniels 1966, 1971, and Hough 1987, 1997.

[10] In the Soviet Union, "provincial level" organizationally was a bit complicated: among the ethnic republics of the Baltics, Caucuses, and Central Asia, "provincial level" meant "republic." Within the larger and more populous republics of Russia, Ukraine, and Belarus, "provincial level" usually meant "oblast," a large subdivision of those republics.

[11] Kotkin 1995.

[12] People forget that an important part of Stalin's Great Purge campaign of 1937–38, which murdered over six hundred thousand party members, was his new constitution, which granted considerable electoral freedom (including the secret ballot) to the lower echelons of the Communist Party. These elections reinforced and fueled denunciations from below.

used "purge and mass mobilization" to attack their own party hierarchy.

A second, less threatening way to mobilize the political pillar for economic reform was for the leader to work through the party hierarchy, not against it. Mao's Great Leap Forward and Stalin's first Five-Year Plan were examples of this.[13] Khrushchev's regional economic councils and Deng Xiaoping's fiscal decentralization were also examples of mobilizing provincial first party secretaries for reform. These cases differed in important details that were consequential for their subsequent evolution, but the point here is that in their constituency politics they are members of a family.

The third political option that dual hierarchy presents to communist leaders interested in reform is mobilization through economic ministries. This modality of reform includes Berliner's categories of Brezhnev-style "conservative" or Andropov-style "reactionary"—which is to say, incremental not radical reform. One should not forget, however, that this was the modality that Stalin shifted into, after his Great Purge, in order rapidly to build the economy for war against Hitler. World War II itself shifted Stalin's heavy-industry-defense approach into hyperdrive. Thus economic mobilization through ministries is not only an antireform approach, although in more recent times it was.[14]

Finally there is the fourth "Hungarian style" of economic reform, which involved leaders reaching around ministries directly down to state enterprises by loosening ministerial control and increasing enterprise autonomy. Typically this involved not privatization but reorienting central planning away from material flows and toward socially regulated prices and profits. Ministries essentially become state banks in such a transformation. In addition to Hungary as a successful example of this approach to economic reform, the Kosygin reforms of 1965 and the Gorbachev reforms of 1987 stand as unsuccessful Soviet examples of this approach.

I do not list private property as a politically viable route to reform under communism because a constituency for that did not exist within dual hierarchy. There were noncommunist constituencies for such a reform. Around the consumer margins of the economy—handicrafts, small consumer goods, small plots in agriculture—a private market might become tolerated.[15] But this would always remain marginal because private property amounts to a dismantlement of dual hierarchy. Any communist leader proposing this would be overthrown.

Deng Xiaoping superficially seems to be the miraculous exception to this political constraint—a communist leader who successfully transformed his central-command economy into a Western-style market. But I will show instead that Deng employed traditional political strategy number two: the mobilization of provincial and local government cadres to lead his reform.[16] As I explain below, the peculiarly decentralized structure of state ownership in China, bequeathed to Deng by Mao's Great Leap Forward and Cultural Revolution, induced Chinese party cadres to behave as precocious entrepreneurs, without owning private property. While it is fair to hold Deng responsible for successfully managing China's economic transformation,[17] it is less widely appreciated that Mao was responsible over the longer run for rewiring the Soviet version into a party-dominated decentralized version of dual hierarchy that Deng then could tip into quasi-markets. Mao made accessible what Deng achieved.

On the Soviet side, Gorbachev, like Deng, wanted to be an economic reformer to strengthen communism, not to unravel it. But the dynamics of the reform process turned him into a political revolutionary, more in strategic style like Stalin and Mao than Gorbachev acknowledged. There are many sides to the dynamics of communist economic reform. One is the politics of reform—how leaders' proposals self-organize alliances to support and oppose them. Another is economic feedback—how alliances and policies spill over into the interaction of economic enterprises. Finally there is biographical feedback—how reaction from dual hierarchy reconstructs the leader over time. Below I highlight these three interlinked dynamics in the communist-reform cases of Joseph Stalin,

[13] It is interesting that Mao's Cultural Revolution followed soon after his Great Leap Forward, just as Stalin's Great Purge followed soon after his first Five-Year Plan. The logic of this sequence will be explored below.

[14] The developmental states of Japan and South Korea, while not communist, are additional apt examples.

[15] NEP in the 1920s under Lenin was an example, though he considered this as transitional.

[16] A fuller description of Deng's strategy will become "robust action" (cf. Padgett and Ansell 1993), once the latent pillar of the People's Liberation Army is taken into consideration.

[17] By this language I do not mean to imply that a great man "did it." All any reform leader can do is to perturb autocatalytic processes into self-reorganization. The complexity of changing a country is beyond anyone's intelligence and foresight.

Nikita Khrushchev, Mao Zedong, Deng Xiaoping, and Mikhail Gorbachev.[18]

To gather data about the co-evolution of reform politics and economics under communism, the empirical cases that I survey in this chapter are as follows: First Stalin, meaning his Five-Year Plans, his Great Purges, and his world war defeat of Hitler. This was the remarkable sequence that created massively centralized dual hierarchy, dominated by ministries. A short interlude on Khrushchev's failed decentralization follows. Then I turn to Mao, meaning his Great Leap Forward and his Cultural Revolution. The outcome of this equally remarkable sequence was party dominance over a decentralized planned economy. Deng Xiaoping's "incremental" economic reforms are analyzed in light of the structure bequeathed by Mao. And finally I discuss Gorbachev's escalation from economic to political reform. The historiographies on these events are vast. I can only hope to identify what I see as the primary causal feedback loops linking economy and politics during these episodes and leave it to others to extend, to modify, or to critique my observations, which are grounded in secondary sources. My main objective in this perhaps overly ambitious comparison is more to get the co-evolutionary topic onto our collective research agenda than it is to provide the impossible last word.

STALIN

I begin with Stalin because he invented dual hierarchy. Lenin made the Bolshevik Party, but Stalin built a central command economy around the party. All other communist leaders, even Mao, worked in Stalin's shadow because they permuted and modified the basic framework that he built.

As is well-known, Stalin's monomaniacal economic priority was heavy industry and defense: to build gigantic modern steel factories like Magnitogorsk and all that supported them.[19] In Stalin's opinion, "we are fifty or a hundred years behind the advanced countries. We must make good this distance in ten years. Either we do it or we shall go under."[20] There was nothing innovative technologically about this; Stalin imported advanced factory designs from the West.[21] What was innovative was the economic organization of central command into which these "high-tech" industrial technologies were inserted. Stalin built the Soviet central-command economy in two major stages: Initially Stalin's central-command system was an economic extension of Lenin's and Trotsky's Bolshevik Party. In the course of his first Five-Year Plan of 1928–32, Stalin organizationally attacked and purged various leftover "class enemies"[22]—kulaks (rich peasants) in agriculture, technical experts in industry, and small traders in commerce—and he tried to reconstruct agriculture, industrial production, and commercial distribution all to be "red." In his second major stage, the Great Purges of 1936–37, Stalin decimated and murdered most of the Leninist party members who had achieved the first stage, and he replaced them with young, better-educated, Stalinist zealots ("the generation of '38"). The economic pillar of central command, which had been subordinated to the political pillar of the party, thereby became the primary, or at least the co-equal, structure within the dual-hierarchy ensemble. The searing events of World War II locked in this ensemble for forty-five years through hyperconcentration in heavy industry.

The driver behind all of this was war. Under Lenin, that had meant World War I, then class war, and then civil war. Under Stalin, that meant class war, then war against surreptitious and ill-defined "enemies of the people," and finally World War II. Science and modernity were important ideological addendums, but at its core the Soviet central-command economy was built for war, both external and internal.

At various points in his career, Stalin appealed to all four of the communist constituencies at his disposal, but in this section I identify the most transformative organizational genesis mechanism that he employed to be "purge

[18] In the section on Gorbachev, the Hungarian case of János Kádár is also discussed en passant. It goes without saying that I cannot possibly cover everything in the vast historiographies on all of these very well-documented leaders. (The historiographies on Gorbachev, Khrushchev, and Kádár, while adequate, are not as high quality as the others.)

[19] Kotkin 1995. Stalin's chosen name reveals much about both him and his economic policies. Joseph Stalin was born as the Georgian Ioseb Besarionis dze Jughashvili. Upon becoming a communist, he renamed himself "Stalin" because *stal'* means steel in Russian. Tucker (1990) discusses psychological aspects of Stalin's identity as a Georgian or a Russian.

[20] Harris 1999, 131. With Hitler soon on the horizon, this ten-year prediction was more accurate than Stalin realized at the time he uttered it in 1931.

[21] In Marxism, after all, socialism was supposed to build on top of capitalism, before then surpassing it.

[22] The original "true" class enemies of nobles, large capitalists and large landlords had already been disposed of by Lenin in 1918. Stalin's class enemies, in contrast, were discretionary selections by him.

and mass mobilization." In the first stage, this meant mass mobilizing both upper and lower echelons of the party to purge noncommunists from economic activities. In the second stage, this meant mobilizing lowest-level young cadres and workers against middle tiers of Stalin's own apparatus, both in the political pillar and in the economic pillar. The organizational transformations achieved by this highly conflictual genesis mechanism were locked in, I shall argue, by the organizational catalysis mechanism of the "circular flow of power,"[23] institutionalized in *nomenklatura* appointments and biographies. On the legal surface and occasionally in fact, this conjunction of genesis and catalysis mechanisms induced supercentralized totalitarianism: namely, almost complete domination by the leader. But more frequently little circular flows of power, in imitation of the leader, reproduced throughout the system.[24] This gave dual hierarchy a bureaucratic-interest dynamic of its own, resistant to control by the nominally all-powerful leader. This stubborn autonomy, in turn, tempted the leader—be it Stalin, Mao, or Gorbachev—to repeat "purge and mass mobilization" in a cyclic manner.

Stalin did not start his career in so dramatic a way. He originally was merely the organization man behind Lenin's and Trotsky's charisma. At that time, "general secretary" meant only that Stalin was Lenin's right-hand person in charge of managing the appointments and promotions of Bolshevik cadres mostly in the provinces, far removed from Moscow. Stalin used his party position in the 1920s to develop a political machine of provincials—especially provincial first secretaries—personally loyal to him. After Lenin's debilitating illness in 1922 and death in 1924, this became the base of political support that Stalin used to defeat Trotsky's more cosmopolitan supporters in Moscow.[25] Upon his succession, therefore, mobilization through provincial first secretaries was the natural political strategy for any policy that Stalin might wish to pursue. This same road to leadership was later followed by Khrushchev and by Gorbachev. Deng also "played to the provinces" late in his life, once Mao became feeble.

The economic context of Stalin's rise to power was Lenin's New Economic Policy (NEP). The NEP economy, which Stalin altered, had consisted of two distinct parts. A core of state-owned industries (the "commanding heights") was the result of the revolution's nationalization of tsarist-era capitalist enterprises. During the chaotic civil war period, money became worthless due to hyperinflation; hence nonmonetary transfer of material supplies among these industries by party cadres was not so much a policy choice as it was a frantic response to wartime meltdown.[26] Surrounding this nationalized industrial core was communist toleration of traditional free markets of peasants, artisans, and petty tradesmen. This also was not so much a policy choice as it was the lack of state capacity to do otherwise. Lenin and his main economic adviser, Bukharin, however, did decide that the time was premature to attack peasants and petty bourgeoisie in the countryside, who vastly outnumbered the beleaguered urbanized proletarians who comprised the bulk of the Bolshevik Party.[27]

It is easy to understand the desire of communists and noncommunists alike to industrialize "backward" Russia. What requires explanation is the breakneck speed at which Stalin pursued this objective. War psychology, rooted not only in looming military threat from antirevolution capitalist countries but also in the narrow class basis of the Bolshevik Party, seems a prerequisite to understanding. Stalin and his supporters (unlike Bukharin and his "rightist" supporters) urgently felt the need to carry forward their "socialist offensive" with dispatch or else they would perish.[28] Violent wartime experiences injected intense emotions into this rational urgency.

But psychology is one thing, and constituency feedback is another. Whatever motivated the Bolshevik elite, vast numbers of people had to be mobilized and crushed in order to achieve breakneck industrialization. The "crushed" half of this equation was class war. The "mobilized" half of this equation was social and political mobility. Put the two halves together and one gets "purge

[23] According to Daniels (1966, 1971) and Hough (1987, 1997), the "circular flow of power" is leaders gradually appointing provincial first secretaries, ministers, and others, who then occasionally collectively assemble into a legislative Central Committee to vote and affirm the leader and his program.

[24] Depending on the context, colloquially these were known as family circles, clans, or troikas.

[25] Daniels (1988) and Medvedev ([1972] 1989) discuss the succession struggle between Stalin and Trotsky.

[26] Malle 1985.

[27] Cohen 1973.

[28] In this, they shared the sentiments of Trotsky and his "leftist" supporters, even though Trotsky by this time had been exiled. The irony was well noted at the time that Stalin had aligned with NEP "rightists" in order to defeat Trotsky, only then to turn on a dime to adopt the "leftist" economic program of Trotsky.

and mass mobilization" as the Bolsheviks' preferred mechanism of organizational genesis, the final product of which was dual hierarchy.

Class warfare was both the ideology and the learned practice of the Bolsheviks, so it is not surprising that they thought that class war, not incentives, was the way to build an economy. Upon seizure and consolidation of power in 1927–28, Stalin launched a first Five-Year Plan for industrialization that has aptly been called a "bacchanalia of planning."[29] Five-year targets for growth rates in heavy-industry production were set at 180–280 percent of current 1927 levels.[30] Behind these fantastic aspired growth rates lay an investment commitment to build gigantic new factories of mass production, indeed not just new factories but new cities of socialism.[31] These new factories and cities were to make regions economically specialized and the country economically interdependent.[32] A language of socialist modernity surrounded these investments. The trick, of course, was where was the massive amount of money (and energy) required to build these modern factories and cities to come from?

The answer to the money question was agricultural collectivization. Peasants were herded into large state-controlled farms in order more efficiently to extract "surplus" from them. Some of this agricultural produce was shipped abroad to gain foreign exchange to pay for imported technology. Most of it was used to feed old and new urban workers at subsidized rates. Agricultural collectivization for state extraction required class war on kulaks and on the private distributional channels that peasants previously had used. Urban Bolshevik cadres were sent into the countryside with orders to expropriate land from kulaks at the point of a gun, with the assistance of any aggrieved poor peasants who had been "exploited" by them.[33] Private traders ("NEP men") were likewise repressed to prohibit peasants from selling more profitably on the private market than to the state at low administered prices.[34] Kulaks and NEP men who resisted this coercive treatment were sent off to newly created gulag labor camps in terrible locations, where they were forced to do manual labor: building canals, clearing forests, and so forth. Famine in 1932–33 was one result of this policy, as peasants killed their livestock to avoid the penal label of kulaks.[35] Flight to the city as uneducated immigrant labor was another. Soviet industrialization, in other words, was built explicitly and self-consciously on the backs of the peasants. As urban proletariat with a monopoly on visions of the future, Russian communists (unlike Chinese communists, who were ex-peasants) experienced little angst about peasant repression.[36]

On the industrial side, "purge" was applied to noncommunist technical experts and engineers, left over from pre-revolutionary tsarist days. Bolsheviks, being mostly workers in background, were not usually very educated; hence they were dependent upon these "class enemies" for managing their desired industrialization. This dependency notwithstanding, Stalin initiated major show trials[37] that loudly accused segments of the technical elite of sympathizing with Germany and of sabotaging budding Russian development from within. These early show trials were the excuse to fire large numbers of needed noncommunist engineers and to demand ideological conversion and fidelity from the rest. Among communists, Bukharin "rightists" were also purged, thereby eliminating NEP-style policy dissent. To replace eliminated technicians, Stalin opened up large numbers of engineering schools for communist youth.[38] Ten years later, once they came on line, these newly educated red youth would become crucial to Stalin's control.

In the meantime, mass industrialization had to proceed another way than through technical experts. Stalin's political power base was provincial first secretaries, so these became the first political constituency of the Five-Year Plan. Stalin's massive industrialization drive promised huge

[29] Jasny 1961.

[30] Zaleski 1962, 54. The target growth rate escalated from 180 percent in March 1927 to 280 percent in April 1929.

[31] Kotkin 1995.

[32] Nove 1969, 144. "On 8 June 1927 a decree by the Council of People's Commissars called for the creation of 'a united all-union plan, which, being the expression of economic unity of the Soviet Union, would facilitate the maximum development of economic regions on the basis of their specialization.'"

[33] Large-scale noble estates had already been expropriated by Lenin, with land disbursed. Kulaks—really just successful peasants—had much smaller landholdings, defined by only a few employees and livestock.

[34] From 1925 to 1931, the annual percentage of trade through legal private channels declined from 42.5 to 42.3 to 36.9 to 22.5 to 13.5 to 5.6 to 0.0 percent. Nove 1969, 136. Unknown volumes of illegal private trade still existed.

[35] Eventually tractors came on line to improve the productivity, if not the misery, of peasants. Manning 1993a, 119.

[36] Kuromiya 1988, 85–86, 110–14; Kotkin 1995, 81–84; Harris 1999, 114–18; Fitzpatrick 2008, 136–41.

[37] E.g., the Shakhty affair in 1928 and the Industrial Party trial in 1930. Kuromiya 1988.

[38] Fitzpatrick 1979b.

factories and economic development for their regions. Project proposals flooded into Moscow with optimistic, even outlandish, promises, as provincial competition for central investment intensified.[39] "D. B. Riazanov quite aptly remarked at the sixteenth party conference in April 1929: 'Every speaker from this platform ends with the conclusion: "Give us a factory in the Urals, and to hell with the Rightists! [*Laughter*] Give us a power station, and to hell with the Rightists! [*Laughter*]."'"[40] To Stalin, industrial giganticism was necessary to win an inevitable war with enemy unknown. To urban youth, industrial giganticism meant modernity and the future. To provincial secretaries, factory investment also meant pork. Some of the pressure for unrealistic bacchanalia of planning came bottom-up from the competing promises of provincial secretaries about what they could achieve in their regions, if only the center would support them. The unrealistic Five-Year Plan, in other words, fueled Stalin's political machine. The race was on to build huge factories, whatever the cost.

These political dynamics had organizational consequences at the factory level. In NEP days, nationalized factories had been run by an onsite collective "troika" of a red director (ideologically correct but often technically unqualified), a technical deputy director (who really ran things), and a trade union representative, working together.[41] Factory cooperation could work in favor of central goals or against them, depending upon interpersonal relations among these three. As Five-Year Plan production targets—backed by provincial secretaries—escalated to unreasonable levels, troika cooperation often turned toward collusive resistance. If this, then troika could be seen by the center as "family circles" and underfulfillment of production orders interpreted (especially after the show trials) as "sabotage." Stalin's response in this first stage of 1928–32 was to make the factory even more red and to put the party in charge. This meant purging technical deputy directors, insisting on dictatorial "one-man management" from the red director, changing the role of trade unions from protecting worker rights to pushing worker discipline, and setting up local party cells within factories to check on all this. The basic Stalinist formula for industrialization was first to import fancy new machines and then simply to make everybody work harder. Soviet workers who responded favorably to this formula (usually the younger ones) were valorized as shock workers and promoted into party cells. Seen as organizational structure, this was a shift from horizontal collective management to vertical top-down control, with the twist that shock troops at the bottom were the whips mostly in charge because they were agents of the party, specifically of the provincial first secretaries. On the whole, this new factory system did improve worker discipline and effort, especially if young shock workers bought into the "Stalinism as civilization" ideology about modernity.[42] This was the birth of dual hierarchy at the factory level.

As should be apparent, the word *plan* in Stalin's first Five-Year Plan was a misnomer. This document was an exhortation for all-out industrial construction and production at any cost. Not only fulfillment but overfulfillment of wild targets was urged. Rapid factory development thereby was achieved by the party but at the cost (among other things) of imbalance, bottlenecks, shortages, and waste: "This Plan, in other words, was not meant to allocate resources or balance demands but to drive the economy forward pell-mell. The Stalingrad tractor plant, for example, could best carry out the Plan by producing *more* tractors than planned, even if this threw the schedules of plants supplying Stalingrad with metal, electric parts, and tyres into total disarray."[43] "Building present-day factories with future bricks," Bukharin scornfully snarled.[44] Impressive economic construction was achieved by the plan, in other words, but economic autocatalysis of input and output supplies smoothly feeding into each other was not. How were interfactory distribution and supply handled, and how did that change?

In the previous NEP days of slow growth, pre-revolutionary factories were assembled into trusts; these trusts contracted among themselves and with intermediate wholesale syndicates for the distribution of their products. The trusts and their contracts were supervised by an economic bureau called Vesenkha, but that superministry had neither the authority nor the administrative capacity to decide product distribution, factory by factory.[45] It was enough of an achievement

[39] Harris 1999 is the best regional study of this.

[40] Kuromiya 1988, 20.

[41] Kuromiya 1984, 1988 are the best studies of changing factory dynamics under Stalin.

[42] Kotkin 1995.

[43] Fitzpatrick 2008, 132.

[44] Cohen 1973, 296.

[45] Nove 1969, 96–102.

clubs of status and privilege for them in the factory. Family circles of factory directors and local party officials had tried to squelch investigations by co-opting and sanctioning their complaining workers, as well as simply by not passing along their complaints. Stalin responded to this by reaching around them directly to the bottom in increasingly demagogic fashion. Hagiographic posters of Stalin and Stakhanov arm-in-arm beaming with armies of workers streaming behind them started to appear everywhere. This worked to the extent that lines of conflict and cleavage could be induced in the workforce: a safe haven for Stalinist zealots, impervious to family-circle control.

Given his growing suspicion of the party channel, Stalin needed to develop a new channel for linking to his loyalists below; this turned out to be the secret police (NKVD). Organizationally this makes sense, but the following numbers always bring one up short: 681,692 people murdered by Stalin in 1937–38;[54] 70 percent of Stalin's own Central Committee murdered;[55] 3.3 percent of delegates to the 27th Party Congress remaining from 1934 to 1939;[56] and almost all obkom first secretaries removed from office in 1937.[57] A bacchanalia of planning in 1929–32 was followed by a bacchanalia of terror in 1937–38. The timing of the brutality seems to have been due to an economic slowdown in 1936–37, which sent Stalin's search for "wreckers" into hyperdrive.[58] The literature on totalitarianism blamed Stalin for all of this,[59] but recently there has arisen a revisionist literature that tries to diffuse the blame.[60] In spite of overwhelming documentation of Stalin's intimate involvement,[61] it seems clear that no single human being could have come up with lists of such magnitude. Stalin's control strategy had to have received strong positive feedback from somebody.

Apart from the secret police themselves, case studies reveal this constituency to have been the lowest party cadres and workers, who denounced their family-circle superiors in droves, once Stalin gave the go-ahead and once the secret police showed up to take names.[62] In 1935–38, in other words, Stalin gave up on his original political base of provincial party secretaries and shifted to mass mobilization of the more rabid bottom levels of the party instead. This matched his economic mass mobilization of the same constituency through the Stakhanovite movement. Stalin's loyal troops below responded, and once denunciations began they escalated, as everyone tried to denounce their neighbor before their neighbor could denounce them. The secret police thereby gathered abundant information on alleged "wrecking." Inconsistencies they ironed out through torture. In addition to violent purges and executions, Stalin positively encouraged his loyalist masses to speak out and to challenge their elders through his Stalinist constitution of 1937, which offered free elections (i.e., open nominations and secret ballots) to low-level posts within the Communist Party. Most of the middle and upper levels of the party disappeared in the name of "democracy" by the masses.

Who was left to run the economic and political machinery? About this time, tens of thousands of communist youth were beginning to pour out of the engineering training schools that Stalin had set up during his earlier purge of noncommunist technical experts.[63] At thirty years of age, new-mint graduates with no experience whatsoever found themselves summoned to be appointed as new factory directors, ministerial officials, and party secretaries. The job openings above them were astronomical in number, so this "generation of '38" experienced the most rapid upward social mobility imaginable. These were the beneficiaries of Stalin's murders.[64] Not surprisingly, along with Stakhanovite workers and Komsomol teenagers, these young educated cadres were grateful and personally very loyal to Stalin, even though of course underlying structural contradictions did not go away. This bulg-

[54] Khlevniuk 2009, 184. According to internal NKVD records, now open to scholars, the NKVD in 1937 and 1938 arrested 1,575,259 people, convicted 1,344,923, and sentenced 681,692 of them to be shot.

[55] Ninety-eight out of the 139 Central Committee members of 1934 were murdered, according to Khrushchev's secret speech (1970, 572). Forty-four of the 62 surviving members of Lenin's old Central Committees were murdered, according to Mawdsley and White (2000, 12). Of the twelve surviving commissars of Lenin's first government, only Stalin himself was not executed in 1937–40 (http://en.wikipedia.org/wiki/Council_of_People's_Commissars).

[56] Gill 1990, 278. Of the 1,966 members of the 27th Party Congress, 1,108 were arrested on charges of counterrevolutionary crimes, again according to Khrushchev.

[57] Gill 1990, 272. "According to Zhdanov, 60% of obkoms, 46% of gorkoms, 41% of raikoms and 35% of PPOs elected in 1938 consisted of people who were elected for the first time. According to Medvedev, 90% of the members of oblast and city committees and republican CCs were liquidated in 1937–38" (414).

[58] Harrison 1985, 6; Manning 1993a.

[59] Khrushchev 1970; Conquest [1968] 1990; Medvedev [1972] 1989.

[60] Getty 1985; Getty and Manning 1993.

[61] Khlevniuk 2009.

[62] Getty 1985; Manning 1993b; Kotkin 1995; Kuromiya 1998; Harris 1999.

[63] Bailes 1978; Fitzpatrick 1979b.

[64] Fitzpatrick 1979a.

ing cohort of young engineers—Khrushchev, Brezhnev, Kosygin, Andropov, and their like—aged together, fought a world war together, and eventually ran the country together as elderly men until Gorbachev succeeded them in 1985. For Stalin a crucial advantage of this cohort, besides its zealous personal loyalty to him, was that these no longer were reds *versus* experts; they were reds *and* experts. Structural contradictions were to be solved through personnel.

The organizational consequence of this vast turnover in cadres was a strengthening of the economic pillar of ministries relative to the political pillar of the party. Almost everybody in administration, ministries, and party was now an engineer. In 1941 the number of ministries grew to forty-three, compared to seventeen in 1933 and nineteen in 1937.[65] Most ministerial proliferation was in the heavy-industry sector. Administrative differentiation implied tighter central supervision and control of industries, even if also greater difficulty in coordination across industries. The percentage of the Soviet GNP devoted directly to military expenditures rose from 7 percent in 1937 to 15 percent in 1940.[66] That was still a far cry from the 55 percent it attained at the height of the war in 1942, but it was a significant escalation in a direction that already had been prepared.[67]

A simplified picture of the autocatalytic economic vision to which Soviet ministries aspired is given in figure 9.2. Input-output planning in the heavy-industry sector of the Soviet economy was supposed to be like a modern, well-engineered machine, smoothly circulating supplies among gigantic factories that were maximally efficient due to specialized mass production. Free markets were not required for this circulation because production orders and transfers cleared through state bank accounts at administered prices, reflecting public not private demand. This "scientifically designed" economic machine was built primarily for war. Agriculture and consumer goods were squeezed mercilessly to feed it, but success was measured in terms of heavy industry, not in terms of those other sectors.

The ultimate test of whether Stalin's grand strategy[68] of "purge and mass mobilization" would work was war itself. I need not review the incredible events of World War II except to emphasize how much those events eventually locked in the system of economic ministries. With Hitler's blitzkrieg into Ukraine, the Baltics, and the Caucuses, about half of the Soviet industrial economy was destroyed.[69] Some crucial machines, technology, and skilled workers were rescued through heroic evacuation from west to east just ahead of the tanks. This was the return of storming, with a vengeance. To say that the regime hung by a thread at Stalingrad, both militarily and economically, is no exaggeration. Even the government was evacuated from Moscow. Thus eventual military victory is an interesting puzzle.

In my reading, the English economist Mark Harrison has looked most deeply into this issue of the surprising resilience of the Soviet military economy. Though factories in the protected Urals always cranked out armaments, Harrison has shown that in 1941 and 1942 Soviet economic planning mostly collapsed. State officials of all types instead scrambled through crisis management to extract every resource in the country and send it to the front—to the point of starving the Russian population. From late 1942 onward, however, the augmented heavy-industry factories in the east and the ministries that ran them roared back on line, producing planes, tanks, and other armaments at rates that exceeded those of the Germans.[70] What accounts for this eventual superiority in Soviet military production? Harrison's answer is mass production. The numbers of (gigantic) factories and armament lines, and their quality, were all much lower than those of the Germans.[71] But the Soviets produced their homogeneous and lower-quality weapons in massive volumes. The Germans emphasized instead more advanced engineering quality and diversity. In the blitzkrieg, quality prevailed, but eventually attrition and sheer quantity won out.

Ever since Kornai and even before, it has been fashionable to denigrate the efficiency of the Soviet planned economy: supply bottlenecks, hoarding, and lack of technical innovation were chronic. Without denying that clear reality, it is too easy thereby to overlook the power and efficiency of the military-industrial complex at the core of the Soviet economy. Part of the economic

[65] Zaleski 1980, 703–4.

[66] Davies and Harrison 2000, 90.

[67] Harrison 1998, 21; Siminov 2000, 220.

[68] The word *strategy* implies rational choice. Tucker (1990) certainly would challenge this assumption, as would the sheer number of Stalin's murders. My presumption is that Stalin was an endogenous learner, like every other human being I know. But I have no privileged access to Stalin's mind.

[69] Harrison 1985, 64.

[70] Harrison 1998, 14–17.

[71] Harrison 2001, 15–16. For the entire war effort, 47 percent of Soviet aircraft and 78 percent of Soviet tanks were manufactured in only four factories each. This is the exact opposite of the guerilla military logic of Mao.

trouble in the Soviet Union was due to informational problems and collusion, inherent in central planning. But part of the trouble was due to the intentional diversion of so many resources to war. In a highly concentrated domain like heavy industry, without too many factory nodes, central planning can work well.[72] The autocatalytic production and supply feedbacks sketched in figure 9.2 are matters of supply-chain topologies and of balanced input-output volumes, not matters of capitalism. In principle they can be attained either by central command or by private markets. In the Soviet Union, I claim, central command did indeed attain self-reproducing autocatalysis in the military-heavy-industry core of its economy.

The organizational lock-ins—that is, the emergent actors—for autocatalysis in heavy industry were the centralized economic ministries. Heavy-industry economic concentration reinforced the political power of central ministries. And the political power of central ministries preserved the centrality of heavy industry in the Soviet economy. It is true that the rest of the economy was exploited to serve that core, but agriculture and consumer goods were not the goals. Whatever the Soviet citizen thought as a consumer, as a patriotic soldier, he or she could feel proud.

That was the emergence of dual hierarchy under Stalin. At first the economic central-command "system" was a projection of the Bolshevik Party. Then the Great Purges gave ministries a relative autonomy from the party (though a subservience to Stalin) that it had not previously possessed. Both stages were induced by the genesis mechanism of "purge and mass mobilization," applied to different targets. World War II provided a powerful stimulus and co-evolutionary lock-in to the central-command system that emerged from the Terror.[73] Organizational catalysis, which routinized all this, was the *nomenklatura* appointment system of social mobility, which made collective biographies for the "generation of '38" and "circular flows of power" for leaders. Family circles were induced by structural contradictions within the system. But they were mitigated by high rates of upward social mobility and returned when rates of mobility slowed down.[74]

[72] This is somewhat like Chandler's (1977) visible hand writ large.

[73] Dunmore (1980) carries the story forward from the end of World War II to the death of Stalin in 1953. Through case studies, he demonstrates the growing power and autonomy of ministries, even from Stalin.

[74] A "wheel of fortune" mobility was also important to the Sultan's control of the patrimonial bureaucracy in the Ottoman Empire. Finley 1980, 37. See also Padgett 1990.

KHRUSHCHEV

My treatment of the other communist cases will not be as extensive as that of Stalin because in my judgment he remains the genetic secret to subsequent communist regimes, even to Chinese communist regimes. Dual hierarchy was pushed in different directions by other leaders, with various results. But it was dual hierarchy to begin with because of Stalin. That founding template shaped and channeled subsequent co-evolutionary trajectories.

After the world war the Soviet Union became an empire as Soviet rule expanded to cover Eastern Europe and to influence China. At home, Stalin ruled as a dictator through ministries and ad hoc committees, with the Politburo and the Central Committee effectively ceasing to meet. Upon his death in 1953, his elite henchmen—Molotov, Malenkov, Khrushchev, Bulganin, Mikoyan, and others—united to eliminate Beria, head of the secret police. With that, the gulag and Terror ended, as did the rapid social mobility that they had produced. Family circles started to flourish again.

A succession struggle pitted the power of Malenkov and Molotov, rooted in the ministries, with that of the earthy Khrushchev—former agricultural cadre and party boss of the Ukraine and Moscow—rooted in the weaker party. Khrushchev imitated the early Stalin by cultivating a party machine of provincial-secretary appointments. After consolidating his base, in 1956 he launched a dramatic factional attack on his colleagues by his secret speech to the revived Party Congress. This aggressive and emotional four-hour speech at midnight documented Stain's crimes and denounced him.[75] Worldwide, this shook Hungary into revolt and alienated Mao. Back home, it pushed the deeply implicated Molotov and Malenkov into retreat while eliding Khrushchev's own guilt.

The reason to classify this succession struggle as "the politics of economic reform" is because of *sovnarhkozy*. This decentralizing economic reform by Khrushchev, implemented a few months after his speech, abolished central ministries and transferred their planning functions and personnel to newly formed regional economic councils under the authority of provincial

[75] Khrushchev did not mention collectivization and the gulag, of which he approved, but focused on the 1937–38 Terror against the party, his audience. The speech was "secret" in that it was not known ahead of time by his colleagues, but it was soon published and widely circulated by Khrushchev.

party secretaries. The political purpose of this reform was transparent to all: namely, to dissolve the power base of his rivals and to increase that of his supporters. His opponents responded in June 1957 with an attempted putsch: the majority of members in the Presidium (the Politburo's name at that time) voted to depose Khrushchev. He stood them down by stalling and insisting on confirmation by the full Central Committee, whose provincial members his supporters frantically flew in from all over the country. This dramatic political counterattack was not only for Khrushchev over his rivals but also for the party over the central ministries. Malenkov et al. were exiled (but not killed). The decentralizing economics of *sovnarhkozy* was central to the politics of Khrushchev's victory.

If co-evolution were as simple as politics-in-command, then that would have been the end of ministry-led dual hierarchy, and Stalinism, more or less, could have been forgotten. What is interesting from the perspective of multiple-network feedback, however, is that soon after Khrushchev's rousing victory, he began to backtrack incrementally toward economic centralization. With no more central economic ministries, the economy went down, as factory supply problems increased. The economic idea of the reform had been that regional economies could develop, with local light industry developing to feed factory behemoths and provincial parties coordinating it all. Not markets exactly but regional autocatalysis (if not autarky) could ensue, and central planning could become a matter only of arranging interprovincial resource transfers.

The problem was not that provincial secretaries did not love this. They behaved just as enthusiastically as had their predecessors under Stalin's first Five-Year Plan, with local economic wheeling and dealing reemerging to substitute for material negotiations with Moscow.[76] The problem was that economic concentration already had gone too far. The specialized behemoth plants to which they needed to link their own specialized behemoth plants were in other geographical locations, whereas they wanted to find supplies locally where they had leverage. Provincial first secretaries resisted giving away prized resources to each other. As a result, supply bottlenecks were worse than ever, no matter how creative the wheeling and dealing of local party officials. Soviet engineers, who preferred living in Moscow to the boonies in any event, began publicly to disparage regional reforms as "Khrushchev's hair-brained schemes." Thus Stalin from his grave defeated the henchman who had denounced him through the vehicle of intense industrial concentration.

There is more to the Khrushchev story, as slow economic recentralization eventually alienated even the provincial secretaries who had been his base of political power. For this reason, Khrushchev was overthrown in 1964, and his successor, Brezhnev, reassembled in Moscow the economic ministries that Khrushchev had dismantled. But that is enough to demonstrate the resilience of the Stalinist system, which could absorb a huge reform perturbation to its core with no long-term effect. Stalinist politics and Stalinist economics reproduced each another in a tight feedback, even with cessation of the Terror and the social mobility that had made them. Administration replaced ideological mass mobilization as the management method of choice. Family circles reproduced widely; that will be discussed in the section on Gorbachev.

MAO

Mao, to say the least, was just as complicated a fellow as Stalin. I will tell only the minimum of the Mao story necessary (a) to show how Mao's choices were also structured by dual hierarchy and (b) to establish the Mao structural legacy that later tipped into so-called capitalism under the leadership of Deng Xiaoping. Maoist economic decentralization similar to *sovnarhkozy*, I will argue, was a crucial prerequisite to the political success of this later transition under Deng.

China's industrial system was set up by Soviet advisers in the early 1950s, so central-command economics, an emphasis on heavy industry, and dual hierarchy came with the package. Even though China inherited a heavy-industry base from the Japanese in Manchuria, China in the 1950s was as overwhelmingly agrarian as Russia had been in the 1920s. The Soviet industrial economy, though a very high priority for Mao, would take a while to grow in Chinese soil. Following Soviet advice, existing Chinese capitalist enterprises (without deposed capitalists of course), mostly on the coast, were agglomerated in a drive toward business concentration. The emphasis in the first Chinese Five-Year Plan

[76] Hough 1969 is an acclaimed study of the economic activity of party secretaries during the Khrushchev era. He emphasizes their very active search for economic supplies for factories in their regions.

trajectory of the Chinese economy, was embraced by China, whereas Khrushchev's *sovnarhkozy* was quickly rejected. The answer has already been adumbrated: by the time of Khrushchev, the Soviet industrial economy was vastly more concentrated than the Chinese economy of the 1950s. China was perhaps on the road to Soviet-style hyperconcentration, but that was still far into the future. The Chinese economy for centuries had been regionally decentralized.[85] Administrative decentralization fit with these traditional "natural" trading patterns in China, and it pushed toward—indeed it accentuated—regional economic autarky, channeling intraregional trade through the party instead of through traditional markets.[86] In my language, existing regional production autocatalyses were harnessed and absorbed into the Chinese party through *sovnarhkozy*, whereas in the Soviet Union those had already been destroyed through hyperconcentration. For synergistic "natural" and *sovnarhkozy* reasons, local Chinese planners gave priority to intraregional supply networks through their party, and they resisted interregional transfers. Conversely, Soviet centralized planning in a deconcentrated economy like China was a nightmare, other than in Manchuria. Chinese central ministries in China protested at the loss of their power, but not too vigorously. Their largest factories were not taken away.

I emphasize these organizational precursors because they channeled the provincial party into the economy. But the real Great Leap Forward was launched in 1958 with the commune movement. This Chinese communist innovation agglomerated village-sized collectives into much larger production units of ten to thirty thousand people. The innovative idea of the commune did not emerge full blown from Mao's brow. It percolated up from provincial secretaries,[87] whom Mao met on his numerous tours of the country. Mao's own speeches at the time emphasized production speed-up, both in agriculture and in heavy industry, not any particular means for doing so. Communes emerged as the magic bullet in a series of three party mobilization meetings in the first half of 1958 that Mao held outside Moscow in the provinces, in Hangchow, in Nanning, and in Chengtu. By the end of these almost revivalist meetings between Mao and "his people," the official decisions of the National Party Conference in May 1958 had been predetermined.

The purposes of the commune were multiple:

1. to break through the bottleneck in agriculture through intensified manual labor more than through mechanization[88]
2. to mobilize millions of peasants in the winter for large-scale agricultural infrastructure projects, like dams and irrigation
3. to mobilize peasants also for rural industrial work, both in light industry and in small-scale versions of heavy industry, like "backyard steel smelting" and local electricity generation
4. to communalize private life through common mess halls, day care, and "happiness homes" for the elderly
5. thereby to put women to work in traditionally male jobs outside the home
6. thereby to free up men to move to cities to work in large-scale heavy industry (with occasional commuting privileges home)

All of this, of course, gave party cadres more power, indeed monopoly control, over peasants' lives.

For believers, this was a passionate rural drive toward the future—an agrarian version of "Stalinist civilization." For nonbelievers, this was a gulag. On the ground, some worked too hard, some not enough. Given the catastrophe in agriculture that it produced, it is often forgotten that the Great Leap Forward was actually a success at industrialization. The number of workers in advanced heavy-industry factories rose from 4.5 million in 1957 to 17.5 million in 1958. Including small backyard furnaces, industrial workers rose from 5.57 million in 1957 to 35.5 million in 1958. This extra effort translated into an increase in steel production from 5.35 million tons in 1957 to 18 million tons at the end of the leap in 1960. Of course offsetting this was a drop in agricultural laborers from 192 million in 1957 to 151 million in 1958. Agricultural production held steady in 1958 but then plummeted from 200 million tons in 1958 to 170 million tons in 1959 to 143.5 million tons in 1960.[89]

[85] Skinner 1964–65.

[86] Donnithorne 1967, 1972.

[87] Especially Li Ching-ch'üan of Szechwan, Wang Jen-chung of Hupeh, and K'o Ch'ing-shih of Shanghai. MacFarquhar 1983, 21.

[88] This included double-cropping and working through the night.

[89] All figures from MacFarqhuar 1983, 327–28. The official statistics, given in the *Statistical Yearbook of China* (1984, 23), paint a rosier picture than this, especially in agriculture.

An enormous famine ensued, which claimed approximately 20 million lives.

In 1961 the Great Leap Forward/Famine was ended. Urban immigrant men belatedly were ordered back to the farms, along with every available cadre, to try to fix the disaster. Mao sulked and withdrew from active leadership to let others, like Liu Shaoqi and Deng Xiaoping (both of whom originally had supported the idea) and Chen Yun (who had not), take charge of repairing the imbalanced economy.[90] Communes were not abolished, but they were hollowed out: common mess halls ended, grain production targets were decentralized to the smaller 10–20 household level of the production team, and 5 percent of land was given over to private household plots. Controversy ensued regarding whether to approve an even further decentralization that had emerged spontaneously in response to famine in many provinces: namely, individual households contracting with their teams for their share of the target, with excess production beyond their contracts to be kept by them.[91] The Liu-Deng-Chen side of the leadership approved of this spontaneous delegation of team targets down to households because that increased production. Mao at first equivocated because of the emergency, but then in 1962 belatedly attacked this extension as right deviationism, capitalism in disguise. Later this emergence was labeled the "household responsibility system."

On the industrial side, ownership decentralization of medium and small enterprises to the provincial and lower levels was not undone, but administrative planning at all levels and statistical infrastructures within enterprises were tightened up, with the consummate bureaucrat Chen Yun in charge. Most important, excessive production targets were eased. The economy slowly recovered through these ameliorative steps.

I spent more time on the Great Leap Forward than I will on the Cultural Revolution because economic issues were more centrally involved in the first event and because I believe that both the Cultural Revolution and Deng's later transformation into "capitalism" were contained in the residues of that earlier event. Take the outcome of Great Leap Forward, in other words, polarize it, and you get both the Cultural Revolution and its opposite, Chinese-style "capitalism." Let me explain what I mean.

In the political domain, the main thing to focus on from a network perspective is the growth of personal networks (*quanxi*) within communism. I start with the comparative puzzle that the literature on Soviet communism mostly emphasizes horizontal "family circles," which emerged to defend provinces and factories from excessive pressure from the center,[92] whereas the literature on Chinese communism mostly emphasizes vertical patron-client relations, which spread from the center down.[93] Walder has made the further interesting observation that Chinese communist clientage was "principled particularism," by which he means that personal loyalties grew up vertically among those who exhibited communist zeal.[94] In other words, ideology and personalism were not contradictory in China, whereas they often were in the Soviet Union.

Assuming these informed impressions are correct,[95] I do not think it is necessary to resort to cultural essentialism to explain them. When vertical pressure coming down from central ministries is stiff, as it was in the Soviet Union, then factory directors need to reach out laterally to provincial party cadres not only to collude to subvert those pressures but also to find supply help in achieving them. But when ministries are decentralized, as they were in China, all the pressure is coming down the party pillar. When that top-down pressure is consistent with increasing the local power of local cadres, then it is most welcome. But when it is not, then effective defense, if there is any, is more to be found through powerful patrons in the center than it is through impotent factory directors in the locale. Chinese local officials went around recalcitrant immediate superiors by end-running to their superiors, if informal *quanxi* ties gave access. Conversely, reaching horizontally to local factory directors accomplished nothing politically in China for local party officials because factory directors were not powerful. Party officials at the center reaped factional benefits from these chronic bottom-up pleas for support.

[90] Curiously Zhao Enlai, who originally was skeptical about the Leap, was so politically humiliated during the provincial meetings that thenceforth he supported everything Mao desired.

[91] Yang (1996, 71–97) discusses these developments in detail.

[92] Fainsod 1958; Berliner 1957; Harris 1999.

[93] Whitson 1969, 1973; Nathan 1973; Pye 1981; Huang 2000; Friedman, Pickowicz, and Selden 2005.

[94] Walder (1986, 123–61) studied Chinese communist factories, but Oi (1989) made similar observations about the rural communes she observed.

[95] I do not question these astute observations by knowledgeable researchers, but it would be nice to have a few quantitative network studies to confirm and make more precise these comparative impressions.

Formal and informal networks therefore interpenetrated in both places, but because the formal was different, so was the counterbalancing informal. Hence, horizontal informal networks of personal assistance cross-cut vertical chains of economic authority in the Soviet Union, and vertical informal networks of political sponsorship cross-cut decentralized formal layers of economic ownership in China.

A second network comment is also helpful to understand the respective co-evolutions. Degree of elite unity shapes how informal networks behave politically. A unified elite, like the Chinese before the Great Leap Forward, gives tremendous mobilization potential to trees of vertical clientage ties. But a fragmented elite, like the Chinese after the Great Leap Forward, causes vertical clientage trees to splinter apart into factions. Conversely, nested layers of family circles, like the Soviet Union, offer to leaders no vertical clientage strings to leverage for breaking through horizontal layers of passive resistance. The main reform option the system offers to such a leader is the more dramatic one of reaching outside the system, to blast horizontal layers from below. Stalin did this through the secret police; Gorbachev did this through democracy. Vertical network factions let Deng avoid these nuclear reform options.

Finally to explain the different trajectories, in the economic domain the regionally autarchic tendencies of the Chinese economy, compared to the Soviet one, cannot be emphasized enough.[96] Regional specialization and enterprise hyperconcentration in the Soviet case meant that economic autocatalysis could be generated by ministries at the national level of gigantic plants in heavy industries. In contrast, the politically decentralized ownership structure of figure 9.3 pushed economic autocatalysis more into regions through connecting the inputs and outputs of local light industries.

The fascinating and painful story of the Chinese Cultural Revolution I will tell only schematically through the lens of this analysis. Instead of the usual "Mao did it," I emphasize that the Great Leap Forward fragmented vertical informal ties into factions as the elite lost its unity. Mao's personal charisma as founder of the nation survived, but his leftist economic mobilization policies were delegitimated in the eyes of many: in the eyes of planners and bureaucrats, in the eyes of the mass peasantry, and most of all in the eyes of his own provincial secretaries, who saw their strenuous efforts blow up in their faces. If Mao had been content just to let the country taxidermy him into big smiling pictures on walls, Liu, Deng, and Chen could have carried through with the policies and more conservative factions that they built from the network ashes of Great Leap Forward discontent. But the Red Army, the PLA, outside the dual hierarchy, gave Mao the political option of avoiding his embalmed fate and of continuing to fight for his dreams and for himself.[97]

Mao's Cultural Revolution was like Stalin's Great Purges. The Red Guards were Mao's shock troops, like Stalin's Stakhanovites, and Mao's Red Army was like Stalin's secret police—namely, a third pillar the leader could use to bludgeon a dual hierarchy that had tried to walk away from him. Like Stalin, Mao defeated his newly discovered enemies and destroyed his own party,[98] but unlike Stalin, Mao did not effectively control his young friends. Perhaps murder is enough to account for this difference,[99] but also the Little Red Book was no substitute for engineering schools to co-opt raging students into something more productive. Instead of cooperating, eventually one of Mao's friends, the Red Army, had to be called in to crush the other of Mao's friends, the Red Guards. The PLA was forced to run the economy once the party had been destroyed. The Cultural Revolution began as a cleansing of the spirit but ended up as a military state.

The Cultural Revolution was not primarily about the economy, but economic consequences were serious nonetheless. Liu Shiaoqi, Deng Xiaoping, and Chen Yun (and of course thousands of others) were all removed from their posts. Economic ministries and central planning collapsed, so even the modest economic recentralization of Chen Yun was rolled back. The Chinese

[96] Donnithorne 1967, 1972; Lyons 1985, 1986, 1987.

[97] At Lushan in 1959, just as Mao was starting to accept the error of his Great Leap Forward ways, his defense secretary Peng Dehuai (who had "won" the Korean war) attacked Mao with an honesty that struck too close to Mao's bone, appearing almost to threaten a coup. Mao reacted passionately not only with a disastrous acceleration of misguided Great Leap Forward policies but also with a purge of Peng in favor of Lin Biao, a fanatic Maoist, as new leader of the PLA. A completely unintended consequence of the Great Leap Forward, therefore, was Mao's personal and ideological control of the army through Lin Biao. One of Lin's first acts as new army commander was to assemble Mao's sayings into the famous Little Red Book to help indoctrinate soldiers.

[98] In 1967 and 1968, twenty-six out of twenty-nine provincial party secretaries were purged. I used the directories in Goodman 1986 to count these.

[99] No matter how serious and life-changing were rectification, public humiliation, and years lost working on farms, they were still not the same as a bullet in the head. Compared to the Terror (or to the Great Leap Famine), not many people in the Cultural Revolution actually lost their lives.

economy, however, did not collapse as badly as did the polity.[100] Regional economic autocatalysis and modularity gave to China a more resilient buffer against political chaos than regional specialization and more efficient interprovincial trade would have done. Too much party governance under the Great Leap Forward destroyed the Chinese economy, but too little party governance under the Cultural Revolution did not. The main thing the Cultural Revolution destroyed was not the economy but political support among cadres for mass mobilization, either by the party or against it. Economic decentralization was reinforced, albeit this time not by design.

DENG XIAOPING

By Western standards, there can be no doubt that Deng Xiaoping was the most successful communist economic reformer ever.[101] Measured solely by economic criteria, the transformation of China he pulled off was little less than miraculous. The attributional tendency post hoc is to anoint him a genius. But unlike Mao, Deng had no utopian vision. His famous declaration of pragmatism was: "I don't care whether the cat is black or white, as long as it catches mice." While there can be no doubt about Deng's shrewdness, the nature of that shrewdness was not a brilliant plan, skillfully implemented. Chinese economists interviewed by Shirk seem to have captured best his and his allies' leadership style when they reported, "When they found loose stones, they pushed through; when stones would not move, they did not waste energy pushing."[102] Deng, in other words, adapted to what he encountered and to what he inherited. He was a leader but an autocatalytic leader, part of the dynamic system he inhabited.[103]

Figure 9.4 presents a simplified overview of the politics underlying Deng's reforms. The columns labeled "leftist faction" and "reform faction" map onto dual hierarchy: the latter was rooted in the provincial parties that Mao had destroyed, and the former's last redoubt was the central ministries after Mao and his Gang of Four had left the scene. The column on the left is the third pillar of the army, which Mao had mobilized politically for the Cultural Revolution against his dual hierarchy and which ran the country at the end. Most westerners saw and remember Deng the economic reformer, who orchestrated the market, but the other face of Deng was Tiananmen Square. Deng toggled between his two political legs of reform faction and army in his struggle against the leftists who previously had exiled him. Deng himself, after Mao's death and once in power, did not occupy any important official position in China—party secretary, economic premier, or chairman—preferring to operate informally behind the scenes through agents. Nor did he issue clear ideological preferences, like Stalin or Mao, instead letting others come to him as the monopoly broker. This governing structure is similar to the "robust action" of Cosimo de' Medici in Renaissance Florence.[104] Like Cosimo, Deng was a sphinx whom others interpreted ambiguously—until, that is, a sword unexpectedly dropped upon them.

How did this politics emerge, and what were its economic consequences? Most commentators stress Deng's economic reform policies in the late 1970s and early 1980s of the household responsibility system, fiscal decentralization, and special international-trading zones, giving uninformed readers the impression of intentional design. From the political perspective, Shirk has called these economic reforms "playing to the provinces." These reforms will emerge in my account as well but as adaptation, not as design. Communist economic reforms, no matter how market-like, need to be understood causally from the perspective of communism, not teleologically from the perspective of postcommunism. New systems are rewirings of pieces from old ones.

Let me begin my survey of co-evolutionary dynamics under Deng, therefore, not with economics but with the army, where Mao left off. Deng's original base of political support after the Cultural Revolution was the PLA. Only after his base of elderly generals chose him did he branch out into economics and playing to the provinces. Two years before he died in 1976, Mao recalled Deng from exile. With the PLA administratively[105] and politically[106] as powerful

[100] *Statistical Yearbook of China* 1984, 23.

[101] Of course, by non-Western standards, Stalin still gets the prize.

[102] Shirk 1993, 6.

[103] Actually all leaders are like this, whether they recognize it or not. Deng, however, accepted this role.

[104] Padgett and Ansell 1993.

[105] In 1968, 17 out of 23 chairmen (and 19 out of 23 first vice chairmen) of the provincial revolutionary committees were military personnel. Harding 1997, 223.

[106] In 1969, 13 out of 25 members of the Politburo were military personnel. Forty-five percent of the Central Committee was military. MacFarquhar 1997, 250–51.

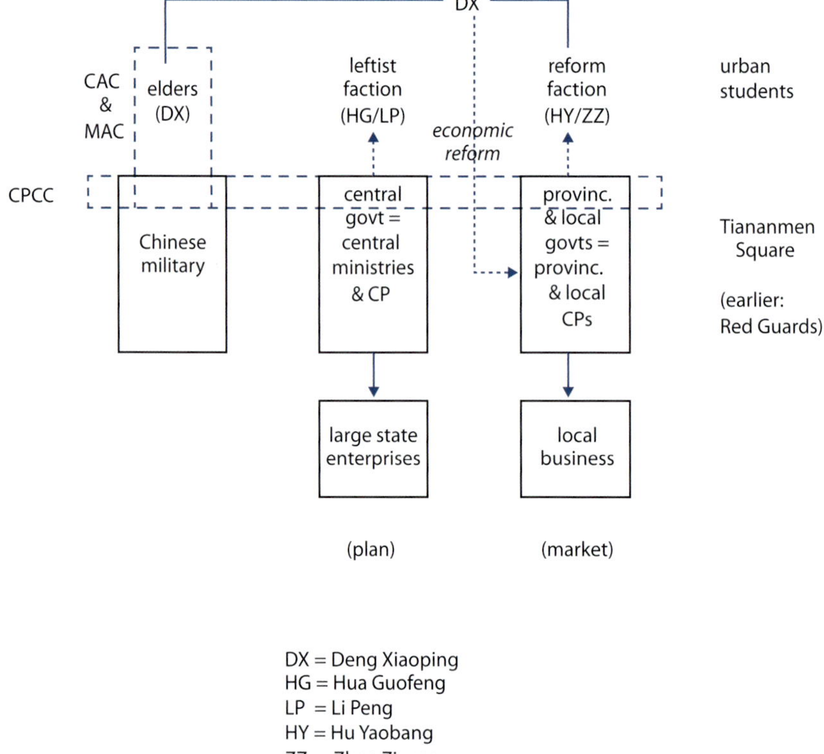

Figure 9.4 The politics of Deng Xiaoping's economic reform.

as it was, and with disorder still rampant, the potential for military coup was high. Indeed in 1971, Lin Biao—that PLA head, fanatic ally, and chosen successor to Mao—tried but failed to assassinate Mao and to pull a military coup before dying in a plane crash in flight from the country. All of Lin's leftist supporters in the military were immediately purged. This purge weakened Mao's control over the remaining more professional army because Lin's red faction had been the instrument of Mao's rule. Instead of an overpowering leader capable of mobilizing millions, Mao at the enfeebled end of his life was reduced to playing off elite factions against each other, in a politics of courtly intrigue.

Mao recalled Deng from Cultural Revolution exile for two reasons: to substitute for a terminally ill Zhou Enlai in running the economy and to enable the simultaneous rotation of eight commanding officers of PLA military regions to weaken their collective potential for a new coup: "The elements of the bargain were clear. In return for giving up political power, the generals were promised that [the premiership] would be put into the responsible hands of a trusted old comrade."[107] Deng only lasted one year before Mao fired him again because Mao distrusted Deng's nonideological approach to his new job.[108] But the incident revealed the popularity of Deng in the post-Lin army. The generals' support for Deng (which was not necessarily anti-Maoist) was rooted in their shared Long March days when Deng himself had been a young general. Struggle for allegiance of the military continued to be the inflection point in the interregnum politics between the death of Mao in 1976 and Deng's accession to power in 1978.

[107] MacFarquhar 1997, 291.

[108] The mechanics of this firing was the first Tiananmen Square incident: An upswell of mass emotional mourning for Zhou, at his death, was interpreted by Mao and the Gang of Four as reactionary political support for Deng, who was seen as stepping into Zhou's vacated shoes. The army was ordered to clear out thousands of milling people and their funeral wreaths with mourning and political-commentary notes attached and to repress this threatening upsurge in sentiment.

The most rabid Maoist faction, the Gang of Four, was arrested a mere month after Mao's death, and most of their Cultural Revolution provincial supporters were purged.[109] No one, especially not the army, wanted them anymore. Deng Xiaoping was recalled again in mid-1977 but not as ultimate leader. Deng and his old friends still had to contend with Mao's appointed successor, new chairman Hua Guofeng, and the remaining leftists in Beijing who supported him. Susan Shirk, in her insightful study *The Political Logic of Economic Reform in China*, makes succession struggles into the main political drivers behind Deng's successful post-Mao economic reforms. I do not reject her analysis, indeed I build on it, but a political contest between Deng and Hua seems imbalanced from the start. Old Guard Deng had deep and wide informal connections to all parts of the apparatus, whereas newcomer Hua had only the resources of formal state office. Too exclusive a focus on post-Mao events risks missing the deeper historical trajectories upon which those contemporary events sat.[110]

Hua Guofeng behaved as one would expect from someone whose power base was the central ministries. He tried to revive Stalinist heavy-industry growth strategies, this time paid for not by agricultural extraction but by petroleum exports. Unfortunately engineers did not find as much oil as they needed to find, so Hua's ambitious five-year central plan was a financial bust virtually from the start. The incident reveals, however, that Stalinism was still alive and well in China.

The second, more dynamic half of Deng's coalition was his famous sequence of liberalizing economic reforms. These emerged through standard communist leadership behavior—namely, reaching out and mobilizing local and provincial party cadres. The main reasons, besides lack of historical perspective, that observers often do not recognize Deng's economic reforms as communist behavior are two twists. The first tactical twist is that usually communist leaders initiated and constituencies responded, whereas with Deng first the constituency responded and then the leader initiated. As a matter of leadership style, this tactic was significant: Deng and his policy goals were inscrutable this way. But as a matter of feedback, the positive reinforcement that political leaders and party constituencies gave to each other was crucial, whoever initiated the feedback cycle.

The second misleading twist is that usually leader-provincial-secretary feedback in communist dual hierarchies led to centralization (the so-called circular flow of power) both in the political and in the economic domains. In the case of Deng, it did lead to centralization (or more accurately to recentralization) in the political domain, but it led to decentralization in the economic domain. Explaining this unexpected divergence in economic outcome from standard communist dynamics is the heart of the Deng puzzle.

My *longue durée* solution to this puzzle is that Deng's robust-action political coalition developed in China on the administrative lattice of figure 9.3, inherited from Mao. In the short run, administrative barriers between central planning at the top of that tree and provincial planning lower down in that tree were deepened by the factional overlay of figure 9.4. As economic reforms developed, the top and the bottom of this territorial "ownership" tree were decoupled (other than through financial transfers)—the center to remain in central planning and the provinces to diverge into local-governments-as-entrepreneurs,[111] free to transact in regional quasi-markets. There were some but not nearly as many tentacles of hyperspecialized factory behemoths reaching from the capital into the provinces as there were in the Soviet Union.

The first step in Deng's economic devolution was the household responsibility system in agriculture. This gave to individual peasant households the right to contract with their production teams, after delivering required grain targets to the state, to sell any surplus production at revived agricultural private markets (i.e., village fairs).[112] This reform in 1978 and 1980 was not Deng's idea; it legitimated rapidly diffusing practices on the ground. Decentralized exchange relations between local party cadres as "landlords" and peasants as "tenants" were revivals of informal institutions that first had appeared sub rosa at the end of the Great Leap Famine.

[109] Eleven of twenty-nine provincial secretaries were replaced in 1977 and eight more in 1978 (Goodman 1986).

[110] I do not want to be critical of Shirk, whose analysis I admire very much. But she like most observers does not couple Deng's economic reforms with his military politics. Because of this common elision, most observers (MacFarquhar is an exception) miss the organizational ambiguity of Deng's robust action.

[111] Walder 1995; Oi 1999.

[112] Tsou, Blecher, and Meisner. 1982; Burns 1986; Oi 1989; Shirk 1993. Informally this was known as "dividing the land" in management, even though legally collective ownership of land, tractors, and livestock remained.

Yang has documented that the household responsibility system spread fastest and widest in 1978–80 in the provinces—like Anhui and Deng's home of Sichuan—that had experienced the worst devastation in the Great Leap and that were physically most distant from Beijing.[113] The elder Deng's first "market innovation" was thus a return to 1962, back to the days right after the Great Leap Forward when the middle-aged Deng and Chen Yun were temporarily in charge.

What was the politics of this first economic reform? The popularity of the household responsibility among peasants seems straightforward because they got personal income. But communist regimes were not known for doing things because peasants liked it. Market diffusion in agriculture occurred precisely at the same time as Deng's succession maneuverings to overthrow Hua. As was his wont, Deng did not propose anything as blunt as "I want this." Rather the centerpiece of his interregnum politics was the epistemological slogan "Practice is the sole criterion of truth."[114] This slogan opposed Hua's "Whatever Mao said is right." Consistent with that red slogan, in agriculture Hua argued strenuously for the revival of Mao's communes. Deng did not oppose this with the household responsibility system; he merely argued for local experimentation.

Agricultural markets for peasants, around the margins of the plan, diffused because local party cadres wanted them. Within their own communes, household responsibility contracts were incredibly valuable goodies that commune party leaders could distribute to local supporters and friends. Especially cadres who had suffered in the Great Leap and who worked far away from Beijing rallied to Deng because his slogan gave them political cover to do what they wanted. More hard-core Maoists nearer to Beijing were not directly threatened by these experiments because they could continue with their red ways if that worked for them. Provincial first secretaries were cagy about this diffusion, as they waited to see how the political winds blew. In general they were open to what their local cadres liked as long as they were not punished by the center for this. Without the hysteria of Mao and Stalin, Deng with his truth criterion in fact was nudging the party, especially local cadres in the provinces, to his side through clientage.

The second politically consequential step in the sequence of Deng's economic reforms was fiscal decentralization. This was the policy reform enabled by the Maoist administrative decentralization shown in figure 9.3. It was this "playing to the provinces" reform that most fully swung provincial first secretaries behind Deng, thereby consolidating the provincial leg of his robust-action coalition.

Fiscal decentralization was the household responsibility system applied to national state finance.[115] All provincial governments would negotiate fiscal contracts with the ministry of finance about the level of tax resources they were to remit to the center, with provincial governments then free to keep any excess that they collected for their own investments. Before this reform, theoretically all provincial taxes and enterprise profits would flow to the center, some of which were then reallocated back down to the provinces through the central state budget. A growing loophole was that provinces sometimes were authorized to keep "extrabudgetary funds" in order to fund territorially dispersed initiatives by Mao. One problem with this loophole, from the perspective of the center, was that provinces often managed to squirrel away much money into this off-budget line item, thereby underpaying the center.[116]

The politics of how this reform of fiscal decentralization developed is similar, on a grander scale, to the clientage politics of household responsibility. In 1977 and 1978 Jiangsu and Sichuan[117] provinces petitioned and received approval from the ministry of finance to try out a variety of new fiscal management and revenue-sharing proposals on an experimental basis. The finance ministry, which normally resisted decentralization, approved these experiments as a way to gain greater predictability on its own portion of the take. These revenue-sharing experiments were judged by both sides to be a success, and fiscal decentralization was officially approved for the country as a whole in 1980. Shirk astutely emphasizes that different provinces received different treatment in the contractual details of these

[113] Yang 1996, 34–42. Yang also presents the most thorough description and discussion of these agricultural reforms in the literature.

[114] Actually the original author of this slogan was Hu Yaobang in a newspaper article that Deng liked. Hu soon was rewarded by Deng with fast promotion to general secretary, with Deng formally remaining behind the scenes.

[115] This can also be analogized to tax farming.

[116] Wang 1995.

[117] Zhao Ziyang was the provincial secretary from Sichuan behind these ideas. Later he was rewarded by Deng by promotion first to economic premier and then, after Hu Yaobang, to general secretary.

fiscal revenue-sharing arrangements—territorial discrimination that she calls "particularistic contracting."[118] The coastal provinces of Guangdong and Fujian and the original provincial innovators of Jiangsu and Sichuan received the best deals, while the central metropolises of Beijing, Tianjin, and Shanghai, the strongholds of Deng's factional opponents, received the worst "experimental" fiscal contracts. Not surprisingly provincial secretaries were enthusiastic about Deng in proportion to the generosity of their deals. From the perspective of economics, Deng's early reforms look like markets; but from the perspective of politics, they were the clientage that built the second leg of Deng's personal faction.

Walder on the urban side and Oi on the rural side have documented the profusion of entrepreneurial state-run businesses that exploded from fiscal decentralization.[119] Just as peasants had rushed to plant more crops and to work their fields harder when they were allowed to reap the profits (even without private ownership), so provincial and local governments invested discretionary revenues in "their own" local enterprises and managed them better when they were allowed to reap the gains from their governance. Some private profit, called corruption, no doubt existed. But field reports show that aboveboard collective profit to local governments was enough to turn governments-as-extractors into governments-as-entrepreneurs. Local and provincial governments competed among themselves, Tiebout or boosterism style, about who could develop their respective clientage enterprises faster, to develop their regions. This was not so unheard of within communism, as the same thing had happened under Stalin's first Five-Year Plan. The difference of course was that under Stalin local governments competed for investments from the center, whereas under Deng local governments competed with "their own" money.

Organizationally what is interesting about these government-sponsored enterprises is that they were ambiguous hybrids: half government, half private—or perhaps more accurately, private-within-government.[120] In Hungary something similar had happened, as Hungarian state employees of communes and large state enterprises formed private partnerships to use state assets off hours, transmitting most of the market profits back to the sponsoring enterprises.[121] In China, the local state kept almost all of the profits, but it used the factional and *guanxi* personal networks of their cadres to develop exchange relationships with (mostly regional) suppliers and consumers of their products. Instead of markets versus the state, this was markets interpenetrating the state—or to call it by its more proper communist label, this was storming all over again, except monetized. The Chinese innovation on that old Soviet theme was that now one got ahead in the party by making money, and one made money by getting ahead in the party, because then one could broker more and wider deals.

Given the abject failure of Gorbachev to achieve anything like this in the Soviet Union, it is worth reemphasizing the structural precondition for economic take-off in China. Administrative decentralization under Mao made the politics of fiscal decentralization possible under Deng. Economically, it reinforced regional autocatalysis and even regional autarky in the various territorial economies of China. Given this setup, local governments could stimulate and guide their enterprises to work harder, and provincial governments could arrange input-output supply synergies within their regional clusters[122] without interference from central ministries. In contrast, Chinese-style fiscal decentralization in the Soviet Union would only have turned matters over to family circles of defensive collusion, which could find not enough supplies locally for their hyperspecialized plants. In addition to different administrative structures, there were different informal network structures, which were adapted to the formal differences. Governmental structures and networks pushed economic development down different trajectories of growth—light industry in China, heavy industry in the Soviet Union.

Over the period from 1979 to 1985, a third liberalizing reform was also implemented: Special Economic Zones in coastal ports to develop international trade. These remind one of colonialist trading zones: special areas of economic contact with foreigners, buffered from contaminating the rest of society. The importance of this for the technological modernization of China hardly needs stress. But the politics of coastal

[118] Shirk 1993, chap. 9, is the primary source for my discussion of fiscal decentralization. The ministry of finance perspective on decentralization was similar to that of Chandler's (1962) multidivisional firms: namely, to delegate operational control downward in exchange for tighter fiscal discipline.

[119] Walder 1995, 1998; Oi 1999. See also Kueh 1983 and Wong 1987.

[120] Walder 1995.

[121] Rupp 1983; Stark 1989, 1996.

[122] Cf. Powell, Packalen, and Whittington, this volume.

provincial support for this reform, and therefore for its sponsor, Deng, was identical to that for fiscal decentralization. In the cases of all three reforms, what from the perspective of economics looks like market liberalization, from the perspective of politics looks like factional clientage: "playing to the provinces." As markets expanded, Deng consolidated his power against Maoist residues, now centered in the ministries. Positive feedback across domains was central simultaneously to the expansion of markets and to the reconsolidation of the Chinese state.

Let me close my analysis of China by returning to the overall political coalition of Deng Xiao ping, which anchored all of this economics. Narrating economic reforms, as I have just done, makes Deng appear to be a liberalizer, which he was even though he also was building a political faction. Playing to local and provincial cadres was the growth leg of Deng's robust action, like the new men for Cosimo de' Medici. But Deng's reform faction was only half of his political coalition, as I tried to make clear in figure 9.4. His original base was the army, so whom one interprets as "the real Deng" depends upon which allies one sees him through. Oddly enough, one occasionally even can see him as representing the central ministries, after his rival Hua Guofeng was deposed from power and his good and old friend Chen Yun was installed in his stead. Like Cosimo de' Medici in Florence, Deng Xiaoping could plausibly be seen as having multiple identities because of the heterogeneous support structure that he supervised. Because of this structurally induced multivocality, which Deng did not destroy by uttering words or policies too clearly, he could be seen as "a friend to all" (except the Maoists) and an honest broker. Because of this, he floated above the system, not beholden to any segment, as I tried to diagram in figure 9.3.

Administratively, Deng's robust action was implemented, like Cosimo's robust action before him, not through holding public office himself but by operating through agents. Deng abolished the title of chairman, which Mao had held. He installed his lieutenant Hu Yaobang as general secretary of the party, in charge of the political half of the dual hierarchy, and he installed another lieutenant, Zhao Ziyang, as premier, in charge of the economic pillar.[123] These lieutenants were hardly lackeys; they along with Chen Yun were the sources, or the messengers, of many of Deng's reform ideas. Indeed Deng's withdrawal to "the second line" behind the scenes, away from day-to-day battles, followed in the footsteps of Mao Zedong, who did the same thing in 1958 without giving up his title as chairman. Policies, vision, and charismatic personality aside, the structure of Deng's political control at its peak mimicked that of Mao at his peak.

Informally, Deng's network position was cemented by the Long March elders, survivors from the founding generation of the communist revolution. Chen Yun, Li Xiannian, Ye Jianying, Peng Zhen, Bo Yibo, and other octogenarians had cycled through numerous positions over their long and tumultuous careers. In 1982 Deng assembled them into an ad hoc Central Advisory Commission, which technically was only advisory but actually was considered to be the power behind the throne in the 1980s.[124] This was the informal glue that knitted together the peaks of all the pillars after Maoists had been purged in three successive waves.[125] Whereas Stalin and Mao had mobilized youth for the future, Deng modernized through the old guard.

Robust action and its structural foundations had dynamic consequences for the management of the developing Chinese economy during the 1980s. Without going into details, rapid economic growth produced by the reforms and by political stability also created problems of inflation and corruption.[126] Robust action by Deng and his old friends allowed them to oscillate in their economic policies, to accelerate or to dampen depending upon the current mix of transitional problems. This oscillatory style of organizational management is like annealing in chemistry: namely, letting explosive components find their own hybrid alloy through raising and lowering the mixing temperature.

In what follows I give only a partial list of examples of this policy oscillation:

1. Large inefficient central plants, which normally would have been the institutional foundation for resistance, were not themselves reformed but rather were bailed out by budgetary subsidies coming from provincial profits. These central-planning plants were never shut down; employees just gradually drifted into more lucrative alternatives.

[123] Chair of the Military Affairs Committee—that is, civilian head of the military—was the only official post that Deng never relinquished.

[124] Shirk 1993, 72–75; Baum 1997, 342–43.

[125] The three waves were Lin Biao, then Gang of Four, and finally Hua Guofeng.

[126] See Shirk 1993; Naughton 1995; and Yang 2004 for this.

2. Local communist cadres, who normally might become jealous of the economic success of their enterprise underlings, were bought off by becoming entrepreneurs themselves and by kickbacks.[127]
3. Restive provincial secretaries who got worse revenue-sharing and export-zone deals than did the Deng clients cooled off as these deals slowly were extended nationwide.
4. Taxes on state enterprises flip-flopped in form from particularistic negotiation of profit sharing in 1982–83 to uniform tax rates in 1983–84 back to particularistic profit sharing in 1985–88.
5. Austerity measures to combat inflation, built around the recommendations of ministry fiscal conservatives like Chen Yun and Li Peng, were imposed in 1988.
6. Most poignantly of all, in reaction to political demands for democracy by students in Tiananmen Square, Deng called in his army to massacre them in 1989.
7. Anticorruption drives were launched after Tiananmen, as central-planning conservatives launched a comeback.
8. But finally Deng reversed the drift of his elderly colleagues toward economic and political retrenchment in his southern tour in 1992, near the end of his life.

Obviously more could be said about these later economic and political developments in China during the 1980s and 1990s. But the period of the late 1970s and early 1980s was the inflection point, which established the oscillating Chinese communist trajectory after Mao. Despite his shrewd maneuvering among Maoist residues, Deng Xiaoping was not the only or the inevitable trajectory of co-evolution out of what Mao had built. If the People's Liberation Army and the Red Guards had been able to coordinate better—as did Stalin's secret police and the generation of '38—then we would have seen a quite different Chinese history.

GORBACHEV

Finally, to complete this comparative survey of reform dynamics within communism, there is Gorbachev and the collapse of the Soviet Union. The original motivation for this chapter was a desire to understand that.

To situate Gorbachev among other communist reformers, not in outcome but in reform style, it is helpful to return to the simple representation of dual hierarchy in figure 9.1. Dual hierarchy offered four possible constituencies to any communist leader interested in reform. Within the economic pillar of the central-command economy, the leader could try to appeal to central ministries at the top or to state enterprises at the bottom. Within the political pillar of the Communist Party, he could try to appeal to upper cadres at regional and provincial levels or to lower cadres in local governments and within enterprises. Combinations were possible, but those were the four basic channels for reform within the system. Given the virtual invulnerability of the communist leader, there was always also the null alternative of appealing to no constituency and ruling only by decree. But that was like talking to yourself in a vacuum: much gesticulation but no response. At the end, after alienating everyone, Gorbachev wound up like that, but he had struggled strenuously to avoid that fate.

Examples of the first reform strategy of mobilizing central ministries include Stalin during the lead-up to World War II and the later technocratic fiddling of Brezhnev. Examples of the second reform strategy of direct mobilization of state enterprises are Kosygin under early Brezhnev and Kádár in Hungary. Both of those reforms tried to loosen the administrative stranglehold of ministries over enterprises to create enterprise autonomy—in the first case unsuccessfully, in the second case successfully. Examples of the third strategy of mobilizing upper party cadres include Deng Xiaoping, Khrushchev, and Stalin early in his career, all of whom used the carrot of patronage. The stern discipline of Andropov was a stick-oriented variant on this third top-down strategy, with the KGB pressuring upper party cadres into following orders.[128] The radical fourth strategy of mobilizing lower party cadres against upper party cadres was epitomized by Mao during the Cultural Revolution. Stalin radicalized even that during his Great Purges

[127] In Chicago, Mayor Daley junior is alleged to have said: "We don't call them bribes anymore, we call them consultant fees."

[128] Although I do not discuss him here, Putin is a young version of Andropov. Both Putin and Andropov were shaped by their careers in the KGB. Putin used a robust-action strategy like Deng, with the KGB in place of the PLA, to reassemble an authoritarian Russian state. Robust-action balancing of KGB and democracy became feasible only after Yeltsin applied "creative destruction" to Russia, as Mao had to China. But Putin is another essay entirely.

by combining mass murder with his mass mobilization. All of these communist leaders were intelligent actors, but they operated within the constraints of reform strategies offered to them by dual hierarchy.

In the first year of his term, Gorbachev was not only like his mentor Andropov, he was the continuation of Andropov, both in economic policies and in reform style. I shall argue in this section that Andropov's and Gorbachev's struggles with the Brezhnev system that they inherited gradually turned Gorbachev into a Stalin, not in policy objectives but in "purge and mass mobilization" reform style. That is, through perestroika and glasnost, Gorbachev first moved from top-down Andropov discipline to purging his own party apparatus and to trying to mobilize the bottom of both dual-hierarchy pillars against the top. Failing to find the desired constituencies within the communist system, Gorbachev then escalated this purge-and-mass-mobilization style to outside the system through plebiscitary democracy, only unintentionally to destroy the Soviet Union. The common driver behind both policy escalations was Gorbachev's vain and futile search for new constituencies as old ones disappeared. Because of this danse macabre with dual hierarchy, Gorbachev became just what he did not want to be—not only a Stalin but a failed Stalin.

Gorbachev was not a true robust actor because of his strong evolution through time, but in the middle of his career as general secretary Gorbachev, like Deng, tried to have it both ways: as a disciplinarian and as a populist. The multivocality of the highly ambiguous words *perestroika* and *glasnost* allowed multiple audiences to read in different meanings to Gorbachev's intentions, and they obfuscated for a while the radical changes in policy actually taking place. In just five years, *perestroika* ("restructuring") changed its practical economic meaning from Andropov-style worker discipline to Kosygin-style administrative reforms and Hungarian-style market socialism to market liberalization. *Glasnost* ("transparency," "publicity," "openness") similarly migrated in meaning from inspections against corruption, to freedom of the press, to communist elections, to public elections. But these sequences in policy are clear only in hindsight. At the time, many reform plans were pursued simultaneously, with Gorbachev zigging and zagging in his emphasis at the moment. This ambiguity was crucial for maintaining an evolving coalition because it gave numerous constituencies, even orthodox communists, room for hope. Robust action is successful when liberals see Gorbachev as representing liberals and the KGB simultaneously sees Gorbachev as representing the KGB. But robust action is a catastrophe when the KGB sees Gorbachev as representing the liberals and liberals see Gorbachev as representing the KGB. Finding the structural reasons for the success of robust action under Deng and its failure under Gorbachev is an analytical focus of this section because that sets the stage for Gorbachev's progressive escalations of purge and mass mobilization and hence for the divergence of China and Russia. Robust action is a knife-edge, which can accomplish much under the right circumstances but can also collapse abruptly.

Throughout the analysis, I refuse to explain regime transition in the Soviet Union through the teleology of reading history backward as convergence to us. Gorbachev did what he did not because he was a westerner but because he was a communist, trying to strengthen Soviet communism.

Gorbachev emerged out of the Andropov faction. This is crucial to understand from the outset in order to disabuse us of the myth, fostered by Gorbachev himself, that he was a westerner in disguise. Andropov—the first elderly successor to Brezhnev,[129] who lasted only a couple of years (1982–84) before he died—spent much of his career in the KGB, fifteen years as its leader. His main claims to fame had been on-the-scene suppression of the Hungarian revolution in 1956 and campaigner for repression of Prague spring in 1968. Together with Marshall Ustinov, head of the Soviet military, Andropov upon his succession in 1982 spearheaded a modernization drive to try to reverse the slow and inexorable decline of the Soviet economy, especially in technologically advanced sectors of interest to the military,[130] which had occurred under Brezhnev. Gorbachev was a dynamic young man who had risen through party ranks from an agricultural and resort district,[131] with no direct experience in

[129] A second elderly successor, who lasted as leader even less (1984–85) before he died, was Chernenko. Chernenko was a brief revival of the Brezhnev regime, whereas Andropov had represented reform.

[130] Reagan's new SDI or Star Wars was of particular concern to Ustinov and Andropov.

[131] The resort aspect was important because that was what enabled young Gorbachev as local party boss to meet, schmooze with, and impress high-ranking Soviet officials on an informal basis. Most important, this is how Gorbachev met Andropov in the very private, informal, and vulnerable medical setting where Andropov was convalescing from illness. The fact that Andropov and Gorbachev were from

industry or the military. Gorbachev became the protégé, even the golden boy, of Andropov. Although he was officially only Politburo secretary for agriculture, Andropov treated Gorbachev as his trusted number-two man, in charge of centralized policy research to develop proposals for economic reform. Kosygin's earlier (1965) failed reforms were revisited and mulled over in this venue. Even more consequentially, Andropov placed Gorbachev in charge of appointments of upper-level cadres, as Lenin had done Stalin. In this potent infrastructural role, assisted by Ligachev, his later rival, Gorbachev began the extended process, initiated by Andropov and continued in his own regime, of replacing provincial first secretaries and others.[132]

Andropov himself died before accomplishing anything. But he "made" Gorbachev, both in the sense of giving to him his original political base and in the sense of giving to him his original economic ideas. Gorbachev was a youthful extension of Andropov and at the beginning of his term as general secretary behaved accordingly.

In Gorbachev's own succession to power in March 1985, Andropov's KGB was one crucial pillar of political support for Gorbachev;[133] another was the new and younger provincial secretaries (like Boris Yeltsin) who had been recently appointed by Andropov.[134] The foreign policy–oriented segment of the old guard, represented by Andrei Gromyko, was a swing vote but gave their blessing to this younger continuation of the modernizing coalition of Andropov. The old guard saw Gorbachev as committed to strengthening their legacy of Soviet military domination. This political alliance of provincial secretaries with KGB-military reminds one of the alliance structure of Deng. The dramatic difference in outcomes between Deng and Gorbachev had more to do with the systems they were struggling against than it did with the content of their original power bases.

Once in power, Gorbachev revealed himself to be a master of the "circular flow of power," invented by Stalin and routinized by Brezhnev. While this did not happen all at once, by August 1987 Gorbachev had replaced 70 percent of the Politburo (14 out of 20), 72 percent of the provincial first secretaries (108 out of 150), 95 percent of commanders of military groups (19 out of 20), 45 percent of the Central Committee (138 out of 307), and 54 percent of republican central committees (1,134 out of 2,089).[135] Part of this was accelerated generational turnover, long deferred under Brezhnev.[136] But no general secretary since Stalin had operated with such ferocious velocity in forcing cadre turnover. Purge was a Stalinist tool that Gorbachev knew well how to use. In the upper ranks of the party, Brezhnev's old men were decimated. The continued voting support that the communist apparatus gave to Gorbachev's proposals, even to the later suicidal ones, is incomprehensible without understanding this lock that he had over appointing the upper echelons of the party. When the party hierarchy belatedly swung against Gorbachev, those for the most part were his own people.

At the beginning, Gorbachev's new appointments were Andropov men, like himself. The first three new full memberships to the Politburo under Gorbachev were Nikolai Ryzhkov, Gorbachev's colleague under Andropov for economic research, Yegor Ligachev, Gorbachev's colleague under Andropov for provincial appointments, and Viktor Chebrikov, head of the KGB. The Brezhnev stalwarts Viktor Grishin, Grigory Romonov, and Nikolai Tikhonov were quickly shown the Politburo door. Centralized formal structure notwithstanding, Gorbachev personally did not so much take over as the Andropov faction assumed power.

Not surprisingly glasnost was an Andropov-style anticorruption campaign at the beginning.[137] Indeed charges of corruption were largely the instrument through which Gorbachev's anti-Brezhnev purges were carried out.[138] At the upper

the same town (Stavropol) reinforced this almost father-son relationship.

[132] Hough (1997, 86–102) points out that Andropov himself had inherited much of the political machine of provincial first secretaries established by Kirilenko. This was the Andropov party base that Gorbachev gradually remolded into his own.

[133] Waller 1994, 48.

[134] Yeltsin 1990, 112; Ligachev 1993, 72–75; Boldin 1994, 60–61.

[135] Hough 1987, 36, 34, 34, 33, 38, respectively. Rutland (1993, 194) adds that 39 percent of new provincial first secretaries in Russia were imported from central jobs in Moscow rather than being promotions of locals, as had been Brezhnev's approach (only 11 percent in non-Russian provinces, however).

[136] In particular, Stalin's famous generation of '38 turned over, of which Brezhnev and his elderly cronies had been members.

[137] Indeed the word first appeared in 1983 in party newspapers discussing Andropov's policies, not Gorbachev's. Gorbachev himself started discussing glasnost in this sense in speeches in 1984, even before he came to power. Gibbs 1999, 12, 22. Even before Gorbachev's takeover, in 1984, major newspapers launched exposés of corruption in Uzbekistan, a portent of more to come. Knight 1990, 95.

[138] Knight 1990, 97; Waller 1994, 49.

echelons of the party, as Gorbachev demonstrated so well, general secretaries pretty much could just fire people as they pleased, as long as they proceeded with an excuse. Hence purging of the top went smoothly. The lower down one went in the party, however, informational and network problems intervened. It was not clear whom to fire, since everyone mouthed the right words, and superiors of derelict clients vouched for their own appointees. The issue was family circles, which as everything goes back to Stalin.[139] Gorbachev himself could fire the top brass, but he could not get the brass that remained to fire their own bases of support. Soviet communists theoretically were supposed to check on each other and to report to the center, but to defend themselves, they often formed collusive cocoons of silences and lies. The hotter the top-down heat, the thicker the horizontal family circles.

Central leaders required extraparty informational channels to combat this. For Stalin, this had been his secret police. For Andropov, this had been the KGB. For Gorbachev, too, this to some extent was the KGB. But Andropov *was* the KGB, whereas outsider Gorbachev merely was backed politically by the KGB. The KGB remained autonomous, as much in control of Gorbachev as he of them.[140] The KGB supported Gorbachev on anticorruption but not necessarily on anything else. Eventually Gorbachev branched out on his own to redefine glasnost as investigative reporting by newspapers. Early in 1986 Gorbachev instituted freedom of the press, not because of the American bill of rights but because of his need for independent exposés to intensify and justify his purges deeper into the apparatus—and to gain an independent lever, more beholden to him personally.[141]

On the economic policy front as well, Gorbachev at first just continued Andropov. In 1985 and early 1986, Gorbachev was more involved in consolidating his power than anything else, but nonetheless he did launch a number of economic initiatives: extension of Andropov's large-scale experiments on enterprise autonomy; acceleration in production in a new five-year plan; increased investments in high technology; prohibition of alcohol to combat laxity at work; a centralized quality-inspection program, modeled on military production; and finally a crackdown on "unearned incomes" (like corruption, embezzlement, and private enterprise).[142] These measures were ad hoc, but they reflected the stern-discipline vision of Gorbachev's mentor from the KGB. Even central ministries could approve of old-school disciplinary ideas like these. Russian workers, however, seethed at having their bonuses and their booze cut.[143]

In the background, policy reform teams of Soviet academics—first established by Andropov (and chaired by Gorbachev) and then continued by Gorbachev (and chaired by Ryzkhov, another Andropov protégé)—laid the seeds for a more comprehensive next step in perestroika: namely, revisiting and updating the Kosygin reforms, which had sought greater autonomy and initiative for enterprise directors outside the "petty tutelage" of ministries.[144] These administrative reforms primarily involved changing economic performance indicators of firms: away from physical production targets, mandated by ministries, and toward financial indicators like profits, calculated on the basis of administered prices. Hungary under Kádár had successfully made this transition in 1968 with his New Economic Mechanism (NEM), whereas Kosygin's own Soviet attempt in 1965 had been foiled by the ministries, whose decision-making monopoly this attacked.[145] These enterprise-autonomy ideas were more threatening to central ministries than the first round of disciplinary policies had

[139] Oliver 1973; Rigby 1981.

[140] "The KGB has not been subjected to the sweeping personnel changes that have been imposed on other institutions, such as the armed forces and the Party. It might have been expected that Gorbachev, like his predecessors, would attempt to assert control over the KGB by bringing in some of his own men, or at least neutral outsiders, to fill top KGB posts. Instead, longtime KGB professionals remain at the helm" (Knight 1989, 24).

[141] "I placed particular value on glasnost when I realized that the initiatives coming from the top were more and more obstructed in the vertical structures of the Party apparatus and administrative organs. Freedom of speech made it possible to go over the heads of the apparatchiks and turn directly to the people, to give them the incentive to act and to win their support" (Gorbachev 1995, 203). See also Gibbs 1999, 21–31. For Stalin parallel, see Harris 1999, 177–83.

[142] For overviews of all of Gorbachev's economic reforms, early and late, see Aslund 1991 and especially Ellman and Kontorovich 1998, whose unusual book is a compilation of testimonies from participants.

[143] The anti-alcohol campaign provoked a crisis in sugar production, as official supplies disappeared into bootleg. It also induced fiscal distress, as the central government lost one of its important tax revenues.

[144] A number of Gorbachev's academic advisers, like Aganbegyan (1988), had been personally involved as youngsters in the earlier Kosygin reforms.

[145] The mechanics of blocking in the 1960s had been the compromise that firms would be evaluated both on physical targets and on profits instead of on profits alone. Soviet ministries implemented this "reform" by insisting that the old physical targets take priority, thereby emasculating profits. In a shortage economy, dependence of enterprises on ministries for supplies was too strong for effective resistance.

been. Kosygin had lost because Brezhnev and the party hierarchy ultimately backed the ministries over him. But now times were propitious for revisiting this Hungarian-style reform: the party was controlled by someone who wanted it. And indeed this reformist track after much internal politicking eventually led to the perestroika flagship Law on State Enterprises in 1987, which destroyed the Soviet economy in 1989.

Starting in earnest in 1986 and carrying through 1987, purges, glasnost, and the second round of perestroika were serious body blows to the core of the Soviet apparatus. Purges and glasnost attacked the declining Brezhnev guts of the party; the second round of perestroika attacked central ministries and underperforming enterprises that had no hope of innovation. It is hardly surprising that these constituencies congealed to resist Gorbachev. Gorbachev counted on the reform constituencies of a new generation in the party, the urban intelligentsia, and better performing enterprises in the economy (which included the military) to carry the day. Weighed strictly as voting blocs, the contest was closer than one might think, knowing the outcome. Gorbachev faced powerful opponents, but he was not without resources. It was cross-domain feedbacks in dual hierarchy, I argue, more than raw political resources that defeated Gorbachev.

It is worth a moment's detour at this point to reflect on why Gorbachev did not go down the reform trajectory of China, especially since that success was known to him at the time. Historically, the Soviet Union went down the economic trajectory of Hungary, with all the political consequences of war on ministries that entailed, because of momentum from Andropov and the military interests he represented. But counterfactually, could Gorbachev have made a different choice? First and foremost, the Chinese approach to economic reform would have been to start with agriculture rather than with large state enterprises. Gorbachev approved wholeheartedly of what the Chinese had done. Gorbachev's own background after all had been in agriculture, not in industry. He knew about agriculture intimately in a way that he did not know about industry. Gorbachev repeatedly urged household leasing for Soviet agricultural cooperatives, pointing explicitly to the Chinese success. In hindsight, it was consequential, and a bit odd, that he did not push agricultural reform more vigorously.

Gorbachev's problem in my view was political. Outside the KGB, Gorbachev's primary power base was new provincial first secretaries, like himself. All provincial secretaries' power bases were the collective farms. Sharply different from Mao, Stalin had taken heavy and light industry out of their jurisdiction, leaving them only with direct control over agriculture.[146] In this structural inheritance, attacking the collective farms for Gorbachev meant attacking his strongest supporters. There was no offsetting plum like light industry to hand to them in exchange, as Deng had done. Ultimately, therefore, it was the decentralized state-ownership system of figure 9.3 (the historical legacy of Mao) that caused mobilizing upper cadres in China to lead to reform in agrarian regions. And it was the centralized state-ownership system of the Soviet Union (the historical legacy of Stalin) that caused provincial first secretaries in the Soviet Union to block the possibility of agricultural reform.[147]

At the deeper level of informal political networks, the difference between the Soviet Union and China was that reform politics under Gorbachev was a war between a mainly unified party center and fragmented but deeply rooted family circles below. In contrast, reform politics under Deng was a war between vertical factions, both of which extended from the top of the party to the bottom. Because of network integuments, Deng's supporters were arrayed in personal factions, loyal to him.[148] Gorbachev never did develop a personal faction within the Communist Party that was loyal to him personally. Because of this, policy appeals by Gorbachev to the bottom of his party had no built-in vertical networks to close the feedback loop back into political support for himself. Many of Gorbachev's actions can be understood as repeated failed attempts to build organizational feedback.

The reason for this absence of vertical networks was structural. *Nomenklatura* appointments meant essentially that superiors appointed their subordinates from centrally approved lists. This meant that Gorbachev had complete control over his own high-level appointments but that they (not he) had control over their own

[146] Khrushchev temporarily reversed this jurisdictional division of labor between provincial secretaries and central ministries, but *sovnarhkozy* had been overturned by Brezhnev.

[147] Valery Yakubovich (personal communication) adds the very reasonable addendum: "I don't think Gorbachev could push a Chinese-style agricultural reform more vigorously, since Russia was much more industrialized than China. Villages were depopulated and full of elders and drunks."

[148] The microfoundations of this are insightfully analyzed in Walder 1986, which describes the "principled particularism" structure of Chinese communist loyalties. See also Pye 1981.

appointments, the next level down. From this perspective, the whole party system can be seen as nested family circles of clientele. The behavioral result of this nesting was obsequious subservience when provincial secretaries faced upward toward their leader but autocratic tyranny when they faced downward toward their underlings. It was not difficult to say one thing in the Central Committee and do another thing back home. Whether this nesting translated behaviorally into centralized obedience or into fragmented resistance depended upon something else, like rates of social mobility and turnover. Gorbachev (like Khrushchev and Kosygin before him) was faced with the challenge of reforming the central-command system through a recalcitrant party structure, upon which his own power was based. Stalin had already showed one way out: extremely high rates of cadre turnover, with massive throughput by newcomers.

More relevant than China as a model for success in the perestroika reform trajectory that Gorbachev was on was Hungary. Janos Kádár in 1968 had successfully implemented the 1965 Kosygin enterprise-autonomy reforms, which Kosygin himself had not. Gorbachev was a student of the Hungarian experience: he visited there in 1986 and began talking up market socialism back home.[149] Gorbachev let his expert advisers focus on the economics of that experience; he focused on the politics.[150] Politically, Kádár's enterprise-autonomy reforms had succeeded because they were embedded in his Alliance Policy of co-opting complaisant noncommunists into the communist government.[151] The administrative side of this gave the Hungarian Communist Party access to the intelligentsia's economic networks and ideas without losing political control. The social side of this Alliance Policy folded collaborative civic organizations into a Patriotic Popular Front. The first aspect reinforced in Gorbachev's mind the potential long-term value of his glasnost policy of artistic freedom. The second aspect reminded Gorbachev of Lenin's soviets, in which workers councils were used by Bolsheviks to mobilize and control trade unions.[152] Legislative soviets remained throughout the Soviet Union, even though Stalin had long since emasculated them into passive institutions that did nothing more than rubber-stamp decisions made by the party. Breathing life into both enterprises and the soviets became Gorbachev's version of Kádár's Alliance Policy. More pregnant ideologically, it became Gorbachev's version of Lenin's NEP. Thereby glasnost escalated considerably beyond anything that Andropov would have approved: from KGB-style inspections in 1985 to newspaper publicity in 1986 to Hungarian artistic openness in 1987.

Elections of low-level communists made their first appearance in this wave of "openness" escalation by Gorbachev. Party regulars hardly went along with this without sabotage and surreptitious manipulation, but in the summer of 1987 secret-ballot elections with multiple communist candidates were held for local-government soviets[153] for the first time since Stalin's brief constitution of 1938. Elections of enterprise directors by factory workers councils were also authorized in the June 1987 Law for Enterprise Autonomy. Why this first step down the democratic road that led eventually and unintentionally to the collapse of the Soviet Union? Realpolitik nudged Gorbachev down his personal pilgrimage toward self-anointed messiah. Communist elections were Gorbachev's way of striking at the *nomenklatura* appointment monopoly of family circles. They were also an outright bid for constituency support from workers councils and from enterprise directors for his economic-autonomy reforms. Kádár had implemented factory-director elections in 1982 in Hungary, as part of his reform package, with positive political benefit to him and no ill economic effects. Factory directors were key political constituents for Kádár, whom Gorbachev desperately wanted as well.

In addition to short-term realpolitik, however, Gorbachev had a utopian side that egotistically wanted to remake history, like Lenin, Stalin, Mao, and other inspirational communist leaders before him.[154] This is evident in his 1987

[149] Aslund 1991, 32–33.

[150] In Gorbachev's speeches, book, and memoirs, there is surprisingly little discussion of economics, in which he was never trained. There is much hortatory discussion of "democratization," however, whatever that might mean.

[151] Berend 1990; Róna-Tas 1997; Seleny 2006. The nicely revealing slogan of this was "He who is not against us is with us." The Alliance Policy was Kádár's attempt to regain some legitimacy for communist rule after the disaster of Soviet repression of the 1956 revolution.

[152] Gorbachev 1987, 25–26, 47–48, 110–13. The Lenin soviets Gorbachev kept alluding to are well described and analyzed in Anweiler 1974.

[153] Hahn 1988.

[154] "In 1986 and 1987, when Gorbachev was strongly under the influence of Lenin's writings, it was my impression that he was anxious to propose some concept that might continue Lenin's thinking and perhaps shake the world as powerfully as anything the founding father of the Soviet Union had done" (Boldin 1994, 96).

book on perestroika from that period.[155] Like his predecessors, Gorbachev believed that the higher purpose of the Communist Party was not just to manipulate economic performance indicators and incentives. It was also to change lives and to make new men. From this utopian but deeply communist point of view, the problem of Brezhnev stagnation was a problem in the Soviet soul. As odd as that sounds to westerners steeped in neoclassical economics, Gorbachev constantly reiterated that the key to economic progress was to reform party cadres. Perhaps this was just propaganda to himself as well as to outsiders, but Gorbachev came to believe that the Andropov panopticon was not enough to get Soviet cadres and workers to work and to care. What looked to his opponents like a drift toward Western-style liberalism looked to him like true communism.

The first counterattack by the forces arrayed against Gorbachev was not really an attack at all. It was paralysis and sandbagging, the simple refusal to obey: "Beginning in 1985 I flew to Moscow three years in a row, immersing myself in the atmosphere of the capital, and met politicians, journalists, artists and writers. What were my impressions? *Perestroika* was going at full speed—a real tidal wave! Then I travelled from the capital into the countryside. Go some hundred or two hundred kilometers away and things were completely different—all quiet, no change."[156]

Party newspapers were ordered by Gorbachev to report on local problems; party newspapers were ordered by local party officials to not. Enterprises were ordered by Gorbachev to increase worker discipline, to accelerate production, and to try to innovate technologically. The response: business as usual. Ministries were ordered to participate in planning for greater enterprise autonomy, but they did so only to subvert that objective.[157] The economic reform process increasingly became planned by a closed brain trust of centralized Gorbachev advisers, without ministerial participation.

To understand what happened next, as a consequence of the perestroika flagship economic reform of the 1987 Law on State Enterprises, it is necessary to describe the Soviet economy in more detail. Figure 9.5 depicts Soviet dual hierarchy in more detail than does the generic figure 9.1. Ignore the third column in figure 9.5 labeled "Soviets" for now, since that represents Gorbachev's last political escalation to full democracy. The dual-hierarchy system he was trying to reform was the first two columns. The figure makes it clear that if direct management by ministries of enterprises is eliminated, then the only other channel available for Gorbachev to reach down to the enterprises is the indirect road through regional and local branches of the party.[158] Of course the hope of the reform was that enterprise directors eventually would learn to cycle around autocatalytic inputs and outputs by themselves—and thereby come to support Gorbachev—but that was in the future. In the meantime, with only obstruction from the ministries, alternative mechanisms had to be found to guide dependent state enterprises toward the alleged nirvana of economic efficiency through maximizing profits. No legal markets were yet in existence, so party was the only tool available.

[155] Here are a few quotes from Gorbachev's book (1987) to give a flavor of his rhetoric at that time: "The life-giving impetus of our great Revolution was too powerful for the Party and people to reconcile themselves to phenomena that were threatening to squander its gains. The works of Lenin and his ideals of socialism remained for us an inexhaustible source of dialectical creative thought, theoretical wealth and political sagacity. . . . Lenin's works in the last years of his life have drawn particular attention" (25). "We have come to the conclusion that unless we activate the human factor, that is, take into consideration the diverse interests of people, work collectives, public bodies, and various groups, unless we rely on them, and draw them into active, constructive endeavor, it will be impossible for us to accomplish any of the tasks set, or to change the situation in the country" (29). "We need wholesome, full-blooded functioning by all public organizations, all production teams and creative unions, new forms of activity by citizens and the revival of those which have been forgotten. In short, we need broad democratization of all aspects of society. That democratization is also the main guarantee that the current processes are irreversible. . . . Since we see our task as unfolding and utilizing the potential of socialism through the intensification of the human factor, there can be no other way but democratization, including reform of the economic mechanism and management, a reform whose main component is promotion of the role of work collectives" (31–32). "The essence of perestroika lies in the fact that it unites socialism with democracy and revives the Leninist concept of socialist construction both in theory and in practice" (35).

[156] The report of American researcher Ed Hewitt to Gorbachev in 1991. Gorbachev 1995, 195–96.

[157] "The main opposition to our [economic] ideas came from the heads of ministries and agencies, firstly the general economic agencies—Gosplan, Gossnab, Minfin, and the government apparatus. Later the opposition joined ranks with the Party bureaucracy. Needless to say, no-one was so bold as to speak out openly against reform; everyone was 'for' the reform process, but many offered half-hearted, ambiguous solutions that left many loopholes and sometimes even a direct opportunity for a roll back to the past. Unfortunately I had clashes with Ryzhkov [Gorbachev's economic ally and agent, in charge of the Council of Ministers] on a number of issues. I could see that he was under strong pressure from his former fellow industrial managers, who were continuously planting an insidious idea: 'The government is required to ensure effective management of the economy and at the same time the dismantling of the plan system is robbing it of the means of control'" (Gorbachev 1995, 227).

[158] As described above, that was what Khrushchev also had been trying to do.

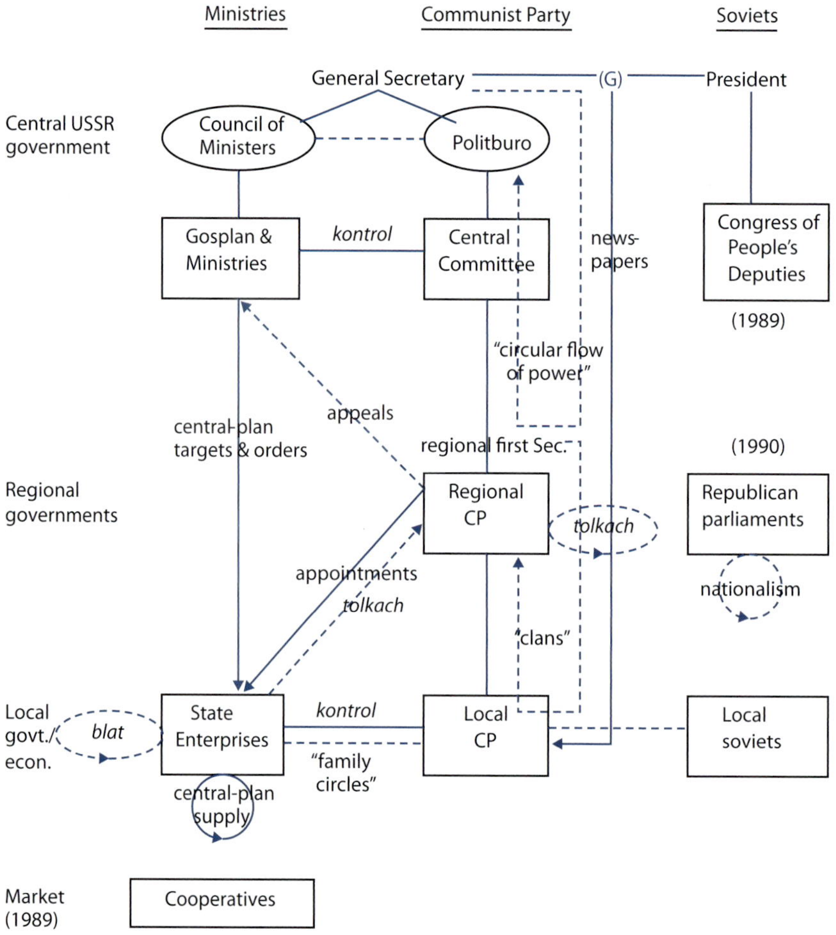

Figure 9.5 Soviet dual hierarchy, including Gorbachev's extension to soviets.

The primary economic side of this dual hierarchy of course was the central-command system, ruled by ministries. Ministries administratively set physical production targets for enterprises and managed the distribution of their products to other enterprises. As discussed in the section on Stalin, this did not work poorly in the heavy-industry and military sectors for which it was primarily intended. But agricultural and light-industry sectors were sucked dry, with shortages there rampant. This resource-extraction explanation does not deny the other problems with central command—information and soft budget constraints[159]—which also contributed to shortages.

[159] Hayek 1944 and Kornai 1980, respectively.

As is well-known,[160] the central-command system was not all that there was to the Soviet economy. Informal resource flows emerged around the margins of central command to deal with the shortages and bottlenecks produced by it. *Blat* was direct reciprocal barter between enterprises, using product inventories that they were not supposed to have had.[161] *Tolkach* were third-party intermediaries who hunted around for supplies in other enterprises, in order to arrange *blat*. Sometimes *tolkach* intermediar-

[160] Berliner 1957; Hough 1969; Rutland 1993; Ellman and Kontorovich 1998.

[161] Orchestrating low targets for one year through intentional underperformance the previous year was one useful way to generate such inventories in the first place. "Theft" of course was another.

ies were employees or private entrepreneurs, but mostly they were party cadres. Local cadres did that when supplies were geographically close at hand, and provincial cadres did it when these were located farther afield. Most of the day-to-day time of provincial and district party secretaries was spent on the phone trying to arrange supplies for "their" enterprises, which theoretically they already had but actually did not. The hoarding necessary to engage successfully in *blat* and *tolkach* exacerbated the shortages that provoked them to begin with. In the dual-hierarchy structure, therefore, Gorbachev's political need to manage perestroika through the party implied increased dependence of the Soviet economy on "corrupt" *blat* and *tolkach*, at least in the short run. New systems always emerge from the chrysalis of old, but in this case that implied building modern economic markets out of family circles.

This analysis makes Gorbachev's task seem difficult, yet Kádár in Hungary had pulled off the trick. How? The political precondition of Kádár's Alliance Policy has already been mentioned. This mobilized political and economic networks beyond the hermetically sealed Communist Party without relinquishing party control. But in addition, Kádár did something creative with his communist enterprises, which was analogous to what Deng had done in China with party cadres. Both leaders legalized entrepreneurial activity within the boundaries of communist organizations. Deng's party-centered approach had been to do this through clientelism: namely, to let party cadres give out permits to other cadres in exchange for kickbacks, mostly corporate but sometimes personal. Kádár's enterprise-centered approach—first with agricultural co-ops in 1968 and then with industrial enterprises in 1982—was to let employees set up partnerships within state-owned enterprises, to use state assets for private gain after hours and on weekends.[162] In both of these organizational innovations, the economic and political interests of multifunctional party cadres and enterprise directors, respectively, were aligned. In both post-reform countries, one got ahead in politics through making money,[163] and one made money by being in politics. By aligning interests across domains, powerful political constituencies emerged to support economic reforms that privatized entrepreneurship without privatizing property.

Gorbachev's problem in adopting either of these known-to-him organizational innovations was twofold. In the short run, he had no legal private markets, even on the edges of the plan, on which to monetize political actions. He had plenty of *blat* and *tolkach* networks, which were nonmonetized markets. And he had plenty of political clans and family circles, which manipulated those markets. But how to bring these existing economic and political networks out into the open and then have them discipline each other, as Deng and Kádár had done?

Gorbachev and his advisers were well aware of this issue, and in their flagship Law on State Enterprises they sensibly proposed wholesale markets for intermediate goods in order to legalize and monetize such socialist markets. This good idea failed for three reasons. First, wholesale presupposes inventories, that is, surpluses. But this was a shortage economy with no surpluses anywhere in sight. Ministries aggressively used the loophole of "state orders," intended to permit the state to be one among many bidders, to soak up surpluses as soon as they appeared. They stepped in and absorbed 90 percent of the goods, to satisfy the plan, before they even made it to market. Kick-starting wholesale markets for intermediate goods required the cooperation of ministries, which they refused to give.[164]

Second, there was the problem of who is a "market." Off-plan distribution around the margins was already handled by *blat* and *tolkach*, most of which was arranged on behalf of enterprises by party cadres. These network managers were the logical ones to manage any transition of their existing economic networks into a "market," through glasnost transparency. But these party cadres were the family circles whom Gorbachev was trying politically to defeat. He ordered them to stop "interfering in the market" through "petty party tutelage." And then he dismantled the party offices through which *blat*, *tolkach*, and *kontrol* had been managed in the past.

The third and deepest problem, which gave ministries so much clout to begin with, was the hyperconcentration of Soviet state enterprises, another legacy of Stalin. To exaggerate only

[162] Rupp 1983; Stark 1989, 1996; Róna-Tas 1997.

[163] In the case of Hungary, Kádár increasingly promoted successful enterprise directors into his Central Committee. This provided him with political support to continue his economic reforms. See Comisso and Marer 1986 and Róna-Tas 1977, 109.

[164] I repeat that had Khrushchev's *sovnarhkozy* reform succeeded earlier, this obstacle could have been overcome, region by region, because then provincial secretaries would have been in charge.

slightly, every industry was a monopoly.[165] "Market competition" has no meaning in such a setting. Releasing prices from administration would have meant astronomical price hikes everywhere. Appeals to neoclassical models of perfect competition only revealed the historical ignorance of their advocates. The best that could be hoped for was some sort of regulated contracting regime, perhaps like Japanese business groups.[166]

In the actual event, perestroika's flagship reform, the 1987 Law on State Enterprises (implemented in 1988), was an utter disaster economically. Annual growth rates in the production of producer-goods industries plummeted from 3.7 percent in 1987 and 3.4 percent in 1988, to 0.6 percent in 1989, to -3.2 percent in 1990, and even lower under Yeltsin. Household income inflated from 3.9 percent in 1987, to 9.2 percent in 1988, to 13.1 percent in 1989, to 16.9 percent in 1990, even as consumer-goods production stayed flat.[167] The *blat* and *tolkach* economic networks of the party were nowhere near strong enough to substitute for the loss of material-supply guidance from central ministries, no matter how frantically party cadres and enterprise directors worked their telephones. Hoarding by state enterprises exploded, and what little consumer goods there were disappeared from retail shelves. In other words, autocatalysis in production was disrupted, and the interdependent system suddenly collapsed.[168] Mainly because of industrial hyperconcentration, the Soviet economy could not be treated like Hungary or China. With his political hand, Gorbachev intentionally was attacking family circles, but with his economic hand he unintentionally was demanding that they save the day. Dissatisfaction spread from ministries and reactionary segments of the party to Gorbachev's own allies in the party. By 1988, Gorbachev was starting to be in trouble.

Overt negative reaction first was expressed publicly in late 1987 and early 1988 under the umbrella of Yegor Ligachev, Gorbachev's own number-two man, his closest partner under Andropov. Ligachev had been Gorbachev's aide in appointing provincial first secretaries and hence drew on Gorbachev's own base of support. The opposition's demands were nailed to the door with the newspaper publication of an inflammatory letter from schoolteacher Nina Andreyeva in March 1988, heavily scripted by Ligachev, which called for restoration of the reputations of Stalin and nationalism.[169] A major grievance of party conservatives was the rough treatment they had experienced in newspaper exposés. Gorbachev aggressively beat back this challenge from Ligachev with more purges, but a gauntlet had been cast.

Perestroika in flames, his party allies starting to doubt him, Gorbachev still tried to save the day through glasnost. After all, the Soviet Union had endured far worse than this in the gulag, the Great Purges, and in World War II, and in those cases the central leader's popularity with the public had soared at the expense of sullen underlings. Secure (some might say barricaded) in the Kremlin, Gorbachev launched his final mass mobilization campaign.

On the economic side, Gorbachev escalated again, this time from his 1987 Law on State Enterprises, which focused on the reform of state enterprises, to his 1988 Law on Cooperatives, which focused on creating a new private market of small production firms.[170] Youth loved this; the elderly hated it.[171] There were both Hungarian and Chinese precedents for market socialism—the coexistence of large state enterprises with small market-oriented firms—although Kádár had been careful to channel his co-ops into the bowels of state enterprises. Workers councils in Soviet state enterprises, however, promptly voted for factory directors who increased their wages.[172] Household incomes went quickly up,

[165] This giganticism, especially in heavy industry, derived from the Soviet engineering understanding of Henry Ford: specialization in mass production is the most efficient and "modern" economy possible. Centralized state investments always were directed toward this. In reality, enterprises could not truly operate this way. Soviet factories did all sorts of "illegal" things on the side to try to push toward self-enclosed autarchy and to improve their position in *blat* and *tolkach* markets.

[166] Business groups were an accessible form of market system to post-Soviet economies, as can be seen in chapters 10 and 12. The Japanese and South Korean variants of business groups were economically successful in part because extensive international trade disciplined them. Needless to say, market discipline has not been a prominent feature of the Russian variant of this organizational form.

[167] In 1987, 4.1 percent; in 1988, 5.4 percent; in 1989, 4.9 percent; and in 1990, 4.4 percent. All figures from Ellman and Kontorovich 1998, 156.

[168] Dare I say, like my models in chapter 3 do, when they die?

[169] Hazan 1990, 39–53.

[170] Aslund 1991, 167–78.

[171] Public opinion polls at the time showed 87.2 percent of those under forty-five approving of private cooperatives, whereas 81.1 percent of those between sixty-one and seventy-five disapproving. Aslund 1991, 177.

[172] "The explosive growth of wages was ignited by the competition on the labor market resulting from the rapid expansion of cooperatives following the adoption of the Law on Cooperatives in May 1988" (Ellman and Kontorovich 1998, 155).

with not enough new to buy. Repressed inflationary pressures drove administered prices and "true market" prices even more out of whack than usual, making prices meaningless as market signals of demand.

On the political side, Gorbachev also escalated dramatically by announcing at the enlarged 19th Party Conference in June 1988 his intention to restructure the national Supreme Soviet into a new, publicly elected Congress of People's Deputies. Radically, this was to contain both communist and noncommunist representatives (but no noncommunist parties).[173] This was Gorbachev's maximal effort to outflank and crush his growing party opposition by co-opting sympathetic noncommunists. The coup de grâce would have been Gorbachev's additional role as president of that national legislature without giving up his old role as general secretary of the Communist Party. Like Lenin's soviets, the idea was not to give up communist control: the electoral rules were carefully jiggered by Gorbachev's team to guarantee a communist majority.

Leading up to this large conference, the first of this size since 1941, elections were held for party conference delegates, following the procedures of the local soviet reforms of the previous year: "Gorbachev's strategy was to outflank entrenched opposition within the party structure by using secret ballot elections to encourage those who supported reform to send sympathetic delegates to the conference."[174] But in neither this nor his enterprise-director elections was he fully successful in getting reformers elected. Family circles defensively manipulated their grassroots networks to control the nomination processes.[175] Gorbachev was reduced to springing his dramatic Congress of People's Deputies idea on the conference at the last minute for a snap vote, almost like a coup. Implementation plans soon followed in a September 1988 Central Committee plenum, in which Gorbachev also unsheathed his "terrible swift sword" of purging Ligachev and his allies from the Politburo.[176] In all this, Gorbachev was countering failure in economics with mass mobilization in politics. Without Stalin in the background, it is hard to understand, in my opinion, what is going on here.

Yeltsin begins to move the story into the next chapter, so I will truncate my discussion of him and the last two years of Gorbachev's reign. As is well-known, Gorbachev failed to maintain control over his own left wing, thereby losing both ends of his coalition. Yeltsin was even more avid a reformer than Gorbachev, with none of Gorbachev's leadership need to compromise occasionally with Ligachev and his ilk. Using the Moscow city government as his party base and glasnost as his cover, Yeltsin repeatedly lashed out at Ligachev in public forums, accusing him of covering up corruption and worse.[177] Famous for his intemperance, Gorbachev used Yeltsin as his attack dog, but this dog proved to be uncontrollable by his master and had to be purged. Freedom of the press gave Yeltsin the opportunity to keep himself in the public limelight, even after his late 1987 demotion from Moscow office. I give Yeltsin no more than facilitative credit for the collapse of the Soviet Union, despite his brave rallying of the Russian people and the army at the very end, which beat back the 1991 coup of party conservatives against Gorbachev. For sure, Yeltsin put himself opportunistically in the position to catch reform-agenda pieces as the communist apparatus fell. But Gorbachev, not Yeltsin, caused the collapse of the Soviet Union.

Economic flameout doomed Gorbachev's desperate mass mobilization strategy—or rather, mass mobilization worked, but not in the way that Gorbachev had intended. The groundswell of public support for true democratic elections was startling after all those years of communist electoral hypocrisy, especially in economically advanced urban areas. Because of the jiggering, Gorbachev and the communists still controlled the 1989 national Congress of People's Deputies, but they now were riding a populist tiger. Instead of channeling populist fever into the party, soviet elections channeled populist fever against the party. In controlled volumes, of course, Gorbachev needed this for his leverage. As the loudly proclaimed sponsor of an economic disaster, however, Gorbachev did not get much credit for himself. Yeltsin stole his reform thunder.

[173] Gill 1994, 63–77; McFaul 2001, 48–53.

[174] Gill 1994, 46.

[175] Gill 1994, 57; Ellman and Kantorovich 1998, 201–3.

[176] Hazen 1990, 66–81. Previous Gorbachev allies under Andropov were targeted: Chebrikov was removed from control of the KGB, and Ligachev himself was demoted from control over ideology and appointments to secretary for agriculture. That last move ensured that economic reform never would touch agriculture. These 1988 purges squelched party opposition in the Politburo, but they hardly did so at deeper levels in the party.

[177] Covering up he may have done, but personally Ligachev was a moral puritan. It had been he who had spearheaded the Andropov-style anti-alcohol campaign against drunkenness.

A jeweler's hammer can break a diamond, but only along the lines of its internal crystal cleavages. When the reform steamroller moved to its logical next stage of republic elections in 1990, populist fever became channeled into the ethnic lines laid down by Lenin when he drew up his federalist constitution of the Soviet Union in the 1920s. Elections in soviet republics meant elections in ethnic regions. Gorbachev was shocked by this unexpected development of ethnic separatism and desperately tried to put on the brakes, but it was too late. Republics in the Baltics and the Caucuses wanted to follow the 1989 lead of their East European brothers in Poland, Hungary, and East Germany. Yeltsin wrapped himself in the Russian flag, and other entrepreneurial provincial first secretaries likewise made quick political calculations about whether they were communist or popular nationalists. Gorbachev had tried to use Stalinist tactics to browbeat a hierarchy of nested family circles into demagogic obedience to him. But with no iron fist at the top, the communist hierarchy fragmented along the lines of its natural cleavages. Some of these family circles stubbornly stuck with communism. Some of them blew with the populist wind of ethnic separatism. Some of them asset stripped their enterprises. Regardless of the heterogeneous responses of local family circles, the top-down internal ligaments of the Communist Party, tying them together, were no more. Skocpol has said that revolutions aren't made; states fall.[178] I take this to mean not that states fall without agency but that they fracture through internal contradictions, otherwise known as destructive feedback.

To conclude this section on Gorbachev, two counterfactuals are worth considering. First, was there any way for Gorbachev to have reformed the Soviet Union without abandoning his Andropov roots? Second, given that Gorbachev launched instead onto the more radical trajectory prefigured by Stalin, could he have succeeded by going all the way to brutality?

There is not much question that Gorbachev could have succeeded politically by sticking to the Andropov formula and faction. That, after all, was what they hired him for. Political support for that program was strong, especially in the next generation of communists. The problem was that more than anticorruption was required to breathe economic life into hyperspecialized industry. For both economic and political reasons, Gorbachev desperately needed factory directors to rise up as a new constituency, and the Hungarian experience told him that market socialism was the way to do that within a centralized system. But he had no organizational channel to them not controlled by his opponents. Ministries were dead-set opponents to an enterprise-autonomy scheme that deprived them of power and of the capacity to fulfill their economic plans. The Communist Party was being purged, quite successfully at the top, but in a way that only strengthened defensive family circles at the bottom, where the factories resided. Under the circumstances, the idea of reviving Lenin's elected soviets was actually a very creative and innovative idea. Had these new organizations worked as planned, by recruiting fresh locals (including factory directors themselves) into the system, that would have become Gorbachev's channel, and Soviet political history might have been different. The problem with this innovative new idea, I believe, was that it was not really clear what existing factory directors were getting out of the deal. Autonomy with no markets to be autonomous within didn't solve factory directors' day-to-day problems.

A deeper issue for Gorbachev, though he did not phrase it this way, was how to make robust action work long enough to allow new channels of any sort to grow. Robust action works by leveraging contradictory forces into alignment through a central, multivocal broker. Multivocality is maintained, as the cases of both Cosimo and Deng show, by finding multifunctional programs and policies that respond to initiative coming from elsewhere. Gorbachev tactically was not unskilled in juggling ambiguous phrases and programs that could be interpreted in different ways. But the feedbacks necessary to move organizational innovation into systemic invention were just not there. On the liberal side, Gorbachev wasn't responding to bottom-up initiative, like Deng and Cosimo were. He was trying top-down to engineer that in order to end-run family circles. When response within the communist system did not come, he broke more and more dual-hierarchy barriers to a democratic autocatalysis that simply was not there, thereby destroying the economic autocatalysis that was. In particular, the KGB, no friends of family circles themselves, understandably became alienated once glasnost shifted in meaning from anticorruption to free speech. A coup attempt became inevitable once Gorbachev's original Andropov base of support (KGB plus provincial secretaries) shifted away from him.

[178] Skocpol 1979, 17–18.

A final counterfactual to consider is what if Gorbachev, with his political back to the wall, had behaved all the way like Stalin. This would have meant unleashing tanks on his own country rather than let ethnic separatism get started. This also would have meant even higher volumes of purges, deeper down, directed at communism itself. Doing these in the name of freedom would have been quite a trick, but Stalin and Mao had shown the way—namely, to declare that existing communism is not true communism and to mobilize a generational war of the young against the old. The soviets and successful market socialism—the expansion of light industry—may have created enough room for youth, if opposition had been more brutally suppressed, perhaps with overt assistance from the KGB and the military. Deng knew how to oscillate between reform and repression; why did Gorbachev not also pull the trigger?

Part of the answer to this question has already been given: at the end, the KGB and the military no longer supported Gorbachev. But the other part of the answer is that this in fact did occur, just in the names of Yeltsin and Putin, not in the name of Gorbachev. Gorbachev laid down the punctuated-evolution trajectory that Yeltsin and Putin, not Gorbachev, completed.

It seems obvious that Gorbachev had no plan when he came to power, certainly not a plan complex enough to cope with the tumultuous contingencies he faced. The preexisting dual-hierarchy structure shaped the reform options that he had, but political and economic feedbacks unleashed by his reforms pulled Gorbachev himself down a road from Andropov to Mao, making him into a radically different leader at the end of his term than he was at the beginning. In the long run, relations make actors, but this long run actually was remarkably brief in time.

SUMMARY AND CONCLUSION

Kremlin, central command, the Brezhnev era, frozen tundra—all combine to give us an image of solidity, structure, and stasis. But that is only to observers and analysts with no sense of evolutionary history. Equilibrium is not the only way to perceive and to think. Another way to perceive and to think is in terms of flows: flows of resources, flows of people, how they move, how they are transformed, how autocatalysis of them can tip.

In economic production, two styles of autocatalysis in product flows were observed in these cases: autocatalysis among large and specialized mass-production enterprises in heavy industry and defense, and autocatalysis among smaller light-industry enterprises within geographical regions. The USSR and China had both styles of economy superimposed and interacting, even though the former dominated in the Soviet Union and the latter dominated in China. Intercalated product flows within these economies were hardly smooth: shortages, bottlenecks, and inefficiencies were pervasive. But whatever the inefficiencies, it is hard to argue that communist economic systems, of whichever version, did not work and did not reproduce. With the prominent exceptions of the Great Leap Forward and Gorbachev's reforms, they mostly achieved what their leaders wanted them to achieve.

But for analyzing dynamics, the key is not these economies sui generis; the key is the overlap between these economic networks of product exchange and political networks of authority and coalition among party cadres. That is what structures feedback and tipping. The mapping is not as simple as central ministries go with the first style of economy and party hierarchies go with the second. Dual hierarchy was foundational in both countries: the Soviet economy needed party brokerage and storming to work out bottlenecks in central plan operation, and the Chinese economy needed ministries to push its cellular structure toward the industrial age.

Stalin's cross-network tipping worked like this: At first, Stalin mobilized provincial secretaries and urban proletariat in his wildly storming first Five-Year Plan. Funded by brutal collectivization of peasants and purging technical experts who got in his way, this "bacchanalia of planning" built huge new mass-production factories and cities at the cost of massive imbalance in input-output supplies. The party struggled mightily to achieve ever-escalating targets, but when they inevitably fell short, factory directors and local party officials formed defensive alliances (family circles) to cover up their inadequacies. Stalin was driven by war and interpreted difficulties in industrialization as due to "sabotage" and "wrecking." He responded to this feedback from the economy politically by repeating his genesis mechanism of purge and mass mobilization on an even grander scale. Hundreds of thousands of party members, in both the economic and the political pillars, were murdered in Stalin's Great Purges, which were leveraged off and fueled by young proletarian zealots in factories and in engineering schools. Organizational catalysis and lock-in of the central-command innovation induced by purge and mass mobilization were achieved by massive upward social mobility (the generation of '38) by Stalin's young Stakhanovites and engineers. Thereby the power balance between the two pillars of dual hierarchy shifted from party to ministries, and the industrialization preference of Stalin for heavy industry and war became institutionalized in the organizational interests of central-command ministries. The previously warlike Communist Party became supportively administrative in response. Hitler was the ultimate natural-selection test, which Stalin passed (barely).

The organizational invention of the Bolshevik Party was achieved by Lenin (and Trotsky), not by Stalin. But Stalin used that to build his own new organizational invention of the central-command economy, at first on the back of the party and then reflecting back to destroy and reconstruct what Lenin had built. This was tipping with a murderous vengeance. The murders, however gripping, should not lead us to overlook the widespread new induced interests that supported and benefited from Stalin's Terror. Murder alone does not create autocatalysis. Reforms, even in centralized communism, must create the interests and the actors to carry them through.

Mao's cross-network tipping worked like this: Mao, like Stalin, also relied on mass mobilization as a genesis mechanism—in the Great Leap Forward only on that, in the Cultural Revolution on that plus purge. But Mao was not as successful as Stalin in catalyzing or locking-in his organizational creations through new flows of reproducing biographies. What he did do repeatedly was to alter cadre and economic networks, which channeled the next stages in Chinese coevolution, including his own. Using the different leadership mechanism of robust action, Deng Xiaoping built on the residues of Mao's networks to make quasi-markets through clientage.

The difference between the Soviet and Chinese communist cases, explaining their diverging coevolutions, is not the basic constitution of dual hierarchy, which they shared. The difference in my analysis is the networks, both formal and informal, that grew on this common constitutional trellis. As part of his anti-Soviet slogan "politics in command," Mao in the economic pillar during the Great Leap Forward (and even a little before that) decentralized the "ownership" of all but the largest communist enterprises to provincial levels of the party, away from control by central ministries. This decentralization the same as Khrushchev's *sovnarhkozy* reforms, which failed to survive in the Soviet Union.[179] The Great Leap Forward was a return (with a rural twist) to the party's storming methods of Stalin's first Five-Year Plan before powerful central ministries had developed in Russia. The failure of the Great Leap Forward led to fracture in the Chinese communist elite at the highest levels and thence to vertical factions: radical Mao versus pragmatist Liu Shao-chi, each with political support reaching down into the Communist Party. In the Soviet Union, informal networks mostly assumed the different form of local horizontal collusions (family circles, clans) for defense. This was because Stalin purged and murdered the pragmatists but also because giant enterprises provided more economic nodes in the Soviet Union for such informal protection networks to cluster upon. Those giant enterprises required informal collusion to get supplies.

Mao's second stage of the Cultural Revolution also bears resemblance to Stalin's second stage of the Great Purges, but here is where organizational outcomes really diverged. Mao again mostly[180] followed Stalin's script: he belatedly purged pragmatist opponents, and he mass mobilized zealous red youth to denounce and humiliate their elders, thereby destroying the party apparatus that was the base of his own power. The "success" of Stalin and the "failure" of Mao over the longer term, therefore, were not due to any deep differences in their leadership styles. They were due to different organizational feedback structures in their constituencies. Stalin's zealous youth denounced their elders to Stalin's secret police, who killed them. But Mao's zealous youth did not turn over their denounced elders to Mao's People's Liberation Army for processing; rather, they did everything themselves. Stalin's secret police closed the feedback loop of mass mobilization back to himself in a way that Mao's PLA did not.

Westerners egotistically like to think that Deng and Gorbachev initiated private markets because the light had dawned and they saw the teleological superiority of our ways. An alternative hypothesis, which explains more of the details of their economic reforms, is that they were communists trying to consolidate their power in communist ways with options, strategies, and

[179] Khrushchev thereby had greater long-term impact on the domestic development of China than he did on the domestic development of the Soviet Union.

[180] The main part of Stalin's script that Mao did not follow was murder. Humiliation and exile yes, but murder no.

networks inherited from the path-dependent past. All of the components of Deng's reform coalition were constructed by Mao. Deng was a member of the Long March generation. Deng's base of power was Mao's PLA, after Mao had purged Lin Biao's reddest supporters. "Playing to the provinces" was a well-established route to communist leadership, followed by Stalin early in his career, by Khrushchev, and even by Mao during the Great Leap Forward. Vertical factions unintentionally had been created by Mao through the failure of his Great Leap Forward. Deng revived Liu Shao-chi's pragmatist faction after Mao had tried to kill it off through the Red Guards. Even the household responsibility system first emerged in the residues of the Great Leap Famine. Indeed all the pieces were in place—except the army and Mao himself—for an economic transition after the Great Leap Forward. It was Mao's awareness of this very real danger that led to the Cultural Revolution. It took a civil war to make this economic transition more or less consensual.

All of these residues notwithstanding, Deng's robust-action style of leadership guided these components into complementarity. Instead of the aggressively charismatic and demagogic style of a Stalin or a Mao, Deng was a sphinx, like Cosimo de' Medici, ambiguous in his policies, in his offices, and in his interests, sitting behind (and above) the scenes adjudicating disputes like a judge. Policy-wise he oscillated, looking like a liberal reformer one moment, like a Tiananmen Square repressor the next, like a conservative disciplinarian the next, but in truth fully committed to none of these faces.

This ambiguity at the top legitimated cadres below to become ambiguous themselves—part communist partisans and part free marketeers. Communists under Deng did not need private property or even to reject communism to become entrepreneurial. They used their preexisting clientelist networks, already well adapted to storming, to become entrepreneurial within the local governments and the local state-owned enterprises that they themselves controlled.[181] In this way, communist cadre networks in China grew outward into society, to broker relations there, rather than inward into Soviet-style administrative *nomenklatura*. This of course is just what Mao had wanted, albeit for the goal of ideological indoctrination, not for the goal of making money. "Communists" now brokered relations among "capitalists," but in truth what was the difference anymore? Markets in China after Mao were the monetization of communist cadre storming, hierarchically still networked into the state.

Gorbachev wanted to do what Deng achieved, namely, to build socialist markets in order to strengthen communism. But as his reform process unfolded, he turned toward behaving more like Stalin and Mao, using democracy as his purge and mass mobilization device. Escalation to this final stratagem proceeded step by step, even though quickly. Faced with a phalanx of family circles suffocating his lethargic factory enterprises, Gorbachev attacked them first through Andropov-style discipline, then through Kosygin- and Kádár-style enterprise autonomy, then through NEP-style liberalization, and only finally through political democracy. The constantly reiterated but ambiguous words *perestroika* and *glasnost* obfuscated somewhat these dramatic switches in approach. What drove Gorbachev to evolve from Deng to Mao? He never could develop a personal faction loyal to him, to slice through the endless horizontal layers of passive resistance that unfolded at every level of the party. Because he had no informal social-network lever to extend beyond the top ranks, Gorbachev was confined to issuing formal thunderbolts from his secure but increasingly isolated Kremlin. Gorbachev knew all about purge from the very beginning. He was a master of Kremlin intrigue and bullying, and indeed was more aggressive at purging than any Soviet leader had been since Stalin. But his most fervently desired constituency for economic reform was the state-enterprise factory directors. In fact no constituency within dual hierarchy arose to respond favorably to his impassioned economic-reform pleas. Feedback lay outside dual hierarchy, not within.

Faced with recalcitrance, the dual-hierarchy system presented him with the limited constituency options discussed at the beginning of this chapter. Ministries were the enemy. Gorbachev tried but failed to arouse enterprise directors. Deng-style clientage mobilization of provincial secretaries at first seemed promising because that had been the original power base of Gorbachev. But they were embedded in and indeed were prime movers in family circles and clans. They would do a lot for Gorbachev—except dissolve themselves. Gorbachev did not have a Mao preceding him, like Deng did, to break the system into parallel vertical factional trees. That left

[181] Bothersome central ministries had already been contained to the "commanding heights" of the plan.

———. 1988. *Stalin's Industrial Revolution.* Cambridge: Cambridge University Press.

———. 1998. *Freedom and Terror in the Donbas.* Cambridge: Cambridge University Press.

Lieberthal, Kenneth. 1997. "The Great Leap Forward and the Split in the Yan'an Leadership, 1958–65." In *The Politics of China: The Eras of Mao and Deng* ed. Roderick MacFarquhar, 87–147. Cambridge: Cambridge University Press.

Ligachev, Yegor. 1993. *Inside Gorbachev's Kremlin.* New York: Pantheon Books.

Lyons, Thomas P. 1985. "China's Cellular Economy: A Test of the Fragmentation Hypothesis." *Journal of Comparative Economics* 9:125–44.

———. 1986. "Explaining Economic Fragmentation in China: A Systems Approach." *Journal of Comparative Economics* 10:209–36.

———. 1987. *Economic Integration and Planning in Maoist China.* New York: Columbia University Press.

MacFarquhar, Roderick. 1983. *The Origins of the Cultural Revolution: The Great Leap Forward, 1958–1960.* New York: Columbia University Press.

———. 1997. "The Succession to Mao and the End of Maois, 1969–82." In *The Politics of China: The Eras of Mao and Deng*, ed. Roderick MacFarquhar, 248–339. Cambridge: Cambridge University Press.

MacFarquhar, Roderick, and Michael Schoenhals. 2006. *Mao's Last Revolution.* Cambridge, MA: Harvard University Press.

Malle, Silvana. 1985. *The Economic Organization of War Communism, 1918–1921.* Cambridge: Cambridge University Press.

Manning, Roberta T. 1993a. "The Soviet Economic Crisis of 1936–1940 and the Great Purges." In *Stalinist Terror: New Perspectives*, ed. J. Arch Getty and Roberta T. Manning, 116–41. Cambridge: Cambridge University Press.

———. 1993b. "The Great Purges in a Rural District: Belyi Raison Revisited." In *Stalinist Terror: New Perspectives*, ed. J. Arch Getty and Roberta T. Manning, 168–97. Cambridge: Cambridge University Press.

Mawdsley, Evan, and Stephen White. 2000. *The Soviet Elite from Lenin to Gorbachev.* Oxford: Oxford University Press.

McFaul, Michael. 2001. *Russia's Unfinished Revolution.* Ithaca: Cornell University Press.

Medvedev, Roy A. [1972] 1989. *Let History Judge.* New York: Columbia University Press.

Nathan, Andrew J. 1973. "A Factionalism Model for CCP Politics." *China Quarterly* 53:34–66.

Naughton, Barry. 1995. *Growing Out of the Plan.* Cambridge: Cambridge University Press.

Nove, Alec. 1969. *An Economic History of the U.S.S.R.* London: Allen Lane.

Oi, Jean C. 1989. *State and Peasant in Contemporary China.* Berkeley: University of California Press.

———. 1999. *Rural China Takes Off.* Berkeley: University of California Press.

Oliver, James H. 1973. "Turnover and 'Family Circles' in Soviet Administration." *Slavic Review* 32:527–45.

Padgett, John F. 1990. "Mobility as Control: Congressmen through Committees." In *Social Mobility and Social Structure*, ed. R. L. Breiger. New York: Cambridge University Press.

Padgett, John F., and Christopher K. Ansell. 1993. "Robust Action and the Rise of the Medici, 1400–1434." *American Journal of Sociology* 98(6):1259–1319.

Pye, Lucian. 1981. *The Dynamics of Chinese Politics.* Cambridge, MA: Oelgeschlager, Gunn and Hain.

Rigby, T. H. 1981. "Early Provincial Cliques and the Rise of Stalin." *Soviet Studies* 33(1):3–28.

Róna-Tas, Ákos. 1997. *The Great Surprise of the Small Transformation.* Ann Arbor: University of Michigan Press.

Rupp, Kalman. 1983. *Entrepreneurs in Red.* Albany: State University of New York Press.

Rutland, Peter. 1993. *The Politics of Economic Stagnation in the Soviet Union.* Cambridge: Cambridge University Press.

Schurmann, Franz. 1968. *Ideology and Organization in Communist China.* Berkeley: University of California Press.

Seleny, Anna. 2006. *The Political Economy of State-Society Relations in Hungary and Poland.* Cambridge: Cambridge University Press.

Shirk, Susan L. 1993. *The Political Logic of Economic Reform in China.* Berkeley: University of California Press.

Siegelbaum, Lewis H. 1988. *Stakhanovism and the Politics of Productivity in the USSR, 1935–1941.* Cambridge: Cambridge University Press.

Siminov, Nikolai. 2000. "*Mobpodgotovka*: Mobilization Planning in Interwar Industry." In *The Soviet Defense-Industry Complex from Stalin to Khrushchev*, ed. John Barber and Mark Harrison, 205–22. London: Macmillan Press.

Skinner, G. William. 1964–65. "Marketing and Social Structure in Rural China." *Journal of Asian Studies.* Part I: 24(1):3–43; part II: 24(2):195–228; part III: 24(3):363–99.

Skocpol, Theda. 1979. *States and Social Revolutions.* Cambridge: Cambridge University Press.

Stark, David. 1989. "Coexisting Organizational Forms in Hungary's Emerging Mixed Economy." In *Remaking of the Economic Institutions of Socialism*, ed. Victor Nee and David Stark, 137–68. Stanford: Stanford University Press.

———. 1996. "Recombinant Property in Eastern European Capitalism." *American Journal of Sociology* 101(4):993–1027.

State Statistical Bureau, PRC. 1984. *Statistical Yearbook of China 1984.* Hong Kong: Economic Information & Agency.

Tsou, Tang, Marc Blecher, and Mitch Meisner. 1982. "The Responsibility System in Agriculture: Its Implementation in Xiyang and Dazhai." *Modern China* 8(1):41–103.

Tucker, Robert C. 1990. *Stalin in Power: The Revolution from Above, 1928–1941*. New York: Norton.

Vogel, Ezra F. 1969. *Canton under Communism*. Cambridge, MA: Harvard University Press.

Walder, Andrew G. 1986. *Communist Neo-Traditionalism: Work and Authority in Chinese Industry*. Berkeley: University of California Press.

———. 1995. "Local Governments as Industrial Firms." *American Journal of Sociology* 101(2): 263–301.

———, ed. 1998. *Zouping in Transition*. Cambridge, MA: Harvard University Press.

Waller, J. Michael. 1994. *Secret Empire: The KGB in Russia Today*. Boulder, CO: Westview Press.

Wang, Shaoguang. 1995. "The Rise of the Regions: Fiscal Reform and the Decline of Central State Capacity in China." In *The Waning of the Communist State*, ed. Andrew G. Walder, 87–113. Berkeley: University of California Press.

Wheatcroft, S. G., and R. W. Davies, eds. 1985. *Materials for a Balance of the Soviet National Economy, 1928–1932*. Cambridge: Cambridge University Press.

Whitson, William. 1969. "The Field Army in Chinese Communist Military Politics." *China Quarterly* 37: 1–30.

———. 1973. *The Chinese High Command*. New York: Praeger.

Wong, Christine P. W. 1987. "Between Plan and Market: The Role of the Local Sector in Post-Mao China." *Journal of Comparative Economics* 11:385–98.

Yang, Dali L. 1996. *Calamity and Reform in China*. Stanford: Stanford University Press.

———. 2004. *Remaking the Chinese Leviathan*. Stanford: Stanford University Press.

Yeltsin, Boris. 1990. *Against the Grain: An Autobiography*. London: Cape.

Zaleski, Eugène. 1967. *Planning Reforms in the Soviet Union, 1962–1966*. Chapel Hill: University of North Carolina Press.

———. [1962] 1971. *Planning for Economic Growth in the Soviet Union, 1918–1932*. Chapel Hill: University of North Carolina Press.

———. 1980. *Stalinist Planning for Economic Growth, 1933–1952*. Chapel Hill: University of North Carolina Press.

10

Deviations from Design

The Emergence of New Financial Markets and Organizations in Yeltsin's Russia

Andrew Spicer

Russian post-communist reform efforts began with a large and concerted effort to design new forms of markets and organizations. By the end of Russia's mass privatization program in June 1994, over seventeen thousand midsized and state-owned enterprises had transformed into joint-stock companies; forty million Russians had became shareholders in newly privatized firms; dozens of new stock markets had been created; and thousands of new financial organizations had entered the new marketplace (Kogut and Spicer 2002). By many measures—whether it is the number of participants or the amount of resources in the market—Russian financial markets could be considered to have "emerged" as early as 1994. One 1995 account of the Russian transition claimed that Russia was already a "market economy" by that date (Aslund 1995).

Yet by limiting the study of market reform to only the successful aspects of its implementation, this design perspective fails to distinguish between the destruction of the old regime and the creation of a new one (Spicer, McDermott, and Kogut 2000). As post-communist research has illustrated in multiple countries, the types of organizational forms that have emerged in these societies do not always match initial designs (Kogut and Spicer 2002; McDermott 2002; Stark 1996; Stark and Bruszt 1998; Stark and Bedres, this volume). In this analysis of the evolution of Russia's post-communist financial markets, I make a similar distinction between design and emergence. I compare the initial design of Russian financial markets at the start of the 1990s to their emergent structure at the end of the decade. On multiple dimensions—whether it is the types of organizational forms authorized to operate on the market, the structure of regulatory agencies, or the pattern of transactional flows—what emerged in these markets differed significantly from what was originally designed.

To explain these deviations from design, I take a broad historical perspective that follows the analytic strategies presented in this volume. Instead of viewing states and markets as separate domains that operate according to independent logics, I examine markets as organizational forms in which public and private activities are inextricably intertwined. Market outcomes are therefore not the result of a "natural" selection process in which organizations survive based solely on their economic functions, nor are they the direct consequence of policy reform. Instead, emergence takes place through the mixing of logics and relationships that cut across economic, political, and social boundaries in a process that is rarely unidirectional or foreseen by economic or political actors. States and markets

I would like to thank Bruce Kogut for his patience in helping me work through the complex story of Russian market development, both as my dissertation adviser and as a colleague and coauthor. I also thank Will Pyle, with whom I wrote an earlier paper on the development of the market for household savings in Russia. Finally, I thank all the participants in the workshops that preceded this publication, particularly John Padgett and Woody Powell. All mistakes and omissions are my own.

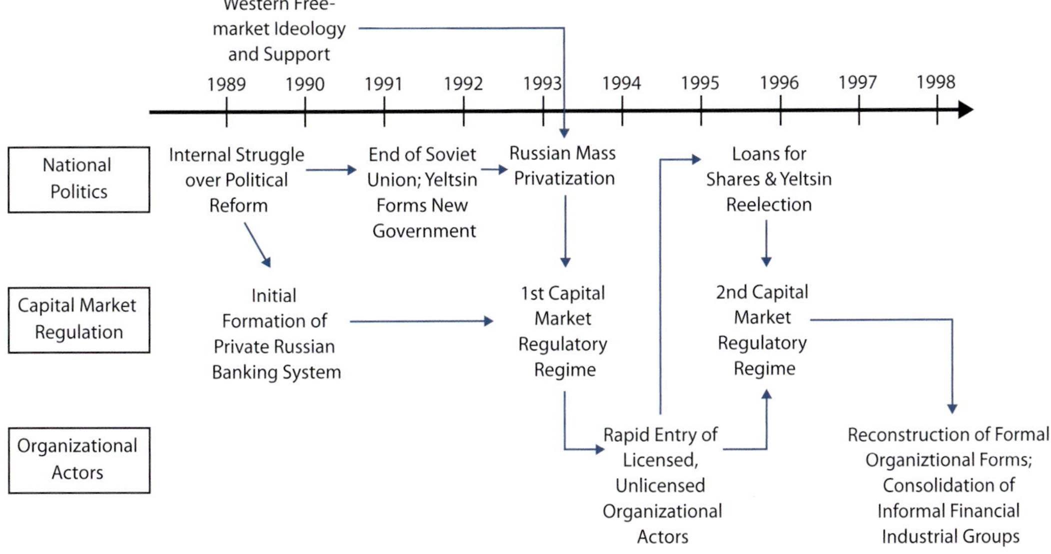

Figure 10.1 Interaction between national, market, and organizational levels of activity.

are co-evolutionary; changes in one domain feedback on the development of the other in an endogenous process of institutional formation and change (Padgett and Powell, this volume).

In my analysis of co-evolutionary dynamics in Russia's post-communist financial markets, I trace the movement of ideas, actors, and resources across three levels of analysis. As figure 10.1 illustrates, the first level examines national politics; the second, market-level regulation and control; and the third, organizational-level strategy and survival.

In stable economic environments, the social and political background to economic activity is usually taken as a given, such that coordination and exchange between organizational entities routinely take place with little active consideration of boundaries between institutional levels and domains. Politically authorized constitutive rules forge "distinctive locations for economic activity that shape the strategic and relative opportunities of economic actors in their mutual economic interactions" (Lindberg and Campbell 1991, 360). In contrast, the constitutive rules of market organization were as yet unformed in Russia. The very definition of what constituted a legitimate market actor, and who should make that determination, quickly became a highly contested political and economic issue. Blurred boundaries between political, regulatory, and organizational spheres of authority created a fluid landscape in which actors and actions frequently crossed institutional levels and domains.

This chapter is structured according to the multilevel chronology illustrated in figure 10.1. In the first half of the chapter, I look at the impact of higher-level political and regulatory systems on the initial emergence of financial organizations in Russia's capital markets. In the first section, I examine the political background of Yeltsin's decision to implement rapid and comprehensive market reforms in post-communist Russia. In the second section, I describe the impact of the political decision to implement reform as rapidly as possible on the choices made to regulate Russia's capital markets. In the third section, I examine the emergence of new organizational forms in Russia's financial markets. Many different types of economic actors emerged to take advantage of the unregulated market environment of the time.

In the second half of the chapter, I move from analyzing the top-down impact of political activity on market activity toward examining the bottom-up processes by which emergent market actors influenced national and regulatory politics. First, I describe the political design of the loans-for-shares deal between the Yeltsin government and the largest Russian banks, which led to massive new resources for Yeltsin's 1996 reelection campaign as well as the vast enlargement of bank ownership in the most profitable natural resource companies in Russia. Next, I explore the way that bankers took advantage of new patronage relationships to gain political control of financial market regulatory structures. I conclude with an analysis of the types of economic actors that populated the market at the end of the 1990s, demonstrating that what emerged at the end of Yeltsin's regime diverged significantly from original design.

My intent in this historical narrative is to focus on the systemic interdependencies that link levels and domains in market emergence. I refer the reader to my own and others' work on the organizational development of the Russian capital markets for fuller historical detail about individual elements of the narrative.[1]

THE POLITICAL CONTEXT OF INITIAL MARKET DESIGN

In terms of speed and scope, Russia's mass privatization exceeded that of other post-communist countries. Developed immediately following the ascendancy of Boris Yeltsin in December 1991 to president of the Russian Republic, the full program was implemented less than one year later in October 1992. Over seventeen thousand midsized and state-owned enterprises were privatized from October 1992 to July 1994, representing 70 percent of Russia's industrial sector. One hundred fifty million privatization vouchers were distributed to the population, and over forty million Russian citizens became shareholders in newly privatized companies. Through the creation of thousands of joint-stock companies, Russian mass privatization created the demand for a new securities market. Thousands of financial organizations flooded Russia's emerging securities market to take advantage of new opportunities to buy and sell privatization vouchers and corporate equities. No other mass privatization program in any post-communist country came close to matching the scale of the Russian privatization experiment (Kogut and Spicer 2002).

The decision to undertake such a radical experimentation in market design needs to first be understood within the political context of the time. Following the failed coup against Mikhail Gorbachev in August 1991, the Communist Party's monopolist control over the political and economic structures of the economy quickly became dismantled. The last remnants of the Soviet system remained the powerful bureaucracies that still had formal control over the vast majority of Russia's industries and enterprises (see Padgett chapter 9, this volume). The struggle to overcome the ministries and their allies shaped the political background to debates over market transition policy and, in turn, strongly influenced the early design of financial markets. In their insider account of Russia's mass privatization policy, Boycko, Shleifer, and Vishny (1995, 11–12) argued that the decision to implement rapid market reform reflected the Yeltsin government's desire to quickly and irreversibly sever ministerial control over economic activity.

The decision to pursue the rapid dismantling of the bureaucratic structure of the old regime is apparent in the political strategies pursued to implement mass privatization. Immediately following the collapse of the Soviet government in 1991, Yeltsin asked Russia's Congress of People's Deputies, a parliamentary body elected in 1990, for emergency powers to implement economic and political reform without legislative oversight for one year. The Russian parliament agreed to Yeltsin's request, and in June 1992 it furthermore voted to support the implementation of a mass privatization program in Russia. The Yeltsin government soon discovered that a critical challenge to implementing the June 1992 privatization accord was that the law required the approval of branch ministries for the privatization of many enterprises. Given obstructionist efforts by the ministries to oppose privatization efforts, a Yeltsin decree on May 8, 1993, authorized the State Committee on Property (GKI), which was accountable only to the executive branch of the government, to circumvent the ministries' authority in implementing privatization policies (Nelson and Kuzes 1995).

In response, the Supreme Soviet appealed the legality of this decree to the newly formed Constitutional Court. Yeltsin argued that the emergency powers that he received from the Supreme Soviet after he ascended to the Russian presidency gave him the authority to run privatization by presidential decree. However, the Supreme Soviet argued that Yeltsin's emergency powers had expired in December 1992 and that the legislature had not renewed them. In July

[1] Kogut and Spicer (2004, 2005) provide further information about the role of Western advice and ideology in Russia's post-communist reform. Spicer (2002) and Kogut and Spicer (2002) describe Russia's mass privatization program in more detail, particularly in comparative perspective. Spicer and Pyle (2002) discuss the failed efforts to create a market for household savings in Russia during this time period. See Johnson 2000 for an excellent overview of the rise of bank-led financial industrial groups in Russia during this time.

1993 the Supreme Soviet called for the transfer of authority to supervise the privatization of federal property from the GKI, part of the executive branch, to the Council of Ministers, part of the legislative branch. This decision was made in direct contradiction of Yeltsin's May 8 decree, which was intended to strengthen executive control over the ministries. In response, Anatoly Chubais, the head of the GKI, presented a new decree that again reiterated the power of his committee to control privatization (Nelson and Kuzes 1995, 23–34).

The battle over the supervision and pace of the privatization process quickly became an important issue in a broader political struggle between the executive and legislative branches. On September 11, 1993, Yeltsin used his executive powers to call for the reelection of the lower parliament. Parliamentary leaders' refusal to obey led Yeltsin to use military force to storm the parliament building. Army tanks fired upon the parliament in October, eventually allowing Yeltsin to dissolve the parliament in time for new elections in December of that year. Following this episode, the entire privatization process was now ruled only through presidential decree with little input from either the branch ministries or the legislative branch of government.

These political contests represent the national-level political backdrop to the decision to pursue rapid and mass privatization in Russia. Reformers feared that the radical reform plans could be stopped politically if not implemented rapidly. They therefore undertook a strategy of introducing reform as quickly as possible before oppositional forces could be effectively mobilized and Soviet structures reconstituted. Egor Gaidar, Russia's first deputy prime minister at the time, expressed this political rationale for implementing market-oriented reform in the following manner:

> At the beginning of their work, a government usually has more freedom for maneuvering. After that, it diminishes under the pressure of responsibility for unpopular decisions. . . . That is why, from January through March [1992], we tried to use in full measure the political time that we had . . . to get the gears of market mechanisms in place. (Nelson and Kuzes 1995, 42)

The tactics of reform centered not only on determining the optimal economic strategy but also on getting the "gears of market mechanisms in place" as quickly as possible before potential opposition could mobilize to oppose their plans.

THE REGULATORY DESIGN OF CAPITAL MARKETS

The regulatory design of Russia's post-communist capital markets resulted from the policy choices made to emphasize speed rather than governance in the implementation of new markets in Russia, particularly in the implementation of mass privatization. Mass privatization uses a simulated capital market model to distribute shares in privatized companies in an effort to achieve speed in the redistribution of ownership rights. The general model entails distributing privatization vouchers to the population at large for free or for a nominal charge as proxies for shares in state-owned companies (Lieberman and Viemetra 1996; Spicer, McDermott, and Kogut 2000). The vouchers transform into actual ownership stakes in companies through state-controlled auctions, whereby individuals—or their agents through investment funds—invest their vouchers in specific firms. The eventual ownership shares in companies depend on a market-clearing "price" based on the number of individuals who invest their vouchers in a particular company. At the end of the mass privatization process, firms are joint-stock companies whose new shareholders hold legal rights to engage in active corporate governance and to receive a portion of the firm's profits through dividends.

A critical issue in the implementation of mass privatization is the design of new financial markets and organizations. While mass and single-firm privatization both involve the transfer of property rights from public to private owners, mass privatization programs face the unique task of having to simultaneously create the market institutions to define, protect, and trade the newly created rights of ownership that are being transferred (Frydman and Rapaczynski 1994, 169). While socialist economies had developed extensive bank and enterprise ties, they had no markets, or institutional experiences, for issuing and trading stocks. The potential to build upon the existing ruins of socialism therefore did not exist for the design of the mass capital markets necessary for the implementation of rapid mass privatization (Kogut and Spicer 2002).

To address this challenge of rapid market design, two distinct mass privatization models had developed prior to the start of the Russian program. In the Czech model, the reliance on market mechanisms in mass privatization was extended to the formation of the capital markets themselves. The Czechs only loosely determined the organizational form that financial activity would take, allowing the market itself to drive the formation of new organizations as well as the rules by which new market competition would develop. The role of the state was limited to stipulating the procedure for establishing privatization investment funds, including the conditions for acquiring a license to operate as a fund manager.

In contrast, the Polish model of mass privatization relied on heavy state intervention in the development of privatization intermediaries. Polish funds were founded by the state but were privatized when shares were issued to the public in return for vouchers. Voucher holders could invest only in investment funds, not directly in enterprise assets. In addition, the composition of the Polish funds was highly regulated. Funds could choose among different companies, but they were required to buy core stakes in a minimum number of companies. They could change the composition of their initial portfolios' transactions on the secondary market, including swaps with other funds. However, their discretion to dispose of the core stakes was limited for several years. The Poles pursued the creation of private incentives through privatization but gave the state an important role in regulating emergent financial actors (Spicer, McDermott, and Kogut 2000).

In choosing a capital market design, the Yeltsin government followed the free-market Czech model rather than the regulated Polish model. Speed was chosen over governance:

> In fact, the Russian privatizers paid a great deal of attention to Poland, where the focus on corporate governance gave rise to a privatization scheme in which firms were to be controlled by large, government-sponsored mutual funds. This scheme was rejected for Russia precisely because of the expectation that any mutual fund created by the government would be politically influenced. It is worth noting that Polish privatization never got off the ground. Perhaps Russia avoided this failure by focusing on the right problems. (Boycko, Shleifer, and Vishny 1995, 13)

To Russian reformers, the "right" problem of privatization referred to the need to quickly depoliticize economic activity in Russia. They argued that they could not support a model of investment fund organization that included strong state oversight.

The political logic behind this choice rested with the desire to implement market reform as rapidly as possible. If the reformers had chosen the more regulated Polish system of investment fund regulation, they would not have succeeded in implementing mass privatization so rapidly. The decree that established the use of vouchers in Russia's mass privatization program was issued in April 1992. The GKI issued the original regulations for voucher investment funds in October 1992. The first voucher fund organizations received their licenses in December 1992. Russian reformers did not have the resources, personnel, or political capital to organize an administrative structure to effectively license and supervise voucher investment fund organizations in the short time frame that they gave themselves. Nor did potential entrepreneurs have the time to engage in extensive organizational activities to establish a voucher investment fund if they wished to found a fund before the start of privatization. Extensive regulatory control over funds and the emergent market system would have delayed the implementation of the entire program, an outcome that the reformers hoped to avoid.

While Russian reformers modeled their program on the Czech model, one critical modification to the Russian privatization model was its insider-ownership component. Managers and employees of state-owned enterprises were allowed to buy up to 51 percent of their company's equity in closed subscriptions before a public privatization auction. The champions of Russian privatization understood that strong insider ownership could hinder firm restructuring, as existing managers would be less likely than outsiders to engage in whole scale reorganizational efforts that included layoffs or managerial change (Boycko, Shleifer, and Vishny 1995). However, insider privatization bought off the support of the managerial elite in Russia, thereby giving market reformers crucial support to counter the opposition of the parliament and the state bureaucracy (McFaul 1995). Another critical modification in the Russian program was the deliberate exclusion of banks from the privatization process. The Czech Republic distributed the equivalent of privatization vouchers to their citizen through the mainly state-owned banking system. For a minimal payment, each citizen received a bank account endowed with a certain number of "points" that individuals used to invest in companies or funds. Secondary trading of initial privatization points was forbidden. In contrast, privatization vouchers in Russia were distributed as bearer certificates issued directly to individuals, which were allowed to be traded without centralized registration or control. By bypassing the banks and allowing the unrestricted sale of privatization vouchers, the Russian model relied more heavily on emergent stock markets in the privatization process than even the Czech model.

FROM STATE TO MARKET: THE EMERGENCE OF NEW ORGANIZATIONAL FORMS

The consequences of the decision to emphasize speed rather than governance in capital market design was that Russian mass privatization created the conditions for massive private market competition before politically determined and accepted rules of market behavior could be established. The implications of these design decisions for the emergence of new organizations in Russia's financial markets are explored below.

Formal Organizational Forms

The legal foundations of Russian capital market design were copied from U.S. securities regulation, placing clear and specific boundaries around the activities of different types of financial organizations allowed to operate on the market. By law, investment funds were divided into two categories: *voucher investments funds*, which were allowed to attract vouchers and cash from the population to create a close-ended mutual fund portfolio; and *cash investment funds*, which were allowed to attract only cash investments to create an open-ended mutual fund portfolio. In contrast, *investment companies* were not allowed to attract investment from the population. However, they were allowed to buy and sell vouchers and securities on their own accounts and on the account of clients. *Financial brokers* were allowed to buy and sell vouchers and securities on the stock exchange, and investment consultants were allowed to underwrite the issuance of new stocks and to provide financial advice to companies. Finally, *commercial banks* could receive a license to act as an investment company if the extent of their activity on the securities market did not exceed 40 percent of total bank assets.[2]

Figure 10.2 shows the number of voucher investment funds and financial brokers with official licenses that operated on the Russian financial markets from the start of mass privatization in October 1992 until October 1995. Over 600 voucher investment fund organizations entered the market during this time period. The minimum charter capital for voucher investment funds was set at 500,000 rubles, which even in October 1992 when the initial voucher law was passed amounted to approximately $1,200. By 1993 an initial charter of $500 was sufficient to start a new fund. Funds and managers had to be licensed by the state, but the licenses were apparently issued to virtually any candidate who applied (Frydman, Pistor, and Rapaczynski 1996, 192). By the end of privatization, the funds had accumulated 34.7 million vouchers, 23 percent of the total 150 million vouchers distributed to the population. Similarly, it is estimated that approximately 23 million Russians became shareholders in the new voucher investment funds, or approximately 15 percent of the entire population. The five largest funds had 500,000–3,000,000 shareholders each, collecting an estimated 27 percent of all vouchers accumulated by the voucher funds (Blasi, Kroumova, and Kruse 1997; Frydman, Pistor, and Rapaczynski 1996).

While voucher funds became the largest outside shareholders in Russia, the attraction of only 23 percent of the voucher total reflected the particular character of the Russia privatization program. First, company managers and employers were allowed to use their vouchers in buying up to 51 percent of their company, the most popular privatization option in the Russian program. In addition, the creation of a secondary cash market for vouchers led to millions of Russians selling their vouchers for cash. These secondary markets created the incentives for the over three thousand entities that entered the market as financial brokerage organizations. As in the case of voucher funds, requirements for registration as a financial brokerage organization were minimal and licenses were issued to virtually any candidate that applied. As figure 10.2 illustrates, thousands of new entrepreneurs entered the market in response to the creation of this new category of economic activity.

[2] Spicer (2002) describes the emergence of Russian financial organizations during this time period in detail; sections of this chapter are drawn from this previous work.

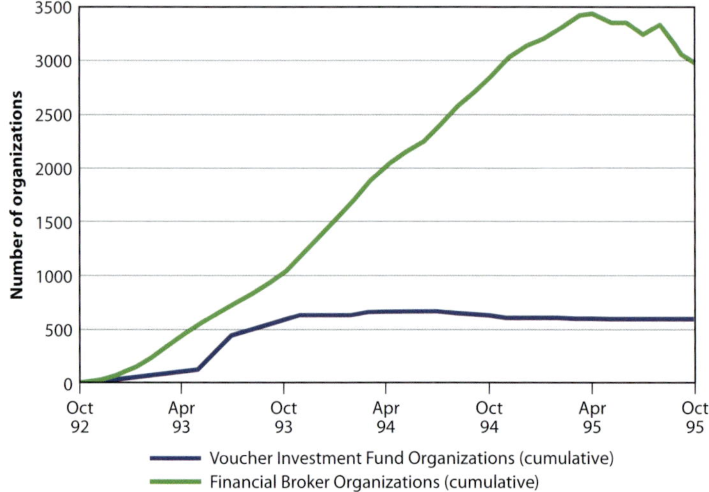

Figure 10.2 Number of licensed financial brokers and voucher investment funds, October 1992–October 1995. Source: Akamatsu 1995; Capital Market Surveillance Unit 1995; Ministry of Finance database on licensed financial broker organizations.

Informal Organizational Forms

The initial demographic data of organizational entry into the Russian financial markets demonstrates the success of mass privatization and market reform in forming new types of market actors in Russian financial markets. Yet the competitive dynamics in Russia's emerging markets did not take place only within the legal categories of proscribed action. Numerous types of competitive action took place in Russia's emerging markets in areas that were illegal, in the sense that competitive behavior contradicted formal laws, and nonlegal, in the sense that competition took place in a way that neither conformed to nor contradicted existing legislation.

I therefore supplement my analysis of legal organizational forms by looking at a third category of financial actors sometimes identified as "unlicensed financial companies" (Federal Commission for the Securities Market 1996a). An "unlicensed" company is (a) a financial company that undertook activities outside its legal scope or (b) a company that operated on the market without any type of government license. A financial company engaged in activity outside its legal scope if it undertook activities that were not included in the rules that defined the organizational form of which it was a member. For instance, a company that has a license as a "financial broker" might offer bank deposits even though it has no license to act as a bank. Another company might open up operations in the absence of any sort of license to engage in financial transactions.

The Russian government estimates that up to 2,000 "unlicensed" financial companies operated on the financial markets between 1993 and 1994, attracting over 50–70 trillion rubles ($5–7 billion) from 80 million Russian investors (Federal Commission for the Securities Market 1996a). Figure 10.3 shows the results of one survey that identified the number unlicensed financial companies in Moscow by month from 1993 to 1994 that promised the equivalent of "bank deposit" contracts with clients (Federal Commission for the Securities Market 1996a). According to Russian law, only organizations with banking licenses had the legal right to offer deposit accounts. Yet, as figure 10.3 illustrates, over one hundred non-bank organizations in Moscow nonetheless offered these types of contracts. The average life span of these fly-by-night companies in Moscow was seven months, and by August 1995 only seven unlicensed financial companies still existed.

While the above examples revolved around unlicensed companies that offered "bank deposits," a second set of unlicensed financial companies offered the equivalent of "stock certificates" without legal permission. These financial companies

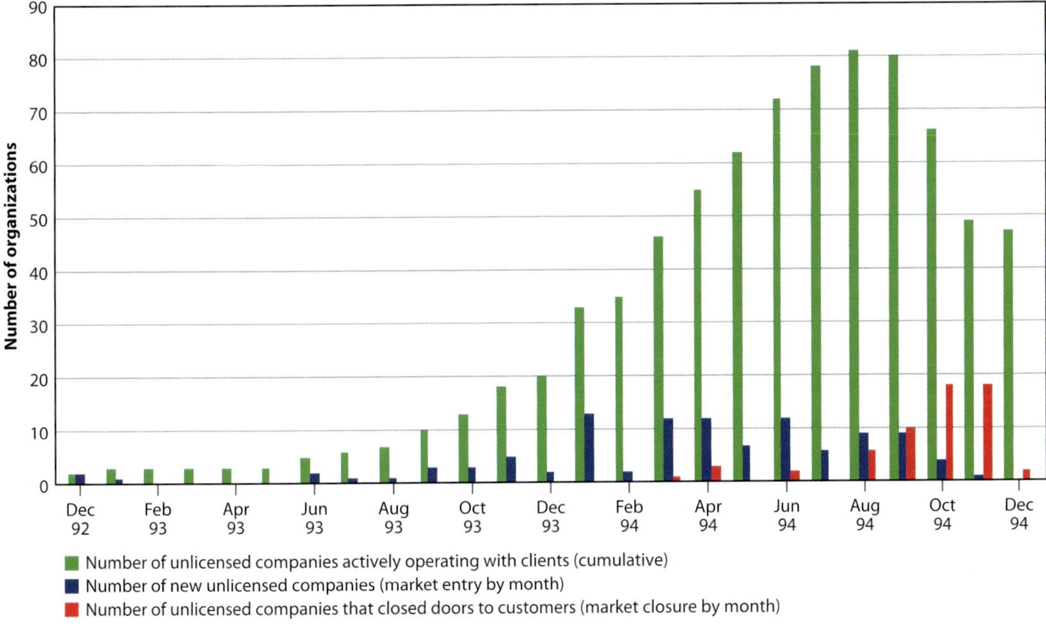

Figure 10.3 Unlicensed financial companies in Moscow, 1993–94.
Source: Federal Commission for the Securities Market 1996.

offered official-looking certificates that stated that a certificate owner was entitled to buy a legal share of the company. Yet since no mechanism was created to allow for the exchange of the certificate, these certificates offered no legal rights to future income streams or any way to monitor their management. These certificates were widely traded on the street, in the subway, and in the official stock markets, but no effort was made to keep an official registry of ownership of the companies that offered these documents. One financial journalist has estimated that 95 percent of the daily trading in securities at the Russian stock exchanges in 1994 took place in these certificates (Baranov 1995). This estimate is especially striking given that it was believed that 90 percent of all trading during this time took place outside the scores of stock exchanges that populated Russia (Morgenstern 1995).

An example of this phenomenon can be found in sales of the "stock" MMM, which dominated the financial markets in Russia during this time period. MMM was not a voucher investment fund but a Ponzi scheme that accepted cash investments from the population. MMM advertised its share prices several days in advance, ensuring that the price increased twice every week. In the six months of its existence, MMM's price increased 6,000 percent on Moscow's stock markets. It is estimated that 5–10 million Russians invested in MMM certificates. In July 1994, the price of MMM fell within two days from a high of $62 on Russian stock exchanges to a low of 50 cents.

The aftermath of the MMM scandal exemplifies the difficulty that the Russian government had controlling fraudulent funds. The MMM directors were not charged with any breach of the securities law because the company argued successfully that it had not broken any part of the Russian legal code. MMM had not registered as an investment company, and the legal rules that applied to such concerns thus did not apply to it. In short, MMM was not illegal but nonlegal: it existed outside the current legal code and could not, or at least would not, be prosecuted under existing regulations. The emergence of new markets and organizations in Russia took place far outside the reach of the law.[3]

[3] See Kogut and Spicer 2002; Spicer 2002; and Spicer and Pyle 2002 for a further discussion of MMM and the consequences of its collapse for financial market development in Russia.

Patronage Networks

The emphasis on speed rather than governance in Russia's reform program also led to the formation of new patron-client networks that quickly bridged public and private domains of capital market activity. In the Soviet Union, patronage relationships had developed within the Communist Party. In one analysis of 933 of the top political elite under Brezhnev, Willerton (1992) estimates that approximately 26 percent (244) had direct patronage ties to Brezhnev and 131 of the remaining elites belonged to the patronage networks of one of the other top leaders in Brezhnev's government. The patron gave economic or political (support, loyalty, protection) resources to a client, who promised reciprocity and loyalty in return.

In post-Soviet Russia, patronage networks expanded to include economic as well as political ties. Emergent bank-led financial industrial groups re-created the logic of Soviet-style patronage networks, although not the actual ties. The actors who became the central nodes in post-Soviet networks were often bankers who had little political or economic power in the Soviet regime. Young entrepreneurs sought out political patrons to build their new banks through access to public power and resources, while politicians sought economic clients that they believed did not have the existing political base to challenge their authority.

The origins of Russia's private banking system predated the onset of market transition policies. In 1988, as a part of Gorbachev's perestroika reform program, the USSR Gosbank (the state bank) was divided into two tiers, a central bank and five specialized banks charged with serving the financial needs of state-owned firms in specific sectors of the economy. Commercial banks spun off from these five state banks following the 1988 Law on Cooperatives, often servicing their former enterprise clients. Other enterprises simply formed their own banks to serve their financial needs, becoming identified as "pocket banks" since their only goal was to service their founding organization.

From 1989 to 1991, the development of the banking system became entangled in the political struggles for independence between the Soviet Union and the Russian Republic. In July 1990 the Supreme Soviet of the Russian Federation had created an independent Russian Central Bank (RCB) to compete with the Soviet Gosbank. The newly appointed head of the RCB, Georgii Matiukhin, took over the Russian Republic branch of the Soviet Gosbank after physically storming the building and demanding that its staff change their allegiance to the Russian Republic. The 1990 resolution similarly declared all branches of the Soviet state banks on Russian territory to be Russian property and provided simple guidelines for their transformation into private, commercial banks. The Russian government hoped to entice the managers of these banks with the prospect of private ownership if they switched their loyalty from Soviet to Russian control. Given the political purposes of the "bank wars," the new RCB accepted the commercialization of any branch of a former Soviet specialized bank with little regulation or supervision. By the end of 1991, the new RCB had registered 775 commercial banks that had spun off from the former specialized banks of the same time and over 1,300 banks overall (Johnson 2000).

The origins of bank-led financial groups in the post-Soviet era arose from the formation of new patronage networks developed in a financial marketplace with little established governance or control. For instance, "authorized" banks appeared in late 1992 and 1993, when commercial bankers persuaded the central government to allow banks other than the state banks—Sberbank, Promstroibank, and Agroprombank—to manage its funds. In return for handling the basic financial services of government organizations, these banks were able to invest government funds on their own account. For instance, the commercial bank Menatep served as an "authorized" bank for the Russian Finance Ministry; loans from the state made up more than half of its lending activity in 1995. As one Menatep employee at the time remarked:

> There was just no point in the painstaking work of investment banking when you could go to have a banya session with your buddy at the Finance Ministry and they would put in $600 million. . . . What Menatep would do was take that $600 million, not pay the ministry anything, and they would delay the start of payment to the regions. When the people came to get the money, they would just delay it for three weeks. Then they would issue not cash but promissory notes—Menatep promissory notes—instead of cash. (Hoffman 2003, 232)

Menatep earned millions by simply delaying payments back to the ministry, using the interval to place the ministry's capital in high-yielding investments for the bank's own profit. By 1995 the largest commercial banks held the accounts of the federal tax authorities, customs authorities, and Finance Ministry, among others. The state Audit Chamber estimated that authorized banks earned about $1.32 billion through access to government funds in 1995–96 (Johnson 2000).

Russian banks similarly used their connections to politicians to earn money in the government bond (GKO) market. The government, looking for cash to finance its growing deficit, introduced GKOs in March 1993 and soon made them extremely attractive to the commercial banks. GKOs yielded consistently high annual returns (an average of 136.8 percent in 1994) and the state made GKO profits tax free (Johnson 2000). The Ministry of Finance chose twenty-six favored banks as primary GKO distributors and kept foreigners out of the first treasury bill auctions.

Banks, as the only Russian commercial entities with access to large amounts of investable cash (especially with access to government cash as "authorized" banks), were the natural customers for this new market. Banks were often accused of delaying payment transfers to play the GKO market or of putting money they held as "authorized" banks toward GKO purchases (in effect, lending the government its own money). Vneshekombank director Anatolii Nosko, for example, was dismissed in February 1996 for "speculating in Russian treasury bills with funds earmarked for repaying foreign debts" (Johnson 2000, 125). According to the State Tax Service, banks invested an average of 60 percent of their credit resources in GKOs. By mid-1995, total trading on the secondary market had reached the equivalent of $136 million per day. In the first six months of 1995, the government issued enough treasury bills to cover 46 percent of the budget deficit, and the total outstanding GKO debt reached 35.7 trillion rubles ($7.9 billion) (Johnson 2000). Authorized banks and the GKO market provided the groundwork for the rise of bankers as powerful political and economic actors in Russia.

FROM MARKET TO STATE: LOANS-FOR-SHARES AND YELTSIN'S REELECTION

While the nature of Russia's rapid market transition policies shaped the organizational structure of its nascent financial markets, the conditions of early market development in turn influenced subsequent efforts to restructure the Russian state. Politicians continued to build on the logic of patronage networks to co-opt economic actors to support their political aspirations. In return, economic actors demanded even stronger control over state agencies and assets. By the end of Yeltsin's presidency, members of a so-called banking "oligarchy" had captured de facto control over the regulatory agencies of Russia's financial markets and had gained ownership of many of Russia's richest natural-resource companies.

The 1995 loans-for-shares deal between Yeltsin and the largest commercial bankers illustrates the increasingly fluid boundaries between states and markets that led to the rise of the banking oligarchy. The economic rationale for the loans-for-shares scheme arose from a growing government budget deficit in late 1995. Since Yeltsin faced general elections in 1996, including his own reelection, he was anxious to shore up the grave shortfalls in his budget in order to stabilize the economy and to provide basic government services and payments. In August 1995, Yeltsin accepted a version of a loans-for-shares program ostensibly designed to fill a growing hole in the government budget. Banks would loan the government money to make up for its budgetary problems, and in return the banks would hold the government shares in a number of blue-chip companies as collateral. Since the privatization of many natural-resource companies had taken place outside the voucher privatization process, the government still had strong equity ownership in many of these strategic enterprises (Lieberman and Veimetra 1996).

In theory, the auctions were to be open to all interested bidders, even foreigners, and the bank that offered the largest loan to the government would win each block of shares. The banks were required to hold the shares until September 1, 1996. If the government did not repay the loan at that time, the banks would be allowed to keep the shares of the companies that they held as collateral.

The loans-for-shares auctions took place in November and December 1995 and were riddled with allegations of fraud. The eventual sale succeeded in raising over a billion dollars of revenue (loans plus payment of fiscal arrears), surpassing the government target. However, the sale was hardly an open competition. The winners were the large banks and the enterprises themselves (for example, Lukoil successfully bid for its own shares, essentially loaning money to

Table 10.1.
Banks and the Loans-for-Shares Deal

Auction Date	Company	Minimum Bid (in millions)	Winning Bid (in millions)
11/95	Norilsk Nickel	$170 (38% stake)	Oneksimbank/MFK $170.1
12/95	Sidanko Oil	$125 (51% stake)	Oneksimbank/MFK $130
12/95	Yukos Oil	$150 (45% stake)	Menatep/Tokobank/ Stolichnii Bank (SBS) $159
12/95	Sibneft Oil	$100 (51% stake)	Menatep/Stolichnii Bank (SBS) $100.1
12/95	Novolipetsk Mettallurgical Combine	$30 (15% stake)	Oneksimbank/MFK $31

Source: Adapted from Johnson 2000, 187.

the government; Surgutneftgas purchased shares through its own pension fund). As table 10.1 illustrates, the bids reflected considerable collusion as the winning bid in almost all auctions was only nominally above the minimum, reserve price identified in a particular auction (and far below the market prices of these valuable assets). Ex post, some of the colluders expressed considerable dismay, leading to outright economic warfare that was widely reported (Lieberman and Veimetra 1996).

If the largest Russian banks had gained initial wealth through the political patronage in "authorized" bank dealings and preferential access to the GKO market, the loans-for-shares deal cemented the economic power of these "oligarch" banks. The loans-for-shares expanded the critical industrial holdings of the leading bankers to such an extent that they were able to amass vast financial industrial groups as the value of their newly acquired natural-resource companies appreciated over time.[4] The bank-led groups complemented their industrial resources with active investment in media holdings.

An examination of the dates of the loans-for-shares program shows how the political design of the program ensured the support of the emergent oligarchs. Discussions about loans-for-shares were initiated in August 1995 and the auctions completed by December 1995. However, the government maintained the right to pay back the "loan" by September 1996. The presidential election took place in June and July 1996. If the Communists won the election, then the new Communist government would be able to pay back the "loans" to regain control over these companies. However, if the Yeltsin team won, then the bankers would be able to keep their new properties. The winners of the loans-for-shares became tied by their own debts to Yeltsin's reelection.

The quid pro quo inherent in a patronage relationship became inherent in the powerful role that the bankers played in the Yeltsin 1996 election campaign. Russia's campaign finance laws officially limited each candidate's campaign spending to $3 million; Yeltsin's campaign team admitted that the banks channeled at least $100 million to his campaign (Johnson 2000). Similarly, the largest banks controlled the major media outlets in Russia and used their influence to support Yeltsin. A study done by the European Institute for the Media found that Yeltsin enjoyed 53 percent of campaign broadcast time in the electronic media during the first round of the 1996 elections, compared to 18 percent for his Communist opponent, Gennadi Zyuganov.

[4] Johnson (2000, 173) identifies the seven banking oligarchs as Vladimir Potanin, the head of Oneksimbank and the MFK bank; Vladimir Gusinskii, the head of Most bank; Mikhail Khodorkovskii, head of Menatep bank; Petr Aven and Mikhail Fridman, heads of Alfa Bank; Aleksandr Smolenskii, head of the SBS-Agro Bank; and Boris Berezovsky, head of the LogoVaz group. She also describes in detail the vast financial-industrial groups that these bankers amassed by the end of Yelstin's presidency.

Positive media references to Yeltsin outweighed negative ones by 247, while Zyuganov's negative references outweighed positive ones by 240 (Rutland 1996, cited in Johnson 2000).

The direct ties between government and business became even clearer when the banking oligarchs were appointed to government posts. Vladimir Potanin, the CEO of Oneksimbank, became a deputy prime minister for the economy. In his new official post, Potanin secured the richest government account for Oneksimbank: the state customs account, into which exporters had to place their customs duties and which generally ran a balance of more than $1 billion (Freeland 2000). Similarly, Boris Berezovsky was named deputy head of the Kremlin's Security Council. During his time in office, Berezovsky secured both access to Aeroflot's accounts as well as an increasing ownership position in the former national airline.

THE GROWING POWER OF THE CENTRAL BANK

The growing capture of the state by increasingly powerful bankers also extended to regulatory control over Russia's capital markets. In response to early financial market scandals, an emergent new regulator, the Federal Commission for the Securities Market, pursued a strategy of implementing strong political control over market actors. The commission hoped to curb the presence of fly-by-night and nontransparent financial scheming that dominated the first period of market development. In response, the Central Bank took up the mantle of "free-market" ideology to oppose the efforts of the commission. The growing power of the banks in Yeltsin's government ensured that efforts to reintroduce regulatory control over economic actors did not extend to banks themselves. Weakly regulated capital markets allowed bank leaders to further consolidate their ownership control in their growing financial-industrial groups.

The Emergence of the Federal Commission as Market Regulator

An independent Securities and Exchange Commission, the Federal Commission for the Securities Markets (FCSM) developed in 1993 as an oversight committee with no formal supervisory powers with representatives from the Ministry of Finance, the State Property Committee, the Russian Central Bank, and the State Anti-Monopoly Committee. In 1994 Yeltsin strengthened the Federal Commission by giving it many formal powers previously held by either the Ministry of Finance or the Central Bank. The commission received authority to issue statutes that had the force of law on members of the securities market (Frye 2000, 172). Anatoly Chubais, the former head of Russia's privatization program, originally headed the FCSM, while Dmitri Vasiliev, Chubais's primary assistant during the privatization program, served as vice chairman and executive director. The leaders of the Russian privatization program now led the new commission responsible for supervising the financial markets that voucher privatization had so quickly developed.

The newly empowered FCSM immediately identified the lack of constitutive rules defining permissible forms of organizational behavior as a primary cause of the entry of so many unlicensed competitors in Russia's capital markets. In turn, they proceeded to redesign the legal rules of market competition in Russia's capital market, requiring all existing organizations to relicense themselves according to a new set of stringent requirements. The Federal Commission's new regulations transformed the competitive environment of both investment funds and financial brokerage organizations.

By the middle of 1996, a new legal category of economic activity, the "unit investment fund," was formed, replacing the voucher investment fund as the primary form of collective investment in the Russian securities market. While voucher investment funds were organized as joint-stock companies with independent legal status, unit investment funds did not have shareholders but were governed by a contractual trust agreement with their investors. Unit investment funds were not subject to corporate tax and therefore did not face the same problems of double taxation that plagued voucher investment funds. Moreover, unlike close-ended voucher investment funds, unit funds were allowed to operate as open-ended funds that granted investors the right to redeem their shares.

While many voucher investment funds wished to transform themselves into unit investment funds, the Federal Commission developed no pathways for conversion (Pistor and Spicer 1997). Since voucher investment funds were not able to transform their legal status, the creation of the unit investment funds meant the de facto end of "voucher investment funds" as a meaningful category of economic organization. The hundreds of voucher funds created in mass privatization simply stopped operating as viable economic actors following the Federal Commission's legal reforms (Spicer 2002).

The complete redesign of the organizational form "financial broker" took place in a similar manner. The original category of "financial broker" developed in 1992 conferred the legal right to conduct transactions with securities on behalf of clients, without any distinction between the types of clients served. In contrast, the 1996 Law on the Securities Market distinguished between broker licenses with rights to conduct business with natural persons and with corporate entities. The capital requirement for a broker organization that wished to obtain a license of "professional securities market participant for brokerage activity excluding operations with natural persons" was 50,000 ECU ($40,000). However, the capital requirement to obtain a license for brokerage activities with natural persons was 450,000 ECU ($360,000). This requirement was more than fifteen times the capital requirements to receive a brokerage license during the initial regulatory regime from 1993 to 1994. Moreover, the new regulations required brokerage organizations to create a role for a "controller," a lawyer who worked for the firm and supervised all financial transactions. As in the case of voucher investment funds, these new legal requirements made it impossible for most of the entrepreneurs who had entered the market during the early 1990s to remain in the marketplace.

The FCSM contended that the reorganization of the securities markets was a necessary response to the initial period of scandals and unlicensed financial competition. The commission estimated that $20–30 billion worth of savings sat outside the financial investment system because the Russian people lacked fundamental confidence in private financial organizations.[5] The commission claimed the formation of highly structured investment funds would inspire confidence in the market as a whole:

> The main goal of the unit investment fund program is to attract new money, including the unused savings of the Russian population, into the Russian capital markets. Studies by the Commission indicate that as much as 10% of domestic savings—or some $2–3 billion—could be drawn into equity investment through well-regulated, reliable investment funds. (Federal Commission for the Securities Market 1996b, cited in Spicer 2002)

In this case, the Federal Commission emphasized the positive role of political institutions in developing new financial vehicles. The commission argued that only "well-regulated, reliable investment funds" would attract the unused savings of the Russian population back into the financial markets.

To increase their control over a new regulated marketplace, the Federal Commission issued a general license in December 1996 to the Central Bank to issue licenses only for operations with government securities. The Central Bank refused to accept this general license because it did not include the power to license banks' operations with corporate equities (Frye 2000). The Federal Commission's power to regulate Russia's capital market activity soon became part of a broader struggle with the Central Bank over the boundaries of jurisdictional authority.

The Central Banks' Response

The Russian Central Bank had been formed in July 1992 after the former head of the Soviet Main Bank (Gosplan), Victor Gerashchenko, became head of the Russian Central Bank. He inherited the administrative staff of the Soviet banking system as well as an organizational structure that operated relatively free of political oversight. To the dismay of the new young economists appointed to run Yeltsin's economic policy, Gerashchenko pursued a loose monetary policy, continuing to issue credits to Soviet enterprises. Yelstin's government tried to gain executive control over the Central Bank but failed after negotiations with the Russian parliament. The compromise position was to keep the Central Bank independent of either executive or parliamentary control. The Russian president gained the authority to nominate the head of the Central Bank but required the confirmation of parliament. However, neither party was allowed to nominate the board of the Central Bank, which was to be drawn from the bank itself. The

[5] For a broader discussion of the role of widespread fraud in financial markets and its subsequent negative impact on the development of a market for household savings, see Spicer and Pyle 2002.

day-to-day decisions of the bank were left to the self-elected board, which had little executive or legislative authority to review or rescind the bank's decisions.

The Central Bank emerged as a powerful and independent power center with strong organizational capabilities and regulatory power that the initial designers of mass privatization hoped to avoid in the implementation of mass privatization policy. The reformers had specifically modeled the original design of capital markets on an Anglo-Saxon model that limited bank participation in securities market activities (Frye 2000). However, politicians revisited the role of banks in market development following the loans-for-shares program. In May 1997 the Central Bank and the Federal Commission signed a resolution in which they agreed to allow banks to participate in the securities markets and, against the wishes of the Federal Commission, to give the Central Bank the power to license banks to engage in these activities. The granting of authority to the Central Bank to license its own members was a major defeat for the Federal Commission in its battle to control Russia's capital markets (Frye 2000).

Anatoly Chubais, the prime minister at the time, signed and orchestrated the 1997 protocol that allowed banks to be exempted from the Federal Commission's supervision of the securities market. The decision was surprising given Chubais's background. Dmitri Vasiliev, the head of the Federal Commission in 1997, was an old political ally of Chubais, having served as his primary assistant in the early 1990s when Chubais had led Russia's privatization program. Chubais had also been the original chairman of the Federal Commission and had appointed Vasiliev to his new role. The decision to limit the power of the Federal Commission was not the result of a technocratic evaluation of the best way to further the economic development of Russia's capital markets. Instead, it reflected the new alliances Chubais had made with a new class of bankers to support Yeltsin's 1996 reelection. The political ties that linked state and market following the loans-for-shares deal extended to the regulatory battle over control of the financial markets, where banks had a vested interest in ensuring a continuation of weak governmental oversight of their activities.

FROM DESIGN TO EMERGENCE: A NEW ORGANIZATIONAL LANDSCAPE

The fluid institutional boundaries between states and markets in Yeltsin's Russia explain the wide divergence between the type of organizational forms that were designed in the early 1990s and what eventually emerged by the end of the decade. As table 10.2 illustrates, the difference did not take place through the selection or survival of individual firms. Instead, the primary difference rests in the very categories of economic actors that were permitted to operate in the market.

The end of voucher investment funds as a viable organizational form provides one illustration of the difference between design and emergence. While the Federal Commission put forth an economic logic for their redesign of investment vehicles, voucher fund managers saw their demise as a result of political rather than economic reasoning. A group of over two hundred voucher investment funds offered the following political explanation of the eradication of their organizational form:

> Today is the moment of choice: either the voucher investment funds become the institutional foundations of economic rebirth in Russia, or they become the victims of the struggle in the aftermath of privatization. Under the banner of the defense of the shareholder and investor rights, it is apparent that a clear intention of the politics surrounding

Table 10.2.
From Design to Emergence

Organizational Actors	Initial Design (early 1990s)	Emerged (late 1990s)
Investment Funds	Voucher funds	Unit funds Bank-led funds
Financial Brokers	Financial brokers	Financial brokers (redesigned) Bank-led brokerage services
Banks	Little role in initial capital market design	Universal banks Bank-led financial industrial groups

> the regulation of the securities market is the liquidation of the voucher investment funds.[6]

Many fund managers believed that they could be economically viable if they were given a chance to compete. They viewed the slow pace of licensing and the extensive requirements of unit investment funds as a political decision to support the members of one organizational form over another.

In this time period, the Central Bank picked up the mantle of free market ideology in their introduction of competing organizational forms. In a 1996 parliamentary debate over a proposed law on investment funds, a bank representative presented the following argument against the Federal Commission's strong control over investment fund activity:

> A law should guarantee above all pluralism. . . . The market, and investors, should choose the [organizational] form that survives. Therefore if there exists the possibility for open investment funds run by joint-stock companies, why should we not write that into the law?[7]

The argument for market pluralism in the formation of new organizations echoed similar arguments about the importance of "depoliticization" in the initial formation of voucher investment funds. Instead of political control over the type of organizational form allowed to survive, the bank representative argued that multiple forms of economic activity should be allowed to compete freely against each other.

To create the desired competition for the unit investment funds, the Central Bank instituted a new form of investment fund, called General Funds of Banking Management, which had little resemblance to the strictly regulated unit funds. Banks were allowed to form investment funds with little direct regulatory supervision by the Central Bank (or the Federal Commission). Banks did not need to hire licensed fund managers to make investment decisions, maintain depositories to safeguard investments, or have specialized registries containing shareholder lists. The bank funds also had far more freedom in deciding where to invest client assets than did the strictly regulated unit funds. As one observer wrote, "Indeed, the requirements for establishing bank funds are so lax that it would appear that, while designing them, the Central Bank's ulterior motive was to eradicate [unit investment funds]" (Peach 1997, 2). The contours of the new economic landscape followed closely the political struggles of regulatory agencies.

More important for many of the banks that participated in the loans-for-shares program, a loosely regulated capital market provided an important means for financial oligarchs to further consolidate ownership control. Many banking oligarchs increased their equity stakes in their newly acquired natural resource companies through schemes such as share dilutions, phony shareholder meetings, and outright fraud to gain the shares of minority shareholders (Johnson 2000). For instance, Vasiliev, after retiring from the Federal Commission, accused the new owners of Sibneft of transferring valuable assets to a holding company and discriminating against small shareholders of subsidiaries in the conversion to a single stock; Sidanko of issuing and placing convertible bonds at a below-market price for placement with affiliated parties; and Yukos of transferring funds from subsidiaries and trying to dilute the shares held by minority shareholders (Vasiliev, Drobyshev, and Konov 2003). While the initial ownership stakes of these companies were gained through the loans-for-shares companies, the subsequent consolidation of control took place in a relatively unregulated securities market.

Given the transitory nature of the banking industry for many of the oligarchs, it is not surprising that following the August 1998 financial crash, these bankers were willing to leave behind the empty shells of their collapsed banks as they moved on to new endeavors. After the government devalued its currency and defaulted on its bond obligations in August 1998, many of the leading Russian banks collapsed. A number of "failed" oligarch banks exploited the weak regulatory environment of the time by quickly transferring their remaining good assets into new legal entities (so-called bridge or shadow banks) with essentially the same set of owners. New "bridge" banks held none of the liabilities of their "daughter" banks, leaving obligations to depositors in the hands of banks that just had many of their best-performing assets stripped from their control (Spicer and Pyle 2002). Bankers were quickly able to manipulate ownership structures so that they were able to leave behind

[6] Resolution of conference of voucher investment funds, Moscow, April 19–20, 1996. Translated from Russian, cited in Spicer 2002, 109.

[7] Russian parliamentary debate on new laws regarding investment mutual funds, June 20, 1996, recorded transcript, p. 15 (translated from Russian), cited in Spicer 2002, 113.

their bank holdings with few consequences, focusing instead on their new roles as leaders of large financial-industrial groups with some of the largest holdings in Russia. Loosely regulated capital markets, a result of the politics of the time, played an important role in both the emergence and survival of financial-industrial groups in Yeltsin's Russia.

DISCUSSION

The boundaries between states and markets that define distinctive locations of economic activity were as yet unformed in Russia during the 1990s, allowing organizations to pursue wealth and power through often unlimited means. In this context, the distinction between action—the everyday behavior taken in market settings—and actors—the entities imbued with the legal or social authority to engage in specific forms of conduct—became critically important to the processes of market emergence. Early hopes that "free" markets themselves could lead to the construction of viable forms of organizational action were quickly discarded as market actors realized that new forms of market order were needed. The subsequent struggle over the reconstitution of the boundaries of permissible organizational behavior quickly moved outside the realm of economics and into the domain of national and regulatory politics. The organizational forms that emerged from these political struggles deviated strongly from their original design.

Aleksander Kolesnikov, the deputy chairman of the FCSM in the mid-1990s, explained the redesign of the Russian marketplace in the following manner when discussing the fate of voucher investment funds:

> Voucher investment funds were to be the middlemen in mass privatization to avoid revolution. In a sense it was successful because it was a bloodless revolution. There are critics of privatization, but there was no revolution. . . . But privatization is now over. The voucher funds no longer play an important role. New functions need to be developed in this stage of development. (Spicer 2002, 104)

Kolesnikov's statement that "voucher investment funds were to be the middlemen in mass privatization to avoid revolution" refers to the political explanation of the choices made in the design of capital markets. Initial organizational forms contributed to a relatively "bloodless revolution" by facilitating the rapid privatization of property before the opposition to such a program could unite. However, Kolesnikov doubted that these organizations could ever grow past their original political purpose. His argument that "voucher investment funds no longer play an important role" and that "new functions need to be developed in this stage of development" reflected the changing economic and political conditions of Russia's financial markets following the implementation of the mass privatization program. A new political situation required new economic actors.

While Kolesnikov used political reasoning to explain the actions of the Federal Commission in redesigning the Russian securities markets, a similar political logic also explains the emergence of bank-led financial industrial-groups during this period. Politicians reached out to new actors in the private sector in an attempt to create new allies, and, in a classic patron-client relationship, these new businessmen supported the political careers of their patrons to ensure continuing access to government largesse. In a co-evolutionary dynamic that shaped the emergence of both states and markets in Russia, the transactional flows between private and public entities worked in both directions: public officials provided the opportunities for private actors to gain wealth, and, in turn, these new private clients provided the resources to support the causes and elections of their political patrons. While the regulatory structure of market activity transformed rapidly during the 1990s in Russia, the underlying political logic of wealth creation remained the same. Economic and political actors relied upon informal agreements rather than a formal rule of law to define the acceptable means of economic organization and market competition. Padgett's (2002) discussion of Renaissance Florence's banking system describes a similar fluidity between states and markets in the emergence of new financial markets and organizations. He posits that a Medician

> financial oligopoly [emerged] in the domain of state finances, with extremely personal and highly politicized linkages between high-level financiers and the emergent Medici court. . . . [I]n the paradigmatic case of Renaissance Florence, it appears to be the centralizing court, not liberal laissez-faire, that spawned the emergence of highly-specialized classes of financiers (both wealthy and impoverished),

differentiated from production and trading, and relating to business through immediate, short-term gains. (2002, 21–23)

Chosen financiers became clients of the new Medici court, gaining access to favored treatment and access to state resources. These "financial oligarchs" withdrew out of the market into the state, leading to the stratification of the market through the development of a few highly successful banking firms.

In Russia markets similarly did not develop according to a laissez-faire logic in which the economic pressures led to the survival of the most efficient producers because financiers were chosen mainly through their connections to the state. The emergent oligarch bankers were young, often in their thirties or early forties, with little previous banking experience or ties to the Soviet regime (Hoffman 2003). In classic patron-client logic, politicians chose young clients who owed their success and loyalty to them. As the bankers grew older and their financial-industrial groups grew more powerful, they shed their original patrons and demanded more direct control over the regulatory system. The Federal Commission's inability to regulate the activities of the banks in the securities markets resulted from the higher-level political alliances developed at the time. While market reform was successful in dismantling the structures of the old regime, it was not successful in designing what emerged in its place. An irony of Russian economic reform was that policies implemented in the early 1990s ostensibly intended to develop free and open markets eventually led to the emergence of a small number of banking "oligarchs" that by the end of the 1990s controlled a disproportionate amount of the inherited wealth of the Soviet system.

Since this chapter is to be understood in comparison to other time periods and countries, it is useful to note that I have examined less than ten years of history in the emergence of Russian financial markets and organizations. Russia's post-communist markets were characterized by the devastation of previous ideologies as well as radical changes in the structural properties of political and economic authority. The history of post-communist Russia described here is short, and it is unclear exactly what type of market system will eventually emerge over the long run. The constitutive understandings of what was a market, how it should be regulated, and who should be allowed to compete were still in formation at the end of Yeltsin's presidency.

REFERENCES

Akamatsu, N. 1995. "Enterprise Governance and Investment Funds in Russian Privatization." In *Corporate Governance in Transitional Economies: Insider Control and the Banks*, ed. M. Aoki. Washington, DC: The World Bank.

Aslund, A. 1995. *How Russia Became a Market Economy*. Washington, DC: Brookings Institute.

Baranov, A. 1995. Otsutstvie zakonodatelnoi basoi sposobstvovalo spekulyatsiyam s tsennimi bumagami na predyavitelya, in Izvestiya, January 19.

Blasi, J., M. Kroumova, and D. Kruse. 1997. *Kremlin Capitalism: Privatising the Russian Economy*. Ithaca: Cornell University Press.

Boycko, M., A. Shleifer, and R. Vishny. 1995. *Privatizing Russia*. Cambridge, MA: MIT Press.

Capital Market Surveillance Unit. 1995. *An Account of Specialized Investment Funds*. Moscow, Russia. September.

Federal Commission for the Securities Market. 1996. "Training Manual for Perspective Unit Fund Managers." Unpublished manuscript translated from Russian.

Freeland, C. 2000. *Sale of the Century: Russia's Wild Ride from Communism to Capitalism*. New York: Crown Business.

Frydman, R., and A. Rapaczynski. 1994. *Privatization in Eastern Europe: Is the State Withering Away?* Budapest: CEU Press.

Frydman, R., K. Pistor, and A. Rapaczynski. 1996. "Investing in Insider-Dominated Firms: A Study of Russian Voucher Privatization Funds." In *Corporate Governance in Central Europe and Russia*, ed. R. Frydman, C. W. Gray, and A. Rapaczynski. Budapest: CEU Press.

Frye, T. 2000. *Brokers and Bureaucrats: Building Market Institutions in Russia*. Ann Arbor: University of Michigan Press.

Hoffman, D. E. 2003. *The Oligarchs: Wealth and Power in the New Russia*. New York: Public Affairs.

Johnson, J. 2000. *A Fistful of Rubles: The Rise and Fall of the Russian Banking System*. Ithaca: Cornell University Press.

Kogut, B., and A. Spicer. 2002. "Capital Market Development and Mass Privatization Are Logical Contradictions: Lessons from the Czech Republic and Russia." *Industrial and Corporate Change* 11:1–37.

———. 2004. "Critical and Alternative Perspectives on International Assistance to Post-Communist Countries: A Review and Analysis." The World Bank, Operations Evaluation Department Background Paper, available at: http://www.worldbank.org/ieg/transition economies/docs/literature_review.pdf.

———. 2005. "Taking Account of Accountability: Academics, Transition Economics and Russia." Working Paper, Paris, INSEAD.

Lieberman, I., and R. Veimetra. 1996. "The Rush for State Shares in the 'Klondyke' of Wild East Capitalism: Loans-for-Shares Transactions in Russia."

George Washington Journal of International Law 29:737–68.

Lindberg, L., and J. Campbell. 1991. "The State and the Organization of Economic Activity." In *Governance of the American Economy*, ed. J. Campbell, J. R. Hollingsworth, and L. Lindberg. Cambridge: Cambridge University Press.

McDermott, G. A. 2002. *Embedded Politics: Industrial Networks and Institutional Change in Postcommunism*. Ann Arbor: University of Michigan Press.

McFaul, M. 1995. "State Power, Institutional Change, and the Politics of Privatization in Russia." *World Politics* 47:210–43.

Morgenstern, C. 1995. "Capital Markets Development and Financing Russia's Transformation." In *Russia: Creating Private Enterprises and Efficient Markets*, ed. I. W. Lieberman and J. Nellis. Washington, DC: World Bank.

Nelson, L. D., and I. Y. Kuzes. 1995. *Radical Reform in Yeltsin's Russia: Political, Economic, and Social Dimensions*. Armonk, NY: M. E. Sharpe.

Padgett, J. 2002. "Organizational Genesis, Identity, and Control: The Transformation of Banking in Renaissance Florence." In *Networks and Markets*, ed. J. Rauch and A. Casella. New York: Russell Sage.

Peach, G. 1997. "Big Competition for PIFs." *Moscow Times*, September 16.

Pistor, K., and A. Spicer. 1997. "Investment Funds in Mass Privatization and Beyond." In *Between State and Market*, ed. I. W. Lieberman, S. S. Nestor, and R. M. Desai. Washington, DC: World Bank.

Rutland, P. 1996. "Independent Monitoring Group: Election Coverage Was Unfair." *OMRI Presidential Election Report* 15 (July 9).

Spicer, A. 2002. "Revolutionary Change and Organizational Form: The Politics of Investment Fund Organization in Russia, 1992–1997." *Research in the Sociology of Organizations* 19:91–124.

Spicer, A., and W. Pyle. 2002. "Institutions and the Vicious Circle of Distrust in the Russian Household Deposit Market, 1992–1999." *Advances in Strategic Management* 19:371–96.

Spicer, A., G. McDermott, and B. Kogut. 2000. "Entrepreneurship and Privatization in Central Europe: The Tenuous Balance between Creation and Destruction." *Academy of Management Review* 25:630–49.

Stark, D. 1996. "Recombinant Property in East European Capitalism." *American Journal of Sociology* 101:993–1027.

Stark, D., and L. Bruszt. 1998. *Postsocialist Pathways: Transforming Politics and Property in East Central Europe*. Cambridge: Cambridge University Press.

Vasiliev, D., P. Drobyshev, and A. Konov. 2003. "Administrative Ethics as a Means against Corruption." Working paper. The Moscow Carnegie Center.

Willerton, J. P. 1992. *Patronage and Politics in the USSR*. Cambridge: Cambridge University Press.

11

The Emergence of the Russian Mobile Telecom Market

Local Technical Leadership and Global Investors in a Shadow of the State

Valery Yakubovich ▪ Stanislav Shekshnia

The first mistake in public business is the going into it.

—Benjamin Franklin

Although Benjamin Franklin's statement in the epigraph warns of the perils of political office, it perfectly summarizes the experience of some of the Russian entrepreneurs of the early 1990s who dared to launch new businesses in the industries perceived to be the natural domain of Soviet monopolies. Cellular telephony is an illustrative case in this regard.

In the 1990s the cellular industry emerged from scratch and grew at an annual rate of 100 percent to serve about thirty-one million customers or roughly one-fifth of the Russian population by the early 2000s (*Handbook "Russia 2004"*). In the same period, the Russian economy as a whole almost collapsed, with inflation reaching 1,000 percent a year, industrial production shrinking more than 40 percent, and the national economy disintegrating into regional subeconomies (Gustafson 1999; Puffer, McCarthy, and Naumov 2000). Major players in the global telecom industry invested in the Russian cellular market despite the hazards of Russia's weak economic institutions, particularly their nontransparency, corruption, and inability to enforce property rights. Foreign direct investments in the telecom sector grew from $520.3 million in 1995 to $819.3 million in 1997, dipped to $310–340 million in the aftermath of the financial crisis of 1998–99, and then jumped to $899 million in 2000, thereby quickly exceeding the pre-crisis level (*Communications and Informatization in Russia* 2001, 444). Miraculously, by the year 2000 Russian society at large came to enjoy a service for which just a decade earlier the country did not have the technology, infrastructure, production base, or management skills to support.

In hindsight, these developments do not look as surprising. Between 1993 and 2000, viable cellular phone services emerged in 102 developing countries (Rouvinen 2006). The limited supply of fixed-line phone services typical of such societies creates virtually insatiable demand, which Western cellular operators and equipment manufactures in collaboration with domestic state-owned fixed-line incumbent and new private operators strived to meet. The resulting structure of the cellular market varied from a monopoly of one or a few subsidiaries, spin-offs, and joint ventures of the fixed-line incumbent to competition among a few independent providers (Gao and Rafiq 2009; Gruber 1999, 2001a, 2001b; Parker and Roller 1997; Schejter 2006). This chapter's research question is: Under what conditions does a monopoly or competition prevail?

Our analysis benefits from the fact that the Russian cellular industry initially emerged relatively independently in the two largest Russian cities, Moscow and St. Petersburg, in the early 1990s and remained regionalized over the whole

Table 11.1.
Relative Market Share of Cellular Operators in Moscow (with Moscow region) and St. Petersburg (with Leningrad region) (%)

		1993	1994	1995	1996	1997	1998
Moscow market	MSA	100	74	41	22	18	14
	MSB			10	22	30	45
	MSC		26	49	56	52	41
St. Petersburg market	SPA	95	47	31	29	34	27
	SPB		29	53	47	49	63
	SPC	5	24	16	24	17	10

Source: Company reports.

decade. The first Russian cellular service provider was officially registered in St. Petersburg in November 1990 and started its operations in September 1991. The first Moscow venture followed in December 1991. In 1992–94 two more operators launched their services in each city. As the customer base data in table 11.1 show, these six companies competed for customers throughout the whole period of our study. We refer to them by three-letter names: the first two letters denote the name of the city, MS for Moscow and SP for St. Petersburg, and the third letter indicates the cellular standard employed. Russian cellular companies initially used three different cellular standards: a European analog standard (standard A), a European digital standard (standard B), and an American analog (later converted into digital) standard (standard C).

By the year 2000, the original structure remained essentially intact in Moscow while a descendant of the former state monopoly emerged as the dominant player in St. Petersburg. This variation in the outcome opens the door to a comparative interregional analysis, a well-developed tool in industry studies (e.g., Saxenian 1994). The analysis is based on fifteen extensive interviews with key industry participants conducted on-site in Moscow and St. Petersburg between December 2002 and March 2004, government statistics and legal reports, the companies' annual reports, and other publications. The respondents included the former Minister of Telecommunications of the Russian Federation, founders and CEOs of cellular companies, executives of Western operators, and shareholders of cellular ventures based in Moscow and St. Petersburg who also held executive jobs at the respective companies themselves. Collectively, the respondents worked at all six ventures or were directly linked with them through their parent companies.

The analysis shows that the subsidiaries of the regional incumbent fixed-line telecoms indeed enjoyed an early advantage in access to cellular licenses and other resources necessary for establishing dominance within the industry. Yet independent operators created regulatory opportunities for themselves by skillfully engaging federalist principles to obtain regional licenses for their services. The realization of these opportunities depended on all the competitors' relative abilities to mobilize tangible and intangible resources that varied systematically with the identities of a firm's owners: Russian co-owners' background in the telecom and adjacent industries and foreign co-owners' identities as telecom service operators, rather than telecom equipment manufacturers, helped secure superior resources. The presence of co-owners with disadvantageous backgrounds and identities coincided with a more proactive role of the state in the firm's emergence. With the federal government exerting more control over the incumbent operator in Moscow, a stronger independent operator was able to emerge there, assuring vibrant competition in the regional market. The opposite was true in St. Petersburg, where the regional government's ineffective attempt to set up a viable independent operator allowed the incumbent telecom company to de facto expand its fixed-line monopoly into mobile services.

The presentation follows closely the logic of the argument. We describe the ownership structure of the cellular industry in the early 1990s, compare and contrast the institutional logics that allowed both incumbent and independent operators to obtain cellular licenses, and examine the role of the various types of founders and owners in providing resources critical to success in the emerging industry. In the discussion section, we summarize these analyses and show

how the involvement of the federal state in shaping the structure of the cellular industry was a double-edged sword.

THE STRUCTURE OF THE CELLULAR INDUSTRY IN MOSCOW AND ST. PETERSBURG

The extensive literature on the emergence of the cellular industry across countries with a varied degree of economic development offers a simple baseline argument for our study (Gao and Rafiq 2009; Gruber 1999, 2001a, 2001b; Parker and Roller 1997; Schejter 2006). The development of a new industry is greatly facilitated by network externalities whereby a product or service becomes more attractive to new consumers as their number grows. In the case of the cellular industry, the number of mobile customers is not the sole driving force behind network externalities, since mobile customers place calls to the users of fixed-line phones as well. In developing economies, where getting a fixed line is often a problem, mobile service represents a more attractive alternative. This externality has one major implication for the structure of the fledgling cellular market: since one telecom company operates the traditional fixed-line phone business, it naturally enjoys a head start in the cellular business while other claimants have to establish access to its land network. This advantage is reinforced further by the utility's preexisting ties to foreign companies as a source of capital and expertise, as well as to the state, with whom it has a regulatory and often ownership relationship. These industry specifics predetermine the traditional operator's ability to secure all the ingredients of a successful entry into the cellular market: an operating license, network equipment, and relevant managerial, technical, and service skills. It follows that the traditional telephone utility itself or its offsprings should dominate and even monopolize the national cellular industry unless the state as a regulator prevents it from doing so.

With this as our background, the Russian case looks like a remarkable exception. Yet we argue that it can be understood systematically if we do not reduce the determinants of market structures to economic forces and competitive advantages but thoroughly explore the relationships between major stakeholders within the telecom industry as well as between the industry and the state, in which all the sides are represented by multiple actors with divergent interests, identities, and multiple logics of action transposed from other institutional domains in a creative manner. To explicate these actors and logics of action, we trace the ownership structure of the mobile companies in Moscow and St. Petersburg in the 1990s and analyze the identities, strategies, and tactics of their owners and operators as those evolved in ongoing interactions with specific state agencies.

Table 11.2 introduces the original owners of the six mobile operators in Moscow and St. Petersburg.

The strikingly similar ownership structures of the two markets include as co-owners incumbent fixed-line operators (initially owned by the federal government), regional government, individual Russian entrepreneurs, foreign telecom operators and equipment manufacturers, and minority shareholders (financial investors). Interestingly enough, the ownership structure aligns well with the technological structure: the two service providers that operated on the European cellular standards A & B were owned by subsequently privatized local branches of the state telecom monopoly, MSA and MSB in Moscow and SPA and SPB in St. Petersburg. The St. Petersburg firms were tightly connected by a network of managers and professionals who "often moved from one company to another as if they were part of the same business group" (Respondent #7).

The third service provider in each city, MSC in Moscow and SPC in St. Petersburg, used the American cellular standard C and was independent from the traditional telecom industry. MSC's dominant owner was a group of entities affiliated with a research institute of the Russian military-industrial complex; the St. Petersburg city government owned a significant stake in SPC.

Each operator had a foreign owner. MSB and SPC were co-owned by foreign phone manufacturers, four firms listed as co-owners foreign cellular operators, and only one, MSC, listed a foreign investment fund. None of the St. Petersburg firms, and yet all of the Moscow firms, listed non-telecom agencies of the federal government among its minority owners (firms listed various state organizations, such as the State Institute of Radio and TV, Railway Ministry, and Ministry of Foreign Affairs as their owners). Likewise, all of the Moscow firms, but only one of the St. Petersburg firms, SPB, listed among their owners firm names preceded by LLPs, and AOZTs, which indicates the possible involvement of individual entrepreneurs whose interests such companies usually represent.

Table 11.2.
Ownership of the Cellular Operators in Moscow and St. Petersburg

	Firm Name	Founding Date	Owners	Stake (%)
Moscow	MSA	1/29/1992	Traditional operator (MTO)	23.5
			Traditional operator (MLIO)	23.5
			U.S. telecom operator (USO)	22
			European telecom operator (EO1)	20
			LLP "Eye Microsergery – MobileCom"	8
			State Institute of Radio and TV	3
	MSB	10/28/1993	European telecom operator (EO2)	35
			Traditional Operator (MTO)	20
			Russian business group (FIG)	19.1
			European equipment manufacturer (EM)	10
			LLP "Vast"	4.9
			Central Comm. Station (Railway Min.)	3
			AOZT "GDSR"	4
			EBRD	4
	MSC	7/28/1993	Radio Institute	11.9
			Interstate AK "Vympel"	10.0
			All-Russia State Radio and TV Comp.	4.3
			Information Transfer Center of MID	0.4
			LLP "Dondo"	6.6
			LLP "KB Impulse"	6.6
			JSC "Region"	6.6
			JSC "Rocico"	6.6
			USE controlled investment fund	47.0
St. Petersburg	SPA	11/12/1990	Traditional operator (PTO1)	57.5
			Foreign telecom operator (USO)	42.5
	SPB	6/17/1993	European telecom operator (EO3)	49
			Traditional operator (PTO2)	17
			Traditional operator (PTO3)	14
			Traditional operator (PTO4)	14
			AOZT "Contact-S"	3
			AOZT "West Link"	3
	SPC	11/16/1992	U.S. equipment manufacturer (USM)	60.6
			St. Petersburg Property Committee	39.4

Note: Some names have been disguised.

In what follows we show how these similarities and differences in owners' characteristics systematically determine their ability to deliver initial material assets, skills, and social relationships that help the firm survive long term as a provider of mobile services. Two firms in Moscow and one in St. Petersburg managed to assemble owners with favorable characteristics, which in turn determined the emergence of a competitive market in Moscow and a monopolistic one in St. Petersburg.

Table 11.3 demonstrates cellular telephony penetration rates in Moscow and St. Petersburg for the period 1993–2000. With an early start, St. Petersburg was slightly ahead at first, but as competition intensified in Moscow and remained minimal in St. Petersburg, the Moscow market took the lead in the number of users.[1]

[1] It is important to note that Moscow had a more prosperous economy than St. Petersburg and, accordingly, a higher GDP per capita throughout the 1990s. But as examples of

Table 11.3.
Cellular Telephony Penetration Rates in Moscow and St. Petersburg, 1993–2000 (% of total population)

	1993	1994	1995	1996	1997	1998	1999	2000
Moscow	0.05	0.2	0.4	1.1	2.2	4.0	6.7	17.3
St. Petersburg	0.08	0.1	0.5	1.1	2.6	3.1	4.7	7.6

Sources: http://www.gortis.info; companies' annual reports.

THE SOCIAL CONSTRUCTION OF COMPETITION IN THE RUSSIAN CELLULAR INDUSTRY: THE FEDERAL STATE AND REGIONAL MARKETS

While mobile phone services are new to Russia, fixed telephony was a major industry of the former Soviet Union, although its consumer component was treated as a poor relative to the state and military. The position of the traditional phone operators at the start of the cellular industry's formation was dominant. They enjoyed a monopoly over the fixed-line communication network of residential and business customers that any mobile operator needed to access. This advantage justified their expansion into the cellular business as well as their demand of a major ownership stake as a precondition for granting such access to new cellular ventures initiated by others. The ownership data on cellular companies in table 11.2 confirm that. The traditional operator in Moscow (MTO) had at least a 20 percent stake in MSA and MSB; another 23 percent stake in MSA belonged to Moscow's traditional long-distance and international carrier (MLIO). The pattern is even more obvious in St. Petersburg where the traditional operator (PTO1) owned more than half of SPA and three other traditional operators (PTO2, PTO3, PTO4) owned about 45 percent of SPB.

Thus traditional fixed-line operators opportunistically converted their monopoly power in the fixed-line phone sector into cellular assets, which is an expected economic outcome. Indeed, traditional telecoms are omnipresent in the cellular industry of developed economies as well as developing ones around the world (Gao and Rafiq 2009; Gruber 1999, 2001a, 2001b; Parker and Roller 1997; Schejter 2006). At the same time, the initially dominant position might dissolve over time if new entrants prove to be more entrepreneurial. For traditional telecoms, this threat is particularly real, as they are accustomed to operating as public utilities protected from competition by government regulation and are often owned by the state.

In the Soviet Union, the government combined the regulatory and production functions in the telecom industry within the Ministry of Telecommunications. The ministry defined the normative framework, issued licenses, and enforced regulations while at the same time directly managed companies by assigning production targets, allocating resources, and hiring or firing managers. The ministry ran thousands of state-owned companies that provided a whole spectrum of telecom services from satellite communication to short-wave radio communication. It had formidable, albeit often troubled, international contacts, including leading European producers of telecom equipment such as Ericsson, Siemens, and Alcatel, and was an active member of the International Union of Telecommunication. In the international arena, "the Ministry had relations with 180 countries and was very close to the global telecom markets" (Respondent #10). With the economic and political reforms of the late 1980s and early 1990s, the situation began to change as the ministry lost its grip on the operating companies, which were first incorporated and later privatized. However, the state maintained a substantial stake in most of such companies and could exercise control through regulation in addition to ownership per se.

Not surprisingly, the top management of the traditional fixed-line operators in Moscow and St. Petersburg, in collaboration with foreign telecom firms, managed to push the cellular industry to the forefront of the ministry's agenda, to obtain the first cellular licenses in the summer of 1991, and to successfully lobby the government for a favorable regulatory framework that would legalize their virtual monopoly in the nascent cellular industry. The document titled *The Conception of the Development of*

---

other Russian regions and other countries demonstrate, this measure of wealth affects more the average revenue per customer rather than the penetration rate, which is a function of the market competitiveness and therefore the availability and affordability of the wireless service.

the General-Use Mobile Ground Networks in Russia until 2010, which summarized and made official early regulatory developments and outlined the national strategy in the area of wireless communication, was made public in February 1994. It recognized two federal standards, A and B, for the mass market and upscale market, respectively, and provided for the issuance of one license per federal standard in each of the eighty-nine administrative regions of Russia. The choice of these particular standards was justified primarily by their European origins, since the government claimed one of its priorities was to make the Russian cellular network compatible with the networks of other European countries. All four federal licenses issued in Moscow and St. Petersburg belonged to MSA, MSB, SPA, and SPB, the joint ventures of the local branches of the traditional state-owned fixed-line operator and foreign businesses with prior dealings with the ministry. In fact, the ministry legislated a monopolistic market structure that did not leave any room for the telecom industry's outsiders SPC and MSC.

In response, SPC and MSC took somewhat different paths, which in hindsight turned out to be complementary. To obtain a license, they needed to solve two problems: to legalize their presence in the market and to find space on radio frequencies appropriate for the cellular standard C. SPC asked for help from the St. Petersburg government which, in fact, had created the firm in the first place as a counterweight to the overwhelming market power of the traditional operator, which controlled both SPA and SPB in addition to enjoying its traditional monopoly over fixed-line services. SPC's antimonopoly argument was rejected by the ministry, which believed that the weak Russian economy could not afford a buildup of two similar and competing networks in the same region. They also pointed to the shortage of appropriate spectrum frequencies due to the needs of the military.

MSC lacked access to the local government but did have a background in and personal ties to the military-industrial complex where the MSC management and engineers had worked previously. To drastically downsize that sector in the late 1980s, the Russian government called for a conversion of its numerous military research and manufacturing facilities to civil uses. The government did not specify what such uses might be, and therefore the call was available to serve as a powerful justification for MSC's agenda. Since the CEO of MSC had founded the company in the first place with the goal of creating jobs for his fellow research scientists, he had plenty of legitimacy and energy to make such an argument. At the same time, his personal ties to the military helped secure radio frequencies:

> I waited for almost a month in the minister's reception room, but he would not see me. I went to see his deputy, the meeting lasted five minutes and he said: "No, the issue is closed." We then came up with the idea of using the theme of military conversion, spent days and nights taking saunas and drinking vodka with the generals [to get much needed frequencies, while his company] invested millions of dollars into test flights and other actions demanded by the military, and found some frequencies there. I went back to the ministry asking to support unemployed military researchers who wanted to develop cellular telephony. (Respondent #12)

> They would show him the door, he'd be back through the window the next day. Finally, he found some guys within the ministry who saw the potential and helped him to get to the minister. (Respondent #15)

Still, the ministry claimed that it could accommodate MSC only within the already adopted regulatory framework, which decreed two federal standards and one license per standard for each region of Russia. MSC and its newfound supporters came up with the idea of a regional standard and justified its introduction by the need to saturate the cellular market quickly. Indeed, standard C, adopted by MSC and SPC, was older and more developed than A and B, which implied substantial savings on equipment and installation. The idea of the regional standard in addition to the federal one fit well with the declared power-sharing principles of the Russian federalist state, which was important at a time when separatist tendencies in the Russian federation were gaining momentum. Unable to ignore or reject these principles, the ministry granted regional governments the right to issue regional licenses. Unexpectedly, the effort of MSC from above converged with the effort of SPC from below in transposing the basic political principle of the federalist state into the economic domain to overcome the resistance of traditional telecoms supported by the ministry and to open the cellular markets in Moscow and St. Petersburg to genuine competition.

REALIZING OPPORTUNITIES FOR COMPETITION

The implementation of the federalist principle in state regulations created the opportunity for competition in the cellular industry on the regional level but did not guarantee competition per se. A contender for either a federal or regional license had to gain support from regulators. Once it obtained the license, it had to prove its viability in the market by providing reliable services and attracting a sufficient customer base, which required physical and financial capital, knowledge and skills, and effective social relationships within the company as well as with key counterparts. Fixed-line operators' traditional monopoly in the communication industry also implied their monopoly over traditional supply channels of such resources. The good news for independent providers was that alternative supply channels were opening up and different skills and expertise, which the old channels could not provide, were required. Thus the relative abilities of the traditional and independent operators to appropriate necessary resources were not clear in advance but, as we show below, varied systematically with the characteristics of their owners.

Russian Owners' Background and Access to Critical Resources

The communications industry is technologically complex and requires sophisticated engineering skills and expertise. In the Soviet Union, these human assets were reproduced within a relatively closed social milieu. To support the vast phone network, industry professionals had to maintain a mobile lifestyle, which was easier if their spouses worked for the industry as well. Exposed to the industry and its specific lifestyle from an early age, the children of its workers often followed their parents' path. Institutions of vocational and higher education subordinated to the Ministry of Communications facilitated the formation of intergenerational dynasties. Moscow and St. Petersburg were home to the ministry's two elite Institutes of Electrical Engineering and Communications, where the vast majority of the industry engineers and managers were educated. Not surprisingly, the wireless subsidiaries of the incumbent fixed-line operators had a well-established exclusive channel to engineering skills, which was reflected in their organizational structures. The Network Development and Maintenance Department was the largest and dominant in MSA, MSB, PSA, and PSB; the head of the department was second in command in each company.

Yet the decline of the military-industrial complex freed up highly qualified engineers, educators, and researchers with a background in military communications who were eagerly seeking opportunities to make a living, could easily grasp new communication technologies, and thus undermined the incumbents' control over the supply of engineering talent. The Russian founder of MSC and his initial team of managers and engineers came to the cellular industry from a military research institute. As the military-industrial complex was losing funding and status, the group was desperate "to put their brains to productive use" (Respondent #12). They had tried many business ideas from radar detectors to satellite television before discovering opportunities in the cellular industry. Their initial intention was to focus entirely on building and operating a cellular network and to leave the provision of the service to an American partner whom the MSC founder met at one of the many meetings on conversion held at his research institute. Since the Soviet military-industrial complex attracted the best talent with the most generous rewards and high status, the workers it was shedding could easily match the traditional telecom's workforce in skills and expertise.

Our evidence shows that engineering skills indeed were held in the highest regard at MSC and became the firm's crucial advantage in the early years of the industry's development. This is how one of the respondents describes MSC's response to the unauthorized access to its network:

> They paid hackers to find a way to penetrate their network and then searched for a defensive algorithm. It is peculiar that the solution found was later sold for big money to the West to be used on more developed networks. The engineering team was completely home-grown and its skill level was in no way inferior, and in many aspects superior, [to the level of its Western counterparts]. The equipment available limited its potential. (Respondent #13)

The engineering and research background of MSC imprinted not only its culture but its organizational structure as well:

> Within the organizational structure, they had a department called "Research Institute," which employed sixty people, all PhDs. They did all kind of highly intellectual work, mostly unrelated to telecom and impractical, but some of their products like billing protection software were pure masterpieces. (Respondent 15).

Although the institute was closed in 2000 and none of its original employees still works for MSC, the company retained the status of the most innovative company in the Russian market.

SPC's origins were problematic in this regard. The initiative to found SPC came from a well-known proponent of free markets who was mayor of St. Petersburg at that time: Anatoly Sobchak. Sobchak put in charge of the fledgling company an industry outsider with limited background and experience in general management as a theater director. That person's complete lack of ties to the telecom and adjacent industries led to severe problems with hiring qualified personnel, getting access to the fixed-line telephony network on competitive terms, and resolving numerous technical and logistical issues. According to one of the insiders, "He [the CEO] graduated from the drama school. I think he had too little business experience, not to mention an absolute lack of telecom experience. . . . It was very difficult for him in the industry, which is a closed old boys' network" (Respondent #5). Unlike MSC, SPC was clearly losing ground to the offspring of the regional fixed-line operator in terms of engineering talent.

While engineering skills could be acquired through the Soviet education and industry channels, service skills were virtually absent in the Soviet Union, where a command economy distributed products and services that were either in abundance and of poor quality or in short supply. Sophisticated marketing and customer service could not help in either circumstance. In addition, post-Soviet engineers were interested exclusively in solving technological problems, sometimes at the expense of the bottom line. As MSC's American founding partner recalls,

> The concept of service was totally foreign to them [Russians]; the engineers would shut down the system if they wanted to do some checks. (Respondent #15)

To overcome such an attitude, the Russian cofounder of MSC "once issued a firm-wide decree obligating all employees to love their customers" (Respondent #13).

Being in short supply in the former Soviet Union as a whole, marketing and customer service were an Achilles' heel of all the cellular service providers in Moscow and St. Petersburg. Getting a foreign partner that was knowledgeable and experienced—and willing to share its knowledge and experience—was the only way of tapping into that area of expertise, which is one reason why foreign co-owners have been present from the get-go in all of the six mobile firms under study here. In addition to access to marketing and customer service expertise, foreign partners also provided access to financial capital and state-of-the-art equipment and technologies. In the next section, we show how these partners were chosen and how the business identity of a partner determined its ability and willingness to provide access to critical resources.

Foreign Owners' Identity and Access to Critical Resources

When a traditional fixed-line operator decided to enter the cellular market and needed a foreign partner, institutional and personal ties with foreign owners that had been established through previous collaborations in fixed-line telephony were major factors in making such decisions. A major U.S. operator (hereafter USO) started its collaboration with the Soviet government in 1988 with a Trans-Soviet Line (TSL) project, a fiber-optic line, which was supposed to connect North America and Europe. The U.S. government under the ConCom regulations later blocked the project, but the initial contacts with the Russian telecom industry were established and allowed USO to explore other opportunities, including cellular telephony:

> Even though we were not ultimately successful in the execution of the TSL project, it was a platform, which gave us enormous credibility and positioning to look at other business opportunities. (Respondent #4)

Not surprisingly, USO became the first foreign entrant to the cellular industry as a cofounder of SPA. However, a similar move in the Moscow market to establish MSA initially stalled. While St. Petersburg traditionally enjoyed some autonomy and the federal government in Moscow sometimes allowed local experiments with risky or ideologically suspicious initiatives, Moscow in the late 1980s was under the close watch of the federal bureaucracy, which had very little enthusiasm for private enterprise (Respondent #7). Western European telecom operator EO1, which had access to the ministry, sought a license similar to the one sought by USO. To overcome the bureaucratic resistance, the two firms agreed to work together and solicited help from one of the first entrepreneurs of perestroika "who had nothing to do with the telecom, but had a high social profile and enjoyed direct ties to Gorbachev" (Respondent #8). That person agreed to participate in founding MSA, became instrumental in winning a license from the ministry, and stayed on as a passive minor co-owner of the company.

Three foreign partners entered the market with some help from informal private contacts. In the first case, a Russian social scientist residing in Europe offered a consortium of European operators (EO3) an introduction to the top management of St. Petersburg's traditional fixed-line operator. The invitation was accepted and eventually resulted in the establishment of SPB in which the intermediary retained a 1.5 percent stake. The second case involved a Russian immigrant in the United States with strong personal ties to St. Petersburg's government who brought to the city the CEO of one of the major American manufacturers of telecom equipment (USM). The two sides negotiated the incorporation of SPC, in which USM contributed capital through an investment firm specifically created for that purpose by the intermediary. In the third case, a Lebanese trader assisted an American entrepreneur (USE) in gaining access to a top-secret defense conglomerate in Moscow. Such an event could have happened only in the context of Gorbachev's policies that encouraged the conversion of the Russian defense firms to civil uses. At a management meeting devoted to conversion, USE met his future Russian partner in MSC. Unlike in the first two cases, the intermediary did not get involved in the partnership.

The actual willingness and ability of foreign co-owners to provide capital and expertise were largely defined by their identity. Telecom operators entered the Russian market with the strategic goal of global expansion of their core business; the cofounders of MSA, SPA, and SPB fall into this category. They brought operational and marketing expertise that Russian companies did not have. The group of manufacturers of telecom equipment included the cofounders of MSB and SPC who were primarily interested in developing new markets for their products and earning a profit from their sales.

A comparison of MSC and SPC clearly demonstrates the drawbacks of investor-manufacturers and the benefits of investor-operators for the development of the venture. USE, the foreign investor in MSC, was both a manufacturer and an operator, an entrepreneur who had a small manufacturing company in the United States and a small cellular network in Latin America. Initially he planned to capitalize on these identities separately by lending his equipment to MSC, which would focus on the maintenance of the cellular network, and running his own service. The service failed for reasons unrelated to this chapter. The equipment, three secondhand base stations and a mini-switch, helped launch the service quickly but turned out to be grossly inadequate for the requirements of the Moscow market. However, as an entrepreneur at large rather than the owner and the operator of a specific business, he was not irreversibly committed to his identity as an equipment manufacturer and to the original business model. He quickly converted the equipment already installed from a loan to an investment, merged his fledgling service into MSC, forged a close partnership with the Russian entrepreneur, helped MSC acquire necessary equipment from a major European manufacturer, brought in $12 million raised from U.S. institutional and private investors to buy out a hostile shareholder, and found a marketing expert to develop the company brand, which later became its major competitive advantage (Respondent #15). In fact, marketing and branding rather than equipment became USE's key contributions to the success of MSC:

> The CEO and his men laughed when I suggested that the company needed a brand, but we managed to change all that and he [the CEO] calls it a "revolution in his mind." (Respondent #15)

This is exactly what SPC's foreign investor USM could never have done, since its business identity was firmly linked to equipment manufacturing. Hesitant to commit significant financial resources, it offered an investment in-kind in the form of its own equipment. This limited SPC's choice of vendors and indirectly increased its cost of capital:

> They [manufacturer-shareholders] achieved their major objective: they sold their equipment

> and made the company fully dependent on them ... they did not allow us to borrow to finance the network's expansion and did not want to supply their base stations free of charge. (Respondent #6)

In a less dramatic form, the story about equipment dumping was repeated in the case of MSB. The difference was that its foreign investor, an equipment manufacturer (EM), recognized its limits and from the beginning involved its close ally, a telecom operator (EO2), as a partner and eventually transferred its stake to that company. For comparison, the only foreign partner of SPB, the telecom operator EO3, brokered for SPB supply contracts with European equipment manufacturers (Respondent #1). Overall, our evidence strongly suggests that as foreign direct investors, equipment manufacturers are detrimental to fledgling cellular operators.

Our findings call for more attention to investors' identities in the literature on foreign direct investment, which primarily focuses on the economic, political, and social characteristics of host countries (Meyer 2001) and sociocultural relations between the home and host countries (Bandelj 2002).

DISCUSSION

In this section, we would like to test the robustness of our conclusions in light of subsequent developments in the industry, recap our empirical findings, and highlight our contribution to the vast literature on the economic, political, and social origins of markets and organizations.

Overall, we show that the structure of the cellular market in Moscow and St. Petersburg is a question of polity and institutions rather than economics and technology. Taking into account exclusively the latter, we would have predicted the dominance of the subsidiaries of the incumbent fixed-line operators in both cities. Instead, we find that independent entrepreneurs created business opportunities for themselves from symbolic resources embedded in the federalist framework of the state (cf. Dobbin 1994).

While symbolic resources are necessary, they are not sufficient for a viable competitive market to take shape. This requires access by all competitors to material and financial capital, knowledge, skills, expertise, and in particular, social relationships within the corridors of power. Our evidence shows how such access varied by the background and identity of a firm's co-owners. Russian co-owners' background in the telecom and adjacent industries became a critical success factor because it allowed the firm to quickly assemble and maintain a strong group of skillful engineers in the absence of a developed job market for them. The telecom industry and military-industrial complex provided skilled engineers to four out of five firms analyzed in this chapter.

At the same time, Russian co-owners alone could not provide the capital and managerial expertise necessary to run cellular businesses. This is where the role of foreign investors became salient. While the literature on foreign direct investments focuses predominantly on the economic and political environments in host countries and the relationships between donor countries and host countries, we show that characteristics of donors are equally important. The equity participation of major foreign telecom equipment manufacturers negatively affected their Russian ventures. Their investments often took the form of overpriced and outdated equipment and were not accompanied by managerial expertise in running cellular services. Both of these factors put the Russian cellular companies created by the manufacturers in a disadvantaged position vis-à-vis the competitors that were co-owned by foreign telecom operators.

In addition to the findings presented above, the robustness of our conclusions is supported by the remedial actions undertaken by some early industry laggards. MSB ended up with a major manufacturer as a foreign co-owner, which forestalled its development at the early stage. However, in 1995 the same business group that helped jump-start MSC (FIG) took a major stake in MSB by acquiring shares from the incumbent fixed-line operator, which that group already controlled. Simultaneously, the European operator and co-owner of MSB purchased the stake of the European equipment manufacturer. The new ownership structure of MSB corresponded closely to the successful model identified in this chapter. The company turned from a sleepy technology house into an aggressive market player with often ruthless but always dynamic and creative tactics. It eventually overtook MSC as the Moscow market leader and later moved on to become the largest national operator in Russia. SPC attempted to move in the same direction and at the same time: a European operator with a stake in MSA bought out the American manufacturer (USM). Thus in all the cases presented, while foreign equipment manufacturers had to give up their ownership stakes in Russian mobile operators rather quickly, foreign telecom operators remained engaged in the long run.

Our observation that foreign co-owners' identities enhance or constrain their willingness and ability to deliver necessary resources to their firms is not entirely new, particularly when one deals with corporate venture capital, that is, start-up investments by established nonfinancial firms. Studies of the fledgling electricity industry in the late nineteenth-century United States show how electric equipment manufacturers had to become in-kind investors in cash-starved central electric stations in order to sell them their product. The arrangement put manufacturers in a precarious position, for as both investors and co-owners, they had to do everything in their power to ensure a central station's success. As manufacturers, they were interested in selling their equipment to any party willing to buy, including isolated stations that produced electricity on industrial and residential premises and vigorously competed with central stations as an alternative organizational form (McGuire and Granovetter 1994). To protect their interests, central station managers sidelined manufacturers within the two national trade associations and drew the industry's boundaries in such a way that excluded both manufacturers and isolated stations. Manufacturers had to withdraw their investments in central stations completely.

The literature on emerging markets and industries suggests that firms might engage in a competition not just for the best product and service or financial and human capital but also for preferential treatment by the state within the logic of patron-client relationships (Eisenhardt and Roniger 1984; Evans 1995; Walder 1986). In the 1990s this was the dominant logic in the Russian economy in general and in the telecom industry in particular. We found that such a competition is not necessarily a zero-sum game; the number of viable competitors within the industry depends on the number of powerful patrons at different levels of the state hierarchy: the central government (Ministry of Telecommunications), local government, military that controlled radio frequencies, and incumbent fixed-line operators. Whether that support came from the participation of firms' founders in the state bureaucracy and its closely linked economic institutions or from mobilization of preexisting or newly established patron-client relationships, the state bureaucrats provided opportunities for the ventures to develop their business and gain tangible and intangible assets (licenses, spectrum frequencies, access to the numbering capacity, etc.) in exchange for resources to support their political careers as well as a share in the material gain. The relationships were continuous rather than transactional and required a significant investment of time and effort on the part of firms' management.

One can argue that we cover a very short early period in the development of the cellular industry; however, some factors we discuss have long-term implications that will determine the industry's structure. The short-term versus long-term considerations are important at an abstract theoretical level but provide little guidance to empirical research. Businesses often act myopically, but this does not necessarily mean that they are doomed to failure in the long run. Multiple new factors come into play over longer periods and may counteract the long-term effects of preceding factors. Most important, there is nothing that automatically prevents organizations from addressing the long-term implications of their actions when those implications surface. For instance, MSC's pick of standard C, determined by necessity rather than free choice, turned out to be beneficial at the early stage but had exhausted its potential by 1998. By then, though, MSC had a vast customer base and strong patronage networks, which helped it obtain a new license for standard B. The customers and the Russian state greatly benefited from the preserved competitiveness of the sector—cellular penetration reached more than 100 percent in 2008, Russians enjoyed one of the lowest costs of communication in Europe, and telephony became a virtually universally available service—a long-proclaimed but never achieved government goal for the fixed-line telephony.

Our findings may not be representative for other businesses. The main distinctive features of the telecom industry are technological sophistication, high fixed costs, and a high level of state regulation. These factors make the economic, political, and technological dimensions crucial determinants of the industry's structure. More research is required to explore the sources of variation across industries.

REFERENCES

Aldrich, E., and C. M. Fiol. 1994. "Fools Rush In? The Institutional Context of Industry Creation." *Academy of Management Review* 19(4):645–70.

Aldrich, H. E. 2003. "Entrepreneurship." In *Handbook of Economic Sociology*, ed. N. Smelser and R. Swedberg. Princeton: Princeton University Press.

Aldrich, H. E., and C. Zimmer. 1986. "Entrepreneurship through Social Networks." In *The Art and Science of Entrepreneurship*, ed. D. L. Sexton and R. W. Smilor, 2–23. Cambridge, MA: Ballinger Publishing.

Arrow, K. 1985. "The Economics of Agency." In *Principals and Agents: The Structure of Business*, ed. J. Pratt and R. Zeckhauser. Cambridge, MA: Harvard Business School Press.

Bandelj, N. 2002. "Embedded Economies: Social Relations as Determinants of Foreign Direct Investment in Central and Eastern Europe." *Social Forces* 81(2):411–44.

Brockhaus R. H., and P. S. Horwitz. 1986. "The Psychology of the Entrepreneur." In *The Art and Science of Entrepreneurship*, ed. D. L. Sexton and R. W. Smilor, 25–48. Cambridge, MA: Ballinger.

Burt, R. S. 1992. *Structural Holes: The Social Structure of Competition*. Cambridge, MA: Harvard University Press.

Campbell, R. W. *Soviet and Post-Soviet Telecommunications: An Industry under Reform*. Boulder, CO: Westview Press.

Chesbrough, H. W. 2002. "Making Sense of Corporate Venture Capital." *Harvard Business Review* 80(3):90–99.

Communications and Informatization in Russia: The Federal Reference Book. 2001. [*Svyaz i Informatizatsiya v Rossii. Federalny Spravochnik*]. Moscow: Rodina-Pro.

Dobbin, Frank. 1994. *Forging Industrial Strategy: The United States, Britain, and France in the Railway Age*. New York: Cambridge University Press.

Dushnitsky, G., and M. J. Lenox. 2005. "When Do Firms Undertake R&D by Investing in New Ventures?" *Strategic Management Journal* 26(10): 947–65.

Economic Newsletter. 2001. Cambridge MA: Davis Center for Russian Studies, Harvard University. April.

Eisenhardt, S. N., and L. Roniger. 1984. *Patrons, Clients and Friends: Interpersonal Relations and the Structure of Trust in Society*. Cambridge: Cambridge University Press.

Evans, P. 1995. *Embedded Autonomy: States and Industrial Transformation*. Princeton: Princeton University Press.

Fama, E. F., and M. G. Jensen. 1983. "Separation of Ownership and Control." *Journal of Law and Economics* 26:301–25.

Gao, Ping, and Adnan Rafiq. 2009. "The Transformation of the Mobile Telecommunications Industry in Pakistan: A Developing Country Perspective." *Telecommunications Policy* 33:309–23.

Gompers, P., and J. Lerner. 2001. "The Venture Capital Revolution." *Journal of Economic Perspectives* 13(2):145–68.

Gruber, Harald. 1999. "An Investment View of Mobile Telecommunications in the European Union." *Telecommunications Policy* 23:521–38.

Gruber, Harald. 2001a. "Spectrum Limits and Competition in Mobile Markets: The Role of Licence Fees." *Telecommunications Policy* 25:59–70.

Gruber, Harald. 2001b. "Competition and Innovation: The Diffusion of Mobile Telecommunications in Central and Eastern Europe." *Information Economics and Policy* 13:19–34.

Gustafson, T. 1999. *Capitalism Russian Style*. New York: Cambridge University Press.

Handbook "Russia 2004." The Statistics Committee of the Russian Federation.

Ledeneva, A. V. 1998. *Russia's Economy of Favours: Blat, Networking, and Informal Exchange*. Cambridge: Cambridge University Press.

Low, M. B., and I. C. MacMillan. 1988. "Entrepreneurship: Past Research and Future Challenges." *Journal of Management* 2(14):139–61.

McGuire, P., and M. Granovetter. 1994. *The Social Construction of Industry: Human Agency in the Development, Diffusion, and Institutionalization of the Electric Utility Industry*. Chapter 10. Working manuscript.

Meyer, K. E. 2001. "Institutions, Transaction Costs, and Entry Mode Choice in Eastern Europe." *Journal of International Business Studies* 32(2): 357–67.

Nee, V. 1989. "A Theory of Market Transition: From Redistribution to Markets in State Socialism." *American Sociological Review* 54:663–81.

Parker, Philip M., and Lars-Hendrik Roller. 1997. "Collusive Conduct in Duopolies: Multimarket Contact and Cross-Ownership in the Mobile Telephone Industry." *RAND Journal of Economics* 28: 304–22.

Peng, Yusheng. 2001. "Chinese Villages and Townships as Industrial Corporations: Ownerships, Governance, and Market Discipline." *American Journal of Sociology* 106(5):1338–70.

Puffer, M., J. McCarthy, and A. I. Naumov. 2000. *The Russian Capitalist Experiment: From State-Owned Organizations to Entrepreneurships*. Cheltenham: Edward Elgar.

Puffer, S. M., and D. J. McCarthy. 2001. "Navigating the Hostile Maze: A Framework for Russian Entrepreneurship." *Academy of Management Executive* 4(15):24–36.

Rouvinen, Petri. 2006. "Diffusion of Digital Mobile Telephony: Are Developing Countries Different?" *Telecommunications Policy* 30:46–63.

Saxenian, AnnaLee. 1994. *Regional Advantage: Culture and Competition in Silicon Valley and Route 128*. Cambridge, MA: Harvard University Press.

Schejter, Amit. 2006. "Israel Cellular Telecommunications Policy." *Telecommunications Policy* 30:14–28.

Schumpeter, J. A. 1934. *The Theory of Economic Development*. Cambridge, MA: Harvard University Press.

Shaver, K. G., and L. R. Scott. 1991. "Person, Process, Choice: The Psychology of New Venture Creation." *Entrepreneurship Theory and Practice* 16(2):23–45.

Thornton, P. H. 1999. "The Sociology of Entrepreneurship." *Annual Review of Sociology* 25:19–46.

Tushman, M. L., and P. Anderson. 1986. "Technological Discontinuities and Organizational Environments." *Administrative Science Quarterly* 31: 297–313.

Walder, A. 1986. *Communist Neotraditionalism: Work and Authority in Chinese Industry*. Berkeley: University of California Press.

———. 2002. "Markets and Income Inequality in Rural China: Political Advantage in an Expanding Economy." *American Sociological Review* 67(2):231–53.

Yang, M. M. 1994. *Gifts, Favors, and Banquets: The Art of Social Relationships in China*. Ithaca: Cornell University Press.

12

Social Sequence Analysis

Ownership Networks, Political Ties, and Foreign Investment in Hungary

David Stark ▪ Balázs Vedres

Can high levels of foreign investment be compatible with interenterprise ownership networks in a developing economy? In addressing this question, this chapter[1] poses a new agenda for the field of economic development: In place of the earlier question of how a national economy is integrated into the global economy, the new agenda asks whether and how foreign investment is integrated into the local networks of host economies. Sustainable growth is more likely, research suggests, where the subsidiaries of foreign companies are embedded in network ties within the host economy, as locals and foreigners alike recognize that business networks can be viewed as a strategic resource (Bair and Gereffi 2003; Dicken, Forsgren, and Malmberg 1994; Kogut and Walker 2001).

Our analysis is conducted in a setting strategically chosen for extraordinarily high levels of foreign direct investment (FDI) in a situation where domestic firms were forming diverse interorganizational ownership networks in response to high levels of uncertainty in their business environment—conditions marking the postsocialist Hungarian economy between 1987 and 2001. Our case represents one of the most rapid and far-reaching transformations of a national economy. During this period, the institutions of the Hungarian economy were fundamentally reorganized from planning to market coordination and the institutions of the Hungarian polity were fundamentally restructured from a monopolistic Communist Party to a system of competing political parties. The system of property was similarly transformed: our data reveal that state ownership of the large-firm sector declined from 98 percent in 1987 to 15 percent in 2001 and the share of the large-firm sector that was foreign owned rose from only 1 percent in 1987 to 53 percent in 2001.

To analyze how the evolution of a national network of interorganizational ownership ties interacts with FDI we gathered data on the complete ownership network histories of 1,696 of the largest Hungarian enterprises from 1987 to 2001. This time frame yields comprehensive coverage of the Hungarian economic transformation, reaching back to the moment when firms could register as corporations and encompassing the institutionalization of private property, market coordination, and foreign investment. Our time frame thus includes the entire period

[1] Research for this chapter was supported by a grant from the National Science Foundation, SES-01-36995. We also acknowledge the support of the Russell Sage Foundation, where Stark was a Visiting Scholar during the initial phase of data analysis, and the Collegium Budapest, where Stark and Vedres revised the chapter while Visiting Fellows. We benefited from discussions at the Santa Fe Institute, INSEAD, Centre de Sociologie de l'Innovation (Paris), the Center on Organizational Innovation at Columbia University, and the Center for the Study of Economy & Society at Cornell University where earlier versions were presented. For assistance in collecting the data, we thank Zsolt Batar. For comments, criticisms, and suggestions on an earlier draft, we are grateful to Laszlo Bruszt, Andrew Buck, Gil Eyal, Amanda Damarin, Neil Fligstein, Geoff Fougere, Istvan Gabor, Paul Ingram, William McAllister, Andrew Spicer, Duncan Watts, Harrison White, and especially Peter Bearman and Monique Girard.

This chapter reprints material from Stark and Vedres, "Social Times of Network Spaces: Network Sequences and Foreign Investment in Hungary," *American Journal of Sociology* 111, no. 5 (March 2006): 1367–1411, modifying that article with additional materials and extending the analysis to include political ties.

in which firms were privatized and new regulatory frameworks were established (governing, for example, banking, bankruptcy, accounting, contracting, and corporate governance). We are therefore able to study, from its inception, network formation across an entire epoch of economic transformation.

We record network formation starting from the very first ownership ties made in a nascent market economy, where the legal possibility of creating an interfirm ownership tie coincides with the starting point of our data collection. We then follow network evolution over the turbulent years of postsocialism into market stabilization and the massive inflow of foreign investment. We will be especially attentive to differences between vertically organized business networks and those with more horizontal patterns of cohesion. We identify the emergence of varieties of both vertical and cohesive structures, and we follow these structures across time to understand their durability and openness to foreign investment. We then augment the ownership data with personnel data on the managers and directors of these firms in 2001. By merging that data set with the list of all political officeholders in Hungary from 1987 to 2001, we can identify a company as having a political tie when one of its economic officeholders is a current or former political officeholder. By utilizing the histories of firm network embeddedness, we are able to model how foreign investment interacts with these network forms.

To do so, we develop analytic tools that reconcile the structural focus of social network analysis with the historical orientation of sequence analysis. In combining the two approaches, we begin with the element that each shares: the notion that meaning is given by context (Abbott 1997). For the network analyst, no tie has meaning in itself. To interpret a tie, the analyst must understand its location in social space. In network analysis, context is topographic. For sequence analysts, as for historical sociologists more generally, no event has meaning in itself. The meaning of an action, an event, a social formation, or a relationship must be understood in its temporal context. In the theoretical approach that we are developing, structure is identified at the intersection of topographic and temporal contexts (see Vedres and Stark 2010). As a parallel to social network analysis, we develop a social sequence analysis. To do so we study variation in the sequences of local network positions. Our combination of network analysis and sequence analysis is, thus, not merely additive: In striving to make network analysis historical we also seek to make sequence analysis relational. At the basis of our project of historical network analysis is a reconstruction of the network sequences of 1,696 firms. Identifying distinctive pathways through a network space, we argue, is a way to understand processes of network evolution.

Our analysis indicates, first, that high levels of FDI are compatible with the persistence of domestic interenterprise ownership networks. Globalization and the reproduction of network embeddedness are not necessarily mutually opposing processes. Second, we find that the Hungarian economy is not a dual-segregated economy composed of domestic firms that are networked and foreign-controlled firms that are isolated. In fact, the proportion of Hungary's mixed economy that is controlled by foreign owners and linked to domestic ownership networks increased from 1991 to 2001. By 2001, only 30 percent of foreign capital was invested in subsidiaries that had never been part of ownership networks. Foreign-owned firms were just as likely to have ties to domestically owned firms as to other foreign-owned firms: we find no evidence for segregation. We find, third, that network forms of "recombinant property" (Stark 1996) are robust throughout the period. Notably, one variant of recombinant property, characterized by cohesive network structures, is most likely to involve the participation of foreign investment. More than a mere legacy of state socialism, these network forms are a viable organizational response to the challenges of an internationalized economy. Fourth, using logistic regression analysis we find that the odds of involving sizable foreign ownership differ significantly across distinctive pathways of network positions. Fifth, we find that the subsidiaries of foreign multinationals are not simply joining existing network structures but are actively participating in network creation and growth. In Hungary, foreign investment and network evolution are intertwined processes. Sixth, we find that social sequence analysis of network topographies provides analytic leverage in understanding how foreign direct investment is related to the ties of firms to political parties. Not as a general rule but through specific histories, firms can be cohesively tied to other firms, closely tied to political parties, and strongly linked to foreign capital.

The first section of the chapter presents the basic contours of our case: the Hungarian economy after the collapse of state socialism, the subsequent emergence of interenterprise networks, the demise of state ownership, and the rise of foreign investment. Following this discussion, we frame our theoretical and methodological contribution as an attempt to model the structure of network practices through combined attention to topography and temporality. After describing our data collection in the second section of the chapter, we chart in the third section the changing proportions of the Hungarian economy that are foreign or domestic, and networked or isolated.

To identify the microprocesses of interorganizational network formation that explain the macrostructural outcomes, we move in the fourth section to modeling that makes sequences of network positions the unit of analysis. The methodological innovation at the core of this study is to combine the tools of sequence analysis and network analysis to yield a sequence analysis of changing network positions. We first define discrete forms of embeddedness. These local network topographies are the building blocks to identify sequences of changes in forms of embeddedness for each of the firms in our population. Next we describe the optimal matching operations for grouping firms on the basis of similarities in sequence patterns through that network space. Using logistic regression analysis we test our proposition that foreign ownership can be explained not simply by the shape of network structures but by the sequencing of network positions. In the fifth section we discuss in detail the typical pathways and their co-evolution with foreign investment. Recognizing that relational resources can be used for different organizing purposes, we interpret the temporal patterns of network properties to understand the interdependent practices of Hungarian managers and foreign investors. In the concluding analytical section, we explore the patterns of firms' personnel ties to political parties, examining these ties first through the lens of the changing proportions of the Hungarian economy identified in the third section. We then present findings that demonstrate the relationship between the network sequence pathways, firms' political ties, and levels of foreign investment.

THE DOMESTIC EMBEDDEDNESS OF FOREIGN INVESTMENT

Emergence of Interenterprise Ownership Networks

The postsocialist economies of Eastern Europe and the former Soviet Union offer a striking laboratory to study processes of network formation in a period of rapid and far-reaching economic change. In their extrication from state socialism, postsocialist firms confronted highly uncertain political, economic, and institutional environments. With the demise of the old COMECON alliance that regulated trade among the socialist economies, firms watched the collapse of their once secure trading partners. Literally within a month, and not at the margin but in overwhelming proportions, they had to seek new suppliers and new customers. They would do so in an institutional environment of extreme complexity. Newly elected democratic governments were dismantling the socialist planning apparatus and launching ambitious programs of privatization.[2] From one month to the next, government agencies promulgated regulations governing banking, bankruptcy, accounting, contracting, foreign direct investment, and corporate governance. For firms remaining in state ownership, for recently "privatized" firms, and for new start-up firms alike, the challenge was to navigate through a maze of new policies in which contradictory regulations and inconsistent enforcement produced ambiguity about which rules and which games were operating.

Writing in the mid-1990s, Stark drew on insights that interorganizational ties might provide means to cope with highly uncertain environments (see Stark 1996). Based on data gathered through complementary research methods (ethnographic research in firms, analysis of government agency documents, and analysis of the ownership records of the two hundred largest Hungarian enterprises and top twenty-five banks in 1994), Stark identified an ensemble of practices that he labeled *recombinant property*. Interenterprise ownership networks, Stark demonstrated, were a response to uncertainty, serving as a strategy to spread risk (see also Johnson 1997; McDermott 1997; Róna-Tas 1998; Spicer, McDermott, and Kogut 2000; Böröcz 2001; Vedres 2000). Like mountain climbers assaulting a treacherous face, postsocialist firms used

[2] For a detailed explication of the debate over privatization at the very outset of the transformation period (late 1988 through mid-1990), see Stark 1990. In Hungary, as elsewhere in the region, the terms of the debate were organized around four themes: foreign versus domestic ownership, spontaneous privatization versus privatization controlled by state agencies, institutional versus natural owners, and concentrated versus dispersed ownership. Hungarian policymakers opted for high levels of FDI, a "bargaining" model in which enterprises proposed and state agencies vetted privatization plans, relatively high levels of institutional cross-ownership but not in the framework of large holdings directed by financial insitutions, and concentrated ownership. That these outcomes might have been otherwise (and indeed in other East Central European countries they were different), see Stark 1992; Stark and Bruszt 1998; and Spicer, McDermott, and Kogut 2000.

networks of cross-ownership as the safety ropes binding them together.

Stark stressed that recombinant property might increase chances of survival without increasing profitability. Some firms were diversifying their portfolio of resources (blurring the boundaries of public and private) to socialize liabilities while privatizing assets (Stark 1996, 1012–15). Similarly, business group networks were a means not only of risk-spreading but of risk-shedding in a context in which policies of creditworthiness and debt forgiveness were highly politicized (Stark 1996, 1009–12). Thus, networked assets could facilitate productive restructuring; but, as Stark demonstrated, they also offered avenues to exploit ambiguities in regulations and offload liabilities to the taxpayer in state-sponsored programs of bank bailouts and debt forgiveness.[3]

Stark's research on recombinant property was conducted while levels of foreign investment were modest, during the period of uncertainty when new regulatory frameworks had been introduced but were not yet institutionalized. Since then, extrication from state socialism has been decisive: the planned economy and the dominance of state ownership have been systematically dismantled. Similarly, the entrance of foreign investment has been massive: the Hungarian economy today is arguably one of the most globalized economies in the world. What, then, happened to organizational ownership networks over the entire period of transformation from 1987 to 2001?

Foreign Investment Meets Postsocialist Networks

The existing literature on foreign investment and network forms in postsocialist settings suggests at least three scenarios for what could happen in a climate such as that of Hungary in 1987–2001. The first is that the shock of system change will produce early patterns of network formation that reach a tipping point to a self-reinforcing dynamic of almost unchecked network growth. Business groups would be strong, partly because they are densely connected and also because they link deeply into the political class. These domestic networks might then lock out foreign capital, perhaps even dispelling some initial foreign investors.[4] In terms of the relative proportions of the economy that are networked or isolated, foreign or domestic, this would be a case where, at the extreme, almost everything is networked and domestically controlled. Even the modest levels of foreign investment would be bound to domestic business groups (table 12.1). This process of network crowding would correspond to the antidevelopmental lines of the contemporary Russian economy analyzed by Burawoy (Burawoy 1996; Burawoy and Krotov 1992) and others (Johnson 1997; Zon 1998).

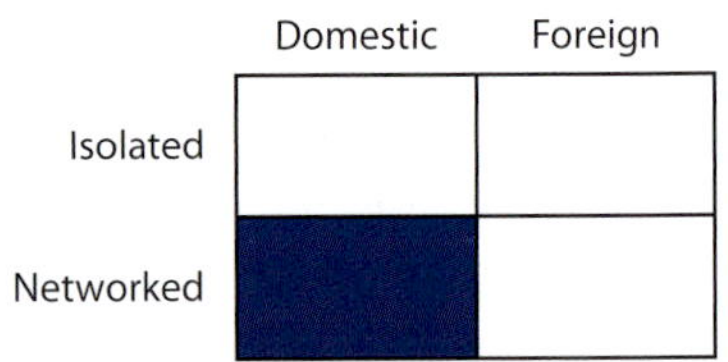

Table 12.1. Scenario 1: domestic networks crowding out foreign capital.

A second possibility is that extraordinarily high levels of foreign investment will lead to the eradication of interenterprise ownership. This expectation corresponds closely to the view of Hanley, King, and Tóth (2002) who, in challenging Stark's approach, argue that interenterprise ownership networks were a transient and fleeting phenomenon, confined to the period immediately following the collapse of state socialism. The eradication of these interenterprise ownership ties, according to Hanley and his coauthors, has been carried out by "private parties" exercising "clear and unambiguous ownership rights" (Hanley, King, and Tóth 2002, 140), in particular by foreign investors who, in their view, desire strong and unambiguous lines of control, undiluted by ownership network ties. Interenterprise ownership links that preceded foreign investment would be broken up when foreigners acquired firms through the privatization process. Moreover, given the powerful influence of foreign firms (rich in resources—financial, managerial, and ideological), their predilection to shun network ties would rapidly diffuse throughout the economy. The result of the direct actions of the foreign multinationals as well

[3] According to Stark, "Centralized management of liabilities will not continue indefinitely, but the organizational dynamics of enterprises formed under the new paternalistic conditions are likely to have strong path-dependent effects" (1996, 1012).

[4] For the Hungarian case, where we know that foreign investment continued to grow, this frst scenario is obviously counterfactual but, nonetheless, heuristically useful.

Table 12.2. Scenario 2: foreign eradication of networks directly and by demonstration effects.

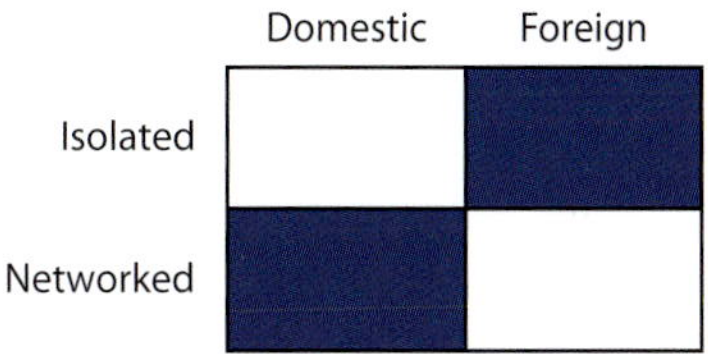

Table 12.3. Scenario 3: a radically dual-segregated economy.

as of these indirect demonstration effects would be, at the extreme, an economy opposite to the first possibility—almost nothing would be networked (see table 12.2).

A third scenario is that of a segregated, dual economy as increasing levels of foreign investment lead to a radical separation between foreign and domestic firms. Foreign investment, in this view, results in "cathedrals in the desert" (Grabher 1994; Hardy 1998; Pavlinek and Smith 1998; Uhlir 1998). These are platform operations importing semi-finished parts to be assembled locally for export. Whereas Hanley, King, and Tóth (2002) take a positive view of the absence of ties, in the dual economy model it is the very absence of connectedness between foreign and domestic firms that is the root of the problem (Comisso 1998). FDI leaves the domestic economy untouched, thereby maintaining underdevelopment. The absence of ties perpetuates a segregated economy, malevolent because its radical separation allows no positive influence across sectors. A case where foreign investors do not make network ties and where the networks of domestic firms grow only among themselves (Zysman and Schwartz 1998) would correspond to a radically segregated, dual economy in which FDI is overwhelmingly isolated and domestic firms are predominantly networked (see table 12.3).

With our data we can chart the proportions of the Hungarian mixed economy[5] that are (1) networked and foreign, (2) networked and domestic, (3) isolated and foreign, and (4) isolated and domestic. The findings, reported in more detail for the entire period in a subsequent section, are at odds with each of the three scenarios depicted in tables 12.1, 12.2, and 12.3: by 2001, large-firm capital was distributed across the four cells in roughly equal proportions. Domestic

[5] In place of the former dichotomy of public versus private, we redefine the term mixed economy along the foreign-domestic and networked-isolated dimensions.

	Domestic	Foreign
Isolated	18%	29%
Networked	26%	26%

Table 12.4. Distribution of large-firm capitalization by type, Hungary, 2001.

networks have not crowded out FDI, and multinationals have not eradicated the networks; but Hungary is also not a radically segregated dual economy (see table 12.4).

This constellation of the macrostructure of ownership suggests that other processes are at play than those outlined in the scenarios above. The challenge, then, is to understand the processes whereby some foreign capital becomes integrated while other foreign capital becomes isolated, and how some network formations survive without foreign capital while other network formations develop with the participation of foreign investors. In short, what are the social processes that produced these macrostructural outcomes?

Business Networks and Political Ties: Political and Economic Competition Reentangled?

In addition to restructuring ties between firms, our case also involves restructuring ties between firms and the political field. Property transformation is only one aspect of this process—for with the emergence of a competitive market economy there was also the emergence of competitive politics among political parties. Our case thus involves the simultaneous transformation of political and economic fields, the separation of state from economy, and a possible repoliticization of the economic field.

To say that the economy under communism was "politicized" would be a misnomer, for to suggest an interaction between one field and another would imply that the two existed as autonomous fields. At the outset of our study, the political and the economic are so tightly entangled they are virtually inseparable (on the lack of autonomy of the communist state, see Stark and Bruszt 1998, esp. chap. 4). As part of the *nomenklatura*, senior managers of the large state-owned enterprises were appointed by and directly accountable to the central authorities. In fact, by virtue of the strategic importance of their positions, many of these enterprise directors were themselves members of the party's Central Committee.

With the collapse of communist rule in the upheavals of late 1989, policymakers of many stripes posited a clear goal in both the economic and the political arena: a market economy of competing firms and a liberal democracy of competing political parties. The means to achieve these goals were also clearly stated: separate the state from the market and sever political ties from the field of economic action.

Although the goals and means were clear, the actual challenges of market competition among firms and political competition among parties led to the establishment of new ties between firms and parties. Restated, the goal of sharply separated fields is undercut by the very logic of competition within each. On one side, to compete in the political field, governing parties need to manage the economy, and all political parties need access to resources. On the other side, to compete in the economic field, firms need access to government contracts and to timely information about government policies. In short, to gain resources to compete for votes, parties compete for firms. At the same time and in parallel, to gain an upper hand in economic competition, firms ally with parties (McMenamin and Schoenman 2007; Schoenman 2005).

In examining newly market-oriented firms and newly competitive political parties, a further question thus arises: What is the relationship between business networks, political ties, and foreign investment?

A Social Sequence Approach to Foreign Embeddedness

Our approach identifies processes that explain the integration of foreign investment in interorganizational ownership networks. We organize the analytical building blocks along two dimensions: topographical and temporal. Along the first dimension, we start from the insight of network analysis that network structures can differ in their topographical properties. Therefore, rather than simply identifying whether a given firm is embedded or not embedded in network ties, we probe for qualitative differences in types of embeddedness. Because we focus on network properties from the perspective of the individual firm, we are interested in variations in local network structures.

In locating the position of a given firm within distinctive local topographies, we distinguish structures that are more vertically organized with greater centralization from those that are more horizontally organized with greater cohesiveness. Recent empirical research on the shape of business networks across a variety of institutional settings has demonstrated that more cohesive, horizontal structures outperform more centralized, vertical forms. In the field of biotechnology, Powell and his coauthors (Powell et al. 2005) found that actors that are embedded in horizontal rather than hierarchical networks were more likely to be innovative. In her study of interorganizational networks in China, Keister (1998) found that nonhierarchical business groups were more buffered from uncertainties and outperformed centralized groups. Similarly, in Russia, whereas defensive strategies of survival correspond to centralized business groups, entrepreneurial groups (often with foreign involvement) were more horizontal in structure (Huber and Wörgötter 1998).

Stark's identification of the two prevalent forms of interenterprise ownership networks in the early part of the 1990s specifically pointed to the emergence of distinctively vertical and horizontal network structures (Stark 1996, 2001). The first form of recombinant property networks involved processes in which large state-owned or formerly state-owned enterprises spun off corporate satellites (some of which were still of considerable size, spinning off their own satellites), resulting in star-shaped networks with the very largest firms at the hubs. Along these vertical ties, firms shifted assets and liabilities in frequently shady arrangements that took advantage of shifting government policies (Voszka 1997). The second type of interenterprise ownership networks involved networks of greater density, resulting in decentered, more cohesive structures. Unlike the simple star-periphery structures, firms in these networks regrouped interdependent assets and restructured enterprises.

Just as domestic firms faced the uncertainties of postsocialism, foreign actors faced uncertainties in entering an emerging market. Our reading of the recent literature on foreign investment (Inkpen and Beamish 1997; Kogut 1988, 1991; Yiu and Makino 2002; Zaheer 1995) suggests that some foreign investors use ownership network ties to learn the rules of play, legitimize their presence, obtain local knowledge, and gain introduction into social networks by having a local partner. Forming a joint venture, for example, means that a foreign investor establishes a strong network tie (in the form of shared ownership) with a local firm to obtain legitimacy in the eyes of domestic economic actors, national policymakers, and local officials. Such network ties are potential avenues to obtain local knowledge, especially under conditions when the regulatory environment is untested, where domestic markets have culturally specific features (e.g., involving tastes or practices in advertising, marketing, packaging, etc.), or where basic infrastructural logistics (e.g., utilities, transportation, etc.) have locally idiosyncratic features.[6]

Following Stark, we posit two distinctive patterns of network formation in the extrication from state socialism: star-periphery structures and cohesive network structures. Following Kogut and others, we posit that a significant number of foreign investors will forge network ties with domestic partners. A key research question, then, is whether and how the vertical and horizontal variants of recombinant property (in network analytic terms, centralized versus cohesive structures) figured in the strategies of foreign investors. Were foreign investors attracted to star-shaped networks because of their structural isomorphism to hierarchical supplier networks, or did they avoid these because of their historical origins as vehicles of asset-stripping and liability management? Did foreign investors avoid entering cohesive and densely networked structures because they are cautious about the entanglements of such embeddedness, or did they prefer these structures because of their managerial entrepreneurialism?

Answering these questions requires that we add a temporal dimension to our topographical dimension. Foreign investment in Hungary was not immediately triggered by the collapse of communism; it was meager at the outset and developed as an incremental process across the entire epoch. To answer the question as to whether foreign owners opted for vertical or horizontal structures, or shunned both, we must therefore first examine whether either or both of these structures had any lasting durability to be available to foreign investment. By adding a temporal dimension to our analysis we can thus make more meaningful inferences about the relationship between network properties and organizing practices. In our study, we identify topography as a static property; we grasp structure as a temporal property identified as a sequence of network positions. In so doing, we respond to Harrison White's challenge to make temporal analysis a key component of structural analysis:

> Social structures often are made to seem the antipodes to, or at least unrelated to details and nuances of, sequencing in timing. This is in part because of the influence of structuralism. Social times should instead be accounted as much part of structure as are network spaces. (White 1992, 77)

Building on recent efforts to bring dynamics into network analysis (Brudner and White 1997; Snijders 2001; Stuart 1998; Watts 1999; Vedres and Stark 2010), we draw on sequence analysis, a recently developed research tool that makes it possible to study historical processes in an eventful way similar to historiography while retaining social scientific abstraction (Abbott and Hrycak 1990; Abbott 1995; Han and Moen 1999; Blair-Loy 1999; Stovel, Savage, and Bearman 1996; Giuffre 1999).

With attention to temporal sequencing, we can pose and answer questions about whether experiences and strategies in the early period of extrication from state socialism had consequences for later developments. This is especially important in Hungary where the challenges facing firms were not of the same kind throughout the time frame of our investigation. In particular, the political and institutional uncertainties of the early 1990s did not continue unabated throughout the entire epoch. Important decisions by the neoliberal socialist government during the

[6] There are indications that the operation of business networks might be compatible with the structure and practices of multinational firms. To cope with the challenges of organizing across geographical and cultural distances, multinationals are increasingly structured as networks (Ghoshal and Bartlett 1990; Morgan, Kristensen, and Whitley 2001), seeking flexibility through empowering subsidiaries and embedding in interorganizational relations (Buckley and Casson 1998). Hedlund (1993), for example, suggests that multinational corporations are more heterarchical than hierarchical.

middle of the decade had emphatic policy outcomes that largely brought ad hoc government subsidies and bailouts to an end.[7] With the institutionalization of regulatory policies of corporate governance, banking, and bankruptcy, for example, uncertainties in the institutional environment were replaced by the "normal" uncertainties of a market environment.

Given this changing historical context, we need to probe the durability of positions in vertical and horizontal topographies. A firm with a durable position in a cohesive structure (C), for example, will evidence a relatively lengthy sequence in the same network position (C-C-C) across a number of years; the sequence of a firm remaining on the periphery (P) of a vertical structure will register as P-P-P; and so on. Because the environment changes during the epoch under investigation, we will be especially attentive to positional durability that begins during the earlier period and survives into the later period. Specifically, we expect to find a significant number of firms in durable positions in vertical and horizontal topographies respectively, and we expect to find such durability extending across the 1995–96 boundary between the earlier and later periods. Moreover, we specifically hypothesize that sequence pathways characterized by durable positions in vertical structures will be significantly less likely to attract foreign owners than firms in durable positions in cohesive structures.

The reasoning behind our hypothesis starts with the observations of Powell, Keister, and others that less hierarchically organized business networks offer real performance benefits over vertically structured networks. Their multiplexity provides greater opportunities to adapt more flexibly to changes in the environment. Although vertical structures might be well adapted to a given environment, they are more prone to "lock-in." That is, their centralized character increases the likelihood of temporally self-reinforcing processes in which patterns that were successful in an initial context persist even though there is no longer a performance advantage.

Foreign investors, we reason, are not averse to centralized, hierarchical structures. But, faced with two already established network structures, they will choose to gain ownership stakes in firms that have durable positions in the less hierarchical, more cohesive network topographies. This choice is especially likely in the Hungarian setting. More horizontally structured business networks can provide resources to cope with the challenges of the initial postsocialist period *and* they can be more easily repurposed if and when the political, institutional, and business environment changes. Firms in positions within such cohesive topographies that endure across the time frame are thus likely to be strong candidates for foreign investment. Vertical structures might seem to offer ready avenues for straightforward command and control, but they are less likely to be repurposed. They will not be targets for foreign takeover. And the more they endure into the later period, the less attractive they will become, leading to yet further temporally self-reinforcing processes that result in a kind of network stasis with little foreign investment.

Thus, although we start from the notion that network ties are strategic resources for firms (Kogut, Shan, and Walker 1992), we do not assume that all firms have the same strategic orientations or that firms participate in network ties in the same way. Network properties vary not only across firms in network space but also across time. As firms make and break ties, they (and those around them in network space) can reproduce or reshape network properties. As they do, they produce distinctive sequences of network structures. That is, just as we will be attentive to variation in the specific shapes of the network properties in a given firm's network locale, we will also be attentive to variation in social times. Network times and network spaces, separately and in their combination, are structuring—they enable and constrain how network ties can be deployed as resources.

We therefore posit that patterns of foreign investment can be explained not simply by the shape of network structures but by the structures of their sequencing. To test this proposition we develop an innovative synthesis of network analysis and sequence analysis.

DATA

Ownership Ties

The data set we have assembled includes the complete ownership histories of the largest enterprises in Hungary during the period 1987–2001. We define a large firm as being in

[7] A key turning point in historical processes was 1995–96. A restrictive package in 1995 ended government bailouts and state paternalism (Stark and Bruszt 1998), and 1996 was the first year GDP started growing after the postsocialist collapse.

the annual ranking of the top 500 firms (based on revenue) in any of the years from 1987 to 2001. Our inclusion rule results in a population of 1,843 firms. For a small country like Hungary, this population of firms accounts for more than a third of all employment, half of the GDP, and the overwhelming proportion of export revenues (Figyelõ 2002). The comprehensiveness of our data set is unprecedented in the literature on changing ownership structures in a transforming economy.[8]

Ownership data were transcribed by our research team directly from the twenty official Courts of Registry where Hungarian firms are obliged to register their owners. For each firm we collected the following: equity in thousand Hungarian forints, the names of the firm's top twenty-five owners, and the percentage stake that each owner holds in the company. We also have information on the date when the firm was founded and the date of filing for bankruptcy, liquidation, or cessation for any reason, that is, the date when the file of the firm was closed at the registry court. Out of the 1,843 firms, 147 ownership files were unavailable or contained little or no information on ownership. Our final data set contains the full ownership histories of 1,696 enterprises. For any given firm in any given month in our data set we can precisely identify the owners and the percentage of the assets each holds.

We define a business tie as an ownership stake that one enterprise in our population holds in another firm in the population. Our definition is restricted to direct ties (representing at least a 1 percent ownership stake) among the largest Hungarian enterprises. It does not include, for example, the numerous ownership stakes that these firms have in smaller companies. Nor do we report two firms as tied if they share a common owner, as in the more inclusive definitions of affiliation networks (Kogut and Walker 2001; Wasserman and Faust 1994). It follows that, in our population of firms, an ownership stake by the state or a foreign owner does not constitute an interorganizational tie. We have also coded owners by type, using the names of owners to classify four categories: state, Hungarian firm, Hungarian person, and foreign owner.

Political Ties

In addition to collecting data on the ownership structure of firms (to examine network ties among them) we also collected personnel data on firms (to examine network ties between firms and political parties). For each firm in our population, we gathered directly from the twenty Courts of Registry the names of all *economic officeholders*, which we define as all senior managers (e.g., CEOs, CFOs, and the like whose signatures are legally binding on the firm), all members of its board of directors, and all members of its supervisory board for the entire length of the firm's existence (with 1987 as the earliest starting point). For each economic officeholder, we record tenure in office as the month and year of accession to office and month and year of exit.

We define *political officeholders* as all elected national and local officials, including all Members of Parliament (MPs) and all local mayors, and all national-level government officials, including the prime minister, all cabinet ministers, and their politically appointed deputies. For the years prior to 1990, we include government ministers, deputies, and members of the Communist Party's Politburo and Central Committee. For the entire period examined, 1987–2001, we gathered the names of each of these political officeholders, recording their party affiliations and any changes in such. As with the economic officeholders, tenure in office is recorded on a monthly time frame.

By merging the lists of economic and political officeholders we can precisely identify (for any given enterprise) whether that company had an economic officeholder who was also a political officeholder as well as identify the party label of that officeholder.

We count a company as having a *political tie* when one of its economic officeholders is a current or former political officeholder. In the schematic shown in figure 12.1, Company A is politically affiliated with Party L because one of its officeholders, p1 , is also a current or former political officeholder in Party L. With no political tie, Company B is without political affiliation.

[8] Research projects on interenterprise ownership networks cover fewer companies, in less depth, over less time. Ferligoj, Prasnikar, and Pahor (2001), for example, have analyzed the networks of the largest Slovenian companies based on ownership and board interlock ties in 1997 and 2000. However, their analysis was cross-sectional, and their sample was limited to the top 150 firms in each of the two years in their study. Several studies outside the East European region examine panel data. Kogut and Walker (2001), for example, study ties among 550 of the largest firms in the German economy from 1994 to 1997. Keister (2001) examines 535 Chinese firms from 1988 to 1996. Her data involve forty named and already identified business groups in which the location of a given firm in a given business group is fixed by lists from 1985.

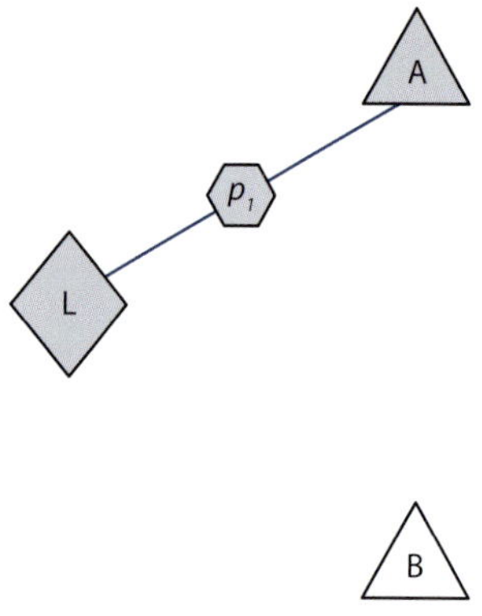

Figure 12.1 Schematic of a political tie between a firm and a party.

THE CHANGING PROPORTIONS OF THE MIXED ECONOMY

Our data set makes it possible to chart the changing configuration of the macrostructure of ownership across fifteen years of Hungary's transforming and globalizing economy. Did domestic networks grow unchecked? Did foreign investment eradicate interenterprise ownership ties? Or is Hungary a dual economy, segregated into two segments of domestically networked and foreign isolates?

To gain a picture of the evolving shape of Hungary's mixed economy, for each year from 1987 to 2001 we computed the proportion of large-firm capital in four categories: (1) firms that are isolated and domestically owned, (2) firms that are isolated and have significant foreign ownership, (3) firms with an interenterprise ownership tie and domestically owned, and (4) firms with an interenterprise ownership tie and significant foreign ownership. A significant foreign owner, in our definition, is a clearly dominant owner or, at least, a coalition partner in ownership.

Figure 12.2 presents the broad contours of the changing shape of Hungary's mixed economy across the period under study. It illustrates that alternative scenarios were open possibilities from 1991. Selective extrapolation from early trends in different categories could yield very different expected outcomes. For example, between 1989 and 1991, the networked-domestic category increased from 27 percent to 57 percent. Selective extrapolation from this dramatic growth could have suggested that networked-domestic firms would crowd out other forms of property including foreign ownership, perhaps along the antidevelopmental lines of the Russian economy (Burawoy and Krotov 1992; Johnson 1997). Similarly, focusing on the growth of the isolated-foreign category, nearly doubling between 1989 (8 percent) and 1990 (15 percent of large-firm capitalization), one could have selectively extrapolated an economy dominated by foreigners and the extinction of domestic-network forms of property (Hanley, King, and Tóth 2002). The high rate of growth of both the isolated-foreign and networked-domestic categories could have encouraged predictions about an emerging segregated dual economy (Comisso 1998).

Our findings indicate that each of the scenarios would fail to account for actual developments. In a segregated dual economy, the overwhelming majority of firm capital would be in two categories: networked-domestic and isolated-foreign. But Hungary is not a segregated dual economy,[9] nor is it an economy dominated by isolates or the networked-domestic. In 2001 the distribution of capital among the four categories was the following: isolated-domestic, 18 percent; isolated-foreign, 29 percent; networked-domestic, 26 percent; and networked-foreign, 26 percent. Although the isolated foreign-owned firms constitute the largest category, this segment of the mixed economy contains only three percentage points more capital than the foreign-owned networked category of firms.

Although the proportion of the economy that participates in interenterprise ownership ties becomes smaller, it does not—in contrast to the arguments of the transition school—dissolve. By the end of our study, 52 percent of capitalization was in firms with at least one interorganizational ownership tie with another large firm in the sample. Moreover, there is evidence indicating that the strength of a given tie has increased. In the first years of our period an average network tie represented a 20 percent ownership stake in a company. By 2001 the average tie strength is 36 percent, suggesting the consolidation rather than the dissolution of the network.

Unanticipated and unexplained by any of the three competing scenarios is the steady growth, between 1991 and 2001, of the networked-foreign category, which eventually comprised half of the networked capital.

[9] We tested the hypothesis that the foreign-owned and the domestically owned segments are not connected by network ties. Chi-square tests of the distribution of ties between and within these segments are insignificant (the smallest p-value for any year is .419). Ties between foreign-owned and domestically owned firms are just as likely as ties within these segments.

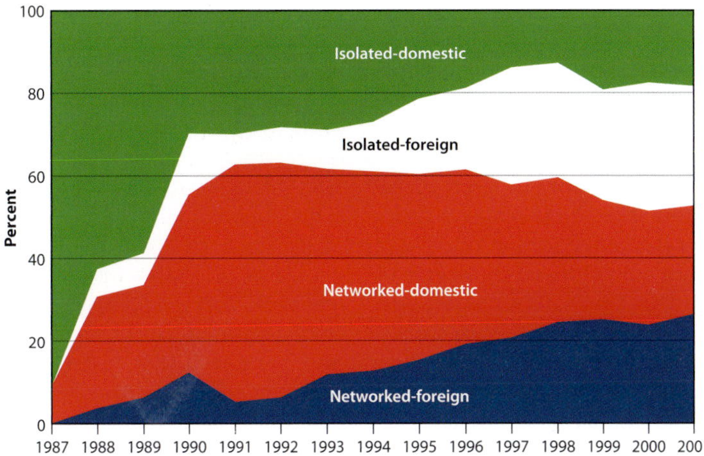

Figure 12.2 Area chart of large firm capitalization: domestic or foreign, isolated or networked.

SOCIAL SEQUENCE ANALYSIS OF NETWORK EVOLUTION

Studies of property transformation in the postsocialist setting typically focus on broad changes in the structure of property in terms of ownership categories such as state ownership, private ownership, foreign ownership, and the like. Although our macrostructural model adopted a similarly categorical approach, the microprocessual models that we develop below examine the structure of property in relational terms, focusing on its network properties. Whereas much of the recent work on network dynamics has focused on topographic properties of the global network, in particular its properties of connectedness, we start from the perspective of the individual firm and analyze its network position within a field of local action. (See also Vedres and Stark 2010.)

To isolate the distinctive processes and the variable social times that might be masked by system-level investigations, we identify patterned variation in sequences of events in the lives of firms. These events are changes in the configuration of the network properties of its local field of action. To proceed, we identify the empirically observable types of local embeddedness and elaborate the methods used to cluster sequences into typical pathways through that network space.

Identifying Local Network Positions

In analyzing the evolution of interenterprise ownership ties in Hungary, we study topography at a socially meaningful level of action. Ownership networks, we reason, differ from networks of flow. In such networks, where electricity, rumors, or contagious disease can spread along any number of steps, the most important task is to understand the global configuration of the network, the redundancy of connecting paths, and the overall structure of reachability. Ownership networks, however, have a shorter range (path distance beyond which there is no interrelatedness). Path distances beyond two steps (the owners of owners) have little importance: whereas the owner of the owner can be important, the owner of the owner of the owner has little influence in the life of a postsocialist firm. Therefore, we focus on the shapes of local network configurations, building up from ties of the focal firm and of its near network neighbors. Accordingly, we ignore the directionality of ties and use the symmetrized ownership network.

In defining local network topographies we do not posit particular *shapes* or configurations in advance. Instead, we begin by defining the *dimensions* along which focal firms' network topographies can vary. Starting from a set of elemental dimensions and applying a clustering algorithm, we identify a finite set of distinctive local network properties. For a given firm, for any year in which it existed, we can then code its position within a local topography. In place of the topographic properties of the global network for each of the fifteen years in our study, our analysis is conducted on 18,073 cases (i.e., one network position for each firm in every year that it existed). The unit of analysis is, thus, the local network position of a given firm in a given year.

We define dimensions of local network topographies in line with findings of the literature on interorganizational networks and business groups. Granovetter (1994), for example, identifies the key structural dimensions of interorganizational network as first of all the size of a firm's network as well as the configuration of its ties, especially the level of cohesion and the degree of centralization. These insights informed empirical research on the shape of business networks. As Powell et al. (2005) found for biotechnology, Keister (1998) found for China, and Huber and Wörgötter (1998) found for Russia, vertical versus horizontal structure is a key dimension of network organizing.

To capture these salient features of business networks, we define four dimensions along which local network topographies can vary. To capture size, we define the first dimension as (1) the number of alters in the focal firm's ego network. To capture the structural configurations of ties, we define three additional dimensions: (2) the average size of all alters' ego networks; (3) the cohesion of the focal firm's network; and (4) the average number of cohesive paths in all alters' ego networks.

Measuring cohesion in ownership networks (dimensions 3 and 4) is less straightforward than measuring size (dimensions 1 and 2). One starting point would be to use a clustering coefficient that measures the proportion of alters connected to one another in ego's network (Watts 1999; Davis 1970). The assumption of this measure is that the basis of cohesion is triadic closure as, for example, when two friends of a third person become friends of each other. However, an ownership network is different from a friendship network: while closed triads are uncommon, firms in cohesive ownership networks are often tied in linked quadruplets (four firms connected by at most two-step paths).[10] Thus, we take both one-step paths (direct ties) and two-step paths into account in estimating the number of alters connected.[11]

It is not the *individual* dimensions but the *patterns* across them that define the discrete shape of a given topography. Therefore, after measuring these four dimensions for each of the firm-years in our population, we ran Ward hierarchical cluster analysis (Ward 1963) on the 18,073 cases to identify patterns in the data. This cluster analysis groups cases according to their similarity across the four dimensions.

Table 12.5 presents the seven typical local network topographies derived by the cluster analysis: isolate, dyad, small star periphery, large star periphery, star center, cohesive cluster, and strongly cohesive group.[12] In the fourth column of table 12.5 we report, for each topography, the mean scores along our four dimensions. There we see, for example, that although the number of ties in the ego networks of small star periphery and large star periphery structures are nearly the same, the mean size of their alters' networks is markedly different.[13] Star centers and star peripheries, of course, lack cohesion, but the cluster analysis further distinguishes a topography that is cohesive from one that has extraordinarily strong group cohesion.

Optimal Matching Analysis of Network Sequences

The particular type of embeddedness for any given firm, in any given year, is now categorized as one of the seven positions. The network history of a firm can now be represented as a sequence of topographies. Figure 12.3 is an example of a firm's history as it moves from one type of embeddedness to another.

This firm starts as an isolate (I). After three years, it becomes the periphery (P) of a small star. In 1992 the topography of the firm's local network is a cohesive cluster (C), and, after three years, these network ties are transformed into a

[10] Ownership networks are, moreover, typically sparser than friendship networks. For a discussion, see Kogut and Walker 2001.

[11] Commonly used clustering coefficients (Davis 1970; Watts 1999) record the proportion of alters that are connected. We decided to use the number rather than the proportion of alters connected because cohesion enters into our cluster analysis along with size—measured as the number of alters. Using the proportion of connected alters as the measure of cohesion in this cluster analysis would seriously underweight this dimension.

[12] We tested the hypothesis that network transformation in this case is a product of a merely random process. This hypothesis is a plausible one, especially given the pace of institutional transformation. Firms might resort to forming ad hoc ties when pressed to hedge against radical uncertainties. Similarly, network ties might be cut at random when, for example, a new owner appears. To evaluate the random network change hypothesis we ran simulations from which we conclude that the observed changes in network ties are not products of a random process.

[13] The breakpoint between these two topographies was not determined a priori. Instead, it was empirically observable in the data. The distribution of star sizes in our data is bimodal with the two modal types represented by the two clusters (small star periphery and large star periphery).

Table 12.5.
Local Network Positions

Network position		N	Percentage of nonisolate	Means of ego network statistics	Graph illustration[a]
I.	Isolate	12,378	-	Size: 0.00 Alters' size: 0.00 Cohesion: 0.00 Alters' cohesion: 0.00	
D.	Dyad member	1,260	22.12%	Size: 1.00 Alters' size: 1.00 Cohesion: 0.00 Alters' cohesion: 0.00	
P.	Small star periphery	1,985	34.86%	Size: 1.22 Alters' size: 3.34 Cohesion: 0.00 Alters' cohesion: 0.00	
L.	Large star periphery	280	4.92%	Size: 1.05 Alters' size: 12.10 Cohesion: 0.00 Alters' cohesion: 0.00	
S.	Star center	543	9.53%	Size: 3.37 Alters' size: 1.35 Cohesion: 0.00 Alters' cohesion: 0.00	
C.	Cohesive cluster member	899	15.79%	Size: 2.84 Alters' size: 6.82 Cohesion: 0.46 Alters' cohesion: 1.20	
G.	Strongly cohesive group member	728	12.78%	Size: 2.71 Alters' size: 9.91 Cohesion: 2.40 Alters' cohesion: 8.55	
Total		18,073	100.00%		

[a] Gray node indicates local network position in graph illustrations.

strongly cohesive group (G). In 1998 the firm becomes a small star periphery again (P). At the end of the period, from 2000, the star shrinks into a dyad (D).

On this basis, we have 1,696 such network histories—sequences of positions—for each of the firms in our population. Some firms' histories, of course, are likely to resemble each other (not because they are tied to each other but because they have similar sequences of network positioning) while differing from others. Using an optimal matching algorithm modified from the analysis of gene sequencing, we construct a matrix of pairwise distances between each of the sequences.

Optimal matching of sequences is a method that historical sociology borrowed from the natural sciences. The use of optimal matching in the natural sciences typically does not involve temporality; instead, the sequences are typically spatial. One important area in the natural sciences in which optimal matching is used is DNA analysis. DNA molecules are considered to be very similar even when large chunks of the molecular sequence are in reverse order (Sankoff and Kruskal 1999). Unlike measures based on vector similarities, optimal matching has some advantages for historical application; but it has been justifiably criticized by Wu (2000) and others (Levine 2000) for its lack of sensitivity to the directionality of time. For example, a firm that is an isolate for eight years and then becomes a small star periphery in 1995 for the next

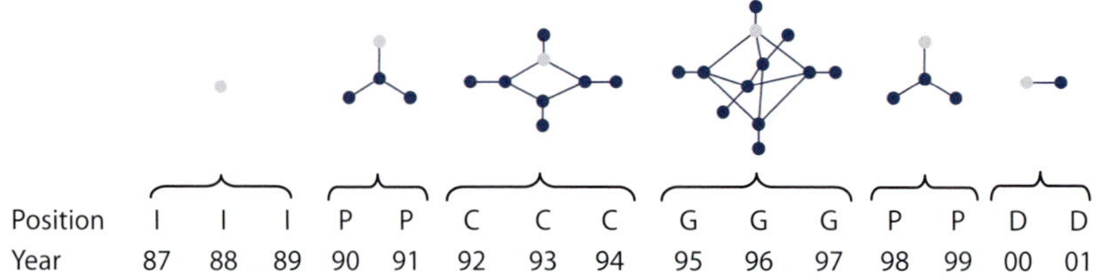

Figure 12.3 An example of a firm's network sequence.

seven years represents a radically different career compared to a firm that is a small star periphery for the first seven years and then becomes an isolate in 1995. Because the default optimal matching algorithm would group these two cases as similar, we make adjustments to the parameters of the method to maximize temporal sensitivity.

We first use optimal matching to find the distance of each sequence from all others. To the resulting matrix we then apply hierarchical clustering that groups sequences so that within-cluster distances are as low as possible and between-cluster distances are high. From among the commonly used clustering methods, we applied Ward's method as the best-fitting clustering solution.[14] The combination of these two algorithms, not unlike the concept of structural equivalence in social network analysis, yields sequential equivalence (Han and Moen 1999, 204).

Using these methods, our social sequence analysis yields twelve distinctive patterns of sequences, or pathways, through the space of local network topographies. Reducing 1,696 firm network histories to twelve pathways, we explain 59 percent of the variance in intersequence distances, indicating that a small number of pathways is a suitable representation of network evolution.

SEQUENCE PATHWAYS AND FOREIGN INVESTMENT

The resulting twelve pathways, grouped as five broad types of pathways, are presented in table 12.6, briefly summarized here, and more fully elaborated later. The first two broad types involve the forms of recombinant property—the star-shaped spin-off structures and the cohesive groupings, respectively. The third type of pathway is marked by start-up firms. Beginning as small star peripheries or dyads, ties are later broken and these firms typically, though not uniformly, exhibit sequences leading toward isolation. The fourth type shows an entirely different sequence. These are pathways in which network formation occurs after the period of greatest institutional uncertainty. Moreover, unlike the pathways in the third family, these ties do not dissipate. In fact, they are not only durable but are evolving from dyads to more complex network topographies. The fifth type comprises firms that are isolates across the entire period. Firms in this final pathway are characterized by a later start and are significantly smaller than firms in other pathways.

Table 12.6 presents, for each of the pathways, the sequence of network positions that best represents firm histories in that pathway. Cell entries (I, D, P, L, S, C, and G) correspond to the local network topographies defined in table 12.5. Enterprise histories are presented in five groups of pathways according to broad similarities in sequence patterns. The number of firms in each pathway is one way to measure their prevalence, but as a better indication of economic importance, we also list the share of each pathway in the total capitalization of the large-firm population in 2001. Recalling the macrostructure of Hungary's mixed economy represented in figure 12.2, in which the growing percentage of the networked-foreign category is the most striking feature that was neither anticipated nor explained by the three competing scenarios, table 12.6 also reports each pathway's share of networked-foreign capital at the close of our study.

To test our proposition that foreign ownership can be explained not simply by the shape

[14] We compare the fit of clustering derived from five algorithms: single link, average link, complete link, Ward (increase in sum of squares) hierarchical clustering, and CONCOR divisive clustering.The *R*-squared of a thirteen-cluster grouping by these methods are .014, .144, .349, .590, and .411, correspondingly. Thus we use Ward's method as the one that best fits our data to identify groups of similar sequences.The clusters that we identify represent a meaningful reduction of the data: the T-test of comparing within-cluster distances to between-cluster distances is -231.300.

Table 12.6.
Pathways' Typical Sequences of Network Positions

Pathways	*N*	Typical sequence of network positions[a]															Share in categories of capital in 2001 (%)	
		87	88	89	90	91	92	93	94	95	96	97	98	99	00	01	All	Networked-foreign
Star-periphery recombinants																		
1	34	I	I	I	S	S	S	S	S	S	S	S	S	S	S	S	7.1	1.4
2	106				P	P	P	P	P	P	P	P	P	P	P	P	3.8	3.0
Cohesive recombinants																		
3	70		I	I	P*	P	C	C*	C	C	C	C	C	P	P	P	18.2	36.1
4	44			C	C	C	G	G	G	G*	G	C	C	C	C	C	4.9	12.2
5	65			C	C	C	G	G	G	G	G	G*	G	I	I	I	3.6	0.6
6	56	I	I	I	I	I	I	I	I	L	L	C	C	G	G	G	7.0	6.7
Start-ups																		
7	63			P	P*	P	P	P	P	P	I	I	I	I	I	I	3.4	0.0
8	97				D	D*	D	D*	I	I	I*	I	I	I	I	I	4.2	0.3
9	70				P*	P	P	P	P	D	D*	D	D	D	D	D	3.9	8.6
Second wave networks																		
10	136	I	I	I	I	I	I	I	I	D*	D	D	D	P	P	P*	9.1	21.6
11	101											D*	D*	P	P	P	3.3	8.7
Isolates																		
12	854						I	I	I	I	I	I	I*	I	I	I	30.7	0.0
Total	1,696																100.0	100.0

Notes: I = Isolate, D = Dyad member, P = Star periphery, L = Large star periphery, S = Star center, C = Cohesive cluster member, G = Strongly cohesive group member. Asterisked figures represent surges in foreign investment when new foreign capital amounted to at least 20 percent of the total capitalization of the pathway in that year.

[a]Cells indicate network positions from table 12.2.

of network structures but by the sequencing of network positions, we use logistic regression to analyze the statistical association between sequence pathways and sizable foreign ownership in 2001. The definition of our dependent variable, sizable foreign ownership, is the same here as in the previous usage. A sizable foreign owner is a clearly dominant owner or at least a coalition partner in ownership.

The first independent variables in our model are the network pathways identified through optimal matching procedures, with the isolate pathway as the reference category. We control for three further attributes of firms, which we expect to be associated with foreign ownership. To rule out that differences between pathways are simply a function of their industrial composition, we first control for branch of industry. Our model uses eleven industry categories: agriculture, food industry, energy and mining, chemical industry, heavy industry, light industry and textiles, construction, wholesale, retail, and finance, with services and transportation as the reference category. Because foreign ownership might be associated with the latest topography rather than the sequence of positions, we next control for local network positions in 2001, with isolation as the reference category. If the inclusion of these variables leads to the loss of significance of pathway coefficients, then our arguments about sequencing become questionable. To rule out that foreign ownership in 2001 is simply a function of early foreign investment, we lastly control for whether there was sizable foreign ownership in a given firm in 1990. In line with how figure 12.2 was constructed, in the logistic regression analysis, we weight firms by their capitalization.

As model 1 in table 12.7 indicates, our sequence pathways are strongly associated with foreign ownership. This statistical association holds and, in fact without exception, becomes stronger when the control variables are included in model 2. Branch of industry and local network position at the end of the study are contributing factors in explaining foreign ownership. The significant association between early foreign ownership and sizable foreign ownership in 2001 does suggest that foreign investment displays considerable stickiness. But the statistical association between pathways and foreign ownership remains robust even when these controls are introduced.

Turning to the sequence pathways, as we saw in the detailed representations of typical sequences in table 12.6, one of the strongest findings of our optimal matching analysis is the persistence of the two forms of recombinant property. But if each of the forms are robust structures that survived the entire epoch, table 12.7 indicates they are strikingly different in terms of their likelihood to attract considerable foreign investment. Pathways in which spin-offs locked into star-periphery structures enlisted hardly any foreign investment. By contrast, two of the pathways with lengthy sequences of cohesion spanning the 1995–96 boundary were likely to have sizable foreign ownership in 2001. (Differences across the pathways in each of the families are elaborated below.)

By themselves, the pathways of the third type might suggest that foreign ownership is associated with the dissolution of network ties. However, the pathways in the fourth type, in which we find a second wave of network formation in the period of institutional stabilization of the market economy, are also significantly more likely than the isolate pathway to involve sizable foreign ownership in 2001. These recently emerging new networks involving foreign owners become organized in small star-periphery structures. As topographies, they are not dissimilar to those of the first type, shunned by foreign investors. The contrast exemplifies that sequence rather than contemporaneous topography matters in explaining foreign ownership.

In the subsections that follow we discuss these findings in greater detail with attention to the co-evolution of network formation and foreign investment.

Spin-off Star-Periphery Recombinants in a Process of Lock-in

The 140 firms in our first group of two pathways (see table 12.6) have distinctive histories of nearly continuous locations in star-periphery topographies. The typical sequences are lengthy episodes either as star centers (S-S-S-S) or as small star peripheries (P-P-P-P). These pathways indicate the process by which state-owned firms spun off corporate satellites in the period of regime change and its immediate aftermath: by 1990, most of the firms in pathways 1 and 2 were stars or the peripheries of stars.

During the period of high institutional uncertainty in the early years of postsocialism, the firms in this first group of pathways follow courses consistent with playing the game of asset-liability management, spinning off satellites, spreading risk, and shedding risk by shifting assets and liabilities among them in attempts to take advantage of state-sponsored programs

Table 12.7.
Sizable Foreign Ownership in 2001: Logistic Regression Estimates

	Sizable foreign ownership in 2001 (Yes = 1)	
Independent variables	1	2
Pathways[a]		
Star-periphery recombinants		
1(I-S)	-5.513**	-5.781**
2(P)	-.422**	-.785**
Cohesive recombinants		
3(I-P-C-P)	-.065**	.622**
4(C-G-C)	.485**	1.112**
5(C-G-I)	1.327**	2.047**
6(I-L-C-G)	-1.091**	-1.341**
Start-ups		
7(P-I)	1.565**	2.087**
8(D-I)	.342**	1.076**
9(P-D)	1.419**	2.756**
Second wave networks		
10(I-D-P)	1.218**	1.752**
11(D-P)	1.184**	1.717**
Industry[b]		
Agriculture		-2.973**
Food industry		2.779**
Energy and mining		.996**
Chemical industry		4.756**
Heavy industry		1.768**
Light industry and textiles		.378**
Construction		-.517**
Wholesale		.391**
Retail		3.695**
Finance		.359**
Local network position in 2001[c]		
D (Dyad member)	-.720**	
P (Small star periphery)	-.097**	
L (Large star periphery)	1.892**	
S (Star center)	.140**	
C (Cohesive cluster member)	-.039**	
G (Strongly cohesive group member)	-2.737**	
Early foreign ownership (1990)		4.326**
Constant	.205**	-.935**
N	1286........	1286........
-2LL	1709.03....	1326.78....
R-squared	.249...	.498...
Percentage correctly classified		66.7......
74.8......		
X^2 (df)	302.45 (11)	684.71 (28)
p-value	.000...	.000...

Notes: I = Isolate, D = Dyad member, P = Star periphery, L = Large star periphery, S = Star center, C = Cohesive cluster member, G = Strongly cohesive group member.

[a]Pathway 12 (Isolates) is the omitted category.

[b]Services and transportation is the omitted category.

[c]Local network position 1 (Isolate) is the omitted category.

** $p < .05$

of debt forgiveness. Of course, not every firm (in the whole population) that starts its network career as a small star or in its periphery stays in that position. Some firms will break off (perhaps as dyads), be sold off (perhaps becoming isolates), or become involved in local networks with more cohesion. If they did, their network histories will show different sequences, and they would not have been clustered in this group of pathways. The point is that the firms in these two pathways did not break off, were not sold off, and, for the most part, did not become involved in more cohesive ties. That is, in these two pathways we see clear evidence of path dependency: having established a pattern of network ties during the period of institutional uncertainty, these firms locked into patterns that endured throughout the epoch even after the organizational environment changed (Arthur 1989; Mahoney 2000).

How did they fare? They survived. Did they thrive? By 2001 these 140 firms (i.e., about 8 percent of the enterprises in the large-firm population) accounted for 10.9 percent of the total capitalization in that population. They are a modest but not negligible segment of the Hungarian economy. The Hungarian economy seems to have room even for path-dependent roads. Did they attract foreign investment? Scarcely. Our findings suggest that foreign investors shunned these firms. Created in the shadow of the state and likely facilitating some shady maneuverings, these ties buffered firms from uncertainty during the extrication from state socialism. But locked into these path-dependent ties, the firms in these pathways were locked out from participating with foreign investors.

Cohesive Recombinants Repurposed

Taken by itself, our first group of pathways might suggest evidence supporting the strong version of the dual economy thesis with domestic firms networked and foreign firms isolated. But that notion is quickly dispelled upon examining the network histories of firms in the second group of pathways. Here we find cohesive structures that were able to attract foreign investors.

The first part of the network history of the firms in pathway 3, like those in the first group, indicates the process of spin-offs and state-owned conglomerates. As separate firms were formed out of the divisions and workshops of the state-owned enterprises, the size of the ownership stars grew. But unlike the pathways in the first group, the firms in this pathway establish cohesion. This is maintained until 1998 when foreign owners begin consolidating their subsidiaries.

The firms in pathway 4 are involved in cohesive structures from the moment of their founding. That is, at the outset of their appearance as a corporate form they are already participating in dense ownership networks. This cohesion, moreover, increases: between 1992 and 1997, the overwhelming majority of the firms are members of strongly cohesive groups. This strong cohesion, however, is not a barrier to foreign investors: by 2001, the firms in this pathway represent 4.9 percent of overall capitalization but constitute 12.2 percent of networked-foreign capitalization.

The enterprises in these two pathways correspond to firms identified by Stark (1996) as parts of characteristically recombinant property networks. Based on comparable data collected from registry courts in 1994, complimented by ethnographic research in 1993–94, Stark's research suggested that for some of these firms, beyond maneuvering in the shadow of the state, these network ties were facilitating an active restructuring of assets. That is, recombinant property could involve creative recognition of resources and their recombination along network lines. From this research conducted during a period of extraordinarily rapid change, it remained an open question whether these network forms of property represented merely a snapshot of a fleeting process. Our findings, based on data gathered across fifteen years, indicate that this organizational form was not limited to the years of turbulent transformation, that it has been robust, and, moreover, that it has been open to a considerable amount of foreign investment. By 2001 almost one-quarter of the foreign-controlled capitalization in Hungary was in enterprises in these two pathways.

Comparing the two processes involving recombinant property forms, we found that foreign investors clearly preferred the durably cohesive structures, reaching into the cohesive groups where restructuring of assets was already taking place. Whereas the more vertical, star-periphery structures locked in, the more horizontal, collaborative, cohesive structures could be repurposed, buffering against the uncertainties of postsocialism in the early period and facilitating further restructuring with foreign participation in the later period.[15] In contrast to the vertical structures in which the relationship of peripheral

[15] Our findings thus offer further support to prior work by Powell et al. (2005) and Huber and Wörgötter (1998) on performance differences between hierarchically and collaboratively organized business groups.

firms was dependent on star centers and firms were insulated from each other, in the horizontal structures affiliated firms were legally separated entities but also interdependent units. These collaborative structures moved opportunistically, in the best sense of the term—reaching out to exploit opportunities to capture niche markets. In the process, they were more likely to be able to reach out to find foreign investors. Paradoxical only on first glance, it was the more cohesive groups that were the more outward looking.

If we had found all firms with cohesive recombinant property forms in pathways 3 and 4, we might conclude that foreign investors who reached in were then permanently captured. Cohesive networks, in that case, would prove entanglements that could not be escaped. Pathway 5 indicates that foreign investment could enter into cohesive topographies and later exit the network. In addition to this late exit another distinctive feature of this pathway is that its sequence shows an abrupt move from cohesive positions to isolation. Recall that large enterprises had spun off firms in the early part of the decade. In 1997 and 1998, some of these firms—and not only those with foreign ownership—dramatically reconfigured their holdings, shutting down or selling off firms to consolidate their positions.

Pathway 6 illustrates that not all formerly state-owned firms used recombinant network strategies to mitigate uncertainties during the period of extrication from state socialism. Unlike the firms in the recombinant pathways, the firms in this pathway, during their long episode of state ownership, are isolated from any network ties. They are privatized in 1995 and simultaneously enter the network as peripheries of large stars. Then, after 1996—exactly when the period of institutional uncertainty is waning—they gain cohesion, which further increases to strong cohesion. Unlike pathways 3 and 4, however, where cohesion could coexist with foreign participation, in this case, cohesion is not compatible with foreign investment. In itself, being in a cohesive network—even being in a cohesive structure at a critical time—does not ensure foreign investment. In 1997–98, pathways 3, 4, 5, and 6 are all in cohesive clusters or strongly cohesive groups. But pathway 6 is considerably less likely to involve foreign investors.

Creating cohesive networks from the outset has a different meaning than creating them after a long episode of clutching onto the state. For the former, dense networks promoted a process of restructuring, a creative cohesion; for the latter, dense ties fostered a defensive cohesion that, while not entirely excluding foreign investment, was not as open to it.

Start-ups Establishing a Foothold

Whereas the first two processes revealed in table 12.6 involve firms that begin their careers as state-owned enterprises or as spin-offs of these, the third process involves start-ups. Many of these new start-ups begin their organizational lives with foreign participation; others acquire foreign investment soon after their establishment. In the transition framework, such new ventures would be unlikely candidates for network participation. But foreign investors were not immune to the uncertainties of postsocialism; as we see in pathways 7, 8, and 9, they, too, use network ties—especially in the earlier period of economic transformation up to the middle of the 1990s—as a buffer against uncertainties in policy preferences and changing institutions.

In these pathways, foreign owners are participating in partnerships with state-owned firms as well as enterprises whose owner is another Hungarian corporation. These three pathways represent best the script expected by the previously discussed recent literature on foreign investment in which the foreign actors use network ties as part of strategies for establishing a foothold in the economy at a time when foreign investors were not yet commonplace. As we see in the sequences through the space of local network positions, some of these ties are long-lasting; but many are temporary, terminating as legitimacy is established, regulatory uncertainties are mitigated, locally specific knowledge is acquired, and operations are running smoothly. In the case of pathway 8, where foreign companies found new ventures, they tend to co-operate for a relatively short episode as dyads before buying out the domestic partner and thus transforming the joint venture into a wholly owned subsidiary. When foreign investors engage in joint venture strategies with firms that are embedded in denser network ties (in pathway 7), they tend to stay in these positions relatively longer before exiting. In pathway 9 the joint venture survives the entire period, becoming dyads after other ties have been cut in 1995.

Foreign-Led Network Formation

Although the overall network tends to lose ties and cohesion after 1995, the firms in our fourth group of pathways go against this trend in a process of foreign-led network formation.

Like the firms in pathways 1, 3, and 6, the firms in pathway 10 have the longest histories, beginning as state-owned enterprises from the period before the regime change. But they also display relatively lengthy periods as isolates in the early stages. That is, these firms are not only relative latecomers to privatization, but they were also not involved in interorganizational ownership ties with other firms while they were state owned. Firms in pathway 10 enter the network after privatization—in marked contrast to the transition framework that expects that severance of state ownership will be followed by severance of interorganizational ties.

The newest firms in our population, representing the latest developments in network processes, are in pathway 11. Although their organizational lives are much shorter than those of the firms in pathway 10, the two pathways are part of a common process. In each case foreign investors establish joint ventures; but then alongside increasing foreign participation comes rearrangement and rebuilding of network ties (in the sequence of their network positions they move from being in a dyad to being a part of a star-shaped group). The networking represented by these pathways is initiated by foreign subsidiaries. These foreign-held companies are establishing ties with each other and are spinning off their own subsidiaries. That is, foreign investors in this case are not consolidating but expanding the firms' networks. By 2001, this process of foreign-led network formation accounted for more than 30 percent of networked-foreign capitalization. In this process, we find FDI not as foreign direct insulation but as foreign-directed embedding.

In the start-up logic, foreign firms create a tie with another company, learn from it, and then typically cut the ties. In the process of foreign-led network formation, however, the sequence goes from a simpler to a more embedded topography. Unlike the earlier, domestic network groups, foreign subsidiaries start building networks from the most elementary form (a dyad) and add ties in a gradual way. The different sequences suggest responses to different environments: Whereas the economic context for the evolution of domestic networks in the late 1980s and early 1990s was radical institutional uncertainty and the formation of joint ventures in the early 1990s represented a strategy to gain legitimacy in a period of political uncertainty, the context of the evolution of foreign-initiated business groups in the mid-1990s is market competition. In contrast to firms whose existence predated the collapse of the state-socialist economy, foreign firms are relatively more isolated and atomized actors in the economy; nonetheless, they take their positions in chains of inputs and outputs. Foreign owners decide to secure some of their inputs by establishing ownership ties to Hungarian firms and start to build business groups similar to those that are integral practices in their home countries (Granovetter 1994; Mizruchi and Galaskiewicz 1994; Podolny 1994; Lincoln, Gerlach, and Ahmadjian 1996).

In doing so, they come into competition with the homegrown networks initiated by postsocialist enterprises. The distinction between foreign-grown and domestically evolving networks is not only an analytic comparison but one that actors in the field note as well. Our interviews with corporate consultants indicate that there is often a manifest competition between foreign firms and domestic business groups to buy shares in a valuable supplier, thereby tying it to either a domestic or foreign-driven group.

Isolation

The fifth process is isolation. Firms in the final pathway are characterized by a relatively late start; none was ever part of the ownership network. Smaller than average, in their capitalization these always isolated firms are only 44 percent as large as the capitalization of the average firm in all the other pathways. Consequently, although about half of the firms in our population are in this pathway, they represent only 30.7 percent of the population's capital.

For the population as a whole, foreign investment increased with almost perfect linearity across the time period.[16] But as the asterisked figures in table 12.6 indicate, this linearity in the overall population masks pronounced punctuation at the level of pathways—a further indication that social sequence analysis is tapping distinctive processes of foreign investment. Cohesive recombinants have early, multiple surges of foreign investment; spin-off star structures have none at all; and the processes of start-ups and foreign-led network formation show yet different punctuations. Firms in isolate pathway 12 received a surge of foreign investment in 1997. Always isolated firms do not have a disproportionate share of foreign capital: at 30.4 percent, their share of total foreign capitalization is al-

[16] As a test of linearity we have fitted regression lines to the trends of decreasing state ownership and increasing foreign ownership. The R-squared of a linear trend line is 0.97 for state ownership and 0.98 for foreign ownership.

most exactly the same as their share of capital altogether (30.7 percent).

NETWORK SEQUENCES AND POLITICAL TIES

Our social sequence analysis was based on the ownership ties among enterprises. But firms can also have ties to other actors, most significantly, if not problematically, to political parties. In this concluding section we briefly examine the role of political ties in explaining patterns of foreign investment.

Recent studies of political cohesion among corporate elites in developed market economies demonstrate that network structures of interlocking directors explain the speed of adaptation of governance practices (Davis and Greve 1997) and that firms that are linked through interlocking directors are more likely to take similar positions on legislative matters (Mizruchi 1992). Burris (2001, 2005) has examined political behavior among the top officers of the 1,050 largest U.S. companies, operationalizing political behavior as contributions to political candidates in the 1980 elections. Using quadratic assignment (QAP) regression on the 289,180 dyads of the 761 presidential contributors in his sample population, Burris finds that social ties through common membership on corporate boards "contribute more to similarity of political behavior than commonalities of economic interests, such as those associated with operating in the same industry or the same geographic region" (Burris 2005, 249).

These studies are part of a wave of empirical research launched after the Federal Election Commission provided machine-readable data, starting in 1978. Widespread availability of these data made campaign contributions the data of choice for political sociologists studying the U.S. corporate elite. Such data are not available for Hungary because political financing in Hungary is not organized around contributions to the campaigns of politicians (Juhasz 2001). Sparing the reader the complexities of Hungarian electoral law, candidates for Parliament do not run as individuals but rather on party lists. In effect, no one contributes to a given politician's campaign.

The absence of campaign contributions to individual candidates does not mean that firms are not a resource for parties. Nor does the absence of data on campaign contributions mean that we cannot find data on firm-party linkages in Hungary. Firms can appoint political officeholders to their boards of directors,[17] compensating them quite handsomely in many cases as well as providing other resources (cars, clerical and other support staff, etc.).[18] Whereas in the United States corporations and their executives contribute to politicians' electoral campaigns, in Hungary companies put politicians on their payrolls. Through the appointment of a particular politician who ran on a party list, a firm creates bonds with a party. Through these directors, firms can influence rule-making and gain access to timely information about government contracts, industrial and trade policies, and changes in regulatory policies and enforcement. The business director/political officeholder thus constitutes a direct link between firm and party.

To examine how political ties are related to foreign investment, we exploit the personnel ties that were a part of our data collection. Recall that in addition to ownership ties among firms, we also constructed the complete list of economic officeholders in our population (the senior managers as well as the members of the boards of directors and supervisory boards of each of the 1,696 firms). We further constructed a complete list of political officeholders in Hungary. That list comprises members of the Politburo and the Central Committee (for the period 1987–90), government ministers, their deputies, and all elected officials including Members of Parliament and every mayor in the country, with party affiliations for each official. By merging the data sets, we can identify a company as having a political tie when one of its economic officeholders is a current or former political officeholder.

Such political ties are far from negligible in the contemporary Hungarian political economy. In 2001, the last year for which we collected data in the current study, 43.5 percent of the large-firm capitalization was in enterprises with at least one such political tie. By analyzing the

[17] Hungarian regulations on conflicts of interest differ from U.S. law. Moreover, such legal regulations change during the two decades of our study. Until the mid-1990s, for example, cabinet ministers were not prohibited from serving as board members. Some restrictions were later placed on sitting politicians.

[18] In interviews with economic and political elites, we learned that a considerable part of the work of the directors of party finance is coordinating such corporate directorships. In party-firm negotiations, parties frequently nominate a list of several of their politicians as candidates for directorship appointments. We inquired about whether it matters that the candidate is a current or ex-politician. The reply, with muted laughter at our naiveté: "In Hungary, there is no such thing as an *ex*-politician."

Table 12.8.
Capitalization in Firms with Political Ties in 2001

	Domestic	Foreign	Total
Isolated	48.4	11.5	25.8
Networked	74.2	44.7	59.3
Total	63.5	27.3	43.5

2001 data on political ties in terms of the two by two table that structured figure 12.1, we can further identify some systematic relationships between the isolated versus networked component and the domestic versus foreign component of Hungary's mixed economy. Comparing the row marginals in table 12.8, we see first that capitalization in firms that were "networked" in 2001 (i.e., firms with at least one direct ownership tie to another firm in the population in that year) was more than twice as likely (59.3 versus 25.8 percent) to have a political tie than capitalization in firms that were "isolated" in 2001 (i.e., without direct ownership ties to any other firm in that year). Having a business tie obviously correlates with having a political tie.

Comparing the column marginals, we see that political ties are much more frequent in domestic firms than in firms with significant foreign ownership: whereas political ties appear among 63.5 percent of the capitalization in firms under domestic control, only 27.3 percent of the foreign-controlled capitalization is in firms with political ties. In general terms, foreign ownership is negatively correlated with political ties.

But we should not conclude from these findings that foreign capital has an absolute aversion to political ties. As the column marginal indicates, more than a quarter of the capital in foreign-dominated firms have an economic officeholder who is also a current or former political officeholder. Most telling is the relatively high proportion of political ties among firms that are networked and foreign. Whereas among the domestically controlled firms the proportion of those with political ties increases from 48.4 to 74.2 percent as we move from the isolated to the networked component, among foreign-dominated firms the networked component is almost four times more likely to have political ties than is the isolated component (44.7 percent compared to 11.7 percent). If, for firms in general, having business ties significantly increases the likelihood of also having political ties, this relationship is even stronger for firms that are foreign dominated.

Our final analytic move repeats the broader architecture of our overall argument. Recall that our analysis started in the third section with the macrostructural overview presented in figure 12.1 based on the dichotomies of isolated-networked and domestic-foreign. In the fourth section we moved from simple notions of embedding-nonembedding to chart the specific properties of local network topographies. And in the fifth section we demonstrated that it was not the topographies themselves but the specific histories, or sequences, of network topographies that explained foreign investment in 2001, summarized in tables 12.6 and 12.7. Thus far, our analysis of political ties has stayed within the framework of dichotomies. In table 12.9 we present our findings about the relationship between FDI and political ties within the framework of the observed network sequences.

Table 12.9 indicates that social sequence analysis of network topographies provides analytic leverage in understanding the complexities of FDI in relationship to the ties of firms to political parties. In the first column of the table, we present the network pathways identified by the modified optimal matching techniques. The second column presents the proportion of capital in each pathway that is involved in firms with political ties, and the third column presents the proportion of capital in each pathway that involves significant foreign ownership.

As table 12.9 indicates, firms of the start-up type, pathways 7, 8, and 9, as well as those of the second wave networks, pathways 10 and 11, conform to the pattern that we might expect if we knew only that foreign-dominated firms generally tend to avoid political ties. In each of these five pathways, relatively low levels of political ties correspond to relatively high levels of foreign ownership. These relationships become somewhat more complex in the two pathways, labeled star-periphery recombinants, where we found that firms locked in very early to a specific topography. The firms in pathway 2 that locked in as the peripheries of stars are about as likely to have political ties as those of the start-ups and the second-wave networks (22.7 percent); and, like those in pathways 10 and 11, they conclude in the peripheral (P) local network topography. But they are significantly less likely to have foreign ownership. In an extreme form, pathway 1 shows that the combination of locking in as star recombinants with high levels of political ties ensures that there will be little foreign investment. Only 5.2 percent of the capitalization

Table 12.9.
Network Sequence Pathways, Political Ties, and Foreign Ownership

Pathways		Capitalization (%)	
		Politicized	Foreign owned
Star-periphery recombinants			
	1(I-S)	7.6	5.2
	2(P)	22.7	44.8
Cohesive recombinants			
	3(I-P-C-P)	75.1	53.6
	4(C-G-C)	70.1	65.8
	5(C-G-I)	5.0	79.3
	6(I-L-C-G)	54.8	29.2
Start-ups			
	7(P-I)	21.7	76.1
	8(D-I)	23.7	61.3
	9(P-D)	19.7	79.0
Second wave networks			
	10(I-D-P)	19.4	79.3
	11(D-P)	19.2	77.1
Isolates			
	12(I)	30.3	55.0
Total	43.5	55.5	

Notes: I = Isolate, D = Dyad member, P = Star periphery, L = Large star periphery, S = Star center, C = Cohesive cluster member, G = Strongly cohesive group member.

of the firms in this pathway is in foreign hands. In fact, we would be justified in speculating that for these firms, having ties to political parties is a substitute for having ties to foreign capital.

That speculation would not, however, be justified for the firms in the cohesively recombinant pathways 3 and 4. Firms in pathway 3 (sequence I-P-C-P) have the highest levels of political ties, with 75 percent of the capitalization in firms with a tie to a political party, but they are just slightly below the average for the entire large-firm population in their levels of foreign ownership (53.6 percent of the capitalization has sizable foreign ownership). Firms in pathway 4, too, are significantly more likely to have political ties (70 percent), and they have high levels of foreign ownership.[19] In these cases, foreign direct investment is compatible with lengthy histories of cohesive business ties *and* with high levels of linkage to political parties. Not as a general rule *but through specific histories*, firms can be cohesively tied to other firms, closely tied to political parties, and strongly linked to foreign capital.

[19] As we observed in the detailed discussion of the pathways in the previous section, the firms in pathway 5 exit the network following a large burst of FDI (with a one-year delay). Firms in this pathway are the least likely among all the pathways to have political ties (only 5 percent of the capitalization) and are among the most likely to have sizable foreign investment (79.3 percent). Recall that pathway 6 represents firms that begin as isolates and are latecomers to cohesion. In 2001 they have above average levels of political ties and below-average levels of foreign investment.

CONCLUSION

By the term *mixed economy* political economists have typically referred to a mix of private and state ownership. Those categories remain meaningful, but it is worth reflecting on the extent to which they were part of the discourse of the cold war. In that context, the very term *mixed economy* pointed to a real possibility that a given national economy might, in actual practice, combine features—of markets and planning, of private and public property—that were portrayed not only as antagonistic but as mutually exclusive.

In this chapter we also use the term *mixed economy*. But here we refer not to a mix of state and private property but to an economy that is a mix of foreign and domestic, of networked and isolated, firms. Yet whereas we have given the term new content, our intent, at another level, shares much with that of the earlier coinage, here signaling limitations of either/or choices in the discourse about globalization. Our findings about Hungary's contemporary mixed economy show that developing economies do not necessarily face a forced choice between networks of global reach and those of local embeddedness. High levels of foreign investment can be integrated into processes of interorganizational ownership network formation in a developing economy. Just as interorganizational ownership networks blurred the boundary between state and private ownership in the early 1990s, from the mid-1990s onward, globally linked and domestically integrated business networks blur the boundary between foreign and domestic ownership.

How distinctive is Hungary? Do other postsocialist economies show a similar profile? Is the large-firm sector in Russia predominantly networked and domestic? Across the region, from the Baltics to the Balkans, what are the national distributions across our four cells of networked-domestic, networked-foreign, isolated-domestic, and isolated-foreign? Our findings invite comparisons among a broader range of cases in various parts of the developing world. A new agenda for the sociology of economic development would call for investigations on the interaction of foreign investment and network evolution comparable to that presented for a fifteen-year period in Hungary (see figure 12.2) in countries such as Argentina, Brazil, Vietnam, the Philippines, and South Africa. In short, our methodology to chart the evolving shape of Hungary's mixed economy provides a strong basis for further comparative research across a broad range of developing economies.

The language of "mixed economy," useful for macrostructural overviews, should give way to concepts that are more relational than categorical when attempting to understand the processes of economic transformation. Our approach to property transformation beyond a simple transition from state to private ownership and instead as restructurings of network properties is an example of this shift from categorical to relational concepts. Similarly, in place of thinking about a simple mix—a whole with identifiably distinctive parts—we think about mixtures in which the units themselves are combinatory and generative.

Our findings about recombinant property are especially instructive in this light. The motivating question of this study has been less whether national ownership patterns can endure than whether they can be adaptive. Networks provide domestic and foreign actors with resources and opportunities to transform structures. As Powell et al. (2005) demonstrate, interorganizational ties not only respond to institutional environments but can also change them (see also Padgett 2001). Our study of pathways of property transformation found that the most cohesive type of recombinant property is most likely to involve the participation of foreign investors. This finding indicates that it would be a mistake to characterize networks of recombinant property as mere holdovers of state socialism, as reactionary or backward-looking agents that freeze action or resist change. If they were a legacy of the informal networks of state socialism, they were not, for that reason, condemned to merely replicate themselves. Network structures, like other social patternings, can be repurposed. The cohesive pathways of recombinant property show such generative reformulation (Sabel and Zeitlin 1997), first as agents of asset restructuring and later, as this study demonstrates, with potential open to foreign investors. Hungary's transformation from state socialism to an emerging market economy with sizable foreign investment did not occur despite its interorganizational property networks but, in part, because of and through these networks.

To produce a sociological account of historical change we developed a social sequence analysis. Network analysis has made important strides in moving from static to dynamic modeling. Our goal in this chapter has been to take the next step—from dynamic network analysis to historical network analysis (Vedres and Stark 2010). We adopt an approach to understanding historical change that is different from categorical studies of transition (e.g., from state ownership to private property) and from dynamic modeling of network systems. In these other approaches, because change is a system-level phenomenon, structure and temporality are both conceptualized at the system level. In our view, by contrast, the transformation of a national economy is not a unitary process obeying a single logic but is formed out of the interweaving of multiple processes with distinctive temporalities (Stark and Bruszt 2001). Instead of collapsing time to before-after dichotomies (as in transition models) or introducing time as a variable (as in dynamic network models), we are alert to the variable structuring of time across different processes.

Thus, in place of properties of the global network, we focus on variation in local properties.

In place of a single system time, we model the processes of social times. In taking up Harrison White's (1992, 77) challenge to make social times as much a part of structure as are network spaces, our contribution to a more historical network analysis does not simply include time as a variable but, instead, recognizes time as variable.

REFERENCES

Abbott, Andrew. 1995. "Sequence Analysis: New Methods for Old Ideas." *Annual Review of Sociology* 21:93–113.

———. 1997. "Of Time and Space: The Contemporary Relevance of the Chicago School." *Social Forces* 75:1149–82.

Abbott, Andrew, and Alexandra Hrycak. 1990. "Measuring Resemblance in Sequence Data: An Optimal Matching Analysis of Musicians' Careers." *American Journal of Sociology* 96:144–85.

Arthur, Brian W. 1989. "Competing Technologies, Increasing Returns, and Lock-In by Historical Events." *Economic Journal* 99(394):116–31.

Bair, Jennifer, and Gary Gereffi. 2003. "Upgrading, Uneven Development, and Jobs in the North American Apparel Industry." *Global Networks* 3:143–69.

Blair-Loy, Mary. 1999. "Career Patterns of Executive Women in Finance: An Optimal Matching Analysis." *American Journal of Sociology* 104:1346–97.

Böröcz, József. 2001. "Change Rules." *American Journal of Sociology* 106:1152–68.

Brudner, Lilyan A., and Douglas R. White. 1997. "Class, Property, and Structural Endogamy: Visualizing Networked Histories." *Theory and Society* 26:161–208.

Bruszt, Laszlo, and David Stark. 2003. "Who Counts?: Supranational Norms and Societal Needs." *East European Politics and Societies* 17(1):74–82.

Buckley, Peter J., and Mark C. Casson. 1998. "Models of the Multinational Enterprise." *Journal of International Business Studies* 29:21–44.

Burawoy, Michael. 1996. "The State and Economic Involution: Russia through a Chinese Lens." *World Development* 24:1105–17.

Burawoy, Michael, and Pavel Krotov. 1992. "The Soviet Transition from Socialism to Capitalism: Worker Control and Economic Bargaining in the Wood Industry." *American Sociological Review* 57: 16–38.

Burris, Val. 2001. "The Two Faces of Capital: Corporations and Individual Capitalists as Political Actors." *American Sociological Review* 66(3):361–81.

———. 2005. "Interlocking Directorates and Political Cohesion among Corporate Elites." *American Journal of Sociology* 111(1):249–83.

Comisso, Ellen. 1998. "'Implicit' Development Strategies in Central and East Europe and Cross-National Production Networks." Berkeley Roundtable on International Economy Working paper. University of California–Berkeley.

Davis, James A. 1970. "Clustering and Hierarchy in Interpersonal Relations: Testing Two Graph Theoretical Models on 742 Sociomatrices." *American Sociological Review* 35(5):843–51.

Davis, Gerald F., and Heinrich R. Greve. 1997. "Corporate Elite Networks and Governance Changes in the 1980s." *American Journal of Sociology* 103(1):1–37.

Dicken, P., M. Forsgren, and A. Malmberg. 1994. "The Local Embeddedness of Transnational Corporations." In *Holding down the Global: Possibilities for Local Economic Prosperity*, ed. Ash Amin and Nigel Thrift, 23–45. Oxford: Oxford University Press.

Evans, Peter B. 1995. *Embedded Autonomy: States and Industrial Transformation*. Princeton: Princeton University Press.

Ferligoj, Anuska, Janez Prasnikar, and Marko Pahor. 2001. "Ownership and Board Interlock Networks of the Largest Slovenian Firms." Unpublished manuscript, Ljubljana University.

Figyelõ. 2002. "Kétszázakklubja 2001." In *Figyelõ Top 200*.

Gereffi, Gary, and Stephanie Fonda. 1992. "Regional Paths to Development." *Annual Review of Sociology* 18:419–48.

Ghoshal, Sumantra, and Christopher A. Bartlett. 1990. "The Multinational Corporation as an Interorganizational Network." *Academy of Management Review* 15:603–25.

Giuffre, Katherine. 1999. "Sandpiles of Opportunity: Success in the Art World." *Social Forces* 77:815–32.

Gnyavali Devi R., and Ravindranath Madhavan. 2001. "Cooperative Networks and Competitive Dynamics: A Structural Embeddedness Perspective." *Academy of Management Review* 26(3):431–45.

Grabher, Gernot. 1994. "The Dis-Embedded Economy: The Transformation of East German Industrial Complexes into Western Enclosures." In *Globalization, Institutions, and Regional Development in Europe*, ed. Ash Amin and Nigel Thrift, 177–96. Oxford: Oxford University Press.

Granovetter, Mark. 1994. "Business Groups." In *The Handbook of Economic Sociology*, ed. Neil J. Smelser and Richard Swedberg, 453–75. Princeton: Princeton University Press.

Guillen, Mauro F. 2000. "Business Groups in Emerging Economies: A Resource-Based View." *Academy of Management Journal* 43(3):362–80.

Han, Shin-Kap, and Phyllis Moen. 1999. "Clocking Out: Temporal Patterning of Retirement." *American Journal of Sociology* 105:191–236.

Hanley, Eric, Lawrence King, and István János Tóth. 2002. "The State, International Agencies, and Property Transformation in Postcommunist Hungary." *American Journal of Sociology* 108:129–67.

Hardy, Jane. 1998. "Cathedrals in the Desert? Transnationals, Corporate Strategy and Locality in Wroclaw." *Regional Studies* 32:639–52.

Hedlund, Gunnar. 1993. "Assumptions of Hierarchy and Heterarchy, with Applications to the Management of the Multinational Corporation." In *Organization Theory and the Multinational Corporation*, ed. Sumantra Ghoshal and Eleanor D. Westney, 211–36. New York: St. Martin's Press.

Hellman, Joel. 1998. "Winners Take All: The Politics of Partial Reform in Postcommunist Transitions." *World Politics* 50(2):203–34.

Huber, P., and A. Wörgötter. 1998. "Political Survival or Entrepreneurial Development? Observations on Russian Business Networks." In *The Tunnel at the End of the Light: Privatization, Business Networks, and Economic Transformation in Russia*, ed. Stephen S. Cohen, Andrew Schwartz, and John Zysman, 51–65. Berkeley: University of California, International and Area Studies Research Series, no. 100.

Inkpen, Andrew C., and Paul W. Beamish. 1997. "Knowledge, Bargaining Power, and the Instability of International Joint Ventures." *Academy of Management Review* 22:177–202.

Johnson, Juliet. 1997. "Russia's Emerging Financial-Industrial Groups." *Post-Soviet Affairs* 13:333–65.

Juhasz, Gabor. 2001. *Partpenzugyek* (Party Finances). Budapest: Aula.

Keister, Lisa A. 1998. "Engineering Growth: Business Group Structure and Firm Performance in China's Transition Economy." *American Journal of Sociology* 104(2):404–40.

———. 2001. "Exchange Structures in Transition: Lending and Trade Relations in Chinese Business Groups." *American Sociological Review* 66:336–60.

Kogut, Bruce. 1988. "Joint Ventures: Theoretical and Empirical Perspectives." *Strategic Management Journal* 9:319–32.

———. 1991. "Joint Ventures and the Option to Expand and Acquire." *Management Science* 37:19–33.

Kogut, Bruce, and Gordon Walker. 2001. "The Small World of Germany and the Durability of National Networks." *American Sociological Review* 66: 317–35.

Kogut, Bruce, W. Shan, and Gordon Walker. 1992. "The Make-or-Cooperate Decision in the Context of an Industry Network." In *Networks and Organizations: Structure, Form and Action*, ed. Nitrin Nohria and R. G. Eccles, 348–65. Boston: Harvard Business School Press.

Kristensen, Peer Hull, and Jonathan Zeitlin. 2004. *Local Players in Global Games: The Strategic Constitution of a Multinational Corporation*. Oxford: Oxford University Press.

Levine, Joel H. 2000. "But What Have You Done for Us Lately?" *Sociological Methods and Research* 29: 34–40.

Lincoln, James R., Michael L. Gerlach, and Christina L. Ahmadjian. 1996. "Keiretsu Networks and Corporate Performance in Japan." *American Sociological Review* 61:67–88.

Mahoney, James. 2000. "Path Dependence in Historical Sociology." *Theory and Society* 29(4):83–94.

McDermott, Gerald A. 1997. "Renegotiating the Ties That Bind: The Limits of Privatization in the Czech Republic." In *Restructuring Networks in Postsocialism: Legacies, Linkages, and Localities*, ed. Gernot Grabher and David Stark, 70–106. Oxford: Oxford University Press.

McMenamin, Iain, and Roger Schoenman. 2007. "Together Forever? Explaining Exclusivity in Party-Firm Relations." *Political Studies* 55(1): 153–73.

Miner, Anne S., Terry L. Amburgey, and Timothy M. Stearns. 1990. "Interorganizational Linkages and Population Dynamics: Buffering and Transforming Shields." *Administrative Science Quarterly* 35(4): 689-713.

Mizruchi, Mark S. 1992. *The Structure of Corporate Political Action: Interfirm Relations and Their Consequences*. Cambridge, MA: Harvard University Press.

Mizruchi, Mark S., and Joseph Galaskiewicz. 1994. "Networks of Interorganizational Relations." In *Advances in Social Network Analysis*, ed. Stanley Wasserman and Joseph Galaskiewicz, 230–53. Thousand Oaks, CA: Sage Publications.

Morgan, Glenn, Peer Hull Kristensen, and Richard Whitley. 2001. *The Multinational Firm: Organizing across Institutional and National Divides*. Oxford: Oxford University Press.

Padgett, John F. 2001. "Organizational Genesis, Identity, and Control: The Transformation of Banking in Renaissance Florence." In *Networks and Markets*, ed. James Rauch and Alessandra Casella, 211–57. New York: Russell Sage Foundation.

Padgett, John F., and Christopher K. Ansell. 1993. "Robust Action and the Rise of the Medici, 1400–1434." *American Journal of Sociology* 98:1259–1319.

Pavlinek, Petr, and Adrian Smith. 1998. "Internationalization and Embeddedness in East-Central European Transition: The Contrasting Geographies of Inward Investment in the Czech and Slovak Republics." *Regional Studies* 32:619–38.

Podolny, Joel M. 1994. "Market Uncertainty and the Social Character of Economic Exchange." *Administrative Science Quarterly* 39:458–83.

Powell, Walter W., Kenneth Koput, Douglas R. White, and Jason Owen-Smith. 2005. "Network Dynamics and Field Evolution: The Growth of Interorganizational Collaboration in the Life Sciences." *American Journal of Sociology* 110(4):1132–1205.

Rohver, Götz, and Ulrich Pötter. 2002. "TDA: A Program for Transition Data Analysis." Ruhr-Universität Bochum, Germany.

Róna-Tas, Ákos. 1998. "Path Dependence and Capital Theory: Sociology of the Post–Communist Economic Transformation." *East European Politics and Societies* 12:107–31.

Sabel, Charles F., and Jonathan Zeitlin. 1997. "Stories, Strategies, Structures: Rethinking Historical Alternatives to Mass Production." In *World of Possibilities: Flexibility and Mass Production in Western Industrialization*, ed. Charles F. Sabel and Jonathan

Zeitli, 1–33. Cambridge: Cambridge University Press.

Sankoff, David, and Joseph P. Kruskal. 1999. *Time Warps, String Edits and Macromolecules: The Theory & Practice of Sequence Comparison*. Stanford: CSLI Publications.

Schoenman. Roger. 2005. "Captains or Pirates? State-Business Relations in Post-Socialist Poland." *East European Politics and Societies* 19(1):40–75.

Snijders, Tom A. B. 2001. "The Statistical Evaluation of Social Network Dynamics." *Sociological Methodology* 31(1):361–95.

Spicer, Andrew, Gerald A. McDermott, and Bruce Kogut. 2000. "Entrepreneurship and Privatization in Central Europe: The Tenuous Balance between Destruction and Creation." *Academy of Management Review* 25:630–49.

Stark, David. 1990. "Privatization in Hungary: From Plan to Market or from Plan to Clan?" *East European Politics and Societies* 4(3):351–92.

———. 1992. "Path Dependence and Privatization Strategies in East Central Europe." *East European Politics and Societies* 6(1):17–53.

———. 1996. "Recombinant Property in East European Capitalism." *American Journal of Sociology* 101:993–1027.

———. 2001. "Ambiguous Assets for Uncertain Environments: Heterarchy in Postsocialist Firms." In *The Twenty-First-Century Firm: Changing Economic Organization in International Perspective*, ed. Paul DiMaggio, 69–104. Princeton: Princeton University Press.

Stark, David, and Laszlo Bruszt. 1998. *Postsocialist Pathways: Transforming Politics and Property in East Central Europe*. New York: Cambridge University Press.

———. 2001. "One Way or Multiple Paths?: For a Comparative Sociology of East European Capitalism." *American Journal of Sociology* 106(4):1129–37.

Stovel, Katherine. 2001. "Local Sequential Patterns: The Structure of Lynching in the Deep South, 1882–1930." *Social Forces* 79(3):843–80.

Stovel, Katherine, Michael Savage, and Peter Bearman. 1996. "Ascription into Achievement: Models of Career Systems at Lloyds Bank, 1890–1970." *American Journal of Sociology* 102:358–99.

Stuart, Toby E. 1998. "Network Positions and Propensities to Collaborate: An Investigation of Strategic Alliance Formation in a High-Technology Industry." *Administrative Science Quarterly* 43: 668–98.

Uhlir, David. 1998. "Internationalization, and Institutional and Regional Change: Restructuring Post-communist Networks in the Region of Lanskroun, Czech Republic." *Regional Studies* 32(7):673–85.

Uzzi, Brian. 1997. "Social Structure and Competition in Interfirm Networks: The Paradox of Embeddedness." *Administrative Science Quarterly* 42:35–67.

Uzzi, Brian, and Jarrett Sprio. 2005. "Collaboration and Creativity: The Small World Problem." *American Journal of Sociology* 111(2):447–504.

Vedres, Balázs. 2000. "The Constellations of Economic Power: The Position of Political Actors, Banks and Large Corporations in the Network of Directorate Interlocks in Hungary, 1997." *Connections* 23:44–59.

Vedres, Balázs, and David Stark. 2010. "Structural Folds: Generative Disruption in Overlapping Groups." *American Journal of Sociology* 115(4):1150–90.

Voszka, Éva. 1997. *A dinoszauruszokesélyei* (The chances of dinosaurs). Budapest Pénzügykutató Rt.

Ward, Joe H., Jr. 1963. "Hierarchical Grouping to Optimize an Objective Function." *Journal of the American Statistical Association* 58:236–44.

Wasserman, Stanley, and Katherine Faust. 1994. *Social Network Analysis: Methods and Applications*. New York: Cambridge University Press.

Watts, Duncan. 1999. "Networks, Dynamics and the Small-World Phenomenon." *American Journal of Sociology* 105:493–527.

White, Douglas. 2004. "Network Analysis, Social Dynamics and Feedback in Social Systems." *Cybernetics and Systems* 35(2–3):173–92.

White, Douglas R., and Frank Harary. 2001. "The Cohesiveness of Blocks in Social Networks: Node Connectivity and Conditional Density." *Sociological Methodology* 31(1):305–59.

White, Douglas R., and Ulla C. Johansen. 2004. *Network Analysis and Ethnographic Problems: Process Models of a Turkish Nomad Clan*. Lanham, MD: Lexington Books.

White, Harrison C. 1992. *Identity and Control*. Princeton: Princeton University Press.

Wishart, David. 2003. Clustan Graphics 5: Cluster analysis program. Clustan Ltd., UK.

Wu, Lawrence L. 2000. "Some Comments on 'Sequence Analysis and Optimal Matching Methods in Sociology: Review and Prospect.'" *Sociological Methods and Research* 29:41–64.

Yiu, Daphne, and Shige Makino. 2002. "The Choice between Joint Venture and Wholly Owned Subsidiary: An Institutional Perspective." *Organization Science* 13:667–83.

Zaheer, Srilata. 1995. "Overcoming the Liability of Foreignness." *Academy of Management Journal* 38: 341–63.

Zon, Hans Van. 1998. "The Mismanaged Integration of Zaporizhzhya with the World Economy: Implications for Regional Development in Peripheral Regions." *Regional Studies* 32:607–18.

Zysman, John, and Andrew Schwartz. 1998. "Reunifying Europe in an Emerging World Economy: Economic Heterogeneity, New Industrial Options, and Political Choices." Berkeley Roundtable on International Economy Working Paper. University of California–Berkeley.

PART IV

Contemporary Capitalism and Science

The sextet of chapters in part 4 examines the emergence and development of contemporary science- and technology-based sectors.The first four chapters examine the commercial field of the life sciences and its consequences for biomedical research, corporate organization, and venture finance. Breakthrough discoveries in genetic engineering in the 1970s helped spawn a new field, which in time had profound, wide-ranging effects. Indeed, some analysts depict this sea change as a major technological discontinuity that triggered a "classic" wave of creative destruction. To be sure, the changes that emerged were far-reaching in terms of new business models, the repurposing of university science, and controversial practices in venture finance. But these changes did not sweep away older models; instead they commingled with them, leaving an imprint in the conservative corridors of research universities and corporate labs. The chapters on the life sciences in this part focus on the genesis of new organizational models and practices, the emergence and growth of technology clusters, the formation of a central core of organizations, dubbed an open elite, and the spread of patenting in the academy.

Chapter 13 by Powell and Kurt Sandholtz analyzes the early years of the first generation of biotechnology companies, which were founded by "amphibious" scientists who simultaneously occupied leadership positions in academic labs and entrepreneurial ventures—and thus introduced academic norms into the start-up world while unwittingly carrying commercial values and metrics into the academy. The result was the creation of a new form—a science-based commercial entity, which emerged from overlapping networks of science, finance, and commerce. The setting is the 1970s, a time when landmark scientific discoveries in molecular biology triggered all manner of perturbations in university science, pharmaceutical research, and venture finance. The novel collection of organizational practices that coalesced into a dedicated biotech firm (DBF) proved highly disruptive. Using historical analysis of archival materials, supplemented by interviews with DBF founders, Powell and Sandholtz piece together the "lash-up" process that melded elements from three separate realms—academic science, venture finance, and commercial health care—into an interactively stable pattern.

Powell and Sandholtz modify received wisdom on organizational genesis in two important ways. First, although novelty routinely involves the reassembly of preexisting elements, it matters greatly whether such recombination results from the rearrangement of recognizable elements within existing or adjacent domains or the introduction and incorporation of foreign elements from previously distant domains. Second, the analysis points to an unexpected paradox: commercial viability and institutional influence may in some cases be inversely correlated. Among the pioneering DBFs were two distinct variants: a handful of businesses founded through recombinatory mechanisms; and a group of firms launched by "trespassers," scientists who naively transposed academic practices and values into a commercial setting. Perhaps not surprisingly, the former proved a more robust business model. Yet the latter—an unusual collision of science and finance—was both disruptive and generative, resulting in a durable rendering of institutional arrangements in both the academy and industry.

A distinctive feature of the chapters in this part is a focus on both failures and successes. Few of the first-generation companies survived as independent entities. But the practices they embraced and refined had long-term consequences, most notably in a small number of communities in the United States. Chapter 14, by Powell, Kelley Packalen, and Kjersten Whittington, examines eleven regions in the United States in the 1980s and 1990s that were all rich in resources—ideas, money, and skills—which might have led to the formation of life sciences clusters. Yet only three of the regions—the San Francisco Bay Area, Boston, and San Diego—developed into robust industrial districts for biotechnology. Most research on the emergence of high-tech cluster samples on successful cases and traces backward to find a developmental pattern. In contrast, rather than read in reverse from a positive outcome, we build networks forward from their early origins, revealing three crucial factors: organizational diversity; anchor tenant organizations that protect the norms of a community and provide relational glue across multiple affiliations; and a sequence of network formation that starts with local connections and subsequently expands to global linkages.

The argument in chapter 14 transcends the nuances of history in each community to specify the mechanisms that foster catalytic growth. The presence of anchor tenants that operated according to principles of openness facilitated diversity in terms of both participants and practices. In such settings, success is readily emulated and improvised on, and failures become the seeds of new efforts. The active presence of for-profit, nonprofit, and public science organizations in the three robust clusters enabled cross-network transposition, where experience, status, and legitimacy in one domain were converted into "fresh" action in another realm. In the "successful" clusters, cross-domain contact became routinized and interorganizational mobility channeled the flow of people, ideas, and resources.

Chapter 15 by Powell and Jason Owen-Smith follows the trajectory of the life sciences into the present day, focusing on the larger question of industry or field evolution. In a field characterized by "gales of creative destruction," how have some types of organizations managed to retain a position of centrality even as others exit and many newcomers arrive? Powell and Owen-Smith analyze the emergence of a core group of organizations, diverse in form and function, which they label an "open elite." The animating question is why this group of organizations, which constituted a structural backbone of the field, did not become ossified gatekeepers but remained active in expansive exploration. The answer is found in their multiconnectivity—the multiple, independent pathways that link research-focused organizations in a wide array of different activities. The organizations in this group amended their initial roles as public or private entities with particular specialist capabilities. They became multifunctional, and in so doing recast the boundaries between public and private science. One consequence of the linkages among this group of interconnected organizations is that practices formerly associated with private entities are now pursued by public science organizations, and private firms have embraced numerous activities that were formerly the sole purview of the academy.

Chapter 16 by Jeannette Colyvas and Spiro Maroulis completes the emphasis on the life sciences and forms a bridge to the modeling efforts in part 2. Drawing on detailed archival work in the Office of Technology Licensing at Stanford, Colyvas and Powell (2006, 2007) analyzed the origins of academic entrepreneurship at Stanford. The process, they found, was contentious and initially highly idiosyncratic to specific faculty laboratories and research programs. Over time, however, consensus was forged and conventions regarding who was an inventor and what was an invention were established. Colyvas and Powell showed that the widely acclaimed Stanford model of academic entrepreneurship was an unanticipated outcome of fortuitous early success and a commitment to serving the interests of faculty and doctoral students. Financial incentives and healthy revenues were an outcome, *not* the motivation for this model of technology transfer. Chapter 16 extends this earlier work with an agent-based model that simulates the rise and spread of patenting by research faculty, drawing on Colyvas's (2007) archival analysis of divergent approaches taken by different lab directors. In so doing, they build on the formal model of autocatalysis developed by Padgett, McMahan, and Zhong in chapter 3, which enables them to disentangle competing explanations. The results are quite surprising.

Incentives or mimicry alone are less likely to account for academic embrace of patenting, whereas preemptive efforts to preserve scientific autonomy do play a large role. The pursuit of safeguards from commercial co-optation by other researchers has the transformative effect of making the emergence of proprietary science more likely.

In each of these chapters, we see vivid examples of how organizational emergence in one domain had unexpected effects in other realms as innovations cascaded across social worlds, producing profound changes in corporate R&D, university careers, and the financing of start-up companies. As careers traversed these multiple domains, scientists, financiers, and ex–corporate executives carried new ideas and organizational practices, resulting in a thorough mixing of different models of organization.

The last two chapters in this part move from the life sciences to information technology, suggesting the generality of cross-network refunctionality across contemporary high-technology industries. In chapter 17, Lee Fleming and colleagues also pursue the topic of regional agglomeration. They look nationwide to discern where technology clusters are located and show the early emergence of Silicon Valley and, three years later, Boston. Much has been made of the cultural differences between Silicon Valley in the Bay Area and Boston's Route 128. Fleming and his coauthors dig beneath this surface portrait, discerning which organizations are most generative. Just as Powell and his coauthors did in earlier chapters, they look at the structural differences between two leading technology hubs. Using patent data that capture inventor networks, they, too, highlight the importance of careers. Their longitudinal analysis reveals much greater information flow and career mobility across organizations and industries in the Valley than in Boston. This movement of people and ideas was spurred by the critical intermediary roles of Stanford University, IBM's Almaden Valley Laboratory, and Xerox PARC, each of which functioned like the anchor tenants that were the pollinators in the biotechnology clusters in chapter 14. Postdoctoral fellowships at Stanford and IBM became both the wellsprings of innovation and a springboard for scientific careers, creating dense overlapping networks that connected inventors throughout the region. This anchoring of diversity is central to the formation of technology clusters. Boston's subsequent emergence as a community occurred only when the network leadership passed from commercial entities, such as GTE, Data General, and Honeywell, to MIT. Fleming and colleagues offer further evidence that public science anchors play a large catalytic role in fostering diversity.

Chapter 18 by Fabrizio Ferraro and Siobhán O'Mahony continues the focus on the public ramifications of private forms of governance. The contemporary open source community is a robust example of private efforts by individuals and organizations to create public resources in the form of free software packages and validation. This widely distributed and decentralized system functions as an alternative to centralized governance and provides broad access to those who want to build on the existing corpus of software code. But how is such pluralism harnessed for productive uses? And how are boundaries maintained in such novel organizational forms? Ferraro and O'Mahony examine the emergence of Debian, a community software project, from 1997 to 2002, showing how select, skilled programmers emerged as the custodians who guided Debian in the context of its highly distributed and pluralistic structure. These stewards functioned in a somewhat comparable fashion to the open elite in biotechnology, ushering in promising newcomers, policing free riders, and maintaining the norms of the community. In such a manner, this small community of gatekeepers helped mobilize resources and commitment to a model of governance that resembled the invisible college of biotech science described in chapter 13. Through the development of key signing practices, a membership process was monitored by a small number of gatekeepers who maintained the openness of the system.

All of the chapters in part 4 address questions about the creation of organizational diversity. Each chapter contributes to our understanding of how practices in one setting travel through networks and are introduced into new venues. As cross-network contacts expand, the ensuing overlay of multiple networks is ripe for the emergence of new organizational forms. This sextet of chapters is replete with rich accounts of such new entities—science-based firms, public science organizations that become the anchors of economic growth, a private company laboratory that develops an influential postdoctoral fellowship program, and an open technological community that develops a self-monitoring gatekeeping system.

REFERENCES

Colyvas, Jeannette. 2007. "From Divergent Meanings to Common Practices: The Early Institutionalization of Technology Transfer at Stanford University." *Research Policy* 36(4):456–76.

Colyvas, Jeannette, and W. W. Powell. 2006. "Roads to Institutionalization." *Research in Organizational Behavior* 21:305–53.

———. 2007. "From Vulnerable to Venerated: The Institutionalization of Academic Entrepreneurship in the Life Sciences." *Research in the Sociology of Organizations* 25:219–59.

13

Chance, Nécessité, et Naïveté

Ingredients to Create a New Organizational Form

Walter W. Powell ▪ Kurt Sandholtz

Where do new practices and models of organization come from? Of course, nothing is entirely new, so the obvious answer is that new things trace their lineages back through earlier incarnations and to the careers of individuals involved in their construction. Such tracing is indeed useful, but it can lead to either a frustrating, infinite regress, with scant analytical purchase, or undue attention paid to the "heroic" role of inventors, without sufficient consideration of the surrounding context in which their creations occurred.

We pursue a different tack, focusing on components of new things and identifying the sources of separable parts, which can be moved, recombined, and translated by inventive humans. We want to account for how and when components are cobbled together. Sociologists of science and technology refer to this assembly process as "lash-up," an idea intended to capture how diverse elements become interactively stable (Law 1984; Latour 1987; Molotch 2003). We are interested in which elements can or cannot fit together, how durable or explosive the resulting amalgam is, and the circumstances under which this occurs. Consider the combination of food and religion. A mother who brings muffins to her Sunday school Bible class combines breakfast and religious instruction, a combination that is commonplace. But a priest would rarely give a sermon at a formal Sunday dinner, and even devout families rarely pray at restaurants, as theology and fine dining are seldom mixed. Our goal is to ascertain which attributes and practices can be combined and when they can be crystallized into something definable and consistent. Put differently, we aim to develop a sociology of compounds.

We explore this process through examination of the earliest biotechnology companies. They were most unusual for their time because they hewed to neither an industrial nor an academic model. Many of their distinctive attributes emerged out of the academy but combined with practices from the realms of finance and industry to produce a new type of science-based firm. Using historical materials, we chart the processes by which this development occurred in the late 1970s and early 1980s and identify the mechanisms that enabled it. In so doing, we show

The title of this chapter comes from remarks by Genentech cofounder Herbert Boyer (2001, 95–96): "I think if we had known about all the problems we were going to encounter, we would have thought twice about starting. I once gave a little talk to a group at a Stanford Business School luncheon, and I took off on the title of a book on evolution by Jacques Monod . . . *Chance et Nécessité*. The title of my talk was 'Chance, Nécessité, et Naïveté.' Naïveté was the extra added ingredient in biotechnology." We thank Tricia Soto, librarian at the Center for Advanced Study in the Behavioral Sciences, and Tanya Chamberlain for assistance in finding archival materials. Our thanks to the Center for Advanced Study for hosting Professor Powell while the chapter was prepared. Martin Kenney was most generous in providing us with the source documents he used in writing his 1986 book, one of the very first studies of the development of the biotechnology industry. We are grateful to Pablo Boczkowski, Matt Bothner, Ron Burt, Jeannette Colyvas, Sally Smith Hughes, Martin Kenney, John Padgett, Paolo Parigi, David Reinecke, and Rebecca Slayton for comments on earlier drafts. We have also greatly benefited from remarks by audiences at the sociology departments at UC–Berkeley, Chicago, Cornell, Hebrew University of Jerusalem, Northwestern, Princeton, and Sciences Po, and the business schools at UC–Berkeley, BYU, Chicago, ESMT, LBS, Mannheim, and MIT. We are grateful to Kathleen Much for her fine editorial hand.

how careers, ideas, and organizational practices crossed significant boundaries and eventually congealed to produce a novel form of organization, which had robust consequences.

We first introduce the scientific, political, and economic context in which the earliest companies were spawned. External forces reshaped the landscape of science and technology in the late 1970s and 1980s, opening up new opportunities. We consider how technological change intersects with organizational innovation and suggest mechanisms that explain how new models of organization develop. We then discuss our data collection strategy for studying the first wave of biotechnology companies, emphasizing that we include those that failed as well as those that persisted. Just four of this original generation are alive in any form today, and only two are independent entities. Our analysis is aimed at characterizing the most notable organizational practices that sprang up at these early companies, whether out of necessity, inspiration, or luck, or simply because the founders did not know any better. Not all of these initial ideas proved durable or productive, but out of a concatenation of alternative and novel means of organizing science, finance, and commerce, a new template for running a science-based company (i.e., a dedicated biotech firm or DBF) was assembled. We conclude with reflections on the consequences of these novel forms for the domains of science and industry.

ATTACK OF THE "CLONERS"

Looking back on the origins of the field of biotechnology, we might think that its growth and development were somehow ordained or predetermined. The science journalist Stephen Hall (1987, 21) captured the transformation and tumult that recombinant DNA research brought to the biological sciences: "It was like the microscope had been reinvented. Everything had to be reexamined, and the molecular biologists roared like Huns through other scientists' turf."

The breakthrough discoveries of the early 1970s attracted enormous attention. At the forefront of this research were scientists at Harvard, MIT, the University of Cambridge, the University of California–San Francisco (UCSF), and Stanford. The initial procedures for making recombinant DNA were developed by the Stanford biochemist Paul Berg and his colleagues Peter Lobban and Dale Kaiser (Yi 2008). At UCSF, William Rutter and his colleagues were at work isolating the gene for insulin. On the East Coast, Walter Gilbert's Harvard lab was exploring chemical methods to identify the base sequences of RNA and DNA. In Cambridge, England, Frederick Sanger and colleagues were also determining the nucleotide sequences of genes.

Into this world of scientific fervor was introduced a cleavage between scientific recognition and legal ownership. Even though Berg, Gilbert, and Sanger would share the Nobel Prize in 1980, the legal award of invention was eventually assigned to two papers on the process for creating recombinant DNA. These seminal papers, written by Herbert Boyer of UCSF and Stanley Cohen of Stanford, appeared in print in 1973 and 1974 (Cohen et al. 1973; Morrow et al. 1974). They were quickly followed by another path-breaking paper that laid the groundwork for monoclonal antibody techniques, written by Georges Köhler and César Milstein (1975), at the Medical Research Council in Cambridge. In its consequences for economic development, the most fateful step was that the Cohen-Boyer papers were followed by patent applications, whereas the Köhler-Milstein work was not. Portending the potential impact of this research, Cohen (1975) wrote an article for *Scientific American* explaining DNA cloning techniques, emphasizing their usefulness to basic science and commercial promise for synthesizing antibiotics, hormones, and enzymes.

Discussions of the prospects of human genetic intervention overflowed from scientific labs and conferences to the media, city councils across the nation, and Congress. Scientists learned an alarming lesson: their own efforts to debate and regulate laboratory safety invited public scrutiny of their research. Controversies arose due to fears raised in the minds of the public, as well as some scientists, about the hazards of recombinant DNA research.[1] An April 18, 1977, *Time* magazine cover story entitled "The DNA Furor: Tinkering with Life" underscored the prospects of great promise and considerable peril. The image of the mushroom cloud of the atomic bomb and the DNA double helix were frequently linked in the popular press. And in the late 1970s, at least sixteen separate bills were introduced in Congress to regulate recombinant DNA research (Wright 1994; Fredrickson 2001). But even as these concerns were bandied about, recognition was growing that recombinant DNA was a scientific tool of enormous potential.

[1] See Hall 1987; Wright 1994; and Colyvas 2007a.

By 1980 many of the concerns about safety had been resolved or silenced, and the commercial, political, and social enthusiasm seemed boundless. The National Institutes of Health research guidelines issued in 1979 were far more permissive than the original restrictive draft legislation of the mid-1970s. And the inviting label "biotechnology" came to replace the more ominous "genetic engineering." A series of new government policies heralded a political sea change from a model of science based on the philosophy of the public domain to one championing ideas about proprietary ownership and control. These federal policies represented a deliberate congressional strategy to alter the landscape of scientific production and innovation and to move universities out of the ivory tower and toward the market. A central component of this reconfiguration was a new alliance between industry and university. Federal policies such as the Bayh-Dole Act of 1980, the Stevenson-Wydler Technology Innovation Act of 1980, and the Economic Recovery Act of 1981 transformed university-industry relations by allowing universities to retain the property rights from innovations arising from federally funded research projects and mandating higher education's participation in technology transfer. With these new patenting capabilities, universities were assigned a central role in the capital accumulation process (Mowery et al. 2004; Rhoten and Powell 2007).

In June 1980, the U.S. Supreme Court decision in *Diamond v. Chakrabarty* recognized that nothing in the U.S. Constitution prevents taking out patents on man-made living organisms. In 1972 a General Electric (GE) scientist, Ananda Chakrabarty, had filed a patent on a living, altered bacterium that could consume oil, which might have proved useful to clean up oil spills. The U.S. patent office declined the application on the grounds that Congress had not passed legislation permitting products of nature to be patented (Kevles 1994, 66). GE appealed the decision, and many years later it reached the Court. A growing backlog of more than one hundred recombinant-DNA patents, including the three patents associated with Cohen and Boyer's research, awaited the outcome of the ruling. Even though this bacterium was created by conventional breeding methods and not through genetic engineering, and GE did not subsequently pursue the technology, the Supreme Court decision proved to be a landmark one. Edward Penhoet, formerly a professor at UC–Berkeley and one of the three founders of the biotech company Chiron, reflected on the impact of the ruling: "if you couldn't protect this intellectual property, then people were not going to invest in this field" (2001, 102). It was one thing to demonstrate that a new technology worked, but the Court decision now made it possible for the new ideas to be owned, traded, and licensed.

The Supreme Court ruling cleared the way for the first initial public offerings (IPOs) of fledgling biotech companies. On October 14, 1980, the young company Genentech had its IPO, which set a record at the time for the fastest run-up in stock price, rocketing from $35 to $89 in just twenty minutes. By day's end, Genentech—without a single product on the horizon—had a valuation of $532 million, and its founders Herbert Boyer and Robert Swanson were fabulously wealthy. This spectacular success, coming in the midst of a steep recession, gave credence to the view that scientific research, infused with start-up firm spunk, could be a critical component of economic growth (Kenney 1986a, 156–57). On the very same day, Paul Berg of Stanford received the Nobel Prize in Chemistry for his "studies of the biochemistry of nucleic acids, with particular regard to recombinant-DNA." The other half of the prize went jointly to Walter Gilbert of Harvard and Frederick Sanger of Cambridge for "determination of base sequences in nucleic acids" (Press release, NobelPrize.org). It was indeed a propitious moment for biotechnology.

The new industry also benefited from changes in tax laws and the regulation of financial markets, which gave start-up firms wider access to equity investments. As anti-tax sentiment welled up across the country in the context of Carter-era stagflation, a bipartisan coalition in Congress cut capital gains taxes in 1978, with the hope that the wealthy would increase their investment in small business. Also in 1978, the Department of Labor issued guidelines for the reinterpretation of the Employment Retirement Income Security Act (ERISA), incorporating the insights of portfolio theory from the field of finance. Subsequently, in July 1979, the Prudent Man Rule was applied to the entire portfolio of a pension fund, allowing institutions to place their funds in the hands of professional investors. This decision opened retirement funds and university and foundation endowments to the financial community for investment in new technology ventures (Berman 2007, chap. 4).

Clearly, then, the emergence of the biotech industry occurred in the context of a number of supportive economic and political changes.

The rapid development of the life sciences and molecular biology as academic disciplines was central, but increased federal funding for biomedical research, a favorable proprietary intellectual property regime, and the expansion of the pharmaceutical and health care industries and their particular modes of conducting industrial research were critical as well. Equally consequential were the emergence and maturation of venture capital organizations and the growing public sense that established U.S. industries were losing ground to foreign competition, most notably the Japanese. There was widespread hope both in the corridors of power and finance and in cities and communities throughout the country that new industries such as information technology and biotechnology would provide engines for industrial renaissance. These broader structural forces turned over the soil for the emergence of biotech, but they did not determine the path of its development, most notably the organizational form in which this new research would be conducted or the places where such research and business activity would eventually be located.

ORGANIZATIONAL AND TECHNICAL CHANGE

Many thoughtful analysts of this era have assumed that the economic opportunities created by biotechnology were transparent to entrepreneurs in the late 1970s and early 1980s and that scientific advances had clearly opened up new markets for companies to exploit (Kenney 1986b; Orsenigo 1989; McKelvey 1996). Seen in this neo-Schumpeterian view, the subsequent organizational transformations in both the academy and biomedical product development followed directly from this technological disruption. We want to challenge, or at least amend, this view in which technological evolution is paramount.

Without question, laboratory advances had outpaced commercial applications. Ron Cape (2006, 16), a cofounder of the first bioengineering company, Cetus, captured the pent-up feeling of the times: "It was like maybe a dam waiting to burst or an egg waiting to hatch, but the fact is, there were a lot of Nobel Prizes in molecular biology, but no practical applications." But the process by which Nobel-quality science is translated into serviceable medicines is by no means trivial; nor does poisedness imply predictability. What retrospectively appears to have been a technologically determined path was, we argue, the result of innumerable social and political choice points, each of which could have radically altered the field's trajectory.

The foundational Cohen-Boyer patent, for instance, was nearly scuttled multiple times. First, consider that at Stanford University, today much celebrated for its successful technology transfer program, the Office of Technology Licensing (OTL) was established in 1968 as only a one-year pilot program; renewal was by no means guaranteed as faculty opposition was considerable. Second, had the OTL director, Nils Reimers, spent more time courting renowned DNA researcher Paul Berg, he would have run headfirst into Berg's opposition to patenting scientific research. Third, Reimers did not even know Professor Cohen; instead he learned about recombinant-DNA research from Stanford's news director, who had read about it in the *New York Times* (Reimers 1987). Fourth, Cohen at first rebuffed Reimers; then he worried that his coauthors would not be included on the patent (Hughes 2001). He was persuaded to proceed with the patenting of their gene-splicing technique only once consensus was reached that any proceeds would be plowed back into research funding (Reimers 1987; Colyvas 2007b).[2] Finally, Stanford then had to decide whether to have an exclusive or open license for the patent. The OTL resisted the then princely offer of $6 million from the pharmaceutical giant Merck for exclusive rights, opting instead for an open license on the principle that it was more in keeping with the standards of public science. Moving away from Stanford to the broader judicial context, the Supreme Court ruling in *Diamond v. Chakrabarty* that permitted the patenting of man-made organisms passed with a narrow 5–4 vote. Had any of these events (or countless others) played out differently, the biotech field may not have spawned a new industry; instead, the scientific discoveries may well have been harvested, albeit much more slowly, by large multinational chemical and pharmaceutical companies. Consequently, although the soil

[2] Cohen's initial response was: "Gee, this can't be patented. This is basic research. How can you patent basic research? And besides, it's dependent on all of these findings that have occurred in molecular biology for the past 15 to 20 years" (Chemical Heritage Foundation 1997, 133). Herbert Boyer's immediate response when Cohen called him about Stanford's effort to patent their recombinant DNA technology was, "That's illegal" (Chemical Heritage Foundation 1997, 126). Paul Berg also had a strong averse reaction to the patent idea: "Hey, wait a minute! I mean, where do Stanford and UC get the entitlement to this whole thing?" (Chemical Heritage Foundation 1997, 129).

might have been fertile for the sprouting of biotechnology, there is little evidence to suggest that it was destined to develop in the organizational form that it did or in the specific places where it flourished.

If technological factors are insufficient to account for the emergence of biotech firms, what other arguments are more promising? A rich scholarly literature analyzes how new combinations of previously existing components are forged (Henderson and Clark 1990; Hargadon and Sutton 1997; Fleming 2001; Baker and Nelson 2005). A complementary strand of work investigates how the prior affiliations of entrepreneurs shape the strategies they pursue when they move into nascent fields (Baron, Hannan, and Burton 1999; Burton, Sorenson, and Beckman 2002).[3] We draw on these lines of work but depart by making a sharp distinction between two types of recombination. To be sure, almost all novelty is "a recombination of conceptual and physical materials that were previously in existence" (Nelson and Winter 1982, 130). We maintain, however, that it matters a great deal whether recombination occurs on a familiar terrain (e.g., an organization in the same or adjacent sector or industry) or in a new or distant setting where the components are foreign. The movement of digital technology from computing to photography, or of an actor from Hollywood to Broadway, or even the current mash-up of the Internet, telephones, and video all represent innovative recombinations that import practices from one sector into a nearby one. The imported practices, however, remain recognizable. In contrast, some recombinations involve the movement of ideas and practices from one domain into another where they are alien and not initially recognized. We label these *transpositions*. For example, moving from the realm of science or religion into the world of commerce or vice versa represents a boundary crossing. Such leaps are much less frequent and less likely to be successful than amalgamations that take place on "safer" ground. But even failures of this sort generate "fresh" action, overcoming the "inherent lethargy of social life" and opening up possibilities that can be exploited by others (White 2008, 279–83).

In order to effect transpositions, individuals must violate institutional boundaries, repurposing old tools or recombining past practices in an unusual manner. Such people have been termed "moral entrepreneurs" or "rule creators" by the sociologist Howard Becker (1963). Symbolic interactionist scholars typically refer to such rule-creating activity as traffic across social worlds. Under such circumstances, participants create new social spaces and synthesize existing cultural practices in these unfamiliar circumstances, resulting in marked departures from the past.[4] Yet, although such trespassings can have a revolutionary effect, transposition need not be radical in its intent. Padgett and McLean (2006), for example, show how the invention of the partnership form in Renaissance Florence, with its unforeseeable transformative reverberations, resulted from the essentially conservative efforts of the ruling elite to retain power by coopting merchant-class bankers into local political positions.

We further suggest that the social synthesis that results from transposition is rarely deliberate, much less visionary. To be sure, such efforts entail considerable social skill and are fruitfully regarded as a form of pragmatic agency.[5] Hence, our theoretical ground does not come from work in strategy and entrepreneurship, with its emphasis on capabilities and resources, as well as "heavyweight" champions. Instead, our argument builds on the ideas of the Carnegie school on premises and routines and on the microsociological insights of symbolic interactionists and ethnomethodologists.[6] Put simply, when the established routines for conducting everyday affairs prove limiting, people begin to search and experiment. In so doing, they draw on their stock of existing knowledge, both formal and tacit, and look around their social worlds for cues about appropriate steps. With this stock of

[3] Beckman and Burton (2008, 3) document how Silicon Valley entrepreneurs "bring important experiences and make critical choices early in a firm's history that leave a lasting imprint." Others have focused on how the founders of spin-off companies inherit ideas and practices from their parent companies (Helfat and Lieberman 2002; Chatterji 2009). Klepper and Sleeper (2005) even employ a genetic metaphor, suggesting that entrepreneurs carry the organizational DNA from their parent firms into new ventures, producing offspring that, although not exact copies of the parent, carry the same traits with some variation.

[4] See Strauss 1978; Fujimura 1987; Clarke 1991; and Rabinow 1996.

[5] Dewey 1939 is the starting point, but also see the useful discussion of skills in Fligstein 2001.

[6] For the Carnegie tradition, March and Simon 1958 is the foundation; for symbolic interactionism, Mead 1934 is the start and Blumer 1969 and Becker 1986 provide rich conceptualizations. The ethnomethodology literature is diverse and somewhat arcane, but we draw especially on Sudnow 1965, Garfinkel 1967, and Cicourel 1968.

information, they may forge new tools for coping with situations without precedent.

The extant literature on organization founding tends to emphasize that entrepreneurs must work especially hard to mobilize the resources required to launch new organizations in new sectors.[7] Clearly the resource aspect of the founding process is critical, but we stress that the creative aspect of coming up with a new template in a new domain might be easier when the canvas has yet to be painted.[8] One advantage that newcomers bring to a distant domain is that they are unencumbered by the baggage of established industry practices (Kaplan and Tripsas 2008). This is not to say that newcomers are baggage free but that their baggage comes from their domain of origin, not the realm they are entering. Moreover, they may not even be aware of such baggage; it is taken for granted, an unquestioned part of their values, expectations, norms, and decision premises. But when transposed into a new realm, these ingrained modi operandi can afford startling possibilities for refunctionality and novelty.[9]

Of course, when identities are too diverse and diffuse, the emergence of a new collective entity is problematic (McKendrick and Carroll 2001), and entities that span too many categories can suffer an "illegitimacy discount" (Zuckerman 1999). Hence the conceptual puzzle: How are truly novel social forms created? As Johnson (2007) puts it, why are certain building blocks, but not others, incorporated into a new enterprise? Our answer hinges on the way that individual attributes and practices attach to one another, forming a particular composite that enables certain activities while precluding others.

The people who built the commercial field of biotechnology lacked any formal blueprint for constructing a DBF, and yet each carried tacit blueprints from the domains they knew well.[10] Scientists, financiers, and businesspeople, drawing on their existing networks and prior skills, came together and managed to create novel organizational forms, obtain new sources of funding for biomedical research, and initiate pioneering work on diagnostic and therapeutic medicines. Some of the companies developed a business model that operated according to quite different principles from the traditional vertically organized corporate hierarchy. In time, a model of a science-based company was constructed, based on horizontal flows of information, porous organizational boundaries, a strong reliance on intellectual capital and collective know-how, and a strategy of pursuing innovation through collaborative ventures with other organizations, some of which were even competitors.

No single early company had all of the elements of the eventual model; in fact, it is clear that few if any of the participants were aware that they were creating a new organizational form. Some, such as Amgen's George Rathmann and Genzyme's Henri Termeer, were motivated by dissatisfaction with existing corporate constraints and practices. Others, such as Ron Cape and Peter Farley at Cetus, seemed determined to experiment with new conditions and rules. Still others simply made it up on the fly, so to speak, inserting new tasks into the confines of existing settings until such arrangements no longer proved viable.[11] One of the earliest firms, Genen-

[7] The initial impetus for this line of work is, of course, Stinchcombe's (1965) classic essay. Freeman, Carroll, and Hannan (1983) develop the idea empirically, and Aldrich and Fiol (1994) expand it conceptually.

[8] Brook Byers, the venture capitalist who was the early CEO of Hybritech, San Diego's first biotech company, aptly illustrated this point when he recalled: "So we were naïve. I think if we had known everything about all the potential huge competitors, we might not have even done it. One of the benefits we had, I suppose, was some combination of naïveté and ambition and this desire to do something on our own . . . I think there was a feeling of a green field, and that we were the first. We didn't know all the answers, but we had time to figure it out" (2006, 21–22).

[9] In music, transposition means to rewrite or play a piece in a different key. When such transposition happens on the fly, as in any type of improvisational music, the musician plays a familiar piece in an unfamiliar tonal environment. This can open up new musical interpretations. Jazz improvisation, for example, always involves recombination. But suppose a jazz musician is asked to play "Take the A-Train" in E-flat instead of the customary key of C. Suppose further that the musician is not used to playing "A Train" in E-flat, and yet she is used to playing other tunes in E-flat. This instantly opens up possibilities (consciously or not) for the crossover, melding, and exchange of musical phrases between the two previously separate domains. Licks and riffs that she tends to use in other E-flat songs are now automatically available for "A Train," and embellishments she has made to "A-Train" in the past become available for future tunes that she plays in E-flat. The analogy is not an exact one, but it helps illustrate the difference between recombination (within domains) and transpositions (across domains).

[10] For example, Brook Byers, venture capital backer and CEO of Hybritech, commented that: "We did not have the business model mapped out, or the ultimate value proposition, which are all things we do today in doing a start-up. We're much more sophisticated now. Back then, we didn't have any of that" (2006, 22).

[11] Hall (1987, 9) captured this sense of excitement in his vivid account of the race to make insulin using the tools of genetic engineering. He observed that the new molecular biologists, especially the younger ones, "had the reputation of being opportunistic, of trespassing onto other scientists' intellectual turf in search of answers." They embraced the tremendous power of the new technology with "unconflicted fervor." A young West Coast biologist, Richard Scheller, commented to Hall, "There was the thought that there were some real key questions and there were a few people who were

tech, which would later turn out to be a bellwether for the industry, was a virtual company for two years.[12] Similarly, Biogen's first breakthrough came from the lab of one of its founders at the University of Zurich. Centocor began by licensing a patent for a monoclonal antibody developed by two of its founders at the Wistar Institute on the University of Pennsylvania campus. Genex's top scientist—a tenured professor at the University of Michigan—was finally persuaded to join the company full-time when he grew weary of constantly defending his "Frankenscience" from campus protestors. Common to all four stories is the tension created by new practices in old contexts. Goffman (1974) has highlighted the process of framing, whereby individuals summarize complex situations into context-specific accounts that enable them to chart a new course of action. When then-current frames—the academic laboratory, the "garage" start-up, the industrial R&D organization—developed stress fractures from attempting to accommodate the odd contours of a fledgling biotech industry, founders had little choice but to create a frame of their own.

We are *not* arguing that the flatter, leaner, and more nimble biotech firms ultimately prevailed over established corporate hierarchies. Indeed, as we argue in chapter 15, they have not. Far from streamlining the process of drug discovery and testing, many of the new firms stumbled through costly clinical trials and underestimated the challenges of scaling up for commercial production (Pisano 2006). Most DBFs ended up deriving the bulk of their financing from venture investments, public stock offerings, and partnerships with large pharmaceutical companies. Only a small number achieved profitability and successfully marketed new biomedical products on their own. Even though the array of new medicines developed with the tools of molecular biology is impressive, the number of failures was considerable. Instead of out-competing the industry giants, the new biotech companies have frequently teamed with them in R&D collaborations, and many small companies had to give away their crown jewels in exchange for financial support. For the established firms, these arrangements provided options on new technologies that they were wary of developing in-house, whereas for the start-ups the collaborations were necessary for survival. Moreover, when scientific and product development successes pushed biotech companies closer to profitability, these accomplishments often made them more visible targets for takeover by larger companies that were eager to expand their product pipelines.

Our concern here is not about the viability of specific small firms. We focus instead on invention: the emergence of a new organizational form, one that in time has become canonical with the knowledge economy. Out of necessity and naiveté, biotech's founding scientists, managers, and financiers improvised an organizational model whose principles were subsequently insinuated into the most unlikely of settings: the conservative corridors of the largest pharmaceutical corporations, and even back into the academy itself.[13] Indeed, the recent reorganizations of biomedical research at almost every major research university have, to some degree, been spurred by the earlier changes ushered in by DBFs (Jong 2008). Moreover, the new biotech firms were not all commercial failures. Companies such as Amgen, Biogen, Chiron, and Genentech brought important novel medicines to market, developed different means for conducting research and clinical trials, and reaped considerable gains in the process. But perhaps of greater import than such achievements was the manner in which they were organized. These firms thrived with fluid boundaries, fostering a model of basic and translational R&D that hinged on close interactions among university, government, and industrial scientists located throughout the world. Over time, this approach supplanted the formerly dominant model of a large, inwardly focused, hermetically sealed industrial R&D lab, as well as the entrenched disciplinary structure of traditional biomedical departments at research universities. As but one illustration of this transformation, the economists Ian Cockburn and Scott Stern (2010, 26) argue that a life sciences innovation system has developed that "ultimately replaced the tradi-

going to answer them, and if you weren't one of them, then you were going to be left out" (ibid.).

[12] In the first two years of its existence, 1976–78, Genentech had no labs or location of its own; instead it had contractual agreements with cofounder Herbert Boyer to pursue research on insulin and human growth hormone in his lab at UCSF and with City of Hope Medical Center researchers in Los Angeles to work on synthetic DNA (McKelvey 1996, 99–107). Although some tensions arose over Boyer's starting a firm inside the university, and an investigation was conducted by the faculty senate committee on rules and jurisdiction, the university administration viewed the relationship in conventional terms as an R&D contract and licensing agreement (ibid., 104).

[13] The changes sparked by this feedback are central to the creation of an "open elite," analyzed in chapter 15.

tional divide between university science and pharmaceutical innovation with a system that depends on interdependent and collaborative knowledge development spanning both public and private organizations."

We are not the first to argue that biotechnology forged a recombination of scientific and commercial cultures, which led to the creation of new organizational practices and forms of discovery.[14] Our contribution is a detailed historical examination of the mechanisms by which traditional institutional boundaries and organizational barriers in both universities and large corporations were transgressed and redrawn. Biomedical research and drug development are inherently interdisciplinary; success is deeply dependent on the ability of organizations to bring together people from different academic backgrounds with those with experience in industry to conduct research and coordinate the work of science and business. The founding teams of the earliest companies embodied such cross-realm contacts, combining and mixing different academic and industrial rhythms and divergent registers of worth. The new spaces were created by trespassers, not by professional managers, university administrators, or government officials; the novel features of the DBF followed no established blueprint. We show that the critical dimensions of this organizational form were rooted in unprecedented recombinations and transpositions of conventions, practices, and bodies of knowledge of basic life science research into the realms of venture finance and corporate management.

To be sure, the new biotechnology firms shared several characteristics found in other high-tech industries in their ways of organizing research and development, and they evinced parallels with consulting and professional service firms in fields as different as advertising and engineering. But none of the other available models from consulting, think tanks, or information technology encountered the types of financial and organizational challenges that biotechnology did. No industry in recent years has been as reliant on basic science for its origins and sustenance as biotech, and no other new-economy industry is subject to such extensive regulatory oversight or has such a lengthy product development cycle. As novel relations were forged between new biotechnology companies and research universities, high-profile scientists began to act as amphibious creatures, moving back and forth as consultants, advisers, and founders of university spin-off firms. We highlight this process of trespassing because those few who traversed the divide between university and industry science remade boundaries and created new interstitial spaces.[15] Over time they received *both* federal research support and industry funding and, in so doing, not only recast the landscape of industrial research but altered the structure of scientific careers and the allocation of professional rewards.[16]

DATA AND METHODS

Using archival and secondary materials, along with oral history interviews, speeches, autobiographical writings, and interviews, we constructed the founding stories of the first era of biotechnology companies. Our sample selection criteria were straightforward. First, we used notable science journalists and historical accounts of the origins of the industry to identify the earliest companies.[17] Second, we drew on key industry analysts and government reports that followed the young industry.[18] Third, we reviewed a number of Ph.D. dissertations that covered the history of biotechnology and its early participants.[19] Fourth, we consulted a database collected by Powell and colleagues to identify the firms with the earliest founding dates.[20] Using this database, we created network visualizations of interorganizational collaborations among uni-

[14] See Powell 1996; Rabinow 1996; and Oliver and Montgomery 2000.

[15] A number of studies have shown that many of these early amphibious creatures were "star scientists," suggesting that their fame made it easier for them to move into these new habitats (Zucker and Darby 1996; Owen-Smith and Powell 2001; Stuart and Ding 2006). Our historical research suggests that many nonetheless felt the pain of "arrows in their backs" from colleagues, experiencing scorn and innuendo from fellow academics.

[16] The process has some parallels with the evolutionary mechanism labeled *exaptation* by Gould and Vrba (1982). Here we have a practice—open science—that was honed for use in one domain that turned out to have an unexpected property in a new domain. Exaptation describes "features that now enhance fitness but were not built by natural selection for their current role" (4).

[17] We found Kenney 1986a, Hall 1987, Teitelman 1989, Wright 1994, Robbins-Roth 2000, and Vettel 2006 particularly useful.

[18] For example, Burrill (2007) dates the inception of the industry to "circa 1973" and notes the first-generation companies were ALZA, Cetus, Amgen, Genentech, and Biogen. Articles in the *New York Times* and the *Wall Street Journal* in the early 1980s routinely referred to the "Big Four"—Cetus, Genentech, Genex, and Biogen. The U.S. Government Office of Technology Assessment produced a widely cited 1984 report on the new industry, also identifying the earliest firms.

[19] For dissertations, Hybels 1994, Porter 2004, Jones 2005, Berman 2007, and Nelson 2007 were especially helpful.

[20] These data provide the basis for the empirical analyses in chapters 14 and 15.

versities, pharmaceutical companies, financiers, and biotechnology firms between 1980 and 1988 and ascertained which DBFs were most central.

The resulting sample is small. Only a handful of firms were created before the early 1980s; fewer still left an available historical record.[21] We believe that the ones that quickly failed had little impact on the subsequent evolution of the field. Those that persisted a few years, we maintain, ultimately had outsize influence, as they provided a template for subsequent generations of biotech firms, as well as a model for new science-based firms more generally. The eleven companies that emerged from this selection process are listed in table 13.1, with their founding year, location, and a short tagline capturing their raison d'être.

Conscious of the potential for survival bias in historical analysis, we find it notable that only one of the eleven firms in our sample has survived as a stand-alone entity (Amgen); another maintained some independence via merger (Biogen Idec). Two of the earliest companies (Cetus and Genex) are portrayed in the literature as failures. As noted earlier, commercial success (or failure) is not central to our analysis. We are much more interested in the events surrounding each firm's founding, the prior experiences and contacts of the groups of founders, and the practices in which the companies engaged. The firms exhibit considerable variation in their founding stories: from a serial entrepreneur who had just sold his packaging company and was looking for his next deal (see Genzyme in appendix, p. 422), to an all-star collection of academic scientists determined to manage their company as a transatlantic research seminar (see Biogen in appendix, p. 412), to seasoned venture capitalists assembling the "next big thing" (see Amgen in appendix, p. 410). We do not view these companies as but the lengthened shadow of a few men; our interest is in identifying the mechanisms that forged novelty.

Capturing the particularities of each company's birth required extensive analysis of archival sources, supplemented by semi-structured interviews with company founders to fill in gaps in the historical record. Of primary interest to us were direct statements by members of each company's founding team regarding their motives, circumstances, and organizational ideas, both pre- and post-founding. A collection of oral history interviews from the Bancroft Library at UC–Berkeley was particularly fruitful; we digested more than 1,800 pages, gleaning insights from the scientists, entrepreneurs, venture capitalists, and earliest employees of the first biotech ventures. We also gathered transcribed interviews with biotech founders from the Chemical Heritage Foundation, the Smithsonian Institution, and the San Jose Tech Museum. Public information was sparse for three of the companies on our list. For each of these companies, we conducted interviews with at least two of the founders, thus enabling us to cross-check individual perceptions and recollections against those of at least one peer. These interviews lasted between forty-five minutes and two hours; all were recorded and transcribed, generating about 150 additional pages of interview data. In all cases, the interview transcripts were reviewed, edited, and approved by the respective informants.[22]

The data from interviews, oral histories, and archival sources were integrated to create case histories of each firm's founding. Brief summaries of the founding stories for each firm are presented in the appendix at the end of this chapter. We focused on attributes of each company—the backgrounds of the founders, how the company was put together and financed, and unique practices that each pursued. We searched for similarities and noted salient differences (Eisenhardt and Graebner 2007). We turn now to a discussion of these practices, but to set the stage, we note here an unexpected outcome of our multicase analysis: With the exception of ALZA—a precursor, really, of the DBF—the eleven firms in the sample divided evenly into two categories, which we label science-centered and commerce-centered variants of the DBF.[23] The former

[21] We are continuing this line of inquiry, searching for news and magazine reports on the companies that we were not able to obtain sufficient information on for this chapter.

[22] To guard against post-hoc impression management, we triangulated accounts from the interviews with real-time archival data, such as company press releases, IPO prospectuses, newspaper and magazine articles, and numerous books written during the mid-1980s on the burgeoning biotech industry. Here again, we sought direct statements from company founders. This allowed us to corroborate their recollections in recent interviews with statements recorded during the time period in question, with the aim of minimizing retrospective bias.

[23] Of the eleven companies, ten should be considered new (or *de novo*) entrants. They were formed for the express purpose of pursuing commercial applications of biotechnology and did not rely on any preexisting corporate structure to do so. Only ALZA is a lateral (or *de alio*) entrant as it moved from the pharmaceutical world of drug delivery into biotechnology. Research has examined how these two types of entrants differ with respect to performance and survival prospects. The general argument is that *de alio* firms are likely to pursue incremental innovation that builds on existing know-how, whereas *de novo* entrants are more likely to generate radical innovations (Anderson and Tushman 1990; Henderson 1993; Christensen and Rosenbloom 1995; Tripsas 1997). On the other hand, prior experience and vastly greater resources are likely to result in *de alio* companies having a

Table 13.1.
Prominent Early Biotech Firms

Company	Founding Year	Location	Founding Model	Currently
ALZA	1968	Palo Alto, CA	"A great place if it were a nonprofit think tank"	No longer in existence
Cetus	1972	Emeryville, CA	Academic playground or "Free Space"; biotech tools would be applied to a host of problems	No longer in existence
Genentech	1976	South San Francisco, CA	"Best of both worlds": serious science and VC funding create a new model for basic research	Subsidiary of Roche
Genex	1977	Montgomery, MD	Low-cost producer: apply biotech methods to the manufacture of industrial chemicals	No longer in existence
Biogen	1978	Geneva, Switzerland	Transatlantic network of world-class scientists	Biogen Idec
Hybritech	1978	La Jolla, CA	New diagnostic tools for the war on cancer	No longer in existence
Centocor	1979	Philadelphia, PA	Bridge between academia and commercial health care	No longer in existence
Amgen	1980	Thousand Oaks, CA	To become a FIPCO (fully integrated pharmaceutical company)	Independent
Chiron	1981	Emeryville, CA	"Get in or lose out": tired of losing top scientists to biotech ventures, UCSF department chair starts his own company	No longer in existence
Genzyme	1981	Boston, MA	Niche collector; "Company of singles rather than home runs"	Subsidiary of Sanofi-Aventis
Immunex	1981	Seattle, WA	Academics find a "pugnacious" entrepreneur willing to back "underdog" scientists	No longer in existence

lower mortality rate than start-ups (Carroll et al. 1996; Klepper and Simons 2000). In the biotech field, many established pharmaceutical companies initially took a wait-and-see approach (Gambardella 1995), thus the number of diversifying incumbents was quite low in the early years (Wright 1994; Zucker and Darby 1997). Over time, once the large pharmaceutical firms no longer reacted defensively and made the choice to transform their technological identity, huge resources were mobilized to do so. (We discuss this transformation in more detail in chapter 15.) Amgen represents an interesting illustration of this contrast, as its first CEO left a large pharmaceutical firm (Abbott Labs) to join Amgen. In an effort to retain him, Abbott offered to set up a biotech subsidiary, which he declined.

represent the movement of practices into an unfamiliar domain; the latter exemplify a mixing of ideas from different commercial settings.

DISTINCTIVE ELEMENTS OF THE EARLIEST FIRMS

Our goal is to account for the origins of the dedicated biotech firm, discerning its diverse sources and explaining how the various elements crystallized. To do so, we culled from the case materials the distinctive organizational features that characterized each company and sorted them according to the three domains—science, finance, and commerce—from which they were borrowed. All of the early companies combined, to differing degrees, resources, personnel, and practices from the academy, venture capital, and the established pharmaceutical and chemical industries. But they varied markedly regarding which elements they used. Moreover, as the components were imported and melded in a new setting, they were transformed by their insertion into a start-up firm context and assemblage with other unfamiliar parts. We begin with a discussion of the individual elements, distilled from the individual case histories. These distinctive features are summarized in table 13.2. The companies are listed chronologically by founding date, with the precursor ALZA in 1968, followed by Cetus, arguably the first in 1972, and then a host of companies from 1976 to 1981.

Several attributes are common to nearly all of the companies, most notably backing from venture capital (VC) firms. In terms of financing, this is a group of "classic" start-up firms that burst onto the scene with the support of VCs. Venture capital was still a cottage industry in the 1970s (Gompers 1994). By then, VC firms had established a presence in Silicon Valley, but they were very much a small circle of insiders, mostly successful past investors in electronics companies, with their headquarters on Sand Hill Road in Menlo Park, California (Kenney and Florida 2000). Kleiner Perkins was the first VC firm founded by partners who came from the world of operations and management rather than pure finance; both Gene Kleiner and Tom Perkins had engineering backgrounds. It was Kleiner and Perkins who led VC investors into biotech, with early investments in Genentech and Hybritech. The first biotech IPO was Genentech's in 1980, and soon thereafter other companies followed suit. To be sure, many of these companies had initial public offerings out of desperation; Amgen was perhaps the most notable as it was running low on cash with no research breakthroughs, revenues, or products in sight (see Amgen in appendix, p. 410). The success of Genentech's IPO spurred Amgen to turn to the public equity markets in hopes that they would realize "gene dreams" as well.

The marriage of venture capital and cutting-edge research in molecular biology is best typified in the long-term relationship between Kleiner Perkins and its biotech investments. In the case of Hybritech, Kleiner Perkins partner Brook Byers became the CEO of the new venture. With respect to Genentech, Perkins (2002, 24) recalls that it was "the most important deal" of his life:

> What was so different about Genentech was the astonishing amount of capital required to do all of this. I know, on day one, if anyone had whispered into my ear that, "for the next twenty years you will be involved in raising literally billions of dollars for this thing," I might not have done it. But in 1979, it occurred to me that for something of this importance, that there was enough money out there for us to do whatever we needed to do. I always viewed my role—my ultimate responsibility—was to make sure that the company didn't run out of money. That was my job. [Genentech cofounder Robert] Swanson's job was to make sure the company deserved more money, at ever-increasing prices. We both had a pretty clear notion of that. It worked for a long time. Hence, all the different things that we did—the private rounds, the research partnerships, the public rounds, and all the deals. It was always more capital than I anticipated. It dawned on Swanson before it dawned on me. I can't remember at what point it dawned on me that Genentech would probably be the most important deal of my life, in many terms—the returns, the social benefits, the excitement, the technical prowess, and the fun. By 1979 I was a total Genentech junkie. I was committed to making Genentech into a huge success. I had signed on for the long haul pretty early.

The second common attribute was the use of research contracts with large pharmaceutical companies, a practice used at all but two of the companies. The two exceptions—Centocor and Genzyme—pursued strategies that were less research intensive, focusing more on the commercialization of existing breakthroughs rather than the pursuit of new ones. For most fledgling biotech companies, however, such contracts were a financial necessity. The founders quickly realized that new biotech products would take many years to bring to market, and in the meantime they desperately needed sources of cash. Cetus pioneered the use of research contracts, agreeing to deals early on with an eclectic mix of partners—oil companies, distillers, cosmetics makers, soft drink bottlers, and drug companies. Genentech, Genex, Biogen, and Amgen cast

Table 13.2.
Distinctive Features of Early Biotech Firms

	Alza (1968)	Cetus (1972)	Genentech (1976)	Genex (1977)	Biogen (1978)
SCIENCE	♦ Assembled an all-star science advisory board ♦ Chose a campus-like setting near a major research university	♦ Assembled an all-star science advisory board ♦ Chose a campus-like setting near a major research university ♦ Offered "free space" for scientists ♦ Scientific founder stayed at the university and consulted with the company	♦ Insisted that staff scientists publish and contribute to public science ♦ Scientific founder stayed at the university and consulted with the company ♦ Launched as a "virtual" start-up: all initial research was conducted by contract with UCSF and City of Hope Hospital	♦ Assembled an all-star science advisory board ♦ Scientific founder stayed at the university initially	♦ Designed as an international consortium of top academic labs (i.e., science advisory board *was* the company) ♦ Launched as a "virtual" start-up: all initial research was conducted in founders' labs ♦ Scientific founders stayed at their respective universities full-time
FINANCE	♦ Went public with no products, breakthroughs, or revenues ♦ Used research partnerships with Big Pharma to generate funds	♦ Used research partnerships with a diverse array of large corporations ♦ Achieved a record-breaking IPO in 1981	♦ Received meager funding until scientific "proof of concept" ♦ Invented "milestone payment" form of incremental financing ♦ Achieved the first biotech IPO (1980): "gene dreams" for Wall Street ♦ Used research partnerships to share costs and risk	♦ Established numerous research contracts with large companies	♦ Received modest initial VC funding ♦ Out-licensed early breakthroughs to Big Pharma
COMMERCE	♦ Founder went on to start numerous biotech firms	♦ Explored a wide range of commercial applications for biotech	♦ Pursued a "swing for the fences" strategy focused on blockbuster medicines	♦ Pursued low-cost, high-volume strategy (e.g., biotech production of industrial chemicals) ♦ Made early investment in manufacturing plant ♦ Scientific founder went on to start additional biotech firms	♦ Targeted blockbuster medicines ♦ Scientific founders ran the company for its first seven years

Table 13.2 *(continued)*

Hybritech (1978)	Centocor (1979)	Amgen (1980)	Chiron (1981)	Genzyme (1981)	Immunex (1981)
♦ Scientific founder stayed at the university full-time and consulted with the company ♦ Talented research assistant played a key founding role ♦ Chose a campus-like setting near a major research university (UCSD) and research institute (Salk)	♦ Pursued aggressive in-licensing of research from public science ♦ Initially located in a business incubator on the University of Pennsylvania campus ♦ Enjoyed a close relationship with research institute (Wistar)	♦ Assembled an all-star science advisory board	♦ Founders stayed at universities initially ♦ Applied the skills of academic administration to business ♦ Insisted that scientists publish and make contributions to public science ♦ Transferred a founder's existing research grant from the university (UCSF) to the company ♦ Used research partnerships with pharma companies and universities as a mode of exploration	♦ Transferred a founder's existing research grant from the university (Tufts) to the company ♦ Talented research assistant played a key founding role ♦ Hired its science advisory board intact (Bio-Information Associates, a consulting firm of MIT and Harvard professors)	♦ Insisted that scientists publish and make contributions to public science ♦ Founding scientists resigned from academic jobs to avoid conflict of interest ♦ Chose a campus-like setting near a major research university (U. of Washington) and research institute (Hutchinson Cancer Center)
♦ VC played dual role as investor and CEO		♦ Went public in a last-ditch effort to save the company, despite no products or patented breakthroughs		♦ Used tracking stocks to compartmentalize risk ♦ Grew through numerous small acquisitions	♦ Out-licensed early patents to Big Pharma, then later reacquired them
♦ Scientific founders became serial entrepreneurs and/or VCs ♦ Recruited senior exec from Baxter to run the company ♦ Focused on diagnostic products; avoided long clinical trials ♦ Introduced the first-ever commercial product based on monoclonal antibody technology	♦ Served as a bridge between academic labs and Big Pharma manufacturing/marketing ♦ Recruited a senior exec from Corning's medical products business to run the company ♦ Focused on diagnostic products	♦ Recruited a senior exec from Abbott's diagnostics division to run the company ♦ Copied 3M's policy of "free time" for researchers to pursue new product ideas	♦ Focused on large potential market underserved by Big Pharma: vaccines ♦ Scientific founders ran the company	♦ Founder was a serial entrepreneur from the packaging industry ♦ Focused on niche markets and orphan drugs ♦ Recruited a senior exec from Baxter to run the company	♦ One of the founders was a proven executive and turn-around artist

similarly wide nets initially but subsequently aligned their portfolios of research partnerships with much clearer scientific direction. Genentech honed this practice by co-developing the idea of a milestone payment with Kleiner Perkins, a form of incremental financing based on demonstrated research progress, not unlike annual progress reports on research grants.

The origins of the "research for hire" mentality are easy to trace. Ever since the post–World War II boom in government funding for basic science, successful academic scientists had grown adept at the pursuit of government grants. For the scientific founders of the early biotechs, the idea of outside funding for one's research program was well established (Kenney 1986a). They merely substituted venture capital and corporate R&D partnerships for government grants. Genentech pioneered by treating the corporate support very much like a multiyear research grant. Indeed, for the scientists at the early companies, securing corporate funding may have involved considerably less rigmarole than applying for federal grants. From the corporate perspective, however, this model of R&D funding did not fit tidily into traditional customer-supplier-competitor categories. Many large companies were deeply challenged in dealing with research funding for multiple start-up companies and even more befuddled in trying to establish relationships with star scientists who had limited understanding of, and even less interest in, corporate organization.

A third widely shared attribute relates to what we earlier termed "amphibious" scientists. In six of the eleven companies, one or more of the academic founders either retained his faculty position while consulting with the new venture or temporarily moved out of the academy only to return later. Companies such as Chiron and Biogen had both types of amphibious founders. Four of the five companies without amphibious founders featured high-powered scientific advisory boards staffed by renowned academics, with arrangements for exclusive consulting relationships and generous stock options. These scientists functioned much more as classic brokers than as amphibians. Straddling domains was a more transgressive act. Many of the scientists associated with the earliest biotech firms—Donald Glaser at Cetus, Herbert Boyer at Genentech, David Jackson at Genex, Ivor Royston at Hybritech, and Wally Gilbert at Biogen—endured the frowns and skepticism of academic colleagues, and some were subjected to formal university investigations of impropriety. Despite this professional discomfort, however, the fact that such accomplished scientists were associated with these new commercial ventures provided a conduit of ideas and values between unfamiliar domains, which later evolved into an accepted, indeed valued, career path for many younger scientists (Stuart and Ding 2006; Colyvas and Powell 2007).[24] In turn, new careers were forged by senior scientists as well: Edward Penhoet was an associate professor when he left Berkeley to cofound Chiron in 1981.While serving as the company's president and CEO, he was advanced to full professor at UC–Berkeley. When he retired from Chiron in 1998, he became Dean at Berkeley's School of Public Health. Such seamless transitions and simultaneous rewards were unprecedented in the life sciences.

If the amphibian image implies the ability to toggle between diverse domains, other new career paths represented more a fusion or melding of domains (including the metamorphic Penhoet who moved from his deanship to a top program at the Gordon and Betty Moore Foundation; at the time of our writing he is a director at Alta Partners, a Bay Area VC firm). A fair number of these founding scientists went on to become either serial entrepreneurs or investors in subsequent bioscience ventures. The combination of scientific stature and start-up experience evidently proved to be both seductive and marketable; the financial independence gained from their first efforts was of course a stimulus as well.

Although clusters of companies shared particular elements, some organizational attributes were unique to individual companies. Centocor was the sole practitioner of its bridge model of business development: find an unlicensed scientific breakthrough, buy the rights to it, develop it into a diagnostic kit for use on existing diagnostic hardware in clinics and hospitals, then sell the kits through the hardware's distribution channels (see Centocor in appendix, p. 414). Genzyme's focus on orphan drugs—treatments for rare but deadly diseases—likewise attracted few imitators as other biotechs went after blockbuster drugs for major unmet medical needs (see

[24] The fault lines between the academy and industry had long been drawn on the principles of openness and autonomy. The academy was purported to be much less constrained in the allocation of scientists' time and attention. The new biotech firms challenged these conventions by offering relief from the burdens of grantsmanship, committees, and teaching, as well as access to exciting new research tools (Kornberg 1995). Cetus was described as a "playground for academic scientists" (Glaser 2006, 105).

Genzyme in appendix, p. 422). For both Centocor and Genzyme, their unique strategies led to predictable cash flow and quicker profitability but failed to find traction in a nascent industry bent on curing the incurable through cutting-edge science.

Among the early companies, only Genzyme and later Amgen would attempt to grow by acquiring other biotech companies. Chiron was founded by noted academics, very much in the vein of Genentech and Biogen, but with a twist. The academic heads of Chiron felt that the skills of running large laboratories and managing researchers could be translated to a start-up firm. In almost every other case, the professors who were founders of start-up companies did not seek the role of top manager. Chiron and Genzyme were alike in that they were initially bankrolled with the migration of a research grant from a university to the company.

Looking at the distinctive elements of each company in chronological order, we find no apparent pattern of temporal diffusion. Nor is there a pattern of regional similarity. It is not the case that early West Coast companies resembled each other more or bore less resemblance to their East Coast counterparts. And though the sample is small, there is little sign of a "founder's effect." Companies whose founders had comparable prior experiences developed in quite divergent ways.[25] Instead of a temporal, regional, or biographical clustering, the attributes appear to cleave with respect to how deep the respective imprints of science and commerce were.

TWO VARIANTS OF THE DBF MODEL: SCIENCE VS. COMMERCE

To explore this distinction between start-up companies that fused science to finance with those that combined commerce and finance, we compare the firms in terms of important attributes that were common to two or more of the companies. Our analysis of the archival and interview materials points to a handful of widely shared features that DBFs borrowed or transposed from the academy, industry, and venture capital. These attributes and their distribution across the companies are presented in table 13.3.

After sorting the companies on each of the eleven key attributes, using a rudimentary blockmodeling technique, a distinctive pattern emerged. Three of the four elements on the science side cohere, most notably: a strong insistence that newly hired scientists be allowed to publish and contribute to public science; a campus-like setting near a university; and a founder who retained his university position. The firms that displayed these attributes most clearly were Cetus, Genentech, Biogen, Chiron, and Immunex. The all-star, high-profile science advisory board was more common to the commerce-oriented firms, which often flaunted such boards as a signal of their credibility but did not display the same commitment to letting scientific considerations shape the organization and direction of their respective companies. At the other end of the spectrum, there was another group of start-ups where science features were less prevalent; instead, they borrowed elements from the world of commerce, including having a founder with a prior business track record and choosing an experienced senior executive from the world of health care to run the company. Often, a restless senior manager was persuaded to leave a second-tier pharmaceutical company and take the risk of being the top executive at a new biotech firm.[26] At this group of companies, the scientific founders left their university positions and many of them went on to become serial entrepreneurs, starting numerous companies. Most of these companies opted initially to pursue non-therapeutic products, rather than novel medicines, in order to have consistent and predictable sources of revenue. The examples here include Genex, Hybritech, Centocor, Amgen, and Genzyme.

[25] For example, Amgen and Hybritech were very similar in founding team characteristics: a well-regarded younger stellar scientist, top-drawer venture capital backing, and an experienced pharma exec in charge. But Hybritech opted for quick growth with monoclonal antibody diagnostics and was bred for sale to Big Pharma, whereas Amgen swung for the fences to develop novel therapeutics and become a stand-alone company. Genex and Immunex were also alike in their respective founders' backgrounds but opted for completely different strategies—Genex chose a highly commercial, low-cost route of producing specialty chemicals, and Immunex went for developing first-to-the-world medicines. In contrast, Biogen and Chiron were similar in having strong scientific credentials in their top leadership, and neither allowed much room for commercial input in their early years.

[26] Interestingly, the execs who took the leap from pharma to take the helm of an unbuilt ship did not come from industry giants such as Merck or Pfizer but instead from Abbott and Baxter. These were second-tier companies organized into entrepreneurial divisions where general managers had considerably more autonomy than in the more hierarchical, giant firms (Higgins 2005). Abbott ended up providing a pipeline of managers to Amgen as well as a successor CEO to Biogen, and Baxter a cadre of senior managers to both Genzyme and later Biogen, replacing its scientist founders.

Table 13.3. Science vs. Commerce: A Continuum

DOMAIN	Cetus 1971	Genentech 1976	Biogen 1978	Chiron 1981	Immunex 1981	ALZA 1968	Genex 1977	Hybritech 1978	Centocor 1979	Amgen 1980	Genzyme 1981
SCIENCE											
Insistence that scientists publish their findings	X	X	X	X	X	X					
Campus-like setting near a major research university	X	X		X	X	X		X	X		
Founder(s) continued at or returned to university or institute	X	X	X	X				X	X		
All-star science advisory board	X		X			X	X			X	X
FINANCE											
Research contracts with large corporations	X	X	X	X	X	X	X	X		X	
Scientific founder(s) *became* VCs or angel investors		X		X	X		X	X			
Active VC involvement in early management		X						X			X
IPO with no products and no predict-able revenue stream	X					X				X	
COMMERCE											
Founder(s) with entrepreneurial track record	X			X			X		X	X	X
Early hiring of senior exec from health care or pharma						X		X	X	X	X
Initial emphasis on non-therapeutic applications	X					X	X	X	X		

We want to stress that we neither view these combinations as an either/or choice of models nor believe that the founders had clear templates in mind. Rather, the distribution of elements in table 13.3 is best viewed as a continuum, ranging from the "pure" domain of science to the "pure" domain of commerce. Finance was blended into both, with its largest imprint at Genentech and Hybritech. We think the various combinations of elements created composite organizational models, which predisposed the participants to act in different ways as a result of both prior experiences and pragmatic responses to new opportunities. Note, in particular, that the science cluster drew less on commercial elements than the commercial cluster built on scientific practices. Unlike in traditional technology start-ups, in which scientific research spawns technological applications that then follow a trajectory that is largely independent of university science, the entire field of biotechnology has drawn on and collaborated with university-based research and depended on basic science for continuing input (Powell 1996).

The commerce-driven companies were clearly more "orderly," in contrast to the "bet the farm" blue-sky approach at the science-dominated companies. Amgen was perhaps the most planned in advance, as experienced venture capitalists set out to "do biotech right" by both recruiting a stellar scientific advisory board and putting a talented, well-regarded pharmaceutical executive in charge. Amgen went on to become the largest biotech firm. Similarly, Hybritech and Centocor had reasonably deep prior founder experience from both the pharmaceutical industry and venture capital. These firms were eventually purchased and absorbed by pharma giants Eli Lilly and Johnson & Johnson, respectively. The fit between the commerce variant and the pharmaceutical world is fairly clear; the disjuncture between the science model and the commercial ethos is vividly illustrated with the case of Biogen.

Consider the contrasting portraits of Wally Gilbert, Biogen cofounder and Harvard professor, given by veteran pharmaceutical executive Hugh D'Andrade and by science journalist Stephen Hall. D'Andrade was an attorney for Ciba-Geigy from 1968 to 1981; he joined New Jersey–based pharma giant Schering-Plough as senior vice president in 1981. He served as Schering's representative on Biogen's board for six years, overseeing their joint interferon project. He described going to the Biogen scientific board meetings in Geneva as follows:

> There would be a two-day scientific board meeting before each board meeting. Two full days. They were real events. . . . Somebody would get up and make a presentation, and then Wally Gilbert [chair of the science board]—I don't know whether Wally tried to humiliate; I couldn't read his mind. And being a non-scientist I couldn't appreciate exactly what was going on. But it looked like the guy presenting wasn't having a lot of fun! Charles Weissman [head of the Zurich lab] is a gentler soul, but could be pretty tough. They'd have the lab scientists present . . . and members of the scientific board would go at them, and then go at each other. So it was very, very rigorous. (2001, 8–10)

From a corporate lawyer's perspective, the science board meetings looked like the Grand Inquisition; moreover, they trumped the board of directors meetings in importance! To a science journalist, however, Gilbert cast a different image:

> To his peers, Walter Gilbert possessed a most desirable array of scientific traits: great intellectual curiosity, rigorous scientific standards, a rich imagination, and a lust for understanding the way life worked in its most microscopic and, in many respects, most intricately beautiful manifestation. "I'm driven by just an intense curiosity," he [Gilbert] would say, his very self-explanation riven by a kind of driving impatience. "I love new things, new ideas, new facts. It goes along with a tremendous impatience. It's very nice to have the old things, but a week or so later, they're all old hat, and you want something new." His was a pursuit of correctness, a kind of intellectual high ground, so focused and astute that temporal distractions—like a caviling colleague—intruded at some peril. (Hall 1987, 29–30)

Different interpretations of intellectual jousting carry over into disparate views of how laboratories should be organized. Hall was attracted by Gilbert's spontaneity and intensity, whereas D'Andrade was alarmed. Hall (1987, 36) describes Gilbert's Harvard lab in this manner:

> The atmosphere in Gilbert's lab reflected the personality of the leader in two important respects: the craving for information was immense, something akin to physical need, and the tone of the place was casual, almost

> fiercely informal. Graduate students would drift into the lab around noon . . . , and often work until the wee hours of the morning or on through the next day. There would be mass excursions to the local Szechwan restaurant for meals, or sandwiches grabbed on the fly. DNA would be chopped and mixed and analyzed to the sounds of Joni Mitchell and the Rolling Stones. At about three or four a.m., the stereos would turn up very loud. People would be working madly.

In contrast, D'Andrade (2001, 10) felt that Biogen, with its amalgam of seven top-tier science labs located at elite universities, was "an organization in constant conflict and turmoil. Because the work was all being parceled out . . . , there was no centralized decision-making structure. There were no regular interactions, other than the scientific board, that would allow the scientists to coordinate their actions, and there was no executive authority."

These differing accounts nicely capture the competing goals of science and industry. Inside Gilbert's lab, the paramount concerns were novel information and speed, guided by both intense curiosity and skepticism about any answer. To a seasoned pharmaceutical executive, this looked like a disorderly debate team, lacking coordination and authority. As a result, resource allocation decisions and project investments were difficult to make. D'Andrade (2001, 12) clearly thought that oversight was needed, and he chafed at the lab operating model transposed to Biogen: "Biogen's unique organizing concept when it set itself up was that it was run by its scientists, not by the venture capitalists or the banks." He felt that Amgen beat Biogen to the release of the earliest biotech medicines because it was able to use "brute force," that is, it was "hierarchically structured and the executives had the scientists in the lab," not the boardroom. D'Andrade (2001, 16) nevertheless recognized the promise in the Biogen model: "I don't know how anybody could have spent as much time as I did with people like Wally Gilbert, Charles Weissman, and Phil Sharp, and not be convinced that they were going to be successful. They were just extraordinarily intelligent people, with more energy and drive than most corporate executives have."[27]

The pharmaceutical-biotech contrast also comes through in discussions of publishing scientific results, which is perhaps the most central divide between the science model and the commerce variant. In the pharmaceutical industry, the open science model of publishing scientific findings was largely eschewed, as freely sharing research was regarded as giving away the crown jewels. Concerns about appropriability and intellectual property took precedence over open science. As a consequence, pharmaceutical scientists were career employees, typically staying with one firm throughout their lives unless they opted to move out of the lab into management, where they might build up a track record of accomplishment that would bring them recognition and capture the attention of other companies. Even scientists who received some recognition by having their name on a crucial patent did not have the kind of currency that would generate attention in the world outside the large corporate R&D lab. Salaried researchers at Big Pharma assumed little personal risk; in return for their efforts they received well-compensated, steady employment.

Genentech, nurtured for its first two years in Boyer's UCSF lab, broke the mold on restricting publishing, transposing the academic invisible college model into the new company as it moved into its South San Francisco headquarters. Cofounder Bob Swanson (2001, 56–57) commented: "it was always clear that we were going to publish our results. Everybody wanted to publish in *Nature* or *Science* or another good journal, and so what we did had to be of a quality that would be published." Here science and intellectual property were put to joint use. Again, Swanson is on point: "So we said, look, let's publish the results; let's make sure we get the patents, and we'll make the patent attorneys work overtime to get them filed before you actually get the papers out. But we'll have to work together on that."

Genentech bet that they could create an alternative to both the academic world and the corporate sector, a setting with more autonomy and opportunity than both. Like industry scientists, their early hires would not have the academic concerns of writing grants. Unlike pharmaceutical or academic scientists, they had a chance to

[27] Later in the interview, D'Andrade (2001, 21) was asked about biotechnology in New Jersey: "I associate pharmaceutical companies with New Jersey, but not biotechnology. The Biogen way of organizing things demonstrated that the people with the techniques to do this early cloning were in universities. You could have gone to every pharmaceutical company in New Jersey and you wouldn't have found a Wally Gilbert."

be owners of the enterprise.[28] They were given equity, and as the company thrived, the value of their stock went up. Such financial opportunity was quite appealing to young scientists at the postdoc and assistant professor career stages. At the same time, publishing was a channel back into the world of university science.[29] Swanson (2001, 57) commented:

> Boyer's philosophy, which I agreed with, was that you gain more from interaction with your academic peers than you give up by telling the competition where you are. So with interaction you can move quicker; you gain more people willing to collaborate with you. We knew then we weren't going to have all the best ideas, and we said, where do the academic scientists go when they have an idea that they think needs to be commercialized? We want them to come to Genentech first, because this is a group of scientists that are well published and that a university scientist would be proud to collaborate with, where they can get a product developed and make it available. So that was a goal from the very beginning.

In contrast to Genentech, Genex made a deliberate decision not to permit its scientists to publish, choosing to pursue more applied work. This strategy was adopted even though its scientific cofounder was an esteemed senior scientist at the University of Michigan and coauthor with Paul Berg of Stanford on a famous 1972 paper that described a new method of generating hybrid DNA molecules using a complementary extension to form a new duplex DNA molecule that could be expressed in mammalian cells (Jackson et al. 1972). We spoke with David Jackson in August 2009, and he evinced some regret about their prohibition against publishing.

> We did make a decision that was different from what Genentech made. They made a deliberate decision that they wanted their people to publish and that they were going to support them and deal with the intellectual property issues that arose, either, hopefully, proactively but if necessary reactively. And I have come to think that Genentech's way is the right way. I think it does help one recruit to let people who you're trying to hire know that they will be able to continue to publish. I think science is such a collaborative and communicative enterprise that you really do need to be connected to a broad, effectively world-wide, community. And the way you do that is by telling people about what you're doing that they're interested in, and you talk to them about what they're doing that you're interested in, and in the long run, everybody benefits from that.

Immunex, the Seattle-based company that spun out of the Fred Hutchinson Cancer Center, also went the science route, encouraging its scientists to publish freely and collaborate with others in the new field. In an August 2009 interview, cofounder Steve Gillis reflected on the relational benefits of publishing:

> We encouraged scientists within the company to publish their findings and speak at meetings. We made reagents freely available to investigators who wanted to play with things that we had invented; again, we weren't totally stupid about that, we had them sign material transfer agreements. But that resulted in spreading the influence of the company, and allowed us to get collaborators who otherwise might not have been open to collaborating with us, because we had this relatively open relationship with academia.

[28] Running through many of the interviews with scientists who moved to biotech labs is the sense that working in these companies was more fun than the academy. David Martin, a professor of medicine and biochemistry at UCSF and a prestigious Howard Hughes investigator, initially declined offers to move to Genentech, but after giving a seminar there he was hooked: "There was a rather broad camaraderie. Everybody was working on the same team, rather than in a series of fiefdoms. I realized that my career opportunities at UCSF, while pretty clear-cut, were not very exciting. At Genentech, however, the opportunities to break out of the mold were tremendous" (quoted in Van Brunt 2000, 3). Martin was cautious, worried that the move would be irreversible. He consulted with colleagues, program directors at the NIH, and even the Howard Hughes people, all of whom encouraged him to "give it a whirl," saying they'd welcome him back. He joined Genentech in 1983 and never returned to academe.

[29] We have highlighted both chance and naïveté, but necessity also loomed large in forging these new companies. Axel Ullrich (2006, 22), one of the first-generation cloners who subsequently cloned insulin, moved from a postdoc at UCSF to Genentech with great trepidation: "How could we know what Genentech would be? Essentially, we made it what it is. And that was made out of concern. The reason Genentech became such a major power in basic research is because of people like me and Peter [Seeburg]. We were worried that if we started doing commercial research we would have problems returning to academia if things wouldn't work out. We were discriminated against at that time. We thought that if we [did] all this applied stuff, we couldn't publish. It would be terrible. We would never get a job if the company failed. If it turned out that this whole thing would never work, we would be in the streets. So we had to publish."

"LASH-UP": THE ASSEMBLY OF ELEMENTS FROM MULTIPLE DOMAINS

Our final step in the analysis is to ask how the various components fit together and became a coherent assembly, and with what ramifications. Analytically, our aim is to capture both *process*—that is, how do elements of science, commerce, and finance flow out of those domains into a new entity—and *feedback dynamics*—that is, the manner in which practices are repurposed and shape the contours of a new field, with potent reverberations back into their domains of origin. We shall see that it is important to keep these two stages analytically distinct, as the commerce model became the more common DBF form, whereas the science model had transformative effects on the world of the academy, the pharmaceutical industry, and venture capital.

Transformative feedback effects, we argue, are often associated with transpositions—or, at least, with those that survive long enough for such reverberations to be felt. At the heart of the transposition process is the disruption or reconfiguration of a domain's fundamental autocatalytic process—that is, the self-sustaining flows of ideas and resources that constitute and reproduce actors and activities within that domain. When a "trespasser" enters a foreign domain, he or she carries cognitive and material resources from her domain of origin. If the trespasser is of sufficient stature to be taken seriously in the new domain, her customary uses of ideas and resources have the potential to intermingle with existing flows within the new domain. This confluence of ideas and resources from previously separate domains holds great potential to generate novel social forms, or what Sewell (1992) calls "structures." And because the novel form remains connected to both prior domains, its new arrangements of schemas and resources are transportable back into these worlds through the flows of ideas and people. Hence, instances of transposition are freighted with the opportunity, but not the guarantee, of transformative feedback effects.

The process of "lash-up" is represented in figure 13.1, juxtaposing a "traditional" high-tech venture with the two variants of the DBF. Technology-based start-ups often drew ideas from university science, as well as human capital in the form of university graduates. If the ideas were sufficiently tangible, they could be licensed as intellectual property. This exchange, however, was a one-way transfer from the academy to industry. Investors were attracted through the public equity markets, and financial analysts evaluated a company's prospects before deciding to invest. The core activity of the firm was the conversion of knowledge into marketable products, which generated revenues, funding the development of additional products, and so on. Note that in the stylized model at the top of figure 13.1, there is *no* overlap between the flow of funding and knowledge in the science domain and the flow of capital and return in the finance domain.

With the emergence of the DBF, autocatalytic flows in the formerly separate domains began to intermingle in a way that was markedly different from either the "industrial science" model of Big Pharma or the "garage start-up" template of information and computer technology ventures.[31] First, traditional pharmaceutical firms

[31] A number of readers have asked whether the DBF model bore any imprint of the mid-twentieth-century industrial R&D labs of large corporations, which were "somewhat insulated from immediate demands yet responsive to long-term company needs" (Reich 1985, 3). Our reading of the business history literature, as well as conversations with the historian Margaret Graham, lead us to believe there are limited parallels.

During the first two decades of the twentieth century, a host of leading U.S. firms—GE, AT&T, DuPont, Kodak, Dow, Standard Oil, Goodyear, and many others—formed internal laboratories to protect their companies' core technologies from being undermined by individual inventors and competitors (Hounshell 1996; Graham 2008). These decisions were prompted by a mix of influences—fear of government antitrust action, a desire to imitate the success of German corporate labs, notably in chemicals, and some degree of faddishness. This bringing of science inside the firm was not without challenges, as many leading scientists and early company lab directors viewed industry R&D as "tainted." James Conant, head of Harvard's chemistry department and university president, regarded DuPont chemists as "a keen lot . . . thought I don't think they compare with us academics. . . .They impress me particularly as lacking in the fine critical judgment of the best teachers, and I wonder whether this is the cause or effect of their industrial relations" (quoted in Hounshell 1996, 27). Conant would not allow his best students in the 1920s and 1930s to go to DuPont for fear his and his students' reputations would suffer, but he was not averse to recommending a "much less able man" for a DuPont job (ibid., 28). During World War II and for decades afterward, many of the corporate labs working in the fields of electronics, aeronautics, and communications became tethered to military funding. This close relationship with the Department of Defense had fateful consequences. The most skilled industrial scientists were assigned to military work, and their research was shrouded in secrecy, largely removing them from regular contact with university science. The corporate labs did not engage much in basic research; in the few cases where they did, such as Bell Labs, the research did not link to application. The labs excelled at systemic development, bundling together disparate work as in the case of color television at RCA. In sum, the DBF model was more the antithesis of the corporate labs than a lineage of them. To be sure, the technology boom of the late 1960s and 1970s did produce some organizational practices that found their way into the DBF model but only after significant modification. Cooperation

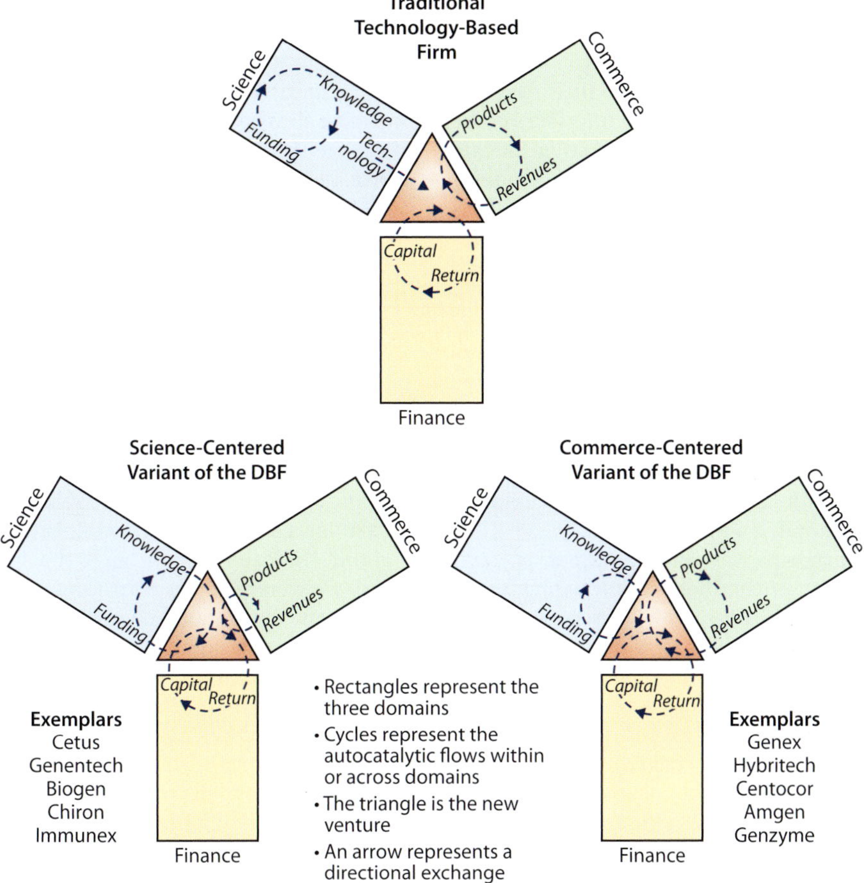

Figure 13.1 The intersection of science, finance, and commerce—three models.

had considerable difficulty accessing the breakthrough discoveries in molecular biology (Orsenigo 1989; Gambardella 1995); moreover, the insular organization of their research labs was unappealing to world-class researchers. When he was a young professor at the University of Illinois, William Rutter (later of UCSF and Chiron) tried to work with a series of pharma companies, including Abbott, Lilly, and Merck, to develop vaccines. But he was unsuccessful in attempts "to broaden their research interests," unable to overcome the view of executives that "there would be only narrow applicability of biotechnology to the pharmaceutical industry," and frustrated by their lack of interest in socially valuable research (Rutter 1997, 58–60). For top-flight university scientists to leave the academy to go to a company, the research opportunities had to be superior. Thus when these elite scientists "trespassed" into the worlds of commerce and finance to start their own companies, they imported (as much out of naïveté as necessity) the invisible college model and searched for alternatives to the cycle of applying for federal grants. This move opened the autocatalytic flow

among competitors was common in the early days of Silicon Valley, for example, but it was a symbiosis of componentry, not core science (Saxenian 1994). Elite universities (MIT and Stanford, primarily) produced raw engineering talent for the tech explosion, but faculty were rarely involved in start-ups; rather, senior faculty placed chosen grad students in the new ventures (Roberts 1991). Finally, the high-tech model was one of a "parent" organization—Fairchild Semiconductor and Hewlett-Packard in the West, various MIT engineering labs in the East—that spawned continuing generations of spin-offs. In contrast, biotech developed a pattern of scientific and commercial collaborations that formed, dissolved, and re-formed (see Powell et al. 2005).

of knowledge production within the science domain to altogether new sources of funding.

The need for funding brought scientists and venture capitalists together, and their meeting triggered notable changes in both. The model of venture capital that had developed in the late 1970s was ill suited for biotech and off-putting to academic scientists.[32] The idea that VCs would ante up start-up capital for a product prototype and increase funding as the prospect of a market opportunity led to an IPO did not map onto the tremendous cost of drug development, the lengthy process of drug discovery, or protracted stages of clinical trials and regulatory review. A handful of venture capitalists began to explore how to signal commercial progress in the absence of prototypes or tangible products and hit upon the idea that scientific accomplishment could be such a marker.

The repurposing of scientific output as a criterion for investment had wide-ranging ramifications. Researchers at the science-oriented biotechs began publishing in top journals, proving that the academic coin of the realm not only retained its value in industry but could be deployed to attract new sources of funding and talent, as young scientists increasingly gravitated to what had previously been considered a second-class career. But just as university researchers moved into industry, industry-spawned ideas also migrated to the academy. Scientists and their universities shifted from the older, traditional model of technology transfer to much more hands-on engagement through university spin-offs, equity participation, and a wide array of research partnerships between universities and companies. In time, the types of arrangements that were previously looked at askance became regarded as appropriate and subsequently were endorsed with enthusiasm (Colyvas and Powell 2006).

But not only university science was transformed. Leading venture capitalists were busy coming up with their own novel practices. Tom Perkins, for example, created two financial innovations in response to the unique requirements of biotech. One was designed to shield a struggling biotech's balance sheet from the enormous costs of clinical trials; the other was a means to retain scientists who were being poached by second- and third-generation companies that could offer equity options as an enticement. Perkins (2002, 9–10) recalled the first of these, the "clinical R&D partnership":

> There had to be a lot of financial engineering in this thing. . . . If you looked at the profit and loss statement, there was no income, no sales. Tremendous expense, big loss. It dawned on me that that was not a viable financial model. Subsequent world events with the Internet have changed that. But in those days, a company was supposed to make earnings, or at least have reasonable prospects of making earnings fairly soon. And we had to fund clinical trials through the FDA. After all, we were making pharmaceuticals. I didn't see how we could take Genentech public and have a decent stock price if that's what our P&L was going to look like. Gallons of red ink for years. So I invented this idea of the clinical R&D partnership. We separated out the clinical trials, the largest expense in any drug development company. We set up a partnership that would fund the clinical trials, and that funding came back to Genentech. So the profit and loss statement is transformed. At the top line, you have hundreds of millions of dollars coming in as revenue. Then the company does the clinical trial under a subcontract, and has that expense. It essentially breaks even on that whole transaction. With a stroke of a pen I was able to change the P&L from just horrific red ink to break-even. . . .These worked very well, until some years later the Securities and Exchange Commission decided it was too aggressive.

The second innovation was a form of "junior common stock," concocted as a means to hire and retain scientists after Genentech had its initial public offering and the financial opportunity to hold shares in a pre-public company had waned. After Genentech's landmark IPO in 1980, Perkins recalled that the retention of key employees and younger scientists became an issue:

> We didn't have a clue how to price the stock. We knew it was going to be a hot issue, and oversubscribed. But Swanson, the board, the

[32] Nobel laureate Arthur Kornberg (1998) described his discomfort when a would-be dealmaker tried to enlist his involvement in an early venture: "After two meetings with them I was completely disillusioned. . . . I don't know how the business prospectus was formulated, but it would encompass recombinant DNA, genetic engineering, microbial hosts, processing, purification, and so on—very vague. Some venture capitalists on Sand Hill Road [Menlo Park] were putting it together, and it was clear that they expected it to be a profitable or marketable enterprise within two or three years. I was a little put off by them and their attitude."

> management, the investment bankers—we were all caught somewhat by surprise. It came out at thirty-five, shot up to eighty-five, then drifted back down. But that spread brought world wide publicity. Everybody knew about Genentech. It established the idea that you could start a new biotechnology company, raise obscene amounts of money, hire good employees, sell stock to the public. Our competitors started doing all of that, so much so that it became an impediment for us to hire and retain employees. We started to lose employees to other biotech start-ups. Our employees had originally acquired our stock as common stock. We were able to justify a ten-to-one difference in price. So if the preferred stock was at thirty-five a share, then employees got common at three-fifty a share. . . . But you can only do that once. Once it becomes a public stock, the preferred shares convert to common and everyone is on the same platform. So how are we going to continue to attract these people? Continue to hold these people? It was a big problem. (2002, 10)

Perkins created a new kind of stock that did not have voting or liquidation rights. In the event of a merger, holders of this stock would be last in line to redeem their shares.

> We got an opinion from the accountants that this stock was only worth one tenth of what the regular common stock was worth, and we called it junior common stock. It would convert to ordinary common stock in case of certain events . . . such as: Genentech had to be earning a certain amount, or some product had to be achieved, events they had to work towards which have a risk factor. By diddling that formula over about four years, we were able to use that form of stock to attract and hold key employees. We were the first company to ever have such a thing. My name and fingerprints were all over it. We were very careful to run these plans through the SEC. They approved it. We never had to retract any of that stock. However, the idea was stolen by all of our competitors and so grossly abused that the SEC made most of our competitors retract and eliminate those stock plans. (2002, 11)

In summary, the intersecting flows of ideas and resources from science and finance rebounded into both domains. Top-tier scientists moved their research into start-up companies, unleashing new career possibilities for younger scientists. Yet these amphibious founders retained their university affiliations—and in turn, universities became much more immersed in the commercial exploitation of basic research. In the venture capital domain, leading VCs had to rethink their investment model to accommodate the protracted and unpredictable timetable of drug discovery and development. In the early years, they converted scientific fame and later notable research papers into evidence of commercial promise. They developed the idea of milestone payments, very much like the renewal of a program project grant. And in a number of cases, the VC partners took the lead executive role, as the scientific founders were either uninterested in such duties or not equipped for them. The result was a thorough mixing of science and finance for commercial purposes, with transformative feedback effects in each realm.

Such mixing was not without contestation, however. For example, Genentech's early existence as a "virtual" company created unprecedented tensions in the academy. The idea of a for-profit company funding and owning the research output of a university lab was not only foreign but offensive to some. Edward Penhoet, subsequently a cofounder of Chiron, spent a sabbatical year at UCSF in 1978 and remembers the infamous day that a senior researcher placed a lock on the freezers where his reagents were stored:

> While I was there, Howard Goodman put locks on all his freezers, because Axel Ullrich and Pete Seeburg had left his lab to go to Genentech. Howard was concerned that they had taken clones with them that belonged to him. . . . So that was a tumultuous time over there, with the locks on the freezers, et cetera, and with those two guys going down the street with the clones. So you couldn't be at UCSF in '78 without sensing all of this foment about what was happening in the field . . . and the controversy around the general issue of shared resources between UCSF and Genentech. (2001, 96–97)

If locking the freezers was new to academia, leaving the labs unlocked was equally out of place in commercial R&D. Yet Arthur Kornberg fought to keep badges and locks out of DNAX, a biotech start-up he cofounded, after it was acquired by Schering-Plough:

> [I]t is conventional or maybe even unfailing that when you enter a pharmaceutical company, you get a badge; you log in, and you carry some indication of who you are and that you're a visitor. . . . At DNAX we'd have none of that. You could come and go as you please, anywhere. I thought that was an essential atmosphere in an academic institution, and DNAX, by its very proclamation of intent, said there were no secrets; we are open; we exchange innovations, etc. Then the current president . . . in response to pressure from Schering-Plough for security agreed that you couldn't enter DNAX by the side or back door without a passkey . . . I objected. I thought this practice was contrary to what we'd established, but I was voted down. (1998)

Of course, secrecy and concern for ownership were not unheard of in academia; scientific recognition has long been built on being first to publish key results. Competition between labs propels scientific progress. The introduction of a direct commercial challenge, however, disrupted longstanding patterns of interaction *within* university labs, a change that was at first contested and then lamented by academic purists (Yoxen 1984; also see Colyvas and Maroulis, this volume). Today, badges and passkeys have become conventional throughout academic science.

The commerce model (depicted in the lower right side of figure 13.1) recombined existing practices and hence produced less novel action. As discussed above, commerce-driven DBFs typically featured mid-career executives from established health care companies who took the plunge to head up new ventures in the unproven world of molecular biology. Not surprisingly, these executives sought ways to attenuate the risks (business and personal) of their unorthodox career moves. First, they focused their firms on more tangible and short-term goals—for instance, specialty chemicals (Genex) or monoclonal antibodies (Hybritech, Centocor) that did not have to go through FDA review, or orphan drugs (Genzyme) where competition was precluded. Only Amgen went after the new-to-the-world medicines similar to those that the science-focused companies pursued, but it organized its laboratories and research program rather more along the lines of a traditional pharma company. Second, the commerce variants developed closer, long-lasting relationships than were typical between hired managers and venture capitalists: Hybritech's first CEO *was* its venture capitalist, Brook Byers, and Genzyme's VCs were actively involved in running the company for much of its first decade.

Science was needed in these companies, too, but typically the scientific founder left the academy, limiting his connections to and influence in the broader community of scientists. Younger scientists who came to work in these well-paid jobs forsook the opportunity to return to the academy as publishing was much less commonplace in the commerce model. These firms also forged research and development partnerships with large pharmaceutical companies, and eventually Hybritech and Centocor were acquired by their larger partners. In contrast, the science-based companies fought to maintain their independence, viewing merger as a loss.[33] Venture capital and law firms played a critical role in negotiating the terms of partnerships with established companies, as the young, commerce-influenced companies did not want to give away their most valuable assets too cheaply. Many of the relationships with Big Pharma turned sour, however. Hybritech was acquired by Eli Lilly in 1986, and within a year all the former Hybritech employees had left. Genex built a close supply relationship with Searle, going so far as to set up a factory, only to have Searle pull the plug on the deal, sending Genex stock on a downward spiral (see Genex in appendix, p. 420). Amgen jointly developed its drug for kidney failure and dialysis with Ortho, a subsidiary of Johnson & Johnson, only to become embroiled in a decade of lawsuits.

In short, the commerce variant involved more of the familiar features of corporate relationships—partnerships that often led to either acquisition or litigation or both. But the commerce model also proved to be a route to success, as the acquisitions of Hybritech and Centocor produced a plethora of well-compensated employees, and Amgen and Genzyme grew into very large firms.

We summarize the development paths in each domain in table 13.6, going through the stages and their consequences. Our takeaway from this analysis is that the transpositions that occurred

[33] When Amgen acquired Immunex in 1991, the Seattle scientists lamented that Amgen did not encourage the publishing of research results, saying that "Amgen is big pharma" with a completely different culture (see Immunex in appendix). In summer 2008, as Swiss giant Roche moved to buy up all of the stock of Genentech, employees of the Bay Area company took to the media to decry a loss of independence and an end of Camelot that would threaten an illustrious thirty-three-year history of research and medical accomplishments. Now that the acquisition is complete, Roche is attempting to leave in place Genentech's research culture (Weintraub 2009).

Table 13.6.
The Creation of Novelty, Step-by-Step

	SCIENCE	FINANCE	COMMERCE
Established routines prove lacking . . .	Traditional corporate R&D model is too insular and proprietary for biotech's purposes; in addition, top-flight researchers are unwilling to leave the academy unless the research (not just economic) opportunities are comparable.	Existing VC approach (i.e., provide small amount of start-up capital, increasing as product goes to market, followed by IPO) is ill suited to the funding needs (in quantity and duration) of biotech development.	Barriers to entry in the pharma business are formidable: clinical trials, FDA approval, creation of distribution channels, scaling up manufacturing. Traditional "bootstrap" model (i.e., start small and channel early revenues into growth) was not feasible. There is no such thing as a credible "low-budget" clinical trial, and cutting-edge life science production processes cannot be easily outsourced to contract manufacturers.
. . . so founders draw on existing knowledge . . .	Scientific founders import the invisible college into a corporate setting, minus the grant chasing and tenure dynamics.	VCs realize that the crucial issue is how to signal commercial progress in the absence of products. Without such signals, the biotech ventures will fail to attract continued investment.	Biotech founders import a proven commercialization model from the world of academia: technology transfer.* In this setting, the transfer is between two for-profit entities, but the resource asymmetries are similar: biotechs have crucial knowledge that big pharma lacks, whereas big pharma has commercialization capabilities.
. . . and scan their social worlds for cues . . .	Top scientists look to each other for validation of commercial involvement and judge the legitimacy of a new model using their customary criteria: quality of scientific output (i.e., publishing in top journals). At the same time, they scan the "new" world of commerce for cues and realize the importance of patenting before publication.	At the intersection of academic science and commercial drug development, VCs see two novel opportunities for demonstrating a biotech venture's worthiness for additional investment: (a) research partnerships with big pharma (validating the eventual product potential of the venture's core science); and (b) the sheer scientific performance of the venture (including stature of founders and/or SAB and publication record of scientific staff).**	To remain viable as commercial entities, however, fledgling biotechs must aggressively negotiate the terms of such technology transfers. Access to legal counsel (typically via their VC's network) becomes crucial, as biotechs learn to "sell" their scientific advances to pharma partners without jeopardizing their future independence.
. . . forging unique elements of a science-based organizational form.	R&D becomes a porous, networked endeavor whose results are published in the top journals. New career paths are established for academic life scientists.	This results in a flowering of inventive financing mechanisms: milestone agreements; research partnerships; initial, second, and third public offerings without any commercial products; tracking stocks; etc.	As a result, a wide variety of partnerships are created between small, science-rich biotechs and large, wealthy product-driven pharmaceutical companies. Many of these bargains prove Faustian, as biotechs forfeit ownership and control in exchange for resources.

*In commerce-driven firms, founders from large pharma drew on existing knowledge and realized the quickest way to make money was to avoid human therapeutics altogether. This was the path taken by Hybritech, Genex, and (initially) Centocor

**Note how mechanisms for dealing with uncertainty were transposed from one domain to another. In science, uncertainty is reduced by reliance on a broader scientific community via publication and peer review. This mechanism was imported into the commercial domain in two ways. First, science-oriented biotech firms organized R&D as an invisible college, based on the idea that isolation from the rest of the scientific world is a bigger risk than disclosing one's own breakthroughs—a fundamentally different approach to uncertainty reduction from the corporate R&D model. Second, and more strikingly, VCs promoted these firms' scientific accomplishments as a way to reduce *investor* uncertainty.

in the science-based company were much more far-reaching in their novel aspects than were the recombinations of the commerce model. The intersection of science and finance produced all manner of "fresh action," whose consequences proved destabilizing for both the academy and industry. Nonetheless, recombinatory activities in the commerce-centered firms also had feedback consequences in the academy. For example, failures at product development reverberated in unexpected ways. Centocor was founded as a product-focused biotech, producing reagents and diagnostics rather than human therapeutics. Seduced by the sexier science-based model, however, the company shifted its focus in the mid-1980s and placed a huge bet on the success of Centoxin, a monoclonal-derived anti-sepsis treatment:

> Our [original] plan was founded as being producers of reagents. We evolved into product development and fully integrated into that side of it, using partners. Then, in the mid-1980s, we decided to take the technology platform and apply it for therapeutics to treat sepsis, septic shock. . . . From 1986 to 1992, we essentially worked on that vision and dream of being a fully independent biopharmaceutical company, essentially built around the success of Centoxin. . . . What happened was that the originating culture got fragmented. From the mid-1980s to 1992, you saw two businesses at Centocor: there was the diagnostic business, which was pretty much of the founding culture; and there was the pharmaceutical business. (Holveck 2001, 46)

In 1992 Centoxin failed to receive FDA approval. Centocor made drastic headcount reductions and barely survived as an independent company. More far-reaching, however, was the blowback of regulatory failure into academic science. Sepsis research had been a prominent and growing area of scientific inquiry in the 1980s. But Centocor's high-profile failure "killed sepsis research for ten years," according to Richard Proctor, Global Director of Scientific Affairs for Infectious Diseases at Merck: "Sepsis research became a pariah—no funding, no projects. It was an enormous setback for an important line of research" (2009). That a commercial and regulatory setback could place such a long-lasting damper on the funding of basic research shows how intertwined the domains of commerce, finance, and science had become by the early 1990s. Although such interconnections had forged a new organizational form, they also had become a conduit for the transfer of evaluation criteria and standards of desirability between domains.

We have emphasized the extent to which transposition uproots the status quo in multiple domains. Perhaps our point is best illuminated by a comparison of the consequences of trespassing versus boundary crossing. The latter implies importing, translating, and brokering ideas across interfaces. In Burt's (2009, 257) language, this is creativity born of the export-import trade. Trespassing highlights the puncturing of boundaries, violating conventions (whether consciously or not), and thereby creating myriad opportunities for unfreezing and repurposing. Most trespassers do not survive. And if they do, the trespassing itself has a short life. Once such movement becomes commonplace, it is no longer inappropriate. Instead it becomes an accepted path for people and also the conduit of ideas, but with unpredictable reverberations through the now overlapping territories. The new biotech firms ushered in a new era: basic science advances were no longer made only in universities, and positions in science-based companies came to be viewed as rich in both financial *and* research opportunities. These alterations proved to have pronounced effects on both the research university and corporate enterprise.

CONCLUSION AND IMPLICATIONS: RESHAPING THE PRODUCTION OF KNOWLEDGE

We began by asking: Where do new organizational practices and forms come from? We are, of course, not the first to take up this issue, but we think our answers are distinctive. We emphasize the collision of divergent domains, where networks were formed between the formerly distant social worlds of the academy and finance. This was not heroic entrepreneurship but pragmatic agency, often the result of serendipity and necessity. The naïve transgressors who founded the early companies forged a new composite in which previously unfamiliar elements from science and finance were combined. This new compound proved consequential as the realms of science, finance, and commerce came to share new attributes. The feedback dynamics of this amalgamation proved highly disruptive to the status quo.

Consider the contrast of our argument with Rao's (1998) excellent work on consumer watchdog organizations and his broader line of research on the role of social movements in advancing new organizational forms (Rao, Morrill, and Zald 2000; Rao and Kenney 2008). The different emphases are perhaps subtle, but they are nonetheless consequential. In his analysis of contestation between rival consumer movements, Rao (1998, 920) argues that a new form becomes established "only when there is a truce amongst the constituents of the organizational field about which frame is used to organize activities." The Consumers Union "strove to import characteristics of trade unions into the consumption sector" (ibid., 948). This model failed to galvanize support and generated much opposition from legislators and the press. Foregoing the activist labor model, Consumers Union later adopted the "rational consumer" ideology of its rival—the Consumers Research Council. The truce produced a new form: the consumer watchdog organization. The analytical purchase in this strand of research comes from a focus on "settlement"—"agreements have to be negotiated among parties before new forms can be institutionalized as codes" (Rao and Kenney 2008, 368).

Our examination of the genesis of new organizational forms in commercial bioscience, however, begins upstream from subsequent settlements or negotiations between competing models. This focus brings us closer to work in the social studies of science that opens up the "black box" of science, as well as studies of the role of social movements in shaping organizational change (Latour 1987; Schneiberg and Lounsbury 2008). We traced how career flows triggered disruption. Moving energy from one realm into another, or converting reputations and resources in one domain into motivating energy in a new arena, unlocked existing social bonds and expectations, creating space for a new form. The "real" action happened prior to the fashioning of any truces in the releasing of new practices whose effects extended well beyond the handful of organizations where they began. Indeed, in a narrow sense, the commerce variant could be seen as the victor in this contest of models, as these recombinations resulted in earlier success and more examples of this model are around today. (We list the eventual "outcomes" for the first-generation companies in table 13.7.) Although the commerce model may have won the initial battles, the science model

Table 13.7.
What Happened to the First Generation?

Alza	Ahead-of-his-time founder creates a prototype for future biotech firms. Acquired by Johnson & Johnson in 2001.
Cetus	First-mover advantage doesn't hold due to lack of focus; acquired in 1991 by Chiron.
Genentech	Science married to finance creates novel model that produces an enviable record of innovation. Despite considerable resistance, became a fully owned subsidiary of Roche in 2009.
Genex	Low-margin business model becomes unsustainable without investment by corporate partners; acquired in 1991 by Enzon.
Biogen	"World class research seminar" makes corporate governance challenging; licensing model proves robust. Merged with IDEC in 2003.
Hybritech	Entrepreneurial scientist finds world-class VC, who recruits a pharma escapee to run the show; bred for eventual sale and acquired by Eli Lilly in 1986.
Centocor	"Academic scavengers" almost lose their company due to grand aspirations to become a fully integrated pharmaceutical company. Acquired by Johnson & Johnson in 1999.
Amgen	Savvy VCs set out to "do biotech right" by recruiting stellar SAB and putting talented pharma escapee in charge; a biopharma titan is born.
Chiron	Scientist-entrepreneurs move the invisible college model to a business setting. Acquired by Novartis in 2006.
Genzyme	VC group goes shopping for a new venture; builds business around orphan drug opportunities. Acquired by Sanofi-Aventis in 2011.
Immunex	Despite stellar scientific record, business success comes late. Acquired by Amgen in 2002, resulting in the loss of local "Immunoid" culture.

ultimately won the war, as it proved to be more influential institutionally in multiple domains. Moreover, the science model had a much deeper influence on research and biomedical product development, prompting more focus on new-to-the-world medicines rather than "me-too" or derivative drugs (Powell and Brantley 1996; Cockburn and Stern 2010).

By influential, we do not mean a "mere" case of one side adopting notable practices of the other. Of course, there are signs of such influences everywhere. Prior research has documented the diffusion of academic practices into the R&D divisions of large pharmaceutical companies (Cockburn, Henderson, and Stern 2000). And industrial science today clearly recognizes the importance of intellectual capital, building university-like campus settings to attract the talent of the creative class and engaging in all manner of partnerships with universities and nonprofit institutes. The insular R&D lab of Big Pharma has dissolved into a lattice-like network of collaborations; publishing by scientists in large firms is not just tolerated but encouraged; and research positions at corporate-sponsored nonprofit institutes are highly sought after by university PhDs.

On the academic front, research universities have become much more businesslike as entrepreneurship is celebrated; compensation has become market based and laden with incentives. But we are not content to make the now obvious point that the formerly separate domains of science, commerce, and finance have become blurred. To be sure, university endowments helped fuel investment in the knowledge economy, and collaboration between industry and the academy has been embraced and encouraged, even evangelized by those in high positions of science policy (Rhoten and Powell 2007). These interminglings and subsequent reshaping of the boundaries of knowledge production have altered both reward systems and career paths. We contend, however, that the transposition of science into commerce was even more unsettling and transformative; it recast the nature of science and industrial work itself and altered the institutional framework for economic growth.

Scientific and corporate work were formerly organized around the twin frames of disciplines and departments. Both were steeped in deep functional expertise—in the academy, specialized knowledge accumulated in an area of scientific inquiry, and in industry, prowess at a skill relevant to a particular product or therapeutic domain was the trademark. The science-based biotech model opened up a project-focused alternative, driven by interdisciplinary and interorganizational collaborations and impelled by an urgent need to solve problems more quickly. This shift to project-based work has the virtue of flexibility as well as the limitation of fragility.

In the academic realm, recall that molecular biology was championed as a revolt against traditional biology. "The Huns" were crashing in, outsiders from physics and biochemistry, even engineering (Hall 1987, 21). Today, every major research university has a large, expansive trans-disciplinary initiative under way, linking the biomedical sciences, engineering, and the physical sciences, with grand synthetic names like "systems biology" and "Bio-X." These programs are generating important work, and as they expand they reshape the activities of traditional science departments.[34] (We discuss them at some length in chapter 15.)

In both the corporate and academic domains, project-based work has become a collaborative enterprise. It transcends department and organizational boundaries, drawing together firms, universities, research institutes, and government labs in fierce research and product development races. Research is no longer a local enterprise, but a coordinated and collective affair. Many scientists view this collaborative model as more engaging than an individualist approach and prefer it.[35] Moreover, as we show in the next chapter, the ability to work across multiple organizational boundaries has had profound consequences for regional economic growth.

Finally, consider that a project also has an endpoint—something tangible is created, an idea is followed through to its resolution, sometimes in a manner that has very real consequences in the lives of ordinary people. This aspect of the remaking of research emphasizes again the effects of careers and multiple networks. Today many scientists and technologists are more tightly aligned with their research goals or the technology they are working on than with their employers. Viewed over the course of the last

[34] A group of us—the Mimir Project at Stanford—are currently studying the impact of large-scale interdisciplinary "supercenters" on the contemporary research university.

[35] Perhaps our early science founders were indeed transitional figures. In retaining their university positions, they may not have been risk averse, as is often thought, but still held a preference for running their own lab according to their goals as opposed to the collectivist endeavors of their new companies, where everyone would drop his own work to join whichever project proved hottest.

four decades, these novel organizational arrangements were generated as much by chance and necessity as by intention, as science-based organizational practices imported into a new space had profound, cascading effects back into the formerly conservative domains of the university and the corporation.

APPENDIX: PROFILES OF FIRST-GENERATION COMPANIES

ALZA: A DBF Prototype

Some might question why ALZA, founded in 1968, belongs among the earliest biotech companies. Like Cetus, it was founded a few years before publication of the breakthrough discoveries of gene splicing (1973) and monoclonal antibodies (1975). ALZA merits inclusion, in our view, because it is an unusual example of a *de alio* biotech entrant. Its origins were in the pharmaceutical industry, but its interest in novel drug delivery mechanisms moved it into bioengineering. ALZA also pioneered many business practices that became common in the new bioscience companies, such as an IPO before it had any marketable products, lucrative (but equity-draining) partnership arrangements with established pharma companies, and reliance on a prestigious board of scientific advisers. Its founder, Alejandro Zaffaroni, was deeply connected to the world of academic science and went on to found numerous biotech ventures.

If Zaffaroni had been able to persuade his then employer, Syntex, to support basic research on novel drug delivery techniques, launching ALZA would have been unnecessary. Zaffaroni spent seventeen years with Syntex, joining in 1951 after completing a Ph.D. and postdoc in biochemistry and endocrinology at the University of Rochester. An immigrant from Uruguay, Zaffaroni was at home in the fast-paced, freewheeling environment of Syntex's Mexico City labs. He joined the company in the thick of its race against world-famous teams from Harvard and Merck to synthesize cortisone. Under the guidance of the renowned chemists George Rosencranz and Carl Djerassi, underdog Syntex won. Most unusual for the time, Rosencranz insisted that Syntex scientists publish their findings in scientific journals; Syntex's publication and research record earned it the label "The University of Steroids" from the eminent Harvard chemist Louis Fieser (Kornberg 1995, 66).

By 1960 Zaffaroni had become president and CEO of Syntex Laboratories. He pressed his board for a U.S. office. Instead of locating in the New York–New Jersey pharmaceutical corridor, Zaffaroni proposed the Stanford Industrial Park for its climate, ambiance, proximity to Djerassi (who had moved to Stanford), and direct flights (from San Francisco) to both Mexico City and New York. The first Syntex research unit established at the new location was called the Institute of Molecular Biology. It was staffed by fifteen scientists and guided by Djerassi and Joshua Lederberg (another Syntex adviser at Stanford). Prompted by his earlier research on gland function, Zaffaroni began asking fundamental questions about drug delivery:

> These small glands have a tremendously important function. They deliver very small amounts of materials that have tremendous impact. . . . How is it possible that these very potent agents are released under highly controlled conditions, and then in medicine we bring the same agents into the body by giving a tablet at a time or an injection at a time? It seemed to me quite evident that the way in which we administer the agents to the body is wrong, and if it is wrong for the hormones, why is it not also wrong for every compound that we throw all at once into the body? (1997)

By the mid-1960s, Syntex had capitalized on its patents in steroid chemistry to create two market-leading products: cortisone skin cream and the birth control pill. Rich but very risk averse, the company was unwilling to sponsor Zaffaroni's foray into drug delivery. So in 1968 Zaffaroni resigned from Syntex, sold his considerable holdings of company stock, and used half of the proceeds to found ALZA, an acronym of the first two letters of his first and last names. Syntex abolished the Institute of Molecular Biology after Zaffaroni left, only a few years before the discoveries of recombinant DNA and the sequencing and cloning of DNA catapulted molecular biology to prominence. Had the early vision of the Institute been preserved, these new technologies almost certainly would have put Syntex years ahead of Genentech and others in the genetic engineering race.

ALZA was not an instant success. One of its first product concepts was a thin polymeric film that could be put on the eye to treat glaucoma. The usual medications had to be put in several times a day, causing blurred vision for the ensuing hour. ALZA's technology would allow the film to release the medication constantly at small enough doses to avoid side effects. Another proposed innovation was the prevention of pregnancy by the release of progesterone from a small T-shaped device placed in the uterus. The essential principle of each product was to diffuse drug molecules through membranes and release them at a controlled rate over an extended period.

These technological advances did not translate into market success, however. Disgruntled analysts began to argue that ALZA's academic culture blinded it to commercial opportunities; it did not help that ALZA had a prestigious scientific advisory board and was close to a university campus. As one critic observed, "ALZA was a university masquerading as a company. You'd go to analyst meetings and [one-time CEO] Marty Gerstel would say, 'We have 2000 patents, hallelujah! We have this technology and we have that technology'" (Longman 1996, 47).

Early in its history, ALZA stumbled into a financing innovation. As part of the original separation agreement between Zaffaroni and Syntex, Syntex was granted 25 percent of ALZA's stock. As it became clear in 1969 that ALZA was developing a birth-control product that would compete directly with Syntex's pill, the two companies agreed that Syntex would distribute all of its ALZA shares to existing Syntex shareholders. The SEC, initially resistant, eventually approved the plan. In effect, ALZA instantly became a publicly traded company with an army of shareholders and market capitalization close to $100 million—all without a single product or any assurance that it would ever have any sales, much less profits. The company consisted of only a handful of employees and Zaffaroni's vision for revolutionizing drug delivery. For ALZA to go public at such an early stage established a precedent followed by many fledgling biotech companies in subsequent years (Kornberg 1995, 80).

ALZA also found it critical to partner with large pharmaceutical and nascent biotech companies when it ran into financial trouble. ALZA's transdermal technology was well suited to delivering the large-molecule peptides and proteins that resulted from biotech advances, which had previously been injectible-only products. After proving the utility of such drug delivery methods in more prosaic settings (such as smoking cessation and motion sickness applications), ALZA was acquired by Johnson & Johnson in March 2001 for $10.5 billion. Over time, ALZA's importance to Johnson & Johnson waned, and in 2005 its operations were closed. By that time, the eponymous Zaffaroni had launched six biotech firms: DNAX (1980), Affymax (1988), Affymetrix (1991), Symyx Technologies (1994), Maxygen (1997), and Alexza (2000).

Amgen: Science Based But Business Led

At the end of the 1970s, the Silicon Valley venture capitalist Bill Bowes saw investment potential in the life sciences. Having served on the board of directors of Cetus from 1972 to 1978 and been privy to the founding of Genentech in 1978, Bowes set out with a handful of fellow investors to assemble a biotech venture that would avoid the missteps of the first companies. His efforts were spectacularly successful on one level: of all the early biotechs, Amgen ranks highest on most commercial measures of success (growth rate, total sales, market capitalization, etc.) and is "only the second fully integrated pharmaceutical company (after Syntex) built from scratch in the post–World War II period" (Kornberg 1995, 206–7). Curiously, despite its success, Amgen did not spawn a strong regional cluster of subsequent biotech activity (see chapter 14).

The seeds of this paradox can be seen in a sequence of early decisions and historical accidents that established Amgen's trajectory. Bowes had been investing in new ventures since the mid-1950s, when he joined Blyth & Co. in San Francisco after earning a Harvard MBA. Following the semiconductor and computer boom of the 1960s, investors were looking for the "next big thing" (Duncan 2005, 16). From his experience on the board at Cetus, Bowes borrowed the idea of an all-star scientific advisory board. He first asked the Stanford geneticist Robert Schimke to join the venture and assemble the advisory board. Schimke declined for personal reasons (his father was seriously ill at the time), suggesting instead the UCLA molecular biologist Winston Salser.

Salser was an entrepreneurial academic who had found a clever way of funding his lab. He bought radioactive tracers in bulk and then sold them to smaller labs in small quantities at much higher prices. He was well-known among West Coast academics, though perhaps less well regarded. He assembled an impressive scientific board by assuring each scientist that the others had already agreed to join, when in fact they had not (Rathmann 2004, 21–22). The board Salser had recruited ended up requesting that he be replaced—an unpleasant task that fell to another of Salser's recruits, George Rathmann.

Rathmann had earned a Ph.D. in chemistry at Princeton in 1952 and spent the first twenty years of his career at 3M. After a two-year detour managing a failing division at Litton Industries (1973–75), he joined Abbott Laboratories as vice president of R&D for the diagnostics division, which he helped build into a market leader. His success, however, was accompanied by restlessness; he had been frustrated by the power of the marketing department at 3M and picayune attention to detail at Abbott (Rathmann 2004, 5, 20). He became interested in the potential of biotechnology to create synthetic antigens and requested a six-month sabbatical from Abbott to explore the idea. On the advice of an Abbott colleague who was a former student of Salser, Rathmann intended to spend the sabbatical in Salser's UCLA lab. But Salser was on leave, involved in starting Amgen. So instead of a research apprenticeship, Rathmann ended up with an offer to be the new venture's first employee and founding CEO. Accepting the position was not easy. Abbott tried to hold on to Rathmann by offering him the opportunity to start a biotech division within the large corporation. In addition, Moshe Alafi (an investor in both Amgen and Biogen and one of the founders of Cetus) tried to recruit Rathmann to run the U.S. operations of Biogen. In the end, Rathmann opted for the freedom and control offered by Amgen. As part of the negotiation, he insisted that the high-powered scientific advisory board report directly to him: "I thought, no way am I going to have a scientific advisory board report to the board of directors and tell them what a crappy job I'm doing. So I said, 'No, if they report to me, that's fine. Otherwise, I'm not going to do this'" (2004, 21). The unforeseen consequence of this was that Rathmann was put in the position of having to fire the person who had brought him into the venture, Winston Salser.

Salser's influence on Amgen extends beyond its illustrious scientific board and CEO. Its location was Salser's choice. He determined that Thousand Oaks, California, was roughly equidistant from three universities from which he drew heavily for Amgen's scientific advisory board (Cal Tech, UCLA, and UC–Santa Barbara), and the town offered cheap housing and smog-free air (Duncan 2005, 31). This geographical isolation is certainly one cause and consequence of Amgen's development as a sort of scientific island, manifest not only in its singular achievement of fully integrated pharmaceutical company (FIPCO) status but also in its aggressive (and, on the whole, successful) legal battles to protect its core patents.

The founding model for Amgen, then, was the audacious vision of a bioscience-based pharmaceutical firm. Dennis Fenton, an early recruit, recalls his first visit to Amgen in 1981: "There was a window in Building 1 and all you could see was just brown California dirt. George said, 'We're going to build a pharmaceutical company as big as Pfizer.' And I looked at him and thought, 'This guy is out of his mind'" (Duncan 2005, 54). Turning that California dirt into an independent biopharmaceutical corporation required a strong managerial hand (and more than a little luck). Having seen the cost of weak management at Cetus, Bowes insisted on experienced business leadership for Amgen. Rathmann recruited a strong team of savvy managers, many of them from his former employer, Abbott Laboratories. Recalls Gordon Binder, Amgen's first CFO and second CEO,

> Much of Amgen's success in raising capital can be attributed to the fact that every one of our senior managers had worked for large corporations. As a result, we had the organizational discipline of a far bigger company, with salary grades, annual performance reviews, monthly reports, and budgets that were taken seriously. All the things that the start-ups rarely do, we did; to us, it was second nature. (Binder and Bashe 2008, 48–49)

In contrast, Amgen's scientific hires (unlike its science advisory board) were predominantly early career PhDs. The message was clear: Amgen was to be science based but not science led. That the business managers were running the show was never in question, as seen in subsequent CEO succession: Rathmann was followed by Binder, a Harvard MBA with an emphasis in finance, who passed the baton to Kevin Sharer, another Harvard MBA with a strong sales and marketing history. In contrast to many other biotech firms, no academic scientist has ever led Amgen.

Still, a large measure of research freedom and "bootleg" spirit, imprinted on Rathmann at 3M, was cultivated at Amgen. The most celebrated example (with overtones of the development of 3M's Post-It note) is Fu-Kuen Lin's dogged quest to clone and express erythropoietin. Despite opposition from management, he succeeded in late 1983, leading to the first bioengineered blockbuster drug (Epogen) and a novel research-management policy: exploratory projects needed approval from only one of three research-related senior executives in order to continue (Berkley and Nohria 1992, 6).

Amgen might not have survived long enough for Lin's breakthrough were it not for a successful, though unusual, financing ploy. Early in 1983 Rathmann calculated that the company would run out of money by September. Binder ran the numbers and figured that with significant layoffs, Amgen might last through the end of the year. Recalls Rathmann (2004, 37), "I looked at that and I thought, Jeez, I just put this team together. To start to send people home, that would just have a devastating effect on the company." Unable to attract additional research partnerships and with current investors unwilling to pony up additional funds for a company that had so far produced nothing, Binder and Rathmann realized that their only option might be to go public. The board of directors' reaction was predictable: "They said, 'You want to go be a public company? Why, we think you're smoking dope!'" (ibid.). Binder and Rathmann moved quickly, however, and by June had prepared the offering, with the help of Bill Bowes's connections at various investment banks. Thus Amgen pioneered a new use for an IPO: a last-ditch effort to save the company. But investors who bought and held those shaky 1983 shares have been handsomely rewarded.

Biogen: A Company Run by Its Scientists

Starting in 1977, Walter Gilbert began to receive unsolicited (and unwelcome) overtures from investors and entrepreneurs who tried to recruit him to bioscience ventures. A physicist-turned-molecular-biologist at Harvard, Gilbert was instrumental in devising a new technique for the rapid sequencing of DNA—work that would earn him a share of the 1980 Nobel Prize in chemistry. To his peers and students, Wally Gilbert was an inspiration, a scientist's scientist who combined brilliance and style (Hall 1987, 29–39). He initially rebuffed all commercial overtures. Relationships with industry were not yet the norm in the biosciences, particularly at Harvard, with its tradition of academic purity. But in late 1977 Gilbert agreed to meet with a pair of venture capitalists in Boston. Still insisting that he was not interested, Gilbert nonetheless remained in their sights.

The VCs were Ray Schaefer and Dan Adams, affiliated with the investment arm of the Canadian mining firm Inco Ltd. The two had been searching for new investment opportunities and, in 1976, had met Moshe Alafi, one of the founders of Cetus and at the time its chairman. Alafi persuaded Schaefer that Inco should make a small investment in Cetus. Inco's shares in Cetus were purchased from VC Tom Perkins, who was involved in funding Genentech; Schaefer also took a 15 percent stake in Genentech on behalf of Inco (Elkington 1985, 61).

Infected by the biotechnology bug, Schaefer and Adams hatched an ambitious scheme to persuade the formidable Gilbert to join them in a start-up of their own. They would recruit an international team of renowned life scientists and ask Gilbert to lead it. Targeting heads of molecular biology departments at leading U.S. and European universities, Schaefer and Adams met with little initial success. Like Gilbert, most academics were wary of commercial endeavors. A turning point came when Schaefer contacted Phillip Sharp, a highly respected molecular biologist at MIT, who in 1977 had been a scientific consultant to Inco on their investment in Genentech. With Sharp along, Schaefer could persuade Gilbert to meet for dinner early in 1978. After an evening of coaxing, Gilbert agreed to attend an exploratory meeting, scheduled for March in Geneva. At a subsequent preparatory meeting with Sharp and Gilbert, the venture capitalists presented their list of the European scientists they were targeting. Essentially a who's who of molecular biologists in Europe, the list impressed Sharp and Gilbert, who suggested a few additional names. Gilbert also agreed to chair the Geneva meeting.

Schaefer was able attract the other eminent scientists by mentioning that "Wally Gilbert will be coming and chairing the scientific meetings" (Hall 1987, 194), a technique akin to that used by Winston Salser in assembling Amgen's scientific advisory board. On March 1, ten top scientists—three from the United States, the rest Europeans—assembled at Geneva's Hotel Le Richemond to discuss forming a company. Unfamiliar with commercial structures and wary of the investors' motives, the scientists drafted a preliminary charter to ensure that critical aspects of control would rest with the company's scientific board. Hugh D'Andrade, a Schering-Plough senior executive and early member of Biogen's board of directors, remembers:

> Biogen's unique organizing concept . . . was that it was run by its scientists, not by venture capitalists, or the banks. . . . The scientific board had the right to elect to the Biogen board quite a few of the scientists. When they went to the scientists, they said, "Look, you don't have to quit your lab and go to work for Biogen like you're working for Genentech, and you don't have to have somebody from some company telling you what to do. The scientists are going to run this company." (2001, 12)

The Geneva meeting ended with no commitments, and a second meeting was scheduled for three weeks later at a Paris airport hotel. The once-reluctant Gilbert assumed the role of go-between: "In a sense, I became a spokesman for the scientists. I also had, in some ways, the greatest sympathy or affinity for the way in which the business side was structured" (Hall 1987, 195). On March 25 the group of scientific luminaries reconvened for two days, with Schaefer and another venture capitalist (Kevin Landry of T. A. Associates) discussing the ins and outs of the potential venture. Recalled Schaefer, "Everything had to be explained in minute detail—every line, every sentence—because they thought there was something hidden there" (Hall 1987, 209).

Before the second meeting, researchers in Gilbert's Harvard lab had successfully cloned and expressed human insulin, an achievement with unmistakable commercial potential. During a break in the meeting, Sharp recalls taking a walk with Gilbert: "He started telling me about his experiments with insulin. . . . I was excited when I heard about it and congratulated him on the achievement, and then I asked him if he was going to patent it. . . . There was a rhythm, a nonspoken feeling, that people were going to try this" (Hall 1987, 210). Near the end of the meeting, Gilbert asked the investors to leave the room. For two hours, Schaefer and Landry waited outside, fearing the venture was doomed. To their surprise, Gilbert emerged with news that all ten scientists had agreed to join the company. Schaefer came up with the name Biogen. Shortly afterward he convened a third meeting in Zurich to iron out financial details and officially incorporate as a Swiss firm, given both opposition to genetic engineering by the city council of Cambridge, Massachusetts, and the purportedly speedier drug approval process in Europe. Joining Inco and T. A. Associates in the $750,000 initial investment were Moshe Alafi and a number of European concerns.

Two unique characteristics of the fledgling company are manifest in this story of its birth. First, although the investors may have brought them together, the scientists were going to call the shots. "This is the only company in the world where scientists have their hands on the company's jugular vein," observed Alafi in 1980 (Bylinsky 1980). Two years later, when Alafi tried to recruit George Rathmann to run Biogen's U.S. operations, Rathmann declined, partly because "the so-called scientific advisory board" was "all-powerful" (Rathmann 2004, 20).

Second, with such meager start-up capital, the company had little choice but to be "virtual" at first. Even after a headquarters lab in Geneva and a research center in Cambridge were established, most of Biogen's research was conducted in the university labs of its founders. Indeed, the founding scientists were expected to advocate and sponsor their own particular projects and were promised shares in proportion to their projects' impact over time (Higgins 2005). Gilbert's leadership style, imported from the world of elite science, turned scientific board meetings into intensely rigorous research seminars. Thus Biogen's global "mini-academy" model created the potential for scientific excellence but some coordination costs as well.

In its first three head-to-head races to bring products to market, Biogen lost out to biotech competitors: Genentech was first to make human insulin, Centocor moved more quickly on hepatitis diagnostics, and Amgen cloned erythropoietin well before Biogen. Trying to gain greater focus, Biogen began shedding its early, Cetus-like pursuit of projects in a wide range of industries (from microbial metal leaching to biofuels) in preparation for its 1983 IPO. Said Gilbert, "The most productive use of the current technology is in the pharmaceutical field. We now concentrate our efforts there because we see it as the new field in which the technology will be the most commercially rewarding over the next ten to fifteen years" (Elkington 1985, 70). Biogen continued to swing for the fences, however. Continued Gilbert, "Unlike a contract research company, our goal is not to make a ten percent return on our research effort. Our goal is quite different. We view our research as an investment on which we want to make a ten- or hundred-fold return" (ibid.).

Under the hydra-headed leadership of its eminent scientific founders, Biogen did not achieve predictable financial returns. Its IPO was underwhelming, and by 1985 the company was on the brink of bankruptcy. Its groundbreaking work in interferons, licensed to Schering-Plough, brought limited royalty revenues. At this point, Gilbert resigned from his post as CEO and returned full-time to Harvard, where he remains (although he has been involved in subsequent biotech ventures). Biogen's board recruited a seasoned pharmaceutical captain to run the ship in a different way: James Vincent, a Wharton MBA ('63) who had built Abbott Laboratories' diagnostics business into an industry powerhouse (where he had been George Rathmann's boss).

Vincent inherited the challenging task of wresting control away from the scientists and focusing the company on commercial products. In his first year at the company, Vincent cancelled dozens of research projects, sold Biogen Geneva to Glaxo and its Belgian operations to Roche, closed a lab in Zurich, and laid off 275 of the company's 500 employees (Fisher 1997). "The perception had been that everything else would take care of itself if we had good science," said Vincent (Feder 1992). And indeed, the company had excellent science. "It was deep, broad, and sound; it had just been misguided," Vincent maintained (Fisher 1997). Over the next four years he replaced the senior management team and focused Biogen's product development efforts on its original scientific breakthrough, alpha interferon. By renegotiating many of Biogen's license agreements with Big Pharma partners, Vincent engineered a financial recovery that by the late 1980s had the company poised to take advantage of numerous promising scientific milestones.

The early 1990s saw two more of Biogen's founding scientists receive worldwide recognition. MIT's Phillip Sharp received the 1993 Nobel Prize in Medicine. (Sharp never relinquished his faculty post at MIT and remains a member of Biogen's board of directors.) Also in 1993, Kenneth Murray of the University of Edinburgh was knighted in England. In 1996 the FDA approved Biogen's Avonex (interferon beta-1a) for the treatment of multiple sclerosis. By 2002 Avonex had reached worldwide sales of $1.1 billion (Biogen IDEC 2003, 6). Biogen had its first blockbuster drug.

Today Biogen is one of the two early biotech firms in our sample that have not been acquired. Maintaining its independence required a 2003 merger with San Diego–based IDEC Pharmaceutical Corporation. It is emblematic of the interwoven nature of the biotech industry that IDEC had been the encore for Hybritech's founders—Brook Byers, Ivor Royston, and Howard Birndorf—after its acquisition by Eli Lilly in 1985. IDEC also jointly developed with Genentech a blockbuster of its own, the anti-cancer drug Rituxan.

Centocor: A Bridge between the Academy and Commercial Health Care

In August 1979 a seasoned entrepreneur/executive and a trio of researchers formed Centocor in Philadelphia to commercialize monoclonal antibody technology. Michael Wall, the entrepreneur, had graduated in electrical engineering from MIT in the 1950s and worked in a series of electronics start-ups. In the mid-1960s he shifted his focus to health care and founded Flow Laboratories, a medical products firm that he and his partners sold in 1969 for $3 million. Wall continued as a senior executive at Flow until the founding of Centocor. One of the scientists was a friend of Wall's: Hilary Koprowski, director of the Wistar Institute and pioneer in the development of improved polio and rabies vaccines. Joining Koprowski was Carlo Croce, a researcher at Wistar and a co-holder of a 1979 Wistar patent on a specific monoclonal antibody, and Vincent Zurawski Jr., at the time a postdoctoral fellow in immunochemistry at Harvard Medical School and Massachusetts General Hospital.

As Wistar director, Koprowski had actively courted Boehringer Ingelheim, a large German chemical and pharmaceutical company, to license the patent, offering a ten-year license in exchange for funding Wistar research to the tune of $500,000 per year. "They dragged the thing out for six or eight months," Koprowski recollects. "Finally their chief of marketing said he saw no future in monoclonal antibodies" (Vaughan 2000, 179). Koprowski turned to Michael Wall, who definitely saw a future in the technology. Koprowski came up with the name Centocor: *cento*, for a literary or a musical composition formed by selections from different authors, and *cor*, the Latin root meaning "heart," reflecting the intent to collaborate with research institutions and established health care companies to bring monoclonal products to market. The company was initially housed in the University City

Science Center, an incubator on the University of Pennsylvania campus near Wistar.

As influential as the original founders was the firm's first executive hire in February 1980: Hubert Schoemaker, an energetic Dutchman with a Ph.D. in biochemistry from MIT. Schoemaker had pursued business rather than research as a career, turning down a postdoctoral position in Stanley Cohen's storied lab at Stanford to work in a friend's low-tech manufacturing company. After absorbing the ins and outs of daily business operations, Schoemaker took a job with Corning Medical, eventually working his way up to head of R&D. Michael Wall at Flow Laboratories had been one of his customers. Schoemaker, in a way, was a mixture of the other founders (Shaw 1997). Like Wall, Schoemaker had ample business and managerial experience; like Koprowski and Zurawski, he had extensive training from an elite institution in a discipline relevant to the new venture's scientific goals.

Centocor's self-proclaimed business model was to be "the bridge from the academic research laboratory to the established health care supplier" (Centocor 1982, 12). Its first license, Koprowski's and Croce's patent for a monoclonal antibody, was not without controversy, however. In granting Centocor an exclusive license to the Wistar patent, Koprowski—at the time still Wistar's director—incurred accusations of conflict of interest from Wistar's board. The issue came to a head in 1982, just before Centocor's planned IPO. With legal action threatening to scuttle the stock offering, Koprowski settled with Wistar. He agreed that he and Croce would resign from Centocor's board of directors and grant the institute 150,000 shares of Centocor stock (Vaughan 2000, 185).

Despite this setback, Centocor's strategy of licensing breakthroughs from academic and nonprofit labs continued. As Schoemaker recalled, "The visionary license agreement with Wistar set the tone. We realized it was a lot cheaper to roam academe and pay a royalty back for what we developed than start our own research facilities. Collaboration was the best way to be competitive" (Vaughan 2000, 186). Wall commented in 1985, "You can have a garage full of PhDs working on a project, and nine times out of ten some guy across the street is going to come up with the discovery that beats them all" (Teitelman 1985, 80). Because Centocor also focused on producing diagnostics, the company could develop assays that would run on equipment manufactured by such health care giants as Abbott Laboratories and Warner-Lambert, avoiding the hassle and expense of its own manufacturing and sales arms.

As Schoemaker transitioned into the CEO role in the mid-1980s, Centocor broadened its focus from diagnostics to therapeutics. Eventually Schoemaker bet the company on FDA approval of Centocor's first drug, Centoxin, making costly investments in proprietary manufacturing and sales capabilities. When the FDA denied Centoxin's application in 1992, Centocor barely survived. Michael Wall, then in semiretirement, came back as chairman and helped Schoemaker cut two-thirds of the company's workforce, regrouping around a pair of promising therapeutics. This marked a return to the "bridge" model of drug development. In 1997 Schoemaker reflected, "Every drug that Centocor has developed has come out of an academic collaboration" (Shaw 1997). After the two drugs (ReoPro and Remicade) received FDA approval, Centocor was acquired by Johnson & Johnson in 1999 for $4.9 billion.

Cetus: An Academic "Free Space"

Incorporated in 1972 in Berkeley, California, Cetus was arguably the first company founded with the intent of commercializing advances in molecular biology and genetics. Its four-person founding team included two would-be entrepreneurs, a Nobel laureate in physics, and a successful Bay Area financier.

Ronald Cape, one of the two entrepreneurs, had just finished a three-year postdoc in molecular biology at UC–Berkeley's Virus Laboratory. He could sense the pregnant condition of the life sciences: "It was like maybe a dam waiting to burst or an egg waiting to hatch, but the fact is, there were a lot of Nobel Prizes in molecular biology, but no practical applications" (2006, 16). Cape's background included a Harvard MBA, followed by a stint managing a family drugstore business in Montreal, during which time he earned a Ph.D. in biochemistry at McGill University to escape the boredom of the job. Upon finishing his postdoc at Berkeley, he had no desire to return to the cold winters of Montreal or the confines of his family's business. He also realized he was more interested in the business of science than in science itself. He met his eventual co-entrepreneur, Peter Farley, in a venture capitalist's office in San Francisco. Farley was an MD who had served as a medic in Vietnam; after the war, he earned an MBA at Stanford. Like Cape, Farley was serving as a consultant and advisor to VCs on medically oriented ventures, biding his time until he could launch his own. Cape and Farley immediately recognized their common interests and formed a partnership.

Donald Glaser, a third founder, was a professor of molecular biology at UC–Berkeley. He had earned the 1960 Nobel Prize in physics for his invention of the bubble chamber, then had taught himself molecular biology. He was applying his physical science savvy to the automation of basic biological research. Having recently lost NIH funding for his project—and with a daughter headed for medical school—he saw Cetus as an opportunity to fund his work and generate some extra income. Glaser's prestige added credibility to the venture, though his expertise in the biological sciences was not deep enough to give him direct influence over Cetus's technical direction: "My job, really, was to interview and hire real molecular biologists who knew how to do genetic engineering" (Glaser 2006, 96). He remained a professor at Berkeley, never spending more than a day a week at Cetus.

The fourth founder, Moshe Alafi, was already a successful investor in the Bay Area and a social acquaintance of Glaser's. Cape (2006, 67) describes Alafi's role: "Moshe Alafi was the chairman of the company, and he had experience in venture capital, had friends in the venture-capital industry. . . . It's hard to say that he was operationally involved, but he was involved in much of the decision-making and we consulted him constantly." Alafi gained crucial (if painful) experience from his involvement with Cetus, going on to fund two subsequent ventures, Biogen and Amgen.

An old adage asserts that true pioneers are easy to distinguish: they are the ones with the arrows in their backs. As the earliest self-proclaimed biotech company, Cetus certainly absorbed multiple attacks, many of which centered on its lack of focus. Investors became frustrated by its "wide ranging, apparently indiscriminate eclecticism" (Vettel 2006, 202), with projects ranging from genetically engineered bacteria for alcohol and fructose production, bioremediation, vaccines, antibiotics, and new approaches to fermenting microbes (Rabinow 1996, 32–33). Cape (2006, 21) describes the company's earliest approach in colorful terms: "The genetic code had been decoded. The field was preparing for something. I mean, it hadn't been exploited *at all*. And we presented ourselves as 'there's got to be a pony in there someplace.'" To "find the pony," Cetus recruited a star advisory board (which in time included six Nobel laureates, Francis Crick among them) and smart scientists, equipped them with state-of-the-art laboratories, then turned them loose to see what they came up with. This "free space" was initially exciting enough to generate a fair amount of hype and garner generous financial support; Cetus's 1981 IPO raised $108 million, then a record. But as time wore on, the charm wore off. As Glaser (2006, 105) expresses it, "We were roundly criticized in some quarters as being a playground for academic scientists. . . . The direction was not very stringent."

The playground allowed such free spirits as Kary Mullis to pursue his work on polymerase chain reaction (PCR), a technique that proved foundational to subsequent research in the biosciences. PCR earned Mullis the Nobel Prize in Chemistry in 1993—the only Nobel Prize awarded so far for work conducted solely in a biotechnology company.[36] Cetus later overcorrected for its lack of focus, investing heavily in Interleukin-2, an immune-system booster. When the FDA failed to approve the drug in 1990, Cetus could no longer support its operations and sold off its PCR franchise to Roche Bio. Its remaining operations were absorbed by its smaller neighbor, Chiron, in 1992. It is notable, however, that three people who played founding roles in subsequent early biotech ventures—Bob Swanson (Genentech), Moshe Alafi (Biogen), and Bill Bowes (Amgen) —were associated with Cetus as investors and learned from its early mistakes.

[36] Mullis joined Cetus in 1979 after obtaining his Berkeley Ph.D. in biochemistry and doing postdoc stints at the University of Kansas and UCSF. During his seven years at Cetus, he did work on nucleic acid chemistry and invented PCR. His opinions about science and business, and the extent to which scientists are usually directed by those who do not understand their work, are pointed and acerbic: "I have never encountered a business person with any true interest in science. Why should he be interested? He had the choice, and he chose business. It is only through good fortune that money ends up in the hands of scientists, who know how to use it for anything other than making money, and it is a sorry situation indeed, since much scientific research is not cheap. Government grants, although offering, in theory, a preferable alternative, have the similar problem of being often administered by scientific incompetents who are after power and personal security, instead of widely useful knowledge. Good scientists don't like administrative jobs, which leaves us exactly where we are. Science is generally directed by non-scientists" (http://www.karymullis.com/pcr.shtml).

Chiron: "Get in or lose out"

Chiron came close to never existing. Its main founder, the distinguished scientist and UCSF research director William Rutter, was one of the early members of Amgen's scientific advisory board. Amgen's founders had initially offered Rutter the CEO post, which he declined (Kornberg 1995, 204). After they had hired George Rathmann as CEO, he moved quickly to keep Rutter in the Amgen fold, proposing that Rutter open an "Amgen North" lab in the Bay Area, staffed with scientists of Rutter's choosing (Rathmann 2004, 34–35). At about the same time, Rathmann (at Rutter's suggestion) had been talking to two of Rutter's former students about joining Amgen. One was Ed Penhoet, an associate professor of biochemistry at UC–Berkeley; the other was Pablo Valenzuela, who was working in Rutter's lab at UCSF. When the "Amgen North" idea derailed, the three researchers realized they could found their own company instead. Penhoet (2001, 102–4) recalls:

> We continued to say to each other: we don't have to do Amgen. Other companies were being formed, and there was a lot of activity in the field at that time. . . . to a point where we said, "Well, if we're going to do this . . . we can get some money, and we have reasonable enough management skills, having managed big labs and people."

Rutter's experience and relationships were the key to the venture. A scientist of broad interests and training—including long-term consulting ties to pharma giants Abbott, Eli Lilly, and Merck—Rutter was the academic equivalent of a turn-around artist. Heavily recruited by the UCSF medical school to take over as department chair of biochemistry, he turned down the offer at least three times before finally agreeing:

> At that time, UCSF was unpopular and considered a mediocre institution. All my friends were saying, "Why leave a great place (Univ. of Washington) to go to a medical school?" . . . Gradually, we consolidated the department to nearly twenty open positions. It was the only significant place in the United States where they had that many open positions. . . . I realized this was a great opportunity. . . . I had gotten all steamed about making a concerted onslaught on human biology. The best way was to bring together people with complementary talents and common interests. (Rutter 1998, 16)

Granted tremendous freedom, Rutter hired a diverse group of top-notch scientists, fought for contiguous space, and transformed the department into an academic powerhouse—a seedbed for numerous scientific breakthroughs and biotech ventures. In fact, it was the poaching of his handpicked team of scientists by upstart biotechs in the late 1970s and early 1980s that eventually convinced him to start his own commercial venture: "The best people in my lab were being recruited by other companies. It became obvious that I had to get in or lose out" (Gannes 1987, 9). Penhoet (2001, 100) corroborates his motivation: "At some point, Bill concluded that he couldn't continue to be competitive on several projects that he was pursuing [at UCSF] . . . because all of the people who worked for him . . . were being offered compelling positions in the budding industry."

Over Easter weekend in 1981, Rutter and Penhoet drafted a preliminary business plan for Chiron and began meeting with venture capitalists in earnest. Rutter had founded and sold a small company earlier in a deal that involved Charlie Crocker (of the Crocker Bank family); Penhoet's wife was a social acquaintance of the Crockers. Crocker assured Rutter, Penhoet, and other scientists who were considering job offers from Amgen that "he would help raise the money for this new company, and it would be fine" (Penhoet 2001, 107). Such assurances were crucial; two-thirds of the company's first twenty scientific hires were from UCSF and the remaining third from UC–Berkeley. By June 1 the founders had lined up enough initial funding to launch the company (based in part on a complex deal to bring a Merck-funded project from Rutter's UCSF lab into Chiron; see Green 2008, 20). Rutter became chairman, Penhoet president, and Valenzuela R&D director. Only Valenzuela left his day job, however; Rutter remained chairman of the department of biochemistry and biophysics at UCSF, and Penhoet stayed on half-time at UC–Berkeley (Penhoet 2001, 109).

Rutter's twelve years as chair of a growing, dynamic, interdisciplinary university department had prepared him for some of the executive duties he assumed at Chiron:

> [The UCSF Biochemistry and Biophysics department] was a little bit like a company, a little bit like Chiron is today. One of the

> reasons why it's been so easy for me to move to Chiron full time is that we have the flexibility [in the department] to make our own decisions and carry them out with no artificial bureaucratic barriers—tremendously important in a competitive scientific environment. (Rutter 1998, 74)

Penhoet, too, had commercial experience, having moonlighted throughout the 1970s in his wife's family's Mercedes-Benz auto leasing businesses (Koberstein 1994, 41). Rutter would remain chairman of the company until 1999, and Penhoet continued as its president and CEO for seventeen years, both remarkably long tenures for scientist-founders.

Chiron's expertise was in vaccines. Indeed, Rutter's belief in the health care benefits and commercial potential of vaccines was what he called a "secondary reason" for founding the company: "I'd gathered that the pharmaceutical industry itself was not interested in protection from disease. . . . Most all the companies began to essentially withdraw from vaccine development. . . . I felt that, in the future, . . . prevention and vaccinology would be a tremendous boon to health care" (Rutter 1997, 65). In addition to its focus on vaccines, Chiron developed successful products in both diagnostics and therapeutics.

William Green (2008, 33), Chiron's general counsel from its founding until 2004, noted that it was more successful than others in partnering with larger pharmaceutical companies and universities:

> Chiron prided itself in having and managing dramatically more collaborative arrangements, both with commercial entities and also with universities, than its peer companies. . . . Chiron's principal advantage was in having a very deep, early-stage research competence, and a view of having this sense of urgency and speed, and being able to move a concept through the very earliest stage of research to create a compound of some sort that would be interesting. Chiron didn't have the downstream skills to move that compound through development process or through pre-clinical or clinical testing . . . so it depended upon its collaborators to execute the more traditional parts of pharmaceutical development processes.

Like Centocor, Chiron partnered with larger pharmaceutical companies to market and distribute its products; unlike Centocor, however, Chiron's own staff of scientists developed most of the company's breakthroughs. Also, like its cross-Bay comrade Genentech, Chiron had a "very high order of belief in academic freedom, and . . . a very low level of concern about loss of trade secrets," which translated into a "very aggressive desire to encourage people to publish" (Green 2008, 28). Chiron's expansive strategy of early stage collaborations with university researchers, which served as initial probes into new areas of medical research, made it one of the most intensively connected of all early biotech firms (Powell, Koput, and Smith-Doerr 1996). Like Genentech, Chiron imported an "invisible college" academic model into its business strategy.

Among Chiron's notable achievements were an IPO in 1983 (a few weeks after Amgen's), the discovery of the hepatitis-C virus, and the bold acquisition in 1992 of biotech pioneer Cetus. Chiron was subsequently acquired by one of its Big Pharma partners, Novartis, in April 2006. It took five years, however, for employees to feel unapologetic about working for the pharmaceutical giant. "For a long time . . . people here would say, 'I'm working for the former Chiron site,'" relates Peter Maag, current president of what is now called Novartis Diagnostics. "Now they can say, 'I'm working for Novartis' and be proud of it" (Morrill 2011).

Genentech: The Best of Both Worlds?

Genentech was neither the first nor the most commercially successful of the early biotech firms, yet arguably it has exerted the greatest influence on what ultimately became the canonical DBF form. Such central practices as boundary-blurring contracts with academic scientists, simultaneous patenting and publishing, milestone payments, and "proof of principle" research evolved from origins that were as simple as they were novel. In the words of founder Herb Boyer (2001, 87), "We tried to set up an atmosphere which would take the best from industry and the best from the academic community, and put them together."

The scope of Genentech's influence would have been impossible to predict in 1976, when the firm was inauspiciously founded by an unemployed would-be entrepreneur and a celebrated molecular biologist on the verge of promotion to full professor. The entrepreneur, twenty-eight-year-old Robert Swanson, had graduated from

MIT with a B.S. in chemistry and an M.S. in management, then spent five years working as an analyst for Citibank's venture investment group (1970–74) and Kleiner Perkins (1974–75). When Kleiner Perkins let him go, Swanson started an active job search. He planned to gain operational experience with an established company then strike out on his own. But job offers were not forthcoming; among the firms that turned him down was biotech pioneer Cetus. Swanson's $410 monthly unemployment check was stretched thin: "My half of an apartment in Pacific Heights was $250, my lease payment on the Datsun 240Z was $110, and the rest was peanut butter sandwiches and an occasional movie" (Swanson 2001, 21). (It is a testament to Genentech's subsequent success that nearly every account of its founding describes Swanson as a venture capitalist.)

Along with pursuing job interviews, Swanson had been reading scientific journals, searching for commercializable ideas. He was intrigued by the burgeoning research on recombinant DNA. More out of desperation than visionary foresight, Swanson began cold-calling academics who had attended the famous Asilomar conference on patenting life forms to explore the possibility of forming a bioscience venture: "So what triggered this [idea of starting a company] was, I needed to get a job. . . . I probably had three [job] interviews a day for three or four months. This was a pretty scary period" (Swanson 2001, 10). The first scientist who actually agreed to meet with Swanson was Herb Boyer at UCSF.

Boyer's academic career was established by the time he met Swanson in January 1976. As coauthor with Stanford's Stanley Cohen on the 1973 papers detailing the methods for recombinant DNA, Boyer was about to be promoted to full professor and made director of UCSF's newly created graduate program in genetics. Perhaps such security allowed him to risk founding a commercial venture; up to that time, distinguished bioscientists had limited their industrial involvement to advisory and consulting roles. In fact, Cohen (who was on Cetus's advisory board) tried to protect Boyer from a career misstep: "Stanley took me to lunch to talk me out of [founding Genentech]. He said, 'I've heard that Swanson's just a gofer anyway'" (Boyer 2001, 82). Boyer stuck with the "gofer," though his initial expectations were very modest: "I thought it would be a good way to fund some post-docs and some work in my laboratory" (2001, 71).

The combination of a renowned and somewhat laid-back scientist with a high-energy, low-experience entrepreneur was oddly powerful. Boyer knew who was doing the best science; he guided Swanson to set up a contract with the City of Hope National Medical Center in Southern California, where Art Riggs and Keichi Itakura had just been denied NIH funding for their work to produce a human protein (somatostatin) in *E. coli* bacteria: "The [NIH] reviewers . . . said the proposal lacked scientific merit and that it could not be completed in the several years for which funding had been sought" (Kiley 2002, 11). With Genentech's funding and help from Genentech-funded postdocs in Boyer's lab at UCSF, Riggs and Itakura produced the protein in nine months. This "proof of concept" research showed that the technology worked. With evidence in hand, Genentech leased its own space, equipped a lab, and hired its first scientists: David Goeddel and Dennis Kleid from SRI in Palo Alto.

Swanson's decision to remain a virtual company until the technology had been demonstrated was heavily influenced by the venture capitalist Tom Perkins (Perkins 2002, 4–6). A second financial innovation stems from the same root: arranging milestone payments from large pharmaceutical partners in exchange for showing progress toward agreed goals, thus obtaining funding without diluting the company's equity (Boyer 2001, 88). Genentech also eschewed prevailing practice and did not set up a scientific advisory board of distinguished (and expensive) biomedical luminaries. Instead, Swanson relied on the opinions of the young scientists he recruited, guided from a distance by Boyer, who never left his full-time academic post at UCSF. As David Goeddel (2003, 21) recalls:

> The stories of some of the other people at that time with other companies were that they [the scientific founders] tried to still be the big-shot professor and tell the companies how to run. . . . I don't think Herb came as often as Bob wanted him there. But when he would come, Herb would come around and say, "Do you have problems or issues? What are you working on?" And he'd try to give advice. Other things he would say, "That's up to you. I can't help you on that. You're better at that than I am." He said, "This is your project; you're going to get credit." He wasn't putting his name on the papers. I think his approach of letting the young scientists do the work really paid off well.

The Nobel laureate and Stanford professor Arthur Kornberg (1995, 200), a consultant to ALZA and scientific founder of the biotech company DNAX, noted the uniqueness of Genentech's approach: "Unlike other biotech ventures, with a seasoned scientist or a distinguished board of scientific advisors for guidance, Genentech relied on its 'Young Turks,' unheralded but talented, industrious, and highly motivated to succeed."

These talented young scientists thrived under another of Genentech's maxims: its insistence that they continue to publish their work in top-tier scientific journals. Traditional pharmaceutical companies shrouded their R&D efforts in secrecy; even biotech pioneer Cetus had adopted a similar approach early on (Rabinow 1996, 32). In contrast, Boyer championed publication, and Swanson ensured that lawyers were ready to file the necessary patents just preceding the submission of the papers. The orientations of the two founders complemented each other, according to Goeddel (2003, 24): "Bob was always a little more worried than Herb about publications and other people knowing what we were doing. There was probably a healthy tension—Bob at one end, Herb at the other. And somewhere in the middle was how the company worked."

As a result, Genentech established a stellar scientific reputation. From 1980 to 2001, Genentech published more highly cited bioscience papers than any other institution except MIT (Levinson 2001). As Kornberg (1995, 201) observed, "The impact of Genentech's success in the ensuing years was felt both in academic and industrial circles. The excellent quality (and large volume) of papers published promptly in the leading journals helped to erase the stigma attached to research careers in an industrial environment." Boyer certainly endured the stigma early on, suffering accusations of impropriety and profiteering from his academic colleagues (Yoxen 1984, 51). Boyer (2001, 98) recalls, "I had a lot of anxieties and bouts of depression associated with this. . . . The way the attacks went, I felt like I was just a criminal. But I always felt that what I was doing was right."

Right or wrong, Boyer's stature and Genentech's rapid ascendance as a premier scientific lab left a lasting legacy for subsequent biotech firms. Boyer, the academic, knew how top-flight science operated; Swanson, the rookie entrepreneur, was unencumbered by any dominant commercial model but tightly linked to the VC network of Kleiner Perkins. Both founders shared values around what motivates people (freedom, ownership) and how companies succeed (focus, fiscal conservatism). Perhaps most crucially, they were unbiased by the conventions of commercial science: "We were so naive we never thought it couldn't be done. . . . I always maintain that the best attribute we had was our naiveté" (Boyer 2001, 96). They were able to create an entirely new hybrid: a world-class research lab funded by commercial means and focused on producing human therapeutic agents.

Genex: Biology as Manufacturing

In April 1977 an employment ad in *Science* magazine sought applicants for the position of CEO of a new genetic engineering venture. The ad was placed by Robert Johnston, a Princeton-based investor who had founded his own firm (Johnston Associates) in 1968 after a career with notable New York investment banks. Among those who responded was Leslie Glick, a thirty-seven-year-old scientist who, at this relatively early point in his career, had earned a Ph.D. in zoology from Columbia, done a postdoc at Princeton, left a department chairmanship at SUNY–Buffalo to start and manage a profitable tissue-culture company (Associated Biomedic Systems Inc.), moved to Washington, D.C., to found a nonprofit institute for scientific accountability, and was consulting with companies large and small on life sciences issues. Thinking that the job posting might provide entrée to a consulting engagement, he called Johnston: "I was curious. I was wondering where did this guy get the capital to set up something like this? Because at that point, there were only two such companies that existed" (Glick 2009). Johnston told him that the goal was to create new medicines from recombinant DNA, and that, in fact, he had not yet lined up the capital to back the venture.

Glick's next phone call was to David Jackson, an associate professor at the University of Michigan whom Glick had met at a conference two years earlier. Jackson's Ph.D. was in molecular biology from Stanford; he was first author on Paul Berg's 1972 paper on recombinant DNA (Jackson, Symons, and Berg 1972). Preceding his Ph.D., Jackson had spent a summer internship in Eli Lilly's research labs in Indianapolis—enough to convince him that he did not want a career in industry. Still, Jackson found Glick's idea intriguing, although both Glick and Jackson believed human therapeutics to be a difficult and distant target. They reasoned that the technology could yield quicker payoff in the manufacture of industrial chemicals:

> I told him [Jackson] my concerns about trying to do this to develop drugs, and he said, "Right. The way to go is to do what you can do right now. We know enough about bacteria; we could develop them to become more efficient at making chemicals and industrial products." That resonated with me. And he gave me some examples, like amino acids. (Glick 2009)

Glick called Johnston back with the idea of focusing the company on biological manufacturing processes. Johnston wanted to know more, so Glick started digging into it:

> I spent two months in the Library of Congress looking into the fermentation industry in Japan. . . . I found out how large the market was for amino acids, and I saw some other chemicals that could be derived from amino acids. I saw there was an opportunity there. So, two months later, I said to Bob Johnston: "Let's do it." (Glick 2009)

The new venture was incorporated in June 1977 and christened Genex (pronounced "gene-x"), with Johnston and Glick contributing $1,500 each, and Jackson earning founder's shares for assembling a scientific advisory board. Jackson was not ready to leave the university, though recent events had undermined his faith in academia. In the early debates over the safety and ethics of bioengineering research, Jackson had been put through the wringer:

> There was this long, drawn-out, dragged-out, convoluted, politicized process that went on for a year-and-a-half to two years at the University of Michigan with teach-ins, meetings of the faculty senate, meetings of the Ann Arbor City Council, the Board of Regents, I mean, it just went on and on about all of this. And I was sort of a central focus in all of this, and had to participate in it, had to defend myself. (Jackson 2009)

Glick and Johnston put together a business plan, and the three founders began visiting VCs. At first no one was interested; the technology was too new and the business opportunity too unproven. At the time, only one recombinant DNA firm, Genentech, had been funded by venture capital. (Cetus was founded before rDNA's invention.) Glick rewrote the business plan and, in early 1978, InnoVen, a New Jersey–based VC backed by Monsanto and Emerson Electric, decided to invest. Genex officially opened its doors in Rockville, Maryland, in May.

Jackson had been involved in pitching the company to VCs and assembling the scientific advisory board; he also consulted for the company one day per week. He remained in academia until 1980, when he left Michigan to join Genex as its vice president and scientific director. Unlike Genentech's Boyer, who had cofounded the company but remained at the university, here a noted scientist resigned his tenured academic post in favor of a commercial venture. Other scientists took notice (Kenney 1986a, 96). Jackson's decision boiled down to a critical question: Where could he do better science? "Even though it was just this incredibly counter-cultural thing to do at that point, [I thought] that if I were at Genex with some significant money available to do R&D, I could actually do more science and have more fun than I was having at the University of Michigan" (Jackson 2009). Jackson never looked back. His subsequent career includes two additional biotech start-ups, ten years in research management at DuPont and a DuPont-Merck joint venture, and subsequent consulting and angel investing. The scientific advisory board (SAB) he assembled for Genex was illustrious, but its role was chiefly symbolic: "Probably the most important role of the SAB was to give the company scientific credibility when it was seeking investment capital" (Glick 2009). Jackson nonetheless worked hard to involve the SAB in identifying and attracting promising young recruits, and in advising on the scientific feasibility of Genex's research contracts. Publishing in scientific journals was never encouraged: "It takes a lot of time to publish stuff, and we were always under enormous time pressure to meet various milestones. And there was a concern about disclosing stuff prematurely, before we'd really had a chance to capitalize on it" (Jackson 2009).

Genex's founding vision—to harness biological processes for manufacturing industrial and commercial chemicals—became a reality in the 1980s and propelled the company to rapid growth. The lion's share of the company's revenues came from a contract with G. D. Searle to manufacture L-phenylalanine (one of two vital ingredients of the artificial sweetener aspartame) using a process developed at Genex.

But Genex also did contract research (ironically, most of it for pharmaceutical companies) and even developed a patented enzyme formulation that it tried to market as a drain unclogger (Elkington 1985, 198). To fulfill the Searle contract, Genex had purchased and extensively modified a manufacturing plant in Paducah, Kentucky, becoming for a time the world's largest supplier of L-phenylalanine. When Searle unexpectedly pulled out of the agreement, Genex was forced to lay off 40 percent of its workers and scramble for new business. Genex's revenues declined more than 80 percent between 1985 and 1986 ("Genex Chief Steps Down" 1987).

By the time Genex was acquired by Enzon Inc. in 1991, it had slipped into obscurity (Feder 1991). But each of its founders was involved in subsequent biotech ventures. Johnston described one of the lessons he had learned from starting Genex: "You have got to go out there with a rifle, not a shotgun." He said he would never again "dream of starting a company as broad as Genex" (Elkington 1985, 43). Johnston's subsequent biotech ventures included Cytogen, Ecogen, Sepracor, i-STAT, Envirogen, and Praelux (JAI 2009). Glick was instrumental in organizing the first biotech industry association, the Industrial Biotechnology Association, founded in 1981.

Genzyme: A Niche Collector

What happens when a successful entrepreneur asks a venture capitalist to find him his next new venture? The unlikely answer is Genzyme. The entrepreneur was Sheridan Snyder, a 1958 graduate in French from the University of Virginia, where he had been the school's top tennis player. Channeling his competitive energies into business, Snyder founded a company in 1964 that manufactured envelope-stuffing equipment and was eventually sold to Pitney-Bowes. His next success was Instapak, a company that pioneered the use of packaging foam for shipping sensitive equipment. Instapak was backed by Ed Glassmeyer, managing partner at Sprout Capital Group at Donaldson, Lufkin & Jenrette. In 1974 Glassmeyer and an associate (Stewart Greenfield) left Sprout with the idea of starting their own fund, Oak Investment Partners. In 1980 Snyder contacted Glassmeyer with an unusual proposition: "I'd like you to help me find a new venture, and as an inducement, I'll pay you a retainer" (Glassmeyer 2009). Ginger More, an associate at Oak, ended up leading the effort.

In their search, More and Snyder were referred to the New England Enzyme Center at Tufts Medical School by 3M (an Oak limited partner). There they met Dr. Stanley Charm, a professor of physiology and director of the center. Charm's research on the detection of penicillin in cow's milk looked promising, but interpersonal differences got in the way of a deal. Instead, More and Snyder convinced a younger researcher in the Enzyme Center to join them: Henry Blair, an enzymologist, who brought with him a grant from the NIH to develop a drug for Gaucher's disease, a rare but debilitating enzyme deficiency. On June 8, 1981, Genzyme was officially launched with Snyder as CEO, Blair as chief scientist, and More as Oak's representative on the board.

None of Genzyme's founding team had expertise in biotechnology. Oak was known for "office of the future" ventures (computers and communications), and Snyder had been successful in commercializing packaging technologies. Blair was a competent researcher but not at the forefront; his work at Tufts was an extension of the research of Dr. Roscoe Brady, an NIH scientist who had been pursuing Gaucher's treatment for more than a decade. Acknowledging Brady's foundational (though not founding) role, Sheridan Snyder recalls, "Dr. Brady is the true father of Genzyme. It was all of his research, scientifically and clinically, which resulted in the Ceradase product for Genzyme" (2009). To add scientific depth, in 1983 Genzyme entered into an exclusive agreement with BioInformation Associates (BIA), a group of eight tenured Harvard and MIT professors from the departments of chemical engineering, biology, biomaterials, and chemistry (Genzyme 1986, 22). In exchange for a 10 percent stake of the company and annual retainers, BIA would provide scientific guidance and opinions, and Genzyme would enjoy exclusive rights to BIA's expertise without the payment of further royalties or consulting fees. "They gave us credibility with all the stellar scientists and they brought us the carbohydrate side of our chemistry," recalls Ginger More (2009). One of the original BIA partners—Charles Cooney, a professor of chemical and biochemical engineering at MIT—remained a member of Genzyme's board until its acquisition by Sanofi-Aventis in early 2011.

In 1983 More initiated a search for a seasoned health care executive to help the company grow. Through Oak's network, they found Henri Termeer, a Dutchman and pharmaceutical veteran from Baxter Travenol. He joined as president, became CEO in 1985, and remained CEO until the recent acquisition. Termeer had been head of the blood fractionating group at Baxter that was looking for new ways to produce proteins and limit reliance on human donors. Also in 1983, the Orphan Drug Act was passed. Genzyme ultimately became well-known as one of the early orphan drug success stories, thanks to its development of Ceredase, a naturally derived enzyme replacement therapy for Gaucher's disease, and a follow-on recombinantly produced version of the enzyme, Cerezyme. Under Termeer's leadership, Genzyme developed orphan drugs for at least four other rare diseases.

Termeer took a significant risk in joining Genzyme. At the time, the company was a far cry from Big Pharma, where he had built a successful and comfortable career. Genzyme's headquarters were in a cramped old building on the edge of Boston's seedy "Combat Zone," and his starting salary was half of what he had been earning at Baxter. But Termeer remembers telling himself, "Biotechnology is going to have an enormous impact on medicine, industry, and the economy. Being in at the beginning is an opportunity that comes just once" (Wilke 1987). Over time, he recruited a number of Baxter alumni to join Genzyme.

At Baxter, Termeer had seen the practical aspects of developing drugs for niche markets. In addition to rare diseases, Genzyme also worked on technologies that would improve the manufacturing of biotechnology drugs. Even before Termeer's arrival, Snyder and More had purchased Whatman Chemicals, a small specialty chemical maker in the U.K., knowing that eventually Genzyme would need the ability to manufacture its own products. From BIA, Genzyme acquired expertise in glycoprotein remodeling, a process that snips away at the large protein chains that constitute most new biotech drugs. It changes their shape and the way they act in the body, potentially reducing side effects, affording a renewed patent position for an improved remodeled compound (Wilke 1987). These and other moves made manufacturing a core value for Genzyme. As one Genzyme alumnus described it, "Henri loves producing stuff. Manufacturing is Genzyme's strategic competitive advantage, not research, which may rub some people the wrong way—but not Henri. Manufacturing has always given Genzyme the upper hand in negotiations because they know how to produce stuff and that's unusual. It's a business, not a research institution" (Higgins 2005, 244).

Termeer and More also inculcated a strong sense of fiscal conservatism at Genzyme. The choice of niche markets reflected a risky bet, but it was very conservatively managed. "Ginger and Henri were a great team," recalls Glassmeyer. "Neither was bet-the-ranch oriented, so they weren't constantly battling over what the strategy should be" (2009). Perfecting the enzyme replacement therapy to treat Gaucher's was hugely expensive and the price of treatment extremely high. The scientific advisory board and other senior managers felt that this focus would bankrupt the company and voted against it. But Termeer saw the advantage of the government's orphan drug category, which gave exclusive rights for seven years. One NIH member was quoted as saying, "I would like to ask Henri how he had the guts to make that decision." Higgins (2005) asserts that Termeer's fortitude stemmed from his deep commitment to maintain the company's independence. Rather than overextend the company or rely on funds from Big Pharma or other partners, Termeer ensured that Genzyme internally generated most of its R&D funding, a strategy that resulted in Genzyme being labeled a small-growth company in an environment where its biotech peers were swinging for the fences. As one analyst put it, "Genzyme is a company of singles rather than home-runs" (Senior 2007, 8). Focusing on hard-to-produce products for tiny (but low-competition) markets allowed Genzyme to survive as one of the few remaining independent biotech entities until its acquisition by pharma giant Sanofi-Aventis in spring 2011. A less successful Termeer innovation was its tracking stocks, intended to raise money for Genzyme's highly autonomous (and often high-risk) divisions without diluting the parent company's stock price. In the end, the ploy was rejected as financial window dressing.

In executing his strategies, Termeer played the role of a portfolio manager, providing financial rather than scientific leadership. Scientific research was never a preeminent value at Genzyme. More (2009) recalls that academic excellence was not a big part of the company's founding culture, and she cannot remember much encouragement for staff scientists to publish their findings: "We weren't out publishing papers. Henry [Blair] . . . was not a scientist who was well-known, not the type who would try to get ahead by publishing a lot of papers. He was just trying to cure Gaucher's." As Jim Vincent, the CEO of Cambridge rival Biogen, explained, "Genzyme is entrepreneurial and fast on their feet. They followed an entrepreneurial technology model, not a deep internal scientific discovery drug model" (Higgins 2005, 249).

Another area in which Genzyme stands apart from most other biotech pioneers is its history of growth through acquisition. Since 1991, Genzyme has acquired twenty-nine companies, compared to a single merger by Genentech, four by Biogen, and eight by Amgen (although Amgen's mergers exceed Genzyme's in total market capitalization). Acquiring companies distinguishes Genzyme, and in 2006 it broke a biotech taboo in successfully completing a hostile takeover of AnorMed, outbidding Millennium Pharmaceuticals, the preferred suitor.

Genzyme became known for its niche focus on narrow markets, emphasis on process development and manufacturing, and decentralized business units—all of which belie the company's roots. In the words of Genzyme's venture capitalist, "This was not a team of blood brothers who met around a round table two or three times a day and pledged allegiance to one another. It was an ad hoc collection of academics (BIA), a project leader (Blair), a founding entrepreneur (Snyder), and a manager (Termeer), who together realized the potential of Genzyme" (Glassmeyer 2009).

Hybritech: Built for Success or Biotech at the Beach?

The oft-told story of Hybritech's founding revolves around a 1978 meeting in the San Diego Airport between UC–San Diego (UCSD) researcher Ivor Royston, his lab assistant Howard Birndorf, and venture capitalists Kleiner-Perkins. When asked how much money they needed to create monoclonal antibodies in a commercially funded lab, Royston and Birndorf are reported to have pulled the number $200,000 out of the air, only to have Perkins reply, "No, I'll give you $300,000. I am sure you underestimated" (Royston 2006). Although his car ran out of gas on the way back from the airport meeting, Birndorf located commercial lab space in La Jolla two days later. Within six months, he and Royston had successfully produced monoclonal antibodies. Hybritech was off and running.

Beneath this charming founding story, however, lies a more complex account of overlapping networks and unique founders' backgrounds. Royston, for example, was neither a typical academic nor a traditional entrepreneur. Born in England in 1945, he immigrated to the United States in 1954. A high school friend recalls, "Ivor wanted to cure cancer when he was five years old" (Gibbons 1989, 2). Along with his drive, Royston exhibited a penchant for risk taking. In high school he joined with sixteen classmates to invest their life savings in commercial real estate; they lost all of their money (ibid.). Undaunted, Royston purchased and operated an ice cream truck to finance his studies, earning a bachelor's in human biology (1967) and an MD from Johns Hopkins (1970). He chose Stanford for his internship and residency, followed by two years studying immunology and virology at the NIH. He returned to Stanford for an oncology fellowship from 1975 to 1977.

Royston was in a position to observe the Bay Area biotech scene during its formative era:

> While I [was] at Stanford . . . I saw Cetus develop, I saw Genentech develop, and my own professor, John Daniels, in the division of oncology at Stanford, was the founder of a company called Collagen—they were the first company to make injectable collagen for smoothing out wrinkles in skin. (2006, 6)

Royston's fellowship at Stanford introduced him to people and ideas that would become crucial. His favorite lab technician was Howard Birndorf, who would follow him to UCSD and then to Hybritech. He also met his future wife, Colette, a nurse at Stanford Hospital who had previously dated another central player in the Hybritech story, venture capitalist Brook Byers (Robbins-Roth 2000, 50). While Royston was at Stanford, Köhler and Milstein's work on monoclonal antibodies was first published. "I read that paper and said, 'Gee, this looks pretty straightforward. . . . This could lead to an entirely new approach for generating highly specific, highly selective antibodies for treating cancer" (Royston 2006). Köhler and Milstein's work had direct impact on Birndorf as well. Dr. Leonard Herzenberg, a genetics professor at Stanford, had spent a sabbatical in Milstein's lab in England, where he had learned how to make hybridomas. "Len came back and taught the technique to a woman in his lab, who taught me," recalls Birndorf. "I started talking with Ivor about how to apply this technique to myeloma [a cancer of the white blood cells]" (Robbins-Roth 2000, 49).

When his Stanford postdoc ended in 1977, Royston accepted a position as an assistant professor of hematology and oncology at rapidly expanding UCSD. He recruited Birndorf to run his lab. Birndorf had spent three years in a biochemistry doctoral program at Wayne State University, but it had been a consolation prize after failing to get into medical school, and he lacked the motivation to finish his degree. Instead, he had moved west and was doing lab work to pay the bills: "I wasn't making a lot as a lab tech—around $15,000—and there was nowhere for me to go without a doctorate. I was trying to figure out whether I should go back to school, or if there was another way to make more money" (B. Powell 1999).

Birndorf's poverty and Royston's drive to cure cancer combined to form a novel business concept: a company that would produce monoclonal antibodies as superior reagents for medical researchers. "All I cared about was I needed these antibodies so I could develop a treatment program at UCSD," remembers Royston (2006). "It was never the idea that I wanted to start a business, make a lot of money and leave the university." In early 1978 Birndorf bought a book entitled *How to Start Your Own Business* and wrote a crude five-page business plan. The two would-be entrepreneurs began the hunt for funding. Royston's efforts to interest established antibody-producing companies met with disbelief: "I was talking about making antibodies in the test tube and they said 'No, antibodies—you must bleed sheep and rabbits and goats,' and it was impossible to communicate with them" (Royston 2006). Birndorf's futile attempts included talking to friends who were commodities traders in Chicago and making the rounds of his parents' wealthy friends in Michigan.

The fund-raising breakthrough came from Colette (Royston's girlfriend at the time, subsequently his wife): she set up an appointment with her one-time beau, Brook Byers. Byers had shared an apartment with Bob Swanson before Swanson founded Genentech; the two were close friends. Having recently joined Kleiner Perkins (investors in Cetus and Genentech), Byers was attuned to the possibilities of life-science-based ventures. Byers did the requisite due diligence (including confirmation that the Köhler and Milstein work had never been patented) and hired an attorney to iron out with UCSD the specifics of Royston's involvement. Not coincidentally, the attorney was Tom Kiley, who had done the legal work for Genentech and had been recommended by Swanson. Byers (2006, 18) also sought Swanson's overall approval of the venture: "[Swanson] thought it was a good idea, and not competitive with Genentech." All of this set the stage for the fateful airport meeting.

Byers's involvement in the new venture went above and beyond that of an active investor. He was Hybritech's first president and CEO—a rare role for a VC at the time:

> People who go into venture capital, for the most part, do it because they love to coach and advise and be an active board member, perhaps, but not to manage something. . . . I had no experience in managing anyone, but perhaps my best qualification for the job was that I didn't want it long term. My first assignment was to go find a president. (Byers 2006, 19)

Byers's search took five months. Before he could recruit an executive of the requisite caliber, Byers felt the fledgling company needed to prove that the technology was practical. He had given Royston and Birndorf a goal to produce monoclonal hepatitis antibodies within six months; they accomplished the "proof of principle" within three months. With these results, Byers was able to persuade Ted Greene from Baxter to join Hybritech as president and CEO in March 1979.

At the time, Greene was looking for a new challenge, having spent five years in various executive positions with Baxter Travenol's diagnostics business (Hybritech 1981, 22). Greene, who had worked for seven years at McKinsey & Co. after earning a Harvard MBA, was intrigued by the commercial potential of monoclonal antibodies and was seriously considering joining a start-up in Orange County. As part of his own due diligence, Greene contacted Byers to quiz the venture capitalist on the feasibility of the technology, unaware that Byers was involved in a similar start-up. Instead of advice, Greene wound up with a job offer (Fikes 1999, 3). As Byers (2006, 25) explains, "It was perfect timing because he [Greene] wanted to leave Baxter and start a company and run it himself. He was what I was looking for. He had a good knowledge of the science, he had worked at the Hyland division of Baxter, which made reagents and components." Greene's business savvy was instrumental in steering Hybritech away from direct competition with Abbott in hepatitis diagnostics, instead focusing on such areas as prostate cancer detection.

Royston remained at the university, which had always been his goal. "[Royston] wanted to stay at UCSD and we respected that," observed Byers (2006, 19). "[He] saw as his role model Herb Boyer at UCSF, who stayed at that institution and was a consultant to Genentech." Like Boyer, Royston endured criticisms and accusations of impropriety from his scientific colleagues. The furor escalated to the point that Royston was formally investigated by the NIH for conflict of interest; he was cleared of any wrongdoing. Unlike Boyer, Royston knew he could be fired for his extracurricular activities: "I had only been there [at UCSD] a year. I wasn't even tenured. I thought it might jeopardize my career, but I also had a gut feeling that this was the right thing to do" (Gibbons 1989, 1).

Hybritech had a successful IPO in 1981 and was sold to Eli Lilly in 1985 for nearly $400 million—the first biotech company to be sold at a premium to an established pharmaceutical company (Robbins-Roth 2000). The acquisition turned out to be a commercial failure, but an overwhelming institutional success: disaffected with corporate life but wealthy, Hybritech's founding executives and scientists went on to found dozens of biotech ventures and establish San Diego as one of the three dominant hubs of biotech activity in the United States (see chapter 14 in this volume).

Immunex: The Biotech Underdogs

In 1981 Steve Gillis was a twenty-eight-year-old investigator at the Fred Hutchinson Cancer Research Center in Seattle (known locally as "The Hutch"). He worked in the lab of Christopher Henney, a forty-year-old professor with a growing reputation in immunology. The two were doing novel work on Interleukin-2 (IL-2) and other immune system hormones, and they wondered about patenting their work. Gillis leafed through the phone book, found an attorney who specialized in patents, and gave him a call. The attorney he sought was out of the office; instead he reached Jim Uhlir, a partner with expertise in patents and business. Uhlir's response was, "Have you thought of forming a company?"

Henney and Gillis had, in fact, considered a start-up but didn't know where to begin. Uhlir arranged a meeting with Bruce Pym, an attorney at another firm who brought a client with him: Steve Duzan, a forty-year-old executive who was looking for a new challenge. A University of Washington graduate, Duzan had spent a year in law school but left it for business. He advanced up the ranks at various companies, and in 1975 he assembled a group of Seattle investors to acquire Cello Bag Inc. Duzan ran the company for five years, then arranged its sale to Atlantic Richfield (ARCO). He stayed on for another six months, enough time to realize he did not want to pursue a career within ARCO. Instead, Duzan was contemplating buying a company of his own to run: "I thought that I would like to start a company, and . . . while I didn't have any idea what it would be, I hoped it would be in some way related to science because I liked that kind of thing" (Duzan 2009).

The meeting in Pym's office on April 6, 1981, was Duzan's first introduction to Henney and Gillis, who also introduced him to Interleukin-2 (a family of molecules known as cytokines and cytokine receptors) and to their vision for its therapeutic possibilities. The three plus Uhlir formally incorporated on August 1, 1981, with Henney and Gillis in charge of the science. Duzan would manage the business and lead the fund-raising; Uhlir would cover the legal aspects and receive founder's shares, though he continued full-time in his law practice. Uhlir and Gillis came up with the name Immunex, a play on Esso's recent rebranding as Exxon (Gillis 2009).

The company's first challenge was to extricate Henney and Gillis from their academic commitments (Wilson and Heath 2001). Recalls Gillis (2009):

> Most of our competitors who were involved in starting companies at the time were . . . staying in academia. We thought that might be a real conflict of interest. We wanted to make a clean break. So in exchange for the intellectual property that we had at the time, the arrangement with the Hutchinson Center was that we would give them some stock in the company, and we transferred our grants to other investigators at the Center, so that the Center would not lose that revenue.

Various faculty colleagues tried to talk the two researchers out of starting a company, warning that they would become pariahs. Gillis remembers going back and forth with Henney on which of them should sever ties with the Cancer Center:

> Chris would come into my office and say, "Look, you're young, you can afford to make a mistake. If you go and do this thing and it doesn't work out, you can always get a job in academia." The next week I would go

into his office and say, "You know, you're ten years older, you have a more established career than I do. Why don't I be the consultant and you go full time? If this turns out to be a mistake you can always get a job back in academia."

In the end, the two decided they were in it together. Duzan, too, had to take care of other obligations before joining Immunex full-time. But by July 1982 all three were working at Immunex in a lab installed in an old waterfront industrial building, and Duzan had lined up a group of investors led by Seattle-based venture capitalists Cable & Howse to provide a modest $1 million in start-up money.

Henney focused on recruiting scientists while Gillis headed up the work in the labs. Like Genentech and Chiron, Immunex had no scientific advisory board, relying instead on the expertise of its own young scientists. In the early 1980s, Seattle was not the technology hub it is today, and an underdog culture developed among the scientific staff. Recalls Duzan (2009):

> We were stuck up in Seattle at a time when Seattle was far less well known in terms of technology of any kind except airplanes. It was us against them. We continuously found as we went around trying to raise money, trying to recruit scientists, trying to do all kinds of things, that we were going to have to be the Avis of this business and try harder and work harder. We were able to foster a culture around that, and everybody who worked there eventually began to call themselves "Immunoids."

Gillis led a work-hard, play-hard culture, epitomizing an informal jeans-and-T-shirt approach to serious science. The research group, an international collection of immunologists, biochemists, and molecular biologists, became known as "Immunex University," and Gillis instituted a "Pons & Fleischmann Award" for lab mishaps, named after the researchers who thought they had discovered cold fusion, which was presented at weekly Friday beer busts (Timmerman 2001). Most of the recruits were young: "In those days, trying to convince established researchers to do what we were doing would have been pretty tough" (Gillis 2009).

Despite the high jinks, the young research team discovered and cloned a series of genes to produce immune-system proteins that could potentially fight cancer, heal wounds, and counter auto-immune diseases. Gillis and Henney strongly encouraged scientists to publish their findings, give talks at scientific meetings, and even share the reagents they created with outside researchers. Genentech led all biotech companies in the number of citations of its scientists' papers, but Immunex "was always second or third," recalls Gillis. Not only was their publication record a source of Immunoid pride, but in the early days Wall Street analysts also paid attention to citation counts as a proxy for commercial potential.

Despite additional rounds of funding and an IPO in 1983, Immunex never had enough money to support expensive clinical trials and bring promising drugs to market. Instead, it continued to fund its research activities by selling its technologies to established pharmaceutical companies for development. Investors worried that Immunex was becoming a research boutique, unable to convert technical breakthroughs into marketable products. "It was a very productive time for science," recalled David Urdal, one of the early biochemists. "I'm not really sure when the connection hit on Immunex becoming a business" (Timmerman 2001). In 1989 Henney left the company to join George Rathmann (Amgen's first CEO) in a new Seattle-based biotech start-up, Icos. Henney has since been involved in founding two more biotech firms.

In 1991 Immunex received FDA approval for its first product: Leukine, a white-blood-cell growth stimulator approved for bone-marrow transplant patients. But a few months earlier, Amgen had introduced Neupogen, a similar product approved for much broader applications. Sales of Leukine were disappointing, and in 1993 Immunex merged with Lederle Oncology, a unit of American Cyanamid, to form a new independent, publicly traded company still called Immunex. American Cyanamid held a majority interest in the new company but was limited to three board seats. Duzan chose to step down as CEO within six months of the merger: "The entrepreneurial phase of Immunex was largely completed with this deal and, frankly, I was a bit burned out" (Duzan 2009). He became an angel investor in five subsequent biotech ventures. Gillis (who had been head of research) served as interim CEO for a few months, then was replaced by Ed Fritzky, an American Cyanamid executive with marketing experience. Although he made significant changes to Immunex, Fritzky tried not to tamper with the culture of the research center. But American Cyanamid was bought by American Home Products (AHP) in mid-1994, and Gillis left Immunex to found another biotech venture, Corixa.

Immunex achieved its hoped-for blockbuster drug with Enbrel, an anti-inflammatory approved by the FDA in 1998 for rheumatoid arthritis. Backed by the manufacturing and sales capability of AHP's Wyeth-Ayerst division, sales of Enbrel skyrocketed, Immunex's stock split multiple times in 1999, and the company began ambitious expansion plans with facilities in Bothell, Washington, a plant in Rhode Island, and an architecturally striking research center in Seattle. Immunex had finally arrived.

Success, however, spelled the end of Immunex as an independent entity. Demand for Enbrel grew spectacularly (Immunex 2001), but it outstripped manufacturing capability. Larger firms also were attracted by Immunex's promising research pipeline, and in December 2001, Immunex was acquired by fellow biotech pioneer Amgen for $16 billion (Fletcher 2002). It is curious to note the reaction among Immunex scientists to the acquisition. One senior-level scientist lamented the fact that he was no longer encouraged to publish his findings: "Amgen sees it [publishing] as giving away the company silver" (Dietrich 2003). Another observer commented, "Morale has been impacted because people finally realized that it's a takeover, they can't keep everybody, and it's not all fun and games. Amgen is Big Pharma, and their culture is so different than Immunex" (ibid.). Mike Widmer, a former Immunex researcher, stated, "A lot of us have concluded there will never be another place like Immunex. It was a magical place" (Timmerman 2004).

REFERENCES

Aldrich, Howard E., and C. Marlene Fiol. 1994. "Fools Rush In? The Institutional Context of Industry Creation." *Academy of Management Review* 19(4):645–70.

Anderson, Phillip M., and Michael Tushman. 1990. "Technological Discontinuities and Dominant Designs: A Cyclical Model of Technological Change." *Administrative Science Quarterly* 35(4):604–33.

Baron, J. N., M. T. Hannan, and M. D. Burton. 1999. "Building the Iron Cage: Determinants of Managerial Intensity in the Early Years of Organizations." *American Sociological Review* 64(4):527–47.

Baker, Ted, and Reed E. Nelson. 2005. "Creating Something from Nothing: Resource Construction through Entrepreneurial Bricolage." *Administrative Science Quarterly* 50:329–66.

Becker, Howard S. 1963. *Outsiders: Studies in the Sociology of Deviance*. Glencoe, IL: The Free Press.

———. 1986. *Doing Things Together*. Evanston, IL: Northwestern University Press.

Beckman, Christine M., and M. Diane Burton. 2008. "Founding the Future: Path Dependence in the Evolution of Top Management Teams from Founding to IPO." *Organization Science* 19(1):3–24.

Berkley, James D., and Nitin Nohria. 1992. "Amgen Inc.: Planning the Unplannable." Harvard Business School Case #9-492-052. Boston: Harvard Business School Publishing.

Berman, Elisabeth Popp. 2007. "Creating the Market University: Science, the State, and the Economy, 1965–1985." Ph.D. diss., UC–Berkeley.

Binder, Gordon, and Philip Bashe. 2008. *Science Lessons: What the Business of Biotech Taught Me about Management*. Boston: Harvard Business School Press.

Biogen IDEC. 2003. "Biogen and IDEC Pharmaceuticals Announce Merger to Create a New Biotechnology Industry Leader." Press release, June 23.

Blumer, Herbert. 1969. *Symbolic Interactionism: Perspective and Method*. Englewood Cliffs, NJ: Prentice-Hall.

Boyer, Herbert W. 2001. "Recombinant DNA Research at UCSF and Commercial Application at Genentech." Oral history conducted in 1994 by Sally Smith Hughes, Regional Oral History Office, The Bancroft Library, University of California–Berkeley.

Burrill, Stephen G. 2007. "Biotech 2007: A Retrospective Look and a Vision for Its Future." Paper presented at Chemical Heritage Foundation, April 19.

Burt, Ronald S. 2009. *Neighbor Networks*. Oxford: Oxford University Press.

Burton, M. Diane, J. B. Sorensen, and C. Beckman. 2002. "Coming from Good Stock: Career Histories and New Venture Formation." In *Research in the Sociology of Organizations*, vol. 19, ed. M. Lounsbury and M. Ventresca, 229–62. Greenwich, CT: JAI Press.

Byers, Brook. 2006. "Brook Byers: Biotechnology Venture Capitalist, 1970–2006." Oral history conducted in 2002–5 by Thomas D. Kiley, Regional Oral History Office, The Bancroft Library, University of California–Berkeley.

Bylinski, G. 1980. "DNA Can Build Companies, Too." *Fortune*, June 16, pp. 144–53.

Cape, Ronald. 2006. "Biotech Pioneer and Co-Founder of Cetus." Oral history conducted in 2003 by Sally Smith Hughes, Regional Oral History Office, The Bancroft Library, University of California–Berkeley.

Carroll, G. R., L. S. Bigelow, M-D. L. Seidel, and L. B. Tsai. 1996. "The Fates of *de novo* and *de alio* Producers in the American Automobile Industry, 1885–1981." *Strategic Management Journal* 17:117–37.

Centocor. 1982. Annual Report to Shareholders. Copy in possession of the authors.

Chatterji, A. K. 2009. "Spawned with a Silver Spoon? Entrepreneurial Performance and Innovation in the Medical Device Industry." *Strategic Management Journal* 30(2):185–206.

Chemical Heritage Foundation. 1997. "The Emergence of Biotechnology: DNA to Genentech." Transcript of June 13 conference.

Christensen, C., and R. S. Rosenbloom. 1995. "Explaining the Attacker's Advantage: Technological Paradigms, Organizational Dynamics and the Value Network." *Research Policy* 24:233–57.

Cicourel, Aaron. 1968. *The Social Organization of Juvenile Justice*. New York: John Wiley.

Clarke, Adele C. 1991. "Social Worlds/Arenas Theory as Organizational Theory." In *Social Organization and Social Processes: Essays in Honor of Anselm L. Strauss*, ed. David Maines, 119–58. New York: Aldine.

Cockburn, Iain M., and Scott Stern. 2010. "Finding the Endless Frontier: Lessons from the Life Sciences Innovation System for Technology Policy." *Capitalism and Society* 5(1), Article 1, available at: http://www.bepress.com/cas/vol5/iss1/art1.

Cockburn, Iain M., Rebecca M. Henderson, and Scott Stern. 2000. "Untangling the Origins of Competitive Advantage." *Strategic Management Journal* 21(10/11):1123–45.

Cohen, Stanley. 1975. "The Manipulation of Genes." *Scientific American* 233(1):24–33.

Cohen, S. N., A.C.Y. Chang, H. W. Boyer, and R. B. Helling. 1973. "Construction of Biologically Functional Bacterial Plasmids in Vitro." *Proceedings of the National Academy of Sciences* 70:3240–44.

Colyvas, Jeannette. 2007a. "Factory, Hazard, and Contamination: The Use of Metaphor in the Commercialization of Recombinant DNA." *Minerva* 45(2):143–59.

———. 2007b. "From Divergent Meanings to Common Practices: The Early Institutionalization of Technology Transfer at Stanford University." *Research Policy* 36(4):456–76.

Colyvas, Jeannette, and W. W. Powell. 2006. "Roads to Institutionalization." *Research in Organizational Behavior* 21:305–53.

———. 2007. "From Vulnerable to Venerated: The Institutionalization of Academic Entrepreneurship in the Life Sciences." *Research in the Sociology of Organizations* 25:345–73.

D'Andrade, Hugh A. 2001. "Regional Characteristics of Biotechnology in the United States: Perspectives of Three Industry Leaders." Oral history conducted in 1998 by Sally Smith Hughes, Regional Oral History Office, The Bancroft Library, University of California–Berkeley.

Dewey, John. 1939. *Theory of Valuation*. Chicago: University of Chicago Press.

Dietrich, Heidi. 2003. "Amgen Shrinks Seattle Operations." *Los Angeles Business Journal*, May 5.

Duncan, David E. 2005. *The Amgen Story: 25 Years of Visionary Science and Powerful Medicine*. San Diego, CA: Tehabi Books.

Duzan, Steve. 2009. Phone interview by Kurt Sandholtz, September 24.

Eisenhardt, Kathleen M., and Melissa E. Graebner. 2007. "Theory Building from Cases: Opportunities and Challenges." *Academy of Management Journal* 50(1):25–32.

Elkington, John. 1985. *The Gene Factory*. New York: Carroll and Graf.

Feder, Barnaby J. 1991. "Biotech's Biggest Sales So Far Are on Wall Street." *New York Times*, November 3, sec. 3, p. 12.

———. 1992. "Biogen Seeks Profits to Call Its Own." *New York Times*. August 15.

Fikes, Bradley J. 1999. "Why San Diego Has Biotech." *San Diego Metropolitan*, April. Available at http://sandiegometro.archives.whsites.net/1999/apr/biotech.html.

Fisher, Lawrence M. 1997. "The Rocky Road from Start-up to Big-Time Player: Biogen's Triumph against the Odds." *Strategy + Business*, July. Third Quarter 1997. Available at http://www.strategy-business.com/press/article/18003.

Fleming, Lee. 2001. "Recombinant Uncertainty in Technological Search." *Management Science* 47(1):117–32.

Fletcher, Liz. 2002. "Amgen's Big-Ticket Play for Immunex." *Nature Biotechnology* 20:105–6.

Fligstein, Neil. 2001. "Social Skill and the Theory of Fields." *Sociological Theory* 19:105–25.

Fredrickson, Donald N. 2001. *The Recombinant DNA Controversy: A Memoir*. Washington, DC: ASM Press.

Freeman, John, Glenn R. Carroll, and Michael T. Hannan. 1983. "The Liability of Newness: Age Dependence in Organizational Death Rates." *American Sociological Review* 48(5):692–710.

Fujimura, Joan H. 1987. "Constructing 'Do-Able' Problems in Cancer Research: Articulating Alignment." *Social Studies of Science* 17(2):257–93.

Gambardella, Alfonso. 1995. *Science and Innovation: The U.S. Pharmaceutical Industry during the 1980s*. New York: Cambridge University Press.

Gannes, Stuart. 1987. "Striking It Rich in Biotech." *Fortune* 116(11):9.

Garfinkel, Harold. 1967. *Studies in Ethnomethodology*. Englewood Cliffs, NJ: Prentice Hall.

"*Genex Chief Steps Down*." 1987. *New York Times*, January 6, p. D2.

Genzyme. 1986. Preliminary Prospectus dated April 16. In possession of the authors.

Gibbons, Ann. 1989. "The Man Who Made Millions by Marketing Monoclonal Antibodies." *The Scientist* 3(5).

Gillis, Steven. 2009. Phone interview by Kurt Sandholtz, October 1.

Glaser, Donald. 2006. "The Bubble Chamber, Bioengineering, Business Consulting, and Neurobiology." Oral history conducted in 2003–4 by Eric Vettel, Regional Oral History Office, The Bancroft Library, University of California–Berkeley.

Glassmeyer, Edward. 2009. Phone interview by Kurt Sandholtz, August 10.

Glick, J. Leslie. 2009. Phone interview by Kurt Sandholtz, September 9.

Goeddel, David V. 2003. "Scientist at Genentech, CEO at Tularik." Oral history conducted in 2001 and

2002 by Sally Smith Hughes for the Regional Oral History Office, The Bancroft Library, University of California–Berkeley.

Goffman, Erving. 1974. *Frame Analysis*. Cambridge, MA: Harvard University Press.

Gompers, Paul A. 1994. "The Rise and Fall of Venture Capital." *Business and Economic History* 23(2):1–26.

Gould, Stephen Jay, and Elisabeth S. Vrba. 1982. "Exaptation: A Missing Term in the Science of Form." *Paleobiology* 8(1):4–15.

Graham, Margaret B. W. 2008. "Technology and Innovation." In *The Oxford Handbook of Business History*, ed. Geoffrey Jones and Jonathan Zeitlin, 347–73. New York: Oxford University Press.

Green, William G. 2008. "William G. Green: General Counsel Chiron Corporation." Oral history conducted in 2005 by Sally Smith Hughes, Regional Oral History Office, The Bancroft Library, University of California–Berkeley.

Hall, Stephen S. 1987. *Invisible Frontiers: Race to Synthesize a Human Gene*. New York: Atlantic Monthly Press.

Hargadon, Andrew, and Robert I. Sutton. 1997. "Technology Brokering and Innovation in a Product Development Firm." *Administrative Science Quarterly* 42(4):716–49.

Helfat, Connie E., and Marvin B. Lieberman. 2002. "The Birth of Capabilities: Market Entry and the Importance of Pre-History." *Industrial and Corporate Change* 11(4):725–60.

Henderson, Rebecca. 1993. "Underinvestment and Incompetence as Responses to Radical Innovation: Evidence from the Photolithographic Alignment Equipment Industry." *RAND Journal of Economics* 24(2):248–70.

Henderson, Rebecca, and K. B. Clark. 1990. "Architectural Innovation: The Reconfiguration of Existing Product Technologies and the Failure of Established Firms." *Administrative Science Quarterly* 35(1):9–30.

Higgins, Monica. 2005. *Career Imprints: How the Baxter Boys Built the Biotech Industry*. San Francisco: John Wiley.

Holveck, David P. 2001. "Regional Characteristics of Biotechnology in the United States: Perspectives of Three Industry Insiders." Oral history conducted in 1998 by Sally Smith Hughes, Regional Oral History Office, The Bancroft Library, University of California–Berkeley.

Hounshell, David A. 1996. "The Evolution of Industrial Research in the United States." In *Engines of Innovation: U.S. Industrial Research at the End of an Era*, ed. Richard S. Rosenbloom and William J. Spencer, 13–85. Boston: Harvard Business School Press.

Hughes, Sally Smith. 2001. "Making Dollars out of DNA: The First Major Patent in Biotechnology and the Commercialization of Molecular Biology, 1974–1980." *Isis* 92(3):541–75.

Hybels, Ralph C. 1994. "Legitimation, Population Density and Founding Rates: The Institutionalization of Commercial Biotechnology in the U.S., 1971–89." Ph.D. diss., Cornell University.

Hybritech. 1981. Prospectus for Initial Public Offering. In possession of the authors.

Immunex. 2001. "Amgen to Acquire Immunex for $16 Billion in Stock and Net Cash." Immunex press release, December 17.

Jackson, David A. 2009. Phone Interview by Kurt Sandholtz, October 5.

Jackson, D. A., R. H. Symons, and P. Berg. 1972. "Biochemical Methods for Inserting New Genetic Information into DNA of Simian Virus 40: Circular SV40 DNA Molecules Containing Lambda Phage Genes and the Galactose Operon of Escherichia Coli." *Proceedings of the National Academy of Sciences* 69:2904.

JAI. 2009. "Robert A. Johnston." Biographical information posted on http://www.jaivc.com .

Johnson, Victoria. 2007. "What Is Organizational Imprinting? Cultural Entrepreneurship in the Founding of the Paris Opera." *American Journal of Sociology* 113(1):97–127.

Jones, Mark Peter. 2005. "Biotech's Perfect Climate: The Hybritech Story." Ph.D. diss., UC–San Diego.

Jong, Simcha. 2008. "Academic Organizations and New Industrial Fields: Berkeley and Stanford after the Rise of Biotechnology." *Research Policy* 37(8):1267–82.

Kaplan, Sarah, and Mary Tripsas. 2008. "Thinking about Technology: Applying a Cognitive Lens to Technical Change." *Research Policy* 37(5):790–805.

Kenney, Martin. 1986a. *Biotechnology: The University-Industrial Complex*. New Haven, CT: Yale University Press.

———. 1986b. "Schumpeterian Innovation and Entrepreneurs in Capitalism: The Case of the U.S. Biotechnology Industry." *Research Policy* 15(4):21–31.

Kenney, Martin, and Richard Florida. 2000. "Venture Capital in Silicon Valley: Fueling New Firm Formation." In *Understanding Silicon Valley: The Anatomy of an Entrepreneurial Region*, ed. Martin Kenney, 98–123. Stanford: Stanford University Press.

Kevles, Daniel J. 1994. "Diamond v. Chakrabarty and Beyond: The Political Economy of Patenting Life." In *Private Science: Biotechnology and the Rise of Molecular Science*, ed. Arnold Thackray, 65–79. Philadelphia: University of Pennsylvania Press.

Kiley, Thomas D. 2002. "Thomas D. Kiley: Genentech Legal Counsel and Vice President, 1976–1988, and Entrepreneur." Oral history conducted in 2000 and 2001 by Sally Smith Hughes, Regional Oral History Office, The Bancroft Library, University of California–Berkeley.

Klepper, Steve, and K. L. Simons. 2000. "Dominance by Birthright: Entry of Prior Radio Producers and Competitive Ramifications in the U.S. Television Receiver Industry." *Strategic Management Journal* 21:997–1016.

Klepper, Steve, and Sally Sleeper. 2005. "Entry by Spinoffs." *Management Science* 51(8):1291–1306.

Koberstein, Wayne. 1994. "Edward Penhoet." *Pharmaceutical Executive* 14(10):40–47.

Köhler, Georges, and Cesar Milstein. 1975. "Continuous Cultures of Fused Cells Secreting Antibody of Predefined Specificity." *Nature* 256:495–97.

Kornberg, Arthur. 1995. *The Golden Helix: Inside Biotech Ventures*. Sausalito, CA: University Science Books.

———. 1998. "Biochemistry at Stanford, Biotechnology at DNAX." Oral history conducted in 1997 by Sally Smith Hughes, Regional Oral History Office, The Bancroft Library, University of California–Berkeley.

Latour, Bruno. 1987. *Science in Action*. Cambridge, MA: Harvard University Press.

Law, John. 1984. "On Ships and Spices: Technology, Power and the Portuguese Route to India." Centre de Sociologie de l'Innovation, Ecole des Mines de Paris.

Levinson, Arthur D. 2001. Introduction to "Robert A. Swanson: Co-founder, CEO, and Chairman of Genentech, Inc., 1976–1996." Oral history conducted in 1996 and 1997 by Sally Smith Hughes, Regional Oral History Office, The Bancroft Library, University of California–Berkeley.

Longman, Roger. 1996. "ALZA Breaks Out of the Ivory Tower." *In Vivo* (January):44–52.

March, James G., and Herbert A. Simon. 1958. *Organizations*. New York: John Wiley and Sons.

McKelvey, Maureen D. 1996. *Evolutionary Innovations: The Business of Biotechnology*. Oxford: Oxford University Press.

McKendrick, David, and Glenn Carroll. 2001. "On the Genesis of Organizational Forms: Evidence from the Market for Disk Arrays." *Organization Science* 12(6):661–82.

Mead, George Herbert. 1934. *Mind, Self and Society*. Chicago: University of Chicago Press.

Molotch, Harvey. 2003. *Where Stuff Comes From*. New York: Routledge.

More, Ginger. 2009. Phone interview by Kurt Sandholtz, August 11.

Morrill, David. 2011. "Pharmaceutical Giant Novartis Emerges from the Shadows." *Contra Costa Times*, April 18.

Morrow, J. F., S. N. Cohen, A.C.Y. Chang, H. W. Boyer, H. M. Goodman, and R. B. Helling. 1974. "Replication and Transcription of Eukaryotic DNA in Escherichia coli." *Proceedings of the National Academy of Sciences* 71:1743–47.

Mowery, David, R. Nelson, Bhaven Sampat, and Arvids Ziedonis. 2004. *Ivory Tower and Industrial Innovation*. Stanford: Stanford University Press.

Nelson, Andrew J. 2007. "Institutional Convergence and the Diffusion of University-Versus Firm-Origin Technologies." Ph.D. diss., Stanford University.

Nelson, Richard R., and Sidney G. Winter. 1982. *An Evolutionary Theory of Economic Change*. Cambridge, MA: Belknap Press of Harvard University Press.

Oliver, Amalya L., and Kathleen Montgomery. 2000. "Creating a Hybrid Organizational Form from Parental Blueprints: The Emergence and Evolution of Knowledge Firms." *Human Relations* 53:33–56.

Orsenigo, Luigi. 1989. *The Emergence of Biotechnology: Institutions and Markets in Industrial Innovation*. London: Pinter.

Owen-Smith, Jason, and W. W. Powell. 2001. "Careers and Contradictions: Faculty Responses to the Transformation of Knowledge and Its Uses in the Life Sciences." *Research in the Sociology of Work* 10:109–40.

Padgett, John F., and Paul McLean. 2006. "Organizational Invention and Elite Transformation: The Birth of Partnership in Renaissance Florence." *American Journal of Sociology* 111(4):1463–1568.

Penhoet, Edward. 2001. "Regional Characteristics of Biotechnology in the United States: Perspectives of Three Industry Leaders." Oral history conducted in 1998 by Sally Smith Hughes, Regional Oral History Office, The Bancroft Library, University of California–Berkeley.

Perkins, Thomas J. 2002. "Kleiner Perkins, Venture Capital, and the Chairmanship of Genentech, 1976–1995." Oral history conducted in 2001 by Glenn E. Bugos, Regional Oral History Office, The Bancroft Library, University of California–Berkeley.

Pisano, Gary P. 2006. *Science Business: The Promise, the Reality, and the Future of Biotech*. Boston: Harvard Business School Press.

Porter, Kelley Anne. 2004. "You Can't Leave Your Past Behind: The Influence of Founders' Career Histories on Their Firms." Ph.D. diss., Stanford University.

Powell, Bonnie Azab. 1999. "Is Eight Enough? Howard Birndorf Can't Stop Starting Biotech Companies." *Red Herring*. September.

Powell, W. W. 1990. "Neither Market nor Hierarchy: Network Forms of Organization." *Research in Organizational Behavior* 12:295–336.

———. 1996. "Inter-organizational Collaboration in the Biotechnology Industry." *Journal of Institutional and Theoretical Economics* 120(1):197–215.

Powell, W. W., and Peter Brantley. 1996. "Magic Bullets and Patent Wars: New Product Development and the Evolution of the Biotechnology Industry." In *Competitive Product Development*, ed. Toshihiro Nishiguchi, 233–60. Oxford: Oxford University Press.

Powell, Walter W., Kenneth W. Koput, and Laurel Smith-Doerr. 1996. "Interorganizational Collaboration and the Locus of Innovation: Networks of Learning in Biotechnology." *Administrative Science Quarterly* 41:116–45.

Powell, W. W., Douglas R. White, Kenneth W. Koput, and Jason Owen-Smith. 2005. "Network Dynamics and Field Evolution: The Growth of Interorganizational Collaboration in the Life Sciences." *American Journal of Sociology* 110:1132–1205.

Proctor, Richard. 2009. Interview conducted by Kurt Sandholtz.

Rabinow, Paul. 1996. *Making PCR: A Story of Biotechnology*. Chicago: University of Chicago Press.

Rao, Hayagreeva. 1998. "Caveat Emptor: The Construction of Nonprofit Consumer Watchdog Organizations." *American Journal of Sociology* 103(4): 912–61.

Rao, Hayagreeva, and Martin Kenney. 2008. "New Forms as Settlements." In *The Sage Handbook of Organizational Institutionalism*, ed. R. Greenwood, C. Oliver, K. Sahlin and R. Suddaby, 352–70. Thousand Oaks, CA: Sage Publications.

Rao, Hayagreeva, Calvin Morrill, and Mayer Zald. 2000. "Power Plays: How Social Movements and Collective Action Create New Organizational Forms." In *Research in Organizational Behavior* 22, ed. B. Staw and R. Sutton, 239–82. Greenwich, CT: JAI Press.

Rathmann, George B. 2004. "Chairman, CEO, and President of Amgen, 1980–1988." Oral history conducted in 2003 by Sally Smith Hughes, Regional Oral History Office, The Bancroft Library, University of California–Berkeley.

Reich, Leonard. 1985. *The Making of American Industrial Research: Science and Business at GE and Bell, 1876–1926*. New York: Cambridge University Press.

Reimers, Niels. 1987. "Tiger by the Tale." *Chem Tech* 17(8):464–71.

Rhoten, Diana, and W. W. Powell. 2007. "The Frontiers of Intellectual Property: Expanded Protection vs. New Models of Open Science." *Annual Review of Law and Social Science* 3:345–73.

Robbins-Roth, Cynthia. 2000. *From Alchemy to IPO: The Business of Biotechnology.* Cambridge, MA: Perseus Publishing.

Roberts. Edward B. 1991. *Entrepreneurs in High Technology: Lessons from MIT and beyond.* Oxford: Oxford University Press.

Royston, Ivor. 2006. Address given to the Von Leibig Forum, June 26, UCTV: University of California, San Diego. Available at http://www.uctv.tv/search-details.asp?showID=11752.

Rutter, William J. 1997. "The Emergence of Biotechnology: DNA to Genentech." Transcript of a presentation at the Chemical Heritage Foundation. Philadelphia, June 13.

———. 1998. "William J. Rutter, PhD." Oral history conducted in 1992 by Sally Smith Hughes, Regional Oral History Office, The Bancroft Library, University of California–Berkeley.

Saxenian, Annalee. 1994. *Regional Advantage: Culture and Competition in Silicon Valley and Route 128*. Cambridge, MA: Harvard University Press.

Schneiberg, Marc, and Michael Lounsbury. 2008. "Social Movements and Institutional Analysis." In *The SAGE Handbook of Organizational Institutionalism*, ed. Royston Greenwood, Christine Oliver, Roy Suddaby, and Kerstin Sahlin-Andersson, 650–72. Thousand Oaks, CA: Sage.

Schumpeter, Joseph. 1939. *Business Cycles: A Theoretical, Historical, and Statistical Analysis of the Capitalist Process*. New York: McGraw Hill.

Senior, Melanie. 2007. "Genzyme: Why Diversification Is Starting to Look Smart." *In Vivo* (December): 8–15.

Sewell, William F. 1992. "A Theory of Structure: Duality, Agency, and Transformation." *American Journal of Sociology* 98(1):1–29.

Shaw, Donna. 1997. "Innovator and Optimist at Centocor: Those in the Industry Call Him an Idea Man and a Mentor. And, He Says, 'I Never Gave Up Hope.'" *Philadelphia Inquirer*, April 2.

Snyder, Sheridan. 2009. E-mail interview by Kurt Sandholtz, August 20.

Stinchcombe, Arthur L. 1965. "Social Structure and Organizations." In *Handbook of Organizations*, ed. James G. March, 142–93. Chicago: Rand McNally.

Strauss, Anselm. 1978. *Negotiations: Varieties, Contexts, Processes, and Social Order*. San Francisco: Jossey-Bass.

Stuart, Toby E., and Waverly Ding. 2006. "When Do Scientists Become Entrepreneurs? The Social Structural Antecedents of Commercial Activity in the Academic Life Sciences." *American Journal of Sociology* 11:97–144.

Sudnow, David. 1965. "Normal Crimes: Sociological Features of the Penal Code in a Public Defender's Office." *Social Problems* 12(3):255–76.

Swanson, Robert A. 2001. "Robert A. Swanson: Cofounder, CEO, and Chairman of Genentech, Inc., 1976–1996." Oral history conducted in 1996 and 1997 by Sally Smith Hughes, Regional Oral History Office, The Bancroft Library, University of California–Berkeley.

Teitelman, Robert. 1985. "Searching for Serendipity: Centocor Combs University Labs for Technology." *Forbes* 135(10):80–81.

———. 1989. *Gene Dreams: Wall Street, Academia and the Rise of Biotechnology*. New York: Basic Books.

Timmerman, Luke. 2001. "Immunex Seeks Genie in a Bottle." *Seattle Times*, August 26.

———. 2004. "Life after Immunex." *Seattle Times*, August 30.

Tripsas, Mary. 1997. "Unraveling the Process of Creative Destruction: Complementary Assets and Incumbent Survival in the Typesetter Industry." *Strategic Management Journal* 18:119–42.

Ullrich, Axel. 2006. "Molecular Biologist at UCSF and Genentech." Oral history conducted in 1994 and 2003 by Sally Smith Hughes, Regional Oral History Office, The Bancroft Library, University of California–Berkeley.

Van Brunt, Jennifer. 2000. "Biotech's Impeccable Lineage." *Signals*, March 22.

Vaughan, Roger. 2000. *Listen to the Music: The Life of Hilary Koprowski*. New York: Springer-Verlag.

Vettel, Eric J. 2006. *Biotech: The Countercultural Origins of an Industry*. Philadelphia: University of Pennsylvania Press.

Weintraub, Arlene. 2009. "Can Roche Leave Genentech Alone?" *Business Week*, December 7, pp. 48–49.

White, Harrison C. 2008. *Identity and Control*. 2nd ed. Princeton: Princeton University Press.

Wilke, John. 1987. "Genzyme Says It Has a Potential Hot Seller." *Boston Globe*, January 6.

Wilson, Duff, and David Heath. 2001. "They Call the Place 'Mother Hutch.'" *Seattle Times*, March 14.

Wright, Susan. 1994. *Molecular Politics*. Chicago: University of Chicago Press.

Yi, Doogab. 2008. "Cancer, Viruses, and Mass Migration: Paul Berg's Venture into Eukaryotic Biology and the Advent of Recombinant DNA Research and Technology, 1967–1980." *Journal of the History of Biology* 41:589–636.

Yoxen, Edward. 1984. *The Gene Business: Who Should Control Biotechnology?* New York: Harper and Row.

Zaffaroni, Alejandro. 1997. "An Interview with Alejandro Zaffaroni." By J. Wolfson and T. Singh. *San Jose Mercury News*, February 2, 1997. Available at http://www.thetech.org/exhibits/online/revolution/zaffaroni/.

Zucker, Lynne G., and Michael R. Darby. 1996. "Star Scientists and Institutional Transformation: Patterns of Invention and Innovation in the Formation of the Biotechnology Industry." *Proceedings of the National Academy of Sciences* 93:12709–16.

———. 1997. "Present at the Revolution: Transformation of Technical Identity for a Large Incumbent Pharmaceutical Firm after the Biotechnological Breakthrough." *Research Policy* 26:429–46.

Zuckerman, Ezra W. 1999. "The Categorical Imperative: Securities Analysts and the Illegitimacy Discount." *American Journal of Sociology* 104: 1398–1438.

14

Organizational and Institutional Genesis

The Emergence of High-Tech Clusters in the Life Sciences

Walter W. Powell ▪ Kelley Packalen ▪ Kjersten Whittington

WHERE DO ORGANIZATIONS AND INSTITUTIONS COME FROM?

Much of the social science literature on institutions resembles a play that begins with the second act, taking both plot and narrative as an accomplished fact. Very little research asks how a play comes to be performed, or why this particular story is being staged instead of some other one.[1] Young (1998, 4) has observed that most social scientists go about their work only after the dust has settled. We thus miss out on seeing where the dust came from or how it settled. Even more important, we may not notice that things are continually moving about, being reshuffled to be used in different ways. The social world is littered, as Meyer and Rowan (1977, 345) remind us, "with the building blocks for organizations," and this "debris" can be used to assemble and create new combinations.

Individuals construct organizations with the social and technical tools they have at hand, fashioning the future with the available tools of the past and present (Stinchcombe 1965). A critical challenge, then, is to explain the genesis of organizations and institutions, particularly why specific elements combine to make distinctive configurations possible only at particular points in time and space. Our goal in this chapter is to tackle this question in the context of the development and growth of regional life science clusters in the United States.

Most research on institutions works backward from contemporary cases to develop a story about how institutions were purposefully created or rationally chosen. This analytic strategy unites actor-centered functionalist accounts by rational

This chapter builds on work we have done with Jason Owen-Smith. We are grateful to Steve Barley, Gili Drori, Neil Fligstein, Hokyu Hwang, Simcha Jong, Martin Kenney, John Lucy, James Mahoney, Johanna Mair, John Meyer, Christine Musselin, Jason Owen-Smith, Charles Perrow, Akira Takeishei, and Marco Zamarian for their suggestions. Ron Burt went well beyond the call of colleagueship in giving rapid and extensive comments across numerous drafts. Michael Storper provided incredibly useful and challenging feedback, which pushed us in very productive directions. Comments by audience members at the Nobel Symposium on Foundations of Organizations, the Academy of Management Distinguished Scholar lecture, the Center for Advanced Study in the Behavioral Sciences weekly seminar, the Universidad de San Andrés, University of Oxford, Imperial College, the University of Chicago, Princeton University, the University of Michigan, Hebrew University of Jerusalem, UC–Irvine, USC, Kyoto University, and the EGOS subtheme on biotechnology greatly aided us in revising the chapter. We thank the D. I. McLeod Term Research Assistantship Program at Queens University for financial support.

[1] Numerous scholars have lamented that the origins of institutions have been largely opaque to social scientists. Kreps (1990, 530) remarked that whereas the economics literature emphasizes the effects of institutions, it "leaves open the question, where did institutions come from?" In an assessment of the sociological literature, Barley and Tolbert (1997) underscore the neglect of how institutional arrangements are created. More recently, in a comprehensive review of organizations research, Greenwood et al. (2008, 26) conclude that "institutional studies have not been overly concerned with how institutions arise."

choice scholars in economics and political science with organizational and sociological analyses that highlight the social and political skills of institutional entrepreneurs.[2] In both forms of explanation, scholars connect the actions of designers to the functions or interests served by institutions (Pierson 2004, chap. 2; Hardy and Maguire 2008). In these accounts, institutions are often portrayed as a solution to collective action problems that enables participants to realize gains from coordination. The challenge with this inventive work is that the results obtained often seem to be the only possible solution. Unsuccessful efforts are rarely examined, and the necessary functions that are asserted always seem to neatly explain the presence of particular institutional structures or policies.

The limitation of such functional or entrepreneurial accounts is that they generally begin with existing practices and activities. Such a retrospective view largely predetermines the outcomes, rendering social and economic change either inevitable or driven solely by external forces. Moreover, there is an implicit assumption of continuity between those who labored to produce institutional arrangements and those who benefit from them. Stinchcombe (1968) has emphasized, however, that the processes that generate an institution are often different from those responsible for its reproduction. Very different sets of activities and participants are likely to be involved in the creation, reproduction, and disruption of institutions (Lawrence and Suddaby 2006). We therefore need arguments that attend to both genesis and change and posit similar mechanisms to account for each.

To be sure, emergence and transformation are thorny questions. Nonetheless, a number of scholars have begun to tackle these concerns and make progress in accounting for when organizations and institutions arise and how they are transformed (Fligstein 2001; Pierson 2004; Thelen 2004). This chapter utilizes our research on the spatial aspects of the life sciences to join the discussion. Specifically, we seek to explain a critical feature of the emergence and development of the biotech field—geographic propinquity.

Today's pattern of pronounced agglomeration was not at all obvious, given initial founding conditions. Distinctive responses to scientific discoveries developed in particular locales, which in turn became self-reinforcing and resilient. Common expectations and knowledge evolved through ongoing contacts, and shared conventions were sustained by members of local technological communities. In this sense we treat a geographic cluster as an entity that became institutionalized. Decisions to locate in particular regions, invest resources, and build a technical community generated increasing returns as a wider number of participants followed suit, developed local norms that guided interaction, and subsequently elaborated on these practices, becoming a community with a common fate. Identities were learned and interests were forged through interaction, producing feedback dynamics that increased interdependence and consensus among the varied participants. Consequently, we argue that the development of a regional technological community offers an apt opportunity to study the origins of institutions. Moreover, this pattern of agglomeration affords comparisons between locales that evolved into productive communities and those that did not.

THE PUZZLE OF SPACE

The pronounced spatial agglomeration of the commercial field of the life sciences in the United States represents an interesting puzzle. Today roughly 50 percent of the U.S. companies in this industry are located in only three regions—the San Francisco Bay Area, Cambridge and Boston, Massachusetts, and north San Diego County. As the field developed in the 1970s and 1980s, two resources were critical to fuel the formation of new science-based companies: money and ideas, both of which are highly fungible and arguably very mobile. Yet the new industry developed deep roots in just two locations and then spread to a third, and only these clusters have evolved to become highly interactive centers for biomedical science and commerce.[3]

[2] Leaving aside important concerns about sampling only successful cases, the burgeoning organizational literature on institutional entrepreneurs portrays these people as uncommonly muscular or endowed with qualities that normal individuals are lacking (R. Meyer 2006; J. Meyer 2008). These "champions" are then contrasted with the rule-following rank and file. Powell and Colyvas (2008) have argued that heroes and cultural dopes are a poor representation of the gamut of individuals who populate organizations and that we need a richer, more relational portrait of individuals and a contextually fuller account of how institutions and fields develop.

[3] One might also ask why the early development of the field took place largely in the United States, even though the relevant scientific knowledge was abundant in many leading research centers of Europe and the United Kingdom. Some who have asked this question stress the favorable public policy in the United States that supported intellectual property

Timing obviously matters for success; being first out of the gate can confer considerable advantage. The Bay Area took the initial regional lead in the 1970s and 1980s. Boston came later and is today arguably a more intensive and spatially dense cluster, and San Diego came third (Powell et al. 2002; Owen-Smith and Powell 2004). More important, as illustrated in the previous chapter, companies in the three established clusters have a mix of founding models, suggesting that a simple copying-and-increasing-returns story is insufficient. Different social, political, and economic circumstances typify these three regions, so the learning and coordination effects that helped reproduce the early successes of these districts stem from divergent origins (for more general reflections on this point, see Mahoney 2000 and Pierson 2000).

Our analysis reveals that although timing is important to understanding development, clear differences exist between nascent and established regions. Despite divergent origins and founding models, the three established regions display similar patterns of organizational diversity and network configurations that sustain regional activity (Whittington, Owen-Smith, and Powell 2009). But at the dawn of the new industry, it was not obvious that the Bay Area, Boston, and San Diego were necessarily the most or the only propitious venues for the field to emerge.

Although many might think of biotech's development in the Bay Area as a Silicon Valley story, the early locations for firms were in South San Francisco and in Emeryville in the East Bay, not in the heart of the information and computer technology world in Santa Clara and Sunnyvale. That early footprint continues today. Biotech blossomed in Cambridge, Massachusetts, in Kendall Square, an area that as late as 1985 was riddled with decaying textile factories. Kendall Square now consists of glass biotech laboratories "as far as the eye can see" (Goldberg 1999, 1). In the 1980s San Diego was home to retired naval personnel and a haven for tourists and fishermen rather than a beacon for high-tech companies. Torrey Pines Road in La Jolla, the epicenter of "biotech beach" in San Diego County, was more widely known for its golf courses and gorgeous beaches than for its laboratories. Interestingly, at the firm level, the odds of survival for new entrants in the established clusters do not differ from the life chances of well-connected firms located elsewhere in the United States (Whittington, Owen-Smith, and Powell 2009). The cluster dynamics are an emergent collective phenomena, as the three regions have become centers where the bar is very high and firms must run faster just to stay in place.

The pattern of strong geographic agglomeration is also peculiar in that the basic science discoveries that led to the field's formation were developed in a number of leading research universities and government institutes in the United States[4] and around the world. To be sure, venture capital firms were concentrated in three regions—New York City, the San Francisco Bay Area, and, later, Boston (Powell et al. 2002; Chen et al. 2009). But financing for biotech start-ups was available not only from venture capital. Many other financial institutions—investment banks, insurance companies, university endowments, and multinational pharmaceutical and health care companies—located throughout the United States, the United Kingdom, Switzerland, Germany, and Japan joined in bankrolling the industry. The standard explanation for geographic propinquity in high-technology sectors stresses spillovers from public science and increasing returns from initial idiosyncratic events (Jaffe 1986; Krugman 1991; Arthur 1994). The path-dependent processes that stem from first moves have a tendency to "lock in," and thus early advantages become magnified. But spillovers and increasing returns are only a partial answer, as they don't explain why an event was a catalyst in one setting but not in another with similar circumstances. Moreover, in the "successful" cases we discuss below, flexibility, switching,

rights for scientific ideas, a financial environment in which equity investments in science and technology companies were encouraged, and private universities interested and engaged in transferring public science into commercial application (Wright 1994; Coriat and Orsi 2002; Rhoten and Powell 2007). To be sure, the United States had these endowments to a much more considerable extent than did their European or British counterparts, who came to the field much later. But cross-national comparative analyses still raise the question of why the new field developed in so few areas within the United States, the issue that we consider here.

[4] Zucker, Darby, and Brewer (1998, 293) report that there were twenty "top quality universities" with very high reputational scores in the biological sciences on the 1982 National Research Council survey of departments. These universities were located on the East Coast in Cambridge, Boston, New Haven, New York City, Philadelphia, Baltimore, and Durham; in the Midwest and mountain states in Chicago, Madison, and Denver; and on the West Coast in Seattle, San Francisco, Berkeley, Palo Alto, Pasadena, Los Angeles, and La Jolla. Zucker and colleagues (1998, 295) also present a U.S. map of active life science "star" researchers in 1990, which shows the heaviest concentrations in the Washington-Boston corridor, the San Francisco Bay Area, and Los Angeles, and in the Midwest at Big Ten campuses.

Table 14.1.
Trends in Biomedical Patenting, by Metropolitan Region

Metro Area	1975–79	1980–89	1990–99
Boston, MA	126	592	3,007
Houston, TX	18	144	634
Los Angeles, CA	106	330	1,399
New York, NY, and northern New Jersey	1,420	3,590	6,800
Philadelphia, PA	679	1,309	3,214
Research Triangle, NC	27	204	796
San Diego, CA	23	210	1,632
San Francisco Bay Area, CA	414	1,173	3,991
Seattle, WA	9	93	770
Washington, DC, and Baltimore, MD	121	470	2,162

Source: Drawn from Cortright and Mayer 2002.

Note: Biological and chemical patents held by pharmaceutical and biotechnology companies.

and disruption were common, whereas lock-in typified the regions that did not flourish.

More critical for the theoretical issues we are tackling, numerous nascent clusters formed in the United States, each with abundant endowments that could have evolved into a robust regional community. A Brookings Institute study (Cortright and Mayer 2002) measured the number of biomedical patents by pharmaceutical and biotechnology companies over the period 1975–99 and found notable stocks of knowledge in many locations. We summarize these data in table 14.1; note that the New York and Philadelphia areas were the initial leaders in number of patents, with the Bay Area third, followed by Boston, Washington, and Los Angeles. San Diego had no stock of patents in the 1970s.

Looked at in terms of organizational resources, the New York City metropolitan area and central New Jersey are both home to leading universities, among them Columbia, NYU, Rockefeller, and Princeton, many wealthy financial institutions, and numerous large multinational pharmaceutical companies. New York City also has an exceptional array of top-tier research institutes and hospitals, such as Sloan Kettering and Cold Spring Harbor. The Philadelphia metropolitan area has the University of Pennsylvania, the Wistar Institute, the Fox Chase Cancer Center, and the Children's Hospital of Philadelphia, all important public research organizations, as well as a number of major pharmaceutical companies. Indeed, Philadelphia was historically "the cradle of pharmacy" in the United States (Feldman and Schreuder 1996, 841). In Washington, D.C., and Bethesda, Maryland, the National Institutes of Health (NIH) constitute the world's most comprehensive research center for the life sciences. Johns Hopkins University in Baltimore has *the* preeminent medical school in the nation and is the leading recipient of NIH funding by a wide margin. Los Angeles, where one of the earliest and most successful biotech companies, Amgen, was founded in 1980, had ample scientific resources at CalTech and UCLA, but a cluster never cohered there. Indeed, by the twenty-first century, Amgen had relocated some of its research activities to Kendall Square in Massachusetts and to its new subsidiary, Tularik, in South San Francisco.

In areas where there was no strong corpus of intellectual property, other resources could have sparked the emergence of biotech. Houston had financial wealth, several medical schools and universities, and M. D. Anderson, a pathbreaking research hospital. The Research Triangle in North Carolina brought together three major research universities and public provision of land for an incubator that attracted multinational pharmaceutical corporations such as Glaxo. In Seattle, computer technology millionaires tried to combine the research prowess of the University of Washington, with its major medical school, and the Fred Hutchinson Cancer Center to start a biotech cluster there. All of these areas saw the spawning of some new science-based biotech companies in the 1970s and 1980s, and each developed various public-private initiatives to build a biotech community. But none of these areas has yet to develop an interactive community of firms and public research organizations that mirrors the dynamics of the Boston, San Francisco Bay Area, and San Diego regions. We can also look beyond the nascent clusters to other areas rich with endowments that never quite catalyzed. For example, Atlanta has the Centers for Disease Control, research universities Emory and Georgia Tech, a wealthy corporate sector keen to invest in new technology companies, and a well-educated middle-class labor force. Cleveland was an early home to venture capital, and the Cleveland Clinic is one of the premier research hospitals in the nation. Neither city today has significant activity in biotech.

Thus the questions that animate this chapter: Why do we see so pronounced a pattern of spatial agglomeration in the emergence of new science-based companies and the creation of a new field? Why does one community with a particular set of participants form and not another? Why did very disparate organizations come together to form clusters in these three locales? What was the developmental sequence that led to the institutionalization of biotech in these three clusters?

THEORETICAL PERSPECTIVE: MULTIPLE NETWORKS AND TRANSPOSITION

Many narratives describing the emergence of the life sciences stress the scientific and technological revolution ushered in by a series of remarkable breakthroughs in molecular biology. Such arguments highlight the discontinuity between the older tools of drug discovery, based in organic chemistry, and the novel methods of molecular biology and genetics (Gambardella 1995; Galambos and Sturchio 1998; Henderson, Orsenigo, and Pisano 1999). This Schumpeterian portrait of a process of creative destruction captures in broad brushstrokes the changed technological landscape, but it does not illuminate where the winds of change would be the strongest.

In the previous chapter, our analysis of the links between science and the economy examined the ramifying effects of scientific and technological change, which led to the creation of new roles and amphibious identities, novel organizational practices, and the invention of the science-based firm. Here we take the next step and argue that changing logics of network affiliation explain both the emergence of organizations and the formation of regional communities. At the core of these developments, we suggest, were new conceptions of both science and finance, which were initially viewed as aberrant but later seen as normal. Central to this transformation was not just statistical reproduction in the sense that something unusual diffused and became widespread but transposition: the initial participants brought the status and experience they garnered in one realm and converted these assets into energy in another domain.

Two features and one mechanism are central to our argument. The core factors are (1) a diversity of organizational forms and (2) the presence of an anchor tenant, and the mechanism is cross-realm transposition. These two factors increase the possibility and salience of transposition so that they have consequences that are linked to, but more consequential than, the initial conditions (Abbott 1990; Mahoney 2000).

Organizational diversity provides a rich soup in which practices, strategies, and rules can emerge. The presence of multiple organizational forms suggests diverse selection environments. This heterogeneity may give a community the resiliency to survive downturns in any one population. But more important, a diversity of forms can generate divergent standards and multiple kinds of rules, resulting in competing criteria for gauging success (Grabher and Stark 1997; Boltanski and Thévenot 2006). The formation of ties in any one domain becomes influenced by structural position in another, as well as by the categories and cognitive classifications that typify each form. These classifications help define eligibility for participation but don't dictate participation itself. Field formation in the context of organizational diversity means that relationships are very much entwined with competing status and identity considerations.

During a period of ferment, some organizations have a foot in several doors, and they may develop the ability to sustain themselves by toggling between different evaluative criteria (Brown and Duguid 2001). Rather than experiencing diversity as flux and confusion, firms can produce new recipes and standards (Lane and Maxfield 1996; Stark 2001). Here the categories and classifications familiar to institutional analysis are not yet taken for granted but are under construction. This emergent process involves search, sense-making, and luck (Weick 1993; Powell and Colyvas 2008).

Rather than unleashed, purposive, instrumental behavior of the kind invoked in agentic stories, we draw attention to an assembly process in the context of organizational diversity, one that resembles microanalyses of "cognition in the wild" (Hutchins 1995) or "on the hoof category construction" (Clark 1993). In this context, recipes and standards emerge within a local community, where interaction among participants both refines practices and facilitates their internalization.

A second crucial feature is the presence of an anchor tenant. The anchor becomes a scaffolding that, either intentionally or unexpectedly, assists subsequent connections and field formation. The anchor tenant is not disinterested, in the sense of being neutral, but it neither directly competes with nor dictates to the other organizations that inhabit the community. We think of anchors in relational terms as a well-connected organization—whether a university, nonprofit institute, venture capitalist, or a firm, which mobilizes others and fosters collective growth. But when central organizations insist that others play only by their rules and do not engage in collective problem-solving, they become "800-pound gorillas" rather than anchors.[5]

The organizations that we dub anchor tenants, drawing on the literature in industrial economics (Pashigian and Gould 1998; Agrawal and Cockburn 2003; Feldman 2003), occupy positions that provide them with access to diverse participants and the legitimacy to engage with and catalyze others in ways that facilitate the extension of collective resources. This ability to span disparate domains has proven valuable in high-velocity environments where resources, power, and wealth are constantly shifting (Cohen 1981; Sabel 1990; Hedlund 1993). In the real estate literature, an anchor tenant is typically the large national department store in a shopping mall that pulls in customers who also patronize smaller, more specialized shops (Eppli and Shippling 1995). In our reformulated use, the anchor tenant sustains multiple principles of evaluation—in this case, world-class science, biomedical discovery, unmet medical need, or financial opportunity—and in so doing continually recombines and repurposes diverse activities.[6]

Relational feedback then generates competitive dynamics as more extensive networks of affiliation are formed, and many participants benefit from the productive friction of cross-fertilization that arises from diverse kinds of affiliations with different partners (Powell, Koput, and Smith-Doerr 1996; Hagel and Brown 2005). Thus, anchor tenants both mobilize a community and serve as a guardian of diverse organizing principles. In contrast, 800-pound gorillas dominate activity and attempt to control the terms of engagement.

Brokerage and diversity alone are usually not sufficient to produce institutional transformation, however. Some form of cross-network alignment is needed in which ideas and models are transposed from one domain to another. To be sure, most cross-network transpositions are selected against because they are likely to fail from at least one perspective, relative to the status quo. The more an idea or activity is multipurpose, the more perspectives from which it can be judged inferior. Indeed, participation in multiple activities is sometimes viewed as an indication of lack of expertise in each, even when this is not true (Zuckerman et al. 2003). But as we saw in the previous chapter, in those unusual circumstances when a cross-network transposition is absorbed by the social system, it creates a new channel that permits activities from one domain to cascade into others, possibly with reorganizing or tipping potential. Feedback from cross-network efforts generates new potentialities, whether in the form of tipping, converging, or descending into chaos.

When one or more social relations are transposed from one network to another and mix with the relations already present, raw material is created for invention. But recombination and interaction are only the first steps. As new careers, practices, ideas, and organizational models cross significant boundaries, they must congeal to produce novel institutional practices and forms in order to have potent ramifications. The challenge is to understand the feedback mechanisms that reinforce these new combinations. How do links that become routine in a statistical sense cascade

[5] Although the phrase 800-pound gorilla is a common one, it is inaccurate. The largest gorillas weigh only around 500 pounds.

[6] In bio-ecology, the concept of keystone species is widely used to point out the crucial importance of a specific species in maintaining the organization and diversity of an ecological community (Paine 1969; Macarthur 1972). Although the term has been used so broadly it has invited criticism, the core idea that one species can have a disproportionate effect on its many associates has clear parallels with our use of the anchor tenant idea. Specifically, two uses of the concept—keystone hosts and keystone modifiers—seem most relevant (Mills, Soulé, and Doak 1993, 220). The hosts, typically plants and fruits, are pollinators and dispersers. Modifiers, of which the classic case is the beaver, alter hydrology and productivity on a wide scale. Beavers transform temperate forests into wetlands, creating a platform that attracts and supports a diverse web of life. The anchor tenants we analyze are pollinators that create an open platform that others can build on for community-wide benefit.

into normative understandings in the prescriptive sense so that participants in a dense network recognize these categorical patterns and start to sustain and reinforce them? As the connective tissue among participants grows, standards develop; even those not involved in their creation aspire to them, and through careers and mobility they transform local standards into more public goals. Cross-realm transposition facilitates the absorption of practices, goals, and status into a new domain. This transposition is made possible by a network of affiliations that bridge social worlds, which were formerly not connected. At a basic level, our argument is relational. Our account is sensitive to local characteristics and the details of history that characterized each region but transcends the cases to make a more general claim that accounts for emergence across multiple particular pathways.

DATA AND METHODS

Biotechnology is a field in which all the relevant capabilities were rarely found under a single organizational roof (Powell and Brantley 1992). The field had its origins in university labs, where research was supported by decades of substantial government investment in R&D. As the new field developed, universities, nonprofit research centers, research hospitals, and start-up companies all had a hand in moving discoveries from the lab into clinical development (Audretsch and Stephan 1996; Zucker and Darby 1996). Large multinational pharmaceutical corporations moved into the field about a decade after its start, as they came to appreciate the merits of new means of targeted drug discovery (Henderson and Cockburn 1996; Malerba and Orsenigo 2002). On the financing side, venture capital firms began to bankroll many start-up companies. Until very recently, however, these diverse types of organizations were not located in physical proximity to one another, so few regional clusters had sufficient access to all of these varied resources; hence there was considerable need for both local and distant affiliations.

This diversity in an emerging field represents more than just novel combinations of organizations. The skills associated with the different parties were distinctive and, as we elaborated in chapter 13, different forms of recombining and repurposing helped generate the first science-based companies with these new capabilities. The participants in the industry became embedded in multiple networks of strategic alliances and gained competitive advantage from continuous scientific, technical, and market innovation (Powell, Koput, and Smith-Doerr 1996). Access to new knowledge and skills was obtained through both local information spillovers and international alliance networks. Our challenge, then, is to understand the relationship between the scale of activity, the diversity of organizational forms, and the nature and timing of the networks and activities that linked the participants within specific geographic locales.

To explore these and related questions, we built a database that includes 661 dedicated biotechnology firms worldwide, and the more than 3,000 partners with these firms, from 1988–2004. The data on firms and their collaborators are drawn from *Bioscan*, an industry publication that reports financial and product information on companies, as well as the formal contractual arrangements they have with collaborators. *Bioscan* covers a wide range of organizations in the life sciences field.[7]

Our focus is restricted to dedicated biotechnology firms (DBFs). These companies are independently operating, profit-seeking entities involved in human therapeutic and diagnostic applications of biotechnology. Companies involved in veterinary or agricultural biotech, which draw on distinctive scientific capabilities and operate in very different regulatory climates, are omitted. Our sample of DBFs covers both privately held and publicly traded firms. Organizations that some might consider DBFs that are wholly owned subsidiaries of major pharmaceutical or chemical companies are not coded as

[7] The first volume of *Bioscan* was released in 1987 by the biotech firm Cetus, but coverage was limited, as many firms were reluctant to share private data with a competitor. Oryx Press issued the first independent directory in 1988, and Oryx eventually sold *Bioscan* to American Health Publishers, which is owned by Thomson. Because the quality of data collection has varied somewhat across years and owners, we supplement *Bioscan* with *Recombinant Capital*, Dun and Bradstreet's *Who Owns Whom?*, and *Standard and Poor's*. For publicly traded companies we use annual reports and SEC filings. Many of the firms in our database were founded before 1988. Indeed, there are 253 firms in our sample in the first year (1988). We have extensive data on firm foundings from the early years of the industry, but the larger alliance data set suffers from left censoring. That is, for firms that were founded *and* disbanded before 1988 we do not have complete network data. We have matched our sample to those developed by other researchers, most notably Steve Barley and John Freeman, Steven Casper, and Martin Kenney and Don Patton. We find one notable early entrant omission in our data set: Hybritech, founded in 1978 in San Diego and acquired by the pharmaceutical corporation Eli Lilly in 1985. Given the important role of Hybritech in the creation of the San Diego cluster, as detailed in the previous chapter, these analyses actually undercount the cohesion in that community. Still, the contrast between San Diego and other clusters will be quite apparent.

biotech firms but are counted as partners. Large corporations, hospitals, universities, research institutes, and government agencies also enter the database as partners that collaborate with DBFs. Our rationale for excluding small subsidiaries and large multinational corporations in the primary database is that subsidiaries seldom make decisions autonomously, and biotechnology may represent only a small portion of the overall activities of international corporations.

Our database includes information on a firm's ownership, formal contractual links to collaborators, founding date, employment, and, for firms that exit, whether they were acquired or failed. Data on interorganizational agreements cover the time frame and purpose of the relationship. We define a collaborative tie or alliance as any contractual arrangement to exchange or pool resources between a DBF and one or more partner organizations. We treat each agreement as a tie and code for both its purpose and duration. A connection exists whenever a DBF and a partner have one or more ties between them. We assign the partner organizations to six categories: public research organizations (PROs, including universities, nonprofit research centers, and hospitals); multinational pharmaceutical and chemical corporations; government agencies and institutes; financial institutions; other biomedical companies (such as agriculture or veterinary biotech, instrument, or medical device companies); and DBFs that are also partners. We collapse the varied types of ties into four major categories: research, finance, licensing, and commercialization. We did not collect data on the ties among the non-DBF partner organizations. In some cases, such connections would be very sparse (e.g., venture capital financing of universities or major corporations). In other cases, they would be commonplace, for example, pharmaceutical company support of clinical trials at a university medical center. The practical problem is that the complete network affiliations of more than three thousand disparate organizations, ranging across multinational firms, huge government agencies, venture capital, and research universities, would be very difficult to collect. Thus we focus on the connections that DBFs have to partners and the portfolio of DBFs with whom each partner is affiliated.[8]

In addition to compiling the quantitative database, we have interviewed hundreds of scientists and managers in biotechnology companies, pharmaceutical firms, university labs, and government agencies over the past two decades. We have done participant observations in university technology licensing offices, biotech firms, large pharmaceutical companies, and university labs. Even though the analyses are drawn largely from data derived from industry sources, much of our understanding of the field comes from direct engagement with its participants.

To address the issue of genesis, that is, why certain regions emerged while others grew rather slowly if at all, we undertake longitudinal comparisons of the organizations in eleven U.S. regions and the links both within and across these clusters and to partner organizations around the globe. Specifically, we focus on 384 DBFs with headquarters in one of the eleven U.S. regions and their alliances with 1,357 partners, each of whom has two or more agreements with these DBFs.

ORIGINS: GEOGRAPHIC PROPINQUITY

The earliest biotechnology companies popped up in a variety of different locales. A precursor of the new field, ALZA, was established in Palo Alto, California, in 1968, followed by Gamma Biologics in Houston in 1970. Cetus Corporation was founded in Emeryville, California, in 1972. In 1976 Enzo Biochem started on Long Island, New York, and Genentech in San Francisco. Genex sprouted in Montgomery, Maryland, in 1977. Biogen appeared in 1978, intended to be based in Cambridge, Massachusetts. Biogen's establishment was contested, however, because of local political opposition to genetic engineering (Watson 2003, chap. 4). Public uproar over "Frankenstein factories" led the founders of Biogen to incorporate initially in Switzerland to avoid the controversies in Cambridge, and cofounder and Nobel laureate Walter Gilbert had to take a leave of absence from Harvard University (Hall 1987, 41–54). Hybritech started in La Jolla, California, in 1978. In 1979 Centocor was founded in Philadelphia and MGI Pharma in Minneapolis. The next year, 1980, saw the advent of Amgen in Los Angeles, Cytogen in northern New Jersey, DNAX in Palo Alto, and Genetic Systems in Seattle. Genentech also had its initial public offering in 1980, fueling interest in the possibilities of this new field (Teitelman 1989; Robbins-Roth 2000). As we showed in the previous chapter, some of these companies lasted just a few years, but several persevered.

[8] This methodological choice results in a 2-mode network representation, which surely overstates the centrality of some DBFs by virtue of their having many ties to other DBFs and downplays the centrality of some partners that are linked to one another without having connections to a common DBF.

Government policies were important to the formation of the industry. Legislation that reduced the capital gains tax and permitted pension funds to invest in venture capital opened the doors for investment in start-up companies (Berman 2007). In 1980, in the *Diamond v. Chakrabarty* case, the Supreme Court, in a close 5–4 ruling, distinguished between a product of nature and a patentable, genetically modified bacterium cell that did not exist in nature, ruling that live, human-made, or genetically modified microorganisms are patentable. In 1987 the U.S. Patent and Trade Office expanded the domain of patentability to any biological material that required human intervention, thus creating fertile ground for intellectual property rights in genetics and biotechnology (Eisenberg 1987). The U.S. Congress passed the Bayh-Dole Patent and Trademarks Act in 1980 (PL 96517), which authorized scientists and universities performing federally funded research to file for patents and grant licenses to others. This legislation replaced what had previously been individual agreements between some universities and companies with a uniform policy and signaled congressional support for the negotiation of licenses between universities and firms (Mowery et al. 2004; Rhoten and Powell 2007). The goal of the legislation was to signal a change in policy away from fear over possible exploitation of public funds toward acceptance of the transfer of federally funded research results and a regime of strong intellectual property rights.[9] The Orphan Drug Act of 1983 was passed to encourage, through seven years of market exclusivity and tax credits, research on "rare" diseases by biopharmaceutical companies. All of these legislative steps were intended to assist in the commercial exploitation of basic research across the nation.

In addition, federal research funding for the life sciences expanded markedly. The NIH increased support for recombinant DNA research by 34 percent per year from 1978 to 1982 (Wright 1994, 94); in the 1990s, research funding burgeoned as the NIH budget went from $8.9 billion in 1992 to $17.08 billion by 2000. Nevertheless, the critical role of the U.S. government in supporting biotechnology tells us very little about why the industry took root in so few places. Indeed, given the capacious scope of the judicial and legislative decisions and the political nature of federal research funding, one might have expected that federal policies would foster a wide distribution of companies across the nation.

Figure 14.1 plots the geographic location of the forty-eight U.S. biotech firms in our database that were active in 1980. The size of the dot reflects the number of firms in a city. The initial groupings of firms were in New York, Boston, and the Bay Area, followed by Philadelphia, Washington, Houston, Los Angeles, and San Diego. A number of other cities, including Minneapolis, Miami, Memphis, Dallas, and Cincinnati, housed some early firms. Fast-forward to 2002, and the distribution of the 368 firms illustrated in Figure 14.2 shows pronounced regional agglomeration. Three clusters—Boston, the Bay Area, and San Diego—have grown dramatically. Other areas, such as New York and New Jersey, persisted, and Washington, Los Angeles, and Philadelphia grew modestly as well. Some new areas, such as the Research Triangle in North Carolina, Seattle, Salt Lake City, and Boulder, appear as well.

The number of companies in a cluster is but one measure of its importance. Perhaps more telling indicators are the cumulative accomplishments of companies located in the Bay Area, Boston, and San Diego. To wit, of the thirty-seven new medicines developed by dedicated biotechnology firms and approved by the U.S. Food and Drug Administration through December 31, 2002, twenty-one came from companies in these three regions. Product sales in biotechnology are heavily skewed toward a few winners, and just six companies have developed the ten most widely sold medicines. Five of the six companies come from the three leading clusters. In our database, 49 percent of the U.S. companies, 60 percent of the biotechnology patents, and more than 50 percent of the formal contractual collaborations involve a company from one of the three largest clusters.

This is not to say that firms located in these regions are universally successful. One of the earliest bellwether firms of the industry, Cetus, located in Emeryville, California, next door to Berkeley, suffered a high-profile rejection of its lead drug by the FDA in 1991 and subsequently failed. The Palo Alto–based ALZA, an early pharma-biotech hybrid, was acquired by Johnson & Johnson in 1994 and closed in 2008 in the course of J&J's corporate downsizing. Our analyses reveal that failure rates for companies inside

[9] Analysts debate whether the Bayh-Dole legislation itself prompted greater university commercialization of research or formalized federal approval of trends that were already well under way (Cole 1993; Zacks 2000; Mowery et al. 2004; Powell, Owen-Smith, and Colyvas 2007).

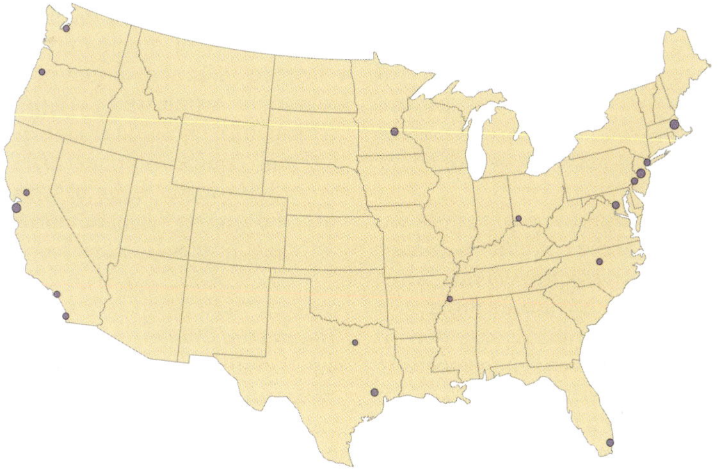

Figure 14.1 Location of U.S. biotechnology companies, 1980 (n = 48).

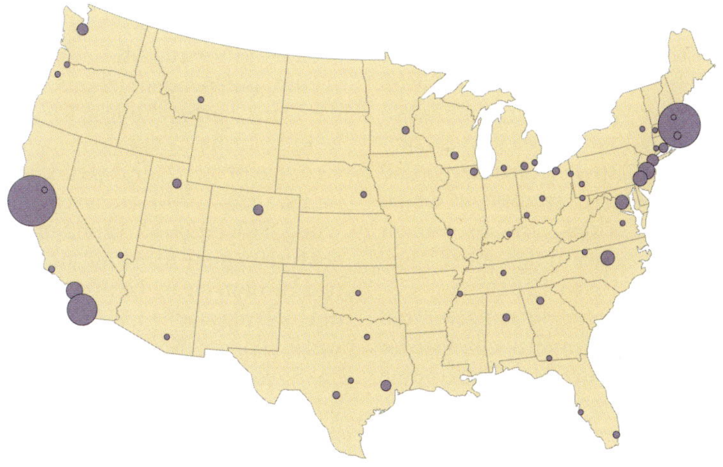

Figure 14.2 Location of U.S. biotechnology companies, 2002 (n = 368).

and outside the three regions show no statistical difference save for San Diego, where firms are actually more likely to fail a bit sooner than in any other locale (Whittington, Owen-Smith, and Powell 2009). Stuart and Sorenson (2003) have shown that success in obtaining venture capital and going public is more challenging for companies in the Bay Area than in other parts of the country. Although the three clusters are notable aggregate producers of innovation and populated by a large number of firms, they are also intensively competitive arenas, and certainly not safe havens. Indeed, it is the indissoluble combination of competitiveness and camaraderie that marks these locales (Portera 2004).

To gain purchase on the pattern of geographic agglomeration, we examine the organizational populations in the early years of the industry in the eleven areas where the earliest firms appeared: Boston, the New York metropolitan area, northern New Jersey, the Philadelphia metropolitan area, Washington, D.C.–Baltimore, the Research Triangle in North Carolina, Houston, San Diego County, the Los Angeles region, the San Francisco Bay Area, and Seattle. The comparative analyses begin in 1990, by which time all eleven regions have a local cadre of companies. We attend to four points of comparison: (1) the organizational diversity in the regions; (2) the effects of anchor tenants; (3) the role of cross-domain networks; and (4) the sequence of network formation. We contend that the character of a region is marked by the diversity of its organizations, the ties among these organizations, and the institutional characteristics of the central nodes in the local network, which shape information flows.

The robustness of a regional economy is enhanced when members of the community pursue science under norms of openness. Thus when public research organizations are anchors in a local ecology, we find a greater circulation of knowledge and more fluid labor markets. PROs, such as universities and nonprofit institutes, increasingly conduct research that is both scientifically advanced and immediately valuable to industry. But this class of organizations has historically differed from research-intensive firms on two important dimensions: their disparate approaches to rules for the dissemination and use of scientific findings, and their position in different selection environments (Dasgupta and David 1987, 1994; Owen-Smith and Powell 2004). New knowledge spreads out of universities much more readily than it does from commercial organizations (Jaffe, Trajtenberg, and Henderson 1993). Similarly, sectors in which noncommercial organizations are prominent in early stage research evince much more open technological trajectories (Dosi 1982).

The evidence for geographically concentrated knowledge flows in research-intensive industries is compelling. Studies drawing on ethnographic research as well as patent citation data have demonstrated the following: (1) ideas travel across organizations more readily when they are co-located; (2) the size and mobility of the scientific labor force increase local information sharing; and (3) strategic alliances among co-located firms augment the stock of common knowledge (Saxenian 1994; Almeida and Kogut 1999; Almeida, Dokko, and Rosenkopf 2003). But it is crucial to recognize that different organizational forms produce varied types of knowledge and resource exchange. Universities and other PROs contribute to technological advance, whereas research hospitals aid translational applications and clinical evidence. Venture capital investors provide a different channel for information transfer, assist in monitoring companies, and help diffuse managerial practices. Large multinational companies and biomedical supply firms contribute by enhancing regional labor markets for scientists and technicians, attracting a deep pool of industry-specific talent. Thus diverse sources of knowledge and skills, along with varied channels of communication and exchange, "irrigate" a local community. But diversity alone is not the whole story. Depth and quality are critical, too. In regions that experience "takeoff," internal competition increases quality; among those who survive, the best ones persist. Diversity and quality become mutually reinforcing in thriving clusters.[10]

The Boston Cluster

We begin by drawing on previous work by Owen-Smith and Powell (2004, 2006) on the Boston biotechnology community, which analyzed how the institutional form of the most central organizations shaped the practices of this regional community, influencing the nature of spillovers and innovation. We initially studied Boston because of its array of PROs, including universities such as Harvard, MIT, Tufts, and Boston University, independent research institutes such as the Dana Farber Cancer Center and the Whitehead Institute (a vital participant in the Human Genome project), and well-known research hospitals, such as Massachusetts General. In earlier work, Powell et al. (2002) observed that local venture capital firms did not become highly active in biotech in Boston until the 1990s; they did not play an early catalytic role. In related work, Porter, Whittington, and Powell (2005) analyzed the founding teams, scientific advisory boards, and co-patenting relationships of Boston biotech firms, finding that most connections in Boston were local. There were numerous connections among Boston-area universities and institutes and Boston DBFs, but very few founding teams involved faculty from outside Boston (Porter 2004). In comparison to the San Francisco Bay Area, the Boston community appeared to be a local "Brahmin" world, whereas the Bay Area was more open to outsiders, a receptivity that has long been a characteristic of California (McWilliams 1949).

We reproduce several of these Boston analyses, as they serve as the model for our inquiry into other clusters. We use graphical representations of the networks at crucial points in their emergence and evolution. The software we employ, Pajek, uses algorithms that represent

[10] We thank Michael Storper for emphasizing this point to us.

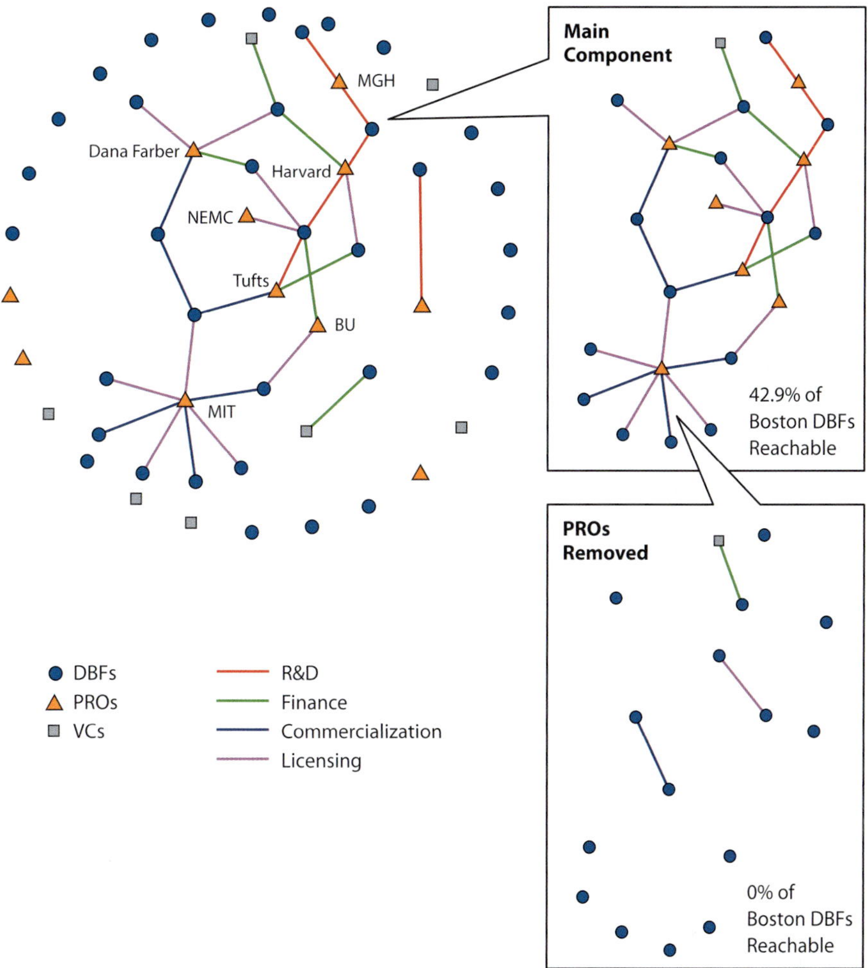

Figure 14.3 Boston local network, 1988. Note: Organizations on the circumference are located in Boston but had no contractual relations with other Boston organizations in 1988. Source: Owen-Smith and Powell 2004.

centrality in a web of affiliations.[11] The nodes are organizations and the lines are types of connections. Nodes repel one another, and lines pull nodes closer. The network maps are stable configurations that reflect a local equilibrium—the overall pattern and density of affiliations in a network are captured at rest. Hence the maps are referred to as minimum-energy drawings. We use the visualizations to discern centrality in regional networks.

Figure 14.3 reprints three images of the Boston biotech community in 1988 (Owen-Smith and Powell 2004). The shape of the nodes reflects organizational form—triangles represent PROs, circles indicate DBFs, and squares are venture capital firms. The color of the lines reflects the type of activity the relationship involved—red is R&D, green is financial, magenta is licensing, and blue represents commercialization activities. All of these ties are based on formal, contractual interorganizational relationships among Boston-based organizations.

Look first at the picture in the upper left. The Boston network was relatively sparse in 1988,

[11] Pajek is a freeware program developed by Vladimir Batagelj and Andrej Mrvar. It is available on the web and in wide use in the biological, physical, and social sciences. Pajek is used to portray meaningful and replicable visual representations of networks. Pajek implements two drawing algorithms based on graph-theoretic conceptions of distance. The images we portray locate isolates on the periphery and situate more connected nodes at the center.

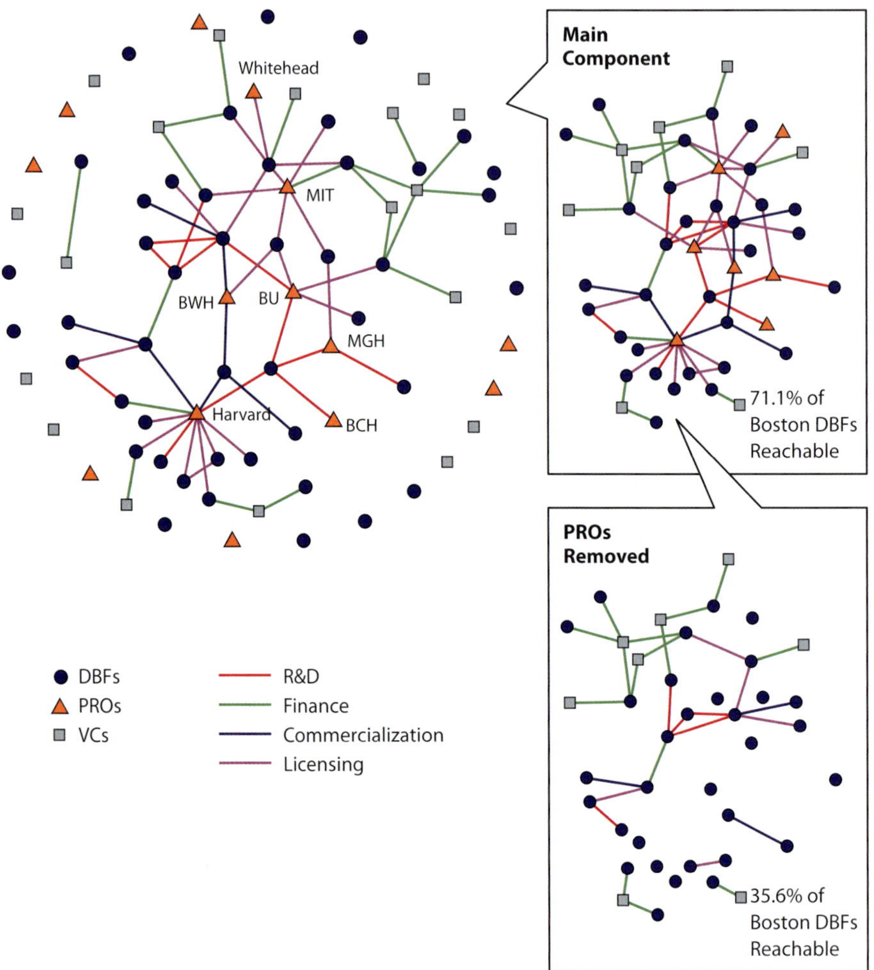

Figure 14.4 Boston local network, 1998. Note: Organizations on the circumference are located in Boston but had no contractual relations with other Boston organizations in 1988. Source: Owen-Smith and Powell 2004.

with the bulk of the organizations located on the outside circle, indicating that they had no formal local connections. Note the critical role of PROs (triangles) in connecting the center of the network. Note also the general absence of venture capital firms. Six public research organizations—MIT, Boston University, Tufts, Harvard, Dana Farber Cancer Center, Massachusetts General Hospital, and the New England Medical Center—are located in the most connected cluster. When we extract the main component—the largest minimally connected cluster[12]—from this network, 43 percent of DBFs in Boston were reachable through connections to this group. But when we remove the PROs and their collaborations from the main component, the network collapses. The most striking feature of the 1988 network was the pronounced dependence of the commercial world of biotechnology on PROs, which provided coherence to the Boston community.

We move forward to 1998 and portray the network in Figure 14.4. The cluster has grown larger and is much more interconnected. PROs continue to be prominent, but now venture capital firms and first-generation companies are also central. When we extract the main component, we find that 71 percent of the biotech firms in Boston were reachable. When the PROs and

[12] For those not versed in network parlance, consider the task of connecting a series of dots. The main component represents only those dots that can be connected without ever lifting a pen.

their ties are removed from the main component, the network no longer dissolves, and 35.6 percent of the biotech firms remain reachable. These figures capture an important transition in the structure of this regional community, highlighting both the continuing impact of public research organizations and the growing role of for-profit entities, notably the local venture capital firms that became intermediaries for Boston companies. We also examined collaborations with partners outside the Boston area but do not include those visualizations here. The "larger" Boston network expanded internationally over time, and the majority of these distant ties were formed with commercial entities. The importance of Boston-based PROs receded, although local centrality remained critical to scientific productivity as it continued to have a positive effect on patenting rates (Owen-Smith and Powell 2004; Whittington, Owen-Smith, and Powell 2009). In sum, basic science acumen was clearly transposed to commercial application in Boston.

As a next step, we compare Boston, the Bay Area, and San Diego at three comparable time points: 1990, 1996, and 2002. The results presented in figure 14.5 show several notable differences between the three leading centers of biotech activity. As with figures 14.3 and 14.4, red lines are R&D, green are financial, magenta are licensing, and blue are commercialization activities. But we switch our representation of nodes from shapes to colors and add additional types of partners: blue nodes are DBFs, pink nodes are biomedical supply companies, gray are financial institutions, brown are government institutes, yellow are pharmaceutical corporations, and orange are PROs.

The San Francisco Bay Area Cluster

The Bay Area is larger, both in the number of organizations—with more biotech companies, several major universities (including Stanford and the Universities of California at San Francisco and Berkeley), and numerous venture capital firms—and its geographic spread. The Boston network is organizationally smaller and geographically denser, with many more PROs and fewer venture capital firms. Whereas the Boston network grew from its early origins with PROs, the Bay Area was heavily influenced by the prospecting and matchmaking efforts of venture capitalists, the multidisciplinary science of the UC–San Francisco (UCSF) medical school, and novel efforts at technology transfer at Stanford (Kenney 1986; Colyvas 2007; Jong 2008).

The biotech community in the Bay Area had its genesis in the partnership of Herbert Boyer, a UCSF scientist, and Robert Swanson, a young, aspiring venture capitalist, who joined together to create Genentech, one of the first biotech companies and long a bellwether of the industry. The organizational model at UCSF fostered by William Rutter, chair of the biosciences there and later a cofounder of Chiron, was interdisciplinary, with a cross-functional approach to medicine and an emphasis on translating basic science into clinical applications (Varmus and Weinberg 1992; Jong 2008). Both Genentech and Chiron adopted and refined UCSF's team model, insisting that their scientists publish in academic journals, but added the impatience of venture capital financial backers with their focus on swinging for the fences. Consequently, the Bay Area network had a strong footprint of venture capital backing (note all the green lines for finance ties in figure 14.5) and an especially important role for first-generation science-based companies Genentech and Chiron. The closely spaced nodes at the center of the 1996 figure for the Bay Area represent the multiple ties between Genentech and other Bay Area organizations. The tightly clustered nodes, reflecting multiple affiliations between two organizations, grow in the 2002 figure. A notable aspect of the Bay Area region, present to a smaller extent in Boston, is the considerable interfirm collaboration among biotech companies that are ostensibly competitors. Here we see the transposition of an invisible college model to the commercial realm, as we detailed in the previous chapter.

Seen broadly, the anchor institutions in Boston and the Bay Area are distinctive, and the type of activity that knits the two regions together also differs. The red lines in the Boston pictures reflect research collaborations, and the blue lines in the 2002 panel typically involve clinical trials. Research hospitals are active participants in Boston. The Bay Area, by contrast, shows a preponderance of green lines, reflecting the imprint of venture capital and the sponsorship role of first-generation companies such as Genentech and Chiron that, over time, became active partners with younger companies. In contrast to Boston, very few local research institutes or hospitals were active in the Bay Area. But the university presence is important in both. The early companies in the Bay Area emerged from academic laboratories, with Chiron started

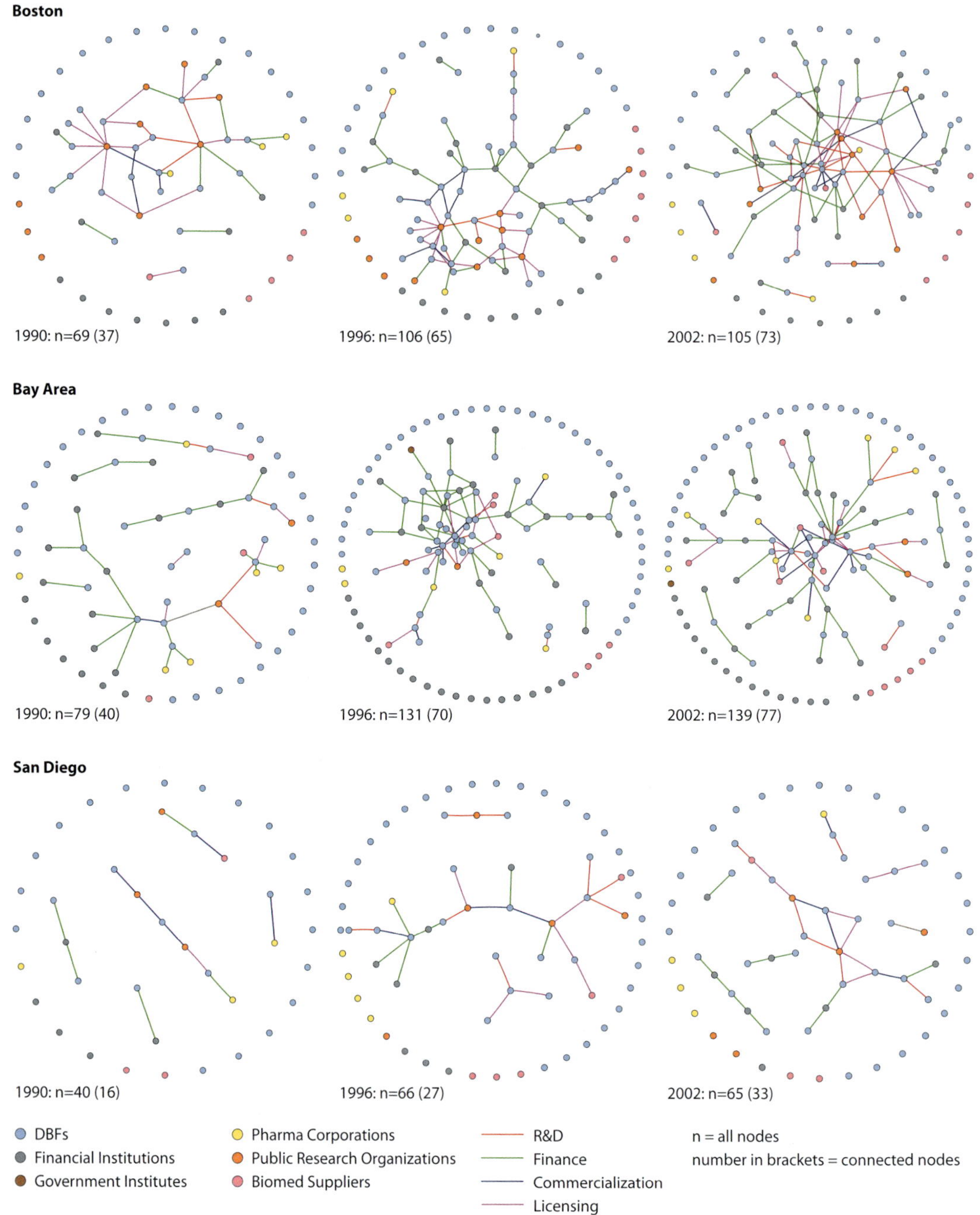

Figure 14.5 Boston, Bay Area, and San Diego, 1990, 1996, and 2002.

by UCSF and Berkeley faculty and Genentech by a UCSF professor. These companies cooperate intensively with local universities, and they adopted academic norms of publishing and collaboration and repurposed them into the world of commerce through extensive affiliations with other biotech companies and universities.[13]

A striking feature of the Bay Area is the extent to which the commercial entities embraced academic norms, while the universities, particularly Stanford, came to venerate and support academic entrepreneurship (Colyvas and Powell 2006). Here we see a cross-realm transposition in which the practices common in one domain are imported into another. In the case of Genentech, transposition can be seen as the infusion of a university lab culture into a commercial firm. This is often cast as the commercialization of the university, but the "academization" of for-profit research in the life sciences is also relevant. Consider comments by Genentech cofounder Herbert Boyer that emphasize firm-level engagement with meritocratic rewards, support for publishing in academic journals, and scientific autonomy:

> We set out with a self-imposed mandate that employees would share in anything that came out of the company, in terms of holding stock in the company. I insisted that we have the scientists publish their research in journals. . . . I felt this was extremely important for attracting the outstanding young scientists in the community that were interested in doing research in an industrial setting. I also wanted to bring in scientists that were outstanding to have them have an opportunity to establish their own reputation, get their own recognition. So we tried to set up an atmosphere which would take the best from industry and the best from the academic community, and put them together. (2001, 87)[14]

[13] Herbert Boyer's research sensibilities are nicely captured in an early interview, where he described his initial motivation to talk with his subsequent cofounder Bob Swanson: "He said he had access to some money, and I thought it would be a good way to fund some post-docs and some work in my laboratory, since we always needed money for that" (2001, 71).

[14] This choice by some early biotech firms to support basic research was consequential because open-ended exploration by U.S. industry has declined markedly over the past few decades, with venues like Bell Labs and central research units either closed or reoriented toward short-term needs of companies.

The San Diego Cluster

Our comparisons of Boston, the Bay Area, and San Diego are buttressed by the excellent work of a number of researchers who have studied the development of biotech in San Diego (Lee and Wolshok 2000; Wolshok et al. 2001; Walcott 2002; Jones 2005; Casper 2007). With our data, we created Pajek images for the San Diego region, which are shown at the bottom of figure 14.5. These analyses reveal a different trajectory from either Boston or the Bay Area. The biotech industry emerged slowly in San Diego. Parallel to our network maps of collaborations, Casper's (2007) analysis of interfirm job mobility among San Diego DBFs between 1978 and 2005 shows that it took about a dozen years for the cluster to take off. Our 2002 representation of local ties in San Diego looks comparable to the 1990 clusters of Boston and the Bay Area.

Interestingly, the trigger for the San Diego cluster was the failed acquisition of an early diagnostics-focused company, Hybritech, by the Indianapolis-based pharmaceutical company Eli Lilly in 1985. Within two years, no Hybritech employees remained with Lilly, but more than forty San Diego biotech firms were subsequently founded by former Hybritech employees (Walcott 2002). A senior female scientist at Hybritech quipped that the merger "was like 'Animal House' meets 'The Waltons.'" She also recalls being told by a Lilly scientist that she was young enough to be his daughter (Fikes 1999, 3). Executives at Eli Lilly have lamented that they are the most successful venture capitalists in San Diego history, only they didn't collect any of the rent.[15]

San Diego is home to numerous first-rate biomedical research centers, including the Salk Institute, Burnham Institute, the Sydney Kimmel Cancer Center, and Scripps Research Institute, all concentrated in the La Jolla area. They are reflected in the multiple red nodes in the bottom row of figure 14.5. In addition to its rapid rise to scholarly distinction in the biological sciences, the University of California–San Diego (UCSD) developed a very strong medical school. Casper (2007, 443) reports that by the early 2000s, these public research organizations were collectively receiving more than half a

[15] The Lilly Corp. did learn from this unsuccessful $300 million investment; as we shall see in the next chapter, it became one of the first of the large pharmaceutical companies to move away from an acquisition and transaction strategy to a more relational one in its dealings with smaller companies.

billion dollars in federal funding for biomedical research; meanwhile, the DBFs pulled in significant private funding as well. San Diego's combination of former employees of its first start-up, who did not want to leave San Diego, and its strong public research community proved to be a lure for venture firms from the Bay Area. These investors set up branch offices in San Diego in the 1990s, and some of the successful VCs became local angel investors.

In the 1980s the San Diego community had a notable lack of financial services and well-connected business networks. To compensate for this, a few business leaders and UCSD officials created a program called CONNECT in 1985, intended as a venue to link academic researchers, budding entrepreneurs, and business support services (Walshok et al. 2001). CONNECT proved to be a highly successful public-private springboard (Lee and Walshok 2000). The blend of the Hybritech spin-offs, the anchor of public research organizations, and the entry of investors from the Bay Area stimulated cluster formation. By the mid-1990s, a number of companies were founded by former Hybritech alums, including Amylin, Gensia, Genta, Idec, Ligand, and Vical. In particular, our data show that Ligand and Neurocrine Biosciences, a spin-off from the Salk Institute, were central in linking San Diego firms (blue) and local PROs (red).

On the surface, the origins of the three robust regions are different, suggesting there is no standard recipe. Rather than a common story of genesis, we see a topology of the possible in which the participants appear to have made do with what they had at hand, following opportunistic, sequential moves, aided by the presence of anchor organizations that fostered the sharing of information, dampened cut-throat rivalry, and enabled cooperative competition. In Boston, PROs played this role. In the Bay Area, venture capital firms were critical. Skilled VCs are very adept at networking, spreading best practices, and gracefully exiting from relationships (Powell et al. 2005). The technology licensing policies developed at Stanford, which focused on relationship building with start-ups rather than maximizing revenue, and the interdisciplinary orientation of UCSF combined to give the Bay Area several anchor organizations, which helped institutionalize a community of like-minded participants. In San Diego, the mismatch between young scientists at Hybritech and senior staff twice their age at Eli Lilly had the unexpected effect of creating a pool of alumni who went on to establish numerous new companies while staying in close touch with one another. Hybritech's failure, unexpectedly, seeded the job market and created a context in which job mobility and information sharing took place. These former employees collaborated with scientists at the numerous research institutes in the La Jolla area and with UCSD faculty.

Nascent Clusters—Lessons from Negative Cases

We turn now to the eight nascent clusters to try to isolate processes and mechanisms that make a cluster self-reinforcing. Earlier, we suggested that in number of participants and available endowments, the broader New York metropolitan area, northern New Jersey, the Philadelphia metropolitan area, the Washington, D.C. metro area, the Research Triangle in North Carolina, Houston, Seattle, and the Los Angeles metro area were plausible candidates for the development of a regional biotechnology cluster. To be sure, each of these areas had a large number of existing industries, and perhaps incumbent sectors acted in some fashion to preclude the formation of new fields. But that explanation doesn't seem to apply to Boston, where insurance and computers preceded biotech, or the Bay Area, where computers and information technology came before biotech, or San Diego, where a large military presence and a tourism industry predated both biotech and an emergent wireless cluster (Simard 2004).

Moreover, each of these nascent regions have strong potential magnets for biomedical research. New Jersey has many major pharmaceutical companies—including Johnson & Johnson and Merck—as well as Princeton University. The New York City metropolitan area has many world-class research hospitals, numerous top-tier universities, leading biomedical research institutes, and, in the 1990s, the world's largest financial sector. Philadelphia also has a major pharmaceutical presence, public research institutes, and universities. Washington and its suburb of Bethesda, Maryland, house the NIH, and northern Virginia has seen the rapid development of an information technology cluster. Houston, Seattle, and Los Angeles all have major research hospitals and medical institutes, as well as leading research universities. The Research Triangle has two state universities and the notable private Duke University, a research park with a major corporate presence in the

British pharmaceutical firm Glaxo, and a state government keen to support high tech. Clearly there were many possible candidates that might have spawned the creation of a biotech cluster in each of these locales.

When we map the local networks in these eight regions, however, we see a marked contrast with the clusters that formed in Boston, the Bay Area, and San Diego. Although there is a diversity of participants, few of the nascent regions developed an extensive pattern of interorganizational affiliations. In contrast to the successful clusters, local ties are rather sparse. The bulk of collaboration occurs with partners outside the regions, suggesting that local knowledge exchange and interorganizational labor mobility are rather limited. Figures 14.6 through 14.8 show the patterns of regional collaboration at six-year intervals, in 1990, 1996, and 2002. The number of organizations in each cluster is listed in the lower left corner of each figure, with the number of local affiliations in parentheses. The eight nascent clusters in 1990 are quite varied. New York has by far the most organizations but very little local activity. New Jersey, Washington, Houston, and Los Angeles are populated by a diverse set of organizations, and some regional links have formed. Philadelphia and Seattle have scant local activity; the Research Triangle cluster has not really formed. In comparison to Boston, the Bay Area, and San Diego (figure 14.5), much less biotech activity is going on *within* these regions.

Moving forward to 1996, Houston and Los Angeles regress, showing even less local activity. More organizations appear in the Research Triangle, New York, northern New Jersey, Washington, D.C., and Seattle, and some signs of cluster formation are apparent. The promise does not pan out, however. All the regions, save for the Research Triangle, are less regionally linked in 2002. Even though organizational diversity was present in each locale, there was no apparent stimulus for creating a regional cluster. Instead, the organizations developed connections to outside parties and largely eschewed local linkages. In sharp contrast, the panels in figure 14.5 show that the three "successful" clusters multiplied. The Boston biotech community became densely interwoven and burgeoned in numbers as well. A similar process characterized the Bay Area, where there are even more regional participants and dense collaborations. San Diego, as the most recent arrival, was not as initially linked locally through formal alliances, but the number of participants and the density of the network increased. Moreover, in related work we have shown that the organizations in the main component of these three high-growth regions are rich in both local *and* global ties, which enable them to recombine well-vetted local ideas with more distant knowledge flows and thus avoid lock-in or myopia (Whittington, Owen-Smith, and Powell 2009).

A comparison of the role of anchor tenants across the different regions affords further insight into their divergent trajectories. Figure 14.9 portrays the percentage of ties from DBFs (located anywhere in the world) to regional partner organizations in each cluster, by type of organizational form. In every case, one party to the formal tie is a dedicated biotech firm and the other is either another biotech firm, a biomedical supply company, a financial institution, a government institute or agency, a pharmaceutical company, or a public research organization. On the left are the three clusters that became institutionalized; on the right are the eight nascent clusters. Two features stand out.

First, note that the three regions on the left had a mix of different types of organizations in 1990. Finance led in the Bay Area and PROs in Boston and San Diego, but there is a considerable variety of types of organizations in each. On the right side, however, with the exception of Los Angeles, a single type of organization dominated in each nascent cluster, responsible for 50–80 percent of all ties. In New Jersey, it was pharmaceutical corporations; in the D.C. area, government institutes; in New York and Houston, financial institutions; in Philadelphia, pharmaceutical corporations; and in the Research Triangle, research universities. In Seattle, DBFs were partners with other biotechs. Although there was an array of different signature organizations in each nascent region, a dominant local presence controlled the bulk of collaborative activity. This hegemony, we suggest, precluded the chance to recombine diverse evaluative criteria and blend practices across different domains.

The second feature is the lack of dynamism in the nascent clusters, compared to the transitions under way in the growing regions. Move down the figure to the panel for 1996. In the three regions on the left side, the anchor tenant spurred activity and passed the baton (reflected by the arrows) to other types of organizations: in the Bay Area to DBFs, in Boston to VCs, and in San Diego to DBFs. In 2002 in Boston there was another hand-off, from VCs to biotech firms. In these three areas, the organizations

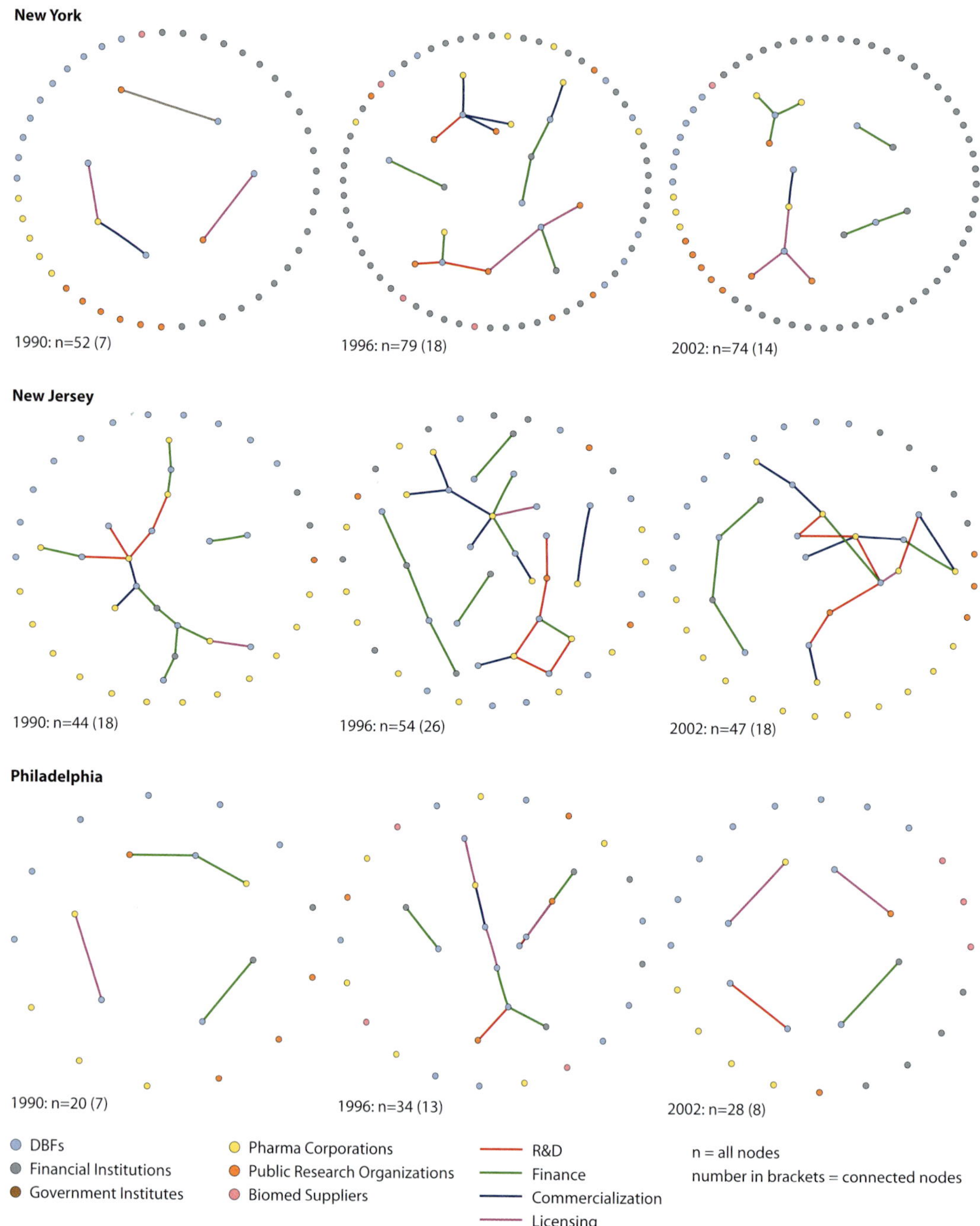

Figure 14.6 New York, New Jersey, and Philadelphia, 1990, 1996, and 2002.

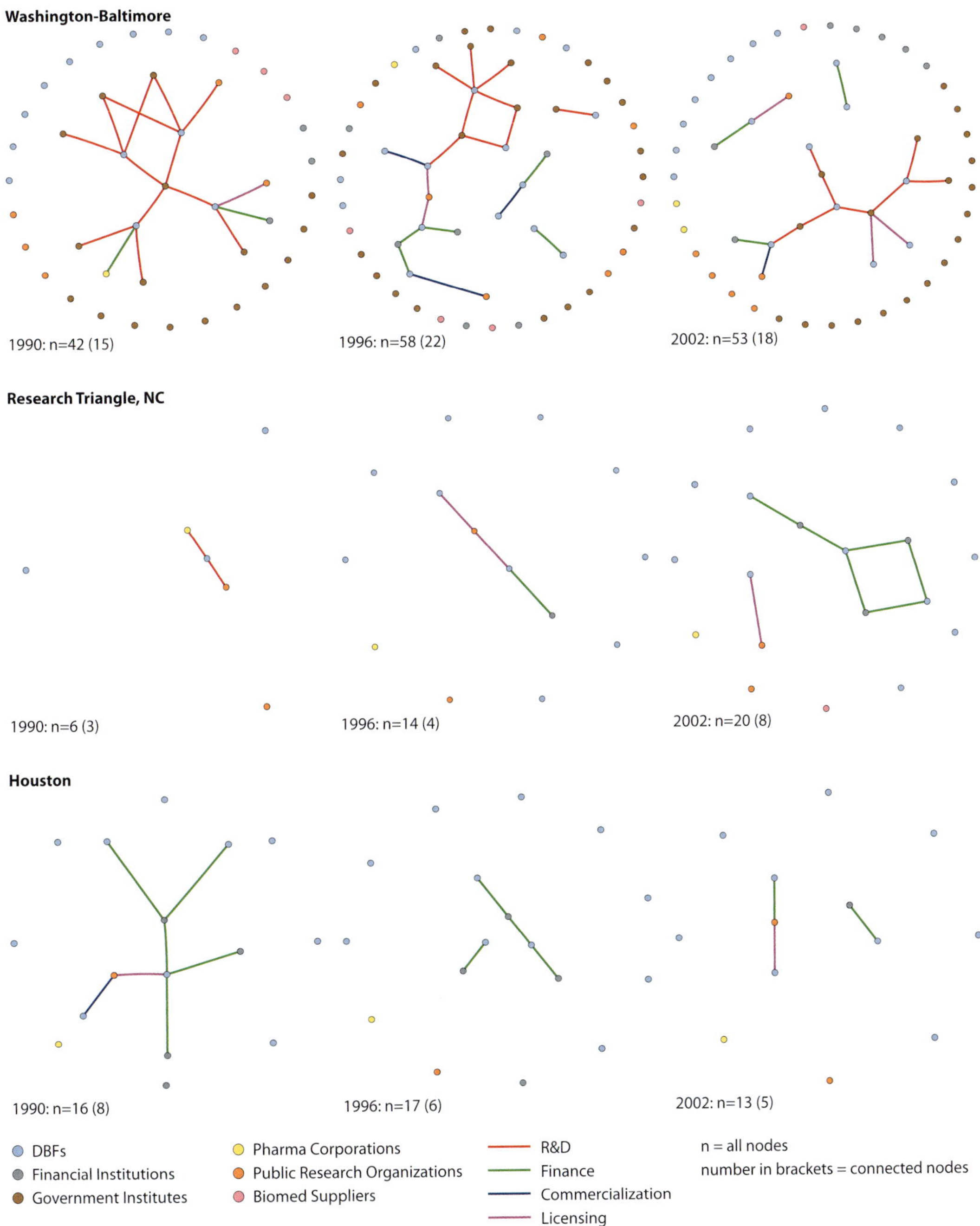

Figure 14.7 Washington-Baltimore, Research Triangle, NC, and Houston, 1990, 1996, and 2002.

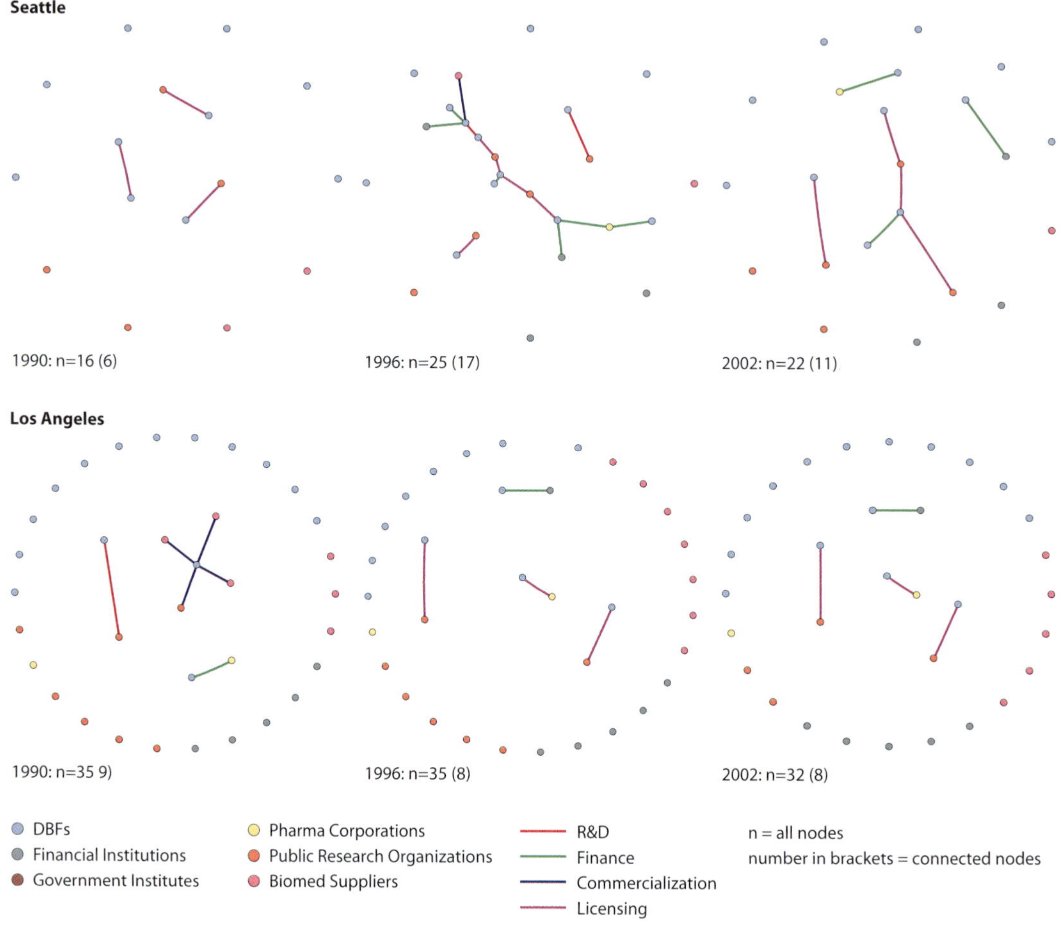

Figure 14.8 Seattle and Los Angeles, 1990, 1996, and 2002.

that initially anchored the community helped create enduring collaborations with other types of organizations, which in turn continued this pattern. In contrast, in 1996, in New Jersey, Washington, Los Angeles, New York, Philadelphia, Seattle, the Research Triangle, and Houston there was no change; the same organizations remained in charge. Pharmaceuticals continued to reign in New Jersey, the NIH in D.C., financial institutions in New York and Houston, research organizations in Los Angeles and the Research Triangle, and biotech firms in Seattle. In 2002 Los Angeles and Houston shifted and there was some reshuffling in Philadelphia, but all three regions also experienced a decline in overall activity. In the other regions, the dominant parties persisted. Rather than acting as a catalyst, the most active partners appear to have operated as 800-pound gorillas rather than anchor tenants.

Digging deeper, figure 14.10 offers a different perspective on the organizational ecologies of these different regions, as well as the diversity of organizations involved in each. Here we focus only on ties within a region and look at the percentage of ties by form of organization. We have dropped Houston and the Research Triangle because there were simply too few local ties to analyze. Note first the range of firms that are involved. In 1990, San Francisco, Boston, and Washington are the only locales with five different types of organizations, while San Diego has four. The rest have but three, except for New York, Houston, and Seattle with only two. Looking down the page, we see that San Diego gains a fifth in 1996 and D.C. drops to four in

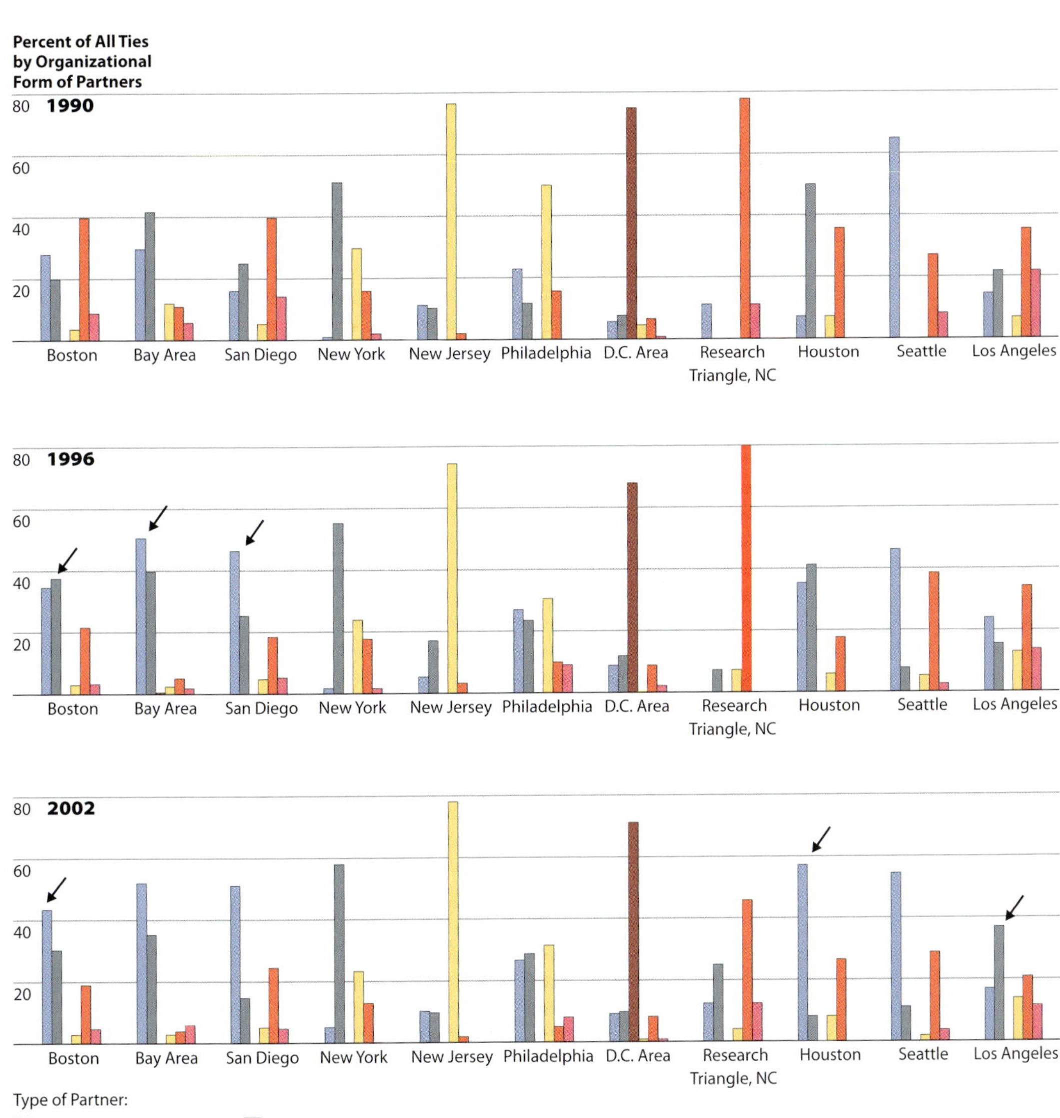

Figure 14.9 Anchor tenant vs. 800-lb. gorilla: percent of all ties by organizational form of partners, 1990, 1996, and 2002.

2002. New Jersey and New York stay the same with three, but Philadelphia and Seattle expand, suggesting some signs of local vitality.

We turn now to regional variation in the role of anchor tenants. Our interest is in examining whether anchors facilitated expansion, drawing in other organizations for mutual benefit. In 1990 venture capital dominated in the Bay Area and public research organizations in Boston and San Diego. In New Jersey, New York, and Philadelphia, pharmaceutical companies were the most active on the local scene, with New York's many financial institutions (apparent in figure 14.9) heavily engaged globally but not regionally. Washington bears the imprint of the NIH, whereas Los Angeles has an unusual number of equipment and supply companies and Seattle a local biotech presence. Move down to 1996. In

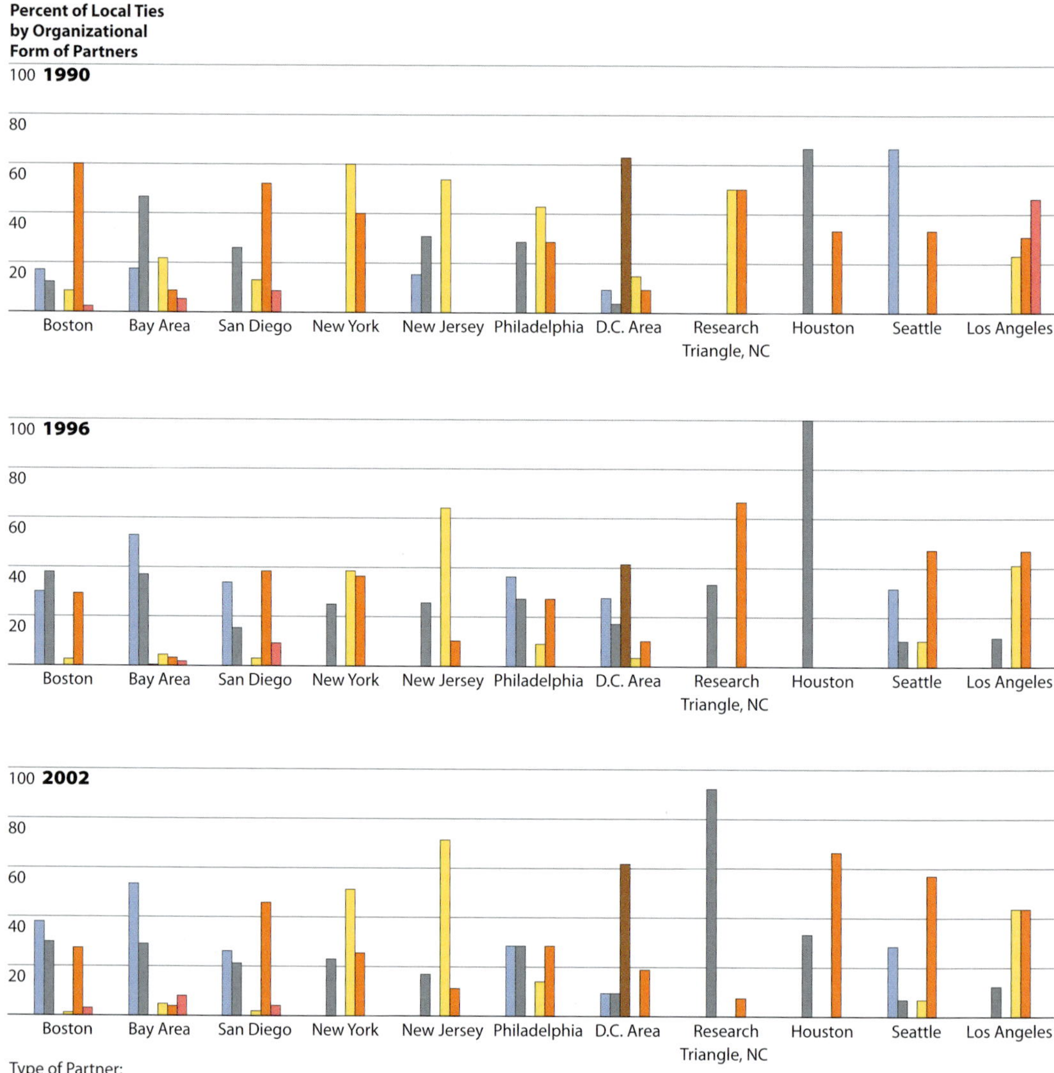

Figure 14.10 Transposition: percent of local ties by organizational form of partners, 1990, 1996, and 2002.

the Bay Area, biotech firms emerge as the community leaders; in Boston, venture capital grows. In San Diego, biotech firms almost reach equivalence with PROs, and in Boston, a further shift occurs as biotech firms assume relational leadership in 2002. But note that in none of these growing clusters does the original catalyst disappear. Instead of a contest for control, we see multiple types of organizations involved, and over time, public research organizations, venture capital, and biotech firms are all deeply involved locally.

In the nascent clusters, very different patterns are apparent. In New Jersey, D.C., and New York, the same type of organization dominates the local scene for all three time periods. Transitions occur via shrinkage in Los Angeles as a result of the departure of the supply companies and in Philadelphia, where the local role of pharma companies recedes. New Jersey, Los Angeles, and New York do not have collaborations among local biotech firms, perhaps the most telltale sign of the absence of a regional community. Philadelphia and Seattle, however, show some signs of emergence, with transitions among their dominant parties and some balancing of engagement, especially in Philadelphia. Although figures 14.6 and 14.8 illustrate that there are only a modest number of participants in these clusters, they do show some indication of the early features that characterized the successful regions back in 1990.

As a check on our assessment of the nascent clusters, we looked to see whether the organizations in these locales eschewed collaboration in favor of internal development. Put differently, this is the issue of unobserved heterogeneity. Are we biasing our arguments by focusing only on collaboration? Perhaps the established organizations chose a different model of drug development in which they focused on vertical integration. Figure 14.11 compares the eleven regions over the same time periods (1990, 1996, and 2002), looking at the number of ties in a region to: (1) biotech firms within the same geographic locale; (2) biotech firms in the Bay Area, Boston, and San Diego clusters; (3) biotech firms in the eight nascent clusters; and (4) biotech firms located elsewhere in the world. Here we simply use a count of the number of ties. The results are striking. In 1990 the most active region in terms of number of ties was D.C., reflecting the expansive national reach of the NIH. New Jersey and New York were also highly engaged, on a relational par with the Bay Area and Boston. Los Angeles, Philadelphia, and San Diego were roughly comparable in volume of collaborations. Note, however, that in New Jersey, D.C., Los Angeles, New York, Philadelphia, Seattle, and the Research Triangle, the local organizations forged more ties externally than within their own clusters. That trend becomes even more pronounced in New Jersey, D.C., Los Angeles, New York, and Philadelphia in 1996 and 2002. Far from foregoing collaboration, the organizations in the nascent clusters were very active partners *but* with outsiders. Moreover, the bulk of those extra-local connections were to DBFs in the three established regions.

The comparison of San Diego with Philadelphia, Los Angeles, and Seattle is intriguing, as all four had sparse connectivity in 1990, but San Diego grew rapidly over the next decade while the latter three did not. In addition to San Diego, the Bay Area and Boston also expanded markedly, and local ties drove the growth, complemented by ties to one another that further fueled the burst of activity. Although collaboration in the nascent clusters grew to varying degrees, it did so by forging alliances to firms in either the successful clusters or around the world and rarely locally or to one of the other nascent clusters. Only Seattle, with its limited activity, shows signs of a regional cluster.

More work is needed to specify carefully the sequence and dynamics of collaboration, but clearly there is no preference for internal development over collaborative production. Moreover, we find an intriguing suggestion of a "virtuous cycle" in the successful clusters: local ties were formed first, then connections were made to the other established clusters, then global linkages were created. In the Bay Area, Boston, and San Diego, local connectivity became the linchpin for global centrality. In contrast, in the nascent clusters external ties came first and connectivity developed outside the region, which appears to dampen local growth. We want to be careful that our argument is not perceived as a recipe for success.[16] The account we are giving is very much a process story: starting points and sequences matter; what types of organizations are involved and where you begin shape where you can go. Moreover, the windows of locational opportunity may be brief, and catalysis may only occur at specific stages in a cluster's evolution (Scott and Storper 2003). Nevertheless, the three burgeoning clusters created local ecologies initially, then expanded globally, whereas the nascent clusters had many more external linkages in their early years.

The three clusters that became institutionalized are characterized by high rates of firm formation *and* dissolution. Unlike the nascent clusters, which never took off and even shrank, organizational formation in the successful clusters occurred at a greater rate than dissolution.

[16] Indeed, an ingredient that many might consider as essential for any successful recipe—federal research dollars—were as or more abundant in the nascent clusters as they were in the successful regions.The list of the top recipients of NIH awards in 1996 has Johns Hopkins first by a wide margin, the University of Washington and UCSF tied for second, and the University of Pennsylvania fourth. The nascent clusters have strong representation throughout the top 50 recipients: UCLA (9th), Duke (11th), University of North Carolina (12th), Columbia (13th), USC (24th), Baylor College of Medicine in Houston (26th), Fred Hutchinson Cancer Center (33rd), Yeshiva Medical Center in New York City (34th), NYU (35th), University of Texas Health Center in Houston (40th), University of Maryland (42nd), and Mt. Sinai in New York (43rd). In contrast, from the successful clusters, Harvard is 8th, Stanford 10th, and UCSD 15th, but UC–Berkeley is 41st and MIT 47th. Clearly differential access to federal research funding is not the explanation.

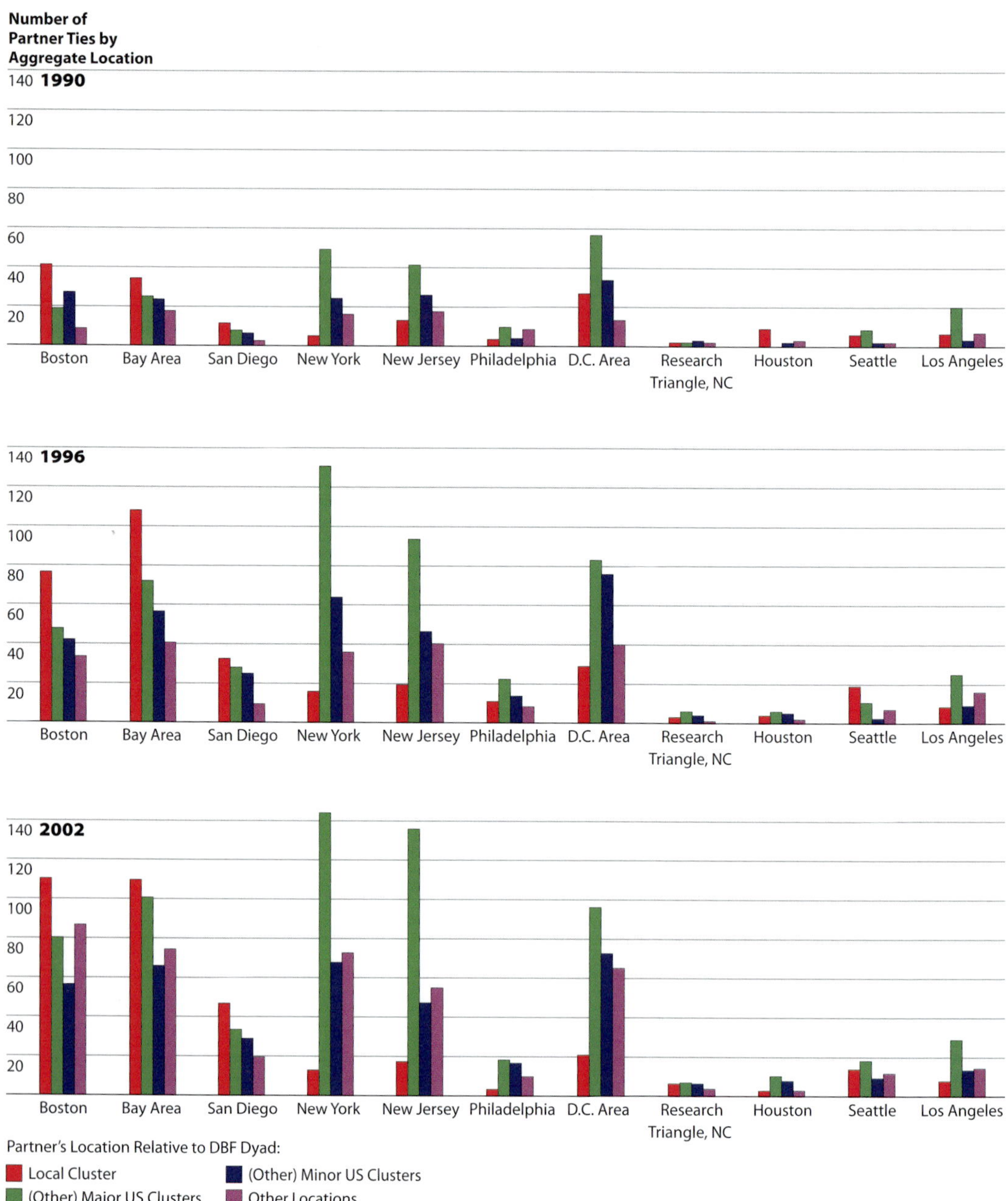

Figure 14.11 Sample selection on networks? Count of partner ties by location, 1990, 1996, and 2002.

This ferment had several consequences. One, labor market mobility became easy. For example, the involvement of early employees of Genentech and Hybritech in starting new companies was quite notable. One report traces eighteen companies founded in the 1990s by scientists and managers who had worked at Genentech during its first decade (Van Brunt 2000). Similarly, MIT faculty and alumni played a big role in the creation of the Boston biotech community (Roberts and Eesley 2011). Two, these personnel flows suggest that the creation of a regional community and the presence of catalytic anchors greatly lessened the risks of starting a new firm. Three, the high rates of founding and turnover point to experimentation with new scientific ideas and business models, which further sustains a cluster.

In sum, several factors distinguish the geographic locales where biotech emerged and grew into an interactive, robust community. All regions possessed some diversity in types of organizations, but the clusters where a local community became institutionalized had anchor tenant organizations that fostered interaction among disparate parties. PROs and VCs appear to have functioned as organization-forming organizations (Stinchcombe 1965). And rather than recede as new entrants joined the scene, these organizations remained active participants.

As a consequence, the norms that characterized interorganizational relations in the three clusters bear the signatures of the anchor tenants. DBFs collaborated with other DBFs in biomedical product development; older DBFs joined in as investors in new start-ups. The older companies took on some of the features of both the PROs and VCs, while the PROs and VCs in these areas became intensively involved in starting companies. Universities took equity positions in start-up biotech companies and facilitated the licensing of university science. Employees at VCs moved to biotech firms to take on founder or executive roles, and biotech company veterans moved on to found VC firms. Whatever one may think of this outcome (with respect to its consequences for corporate governance or public science), in the three regions where cross-network transposition occurred, we see a thorough mixing of participants from formerly separate domains.

In contrast, the regions that did not develop local clusters were dominated by one type of organization that may have been more inclined to "call the shots," asserting its own primacy and dictating the rules of the game. In some cases, these 800-pound gorillas were giant pharmaceutical companies; in others, the local leader was either a large government institute or local university or research hospital. In Los Angeles and Seattle, first-generation biotechs did not spawn subsequent companies. Our aim is not to point a finger at particular organizations for not being generative but to emphasize that the continuing predominance of a single type of organization hinders community emergence.

CONCLUSION AND IMPLICATIONS

The genesis of the life sciences field offers an opportunity to reflect on the process of institutionalization. The core question in studies of field formation concerns how a collection of organizations coheres into a community, engaged in common activities and subject to similar reputational and regulatory processes (DiMaggio and Powell 1983; Bourdieu and Wacquant 1992; Martin 2003). To be sure, the origins of biotech have some idiosyncratic features. The crucial role of university research in creating and sustaining the science, the importance of intellectual property and patent law, and large-scale public financing of R&D all render biotechnology distinctive, at least in comparison to many twentieth-century manufacturing industries. It remains to be seen whether these factors prove to be standard building blocks for twenty-first-century science-based fields. Nonetheless, the processes we have analyzed shed light on invention and institutionalization more generally.

Our argument hinges on two main factors: one, the presence of a diversity of organizations, and two, connections mediated through anchor tenants, some of which prompted the boundary crossing we have termed transposition. This combination produced relational density in a very small number of geographic locales and not in other venues that also had an enviable set of initial endowments. Relational density in the context of geographic proximity generated shared expectations. Local norms for collaboration and knowledge exchange developed. Both competition and cooperation coexisted through repeated exchanges and fluid labor markets. The three clusters became intense incubators for scientific ideas and business models, so that jockeying for success occurred on more meritocratic (or at least publicly transparent) grounds.

The diversity of organizations provided multiple means for information exchange, varied organizational strategies, and divergent criteria for success. In each of the three communities, a distinctive model of information diffusion developed to enable relational contracting (Macneil 1985; Powell 1990). Public research organizations were most influential in Boston, but they were clearly important in the Bay Area and San Diego, too. PROs are unusual because they are very "leaky" institutions, as information flows out of them readily. But they are also venues for the rapid dissemination of standards and evaluative criteria, as well as high-speed gossip networks to carry stories of malfeasance.

Venture capital was a spark plug in the Bay Area, most notably because it provided the bridge to transport basic science into the commercial realm. To be sure, academic biological science had become "big," and running a successful lab at a top-tier university had taken on many elements of managing a small business. But as we showed in chapter 13, few faculty members were prepared back then to be biotech executives—or even wanted to. VCs functioned as stand-in executives and advisers to new biotech firms, and they translated managerial practices from the semiconductor and computer worlds to biotech.

San Diego saw the unusual case of a failed merger that generated numerous spin-offs. There are many historical cases of spin-offs driving industry evolution, in such areas as autos in Detroit and the tire industry in Akron (Klepper 2008), and in the footwear industry as well (Sorenson and Audia 2000). Many of the more famous examples, such as Olds in cars and Fairchild in semiconductors, led to disgruntled employees who exited and formed competitors. The Hybritech example seems to have a different twist. The many alumni appear to have treated the unsuccessful acquisition of their young firm as a signal that they could collectively build a biotech industry in San Diego. Rather than becoming competitors with one another, they cooperated, and a number of alums went on to become serial entrepreneurs. Meanwhile, the acquiring multinational, Eli Lilly, eventually became one of the first big companies to be an engaged collaborator with start-ups and PROs, after writing off the losses from the Hybritech acquisition in 1994.

The role of first-generation biotech companies in partnering with smaller companies changed the model of competitive spin-offs to a more relational one. The scientists who moved from university to firm or from firm to nonprofit (dubbed "sector switchers" by Whittington [2007] in her analysis of Boston life scientists) transferred research ideas and business blueprints. In sum, interfirm job mobility was crucial to the cross-network transfer of knowledge in all three locales.

Extending beyond these cases, the sequencing of network ties significantly alters the practices and relationships that become institutionalized (Stark and Vedres 2006). Starting points matter a great deal in institutional formation. We have emphasized that the industry's origins were characterized by an asymmetric distribution of resources and capabilities. This initial variation may have been one of the drivers for change, as start-up firms and research organizations looked to alter the status quo. For organizations in the three clusters, the creation of a local community, as well as affiliations with organizations in the other "successful" regions, led to a more diverse portfolio of distant partnerships. In the successful clusters, biotech firms occupy a dual position: both as a member of a cluster and as a conduit to external activity.[17] In contrast, in all of the nascent regions, save for Seattle, which remains small, local DBFs have to make do with distant ties. Put differently, densely connected local communities grew to become cosmopolitan, but regions where a few key organizations had cosmopolitan connections never developed a local cluster.

Some might contend that the analysis we have offered is "just" a case of brokerage, albeit one in which the brokers (i.e., the anchor tenants) acted to coordinate and distribute resources rather than benefit from arbitrage.[18] Certainly, as the field developed, the distribution of resources and benefits shifted to privilege different groups over others. But the transition from somewhat sparse local networks to a densely connected field reflected not just the brokerage role of PROs, VCs, and DBFs. Cross-network feedback is an essential part of the story. The catalyzing effects of combining the tools of one sector with those of another transformed the life science business in ways that no strategic broker or entrepreneur could ever have anticipated. Brokerage certainly forged contacts among a diverse collection of organizations, but the ramifications of these collaborations led to an important institutional transformation. To be sure, the prior experiences of the founders of DBFs (university researchers, venture capitalists, or refugees from established companies) shaped the way in which they thought about how a science-based company could be organized and how organizations in the same field might interact with one another.[19]

[17] Multivocality can be a risky strategy early in a career or in a field's formation (Zuckerman 1999). Put differently, a multivocal categorization may pose obstacles at certain moments in a field's evolution. But as cross-network transpositions occur and ramify, a multivocal persona may become venerated, as the ability to tap a wider pool of resources is translated as richness and generativity.

[18] Ron Burt has commented to us that this process of managing diversity could be regarded as sponsored "collateral brokerage."

[19] The first CEO of Amgen, George Rathmann, had three decades of experience as a manager at 3M, Litton Industries, and Abbott Laboratories, all of which left him discouraged about the ability of most large firms to pursue R&D: "Deciding to decompartmentalize and fragment R&D is just plain wrong! The whole tenor of Abbott was grind it out, grind it out, make sure you have all your details right. Make sure you execute it properly. I hated the word execution; I liked the word innovation that I had brought from 3M. . . . But at 3M, just about the time when things started to move, the marketing guys would move in, and they would take over to run the business." With Amgen, Rathmann was determined to do things "right": "If you're going to be a science-based business,

But the outcome of this recombinatory process generated a landscape that was unanticipated by all—and not necessarily in any one group's interest. Moreover, in the successful clusters, spillovers extended further, into the architectural, financial, legal, medical device, and biomedical supply fields that supported the burgeoning life sciences community.

Cross-network transpositions operated as the means by which ideas and skills were transferred into new domains, where they recombined with existing practices. This mixing created new possibilities in organizational practice and strategy, to be sure, but in identity as well. These new clothes may fit somewhat awkwardly, however. Identities change as individuals and organizations move from one domain to another, and as they do, original meanings can be lost (White 1992). Consider how the blurring of basic and applied research, or public and private science, has subtly transformed the identities of the public institutions that carry out basic research.

Thoughtful current discussions of the innovation process emphasize the need for "collaborative public spaces" to facilitate creativity and search (Lester and Piore 2004). Sometimes, however, such admonitions can be couched in a language that vastly overstates the ability of public research organizations to contribute to new product development. Recall that the PROs in this field were critical for successful cluster formation precisely because they acted as research organizations contributing to the continuing advance of science and technology rather than as commercial entrepreneurs (Owen-Smith and Powell 2004). Today many U.S. research universities are burdened with the demands of regional job creation and economic development, sometimes at the expense of scientific advance. Moreover, the tendency for many large corporations to wait until technologies are vetted by public science before investing in them does not necessarily bode well for continuing technological advance.

It is important not to view the transformations we have outlined as the necessary or desirable route for the trajectory of science and industry. Our goal was not to offer a recipe for how a science-based industry develops. Instead, our aim is to illuminate how institutions emerge from the interactions of organizations with divergent skills and resources and explain how transpositions across a multiplicity of networks triggered change in the organizing logic of this field.

Multiple-network combinations can be regarded as legitimate, as a compromise, or as deviant. Four decades ago, the interface of public science and private finance was highly contested. The challenge of meeting evaluative standards in distinct domains is considerable, but this threshold is lessened when practices in one domain satisfy the standards of those in others. In this field, practices sculpted for the use of science and medicine turned out to have unexpected utility in a new domain. In these unusual circumstances of exaptation, cross-talk generated innovation through new models of behavior (academic scientist as entrepreneur, venture capital tycoon as public policy activist), new organizational practices (proprietary firm rewarding publication of public science, public research organizations pursuing licensing deals and equity shares, venture capital firms creating entrepreneurs in residence programs), and new modes of financing (venture capital funds and research grants combine to fund start-up companies). These varied innovations reverberated to transform all the participants and concatenated to produce novel institutions. Such cascades are quite unusual. When they do occur and are reinforced by the most central organizations and authorized by law and public policy, the potential for systemic change—either positive or negative—is considerable.

for gosh sakes recognize who's essential to that business! It's the scientists" (2003, 6, 20).

REFERENCES

Abbott, Andrew. 1990. "Conceptions of Time and Events in Social Science Methods." *Historical Methods* 23(4):140–50.

Agrawal, Ajay, and Iain Cockburn. 2003. "The Anchor Tenant Hypothesis." *International Journal of Industrial Organization* 21:1227–53.

Almeida, Paul, and Bruce Kogut. 1999. "Localization of Knowledge and the Mobility of Engineers in Regional Networks." *Management Science* 45:905–17.

Almeida, Paul, Gina Dokko, and Lori Rosenkopf. 2003. "Startup Size and the Mechanisms of External Learning: Increasing Opportunity and Decreasing Ability?" *Research Policy* 32(2):301–15.

Arthur, W. Brian. 1994. *Increasing Returns and Path Dependency in the Economy*. Ann Arbor: University of Michigan Press.

Audretsch, David B., and Paula Stephan. 1996. "Company-Scientist Locational Links: The Case of Biotechnology." *American Economic Review* 86(3): 641–52.

Barley, Stephen R., and Pamela S. Tolbert. 1997. "Institutionalization and Structuration: Studying the

Links between Action and Institution." *Organization Studies* 18(1):93–117.

Berman, Elizabeth Popp. 2007. "Creating the Market University: Science, the State, and the Economy, 1965–85." Ph.D. diss., University of California–Berkeley.

Boltanski, Luc, and Laurent Thévenot. 2006. *On Justification: The Economies of Worth*. Princeton: Princeton University Press.

Bourdieu, Pierre, and Loic Wacquant. 1992. *An Invitation to Reflexive Sociology*. Chicago: University of Chicago Press.

Boyer, Herbert W. 2001. "Recombinant DNA Research at UCSF and Commercial Application at Genentech." Oral history conducted in 1994 by Sally Smith Hughes, Regional Oral History Office, The Bancroft Library, University of California–Berkeley.

Brown, John Seely, and Paul Duguid. 2001. "Creativity versus Structure: A Useful Tension." *MIT Sloan Management Review* 42:93–95.

Casper, Steven. 2007. "How Do Technology Clusters Emerge and Become Sustainable? Social Network Formation within the San Diego Biotechnology Cluster." *Research Policy* 36(4):438–55.

Chen, Henry, Paul Gompers, Anna Kovner, and Josh Lerner. 2009. "Buy Local? The Geography of Successful and Unsuccessful Venture Capital Expansion." NBER working paper #15102.

Clark, Andy. 1993. *Associative Engines: Connectionism, Concepts, and Representational Change*. Cambridge, MA: MIT Press.

Cohen, Michael D. 1981. "The Power of Parallel Thinking." *Journal of Economic Behavior and Organization* 2(4):285–306.

Cole, Jonathan. 1993. "Balancing Acts: Dilemmas of Choice Facing Research Universities." *Daedalus* 122(4):1–36.

Colyvas, Jeannette. 2007. "From Divergent Meanings to Common Practices: The Early Institutionalization of Technology Transfer at Stanford University." *Research Policy* 36(4):456–76.

Colyvas, Jeannette, and W. W. Powell. 2006. "Roads to Institutionalization: The Remaking of Boundaries between Public and Private Science." *Research in Organizational Behavior* 27:305–53.

Coriat, Benjamin, and F. Orsi. 2002. "Establishing a New Intellectual Property Rights Regime in the United States: Origins, Content and Problems." *Research Policy* 31(8–9):1491–1507.

Cortright, Joseph, and Heike Mayer. 2002. "Signs of Life: The Growth of Biotechnology Centers in the United States." http://www.brookings.edu/es/urban/publications/biotech.pdf..

Dasgupta, Partha, and Paul A. David. 1987. "Information Disclosure and the Economics of Science and Technology." In *Kenneth Arrow and the Ascent of Economic Theory*, ed. G. R. Feiwel, 519–42. New York: New York University Press.

———. 1994. "Toward a New Economics of Science." *Research Policy* 23(5):487–521.

DiMaggio, Paul J., and Walter W. Powell. 1983. "The Iron Cage Revisited: Institutional Isomorphism and Collectivity Rationality in Organizational Fields." *American Sociological Review* 48(2):147–60.

Dosi, Giovanni. 1982. "Technological Paradigms and Technological Trajectories." *Research Policy* 11(3):147–62.

Eisenberg, Rebecca. 1987. "Proprietary Rights and the Norms of Science in Biotechnology Research." *Yale Law Journal* 97(2):177–231.

Eppli, M. J., and J. D. Shilling. 1995. "Large-Scale Shopping Center Development Opportunities." *Land-Economics* 71(1):35–41.

Feldman, Maryann. 2003. "The Locational Dynamics of the U.S. Biotech Industry: Knowledge Externalities and the Anchor Hypothesis." *Industry and Innovation* 10:311–28.

Feldman, Maryann, and Yda Schreuder. 1996. "Initial Advantage: The Origins and Geographic Concentration of the Pharmaceutical Industry in the Mid-Atlantic Region." *Industrial and Corporate Change* 5(3):839–62.

Fikes, Bradley J. 1999. "Why San Diego Has Biotech." *San Diego Metropolitan*. (March):1–7.

Fligstein, Neil. 2001. *The Architecture of Markets: An Economic Sociology of Capitalist Societies*. Princeton: Princeton University Press.

Galambos, Louis, and J. Sturchio. 1998. "Pharmaceutical Firms and the Transition to Biotechnology." *Business History Review* 72(2):250–82.

Gambardella, Alfonso. 1995. *Science and Innovation: The U.S. Pharmaceutical Industry during the 1980s*. Cambridge: Cambridge University Press.

Goldberg, Carey. 1999. "Across the Country, Universities Generate a High-Tech Economic Boom." *New York Times*, October 1, pp. 1, 22.

Grabher, Gernot, and David Stark. 1997. "Organizing Diversity: Evolutionary Theory, Network Analysis, and the Postsocialist Transformations." In *Restructuring Networks: Legacies, Linkages, and Localities in Postsocialism*, ed. Gernot Grabher and David Stark, 1–32. London: Oxford University Press.

Greenwood, Royston, Christine Oliver, Kersten Sahlin, and Roy Suddaby. 2008. Introduction to *The Sage Handbook of Organizational Institutionalism*, ed. R. Greenwood et al., 1–47. London: Sage.

Hagel, John III, and John Seely Brown. 2005. "Productive Friction: How Difficult Business Partnerships Can Accelerate Innovation." *Harvard Business Review* 83(2):82–91, 148.

Hall, Stephen S. 1987. *Invisible Frontiers: The Race to Synthesize a Human Gene*. New York: Atlantic Monthly Press.

Hardy, Cynthia, and Steve Maguire. 2008. "Institutional Entrepreneurship." In *The Sage Handbook of Organizational Institutionalism*, ed. R. Greenwood et al., 198–217. London: Sage.

Hedlund, Gunnar. 1993. "Assumptions of Hierarchy and Heterarchy, with Applications to the Management of the Multinational Corporation." In

Organization Theory and the Multinational Enterprise, ed. S. Ghoshal and E. Westney, 211–36. London: Macmillan.

Henderson, Rebecca, and Iain Cockburn. 1996. "Scale, Scope, and Spillovers: The Determinants of Research Productivity in Drug Discovery." *Rand Journal of Economics* 27(1):32–59.

Henderson, Rebecca, Luigi Orsenigo, and Gary Pisano. 1999. "The Pharmaceutical Industry and the Revolution in Molecular Biology: Interactions among Scientific, Institutional, and Organizational Change." In *Sources of Industrial Leadership*, ed. D. C. Mowery and R. R. Nelson, 267–311. New York: Cambridge University Press.

Hutchins, Edwin. 1995. *Cognition in the Wild*. Cambridge, MA: MIT Press.

Jaffe, Adam B. 1986. "Technological Opportunity and Spillovers of Research-and-Development: Evidence from Firm Patents, Profits, and Market Value." *American Economic Review* 76(5):984–1001.

Jaffe, Adam B., Manual Trajtenberg, and Rebecca Henderson. 1993. "Geographic Localization of Knowledge Spillovers as Evidenced by Patent Citations." *Quarterly Journal of Economics* 108(3):577–98.

Jones, Mark Peter. 2005. "Biotech's Perfect Climate: The Hybritech Story." Ph.D. diss., University of California–San Diego.

Jong, Simcha. 2006. "How Organizational Structures in Science Shape Spin-Off Firms: The Biochemistry Departments of Berkeley, Stanford, and UCSF and the Birth of the Biotech Industry." *Industrial and Corporate Change* 15(2):251–83.

———. 2008. "Academic Organizations and New Industrial Fields: Berkeley and Stanford after the Rise of Biotechnology." *Research Policy* 37(8): 1267–82.

Kenney, Martin. 1986. *Biotechnology: The University-Industrial Complex*. New Haven: Yale University Press.

Klepper, Steven. 2008. "Silicon Valley: A Chip Off the Old Detroit Bloc." Paper presented at the DRUID Conference, Copenhagen Business School, Copenhagen, Denmark.

Kreps, David. 1990. *A Course in Microeconomic Theory*. Princeton: Princeton University Press.

Krugman, Paul. 1991. "Increasing Returns and Economic Geography." *Journal of Political Economy* 99(3):483–99.

Lane, David, and Robert Maxfield. 1996. "Strategy under Complexity: Fostering Generative Relationships." *Long Range Planning* 29(2):215–31.

Lawrence, Thomas B., and Roy Suddaby. 2006. "Institutions and Institutional Work." In *Handbook of Organizational Studies*, S. Clegget et al., 215–54. London: Sage.

Lee, Carolyn, and Mary Walshok. 2000. *Making Connections: The Evolution of Links between UCSD Researchers and San Diego's Biotech Industry*. A report for the University of California's Industry-University Cooperative Research Program.

Lester, Richard K., and Michael J. Piore. 2004. *Innovation: The Missing Dimension*. Cambridge, MA: Harvard University Press.

Macarthur, R. 1972. "Strong, or Weak, Interactions?" *Transactions of the Connecticut Academy of Arts and Sciences* 44:177–88.

Macneil, Ian. 1985. "Relational Contract: What We Do and Do Not Know." *Wisconsin Law Review* 3: 483–526.

Mahoney, James. 2000. "Path Dependence in Historical Sociology." *Theory and Society* 29(4):507–48.

Malerba, Franco, and Luigi Orsenigo. 2002. "Innovation and Market Structure in the Dynamics of the Pharmaceutical Industry and Biotechnology: Towards a History-Friendly Model." *Industrial and Corporate Change* 11(4):667–703.

Martin, John Levi. 2003. "What Is Field Theory?" *American Journal of Sociology* 109(1):1–49.

McWilliams, Carey. 1949. *California, the Great Exception*. New York: Current Books.

Meyer, John W. 2008. "Reflections on Institutional Theories of Organizations." In *The Sage Handbook of Organizational Institutionalism*, ed. R. Greenwood et al., 790–812. London: Sage.

Meyer, John W., and Brian Rowan. 1977. "Institutionalized Organizations: Formal Structure as Myth and Ceremony." *American Journal of Sociology* 83(2): 340–63.

Meyer, Renate. 2006. "Visiting Relatives: Current Developments in the New Sociology of Organization." *Organization* 13(5):725–38.

Mills, L. Scott, Michael E. Soulé, and David F. Doak. 1993. "The Keystone Species Concept in Ecology and Conservation." *BioScience* 43(4):219–24.

Mowery, David C., Richard R. Nelson, Bhaven Sampat, and Arvids Ziedonis. 2004. *Ivory Tower and Industrial Innovation*. Stanford: Stanford University Press.

Owen-Smith, Jason, and W. W. Powell. 2004. "Knowledge Networks as Channels and Conduits: The Effect of Spillovers in the Boston Biotechnology Community." *Organization Science* 15(1):5–21.

———. 2006. "Accounting for Emergence and Novelty in Boston and Bay Area Biotechnology." In *Cluster Genesis: The Emergence of Technology Clusters and Their Implication for Government Policy*, ed. P. Braunerhjelm and M. Feldman, 61–83. Oxford: Oxford University Press.

Paine, R. T. 1969. "A Note on Trophic Complexity and Community Stability." *American Naturalist* 103: 91–93.

Pashigian, B. Peter, and Eric D. Gould. 1998. "Internalizing Externalities: The Pricing of Space in Shopping Malls." *Journal of Law and Economics* 41:115–42.

Pierson, Paul. 2000. "The Limits of Design: Explaining Institutional Origins and Change." *Governance* 13(4):475–99.

———. 2004. *Politics in Time*. Princeton: Princeton University Press.

Porter, Kelley. 2004. "You Can't Leave Your Past Behind: The Influence of Founders' Career Histories on Their Firms." Ph.D. diss., Stanford University.

Porter, Kelley, Kjersten Whittington, and W. W. Powell. 2005. "The Institutional Embeddedness of High-Tech Regions." In *Clusters, Networks, and Innovation*, ed. S. Breschi and F. Malerba, 261–96. Oxford: Oxford University Press.

Portera, Carol. 2004. "Serious Research in Biotech Beach Corridor." *Genetic Engineering News* 24(1):46.

Powell, W. W. 1990. "Neither Market nor Hierarchy: Network Forms of Organization." *Research in Organizational Behavior* 12:295–336.

———. 1996. "Inter-organizational Collaboration in the Biotechnology Industry." *Journal of Institutional and Theoretical Economics* 120(1):197–215.

Powell, W. W., and Peter Brantley. 1992. "Competitive Cooperation in Biotechnology: Learning through Networks?" In *Networks and Organizations*, ed. R. Eccles and N. Nohria, 366–94. Boston: Harvard Business School Press..

Powell, W. W., and J. A. Colyvas. 2008. "Microfoundations of Institutional Theory." In *Handbook of Organizational Institutionalism*, ed. R. Greenwood et al., 276–98. London: Sage.

Powell, W. W., K. W. Koput, and L. Smith-Doerr. 1996. "Interorganizational Collaboration and the Locus of Innovation: Networks of Learning in Biotechnology." *Administrative Science Quarterly* 41(1):116–45.

Powell, W. W., J. Owen-Smith, and J. A. Colyvas. 2007. "Innovation and Emulation: Lessons from American Universities in Selling Private Rights to Public Knowledge." *Minerva* 45:121–42.

Powell, W. W., K. W. Koput, J. I. Bowie, and L. Smith-Doerr. 2002. "The Spatial Clustering of Science and Capital: Accounting for Biotech Firm-Venture Capital Relationships." *Regional Studies* 36(3):291–306.

Powell, W. W., D. R. White, K. W. Koput, and J. Owen-Smith. 2005. "Network Dynamics and Field Evolution: The Growth of Inter-organizational Collaboration in the Life Sciences." *American Journal of Sociology* 110(4):1132–1205.

Regional Oral History Office, University of California–Berkeley Bancroft Library. 1997. Available from the online archive. Interviews by Sally Smith Hughes with Herbert Boyer, 1994, George B. Rathmann, 2003, Robert A. Swanson, 2000.

Rhoten, Diana, and W. W. Powell. 2007. "The Frontiers of Intellectual Property: Expanded Protection vs. New Models of Open Science." *Annual Review of Law and Social Science* 3:345–73.

Robbins-Roth, Cynthia. 2000. *From Alchemy to IPO*. Cambridge, MA: Perseus Publishing.

Roberts, Edward B., and Charles Eesley. 2011. "Entrepreneurial Impact: The Role of MIT." *Foundations and Trends in Entrepreneurship* 7(1–2):1–149.

Sabel, Charles. 1990. "Moebius-Strip Organizations and Open Labor Markets: Some Consequences of the Reintegration of Conception and Execution in a Volatile Economy." In *Social Theory for a Changing Society*, ed. Pierre Bourdieu and James Coleman, 23–54. Boulder, CO: Westview Press.

Saxenian, Annalee. 1994. *Regional Advantage: Culture and Competition in Silicon Valley and Route 128*. Cambridge, MA: Harvard University Press.

Scott, Allen J., and Michael Storper. 2003. "Regions, Globalization, and Development." *Regional Studies* 37:579–93.

Simard, Caroline. 2004. "From Weapons to Cell Phones: Knowledge Networks in San Diego's Wireless Valley." Ph.D. thesis, Stanford University.

Sorenson, Olav, and Pino Audia. 2000. "The Social Structure of Entrepreneurial Activity: Geographic Concentration of Footwear Production in the US, 1940–1989." *American Journal of Sociology* 106(2):424–61.

Stark, David. 1996. "Recombinant Property in East European Capitalism." *American Journal of Sociology* 101(4):993–1027.

———. 2001. "Ambiguous Assets for Uncertain Environments: Heterarchy in Postsocialist firms." In *The Twenty-First Century Firm: Changing Economic Organization in International Perspective*, ed. Paul DiMaggio, 69–104. Princeton: Princeton University Press.

Stark, David, and Balázs Vedres. 2006. "Social Times of Network Spaces: Network Sequences and Foreign Investment in Hungary." *American Journal of Sociology* 11(5):1367–1411.

Stinchcombe, Arthur. 1965. "Social Structure and Organizations." In *Handbook of Organizations*, ed. James G. March, 142–93. Chicago: Rand McNally.

———. 1968. *Constructing Social Theories*. New York: Harcourt, Brace World.

Stuart, Toby E., and Olav Sorenson. 2003. "The Geography of Opportunity: Spatial Heterogeneity in Founding Rates and the Performance of Biotechnology Firms." *Research Policy* 32:229–53.

Teitelman, Robert. 1989. *Gene Dreams: Wall Street, Academia, and the Rise of Biotechnology*. New York: Basic Books.

Thelen, Kathleen. 2004. *How Institutions Evolve*. New York: Cambridge University Press.

Van Brunt, Jennifer. 2000. "Biotech's Impeccable Lineage." *Signals Magazine*, March 22, pp. 1–10.

Varmus, Harold E., and Robert A. Weinberg. 1992. *Genes and the Biology of Cancer*. New York: Scientific American Press.

Walcott, Susan M. 2002. "Analyzing an Innovative Environment: San Diego as a Bioscience Beachhead." *Economic Development Quarterly* 16(2):99–114.

Walshok, Mary L., Carolyn Lee, Ed Furtek, and Pat Windham. 2001. *Networks of Innovation: Contributions to San Diego's Telecommunications and Biotechnology Clusters*. A report for the University of California's Industry–University Cooperative Research Program.

Watson, James D. 2003. *DNA: The Secret of Life*. New York: Knopf.

Weick, Karl. 1993. "The Collapse of Sensemaking in Organizations: The Mann Gulch Disaster." *Administrative Science Quarterly* 38(4):628–52.

White, Harrison C. 1992. *Identity and Control.* Princeton: Princeton University Press.

Whittington, Kjersten Bunker. 2007. "Employment Sectors as Opportunity Structures: The Effects of Location on Male and Female Scientific Dissemination." Ph.D. diss., Stanford University.

Whittington, Kjersten Bunker, Jason Owen-Smith, and W. W. Powell. 2009. "Networks, Propinquity and Innovation in Knowledge-Intensive Industries." *Administrative Science Quarterly* 54(1):90–122.

Wright, Susan B. 1994. *Molecular Politics Developing American and British Regulatory Policy for Genetic Engineering, 1972–1982.* Chicago: University of Chicago Press.

Young, Peyton. 1998. *Individual Strategy and Social Structure.* Princeton: Princeton University Press.

Zacks, Rebecca. 2000. "The Technology Review University Research Scorecard 2000." *Technology Review* 103(4):88–90.

Zucker, Lynne G., and Michael R. Darby. 1996. "Star Scientists and Institutional Transformation: Patterns of Invention and Innovation in the Formation of the U.S. Biotechnology Industry." *Proceedings of National Academy of Science* 93:709–16.

Zucker, Lynne G., Michael R. Darby, and Marilyn Brewer. 1998. "Intellectual Human Capital and the Birth of U.S. Biotechnology Enterprises." *American Economic Review* 88(1):290–306.

Zuckerman, Ezra. 1999. "The Categorical Imperative: Securities Analysts and the Illegitimacy Discount." *American Journal of Sociology* 104(5):1398–1438.

Zuckerman, Ezra, Tai Kim, Kalinda Ukanwa, and James von Rittman. 2003. "Robust Identities or Nonentities? Typecasting in the Feature Film Labor Market." *American Journal of Sociology* 108(5): 1018–74.

affiliating with partners that are already rich in connections creates a topology centered on well-connected "hubs" (Barabási and Albert 1999). A structure of highly connected nodes is quite robust in the face of random error but also susceptible to deliberate attack (Albert, Jeong, and Barabási 2000). In contrast, adding just a small number of random connections to a lattice structure, which has a fixed number of equidistant participants, fundamentally alters path lengths and local clustering, reshaping patterns of diffusion (Watts and Strogatz 1998). Consequently, the manner in which networks evolve by adding or subtracting connections has significant consequences for how they work (Watts 2004). Mixed strategies and emergent structures are particularly characteristic of social and economic networks, which differ from physical and biological topologies—such as metabolic networks or the World Wide Web—in that they tend to be assortative, meaning that nodes with many connections are more likely to be linked to other nodes with numerous connections. By contrast, physical and biological networks tend to be disassortative (Newman 2002; Newman and Park 2003). Blended logics of partner selection generate hybrid structures, which often prove to be durable precisely because they constrain future attachments (Bearman, Moody, and Stovel 2004; White et al. 2004).[3]

Although social and economic networks generate prominent hubs as they grow, these central nodes vary internally and through time with respect to how they connect to one another. When the most prominent participants in a network establish ongoing linkages among themselves, the resulting "core" group can dictate the developmental pattern of an overall network. Such an elite group of multiconnected organizations may act as *gatekeepers* (because newcomers typically want to connect to one of the central incumbents) or as *arbiters* (who influence the direction and behavior of a field). They can also serve as *catalysts* (by ushering in new participants through sponsorship and igniting new lines of activity). These differing roles may be conditioned by either local circumstances or the wider environment. And, we emphasize, the execution of these roles may not be strategic or visionary. Conservative motives can trigger a search for new partners, whereas the intention to be innovative can lead to protectionist moves.

Collectively, the distributional and structural features that characterize elite clusters afford the most central nodes considerable influence. The most highly connected may operate as gatekeepers by virtue of their foundational role in the formation of new ties, their small numbers, their longevity and robustness, and the accompanying barriers those features erect to newcomers seeking to join their ranks. Newcomers continually seek the relational imprimatur of existing elites, but it is the elites that do the selecting.

The core players in a network also serve as arbiters for the direction of a field. Their decisions—taken independently but felt collectively—shape the macrodynamics of a field. When, for instance, elites turn their attention inward and close the palace gates by emphasizing ties only to other top-tier partners, they, wittingly or not, limit access for newcomers. When the core grows more closed and convergent, rebuffed outsiders may turn to one another, possibly sowing the seeds of a new cohesive cluster that may someday sweep out the old guard. Alternatively, when elites prospect for new and diverse partners, they may do so at the expense of connections to established rivals. Taken to the limits, an elite cluster could fade of its own accord as access to newcomers comes to trump connections to incumbents. Consequently, even a group with the power and influence of an elite faces a balancing act—too much attention focused on other elite members produces a rich-get-richer dynamic that leads to consolidation and eventual stagnation, whereas using one's status and influence to prospect for novel information can lead to elite disintegration when the new phenomena are not well understood.

We use these insights about network growth and topology to study the emergence and development of central nodes, those core participants at the apex of a field who through their multiple linkages influence its direction. We argue that the structure of a network and its influence on all the participants depend intimately upon the mix and character of gatekeepers, arbiters, and catalysts at its core. Systematic differences in the patterns of connection that link the most prominent members of a system to one another and to less well-positioned alters have potent implications. Two stylized patterns representing end points of a continuum running from adaptability to ossification capture features of networks dominated by assortative mixing and degree-biased attachment.

[3] The adaptability of community structures is contingent on the rate of turnover of members. In smaller social communities, stable membership is key to longevity but the persistence of larger communities is increased by membership turnover (Palla, Barabási, and Vicsek 2007).

When the central nodes in a network turn their finite energies inward to connections with other central players, new ties will serve primarily to consolidate the position of those who are already prominent. Network growth thus generates an increasingly closed elite. Put more formally, a strong tendency toward assortative mixing will create a relatively impermeable, interconnected cluster of nodes whose stability comes at the price of insularity. Social and economic systems dominated by such an inward-looking core create a stratification order that limits the mobility of "commoners" and conserves the power of incumbents at the expense of adaptability and novelty.

Alternatively, prominent participants may look outward by linking with promising newcomers and less well-connected members who seek the resources and legitimacy that accrue from affiliations with central players. Rather than calcifying, expansive systems can promote responsiveness and mobility as those at the center become pacesetters. Although this flexibility may enhance the overall resilience of a network in the face of abrupt change, the lack of coherence can also rob core members of their influence. Moreover, a network growth regime dominated solely by new ties that reach out from the system's center may never cohere. Stated in organizational terms, networks that grow largely by consolidating position are a recipe for oligarchy, whereas networks that grow through outreach are more characteristic of free-wheeling markets.

Actual social and economic systems manifest a mix of consolidating and expansive growth and thus exhibit varying levels of responsiveness, stability, and mobility. Some cohesive structure is necessary for network position to have real effects on social and economic outcomes (Moody and White 2003; Newman and Girvan 2004), whereas some openness is required if networks are to adapt to changing environments (Owen-Smith and Powell 2004). We hope to demonstrate that a fruitful approach to understanding the emergence and ramifications of complex social and economic networks is provided by an analysis of tie formation in terms of expansion and consolidation of a system's core. We apply these ideas to the evolution of the biotechnology industry over the past four decades.

DATA AND METHODS

The database used for this chapter covers 661 dedicated biotechnology firms worldwide and more than 3,000 partners with these firms over the period 1984–2004.[4] Our focus has been restricted to dedicated biotechnology firms (DBFs) and the formal contractual arrangements they have with collaborators. Our sample of DBFs covers both privately held and publicly traded firms. Large corporations, hospitals, universities, research institutes, and government agencies enter the database as partners who collaborate with DBFs; thus our network consists of both ties among DBFs and ties from DBFs to partner organizations. For the purposes of this chapter, we use the full sample, including companies from the United States, Canada, Australia, Europe, and Asia. Included among the partner organizations are more than 450 public research organizations (e.g., universities, nonprofit institutes, government labs), 750 venture capital firms (VCs), and 500 pharmaceutical, chemical, and health care companies.

The data on interorganizational agreements cover the time frame and purpose of the relationship. In this analysis, we define a collaborative tie or alliance as any contractual arrangement to exchange or pool resources between a DBF and one or more partner organizations.[5] A connection exists whenever a DBF and a partner have one or more ties between them. We assign the partner organizations to one of six categories: public research organizations (including universities, nonprofit research centers, and research hospitals), government institutes, multinational pharmaceutical and chemical corporations, financial institutions, biomedical companies (such as agriculture or veterinary biotech, instrumentation and supply companies), and other DBFs. We collapse the varied types of ties into four general categories: science, finance, licensing, and commercialization. Our initial descriptive analyses chart the pattern of collaborations by both type of activity and partner over time. We pay particular attention to the dynamics of new ties, as we have previously shown that tie formation was the undercurrent that pulled the overall network (Powell et al. 2005).

To identify the most connected members of the biotechnology network, we use the method of k-core decomposition (White and Harary 2001; Moody and White 2003). This approach

[4] See chapter 14, footnote 6 for further discussion of the database.

[5] All collaborations are coded according to their starting date and ended when the relationships concludes; that termination could reflect either the closing of a relationship or the exit of one or both of the parties from the industry.

has proven particularly fruitful for the study of large-scale networks, where definitions of centrality and structural characteristics are hindered by the complex interplay of multiple types of linkages. The k-core method is based on identifying particular subsets of the graph, called k-cores, with each one obtained by iteratively removing all the vertices of degree smaller than k until the degree of all remaining vertices is larger than or equal to k. More specifically, we analyze the architecture of the biotechnology network as a set of successively enclosed substructures. A k-core decomposition is a means to identify the fingerprints of a network's elite. This method has been used effectively on a robust array of problems, including protein interaction networks, disease transmission networks, friendship cliques, kinship lineages, and linkages on the World Wide Web.[6]

Put differently, a k-core decomposition is like peeling an onion layer by layer, revealing the structure of the different shells from the outmost skin to the inner bulb (Alvarez-Hamelin et al. 2006). By pruning the overall network of its least connected members, we can discern the hierarchical structure of the field and focus on its most central members. Identification of k-cores is implemented in a number of software packages. We use Pajek to calculate a partition of core membership on a network of binarized edges for each year.[7] Hence our measure is structural, based on the presence or absence of any connection between pairs of organizations in the network. For the purposes of k-core identification, we use the presence of a single connection and do not focus on multiple ties between pairs of organizations.

We analyze the dynamics of consolidation and expansion in the field by examining three types of affiliations:

1. Conserving ties, where a member of the most connected subgroup makes a tie to another member of this elite. Such ties contribute stability at the risk of calcification.
2. Closure ties, where a member of the most connected group forms a tie to a party that is not a member of the core but has at least one previous tie to another elite member. These ties promote transitivity and consolidate influence.
3. Expansive ties, where a member of the most connected subgroup forges a tie to a newcomer with no prior elite connections. These ties enhance diversity and add flexibility but at the risk of too much exploration and cognitive distance.

Our focus on the evolving mix of different types of ties allows us to reconstruct network structure and its relational implications during phases of birth, expansion, maturation, and consolidation. Rather than seeing network structure as time independent, we can discern how variation in types of ties and partners is associated with different periods.

MARKET STRUCTURE AND THE DIVISION OF INNOVATIVE LABOR

The pharmaceutical industry has been the subject of in-depth study by many leading business historians and social scientists.[8] We draw freely on this rich stream of work to situate the pharma industry in the context of the emergence of biotechnology, which we covered in detail in the two previous chapters. This overview of key features of the market and scientific terrain helps reinforce a central point: even though the pharmaceutical sector underwent a radical technological discontinuity with the development of molecular biology, alongside notable organizational challenges with the entry of science-based, dedicated biotech firms, there was no wave of wholesale replacement of older firms by newer ones. On the contrary, we will show that incumbents eventually adopted the scientific and organizational tools of the new entrants. Thus the pattern of industry evolution involved a great deal of recombination and crosstalk spanning multiple domains.

For much of the twentieth century, the search for new compounds was a very slow process, and serendipity played a big role in discovery. The mechanism of action for most drugs was

[6] See Tong et al. 2002 for protein networks, De et al. 2004 for disease transmission, Moody 2001 for friendship cliques, White and Harary 2001 for kinship networks, and Dorogovtsev, Goltsev, and Mendes 2006 for web links.

[7] Pajek is a freeware package for the analysis and visualization of complex networks (http://vlado.fmf.uni-lj.si/pub/networks/pajek). This program is particularly good at representing the tensile strength of relations among multiple parties (deNooy, Mrvar, and Batagelj 2005).

[8] On the business history side, see Galambos and Sewell 1996 and Galambos and Sturchio 1996, 1998. Among the many social science analyses, we have found the following most helpful: Orsenigo 1989; Gambardella 1995; Henderson and Cockburn 1996; Malerba and Orsenigo 2002; Cockburn 2004; and Scherer 2004.

poorly understood, hence finding a treatment for one disease while searching for another was not unusual. The organizational, market, and regulatory ramifications of this random-screening search process were considerable (Cockburn, Henderson, and Stern 2000). This "brute force" model entailed testing thousands of chemical compounds for evidence of a physiological reaction in cell cultures, assays, and laboratory animals. Pharmaceutical companies had to maintain immense libraries of chemical compounds. But success on one front did not offer insights into other diseases or provide clear understanding of mechanisms and targets.[9] The discovery process required large resource outlays as science was a poor guide to whether a compound would prove safe and efficacious.

Patent protection was critical as it gave pharmaceutical firms a fixed amount of time to embark on the costly and protracted process of drug development without incursion from imitators. For much of the post–World War II era, drug discovery involved a series of discrete phases, and after the completion of each step, a choice was made whether to continue the project. If approved, the drug was handed off to a different team to continue development. This sequential process was a way to conserve on the costs of each phase. Much has been made of the high cost of developing new medical entities, and consumers certainly feel the brunt of these expenses. But the success rate for creating new drugs was very low and the risk of failure in the early stages exceptionally high. A small army of analysts have devoted a great deal of attention to calculating the costs of drug development. Suffice it to say, a period of eight years from laboratory bench to doctor's office would be regarded as timely, and development costs on the order of $300 to $800 million would be considered standard, varying according to whether extensive testing is necessary to identify long-term effects, as in the case of drugs for chronic diseases (Scherer 2004).

If a new drug was eventually approved by the U.S. Food and Drug Administration, marketing it directly to doctors through sales representatives was the route to reach patients. The ubiquitous drug advertising that we endure today was uncommon until the mid-1990s. Successful firms rode the fortunes of new drug releases and became deeply reliant on a few successful blockbusters.[10] Revenues were plowed back into research, but prior success afforded little cumulative guidance as to where to search next. In time, competitors developed and released similar drugs, and after patent protection expired, generic drug manufacturers moved in, eroding sales. Consumer recognition and loyalty accrued to a treatment regimen, not to any company.[11]

The advent of molecular biology and genetic engineering in the late 1970s dramatically altered the search process with profound ramifications for drug discovery, organizational design, and market dynamics. Scientific breakthroughs enabled much greater understanding of the mechanisms of how a drug worked, deeper insight into the molecular roots of diseases, and greater specificity of targets. Progress in a therapeutic area had much broader spillover effects. Rather than searching randomly, researchers could design molecules for specific therapeutic effects. And, unlike in the past, success shed light on a host of related possibilities. Nonetheless, although these scientific advances led to some significant successes in mitigating several leading causes of death, most notably heart disease, HIV, and some cancers, a number of the promised cures have proved elusive due to the complexity of many diseases. Instead, more progress has been made with new medicines that prolong and improve the quality of life for patients.

The gains in knowledge accumulation afforded by biotechnology also opened up the possibility for new modes of organizational design. Partly out of necessity but also as a result of influence from patient groups, start-up biotech

[9] To be sure, many successful and profitable new drugs were produced through this approach. Carlsson (1983, 35) comments on how much medicinal chemistry could accomplish without any knowledge of the biological system. "The narcotic analgesics may serve as an example." By means of rather simple screening methods an enormous number of potent analgesics were developed.

[10] The development of anti-ulcer medicines, excellently depicted by Berndt et al. (1995, 1997), provides an apt illustration of product development in the traditional chemical era. Tagamet was introduced in 1977 as the first drug to relieve ulcers by blocking histamine 2 receptors in the stomach from stimulating acid production. Six years later, Zantac was approved. It was a second H_2-antagonist and it went on to become the largest-selling drug in the world. This success attracted more entrants, as Pepcid and Axid were soon released. Thus four substitutable, competing drugs using the same therapeutic mechanism, with minor, but patentable, pharmacological differences, were released. This marketing of "me-too" drugs captures the dominant pharmaceutical strategy of the twentieth century.

[11] Interestingly, this "modularity" probably heightens innovation. Unlike many products, patients experience very few "switching costs" if they change their course of therapy. And new product introductions require no systemic revamping of health care delivery, payment and reimbursement, or training of medical professionals. This ease of movement from one product to another facilitates entry of new medicines.

firms brought in physicians to advise on discovery efforts. Rather than the linear, baton-passing design sequence of the large pharma companies, biotech firms brought scientists, physicians, and even patient groups together at an early stage and throughout the development process. Among the new entrant biotech companies, many chose to specialize and focus on particular mechanisms, targets, or modes of delivery. Start-up firms were guided by scientific hypotheses to look in new domains; thus few newcomers were imitators. In the context of this classic exploration versus exploitation scenario (Holland 1975; March 1991), the division of innovative labor shifted to reward innovators rather than copycats.

In the early years of the molecular biology revolution, from the late 1970s to the early 1990s, most biotech companies were small fry and had to rely heavily on external support. As Herbert Boyer, cofounder of Genentech, remembered, venture capitalists were initially leery of funding the unproven technology of genetic engineering, and so to meet their goal of positive cash flow from day one, Genentech had to set up deals with established pharmaceutical companies, such as Eli Lilly and Kabi.[12] None of the new dedicated biotech firms had the full range of skills or resources to bring a novel medicine from the lab bench to the doctor's office. Out of necessity, they became involved in relationships with universities, hospitals, and a handful of large multinational companies. During this early period, most large pharmaceutical companies either were reluctant to incur the considerable expense of developing internal scientific competencies in genetic engineering or were skeptical about its value. But some pharma firms were drawn to the biotech start-ups as a means of outsourcing or prospecting (Henderson, Orsenigo, and Pisano 1999).

Early on, then, the different members of the new field had fairly specialized competencies. Universities and public research organizations were skilled at basic science for the early stages of drug discovery. Biotechnology start-ups, many of which were offshoots of academic laboratories, had capability in both basic research and translational science. Large multinational firms had decades of experience with chemical-based drug discovery, very deep pockets, extensive knowledge of the regulatory approval process, manufacturing capability, and vast sales and marketing resources.

This brief portrait is intended to give context for our analysis of the relational changes in the division of innovative labor. Because of the asymmetric distribution of technological skills and organizational resources, the life sciences have been marked by a heavy reliance on dense interorganizational networks (McKelvey 1996; Powell and Brantley 1996). Far-flung formal connections among diverse organizations comprise the industry's skeleton as well as its locus of innovation (Powell, Koput, and Smith-Doerr 1996). This network is not stable, however; it shifts markedly through both the addition of participants and the exit of those unable to keep pace. Relationships are also quite dynamic, as alliances are ended, partners merge, and businesses fail. We analyze patterns in the formation of ties between biotechnology firms and different partner organizations to show an important feature: the development and coherence of a stable, structurally defined, elite whose members garnered significant returns to their position while they set the pace for the entire field. We turn now to examine these interorganizational agreements as a key to industry evolution.

SHIFTING PATTERNS OF AFFILIATION

We begin with a general portrait of the trends in collaborative agreements for the years 1985–2004, portrayed in figure 15.1 with data on the number of new and continuing ties annually for all the organizations in the sample. These formal contractual affiliations are coded according to their primary activity, reflected in four general categories: science, finance, licensing, and commerce. The commerce category is the broadest, and includes clinical trials, manufacturing, sales and distribution, and multistage partnerships that involved both R&D *and* manufacturing. A science tie entails some form of a R&D partnership, and a financial relationship involves funding a DBF in exchange for equity or product options. Up until 1991, the most frequent form of collaboration was a commercial partnership.

During the 1980s, venture capital financing of biotech was still rather limited. The capital requirements of drug development rapidly outgrew the amounts that venture funds were able to raise. Even after multiple rounds of financing,

[12] Boyer comments that his fledgling start-up, Genentech, needed to "have established pharmaceutical companies fund what we are doing in order to defray the costs." Venture capitalists "were still treading water with respect to their comfort factor. So we went to KabiGen in Sweden and got them involved, because they were the world's largest supplier of human growth hormone outside of NIH." Interview with Herbert Boyer by Sally Smith Hughes, Regional Oral History Office, University of California–Berkeley, 1994, p. 79.

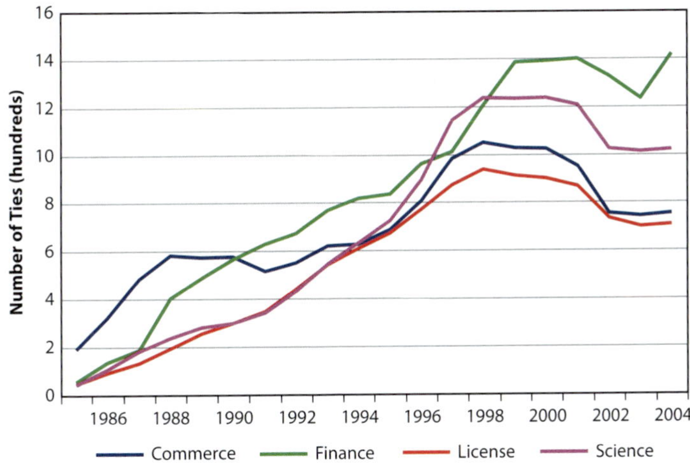

Figure 15.1 Trends in collaborative activity, 1985–2004.

the voracious DBFs needed more cash but lacked the usual collateral associated with tech startups (i.e., prototypes, balky first-generation products, beta customers, etc.). Without such tangible indicators of potential revenues, venture funds grew leery of pouring more money into biotech. This forced DBFs into selling their lead products to the large pharmaceutical corporations, who guided them through the regulatory approval process and subsequently marketed them, pocketing the lion's share of the revenues. A handful of emerging biotech firms with strong translational research abilities became highly sought after as collaborators by large pharma companies.

The organization of innovation began to change in the 1990s. We see in figure 15.1 that financial partnerships surpassed commercial ties by 1991, and by 1994, research alliances also outgrew commercial relations. As the science undergirding biotechnology deepened, the intellectual property (IP) rights associated with it became more codified and legally secure. This IP protection attracted keener interest from venture capital. The National Institutes of Health (NIH) funded research at universities and, through the Small Business Innovation Research program, biotech firms at an increasing clip, as progress was realized on a host of new therapeutic treatments. Thus, by the early 1990s, biotech firms not only had prestigious scientists and publications in top-tier journals but intellectual property in the form of patents. Our data on patterns of affiliation signal this shift.

The support and involvement of the NIH in the life sciences field cannot be overemphasized. Much of the initial work that led to the development of gene splicing was done by scientists with NIH funding. Aside from this direct support, there were two additional aspects of public funding of R&D. We will see below that private money, whether from the equity markets or pharma companies, had a "surge and retreat" character. The prospects of breakthroughs and magic bullets would attract huge interest that would subsequently subside once the reality of the hard work set in (Powell and Brantley 1996). In contrast, the steady pace of increasing federal support of biomedical research, from Nixon's War on Cancer through the Clinton years, meant that universities and research-intensive firms could count on a countervailing public sector anchor in the face of private sector volatility.

The second feature of NIH and National Science Foundation (NSF) funding was its mode of award. The allocation of grants was based on competition among applicants from universities, medical centers, nonprofit institutes, and small firms. The decision to apply for funds was investigator initiated, and projects were supported on the basis of peer review. This focus on scientific merit created a bottom-up process in which diversity, creativity, and autonomy were rewarded.[13] This mode of resource allocation proved to be highly compatible with the

[13] Of course, there has been earmarked attention to specific diseases, and some institutions, as we noted in chapter 14, have been hugely successful in obtaining federal funds. But in contrast to a top-down approach, whether in the form of corporate decision making or government policy, the investigator-driven process rewards heterogeneity.

public-private interfaces pursued by many biotech firms.

To be sure, all types of interorganizational collaboration show an upward trend throughout the 1990s. Commercial affiliations show less ascendance, however. In 1988 there were 684 commerce ties, 458 finance, 212 licensing, and 292 science. Commerce alliances rose to a high of 1,051 in 1998 but declined to 754 in 2004. Licensing escalated to a high of 937 in 1998 and fell more modestly to 709 in 2004. Finance investments doubled to 961 by 1996 and continued to expand to 1,420 in 2004. Note, however, that the nature of finance ties shifted from being largely the province of venture capital to also include investments by larger biotech firms and pharma companies in new start-ups. Science partnerships mushroomed, increasing threefold by 1996, surging higher to a peak of 1,237 in 2000 before declining somewhat to 1,022 in 2004. Clearly the trend reflected in figure 15.1 is that finance and science ties supplanted commercial affiliations as the primary locus of collaborative activity in the 1990s.

The 1990s were a period of intense activity in biotech, with new collaborations being forged and relationships ended at a fast clip. Figure 15.2 illustrates this hurly-burly pace, showing trends for new and concluded ties annually, again for the full sample, for 1988–2004. The termination of a relationship can reflect diverse outcomes, from a successful initial public offering or the conclusion of a research project to a failed clinical trial. New and concluded ties increased sharply from 1991 to 1997, then both began to decline and fall precipitously from 1999 to 2001. New tie formation subsequently stabilized at a pace comparable to that of the late 1980s.

Differing accounts can be given to understand this change in the organization of production. Some are agentic and instrumental, whereas others emphasize process and sequence. All have some credibility. Some multinational firms were willing to relinquish tight control over product development in order to gain fuller access to, and understanding of, new research frontiers. Most multinational pharmaceutical companies were pressured by the lagging performance of their own internal research labs and the thinness of their product pipelines. Consequently, pharma companies turned to either mergers with one another or new forms of collaboration with science-focused organizations, or both. Moreover, dedicated biotech firms were anxious to get out from under the thumb of giant pharmaceutical companies and partner on a more even keel. Researchers in university labs, government institutes, and biotech companies avidly pursued molecular biology and genetics as the new means to uncover first-to-the-world medicines. Venture capital support of biotech was critical to a division of innovative labor in which DBFs pursued risky R&D aimed at proving the value of university discoveries. Finally, the thirteen-year race between two rival consortia to map the human genome, concluded in 2003, brought worldwide attention to genetics research. All of these factors combined to shift attention to the science of drug discovery and its financing.

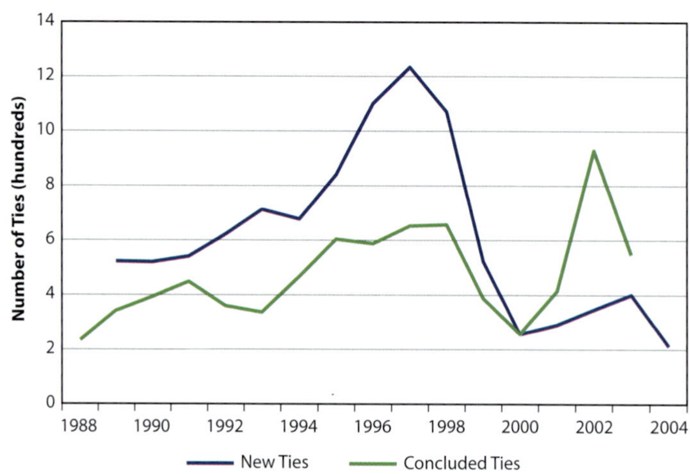

Figure 15.2 Annual counts of newly formed and concluding ties, 1988–2004, full sample.

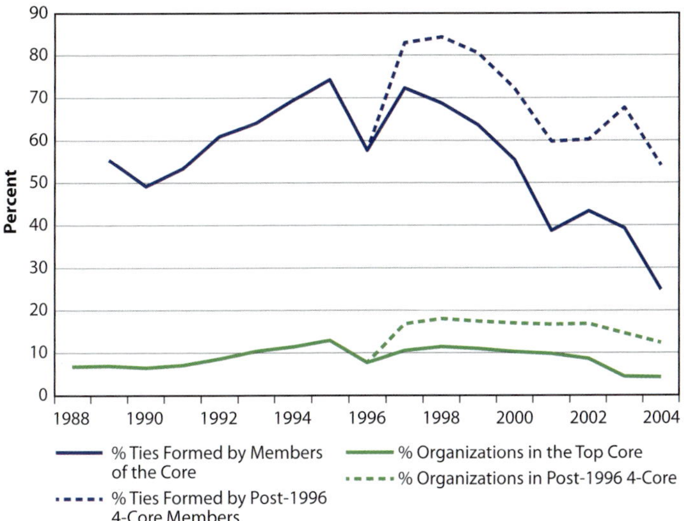

Figure 15.3 Distributional features of the elite, 1988–2004.

Our perspective on this metamorphosis builds on the idea of multiconnectivity. When organizations are linked to multiple domains with different evaluative criteria, interactions across them are more likely to prompt unanticipated changes in the distribution of power. If the registers of worth across domains are not highly correlated, then jockeying for position, rather than clear alignment, ensues. To explore this argument, we turn to examine the collaborative portfolios of the organizations that were the most connected members of the field. Our earlier work underscored the finding that even as the field expanded in terms of number of organizations and grew markedly in terms of collaborations, the most central organizations become more densely and intricately embedded (Powell et al. 2005).

Our first concern is with how much of the overall activity in the global network is driven by the actions of its most connected subcomponent of organizations. Are the general trends guided by this select group, and are they more able to shape these patterns and, possibly, stay ahead of them? Our second question looks to identify the targets of elite activities. Which organizations are enrolled and pulled into this new arena? After considering these questions, we examine both the shape of the core and the relations that flow through it.

The activities of the most connected organizations are indeed fateful. The group that constitutes the elite, as measured by the most connected k-core, never represents more than 10 percent of the organizations in the field, but it had a huge impact on overall activity. For more than a decade, from 1988 to 2000, at least 50 percent of new tie formation involved a collaboration with at least one member of the most connected core. Figure 15.3 documents the strong footprint that the elite leaves on the overall field. Note that 1988 is the first year that a 4-core forms, that is, a group of organizations with at least four collaborations with one another. The impact of this select group grows sharply, rising to more than 70 percent of all collaborations by 1995. The elite consolidates further in 1996, forming an even more cohesive 5-core. Not surprisingly, the reach of this more select group is not as extensive. (We show the continuing imprint of the organizations in the 4-core with dotted lines.) The percentage of ties involving an elite member begins to decline notably after 2001.[14]

These central organizations weave multiple strands together to form an elite. In terms of demography, this small group accounts for the bulk of new tie formation annually. Simply put, they are where the action is, as their role in creating and maintaining the network is highly disproportionate to their numbers. They are the

[14] We caution against reading too much into the sharp new tie dip in 2004, as the data source is somewhat right censored as reports of alliances sometimes do not appear until one or two years later.

arbiters of the field's direction. Moreover, this elite is very cohesive. Members are connected to each other by many indirect network paths. Consequently, membership in the elite requires ties to multiple participants who are themselves interconnected. This level of cohesion has numerous consequences. First, barriers to entry are significant as newcomers must forge and maintain connections to multiple (at least four or five, depending on the year) existing elite members. Second, these interconnected clusters are very robust. In order for any single core organization to be disconnected from the group, ties to many other elites must be broken. Put differently, once an organization enters the club it is likely to remain, unless it is consumed through acquisition by another elite member. In this respect, this group also plays a strong gatekeeping role. Third, and perhaps most consequential, multiconnected clusters offer numerous paths for information flow between organizations, speeding the spread of news as well as word of defections or malfeasance. Reputation looms large in dense clusters as all members are at most a few network steps removed from one another.[15] In a field such as biotechnology, where scientific competition is intense and product development challenges considerable, these features of an elite become particularly salient.

We next assess the direction of elite activity. With whom do the most central organizations ally? We partition the new ties for three time periods (1990, 1996, and 2002) and in two ways: (1) by type of tie partner; and (2) by type of activity. With respect to the organizations that our elite members affiliate with, we distinguish among *conserving* ties that link two current members of the core; *closure* ties between an elite member and a non-elite participant with an existing tie to another member of the core; and *expansive* ties by an elite member to an outsider. The type of activity refers to our four stages in the production process. Given the small number of universities involved, we have combined universities, nonprofits, and government as public research organizations in contrast to for-profit private science.

The choice of these three years—1990, 1996, and 2002—is motivated by several considerations. One, we wanted comparability with the years used for the analysis of regions in the previous chapter. Two, these years provide fascinating contrasts. In 1990 the industry was still in its adolescence, as many first-generation companies were either about to release major new products or had received discouraging reviews from the U.S. FDA on their initial product launches. In 1990 the commercial logic associated with pharmaceutical dominance was at its apex. By 1996, a high-water mark of excitement over biotech was reached, with active venture capital participation, many new firms being formed, and ample research funding during the Clinton era from the NIH. The tide had turned again by 2002, a down year coming on the heels of the dot com crash, the souring of interest in the public equity markets, and the broader financial retreat in 2001 in the aftermath of September 11. Thus these three years offer windows into the activities of the elite during markedly different periods. Finally, just to check that we have not focused too much on features of unique years, we ran the results for both years on either side of 1990, 1996, and 2002 and do not find sharply divergent trends.

We summarize trends across the years first, then we dig down and assess the divergent activities of members of the elite. In 1990, 234 new affiliations were launched where at least one party was a member of the elite. The types of ties—conserving, closing, or expanding—forged were roughly equal. The core group in 1990 engaged

[15] We have analyzed membership in the elite in a number of ways and discussed these maps with executives in several of the most connected firms. Technically, we find that our measure of k-cores maps perfectly onto k-components (we thank Mario Diani for that suggestion). We also find no differentiation within the elite using Mark Newman's community-finding algorithms. Conversations with members of this group, and recognition of the differential skills and locations of the participants, raise the question of whether there is an "inner circle" (to use the phrase of Useem 1984) within this already clustered group.

Consider that some organizations, such as VCs, do only certain "specialist" tasks, whereas others, such as DBFs and increasingly elite universities, can be involved in multiple types of alliances. An established DBF can financially support a smaller firm, engage in a research partnership with it, and distribute a jointly developed new medicine. Universities now do much more than license discoveries. They may jointly do research with a firm, have an equity stake in a company, and/or run a clinical trial. Such multiple affiliations, especially with different partners, afford greater access and shared fate. To be sure, these affiliations may not be as consequential as venture capital financial backing and the accompanying executive and strategic advice. But we have an analytical challenge here with different partners playing different roles.

In addition, there are important locational differences among the elite, which we explore below, following the insights garnered in chapter 14. The upshot of these factors is that some members of the "core" know one another better. And some members have a much broader scan of their environment. When we use network distance to partition the elite, we do find some internal differentiation. Several organizations, e.g., Biogen, Genentech, the NIH, and Novartis, are closer on average to all other members of the core, whereas others, e.g., smaller VCs, pharmas without connections to the three geographic centers, and universities, are on average further away.

in partnerships with other central members that consolidated their positions of influence, ushered in those who had a previous tie to another elite member, and reached out to prospect for newcomers.

The level of new collaborative activity snowballs through the 1990s. In 1996 there were 597 new alliances involving at least one member of the elite. The core group becomes more interconnected as the rate of growth for ties that conserve elite cohesion develops threefold. Closure ties, which draw newcomers closer, grow by two and half times and expanding ties that reach out to new prospects double. The pace of activity withers in the new century, however, with the pace of growth shrinking to only 136 new collaborations in 2002. Closure ties show the sharpest decline, with an eightfold drop. In the difficult climate of the early 2000s, members of the most connected cluster divided their relational efforts almost equally between conserving connections to other members of the elite and alliances that allow them to prospect with organizations that previously lacked elite sponsorship.

The content of new elite ties also changes, as do the relational networks of the different types of elite organizations. Science and licensing connections are the bedrock of the biotechnology field and remain constant across the years as a proportion of new elite ties. In contrast, the role of finance grows over time. In 1990 finance ties accounted for 29.5 percent (69/234) of new connections involving the elite. By 1996 that number climbed to 36.5 percent (218/597), a statistically significant expansion ($z = 1.917$, $p < .05$ one-tailed test of proportions). The relative growth in finance ties continued even through 2002, where fully 50 percent (68/136) of new ties involving the elite were investments. This change too represents a significant increase from 1996 ($z = 3.939$, $p < .0001$ one-tailed test of proportions).

As finance ties grew, the role of commercial connections shrank. In 1990, 27.1 percent (64/236) of new ties involved commercialization efforts. By 1996 that percentage had shrunk to 20.1 percent (120/597), a statistically significant decline ($z = 2.264$, $p < .05$ one-tailed test of proportions). In 2002 commerce ties declined further with just 10.3 percent of new elite ties focusing on commerce ($z = 2.670$, $p < .01$ one-tailed test of proportions). In short, as the elite's role as a motor of network growth surged, leveled off, and faded across the period we observed, both the structural (expansion, closure, conservation) and the relational (science, commerce, licensing, finance) features that characterized its collective efforts changed.

We now examine whether these changes were based on shifts in the activities of particular types of elite organizations. We do so by focusing on the combinations of activities and partners that dominate relationships that expand to newcomers, induct new elites (closure), and conserve the power of incumbents. Figure 15.4

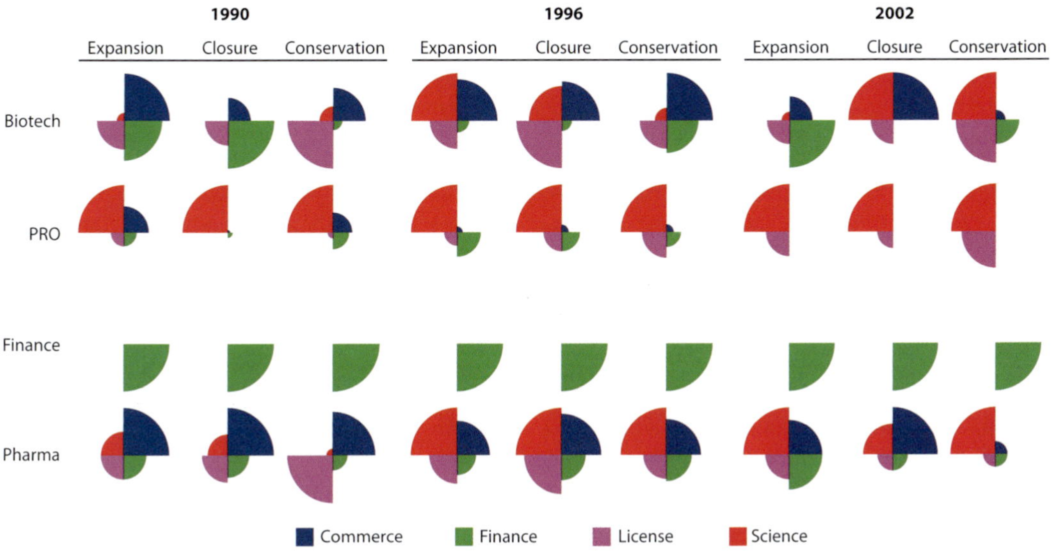

Figure 15.4 New elite ties, 1990, 1996, 2002.

illustrates activity type by partner combinations across the structural locations of elite partners over the three time periods. In each panel of figure 15.4, rows represent types of organizations and columns reflect the three structural types of ties. The activities that make up each category are captured by the "roses" where each colored "petal" depicts a different type of relationship. The relative size of a petal reflects the number of ties of that type. In 1990, for example, the large blue petal on the first rose (new expansion ties from elite biotechnology companies) represents seven new connections, while the smaller magenta petal opposite it reflects four licensing ties.

When elites acted as catalysts for expansion, the primary activities that connected newcomers and incumbents were financial (37/87 = 42%) and commercial (20/87 = 23%). Green and blue dominate all but PRO activity in the first column of figure 15.4. These moves reflect a year that was the inflection point between a commercially driven era dominated by pharmaceutical firms and a more VC-fueled and science-powered period in subsequent years. Indeed, elite VC firms are the primary motor of expansion. The new financial connections forged by VCs to non-elite biotech firms account for more than 26 percent (23/87) of all expansive ties in 1990.

Pharmaceutical firms were important catalysts, too, as they pursued their efforts to fill out their product pipelines. Their new commercial connections with non-elite biotechs accounted for nearly 15 percent (13/87) of expansive relationships. Pharmaceutical firms forming commercial alliances also play important roles as both gatekeepers—17.7 percent (11/62) of closure ties represented commercial affiliations of elite pharmaceuticals with DBFs—and arbiters—17.6 percent (15/85) of conserving ties were new commercial alliances connecting elite pharmaceutical firms to elite biotech companies. Even though commercial new ties were paramount for pharma, licensing from established biotechs was also consequential. The overall story reflected in the 1990 rose plots captures the commercial power of elite pharmaceuticals and the emerging catalytic role of elite VCs. Meanwhile, public sector organizations function as arbiters, and in so doing they helped shift the overall field toward a science and finance logic. Nearly a third (30.6 percent) of new connections that pulled non-elite biotechs into the orbit of the elite were science partnerships forged with elite government institutes and universities. These are depicted by the large red petals for PRO expansion and closure ties. Public sector science ties were 14 percent (12/85) of new conserving ties, trailing only the commercial relationships of pharmaceutical firms.

The bountiful year of 1996 sees three important changes. Note how much the biotech and pharma roses fill out. And note also the changes in the color of the petals. Most notably, the change in relational logics presaged in figure 15.1 is now fully apparent in the new connections forged by elite members. Finance (green) and science (red) connections dominate all three panels. But a closer look at the types of organizations pursuing those ties tells a more complex story. First, consider expansive ties. Note that elite VCs do an even greater share of prospecting through financial investments (30.4 percent, or 59/194). New science ties, too, are an important source of elite expansion. Biotech companies, PROs, and pharma now pursue them in about equal measure. In 1990 biotechnology firms formed new science ties at a relatively slow pace. Just 9.1 percent (4/44) of new ties involving elite biotechs in this period were science connections. By 1996 a significant shift occurs as the red petals in the biotech row account for 23.5 percent of new ties ($z = 2.072$, $p < .05$ one-tailed test of proportions). Although the overall proportion of new science ties stayed stable from 1990 to 1996, the percentage of new science ties in the portfolio of elite biotechs grew. Elite pharmaceutical companies also saw a rise in their relative proportion of science connections. In 1990, 13.7 percent (13/95) of new ties forged by elite pharmas were science oriented. By 1996 that number escalated to 34.2 percent (82/240, $z = 2.430$, $p < .01$ one-tailed test of proportions). Clearly elite pharmas were learning to engage in new types of relationships with DBFs.

In a time of fast growth, prospecting happens in many veins. The larger story in closure and conserving ties, however, has to do with private sector science ties surpassing public sector R&D connections. In 1996 both biotech and pharma elites use their science ties to draw promising outsiders closer and to deepen core interconnections. In the context of the shift toward finance and science logics of attachment, private sector research support increased, and there was an impressive degree of congruence in the new connections forged by both biotechs and pharmaceuticals. By the mid-1990s, the biotech model of organizing that was so disruptive to early pharmaceutical giants was being adopted with gusto by the pharmaceutical companies that remained in the game.

Finally, in the wake of the terrorist attacks on September 11, a decline in federal funding, and dramatic market uncertainty, 2002 marked a period of obvious retrenchment. Relatively few new ties are forged by members of the elite. Connections that were made remain focused on science and finance, but the role of public sector and pharmaceutical elites was very small. Private sector science anchored by elite biotechs formed the bulk of elite conservation, while VC investments were the most prominent new connections across expansive, closure, and conserving ties.

The pattern of affiliations across the time periods clearly shows the central role of the most connected organizations in driving the shifting locus of innovation. Venture capital and PROs laid the groundwork for the decline of the commerce model, and select biotechs and pharmas learned to collaborate in new and varied ways. Which organizations were involved and where were they located? To answer these questions and further examine elite influence, we turn our attention to membership in the core and the relational profiles of its most connected organizations.

THE INTERNAL DYNAMICS OF THE CORE

We turn now to network "X-rays" of the elite. We take four time periods—1984, 1990, 1996, and 2002—and drill down, extracting the most highly interconnected k-component from the global network. We start with the first year in which a giant component formed. This was 1984, and the map of this newly formed group is presented in figure 15.5. This is the first time we have presented network data for this early period. Recall that our network ties are left censored; hence any organizations that exited the network before 1988 and any ties from this period that were terminated before then are not captured here.[16] But we think this figure is useful in a number of respects. It provides a glimpse into the formation of an elite. A little more than a decade after the landmark papers were published in 1973, a structure emerged that linked fledgling biotech companies, government institutes, and global corporations. Among the most active members of this group of 106 organizations were two government institutes—the NIH (#20) and its branch, the National Cancer Institute (NCI, #28), both of which were involved in funding research at several early biotech firms. Among the early entrant biotechs, Immunex (#29, Seattle), Centocor (#1, Philadelphia), Biogen (#10, Boston), Repligen (#2, Boston), and Genentech (#34, Bay Area) have the most alliances, nearly all of which are with pharmaceutical companies, save for the PRO linkages that Centocor has developed. Amgen (#13, Los Angeles) is on the far right, with its unusual ties to Texaco (#15) and Japanese brewer Kirin (#14). On the left side, Chiron (#24, Bay Area) has linkages with Merck (#25) and Novo Nordisk (#26) on some of its early vaccine research.The most connected multinational at this time is the Swiss firm Hoffman La Roche (#33).[17]

This image of the field at its earliest stage of cohesion captures the exploratory nature of the initial alliances. Both Amgen and Genentech are partnering with large corporations (Kirin, Texaco and Kodak, Lilly, Boehringer Ingelheim, respectively) that are intrigued by this new science. Early entrant PROs—Massachusetts General Hospital, Sloan Kettering Hospital, Wistar, Dana Farber Cancer Center, Duke, NYU, MIT—have allied with DBF Centocor, which you will recall from chapter 13 is a prospector that scoured hospitals and universities across the mid-Atlantic and New England for promising licenses and projects. The NIH has gotten involved with several early firms. And out West, Immunex has developed R&D partnerships with several European multinationals. The majority of these relations are high risk and very uncertain efforts to search for new opportunities.[18] These relationships are overwhelmingly dyadic ties, hence the

[16] We have debated the utility of this figure at some length. We verified it with annual reports from companies that had gone public by 1984. The information is accurate for these organizations; moreover, very few relationships were concluded by 1988. But we know that at least two important early companies—Hybritech and DNAX—were acquired before 1988 and are thus missing.

[17] In this early main component, 22.6 percent of the organizations are from the Boston, San Francisco, or San Diego regions. And 23.6 percent of the 254 organizations in the full sample are from one of these regions; thus the proportion in the core is not significantly different than the percentage in the full network ($z = -0.200$, $p = .8411$). This confirms our argument from the previous chapter that regional advantage was not baked into the field at the outset but was emergent.

[18] Indeed, it is striking how diffuse the participants were in this early period of "gene dreams." Nearly 10 percent of the nodes are biomedical supply and instrumentation companies. There is a solid foreign presence—BASF, Knoll AG, Hoechst, Boehringer Ingelheim from Germany, and Kirin, Kabi, and Green Cross from Japan. Texaco, Kodak, and Du Pont tried to get in on the new game as well. None of the supply companies and few of the non-pharma or chemical companies managed to remain highly connected as the field evolved.

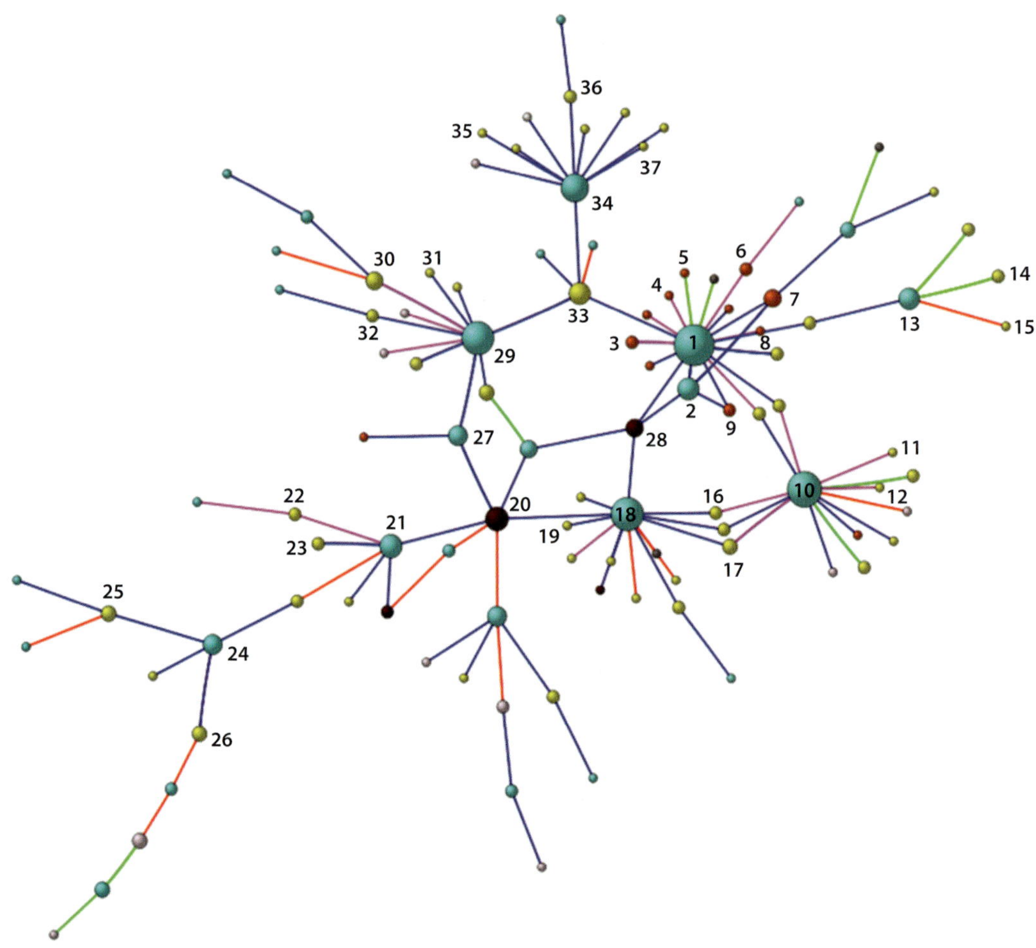

Activity	Tie Color	# Ties	%
Commerce		87	64.9
Finance		13	9.7
Licensing		18	13.4
Science		16	11.9
Total		**134**	

Organization	Node Color	# Nodes	%
DBF		30	28.3
Finance		3	2.8
Government		4	3.8
Pharmaceutical		47	44.3
PRO		12	11.3
Biomedical		10	9.4
Total		**106**	

Influential Members

1. Centocor
2. Repligen
3. Massachusetts General Hospital
4. Memorial Sloan Kettering
5. Wistar Institute
6. Dana Farber Cancer Center
7. MIT
8. New York University
9. Duke University
10. Biogen
11. BASF
12. Knoll AG
13. Amgen
14. Kirin Brewery
15. Texaco
16. Green Cross
17. Kabi AB
18. Genex
19. Bristol Myers Squibb
20. NIH
21. Oscient
22. Ciba-Geigy
23. Sandoz
24. Chiron
25. Merck
26. Novo Nordisk
27. Genzyme
28. NCI
29. Immunex
30. Syntex
31. Hoechst
32. Marion Merrill Dow
33. Hoffman La Roche
34. Genentech
35. Eastman Kodak
36. Eli Lilly
37. Boehringer Ingelheim

Figure 15.5 Main component with an embedded 2-core in 1984, all ties.

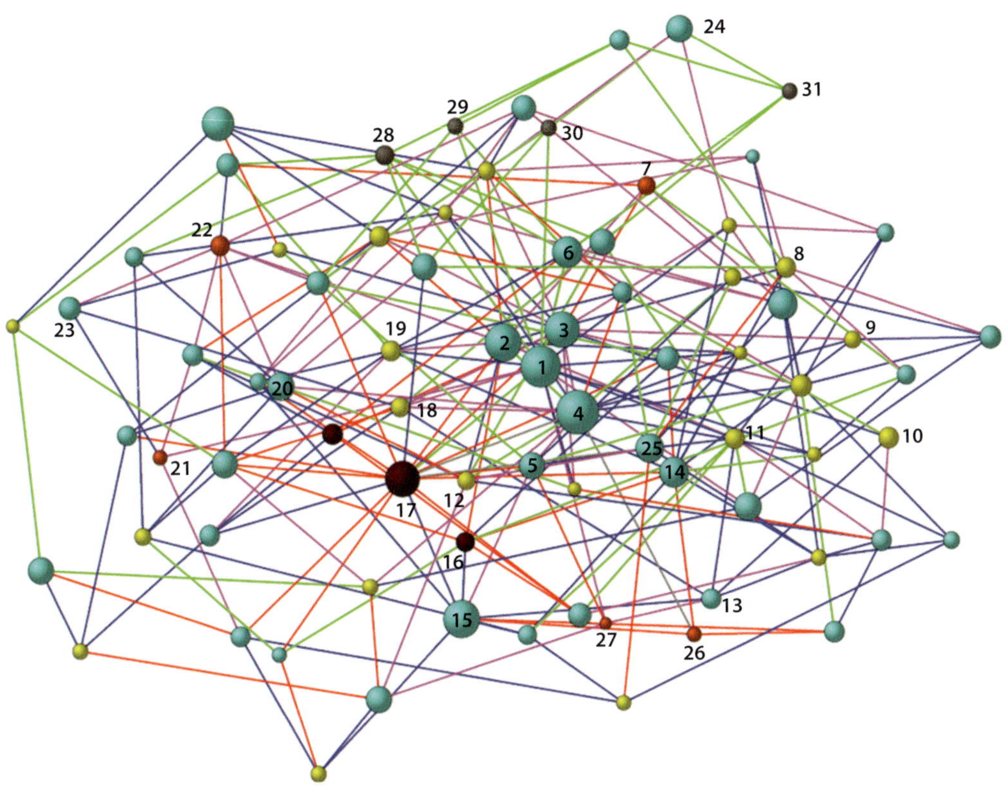

Activity	Tie Color	# Ties	%
Commerce	purple line	93	37.7
Finance	green line	50	20.2
Licensing	pink line	57	23.1
Science	red line	44	17.8
Other	gray line	3	1.2
Total		247	

Organization	Node Color	# Nodes	%
DBF	teal	43	54.4
Finance	gray	4	5.1
Government	dark red	3	3.8
Pharmaceutical	yellow	24	30.4
PRO	orange	5	6.3
Total		79	

Influential Members

1. Centocor
2. Scios
3. Biogen
4. Genentech
5. Genetics Institute
6. Repligen
7. Harvard University
8. Merck
9. Ciba-Geigy
10. Hoffmann-La Roche
11. Johnson & Johnson
12. Pfizer
13. Amgen
14. Chiron
15. Cetus
16. NCI
17. NIH
18. SmithKline Beecham
19. DuPont
20. Genzyme
21. Stanford University
22. MIT
23. Immunex
24. IDEC
25. Celltech
26. University of California
27. Memorial Sloan Kettering
28. Biotech Investments
29. Hambrecht & Quist
30. Venrock
31. Abingworth

Figure 15.6 The elite (4-core) in 1990, new and continuing ties.

network structure stretches and resembles weak connections among small clusters.

Let us move ahead to 1990, where we have complete affiliation data for all of the DBFs and no concerns about left-censoring. A very cohesive cluster of 79 organizations has been forged, all of which have four or more ties to one another. Figure 15.6 shows this tightly linked 4-core. The respective size of the circles reflects network degree, calculated as the number of affiliations that an organization has in the full network.[19] The picture is very different from that of 1984—much more clustered and tight, and many of the early participants have dropped out. This structurally cohesive group consists of first-generation biotech firms (the larger cyan circles), including Amgen (#13), Biogen (#3), Centocor (#1), Cetus (#15), Chiron (#14), Genentech (#4), Genzyme (#20), and Immunex (#23) (all in the United States). There are a few foreign DBFs, such as Celltech (#25, England) and AGEN Biomedicine (Australia). There is a significant presence of pharmaceutical corporations (yellow circles); the ones from the United States include Johnson & Johnson (#11), Merck (#8), Pfizer (#12), and Abbott, and from Europe, Hoffman La Roche (#10), Boehringer Ingelheim, Ciba-Geigy, SmithKline Beecham (#18), and Hoechst. A few chemical companies are in this inner circle, including Kodak, DuPont (#19), Takeda, and Mitsubishi. Moving ahead in time, the chemical companies drop out of the core as they are less able to exploit the tools of genetic engineering. Looking back, a very striking feature of this 1990 core is the subsequent pattern of intermarriage: many of the pharma companies merge or acquire one another and a number of the biotech firms are absorbed by the pharma giants.[20]

There are four venture firms (gray circles) on the north edge of this 1990 core—Hambrecht & Quist (#29) from the Bay Area, Venrock (#30) from New York, and Abingworth (#31) and Biotech Investments (#28) from the United Kingdom. Venture capital had not yet jumped firmly on the biotech bandwagon, and these were the early movers in terms of having multiple investments in DBFs. The largest blue nodes in the center are the early biotech firms. The brown circles are branches of the NIH, and the smaller orange circles represent PROs. Here we see several new PRO entrants into the field, including Stanford (#21), Harvard (#7), and the University of California–San Francisco (#26), along with MIT and Memorial Sloan Kettering Hospital (#27, New York) from the 1984 figure.

These organizations are internally connected through 247 partnerships, 93 of which are commercial relationships. The remaining affiliations are divided almost equally among finance, licensing, and science ties. The preponderance of blue lines reflects the connections between pharma and biotech, where new firms licensed their lead molecules to the established companies. Note that almost all the links between cyan and yellow circles are either blue or green, reflecting either this co-production model or equity investments. The red lines (research) extend almost exclusively from the NIH or PROs. This network image captures the shift we saw in the rose plots in figure 15.4, where the conserving and expanding ties of DBFs and pharma were predominantly blue. Clearly the dominant coalition in the field in 1990 pursued a commercial logic, reflecting the asymmetric power of pharma over fledgling biotechs.[21]

Moving ahead six years to 1996, we see in figure 15.7 a sharp change in the most central group. The members of the core are now more connected with one another, with five or more ties among them. Although this central group has become more structurally cohesive, it has also burgeoned in size to 140 organizations with 542 affiliations. This is a notable shift—a more tightly linked 5-core elite that has more members, suggesting mobility and openness, too. The most common relationship is financial, and venture capital firms have become a major presence, with 23 VCs now in the core and nearly 39 percent of the ties. The left side of the figure is entirely colored by green linkages, connecting biotech and VC firms. The most connected and central VC is Kleiner, Perkins, Caufield, and Byers (#26), an early funder of both Genentech and Hybritech. Clearly venture capital firms have become important participants.

Finance is not the only story here, however. Research partnerships have also moved ahead of commercial ties in frequency. Moreover, red lines now criss-cross with green, magenta, and blue, illustrating that the most central organizations are engaged in several different types of activity. Here we see the indication that multiple

[19] Recall that the database is organized as a two-mode network, with biotech firms and their partners as the focus. We do not collect data on linkages among the partners. Consequently, the largest nodes are necessarily more likely to be biotech companies.

[20] The Swiss firms Ciba-Geigy and Sandoz merged in 1996 to form Novartis. The German firm Hoechst merged with French multinational Rhone Poulenc in 1998 to create Aventis, which merged with Sanofi in 2004. The British multinational Glaxo Wellcome (formed in 1995 when Glaxo acquired Wellcome, a venerable British firm and trust) merged with the Philadelphia-based company Smithkline Beecham (which was formed in 1989 through merger with the British company Beechman Group plc) in 2000, creating the then largest drug company in the world.

[21] Again, there is no evidence of a settling on just three regions. New York, Philadelphia, and Seattle-based companies and PROs are quite active.

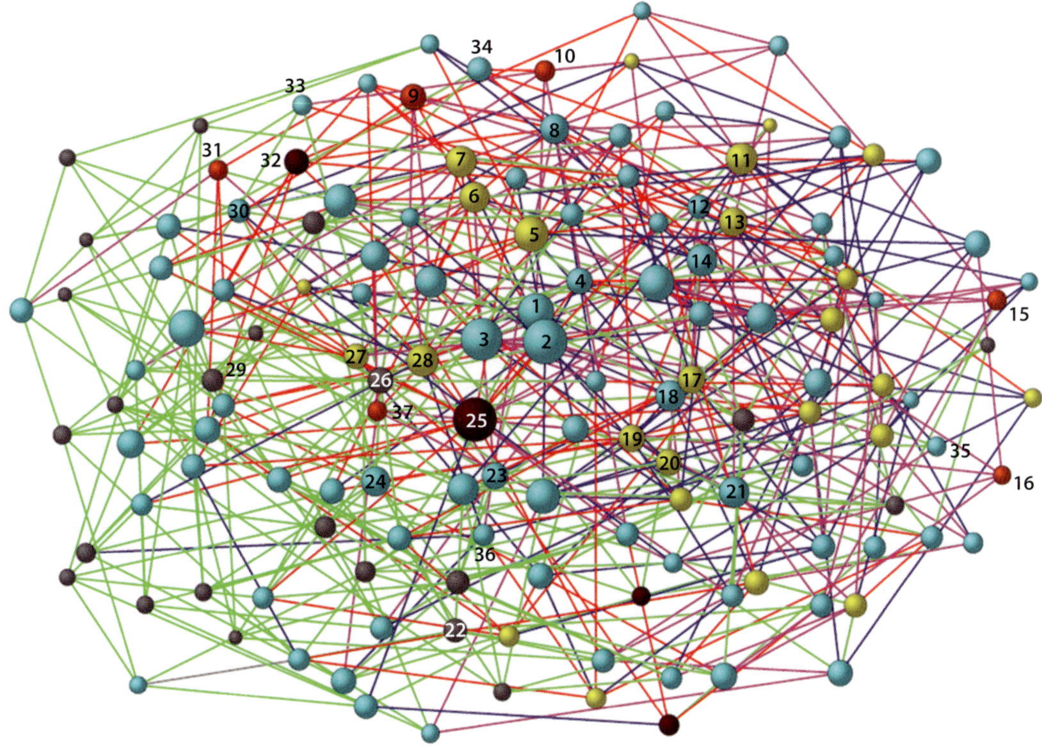

Activity	Tie Color	# Ties	%
Commerce		111	20.5
Finance		211	38.9
Licensing		105	19.4
Science		114	21.0
Other		1	0.1
Total		**542**	

Organization	Node Color	# Nodes	%
DBF		83	59.3
Finance		23	16.4
Government		4	2.9
Pharmaceutical		24	17.1
PRO		6	4.3
Total		**140**	

Influential Members

1. Centocor
2. Chiron
3. Genentech
4. Ligand
5. Boehringer Ingelheim
6. SmithKline Beecham
7. Hoffman La Roche
8. Genzyme
9. University of California
10. Stanford University
11. Merck
12. Biogen
13. Johnson & Johnson
14. IDEC
15. Harvard University
16. MIT
17. Eli Lilly
18. Genetics Institute
19. Schering-Plough
20. Ciba-Geigy
21. Incyte
22. Hambrecht & Quist
23. Repligen
24. Athena Neurosciences
25. NIH
26. Kleiner, Perkins, Caufield & Byers
27. Glaxo
28. Pharmacia & Upjohn
29. New Enterprise Associates
30. Gilead Sciences
31. Memorial Sloan Kettering
32. NCI
33. Neurocrine
34. Vical
35. Corvas
36. Gensia
37. Johns Hopkins University

Figure 15.7 The elite (5-core) in 1996, new and continuing ties.

affiliations involving different activities are a catalyst. Both the demography and structure of this elite group has changed, too, as the NIH is more central and VC participation has increased eightfold. The number of pharma companies has stayed constant, while the number of DBFs has nearly doubled.

Among the new DBFs are a healthy crop of nine San Diego firms, including Corvas (#35), Gensia (#36), Ligand (#4), Neurocrine (#33), and Vical (#34), along with an influx of Boston and Bay Area companies, among them Alkermes, Athena Neurosciences, Geron, Gilead Sciences (#30), Incyte, Millennium, and Vertex. Familiar names from the VC world also join—New Enterprise Associates (#29), Morganthaler, Oak Investment, Advent Group, Oxford Partners, and Avalon Ventures are now heavily invested in biotech. Johns Hopkins University (#37) enters the inner circle of PROs. The chemical companies depart, replaced by more large pharma firms such as Glaxo (#27), Eli Lilly (#17), American Home Products, Rhone-Poulenc, and Pharmacia and Upjohn (#28).

The k-core decomposition documents an important change in the character of the elite, both in terms of the diversity of organizations and the types of activities they engage in. Even as the field expanded, growing in both number of members and types of partnerships, with a healthy increase in both VC and U.S. government funding, the most central organizations become more densely linked. The older model of large multinationals turning to small firms as R&D boutiques was a restrictive one, especially for DBFs but also in terms of its generative potential. Commercialization agreements are downstream activities. One might consider them the last dance in the product life cycle. In contrast, financing is an upstream activity, which funds R&D, licensing, and subsequent commercialization. Consequently, the shift from commercial dominance to financial and scientific ties enrolled many more participants engaged in multiple efforts of exploration and information transfer. This growth does not, however, appear to represent an influx of challengers. Instead, it is the result of a well-connected and open elite, comprised of select global multinationals, first-generation biotech companies, government agencies, and a handful of research universities that are allying with promising second-generation DBFs. The door is certainly ajar, but admission remains selective.

These central organizations pull in new participants through sponsored mobility. The effect of this entry into the core and on the larger field is a change in the mode of collaboration. This feedback effect is one form of endogenous institutional change. With the addition of more participants, a wider array of organizational forms is entwined in the center, and the logic of attachment shifts. Diversely anchored, multiconnected networks are much less likely to unravel than networks that are reliant on a few organizations, and the organizing practices of multiconnected networks are more likely to become institutionalized because they diffuse through multiple channels.

Fast forward to 2002, presented in figure 15.8. Here we see how thorough the transformation from 1990 is. The visual image alone tells a great deal. The predominant colors of the lines that represent alliances are green and red. Blue lines are much less prevalent (only 16.6 percent). The NIH (#23) is at the center of the image, and red linkages dominate the middle of the figure. In terms of number of affiliations, finance and science are roughly equal, accounting for nearly 60 percent of the alliances. Licensing deals have also passed commercial ties in frequency. More PROs are present, with the addition of the Salk Institute from San Diego (#30). There is now a notable regional concentration as 39 percent of the core organizations are from Boston, San Diego, and San Francisco, whereas only 23 percent of the organizations in the full sample come from these locales. Much of that infusion comes from the new genomics companies, Affymetrix (#26), Arqule (#28), and Human Genome Sciences (#29). That this regional proportion in the three clusters is significantly higher than the full population ($z = 4.733$, $p < .001$, one-tailed test of proportions) is particularly striking when you consider that at the outset of 2002, no pharma companies (who make up 18 percent of the core) were located in these three areas. The regional concentrations consist entirely of DBFs, PROs, and VCs.

In terms of activities, there are now 184 organizations in this 5-core, connected by 791 ties. This increasing cohesion occurred even as the overall field experienced gyrations in the formation of ties. Members of the elite maintained their existing ties and continued to add conserving connections. The composition of the elite shifted from 1990 to 2002, as the pharmaceutical presence declined from 30 to 18 percent, and venture capital increased from 5 to 16 percent.[22] But much more consequential than the numbers are the portfolio of activities. Look at the small number of yellow nodes at the center of the figure. Here are a small handful of multinational pharmaceutical companies—Eli Lilly (#10), Bristol Meyers Squibb (#21), Novartis (#15), and Hoffman La Roche (#4) —deeply involved in research collaborations. The key takeaway from this figure is that the era of specialization

[22] Mergers continued apace in the pharmaceutical world, as consolidation continues with many second-tier companies, who were active back in 1984, were gobbled up by the giant firms.

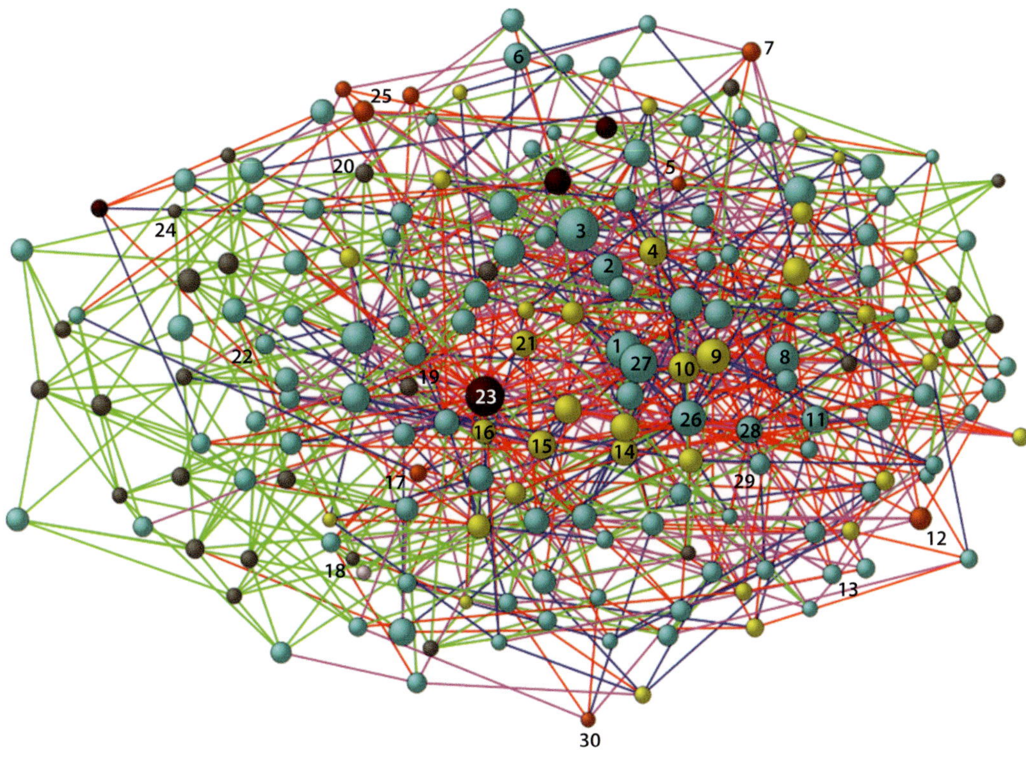

Activity	Tie Color	# Ties	%
Commerce		131	16.6
Finance		237	29.9
Licensing		188	23.8
Science		231	29.2
Other		4	0.5
Total		**791**	

Organization	Node Color	# Nodes	%
DBF		112	60.9
Finance		26	14.1
Government		4	2.2
Pharmaceutical		33	17.9
PRO		8	4.3
Biomedical		1	0.5
Total		**184**	

Influential Members

1. Genentech
2. Genzyme
3. Chiron
4. Hoffmann-La Roche
5. Stanford University
6. Amgen
7. MIT
8. IDEC
9. Schering-Plough
10. Eli Lilly
11. Biogen
12. University of California
13. Immunex
14. SmithKline Beecham
15. Novartis
16. Johnson & Johnson
17. Massachusetts General Hospital
18. Kleiner, Perkins, Caufield & Byers
19. Biotechnology Venture Fund
20. Hambrecht & Quist
21. Bristol Myers Squibb
22. Gilead Sciences
23. NIH
24. Alta Partners
25. Harvard University
26. Affymetrix
27. Incyte
28. Arqule
29. Human Genome Sciences
30. Salk Institute

Figure 15.8 The elite (5-core) in 2002, new and continuing ties.

has ended, and the commercial firms, government institutes, and PROs that are most central are now engaged in multiple lines of activity.

Pharmaceutical companies recognized that they had to learn skills other than product development in order to compete with both university scientists and venture capitalists for access to cutting-edge ideas. Established biotech firms began to act like older siblings to younger, smaller biotech firms, some of which were spin-offs from their own companies. Once the new model of affiliation took hold and the older specialist approach declined, the key participants became generalists, adopting a logic we term *multivocal*. Neither money, market power, nor the sheer force of science dominated the production process. Rather, organizations with diverse portfolios of well-connected collaborators became the most cohesive participants in the field. This change in the structure of the network and the shift from a specialized form of collaboration to one on a more equal footing on a broader array of tasks triggered a transformation in the way in which medicines were developed and produced. The dynamics driving this change were the increasing diversity of organizational forms and an elite of densely connected participants that was open to new entrants and able to move across a range of activities.

What do we learn from this exercise of k-core decomposition with respect to questions of openness versus closure? The broad pattern that combines network growth and preferential attachment by central incumbents to promising newcomers generates a network core comprised of a relatively small percentage of organizations. In addition to being key participants, as defined by network centrality, the core is also characterized by its cohesiveness, a robust pattern of independent pathways that connect each member of this "elite" to the others (White and Harary 2001). Whereas the bulk of organizational participants can be separated from the overall network by the simple expedient of severing one or two ties, organizations at the field's core were connected to each other by either four (in 1990) or five (1996 and 2002) node-independent pathways.[23] Put differently, the elite that developed as this field grew was both highly robust (separating an organization from the group requires that at least five ties be broken or five connecting nodes removed) and difficult to enter (a challenge that requires newcomers to forge multiple ties to many well-connected insiders).

The level of cohesion that defines this structural elite increased with time: in 1990, 79 organizations represent a 4-core whose coherence depends on four node-independent pathways connecting its members. In 1996, 140 organizations constituted a 5-core, and that group grew to 184 by 2002. The share of this elite remains relatively constant, however, including less than 10 percent of the organizations in the overall network. Whereas the size of the elite remains comparable in percentage terms, the bar for entry was raised as the participants at the center had to become more adept at engaging in multiple activities with varied partners.

In some respects, this pattern of elite formation is endemic to a model of growth that combines degree-biased (hub-creating) tie formation with an assortative mixing (hub-connecting) process. In situations where individual nodes (be they organizations or people) can only accommodate a finite number of partners, this process seems to contain a built-in bias to turn inward, restricting access and stagnating. No serious student of networks or politics would be surprised at this general phenomenon of eventual restriction and calcification. The interesting question is, what has kept this field relatively open?

Purely from the perspective of network dynamics, the picture suggested by the k-core decomposition is that the most central organizations not only prospected for new resources, information, and partners; they also embarked on new activities. No single skill or activity defined the elite; instead mobility was multivalent. The combination of multiple ties and different types of activities added restlessness to the system, ensuring that there was turnover in the composition of the elite. The transformation from 1990 to 1996 is particularly telling here, as older chemical firms exited and younger biotechs and PROs moved in. At the same time, pharmaceutical companies began en masse to acquire one another. Organizations unable to engage in both multiple ties and diverse activities dropped out of the most connected core. This adaptability persisted, even in the face of a decline in the industry's fortunes in the early years of the twenty-first century as the financial picture turned gray and the scientific prospects more complex.

THE ROBUSTNESS OF THE ELITE?

The first decade of the twenty-first century was an unusual period for the life sciences—a time of scientific progress but also financial turmoil and organizational disruption. In some respects, biotechnology lost its ability to capture the public imagination, as enthusiasm jumped to media companies like Google, Facebook, LinkedIn, and Twitter, which appealed to anyone with a cell phone or Internet connection. But even underneath the surface transformation in public

[23] Two indirect paths between nodes *i* and *j* are *node-independent* if they share no intermediate nodes in common.

attention, there were deeper currents of change. We briefly review these developments with two aims in mind: (1) How robust was elite membership in the face of such pronounced shifts in the landscape? (2) Does the catalytic recombination of science and commerce persist in generating new organizational models?

The scientific and commercial developments of the last decade cannot be readily divorced from one another, but the interplay is sufficiently intricate that it best serves the exposition to pull them apart initially. The financial turmoil is, of course, better known but its consequences merit discussion. Access to capital became considerably more difficult for DBFs as a confluence of factors came together. The financial turmoil after September 11 and again after the 2008 banking meltdown soured the public markets. Investor attention, such that it was, turned to clean tech and social media. There was intense competition from other sectors for a smaller pool of money, and the number of new entrant biotech firms consequently declined.

Research funding also slumped, and competition increased there, too. Pressure to rein in health care costs changed the regulatory ground, as new medicines needed to demonstrate improvements in health outcomes beyond existing therapies. To many DBFs and pharma companies, the finish line was suddenly moved farther back. Other rules of the game were altered as well. Venture funding that had operated as milestone payments morphed into "drip funding" as "mere" scientific progress was no longer sufficient. The combination of a lapse in investor enthusiasm and stagnation and decline in research funding meant a sharp loss in negotiating leverage for DBFs in their dealings with Big Pharma.

As recognition became pervasive that biotech drug development was expensive, time-consuming, and risky, the excitement of the early years faded. Organizational consolidation, retrenchment, and failure became the order of the decade. Large pharma companies continued to absorb one another, but in so doing, they pruned redundant affiliations and in some cases reduced their reliance on alliances altogether.[24] Some of the largest pharmas acquired their biotech partners, sometimes through hostile takeovers, which were previously thought to be unworkable for science-intensive companies where the human capital is highly mobile.[25] As many of the first-generation stalwarts, including Chiron, Genentech, and Genzyme, disappeared, there was both a shrinkage in the pool of available partners and serious questioning as to whether new companies like Genentech or Amgen would ever again be created (Janeway forthcoming).

Although financial and regulatory realities were paramount, advances continued on the science frontier. To be sure, there was recognition that the lowest-hanging fruit had been picked and complex questions remained. The gains from the mountains of information obtained through the mapping of the Human Genome Project proved to be challenging to realize. But the break with chemical-based drug discovery approach was clear, and movement toward a systems biology where knowledge would be complementary and applicable across multiple diseases and biological processes was well under way.

How did the organizations at the core of the field react to these challenges and opportunities? We saw earlier that the center was responsive to novelty in absorbing San Diego–based companies in 1996 and many of the new genomics companies in 2002. But entry does not guarantee that the center will hold; indeed, it could represent the first steps toward either replacement or dissolution. And clearly the increased pace and scale of the mergers of the last decade were signs of the elite turning on itself. But the adoption of a science logic over a commerce logic, which was captured so clearly in the shifting

[24] Consider how many fewer collaborations resulted from the string of consolidations that led to today's giant company, Pfizer. The Swedish company Pharmacia merged with Upjohn in 1995, and the new entity acquired Searle and a portion of Monsanto in 2000. In the same year, Pfizer acquired Warner Lambert, which had previously bought the San Diego biotech company Agouron in 1999. Pfizer then merged with Pharmacia in 2003. In 2008 Pfizer acquired Wyeth, another large company, and one with deep roots in biotech from its acquisitions in the 1990s of early biotech companies, Genetics Institute and Elan. The "new" Pfizer has now absorbed three major corporations, their subsidiaries, and all their affiliations in less than a decade. Critics have argued that the work of integrating Pharmacia and Warner Lambert stalled Pfizer's research efforts for years (Johnson 2009). The "new" Pfizer has two separate R&D organizations, one for small molecules and one for large, and nine distinct business units.

[25] Roche took over its partner, Genentech, in 2009 after months of opposition from Genentech employees and widespread criticism that such a move would "kill the goose that laid the golden egg." But Roche did not just acquire its partner of two decades. After eight decades of having its U.S. headquarters in Nutley, New Jersey, the firm closed most of its operations there and moved them to South San Francisco to the Genentech campus. The Swiss drugmaker also shortened its century-old name from Hoffman LaRoche to Roche. Gilead Sciences, now the dominant independent Bay Area biotech firm, has recently embarked on an active acquisition binge, buying up fledgling companies at a fast clip, in order to diversify its research and product portfolios. Mergers among pharma giants have continued as well, as Merck acquired Schering Plough in 2009, creating an even larger firm.

affiliations, is crucial. Many industries consolidate after early years of openness and fluidity (Utterback 1994). In the life sciences, however, the acceptance of many features of academic science (e.g., publication, peer review, investigator autonomy, diverse sources of research funding, multiple research collaborations across organizational boundaries) served as a buffer against rigidity and conformity by ensuring that a wide range of investigations are explored. The scientific norm of priority disclosure further ensured that any "news" was rapidly transmitted (Merton 1973; Dasgupta and David 1994).

Openness is also apparent in moments of transposition. Several members of the core have further moved to mix practices and cross domains that were previously not bridged. No clear template is at yet present, but a number of new research institutes have been established by members of the elite. In various ways these institutes incorporate elements from venture finance into academic settings and transplant norms of open access to research findings into industrially oriented settings.[26] Interestingly, there is no consistency to their ownership status—some are nonprofit, others are housed at universities, and one of the most notable is the research arm of a Swiss multinational. Moreover, many of the individuals involved in the founding of first-generation biotech companies had a hand in the development of these new centers. They are also located in precisely those regions where we showed in chapter 14 that robust clusters had formed—the Bay Area, San Diego, Cambridge/Boston, as well as Seattle, which was a nascent district. Efforts at replication of these centers are now under way at universities, government labs, and corporate research facilities around the world. But this first generation has at least a decade head start in weaving together knowledge and techniques from multiple domains. With their creation and replication, we see another sign of elite influence as the behavior of the few at the center becomes the aspiration of many in the field.

In the sections that follow we provide select overviews of several of the earliest institutes, all founded by members of the core, emphasizing the commingling of practices and commitment to open access and translation. These examples provide further evidence for the transformative feedback dynamics unleashed by the creation of a new organizational form—the science-based company—and the open science role of select elite members of the network.

Bio-X, Stanford University

This interdisciplinary research and teaching facility had its origins in spring 1998 when a group of Stanford faculty from medicine, engineering, and the biosciences hatched a plan to develop the Bio-X program. The centerpiece is a radical new building, the James H. Clark Center, completed in 2003, which currently houses more than nine hundred researchers from a wide range of disciplines and departments. The residents are co-located in a glass building with virtually no natural barriers, with shared access to state-of-the-art molecular imaging equipment and a large, appealing cafeteria space. Physically, the building represents a new era—all glass, few walls, modernist in design, and appealing eating options available throughout the day.[27] The floor space is completely open, and furnishings are mobile. The Clark Center is designed to annihilate the intellectual and physical barriers imposed by disciplines and maximize opportunity for serendipitous encounters.

Bio-X combines basic science and advances in imaging technology with a focus on the design of therapeutic devices and molecular machines. Some of the most acclaimed work out of BioX, for example, Karl Deisseroth's work on optogenetics, which bridges the fields of psychiatry, neuroscience, and bioengineering, renders the line between fundamental science and its application moot.[28] Funding is offered through seed grants, based on promising proof of concept. Using a model drawn from venture capital, the idea is to provide seed and bridge funding for research that would not be funded by the NIH or NSF, which typically reserve their scarce funds for work that has already demonstrated feasibility. Moreover, federal research funds are allocated by disciplinary panels that often look askance at novel work

[26] Evans (2010, 152) quips that nonprofit research institutes were, historically, companies without products that evolved into universities without students. But these newer entities have active doctoral and postdoctoral fellowship programs and are keenly concerned with translating research into biomedical designs and new forms of treatment.

[27] The building received *R&D Magazine*'s Lab of the Year award in 2004. Gieryn (2008, 796) has observed that it is "a laboratory building not quite like any other," designed for maximal visibility and observability.

[28] *Science* cited Deisseroth's efforts to perturb and re-engineer brain circuits as one of the "big ideas of the past ten years" in their survey of influential research over the past decade (330 [December 17, 2010]: 1612–13).

that transcends departmental lines. New fellowship programs have been developed to attract graduate students and postdoctoral fellows, and those fellows are routinely exposed to researchers throughout the center, to venture capitalists, and to scientists from Bay Area biotech firms. There is a clear effort to remake the trajectory of scientific careers as part of the initiative.

Among the founding members of the Bio-X advisory council are several key people who were deeply involved in the birth of the biotech industry. Franklin "Pitch" Johnson was an early funder of Amgen, Brook Byers an early investor in Genentech and the first CEO of Hybritech, William Bowes an investor in Cetus and the founding shareholder and first chairman of Amgen, and Dr. Richard Scheller a part of the first generation of scientists who left UC–San Francisco to join the scientific staff at Genentech.

The Genomics Institute of the Novartis Research Foundation, La Jolla, California (GNF)

GNF was created in 1999 to advance research in drug discovery using high throughput techniques from structural biology, combinatorial chemistry, and computational biology. The institute was funded through the Novartis Foundation and set up as a nonprofit organization. It presently has six buildings that house over 550 employees. The physical space is also notable here as the buildings are connected by a central circulation spine and, most unusual for Southern California, are in walking distance of the Scripps Institute, the Salk Institute, Sanford-Burnham Medical Research Institute, and UC–San Diego (UCSD). GNF represents an effort to combine bioengineering and bioinformatics to identify new biological processes and develop new therapeutics.

Full access to research results and all publications are available on the institute's Web site, as well as open access to research tools and databases. The public dissemination of results fits a nonprofit science model, but the institute is also a branch of a global corporation, Novartis. GNF has a highly popular postdoctoral fellowship program, whose graduates have gone on to careers in universities, research institutes, and industry. There is no requirement that fellows subsequently work for Novartis. The institute is a member of the Joint Center for Structural Genomics, along with Scripps, Burnham, and UCSD. This center is funded by the NIH. Much of the research at GNF is supported by various disease foundations.

The GNF model is an unusual hybrid with its mix of funding from a corporate sponsor, the U.S. government, and nonprofit foundations. It is co-located with other nonprofit research institutes and a leading public research university. Not surprisingly, the first director of GNF embodied all the characteristics of an amphibious scientist. Peter Schultz made his reputation as a chemistry professor at the University of California–Berkeley and later joined the Scripps Institute. He became the first director of GNF while maintaining a laboratory of about forty people at Scripps. Schultz was a pioneer in the field of combinatorial chemistry, a methodology for rapidly generating and screening chemicals for potential therapeutic properties. During his time at Berkeley, he connected with Alejandro Zaffaroni, the founder of both ALZA and the gene chip maker Affymetrix. Although Schultz had turned down numerous offers from venture capitalists to develop his research into a company, Zaffaroni was persuasive, and together they founded Affymax. Schultz went on to start several biotech firms and has been involved in more start-ups that have sprung out of work at Scripps and GNF. He straddles the world of academic, nonprofit, and commercial scientists and maintains an active hand in all three. Schultz was the director of GNF for its first decade.

Novartis Institutes for Biomedical Research, Cambridge, Massachusetts (NIBR)

In 2002 the Swiss pharmaceutical giant decided to reorganize its global research laboratories and relocate a sizable portion of its R&D facilities in Cambridge, Massachusetts. The cost of acquiring space close to MIT, the Whitehead Institute, and Biogen was considerable, and there were many questions as to whether a pharmaceutical research operation would even fit, much less thrive, in this academic hotbed. Novartis made the unusual choice of hiring an outsider, Mark Fishman, a cardiologist from Massachusetts General Hospital, as president of NIBR. Today the research center in Kendall Square is quite large, with more than two thousand employees, and its operations are markedly different from those of any other pharmaceutical corporation.

NIBR's goal was to integrate its commercial research operations into the local scientific community in order to benefit from extensive interaction and career mobility. To accomplish this, Fishman has insisted that discovery research is guided by science, not the market. According to Douglas Melton, a Harvard professor on NIBR's scientific advisory board, Fishman "didn't want to let the marketers define the disease targets" (Weisman 2011). Fishman contends that "the decision to pursue one type of molecule as compared with another cannot be a strategic one; it must be based on outcomes that are dictated by how the science goes. We will go wherever the science takes us" (Mintz 2010). Such an approach met with a great deal of initial skepticism, both from more business-oriented staff at Novartis and academics initially suspicious of a pharma giant's commitment to basic science. Fishman recruited department heads from both the academy and small biotech companies and set up postdoctoral fellowship programs that have attracted promising researchers who pass through Novartis and leave an imprint. All NIBR staff are encouraged to publish. Today Novartis is perhaps the most science-based company in Cambridge[29] and one of the anchor tenants of the Boston region.[30] Novartis's strategy reflects the idea that internal research and external collaborations complement each another in that they enhance absorptive capacity and infuse a strong scientific vision regarding the direction of drug discovery (Cohen and Levinthal 1990; Powell, Koput, and Smith-Doerr 1996). To that end, NIBR maintains an open repository of its publications so that they are accessible to the broader scientific community.

Institute for Systems Biology, Seattle (ISB)

Recall from the preceding chapter that Seattle was a nascent technology cluster. The Seattle region had several notable endowments, including the large, well-funded medical school at the University of Washington, the Fred Hutchinson Cancer Center, and Immunex, one of the first-generation, science-based firms. Our analysis of Seattle pointed out that in the 1980s and 1990s, during biotechnology's emergence and expansion, Seattle lacked both a density of organizations and diversity of affiliations. Although many pieces were in place, a number of factors combined to make it challenging for a robust cluster to form there. Not the least of these was the fact that Immunex, an elite-connected firm with a strong research and publication record, did not meet with commercial success during its early years and was eventually acquired by Amgen. One takeaway is that windows of opportunity for emergence may be relatively short-lived, and if catalysis does not take place during such periods, it may have a limited ability to occur at a later date. Now that the momentum for biotechnology start-ups has faded with the financial crises of the past decade, Seattle's status as a nascent cluster may not change. Nonetheless, there has been considerable scientific ferment in the Northwest for some time and a new focus on global health.

In the early 1990s the University of Washington (UW), with funding from Bill Gates, lured the world-renowned chemist Leroy Hood away from Cal Tech in the hope that Hood would be the springboard to new research initiatives at UW. In 2000 Hood bolted from UW and, along with Alan Aderem, an immunologist, and Ruedi Aebersold, a protein chemist, cofounded the Institute for Systems Biology. Today, the institute has more than three hundred staff members. The nonprofit center has a postdoctoral fellowship program, and its publications and data sets are downloadable on its website, which details ISB's hybrid status as an independent organization poised between academia and industry. The advisory board includes several directors who had a strong hand in the creation of biotech, including Bill Bowes, George Rathmann, the first CEO of Amgen, and Louis Lange, the founder of CV Therapeutics.

The departure of Hood and his colleagues from the University of Washington was a rocky one, but they contended that new ideas required new organizational structures, arguing that "traditional universities are too rigidly departmentalized for a field that integrates many disciplines and too hesitant about transforming their findings into products. Even traditional corporations are too constrained by organizational processes

[29] During a presentation of an early draft in 2009 at an MIT seminar, Fiona Murray commented that, "Curiously, the most science-oriented firm in Cambridge today is Novartis." The acquisition of Genzyme, long one of the pillars of the Cambridge biotech community, in 2011 by Sanofi-Aventis has further shifted scientific leadership to Novartis (Ledford 2011a). Genzyme was, as we detailed in chapter 13, the first biotech firm to focus on rare diseases. It learned to develop extensive registries of its patients worldwide and to build relationships with patients and payers. More than two decades later, NIBR has also chosen to focus on rare diseases, arguing that the mechanisms that underlie such diseases are better understood. Progress on these mechanisms of disease action rather than symptoms is the cornerstone of the NIBR approach.

[30] MIT president Susan Hockfield has remarked that "Novartis has been a tremendously powerful catalyst to the whole biomedical enterprise in the region" (Weisman 2011).

and boundaries and too focused on quarterly profits."[31] Defining systems biology is an elusive task (Cowley 2004), but ISB provides an in-depth tutorial detailing its premise, promise, and methodologies.[32] The institute brought together an unusual assortment of scientists, including biologists, mathematicians, computer scientists, physicists, and oceanographers. Recently ISB has moved across Lake Union, to the south shore, where it is close to the Hutchinson Cancer Center and Seattle Biomed.[33] ISB's hybrid status is further reflected in its funding structure. In its early years, Leroy Hood helped self-fund it with $5 million of his own money. More recently, ISB has received large research grants from the NIH and the governments of Luxembourg and Sweden. Four companies have been spun out of ISB thus far.

Although fascinating and consequential in their own right, these institutes are important for a larger reason. They are the leading edge of organizational variety. The life sciences field has been characterized not only by its extensive—and unusual for its time—interorganizational collaboration but also by experimentation with new organizational forms. We chronicled the emergence of the dedicated biotech firm in chapter 13, but now we find an even wider array of new species. Alongside private sector academic institutes such as NIBR and the other hybrids discussed above, there are a plethora of new forms. Philanthropies such as the Cystic Fibrosis Foundation, the Gates Foundation, the Muscular Dystrophy Association, and the Wellcome Trust are acting like venture firms, investing large sums in early stage, high-risk research in return for a stake in any eventual returns if new medicines are developed (Ledford 2011b). VCs have become academic advisers, and private firms and public organizations have formed consortia to tackle thorny diseases such as autism and malaria (Allarakhia and Walsh, 2011). A leading nonprofit mouse repository, Jackson Laboratory, which supplies scientists worldwide with research mice, has also developed a strong research and teaching program in mammalian genetics. One World Health (OWH) is a nonprofit pharmaceutical company developing medicines for sick children in the poorest countries in the world. OWH is supported by funding from the Gates Foundation and the U.K. Department for International Development (DfID), patent donations from universities, DBFs, and pharma firms, and savvy use of orphan drug regulations. And Gilead Sciences, now the largest independent DBF in the Bay Area and the world's largest seller of HIV medicines, has developed a creative alliance with generic manufacturers in the developing countries and a patent-sharing body at the United Nations to sell its antiviral medicines on a nonprofit basis to poor populations. This diversity of forms enhances the cross-fertilization of ideas and approaches. Moreover, these different organizational models operate according to different rules and registers of worth, even when they are engaged in similar activities.

The spillovers across these hybrid forms do not just reflect interdependencies. Many industries, from aircraft and autos to renewable energy to winemaking, deal with considerable interdependence among the participants with respect to technology, financing, and regulations and thus turn to forms of collaboration. But it is not only resources that are flowing through the organizations at the core of the life sciences network; people are moving through these organizations as well. As career circulation becomes commonplace, the mores and practices from one arena move to another. The unexpected and contested moves of the amphibious scientists of the late 1970s have become routine for a new generation of researchers.

This blending of careers and practices has the consequence that some of the most interesting organizations doing science today have hybrid features. Even though they may be under the auspices of universities, global corporations, or nonprofit organizations, their activities recast the boundaries of public and private science, just as the first-generation biotech companies did in the late 1970s and early 1980s. In short, even though the science-based, dedicated biotech firm has declined in its prevalence, the organizing principles that DBFs created have spread to the most central members of the life sciences field, forming a new center of gravity.

[31] Quotation from ISB website: http://www.systemsbiology.org/Introduction_to_the_Institute/Our_History.

[32] It is intriguing to see the parallels between ISB's description of the core features of systems biology and the multiple-network approach that we pursue in this book. ISB argues that the concept of emergent properties is central to the study of systems. Any function performed by a system that is not the result of a single part in the system but is the result of interacting parts in the system is an emergent property. Systems that have emergent properties are said to be irreducible. They cannot be reduced to their individual parts or studied one part at a time ("Intro to Systems Biology, Why Systems Matter," 2001, http://www.systemsbiology.org/).

[33] The new head of Seattle Biomed is Alan Aderem, one of ISB's cofounders. He and a team of forty-two researchers have recently moved out of ISB to become part of an initiative on global health funded by the Gates Foundation.

DISCUSSION AND CONCLUSION

We began by posing questions regarding why the organization of production in the biopharmaceutical field has changed so markedly over the past four decades. We wanted to understand the dynamics of this transformation, as well as its causes and consequences.The field developed through overlapping linkages that brought together university labs, start-up companies, huge multinational firms, government institutes and regulatory agencies, and law and venture capital offices. Rather than locking in early on a dominant design in which small firms served as boutiques for the established incumbents, there was considerable recombining of skills and resources that altered the roles and identities of the participants. Over time, the pursuit of alliances with new parties changed the routines and skills of all the surviving participants.

This search for novelty suggests both skill at prospecting for new partners and an ability to interact with a heterogeneous set of participants. When such relationships are also structurally cohesive, as was the case in the highly interconnected k-core elite, there are plural pathways through which the organizations are fatefully linked. The larger the number of reliable paths for communication and exchange, the more rapidly news percolates through a network. And when more knowledge is exchanged, participants attend to their partners more intensively. The cohesive features of the core help ensure that tacit information is exchanged and advanced and that the expansive ties bring in new sources of diversity. Thus, network cohesion and organizational diversity operate as countervailing forces, with the former enhancing the reliability of exchange and the latter pulling in newcomers that aid in exploration.

Throughout this book, we have invoked the phrase "actors make relations, but relations make actors." Here we see vivid illustration of this process. The first-generation, amphibious scientists depicted in chapter 13 helped establish, often unintentionally, a new model of a science-based company. These companies became involved in an intricate array of relationships with universities, government institutes, VCs, and pharmaceutical and chemical companies. Together, this group of organizations formed a densely connected elite at the apex of the field, which we have closely analyzed in this chapter. Keeping pace with this group was immensely challenging, and many dropped by the wayside even as newcomers joined the race. As the type of ties pursued by surviving members of the elite shifted, the skill set of these participants changed. Moving from commercialization activities to a science and finance logic required participants to interact more intensively and on a more common ground. The mutualism that evolved altered the identities of many of the most connected players. As the DBF model of organizing (i.e., the combination of basic science, multiple funding sources, external collaboration, and engagement of physicians and patient groups in drug discovery) spread to more participants, the overall direction of the field shifted as well. But those in the core were among the first to derive benefits from this fresh action.

Our analysis of the collective dynamics of biotechnology's elite highlights the purchase gained from studying multiple network affiliations. Through the multiple network lens, we have identified three features of a network elite that contribute both to the character of a field's central participants and to its overall poisedness in the face of exogenous shocks and endogenous shifts.

Network elites can be distinguished along three dimensions. In *structural* terms, the connections they forge can favor conservation of their position or expansion of their reach. When conserving ties that enhance elite cohesion trump relationships that allow prospecting via connections to newcomers, the result is a system that tips toward oligarchy. Where prospecting overwhelms conservation, something more akin to the ideal typical spot market of economic theory results. In the language we have used, when elites primarily emphasize their gatekeeping rather than catalyzing roles, calcification follows.

Similarly, elites can be understood *relationally* through an analytical lens on the type and range of activities that central members undertake. When the majority of members of an elite are relational generalists, capable of multivocal interactions that span many activities, there is little need for them to reach beyond their existing orbit. Such enclosure of a field tips it toward oligarchy. In contrast, when the most central players in a field are specialists in a regime with a complex production function, success requires constant outreach and rewiring, thus tipping the field toward the market end of the spectrum. In our terms, the extent to which elite arbiters develop multiple parts in common helps explain when fields tip.

Finally, network elites should be also considered *compositionally* in terms of the types of organizations that comprise a cohesive cluster. Despite similarities in structural positions and relational portfolios, different types of organizations exist in varied selection environments and work under different sets of institutional rules and conventions. Put another way, universities and biotech companies might both occupy the cohesive core and maintain multivocal portfolios of relationships that focus on collaborative R&D; but the implications of their activities differ for the simple reason that well-connected research universities seldom go out of business and even more rarely engage in mergers and acquisitions. In contrast, well-connected pharmaceutical firms and DBFs are often targets for acquisition. More sociologically, even as universities adopt practices from private industry and become hybrid entities, the rewards to, say, publishing a paper in a top-echelon journal are different for professors and researchers at firms. When the most connected core of a field's network is composed of homogeneous organizations competing for the same resources under similar rules and conventions, oligarchy results from concentration and gatekeeping. In contrast, if the members of an elite have few rules or resource environments in common, there is little to hold them together and a more free-wheeling field develops. In sum, how elites enact gatekeeper, arbiter, and catalyst roles influences the dynamics of fields, but who they are matters as well.

We argue that the overall poisedness of fields anchored by complex, dynamic networks is a function of an elite's ability to balance between relational, structural, and combinatorial extremes. In biotechnology, a mix of conserving and prospecting connections that spanned the industry's entire network, an increasingly varied array of activities, and diverse types of organizations has resulted in an open elite that neither calcified nor collapsed despite significant scientific, financial, and regulatory changes that shook the system and competitive dynamics that prompted widespread consolidation. The key to this balancing act is the adaptability of long-standing members of the elite in the face of both exogenous and endogenous pressures. This organizational flexibility, in turn, is a function of the "compounds" that were the building blocks of these organizations (see chapter 13) and their location in robust regional communities (chapter 14). The new efforts to house cutting-edge and commercially relevant life sciences research in institutes that span public and private sector rationales situated in the world's most productive biopharmaceutical regions are evidence of the open character of this elite.

Just how durable are these organizational arrangements? In one respect, they have proven quite resilient as the nature of collaboration has shifted notably with respect to both form and content. Alliances are useful precisely because they are neither permanent nor exclusive. We saw a high rate of formation and dissolution of partnerships over this time period, which means that the mix of central participants was changing. But clearly the resilience of this model of cohesive exploration is deeply dependent on the generation of novelty, which requires continual technological dynamism and discovery. When there is a thinning of the population or funding grows scarce, the search process narrows. Under such circumstances, a few scenarios seem likely. One, the most connected group could turn inward on itself, relying only on its most prominent partners for new ideas and resources. This is an eventual recipe for stagnation, which thus far has been avoided. Two, partnerships and collaborations can become a transitional phase in which the more powerful participant can use the relationship as a type of lease arrangement. Although the stronger partner may wish to purchase the other party at some point, such relationships are not always optimal for the generation of new ideas. Moreover, integration in this field has proven to be exceedingly thorny to manage. The last decade of high-profile pharma mergers and biotech acquisitions suggest this trajectory is being pursued by some of the core participants. Three, a handful of the most well-connected participants could use their position and contacts to create new organizational models, as we see with the creation of research institutes. The future evolution of the field will be shaped by the interlinked influences of scientific advance and organizational designs for accessing knowledge and resources. Our contribution has been to demonstrate the imprint of network dynamics on this industry's evolution by demonstrating how the collaborations of the most connected set of participants aggregate into a structure that, in turn, shaped both the direction of the industry and its modes of organizing.

REFERENCES

Albert, R., H. Jeong, and A. L. Barabási. 2000. "Error and Attack Tolerance in Complex Networks." *Nature* 406:378–82.

Allarakhia, Minna, and Steven Walsh. 2011. "Managing Knowledge Assets under Conditions of Radical Change: The Case of the Pharmaceutical Industry." *Technovation* 31:105–17.

Alvarez-Hamelin, José Ingacio, Luca Dall' Asla, Alain Barat, and Allesandro Vespignani. 2006. "Large Scale Networks, Fingerprinting, and Visualization Using the k-core Decomposition." In *Advances in Neural Information Processing Systems* 18, ed. Y. Weiss, B. Schölkopf, and J. Platt, 41–50. Cambridge MA: MIT Press.

Barabási, A. L., and R. Albert. 1999. "Emergence of Scaling in Random Networks." *Science* 286:509–12.

Bearman , Peter S., James Moody, and Kate Stovel. 2004. "Chains of Affection: The Structure of Adolescent Romantic and Sexual Networks." *American Journal of Sociology* 110:44–91.

Berndt, Ernst, Linda Bui, David Reiley, and Glen Urban. 1995. "Information, Marketing and Pricing in the U.S. Anti-Ulcer Drug Market." *American Economic Review* 85(2):100–105.

———. 1997. "The Roles of Marketing, Product Quality, and Price Competition in the Growth and Composition of the U.S. Antiulcer Drug Industry." In *The Economics of New Goods*, ed. T. Bresnahan and R. Gordon, 277–322. Chicago: University of Chicago Press.

Carlsson, Arvid. 1983. "The Role of Basic Biomedical Research in New Drug Development." In *Decision-making in Drug Research*, F. Gross, 35–42. New York: Raven Press.

Cockburn, Iain M. 2004. "The Changing Structure of the Pharmaceutical Industry." *Health Affairs* 23(1): 10–22.

Cockburn, Iain M., and Scott Stern. 2010. "Finding the Endless Frontier: Lessons from the Life Sciences Innovation System for Technology Policy." *Capitalism and Society* 5(1): Article 1. http://www.bepress.com/cas/vol5/iss1/art1/.

Cockburn, Iain M., Rebecca Henderson, and Scott Stern. 2000. "Untangling the Origins of Competitive Advantage." *Strategic Management Journal* 21: 1123–45.

Cohen, Wesley, M., and D. A. Levinthal. 1990. "Absorptive Capacity: A New Perspective on Learning and Innovation." *Administrative Science Quarterly* 35:128–52.

Cowley, Allen W. 2004. "The Elusive Field of Systems Biology." *Physiol. Genomics* 16:285–86.

Dasgupta, Partha, and Paul A. David. 1994. "Toward a New Economics of Science." *Research Policy* 23(5): 487–521.

De, P., A. E. Singh, T. Wong, W. Yacoub, and A. M. Jolly. 2004. "Sexual Network Analysis of a Gonorrhea Outbreak." *Sexually Transmitted Infections* 80:280–85.

deNooy, Wouter, Andrej Mrvar, and Vladimir Batagelj. 2005. *Exploratory Social Network Analysis with Pajek*. New York: Cambridge University Press.

Dorogovtsev, S. N., A. V. Goltsev, and J.F.F. Mendes. 2006. "*k*-core Organization of Complex Networks." *Physical Review Letters* 96(040601):1–4.

Evans, James A. 2010. "Nonprofit Research Institutes: From Companies without Products to Universities without Students." In *Politics and Partnerships*, ed. E. S. Clemens and D. Guthrie, 151–82. Chicago: University of Chicago Press.

Galambos, L., and J. E. Sewell. 1996. *Network of Innovators: Vaccine Development at Merck, Sharp & Dohme and Mulfor, 1895–1995*. Cambridge: Cambridge University Press.

Galambos, L., and J. Sturchio. 1996. "The Pharmaceutical Industry in the Twentieth Century: A Reappraisal of the Sources of Innovation." *History and Technology* 13:83–100.

———. 1998. "Pharmaceutical Firms and the Transition to Biotechnology: A Study in Strategic Innovation." *Business History Review* 72:250–78.

Gambardella, Alfonso. 1995. *Science and Innovation: The US Pharmaceutical Industry during the 1980s*. Cambridge: Cambridge University Press.

Gieryn, Thomas F. 2008. "Laboratory Design for Post-Fordist Science." *Isis* 99:796–802.

Hagedoorn, John, and Nadine Roijakkers. 2002. "Small Entrepreneurial Firms and Large Companies in Inter-Firm R&D Networks: The International Biotechnology Industry." In *Strategic Entrepreneurship*, ed. M. A. Hitt et al., 223–52. Cambridge, MA: Blackwell.

Henderson, R., and I. Cockburn. 1996. "Scale, Scope and Spillovers: The Determinants of Research Productivity in Drug Discovery." *RAND Journal of Economics* 27:32–59.

Henderson, Rebecca, Luigi Orsenigo, and Gary P. Pisano. 1999. "The Pharmaceutical Industry and the Revolution in Molecular Biology: Interactions among Scientific, Institutional and Organizational Change." In *Sources of Industrial Leadership: Studies of Seven Industries*, ed. D. C. Mowery and R. R. Nelson. Cambridge: Cambridge University Press.

Holland, John H. 1975. *Adaptation in Natural and Artificial Systems*. Ann Arbor: University of Michigan Press.

Janeway, William H. Forthcoming. *Cash and Control: Doing Capitalism in the Innovation Economy*.

Johnson, Avery. 2009. "Pfizer Outlines R&D Leadership, Integrating Wyeth Researchers." *Wall Street Journal*, April 7. http://online.wsj.com/article/SB123910921156696767.html.

Ledford, Heidi. 2011a. "Genzyme Deal Set to Alter Biotech Landscape." *Nature*, February 22, 2011. http://www.nature.com/news/2011/110222/full/470449a.html.

———. 2011b. "Charities Seek Cut of Drug Royalties." *Nature* 475(July 21):275–76.

Lundvall, Bengt-Ake. 1992. *National Systems of Innovation: Towards a Theory of Innovation and Interactive Learning*. London: Pinter Publishers.

Mahoney, James, and Kathleen Thelen, eds. 2010. *Explaining Institutional Change*. New York: Cambridge University Press.

Malerba, Franco, and Luigi Orsenigo. 2002. "Innovation and Market Structure in the Dynamics of the Pharmaceutical Industry: Towards a History Friendly Model." *Industrial and Corporate Change* 11(4):662–705.

March, James G. 1991. "Exploration and Exploitation in Organizational Learning." *Organization Science* 2(1):71–87.

McKelvey, Maureen. 1996. *Evolutionary Innovations*. Oxford: Oxford University Press.

Merton, Robert K. 1973. *The Sociology of Science*. Ed. Norman W. Storer. Chicago: University of Chicago Press.

Mintz, Cliff. 2010. "Fostering Pharma R&D." *Life Science Leader*. http://www.lifescienceleader.com/index.php?option=com_jambozine&layout=article&view=page&aid=4067&Itemid=68.

Moody, James. 2001. "Peer Influence Groups: Identifying Dense Clusters in Large Networks." *Social Networks* 23:261–83.

Moody, James, and Douglas R. White. 2003. "Social Cohesion and Embeddedness: A Hierarchical Conception of Social Groups." *American Sociological Review* 68(1):103–28.

Nelson, Richard R. 1993. *National Innovation Systems A Comparative Analysis*. New York: Oxford University Press.

Newman, Mark. 2003. "Mixing Patterns in Networks." *Physical Review E* 67:026126 (13 pp.).

Newman, M.E.J. 2002. "Assortative Mixing in Networks." *Physical Review Letters* 89:20871.

———. 2003. "The Structure and Function of Complex Networks." *SIAM Review* 45:167–256.

Newman, M.E.J., and M. Girvan. 2004. "Finding and Evaluating Community Structure in Networks."*Physical Review E* 69 (article number 026113).

Newman, Mark E. J., and Juyong Park. 2003. "Why Social Networks Are Different than Other Types of Networks." *Physics Review E* 68(4):036122.

Orsenigo, Luigi. 1989. *The Emergence of Biotechnology*. New York: St. Martin's Press.

Owen-Smith, Jason, and Walter W. Powell. 2004. "Knowledge Networks as Channels and Conduits: The Effects of Spillovers in the Boston Biotechnology Community." *Organization Science* 15(1):5–21.

Palla, Gergely, Albert-László Barabási, and Tamás Vicsek. 2007. "Quantifying Social Group Evolution." *Nature* 446:664–67.

Pierson, Paul. 2004. *Politics in Time*. Princeton: Princeton University Press.

Powell, W. W., and Peter Brantley. 1996. "Magic Bullets and Patent Wars: New Product Development in the Biotechnology Industry." In *Managing Product Development*, ed. T. Nishiguchi, 233–60. New York: Oxford University Press.

Powell, W. W., K. W. Koput, and L. Smith-Doerr. 1996. "Interorganizational Collaboration and the Locus of Innovation: Networks of Learning in Biotechnology." *Administrative Science Quarterly* 41:116–45.

Powell, W. W., D. R. White, K.W. Koput, and J. Owen-Smith. 2005. "Network Dynamics and Field Evolution: The Growth of Inter-organizational Collaboration in the Life Sciences." *American Journal of Sociology* 110:1132–1205.

Regional Oral History Office, University of California Berkeley Bancroft Library. 1997. Available from the online archive. Interviews by Sally Smith Hughes with Herbert Boyer, 1994, George B. Rathmann, 2003, Robert A. Swanson, 2000.

Scherer, Frederick M. 2004. "The Pharmaceutical Industry: Prices and Progress." *New England Journal of Medicine* 351(9):927–32.

Schumpeter, Joseph. 1936. *Capitalism, Socialism, and Democracy*. New York: Harper and Brothers.

Thelen, Kathleen. 2004. *How Institutions Evolve*. New York: Cambridge University Press.

Tong, Amy, B. Drees, G. Nardelli, G. Bader, B. Brannetti, L. Castagnoli, M. Evangelista, S. Ferracuti, B. Nelson, S. Paoluzi, M. Quondam, A. Zucconi, C. Hogue, S. Fields, C. Boone, and G. Cesareni. 2002. "A Combined Experimental and Computational Strategy to Define Protein Interaction Networks for Peptide Recognition Modules." *Science* 295(5553):321–24.

Useem, Michael. 1984. *The Inner Circle: Large Corporations and the Rise of Business Political Activity in the U.S. and U.K.* New York: Oxford University Press.

Utterback, James. 1994. *Mastering the Dynamics of Innovation*. Boston: Harvard Business School Press.

Watts, Duncan J. 2004. "The 'New' Science of Networks." *Annual Review of Sociology* 30:243–70.

Watts, D. J., and S. H. Strogatz. 1998. "Collective Dynamics of 'Small-World' Networks." *Nature* 393:440–442.

Weisman, Robert. 2011. "At Novartis, a Winning Formula." Boston.com. http://articles.boston.com/2011-01-04/business/29348116_1_novartis-research-drug-discovery-big-pharma.

White, D. R., and F. Harary. 2001. "The Cohesiveness of Blocks in Social Networks: Node Connectivity and Conditional Density." *Sociological Methodology* 31:305–59.

White, D. R., J. Owen-Smith, J. Moody, and W. W. Powell. 2004. "Networks, Fields, and Organizations: Micro-Dynamics, Scale, and Cohesive Embeddings." *Computational and Mathematical Organization Theory* 10:95–117.

16

Academic Laboratories and the Reproduction of Proprietary Science

Modeling Organizational Rules through Autocatalytic Networks

Jeannette A. Colyvas ▪ Spiro Maroulis

The introduction to this volume emphasizes the origins and emergence of new forms as a collective blind spot in the social sciences. Few analyses capture the relationship among all three features of social and economic life—the origin of new practices, their emergence as broader self-reproducing structures, and the form that they take as a result of this process. Our approach to this question examines how disparate elements of the social organization of academic science were assembled, transposed, and recombined to define a new regime of public and proprietary knowledge production.

Our aim is to illuminate the feedback dynamics of crossing boundaries and emergent institutional change. As the "amphibious" life scientists described in previous chapters came into contact with the world of commerce, how did their experiences reverberate into the conservative halls of academia? We explain this process through the recombination of meanings and practices within the existing social structure of science. We demonstrate how anticipatory efforts to maintain autonomy and expand the reach of one's research program fueled change, despite the fact that these actions were part of concerted struggles to preserve the academic system. Consequently, our analysis shows that efforts to operate within the social structure of science generated the mechanism that transformed it.

From this perspective, emergence is a bottom-up process as repeated social interactions give rise to vocabularies of motives that come to define what is standard and appropriate. New forms are built by participants situated in the cultural routines of their past. Opportunities and constraints, both new and old, make some participants receptive to alternatives from other domains, which remain invisible to others. When transposition happens, new practices are assembled selectively rather than adopted wholesale, and as they become integrated into the social order, these practices can also alter the domain in which they are transposed. Furthermore, emergence is built on a scaffolding of networks that transform rather than transmit.

To better understand the feedback dynamics of assembly and recombination in the origins and emergence of new practices, we combine detailed archival analysis with computational,

We are grateful to Woody Powell and John Padgett for extensive comments. We would also like to thank Michelle Wilkerson and Rick Orlina for their assistance on the implementation and testing of the agent-based model, as well as for conversations that have substantially improved several aspects of this chapter.Support for this project came from the Northwestern University Research Grants Committee, the National Science Foundation (#0849036), and the Center for Connected Learning and Computer-Based Modeling.

agent-based modeling (ABM). We examine the introduction and spread of proprietary science in the academy, specifically as a set of routines that shaped the production and disclosure of university-based research. The preceding chapters have demonstrated how scientific skills and status shaped the genesis of life science firms by transposing tools from one domain into new uses in others. We take up the academic counterpart of this process, whereby scientists in open science developed models of how their research programs would interact with commerce while navigating the existing social structure of academic science.

We take inspiration from two sources to show how proprietary science developed in a university system where patenting was rare and illegitimate and became one where ownership of one's research findings was common and appropriate. First, we utilize findings from extensive documentary records of the early introduction of patenting practices to life science labs at Stanford University, which, along with the University of California–San Francisco (UCSF), served as one of the fountains of early Bay Area biotechnology (Powell and Sandholtz, this volume). This approach enables us to distinguish among different approaches to commercializing academic research, specifically in terms of how social and technical categories of invention and inventor were defined as well as what kinds of boundaries with firms would be established and how pecuniary rewards would be appropriately utilized. Second, we build on autocatalytic models of emergence, reinforcement, and reproduction described in part 2 of this volume. Since some type of feedback is necessary for a new regime to emerge to both replicate practices and maintain their combinations as patterned interaction sequences, autocatalysis provides an apt imagery for examining emergence and reproduction.

Proprietary science in the academy is a strategic setting for examining these processes. When introduced to academic settings, proprietary knowledge disclosure was largely contradictory to the existing norms of open science. This new practice conflicted with established ones, rendering the establishment of patenting a much more interesting and rich process than the adoption and diffusion of a new practice into a blank slate. Instead, the contradictions between these two regimes made the acceptance of proprietary science a problem of interpretation. Identifying how commercializing academic research could be done legitimately entailed the conversion of proprietary science into practices and understandings that matched particular discoveries to academic identities.

ABM affords the ability to operationalize insights from empirical settings and to study alternative and competing ways in which dynamic microprocesses lead to macro-level outcomes. Our contribution in utilizing such an approach is in disentangling the mechanisms that are responsible for the emergence of an institution. We identify inductively three potential explanations for the emergence of proprietary science through an archival analysis of the origins of commercial practices in the academy: (1) a population-level mode of learning, reflecting how scientific labs produce both knowledge and scientists; (2) a lab-level, participatory form of adaptation through engagement in a chain of knowledge production; and (3) a lab-level preemptive form of adaptation through anticipation of others' actions. We examine our mechanisms under three different reward conditions that represent the relative value of patenting compared to publishing in reinforcing academic science. In doing so, we emphasize the transformative aspect of self-reinforcing processes in recasting networks, shaping routines, and guiding science.

We proceed as follows. First we provide further detail on our empirical setting and then discuss our research approach, which combines archival analysis and ABM. Next we highlight the ways in which the findings from the archives informed our model. After that, we delineate the core components of the scientific production model, explaining the outcomes of interest and experimental conditions. The findings of our model are presented in the section that follows, and then we conclude with a discussion of this application theoretically and empirically.

THE INTERSECTION OF SCIENCE AND COMMERCE IN THE ACADEMY

Research on the production of science has emphasized the strong normative basis of how science is conducted and rewarded. Dasgupta and David (1994, 494) have made this point vivid in distinguishing science and technology on the basis of its normative and social organization rather than its material character, specifically legitimate goals, forms of knowledge disclosure, and definitions of rewards.

In the years following World War II, academic research was largely conditioned on this "republic of science," characterized by norms of open disclosure that were reinforced through publication, citations, and peer review. Monetary rewards from scientific findings came only episodically through public awards and grants for further research. The adoption of patenting practices by academic scientists, initially in the 1970s and in greater numbers by the 1990s, reflected a contrasting norm of disclosure with its conferral of the right to exclude others from using a research finding and the reaping of direct monetary benefit to oneself and one's place of employment. The broad-based acceptance and proliferation of patenting in the academy reflects how the once disparate domains of public and proprietary science became a hybrid regime, combining elements of both (Rhoten and Powell 2007).

The development of commercial practices at the level of scientists and their labs is often linked to federal legislation in the 1980s that mandated a shift toward closer engagement with industry. Historians of science, however, have argued that the worlds of industry and science were much closer in the early postwar period than is generally recognized (Shapin 2008). In many universities, particularly among the more successful and widely emulated ones in the United States, commercial practices were already in place (Mowery et al. 2004). In the late 1960s and early 1970s, faculty contact with companies through consulting and professional conferences was not uncommon, particularly in the chemistry, engineering, and biomedical fields. But claims for proprietary ownership of scientific findings and tools by university science were rare indeed. Hence the codification of scientific findings as patents prompted a profound rethinking of general practices of property, credit, and rewards.

How did these formerly separate, contradictory realms become intermingled to produce new practices for the production and disclosure of knowledge? Many scholars conceptualize this question as the adoption and diffusion of entrepreneurial practices in the academy. Some emphasize how the procedures and reward systems became aligned to encourage commercialization (Shane 2004). From this view, the heavy reliance of new industries, such as biotechnology, on university-based research generated incentives for faculty to commercialize their research findings. For example, Lach and Schankerman (2003) argue that universities with policies that provided revenues to individual scientists attracted more faculty to engage in the commercialization of their research.

Others emphasize the relational aspects of scientific work through exposure to firms or colleagues with industry experience. Scientists who trained at entrepreneurial universities, with coauthors who have patented or coworkers who commercialize their research findings, are more likely to engage in proprietary practices (Stuart and Ding 2006; Bercovitz and Feldman 2008). Experience in the lab also plays an important role. Colyvas and Powell (2007) show how the first generation of life scientists at Stanford University who engaged in technology transfer influenced graduate students who were members of their collaborations, who then continued to patent on their own. This relational approach suggests that diffusion takes place through social contagion, either at the organizational or project level, and is highly conditioned by the life course of academic training.

Other researchers have analyzed how organizational routines are linked to broader cultural frames, generating a form of legitimacy that links practical, everyday action and higher-order institutions that shape the range of acceptable behavior (DiMaggio and Powell 1991; Suchman 1995; Ruef and Scott 1998; Colyvas and Powell 2006). From this view, incentives systems that purportedly function to attract scientists to commercializing science are the outcome, not the input, to the institutionalization of proprietary science in the academy. Colyvas (2007a) has shown that the earliest stages of institutionalization at Stanford University involved considerable ambiguity, case-by-case review, and procedural flexibility on the part of administrators involved in applying new technology transfer policies within the context of established norms and routines of academic science. The normative order of science was not fixed but offered room for diverse interpretations that defined what was possible, how credit applied, and how careers were pursued. These differences were very much tied to the organization of scientific research, such as employing skills to publish findings, and the reproduction of scientific careers, notably the training of graduate students who move on to create their own labs. In the interactions between senior faculty, their research teams, and the technology transfer office, conventions about technology transfer policy developed.

Our approach treats the amalgamation of public and proprietary science as a problem of transformation and the emergence of institutionalized routines. We emphasize the organizational aspects of the production of knowledge as well as the participatory aspects of scientists in disclosing their research findings as patents in the process of their academic work. We make a key distinction between the diffusion of practices and the origins and emergence of an institutional regime comprised of those practices. By origins we refer to the character and operation of a setting in which a new practice or organizational form is observed. Analyzing the origins of proprietary science requires examining the earliest introduction of patenting in the day-to-day work of the production of academic science. Few empirical analyses have taken up this exercise, save several notable exceptions (Berman, 2012). Colyvas (2007a, b) has examined the microprocesses inside labs and technology transfer offices, and we draw on her archival materials for this chapter. In using the word *emergence*, we refer to a social and behavioral pattern that arises temporally from "nothing" through some means of reinforcement and reproduction.[1] Analyzing emergence entails identifying the factors that explain the form of what is institutionalized in the context of how such factors operate as mechanisms—the set or sequences of actions or abstract relations that take place at a lower order of complexity and bring about an effect in higher-order social relations (Gross 2009).

Emergence is not reducible to its constituent parts and requires understanding the non-linear dynamics and complexity of a system. Thus one would expect that while the origin of a phenomenon provides guideposts to the analysis of emergence, it does not determine it. In turn, an emergent outcome provides a terminus and boundary around the form of what is to be explained but does not necessarily result from serving a particular function. Our challenge is to mobilize a theoretical lens that parses out the character and operation of a setting in a way that can be operationalized in a simple dynamic model that explains the outcome under counterfactual conditions. We draw from theoretical and empirical arguments that explain the diffusion of practices among individual scientists and how they combine to those that explain their institutionalization within universities and the profession of science. We compare these arguments to what we are able to observe in the lesser examined context of origin and develop constructs that we can operationalize in a formal model.

DATA AND METHODOLOGY

We combine careful comparative, archival, and longitudinal analysis with computational ABM. The two approaches are complementary: The empirical portion provides a grounded basis for theory development, including the scope and conditions to be incorporated in a dynamic explanation of the emergence of proprietary science. The computational modeling provides additional insight into the role of different mechanisms in this explanation through the clarity and conceptualization brought about by (1) forcing a precise translation of qualitative findings into "runable" code; and (2) providing a platform to explore counterfactual scenarios that are impossible to investigate with historical records. At one level, the effort is exploratory in that little work has been done to analyze the emergence of commercial science as part of a formal model of knowledge production. We seek fresh insight into the relationship between commerce and science by focusing on the transformation of organizational routines. Through simulation, we deepen our ideas by operationalizing qualitative findings in a way that can be connected to macro-level outcomes.

Archival Setting and Methodology

The archival research draws on a data set that examines the development of technology transfer at Stanford University and the diffusion of related practices across life scientists (Colyvas 2007a). We focus on a single biomedical department at Stanford University, between 1968 and 1982, reflecting the initial introduction of a formal technology transfer program to the university and a group of academics up through the passage and implementation of federal and legislative initiatives in the 1980s.[2] Stanford is

[1] Emergent patterns are often examined by identifying a settled or institutionalized outcome.We stress the theoretical possibility that institutions can be in flux (Padgett and Powell, this volume). We also emphasize the analytic purchase gained from a framework that can accommodate institutionalization as a process and a failed outcome (Colyvas and Jonsson 2011).

[2] The time period is the same as the years covered in chapter 12. A more detailed account of this analysis is reported in Colyvas 2007a.

known both for its high-quality science and for establishing one of the earliest and most organizationally emulated formal technology transfer programs. By the 1990s, commercialization efforts became fully integrated into the production of academic science.

The archives included two main sources: the administrative records of the university's Office of Technology Licensing (OTL) and files of individual inventions. A rich corpus of correspondence between inventors and university administration provided insight into the practices and rationales that emanated from labs. OTL records were organized as "subject files" covering the formation, operation, and reporting of the activities of the office. Invention records were organized as individual "dockets" that contain the initial disclosure form that scientists must submit in order to pursue commercializing a research finding, as well as any documentation related to patenting, marketing, and licensing a scientific product. OTL records were reviewed to obtain a chronology of the formal policies and compared to evidence of informal practices. Docket files provided a basis to profile individual labs and observe the introduction and successive engagement in commercializing research findings. A sample of forty-one inventions from the basic life science department was identified and linked to a laboratory of origin. The dockets were organized chronologically for each lab and coded for points where discussion and conflict took place around the blending of academic and proprietary practices.

Four core areas were identified where conceptions of academic science and commerce came into contact:(1) when a scientific finding constituted an invention; (2) which individuals were the "actual" inventors; (3) how any licensing revenues would be shared; and (4) debates over the boundaries between business and science. These points of contact were utilized as a basis for comparison over time. Each individual invention was treated methodologically as an "event" whereby commercialization practices were enacted and subject to change.

Agent-Based Modeling

We use the NetLogo Programmable Modeling Environment (Wilensky 1999) to develop agent-based models that operationalize and extend insights from the archival analysis. NetLogo models—and agent-based models in general—are usually comprised of three components: agents, environment, and rules.In the context of a social system, agents are usually people with heterogeneous attributes. The attributes can be fixed characteristics (e.g., race, gender) or can change over time (e.g., knowledge, wealth, preferences). The environment often takes the form of a lattice of sites or "patches" that themselves can be viewed as agents with attributes. For example, a patch in an agent-based model may represent a geographical location for a scientific laboratory. Importantly for social systems, the environment can additionally, and more broadly, be conceived as including a network of social relations taking the form of "links" between the agents. Similar to patches, the links themselves can be thought of as agents with attributes (e.g., strength of tie). Rules govern the behavior of the agents, the patches, and the links.An example of an agent rule might be something like "always allocate resources to maximize your utility." For patches or links, a rule might govern some underlying rate of growth or decay of the resources at a site or the strength of a relation. Rules can also govern the interaction between agents and their environment ("move to the most prosperous patch"), the interaction between agents and agents ("transfer knowledge only to my closest social relations"), and the dynamic formation of the network topology ("you are more likely to help a friend of a friend than a stranger"). In our models, the primary agents are scientific labs governed by rules of knowledge disclosure whose interaction topology is defined by the collegial ties between labs.

ABM is well suited for analyzing the interaction between individuals and higher order environments that is foundational in institutional approaches to the study of science and organizing. As Epstein and Axtell (1996) note, "[W]e give agents rules of behavior and then spin the system forward in time and see what macroscopic social structures emerge . . . we believe that the collective structures, or 'institutions,' that emerge can have feedback effects in the agent population, altering the behavior of individuals." Another advantage of ABM is that unobserved phenomena may be examined, such as counterfactual forms of organizing, where data or combinations of variables are not empirically available but distinctive mechanisms are known to matter. For our purposes, the primary advantage of agent-based modeling is that it provides an opportunity to reveal macro-level outcomes stemming from micro-level processes—for example, what we describe as emergence.

We utilize agent-based modeling in the following manner. First, we characterize our research question in the form of an emergent "reference pattern"—a macro-level change in a key outcome of interest. Identifying such reference patterns is a crucial step in defining the scope of a computational model and grounding it in a real world problem (Sterman 2000). In our case, that reference pattern is a shift in the distribution of scientists' willingness to patent a broader range of scientific findings (from few scientists patenting only certain types of findings to a much more widespread deployment of patenting of more basic scientific output). Second, we use the archival analysis to identify the most salient micro-level features and mechanisms of the real world system that may have given rise to that emergent pattern. Third, we operationalize those features with the specificity required to develop a computational, agent-based model that can give rise to the reference pattern of interest, as well as alternative ones. Fourth, we experiment with that model to better understand the systemic implications of the micro-level mechanisms identified in the archival analysis. In particular, we pay special attention to which mechanisms provide the most leverage in shifting the threshold of which labs are willing to patent. We turn now to an explication of the archival portion of our analysis.

ARCHIVAL EXAMINATION OF THE EARLY INTRODUCTION OF COMMERCIAL PRACTICES

The technology transfer archives were replete with detailed discussion of issues at the intersection of professional norms and the prospect of commercializing academic findings. From the archives, we derived four insights that motivate our formal characterization of the emergence of proprietary science.

First, despite all the attention given to national and local policies, approaches toward commercializing research emanated more from individual labs than government, legal, or university sources. The OTL had formed in 1968 as a pilot program with the idea that scientists could participate voluntarily in formal technology transfer efforts unless patenting was required by a funder. As early as the 1960s federal policies were in place that required the reporting of patentable inventions resulting from government-funded research. Application of the policy, however, was inconsistent, as the wording was vague enough to allow for anything and nothing to be patented. A piece of correspondence to a faculty member from the sponsored research office provides an apt example: "We are required to submit a disclosure on any 'subject invention,' which means any process, machine, manufacture, composition of matter or design, or any new or useful improvement thereof, which is or may be patentable."[3]

The newness of technology transfer, along with the university's dependence on scientists to build relationships with firms, made early commercialization efforts ambiguous and flexible. Scientists often opted not to report findings at all, simply stating that the particular research output was not an "invention" or even inappropriate to patent. Some scientists declined to list themselves as inventors, reasoning that inventors were engineers or technicians who built prototypes rather than the principal investigators or authors themselves. What kind of findings were an invention, who would be an inventor, or how rewards would be shared differed remarkably among labs and were only loosely related to legal definitions and formal policies. Table 16.1 summarizes characteristic approaches reflected in the archival records, distinguished by labs (columns) and four points of variation (rows) around invention, inventor, resources, and boundaries. Each lab is given a summary label—"Team Effort," "Clear Boundaries," "Non-Faculty Career," and "Fair Share"—which captures the orientation of major life science laboratories at Stanford. These local lab cultures are further detailed later in the chapter.[4]

This observation of multiple practices emanating from labs guided our thinking in developing a bottom-up model that would focus on the lab as the unit of analysis and capture qualitative differences in a lab's willingness to patent. This approach makes disclosure of knowledge an endogenous decision, building on the observational insight that local options drove the process rather than scientists' conformity to regulatory mandates. Further, we recognize that Stanford University policies emerged in response to scientific discoveries and opportunities.

[3] OTL Disclosure Files: OTL letter to inventor, March 26, 1979.

[4] In prior reporting of this research (Colyvas 2007a), labs were characterized as having organizational models, similar to characterizations of employment models in firms (Burton 2001). For the purpose of clarity with our computational methodology, we refer to labs as having approaches so as not to confound the uses of the term *model*.

Table 16.1.
Laboratory Approaches to Commercializing Research, 1970–82

	Laboratory I "Team Effort"	Laboratory II "Clear Boundaries"	Laboratory III "Non-Faculty Career"	Laboratory IV "Fair Share"
Invention				
Meaning	Patenting attracts industry expertise to advance research program	Patenting is appropriate for applications, not basic science	Patenting is an admission ticket to industry work	Patenting protects university science from exploitation by industry
Practice	Patent devices, not biological materials	Patent consumer applications, not basic science	Patent industry science, publish academic science	Patent basic research findings or methodologies
Inventor				
Meaning	Inventorship is a legal technicality, not credit for the scientific advance	Inventorship narrowly defined reflects credit for scientific advance, not the technical work	Inventorship is a legal definition and signals individual ownership to industry	Inventorship reflects academic ownership vis-à-vis industry
Practice	Staff technicians or engineers on disclosure, not Principal Investigator	Principal Investigator on disclosure, not technical or scientific staff	Legally determined collaborators on disclosure, not Principal Investigator	Principal Investigator and all collaborators on disclosure
Revenues and Rewards				
Meaning	Development is a "team effort" and revenues should support the lab; the reward is advancing the research program	Science is cumulative, personal wealth is inappropriate; the reward is credit for the discovery	Patents are portable and revenues to the individual are welcome; the reward is an industry career	Wealth from science should go to the loci of research; the reward is credit for the discovery
Practice	Assignment goes to university; inventor shares go to the lab	Assignment goes to university, inventor shares are donated	Assignment goes to the individual; inventor shares go to individual	Assignment goes to the university; inventor shares go to individual
Boundaries between Science and Business				
Meaning	Industry is a tool for furthering research and enhancing scientific reputation	Commerce is separate from science; use boundaries to preserve reputation and make commercializing legitimate	University affiliation is a platform to freelance and consult; use patents to increase currency in industry	Industry science depends on academic discovery; use tools of IP to protect science from industry
Practice	"Hands-on" to develop invention; consulting is integrated to mobilize industry and expand science	"Hands-off" in details of technology transfer; consult as a sideline activity	"Hands-on" in technology transfer; consulting is integrated to enhance freelance career	"Hands-on" in technology transfer; consult and interact with industry to 'beat them at their own game"

Source: Adapted from Colyvas 2007a, figs. 1, 2.

Second, engagement in commercial science was shaped by the production process and reward system of science. We find that from the perspective of principal investigators, the willingness to patent academic findings was highly contingent on the character of the scientific finding. For example, one scientist (Lab I:"Team Effort") opted to commercialize a device that became quite lucrative, yet later declined to patent a biological target, reasoning that scientific materials or processes were not appropriate to patent. Another laboratory principal investigator (PI) (Lab II: "Clear Boundaries") argued that patenting was appropriate for commercial applications but not basic science. Still another lab (Lab IV: "Fair Share") sought to patent all research findings intended for further research, less as a form of gaining profit but as a means of protecting science from exploitation in industry. A scientist's correspondence with a local start-up illustrates this sentiment:

> Although many of us are not in a position to exploit our discoveries, we do feel that universities and university-based research should benefit from profitable applications of our findings. I had hoped that an industry so recently spawned by university research would be enlightened in its recognition of who is responsible for its existence. . . . Your comments leave me and other academicians no alternative but . . . to patent or make exclusive arrangements for whatever we develop. I can assure you that I will alert my colleagues throughout the world to guard against what I consider exploitation.[5]

These differences also extended to how monetary resources would be distributed. According to university policy, scientists were entitled to one-third of the revenues from inventions that were licensed to firms. Yet three of the four lab directors refused personal revenues and even declined to list themselves as inventors, despite profits generated already in two of the labs. The principal investigator in Lab I initially assigned all patents to the university and established a lab-wide policy that revenues from any inventions coming from his group would be directed back to research in the lab. Lab II chose to donate his revenues to a fellowship fund and to his alma mater, while Lab IV chose to distribute revenues to the inventors themselves. The PI of Lab III viewed patent ownership as something for individuals who sought a career outside the academy, declining to list himself as an inventor when the legal criteria for inclusion were ambiguous.

These multiple approaches to commercializing science prompted us to examine heterogeneity among labs not only in terms of a scientist's willingness to patent as a discrete attribute of a lab but in terms of which circumstances deemed patenting acceptable. This insight makes patenting highly contingent on the correspondence between a PI's stance on proprietary science and the character of a research finding. For most scientists, the debate hinged on how basic or exclusively fundamental to science a particular finding was. In such cases, excludability could both hinder the application of the research and preclude further discoveries. In contrast, some scientists viewed patenting as a means of preserving the ability to disseminate one's science when threatened by others patenting similar or related work.

Third, revenue and ownership of patents were very much entwined with authority over the science rather than the prospect of making money. A memo from the OTL director in 1972 articulates this sentiment:

> There is a strong feeling by many, if not most inventors, that as they are responsible for bringing in the royalty funds, they should have a strong (if not the only) voice in controlling distribution of income. . . . A royalty income fund under control of a PI would allow the PI to get a piece of equipment for general laboratory use, to send people to important technical society meetings for which grant or other funds are not available, etc.[6]

The role, meaning, and use of revenues prompted considerable attention from the scientists. Commercializing research was indeed valuable to scientists, as it provided an opportunity to extend the research programs of faculty. For example, the PI of Lab III viewed patenting as a currency for mobility outside academia, particularly for scientists who chose not to pursue a career in university-based research. Lab I clearly indicated the role of commercializing as a means of expanding his research program by joining with a company to build his device with

[5] OTL Disclosure Files: October 7, 1980.

[6] OTL Subject Files: "Inventions, Patents and Licensing at Stanford," February 1972.

commercializable parts. This effort promoted the adoption of his technology to other labs and made his research technique ubiquitous.

We thus sought to consider different forms of enrollment into commercializing science in the context of the goals accepted as legitimate among academic scientists—largely to advance their research programs and ensure the prosperity of their labs. Through this lens, reward rests on incremental scientific advance (i.e., through generating findings and having others build on those findings), which feeds back into the labs through the ability to develop and support capacity.

Finally, despite the conviction and authority of many of these scientists, laboratory approaches were neither coherent nor stable. As technology transfer expanded, no one laboratory approach survived in its original form. Rather, each lab changed its practices in some fashion. By 1982 a common set of practices emerged as illustrated by the labs summarized in table16.2. The practices developed in this department played a potent role in shaping university-wide policies. Patenting basic research findings became the norm and the practice of donating revenues disappeared, as taking individual monetary rewards from successful licenses became common. This standardization reflected both a selective retention of some features of early approaches and the demise of others.

What accounts for these changes? The normative structure of science initially influenced each model, both in shaping the faculty members' positions with regard to rewards and industry involvement and opening up diverse responses to opportunities. But these divergent interpretations also contributed to their variation. Lab I's relegation of inventorship to technicians and Lab III's perception that patenting was a currency for industry mobility both reflected a view that university and industry science remain separate. The career structure of science was also important because the mobility of graduate students and postdocs afforded younger inventors the space to advocate for their own research and rewards. In 1981 a postdoc in Lab I who was leaving the university elected to take her inventor shares, defying the terms that the lab PI had set for everyone in his research program. Much controversy ensued over this withdrawal from the "team effort" approach. Eventually, the university supported her claim, markedly weakening the esteemed senior professor's ability to maintain laboratory-wide policies. Consequently, the PI listed himself as inventor on subsequent inventions. Being formally listed as an inventor became a means of asserting credit and control over the science, a claim that had previously been asserted solely by publication.

The character of the science, although critical in shaping initial approaches to commercialization, was also responsible for triggering a reconsideration of whether to patent. Novel forms of science, such as developing monoclonal antibodies, generated opportunities for students and postdocs to become co-inventors, extending patenting to more junior-level scientists. The importance of these new research tools also prompted debates over ownership of the science, as the tools could be exploited by both industry and the academy. This dual-use reinforced the approach of Lab I's PI toward patenting to generate industry interest that would advance his research program, as well as the premise in Lab IV of patents representing credit for the university and research colleagues. Patenting became a tool for those situated squarely in "pure science" (Labs II and IV), as well as a strategic opportunity for expanding one's research enterprise (Lab III). The same practice of patenting facilitated different agendas of advance and reputation.

Resources were consequential in facilitating commercialization, shaping initial approaches, and contributing to their standardization. Ample research funding made a corpus of science possible for commercialization. For example, based on the scale of research expenditures, Labs I–III had the largest research operations in the entire department. Yet debates over rewards also triggered change. The prospect of reward underscored the importance of Lab IV's fair-share policies, making clear definitions of invention and inventor consequential. Inclusion on a disclosure mapped directly onto which departments, schools, and labs would benefit, even if individuals did not directly. With real returns coming in for novel science, no longer did Lab III's routine of donating back suffice as a gesture of team effort because it deprived others of income.

One might argue that anticipated returns motivated faculty to pursue technology transfer. Indeed, by 1982, two of the labs in the sample would garner roughly \$2.3 and \$1.8 million, respectively, for inventions that continued to be lucrative through the mid-1990s. But the case for profit as the motivator is quite weak. Most life scientists did not patent. Six of the ten faculty in the department did not disclose at all

Table 16.2.
Recombined Laboratory Approaches to Commercializing Research, 1970–82

	Laboratory I "Team Effort"	Laboratory II "Clear Boundaries"	Laboratory III "Non-Faculty Career"	Laboratory IV "Fair Share"
Invention				
Meaning	Patenting attracts industry expertise to advance research program	Patenting is appropriate for applications, not basic science	Patenting is an admission ticket to industry work	Patenting protects university science from exploitation by industry
Practice	Patent devices not biological materials	Patent consumer applications, not basic science	Patent industry science, publish academic science	Patent basic research findings or methodologies
Inventor				
Meaning	Inventorship is a legal technicality, not credit for the scientific advance	Inventorship narrowly defined reflects credit for scientific advance, not the technical work	Inventorship is a legal definition and signals individual ownership to industry	Inventorship reflects academic ownership vis-à-vis industry
Practice	Staff technicians or engineers on disclosure, not Principal Investigator	Principal Investigator on disclosure, not technical or scientific staff	Legally determined collaborators on disclsure, not Principal Investigator	Principal Investigator and all collaborators on disclosure
Revenues and Rewards				
Meaning	Development is a "team effort" and revenues should support the lab; the reward is advancing the research program	Science is cumulative, personal wealth is inappropriate; the reward is credit for the discovery	Patents are portable and revenues to the individual are welcome; the reward is an industry career	Wealth from science should go to the loci of research; the reward is credit for the discovery
Practice	Assignment goes to university; inventor shares go to the lab	Assignment goes to university, inventor shares are donated	Assignment goes to the individual; inventor shares go to individual	Assignment goes to the university; inventor shares go to individual
Boundaries between Science and Business				
Meaning	Industry is a tool for furthering research and enhancing scientific reputation	Commerce is separate from science; use boundaries to preserve reputation and make commercializing legitimate	University affiliation is a platform to freelance and consult; use patents to increase currency in industry	Industry science depends on academic discovery; use tools of IP to protect science from industry
Practice	"Hands-on" to develop invention; consulting is integrated to mobilize industry and expand science	"Hands-off" in details of technology transfer; consult as a sideline activity	"Hands-on" in technology transfer; consulting is integrated to enhance freelance career	"Hands-on" in technology transfer, consult and interact with industry to "beat them at their own game"

Source: Adapted from Colyvas 2007a, figs. 1, 2.

during this early period, and only two did so with a biological invention. Thus the sharp divide between academic and industrial science loomed large from the perspective of scientific careers. The 1970 disclosure from this department was among the first from the medical school or a biological science department. Before 1978, only one department faculty member (Lab I) participated in formal technology transfer. The new chair (Lab II) appointed that year brought with him a few inventions, and two assistant professors would disclose after 1980. The market was nonexistent for the device in Lab I, and the PI of Lab II chose to disclose a breakthrough technology only after considerable prodding by the OTL.

The PIs of Labs I and II signed back their inventor shares, which amounted to over half a million dollars each. A 1972 OTL report echoes this sentiment: "it is not infrequent that inventors will . . . forego their personal share."[7] Initially research funding for one's lab was a much more salient concern than the prospect of personal profit. If money played a role in the first decade of technology transfer, it served to enhance the survival and expansion of research programs rather than line the pockets of individuals.

Accordingly, we sought a model that enabled us to investigate the mechanisms that explained the expansion of commercial practices among labs in the context of the then acceptable goals and perceived rewards of academic science. Guided by these dimensions and informed by the experiences of the observed labs, we addressed three mechanisms that might account for the emergence of proprietary science. First, we introduced a means of population-level reproduction that was inspired by the instrumental role of graduate students and postdocs in prompting a rethinking of practices as they left their advisers' labs to establish their own labs. Second, we included a means of social influence that incorporated the ways in which scientists' engagement in transferring their knowledge to more commercially minded partners prompted a rethinking of their own practices. Third, we incorporated a form of adaptation for scientists that captured the ways in which the prospect of others patenting and claiming the right to exclude others from further developing an area of science provoked them to take up patenting themselves.

[7] Ibid.

AN AGENT-BASED MODEL OF KNOWLEDGE PRODUCTION AND PROPRIETARY SCIENCE

As a starting point, we build on an existing agent-based computational model developed by Padgett and colleagues and drawn froma chemistry-inspired view of economic production (Padgett 1997; Padgett, Lee, and Collier 2003; Padgett, McMahan, and Zhong, this volume). In their model, firms are assemblages of skills that transform inputs into outputs that can be used by other firms, much like chemical reactions convert products into other products. Firms "learn by doing" in the sense that the skills (which are product transformation rules) used often by firms are strengthened relative to those that are not. Padgett and colleagues use this basic formulation to examine the conditions under which networks of such skills, in the face of environmental selection pressures, can self-organize and sustain themselves through self-reinforcing feedback,[8] or, stated differently, how self-sustaining "economic life" can emerge from initially randomly distributed production activity in a way organic life has been theorized by some to emerge from randomly distributed chemical activity.

For our purposes, such a model maps closely with the goals of our modeling effort. First, it provides a well-tested evolutionary engine for knowledge production and, moreover, one where skills and/or routines can co-evolve with knowledge. Second, for patenting to become institutionalized, some type of positive feedback is necessary to both replicate practices and maintain their combinations as patterned interaction sequences—a purpose readily served by the autocatalytic networks in Padgett and colleagues' model. Indeed, to take the connection even further, one way to view the goal of our modeling is that we are trying to explain the "origin of life" problem for proprietary science—that is, how did we go from nothing to something?

Our model is made up of three parts: scientific products, scientific labs, and routines. The basic idea of the model is that scientific labs use routines to transform knowledge. In a manner that follows the chemistry-inspired model presented by Padgett and colleagues, this transformation process can result in self-reinforcing chains of production. We made several important adaptations and extensions of the model to account

[8] E.g., one firm can transform a "1" to a "2," a neighboring firm a "2" to a "3," and a third common neighbor a "3" to "1," creating a self-reinforcing loop of production.

for our context and insights from our archival analysis (see table 16.3). The primary one is layering organizational routines that govern decision making about commercialization on top of the knowledge production process—that is, scientific labs also own decision-making routines that determine whether to produce proprietary or non-proprietary science, which in turn recasts networks and shapes the profile of laboratories. Other major extensions include incorporating mechanisms for laboratory-level adaptation and learning (not just population-level learning) and endogenous network formation driven by the work labs share. Consequently, we are able to set forth and experiment with an evolutionary process that reflects a core insight of the archival analysis: the idea that organizational routines in a field—the patenting practices in scientific labs—did not evolve independently from the actual work of the field—the production of knowledge.

Description of the Model

Scientific Products

Scientific products are the raw material of the knowledge production process in the model, reflecting the tangible and intangible ideas, tools, or findings that are produced in the research process. We represent them as balls sitting in an urn, waiting to be used by labs. Each ball has two primary characteristics. The first is its type, as indicated by a number from 1 to *n*. The second is its degree of importance to science as a number from 1 to 100, which represents the extent to which the scientific product is valuable to the further advance of basic science. A scientific product is also characterized by an additional attribute of whether or not the product is only patented or published as well.

Scientific Labs

Labs are modeled simply as repertoires of routines. A key dimension in which they vary is on the patentability threshold of the disclosure routine—a number from 1 to 100 that determines the level of importance of a product to science, beyond which a lab is unwilling to patent. For some experimental variations of the model, labs will have the ability to change their disclosure routine (i.e., adapt through some form of learning); in others they will not.

Labs are arrayed spatially on a grid with wrap-around borders and connected to each other via collegial ties. The pattern of collegial ties defines the interaction topology for the labs. For any given lab, we refer to the other labs with whom it shares collegial ties as its set of "network neighbors." In the initial time period of the model, "network neighbors" correspond to spatial neighbors on the grid (e.g., Moore neighborhoods).

Routines

Routines encode the knowledge production and decision-making rules of a lab. In our model, there are five types that reflect the production of knowledge, ways of disclosing that knowledge, and mechanisms that explain change:

1. Knowledge advancement routine. This routine characterizes the core competencies or skills of a particular lab. It describes the ways in which a particular lab "advances" scientific knowledge by transforming a product of one type to another. For example, if a lab contains a routine 1 → 3, it has the ability to transform a scientific product of type 1 to one of type 3. In the context of the life sciences, one can consider these knowledge advancement competencies in terms of subdisciplines such as immunology, bioinformatics, or cell biology that may differ in the kinds of findings they build upon as well as the knowledge they produce. With the exception of self-transformations (e.g., 1 → 1), all possible one-to-one combinations of *n* types are possible. This results in n(n-1) different types of knowledge advancement routines.[9]
2. Disclosure routine. A lab determines whether it deems a particular scientific product patentable by comparing its patentability threshold to the science value score of the product it is evaluating. If the science value score of the product exceeds its patentability threshold, the lab does not deem that particular product appropriate for patenting. In experimental variations of our

[9] In this volume and elsewhere (1997, 2003), Padgett and colleagues discuss the implications for the complexity of the production process that emerges when making different assumptions about the rule sets, or "chemistries," are specified in the model. Our own experimentation with different chemistries did not similarly examine the complexity of knowledge production but focused on whether specifying different rule sets altered the conclusions when comparing change mechanisms. With the exception of the case where hypercycles were not theoretically possible (which brought the evolutionary process to a halt), the chemistry we specified did not alter the fundamental conclusions of the comparisons we present.

Table 16.3.
Empirical Claims about Science Production and ABM Mechanisms

Theoretical and Empirical Claims	Operationalization in the Model
Characterizing the Knowledge Production Process	
• The social system of science is prefaced on the cumulative production of knowledge, whereby scientists build on each other's work, often in self-reinforcing ways. Scientific advance is highly complex as it relies on the combination of skills and tools distributed across scientists, which creates networks of science and scientists.	• We build on existing autocatalytic models of economic production where scientific labs are comprised of skills that transform scientific products into other products in the form of a *knowledge advancement routine*.
• Features of the reward system rely on peer review, publication, and citation. Lab success depends on others using the knowledge they produce.	• Lab survival depends on having skills that are replicated when knowledge is successfully transformed and advanced to another lab.
• While publication is critical, an important form of knowledge transfer occurs through training and mobility of PhDs. Successful labs imperfectly reproduced their practices through the training of PhDs.	• Each lab is given a *lab reproduction routine*, whereby new labs are "hatched" from *successful* parents with some amount of random mutation.
Characterizing Forms of Disclosure	
• Approaches toward commercializing research emanated more from labs and everyday scientific work than government, legal, or university policies. Opportunities to change disclosure practices and opportunities to produce science are strongly linked.	• Each lab is given a *knowledge disclosure routine* that is activated by the knowledge production process.
• Patenting was a contingent choice that varied across scientists, depended on characteristics of particular findings, and were subject to change at each disclosure opportunity. Decision whether to patent involved considering both one's own perceptions of patenting and one's own perception of how important to science the idea produced was.	• Each lab agent in the model has a different *patenting threshold* and each scientific product has a different *science value on a* scale of 1–100. During the disclosure routine, the lab compares its *patenting threshold* to the *science value* of the finding.
Characterizing the Adaptation of Labs	
• Scientists were influenced by what others were doing with their science. Labs learned from the ability of others to patent downstream developments of their work.	• Each lab is given a *participatory adaptation routine:* labs update their individual thresholds as a weighted average of one's own threshold and that of successful colleagues.
• Scientists were aware of the increasing commercial opportunities of their science. Labs reacted to the patenting taking place among their peers over the same kind of science by choosing to patent themselves.	• Each lab is given a *preemptive adaptation routine:* labs update their individual thresholds based on the existence of more liberal thresholds among colleagues.

model, we allow labs to learn and adapt their patentability threshold.

3. Participatory adaptation routine. In some experimental variations of the model, labs update their patentability threshold after every knowledge advancement transaction where its transaction partner was rewarded more than they were. In such cases, a lab's patentability threshold is recalculated as the weighted average of its current threshold and the threshold of the more successful transaction partner. The weight given to the

more successful partner is determined by a tunable parameter, α, and the weight given to the current threshold is 1 – α.

4. Preemptive adaptation routine. In some experimental variations of the model, even if a lab does not deem a product patentable according to its disclosure routine, a lab may patent a product out of concern that it will lose control of it. More precisely, if a lab has a network neighbor whose disclosure routine would lead to the patenting of the product, the lab will adjust its patentability threshold to the minimum level that allows it to patent the product itself.
5. Reproduction routine. If a lab is chosen to reproduce, it will do so by executing its reproduction routine. The reproduction routine specifies the patentability threshold of the offspring, which is given by a random draw from a normal distribution with the mean equal to the patentability threshold of the parent and the standard deviation equal to an exogenously determined parameter that governs the amount of random mutation in the process. It also specifies the likelihood, *plink*, that the child will inherit any given link to a parent's network neighbors, including the parent themselves.[10]

Knowledge Production and Patenting Process

Every time period of the model consists of the following steps, also illustrated in figure 16.1.

1. A knowledge advancement routine is chosen at random from all possible routines. The labs containing that routine in their repertoire pick a scientific product (a ball) to evaluate for use from the urn of all existing scientific products.
2. The labs apply their knowledge advancement routines to determine whether the scientific product they are evaluating is something they can advance. If so, they then apply their disclosure routine to see if this is something they can patent.
3. If "preemptive adaptation" is on, labs apply their preemptive adaptation routine.
4. The following outcomes are possible from this evaluation process:
    a. If the input product is not advanceable, the lab returns the product to the urn.
    b. If the input product is advanceable but not patentable, the lab transforms the scientific product accordingly and passes the product on to one of its randomly selected network neighbors. One might consider this a product that was published but not patented.
    c. If the input product is advanceable and patentable, the lab transforms the scientific product accordingly, patents the product, and then passes the product on to one of its randomly selected network neighbors.
5. The selected network neighbor then evaluates the transformed scientific product in the same manner as if she had pulled the ball from the urn. The result of this evaluation can lead to one of five types of transactions with the sender of the product:
    a. If the product is not advanceable for the receiver, the receiver returns the product to the urn.
    b. If the product was not patented by the sender but patented by the receiver, we mark the transaction a successful *publication-patent* transaction.
    c. If the product was not patented by the sender and advanced and not patented by the receiver, we mark the transaction a successful *publication-publication* transaction.
    d. If the product was patented by the sender and by the receiver, we mark the transaction a successful *patent-patent* transaction.
    e. If the product was patented by the sender but advanced without being patented by the receiver, we mark the transaction a successful *patent-publication* transaction.
6. If a product is advanceable, the recipient labs will then also pass the now twice-transformed scientific product on to one of their randomly selected network neighbors. At the point where a lab does not deem a scientific product useable (i.e., does not have an advancement routine that can act on what it receives), the scientific product is returned to the product urn.
7. Knowledge advancement routines associated with successful transactions are rewarded

[10] Note that the total number of network neighbors is not allowed to exceed the initial maximum number of eight. In cases where the reproduction process leads to some labs having more than eight network neighbors, the lab kills off the links over which it has had the fewest successful transactions.

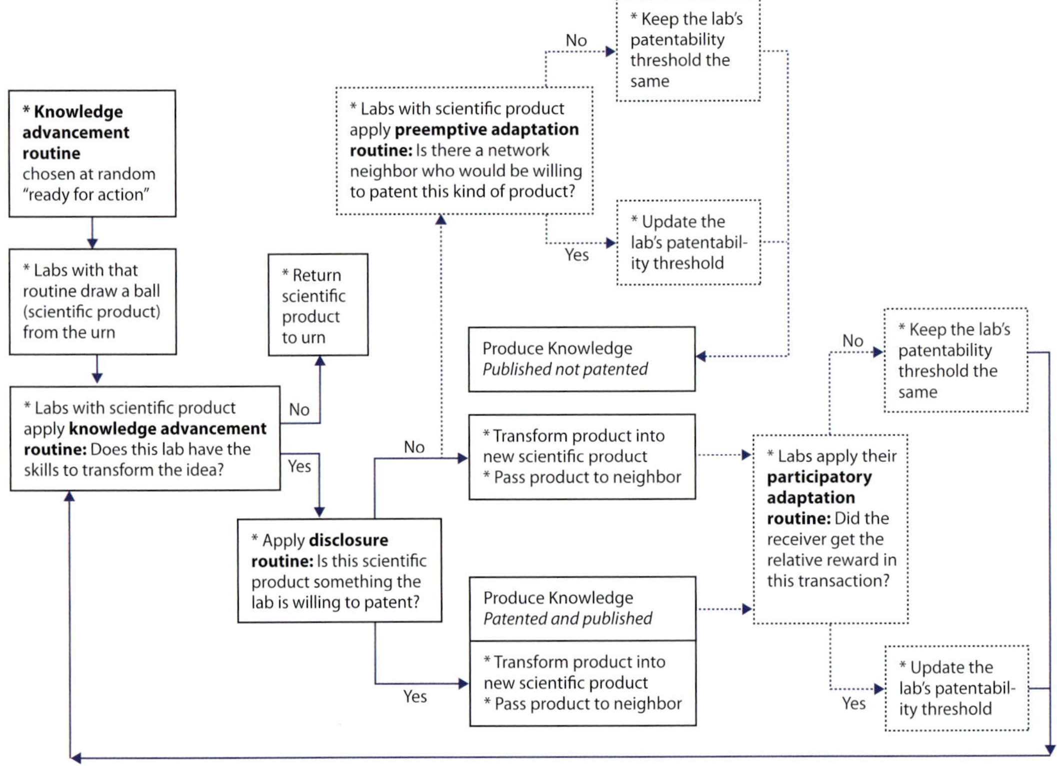

Figure 16.1 Schematic representation of scientific knowledge production. Dotted lines represent adaptation routines that can be turned on or off.

with duplication based on relative benefit in the following manner:

a. For successful *publication-publication* transactions, the sender's knowledge advancement routine is duplicated. It reflects the benefit to the sender of being cited by the work of another lab. The intuition here is that the receiver is rewarded insofar as someone can use the knowledge.[11]
b. For successful *publication-patent* and *patent-publication* transactions, the receiver's knowledge advancement routine is duplicated. In the former case, the recipient benefits from a patent, but the sender neither participates in the patent nor benefits from an academic citation. In the latter, the recipient benefits from a publication but the sender does not benefit from the right to exclude others from using it. Rewarding the receiver in either of these situations makes survival chances greater for those who counter the previous form of disclosure—essentially taking advances in one domain and utilizing them to capture benefits in another.[12]

[11] Consider that most publications are seldom cited (deSolla 1965).

[12] For example, thousands of university scientists around the world utilized recombinant DNA technologies in the 1980s and 1990s without ever taking out a license for active Stanford patents on this work when research results were only published. In a legal sense, scientists have the opportunity to utilize patented technologies if solely for experimental purposes. Experimental use, as defined by the courts, however, is much more strict than would be understood from the perspective of many scientists. Even when they are in any kind of violation of infringement in a legal sense, the potential damages from the court's perspective are so low that most cases of infringement are never realized. From the perspective

c. For successful *patent-patent* transactions, both the sender's and receiver's knowledge advancement routines are duplicated, as both benefit from the patent. We chose to reward this scenario mutually because building on a previously patented finding incurs resources to the sender and excludability to the receiver.

8. Every time a routine is duplicated, another routine chosen at random is killed off.
9. If "participatory adaptation" is on, labs apply their participatory adaptation routine.

Labs with no advancement routines left will die. Every time a lab dies, a new lab is created to replace it by choosing an existing lab to execute its reproduction routine so as to keep the number of labs constant over a run. The probability of a lab being chosen to reproduce is proportional to the total number of advancement routines it contains (i.e., the "stronger" labs reproduce more).

MODEL ANALYSIS

Embedded in the model are three specific mechanisms (defined as routines) that can lead to a shift in patenting practices:lab selection and reproduction, participatory adaptation, and preemptive adaptation. In the real world, as captured in our archival analysis, one can observe all three mechanisms simultaneously taking place. Simulation provides a methodological advantage in enabling us to design hypothetical experiments that investigates how these mechanisms operate in isolation (i.e., they can be "turned off"). This approach allows us to examine whether any of our three mechanisms has more leverage than another in explaining the emergence of proprietary science.

First, to further describe the model and illustrate the type of data collected, we present sample results from a representative run of the model. Second, we present the results of an experiment that suggests that moving from a very low to very high mean patentability threshold in a population of labs is more likely to occur when reproduction is coupled with preemptive adaptation than it is when reproduction coincides with participatory adaptation. Third, we present our attempts to better understand the boundary conditions of these results and include a discussion of model parameters and stability of results.

Representative Results

Figure 16.2 illustrates a representative run in the NetLogo modelwhere the reproduction and preemptive adaptation routines are turned on and the participatory adaptation routine is turned off. The boxes represent labs. The gray lines linking labs are collegial ties among the labs.The small circles within the labs represent production rules (or "skills"). The model is initialized as described above with the labs arrayed spatially on a grid. Initially all labs had exactly eight collegial ties to neighbors—the eight closest labs geographically—and skills randomly distributed across all labs. As the model runs, labs with unused skills die off and are replaced by offspring who develop a network tie back to their parent lab (and, for the sake of our visualization, geographically proximate to the parent lab). Consequently, the network is transformed into something new—a new structure that is a result of the simultaneous execution over time of the reproduction routine and the routines that govern the production of knowledge. Figures 16.2A through 16.2D show the evolution of the model over time (defined as the number of transactions taking place).

Figure 16.3 further characterizes what is happening "beneath" these visualizations, from a network-level perspective. Specifically, it provides a snapshot of the lab and skill networks that emerge after fifty successful transactions within the process. The picture on the left-hand side depicts the lab-to-lab ties described above. These are collegial ties among labs—ties to "network neighbors" who are more likely than others to learn about the focal lab's scientific production. The right-hand side of figure 16.3 depicts a substantively different kind of network related to the *work* of the labs—that is, the network of complementary skills responsible for the production of knowledge. More specifically, a node in this network is an instance of a skill in a lab (e.g., 12 represents skill 1-> 2), with the size of the node proportional to the strength of that skill. A link from one skill to another indicates that (a) the skills reside in labs that could potentially pass transformed products to each other; and (b) the output of the first skill can be used as input for the second skill. Note that

of administration and everyday academic science, the practice resembles one of "asking forgiveness rather than permission."

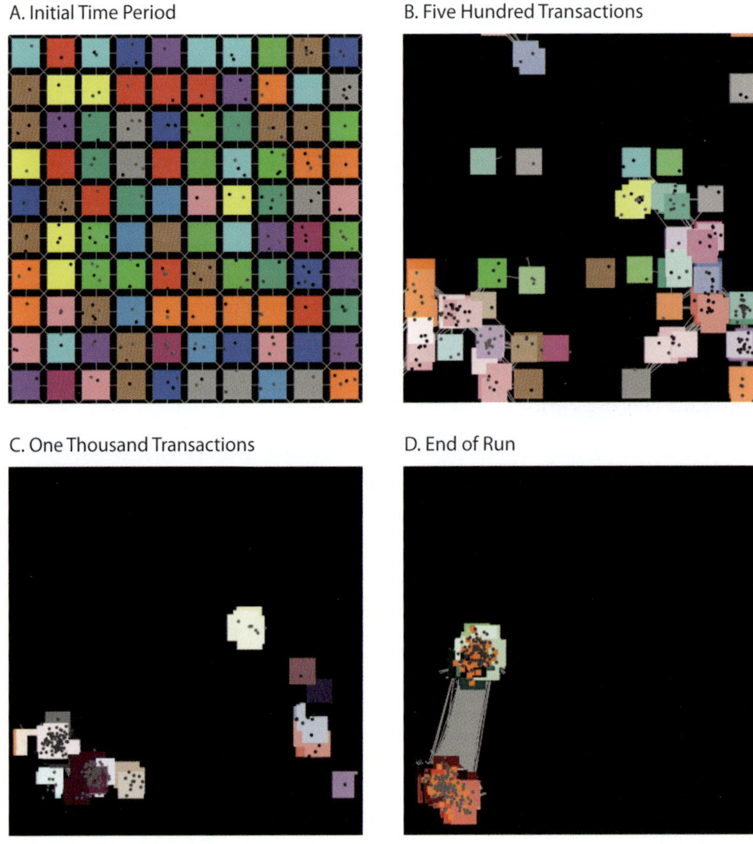

Figure 16.2 Evolution of agent-based model over time. A. Initial time period. B. Five hundred transactions. C. One thousand transactions. D. End of run.

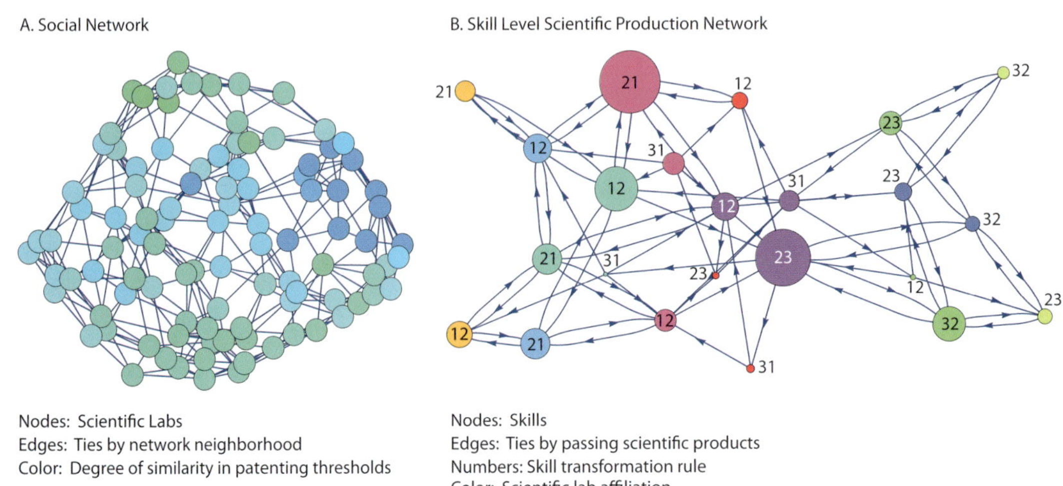

Figure 16.3 Multilevel scientific production networks. A. Social network. B. Skill level scientific production network.

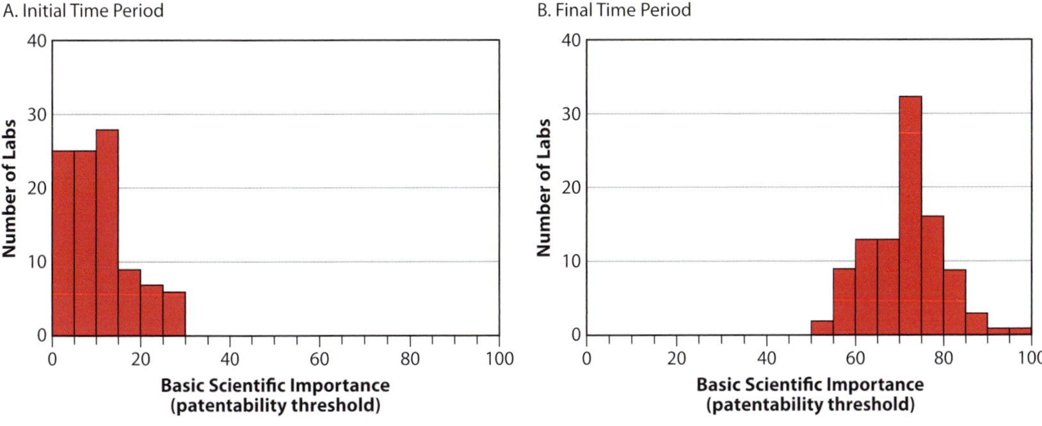

Figure 16.4 Distribution of patentability thresholds. A. Initial time period. B. Final time period.

autocatalytic relationships exist in many places in this network; for example, instances where "12" nodes point to "21" nodes and where those same "21" nodes point back to the "12 nodes." In this particular example, the length of the cycle is 2 nodes. In other cases, the cycle is more "complex" in the sense that a larger number of nodes is involved.[13] Like the potential collaboration network on the left, this network has also undergone change since its initial state—a collective result of reproduction, adaptation, and production routines.

Figures 16.4A and 16.4B illustrate the consequences of these organizational and production process changes on the type of science being produced over time. More specifically, the plots in figures 16.4A and 16.4B show the fraction of the trailing 500 transactions where either (a) both partners in a transaction patent their scientific output (pat-pat); (b) both partners in a transaction do not patent their scientific output (np-np); or (c) one partner patents and the other does not (mixed). The differences between figure 16.4A (where preemptive adaption is on) and figure 16.4B (where it is not) foreshadow the finding to come: all other things equal, moving from a world of little to ubiquitous patenting is more likely the consequence of a lab-level preemptive adaptation mechanism than a lab-level participatory learning mechanism.

[13] For the results presented in this book, the typical longest cycle length in the final state of the model is 2. See chapter 3 in this volumefor a deeper examination of the conditions under which such an autocatalytic process can yield more complex chains of production in equilibrium.

Figure 16.5 shows the distribution of patentability thresholds—our key outcome of interest—at the beginning and end of the run corresponding to figure 16.4B. Note that in this case the distribution shifts substantially from a world where most labs are willing to only patent products of low basic scientific importance to one where a much larger range of scientific importance is considered patentable. Under other experimental conditions, the distribution changes in different ways, perhaps with a smaller shift or greater flattening of the distribution. In the experiments that follow, we summarize the difference in final distributions across experimental conditions by comparing the means of their end-of-run patentability distributions.

Comparing Change Mechanisms

The model contains three distinct mechanisms for change: reproduction, participatory adaptation, and preemptive adaptation. To better understand the connection between each mechanism and the emergence of patenting by academics we conducted a computational experiment comparing (a) the baseline case of reproduction only;(b) reproduction plus participatory adaptation; and (c) reproduction plus preemptive adaptation. Our primary outcome of interest was the mean of the patentability thresholds across labs at the end of a run.Each incidence of running the model reflects a process with multiple stochastic elements. We therefore repeated each run fifty times under each experimental condition.This

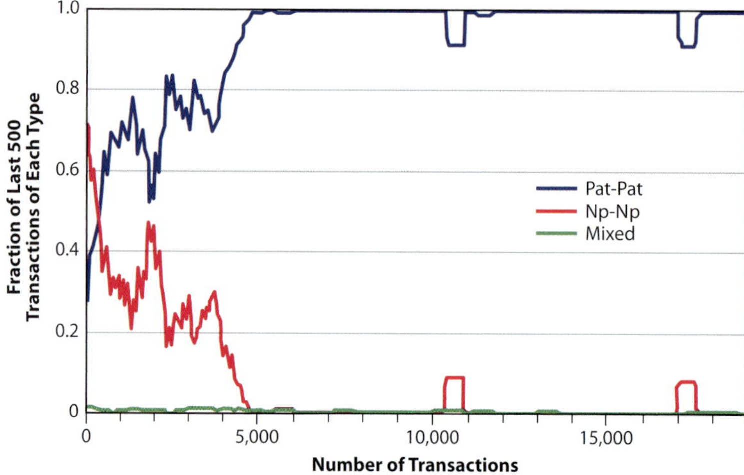

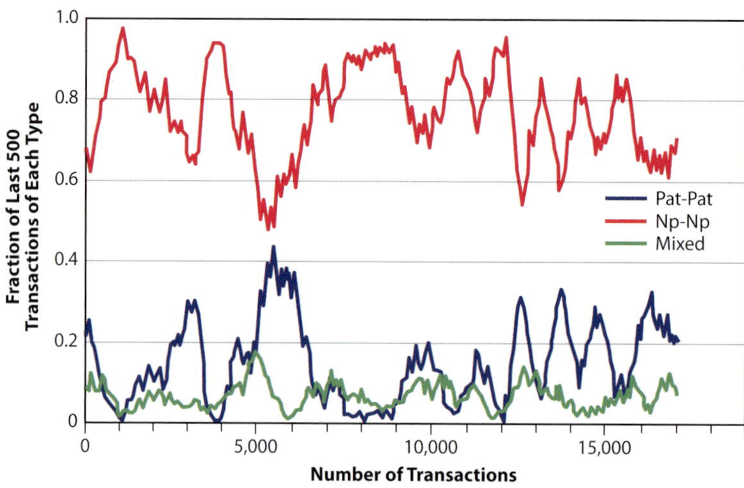

Figure 16.5 A. Transaction types over time with preemptive adaptation on. B. Transaction types over time with preemptive adaptation off.

approach created a distribution of outcomes for analysis.[14]

We present our results as a set of box and whisker plots, each representing an experimental condition for fifty runs, depicted in figure 16.6. The y-axis represents the distribution of the mean patentability threshold across the labs in the final time period of a run. The x-axis reflects the mechanisms that were "turned on" for each experimental condition. The initial lab mean patentability threshold for all runs and

[14] Unless otherwise noted, each run was parameterized in the following manner: 100 labs were spatially arranged on a 10 × 10 spatial grid with wrap-around boundaries and initially networked to their eight nearest (Moore) neighbors; the patentability threshold of each lab's disclosure routine was randomly determined by a draw from a normal distribution with mean 15 and standard deviation 2; scientific products (the balls in the urn) come in 4 types (1 to 4), yielding 12 possible unique transformation rules; 200 instances of those 12 transformation rules were uniformly distributed across the 100 labs; the urn was populated with 50 balls, none of which were initially patented, and each ball was randomly assigned a science value score from 1 to 100; $\alpha = 0.2$ in the participatory adaptation rule; offspring always create a link to their parent lab in the reproduction routine ($p_{link} = 1$); an offspring's patentability threshold is determined by a random draw from a normal distribution with a mean equal to the threshold of the parent and a standard deviation of 5.

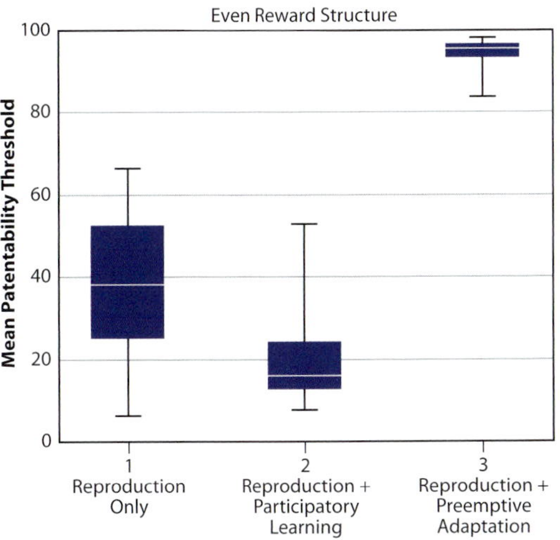

Figure 16.6 Final patentability thresholds (50 runs) even reward structure.

under all conditions was set at fifteen. Under the baseline case of "reproduction only" the mean threshold across labs shifted only to approximately thirty-eight. This moderate increase is a consequence of the initial thresholds, which are very low and unable to decline below zero. The result of this simulation process is that random mutation will more often than not lead to an overall increase in the patentability threshold. The second experimental condition demonstrates, however, that adding the participatory adaptation mechanism actually keeps any increase in check. This result has to do with the initial state of the simulation, whereby the participatory adaptation mechanism is actually reinforcing the extant norm of low patentability thresholds already in place.

In contrast, the "preemptive adaptation" mechanism does not seem to be hindered by the initial norms of the system. Instead, the results in that case most closely match the reference pattern we are trying to understand—a very large shift in the distribution of patentability thresholds. All other things being equal, it appears that preemptive adaptation provides more leverage from the shift. The intuition may seem surprising at first but makes sense given the system already in place. Whereas the participatory adaptation mechanism requires a successful lab with a high patentability threshold to emulate, the preemptive mechanism only needs a socially proximate lab with a threshold that is slightly higher than the "susceptible" lab. Once the "susceptible" lab changes its own patentability threshold, that lab is more likely to become "contagious" to other susceptible labs, which in turn may need to take preemptive adaptive action themselves. Stated differently, the preemptive adaptation mechanism only needs small variation in thresholds nearby to prompt change, whereas the participatory adaptation mechanism needs a high threshold "seed" to diffuse in the population. Preemptive adaptation, however, is not the only way to achieve our outcome of interest in our simulation process. We modified the parameters of the model to understand whether other conditions besides preemptive adaptation might bring about our reference pattern and, similarly, whether other conditions could dampen the effect of preemptive adaptation. Figure 16.7 addresses the first question—alternative conditions that may lead to a large shift in patentability thresholds by altering the reward conditions to strongly favor patenting. This change was implemented by having the skills rewarded for being involved in successful transactions as a result of patenting replicated ten times instead of only two as in the baseline case (and leaving the rewards for non-patenting the same). In this scenario, all adaptation mechanisms appeared to produce our outcome of interest.

The results, however, are rather robust when considering attempts that we designed to mitigate the effects of preemptive adaptation (figure 16.8). Our experiment with an inverse environment—one that replicates the skills rewarded

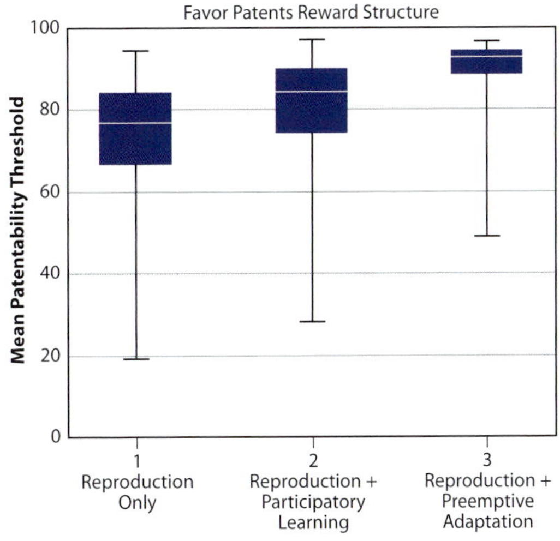

Figure 16.7 Final patentability thresholds (50 runs) favor patents reward structure.

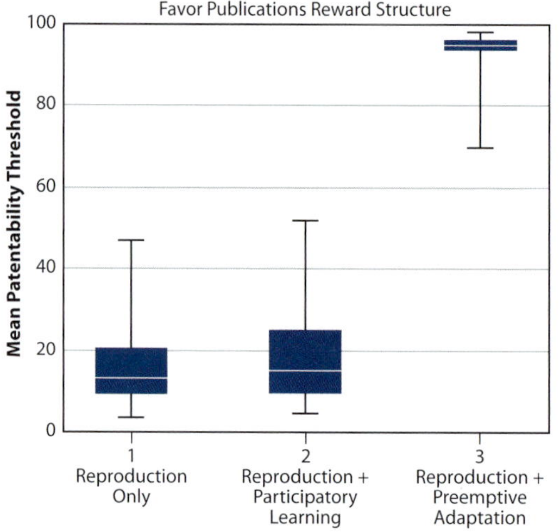

Figure 16.8 Final patentability thresholds (50 runs) favor patents reward structure.

for being involved in successful transactions as a result of not patenting ten times—still does not prevent the preemptive mechanism from bringing about a large shift in thresholds. Figure 16.9 similarly shows that the result is not sensitive to the precise parameterization of the participatory observation mechanism. Changing the weight put on this mechanism does not seem to change the basic story.

CONCLUSION

Utilizing a combination of ABM and empirical analysis provides the opportunity to link a formal operationalization of organizational reproduction to theoretical claims about the emergence of practices and their concrete instantiation in institutions and to refine both through the application to knowledge production. In

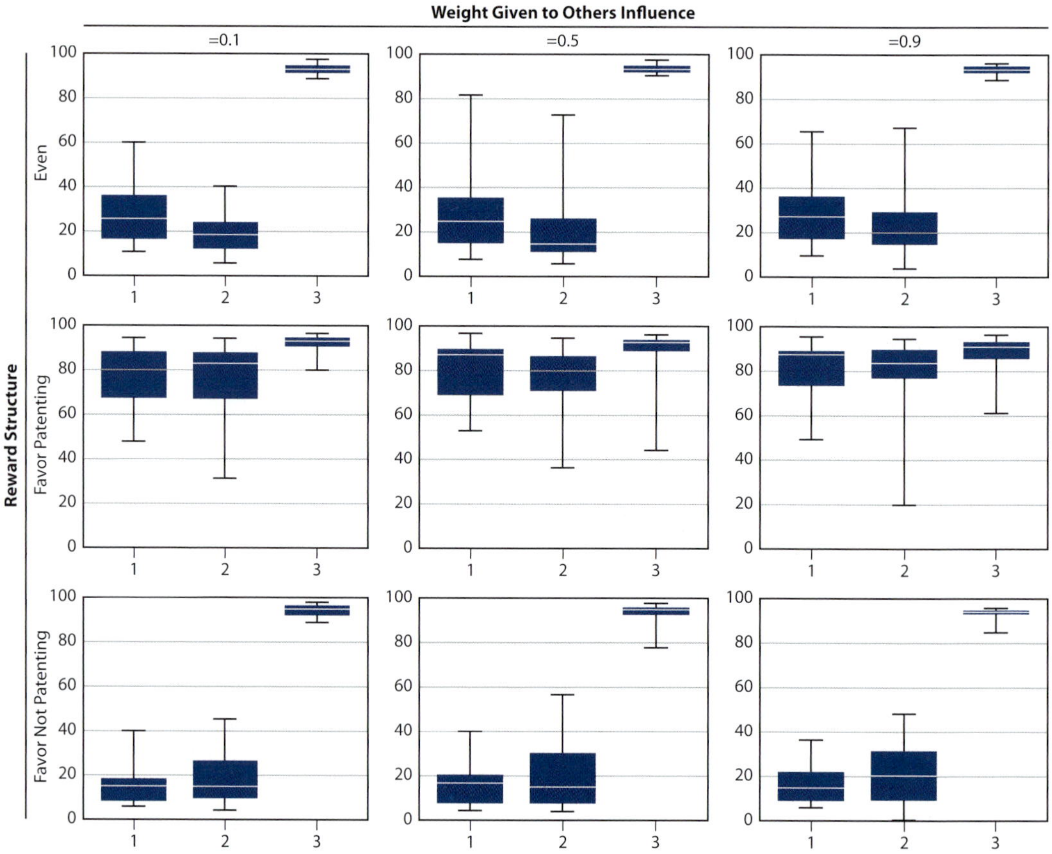

Figure 16.9 Final patentability thresholds by alpha and reward structure (50 runs).

adapting the autocatalysis framework to the setting of proprietary science, we extend an existing model of the emergence of economic "life" to the emergence of disclosure regimes that govern the production of knowledge. We demonstrate accommodations to the model to address the production of routines and proprietary science. In doing so, we further refine existing arguments about the ways in which institutions of science combine with resources,skills, and technologies to shape laboratory-level practices.

Our analysis results in several insights. First, our investigation sheds new light on the dynamics of emergence. By examining life scientists at the origins of patenting, we demonstrate how commercializing academic science was a contingent and relational decision and not only a matter of whether scientists were willing to accept the practice of patenting in their labs. Inventions that culminated in attempts to patent were the result of multiple factors: the process by which scientists conducted their work, their perceptions about appropriate ways to relate to colleagues in both universities and firms, and particular research findings under consideration. Debates emerged at points of contradiction between science and commerce, prompting seemingly similar problems of control over resources and organizational survival despite very different rationales. Returns to research and development for academic labs meant extending one's research program and enhancing the prospects of the rewards of academic science rather than personal profit as reflected in the codified incentive structure of the university.[15] Scientists were very much proprietary about their research programs, as credit and priority of discovery relied on the continued trajectory of their work. In practice, however, the meaning of proprietary differed substantially under a regime where open disclosure reflects the linchpin to reinforcing science. For scientists, standing on the shoulders of giants meant taking part in self-reinforcing chains of discoveries and was fundamental to their success.

Second, even without centralized control—that is, exogenous regulations such as laws or policies that promote individual rewards—we establish ways in which proprietary science can emerge in the form of more labs patenting a broader range of science. We show how rules can develop and persist in particular forms without top-down coordination such as policy incentives. Moreover, we demonstrate the difficulty entailed in attaining high levels of patenting through basic processes of selection and reproduction. Adaptation and interdependence in lab decision making appear necessary to generate the emergence of a regime where patenting is commonplace. Stated differently, in order to get self-reinforcement and reproduction of new routines, labs have to interact and be willing to change their rules and conceptions about invention. This finding corresponds to our archival investigations, where scientists exhibited considerable discretion around what findings would be patented or how resources would be utilized.

Third, although both participatory and preemptive adaptation mechanisms are consistent with the empirical association between the likelihood of patenting and having colleagues who patent (Stuart and Ding 2006; Bercovitz and Feldman 2008), our model illustrates that they have different implications if one is concerned with the emergence of a new practice instead of the diffusion of an existing one. By distinguishing between learning from one's own experience (participatory adaptation) and changing from anticipating the actions of others (preemptive adaptation), we find that the latter mechanism is more likely to produce outcomes one could characterize as emergence—that is, moving from a world where patenting was rare and unacceptable to one where it was desirable and appropriate. This finding points to a larger benefit of the general approach of this chapter. By combining computational methods and archival analysis in the context of proprietary science, we are able to make more explicit how the mechanisms that give rise to an institution can be quite different from those that reinforce it (Stinchcombe 1968; Mahoney 2000).

Finally, our research approach provides rich insight into the origin and emergence of proprietary science from the perspective of a successful research university. Previous work has suggested that the emergence of proprietary science was not entirely a reaction to regulatory changes or external incentives but the result of micro-level assembly of practices drawn from the perspective of academic science (Colyvas 2007a, 2007b). Using archival data alone, however, it is difficult to discern to what extent those

[15] The latter motivation of enhancing one's personal salary would emerge as a legitimate practice many years later, often much to the disappointment of less experienced administrators and scientists who witnessed how the vast majority of inventions make no money at all. Even when they do, most disbursements result in a rather small amount once expenses and university and department shares are removed (Colyvas and Powell 2007).

bottom-up processes could collectively or individually account for the current disclosure routines and norms currently in practice at Stanford. By translating the insights of that work into an agent-based model, we can now show that (a) it was possible that bottom-up processes alone could give rise to the system we observed; and (b) some observed social mechanisms alone were not enough to account for the emergence of the current system. Moreover, in previous chapters in this volume, we saw sharp regional variation in the role and success of anchor tenants despite comparable material endowments (e.g., Powell, Packalen, and Whittington, this volume). Early biotechnology ventures arose through networks of affiliation where scientists could apply the tools and conceptions of their prior experience in labs to shape the form that private biotechnology enterprises would take. The academic life sciences provide an important parallel as engagement in patenting as a new and contradictory form of disclosure required a requisite level of mutability in social and technical categories, such as invention and inventor, for emergence to take place. A university of a different character, for example, one that was much more rigid and imposing in the application of norms and policies, would have made laboratory-level assembly and flow of practices difficult. Our counterfactual inquiry focused on comparing different mechanisms that would explain a shift in two distributions of labs patenting certain kinds of science, reflecting the change we observed at Stanford. Other universities or fields may have exhibited different starting points and emergent distributions. This approach lays the groundwork for comparative analysis across regions as well in characterizing different reference patterns from origin to emergence and extending the counterfactual to different forms that the emergent outcome may take.

REFERENCES

Bercovitz, J., and M. Feldman. 2008. "Academic Entrepreneurs: Organizational Change at the Individual Level." *Organization Science* 19(1):69–89.

Berman, Elizabeth Popp. 2012. *Creating the Market University: How Academic Science Became an Economic Engine*. Princeton: Princeton University Press.

Burton, D. M. 2001. "The Company They Keep: Founders' Models for Organizing New Firms." In *The Entrepreneurship Dynamic: Origins of Entrepreneurship and the Evolution of Industries*, ed. C. B. Shoonhoven and E. Romanelli, 13–39. Stanford: Stanford University Press.

Colyvas, J. A. 2007a. "From Divergent Meanings to Common Practices: The Early Institutionalization of Technology Transfer in the Life Sciences at Stanford University." *Research Policy* 36:456–76.

———. 2007b. "Factories, Hazards, and Contamination: Metaphors and Recombinant DNA in University and Biotechnology." *Minerva* 45:143–59.

Colyvas, J. A., and S. Jonsson. 2011. "Ubiquity and Legitimacy: Disentangling Diffusion and Institutionalization." *Sociological Theory* 29(1):27–53.

Colyvas, J. A., and W. W. Powell. 2006. "Roads to Institutionalization: The Remaking of Boundaries between Public and Private Science. *Research in Organizational Behavior* 27:315–63.

———. 2007. "From Vulnerable to Venerated: The Institutionalization of Academic Entrepreneurship in the Life Sciences." *Research in the Sociology of Organizations* 25:219–59.

Dasgupta, P., and P. David. 1994. "Toward a New Economics of Science." *Research Policy* 23(5): 487–521.

deSolla, P.D.J. 1965. "Networks of Scientific Papers: The Pattern of Bibliographic References Indicates the Nature of the Scientific Research Front." *Science* 149:510–15.

DiMaggio, P., and W. W. Powell. 1991. Introduction to *The New Institutionalism in Organizational Analysis*, ed. Walter W. Powell and Paul J. DiMaggio, 1–36. Chicago: University of Chicago Press.

Epstein, J. M., and R. Axtell. 1996. *Growing Artificial Societies: Social Science from the Bottom up*. Washington, DC: Brookings Institution.

Gross, N. 2009. "A Pragmatist Theory of Social Mechanisms." *American Sociological Review* 74:358–79.

Jepperson, R. 1991. "Institutions, Institutional Effects and Institutionalism." In *The New Institutionalism in Organizational Analysis*, ed. Walter W. Powell and Paul J. DiMaggio, 143–63. Chicago: University of Chicago Press.

Lach, S., and M. Schankerman. 2003. "Incentives and Invention in Universities." NBER working paper no. W9727.

Mahoney, J. 2000. "Path Dependence in Historical Sociology." *Theory and Society* 29:507–48.

Mowery, D., R. Nelson, B. N. Sampat, and A. Ziedonis. 2004. *Ivory Tower and Industrial Innovation*. Stanford: Stanford University Press.

Nelson, R., and S. Winter. 1982. *An Evolutionary Theory of Economic Change*. Cambridge, MA: Harvard University Press.

North, D. 1990. *Institutions, Institutional Change, and Economic Performance*. New York: Cambridge University Press.

Padgett, J. F. 1997. "The Emergence of Simple Ecologies of Skill: A Hypercycle Approach to Economic Organization." In *The Economy as an Evolving Complex System II*, ed. W. Brian Arthur, Steven N.

Durlauf and David A. Lane. Reading, MA: Addison-Wesley.

Padgett, J. F., J. F. Doowan Lee, and N. Collier. 2003. "Economic Production as Chemistry." *Industrial & Corporate Change* 12(4):843–77.

Pierson, P. 2004. *Politics in Time: History, Institutions, and Political Analysis*. Princeton: Princeton University Press.

Rhoten, D., and W. W. Powell. 2007. "The Frontiers of Intellectual Property: Expanded Protection vs. New Models of Open Science." *Annual Review of Law and Social Science* 3:345–73.

Ruef, M., and W. R. Scott. 1998. "A Multidimensional Model of Organizational Legitimacy: Hospital Survival in Changing Institutional Environment." *Administrative Science Quarterly* 43(4):877–904.

Shane, S. 2004. *Academic Entrepreneurship: University Spinoffs and Wealth Creation*. Northampton, MA: Edward Elgar.

Shapin, S. 2008. *The Scientific Life: A Moral History of a Late Modern Vocation*. Chicago: University of Chicago Press. http://www.amazon.com/Scientific-Life-History-Modern-Vocation/dp/0226750248/ref=sr_1_1?ie=UTF8&s=books&qid=1239403582&sr=1-12008.

Sterman, J. 2000. *Business Dynamics: Systems Thinking and Modeling for a Complex World*. New York: Irwin/McGraw-Hill.

Stinchcombe, A. 1968. *Constructing Social Theories*. New York: Harcourt, Brace, and World.

Streek, W., and K. Thelen, eds. 2005. *Beyond Continuity: Policy Change in Advanced Political Economies*. Oxford: Oxford University Press.

Stuart, T. E., and W. Ding. 2006. "When Do Scientists Become Entrepreneurs? The Social Structural Antecedents of Commercial Activity in the Academic Life Sciences." *American Journal of Sociology* 11: 97–144.

Suchman, Mark C. 1995. "Managing Legitimacy: Strategic and Institutional Approaches." *Academy of Management Review* 20:571–611.

Thelen, K. 2004. "How Institutions Evolve: Insights from Comparative Historical Analysis." In *Comparative Historical Analysis in the Social Sciences*, ed. J. Mahoney and D. Rueschemeyer. New York: Cambridge University Press.

Weingast, B. 2002. "Rational Choice Institutionalism." In *Political Science: The State of the Discipline*, ed. I. Katznelson and H. Milner. New York: Norton.

Wilensky, U. 1999. NetLogo. [computer software]. Evanston, IL: Center for Connected Learning and Computer-Based Modeling, Northwestern University. http://ccl.northwestern.edu/netlogo.

Wilensky, Uri, and William W. Rand. 2007. "Making Models Match: Replicating Agent-Based Models." *Journal of Artificial Societies and Social Simulation* 10(42):42.

Winter, S. G. 1990. "Survival, Selection and Evolution." In *The New Palgrave of Economics*, ed. J. Eatwell, M. Milgate, and P. Newman, 3:614–17. London: Macmillan.

17

Why the Valley Went First

Aggregation and Emergence in Regional Inventor Networks

Lee Fleming ▪ Lyra Colfer ▪ Alexandra Marin ▪ Jonathan McPhie

It has become increasingly fashionable to identify social networks as crucial contributors to regional innovative capacity (Marshall 1920; Piore and Sabel 1984; Krugman 1991; Stern and Porter 2001). Networks have been argued to offer improved customer-supplier relations, more efficient venture capital and legal infrastructure, and increased knowledge spillovers between firms and regional institutions. Knowledge spillovers are thought to be particularly crucial to fast-developing technologies such as semiconductors and, more recently, biotechnology. Spillovers correlate with increased labor mobility (Angel 1989), relaxed enforcement of non-compete covenants (Gilson 1999), and increased labor mobility and brain drain (Marx et al. 2009, 2011). Saxenian (1994) makes the functional argument connecting networks and innovative capacity, proposing that Silicon Valley's rapid labor mobility, collective learning, interfirm relationships, and informal knowledge exchange gave it a decisive edge in competing against the more secretive and autarkic firms of Boston.

Nevertheless, there is still skepticism about the causal influence of networks in regional innovative productivity. For example, Kenny and Burg (1999) acknowledge that "all business activity is dependent upon networks" but contend that a region's network(s) will adjust to suit its technological competencies over time. Where Saxenian (1994) sees causal differences in Silicon Valley and Boston networks, Florida and Kenney (1990, 98–118) see indeterminate similarity and propose that technological trajectories drive regional advantage. Turning the argument on its head, the skeptics propose that networks result from—and do not necessarily improve—regional innovative advantage (Feldman 2001).

These opposing arguments for and against causality immediately raise the suspicion of coevolution. Surely networks influence regional advantage and are in turn shaped by regional success or failure. But much of the current discussion about networks and regional advantage remains static (for important exceptions, see Owen-Smith and Powell 2004), implicitly assuming that networks differ across regions but remain essentially unchanged within them. If this assumption were untrue—and could be cleanly unpacked—the discussion could be greatly enriched.

With these goals in mind, this chapter has two objectives: first, to understand how isolated clusters of regional inventors become connected, and in particular, why Silicon Valley aggregated earlier than Boston; and second, to describe the information flows and creative ecologies of such networks. We begin by comparing the structural histories of the patented inventor coauthorship networks of Boston and Silicon Valley from 1975 through 1999. Following Fleming, King, and

We would like to thank Ivin Baker, Jeff Chen, and Adam Juda for their help with matching algorithms and illustrations; Christine Gaze for her editing; and the Harvard Business School Division of Research for support. Most important, we would like to thank all the inventors who spent a great deal of time with us discussing their careers.

Juda (2007), we first demonstrate that the largest connected network component in Silicon Valley underwent a dramatic transition in the early 1990s.[1] Although small at first—and similar in size to Boston's largest connected component in 1989—it grew rapidly from 1990 on, encompassing almost half of Silicon Valley's patenting inventors by 1999. Boston did not undergo a similar transition until the mid-1990s, and even recently its largest connected network component remains proportionally smaller, containing approximately a quarter of its inventors. We investigated this historical divergence by focusing on the actual ties that inventors created—or failed to create—across the dominant network components in their regions. To fulfill our second objective, we asked the inventors about the knowledge flows in their careers, both within and across the observed clusters, and how such flows influenced their creativity.

While inventors move from job to job and create collaborative ties for a wide variety of reasons (Gulati and Gargiulo 1999), our data highlight the importance of "academic" institutions in the creation of ties across regional organizations. Much of the difference in aggregation[2] can be traced to Stanford doctoral students taking local employment, in contrast to MIT students leaving the Boston region. We also find that a single institutional program—the postdoc fellowship at IBM's Almaden Valley Labs—was responsible for 30 percent of the Valley's initial aggregation. Young inventors play a particularly important role in the process of regional aggregation; while older inventors move to start-ups (and are less likely to move in general; see Angel 1989), young inventors move from graduate school through private firm postdoc programs and other positions within large network components, bridging technological communities and generating new technological combinations.

With respect to the competing comparisons of the two regions (Saxenian 1994; Florida and Kenney 1990; Kenney and Burg 1999), we found that Silicon Valley's patenting coauthorship networks are indeed more connected—but in some cases less robustly so—than those of Boston. While our interviews indicate that information flowed more freely between firms in the Valley, there were plenty of engineers and scientists in Boston who were also willing to risk management stricture and talk to their colleagues across organizational boundaries. Willingness to share information appears to be more strongly correlated with a managerial versus technical profession than with location.

DATA AND METHODS

To gain empirical traction on the issue of how the social structures of Boston and Silicon Valley differed and the effect this had on the development of their innovative capacity, we consider all patented inventors and their coauthorship relations in the two regions. For our purposes, there is a relationship between patented inventors if they have coauthored any patent over a five-year moving window (alternate window sizes also demonstrated a qualitatively similar emergence phenomenon). This relational definition results in many disconnected components that demonstrate a skewed distribution, with most components of small size and fewer and fewer of larger size. We refer to the largest and right-most component on this distribution as the "largest component." Appendix A contains a description of the matching algorithm we used to identify individual inventors over time (for a later version of this algorithm, see Lai et al. 2011).

Figure 17.1 illustrates the proportion of patented inventors encompassed within a region's largest component.[3] For example, if there were ten inventors in a region and six of them coauthored any patents together in the prior five years, then the proportion in that region would be 0.6 or 60 percent. Note that the relationship is transitive—if inventor A and B worked together on one patent, and B and C on another, then A and C can trace an indirect coauthorship to one another and lie within the same component. If

[1] We define "component" as a cluster of inventors connected by at least one patenting coauthorship tie in the previous five years.

[2] We define the coming together of isolated inventor networks into larger networks as a process of network "aggregation." The term is intentionally dissimilar to the word *agglomeration* used in the economics literature, which refers to economies that firms gain by clustering together and sharing pooled labor availability, infrastructure, suppliers, and other services.

[3] We define a patent as being in a region if at least one inventor lives within that region, as determined by the hometown listed on the patent. Hometowns are classified within Metropolitan Statistical Areas (MSAs) by the U.S. Census Bureau (Ziplist5 MSA 2003). Note that this definition enables inventors from outside Silicon Valley or Boston to be included as regional inventors if they worked with someone who did live within the region. We analyzed a more restricted definition and found only minor qualitative differences in the processes . All graphs include all 337 U.S. MSA regions for comparison and illustrate five-year moving windows.

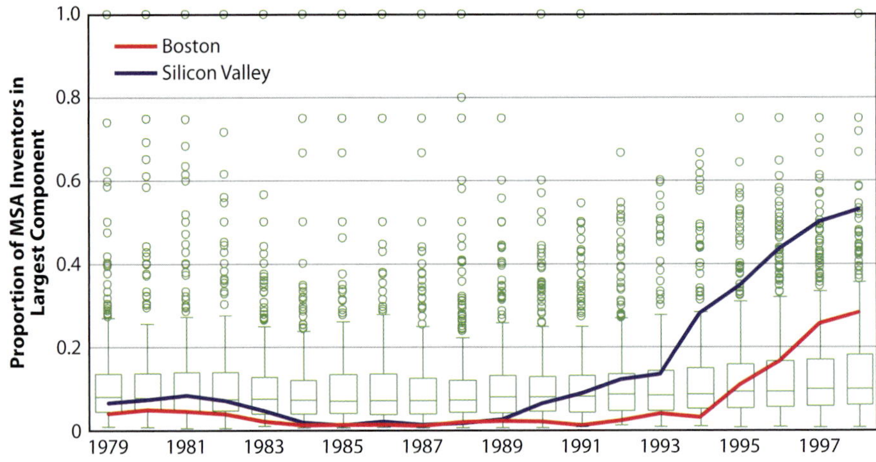

Figure 17.1 Box plots of the size of the largest connected component relative to the entire network of patented inventor collaborations by U.S. Metropolitan Statistical Area (x-axis indicates last year in five-year moving window).

four of the ten inventors had coauthored patents and no other group of coauthors was bigger, then the proportion would be 0.4 or 40 percent. The interesting feature of figure 17.1—and the original motivation for this chapter—is the aggregation process in Silicon Valley. It began in 1990, and by 1998 almost 50 percent of the Valley's inventors had aggregated into the largest component. Boston's aggregation, by contrast, did not begin until 1995, and by 1998 its largest component had only reached 25 percent of the region's inventors.

The histograms of figure 17.2 show which of the prior year's network components aggregated to form the following year's largest component, from 1988 to 1992. Note that the size of any given component is simply the number of inventors it includes. Each region contains thousands of components of varying sizes in any given year (most of which contain just twenty or fewer inventors and therefore fall above the frequency cutoff used for the y-axes in figure 17.2).

Figure 17.2 illustrates the early similarity in the distributions of the two regions' components. In 1988 Boston had a larger largest component (although figure 17.1 obscures this because it illustrates the proportion of inventors and Boston had slightly more inventors in that time period). In 1989 the distributions of the larger components across the two regions were similar. Yet as the 1989 panels of figure 17.2 illustrate, the 1st, 2nd, and 6th largest components merged in the Valley to form its largest component in 1990, while in Boston, only the 3rd, 13th, and 384th largest merged to form its largest component in 1990. By 1992 the largest component in Silicon Valley had over 1,600 inventors, in contrast to Boston's approximately 330 inventors. Furthermore, figure 17.2 shows the extent to which Silicon Valley saw a greater number of smaller and distinct components from one time window merging to form its largest component in the subsequent time window. Even though the process begins with the linkage of larger components, it reaches a critical mass at which the largest component begins to suck in components of all sizes.

Qualitative Methods

We conducted in-depth interviews with key inventors in both regions to understand the historical and social mechanics of the aggregation process. We identified these inventors in two rounds. First, we graphed the largest component of 1990 in both regions to pinpoint the inventors who provided crucial linkages from the previous year's components. For example, drawing on the histograms in figure 17.2, we identified the inventors who connected the 1st, 2nd, and 6th largest components together in the Valley and the 3rd, 13th, 384th, and 707th largest in Boston. We then identified similar inventors who

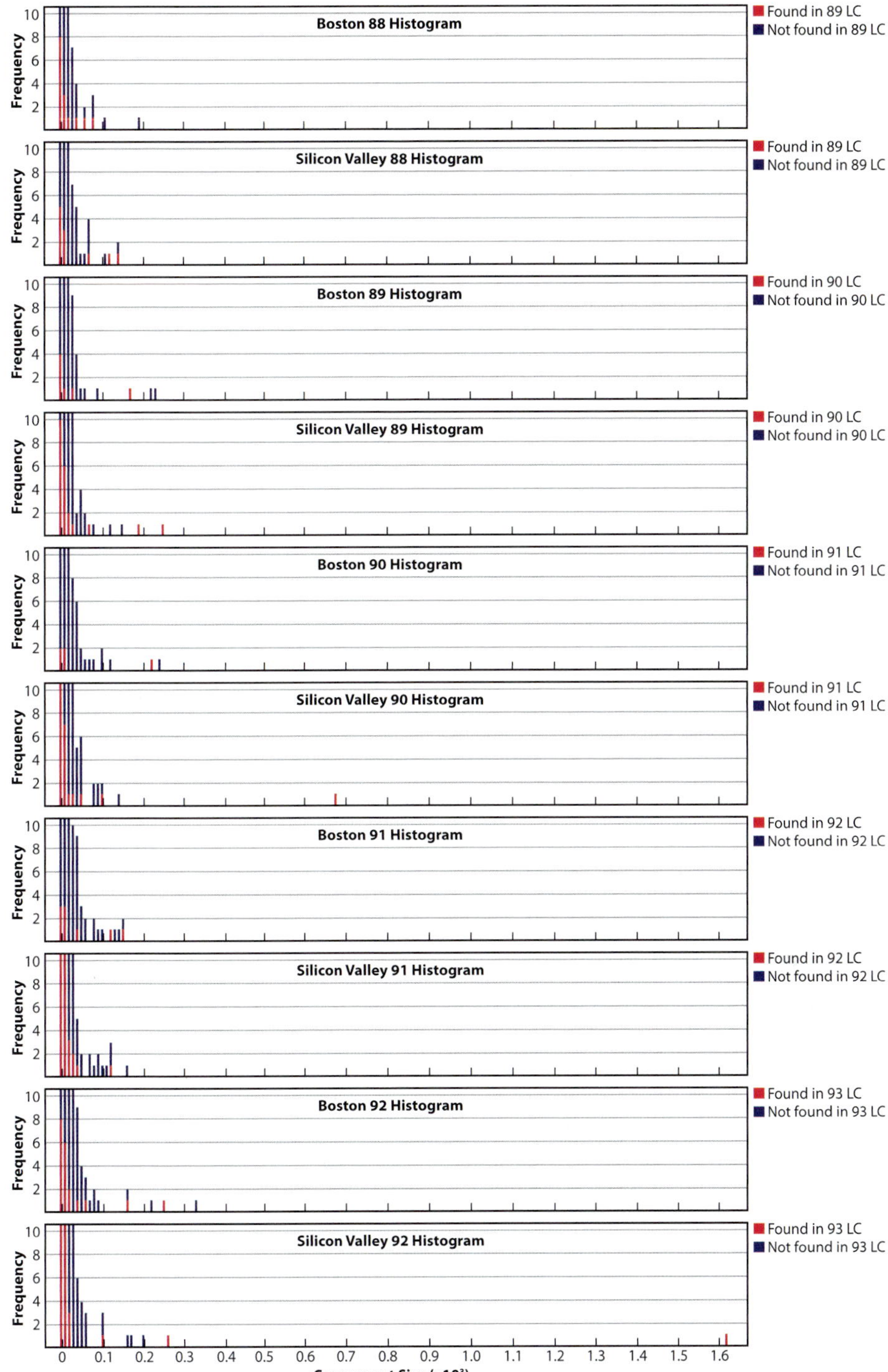

Figure 17.2 Time series of histograms of component size frequency of Boston and Silicon Valley. The x-axis identifies the range of possible sizes (in number of inventors) for network components (demarcated into bins of 10 for readability), while the y-axis reflects, in blue, the number of connected components of a given (bin) size found in that region during that year (truncated to 10 to allow for visibility of the red bars described hereafter) and, in red, the number of those components which merged to become a part of the single largest connected component of that region in the following year. Because of space constraints and to emphasize the right-skewed outliers, we truncated the y-axis of each histogram. Boston generally has a larger number of inventors in the first category—that is, its distribution is more left-skewed—over all the time periods.

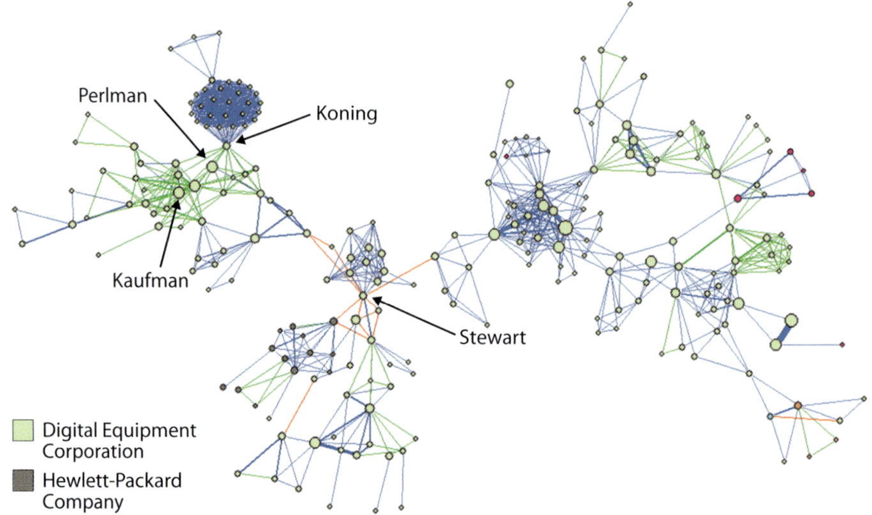

Figure 17.3 Largest component of Boston, 1986–90, by assignee and importance of inventions. The DEC component did not aggregate into the 1990 largest component. (Previously published in Fleming, King, and Juda 2007.)

did not create such linkages between other large components—for example, the 3rd, 4th, and 5th largest components in the Valley and the 1st, 2nd, 4th, and 5th largest in Boston.

We chose this second set of control inventors based on its similarity to the first set of linking inventors. All inventors from components that did not aggregate into the 1990 largest component but were similar in size to those that did were at risk of control selection. We ran a Euclidean distance-matching algorithm (the compare command in STATA) with variables that measured the linking inventor's patenting history. We included variables to measure the inventor's access to information and likelihood of career movement opportunities, such as the mean degree of collaborations, clustering of the inventor's collaborators (a density measure of the actual number of ties between alters, divided by the possible number of ties), number of patents by time period (or basic inventive productivity), and future prior art citations by the time period (since citations have been shown to correlate with patent importance; see Albert et al. 1991). Finally, we interviewed Robert Stewart because of his compelling position at the center of the disintegration of Boston's largest component, as illustrated in figures 17.3 and 17.4.

We were able to contact many of the linking and control inventors we identified. We interviewed them mainly during July and August 2003, presenting the inventors with the histograms shown here and illustrations of their own network components with all of their coauthors identified. We asked them about their careers, what was happening within their component during the time period under study (especially with regard to job mobility), and where their collaborators were now. We asked specifically about the collaborators in their patent networks and about any other networks, such as social or scientific networks.

Follow-up questions probed for inaccuracies in our illustrations and name-matching algorithm and for sampling bias caused by failed patent attempts or by technical efforts that were not intended for patenting. None of our inventors indicated an inaccurate name match or colleagues, and all felt that the illustrated network reflected their patent coauthors accurately. For example, Salvador Umatoy of Applied Materials indicated that a failed project had not been patented but that his collaborators on successful patents were all reflected; Jakob Maya, a lighting scientist, noted that some of his projects concluded with published papers rather than patents, as did Radia Perlman and Charles Kaufman (both computer engineers originally with Digital Equipment Corporation [DEC]), but none recalled any patent collaborators who

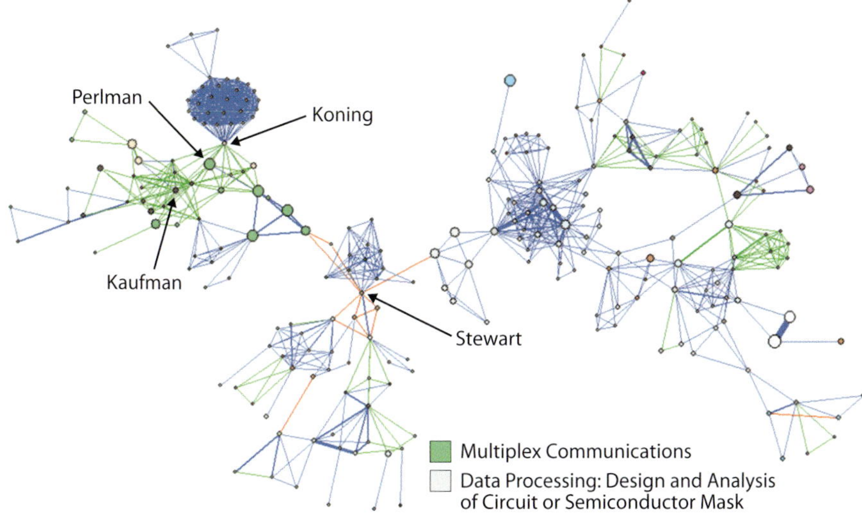

Figure 17.4 Largest component of Boston, 1986–90, by technology type and usage of scientific literature. The DEC component did not aggregate into the 1990 largest component.

were not represented in his or her network component as illustrated. Given evidence from patent citation data that information flows across indirect linkages (Singh 2005) and that aggregation processes improve regional inventive productivity (Fleming, King, and Juda 2007), we also asked the inventors about information flow across the illustrated linkages (the second motivation for this chapter). Finally, we simply asked them what they thought might have caused the aggregation processes we observed.

To supplement these detailed analyses of the individual components, we also investigated plausible alternatives. Additional analyses of the patent data (available from the first author) showed that Boston inventors were slightly more likely to work alone, be self-employed and therefore own their own patents, and work with a fewer number of collaborators. There were only slight differences in tie density over time for the two regions, in the age and diversity of technology, and in the number of assignees per inventor for the two regions. Fleming and Frencken (2006) explicitly investigated inventor mobility between the regions and found that mobility was slightly higher in the Valley in 1975. The difference in mobility steadily reversed, however, such that differences were negligible in 1990.

Most important, none of these potential causes demonstrates an abrupt transition around the time of study that might have caused the aggregation processes we observed. Finally, even though universities as a whole were patenting more over the time period than they had before, the elite schools such as Stanford and MIT did not change their patenting rates very much (Mowery et al. 2001). Also, given that Boston had more university patents than the Valley did, this may well have increased aggregation in the region, as inventors left school and took local employment.

Qualitative Data

Our interviews with the Valley and Boston inventors revealed both common and region-specific reasons for aggregation and non-aggregation. We organized these reasons by regions and whether the cause was specific by region. These reasons are summarized in table 17.1. We did not hear of any exactly similar aggregation processes, although we will discuss the obvious similarities among the stories that follow. The Silicon Valley–specific reasons for aggregation included an IBM postdoc program and local hiring of local graduates. Boston-specific reasons included internal collaboration within DEC. Common non-aggregation reasons between the regions included the instability of big

Table 17.1.
Summary of Reasons for Aggregation and Non-aggregation in Silicon Valley and Boston

	Aggregation	Non-aggregation
Silicon Valley	Local graduate employment IBM postdoc program	Internal labor markets Start-ups Big firm instability Self-employment
Boston	Internal collaboration	Internal labor markets Start-ups Big firm instability Non-local graduate employment Lack of internal collaboration Non-local internal collaboration Patenting/publication policies

firms, internal labor markets, and the movement of personnel to start-ups. Valley-specific reasons for non-aggregation included the movement of personnel to self-employment, while Boston-specific reasons included non-local graduate employment, lack of internal collaboration, internal firm collaboration that was non-local, patenting policies, and product life cycles.

Valley-Specific Reasons for Aggregation

We identified two aggregation processes unique to Silicon Valley, both driven by IBM. The company hired local doctoral graduates, connecting it with Stanford components, and it sponsored a postdoctoral fellowship program, connecting it to the large pharmaceutical and biotech component in the Valley. Figures 17.5 and 17.6 illustrate the largest component of the Valley from 1986 through 1990.[4]

IBM's Almaden Valley Research Lab provided the stable backbone of the 1990 Silicon Valley aggregation. IBM constituted the largest component in the Valley by 1987 and remained the largest component in 1988 and 1989 (in contrast to the unstable backbone of the Boston aggregation process, a point to which we will return later). Stanford's Ginzton Applied Physics Lab network joined the Valley's largest component in 1989 through the career of William Risk. Upon graduation from Stanford with a Ph.D. in electrical engineering, Risk accepted employment (and obviously patented) at IBM.[5] Further Stanford aggregation occurred in 1990 with William Kozlovsky's graduation and departure from Professor Robert Byer's lab. Hence these multiple ties created a robust conduit of inventors and ideas from Stanford to IBM.

William Risk and Professor Gordon Kino[6] elaborated on the mobility of students and the resultant knowledge flows.[7] Kino reported that his students of that era had gone on to a variety of academic and technical positions, including start-ups in the Valley and in Oregon, self-employment as an entrepreneur in Wyoming, academic positions at Stanford, UC–Santa Barbara, and Wisconsin, and employment at Tektronix, Bell Labs, AT&T, and IBM New

[4] Each node corresponds to an inventor and network ties correspond to coauthorship of at least one patent. A1 colors the nodes by firm and A2 colors them by technology (only A2, A7, and A14 are in full color; other pictures are grayscale. Node size in A1 corresponds to future prior art citations to the inventor's patents over the five-year time period and can be interpreted as the importance of the patent holder's inventions (Albert et al. 1991). Node size in A2 indicates the number of non-patent (generally scientific) references. Tie strength corresponds to coauthorship strength, as measured by the number of coauthored patents, normalized by the number of inventors on the patents. Tie color corresponds to tie age: green ties were formed in the prior year, blue ties in the second through fourth prior years, and red ties were formed five years prior. All network diagrams were plotted in Pajek with a directed force algorithm (Batagelj and Mrvar 1998).

[5] William Risk is still at IBM Almaden Research Laboratory and has done research in applied physics, optics, and photonics.

[6] Gordon Kino received his Ph.D. from Stanford University in 1955 and has done research in nondestructive testing, fiber optics, fiber-optic modulators, fiber-optic sensors, and optical, acoustic, and photo-acoustic microscopy. He is a member of the National Academy of Engineering.

[7] Technically the agglomeration between Gordon Kino of Stanford and William Risk of IBM occurred one year earlier than the 1986–90 window. Given that we were unable to meet with William Kozlovsky and Robert Byer and given that the Stanford-IBM inventors knew each other well and corroborated the processes described here (Kozlovsky did so in a phone interview), we report from Kino and Risk. Given that a very similar process occurred twice over two years, it would appear to be a robust and frequent occurrence.

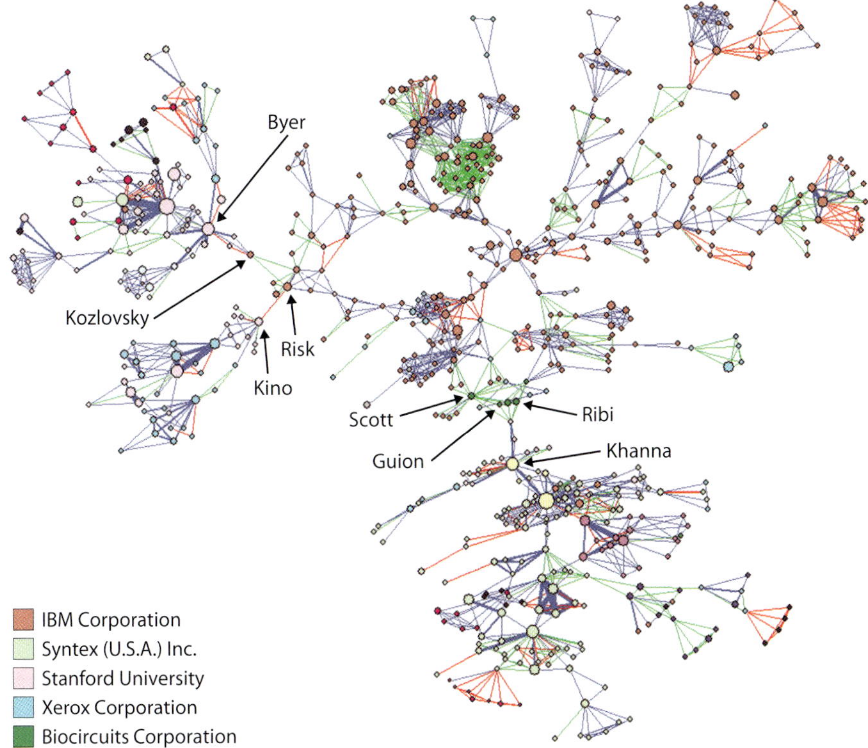

Figure 17.5 Largest component of Silicon Valley, 1986–90, by assignee and importance of inventions. Node sizes indicate the number of future prior art cites to an inventor, normalized by the number of collaborators. Tie width reflects the number of collaborations, tie color indicates age of tie (red is five years prior, blue is two to four years prior, and green is prior year), and colors indicate assignee (generally a firm or university). Yellow nodes in lower right indicate Abbott Laboratories, to which Pyare Khanna (along with Edwin Ullman) moved to late in the time period. Graphed in Pajek with Kamada-Kawai/Free algorithm (Batagelj and Mrvar 1998). (Previously published in Fleming, King, and Juda 2007.)

York. He and his students studied microscopy, acoustics, photonics, and microwave phenomena, and his students went on to work in a wide variety of industries, including medical instrumentation, electronics, optics, and scientific instrumentation. Professor Kino's description of local employment for Stanford graduates appears to be the flip side of Professor Richard Cohen's description below of non-local employment for MIT graduates. As such, the processes of local and non-local employment of graduates surely operate similarly across regions—when appropriate local firms are hiring, graduates are more likely to stay, and when they are not, or if the region lacks such firms, graduates emigrate. For example, William Risk stressed the importance of optics to a wide variety of industries and how the Valley provided a great diversity of technological applications and industrial opportunities.[8]

Kino and Risk renew old ties at conferences and visits (Risk had visited Stanford the week prior to the Kino interview). The former students and their professors discuss technical work at conferences even though they work for different firms. With the exception of Kino's formal consulting relationships, neither Kino nor Risk remembers other substantial or formal technical information flows. Both agreed that the technical information only flows through a strong,

[8] Even though Angel (1989) provides some evidence that Valley firms are more likely to hire local graduates than are firms in other regions, our categorization of such local hiring processes as Silicon Valley–specific is mostly an expositional convenience, based on our interview sampling and the economic conditions at the time.

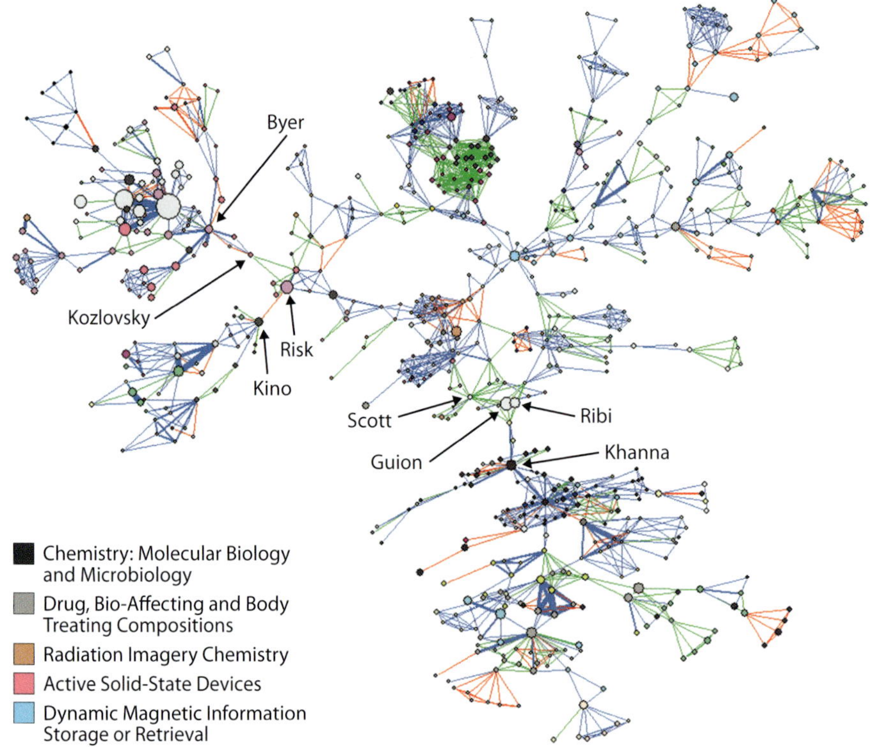

Figure 17.6 Largest component of Silicon Valley, 1986–90, by technology type and usage of scientific literature. Node sizes indicate the number of references to non-patent literature by an inventor (mainly peer reviewed science), normalized by the number of collaborators. Tie width indicates number of collaborations, tie color indicates age of tie (red is five years prior, blue is two to four years prior, and green is prior year), and colors reflect U.S. Patent Office technology class. Graphed in Pajek with Kamada-Kawai/Free algorithm (Batagelj and Mrvar 1998).

informal social network. In particular, they felt that graduates from the Ginzton Applied Physics Lab at Stanford had maintained particularly close contact since leaving Stanford.

The largest aggregation occurred with the linkage of the second-largest component in the Valley—Syntex (a research-intensive pharmaceutical firm) and smaller biotech firms—with IBM in 1986–90.[9] The actual connection was indirect and occurred indirectly through the career of John Campbell Scott[10] and the (now failed) start-up of Biocircuits.

Scott described how the Almaden Lab hired postdocs straight from school (generally PhDs but other degrees as well) with the intention that they would leave for employment with another private firm after one or two years. Modeled after academia and similar programs at Bell Labs, the practice was intended to seed the technological community with experienced IBM-friendly scientists. Such a process would obviously create observable ties between IBM and a wide variety of other firms. Unlike the departure of senior inventors from large and established firms for start-ups (which does not create ties between

[9] Even though Silicon Valley is known in this time period as a center of semiconductor and computer technologies, only the 1st and 5th largest components covered such technologies, namely magnetic media (computer disks at IBM) and semiconductor manufacturing equipment (at Applied Materials). The 2nd, 3rd, and 4th largest components consisted of pharmaceutical (Syntex), polymer chemistry (Raychem), and optical (Xerox PARC/Spectra Physics, Hewlett Packard) technologies.

[10] John Campbell Scott still works at IBM Almaden Research Laboratory. He earned his Ph.D. in solid state physics at the University of Pennsylvania and has worked in materials science for most of his career.

large components), the postdocs found future employment across a variety of firms. Hence the IBM postdoc program played a crucial role in the initial and continuing aggregation processes in the Valley because it linked large components to other large components.

While the connection of the Syntex and IBM components relied on the postdoc program, it actually occurred through the career of a young inventor at Biocircuits, an early (and ultimately failed) electronics-biotech start-up that developed biosensors.[11] Todd Guion, a Stanford graduate in chemistry, worked for Scott during his postdoc at IBM and then took a job at Biocircuits. Victor Pan took a similar path from San Jose State and Santa Clara University through IBM to Biocircuits. Biocircuits was attempting to build a biosensor based on polymeric material and wanted to get a charge through a polymer. Guion thought that optical technology might help and recommended to Hans Ribi,[12] the CEO of Biocircuits, that he contact Scott for help. After some initial difficulty, Scott secured permission from IBM management to act as a scientific adviser, given that there were no apparent conflicts of interest. Scott spent many days at Biocircuits and interacted with most of its employees. He suggested the use of bio-refringence associated with specific binding to solve the problem. He reported that he "definitely learned a lot of interesting things" that he is now, many years later, applying as IBM moves into biological technologies. He had no interaction with Pyare Khanna,[13] however, the prominent pharmaceutical inventor on the other side of the Biocircuits bridge.

Hans Ribi, a Stanford graduate in biochemistry and the owner/CEO of Biocircuits, had a much less positive view of information flow across collaborative linkages, believing that it should not and generally does not occur. He argued that patents are used to protect proprietary property and that coauthorship did not indicate a higher probability of information flow. Interestingly, the manager on the other side of the IBM-to-biotech/pharma connection, Pyare Khanna, also complained about the possibility of information flow. Both Ribi and Khanna were managing start-ups at the time of the interview and felt much more vulnerable to the loss of proprietary information and key individuals, in contrast to the IBM scientists who, as "good corporate citizens," felt resigned to the possibility of such loss.

Boston-Specific Reasons for Aggregation

We identified only one Boston-specific reason for aggregation. The largest component in 1990 resulted from internal collaboration—newly initiated interaction of smaller work groups—within Digital Equipment Corporation, as illustrated in figures 17.3 and 17.4. We describe the integration of the DEC component through the careers of Charles Kaufman, Paul Koning, Radia Perlman, and Robert Stewart.[14]

Charles Kaufman, discussing his own role as a "point of connection" in these processes, noted that he was particularly likely to be responsible for information flow across multiple departments of DEC for two reasons. First, he was one of "the gang of four" chosen from four distinct working groups to design DEC's "next generation of security." Second, while he was a software engineer by trade, he often socialized with those working in hardware. Paul Koning, addressing the same question, noted that his shifting collaborators usually corresponded to shifting task assignments but that two exceptional features of working at DEC could explain some of his more interesting collaborations. First, his working group's manager

[11] The start-up might be described as a forerunner of today's combinations of biological and digital technologies, seen in products such as Affymatrix's combination of assay and semiconductor technology into a gene array chip; in publications, such as *BIO IT World*, that focus on the application of computing power to biological and genomic problems; and in research laboratories, such as Stanford's BIO-X, that hope to encourage collaboration between chemistry, engineering, biological, and medical research. Pyare Khanna felt that Biocircuits failed because it was too early and the integration was too difficult.

[12] Hans Ribi received his Ph.D. in biochemistry at Stanford University in 1988 and was the CEO of Biocircuits at the time that Todd Guion suggested that John Campbell Scott work with the firm.

[13] Pyare Khanna worked at Syntex as a senior scientist during the period of the study. He is currently the CEO of Discoverx, a drug target company in Fremont, California.

[14] Charles Kaufman attended Dartmouth for mathematics and worked with a Dartmouth-related technology venture prior to accepting a position in the network architecture group at DEC. Paul Koning worked with Charles Kaufman and Radia Perlman at DEC before moving to smaller start-up ventures. He is currently the founder and CTO of a successful VC-backed start-up just outside the Boston area. Radia Perlman earned her Ph.D. from MIT while employed by DEC. She is currently a Distinguished Engineer at Sun Microsystems and serves on the Internet Architecture Board of the Internet Engineering Task Force. Robert Stewart earned undergraduate and master's degrees in electrical engineering from MIT. He took employment with DEC upon graduation and remained with the firm until its purchase by Compaq. We interviewed Stewart because he was so central to the disintegration of DEC in 1990. He did not meet our typical criteria of being either a bridging node that caused aggregation or a bridging control node.

routinely sought brainstorming solutions from a wide distribution of engineers. Second, co-inventor Radia Perlman's collaborative style of brainstorming made her a particularly strong candidate for generating information flow during this process (as much with him as with other individuals), as did her tendency to prefer topics and projects "at the boundary of academic research and engineering." On the other hand, Koning also noted that Perlman was probably unable to patent much of this work when the participants spanned company boundaries. Both Kaufman and Perlman independently confirmed this viewpoint, enumerating several bureaucratic obstacles they have had to surmount in order to work together since leaving DEC. One particularly interesting example required both parties to persuade their respective employers that their joint invention, while worthy of patenting, was not worthy of commercial sale.[15] Like Scott in the Valley, these Boston inventors overcame legal, managerial, and strategic obstacles to collaboration across organizational boundaries.

Koning and Kaufman both reported switching job functions within DEC several times,[16] typically to new technologies where the knowledge of earlier collaborators proved less useful. Koning often maintained loose ties with prior collaborators throughout this process, occasionally passing back information about old projects but rarely requesting help or technical advice from his old network. On the other hand, he also noted that he and Perlman are a significant exception to this trend because they have continued to collaborate in new ways (e.g., on multiple academic papers and publications) for well over a decade now, despite working for different employers since 1993.[17]

Common Reasons for Non-aggregation

Some of the explanations we heard for non-aggregation between components were common to both regions. First, large established firms with internal labor markets generally retain their employees (Angel 1989). Second, successful inventors from established firms generally go to start-ups rather than to other large established firms. This implies that they will link established firms with large components to start-up firms with small or nonexistent components rather than linking large components to other large components. Finally, when established firms become unstable, they do not hire and their current inventors often spend more time protecting their jobs or seeking new ones than they do inventing. This will be reflected in a decreased rate of patenting and thus in smaller components.

Salvator Umatoy's[18] career matched the explanation for Applied Materials' (the fourth largest component in the Valley) failure to aggregate. The firm's business boomed during the time period under study and there were many internal technical and managerial opportunities for its employees. (Even now, during much tougher times, it retains a strong internal labor market and hires mostly new college graduates.) Applied Materials provided its employees with generous incentives, such as stock options, to stay within the firm. Most of the colleagues in Umatoy's network there (figure 17.7) remained with the firm and—at the time of our interviews—were still technical contributors or had become senior managers, working in close proximity to each other ("he works down that aisle . . . he works in the building next door"). Umatoy commented that only managers went to other large firms; senior engineers went to start-ups (which further inhibited aggregation). When asked about people in his network with whom he had not patented at the time and who had left (part of our concern about sampling bias), he mentioned an engineer who left technology and the Valley altogether and a technology process manager who left for IBM. Umatoy did not work directly with this manager (he was not illustrated in the figures). This memory serves to bolster Umatoy's earlier conjecture that engineers left for start-ups and only managers left for other large firms. Umatoy expressed mixed opinions about information transfer across firms. He also felt that Applied Materials did not "give you time for any outside life [that would enable knowledge transfer]." Yet he reported that before starting a project, Applied Materials engineers do call their

[15] This joint invention was a strong password protocol they created specifically to serve as a free alternative to two patented protocols. Both of their employers agreed not to patent it and they published a paper to place the protocol into the public domain.

[16] Koning reported switching firms several times, choosing one start-up after another, two of which he founded.

[17] Lotus Development acquired Koning's employer, Iris Associates, in 1994; IBM acquired Lotus Development in 1995. Despite these changes, Kaufman continues to work with the same group, now under the IBM umbrella.

[18] Salvador Umatoy (control to Glenda Choate, a bridging inventor at Biocircuits whom we were unable to locate) worked in the medical instrumentation industry before coming to Applied Materials in the early 1980s. He remains there and currently manages mechanical engineers designing wafer fabrication equipment.

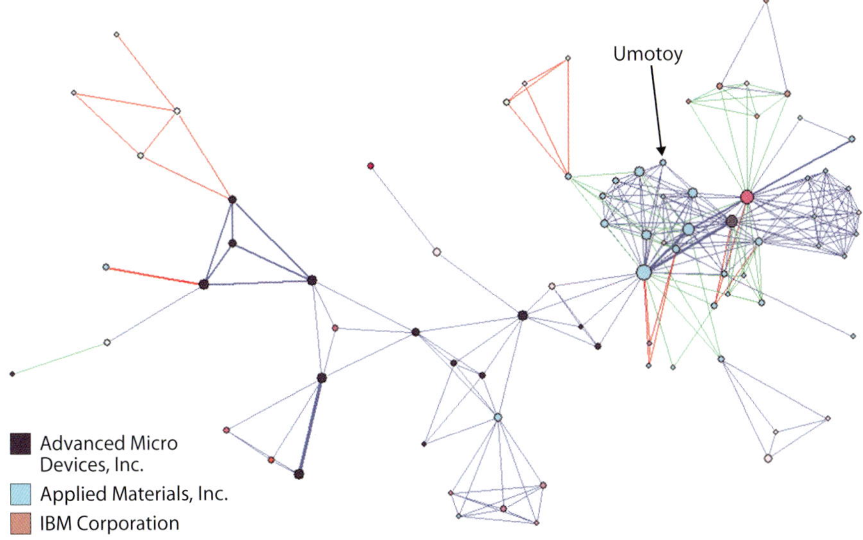

Figure 17.7 Applied Materials component, Silicon Valley's fifth largest component in 1989, by assignee and importance of inventions. Applied Materials did not aggregate into the 1990 largest component.

friends (including colleagues at other firms), contact professors at universities, and read the patent and scientific literature.

In contrast to the seeming lifetime employment at Applied Materials, most of the inventive colleagues of Robert Sprague[19] have left the legendary Xerox PARC. He listed a variety of destinations for his coauthors during the period of study, including Spectra Diode Labs (figure 17.8), Komag, Exxon Enterprises, Canadian Research Corporation, and a variety of start-ups. Most became CEOs, CTOs, or chief scientists, and they often left with the core technology they had invented at PARC. He could not remember any colleagues who left for an established firm, mainly because the start-ups provided stock opportunities. He divided the movement of technology out of PARC into three categories: disgust, opportunities, and friendly, the last category being sponsored and supported by Xerox. He included Spectra Diode Labs and his own, Michigan-based start-up, Gyricon, in the last category. While Xerox might have done a better job in commercializing its PARC technologies, Sprague did not express resentment at the mobile inventors and the spillovers they caused.

We heard similar stories about the power of internal labor markets from our Boston inventors. In addressing why the DEC component did not remain the largest after 1993,[20] Charles Kaufman observed that DEC was not hiring, due to its economic concerns,[21] and that leaving was considered "kind of 'traitorous.'" In fact, he noted that DEC had an explicit policy that employees who left were not to be rehired and he recalled few people leaving before formal layoffs began in 1991.[22]

Despite the increasingly gloomy economic climate along Route 128 during the latter half of the 1980s, the DEC inventors did not recall perceiving any risk to their own careers at the time. They recalled many alternative opportunities available to them, both in Silicon Valley and along Route 128, but they preferred staying at DEC for several reasons. While Kaufman noted

[19] Robert Sprague (control to Pyare Khanna) earned his Ph.D. in physics from the University of Rochester. He has worked at Xerox PARC since the period of study and is CEO of Gyricon, a Xerox PARC spinout.

[20] As mentioned in an earlier footnote, the GTE/Siliconix component displaced the DEC component to become the largest in Boston in 1991. Thereafter, the DEC component resumed its rank as largest in 1992, only to be displaced a final time in 1993. All three of the bridging inventors at DEC with whom we spoke departed in 1993.

[21] At the same time, he also pointed out that he himself had been hired during a freeze and perceived that such exceptions were not particularly rare.

[22] Drawing on the first author's anecdotal experience at Hewlett Packard, he remembers many of his lab's best engineers leaving for an early pen-computing start-up. They were rehired following the start-up's failure and given a party upon their return.

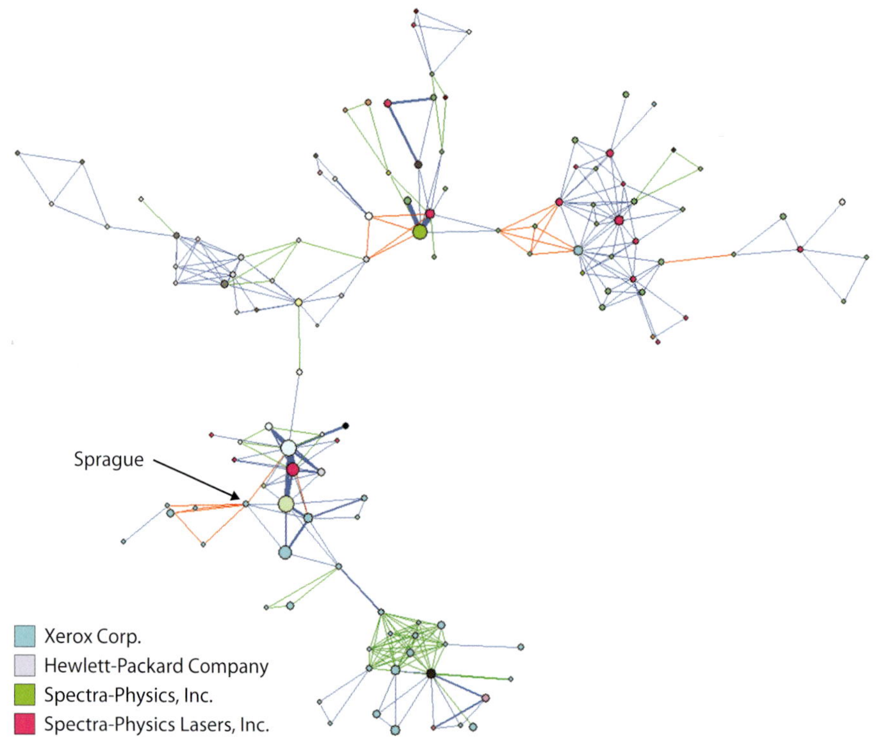

Figure 17.8 Xerox PARC and Hewlett Packard component, Silicon Valley's fourth largest component in 1989, by assignee and importance of inventions. This component did not aggregate into the 1990 largest component.

that DEC had a reputation for treating its engineers particularly well and that no other offers he received at the time could match DEC's compensation, Koning and Perlman also emphasized that their collaborators were still sharp, their work was still innovative, and they were still being given opportunities with the potential for large-scale impact. In fact, both Koning and Perlman specifically described their small work groups within DEC as being rather "start-up like," explaining that despite suffering its share of bureaucratic dysfunction, DEC had "portions" that were still very successful and exciting, at least technologically speaking, even then. All three remained at DEC until 1993, acknowledging that they had stayed on well after the headlines on the business pages of the *Boston Globe* had soured.

Valley-Specific Reasons for Non-aggregation

Michael Froix[23] provided the most interesting career story and uncovered the one Valley-specific story explaining non-aggregation. Raychem—neither a semiconductor firm nor a computer firm but a large and established polymer chemistry firm—had been the Valley's largest component until it was overtaken by IBM in 1987. Froix took his first job in the Valley with Raychem as a senior scientist in 1979 and left in 1985 as a lab director. According to Froix, the firm had initially provided an environment where inventors could work on anything that would lead to a business. This changed in 1983, however, when non-technical management assumed control. Without technical foresight from management, Froix felt that politics became rampant and this caused many senior inventors and scientists to leave. Destinations included medical device and fiber-optics firms, small start-ups, and medium-sized firms such as JDS Uniphase. This was unfortunate for Raychem because it was the only large company in the Valley with polymer expertise at a time when polymer applications were "exploding" in the medical, optical, and

[23] Michael Froix (control to William Risk) earned his Ph.D. in physical chemistry from Howard University. He has worked at Xerox, Celanese, Raychem, Cooper Vision, and Quanam, and has been a very successful independent inventor.

chip and board fabrication industries. In Froix's opinion, Raychem's management repeatedly failed to seize these opportunities. For example, Advanced Cardio Systems asked for help in applying Raychem's electron beam techniques to the medical pacemaker market—which was unrelated to Raychem's current markets—yet Raychem management turned down the request for the purported fear of losing advantage in their current markets.

Froix left Raychem in 1985 out of frustration with no job but a part-time teaching position at the University of San Francisco (USF). He decided to invent a material that would decrease the clotting that occurred on the surface of an artificial heart (recipients of such hearts would generally survive the first few weeks, only to suffer strokes caused by such clots). He worked after hours in a friend's corporate lab. He had approval, since his friend was the founder, but Froix supplied all his own materials, had no access to proprietary information, and did not interact with the employees. He also worked in the lab of a supportive professor at USF. He then read about an analytic technique to measure the effectiveness of his material, developed by Channing Robertson at Stanford. He contacted Professor Robertson in 1986 and asked for help. Robertson replied that he would leave the decision to his best graduate student, Seth Darst (now a professor at Rockefeller University). Darst agreed to help but, like a typical graduate student, didn't begin working until midnight. Undeterred, Froix would sit on the stairs next to the lab from 6:00 P.M., when the building was locked, until Darst arrived many hours later. The collaboration worked well and Froix perfected his invention,[24] sold his technique to Cooper Vision, and helped implement its application to a corneal implant product. He was then introduced to a Stanford cardiologist, Simon Stertzer, and began working on a drug-delivery stent in his garage in Mountain View and at Stanford. He formed a start-up, Quanam, which has been bought by Boston Scientific.[25] According to Boston Scientific's chief technology officer, the technology has become an important part of the firm's product portfolio (Cohen 2003). Froix is now working with a molecular biologist on tissue generation with stem cells.

As can be seen in figure 17.9, Froix did not have many collaborators at Raychem, but he has stayed in touch with them and other former colleagues over the years. Although this was mainly for job searches, he has also discussed technical matters within this network over the years. Froix's experience provides a compelling story of inventive tenacity in the interstices of a technological ecosystem. It is difficult to understand how representative his experience was, however, without a better understanding of the sampling distribution of inventors and their likelihood of their bending corporate and university rules. The Valley might be more supportive of such inventors, but Boston inventors may also have had after-hours access to corporate and university laboratories and there may have been professors at MIT or Harvard who were willing to support their research. Determining how widespread such practices are, in Boston or any other region, would require inventors to admit to violations of corporate and university rules, possibly putting their jobs at risk. Hewlett Packard had an oft-repeated story (told by the protagonist in Packard 1995) about the founders coming in on the weekend and finding the central lab supplies locked. They sought out a security guard, had the padlock cut, and ordered that lab supplies should never again be locked. They felt that supporting an inventor's creativity outweighed any employee theft that might occur. Such stories remain anecdotal, but they consistently suggest that strong engineering and science cultures (wherever they might be) place creativity before financial and proprietary concerns.

Paul Koning expressed skepticism regarding such a generous flow of information or resources across collaborative linkages; he specifically felt that Froix's story was incomplete. In comparing his own more mundane stories of cooperative exchange with accounts of fledgling entrepreneurs slipping into the offices of established firms to borrow slack resources on the late shift, Koning doubted the underlying truth of these anecdotes. While such stories might be true to a point, he contended, surely there was always some form

[24] Professor Robertson, now a dean in the Stanford School of Engineering, did not recall Froix specifically. "There were so many people who contacted me over the years," he explained, "I can't remember them all. I have no reason to believe the story isn't true." Darst corroborated Froix's description via email.

[25] Froix supported other inventors as he had been supported. "When I was running Quanam, I met a physicist on the tennis courts. He had some ideas about a new approach to a surgical cutting device. I made the Quanam labs available to him to carry out some of his experiments and to evaluate prototypes of his devices. My view on this was, and still is, it's always a lot of fun and it is very stimulating to have bright creative people around. Neither I nor Quanam had any proprietary interest in his technology, nor did we desire any such interest. Understanding the science of what he was doing and being in a position to help him was the only consideration."

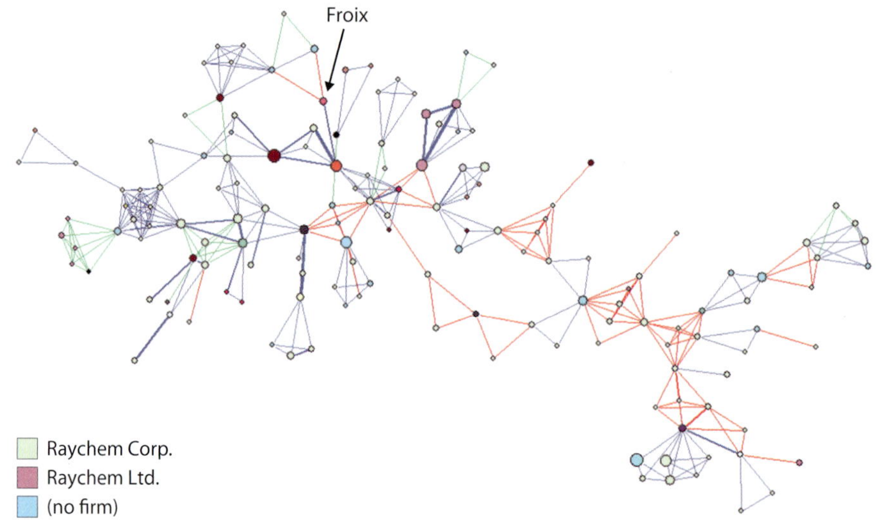

Figure 17.9 Raychem component, Silicon Valley's third largest component in 1989, by assignee and importance of inventions. Raychem did not aggregate into the 1990 largest component.

of unseen equity relationship underlying this seemingly informal cooperative behavior.

Boston-Specific Reasons for Non-aggregation

We found seven reasons for Boston's non-aggregation. First, MIT graduates tended to take academic and private sector jobs outside the Boston area, despite the wide variety of academic opportunities available there. Second, MIT graduates went to smaller firms in the medical device industry, so their mobility did not link large clusters.

Third, continued aggregation of the DEC component was hampered by management's encouragement of internal rivalry and competition. Fourth, engineers at Honeywell, another large component in the time period, only collaborated with Intel inventors and other Honeywell inventors outside the region. Fifth, the pensions at older firms penalized mobility. Sixth, the heavily academic focus of the Boston area resulted in less emphasis on patenting and more on the publication of scientific papers. Finally, some firms patented reluctantly in order to control costs.

Whereas the IBM component emerged by 1987 to serve as the underlying foundation of the largest Valley component in all subsequent years, the composition of the largest Boston component shifted from one year to the next until 1993.[26] The immediate cause of this instability is dramatically illustrated by the career of Robert Stewart in figures 17.3 and 17.4. Stewart is the only inventor who integrates the three major subcomponents at DEC. He (2004) indicated that his integrating role arose from his popularity as a design reviewer across different DEC product lines. While these design reviews did not create the observed ties, they made Stewart and other technical leaders aware of where the experts were located in the corporation. When Stewart or other smart colleagues had a question or problem that might benefit from collaboration, they knew whom to contact. These contacts then resulted in the observed ties. As illustrated by the red color of Stewart's ties, however, they are all five years old. The abruptness of DEC's structural disintegration was caused by the product life cycle. DEC's lawyers generally filed all necessary patents the night before a product shipped. In this case, the upper and right ties had been created with the shipment of the Nautilus project in early January 1986. In addition to the Nautilus project ties, the lower left tie had been one of many collaborations between Stewart

[26] The GTE/Siliconix component, which was 2nd largest in 1989 and 1990, actually displaced the DEC component to become the largest in Boston in 1991. Thereafter, the DEC component resumed its rank as largest in 1992, only to be displaced a final time in 1993 by the merging of one portion of the former 1989 largest component with several other mid-sized components to create a single aggregation of inventors across organizations as diverse as MIT, Polaroid, Reebok, Kopin Corp., Motorola, Mobile Oil, and United States Surgical Corporation, among many others.

and the R&D and networking groups and just happened to expire at the same time.

During the 1985–89 window, the largest component in the Boston network consisted primarily of MIT affiliates. Richard Cohen[27] of the Division of Health Sciences and Technology served as a key bridging point among these individuals. Reflecting on his involvement on a 1985 "cut-patent"—a patent for which collaborator ties were *not* renewed or reinforced by subsequent patenting activity within the next five-year window—Cohen observed that nearly all of his collaborators on patents between 1985 and 1990 were graduate students from his lab who left the Boston region altogether on completing their degrees and research responsibilities at MIT. Their employment destinations included universities, hospitals, and, less frequently, businesses across the country and abroad. Cohen acknowledged that his particular division of MIT had not kept many of its own graduates, despite the fact that they often proved to be some of the most compelling candidates on the job market several years later (when they had become too senior and well compensated to be drawn back). Cohen's comments imply that elite universities might actually have less influence on local aggregation than non-elite universities, since their graduates are more likely to leave the area in search of comparably elite positions.

Nonetheless, based on his experiences at MIT and as the founder of Cambridge Heart, Inc., Cohen reported that because biotech information flows quite freely within the academic community, it is a particularly fertile environment for "proof of concept" research. Given that Boston technology relies to a much greater extent on university patents and published science, its technical social networks might actually be more connected than the Valley's. On the other hand, Cohen also believed that academic interest in new ideas tended to shift from the successful proof of one concept to another without sustaining the creation or exchange of knowledge through the subsequent design or development of commercial products. Compounding this problem, according to Cohen, the businesses that did bring such products to market inhibited any information flow specific to their commercialization processes.

Moreover, within the larger biotech industry, Cohen felt that the medical device business was quite distinct from the pharmaceutical business. The smaller end market for devices tended to sustain much smaller, less generously funded, and perhaps more insular companies. The smaller scale of medical device efforts is consistent with Froix's Valley experience, where he was able to commercialize breakthrough medical technology without the complete resources of a large firm. As a result of the typical transfer and development into smaller firms, we would expect less aggregation.

Patenting policies also influenced the second-largest connected component in Boston—composed largely of scientists and engineers at General Telephone and Electric (GTE)—during both the 1985–89 and 1986–90 windows. We asked GTE inventors Alfred Bellows and Jakob Maya[28] why the GTE component did not aggregate to rise in size rank from 1989 to 1990 and, more significantly, why it did not persist as the largest connected component after displacing the DEC component in 1991. They explained that people at GTE (and in the lighting technology field more broadly) typically view patents as very costly (for example, one quarter of a million dollars to internationally patent a single invention on an ongoing basis), so the culture of the industry is to limit them to genuinely innovative work for which the protection is thought absolutely necessary. Success in research on lighting technology has been carried out with and benefited from a high level of cross-fertilization between scientists in industry and academia (especially for government-contracted research and development). This work routinely generates papers, however, rather than patents.[29] Maya estimated, based on his own patent collaborator network graph from 1985–89, that the true size of his portfolio of collaborative relationships at the time was about three times what we had depicted, noting specifically that he had as many

[27] Richard Cohen (control to Radia Perlman) holds an M.D. and Ph.D. Dr. Cohen applies physics, mathematics, engineering, and computer science to problems in medicine and health. He helped found Cambridge Heart and is the Whitaker Professor in Biomedical Engineering at MIT.

[28] Alfred Bellows (control to Charles Kaufman) is currently working with OSRAM Opto Semiconductors. At GTE, Bellows was engaged in R&D projects relating to inorganic chemistry and the properties of materials such as ceramics and silicon nitride. Jakob Maya (control to Paul Koning) holds a Ph.D. and is currently leading research in lighting technology at Matsushita Electric Works R&D Lab. Before joining Matsushita, Maya was a director of R&D at GTE.

[29] Our patent data support this assertion. Patents also cite non-patent references, and these are mostly peer-reviewed scientific papers (Sorenson and Fleming 2004). Since 1975, Boston patents cited 30 percent more science papers on average than Valley patents did. Boston also had a greater proportion of academic patents over the entire time period as well.

papers with other authors (and at times not in the same firm) as he did patents. Second, the GTE component in Boston, already relatively weak, was probably made even weaker when GTE Sylvania sold its lighting business to Siemens's Osram in 1992, though this might have temporarily connected Siemens and GTE. Consistent with Froix's description of Raychem's implosion, Maya reported that people spent several years thereafter worried far more about simply keeping their jobs than about the quality, rate, or volume of their inventive work.[30]

The trade-offs between public science and private technology also influenced the collaborative linkages of Honeywell, the sixth largest connected component, though explicit career considerations also mattered. Thomas Joyce,[31] a lifetime employee at Honeywell (1960–2000), provided three reasons why the Honeywell component did not aggregate to rise in size rank from 1989 to 1990. (In fact, it dropped from fifth to sixth in the following year.) First, collaboration at Honeywell tended to be global rather than local; Joyce recalls working with a number of European Honeywell employees at the time but never exchanging information with anyone outside Honeywell, regardless of region. He attributed this fact partly to the nature of Honeywell's technology and partly to his own personal situation, as both his own skill set and Honeywell's development opportunities were constrained by the distinctly proprietary nature of the chip design work being done there.

Second, Joyce noted that he was linked to a comparatively more mature cohort of inventors, "older hangovers from the 1960s and 1970s," many of whom had more pressing family concerns or were nearing a reasonable age for retirement. Honeywell, like other Boston firms, made its pensions contingent on retirement with the firm, which certainly would have inhibited these older employees from leaving and thereby served as bridges to link the Honeywell component to other Route 128 components.[32]

Third, Joyce added that Honeywell's chip designers found themselves "under the secrecy cloak of Intel by the early 1990s"; collaborating with Intel prevented Honeywell from sharing knowledge elsewhere (publicly or otherwise). Our patent data strongly support Joyce's description of Honeywell's insularity. Of the eighty-one inventors in the 1986–90 window, eleven had collaborated on one or two of three non-Honeywell patents, while Honeywell held the ninety-one remaining patents linking this component.

Kaufman, Koning, and Perlman also emphasized how organizational culture influences the level of patenting, noting that DEC's explicit patenting policies motivated them to identify their patentable work proactively. They felt that these policies implicitly encouraged employees to identify other collaborators for each of their patents, partly because DEC awarded the full patent bonus amount of $500 to as many as three inventors per patent. So those with ideas to patent were often inclined to seek out collaborators (whether needed or not) in order to "share the wealth" and to encourage others to "return the favor." Additionally, DEC granted a steeper set of awards for cumulative patenting ($5,000 for 5 patents, $10,000 for 10, up to as much as $20,000 for 20, or perhaps even $25,000 for 25), and these awards allowed for any number of collaborators per patent. Kaufman also noted that DEC displayed a cyclical pattern based on patenting objectives that were established in response to a cross-licensing relationship with IBM, which would grant a company the use of all IBM-patented technologies in exchange for IBM's right to use that company's patented technologies. Because IBM's fee for this arrangement was inversely proportional to the size of the company's portfolio of patents, DEC business managers recognized a value to patents exceeding licensing revenue or protection from imitation.

It would seem that these policies would have increased collaborations and made the DEC component larger and more robust. Saxenian (1994) and others, however, have commented on the less collaborative norms within and across Boston firms. Paul Koning confirmed this reputation, describing how Ken Olsen, DEC's founder and CEO, routinely created competing internal groups as a means of fueling rapid progress. Koning went on to note that the practice severely strained internal morale and interdepartmental cooperation. Furthermore, given that patent law clearly stipulates that only contributing inventors be listed on a patent, the collaborative awards policy may have been of limited effectiveness. This might account for the persistent fragility in the DEC's networks and is consistent with its reputation for fostering competition between work groups.

[30] Maya left GTE just prior to this change because he anticipated it; he would have stayed otherwise.

[31] Thomas Joyce (control to Radia Perlman) worked as a logic designer and patented repeatedly at Honeywell, Honeywell Bull, and Bull until his retirement.

[32] Preliminary conversations with two Harvard Business School accounting professors, Paul Healy and Greg Miller, indicated great plausibility for this argument, although they were unaware of any specific citation in the accounting literature.

Taken collectively, these inventors' comments broadly suggest that the corporate policies and strategies of the dominant firms in the Boston region at the time often served to blunt aggregation both *within* and *across* firms. However, invention also stagnated at these firms due to more sweeping strategic business decisions—pursuing proprietary technologies (at DEC, Data General, and Honeywell) and selling ownership to an acquiring firm (at GTE and Honeywell). In the cases of proprietary technology, invention suffered as firms struggled with the negative economic outcome of their decision, while inventors were constrained in their careers by proprietary skill sets. In the cases of acquisition, it is reported that many inventors left their respective fields, retired, or focused more effort on keeping their jobs than on inventing. In the Valley, by contrast, inventors entered the external labor market with sellable skills because technologies were less proprietary (Angel 1989; Fallick et al. 2006).

At the same time, the slow pace of intra-organizational job movement was certainly not a function of limiting proprietary skill sets or organizational upheaval alone. The majority of Boston region inventors stressed firmly that their decision to remain in the same firms was primarily due to their satisfaction with both their work opportunities in those organizations and the way in which those organizations treated them as engineers and scientists. In fact, when these individuals finally left their firms (and any others subsequently in their careers), they reported that it was almost *always* because they saw no viable alternative; the organizations were either changing ownership or failing visibly. Naturally, many of these economic failures can be attributed in part to these firms' proprietary technological strategies. Thus there are two distinct ways in which the decision to remain with proprietary development hindered the growth of collaborative inventor networks in the Boston region. At the individual level, proprietary technology limited the job mobility of some, and at the organizational level, it contributed significantly to the ultimate failure or disruptive acquisition of at least three dominant firms in the area—DEC, Data General, and Honeywell.

DISCUSSION

As with all qualitative data, our presentation and analysis remain inseparable. Nonetheless, we wish to highlight three issues in our discussion. First, we are struck by the importance of institutions in the aggregation of regional inventor networks. Consistent with the themes of this volume, universities and postdoc programs play a catalytic role in the initial connections between components. This catalytic role creates opportunities for inventors (particularly young inventors) to forge bridging opportunities. Second, we are not struck by any fundamental differences in the network structures of Silicon Valley and Boston. To quantify these impressions, we explore and demonstrate that the micro-level structure of collaboration in the Valley is on average similar and sometimes less robust than that in Boston. Finally, we will collect our impressions of the differences between Boston and the Valley and comment on the Saxenian argument that the Valley is more networked.

IBM's postdoc program enabled young inventors to move across inventor components and explore new combinations of technologies and ideas. IBM modeled its program on Bell Lab's postdoc program (which, after the breakup of AT&T, no longer exists). When asked why IBM supported such a program, William Risk and John Campbell Scott provided a variety of reasons and motivations. First, the postdocs provided cheap labor. Second, new people with fresh ideas were seen as valuable. Third, IBM assumed that such people would depart as ambassadors for the firm. Risk and Scott did not mention the concerns about loss of proprietary information expressed by Hans Ribi and Pyare Khanna. Part of this reflects IBM's academic and admittedly "ivory tower" attitudes at the time. It also reflects founder and time period effects for the Almaden Lab in the 1960s. IBM operated as a virtual monopoly then. According to Scott, "the research division was set up by scientists with foresight." Their foresight had an impact well beyond IBM. (IBM has since reduced the postdoc program due to the firm's financial problems in the early 1990s. Other firms, however, such as Hewlett Packard, have begun similar programs [Fleming et al. 2005]).

The institutional support of mobility by young inventors appears to have greatly fostered their careers and, in turn, knowledge flow across firms in the Valley. Modeling at the inventor level of analysis also indicates that brokerage opportunities are most fruitful for young and relatively inexperienced inventors (Fleming, Mingo, and Chen 2007). After an inventor has gained a breadth of creative experience, she gains greater marginal benefits by collaborating cohesively because she brings non-redundant information that offsets the insularity of closed networks. It

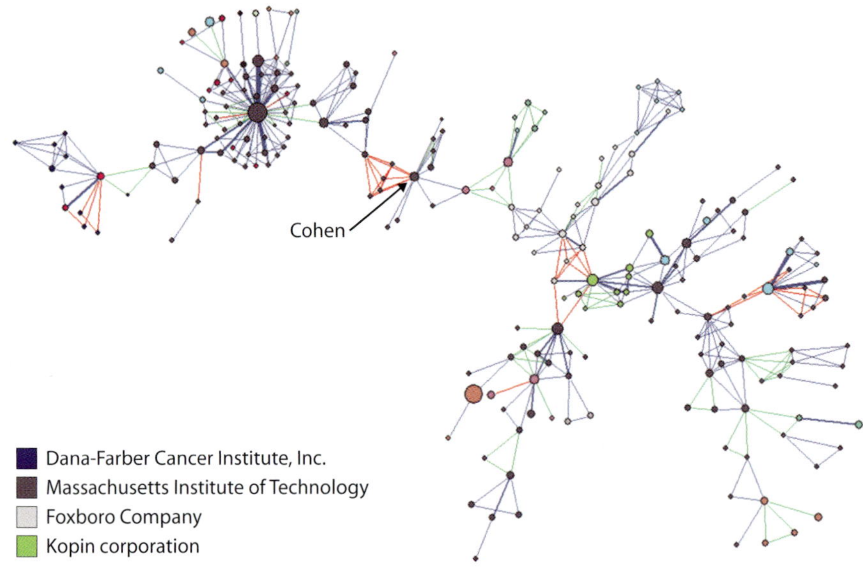

Figure 17.10 Boston's largest component in 1989, by assignee and importance of inventions. The MIT component did not aggregate into the 1990 largest component.

is interesting, though probably non-causal, that inventors are most mobile early in their careers, when they can most benefit from exposure to new ideas and technologies.

In the course of our interviews and graphical exploration of collaboration networks, we also perceived that Boston networks were less dense and robust than Valley networks. Whereas the IBM component emerged by 1987 to serve as the underlying foundation of the largest component in all subsequent years in the Valley, the composition of Boston's largest component continued to shift from one year to the next until 1993 when the Digital component was permanently displaced. Figure 17.10 illustrates another dramatic example of this process, the disintegration of the MIT/Foxboro/Dana-Farber component, Boston's largest component in 1985–89. Its red ties mark the patents that had expired by the following year (basically, patents that had been applied for in 1985). This illustrates how the component lost important bridging ties and completely fell apart. Given that this disintegration process would support the Saxenian arguments for Silicon Valley's more densely networked social structure, we tested the hypothesis that the Valley components were indeed more robust. Surprisingly, we found the opposite: paired comparisons across similarly ranked components indicate little difference, except that the second-largest component is more robust in Boston (GTE) than in the Valley (and, indeed, is by far the most robust of any component we analyzed). Appendix B describes the robustness analyses in detail. The analyses suggested that the Valley's greater degree of aggregation was not caused by a fundamental difference in the microsocial structure of its collaborative network. Indeed, the analyses (and even a visual comparison of the figures) indicated that the top six components of the two regions were quite similar, with the exception that the GTE/Siliconix component was more densely networked than its Valley counterpart.

Finally, we sought to understand whether Boston and the Valley had different information flows. We are struck by the bi-modal distribution of attitudes on the issue, mainly along professional lines and independent of the region. Most of the inventors from both regions expressed similar laissez-faire, open, and positive attitudes toward information flow. Many of their stories described an effort to evade efforts by management to contain their boundary-crossing collaborations. The most strident concerns about the leakage of proprietary information through collaborative relationships and extra-firm networks actually came from three Valley interviewees—Hans Ribi, Pyare Khanna, and (to a lesser extent) Salvador Umatoy.

Khanna explicitly described spillovers as bad, saying that it took one year to train a scientist, after which he preferred to keep the scientist in isolation. He felt that the important connections across the firm boundary were at his level and that scientists should work in silos. He sends his people to conferences, but only outside the Valley, to prevent poaching by rival Valley firms. At one time his firm had been in Concord, California, outside the traditional commuting distance of Silicon Valley. He preferred this location because salaries were 20–30 percent lower and people were less likely to leave. He remained noncommittal about why he subsequently moved his firm to Fremont (a city considered within the confines of the Valley), merely commenting: "Here there is the nucleus of growth." He opined that Kendall Square (a popular public plaza near MIT in Cambridge) in contrast, had no industry, only universities.[33] Khanna also remained noncommittal about the classic argument for location in technologically dynamic regions, namely the availability of technical personnel (Angel 1989).

The inventors in the Boston region noted a similar tension between managers and engineers regarding the decision to share information. "At Digital," Kaufman explained, "management thought we had all these great secrets to conceal; the engineers knew that the value was in collaboration." Koning felt that the core of the issue could be found in the underlying multiplicity of purposes for patenting. For example, an inventor might wish to patent a technology as a means to block its development by others in order to monopolize its sale or licensing. Alternatively, an inventor might patent as a means to steer the technology's subsequent development by others via "licensing on very generous terms" in order to acquire a first-mover/first-to-market advantage. (The latter motive is far more common for inventions that lend themselves to open standards and/or enjoy network effects, such as the computer networking hardware and software with which Koning is most familiar.) As both an engineer and an entrepreneur himself, Koning believed that in most cases, *both* motivations reflect the same basic principle: "You disclose x or license y because you make a business or engineering decision that the gain is greater than the loss." Naturally, this heuristic may not adequately address situations where business and engineering interests are at odds. Likewise, there is always a delicate balance between the desire to rely on public standards to protect proprietary decisions and the need to disclose proprietary decisions in order to institute those standards in the first place. As Koning put it, "It gets to be a very interesting dance. Sometimes it feels more like diplomacy than engineering."

Taken collectively, these inventors' comments suggest that simple characterizations of Boston secrecy and autarky versus Silicon Valley cooperation and interdependence fail to reflect the tension between managers and engineers on both coasts. Both communities struggled as they sought a practical and productive balance between making money, promoting public standards, and collectively solving problems. While unwanted spillovers certainly detract from the value of location in fast-paced technological regions like Boston and Silicon Valley, there are clearly many counterbalancing attractions. Managers can identify and attempt to keep their firm's mobile gatekeepers, but ultimately, and particularly in regions that do not enforce noncompetes or trade secret law, their options remain limited (Fleming and Marx 2006).

CONCLUSION

Why do regional inventor networks aggregate or disintegrate? And what influence does such aggregation have upon knowledge flows and creativity? We found many mechanisms that hamper aggregation, including the breakup of firms and the related uncertainty that saps morale and productivity; the dispersal of graduates to jobs outside the region; the departure of senior inventors to start-ups and self-employment rather than to other established firms; company policies that discourage collaboration; discrete product life cycles; and proprietary strategies that make collaboration unproductive. We found fewer influences that enhance aggregation. These include collaboration across academic and firm boundaries; collaboration within large firms; hiring local university graduates; and postdoc fellowships that seed local businesses with technically trained personnel. In the particular case at hand, Silicon Valley aggregated before Boston because Stanford graduates took employment at IBM's Almaden Valley Labs and because IBM sponsored a postdoctoral program that seeded the Valley with IBM patent coauthors. In contrast,

[33] An observation that is out-of-date, as any stroll through Kendall Square would reveal.

MIT graduates did not take employment at GTE, DEC, Data General, or Honeywell, and none of those firms sponsored collaborative programs like that at IBM. These differences were reflected in the generative ecologies of the two regions: Silicon Valley mobility increased the possibility of knowledge spillovers between firms and technologies. We found the attitudes of engineers toward spillovers to be remarkably similar in the two regions, however. Engineers appear eager to share ideas and facilitate creativity, independent of their location.

APPENDIX A: MATCHING ALGORITHM

We extracted source data on all granted U.S. patents from 1975 through 2002 from the United States Patent Office (USPTO) Cassis product, and MSA data for 2003 (ZIPList5 MSA 2003). Every patent includes all inventors' last names (with varying degrees of first and middle names or initials), inventors' hometowns, detailed information about the invention's technology in subclass references (there are over 100,000 subclasses), and the owner or assignee of the patent (generally a firm and less often a university, if not owned by the inventor). Since the USPTO indexes source data by patent number, we devised an inventor-matching algorithm to determine each inventor's patents and the other inventors with whom the focal inventor has coauthored at least one patent. The database includes 2,058,823 inventors and 2,862,967 patents (for description of more sophisticated algorithms and public accessible database, see Lai et al. 2011).

The matching algorithm refines previous approaches (Newman 2000). If last names match, first initials and middle initials (if present) must then match. Whole first names and whole middle names (if present) are then compared. If all these comparisons are positive, the algorithm then requires an additional non-name similarity: hometown and state, corporation (via assignee codes), or technology (via technology subclassifications). We also implemented a common name parameter that ignored the additional match requirement if the last name made up less than .05 percent of the U.S. population, as determined by the U.S. Census Bureau.

For 30 randomly selected inventors, the algorithm correctly assigned 215 of their 226 patents (as determined by résumé searches and personal contact). The 11 incorrectly determined patents were assigned to four isolated nodes (i.e., they did not create spurious cutpoints). Given the sensitivity of the measures to cutpoints, generating false negatives remains preferable to generating false positives or to incorrectly matching two different inventors.

The analyses presented relied on all patents with at least one inventor within the region. Thus if inventors from inside and outside a region coauthored a patent, the patent (and both inventors) would appear in each region. To explore the sensitivity of this definition, we regraphed all data with the more exclusive definition that did not include inventors from outside the region. While the graphs and network diagrams were generally smaller (as might be expected, since there will be at most the same number of inventors in each), the qualitative results were unchanged.

APPENDIX B: PATENT ROBUSTNESS ANALYSIS

One obvious explanation for the greater aggregation in the Silicon Valley network is that its components were more robust. We tested this hypothesis at the inventor level of analysis and then at the patent level of analysis. Figures 17.11 and 17.12 illustrate the inventor level of analysis for the largest and second largest components in the regions. (Illustrations for the third through sixth largest component comparisons looked qualitatively similar to those for the largest component and are not shown.) The y-axis of these illustrations is the proportion of nodes that remains connected in the largest resulting component after a proportion of the original nodes have been removed.The x-axis represents the proportion of original nodes that is removed.

Consider figure 17.12 first, illustrating the second largest components. The point 0.05 on the x-axis indicates that 5 percent of the nodes have been removed from what were originally the second largest components of Boston and the Valley. At this point, the y-axis indicates that the minimum proportion of nodes that remain connected in the reduced largest component is about 30 percent for the Valley and well over 40 percent for Boston. The graphed points are summary statistics (minimum, median, and maximum) of 50 samples for each data point. We sampled to avoid the combinatorial explosion of exhaustively calculating all possible choice combinations.

Figure 17.11 reveals very similar robustness for the two regions. Figure 17.12, however, illustrates that the Valley component is more

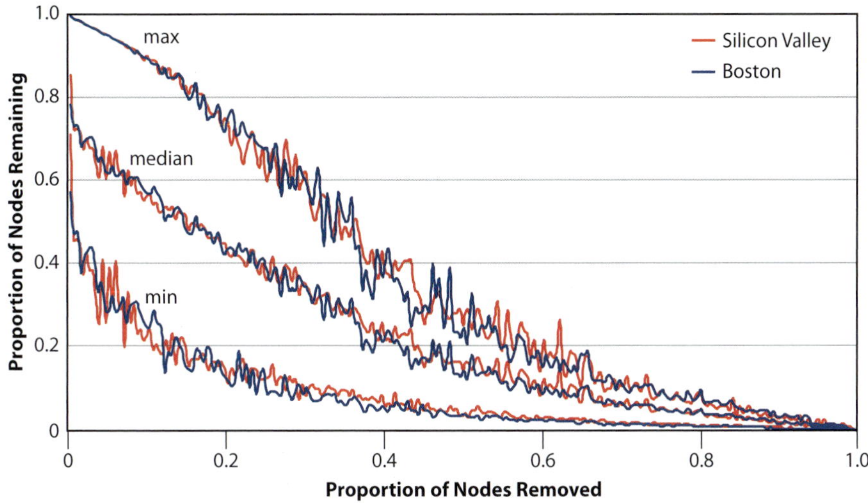

Figure 17.11 Size of component after removal of specified proportion of component's nodes, for Boston and Silicon Valley's largest components in 1989. The x-axis represents the proportion of original nodes that is removed. The y-axis illustrates the proportion of nodes that remains connected in the largest resulting component after a proportion of the original nodes have been removed.

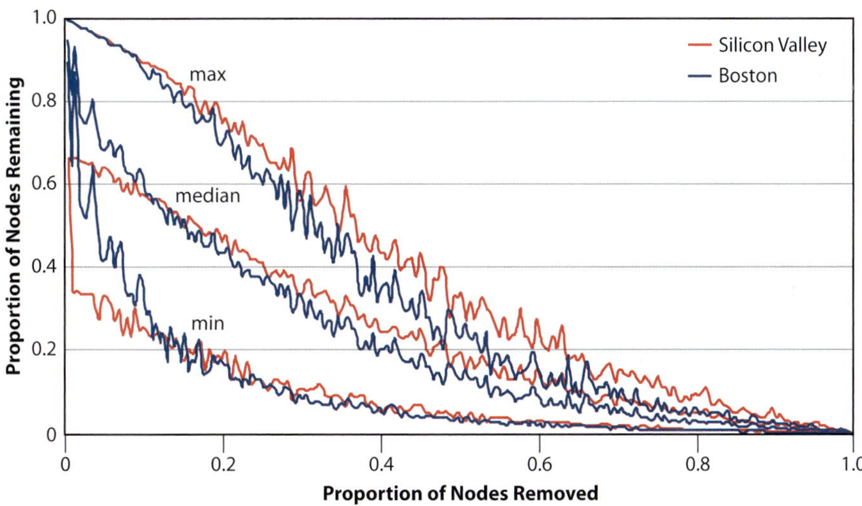

Figure 17.12 Size of component after removal of specified proportion of component's nodes, for Boston and Silicon Valley's second largest components. The x-axis represents the proportion of original nodes that is removed. The y-axis illustrates the proportion of nodes that remains connected in the largest resulting component after a proportion of the original nodes have been removed. As can be seen on the lower left, Silicon Valley was more vulnerable to node removal than Boston.

vulnerable to the loss of a few nodes. The steep initial drop in figure 17.12 for Silicon Valley indicates that the loss of a few key inventors quickly breaks the component up into much smaller pieces—similar to what is illustrated in figures 17.3 and 17.4. Silicon Valley appears to be simply more dynamic, breaking and re-forming nodes much more quickly, which is probably a reflection of its greater career mobility.

To confirm our results, we repeated the analysis at the patent level. For each of the components, we examine the extent to which the component would be disconnected by the removal of each patent. We define the extent to which a component is disconnected by the proportion of inventor dyads in that component that would no longer be able to reach one another after the patent is removed. We find this measure by considering each of these components individually and then calculating for each patent:

$$\sum_{c=1}^{K} (n/N)^2,$$

where N is the number of inventors in the original component, c is a component created by the removal of a patent, n is the number of inventors in a component c existing after a patent is removed, and K is the number of components in the post-removal network.

This measure yields a high value when the removal of a patent results in the creation of many new components and the inventors are divided equally among components. For example, if the removal of a patent divides a component into ten smaller components with one-tenth of the inventors in each component, this results in 0.9 of dyads being disconnected. However, if the removal of a patent results in a similar number of components but with inventors less evenly spread among them, the value generated by this measure will be smaller. For example, given a component of 100 inventors, if the removal of a patent breaks the component into 10 components with 9 of these being isolates and 91 inventors in the remaining component, then 0.171 of dyads are disconnected, indicating far less damage to the connectivity of the network. The maximum possible value would exist in a component where all inventors were coauthors on one patent and no other coauthorships existed. In this case the removal of the one shared patent would result in the disconnection of all inventor dyads.

We measure the vulnerability of each network by taking the mean proportion of inventor dyads disconnected by each patent. As stated earlier, the maximum value of this number is 1.0 for individual inventors. Calculating the maximum value for the mean of patents in a component is considerably more complex and beyond the scope of this chapter. However, since the maximum possible value will be related to the component size, caution should be exercised when comparing mean values across components of different sizes.

Table 17.2 illustrates robustness results. As the low numbers suggest, most patents within each component can do only minimal damage to the network. What is most striking is the lack of systematic difference across the two regions. The mean vulnerability over all the Boston components is 0.0241; over all Silicon Valley components it is 0.0272. Consistent with the inventor-level analysis, the second component appears to be much more robust in Boston, relative to all other components in both Boston and the Valley.

Both of these analyses suggest that the Valley's aggregation did not occur because its components were more robust and able to merge with other components.

Table 17.2.
Patent Analysis of Component Robustness

Component	Component Vulnerability	No. of Patents	Maximum
Boston 1	.0212 (.0763)	208	.52
Boston 2	.0074 (.0231)	345	.20
Boston 3	.0301 (.0762)	123	.49
Boston 4	.0179 (.0806)	182	.65
Boston 5	.0226 (.0610)	116	.35
Boston 6	.0451 (.0989)	45	.46
Silicon Valley 1	.0311 (.0757)	159	.49
Silicon Valley 2	.0208 (.0552)	161	.45
Silicon Valley 3	.0209 (.0477)	107	.38
Silicon Valley 4	.0330 (.0950)	131	.52
Silicon Valley 5	.0338 (.0729)	60	.49
Silicon Valley 6	.0237 (.0712)	78	.54

Note: Component vulnerability is the mean number of the proportion of inventor dyads disconnected by the removal of each patent within a given component (higher values indicate more vulnerable components). Standard deviations in parentheses.

REFERENCES

Albert, M. B., F. Narin, D. Avery, and P. McAllister. 1991. "Direct Validation of Citation Counts as Indicators of Industrially Important Patents." *Research Policy* 20:251–59.

Almeida, P., and B. Kogut. 1999. "Localization of Knowledge and the Mobility of Engineers in Regional Networks." *Management Science* 45:905–16.

Angel, D. 1989. "The Labor Market for Engineers in the U.S. Semiconductor Industry." *Economic Geography* 65(2):99–112.

Angel, D., and J. Engstrom. 1995. "Manufacturing Systems, and Technological Change: The U.S. Personal Computer Industry." *Economic Geography* 71(1):79–102.

Batagelj, V. and A. P. Mrvar. 1998. "A Program for Large Network Analysis." *Connections* 21:47–57. Pajek version 0.91, 2003, http://vlado.fmf.uni-lj.si/pub/networks/pajek/.

Beam, A. 1989. "Our Technology Graveyard." *Boston Globe*, July 26, p. 21.

Burt, R. 1992. *Structural Holes*. Cambridge, MA: Harvard University Press.

Clark, D. 1991. "Newcomers Put Stamp on Silicon Valley." *San Francisco Chronicle*, July 8, p. B1.

Cohen, F. 2003. Personal interview. February 13, Natick, MA.

Cohen, W., and D. Levinthal. 1990. "Absorptive Capacity: A New Perspective on Learning and Innovation." *Administrative Science Quarterly* 35:128–52.

Fallick, B., C. Fleischman, and J. Rebitzer. 2006. "Job-Hopping in Silicon Valley: Some Evidence Concerning the Micro-Foundations of a High Technology Cluster." *Review of Economics and Statistics* 88:472–81.

Feldman, M. 2001. "The Entrepreneurial Event Revisited: Firm Formation in a Regional Context." *Industrial and Corporate Change* 10(4):861–92.

Fleming, L. 2001. "Recombinant Uncertainty in Technological Search." *Management Science* 47(1):117–32.

Fleming, L., and K. Frenken. 2006. "The Evolution of Inventor Networks in the Silicon Valley and Boston Regions." *Advances in Complex Systems* 10(1): 53–71.

Fleming, L., and M. Marx. 2006. "Managing Creativity in a Small World." *California Management Review* 48:6–27.

Fleming, L., D. Chen, and S. Mingo. 2007. "Collaborative Brokerage, Generative Creativity, and Creative Success." *Administration Science Quarterly* 52:443–75.

Fleming, L., C. King, and A. Juda. 2007. "Small Worlds and Regional Innovation." *Organization Science* 18(2):938–54.

Fleming, L., M. Thursby, and J. Quinn. 2005. "HP Nanotech: Partnership with CNSI." Harvard Business School case 606-045. http://hbr.org/product/hp-nanotech-partnership-with-cnsi/an/606045-PDF-ENG.

Florida, R., and M. Kenney. 1990. *The Breakthrough Illusion*. New York: Basic Books.

Gilson, R. 1999. "The Legal Infrastructure of High Technology Industrial Districts: Silicon Valley, Route 128, and Covenants Not to Compete." *New York University Law Review* 74(3):575–629.

Glaeser, E., H. Kallal, J. Scheinkman, and A. Shleifer. 1992. "Growth in Cities." *Journal of Political Economy* 100(6):1126–53.

Graham, R. 1989. "'Miracle' Proves a Mirage: New Arrivals Find Too Little of High-Tech Boom, Too Late." *Boston Globe*, July 28, p. 13.

Granovetter, M. 1973. "The Strength of Weak Ties." *American Journal of Sociology* 78:1360–80.

Grove, A. 1990. "The Future of the Computer Industry." *California Management Review* 33(1):148–61.

Gulati, R., and M. Gargiulo. 1999. "Where Do Interorganizational Networks Come From?" *American Journal of Sociology* 104(5):1439–93.

Gura, T. 2004. "Joining a Trend, Scientists Increasingly Say 'Call My Agent.'" *Science* 303:303–5.

Henderson, V. 1997. "Externalities and Industrial Development." *Journal of Urban Economics* 42: 449–70.

Henderson, V., A. Kuncoro, and M. Turner. 1995. "Industrial Development in Cities." *Journal of Political Economy* 103(5):1067–90.

Jacobs, J. 1970. *The Economy of Cities*. New York: Random House.

Kenney, M., and U. von Burg. 1999. "Technology, Entrepreneurship, and Path Dependence: Industrial Clustering in Silicon Valley and Route 128." *Industrial and Corporate Change* 8:67–103.

Krugman, P. 1991. "Increasing Returns and Economic Geography." *Journal of Political Economy* 99(3):483–99.

Lai, R., A. D'Amour, A. Yu, Y. Sun, and V. Torvik. 2011. "Disambiguation and Co-author Networks of the U.S. Patent Inventor Database." Working paper, Harvard Business School.

Leslie, S., and R. Kargon. 1996. "Selling Silicon Valley: Frederick Terman's Model for Regional Advantage." *Business History Review* 70:435–72.

Marshall, A. 1920. *Principles of Economics*. 8th ed. London: Macmillan.

Marx, M., J. Singh, and L. Fleming. 2011. "Regional Disadvantage: Non-Competes and Brain Drain." Working paper, MIT Sloan School of Management.

Marx, M., D. Strumsky, and L. Fleming. 2009. "Mobility, Skills, and the Michigan Non-Compete Experiment." *Management Science* 55:875–89.

McCormick, J. 1999. "Asia's Best and Brightest Flock to Silicon Valley." *Electronic Business*, http://www.reed-electronics.com/eb-mag/index.asp?layout=article&articleid=CA65539&rid=0&rme=0&cfd=1.

Mowery, David C., Richard R. Nelson, Bhaven N. Sampat, and Arvids A. Ziedonis. 2001. "The Growth of Patenting and Licensing by U.S. Universities: An Assessment of the Effects of the Bayh-Dole Act of 1980." *Research Policy* 30(1):99–119.

Newman, M. 2000. "The Structure of Scientific Collaboration Networks." *Proceedings of the National Academy of Sciences of the United States of America* 98:404–9.

Nohria, N. 1992. "Information and Search in the Creation of New Business Ventures: The Case of the 128 Venture Group." In *Networks and Organizations: Structure, Form, and Action*, ed. N. Nohria and R. Eccles. Boston: Harvard Business School Press.

Owen-Smith, J., and W. Powell. 2004. "Knowledge Networks as Channels and Conduits: The Effects of Spillovers in the Boston Biotechnology Community." *Organization Science* 15(1):5–21.

Packard, D. 1995. *The HP Way: How Bill Hewlett and I Built Our Company*. New York: HarperCollins.

Piore, M., and C. Sabel. 1984. *The Second Industrial Divide: Possibilities for Prosperity*. New York: Basic Books.

Robertson, P., and R. Langlois. 1995. *Firms, Markets, and Economic Change: A Dynamic Theory of Business Institutions*. New York: Routledge.

Rosegrant, S., and D. Lampe. 1992. *Route 128: Lessons from Boston's High-Tech Community*, New York: Basic Books.

Saxenian, A. 1990. "Regional Networks and the Resurgence of Silicon Valley." *California Management Review* 33(1):89–113.

———. 1994. *Regional Advantage: Culture and Competition in Silicon Valley and Route 128*. Cambridge, MA: Harvard University Press.

———. 1999. "Comment on Kenney and von Burg, 'Technology, Entrepreneurship, and Path Dependence: Industrial Clustering in Silicon Valley and Route 128.'" *Industrial and Corporate Change* 8:105–10.

Schweikart, L. 2000. *The Entrepreneurial Adventure: A History of Business in the United States*. Fort Worth, TX: Harcourt College Publishers.

Simon, J. 1989. "Job Chill on 128: With Cutbacks and Slowed Growth, the Hiring Sizzle Is Gone." *Boston Globe*, April 30, p. A1.

Singh, J. 2005. "Collaborative Networks as Determinants of Knowledge Diffusion Patterns." *Management Science* 51(5):756–70.

Sorenson, O., and L. Fleming. 2004. "Science and the Diffusion of Knowledge." *Research Policy* 33(10): 1615–34.

Stein, C. 1989a. "128: Why It Will Never Be the Same." *Boston Globe*, January 3, p. 21.

———. 1989b. "Along Route 128, High Tech Hits Lows." *Boston Globe*, August 1, p. 1.

Stern, S., and M. Porter. 2001. "Innovation: Location Matters." *Sloan Management Review* 42(4).

Stewart, R. 2004. Personal interview, June 17, Cambridge, MA.

Watts, D., and S. Strogatz. 1998. "Collective Dynamics of Small-World Networks." *Nature* 393:440–42.

ZIPList5 MSA. 2003. Downloaded April 24 from CD Light, LLC: http://www.zipinfo.com/products/z5msa/z5msa.htm.

18

Managing the Boundaries of an "Open" Project

Fabrizio Ferraro ▪ Siobhán O'Mahony

Both scholars and observers of the rise of Wikipedia and open source software projects such as Linux often wonder how collectively managed projects that are open to any and all manage the production of complex knowledge goods. If the boundaries of public collective projects are open to any volunteer, how can the quality of complex knowledge goods be sustained? Without the credentialing of knowledge, appropriate organizational controls, and adequate financial incentives, surely such settings are ripe for malfeasance, co-optation, or just inferior work products. Yet empirical studies demonstrate modest discrepancies between encyclopedia texts produced by credentialed experts and those of Wikipedia's motivated body of volunteers (Giles 2006), and industries continue to clamor over the "open" approach to innovation (Chesborough 2005, 2006). Furthermore, since these two collective projects have become world renowned, the public and open approach to producing other types of goods has become increasingly popular (e.g., von Hippel 2005; Jeppesen and Lakhani 2010).

Despite the fact that determining an organization's boundaries with the environment is fundamental to economic (Williamson 1975, 1981), sociological (Lamont and Molnar 2002), and organizational theories (Santos and Eisenhardt 2005), little research has examined how seemingly open projects create or manage organizational boundaries. Do collectively managed projects remain open to all, or do they funnel and narrow over time, becoming increasingly closed to a select population of elite incumbents? If project boundaries remain open, how do they ensure that incoming contributors do not violate the project's mission? If project boundaries close, who become the gatekeepers of such forms? Our research draws upon both field and network methods to explore how social networks affect the emergence of organizational boundaries in novel collective forms, focusing on membership as a core boundary of interest. With qualitative data, we unpack the threats faced by open projects and the membership mechanisms designed to manage these threats. With quantitative data, we analyze the structure of the project's network to predict who designs the new membership process, thereby becoming gatekeepers to the project. In doing so, we explain how networks and social structures coevolve to affect organizational boundaries in novel forms.

This research was supported by Stanford University Center for Work, Technology, and Organization, the Social Science Research Council Program on the Corporation as a Social Institution, the Harvard University Business School Division of Research, and a Spanish Government Research Grant (Ministerio de Educación y Ciencia-ECO2009-08799). We thank the attendees of the Santa Fe Workshop on the Network Construction of Markets and the Schenna Workshop on the Emergence of Organizations and Markets for their helpful comments, in particular the guidance of Woody Powell, John Padgett, Steve Barley, Lee Fleming, Jeannette Colyvas, Kelley Packalen, and Ben Adida. The data collection and processing efforts of John Sheridan, Vikram Vijayaraghavan, and Jordi Torrents were much appreciated. All errors or omissions are our own. Neither author has any financial interest in Linux or open source companies.

MANAGING BOUNDARIES IN KNOWLEDGE COMMUNITIES

Although the examination of organizational boundaries was once dominated by transaction cost economics (Williamson 1978, 1981), organizational theorists are starting to consider power, competence, and identity as underappreciated and critical elements to providing a holistic view of organizations and their environment (Santos and Eisenhardt 2005). For example, in their research comparing the Burning Man and open source communities, Chen and O'Mahony (2009) identified two boundaries that were critical to the creation of new organizations: the boundary between individuals and the organization (determining what the organization could and could not do) and the boundary between the organization and the market (determining the degree to which community efforts could be commoditized). Santos and Eisenhardt might argue that the first boundary is one of power, demarcating an organization's domain of influence, while the second boundary is one of identity, enabling sensemaking among organizational members and inspiring attachment. Establishing both boundaries proved to be important to the ability of the Burning Man and open source communities to represent the interests of their growing membership base and sustain the motivation of volunteer contributors (Chen and O'Mahony 2009).

To advance theory, Santos and Eisenhardt urge scholars to move beyond efficiency arguments such as make or buy decisions to "problem-driven boundary phenomena" that are less atomistic in nature. New boundary choices in nontraditional settings or boundary decisions in nascent industries and organizations are likely to generate much-needed new thinking in this area (Santos and Eisenhardt 2005). One example of a problem-driven boundary decision is deciding who can legitimately participate in, contribute to, and join in an organization's activities. When organizations establish criteria for recruiting and selecting new members, they are simultaneously selecting the talents and values that will permeate the organization and who will gain a say on guiding the organization's mission. Determining membership is a critical function by which organizations can sustain themselves when facing any type of natural attrition. This is especially true in professional and knowledge-producing communities where contributors to knowledge projects are also trying to exert control over their work through setting boundaries.

For example, the literature on the professions shows how professions collectively determine criteria to keep "unqualified" members out of the profession and lay claim to a specific knowledge base (Sarfatti-Larson 1979). Boundaries help distinguish laymen from experts, science from non-science (Lamont and Molnar 2002). Scientists engage in "boundary-work" to distinguish "true science" from "non-science" and thus retain authority over their expertise (Gieryn 1983, 1999). This is particularly the case when scientists strive to distance their work from political or commercial aims (Moore 1996; Guston 2000).

To develop more generalizable theories on boundary processes that may be common across apparently unrelated phenomena, Lamont and Molnar (2002, 168) suggest that scholars "undertake the systematic cataloging of the key mechanisms associated with the activation, maintenance, transposition or the dispute, bridging, crossing and dissolution of boundaries" (2002, 187). Boundary disputes in particular offer a critical empirical entrance point to understanding processes of boundary activation and revision. A boundary dispute may question the blurring, penetration, or division of two previously distinct social worlds. To inform our present inquiry, we identified two critical boundary disputes in science and knowledge-producing communities: (1) managing the boundaries between open and commercial science; and (2) managing the boundaries between open source software and industry.

Open Science and Commercial Science

Many scholars have become concerned that the boundaries between public (or "open" and academic) and commercial science have become blurred to detrimental effects. The open and commercial science communities are interdependent in the creation of new knowledge but diverge in their reward systems and in their dissemination and use of that knowledge (Dasgupta and David 1994). The logic of open science assumes that the production of science is a public endeavor (David 2001, 2003) and encourages universalistic standards based on competence or merit (Merton 1973). The practice of open science demands full and timely disclosure of methods and findings in order to allow scientists to replicate and verify each other's work (Merton 1973; Latour and Woolgar 1979). While the goal of commercial science is to increase the stream of rents that can accrue from rights to private knowledge, the goal of open science is to add to the stock of public knowledge (Dasgupta and David 1994).

Instead of property rights, scientists are granted priority for discoveries made. This provides scientists with an incentive to share their discoveries early, helping scientists avoid duplication and advance the field more rapidly. David argues that the institutional framework supporting public science can be undermined if too great an emphasis is placed on property right protections (2001). Thus many scholars have examined how the Bayh Dole Act, which permits universities to take an expanded role in licensing academic research for commercial purposes, has affected the funding, conduct, use, and dissemination of university research (Owen-Smith 2003; Owen-Smith and Powell 2003; Mowery and Sampat 2001, 2004; Mowery and Ziedonis 2002). Of concern is whether the norms of open science are compromised when university endeavors cross commercial boundaries.

There is suggestive evidence that the blurring of commercial and university science boundaries has, in the last twenty years, had some effects (Owen-Smith 2003; Owen-Smith and Powell 2003; Huang and Murray 2009). Universities well connected to industry had patent portfolios with greater impact, but these relationships reached a point of diminishing returns. Technology licensing offices that were too closely tied to industry had less innovative patent portfolios (Owen-Smith and Powell 2003). The suggestion that university research has become more applied due to close relationships with commercial entities highlights both the importance and the fragility of managing boundaries between public and private organizations as these relationships can actually affect the type of knowledge produced. Most scholars agree that commercial support of university research is imperative as public support for it has declined (Mowery and Sampat 2004). The question is how a more integrated commercial and academic relationship can prosper without unduly influencing the direction of open science. Sustaining openness and pluralism without risking co-optation from commercial entities is a central concern. This is also a boundary dispute to which open source software projects are starting to gain exposure.

Open Source Software and Commercial Software

The production of open source software is often compared to the "open science" process of peer review (Dalle and David 2005; Kogut and Meitu 2001; Raymond 1999) where work and method are critically evaluated by peers with informed skepticism (Merton 1973; Latour and Woolgar 1979). This comparison is only partially true—for example, academia has a long history of indoctrinating graduate students to the norms of science that open source projects do not share. Open source software projects do embrace open science principles and are guided by powerful norms that reinforce or discourage certain types of behavior. O'Mahony (2007) defines community-managed open source software projects as embracing principles of: (1) independence, (2) pluralism, (3) representation, (4) decentralized decision making, and (5) autonomous participation. Most important, project organization and decision making occurs in public forums independent of any one firm and is not influenced by authority relations that stem from employment (O'Mahony 2007). However, these community projects lack the socialization, institutional, and professional structures academe provides to guide training and access to the production of new knowledge.

Both open science and open source software are similar in the challenge they face with respect to boundary disputes between the open and public production of knowledge and the commercial capturing of value. Since the term *open source* was created in 1998, open source software has attracted a more diverse group of supporters interested in commercializing open source software despite the fact that it is produced in public forums and distributed with open source licenses. Some open source software projects have been receptive to a commercial audience and engaged in synergistic relations with firms but remain wary that their culture, practice, and code may be compromised. Sponsorship from industry dominants has introduced a new challenge: how to maintain independence and neutrality in the face of industry support (O'Mahony 2002; O'Mahony and Bechky 2008).

While open communities producing new knowledge benefit from the diversity of their contributors, contributors must share a common goal in the project's success as a noncommercial entity for the project to sustain itself.

In a completely open environment, not all contributors may have the project's best interests in mind. As the number of contributors to open source projects grows, so does the diversity of contributor skill and motivation. The potential for someone to co-opt or hijack a project or unwittingly introduce code owned by someone else looms large. Good intentions without skill can be equally dangerous. For quality in this context is not merely technical but also legal, referring to code that is free of proprietary licenses. Open source projects do not want to unknowingly accept code that might conflict with open source licenses. Thus project members want to ensure that potential contributors share the project's values and do not introduce code that might jeopardize the project's boundary with proprietary software. In this sense, managing project membership not only affects the boundary of the project itself but also helps preserve the project's legal boundaries with the commercial world.

Recent research has attended to ways in which open projects are becoming more bounded. For example, despite the popular belief that open source contributors give their work away, many contributors to open source software projects now assign copyrights to a nonprofit foundation designed to hold the group's efforts in trust (O'Mahony 2003). With growth in the scale of code, contributors, and industry sponsors, several open source projects have sought to make clearer determinations of membership and rights (von Krogh, Spaeth, and Lakhani 2003; Michlmayr and Hill 2003). In their study of the FreeNet project, von Krogh and colleagues (2003) discovered that potential contributors with particular "joining scripts" and contributions of code were more likely to be awarded developer status. O'Mahony and Ferraro (2007) have shown how one community's conception of leadership changed over time as the project scaled and became unwieldy. Thus the question is, how do open source communities manage the boundaries of an open project? Powell (1990) predicted that network forms would face novel problems of control and that membership in a community would require new organizational practices (Powell, Koput, and Smith-Doerr 1996, 142). Our research explores how one project managed these exact challenges by examining the design of their new membership system. We then examine who became the gatekeepers of this system, revealing how the project's social network and organizing structure co-evolved over time.

METHODS

Research Setting

Despite the fact that the distributed setting of an open source project implies the existence of powerful social networks, a social network approach has yet to be used to explain the evolution of a project's social structure. With unique longitudinal network data, we examined the evolution of the Debian Linux project's social network over a five-year period (1997–2001) to assess how changes in the network structure affected the design of membership mechanisms. Debian produces the largest and most popular noncommercial Linux operating system distribution and has been in existence for over fifteen years. Like other commercial distributions such as Red Hat™ (www.redhat.com), Debian integrates the Linux kernel maintained by LinusTorvalds and other kernel hackers (www.kernel.org) with thousands of other software packages to create a complete self-installing distribution. Unlike Red Hat, Debian is not a commercial entity and does not sell its code or pay its programmers. Debian has over a thousand volunteer programmers[1] in over forty countries who collectively maintain over eight thousand software packages. The vast majority of coding activities are publicly accessible and the software produced can be downloaded for free. But access rights to the code base must be managed so as not to jeopardize the project's security.

Unlike online communities with fluid boundaries and potentially anonymous, shifting members and identities, the Debian project needed a way to trust the identity of project contributors in order to grant them the right to contribute directly to a project's code base. Membership could be fluid, but it could not be *indeterminate*—the allocation of access rights had to be known and distinguishable. Since contributors may never meet each other, they faced a unique problem: how to verify the identities of individuals around the world. Thus the Debian project began using public key encryption as a way to build trust and authenticate member identities in 1994. This method became, in the spring of 2000, a condition for becoming a project member.

[1] Some developers engage in wage-earning activities that allow them to work on Debian as part of their paid work: they are what we define as sponsored contributors. Others are volunteers. Participation in the project is always voluntary.

A key is merely a large number that, with the help of a particular cryptographic algorithm, like one offered by "Pretty Good Privacy" (PGP) or GnuPG (GPG), allows text to be encoded and decoded only by the intended recipients. Some cryptography methods, called symmetric key algorithms, use the same key to encode and decode data. This presents a complicated key distribution problem: how can a distant sender and recipient exchange this secret key without compromising each other's security?

Public key encryption uses cryptography to solve this problem by using asymmetric keys: a public key encodes the data and a completely different private key decodes the data, allowing a sender and recipient to exchange private information without secret key distribution. Thus a user's private key is never revealed (Network Associates 1990). Asymmetric cryptography does not, however, solve the problem of certifying a key holder's identity. Public key cryptography secures the authenticity of the contents of the communication but not the link between the key and the sender's identity. To make public key cryptography useful, a real-world identity must be linked to a given public key.

The Debian project uses "key signing" practices to link individual identity to key ownership. A key is certified when one person digitally signs the public key. A key certification is an expression of trust: the signer believes that the public key she signs belongs to the cited person. Some form of identification documentation (usually government issued) demonstrates that a public key belongs to its owner and is represented by the user ID packet (Brennen 2003). This certification does not provide assurance as to the authenticity of identification documents but does provide assurance that a particular identity is assigned to a particular key (Network Associates 1990).

In a globally distributed environment like Debian, where everyone cannot meet everyone else, responsibility for validating public keys is delegated to trusted others. Key signers are explicitly encouraged to consider not only their own security requirements but the interests of others who may rely on their judgment.

> Key signing has two main purposes: it permits you to detect tampering on your keyring, and it allows you to certify that a key truly belongs to the person named by a user ID on the key. Key signatures are also used in a scheme known as the web of trust to extend certification to keys not directly signed by you but signed by others you trust. (Free Software Foundation 1999, 13)

Certificates provide validation, but people are trusted to be judicious when validating the certificates of others. A "web of trust" is a collection of key signings that allows people to rely upon third-party verification of others' public keys. The web of trust assumes that the more people who have signed each other's key (the greater the density of the network), the more reliable is the information authenticated: "The more deep and tightly interlinked the web of trust is, the more difficult it is to defeat" (Brennen 2003). There is no limit to the number of people who can sign a key.

Debian contributors have their keys signed by hosting or attending "key-signing parties"—get-togethers for the purpose of signing each other's keys. At a key-signing party, a small group of individuals will bring a copy of their public key and valid photo identification and certify each other's public keys. After a key is signed it can then be placed on a central key server that may be maintained by a "keyring coordinator." Key-signing parties are viewed as critical to enhancing the web of trust, to teaching people about the benefits of cryptography, and to building technical communities (Brennen 2003).

> [P]lease don't sign keys of people you did not personally identify. If you don't take this process seriously, you are a weak link in the Web of Trust. If I see that you signed the key of someone who wasn't at the event, I won't sign your key, and I'll suggest that others don't either. (Key Signing Party Organizer, July 8, 2001)

As this party organizer explains, violating key signing protocols can lead to sanctioning and possible estrangement by other project members. Signing someone's key without physical verification of his or her identity breaches the norms of the community and threatens the web of trust. If someone is viewed as lax in his security requirements, his ability to maintain the respect of his peers will be compromised.

Since each key signing is dated and requires a face-to-face meeting, these data indicate when individual project members met each other and provide a unique longitudinal network data set. We analyzed these data to determine if an individual's structural position in the network affected the attainment of gatekeeper positions. With qualitative data on the project's evolution, we examined how the Debian project managed a membership crisis where an influx of contributors new to the project's norms, methods, and values began to overwhelm the project. Together, these two empirical approaches show how organizational design and social network dynamics are intertwined and that the former cannot be ignored when attempting to understand the emergence of new social orders.

Data Collection and Measures

The data we collected from the Debian keyring consist of GPG and PGP keys signed by dyads between 1994 and 2002. The keyring network was only minimally active during the project's first two years (1994–96). Thus we begin our analysis at the beginning of 1997 when key signing started to become more widely adopted. Table 18.1 reports the number of developers in the keyring, rate of growth of the nodes in the network, number of ties between members, average degree (number of keys signed or people met), standard deviation of degree, number of components, and density of the network from 1997 to 2002.

Statistical Model

From the project developer database, we identified the continent of residence for each developer and leadership positions, if any, held over time. In Table 18.2 we summarize data on the continent of residence with three dummy variables (Europe, North America, and Other), as well as other descriptive statistics such as packages maintained, postings to the mailing list, tenure, and degree centrality. As a measure of each developer's contribution to the project, we collected data from the project's bug tracking database on the number of software packages each developer

Table 18.1.
Growth in the Debian Keyring Network

	1997	1998	1999	2000	2001	2002
Number of developers in network	13	82	176	298	532	671
Growth rate	-	530.77%	114.63%	69.32%	79.32%	26.13%
Number of ties	11	111	239	543	1212	2014
Average degree	2.46	2.71	2.72	3.64	4.56	6.00
S.D. degree	1.60	3.04	3.22	4.67	6.57	8.84
Number of components (min. 2)	3	19	29	31	39	33
Density	0.124	0.033	0.015	0.012	0.009	0.009

Table 18.2.
Descriptive Statistics of Debian Developers, 2001–2

	2001		**2002**	
	All Developers (N = 532)		All Developers (N = 671)	
	Mean	S.D.	Mean	S.D.
Dependent Variable				
New Maintaner Committee[a]	.010	.005		
Independent Variables				
Number of packages maintained	6.68	9.01	7.23	9.87
Package popularity	299.5	809.8	270.9	749.6
Tenure (in months)	18.54	15.50	22.89	16.41
Europe (reference category)[a]	.46	.47		
North America[a]	.31	.31		
Other continent[a]	.12	.13		
Tie to leader[a]	.11	.12		
# of mailing list postings	12.24	28.43	13.54	42.35
Degree centrality	4.56	6.58	6	8.85

[a] Dummy variables

Table 18.3.
Correlation Coefficients in 2001

Variables	(1)	(2)	(3)	(4)	(5)	(6)	(7)	(8)	(9)
(1) New Maintainer Committee	-								
(2) # of packages maintained	0.1568	-							
(3) Package popularity	0.1134	0.3759	-						
(4) Degree centrality	0.3152	0.1359	0.1203	-					
(5) Tie to leader	0.1383	0.0540	0.1017	0.4655	-				
(6) # of mailing list postings	0.1069	0.2852	0.3754	0.3199	0.1359	-			
(7) Tenure (months)	-0.0548	0.0075	0.1501	0.2781	0.2014	0.1021	-		
(8) North America	-0.0161	-0.0652	0.0176	-0.1058	-0.0477	0.0489	-0.0918	-	
(9) Other	-0.0071	0.0786	0.0405	-0.0724	-0.1022	0.0166	-0.0518	-0.2506	-

Table 18.4.
Correlation Coefficients in 2002

Variables	(1)	(2)	(3)	(4)	(5)	(6)	(7)	(8)	(9)
(1) New Maintainer Committee	-								
(2) # of packages maintained	0.0846	-							
(3) Package popularity	0.0751	0.3738	-						
(4) Degree centrality	0.0725	0.0796	0.0892	-					
(5) Tie to leader	0.0076	0.0177	0.0982	0.3513	-				
(6) # of mailing list postings	0.0641	0.2208	0.3752	0.2787	0.0410	-			
(7) Tenure (months)	-0.1145	-0.0364	0.1552	0.1805	0.2396	0.0430	-		
(8) North America	0.0568	-0.0391	0.0180	-0.1453	-0.0385	-0.0172	-0.0710	-	
(9) Others	-0.0422	0.0804	0.0361	-0.1035	-0.0752	0.0608	-0.0647	-0.2630	-

maintained in 2001 and 2002 (the only years available). In both years, developers maintained an average of 7 packages (with a standard deviation of 9 in 2001 and 10 in 2002). Similar to prior studies of the Apache, FreeNet, and GNOME projects, a small fraction of maintainers contribute the majority of the work (von Krogh, Spaeth, and Lakhani 2003; Mockus, Fielding, and Herbsleb 2002; Koch and Schneider 2000). Under 8 percent of maintainers managed more than 20 packages in 2001 and 2002. The maximum number of packages maintained by any one person was 81 in 2001 and 101 in 2002.

Since the number of packages maintained provided only a raw measure of quantity of effort, we created a measure of the criticality of a developer's work on the project by computing the *package popularity*. Since early 2003, Debian users could install a "popularity-contest package" that automatically calculates the number of people that use a particular package regularly. We computed the raw sum of the votes for all packages maintained by individual developers to measure the criticality of their work to others. We also included a variable to measure other forms of participation that did not involve direct coding by measuring the number of mailing list postings each developer contributed to the project's primary mailing list focused on development: "debian devel."

For each year we computed a measure of developer project tenure, counting the months since they first signed a key. We used the keyring data to measure the degree centrality of each developer, which is the number of other developers each one of them has met face-to-face at least once.[2] Finally, we created a variable to measure ties to the project leader indicating which developers signed the project leader's key. We wanted to control for any effect that the project leader might have on the final composition of the new maintainer committee: our dependent variable of interest. As described in more detail in the next section, the New Maintainer Committee was established to design the new membership process and the rules that would admit new entrants to the project. This group in essence becomes the project gatekeepers once new boundaries are established. Tables 18.3 and 18.4 present the

[2] We also computed betweenness centrality, which measures the extent to which an actor can broker communication between other actors (Freeman 1979; Wasserman and Faust 1994), but since this measure was highly correlated with degree centrality, we only used the latter in our analysis.

correlation coefficients of all the variables considered, for 2001 and 2002.

To show how the structural position of the developers affected the composition of the New Maintainer Committee, we estimated a logistic regression model (Long 1997), testing whether degree centrality in the network (1997–2000) affected the composition of the new maintainer committee in 2001–2 after controlling for the level and criticality of contribution, ties to the project leader, tenure in the project, and geographic location.

Field Research

In order to understand these data in the context of the project's evolution, seventy-six informants from the open source community at large were interviewed, six of them in leadership positions within Debian. Online documentation such as mailing list archives, meeting notes, and other formal project documents offered an additional source of data. With these data, we analyzed the project's evolution along six critical phases: (1) project initiation; (2) success and new vulnerabilities; (3) membership crisis; (4) designing the membership process; (5) emergence of gatekeepers; and (6) narrowing the pipeline. We analyzed how project members' conceptualization of membership evolved over time and how this affected the project's boundary with the very open and public environment in which the project operated.

DESIGNING A MEMBERSHIP PROCESS

Project Initiation

On August 16, 1993, the founder of Debian proposed developing an easily installable packaged version of the GNU[3]/Linux operating system to a Usenet newsgroup. He wanted to create a complete operating system that would be "commercial grade" but not commercial and be managed differently from the Linux kernel project.

> Rather than being developed by one isolated individual or group, as other distributions of Linux have been in the past,[4] Debian is being developed openly in the spirit of Linux and GNU. The primary purpose of the Debian project is to finally create a distribution that lives up to the Linux name. . . . It is also an attempt to create a non-commercial distribution that will be able to effectively compete in the commercial market. (Murdock 1994)

About two dozen people responded to the posting and the founder created a new mailing list specifically for this project, named "Debian."[5] Between 1993 and 1996, the founder, with the help of Usenet respondents, collectively designed a modular package management system.

A package is a unit of code that can be maintained independently from the rest of the operating system but has a standardized interface that allows integration with other packages. To maintain a package is to manage the receipt and review of code contributions from other contributors (called "upstream maintainers") and "package" these smaller contributions into a discrete module. A modular package system enables many people who are not physically co-located to contribute to the project by permitting different development activities to be conducted in parallel. From 1994 to 1995, the Free Software Foundation supported the founder in designing a technical infrastructure that could handle a large number of contributors. The first whole number release (1.1), announced in June 1996, had 474 packages.

In the months leading up to the project's first official release in July 1997, members debated how to manage the project's status as a noncommercial entity. Five issues were critical to establishing boundaries with the business world: (1) garnering legitimacy as a noncommercial entity; (2) determining how to logistically distribute their software; (3) raising funds to support the project's legal expenses as a nonprofit; (4) distinguishing "official" copies of Debian from versions modified for commercial purposes; and (5) determining how, if at all, commercial entities should contribute to the project. Exploration of these concerns challenged the meaning of "noncommercial" as it was initially conceived and reflected competing goals among members to both control their product and disseminate it broadly.

[3] GNU is a recursive acronym that represents the phrase "GNU is Not UNIX." The GNU system pioneered by Richard Stallman was designed in opposition to the proprietary restrictions associated with UNIX.

[4] This reference to other Linux distributions managed by one person likely refers to the Linux kernel managed by Linus Torvalds.

[5] The origins of the project's name stems from a combination of the names of the founder and his wife.

> We don't want to be in the CD manufacturing business, the import-export business, or the order fulfillment business. We want to get Debian into as many people's hands as we can, for as little money as possible. (Posting to Debian Development mailing list, January 17, 1997)

Project members wanted to acquire the legitimacy associated with shrink wrap software, but Debian did not have the capital to manufacture a physical distribution. Commercial involvement would help them establish a larger market share than Internet downloads would permit, but they did not want to sell their work.

One proposal to contract with firms to distribute Debian for two dollars was perceived by others as crossing the "noncommercial" line. Project members questioned whether it was within their charter to ask, mandate, or suggest contributions from firms. The project leader who informally took over the project when the founder resigned at the end of 1996 angrily defended the commercial appeal of the project in the following post.

> I AM NOT TRYING TO TURN THE PROJECT INTO A COMMERCIAL ORGANIZATION. IT IS A NON-PROFIT. I WANT TO RAISE OUR PERCEPTION IN THE PUBLIC BY MAKING OUR PRODUCT _ LOOK_ COMMERCIAL. (Posting to Debian Development mailing list, January 19, 1997, original format)

What constituted a noncommercial distribution was hotly contested, and in the end, a consensus agreed that Debian would not sell its code. Individuals and firms could freely download and resell the Debian distribution with no fee. In return, some firms could, at their choice, donate a portion of their proceeds to Debian.

Success and New Vulnerabilities

With these agreements in place, the project released the first "official" distribution (1.3) with 974 packages contributed by 200 developers. This event also marked the growth of the keyring network. Although the keyring was initiated in 1994, only 13 project members had signed each other's keys at the start of 1997. The keyring network grew to 82 people in 1998 and 176 in 1999 (table 18.1). This rapid growth may have been stimulated by media coverage that began after the first release (figure 18.1) but also reflected concerns over the threat of "Trojan" contributors. A Trojan contributor would be a volunteer or "malicious contributor" who purposely introduced bugs or viruses to the project.

Debian's technical success in building a complete distribution and its subsequent popularity meant that, like other Linux distributions, it was now a threat to other commercial operating systems, making Debian vulnerable to anticompetitive tactics. However, well-intentioned but unskilled developers could create equally

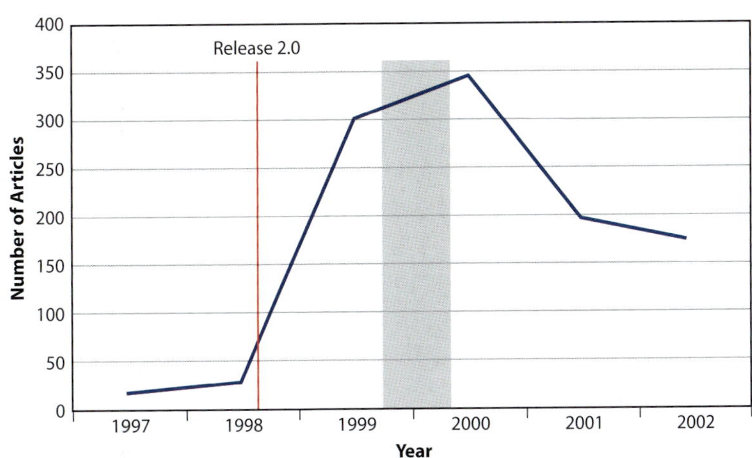

Figure 18.1 Media citations of Debian GNU/Linux, 1997–2002. The shaded area indicates the time during which the Debian project closed its doors to new members. *Source:* Data on articles citing "Debian Linux" were collected from ABI/Inform database in Proquest and the Factiva database in 2003.

detrimental effects. Debian developers all have the same access rights and can upload anything into the project's code archive. This has the potential to affect all other packages. Typically the official maintainer of a package makes such an upload. Changes made by a non-maintainer will not carry the same status as those made by someone listed as the maintainer.[6] If someone fixes a bug in another person's package, that bug will be tagged and fixed, but the maintainer will have to close the bug in the database herself, signaling that the person responsible has reviewed the work of the non-maintainer. Newcomers to Debian who were not fully cognizant of Debian procedures could wreak havoc with Debian's detailed code formats and operating procedures. Members were torn between reconciling the need to welcome people interested in Debian with the need to protect the project from potentially destructive outsiders.

Mailing list archives indicate that the idea of using a keyring to authenticate contributor identity was proposed by the person who initiated the keyring network in 1994.

> I think that at least one of our objectives should be to establish a socio-legal comeback in the case of a malicious developer. This means that we need to verify the real-world identity of the developer somehow. There are several ways to do this, including personal introduction by an existing developer, commercial key-signing, attempting to use PGP web of trust, telephone verification of some kind. (Posting to Debian Development mailing list, February 28, 1997)

At the time, there was no formal standard membership process and little preliminary screening. As the informant below describes, the ability to articulate areas for contribution was considered evidence of one's capability to work on the project.

> When I applied, I told [the Debian Project Leader], "Here are the packages I want to work on." Back then it was pretty easy and we didn't do the identity check at that point. It was pretty easy to assume that if you knew about Debian back then, you were fairly competent and probably understood the basics of what free software was about. It was a new thing back then—free software particularly. (Sponsored Contributor, former volunteer, November 9, 2000)

Several mailing list threads discussed ways to secure the identities of contributors, ascertain membership, and determine project decision rights: "There are enough psychos out there to make sure that groups such [as] Debian do not succeed" (Posting to Debian Development mailing list, October 25, 1997). This discussion persisted for some years.

How could Debian keep the project "open" but ensure that contributors were not only well intentioned but skilled enough not to inadvertently harm the project? Members were reluctant to articulate a formal set of skill requirements or make too many demands of volunteers: "I'm not sure about competence or integrity requirements [to acquire maintainer status]; somehow it goes against the grain for someone who is not issuing my paycheck" (Posting to Debian Development mailing list, February 27, 1997).

The second whole number release (2.0), announced in July 1998, had 1,500 packages and over 400 developers. As figure 18.1 shows, this release coincides with a sharp increase in media attention devoted to Debian. Shortly after Debian's fifth birthday, the third leader initiated the collective drafting of a constitution to outline the roles and rights of the project leader and project members. The constitution delimits the authority of the Debian leader and bounds the group's authority over each other. Members have the right to: (1) make technical or nontechnical decisions with regard to their own work; (2) propose or sponsor draft resolutions; (3) run as a project leader candidate in elections; and (4) vote for resolutions and leadership elections. The constitution details specific privileges for members but does not articulate how one becomes a member. The question of how to prevent a "Trojan" was left unresolved as Debian's public presence continued to grow.

Membership Crisis

In August 1999 several package maintainers who were not yet full developers began complaining about the wait to obtain a developer account. Contributors who proved their ability to maintain a package could become maintainers, but they did not necessarily become developers or project members. Only developers had accounts to access

[6] See Michlmayr and Hill 2003 for more description of the new maintainer upload process.

the code repository and in order to upload a package directly as the project now required members to sign the package with their key.

> If anyone could upload to Debian . . . [twisted facial expression]. We had to guarantee that it actually comes from a trusted source, and that it hasn't been changed along the way. That is how what we achieve this—by signing the packages. . . . First of all it shows that it is from a trusted source. It is signed by a key, which is a developer. The other thing is it shows that the package hasn't been modified. Like during the upload someone could come and change the package perhaps. (Volunteer contributor, Debian Project Leader, June 20, 2003)

The Developer Accounts Manager (DAM), who was authorized to assign new accounts, faced a backlog of people interested in the project and had no real way to ascertain the qualifications of a particular maintainer. A few candidates resigned in frustration.

To avoid losing contributors, some developers began "sponsoring" member candidates by uploading their packages for them and signing them with their keys. Postings to the list and interviews with informants suggest that the delay in accepting new maintainers was partly due to a heavy workload for volunteers but also due to their concerns that recent entrants to the project were actually hindering the project more than they were helping.

> The problem is they [new maintainers] are not contributing. And some of them are contributing bugs. They are actually adding bad packages. And there was a lot of kicking from old developers about the new people and how they are not reading anything and doing things, it is always old versus new. So we closed being a new maintainer for a while because there were so many new packages coming in that they were not helping with anybody else's packaging, they were just uploading their own. So what we were seeing is 1,000 new packages a year and that many more bugs per package showing up. But no change right? It was not getting better, it was getting worse. So we closed it off for a year. Then we sat down and wrote up how we wanted it to work. (Sponsored Contributor, March 20, 2001)

After doubling in size, project members were frustrated by the growth in bugs relative to contributions from new members and, in particular, the age of unaddressed bugs. New maintainers wanted to work on areas of their interest, not debug existing bugs.

To address the problem, the fourth project leader (newly elected by the powers of the constitution) made a controversial decision: he closed the project to new maintainers until a new membership process could be designed. Membership would remain closed until April the following year—almost six months. As table 18.1 shows, Debian's contributor and package growth experienced a plateau during this period.

> Debian's new maintainer team is currently not processing requests. The team wanted to resolve some problems they observed with the way Debian maintainership is currently handled, and decided to close new-maintainer until these have been fixed. We are currently working on a new structure for handling new-maintainer requests, and hope to have this finished as soon as possible. (Debian Project Leader, posting to mailing list, October 11, 1999)

This announcement was followed by a recruiting call outlining criteria for a new membership committee: the New Maintainer Committee (NMC). Developers were invited to e-mail the leader (privately) and were told that committee members would be selected according to the following criteria:

> [T]he following guidelines will be used in selecting new members to the new-maintainer team:
>
> needs to have a *strong* opinion for free software
>
> he needs to be able + willing to make long distance phone calls
>
> He needs to know what he's doing, that new people need some guidance, we have to prevent ourselves from trojans etc.
>
> we need to trust him—more than we trust *any* other active person
>
> He *has to* understand that new-maintainer is *more* than just creating dumb accounts on machines. (New Maintainer Proposal, October 19, 1999)

The need to "trust committee members more than any other active person" suggests that the project leader understood that this committee would become gatekeepers for the project and wanted confidence in their philosophical commitment above and beyond their effort on the project.

Designing the Membership Process

While there had always been some identification process before granting new developer accounts, it was not standardized. The committee initially proposed a four-stage process: initial contact (with possible phone interview), checking identification, internship, and acceptance. Identity authentication would ensure that members "know that the person actually exists as the person that they say they are, that there is a known location for that person where they can be spoken to" (New Maintainer Proposal, October 17, 1999). Project members engaged in this debate recognized that face-to-face meetings could help instill greater collegiality, trust, and respect among members.

> Maybe the "meet a developer approach" combined with a brief phone interview is better than a lengthy call from some faceless developer. Plus it gives new maintainers an opportunity to have their key signed, which helps build our web of trust, and the personal contact might socialize against flame mongering. (Posting to Debian Project mailing list, October 18, 1999)

The "internship" would allow applicants to prove themselves by testing the candidates' technical competence, knowledge of organizational procedures, collegiality and commitment, and philosophical agreement with the principles of the project.

> It [the internship] allows us a good method to help a new maintainer with his new work and teach him about the Debian system (both technical and organizational). It allows us to get to know the person: is he responsive to bug reports or other requests, is he able to produce a quality product, and also very important: does he agree with our philosophy? (New Maintainer Proposal, October 19, 1999)

Agreement with the project philosophy was critical to ensuring that people did not introduce code licensed under legal terms that differed from the project's open source license. This proposal led to a discussion of what it meant to be an "open project." Some wondered whether these requirements were too onerous for an open project that valued freedom.

> What are the reasons for ever not letting new maintainers in? There are none, I agree. I'm very disappointed that [Debian Project Leader #4] has failed to reopen New Maintainer. This is the biggest failure of his tenure thus far, IMHO [In my humble opinion]. (Posting to Debian Project mailing list, December 29, 1999)

Ready and willing would-be contributors posted their frustrations with the closed process and the lack of clear criteria for membership.

> My understanding is that the addition of new maintainers is not merely slow, but has been officially stopped. Why? What IS the motivation? Here I am, a highly competent person, a happy and satisfied Debian user, and someone who thinks it's my duty to contribute back to Debian with some of my labor and talent. (Posting to Debian Project mailing list, December 20, 1999)

However, the new maintainer process did not reopen before the year's end.

The final stage in the membership process required not only identity verification through face-to-face exchange of keys but sponsorship by an existing member, demonstrated understanding of the community's philosophy and procedures, demonstrated technical capability, and a written recommendation from an application manager. The first new Debian member formally admitted after October 1999 was admitted in April 2000.

Members of the NMC worked diligently throughout the spring of 2000 to get through the backlog of applicants. By November 10, 2000, one hundred people had passed the new maintainer process and several hundred were in progress.

Emergence of Gatekeepers

The NMC effectively modified the future structure of the project by developing a process that would regulate the flow of new members: in

Table 18.5.
Logistic Regression Coefficients for the Regression of New Maintainer Committee Membership on Selected Independent Variables in 2001

	(1)	(3)	(5)
Number of packages	0.035** (1.036)	0.033** (1.034)	0.033** (1.033)
Package popularity	0.0002 (1.0002)	0.0003 (1.0003)	0.0004* (1.0004)
Tenure in the project	−0.027** (0.974)	−0.028** (0.973)	−0.049*** (0.952)
Tie to leader (year t − 1)	1.194*** (3.299)	1.166*** (3.211)	0.170 (1.186)
North America[a]	−0.095 (0.910)	−0.133 (0.876)	0.153 (1.165)
Other continent[a]	−0.139 (0.870)	−0.152 (0.859)	0.138 (1.147)
Number of postings (year t − 1)	0.003 (1.003)	−0.001 (0.999)	
Degree centrality		0.142*** (1.152)	
Intercept	−2.292***	−2.303***	−2.686***
Log-likelihood ratio for model estimated:			
vs. null model	23.73††	24.89††	57.63††
(df)	(6)	(7)	(8)
vs. previous model	1.16	32.74††	
(df)	(1)	(1)	
Observations	515	515	515
Pseudo R-squared	0.07	0.07	0.17

Note: Odds ratios in parentheses.

[a]Compared to developers located in Europe

† $\chi 2$ significant at the level (p = < .05)

†† $\chi 2$ significant at the level (p = < .01)

* = p < .1

** = p < .05

*** = p < .01 (one-tailed tests)

Table 18.6.
Logistic Regression Coefficients for the Regression of New Maintainer Committee Membership on Selected Independent Variables in 2002

	(1)	(2)	(3)
Number of packages	0.025 (1.025)	0.022 (1.023)	0.024 (1.024)
Package popularity	0.0004* (1.0004)	0.0003* (1.0003)	0.0004* (1.0004)
Tenure in the project	−0.060*** (0.942)	−0.060*** (0.942)	−0.069*** (0.933)
Tie to leader (year t − 1)	0.662 (1.939)	0.673 (1.959)	0.381 (1.463)
North America[a]	0.397 (1.487)	0.398 (1.489)	0.616 (1.852)
Other continent[a]	−0.799 (0.450)	−0.817 (0.442)	−0.556 (0.573)
Number of postings (year t − 1)	0.002 (1.002)	0.001 (1.001)	
Degree centrality		0.044** (1.045)	
Intercept	−2.442***	−2.481***	−2.717***
Log-likelihood ratio for model estimated:			
vs. null model	21.52††	22.31††	27.11††
(df)	(6)	(7)	(8)
vs. previous model	2.37	4.8†	
(df)	(1)	(1)	
Observations	647	647	647
Pseudo R-squared	0.09	0.09	0.11

Note: Odds ratios in parentheses.

[a]Compared to developers located in Europe

† χ^2 significant at the level (p = < .05)

†† χ^2 significant at the level (p = < .01)

* = p < .1

** = p < .05

*** = p < .01 (one-tailed tests)

effect becoming architects of the future network. We used statistical analysis to examine how the structure of the network affected who became gatekeepers of the project. Tables 18.5 and 18.6 present the logit coefficients for models predicting membership on the NMC based on the number and popularity of packages maintained, tenure, geographic location, the number of mailing list postings, and the number of ties (degree centrality) of developers in the network, in 2001 and 2002.[7] We also controlled for ties to the project leader who had final approval authority of the committee.

In the base model, which does not include degree centrality or mailing list postings, only the number of packages maintained and ties to the project leader had a significant positive effect on the likelihood of joining the NMC in 2001, while tenure had a negative effect. In the second model for 2001, we included the number of mailing list postings made the year prior and found little effect. In the third model for 2001, we included degree centrality and found a significant positive effect that is larger than any other variable. Controlling for ties to the project leader, developers

[7] The correlation coefficients of the variables are reported in tables 18.3 and 18.4 for 2001 and 2002, respectively.

with a greater degree centrality were much more likely to become a member of the NMC in 2001. The number and popularity of packages maintained continue to have a positive effect, while tenure continues to have a negative effect.

Our findings show that technical contributions are predictive up to a point, but degree centrality has a significant and positive influence on becoming a project gatekeeper. These findings are consistent with the findings of prior research on the Debian leadership team (O'Mahony and Ferraro 2007) and with Fleming and Waguespack's (2007) study of leadership on the Internet Engineering Task Force (IETF).

Maintaining one more package increased the likelihood of becoming a member of the NMC by 3.3 percent.[8] Meeting five more people (one standard deviation increase in degree centrality) increased the likelihood of becoming a member of the NMC by 76 percent. The popularity of one's package is also marginally predictive of NMC status. For every one hundred people who use a developer's package, he or she is 4 percent more likely to become a NMT member. In 2002 these results are confirmed, even though the magnitude of the effect of degree centrality is smaller (Odds ratio = 1.045).[9] However, the number of packages and ties to the project leader are not significant in either model in 2002.

The negative effect of tenure may seem counterintuitive, but those who joined the project more recently were more aware of the problems of admitting new members. Interviews with informants suggested that members who joined the project earlier were less likely to be interested in administration and more likely to be "hard core" programmers interested in Linux prior to its commercialization.

Narrowing the Pipeline

Some members felt that the membership requirements established by the NMC were too onerous and undermined the freedoms Debian espoused. One informant expressed his gratitude at having joined the project before the new maintainer process was in place.

> Raising the threshold too high, or even just the perceived notion, whether justified or not, that many NMs [New Maintainers] are unskilled, could make Debian more and more like an elitist society. . . . As for me, I am just glad that I became a Debian developer over 3 years ago, long before this was even an issue. (Posting to Debian Project mailing list, January 7, 2001)

However, the process would become stricter yet. When processing candidates for membership, application managers found that many applicants were no longer interested or responsive. The head of the NMC proposed narrowing the pipeline of candidates by requiring applicants to obtain a sponsor before submitting their application.

> An increasing number of applicants are either not serious about joining Debian and contributing to the project or not well prepared for the new maintainer process yet. A proposal is made to require all potential developers to maintain the recommendation of an existing developer. . . . Those not very serious in joining are thus not able to apply in the first place. (Changes to the New Maintainer System, February 5, 2001)

This change, accepted as a means for members of the NMC to save time, effectively eliminated the possibility of newcomers without prior attachment to a network incumbent.

One project member (in the top 5 percent of maintainers in terms of the number of packages managed) running to become the fifth leader argued that the difficulties that underlay the new maintainer process were the product of Debian's unusual success.

> The biggest frustrations I see with Debian are, in fact, all related to this success. We have more developers than ever, more packages soaking more bandwidth to mirror than ever, more open bugs than ever, and our user community is broadening into areas where the criteria for success may be different. This puts enormous pressure on our organization, forcing us to continue to evolve. (Debian Project Leader Candidate Platform, February 23, 2001)

[8] To help the interpretation of the logit coefficients, the odds ratios are reported in parentheses. Odds ratios are computed by taking the antilogarithm of the logit coefficient; thus for the effect of the number of packages in 2001, we can simply compute: $e^{.04} = 1.04$. Values exceeding 1 indicate an increased likelihood of becoming a member of the NMC, while values less than 1 indicate decreased odds.

[9] We also estimated other logit models using betweenness centrality, rather than degree centrality, and the results are consistent with the ones we obtained for degree centrality. These models are not reported here but are available from the authors upon request.

The winner of the 2001 election also proposed "adding more structure to the project," namely to improve the new maintainer process. He noted that the NMC was under incredible pressure to protect Debian from "Trojans" and that the current process was still not robust enough to handle further growth.

> [W]e all have the same permissions to upload packages, we all have just as much right to screw up the archive as anyone else. In there lies the problem. Maintainer count is on the rise all the time. It may not seem to be a problem now, but increasing administrative and security work to keep this increase on a good footing is not going to remain easy (well, it isn't easy now). Stopping developer entrance all together is not an alternative either. Some may argue that this makes Debian less "open." Well, I don't think Debian is closed at all. . . . Now I know this isn't the same as having one's own packages, and that sponsorship is not turning out to be the godsend that we had hoped. However, allowing more levels of maintainship will likely make it easier for people to contribute. (Debian Leadership Platform, February 20, 2001)

The Debian Project Leader's approach to keeping Debian open but managing its boundaries was to create differentiated levels of access to the code base, a change that was not implemented by the NMC.

Analyzing Network Expansion

With the implementation of the new maintainer process in 2001, the keyring network doubled in size to 532 nodes with 1,212 ties. As entrance into the keyring required a face-to-face meeting, events such as the first project meeting held in France helped grow the keyring network. Several firms hired programmers to work on Debian and sponsored their travel to trade shows and conferences. Informants reported that greater support for travel was a positive side effect of the growing commercial support for Linux. Since developers do not live equidistantly and do not all receive corporate sponsorship, they likely face different probabilities of meeting each other. Thus the Debian keyring network may not grow randomly. By analyzing the distribution of degrees (the number of people developers have met), we can determine if the Debian network is a random network.

If the network grows randomly, we would expect the degree distribution to approximate a Poisson distribution. If the network grows through a process of preferential attachment, where each new node is more likely to attach to a node with a higher degree, then it may follow a power-law degree distribution where a large number of nodes has very few ties and a small number of nodes has a large number of ties (Albert and Barabási 2002; Clauset, Shalizi, and Newman 2009). Figure 18.2 reports the degree distribution of the Debian network. In 1998, 77 percent of developers had met only one or two people and 6 percent had met over ten. In 2002, 50 percent of developers had met one or two people and 4.8 percent had met over twenty-five. Table 18.1 shows that the average degree of developers, stable from 1997 to 1999, increased to 3.64 in 2000 with a standard deviation of 4.67. This was much higher than the standard deviation in the two previous years. After 2000 the average degree of the network and its standard deviation increase every year. Figure 18.3 presents the log-log plot cumulative degree distributions of the Debian keyring from 1997 until 2002 and confirms that the network does not follow a Gaussian or a Poisson distribution but could be better described as a power-law distribution with an exponential cutoff.[10] Our research helps explain why this network follows this distribution: the NMC's decision to require new members to be sponsored by an incumbent encouraged new members to attach to members with higher degree centrality. This means that the gatekeeping position acquired by some developers and institutionalized by the NMC is reinforced with the entry of new participants. At the same time the elite created by this process is not closed, and new contributors can become more central in the network and in the project.

Debian as a Bounded Entity

In 2001 Debian was regarded by the press as technically sophisticated but lacking the reliability

[10] If the network followed a power-law distribution, a plot of the log number of degrees on the x-axis and the log of the number of developers on the y-axis would result in a straight line, and we can see from figure 18.3 that over time the log-log plots approximate this distribution. This plot does not rule out a number of other types of distributions (log-normal, weibull), but it is enough to argue that the tails of the distributions are "heavy" (Clauset, Shalizi, and Newman 2009).

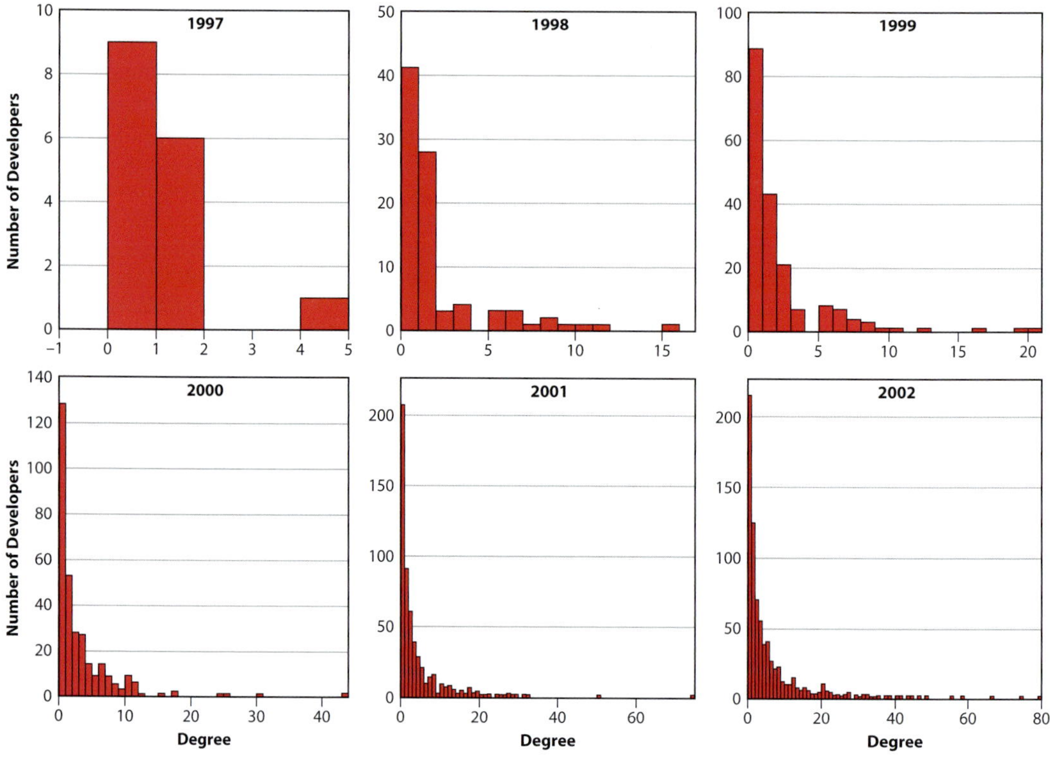

Figure 18.2 Degree distribution of the Debian Network, 1997–2002.

of a company. When reviewing Release 2.2, the editors of *PC Magazine* reported that "From a corporate standpoint, Debian's main drawback is the lack of a company to support it. . . . Debian's developer community is very active, open and approachable, and Usenet groups and mailing lists are abundant, but don't expect a lot of novice-level explanations. Commercial technical support for Debian is only available through third parties" (Ulrich 2001). Debian remains noncommercial, but third parties can provide support and value-added services.[11] Qualified developers can work on packages of their choosing, conditioned only by what their colleagues are doing. Debian's development environment and source code remain publicly accessible. However, becoming a developer is no longer as easy as it once was. A Debian leader in 2003 agreed that it was much harder to become a member now than when he first joined the project, recounting the many tests a new member candidate must now pass to become member.

> At the time new maintainer was not as formal or anything as it is now. . . . [W]e are asking many more questions, and we're doing more checks and everything. It is much more complicated now . . . for example you have to also look at a [traditional] license and say why that is not free software. We look at the different points in the Debian free software guidelines that it [a traditional license] violates. . . . [Y]ou have to agree that you comply with it [the GNU General Public Licence], and that you understand it. . . . You have to summarize it and then you have to state explicitly that you agree to the social contract, and you have to explicitly agree that all that you do as part of Debian is free software as defined by the free software guidelines. (June 20, 2003)

It can now take six months or more for a new maintainer to become a developer.[12] Candidates are strongly encouraged to ask Debian

[11] One such firm is www.projeny.com.

[12] In 2003 the NMC designed improvements to the New Maintainer Process to move registration, philosophy,

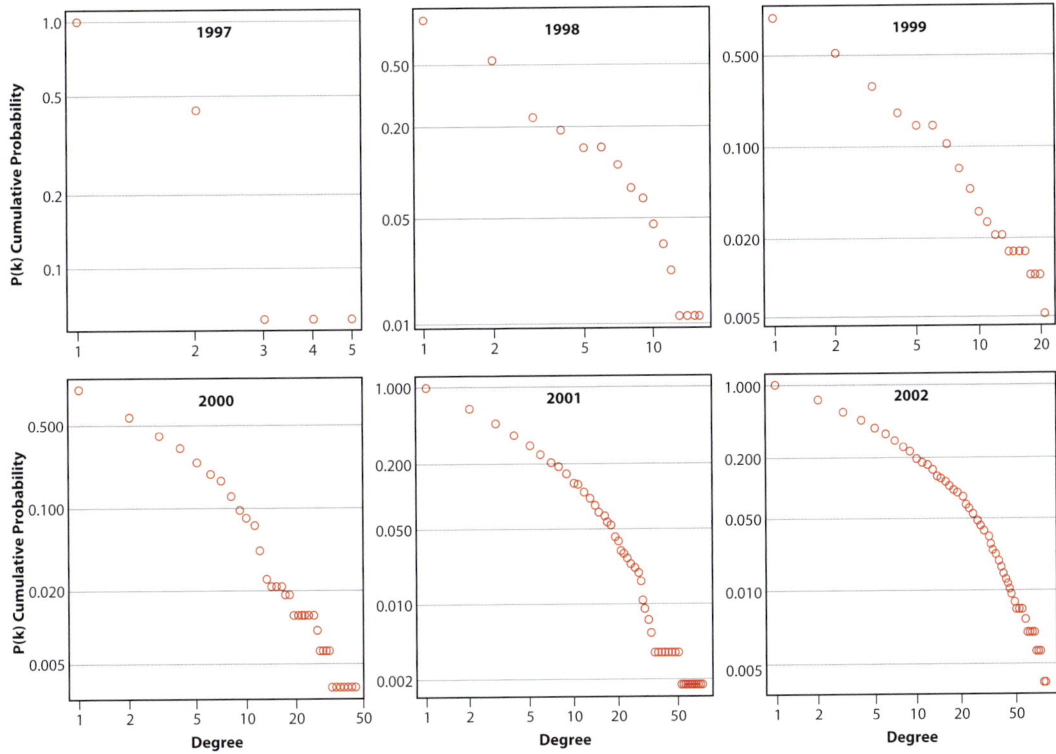

Figure 18.3 Log-log plot of the cumulative degree distribution of the Debian Network, 1997–2002.

developers to write a letter of reference for them, just as they would for a traditional bureaucratic organization. Applications are discussed in private and three types of rejection are possible: weak, strong, and ultimate. An application manager's decision to issue a weak rejection can be overturned by the NMC with a one-fourth vote; a strong rejection can be overturned by a two-thirds vote; and an ultimate rejection cannot be overturned.[13] As of January 2009, 934 members have gone through the new process, 159 applications were in progress, and 24 applications were on hold.[14] Forty-six application managers oversee this process. Fifty-nine people in 23 countries[15] were looking to have their key signed despite the fact that 282 people in 39 countries offer to sign keys.[16]

The new membership process reinforces conditions for network expansion through preferential attachment. Thus new nodes will not enter randomly but most likely attach to a node that already has a large number of ties. This can result in a sustained power-law distribution where a small number of nodes become even more highly connected and the bulk of nodes are only loosely connected. Since developers are more likely to attain gatekeeper positions if they are more connected, and new members tend to create new ties with developers with higher degree centrality, this pattern of growth and preferential attachment reinforces stability in gatekeeper positions. As suggestive evidence of this pattern, the leader of the NMC was elected project leader the following year.

procedures, task, and skills test online. These improvements are expected to considerably speed the process.

[13] Unfortunately, application rejection data were not available.

[14] See http://nm.debian.org/ for more information.

[15] These countries included Armenia, Argentina, Belgium, Brazil, Canada, Chile, China, Columbia, Germany, Denmark, Spain, Italy, Norway, Philippines, Poland, Portugal, Russian Federation, Singapore, Turkey, Ukraine, United States, Vatican City State, and South Africa.

[16] See http://nm.debian.org/gpg_offer.php and http://nm.debian.org/gpg_need.php for more information.

DISCUSSION

"No topic more deeply engages scholars in the fundamental attributes of organizations" than the creation and revision of organizational boundaries (Santos and Eisenhardt 2005, 505). Despite the fact that managing organizational boundaries is central to economics, organizational theory, and sociology, observers of open communities producing complex knowledge goods have been overly fascinated with the very "openness" of these communities and neglectful of the ways in which these communities must somehow bound their activities in order to sustain their form. Organizational theorists have acknowledged that postindustrial organizations are no longer meaningfully bounded entities but comprised of porous and often shifting boundaries and that this has widened the gap between theory and postindustrial modes of organizing: "Explanation through counting misses the major dynamics of the new economy" (Davis and McAdam 2000, 205). Thus our methods, approaches, and vocabularies need to be enriched in order to better understand and explain emerging organizing phenomena that may not depend upon a shared place or context to support production (Barley and Kunda 2001).

One empirical strategy is to examine processes held in common across a variety of new organizing contexts (Lamont and Molnar 2002). We pursued such an approach by focusing on a particular boundary dispute: how to ascertain who becomes a member in a new organization. This dispute is one that is central to collectively managed organizations: "How is collective action coordinated when participation by 'members' is impromptu and impermanent?" (Davis and McAdam 2000, 214). Our research examined this boundary decision in the context of a collectively managed open source software project that had no prior structures in place to help determine how new members should be brought into the organization. By observing how the Debian community confronted this challenge, we (1) learned how one type of organizational boundary is established; (2) identified the behaviors that are likely to predict who becomes a gatekeeper of this system; and (3) identified a critical mechanism that affects future growth of the project's social network. Our research helps deepen our understanding of how social networks and new organizing structures co-evolve.

Explosive growth in contributors to the project led to an organizational crisis upon which the project closed its doors to all new members—until a group of project incumbents could design a new process that would ensure that prospective members' skills, goals, and ideology were aligned with the collective. Even though some within the project displayed reluctance to "close" the project in any way, our field research shows how the community came to terms with this crisis—forming a New Maintainer Committee to establish rules and a process for membership and thus becoming future gatekeepers to the project. This new process makes organizational boundaries more difficult to penetrate over time—narrowing but not closing. With statistical analyses, we discovered that project contributors that had met more people face-to-face and were more central in the project's social network were more likely to become gatekeepers to the project. While project members coordinate their work almost solely online, when choosing individuals to manage organizational boundaries, they trust those they have met.

Further analysis of the network's expansion shows that the project's network does not grow randomly but develops through preferential attachment, leading to a power-law distribution. Our field data help explain how preferential attachment operated in this community. The NMC designed a process that required sponsorship from a project incumbent and a face-to-face meeting. These rules set in motion a process whereby new entrants are more likely to connect with project members who are more central than with any random project member. Thus the committee designed a membership process that reinforced their role as gatekeepers who would guide future expansion of the network. The boundary dispute, in essence, was resolved with a membership process that reshaped the subsequent social structure of the community.

Together, these three contributions help explain the mechanisms that permit scale-free social networks to come into existence. Our research approach shows that, as suggested by Lamont and Molnar (2002), there is value in studying boundary disputes. However, we took this charge a step further by using boundary disputes as way to unpack our understanding of how networks and organizational structures co-evolve over time. Network processes shape who emerges to define organizational boundaries; how those boundary rules are set then affects the project's future network structure. Our research shows how networks evolve to affect the design of organizational practices and policies that can then, in turn, affect the future structure of the network.

Prior research on the evolution of networks in the biotechnology industry found that no single rule of attachment dominated the creation of new ties. The recombinative nature of innovation in the biotechnology field demands a constant quest for new partners and ideas, with actors in this field preferring diverse ties as opposed to connecting with incumbents or similar others (homophily) (Powell et al. 2005). However, this same study tracked the emergence of an "open elite" where those that were more central continuously refreshed themselves by welcoming new entrants. Similarly, our research of Debian's evolving organization shows that elites define the terms of admittance. In doing so, they help the project stay open, but bounded, sustaining their own structural advantage. In terms of the ongoing boundary dispute between open and commercial science, our research suggests that those in the position to make boundary rules can affect the networks and social structure that follow. For example, if patent holders acquired more gatekeeper roles in academia, our research suggests that this would likely shape the management of boundaries between open and commercial science.

This research has broader implications for researching collectively managed knowledge communities. First, it suggests that literature on virtual communities and new organizational forms remains naïve to the realities and challenges of producing complex knowledge goods in a distributed community. New organizational forms and virtual organizations are often depicted as nebulous and constituted by a shifting and ever-changing body of members. However, volatility and turnover in new organizational forms are not the same as indeterminacy; flow is not the same as ambiguity and these distinctions have different implications for the study of organizational boundaries.

Boundary definition and management are likely to be critical for any type of community that strives to remain open while producing knowledge goods without jeopardizing the security and stability of their work, as David and Foray so presciently predicted. "What is at stake here is the entire range of mechanisms that will facilitate interpersonal and inter-organizational transactions, given the new conditions for knowledge transactions and exchanges. . . . Clearly new methods need to be devised to "certify" the knowledge circulating on the Internet" (2003, 42). If knowledge-producing communities that cross or exist outside established organizational boundaries are to survive, innovations in trust and reliability mechanisms will continue to emerge and require further comparative study.

More research on mechanisms that help carve a protected and common informational space for collaboration (O'Mahony 2003) is needed to understand not only the emergence of such mechanisms but their contribution to project security and effectiveness. We should point out that security and effectiveness can be measured in multiple ways. In the case of Debian, new membership criteria tested not only technical quality but new entrants' knowledge of software licenses in order to ensure that contributions received from new members would comply with the project's legal boundary with the commercial world (see also Chen and O'Mahony 2009). In this sense, the membership boundary is one way in which the larger open source and industry boundary dispute is managed.

Research on mechanisms should attend to the crises such communities confront, the triggers of such crises, and the range of solutions from which communities draw to address them. Research on how communities scale is not popular but, as David and Foray point out, the challenge of knowledge production "become[s] greater as a community expands" as do "costs of data search, the risk of congestion and anonymity amongst members, which can in turn, represent a source of acute problems of trust" (2003, 30). Our research shows that problems of trust and malfeasance are real and that the design of new mechanisms to manage them will co-evolve with the social networks that underlie knowledge-producing communities.

REFERENCES

Albert, R., and A.-L. Barabási. 2002. "Statistical Mechanics of Complex Networks." *Review of Modern Physics* 74:47.

Barabási, Albert-Laszlo, and Reka Albert. 1999. "Emergence of Scaling in Random Networks." *Science* 286:509–12.

Barley, Stephen R., and Gideon Kunda. 2001. "Bringing Work Back in." *Organization Science* 12:76–95.

Batagelj, V., and Andrej Mrvar. 1998. "Pajek: A Program for Large Network Analysis." *Connections* 21 (2):47–57.

Brennen, Alex V. 2003. GnuPGKeysigning Party HOWTO. http://www.cryptnet.net/fdp/crypto/gpg-party.html.

Chen, Katherine, and Siobhan O'Mahony. 2009. "Differentiating Organizational Boundaries." *Research in the Sociology of Organizations* 26:183–220.

Chesborough, H. 2005. *Open Innovation*. Boston: Harvard Business School Press.

———. 2006. *Open Business Models: How to Thrive in the New Innovation Landscape*. Boston: Harvard Business School Press.

Clauset, A., C. R. Shalizi, and M.E.J. Newman. 2009. "Power-Law Distributions in Empirical Data." *SIAM Review* 51:661–703.

Coriat, Benjamin, and Fabienne Orsi. 2002. "Establishing a New Intellectual Property Rights Regime in the United States." *Research Policy* 31:1491–1507.

Dalle, Jean-Michel, and Paul A. David. 2005. "Allocation of Software Development Resources in Open Source Production Mode." In *Perspectives on Free and Open Source Software*, ed. Joseph Feller, Brian Fitzgerald, Scott A. Hissam, and Karim R. Lakhani, 297–328. Cambridge, MA: MIT Press.

Dasgupta, Partha, and Paul A. David. 1994. "Toward a New Economics of Science." *Research Policy* 23: 487–521.

David, Paul A. 2001. "Tragedy of the Public Knowledge 'Commons'? Global Science, Intellectual Property and the Digital Technology Boomerang." MERIT Research Memoranda 2001-003.

———. 2003. "The Economic Logic of 'Open Science' and the Balance between Private Property Rights and the Public Domain in Scientific Data and Information: A Primer." Stanford Institute for Economic Policy Research Discussion Paper No. 02-30.

David, Paul A., and Dominque Foray. 2003. "Economic Fundamentals of the Knowledge Society." *Policy Futures in Education*. 1(1). http://www.wwwords.co.uk/pfie/.

Davis, J., and D. McAdam. 2000. "Corporations, Classes, and Social Movements after Managerialism." *Research in Organizational Behavior* 22: 193–236.

Fleming, L., and D. M. Waguespack. 2007. "Brokerage, Boundary Spanning, and Leadership in Open Innovation Communities." *Organization Science* 18:165.

Free Software Foundation. 1999. *The GNU Privacy Handbook*. http://www.gnupg.org/gph/en/manual/book1.html.

Freeman, Linton. 1979. "Centrality in Social Networks: I. Conceptual Clarification." *Social Networks* 1:215–39.

Gallivan, M. J. 2001. "Striking a Balance between Trust and Control in a Virtual Organization: A Content Analysis of Open Source Software Case Studies." *Information Systems Journal* 11:277–304.

Gieryn, T. F. 1983. "Boundary-Work and the Demarcation of Science from Non-Science: Strains and Interests in Professional Interests of Scientists." *American Sociological Review* 48:781–95.

———. 1999. *Cultural Boundaries of Science: Credibility on the Line*. Chicago: University of Chicago Press.

Giles, J. 2006. "Internet Encyclopedias Go Head to Head." *Nature* 438:900–901.

Guston, D. H. 2000. *Between Politics and Science: Assuring the Integrity and Productivity of Research*. Cambridge: Cambridge University Press.

Hellstrom, Tomas. 2003. "Governing the Virtual Academic Commons." *Research Policy* 32:391–401.

Huang, K., and F. Murray. 2009. "Does Patent Strategy Shape the Long-Run Supply of Public Knowledge?" *Academy of Management Journal* 52:1193–1221.

Jarvenpaa, S., and D. Leidner. 1999. "Communication and Trust in Global Virtual Teams." *Organization Science* 10:791–815.

Jeppesen, Lars B., and Karim R. Lakhani. 2010. "Marginality and Problem Solving Effectiveness in Broadcast Search." *Organization Science* 21(5) 1016–33.

Kamada, T., and S. Kawai. 1989. "An Algorithm for Drawing General Undirected Graphs." *Information Processing Letters* 31:7–15.

Koch, S., and G. Schneider. 2000. *Results from Software Engineering Research into Open Source Development Projects Using Public Data*. http://opensource.mit.edu/papers/kochossoftwareengineering.pdf.

Kogut, Bruce, and Anca Metiu. 2001. "Open-Source Software Development and Distributed Innovation." *Oxford Review of Economic Policy* 17: 248–64.

Lamont, Michelle, and Virag Molnar. 2002. "The Study of Boundaries in the Social Sciences." *Annual Review of Sociology* 28:167–95.

Latour, Bruno, and Steve Woolgar. 1979. *Laboratory Life: The Social Construction of Scientific Facts*. Beverly Hills, CA: Sage Publications.

Long, J. S. 1997. *Regression Models for Categorical and Limited Dependent Variables*. Thousand Oaks, CA: Sage.

Merton, Robert K. 1973. *The Sociology of Science*. Ed. Norman W. Storer. Chicago: University of Chicago Press.

Michlmayer, M., and B. Mako Hill. 2003. "Quality and the Reliance on Individuals in Free Software Projects." Presented at *Taking Stock of the Bazaar: 3rd Workshop on OS SW Eng*, May 3–10, Portland, OR. http://opensource.ucc.ie/icse2003/.

Mockus A., R. T. Fielding, and J. Herbsleb. 2002. "Two Case Studies of Open Source Software Development: Apache and Mozilla." *ACM Transactions on Software Engineering and Methodology* 11(3):309–46.

Moore, K. 1996. "Organizing Integrity: American Science and the Creation of Public Interest Organizations, 1955–1975." *American Journal of Sociology* 101:1592–1627.

Mowery, David C., and Bhaven N. Sampat. 2001. "Patenting and Licensing University Inventions: Lessons from the History of the Research Corporation." *Industrial and Corporate Change* 10:317.

———. 2004. "The Bayh Dole Act of 1980 and University Industry Technology Transfer: A Model for

Other OECD Governments?" In *"Ivory Tower" and Industrial Innovation: University-Industry Technology Transfer before and after the Bayh-Dole Act*. Palo Alto: Stanford University Press.

Mowery, David C., and Arvids A. Ziedonis. 2002. "Academic Patent Quality and Quantity before and after the Bayh-Dole Act in the United States." *Research Policy* 31:399.

Murdock, I. 1994. "A Brief History of Debian: Appendix A—The Debian Manifesto." Rev. January 6. http://www.debian.org/doc/manuals/project-history/ap-manifesto.en.html.

Network Associates. 1990. "An Introduction to Cyptography." http://www.pgpi.org/doc/guide/6.5/en/intro/.

Nohria, Nitin, and Robert G. Eccles. 1992. "Face-to-Face: Making Network Organizations Work." In *Networks and Organizations: Structure, Form, and Action*, ed. Nitin Nohria and Robert G Eccles. Boston: Harvard Business School Press.

O'Mahony, Siobhán. 2002. "Community Managed Software Projects: The Emergence of a New Commercial Actor." Ph.D. diss., Stanford University.

———. 2003. "Guarding the Commons: How Community Managed Projects Protect Their Work." *Research Policy* 32:1179–98.

———. 2004. "Managing Community Software in a Commodity World." In *Ethnographic Reflections on the New Economy*, ed. Melissa Fisher and Greg Downey. Durham: Duke University Publications.

———. 2007. "The Governance of Open Source Initiatives: What Does It Mean to Be Community Managed?" *Journal of Management and Governance* 11: 139–50.

O'Mahony, Siobhán, and Beth A. Bechky. 2008. "Boundary Organizations: Enabling Collaboration among Unexpected Allies." *Administrative Science Quarterly* 53:422–59.

O'Mahony, Siobhán, and Fabrizio Ferraro. 2007. "The Emergence of Governance in an Open Source Community." *Academy of Management Journal* 50: 1079–1106.

Owen-Smith, Jason. 2003. "From Separate Systems to a Hybrid Order: Accumulative Advantage across Public and Private Science at Research One Universities." *Research Policy* 32:1081–1104.

Owen-Smith, J., and W. W. Powell. 2003. "The Expanding Role of University Patenting in the Life Sciences: Assessing the Importance of Experience and Connectivity." *Research Policy* 32: 1695–1711.

Powell, Walter W. 1990. "Neither Market nor Hierarchy: Network Forms of Organization." Ed. Barry M. Staw and L. L. Cummings. *Research in Organizational Behavior* 12:295–336.

Powell, Walter W., and Jason Owen-Smith. 1998. "Universities and the Market for Intellectual Property in the Life Sciences." *Journal of Policy Analysis and Management* 17(2):253–77.

Powell, Walter W., Kenneth W. Koput, and Laurel Smith-Doerr. 1996. "Interorganizational Collaboration and the Locus of Innovation Networks of Learning in Biotechnology." *Administrative Science Quarterly* 41:116–45.

Powell, W. W., D. R. White, K. W. Koput, and J. Owen-Smith. 2005. "Network Dynamics and Field Evolution: The Growth of Interorganizational Collaboration in the Life Sciences." *American Journal of Sociology* 110:1132–1205.

Raymond, Eric S. 1999. *The Cathedral and the Bazaar: Musings on Linux and Open Source by an Accidental Revolutionary*. Sebastopol, CA: O'Reilly & Associates.

Santos, F. M., and K. M. Eisenhardt. 2005. "Organizational Boundaries and Theories of Organizations." *Organization Science* 16(5):491–508.

Sarfatti-Larson, M. 1979. *The Rise of Professionalism*. Berkeley: University of California Press.

Stallman, Richard. 1999. "The GNU Operating System and the Free Software Movement." In *Open Sources*, ed. Chris DiBona, Sam Ockman, and Mark Stone. Sebastopol, CA: O'Reilly.

Tuomi, Ilkka. 2003. *Networks of Innovation: Change and Meaning in the Age of the Internet*. Oxford: Oxford University Press.

Ulrich, Bill. Debian GNU/Linux 2.2 (Potato). 2001. *PC Magazine*, November 13, http://www.pcmag.com/article2/0,4149,16093,00.asp.

von Hippel, E. 2005. *Democratizing Innovation*. Cambridge, MA: MIT Press.

von Krogh, Georg, Sebastian Spaeth, and Karim R. Lakhani. 2003. "Community, Joining, and Specialization in Open Source Software Innovation: A Case Study." *Research Policy* 32:1217–41.

Wasserman, Stanley, and Kathleen Faust. 1994. *Social Network Analysis: Methods and Applications*. New York: Cambridge University Press.

Wayner, Peter. 2000. *Free for All: How Linux and the Free Software Movement Undercut the High-Tech Titans*. New York: HarperCollins.

Williamson, O. E. 1975. *Market and Hierarchies: Analysis and Antitrust Implications*. New York: Free Press.

———. 1981. "The Economics of Organizations: The Transaction Cost Approach." *American Journal of Sociology* 87(3):548–77.

Coda

Reflections on the Study of Multiple Networks

Walter W. Powell ▪ John F. Padgett

The early origins of this book date back to June 2000 when a working group was formed by Padgett at the Santa Fe Institute (SFI).[1] The working group later evolved into a funded project by Padgett and Powell, The Co-Evolution of States and Markets. Over the years we met annually at SFI, and many different colleagues participated in our sessions. We invited colleagues who were our peers and younger scholars who were students or kindred spirits, and SFI fellows and visitors also joined in. It was through careful comparison of the biographies of medieval Florentine families and twentieth-century life scientists that we saw parallels in the way ideas and practices traveled across multiple networks, reverberating to alter relations in their domains of origin. The recognition of the far-reaching ramifications of crossing social worlds prompted the workshops, meetings, and essays that constitute this volume.

In 2000 networks were a relatively new topic; at SFI there was almost no research on networks, and ours was one of the first social science projects at the institute. Over the past decade, network research has become ubiquitous at SFI, and researchers in biology, chemistry, and physics have assumed leadership of this line of research.[2] In many respects, this has been a salutary development, even if at times we have chafed somewhat at the assumption that one dominant mechanism, typically a power law, explains all network growth. Nevertheless, the adoption of network ideas by our colleagues in the physical and biological sciences has led to an extraordinary interest in the topology of phenomena as different as protein interaction networks, contributions to Wikipedia, animal social relations, food webs, epidemiological contacts, virus life cycles, and signaling pathways. These varied inquiries all have a common signature of analyzing how information is accessed, transmitted, stored, replicated, and transformed. In many respects, networks have become sociology's most successful export.

The study of how networks evolve through time remains less examined than research on topographic structure. The idea that one needs to gather fine-grained relational data over a number of years and analyze the dual evolution of persons or organizations and their biographies

[1] One might date the project's inception back further, to spring 1992, when Padgett was a fellow at the Center for Advanced Study in the Behavioral Sciences, and Powell visited at Stanford. Padgett's work on Florence at that time led to his and Chris Ansell's paper on robust action and Cosimo d' Medici. Powell was doing interviews at biotech companies, and this led to his paper with Ken Koput and Laurel Smith-Doerr on networks as the locus of innovation paper in technolgically fast-moving fields. As we watched our young children and a very large dog play in the evenings, we swapped ideas about how to build relational databases.

[2] In summer 2002, Doug White and Woody Powell presented a very primitive network "movie" of the evolution of a decade of alliances in biotech, cobbled together from yearly images, drawn with an early beta version of Pajek. Approximately forty SFI staff gathered, and popcorn and lemonade were served. The reactions of physicists, chemists, economists, and biologists were surprisingly enthusiastic, as all manner of generative questions were posed and ideas flew across disciplinary borders.

is daunting to many. To be sure, the data collection challenges are considerable and the requirement to have deep substantive knowledge of the phenomena under study is demanding. Indeed, at one of our early research meetings, our colleague Elisabeth Clemens asked us if it was necessary to spend two decades poring over records or archives in order to effectively do this kind of work on historical networks.[3] Today we are pleased to say that many more historical studies of networks are available. Our contributors Lee Fleming, David Stark, and Balázs Vedres provide ample evidence of the benefits of such research, and others who joined us at various times at Santa Fe, including Bruce Kogut, Dan McFarland, Paul McLean, Douglas White, and Brian Uzzi, have produced valuable longitudinal accounts of network evolution. Our younger colleagues who have contributed chapters to this volume have explored network histories—without having to invest the bulk of their careers in such efforts. Improved access to historical records, extensive bibliometric records, use of digital archives, the ability to scrape the web and access linguistic networks, and other uses of computational social science have given researchers much greater entree to large-scale, longitudinal network data sources. Thus, with regard to the incorporation of time into network studies, considerable progress has been realized.

Another aspiration of our SFI project was insight into the dynamics of multiple networks, their interpenetration, and the long-term feedback consequences of such contacts. We have shown throughout this volume how behavior from one realm often spills over into another, sometimes with dramatic consequences. Exactly when such perturbations happen and with what consequences are a research agenda for the future, which we discuss below. But to begin, let us start with a clearer specification of different types of spillovers. The critical element is that parts of life from one domain find a commonality, utility, or simply a resonance in a different and unexpected domain. Consider the following simple illustrations of different forms of multiple networks. First, there are circumstances in which very similar persons are engaged in the same relationships but with people from different social worlds. The friendship networks found on many Facebook pages are an apt illustration, as one's friends from work, college, high school or elementary school, church, and sports intersect and become linked through mutual access. Sometimes a good deal of code switching is necessary to move across these different social worlds, even when one has the same type of relationship, albeit at different depth, with everyone. Here we see the intersection of multiple networks of friends and the potential cross-talk, surprise, and opportunities that can develop. Ideas from friends at work may end up getting used at church, or an old friend may prove helpful in finding a new place to live. This moving across networks reflects the classic strength-of-weak-tie argument.

A second type of spillover occurs when the persons are in some respects similar but engaged in different pursuits. Take, for example, the role of a faculty member and one's varied affiliations with departmental colleagues, coauthors, graduate and undergraduate students, staff, administrators, and persons in units on campus other than one's own. All such people are linked through common membership and identification with a university, but one's responsibilities may condition much of the content of affiliations. Indeed, there are even rules or norms of propriety about how close relationships can be among members of the community who have different statuses. But when a problem needs to be solved, a deadline presents itself, or funding opportunities pop up, one might well jump across these formal lines to enroll someone in accomplishing a task. People who are able to make such leaps consistently become, over time, the movers and shakers of the university, as well as the carriers of a great deal of tacit institutional knowledge.

A third type of spillover involves different persons, alternate relationships, and divergent activities but in the context of a social or physical boundary that brings people into contact. Consider the separate micro worlds of the family, the polity, and the market in Renaissance Florence or the domains of science, finance, and public health in the contemporary life sciences. The typical people who inhabit each of these domains and their associated affiliations within them are fairly well understood. But when interchange and possible synergy draw together the different domains, things that are not immediately commensurate get moved from one setting to another, often with unexpected outcomes. Such turbulence has to be stabilized or those

[3] She clearly had in mind the more than two decades that Padgett and Powell had spent on their respective projects. We are not sure if Clemens recalls how profoundly depressing her question was, and it was only the encouragement of our students that persuaded us that this line of inquiry was indeed portable.

who created it have to become new role models. In this way, the aspirations of the few become the goals of many. Mapping these interactions has been the goal of this book.

It is possible to portray these three stylized examples of multiple networks with Venn diagrams and assess what parts are shared across the different communities. This exercise is valuable because it is through these common elements that flows move through networks. This is where the action is because these spillovers can become multifunctional. The obvious example is resources, where one might use a family tie in a business setting or a professional or social affiliation to muster political mobilization. Such efforts may well be consequential, but they are not necessarily transformative. When routines and rules move across multiple networks, interdependencies are created that draw the two different social worlds closer together. This is only step one, however, and although it may have consequential local effects, interdependence rarely triggers large-scale changes. More consequential is when persons move across these domains; with this mobility biographies and careers are transformed. Such movement can lead to the creation of new identities. And once rules, skills, careers, and persons become regular inhabitants of two different networks, the stronger the effects of formerly foreign practices on each domain. This type of transposition creates a new set of circumstances with which both domains must contend.

Interactions of this kind with commonly shared parts are not at all unusual. But as we argued in the introduction, it is remarkable how little awareness the social sciences evince of such boundary-crossing behaviors. We lack a good social science conception of the relational person. Much network research treats relationships as tools for access and control. To be sure, brokerage activities are commonplace, hence the popular use of networking as both a verb and a noun. Other scholars have emphasized the affinity group aspect of relationships. Indeed, Harrison White, to whom we have dedicated this volume, broke new ground in the 1960s by emphasizing structural affinities: the ways in which individuals who did not know one another but were located in common structural positions shared equivalent demands. We want to move beyond these somewhat limited conceptions of a relational person, however. Our expanded conception of a relational person would certainly include the familiar ground of emotions, routines, politics, and search behavior. But missing from view thus far is a conception of relationships as signs of discernment.

How does discernment enter into the formation of relations and the creation of persons? The world of brokerage is a world of weak ties, with low cohesion, little closure, much novelty, and high turnover. Affinity ties are stronger, more durable, and multiplex. But we need a conception that is more interpretive, expansive, and robust. One might imagine George Herbert Mead's looking-glass self but as a two-way mirror, in which relations are a lens for both parties and a prism for others. We think of discernment as more dynamic than status, as status quickly devolves into instrumentality or peer groups. In a number of our chapters we have emphasized that rather dramatic changes in economic, political, and scientific orders came about largely unintentionally, often through conservative motives, when individuals had the insight or luck that a card in their everyday deck might be played at a different table. Multipurpose ideas are always risky because they can be shot down from multiple directions. But sometimes such ideas are accepted by others for different reasons. And when they are absorbed by multiple domains, they have the potential for transformative effects.

How does one go about collecting multiple network data, and how do we assess when spillovers across multiple networks are not only repurposed in a new domain but have transformative effects? We have provided numerous illustrations in this volume that suggest ways in which networks can be analyzed and compared to one another. Whether as horizontal planes or complex network maps, one can array the set of relationships within a social, political, or economic system and examine how those relations evolve through time. One can then do the same analysis for a companion system, be it politics and markets, religion and politics, or science and commerce. As one collects the network data, always be on the lookout for linkages of any kind—through persons, committees, or practices—that are exchanged or travel across the different domains. These shared elements may be the loci for transformative relations. Finding such linkages enables one to trace spillovers and to see if such spillovers increase over time, prompting chain reactions. Reactions of this sort may well provoke opposition, induce contradictions, and thus be rebuffed. Finding such examples is a critical step toward mapping the interactions of multiple networks. And studying failures at transposition is essential to learning about the vulnerability of social systems.

Recombinant practices, generative disruptions, and hybridization are all forms of multiple network spillovers that can lead to organizational innovation. This volume is rich with examples of the absorption of distant practices into new domains, which in turn altered the terrain that parties had to traverse. We had less to say about system poisedness or vulnerability, however. When do perturbations have lasting consequences? Put differently, can these innovations find enough traction and support such that they are more than short-term solutions to unanticipated problems? A central question for future research to explore is what turns fragile responses or transitions into more systemic innovations. This issue of matching the character of innovative transpositions to the structural features of the system into which they were introduced is, to our minds, the research frontier. We need to explain the architecture of systems that are most poised to tip in response to disturbances. When do new practices cause an existing order to unravel and when are systems resilient and able to accommodate, and even prosper, from the introduction of novel elements?

To our way of thinking, reproductive fidelity is central to stability. To the extent that networks are dense and interconnected, new elements are more readily absorbed. We saw confirmation of this in chapter 15 when the intricately interconnected core of the biopharmaceutical community was able to absorb new entrants, as well as take on new skills, without unraveling. This elite group was buttressed by multiple relations among themselves involving different activities, giving them redundancy in terms of both connections and expertise. But when relations among the members of a field are thinner and the range of skills leaner, then the march-in of new elements may have more transformative effects. And if the connectivity among the core is more a Potemkin Village, new entrants may well take over leadership of the system.

What kind of events can reduce reproductive stability, thus leaving the status quo vulnerable? Obviously crises of various kinds can threaten a system's ability to replicate its organizing routines. In Renaissance Florence, disease and war robbed families of their young men, making it challenging to pass on family wealth and power. In the contemporary knowledge economy, technological change can pull the rug out from under incumbents, leaving them vulnerable. But crises are too simple an answer, as our cases of Florence and the contemporary life sciences show. Change and tumult were ever-present in both worlds and challenges to incumbents continuous. Much of the time these threats were absorbed without too much damage to the existing order. But when crises led people to vote with their feet, so to speak, and flock to new affiliations or careers at alternative sites, the external challenges rendered existing practices brittle. Here the choice is no longer to resist or absorb but to see how quickly an incumbent can take on new alliances or pursue new kinds of practices, rules, and personnel in order to maintain its position of importance. When rates of defection and turnover exceed the incumbent's ability to learn new procedures, then collapse is the likely outcome.

The example of the pharmaceutical and biotech responses to external challenges may be illustrative. Big Pharma companies had deep pockets and skills but lacked real access to university science and top-tier scientists. Biotechs, born out of universities, had such access and knowledge but were weak on organizational skills and starved for cash. Their twin responses did not involve adopting the other's capabilities but partial absorption and blending, depending on external options. This oscillation between adopting hybrid responses and maintaining sufficient skill at what they were best at enabled organizations to be responsive. Taken too far, however, such oscillation leaves organizations with no competitive advantage.

The distribution and accessibility of resources are two additional elements of system poisedness. When resources are widely distributed, a skilled politician such as Bismarck could rise to prominence by deftly pulling the strings and playing off disparate participants. But as the very system of state power that he helped create congealed into a few powerful players, his room to maneuver was reduced and his influence waned. Technological systems where the sources of knowledge are diffusely located and developing rapidly are also ripe for cross-network transpositions. But this opportunity for catalytic feedback is contingent on the pace of scientific advance. If the knowledge matures or funding becomes scarce, incumbents will dominate. In such cases there is little opportunity for tipping, unless those in control become too recalcitrant to continue to advance.

The authors in this volume use an eclectic array of methods to study emergence, ranging from examining archives to constructing relational databases with centuries of detailed records to doing ethnographic observations of technical communities. A similar variety is needed to study poisedness, and we urge the same openness to the creative use of multiple methods as is shown in this volume. We emphasize that we view deductive modeling and inductive social histories as complements to, not substitutes for, understanding social processes. Creative blending of quantitative and textual evidence is essential to progress on this front.

Consider, for example, the Colyvas and Maroulis's use of Padgett et al.'s hypercycle model in chapter 16. Here the modeling offers an opportunity to test counterfactual alternatives to observations steeped in careful historical analysis of Stanford's archives. The effort is a valuable lesson to many who misread the takeaways from universities, such as MIT and Stanford, who reaped early benefits from the commercialization of their basic science. Some later imitators look back on the first movers and assume they somehow got the incentives and rules right. They believe there must be a recipe that can be emulated. But Colyvas and Maroulis confirm earlier research by Colyvas and Powell, which documented that faculty were not spurred by the prospects of great wealth, nor were there well-codified routines. Instead, faculty responded to the local exigencies of their research programs and the organization of their labs, looking to translate their research into tangible outcomes in order to advance science and medicine. The modeling effort points out a plausible mechanism: the fear that patenting by colleagues would restrict scientific autonomy prompts a shift to a proprietary regime.

In this analysis, we see the great value of multiple methods, combining historical research with formal modeling. A similar approach will prove valuable to examining the architecture of systems in order to uncover the mechanisms that illuminate vulnerability. For example, the combination of interviews or ethnography with network analyses of elite structures would afford insight into the extent to which incumbents are absorbing new skills or are fundamentally challenged by them and reveal just how aware groups are of their connectivity. Several of the chapters in this volume present network X-rays that are sharp depictions of the structure of community relations. When these carefully drawn cartographic examinations are combined with interviews that allow participants to tell their version of how they believe they fit into a larger social order, one gathers purchase on just how formidable the advantages of position are.

Many of the chapters in our volume draw on rich relational databases that permit linking individuals or organizations across multiple relations and data sources. We have largely used these programs to track the relational profiles of individuals and organizations. But there are suggestive hints in chapters 12 on Hungary and 14 on regional innovation of how to think about the system-level changes that render particular ecologies robust or susceptible in the face of challenges. For example, in their examination of successful biotech clusters, Powell et al. find that the three regions where robust clusters grew all started with dense local connections, then expanded outside the respective regions. In the eight communities where clusters did not develop, the most influential local participants built external connections first. Neither the biotech nor the Hungarian case goes on to explore the larger question of system vulnerability, but both strongly suggest that the sequence of tie formation and the manner by which new skills were incorporated are crucial to understanding the robustness of networks..

These negative cases point to our final word. To build a relational and historical understanding of system vulnerability does not mean looking only at cases when the walls came down. Throughout this volume, there have been bankers, politicians, scientists, and engineers who moved between stations in life, seemingly in worlds without walls. Our efforts have been focused on detailed reconstruction of the options that individuals and organizations pursued and did not consider at particular points in history. We have dug deep into the details of different cases to produce grounded causal accounts, sensitive both to context and to the possibility that alternative accounts can be ruled out. The horizons of possibilities we have sketched are the architecture of systems, not walls of concrete but self-reproducing chains of interaction, amenable to analysis in the manner we have undertaken here.

Index of Authors

Page numbers in italics indicate figures and tables.

Index of Subjects

Page numbers in italics indicate figures and tables.